Thesaurus of

Book Digests

Thesaurus of Book Digests

LIST OF EDITORS

BIBLE
Samuel Terrien, *Union Theological Seminary*

EAST EUROPEAN
Clarence Manning, *Columbia University*

FRENCH
William Frohock, *Columbia University*

GERMAN
Claude Hill, *Rutgers University*

GRAECO-ROMAN
Lloyd Daly, *University of Pennsylvania*

HEBREW-YIDDISH
Abraham Burstein, *Sec. Jewish Academy of Arts and Science*

ITALIAN
Ronald Del Monte, *Brooklyn College*

NETHERLANDS
Benjamin Hunniger, *Columbia University*

ORIENTAL
Younghill Kang, *New York University*

PHILOSOPHY
Henry Magid, *College of the City of New York*

RELIGION
Florence Mary Fitch, *Oberlin College*

RUSSIAN
John Cournos, *author, translator, reviewer*

SCANDINAVIAN
Adolph B. Benson, Professor Emeritus, *Yale University*

SCIENCE
Carl B. Boyer, *Brooklyn College*

SPANISH, PORTUGUESE, LATIN AMERICAN
Angel Flores, *Queens College*

Thesaurus of Book Digests

Digests of the World's Permanent
Writings from the Ancient
Classics to Current Literature

COMPILED UNDER THE EDITORIAL SUPERVISION OF
Hiram Haydn & Edmund Fuller

AVENEL BOOKS

NEW YORK

Copyright MCMXLIX by Crown Publishers, Inc.,
Copyright © MCMLXXVII by Crown Publishers, Inc.
All rights reserved.
This edition is published by Avenel Books,
distributed by Crown Publishers, Inc.
a   b   c   d   e   f   g   h
AVENEL 1978 PRINTING

Library of Congress Cataloging in Publication Data
Haydn, Hiram Collins, 1907-1973, ed.
    Thesaurus of book digests.
    Includes index.
    1. Literature—Stories, plots, etc.   2. Books—
Reviews. I. Fuller, Edmund, 1914-   II. Title.
PN44.H38   1949b   803   78-19147
ISBN 0-517-00122-5

Contents

Acknowledgment

Special acknowledgment should be made of the services of various people who have contributed substantially to one or another stage of work on the book —first of all, to the late Will D. Howe, under whose supervision the project was started some eight years ago. Thanks are also due to Samuel H. Post and Patricia Vos, for extensive and valuable editorial work, and to H. Robinson Shipherd, for his creative job of proofreading.

Introduction

It was our intention to include in this work a concise digest and discussion of every book ever published that has achieved a permanent place in world literature. Selecting the *candidates* for this accolade was simply a matter of sufficient diligence and the exercise of informed intelligence.

We examined all existing reference works, and all the "classic" series like Modern Library, Everyman's, Oxford World Classics, Grosset & Dunlap reprints, etc. We combed over carefully every available list of outstanding books: "The University of Chicago's Great Books List," "100 Great Books," "1000 Best Books," "Best Books of Our Time," basic stock lists, basic library lists, etc., and it was startling to learn how many such lists have been issued. We made a preliminary selection from these works and series and lists, and then divided them into major classifications by language, literature and subject matter.

The next step was to consult the specialists we had retained. Each examined, revised and added to the list in his field. When all this was done, we were confident that no worthy book could have been omitted because of oversight.

At this point the question of definition of standards entered. What is a permanent place in world literature? No one can define such a phrase precisely, but we found useful criteria: Is the book still in print in any kind of edition? Are there still calls for it at libraries? Is it still discussed or studied in schools and colleges? Does it have historical importance? Is it read, talked about or referred to any more?

If a book could not pass *any* of these tests it was out, regardless of whatever nominations for greatness it may have received. On the other hand, a book might be completely out of print and still live on in the memory of readers and by reason of discussion of it and reference to it in other books.

We could not, of course, eliminate entirely the elements of personal opinion and editorial judgment, but by means of these tests we did reduce those subjective standards to a minimum, particularly with regard to the older books.

The real dilemma came with the decision about books of the twentieth century. Here our criteria could not be applied so effectively. How to judge whether the widespread popularity of a given book was the harbinger of a continued and deserved recognition, or merely the condition attendant on those evanescent best sellers which make a big splash but shortly thereafter leave not even a ripple?

The only thing we could do was to get the cooperation of as many trained and experienced intelligences as we could. That we have done, and on that our case must rest.

Besides the books selected for full treatment, there were as many again that we felt deserved a mention or a short description, but not the full-length treatment. Each of these books is discussed in conjunction with, or at the foot of, the article about some more important book by the same author. But in every case the book is *listed* alphabetically with its appropriate cross-reference.

This is a book of *books;* no separate treatment is given to *authors.* However, there have been and are some writers whose writings have endured; who are remembered, not for one or two particular books, but rather for the body of their work. This is notably true in the cases of short story writers, philosophers and lyric poets. Who, except the specialists, remembers particular *volumes* of John Keats? It has seemed to us appropriate, therefore, to list the work of such writers under the author's name (incorporated alphabetically under his last name) rather than by the titles of individual books. Therefore, for example, the reader will find no separate and single description of *a book* by Yeats, but instead cross-references to particular titles, all leading him back to the entry headed YEATS, WILLIAM BUTLER, which covers Yeats' work in toto.

Some authors are remembered for one, two, or more particular books *and also* for the body of their work. In such cases, the books that have endured are given full treatment by themselves and there is also a comprehensive article about the author's other works. For example, Chekhov's most important plays are listed and described separately, but his short stories are treated in an article under the author's name.

Every author who is represented is listed in the Author Index, which directs the reader to all pages containing descriptions of his work.

There is another index, which is, we believe, unique. It is a Character Index, listing alphabetically and with page references the major fictional characters mentioned in the entire book. And, by way of extension, it may fairly be said that this Character Index is a cross-reference to those fictional characters who have achieved a permanent place in world literature.

We believe we have made the book very easy to use. If you know the name of the book, simply look it up in its alphabetical order. If you don't know the name of the book, but do know the name of the author, consult the Author Index for the appropriate references. If you can't think of the author's name or the name of the book, perhaps you can think of a major character. If so, you will be led to the particular pages by the Character Index. These are the three simple keys to the book. But it would be wrong to conclude this brief foreword to the THESAURUS OF BOOK DIGESTS without directing the reader's attention to the richness of its content. Its pages are amazingly high in sheer interest. Planned and produced as a reference book for the seeker-after-facts, it will gratify and reward the seeker-after-reading-enjoyment.

Hiram Haydn

ABC OF AESTHETICS, THE (1927), by Leo Stein. See APPRECIATION: PAINTING, POETRY AND PROSE, by Leo Stein.

ABE LINCOLN IN ILLINOIS (1938), by Robert E. Sherwood. This Pulitzer Prize play is a carefully documented series of twelve scenes chronicling the life of Lincoln from unsuccessful storekeeper, to lawyer, to President-elect of the United States. In the beginning, the young man is being tutored in grammar and rhetoric by Mentor Graham. Inspired by love for Ann Rutledge of New Salem, he runs for State Assembly, with the encouragement of his brother-in-law Ninian Edwards, and Joshua Speed. After the tragedy of Ann's illness and death, Edwards introduces Lincoln to his sister-in-law, Mary Todd. Mary recognizes the potentialities of the man, so different in background from herself, and artfully manages to have him propose marriage. Influenced strongly by her ambition, and the sincere friendship of his law partner Billy Herndon, Lincoln enters the political lists in earnest. He debates against the popular Stephen Douglas, and is at length elected President. Never desirous of this honor, Lincoln then faces his responsibilities with lofty ideals.

ABENCERRAJE, THE (1551), by Antonio de Villegas. The Moor Abindarráez, belonging to the famous Abencerraje family, is on his way to Coin to a secret marriage with the governor's daughter, the beautiful Jarifa, when he is met by some Christian knights. A fight ensues, and in spite of his bravery, Abindarráez is taken prisoner by Rodrigo de Narváez, governor of Antequera and Alora. Upon learning, however, the object of the Moor's journey, the Spanish knight, like a true cavalier, sets him free, on condition that he return to captivity after three days. Abindarráez keeps his word, bringing with him the stolen bride. Rodrigo de Narváez generously grants them their freedom and intervenes with the King of Granada, who succeeds in reconciling Jarifa's father with her. Prepared for the press about 1551, though not published until 1565, this short and simple novelette opened a new era in the history of the Spanish novel, for it contains all the essential characteristics of the historical novel and is distinctly different from the novel of chivalry.

ABRAHAM AND ISAAC (ca. 15th c.). This medieval English miracle play is based on the Biblical story of the sacrifice of Isaac. Of six extant treatments of the theme, the best is this of the Brome Manuscript (ca. 1475). It depicts the emotional conflict in both father and son. Abraham's struggle is between his submission to God's will and his natural love for his son. Isaac, on the other hand, is torn between his fear of death and his desire to obey his father. At the climax of the drama, Abraham lifts his sacrificial knife and is about to strike, when Isaac prays:

Ah! Father of Heaven to thee I cry,
Lord receive me into thy hand.

Then the miracle happens: an angel appears, carrying a ram to be substituted for the sacrifice of the boy Isaac. The play is generally regarded as the finest specimen of its kind in the language, a masterpiece of suspense and pathos.

ABRAHAM LINCOLN (1926–1939), by Carl Sandburg. This massive biography, six volumes in all, is divided into two main sections. The first of these, in two volumes, is *Abraham Lincoln: The Prairie Years* (1926). It traces the life of Lincoln from birth to departure from Springfield as President-elect of the United States. This portion is especially distinguished by the richness of its portraiture—the man depicted in his world, with full use of the wealth of folk material of Lincoln's environment.

The second section, in four volumes, is *Abraham Lincoln· The War Years* (1939). The work might be called more properly an epic history than a biography. In exhaustive detail, documentarily authentic, it covers Lincoln's presidential career from the 1861 rambling trek to Washington through the tragic funeral cortege of 1865, slowly retracing the same route. Speeches, letters, state papers and anecdotes are quoted. There are fruitful character studies of cabinet members, senators, representatives, military men, and other prominent figures—the study of whose complex relationships and activities is a political education.

From this great mass of material, skillfully and objectively selected and assembled, emerges a unique portrait. An extraordinary sense of the living presence of Lincoln is produced without any intrusion or literary "art." This is the genius of the work. Yet always, the mark of Sandburg the poet underlies Sandburg the historian.

Abraham Lincoln was quickly recognized as one of the monuments of contemporary letters, transcending any single classification. *The War Years* was awarded the Pulitzer Prize for American History in 1940.

ABRAHAM LINCOLN, THE BACKWOODS BOY (1883), by Horatio Alger, Jr. See ALGER, HORATIO, JR.

ABSALOM AND ACHITOPHEL (1681–1682), by John Dryden. See DRYDEN, JOHN.

ABU TELFAN (1865–1867), by Wilhelm Raabe. See RAABE, WILHELM.

ACADEMICS, by Cicero. See PHILOSOPHICAL ESSAYS, by Cicero.

ACROSS THE WIDE MISSOURI (1947), by Bernard DeVoto. See DEVOTO, BERNARD.

ACT OF FAITH (1946), by Irwin Shaw. See SHAW, IRWIN.

ACTION AT AQUILA (1938), by Hervey Allen. See ANTHONY ADVERSE, by Hervey Allen.

ADAM (LE JEU D'ADAM) (12th c.), Anonymous. This five-act miracle play presents the stories of Adam, Eve, the Fall and the murder of Abel. Following these, the prophets Abraham, Moses and Isaiah—and with them, strangely, King Nebuchadnezzar—appear and foretell the Redemption. Arranged for outdoor presentation under Church auspices, *Adam* is read largely by those interested in the religious origins of French drama.

ADAM AND EVE (1930), by Karel Čapek. See R.U.R., by Karel Čapek.

ADAM BEDE (1859), by George Eliot. Adam Bede, a young carpenter, is in love with Hetty Sorrel, a pretty, empty-headed girl who lives on the farm of Martin Poyser. Arthur Donnithorne, the village Squire's son, is unaware that Adam, his best friend, cares for Hetty; since he is attracted to her himself, he makes secret rendezvous with her in the woods. As Hetty's fondest dream is to become lady of the manor, she encourages Arthur. One day Adam surprises the lovers in the woods and forces Arthur to fight. The bewildered Arthur tries vainly to make light of the situation. Conscience-stricken, he writes a farewell letter to Hetty and goes off with his regiment. Hetty agrees to marry Adam in the spring to make the best of a bad bargain. But as the wedding day approaches, her pregnancy can no longer be concealed. She thinks of suicide and vainly goes in search of Arthur. On the way, she gives birth to her child; in despair she murders it and is arrested. At the trial her stubborn silence arouses general indignation. She is found guilty of infanticide and condemned to death. At the last moment, Arthur arrives with a reprieve: her sentence is commuted to transportation. Later, Adam marries Hetty's friend, the gentle Dinah Morris, a lay preacher, who is interested in saving souls. Adam's brother, Seth; Bartle Massey, a school-master; Mr. Irvine, the vicar; and Mrs. Poyser, are among the other notable characters of the story.

ADAM IN BALLINGSCHAP (1664), by Joost van den Vondel. See VONDEL, JOOST VAN DEN.

ADDING MACHINE, THE (1923), by Elmer Rice. See STREET SCENE, by Elmer Rice.

ADDRESS TO THE GERMAN NATION (1807–1808), by Johann Gottlieb Fichte. See FICHTE, JOHANN GOTTLIEB.

ADE, GEORGE (1866–1944). George Ade of Indiana was a regional humorist, and it is for his piquant use of an "American" vernacular that he is famous.

Fables in Slang (1899), his most popular work, is a collection of twenty-six sketches modeled after *Aesop's Fables*. The country characters, sympathetically portrayed, and the everyday occurrences in their everyday lives, suggest humorously perverse morals to Ade. Thus, a phrenologist plies his trade by telling customers what he knows they want to hear—and the author remarks, "A good jolly is worth whatever you pay for it." Other tales concern a young girl who looks for her ideal man and finally marries a janitor; returning heroes; a preacher; vaudeville performers; the politician; a caddy who wonders if he has a soul; a Bohemian writer; and typical college boys.

In dealing with this last group, Ade was a master satirist. He wrote farces of student life, such as *Just Out of College* (1905), and *The College Widow* (1904). The "College Widow" is Jane Witherspoon, daughter of the President of Atwater, a small Presbyterian college. Jane "buries one sweetheart every commencement." She consents to entice Billy Bolton, on his way to a Baptist school, to attend Atwater and play football for them. Although Bolton's irate father shows up and tries to stop the big game of the season, exposing Jane's motives, love conquers all.

Ade wrote many musicals, the best known of which is *The Sultan of Sulu* (1902). He also wrote sequels to his *Fables in Slang: People You Knew* (1903), and *Hand-Made Fables* (1920).

ADMIRABLE CRICHTON, THE (1902), by Sir James M. Barrie. See BARRIE, SIR JAMES MATTHEW.

ADONAIS (1821), by Percy Bysshe Shelley. See SHELLEY, PERCY BYSSHE.

ADVANCEMENT OF LEARNING, THE (1605), by Francis Bacon. Except for the *Essays* (q.v.), this is Bacon's best known work. It is the original English model for the later, longer, Latin *De Augmentis Scientiarum.* An exalted statement of the dignity of knowledge, it reviews what has been achieved in the various fields so far and takes note of obstacles to the further expansion of knowledge. Bacon's assumption that all knowledge was his province is less important than his concern with principles and methods. Although failing to present a key, it offers a general solution. Written before the *Novum Organum* (q.v.), this is actually an introduction to it. The First Book is a prologue, showing how learning became discredited by the inadequacies of scholars and critics. Testimony of its real excellence is submitted from divine and human sources. The Second Book notes "What has been done for the Advancement of Learning, human and divine, with the Defects of the same." Bacon points out the weaknesses of universities, the neglect of science by peoples and governments, and the lack of contact between the scholars of different countries. Learning he divides into three elements: history, which corresponds to memory; poetry, which corresponds to imagination; and philosophy, which corresponds to reason. There is a triple division and subdivision of each branch and sub-branch of knowledge, along traditional lines. Knowledge, insisted Bacon, was meant to be used in practical life: "But men must know that in this theatre of man's life it is reserved only for God and the angels to be lookers-on."

ADVENTURES OF GIL BLAS, THE (1715), by Alain René Le Sage. See GIL BLAS, by Alain René Le Sage.

ADVENTURES OF HUCKLEBERRY FINN, THE (1884), by Mark Twain. See HUCKLEBERRY FINN, THE ADVENTURES OF, by Mark Twain.

ADVENTURES OF SHERLOCK HOLMES (1892), by Sir Arthur Conan Doyle. See SHERLOCK HOLMES, by Sir Arthur Conan Doyle.

ADVENTURES OF TELEMACHUS, THE (1699), by François de Salignac de la Mothe-Fénelon. In a story following the essential pattern of the *Odyssey* (q.v.), Telemachus, a young prince animated by love of his country, has been shipwrecked on the island of Calypso while in search of his father, Ulysses, whose long absence has brought many misfortunes to his family and nation. Telemachus runs the gamut of dangers, and rejects the offer of kingdoms more substantial than his own. In his arduous passage through a series of unknown countries, he learns everything necessary to the proper government of his own domains, principles that spring from the wisdom of Ulysses, the piety of Aeneas, and the valor of both. At the conclusion of wanderings leading all the way into Hades, the youth returns to Ithaca, where he finds his father safely awaiting him. Written by a bishop for the moral and intellectual guidance of the French princes of the late seventeenth century, the work is an argument in favor of piety, virtue and good government.

ADVENTURES OF TOM SAWYER, THE (1876), by Mark Twain. See TOM SAWYER, THE ADVENTURES OF, by Mark Twain.

ADVENTUROUS HISTORY OF HSI MEN AND HIS SIX WIVES (1580), by Hsu Wei. See CHIN P'ING MEI, by Hsu Wei.

AENEID (ca. 19 B.C.), by Virgil (Publius Virgilius Maro). Virgil's epic of the beginnings of the Roman state is the most celebrated work in Latin literature. Its materials are drawn from the Trojan legend and earlier Roman poets and its form from Homer, but the *Aeneid* reflects the more deliberative and personal spirit of the literature of the sophisticated Augustan age. It retells the story of Aeneas' flight from fallen Troy and his final settlement in Latium. There are twelve books, the first six modeled on the *Odyssey* (q.v.) and the last on the *Iliad* (q.v.). Book I tells how Aeneas and his followers were driven ashore at Carthage and there hospitably received by Queen Dido. In Book II Aeneas relates to Dido how Troy was captured by the ruse of the wooden horse; how he himself escaped from the burning city bearing his aged father, Anchises, on his back and leading his little son, Ascanius, by the hand; and how he lost his wife on the way and finally reached the slopes of Mt. Ida, where he joined other refugees. In Book III he continues with the narrative of his voyage and many adventures as leader of the Trojan exiles, and how he lost his father and finally reached Carthage. In Book IV Dido has fallen desperately in love with Aeneas, but the restless hero feels himself led by the will of the gods to pursue his quest for the fated goal of his travels. He sails away from Carthage, and the heart-broken Dido immolates herself upon a pyre. Book V tells of his arrival at Sicily, where funeral games are celebrated in honor of Anchises, and how he sailed on and reached Cumae in Italy. Book VI is an account of his descent to the infernal regions under the guidance of the Cumaean Sibyl. There the shade of Anchises foretells the future of his line and the destined greatness of Rome. In Book VII Aeneas reaches Latium at the mouth of the Tiber and is welcomed by Latinus, who offers him the hand of his daughter Lavinia. This princess had already been betrothed to Turnus, king of the Rutulians, who now raises an army of allies against Latinus and Aeneas. Book VIII tells how Aeneas visited the neighboring king Evander and enlisted his aid and that of the Etruscans. Books IX-XI describe the war with the forces of Turnus, and XII, the single combat between Aeneas and Turnus, resulting in the death of Turnus and the victory of Aeneas.

The purpose of the poem is to celebrate the high destiny of the Roman state in general, and in particular of the reign of Augustus, for whom descent is claimed through Aeneas from the Trojans on one side and on the other the gods.

AESOPIC FABLES. See FABLES, by Aesop.

AETHIOPICA (ca. 3rd or 4th c.), by Heliodorus of Emesa. Theagenes, a descendant of Achilles, falls in love with Chariclea, a priestess of Delphi. The two lovers flee to Egypt and after many adventures reach Ethiopia.

The wild people of that dark land prepare to sacrifice them as burnt offerings to the sun god and the moon god, when it is revealed that Chariclea is not a white Greek at all, but the daughter of the King of Ethiopia, born white through the pre-natal effect of a marble statue upon her mother. Exposed in infancy, she had been rescued and given into the guardianship of the priest of Apollo. Saved from death, the lovers are married. The work is one of the earliest specimens of the "romance." The author is said to have been Bishop of Trikka in Thessaly; there is a story that he was stripped of his bishopric because he refused to disclaim authorship of the *Aethiopica,* which led the Synod of the Church to ban and burn his popular book. The first Greek manuscript known to modern times was discovered in the sack of Budapest in 1526. The French translation of Amyot (1547) introduced the work to western Europe and gave it a great popularity.

AFTER STRANGE GODS (1934), by T. S. Eliot. See ELIOT, THOMAS STEARNS.

AGAINST THE GRAIN (1884), by Joris-Karl Huysmans. This is the story of an effete character who turns to artificial pleasures as an escape from life's monotony. Des Esseintes, the hero, is fastidious, rich, disillusioned and lost in a world composed, "for the most part, of imbeciles and knaves." He feels a great scorn for humanity, and combines many features of Romantic heroes like Werther, Obermann and René. Women he finds boring, stupid and vain. He goes to a remote place in the country, and organizes his life "against the grain." He sleeps by day, lives by night. His living room is decorated with dark draperies; the paths of his garden are powdered with coal; his plates are bordered with black; he drinks dark wines from dark cups; grows monstrous artificial flowers, reads decadent literature, and delights in abnormalities. This continues till his health fails, and he has to resume ordinary living. The book is regarded as a classic of late nineteenth-century "decadent school" literature.

AGAMEMNON (458 B.C.), by Aeschylus. This is the first tragedy of a trilogy, including also the *Choephori* and the *Eumenides,* which is based on the story of Orestes and concerned with the blood guilt and purification of the royal house of Atreus. The action takes place before the palace of Agamemnon in Argos at the time of his victorious return from the Trojan war. As the play opens, a watchman announces the fall of Troy, of which he has learned from beacon fires. The queen, Clytaemnestra, a strong-willed woman, who hates Agamemnon for having sacrificed their daughter, Iphigenia, to appease the gods, makes preparation for his return. The chorus senses impending disaster and broods over the past of the ill-starred house. A messenger announces Agamemnon's approach, but tells how he had wantonly desecrated captured Troy. Upon his arrival, after tricking the king into a final act of insolence in treading upon a purple carpet like a very god, Clytaemnestra welcomes him to his halls. Cassandra, a captive Trojan princess with prophetic powers, whom Clytaemnestra despises as her husband's concubine, refuses to approach the palace, and in the throes of inspiration darkly predicts the impending murder of Agamemnon. Soon Clytaemnestra reappears with bloody hands to tell triumphantly how she has slain her husband

and avenged the death of her child. Any tendency on the part of the chorus, representing the people, to rebel, is quelled by the appearance of Clytaemnestra's paramour, Aegisthus, with armed attendants. The chorus, which has about half the lines in the play, is omnipresent and sets the tone in its brooding reflections upon the fate of the accursed house. The remaining plays of the trilogy, which is called the *Oresteia,* deal with the murder of Clytaemnestra by her own vengeful son, Orestes, and his justification and purification in the sight of the gods.

AGAMEMNON, by Seneca. See TRAGEDIES, by Seneca.

AGAR (1883), by Hviezdoslav. See HVIEZDOSLAV.

AGATHON, THE HISTORY OF (1767), by Christoph Martin Wieland. See WIELAND, CHRISTOPH MARTIN.

AGE OF ANXIETY, THE (1947), by W. H. Auden. See AUDEN, WYSTAN HUGH.

AGE OF CONFIDENCE, THE (1934), by Henry Seidel Canby. See CANBY, HENRY SEIDEL.

AGE OF DESPOTS (1875), by John Addington Symonds. See HISTORY OF THE RENAISSANCE IN ITALY, by John Addington Symonds.

AGE OF INNOCENCE, THE (1920), by Edith Wharton. The story begins in New York in the 1870's. Ellen Oscnka, a former society girl, has left her titled Polish husband abroad because of his dissipation and returned to New York. Here she meets Newland Archer, a young lawyer engaged to her pretty cousin, May Welland. Archer and Ellen realize a communion of ideas and a stimulation of thought in each other's company, but Archer feels that he cannot with integrity break with his shallow young fiancée May, and marries her. Ellen's family becomes deeply concerned with her refusal to respond to the overtures of her husband because they dread, above all things, the scandal of a divorce. Archer is enlisted to persuade Ellen not to go to court. She consents, but realizing the hopelessness of her situation, decides to go to Paris to live. At May's farewell party for her, Archer sees that the family secretly suspects him of being Ellen's lover. He is disgusted by the artificial standards of his society, but determines never to see Ellen again. Years later, he visits Paris with his son, but does not see her, preferring his memories. Mrs. Wharton received the Pulitzer Prize for this novel.

AGE OF LOUIS XIV, THE (1751), by Voltaire. Voltaire's history of the French Golden Age is valuable less for what it shows of its subject than for what it reveals about Voltaire. He was tired of "heroic" histories and wanted to write one which would assess the whole culture of a time, covering not only its political and military fortunes, but also its achievements in art and industry; in other words, he wanted a history satisfactory to the philosopher. What he wrote is serious without being solemn, but somewhat too abstract and analytical to please modern readers. Students of historiography insist that Voltaire lacked the historic sense—meaning that he was not sufficiently aware of the differences between men of one time and men of another. In its own time his history was universally admired.

AGE OF REASON, THE (1794–1795), by Thomas Paine. See COM-
MON SENSE, by Thomas Paine.

AH, WILDERNESS! (1933), by Eugene O'Neill. This pleasant comedy
of New England during the first decade of the twentieth century is quite unlike O'Neill's other works. Richard Miller, rebellious high school senior, is in
love with his neighbor, Muriel McComber, with all the passion of adolescence.
Muriel's father, David, is apprehensive of Richard's wild tendencies, and
breaks up their relationship. The sensitive youth wanders into a saloon and
meets Belle, a young college town flirt. Getting drunk for the first time in
his life, he tries to fight with a salesman who picks her up, and is ejected
from the saloon. Richard's father, sympathetic to his son's predicament, when
he sees that no damage has been done, helps him to regain his balance. Young
Richard determines to wait for Muriel, anyhow, having learned by a secret
message that she does love him.

AIKEN, CONRAD (1889–   ). Conrad Aiken was born in Georgia.
After graduating from Harvard University, he began to travel in Europe, and
now divides his time between England and New England. His writings have
been distinguished in the fields of poetry, fiction and criticism. Aiken's poetry, with its subtle rhythms, shows his characteristic interest in human psychology. *Selected Poems* (1929) won the 1930 Pulitzer Prize. More clinical
in their characterizations are Aiken's short story collections, such as *Bring!
Bring!* (1925), and *Costumes by Eros* (1928); and his novels, such as *Blue
Voyage* (1927), written in the stream-of-consciousness technique; *Great Circle*
(1933), *Conversation* (1940), a chronicle of crises in marital relations, and
King Coffin (1935), the story of a criminal. Aiken has contributed to many
literary magazines, but has always considered himself an independent critic.
He has commented on contemporary poets in *Scepticisms* (1919), being espe-
cially interested in Emily Dickinson.

AJAX (ca. 445–440 B.C.), by Sophocles. Ajax, son of King Telamon of
Salamis, was considered second in courage only to Achilles of all the Greek
heroes before Troy. After Achilles' death Ajax had disputed the possession
of his arms with Odysseus, but had lost them to him by the decision of the
leaders. Infuriated at what he felt was rank injustice to his valor, Ajax set
about to murder them all at night. Athena, whose aid he had scorned in his
overweening pride, cast upon him a fit of madness in which he mistook a
flock of sheep, part of the spoils, for his enemies. Under this delusion he had
slaughtered some of the sheep and driven others to his tent for torture. As
the play opens, Ajax is still in his tent and still under Athena's spell. His
followers, the Salaminians, enter with his concubine, the Phrygian princess,
Tecmessa. Ajax quickly recovers from his insanity and realizes what he has
done. To the chorus he reviews his misfortunes. He fears he will become the
laughingstock of the army and bring disgrace upon his father. Resolving to
end his life, Ajax cannot be swayed by the entreaties of Tecmessa and the
Salaminians, but allays their fears. In a moving and ambiguous monologue,
he takes leave of Tecmessa, their son Eurysaces, and his companions. Then,
taking the sword of Hector, he leaves the tent. Teucer, Ajax's half-brother,
sends a belated warning to the Salaminians, ordering them to keep Ajax in his

tent since Calchas, the seer, had prophesied this would be a day of evil for him. Ajax, however, has already destroyed himself by falling on his sword. The last part of the play is concerned with Teucer's attempt to secure a proper burial for his brother, contrary to the stern injunction of Agamemnon and Menelaus. Though in life Ajax had been his bitter foe, Odysseus nobly intercedes and secures permission for the burial of the warrior whose self-sufficient haughtiness had been his undoing.

A LA RECHERCHE DU TEMPS PERDU (1913–1927), by Marcel Proust. See REMEMBRANCE OF THINGS PAST, by Marcel Proust.

ALADDIN, or THE WONDERFUL LAMP (1805), by Adam Gottlob Oehlenschläger. Brandes called this work the "corner-stone of Danish literature during the first half of the nineteenth century." It is an extensive Romantic drama in five acts, with songs and choruses, based on the famous tale from *Arabian Nights* (q.v.), about an indolent but innocent poor tailor's son who through innate honesty, faith in the power of his lamp, and divine favoritism, becomes in Persia first the husband of the Sultan's daughter and eventually, upon the death of her father, his successor. *Aladdin* represents the goal of all yearning. It is the acme of the Oriental or European Romantic idea; the youth of fortune and the acquisition of magic power symbolize that the "poet alone can penetrate into the spiritual realm of reality" and fantasy. And there is the omnipresent ethical side: the selfish sorcerer is discovered and eliminated: virtue conquers. Today the author is best known for his numerous works on themes of national historical import. Best are his tragedies *Hakon Jarl* and *Palnatoke,* both of 1807 and both localized at the dawn of Christianity.

ALASTOR (1815), by Percy Bysshe Shelley. See SHELLEY, PERCY BYSSHE.

ALCAEUS (7th–6th c. B.C.). One of the canon of nine lyric poets, Alcaeus, like Sappho, was a native of the island of Lesbos. His ten books of poems are preserved only in fragments, many of which have been recovered in recent years from Egyptian papyrus. They are of great formal beauty and are frequently, though not exclusively, written in the stanzaic form named after their author. His range of subject matter is wide, from hymns to the gods to love and drinking songs. The latter especially are inspired with fine zest for living. His so-called stasiotic songs are full of the bitterest hatred for the tyrant who overthrew the aristocracy to which Alcaeus belonged. Typical of these for its political zeal is the poem in which he compares the state to a storm-wracked ship, the first appearance of the metaphor of the ship of state in literature. This poem and many others of Alcaeus were imitated by the Roman Horace.

ALCALDE DE ZALAMEA, EL (1651), by Pedro Calderón de la Barca. See MAYOR OF ZALAMEA, THE, by Pedro Calderón de la Barca.

ALCESTIS (438 B.C.), by Euripides. One of Euripides' earliest dramas, this is the fourth play of a tetralogy which the poet had entered in competition for the tragedy award of the year. The scene is at Pherae, outside the palace of Admetus, King of Thessaly, who is doomed to die. Apollo, who has worked for Admetus as a mortal to atone for an offense to Zeus, tricks the Fates, who then pledge that Admetus shall escape immediate death, if he can find someone to die for him. The King has asked both his old father and mother, and has been refused. However, his young wife, Alcestis, is willing to make the sacrifice. Resigned to her fate, she begs her husband not to marry again and to look after their motherless children; then falls back dead. Shortly thereafter Heracles arrives, wearing his lion skin and carrying his great club. He is going in quest of the horses of Diomedes at the bidding of Eurystheus of Tiryns. The funeral procession of the queen is leaving the palace, but Admetus, according to the laws of hospitality, dissembles his grief before Heracles. He tells him he is following the body of a stranger to the grave, and invites Heracles to make use of his guest quarters. Pheres, Admetus' father, enters to make his funeral offering to the dead queen, but Admetus furiously turns on his parent who would not die for him. The ancient, in his turn, points out that Admetus had acted the part of a coward in allowing his wife to make such a sacrifice. Heracles hears the story of Alcestis from a servant and, sobered from his revelry, determines to rescue her. Admetus, in the meantime, has come back from the tomb, and, overcome with grief, he cannot bear to enter his palace, where everything is associated with the memory of his departed wife. Thereupon Heracles returns, leading a veiled woman, Alcestis, whom he has won from Death in personal combat.

ALCHEMIST, THE (acted 1610; printed 1612), by Ben Jonson. One of Jonson's best known and most robust comedies, this play relates the search for the philosopher's stone, satirizing human gullibility and duplicity. Lovewit, a London gentleman, leaves the city to escape the plague, placing in charge of the house his butler, Face. That rogue brings in Subtle, an alchemist, and his accomplice, Dol Common; among them, they set in motion a complicated program of swindles. Sir Epicure Mammon, a knight who dreams of turning all base metals into gold, and who has an amorous eye for the ladies, is a ready client for the trio. Other victims include Tribulation Wholesome and Ananias, two hypocritical Puritans; Dapper, a clerk who desires a magical skill at gambling; Abel Drugger, a tobacconist wishing a device to fascinate customers (a role often played by David Garrick); Kastril, an aggressive country lad aping court manners; his sister Dame Pliant, a pretty young widow who wishes to marry again; and Surly, a gamester friend of Mammon who alone suspects the proceedings. Lovewit unexpectedly returns, at a critical moment. The charlatans flee; Lovewit marries Dame Pliant, and forgives Face because he was the matchmaker.

ALEXANDERPLATZ, BERLIN (1929), by Alfred Döblin. This novel deals with the ideas, dreams, associations and experiences of a simple man, Franz Biberkopf, who is trying to adjust himself to a normal life after his release from jail. The title suggests both the famous police headquarters and the hunting grounds of the demi-monde in Berlin where the hero is at home. The book is the earliest and strongest proof of James Joyce's influence on modern German literature. Its author, Alfred Döblin, a psychiatrist and novelist, was one of the foremost expressionistic prose writers during the Weimar Republic.

ALF LAILAH WA-LAILAH (ca. 1440–1550). See ARABIAN NIGHTS' ENTERTAINMENTS.

ALGEBRA, THE GREAT ART (1545), by Jerome Cardan. See ARS MAGNA, by Jerome Cardan.

ALGER, HORATIO, JR. (1834–1899). After Horatio Alger had experienced a Bohemian existence in Paris, then become a Unitarian minister, he moved to New York and began his famous literary career. He wrote about 130 books for boys. All of a single theme, they chronicled the perseverance of a central character against poverty and temptation. The character, liberally aided by lucky events, would eventually attain fame and fortune. This formula sold upwards of 20,000,000 books. The most famous of the Alger success stories are the *Ragged Dick* series (1867ff.), *Luck and Pluck* (1869ff.), and *Tattered Tom* (1871ff.). Alger also wrote biographies of self-made statesmen whose lives seemed to fit his own literary pattern, such as *Abraham Lincoln, the Backwoods Boy* (1883).

ALGORISMUS (printed ca. 1490), by Joannes de Sacrobosco. See SPHAERA MUNDI, by Joannes de Sacrobosco.

ALICE ADAMS (1921), by Booth Tarkington. The heroine of this novel of provincial snobbery is Alice Adams, a twenty-two-year-old who knows she is pretty, and supposes herself very clever. Unfortunately for her ambitions of a wealthy marriage or a stage career, her family is plain, poor and undistinguished. Alice meets socially prominent Arthur Russell, and they fall in love. Apprehensive about his probable disillusionment with her family, she practices endless strategems to prevent his meeting them. Eventually, however, Arthur does meet the Adamses at a dinner party, which turns out to be quite painful for the young couple. Alice's father, Virgil, and her brother, Walter, have become involved in serious financial difficulties because of the nagging of ambitious Mrs. Adams. She is forced to run a boarding house at last, to support her husband in his failing health; and Alice makes a sensible decision to register at a business school.

This realistic novel won the Pulitzer Prize for 1922.

ALICE'S ADVENTURES IN WONDERLAND (1865), by Lewis Carroll (Charles Lutwidge Dodgson). This is a story for children, about Alice's wonderful dream. Chasing a watch-carrying White Rabbit, Alice tumbles down a rabbit-hole into a marvelous land of adventure. Here she grows alternately tall and short from drinking a magic potion and eating a magic cake, in her effort to enter a wonderful garden. In a pool of her own tears she meets Mouse, Duck, Dodo, Lory and Eaglet. Three inches high, she philosophizes with the Caterpillar. She meets the Ugly Duchess and watches a baby turn into a pig. After taking advice from a vanishing Cheshire Cat, she has a wild tea-party with the March Hare, the Mad Hatter, and the Dormouse. With the King and Queen of Hearts, Alice plays croquet, using flamingos for mallets and hedgehogs for balls. She watches the Mock Turtle, the Gryphon and the Lobster dance. The final episode tells of an hilarious trial to determine who stole the tarts from the King and Queen. Alice, in dismay, accuses the characters of being nothing but a pack of cards. They rise up and fly at her, and she awakens.

This immortal story, with original illustrations by Sir John Tenniel, has been cherished for generations. It was followed by a sequel, *Through the Looking Glass* (q.v.), and there have been stage and motion picture versions.

ALISON'S HOUSE (1930), by Susan Glaspell. See GLASPELL, SUSAN.

ALL FOR LOVE, or THE WORLD WELL LOST (1678), by John Dryden. This is a version of the well-known story of Mark Antony and his fatal love for Cleopatra. The play opens with the attempt by Ventidius to break Antony away from Cleopatra. To counter her wiles, he brings Antony face to face with Antony's virtuous wife Octavia, the sister of Octavius (Augustus) Caesar. For a little while she manages to win back her husband's loyalty, but his jealous suspicions of his friend Dolabella make him realize he cannot live without Cleopatra. Octavius Caesar marches on Alexandria, and when Antony is falsely told that Cleopatra is dead, he kills himself. Cleopatra completes the tragedy by permitting a deadly asp to bite her. The play is an adaptation of Shakespeare's *Antony and Cleopatra* (q.v.), simplified in plot. In it, Dryden forsook his customary heroic couplets and observed the unities of blank verse.

ALL MEN ARE BROTHERS (Eng. tr. 1937), by Shih Nai-an. See SHUI HU CHUAN, by Shih Nai-an.

ALL QUIET ON THE WESTERN FRONT (1929), by Erich Maria Remarque (Erich Maria Kramer). The power of this realistic novel of World War I lies in its passionate hatred of war. The gripping, muscular style, characteristic of the best type of narrative journalism, gives the story pace and terror. Remarque was a veteran who had lived through the hell that he described. "We learned," comments Paul Bäumer, the German narrator of the story, "that a bright button is more important than four volumes of Schopenhauer." Disenchantment about the war and the Kaiser came early to Paul and his comrades: Stanilaus Katcyinsky, who was "the greatest glutton in the army," Muller, the argumentative ass, Kemmerich, who traded his mortality for a more permanent peace, Tjadens, and Albert Kropp, the only one besides Paul who was still alive when the Armistice was signed. The story is packed with searing incidents of terror and grandeur under fire, of the filth and meanness in the trenches, of the desperate searching among all decent soldiers within themselves and within one another for the least glimmer of light or hope, so that they might wish to survive the nightmare of war. The pathos of young lives, building dreams of a better kind of world to live in "after the war will be over," is made unbearable by the background of continuous agony and slaughter. When Paul finally is demobilized and returns to the ruins of his life, he find his mother dying of cancer. Symbolically, this is the returning soldier's reunion with a tortured life.

Having attained sudden world fame with his war novel in 1929, the young author later moved to Switzerland after the German right-wing press had subjected him to a campaign of vitriolic hatred and vicious abuse. During World War II he came to the U.S.A., where he wrote his best-selling *Arch of Triumph* (1946), dealing with the fate of the Hitler refugees in Paris. Another novel by Remarque, *Three Comrades,* like most of his books, has been translated into many languages.

ALL THE KING'S MEN (1946), by Robert Penn Warren. See WARREN, ROBERT PENN.

ALL'S WELL THAT ENDS WELL (ca. 1602?), by William Shakespeare. The play opens at the palace of young Count Bertram of Rousillon. Bertram is about to leave for the court of the King of France. Helena, a young gentlewoman, who had been brought up by his mother, the Countess, is in love with him. Her father had been a famous physician, and she begs the Countess to let her attend the King, who is suffering from a supposedly incurable malady, as she thinks one of the remedies her father willed her on his death-bed will effect a cure. The King hesitates at first, as his physicians despair of his condition, but Helena's remedy proves effective; he recovers, and she requests as reward that he let her select a husband from among his eligible nobles.

She chooses young Bertram, who is forced to marry her, much against his will.

Urged on by his follower Parolles, a bragging knave, Bertram leaves Helena and goes to Florence to fight for the Duke. He sends Helena a letter, saying that until she can obtain a certain ring from his finger, and show him a child of which he is the father, he will not return. Helena follows him to Florence, disguised as a pilgrim, and meets a worthy widow and her daughter, Diana, to whom Bertram has been making advances. She proves to the widow that she is Bertram's wife, and promises Diana a dowry if they will do just as she requests. Diana is to consider yielding to Bertram's advances, but is first to request his ring, and offer him in exchange a ring which the King had presented to Helena. Helena takes Diana's place that night, receiving the ring, and the next day Diana repels Bertram's advances, but refuses to take back the other ring. In the meantime, Helena has circulated a report that she is dead.

Bertram returns to France with excellent letters from the Duke of Florence. The King, who had been angry at his behavior, forgives him and arranges for him to marry the daughter of Lafeu, an old lord. The King notices the ring on Bertram's finger and asks him how he came by it; and, as he can give no satisfactory explanation, has him arrested on suspicion of having made away with Helena.

Diana and her mother arrive, and Diana produces Bertram's ring claiming him as her husband. She calls on Parolles, who had been the go-between, to bear witness. When the King demands an explanation of the rings, she refuses to answer. The widow then introduces Helena, who is with child, and has now fulfilled her husband's terms to the letter. Bertram is reconciled to her, and so, "All's Well That Ends Well."

The story derives from the *Decameron* through Painter's translation in the *Palace of Pleasure.*

ALLEGORICAL INTERPRETATION OF THE LAWS, by Philo Judaeus. See PHILO JUDAEUS.

ALLERZIELEN (1903), by Herman Heijermans. See OP HOOP VAN ZEGENS, by Herman Heijermans.

ALMA MATER (1947), by Henry Seidel Canby. See CANBY, HENRY SEIDEL.

ALMAGEST (ca. 125–150), by Ptolemy of Alexandria. Ptolemy composed a number of works (including one on astrology), but two in particular have remained as classics in the history of science. One is his *Geography,* printed in 1462 and many times thereafter; the other is the *Almagest,* printed in part in 1496, with complete editions in 1515 and subsequently. In spite of the popularity of the *Geography,* the *Almagest* is in reality a greater work, for Ptolemy was primarily an astronomer. Little is known about his life, apart from his scientific work, but he remains one of the two most famous astronomers of antiquity, Hipparchus being the other. The Egyptians and Babylonians had made and preserved numerous observations of the celestial bodies, and these were used by the Greeks to build up their astronomical systems. The first mathematical theory was that of Eudoxus, in which the sun, moon, planets and fixed stars revolved in a system of circles or spheres with the earth at the center—the so-called "homocentric spheres." This scheme was found not to agree sufficiently closely with observations, and so a system was devised in which the planets moved in circles (epicycles) the centers of which themselves moved along the circumferences of other circles (deferents), the centers of which generally were at the earth. This geocentric system of cycles and epicycles was elaborated mathematically by Hipparchus (ca. 150 B.C.), but his work has been lost. Fortunately, however, his results were known to, and freely used by, Ptolemy of Alexandria two and a half centuries later. The Ptolemaic system, presented in the *Almagest,* is basically the same as that of Hipparchus, but it includes new observations and devices. It is the climax of Greek astronomy, for Ptolemy had no noteworthy successor in antiquity.

The *Almagest* or *Great Syntaxis,* so-called to distinguish it from a collection of works known as the *Lesser Astronomy,* is divided into thirteen books. The first is introductory and reviews the work of his predecessors, although Ptolemy is not always careful to acknowledge his indebtedness to earlier men. The next several books present the apparent motions and distances of the sun and moon by means of excentrics and epicycles. Book VI deals with eclipses; Books VII and VIII contain a star catalogue based upon that of Hipparchus; and the remaining books are devoted to the motions of the planets. Ptolemy concludes the work by saying that he has included in it everything of practical utility, the whole being treated by "the sure methods of geometry and calculation." The fame of the work spread rapidly, and the *Almagest* became the subject of numerous commentaries, both in Greece and later among the Arabs. It was translated into Latin in the twelfth century, and in the following century it became the basis for the well-known *Sphaera* (q.v.) of Sacrobosco. For fourteen hundred years (i.e., until the time of Copernicus) the *Almagest* was almost universally accepted as the foundation of astronomical science.

ALSO SPRACH ZARATHUSTRA (1883–1891), by Friedrich Nietzsche. See THUS SPAKE ZARATHUSTRA, by Friedrich Nietzsche.

AMBASSADORS, THE (1903), by Henry James. This delightful novel narrates the reactions of several Americans to a European environment. Lambert Strether is sent as "ambassador" to Paris by his fiancée, the wealthy Mrs. Newsome. She wishes her son Chadwick to return to Woollett, Massachusetts, and carry on the business he has inherited. Chad is, moreover, reportedly entangled with a Parisian woman. Strether becomes acquainted with Waymarsh, another American traveling in Europe; Maria Gostrey, a sympathetic expatriate with whom he has a mild flirtation; Chad's mistress, the lovely Countess de Vionnet; and her daughter Jeanne. He becomes enchanted with the city himself, and stays on. As a result, Mrs. Newsome sends more ambassadors: her daughter and son-in-law, Sarah and Jim Pocock; and Jim's sister, the ingenuous Mamie, who had hoped to marry Chad. Although Strether finds comical the inability of these new ambassadors to appreciate Paris and its old-world air, he realizes he must return home. The established strain is too strong in him; but he advises Chad to remain and continue the fuller kind of life which he has been denied.

Novels by James which touch on a similar theme are *The American* (1877), and *The Europeans* (1878).

In *The American,* Christopher Newman, a wealthy American, visits Paris and falls in love with the aristocratic Claire de Cintré. Her family, particularly her brother, Count Valentin, and her mother, the Marquise, are much upset by their engagement. Valentin is killed in a duel over the daughter of Newman's French teacher; and Claire, having renounced the engagement, determines to become a nun. Through Mrs. Bread, an English maid, Newman learns that the proud old Marquise had killed her husband. Even when he threatens her with the evidence, however, she refuses to approve the marriage, and Newman, too disgusted with himself to reveal the crime, resigns himself to defeat by the mores of a culture he can neither understand nor combat.

In *The Europeans,* Eugenia, Baroness Münster, is the wife of a German prince who is about to repudiate the marriage for reasons of state. She goes to America with her brother, Felix Young, staying in Boston with her uncle, Mr. Wentworth. Wentworth's children, Gertrude, Charlotte and Clifford, and his sophisticated friend Mr. Acton, become friendly with the Europeans. Eugenia tries to entice Acton and Clifford, but fails; Clifford marries Acton's sister Lizzie, Gertrude marries Felix, Charlotte marries a minister, and Eugenia returns to Europe, discouraged by her unsuccessful fortune hunting.

AMELIA (1751), by Henry Fielding. This novel exposes the wickedness of the law courts and the evils of the English prisons of the eighteenth century. While confined in debtor's jail, William Booth, a simple-hearted, weak soul, innocently narrates his love and courtship of Amelia Harris, to a fellow prisoner, a Miss Matthews, an adventuress and murderess. Amelia's mother's opposition to the match had precipitated an elopement. An army lieutenant, William was soon ordered to take part in the siege of Gibraltar. He was severely wounded, and Amelia took him to Montpélier in France to recuperate. There they lived in the direst poverty until William was seized and flung into the debtor's prison. Miss Matthews seems sympathetic to his woes, and lures him into an amour which leaves him conscience-stricken. In the meantime Amelia, innocent in the ways of the world, is being preyed upon by many men, including William's false friend, Colonel James. But Amelia's purity is her shield. After the happy reunion of William and Amelia, despite the evil plottings of Miss Matthews, they again struggle with poverty. Amelia has generously forgiven his infidelity. A certain lord who has evil designs on Amelia induces Colonel Trent to gamble with the now desperate William and win fifty pounds from him. Unable to pay, William is again flung into the debtor's prison. But in the end virtue is triumphant. Amelia receives an inheritance through the true interpretation of a forged will, and she and William retire to the country to lead a serene life.

AMERICA (1918), by Sholem Asch. See NAZARENE, THE, by Sholem Asch.

AMERICA IN MIDPASSAGE (1939), by Charles A. Beard. See BEARD, CHARLES A.

AMERICA'S COMING-OF-AGE (1915), by Van Wyck Brooks. See FLOWERING OF NEW ENGLAND, THE, by Van Wyck Brooks.

AMERICAN, THE (1946), by Howard Fast. See CITIZEN TOM PAINE, by Howard Fast.

AMERICAN BEAUTY (1931), by Edna Ferber. See SHOW BOAT, by Edna Ferber.

AMERICAN COMMONWEALTH, THE (1888; revised 1910), by Viscount James Bryce. This monumental work is divided into six large sections. It deals with the social, economic, professional and political aspects of the American scene. Written in a straightforward style, the book is intelligible even to those uninitiated in government affairs. Parts of the book are used in American universities as supplementary reading in economics and sociology. The main divisions treat of the federal government, its judiciary, executive and legislative branches; county, state and municipal governments; political parties and machines; public opinion and its control; the strong and weak aspects of democracy; and the non-political institutions of "the nation of the future."

AMERICAN CRISIS, THE (1776–1783), by Thomas Paine. See COMMON SENSE, by Thomas Paine.

AMERICAN FOLKLORE, A TREASURY OF (1944), by Benjamin A. Botkin. See BOTKIN, BENJAMIN A.

AMERICAN FOREIGN POLICY IN THE MAKING: 1932–1940 (1946), by Charles A. Beard. See BEARD, CHARLES A.

AMERICAN LANGUAGE, THE (1919, 1945, 1948), by H. L. Mencken. A remarkable work of philology, this book refutes those who contend that there is no such thing as an American language. Mencken easily proves that there is, and that its evolution from "English English" to our own tongue has been so far-reaching that when an American and an Englishman meet, they are conscious of employing different languages. Supplements to *The American Language* appeared in 1945 and 1948. Mencken, during his long editorial and critical career, has exerted a profound influence upon the literary taste of the country, often working with George Jean Nathan. The two founded *The American Mercury* in 1923, and Mencken left the magazine in 1933. He sponsored such authors as Sinclair Lewis, Sherwood Anderson, Willa Cather, Ruth Suckow and Theodore Dreiser. For a long time, Mencken was an influential social critic as well. His *Selected Prejudices* (1927) ridiculed contemporary errors of opinion, and in general regarded with extreme skepticism all aspects of human behavior not condoned by enduring, scientific evidence. The author considered such diverse matters as politics, birth control, and writing as a profession. In 1949 he produced a volume of his collected works, the *Mencken Chrestomathy*.

AMERICAN MEMOIR (1947), by Henry Seidel Canby. See CANBY, HENRY SEIDEL.

AMERICAN SONGBAG, THE (1927), by Carl Sandburg. See SANDBURG, CARL.

AMERICAN TRAGEDY, AN (1925), by Theodore Dreiser. Clyde Griffiths has been raised in poverty by Kansas City street evangelists. Longing for wealth and social freedom, he first glimpses the excitement of a different world as a hotel bellhop. He does not perceive its moral shabbiness, however, and allows undesirable company to lead him into personal difficulties which force him to leave the city. Samuel Griffiths, a wealthy uncle, gives Clyde a humble position in his collar factory in Lycurgus, New York. The Griffiths do not accept him socially, and Clyde finds intimate companionship with Roberta Alden, an employee in his department. Clyde still has social aspirations, and presently falls in love with wealthy Sondra Finchley, who is ignorant of his background. He becomes frantic when Roberta, who is pregnant, demands that he marry her. The thought of Roberta's death becomes an obsession with Clyde. Finally, he plans a trip to a lake resort with her. At the last moment, he is unable to carry out his intention of drowning Roberta, but when the boat accidentally upsets, he lets her sink, and escapes. The remainder of the novel details his detection, arrest and trial. Clyde is sentenced to death, and at the end gropes toward a spiritual understanding of his anguished life.

Dreiser, brought up in a poor but religious background, became a famous figure with the publication of his first novel, *Sister Carrie* (q.v.). He was a literary giant after *Jennie Gerhardt* (q.v.). There followed the Cowperwood trilogy (q.v.); *The Genius* (1915), story of a midwestern artist, Eugene Witla, who climbs the ladder of New York social and financial success only to suffer a breakdown due to intemperate living, and finally again devotes himself to creative painting, and the education of the child of his dead wife, Angela Blue;

and *The Bulwark* (1946), a novel concerning spiritual values in modern life.

Dreiser, traditionally characterized as a technically clumsy, but realistic and forceful writer, has also produced poetry, short stories, essays, plays, autobiography, and books about contemporary politics.

AMERICANS, THE (1877), by Henry James. See AMBASSADORS, THE, by Henry James.

AMERICANIZATION OF EDWARD BOK, THE (1920), by Edward Bok. This autobiography of the little Dutch immigrant who came to New York at the age of seven and at the age of 26 was Editor of the *Ladies' Home Journal* is a rambling chronicle of Bok's life, his influential editorial and business affairs, and the eminent people he met in a long and prosperous career. The author adopts the literary device of third person narration. This book, which was awarded the Pulitzer Prize in 1921, is often held up as an example of the opportunities which America offers to all.

AMERIKA (1928), by Franz Kafka. See TRIAL, THE, by Franz Kafka.

AMICA DELLE MOGLI, L' (1927), by Luigi Pirandello. See PIRANDELLO, LUIGI.

AMIEL'S JOURNAL (1882), by Henri Frédéric Amiel. Not written for publication, and published posthumously, the *Journal* is the story of Amiel's failure and disillusion. "What interests me in myself," he writes, "is that I find in my own case a genuine example of human nature, and therefore a specimen of general value." Actually, the value of the *Journal* lies in the account it presents of an unusual pursuit of an inaccessible ideal. Amiel aspires to perfection, nothing less—and knows that he has not attained it. "The real disgusts me," he writes, "and I cannot find the ideal." The thought, all the more because Amiel possesses a profound critical faculty, paralyzes his ability to act. Yet it is clear that he is no mere sour misanthrope, but a kindly, amiable, unduly sensitive man who loves mankind. He confesses to having "too much imagination, conscience, and penetration, and not enough character." He is the classic case of frustration in a modern world, which seems to him barbarous, materialistic, noisy, greedy. He believes much of the solution lies in religion. Otherwise his book, very much like Henry Adams' *Education* (q.v.), foresees disaster, for man's moral energy has not kept up with the mechanistic progress he has devised.

AMORE DELLE TRE MELARANCIE, L' (1761), by Carlo Gozzi. See GOZZI, CARLO.

AMORETTI (1595), by Edmund Spenser. In this, one of the three most important (along with Shakespeare's and Sidney's) Elizabethan sonnet-sequences, Spenser was apparently recounting his courtship of Elizabeth Boyle, the lady he married. The lover is desperate but importunate, the mistress conventionally proud: "Sweet warrior, when shall I have peace with you?" The contest is carried on through eighty-eight sonnets that are unusually musical by virtue of their interlinked quatrains reminiscent of the Spenserian stanza.

AMPHITRYON, by Plautus (Titus Maccius Plautus; 254–184 b.c.). Plautus' comedy is the earliest dramatic version of the Amphitryon story, so persistently popular and played in many adaptations in the theatre, from his time down to our own. It actually antedates the Roman dramatist who based his works upon Greek comedies. But as the Greek original is no longer extant, it is Plautus to whom we are indebted for the standard version. The story is simple. Jupiter, inexhaustibly amorous and versatile beyond imagining in his modes of courtship, presenting himself in forms varying from swans to cattle to showers of gold, fastens his eye upon the lovely Alcmena, wife of Amphitryon, a general of Thebes. As the good lady is incorruptible to a degree, he resorts to a stratagem while Amphitryon is away at the wars. Jupiter assumes her husband's form and presents himself to Alcmena on the pretext that he is home on a brief visit from the front. Accordingly, he spends a night with her, resorting to Joshua's stratagem of stopping the movement of the sun and the stars, but for the less worthy purpose of lengthening the night instead of the day. Under these circumstances he begets the demigod Hercules. Amphitryon himself now returns, but finds Alcmena surprisingly cold and, convinced she has been unfaithful, he sets out to denounce her to her kinsmen. Returning again, he finds Jupiter closeted with Alcmena and himself locked out. Beside himself at this insult, he becomes violent and must be silenced by a thunderbolt. Subsequently he learns the truth, but with the customary respect of a devout mortal for the father of the gods, does not attempt to make anything of it, inasmuch as a bit of divine infiltration in the family stock was a point of honor and pride among the noble families of Greece. A subordinate line of low comedy follows the antics of Mercury, who aids and abets his master in the guise of Amphitryon's servant, Sosia. Among the many adaptations, that of Molière is notable. The most recent is by Jean Giraudoux under the title *Amphitryon 38* (ostensibly because it is the 38th version) which was produced in this country with Alfred Lunt and Lynn Fontanne in an American version by S. N. Behrman.

ANABASIS (ca. 400 B.C.), by Xenophon. In seven books the work recounts in dramatic narrative form the luckless expedition of Cyrus the Younger from Sardis to the Euphrates, and the retreat of the "Ten Thousand" Greek mercenaries who accompanied him. Xenophon, who belonged to the Athenian order of knights, had been an admirer of Socrates. When his friend Proxenus, a military adventurer, organized his contingent of the Ten Thousand to fight with Cyrus, who wished to dethrone his brother Artaxerxes, Xenophon accepted the invitation to accompany him. This expedition occupied him from 401 to 399 B.C. The *Anabasis,* which in Greek means "the march inland," tells how Cyrus was killed in battle near Babylon and the Greek force left without an employer. During negotiations with Artaxerxes, five of the Greek generals were treacherously killed. Thereupon the Ten Thousand, with Xenophon now one of its new generals, began their epic retreat, fighting almost every inch of the way through hostile territory in Kurdistan, Armenia and Georgia, to the Black Sea. They continued their desperate struggle through Byzantium and Thrace, by which time they had already been reduced to six thousand men. Memorable is Xenophon's description of the manner in which he and his exhausted compatriots first caught sight of the sea which meant safety and home at last, after their terrible experiences: "Presently they could hear the soldiers shouting and passing on the joyful word, 'The sea! The sea!' Thereupon they began running, rearguard and all, and the baggage animals and horses came galloping up. But when they had reached the summit, then indeed they fell to embracing one another—generals and officers and all—and the tears trickled down their cheeks." The *Anabasis* drew attention to the many vital weaknesses of the great Persian Empire. A Greek writer commented several centuries later: "Alexander the Great could not have been great had not Xenophon been."

ANACREON (6th-5th c. b.c.). A native of Ionia in Asia Minor, Anacreon fled before the Persians and lived as a court poet with Polycrates of Samos and Hipparchus of Athens. Of his genial poetry of wine, love and good fellowship, we have only a few fragmentary bits. For the ancients he came to typify the bibulous and amorous oldster who has outlived his gayer days but still casts a nostalgic if good humored eye on wine and women in his songs. His style was much imitated, and we still have a collection of sixty so-called *Anacreontics,* which were written at various dates from the Alexandrine to the Byzantine eras. These *Anacreontics* were long popular with English readers in the translations of Cowley and Moore, and were supposed to be true works of Anacreon.

ANATHEMA (1909), by Leonid Andreyev. Anathema is the name given to the Devil in this tragedy in seven scenes. The drama is charged with the spirit of revolt against all accepted dogmas of good and evil, reward and punishment. In the Prologue, Anathema calls upon the Guardian of the Gates of Eternity to give him but a glimpse of the eternal mysteries, for he, Anathema, is in the same state of troubled confusion as mankind. He wants to be enlightened in order that he might be able to help man understand all absolute values. But the Gates remain closed and the question unanswered. In the guise of a crafty lawyer, Anathema seeks out a pious old Jew, David Leiter, who is slowly dying of hunger and misery in a wretched Russian town. Nevertheless, the old Jew remains righteous. Anathema showers millions of rubles upon him. Old David cannot be tempted; he distributes all this money to the poor. Foiled in his cynical designs, Anathema summons all the outcasts and miscreants on earth, who rob David of his last kopek and, because he cannot provide for them by means of a miracle, they stone him to death. In an Epilogue, Anathema once more comes before the Gates of Eternity and hurls his challenge at the Guardian, to explain to him where God's justice is. Did not David demonstrate by the failure of his virtuous life the sterility of love? The Guardian denies his accusation. Old David, he says, will forevermore live in the memory of man and in the deathlessness of his virtue. As for Anathema, never will he succeed in comprehending the radiant *raison d'être* of goodness and life. Anathema, eternally in revolt, replies to the Guardian with cries of defiance and maledictions.

ANATOL (1893), by Arthur Schnitzler. See SCHNITZLER, ARTHUR.

ANATOMICAL DISQUISITION ON THE MOVEMENT OF THE HEART AND THE CIRCULATION OF THE BLOOD, AN (1628), by William Harvey. See DE MOTU CORDIS ET SANGUINIS, by William Harvey.

ANATOMY OF MELANCHOLY, THE (1621), by Robert Burton. Published at Oxford, this remarkable work of rambling philosophic-scientific reflections has as its full title: *The Anatomy of Melancholy, What it is. With all the Kindes, Causes, Symptomes, Prognostickes, and severall Cures of it. In Three Maine Partitions, with their severall Sections, Members, and Subsections. Philosophically, Medicinally, Historically, opened and cut up. By Democritus Junior. With a Satyricall Preface, conducing to the following Discourse. Macrob. Omne Meum, Nihil Meum.* The Latin motto refers to Burton's penchant for working quotations, usually in Latin, into his own long sentences. ("It's all mine and none mine.")

The book discusses diseases in general, and diseases of the mind in particular. Burton discourses on the anatomy of the body and the anatomy of the soul. After that he proposes to "perspicuously define what this Melancholy is," its major causes, love and religion. The author's juxtaposition of satire and earnestness leaves one in doubt whether he was at all serious about his project. Burton concludes that the whole world is more or less mad. Undeniably *The Anatomy of Melancholy* is one of the oddest, wittiest and most learned books in English literature.

ANATOMY OF WIT, THE (1579), by John Lyly. See EUPHUES, by John Lyly.

ANCIENT MARINER, THE RIME OF THE (1798), by Samuel Taylor Coleridge. This strange melodic ballad in 625 lines tells of a mariner with hypnotic eye who stops one of three wedding guests and compels him to listen to his story of lost and returned grace on board ship. The mariner, when his ship had been driven by a storm toward the South Pole, killed the bird of good omen, the albatross, and that is the start of all his troubles—the becalmed ship, the specter-woman and her death-mate, the crew's dropping dead one by one, until the mariner is "alone on a wide wide sea." But he blesses the water-snakes, and that is the beginning of better luck. Angelic spirits guide the ship back to the mariner's own country, and ever since, for penance, he has been compelled to journey from land to land, teaching by his example love and reverence to all God's creatures.

ANCIENT REGIME, THE (1875), by Hippolyte Taine. See ORIGINS OF CONTEMPORARY FRANCE, THE, by Hippolyte Taine.

ANCRENRIWLE, or RULE OF NUNS (13th c.). An unknown ecclesiastic was the author of this treatise on the duties of convent life. It was written for the guidance of three nuns of noble rank who presided over a convent in Dorsetshire. In eight parts, it presents a daily schedule of activities: prayer, work and charity. It warns against the seven deadly sins, prescribes a program for the discipline of the heart and the senses by confession and penance. The author warns the "anchoresses" against having too much commerce with the sinful outside world: "Make ye no banquetings, nor allure ye not to the gate no strange vagabonds . . . it would other while hinder heavenly thoughts . . . An anchoress ought not to have anything that draweth outward her heart." What then was the ideal she should follow? "A good nun is silent like Our Lady, not a hen like cackling Eve." Versions exist in French and Latin.

ANDROCLES AND THE LION (1916), by George Bernard Shaw. Androcles, a humble Greek tailor converted to Christianity, has a love for animals. While he and his querulous wife, Megaera, are journeying through a jungle in North Africa, they encounter a savage lion with a wounded paw, from which Androcles extracts a large thorn. Later, Androcles is seized with other Christians and brought to Rome to be thrown to the beasts. The band of prisoners sing hymns and joke about their fate, to the annoyance of their captors. A handsome Captain of the Guard is in love with Lavinia, one of the prisoners, and tries to persuade her to recant, but she remains steadfast. Ferrovius, a blacksmith, is afraid he will forget himself in an un-Christian manner and resist the gladiators, and this is just what happens in the arena. He kills six gladiators single-handed, much to the admiration of the Emperor. Androcles finds himself face to face with his jungle friend, who saves his life. The Emperor is so amazed that he pardons Androcles along with the other prisoners. This has been called "a comedy of saintliness" by the critic, John Gassner, who observes that it demonstrates, sympathetically and affectionately, that "Saints differ as much as other men, for saintliness can be sought by both the weak and the courageous, by the most intelligent thinkers and the most innocent of heart." The Preface, on Christianity, is one of the most searching of Shaw's prefaces, almost dwarfing the play.

ANDROMACHE (ca. 426 B.C.), by Euripides. One of Euripides' lesser tragedies, the story falls into two loosely connected parts. The characters are singularly savage and cruel. In Menelaus and his daughter, Hermione, Euripides has embodied all the most detestable Spartan characteristics which roused the hatred of the Athenians. The scene is laid in Thessaly before the temple of Thetis. Trojan Andromache, Hector's widow, is now the slave and concubine of Neoptolemus (Pyrrhus), son of Achilles. Neoptolemus, who is absent on a trip to the oracle at Delphi, has married Hermione, daughter of Menelaus. The latter is jealous of Andromache, because she has borne Neoptolemus a child, Molossus, while the Queen herself is childless. Hermione and her father plan to kill Andromache and Molossus while Neoptolemus is away. Menelaus has his guards seize and bind Andromache, but fortunately Neoptolemus' grandfather enters at this moment. He orders that Andromache be freed, and takes her and Molossus under his protection. In the second part, Hermione is in dread of Neoptolemus' return and his reaction when he learns of her attempt to kill Andromache and Molossus. Orestes, Hermione's cousin to whom she had been betrothed, stops in Thessaly on his way to the oracle at Dodona. Hermione tells him her fears and begs him to take her to her father, which he does. The grandfather of Neoptolemus, Peleus, comes to verify the rumor of their departure. A messenger arrives with news of the death of Neoptolemus, who has been killed by the citizens of Delphi. They had risen against him under the influence of Orestes. The goddess Thetis visits her husband, Peleus, and tells him to send Andromache and her child to Molossia, and to bury Neoptolemus in Delphi.

ANDROMAQUE (1667), by Jean Baptiste Racine. Racine opens his drama with the arrival of Orestes at Buthrotum to request Pyrrhus to give up Andromache's son by Hector, Astyanax, to the Greeks. Orestes is hopelessly in love with Hermione, the daughter of Menelaus and Helen, who in turns loves Pyrrhus, to whom she is betrothed. But Pyrrhus postpones the marriage because he is now in love with his captive, Andromache. She refuses his suit. Promising Andromache he will not give up Astyanax, he now prepares to marry Hermione, inviting Orestes to be present at the ceremony. After Andromache has appealed to Hermione to protect her son and is scornfully refused, she learns that Pyrrhus, for reasons of policy, intends to give Astyanax to the Greeks, and, overcoming her hatred, promises to marry him in order to save her son. Pyrrhus breaks off his match with Hermione, telling her he must follow the dictates of his heart and marry the beautiful Trojan. Hermione, in a jealous rage, appeals to Orestes to avenge her by killing Pyrrhus at the altar. When he does so, her rage turns to remorse, and she stabs herself on the body of Pyrrhus. Orestes, now insane, is borne out unconscious by his friends. *Andromaque* is considered one of the most successful of Racine's stately psychological tragedies. Others are *Phèdre* (q.v.), *Bérénice* (1670), *Britannicus* (1669), *Athalie* (q.v.) and *Esther* (1689). All are written in a subtle verse which consistently baffles his translators.

ANECDOTA (ca. 575), by Procopius of Caesarea. See HISTORY OF THE WARS, by Procopius of Caesarea.

ANGLO-SAXON CHRONICLE, THE (ca. 10th c.). Amplified toward the end of the tenth century by order of Alfred the Great, in his attempt to revive English civilization after he had defeated the Danes in the field, this ancient record, or rather, set of records, is pagan in feeling, and some of it dates from pre-Christian times. Its language is rude and its style is formless. It was written for the greater part by the monks of the monasteries at Winchester, Canterbury, Abingdon, Worcester, and later at Peterborough. That part of the *Chronicle* which had been written up to the time of Alfred was nothing more than a genealogy of the West Saxon kings until the death of Aethelwulf. Alfred caused it to be expanded to include the events of his own reign. He thus converted the genealogical record into the beginnings of a history of the English people.

ANIMAL KINGDOM, THE (1932), by Philip Barry. See BARRY, PHILIP.

ANIMAL KINGDOM, THE (1817), by Georges Cuvier. See RÈGNE ANIMAL, LE, by Georges Cuvier.

ANN VERONICA (1909), by H. G. Wells. Wells has explained: "My book was written primarily to express the resentment and distress which many women feel nowadays at their unavoidable practical dependence upon some individual man not of their deliberate choice, and in full sympathy with the natural but perhaps anarchistic and anti-social idea that it is intolerable for a woman to have sexual relations with a man with whom she is not in love, and natural and desirable and admirable for her to want them and still more so to want children by a man of her own selection." This, in brief, is the theme of this thesis novel.

Ann Veronica Stanley, twenty-one and intelligent, who always had been obedient to the direction of her father and aunt, suddenly decides to break out of the loving confinement of her home and learn what life is like. She goes to London and devotes herself to the study of biology. Soon, however, she finds herself hampered in her career by a lack of funds. She begins to realize that it is a man's world and that, without her family's aid, she is quite helpless. Determined to alter matters, Ann Veronica joins the Women's Suffrage movement and is sent to jail for her loyalty to it. Later she falls in love with Capes, a married man. She frankly confesses her love. To avoid trouble with malicious "Mrs. Grundy" she and Capes go abroad together and find happiness, despite the gossip and scandal. In the end they are able to get married and return to England to satisfy the moral-legal sanctions of society.

The other characters are Ann Veronica's father, Peter Stanley, a smug solicitor; Tedd Widgett and his badminton-playing sisters; the wealthy broker, Ramage; Miss Miniver; Lady Palsworthy and her nephew, Mr. Manning; Ann's sisters, Gwen and Alice; and Miss Klegg.

ANN VICKERS (1933), by Sinclair Lewis. See ARROWSMITH, by Sinclair Lewis.

ANNA CHRISTIE (1921), by Eugene O'Neill. Old Chris Christopherson, captain of a coal barge, welcomes his daughter Anna, whom he has not seen in fifteen years. During a voyage from New York, she begins to forget all the tawdry developments which have coarsened her life since seduction by a cousin at the age of sixteen. Among shipwrecked sailors whom the barge picks up is Mat Burke, a great-hearted stoker, who falls in love with the girl. When Anna reveals her former life, and both Chris and Mat are crushed, she despairs; but Mat, after a drinking bout with Chris, returns to her. She promises to wait for the two men, who have signed up for a voyage on the same ship.

ANNA KARENINA (1874–1876), by Count Leo Tolstoy. Of *Anna Karenina*, one of the great novels of the world, Matthew Arnold has said: "We are not to take *Anna Karenina* as a work of art; we are to take it as a piece of life." It is a chronicle of Russian life, passionate and moving, and written with a simplicity which defies analysis. It confirms Tolstoy's deserved reputation as the master portrayer of the normal.

The story is woven in two strands. One concerns Anna Karenina and Count Vronsky; the other, Kitty Oblonsky and Konstantin Levin. The latter is more or less the mouthpiece for Tolstoy's own ideas about what life should be. Indeed, it is generally conceded that Levin is drawn from the author himself. These two strands are knotted at the outset when Levin comes to Moscow to propose to Kitty. Kitty rejects him, for she is in love with Vronsky. But Anna, who is the wife of Aleksey Aleksandrovitch Karenin, a Minister of the Government, is also visiting Moscow, and Vronsky falls in love with her. Her relationship with her husband is cold and unhappy. She returns Vronsky's love and is too forthright and passionate to dissemble. She breaks with her husband, even though it means losing her beloved child. Later she bears an illegitimate daughter to Vronsky. Anna and her lover are both persons of integrity and high character, but the inexorable pressures of society, the reminders of the opportunities lost by each, insidiously prey upon each of them. It is the impulsive, brooding Anna who first finds the strain unendurable and who flings herself under the wheels of a train.

The story of Levin and Kitty is the antithesis of this tragic history. Levin is over-serious, amiable, but rather tedious in his obsession with the revolution in living standards; he harps on social theories and religion. His courtship of Kitty is a somewhat clumsy affair, requiring as it does first his slow recovery from the wound of her initial rejection, and the mending of Kitty's vanity from the jilting by Vronsky. They settle down to a dull and commonplace existence.

The transcendent portions of the book are to be found in the observation of the progressive deterioration of the relationship between Anna and Vronsky. We see them fly from pillar to post, from Petersburg to Moscow, to Italy, to Vronsky's country estates; from dabbling in art to community good works—all in the effort to settle themselves in a free life. But society will not tolerate their honest relationship. It requires of them deceit, and pretense—the one price their natures forbid them to pay. Tolstoy makes it clear that their doom is foreordained with a positiveness in direct ratio to their honesty.

The book is rich in character studies. None of its figures is more complex than the lonely, tragic, well-meaning, exasperating, fumbling, pompous and frightened Karenin. In spite of the hateful and neurotic mannerisms of his personality, he attains at times a magnanimity of the highest order. With his peculiar genius Tolstoy reveals Anna's self-responsibility for much of the consequences of her social defiance. Nothing but her own pique and perverse contrariness prevent her from obtaining a divorce and freedom to marry Vronsky. That Karenin later vacillates and is hardened by the pressure of malicious friends, need not have made the debacle inevitable.

ANNALS (ca. 115-117), by Gaius Cornelius Tacitus. Nominally a history of the early Roman Empire (14-68), this is actually a series of psychological biographies of the several Roman emperors, their families and courtiers, from Tiberius to Nero. Although this work consisted originally of sixteen books, VII-X are lost entirely and we have only portions of V, XI, and XVI. The first six books deal with the reign of Tiberius, the next four cover those of Caligula and Claudius, and the last six books are concerned with that of Nero. Tacitus was inspired in his writing, with great moral fervor and a bitter hatred of the despotism and corruption of the reigns of these four emperors. With his concise, pungent and dramatic style he subtly builds up prejudice which, as in the case of Tiberius, requires considerable correction. Typical of his dramatic style is the description of the violent death of Nero's mother at the hands of her son's emissaries in Book XIV. Most celebrated is the account of Nero's persecution of Roman Christians to divert attention from the conflagration of Rome for which he was suspected of being responsible. Tacitus had a high conception of his duty as a historian. He says, "My purpose is to relate a few facts about Augustus—more particularly his last acts, then the reign of Tiberius, and all which follows, *without either bitterness or partiality . . .*"

But his moral convictions and bent for dramatic writing result in impressionistic sketches rather than cold, factual history.

ANNUS MIRABILIS (1667), by John Dryden. See DRYDEN, JOHN.

ANOTHER PART OF THE FOREST (1947), by Lillian Hellman. See HELLMAN, LILLIAN.

ANTHOLOGY OF KOREAN POEMS (1923), edited by Choi Nam-Sun. See SHIJO-YUCHIP, edited by Choi Nam-Sun.

ANTHONY ADVERSE (1933), by Hervey Allen. Anthony Adverse is the illegitimate son of Maria, Scotch wife of Don Luis da Vincitata, and Captain Denis Moore. Don Luis kills Moore when he discovers the truth, and Maria dies in childbirth. The orphaned boy is educated at an Italian convent; and his adventures begin when he is apprenticed to John Bonny-feather, a wealthy Leghorn merchant, and Maria's father. A romantic story unfolds against an international historical background. Anthony meets Napoleon in Italy; travels to Havana, where a "miracle" is performed; meets and loves Dolores; visits Africa as a slave trader, and has a love affair with Neleta, a half-breed; goes to France with Napoleon on business; then to England, Holland, Spain and America.

Anthony falls in love with Angela Guessippi, a singer and childhood friend from Leghorn, but she prefers to continue her career. The lovers meet seven years later in Paris, and Anthony finds that he has a son. Angela, now famous, is one of Napoleon's favorites. Anthony leaves his son with a friend, Vincent Nolte, and travels on to New Orleans. In the new world, he marries Florence Parish and finds contentment at their ranch, Silver Ho.

With the tragic deaths of his wife and daughter, Anthony's fortunes begin to decline. He meets Don Luis, now Military Governor of Northern Mexico, and as a prisoner is exposed to the old man's hatred. In Mexico, he meets Dolores again and marries her. He is accidentally killed while felling trees; his last words are prayers to the little Madonna, which had belonged to his mother, Maria, and from which he never parted.

The publication of Allen's nineteen-pound manuscript, which had taken him four years to write, started a new craze for historical romances in the 1930's. He himself wrote another, *Action at Aquila* (1938), a novel of the Civil War, and is engaged at present in a five-novel sequence of eighteenth century frontier life (*The Forest and the Fort,* 1943; *Bedford Village,* 1944; *Toward the Morning* 1948); but he regards himself primarily as a poet. Indeed, from his earliest work in the post-war poetry movement, he was a popular writer.

Allen also published a record of war experiences, *Toward the Flame* (1926), and a biography of Edgar Allan Poe, *Israfel* (1926). This latter is documented by long-neglected and somewhat unromantic sources, and gives a new portrait of Poe. The pathetic details of Poe's struggle for existence are indeed more valuable than the usual psychological-romantic "Poe mystery." This is an unprejudiced account of the poet's personality and career, written by a serious man of letters.

ANTIC HAY (1923), by Aldous Huxley. Says one of the characters in *Antic Hay,* "I am interested in everything," to which the reply is made,

"Which comes to the same thing as being interested in nothing." In this sense *Antic Hay* may be called a book about everything and nothing. It is a pure product of post-World-War I intellectual nihilism. This is the world in which there came ultimately the sharp cleavage between those who shook off despair and stepped out toward a progressive world and those who embraced the decadence and moral bankruptcy of which Fascism became the political ideal.

This book precedes the more mature *Point Counter Point* (q.v.), in which Huxley was able to isolate sharply the symptoms of this ultimate division. *Antic Hay* is a rotation in the orbit of an aimless and deteriorating society seen primarily through the eyes of the young idler Theodore Gumbril. It is peopled by a Huxleyesque galaxy of characters, fascinating in themselves, ranging from the absent-minded scientist Shearwater and the degenerate Coleman, who can be compared only to the more highly developed Spandrell of *Point Counter Point* to the grotesque Casimir Lypiatt with his unfounded genius complex.

ANTIEK TOERISME (1911), by Louis Couperus. See COUPERUS, LOUIS.

ANTIGONE (ca. 440 B.C.), by Sophocles. A sequel to the tragic story of Oedipus, King of Thebes, who had surrendered his throne to his two sons, Eteocles and Polynices. By agreement between them, the sons were to rule alternately, but the first refused to yield to the second in his turn. Polynices, thus betrayed, brought the armies of seven allied chieftains against Thebes to fight for his rights. The war was bitter and in the course of it, although the invaders were repulsed, the brothers met in personal combat and slew one another. Thereupon their uncle, Creon, became king. At the opening of the play Creon has issued a decree forbidding anyone upon pain of death to give burial to the body of Polynices, a decree which flouted the most sacred duty of a family to bury its dead. Antigone, a sister of Polynices, who is imbued with a high sense of family duty and piety and endowed with a will and determination that is inflexible to a fault, flies in the face of the despotic decree. When her more feminine sister, Ismene, refuses to stand with her, she goes alone at night and performs the symbolic burial by sprinkling a few handfuls of dust on the body before she is apprehended by Creon's guard. Creon is swift to inflict punishment and orders Antigone shut up in a cave to die. An appeal from his son, Haemon, to whom Antigone is betrothed, is of no avail, but his will is finally bent by the words of the prophet Tiresias. While Polynices is being buried, it is discovered upon opening the cave that Antigone has taken her own life. Haemon, after driving his father away, falls on his sword and dies by Antigone's side. When this word is brought to Haemon's mother, she too takes her life and fills Creon's cup of remorse.

ANTIQUITIES OF ROME, THE (1558), by Joachim du Bellay. See DU BELLAY, JOACHIM.

ANTIQUITIES OF THE JEWS (93), by Flavius Josephus. The twenty books into which Josephus' Greek history of the Jews is divided were not written by the Jewish historian for Jewish readers, but for the Graeco-Roman world. Although Josephus takes his readers down the long corridors of Jewish history, beginning with the Creation, the really significant part of his chronicle concerns the events in Palestine that took place in his own day: ". . . for since I myself had witnessed the war which we Jews had with the Romans, and knew its particular actions, and conclusion, I felt forced to give the history of it, because of those who perverted the truth in their writings." This "perversion" of the truth was due to the fact that many Jews accused Josephus, who had earlier been a Jewish general and priest, of betraying Jerusalem to Titus. The warm welcome he found at Rome under Vespasian and his long residence there as a court pensioner only strengthened this belief.

Book I: Interval of 3,833 years, from creation to the death of Isaac. Book II: Interval of 220 years, from the death of Isaac to the Exodus from Egypt. Book III: Interval of two years, from the Exodus to the rejection of that generation. Book IV: Interval of 38 years, to the death of Moses. Book V: Interval of 476 years, to the death of Eli. Book VI: Interval of 32 years, to the death of Saul. Book VII: Interval of 40 years, to the death of David. Book VIII: Interval of 163 years, to the death of Ahab. Book IX: Interval of 150 years, to the captivity of the ten tribes. Book X: Interval of 182 years, to the first year of Cyrus' reign. Book XI: Interval of 253 years, to the death of Alexander the Great. Book XII: Interval of 170 years, to the death of Judas Maccabeus. Book XIII: Interval of 82 years, to the death of Queen Alexandra. Book XIV: Interval of 32 years, to the death of Antigonus. Book XV: Interval of 18 years, to the finishing of the temple by Herod. Book XVI: Interval of 12 years, to the death of Alexander and Aristobulus. Book XVII: Interval of 14 years, to the banishment of Archelaus. Book XVIII: Interval of 32 years, to the departure of the Jews from Babylon. Book XIX: Interval of 3½ years, to Fadus, the Roman Procurator. Book XX: Interval of 22 years, to Florus, the 56th year of Josephus' own life.

ANTIQUITY OF MAN (1863), by Sir Charles Lyell. This is one of the earliest works on anthropology. Lyell had been an early advocate of the geological doctrine of "uniformitarianism," and his *Principles of Geology* (1830–1833), show that, geologically, ancient conditions were in essence similar to those of our time. This book appeared in more than a dozen editions. His *Elements of Geology* (1838), a work on paleontological geology, went through half a dozen editions in his lifetime. (It was Lyell who introduced the word "paleontology" into English.) Lyell had studied the biological theories of Lamarck and held to the view that land animals were derived by "gradual evolution" from "certain organisms of the ocean." He had studied tertiary fossils in Italy and coal formations in Nova Scotia. Lyell was responsible for the recognition and naming of the ages known as Eocene, Miocene, and Pliocene. It was after reading Darwin's *Origin of Species* (q.v.) that he resolved to investigate the early existence of mankind. The result was Lyell's third great work, *The Antiquity of Man,* in which he gathered together all available evidence of prehistoric man. He was the first to study the descent of man from the standpoint of comparative anatomy and geologic age.

The author's final acceptance of Darwinism is indicated by the full title— *Geological Evidences of the Antiquity of Man with Remarks on Theories of the Origin of Species by Variation*—and the author's temperate presentation did much to mitigate the bitterness of the evolution controversy. In this book the succession of cultures, crafts and arts from Paleolithic Man to Neolithic Man are linked with geographical and geological changes. Lyell gave a survey of the arguments for man's early appearance on the earth, derived from the study of artifacts discovered in post-Pliocene strata; and he discussed flint implements found in deposits of the glacial epochs. *The Antiquity of Man* appeared in numerous editions, running through three editions in the first year. Since his time the cultures of the "stone ages" have been the subject of numerous studies.

ANTONY AND CLEOPATRA (1606–1607?; printed in 1623), by William Shakespeare. Antony, one of the Triumvirate of Rome, is wholly absorbed in an affair with Cleopatra in Alexandria, when a messenger brings news that Fulvia, his wife, is dead. He feels that he must return to Rome to look after his affairs. The other two triumvirs, Octavius Caesar and Lepidus, are fighting Pompey. Antony joins them, and to cement their friendship he and Caesar agree that he shall marry Caesar's sister, Octavia. When Cleopatra hears the news of Antony's wedding, she strikes the messenger in a rage. The triumvirs make peace with Pompey, and Antony and Octavia leave Rome for Athens. Caesar's speeches have offended Antony. When Octavia goes to Rome to act as mediator, Antony returns to Cleopatra and assembles a large force of men for war. Cleopatra foolishly visits his camp at Actium. He hopes to fight Caesar at sea, but his friend, Enobarbus, warns him that his ships are poorly armed, that Cæsar's sailors are veterans of the war with Pompey.

In the sea fight that follows, Cleopatra flees in her ship at the critical moment; Antony loses his head and follows her. He is defeated and reduced to sending his schoolmaster, Euphronius, as ambassador to Caesar. He sees Thyreus, Caesar's special messenger to Cleopatra, kissing her hand, and has him whipped for his impudence, sending him back to his master with a scornful message. Realizing that his star is waning, Antony bids an affectionate farewell to his retainers. He finally loses to Caesar in another sea fight, and the Egyptian fleet yields to the Romans. Miserable, he turns on Cleopatra. In retaliation, she causes him to be informed that she is dead. The grief-stricken Antony asks his friend Eros to kill him; when he refuses, Antony falls on his sword. Cleopatra sends word, too late, that she is alive; the dying Antony is brought to her. In the end, to escape being taken to Rome in triumph by Caesar, Cleopatra commits suicide, by allowing herself to be bitten by an asp.

It is one of Shakespeare's maturest plays, though difficult to stage because of the multitude and diversity of its scenes.

APARTMENT IN ATHENS (1945), by Glenway Wescott. See GRANDMOTHERS, THE, by Glenway Wescott.

APHORISMS (ca. 415 B.C.), by Hippocrates. This is probably the best-known of the body of works called "the Hippocratic Collection." Culled from his medical treatises, especially "The Prognostics," "On the Articulations," and "On Airs, Waters, and Places," the *Aphorisms* of the founder of Greek medical science achieved such wide acceptance and circulation that numerous interpolations inevitably crept into them, as they do frequently into works of great popularity. The work is divided into seven sections, containing from twenty-five to eighty-eight aphorisms each. The first aphorism in Section I has become proverbial: "Life is short, the Art long; opportunity fleeting; experience treacherous, and judgment difficult. The Physician must be prepared not only to do what is right himself, but also to make the patient, the attendants, and externals cooperate." The twenty-five aphorisms that follow relate principally to dietetics and to gastro-intestinal conditions, i.e., Aphorism Four: "A diet brought to the extreme point of attenuation is dangerous; and repletion, when in the extreme, is also dangerous." Section II is devoted largely to prognosis; Section III to the temperatures of the seasons and the diseases associated with them, the different ages and the diseases peculiar to them; Section IV concerns purgings, sweats and fevers, and is principally drawn from "The Prognostics" and "The Coan Praenotions." Section V considers diagnostic and prognostic rules; Sections VI and VII relate to a class of cases which, in the ancient system of prognostics, were called superventions, i.e., those supervening or coming on another disease, as a fever upon pleurisy. Medical scientists of today look back with respect upon the advanced knowledge Hippocrates possessed for his time. These precepts, observations and summations represent the culmination of Greek inquiry into the problems of healing and of maintaining health. The Hippocratic Oath, which all physicians take on graduation from medical school, pledges the doctor to unselfish service in his profession.

APHRODITE (1896), by Pierre Louys. In the year 58 B.C. Queen Berenike of Egypt falls passionately in love with the handsome Greek sculptor, Demetrios of Alexandria. But the love, honors and power she offers him are useless. He is enamored of his statue of Aphrodite. Berenike pleads for his love. He spurns her. Then, one night on the streets of Alexandria, Demetrios meets the beautiful courtesan, Chrysis of Galilee, and falls in love with her. She remains elusive, and to torment him and turn him completely to her, she asks him to fulfill three of her wishes: he must steal the mirror of Rhodopis from her friend Bacchys, whom she hates; kill the beautiful widow, Tounis, at her wedding to the new High Priest, and take from her the comb of Queen Nitocris; and steal the necklace of seven strings of sacred pearls from Aphrodite's lifted hands in the Temple of Love. He fulfills all her wishes, but afterwards he is filled with remorse. When Chrysis offers herself to him, he will not have her. Later the city is alarmed. The comb, mirror and necklace must be restored or great disaster will befall the country. Naked, and carrying all three stolen treasures, Chrysis ascends to the top of the great beacon of Alexandria. The people take her for the goddess Aphrodite. When she is brought down, the sculptor murmurs: "My Aphrodite! Blind was I—I did not know that you, Chrysis, were the reincarnation in life of all that I had worshipped in the ideal!" But it is too late—Chrysis has taken poison and dies. This work has long been considered one of the minor classics of erotic literature.

APOLOGIA PRO VITA SUA (1864), by John Henry (Cardinal) Newman. Charles Kingsley, the English novelist and clergyman, in an article in *Macmillan's Magazine* had observed, with specific reference to Father Newman, that: "Truth for its own sake has never been a virtue with the Roman clergy. Father Newman informs us that it need not be, and on the whole ought not to be; that cunning is the weapon which Heaven has given to the Saints wherewith to withstand the brute male force of the wicked world which marries and is given in marriage. Whether his notion be doctrinally correct or not, it is, at least, historically so." Cardinal Newman demanded a retraction, and upon refusal, sat down to write a vindication of his religious life and latter-day espousal of the Roman Church. He wrote in a white passion and in great spiritual turmoil, "constantly in tears, and constantly crying out with distress." He composed seven pamphlets and published them finally in book form, precipitating lively public discussion. The *Apologia* is divided into seven parts and an appendix. The divisions are as follows: "Mr. Kingsley's Method of Disputation; True Mode of Meeting Mr. Kingsley; History of My Religious Opinions up to 1833; History of My Religious Opinions from 1833 to 1839; History of My Religious Opinions from 1841 to 1845; General Answer to Mr. Kingsley; Appendix; Answer in Detail to Mr. Kingsley's Accusations." Cardinal Newman writes with eloquence and fire in the polemical parts, and in the calm discursive passages reveals his refinement, culture and sincerity. The work has become an established classic in modern apologetic literature.

APOLOGIE FOR POETRIE (ca. 1580; published 1595), by Sir Philip Sidney. The author wrote this treatise to support the claim of poetry to the eminence to which the ancients raised it. He regarded poetry as an instrument of education. The first argument in its favor was its antiquity; the earliest philosophers, such as Thales, Empedocles and Plato, were poets. Besides having a prophetic character, and being superior to all science, poetry was universally exalted above all branches of knowledge. Philosophy presented precepts, history gave examples, but poetry did both and was a greater incentive to virtuous action than either of the others. Conversely, the author examined all objections made against poetry, such as that it "abuses men's wits" or "that poets are liars." He demolished these gracefully. He partially blamed poets themselves for the ill repute of their art. His own opinion was that "poesie is full of virtue-breeding delightfulness."

APOLOGY, by Plato (427–347 B.C.). This *Apology* purports to be the defense of Socrates on trial for his life before an Athenian court on a charge of introducing religious innovation and corrupting the youth. Plato does not apparently try to give a verbatim report of his master's actual defense, but rather to represent the spirit in which Socrates faced his accusers. Socrates shows first that the prosecution is relying upon a long-standing popular misapprehension of the nature of his interests, to create prejudice against him in the court. He also shows that at least one of the three accusers has no clear understanding of the charges and is actually aiming at something which is not punishable under existing law. The rest of the speech is a true *apologia pro vita sua* in which Socrates explains the moral basis of the unconventional life of inquiry which has caused such strong prejudice against him, and the reasons why he cannot abandon his search for truth. He refuses to throw himself on the mercy of the court and declares his reliance upon the gods. After the court has declared him guilty, he refuses to suggest, as he might have done, any substantial penalty as an alternative to death, since he is conscious only of having benefited and not of having harmed the city. Finally, after the death sentence has been pronounced, he speaks again formally to those who had voted against him, pitying them, and to those who had voted for him, encouraging them and saying that one should be of good cheer in the face of death and keep in mind the one truth, that nothing is evil for a good man, either alive or dead, and that his lot is not a matter of unconcern to the gods. In judging the *Apology,* it is difficult to separate sympathy with the noble character of Socrates from admiration for the skill with which Plato presents it. Plato's real achievement can best be appreciated by comparing this *Apology* with that of Xenophon.

APOLOGY (ca. 197), by Tertullian (Quintus Septimius Florens Tertullianus). Addressed to the Roman magistrates, this tract is a vigorous, colorful defense of Christianity and Christians, in answer to the criticisms of the cultured Roman pagans of that period. It has the fresh ring of a new faith, a new fervor, a revelation of hitherto undiscovered religiosity. It proclaims the principle of religious liberty as an inalienable right of man. It demands of the dominant pagan class a fair trial for Christians before condemning them to death. Tertullian refutes the inflammatory charges that Christians sacrificed Roman infants at the celebration of the Lord's Supper. He presents the testimony of Pliny that Christians are pledged not to commit murder or other crimes. He counters with the accusations that pagans commit savage outrages by throwing gladiators to the wild beasts in the circuses. Christians, he continues, do not engage in foolish worship of the Emperors as gods; they do better, they pray for them. He concludes his vehement argument with a challenge to Christian detractors, stating that the followers of Christ are not to be intimidated by threats of death or torture. The more they are killed, the more they increase: "the blood of Christians is seed." Tertullian, whose vigorous personality and abilities led to a stormy theological career, is one of the group known as the ante-Nicene Founding Fathers of Christianity. He is among the first of the great Latin Christian writers and was the teacher of St. Cyprian, who in turn taught the great Augustine, pillar of Roman theology.

APOLOGY FOR THE LIFE OF MR. COLLEY CIBBER, COMEDIAN (1740), by Colley Cibber. The famous eighteenth-century English wit and playwright wrote this book in answer to his critics. In it he reviews his long and colorful career on the stage and sketches his own character (favorably) in order to refute his enemies' slanders. Without excessive modesty, he records his not inconsiderable theatrical achievements at the Drury Lane, and advances persuasive proofs that through most of his long life, he had worked indefatigably to bring the London stage to its highest artistic development and popularity. The book is chatty, discursive, anecdotal and witty. More than an apology for himself, it is a priceless history of the London stage, of actors, playwrights, critics, audiences, life and manners during this lively century.

APOSTLE, THE (1943), by Sholem Asch. See NAZARENE, THE, by Sholem Asch.

APPOINTMENT IN SAMARRA (1934), by John O'Hara. Julian English is an aristocratic drunkard. He is neither malicious, nor degenerate, but a victim of psychological and moral flabbiness. He outrageously mistreats his wife Caroline, although he loves her; he becomes concerned in needless altercations with strangers, and even with friends toward whom he feels a moral obligation. His tragedy begins on Christmas Eve, after a drinking bout. By the next day, he is so overwhelmed by his grossness and futility that he commits suicide. The only seemingly normal people in the story are Luther Fliegler, a salesman, and his wife. But they, too, are condemned to suffer from Julian's acts, as are Al Grecco, a bootlegger, the inoffensive Harry Reilly, and many others whose lives become involved in a casual way with Julian's. The novel is written episodically, but achieves integration by its hard-boiled theme of the destructive effects of fast living.

John O'Hara has written much realistic material about the sordid and banal events in the lives of ordinary people. *Butterfield 8* (1935) is a novelization of the sensational lives of the night-club set involved in an actual New York scandal. Young Gloria Wandrous is one of several characters in New York's fabulous, immoral prohibition period, whose lives become interrelated. Her influence sets up a chain reaction of passion and violence, ending with her death. Gloria falls overboard from a cruise ship she had sailed on to run away from Weston Liggett, the only man she has ever loved. Liggett had broken up his marriage because of her.

Pal Joey (1940) a sequence of letters from an entertainer, was produced as a musical comedy. O'Hara's collections of short stories have been most popular. His most recent novel, *A Rage to Live* (1949), is a long, ambitious work about which critical opinion is divided.

APPRECIATION: PAINTING, POETRY AND PROSE (1947), by Leo Stein. This book, "a little debauch in the realm of ideas," is the rich human document of an independent mind challenging the conventional aesthetic ideas of his time. From years of experience and productivity in the arts, and reminiscences of personal friendships with great artists, the author produces provocative criticism of the arts and fresh definitions of poetry and prose. An American by birth, Leo Stein, brother of Gertrude Stein, lived in Paris before World War I, and after a brief return to this country settled in Settignano, Italy, where he died a few weeks after the publication of *Appreciation*. His first book was *The ABC of Aesthetics* (1927).

APPRECIATIONS, WITH AN ESSAY ON STYLE (1889), by Walter Pater. Eleven critical essays (variously titled "Style"; "Wordsworth"; "Coleridge"; "Charles Lamb"; "Sir Thomas Browne"; *"Love's Labour 's Lost"*; *"Measure for Measure"*; "Shakespeare's English Kings"; "Dante Gabriel Rossetti"; "Feuillet's *La Morte*," and "Postscript") are in this book. In objective manner, Pater analyzes style, background, personalities, and reasons for writing. In the first essay, he states the differences between prose and poetry, selection of words, etc., subjects that become important in the rest of the book.

In the last essay, he compares the Classical and Romantic literature of England with the literature of other countries, and defines the romantic quality as coming from "the addition of strangeness to beauty." Not the least of Pater's gifts was his ability to single out apt quotations.

ARABIA DESERTA, TRAVELS IN (1888), by Charles Montagu Doughty. This is the remarkable record of a man, in ill health and of slight means, impelled somewhat unaccountably, even to himself, to undertake a difficult nomadic existence among strangers in the Arabian wilderness. His was a stern, ascetic nature, made passionate by frustration. For ten years he worked over his *Arabia Deserta,* "wherein," to use his own words, "I have set down that which I saw with my eyes and heard with my ears and thought in my heart, neither more nor less." No better appreciation of the book can be cited than that of T. E. Lawrence (of Arabia) in 1921: "I have talked the book over with many travelers, and we are agreed that here you have all the desert, its hills and plains, the lava fields, the villages, the tents, the men and animals. They are told of to the life, with words and phrases fitted to them so perfectly that one cannot dissociate them in memory. It is the true Arabia, the land with its smells and dirt, as well as nobility and freedom. . . . Doughty's completeness is devastating. . . . He took all Arabia for his province. . . . We may write books on parts of the desert or some of the history of it; but there can never be another picture of the whole, in our time, because here it is all said, and by a great master."

ARABIAN NIGHTS' ENTERTAINMENTS (ca. 1440–1550), by Sir Richard Burton (1885–1888). Antoine Galland's translation of the *Arabian Nights' Entertainments* or *The Thousand Nights and a Night* from the Arabic to French in 1704–1717 brought this imaginative collection of tales before the Western world. In 1840 Edward William Lane translated the stories into English, omitting some. Sir Richard Burton published the first complete English translation. The story of Scheherazade's ingenuity is of Persian origin. Mas'udi speaks of it in 944, and it is also referred to in the *Fihrist* (987) as appearing in the *Hezar Afsane* (Thousand Tales) which was attributed to the Princess Homai, daughter of Artaxerxes I. However, the tales are more Arabian than Persian in flavor. It is possible that they were collected in Cairo by a professional story-teller around the fifteenth century. The involuted form of the *Arabian Nights' Entertainments* has been a source of admiration as a miracle of narrative architecture. Boccaccio's *Decameron* (q.v.), Chaucer's *Canterbury Tales* (q.v.), and the *Fables of Bidpai* are all similar to them in construction, in that they are collections of stories within stories, but the Arabian work is infinitely more complicated.

The frame of the work consists of the following whimsical plot arrangement: Shahriyar, King of India, is inflamed with jealousy by his wife's wanton ways, and after executing her, he resolves to take his revenge on all womankind. Night after night he marries some beautiful girl, only to order her beheaded the next morning. But at last he meets Scheherazade, the beautiful and clever daughter of his vizier. She is resolved to preserve her head by means of her intelligence. Knowing that Shahriyar loves a good story, she begins, on the night of their wedding, to spin a bewildering number of yarns which, like an expert serialist, she suspends just as the climax is being reached. Devoured by curiosity to know the end of each story, Shahriyar is constrained, against his own judgment, to stay the hand of the executioner. After a thousand and one nights, the king is cured of his mania.

Such stories as "Aladdin's Lamp," "Sindbad the Sailor," "Ali Baba and the Forty Thieves" are well known. They have become common heritage.

ARAUCANAID, THE (1569, 1578, 1589), by Alonso de Ercilla. This long heroic poem in thirty-five cantos deals with the conquest of Chile by the Spaniards. Parts of it were written on the battlefield by a doughty warrior, the noble Alonso de Ercilla, on scraps of paper and on the parchment of drums. The first part, which was published in 1569, is primarily a versified chronicle of the early stages of the war, accurate in its topography and chronology. For the first time, the landscape of America appears in all its majesty in a literary work of the first magnitude, but, even more notable, for the first time the American Indians—in this case, the Araucanians—are treated with dignity and respect. Years later Ercilla resumed his work (Part II was published in 1578 and Part III in 1589), but he interspersed it with more interesting and poetical incidents, dreams and visions and the lofty events of his contemporary Spain—the battles of Saint Quentin (1557) and Lepanto (1571), the conquest of Portugal (1578), etc. Thus the main thread of the narrative is broken, and with it the original epic grandeur of the poem. Despite the sudden transitions and supernatural machinery, *La Araucana* will be remembered for its vivid descriptions of battles and of nature, for its remarkable dramatic speeches (one by the Indian Colocolo rivals in power that of Ulysses in the *Iliad*), and for its precise delineation of character.

ARCADIA (printed 1590), by Sir Philip Sidney. Written originally for the Countess of Pembroke, Sidney's sister, *Arcadia,* a prose romance with eclogues at the ending of each book, was later revised considerably, with the exception of the fourth and fifth books.

Two young heroes, Pyrocles and Musidorus, are shipwrecked off the coast of Laconia. Musidorus is abducted by pirates and Pyrocles is taken by shepherds to Arcadia. Basilius, King of Arcadia, in fulfillment of the words of the oracle, has retired to the forest with his charming wife, Gynecia, and his beautiful daughters, Pamela and Philoclea. Pyrocles falls in love with Philoclea and, disguising himself as a woman, takes service in the king's household. Basilius is deceived by the disguise and falls in love with "Zelmane" as Pyrocles is now called. Gynecia pierces the disguise and also falls in love with him, as does Philoclea. Musidorus arrives in search of Pyrocles and finds himself in love with Pamela. He also takes service in the house and makes love to Mopsa, the uncouth daughter of Dametas, a servant, in order to conceal his love for Pamela.

Pamela, Philoclea, and Pyrocles are kidnapped by Cecropia, a woman who hopes to attain the crown of Arcadia by forcing one of Basilius' daughters to marry her son, Amphialus. After many hazardous adventures, including a siege of Cecropia's castle, the three escape. Musidorus runs off with Pamela, and Pyrocles, hoping to rid himself of their advances, grants both Gynecia and Basilius a love-tryst in the same place and at the same time. In the meantime, he goes to Philoclea's chamber, where he is captured and arrested. Basilius, after drinking a love-potion intended by his wife for Pyrocles, goes into a deathlike trance. Gynecia confesses what she has done, thinking she has killed her husband. All are tried, and Pyrocles and Musidorus are sentenced to die, Philoclea is consigned to a convent, and Gynecia is to be entombed alive. At this point Basilius revives, and a messenger arrives with the news that the two youths are princes, Pyrocles of Macedon, and Musidorus of Thessaly. All are pardoned.

ARCANA COELESTIA (1749–1756), by Emanuel Swedenborg. See HEAVENLY ARCANA, by Emanuel Swedenborg.

ARCH OF TRIUMPH (1946), by Erich Maria Remarque. See ALL QUIET ON THE WESTERN FRONT, by Erich Maria Remarque.

ARCHIMEDES (287–212 B.C.). Trained in the Alexandrian school, the great mathematician of Syracuse lived a life entirely devoted to mathematical research. He became celebrated for a number of ingenious inventions, but these things, he said modestly, were merely "the diversions of geometry at play." Plutarch says, "He possessed so high a spirit, so profound a soul, and such treasures of scientific knowledge that, though these inventions had obtained for him the renown of more than human sagacity, he yet would not deign to leave behind him any written work on such subjects, but, regarding as ignoble and sordid the business of mechanics and every sort of art which is directed to use and profit, he placed his whole ambition in those speculations in whose beauty and subtlety there is no admixture of the common needs of life." Archimedes regarded his work *On the Sphere and Cylinder* as his most important. He requested his friends and relatives to place upon his tomb a representation of a cylinder with a sphere within it, together with an inscription giving the ratio which the cylinder bears to the sphere (with respect both to volume and surface area), an achievement which he regarded as the crowning point of his mathematical activity. According to the Greek scientist Pappus, it was in connection with his discovery of the solution of the problem, *To move a given weight by a given force,* that Archimedes uttered the famous saying: "Give me a place to stand on, and I can move the earth." According to Plutarch, the tyrant Hieron was struck with amazement at this boast. He "asked him to reduce the problem to practice and to give an illustration of some great weight moved by a small force." Archimedes thereupon chose a three-masted royal ship "which had only been drawn up with great labour and many men; and loading her with many passengers and a full freight, sitting himself the while far off, with no great effort but only holding the end of a compound pulley quietly in his hand and pulling at it, he drew the ship smoothly and safely as if she were moving through the sea." The extant works of Archimedes include the following: *On the equilibrium of planes; Quadrature of the Parabola; On the Sphere and Cylinder; On spirals; On Conoids and Spheroids; On floating bodies; Measurement of a circle;* and *The Sand-reckoner.* Unfortunately, many of Archimedes' great works are lost. Among these are: *On balances or levers; On centers of gravity; Principles* (arithmetical); *Optics; On sphere-making; On the Calendar.* Many legends are attached to Archimedes' name concerning the solution of challenging problems: the raising of water by his water screw, or inclined plane confined within a cylinder; the weighing of elephants; and the destruction of the ships of a Roman fleet in the harbor of Syracuse by means of a burning glass. There is a household tale of his leaping naked from a tub and rushing forth, crying "Eureka" ("I have found it!") upon perceiving, in the buoyancy of water and in the displacement which had caused the tub to overflow, the means of testing the genuineness of a gold crown by specific gravity. According to tradition the Roman general, Marcellus, invading Syracuse, had ordered the sparing of Archimedes' life. But the mathematician, engrossed in a problem he had diagrammed on the sands of the beach, failed to hear and obey the order of a soldier and was struck down, his identity not realized.

archy and mehitabel (1927), by Don Marquis. Two new characters introduced into American humorous literature are archy, a literary cockroach, and his sweetheart mehitabel the cat, whose motto is "toujours gai." Despite the latter's numerous indiscretions, she manages to maintain an unruffled dignity throughout all her misadventures—which afford the author an opportunity to make satiric comments about the world. Most of the book is written in chatty, jazzed-up free verse, without benefit of capitalization because archy types by butting his head against the keys and cannot use the shift lever. The saga of these two is extended in later volumes, *archys life of mehitabel* (1933), and *archy does his part* (1935).

Don Marquis wrote, during Prohibition days, a humorous diary (later dramatized) called *The Old Soak* (1921), whose central character sighs sadly after the rummy virtues of the old barroom. Attached to this narrative are a number of verses such as "A Last Drink," "The Last Case of Gin," and "A Kansas Tragedy." The author was less successful with his novels and serious books.

AREOPAGITICA: A SPEECH OF MR. JOHN MILTON FOR THE LIBERTY OF UNLICENSED PRINTING TO THE PARLIAMENT OF ENGLAND (1644), by John Milton. An answer to the Order of Censorship imposed on printing by Parliament in 1643, the pamphlet (only figuratively a speech) is one of the most inspiring pleas for free thought ever uttered. It is modeled after the *Areopagiticus* of Isocrates (355 B.C.), in which the Greek philosopher-orator urged the restoration of the old freedom of the Areopagus, the place of public meeting and debate in Athens. Though the Order of Censorship remained in force under the Commonwealth and until 1695, its effectiveness was largely broken by this bold pamphlet. The work can be split into six divisions: Introduction; the origin of restrictions on printing; the use of books generally; the negative argument against the Order; the positive argument, and Conclusion. There are many unforgettable and widely quoted passages, such as the statement: "As good almost kill a man as kill a good book. Who kills a man kills a reasonable creature, God's image; but he who destroys a good book kills reason itself, kills the image of God as it were in the eye. Many a man lives a burden to the earth; but a good book is the precious life-blood of a master spirit, embalmed and treasured up on purpose to a life beyond life." Milton argues cogently: are twenty men enough to estimate all the genius and the good sense of England? Is there to be a monopoly of knowledge; are the products of all English brains to be stamped like broadcloth and woolpacks? The affront is not to the educated alone, but also to the common people who are maligned by the view that they are too brainless to be trusted with judgment. Furthermore, the Order was hostile to truth. "The waters of truth have been likened to a fountain," says Milton, "but they will stagnate now into a muddy pool of conformity and tradition." Finally, Milton warns the Parliament, if it wishes to crush knowledge, it might as well suppress itself, for only a free government makes a free spirit, and, "If you would have us slaves, you must be tyrants."

ARGONAUTS, THE (1820), by Franz Grillparzer. See GOLDEN FLEECE, by Franz Grillparzer.

ARGONAUTICA, by Apollonius of Rhodes (ca. 295-215 b.c.). This epic is one of the few complete remnants of Alexandrian Greek literature. Apollonius was one of the leading lights of the great circle of court poets assembled by the early Ptolemies. He was firmly convinced that epic poetry was not *démodé* and could still be successfully written. His poem is the vindication of his theory. The legend upon which the poem is based is the age-old tale of Jason and the quest for the Golden Fleece. The first two books recount the adventures of Jason and those who sailed in the Argo until they reached the land of Colchis. The third book tells of Jason's yoking the fire-breathing oxen of Aeetes with the aid of Medea, and the fourth narrates how she helped him carry off the Golden Fleece and fled with him to Greece. In diction and meter, Apollonius followed Homer as the only possible model, but his style is his own, or rather that of his age. The tone of the poem is romantic rather than heroic. The central point of interest is the love of Medea for Jason, and this is developed with a depth of psychological analysis that had been learned from Euripides, to which is added a sensitivity for the feelings of romantic love which is truly Alexandrian and courtly. A modern parallel to the *Argonautica* is William Morris' *Life and Death of Jason*.

ARIA DA CAPO (1919), by Edna St. Vincent Millay. See MILLAY, EDNA ST. VINCENT.

ARIADNE OF NAXOS (1912), by Hugo von Hofmannsthal. See HOFMANNSTHAL, HUGO VON.

ARISTODEMEUS (1786), by Vincenzo Monti. See MONTI, VINCENZO.

ARITHMETICAL RESEARCHES (1801), by Karl Friedrich Gauss. See DISQUISITIONES ARITHMETICAE, by Karl Friedrich Gauss.

ARMS AND THE MAN (produced 1894; published 1898), by George Bernard Shaw. The action takes place in a small town in Bulgaria in 1885–1886. The Petkoffs are one of the wealthiest families in Bulgaria and live in a house with a library and an electric bell. Catherine Petkoff comes to her daughter Raina's room as the latter is going to bed, and tells her that her betrothed, Sergius, in the Bulgarian army, has led a heroic cavalry charge against the Serbians, who are in full retreat, and that some of the stragglers may flee through their town.

Later, Captain Bluntschli, a Swiss officer in the Serbian army, climbs in at Raina's window and threatens her with a pistol. He is exhausted, nervous, and eats chocolate creams greedily, being accustomed to chocolate rations. He recognizes a picture of Sergius and tells Raina the cavalry charge succeeded only because the Serbians had no cartridges. He is a debunker of battle and outrages the romantically inclined Raina by declaring that a soldier's first duty is to save his own skin. Raina and Catherine protect him and finally send him off in Major Petkoff's old coat.

Peace is made, and Petkoff and Sergius return. Petkoff is glad to be at home and comfortable. Sergius finds heroic love with Raina trying, and flirts with her pretty maid, Louka, who is plighted to Nicola, the middle-aged manservant. Petkoff keeps asking for his old coat, and tells a story he has heard about two Bulgarian women who had hidden a Serbian and sent him off in the master's coat, not realizing they are his own wife and daughter. Captain Bluntschli calls to return the coat, and Petkoff thinks he has come to see him. The practical Swiss had pawned the coat for safe-keeping. Raina, who had put a picture of herself, dedicated to the chocolate soldier, in the pocket, manages to retrieve it. Louka, jealous of her mistress, tells Sergius that Bluntschli had been in Raina's room. He wishes to fight the Swiss, who talks him out of it. Sergius at last becomes aware that he really loves Louka. Bluntschli at this point inherits nine hotels in Switzerland and leaves with the understanding that he is to return and marry Raina.

The play is a witty satire on the heroics of war, with fine character contrasts. The calm, efficient and disillusioned professional attitude toward war on the part of Bluntschli ludicrously emphasizes the empty bombast of Sergius and the blundering incompetence of the old Major. The popular light opera, *The Chocolate Soldier,* by Oscar Straus, was adapted from the play.

ARMANCE (1827), by Stendhal. See CHARTERHOUSE OF PARMA, THE, by Stendhal.

ARMORER, THE (1891), by Viktor Rydberg. See LAST ATHENIAN, THE, by Viktor Rydberg.

AROUND THE WORLD IN EIGHTY DAYS (1873), by Jules Verne. One day at the Reformers' Club in London, Phileas Fogg, a cold-blooded, methodical Englishman, takes up a wager to journey around the world in eighty days and, with clocklike precision, to report at the Club at a specified time. Accompanied by his French valet, Passepartout, and by Detective Fix, assigned by the Club to check up on his movements, Fogg starts out on his impossible voyage. Adventure is piled on adventure. Being the cool and intrepid Englishman of popular legend, he overcomes the most forbidding obstacles with endless resourcefulness. In China he saves Passepartout from a hostile mob. In India, despite his terrific hurry, he takes time to rescue Aouda, a beautiful widow, from being burned alive on the funeral pyre of her dead husband—and more time still to marry her. The book ends as Phileas Fogg nonchalantly walks into the Reformers' Club, ten minutes ahead of schedule, as the waiting members look at their watches. "Here I am, gentlemen," he drawls. . . . The story has survived the development of transportation facilities much faster than those available to its hero.

ARROWSMITH (1925), by Sinclair Lewis. The story of Martin Arrowsmith begins with his boyhood fascination with medicine. It is during his work as a medical student that he is first confronted with the choice between the careers of the doctor-healer and the doctor-research scientist. He is first influenced by Dean Silva of the medical school, but later comes under the spell of Dr. Max Gottlieb, harsh mentor, but brilliant researcher. Arrowsmith goes into private practice in South Dakota, with the companionship of his wife Leora, a former nurse. His practice remains small, however, and he takes a position as Public Health Director in Nautilus, Iowa. After further disappointment, he finds his real place with his old master Gottlieb in the laboratories of the McGurk Institute in New York. Martin really begins to develop as a bacteriologist. At length he goes to the West Indies in a fight against the bubonic plague. Leora and Martin's associate Gustaf Sondelius die of the disease. Martin partly fails in his mission by breaking the ruthless scientific limit for serum administration, and dispensing more than his quota. The rest of the book traces his struggle, through self-doubts and a second, ill-fated marriage, to final harmony with himself in the pursuit of pure science on a Vermont farm.

The book was awarded the 1926 Pulitzer Prize, but Mr. Lewis declined the honor. In 1930, however, he accepted the Nobel Prize for Literature.

Lewis has written many novels. After several minor ones, *Main Street* (q.v.) brought him recognition. *Babbitt* (q.v.) and *Arrowsmith* followed. These are usually considered his best works.

Lewis' forte is good-natured satire of various elements of American middle-class society, such as religious hypocrisy in *Elmer Gantry* (1927), and dishonest philanthropy in *Gideon Planish* (1934). But he has also turned his eye upon many serious problems: social reform and the place of women in our society in *Ann Vickers* (1933), the threat of fascism in *It Can't Happen Here* (1935), marital problems in *Cass Timberlane* (1945) and *Dodsworth* (q.v.), and racial prejudice in *Kingsblood Royal* (1947).

ARS MAGNA (1545), by Jerome Cardan. The *Ars Magna* of Cardan occupies much the same place in mathematics as does the *De Revolutionibus* (q.v.) of Copernicus in astronomy and the *De Fabrica* (q.v.) of Vesalius in anatomy. It, too, marks the beginning of the modern age. As early as 2000 B.C. the Babylonians had solved equations of the first and second degree, using methods not differing in essentials from those of modern algebra; but the peculiar characteristics of Greek mathematics had led them to substitute geometric solutions for such equations, as well as for equations of the third degree. Much later, the Persian poet, Omar Khayyam, boasted that he could solve all cubic equations geometrically by means of conic sections; and he expressed the belief that algebraic solutions of cubics are impossible. This view continued until early in the sixteenth century when an algebraic solution of the equation $x^3 + m x = n$ was discovered by Scipione del Ferro and imparted to one of his students. The solution seems to have remained a secret; but another mathematician, Tartaglia, worked out independently the solution of this and other cubic equations. Cardan importuned him to divulge his method; and upon receiving Cardan's solemn pledge of secrecy, Tartaglia consented. In 1545, however, Cardan published the rule for the first time in his *Ars Magna*, a comprehensive treatise on algebra. Cardan thus broke his vow, although he did acknowledge his indebtedness to Tartaglia; and the solution since then has been known either as the "formula of Tartaglia" or the "formula of Cardan." The solution of the cubic equation served to spur mathematicians on to seek the roots of equations of still higher degree; and Cardan in the *Ars Magna* published the rule for quartics which his follower, Ferrari, had discovered. For almost three centuries men searched in vain for solutions of equations of degree more than four, only to find, through the work of Abel and Galois, that these are impossible in the ordinary sense.

The *Ars Magna* exerted a tremendous influence on the development of algebra, and today this is the best known of Cardan's numerous works. In his day, however, he enjoyed a wide reputation in medicine and science, as well as in mathematics; and his collected works, published in ten folio volumes in 1663, cover a wide field. Two of his books on natural science, *De Subtilitate Rerum* (1551) and *De Varietate Rerum* (1557), at that time rivaled the *Ars Magna* in popularity, but they have had less lasting value. This undoubtedly is due in part to the then primitive state of knowledge in chemistry and physics. Cardan believed that the inorganic world, like the organic, is subject to progressive development, and hence that gold is produced from the inferior metals by gradual perfection. He believed in astrology, as well as in alchemy, and he cast the horoscope of Edward VI of England. In mathematics, however, Cardan's contributions have had positive and lasting value, and the *Ars Magna* thus remains a landmark in the development of algebra.

ART AS EXPERIENCE (1933), by John Dewey. See DEWEY, JOHN.

ART OF HEALING (Early 16th c.), by Paracelsus (Theophrastus Bombast von Hohenheim). Because of conflicts with followers of Galen and Avicenna who did not relish his ideas, Paracelsus (1493–1541) became a wandering doctor. He traveled all over Germany on foot, like the veriest beggar, and went wherever he expected to find something that might be useful to know. "I went in search of my art, often risking my life. I have not been ashamed to learn that which seemed useful to me even from vagabonds, executioners, and barbers. I know that a lover will go a long way to meet the woman he adores: how much more will the lover of wisdom be tempted to go in search of his divine mistress." And concerning medicine he had this sage reflection: "Reading never made a doctor. Medicine is an art and requires practice. . . . I began to study my art by imagining that there was not a single teacher in the world capable to teach it to me, but that I had to acquire it myself. It was the book of Nature, written by the finger of God. . . . My accusers complain that I have not entered the temple of Knowledge through the legitimate door. But which one is the truly legitimate door? Galenus and Avicenna or Nature? I have entered through the door of Nature: her light and not the lamp of an apothecary's shop, has illuminated my way."

Paracelsus presents a strange combination of lofty concepts of medical practice with much poor observation and metaphysical nonsense. He denounced the association of astrology with medicine; but he substituted a theory just as fanciful when he asserted that the "Archaeus," rather than the stars, controls man's destiny. The Archaeus is a sort of mystical alchemical spirit presiding in the various organs of mankind and regulating their operation. Disease results when the Archaeus fails properly to regulate the organs in the harmonious discharge of their functions. There is in the works of Paracelsus much allegory, pretense and superstition; but he made several very significant contributions to medicine and science. His iconoclasm did indeed lead him to excesses, but his rejection of authority in favor of the direct observation of nature was clearly in the direction of modern science. In medicine he introduced a great number of new drugs, especially recently-discovered inorganic chemical compounds. It is largely because of Paracelsus, for example, that preparations of antimony were highly popular in the sixteenth and seventeenth centuries. He helped to spread the use of mercury in the treatment of syphilis, and he prescribed medicines containing copper, iron and lead.

The widespread use of new preparations in medicine marks Paracelsus as the founder of a new era in chemistry. For the aims of the alchemist, he would substitute the application of chemistry to medicine: "Many have said of alchemy that it is for making gold and silver. But here such is not the aim, but to consider only what virtue and power may lie in medicines." The new period thus initiated is referred to as that of iatrochemistry, and the awakened interest in the subject is taken by some to mark "the true commencement of chemical investigations." The influence of Paracelsan literature was, however, not always in the direction of progress. There are several hundred works attributed to him, some of dubious authenticity; and in this mass of writings there is much of credulity, obscurity and charlatanism. Paracelsus nevertheless remains a great physician, a pioneer in chemistry, and a herald of the new spirit in science.

ART OF LOVE (ca. 2 B.C.), by Ovid (Publius Ovidius Naso). In these three books of elegiac verse Ovid expounds the niceties of amorous adventure in graceful and elegant language for the sophisticated society of Augustan Rome. The first two books contain advice for the predatory male, but the third Ovid devotes to the opposite sex, to avoid, as he affects to say, any charge of partiality. The whole is in the convention of the erotic Alexandrian elegy, but has a special flavor of Ovid's wit. To write an *Art of Love* is comparable to writing, e.g., an *Art of Speech*, and the poet is then posing in mock seriousness as the professor. There was at this period a great deal of what struck the more serious-minded citizen as gross moral laxity in Roman society. In this work Ovid gives a sympathetic insight into this society which Horace, on the other hand, censures from the point of view of a moralist in his *Satires*. The Emperor Augustus was trying to effect a moral regeneration at Rome and could hardly look with favor on such poetry. At any rate Ovid was exiled for life to the coast of the Black Sea, and felt his poetry was partially responsible for his misfortune.

ARTS, THE (1937), by Hendrik Willem van Loon. See STORY OF MANKIND, THE, by Hendrik Willem van Loon.

ARTEMUS WARD: HIS BOOK (1862), by Artemus Ward (C. F. Browne). "Artemus Ward," a traveling showman, had many adventures among backwoods characters. It was his opinions on current events which helped bring him fame. *His Book* was the foremost volume of Civil War humor, and achieved a prompt sale of 40,000 copies. It satirized at large the foibles of the people of the Union in their struggle against the seceded South. Much affectionate humor was lavished upon the person of "O. Abe," as Ward abbreviated his references to Lincoln, and criticism was leveled at the administration's opponents.

ARUNDEL (1930), by Kenneth Roberts. See NORTHWEST PASSAGE, by Kenneth Roberts.

AS I LAY DYING (1930), by William Faulkner. See FAULKNER, WILLIAM.

AS YOU LIKE IT (ca. 1599), by William Shakespeare. The direct source of this popular comedy was Thomas Lodge's romance *Rosalynde* (1590). The story, a pastoral formula, revolves around the roving court of a banished Duke in the Forest of Arden. Rosalind, daughter of the Duke, and Orlando, unjustly disinherited son of one of his friends, pursue a conventional but sometimes confused romance with the maiden disguised as a youth for the greater part of the play. She has taken man's apparel and called herself Ganymede when banished from the usurping Duke Frederick's court, and her best friend, Duke Frederick's daughter Celia, goes with her as a sister under the name of Aliena. Phebe, who has scorned her swain Silvius, falls in love with the pretended man, while the latter persuades Orlando to woo as if he were wooing Rosalind. Oliver comes to the forest with the intention of killing his brother Orlando, but instead is saved from a lioness by him, and repents. Oliver falls in love with Celia, and in the end disguises are cast aside, and the way is paved for reconciliation and reinstatement of Orlando's inheritance. All is capped by the timely conversion to religious life of the usurping Duke, who restores the dukedom to its rightful lord. The play closes with all romances happily crowned in the celebration of a mass wedding. Notable are the clown Touchstone and the melancholy Jaques, who speaks the lines about "All the world's a stage . . ."

ASCENT TO THE HEIGHTS (1895), by José María de Pereda. Marcelo, a fashionable, well-to-do young man from Madrid, is summoned to the manorial house of his old, childless uncle, Don Celso, who feels he has not long to live and wants to see his only relative before he dies. Don Celso's ancestral home is located in a remote village, perched on the loftiest peak of the Cantabric range, near Santander. Marcelo does not relish the idea in the least, but he feels obliged to comply with the request, so he visits his uncle's mountain retreat in the dead of winter. It is an excruciating experience for the pampered city fellow, comfortably housed in Madrid, to live in the desolate wintry mountains; he feels he can endure it only for a short while. However, he does succeed in acclimating himself, and this process of adaptation is remarkably conveyed by the author in his inimitable descriptions of the beauties of nature, of rural life, of the chores and the sports and the clean, healthy cordiality of the peasants. In compliance with Don Celso's request before his death, Marcelo comes to live in the village and carries on his uncle's patriarchate; he settles down and marries one of the village girls.

ASH WEDNESDAY (1930), by T. S. Eliot. See ELIOT, THOMAS STEARNS.

ASHES (1904), by Stefan Żeromski. Stefan Żeromski (1864–1925) ranks as one of the leading writers of his generation in Poland. He feels and emphasizes the evils of human nature which weigh so heavily upon the life of the oppressed people of a Poland which had lost its independence. The performance of one's duty must take the place of hopes of success. It is with this point of view that he approaches the history of Poland during the Napoleonic period in *Ashes.* His leading characters, Rafal Olbromski, Krzysztof Cedro, and Prince Gintult, all represent various aspects of the Polish national character, and they range from men of action to men of thought, from ardent patriotism to intellectual indifference and cynicism in the name of idealism. The scene is laid among the Polish Legions which, organized to aid Napoleon recover Polish independence, marched here and there, fighting incessantly for all other causes. The story with its many lyric episodes covers the career of these Legions and their commanders from 1797 to 1812. In space it touches all strata of Polish life, the palace and the cottage, the campaigns in Italy, in France, in Spain, in Santo Domingo, where a large part of the force perished. There are scenes of love and hate, of courage and cowardice, of the old splendor and the new misery. The verdict of history upon the whole is the title of the book, *Ashes.* It is an unromantic romanticism, as it has been called, quite unlike the method of Sienkiewicz with his strong tendency to emphasize the story and to inspire the people. Zeromski sees the history of the past as a thing of bitterness and failure, and yet it is the task of man to press on to his goal despite his suffering and his misery. The book ranks among the greatest of its kind—historical novels in which the mood and the delineation of character are more important than the frame of events within which they are represented.

ASMODEUS (1707), by Alain René Le Sage. A young student of Alcola, Don Cleofas Leandro Perez Zambullo, is visited one night by Asmodeus, a demon who cheerfully introduces himself as the most active and indefatigable devil in hell. To bolster this claim he asserts: "It is I that have introduced into the world luxury, debauchery, games of chance, and chemistry. I am the inventor of carousels, dancing, music, plays, and all the new French fashions." Catching hold of the cloak of the *diable bon homme,* Don Cleofas flies with him to the high steeple of St. Saviour in Madrid. With one wave of the hand Asmodeus lifts the roofs of all the houses, and reveals everything going on inside. The devil then commences the narration of a number of tales concerning some of the people they see, in order to give him a comprehensive picture of Madrid society. Several of the principal stories are: "The History of the Amours of the Count de Belflor and of Leonora de Cespides," "The Power of Friendship," "Of the Broil Betwixt a Tragic and Comic Author," "Of Dreams," "Of the Confined Mad People," "Of the Prisoners," "Of the Tombs, the Ghosts and Death." Beneath the fantasy lies a wealth of shrewd social observation. Among its early admirers was Tobias Smollett, whose translation, *The Devil on Two Sticks,* was immensely popular.

ASSUMPTION OF HANNELE, THE (1893), by Gerhart Hauptmann. See HANNELE, by Gerhart Hauptmann.

ASTRÉE(1610–1627), by Honoré d'Urfé. D'Urfé's romance is really a collection of pastoral or chivalric episodes. There is no sustained plot, and the central character, Celadon, a gentleman soldier, is merely a peg on which to hang various gallantries. The episodes treat a variety of amorous states: the love of Hylas is hedonistic; Damon's is violent; Chryseide's is self-assertive; Valentinian's lusty, Tirois' platonic, and Sylvandre's subtle and worldly. Characters and action alike are completely stylized. Many read this book, in its time, as a manual of polite conduct.

ASTRONOMIA NOVA (1609), by Johann Kepler. The early years of Kepler were marked by ill-health and poverty, but, thanks to the Duke of Württemberg, he received a university education. His early studies were theological, but at Tübingen Kepler came under the influence of Michael Mästlin, professor of mathematics and astronomy, who converted him to the Copernican doctrine. The increasing heterodoxy of his opinions precluded his achieving a career in the church, and Kepler henceforth devoted himself to mathematics and astronomy. He wrote voluminously, but he had such strong mystical leanings that a large proportion of his writings strike a modern reader as utter foolishness. He adopted the Pythagorean doctrine of the harmony of the celestial spheres, for example, and his *Harmonices Mundi* (1619) contains many bars of music purportedly giving the tones (not, however, having audible existence) emitted by the planets in their courses. Nevertheless, in all of his works one finds discoveries in astronomy, optics and mathematics which are among the greatest; and of his many treatises none had greater influence and significance than the *Astronomia Nova*.

Kepler's poor eyesight prevented him from achieving fame in observational astronomy, but he became instead a great theoretician—the "law-giver of the heavens." As a young man he served as mathematical assistant to the keen-eyed Tycho Brahe, and he fell heir to Tycho's invaluable observations. So accurate were these astronomical data that Kepler found it impossible to reconcile the observations on the planet Mars with any of the celestial schemes of the time, Ptolemaic, Copernican, or Tychonic. After years of calculation and recalculation, Kepler finally decided to abandon systems of circles and try some other curve. After trying many ovals, it occurred to him to try an ellipse, the simplest of ovals and a curve of which the Greeks had developed the mathematical properties. Kepler was delighted to find that an elliptical orbit for Mars satisfied the data of Tycho, and he published in the *Astronomia Nova* the first two of the three so-called "Laws of Kepler." (1) The planet describes an ellipse about the sun at one focus. (2) The radius vector drawn from the sun to the planet describes equal areas in equal times.

In later works, notably the *Epitome Astronomiae Copernicanae* (1618–1621), he applied these important laws to the other known planets. Kepler's third law appeared first in his *Harmonices Mundi*.

Kepler's laws were not immediately accepted by his contemporaries, but in 1687 they became the basis of the famous Newtonian synthesis through the law of gravitation. The idea of universal gravitation was in part anticipated by Kepler himself, for in the important *Astronomia Nova* he suggests that two bodies exert upon each other an attraction similar to magnetism. This book undoubtedly is the greatest book on mathematical astronomy between the *De Revolutionibus* (q.v.) of Copernicus and the *Principia* (q.v.) of Newton.

ASTROPHEL AND STELLA (1591), by Sir Philip Sidney. This sequence of 108 sonnets (with 11 songs interspersed), mostly Petrarchan in form, is thought to express Sidney's disappointed love for Penelope Devereux, daughter of the first Earl of Essex. She was married against her will to Lord Rich, but later divorced him to marry Charles Blount who, apparently, had always been her choice. The first, and possibly most famous sonnet, punctuates Sidney's description of himself in the painful throes of composition with his Muse's advice— "Fool . . . look in thy heart and write!" Strongest evidence for the accepted identification of Stella (Star) with Penelope lies in Sonnet XXXVII wherein the word *rich* occurs seven times. Astrophel (Star-Lover) is, of course, Sir Philip.

A TOIT (1909), by Zalman Shneiur. See SHNEIUR, ZALMAN.

AT HEAVEN'S GATE (1943), by Robert Penn Warren. See WARREN, ROBERT PENN.

AT SUNSET (1906), by Zalman Shneiur. See SHNEIUR, ZALMAN.

AT THE BOTTOM (1903), by Maxim Gorky. See NIGHT'S LODGING, THE, by Maxim Gorky.

AT THE SIGN OF THE REINE PÉDAUQUE (1893), by Anatole France. See REVOLT OF THE ANGELS, THE, by Anatole France.

ATALA (1801), by François René de Chateaubriand. Captured by enemy Seminoles, the young Natchez brave Chactas is about to be tortured when the Seminole Princess Atala makes possible his escape. Together they brave the colonial American forest, evade their pursuers, and travel westward until they are caught by a tremendous storm. They are rescued by Father Aubry, a hermit who has established a community of Christian Indians in the wilds. Chactas and Atala are ardently in love, and it now appears that if Chactas will abjure his heathen beliefs the hermit will seal a happy marriage. But Chactas and his rescuer return from early morning mass to find Atala dying of a poison. She confesses that to please her dying mother she has vowed eternal virginity, and, caught between her vow and her great love, in her ignorance she has chosen suicide.

Atala is less noteworthy for its romantic story than for spectacular descriptions, three of which—the storm, the Mississippi River, and the mass at daybreak—are famous. Conceived as part of Chateaubriand's *Genius of Christianity* (q.v.) to illustrate the beauty of Catholicism, it forms a series with *Les Natchez* (1826) and the once celebrated, Wertherian *René* (1802). These, with the *Memories from Beyond the Tomb* (1811–1846), now overshadow such other writings of Chateaubriand's as *The Martyrs* (1809) and *Itinerary from Paris to Jerusalem* (1811).

ATALANTA IN CALYDON (1865), by Algernon Charles Swinburne. This is a drama in the classical Greek manner. The three Fates prophesy at the birth of Meleager, son of Althaea and Oeneus, king of Calydon, that he shall die when the log then burning is consumed. Althaea snatches up the burning stick and preserves it. Meleager becomes a great warrior, slays a wild boar and presents its horns and hide to Atalanta, priestess of Artemis, whom he loves. Defending Atalanta's trophies, he slays his mother's brothers. Althaea then burns the prophetic stick, and Meleager dies. The choruses, masterpieces of musical poetry, brought Swinburne fame.

ATHALIE (1691), by Jean Baptiste Racine. The story is from Second Kings and Second Chronicles. Joram, king of Judah, has married Athaliah, daughter of Ahab and Jezebel, rulers of Israel. Athaliah has persuaded Joram to build a temple to Baal in Jerusalem. Joram dies, and his son, Ahaziah, succeeds him, only to be murdered by Jehu, who has been trying to exterminate all the descendants of Ahab and the wicked Jezebel. To revenge her son's death, Athaliah has attempted to wipe out the race of David by slaying all the children of Ahaziah. However, Johosheba, sister of Ahaziah and wife of Jehoiada, the high priest, has rescued one child, Joash, and concealed him in the Temple. When the play opens, Abner, one of Athaliah's soldiers, comes to warn Jehoiada that Mattan, the priest, has gone over to Baal, and is urging the queen to destroy the Temple. Jehoiada confides in Abner that Joash is alive. He then enlists the help of the Levites in the defense of the Temple and of David's line. Athaliah visits the Temple with Mattan, meets Joash and likes him. When he tells her he is an orphan, Athaliah tries to persuade him to return to the palace with her. The boy refuses, and she sends Mattan to Johosheba, demanding him. This brings matters to a crisis. Jehoiada and the Levites reveal Joash's true identity and proclaim him King of Judah, thus ensuring the survival of the line of David. Racine wrote the play for presentation by students of the convent school at Saint-Cyr, after he had abjured the professional theater.

ATHERTON, GERTRUDE (1857–1948). Gertrude Atherton, during a long literary career, produced books with settings in her native California, although her own preference was for the many novels of foreign lands and ages which she also wrote. Honored by many academic distinctions, she is best remembered for *Black Oxen* (1923).

This study of feminine psychology concerns Mary Ogden, who arrives in New York from Europe. She meets the young columnist Lee Clavering, whose elderly cousin Charles Dinwiddie tells him that the woman greatly resembles his former sweetheart. Mary tells Lee that she is indeed that woman's cousin, but wishes to conceal her identity. After the two fall in love, however, Mary confesses that she is Charles' former sweetheart, who had disappeared thirty years earlier; but has been restored to physical youth by gland treatments. Lee is shocked, but still wishes to marry her. When Mary's lover, Prince Hohenhauer, arrives in New York on a diplomatic mission, and asks her to return to Austria for political reasons, her love for power overcomes her love for Lee. She agrees to go, and leaves Lee brokenhearted.

The Conqueror (1902), though subtitled "The true and romantic story of Alexander Hamilton," often distorts the truth in an effort to create an interesting fictionalization, especially in the character studies of Hamilton, Jefferson and Madison.

ATLANTIS (1912), by Gerhart Hauptmann. See HAUPTMANN, GERHART.

ATOMIC ENERGY FOR MILITARY PURPOSES (1945), by Henry De Wolf Smyth. This republication of the official report issued by the Manhattan District U.S. Corps of Engineers (the atomic bomb project) is an administrative history. It chronicles the efforts of many cooperating groups, and the scientific knowledge upon which the enterprise was based. Specifically, it describes America's scientific development between 1940 and 1945 toward the military use of energy from atomic nuclei. The report explains—as far as national security allows—radioactivity, nuclear structure and reaction, and the discovery of uranium fission. It makes clear that the development of atomic energy was based upon the known laws of the indestructibility of mass and energy, and their equivalence. The problems of organization are stated, and the various projects described, through the establishment in 1943 of an entirely new laboratory at Los Alamos, New Mexico, under the scientific direction of J. Robert Oppenheimer. There, theories and techniques were improved, materials purified, and finally workable atomic bombs were designed and constructed. The report closes with a prediction of important scientific progress to follow.

ATOMIC THEORY AND THE DESCRIPTION OF NATURE (1934), by Niels Bohr. For his application of the quantum theory to the problem of atomic structure, the Danish scientist Niels Bohr in 1922 was awarded the Nobel prize in physics. In 1913 physicists had been faced with a dilemma in their interpretation of atomic constitution. Rutherford had pictured the atom as consisting of a relatively heavy nucleus, positively charged, surrounded at a distance by tiny negatively charged particles or electrons. But if the surrounding electrons are assumed to be stationary, they should fall toward the center under the mutual attraction of the electric charges; if, on the other hand, they are regarded as moving in orbits about the nucleus, they should (under classical electromagnetic theory) radiate energy and hence not have permanent existence. To resolve the paradox, Bohr rejected the classical theory and postulated that certain orbits do exist in which the electron can continue to move without radiating energy. Since Planck had shown that energy is emitted discontinuously in quanta, Bohr concluded that the possible orbits are not unrestricted, but are determined in accordance with the quantum principle. That is, an electron can jump from one of these possible orbits to another, but it cannot occupy an intermediate position. If an electron falls from an outer to an inner orbit, radiation is emitted; if it goes from an inner to an outer position, energy is absorbed. Bohr reconciled his atomic theory with the known facts concerning spectral lines, and in 1916 Einstein deduced Planck's radiation law from a generalized Bohr atomic model.

Despite its initial success, the Bohr model of the atom was criticized as a mixture of classical, quantum, and relativity concepts. The mysterious nature of the jump of an electron from orbit to orbit has been another stumbling block. The philosophical implications have been serious, leading to Heisenberg's principle of indeterminacy and to some skepticism about the law of causality itself. These problems were discussed by Bohr in four articles appearing from 1925 to 1929, which were collected in the present volume in 1934.

ATTA TROLL (1847), by Heinrich Heine. See HEINE, HEINRICH.

AU PAYS DU MATIN CALME (1931), by Younghill Kang. See GRASS ROOF, THE, by Younghill Kang.

AUCASSIN AND NICOLETTE (13th c.), Anonymous. The scene is the south of France, in the country near Beaucaire. Aucassin, the count's son, is desperately in love with Nicolette, a Saracen captive, the daughter of the "King of Carthage." Count Gorins is planning a different match for his son and imprisons the lovers. They escape and encounter numerous perils in flight, become separated, and are captured by Saracen pirates. Finally their reunion is effected by the courageous Nicolette, disguised as a jongleur.

Written in Picard dialect by a sophisticated craftsman, who was familiar with the courtly romances of Christian of Troyes, this *chante-fable* is a masterpiece marked by a naïve beauty produced by a nice calculation of effects. It is written in mixed prose and verse, for recitation to a musical accompaniment.

AUDEN, WYSTAN HUGH (1907–   ). Born and educated in England, Auden has been living in the United States since 1939. He is widely considered the most important and original poet writing in English of the generation younger than T. S. Eliot. His first American publication, *Poems* (1934), caused him to be associated with Stephen Spender, from whom, however, he differs, being a satirist and experimenter, where Spender carries on the romantic tradition. Auden often uses private symbols difficult to interpret, but on the other hand can be very colloquial in style, as in *On the Island* (1937). *The Double Man* (1941) resorts to Swift's favorite measure, the octosyllabic couplet, to take a bleak view of the modern world. Among the *Collected Poems* (1945) was "In Memory of W. B. Yeats," notable for its estimate of what poetry can do in a world literally or spiritually at war. *The Age of Anxiety* (1947), a "baroque eclogue," is probably Auden's most significant work to date. On All Souls' Night, the evening of a day of prayer for those in Purgatory, four strangers meet in a bar: Quint, a tired widower whose mind is filled with mythology, imagines he seeks a Utopia while actually pursuing Eternal Life; Emble, a Navy enlistee who is oppressed by mental conflicts; Malin, an intelligence officer on leave from Canada, who is in search of a good time—but really in search of Goodness, though he little suspects it; and Rosetta, a woman buyer from a large department store who dreams of her own true love, eventually to discover that what she seeks is divine love. In subtle cadences, Auden relates these soulsearchings. He sings of fear and lust, but bids us be of good cheer; not to be frightened, but to cease self-analysis. Though we "appear dejected," we may be "self-resurrected" by a reliance on the strength and love outside ourselves.

AULULARIA, by Plautus. See POT OF GOLD, THE, by Plautus.

AURORA LEIGH (1865), by Elizabeth Barrett Browning. In this sociological novel in blank verse, Mrs. Browning aims at a bold, truthful delineation of the life of the poor in the rookeries of St. Giles, London. With a poetic realism rare for her day she does not hesitate to expose the social injustice of the society in which she lives. She defends her concern with the ugly realities:

> "Nay, if there's room for poets in this world . . .
> Their sole work is to represent the age."

Aurora Leigh has a passionate interest in social questions. She longs for knowledge and freedom and seeks both with Romney, her husband, who has founded a phalanstery in Shropshire.

AUSTRALIA FELIX (1917), by Henry Handel Richardson. See FORTUNES OF RICHARD MAHONY, by Henry Handel Richardson.

AUTOBIOGRAPHIES (1938), by William Butler Yeats. See YEATS, WILLIAM BUTLER.

AUTOBIOGRAPHY, by Benvenuto Cellini (1500-1570). Cellini's *Autobiography* is the story of one of the greatest goldsmiths, engravers and sculptors of the Italian Renaissance. The book relates with vivacity the most picturesque episodes of a life which was typical of that adventurous period. The author's character, as revealed by the book, is vain, vindictive and dominated by art. The *Autobiography* is the story of a man who was at the same time an artist, a boaster, a bully, a libertine, a duelist and an assassin. When Rome was besieged, Cellini, as a soldier, killed the Marshall of Bourbon, and was taken prisoner to the gloomy Castel St. Angelo. Later the reader finds him in Paris, where Cellini lived under the patronage of Francis I. He then returned to Florence to produce, in 1545, the famous statue of Perseus, now admired in the Piazza della Signoria. Cellini's *Autobiography* gives a clear idea of the general atmosphere prevailing in Italy during the sixteenth century. The author moves especially among princes and nobles, outraging their forbearance by his turbulent actions and, when he has exhausted their patience, revenging himself with malicious truth or reckless calumny. Although many of Cellini's statements seem today grossly exaggerated, especially at points when his vanity is concerned, the inaccuracy of particular facts and impressions does not affect the fidelity of the general picture.

AUTOBIOGRAPHY (published in 1796), by Edward Gibbon. Compiled by Lord Sheffield from six different sketches found among Gibbon's papers, this work, though fragmentary, amply reveals its author's personality and is stocked with memorable anecdotes of his private life. After a sickly and precocious childhood, he studied at Oxford and then Lausanne, with scant satisfaction. "Every man who rises above the comomn level has received two educations: the first from his teachers; the second, more personal and important, from himself." The young Gibbon, in his "thirst of improvement," read enormously, and, while in Switzerland, began "a literary correspondence with several men of learning." He also fell in love, but his father forbade the marriage. "After a painful struggle I yielded to my fate; I sighed as a lover, I obeyed as a son." He never married, but continued his bookish life and his travels. "It was at Rome, on the 15th of October 1764, as I sat musing amidst the ruins of the Capitol, while the barefooted friars were singing vespers in the temple of Jupiter, that the idea of writing the decline and fall of the city first started to my mind." The rest of the *Autobiography* is notable mainly for its account of the preparation, the composition, and the reception of the great work, of the unrivaled merits of which the author does not pretend to be unaware.

AUTOBIOGRAPHY (1913-1923), by Maxim Gorky. A landmark in the literature of self-revelation, Gorky's work consists of three books: *My Childhood* (1913), *In the World* (1917), and *My Universities* (1923). The events recorded in the first are seen through the eyes of a little boy who is keen, curious and brooding. He is little Alexey Peshkov, who as a writer adopted the *nom de plume* of Maxim Gorky. By and large, his was a joyless, sordid life, poverty, ignorance and drunkenness forming the sensitive boy's environment in the city of Astrakhan. It was relieved by the presence of his wonderful grandmother. She was dark, odd-looking and witty. Her life was made unbearable by her two savage sons, Mikhail and Yakov, who seemed destined for a bad end. His mother's second husband, Eugene Maximov, a profligate college student, humiliated her constantly. She died of tuberculosis. Unforgettable is the scene in which the six-year-old Gorky attacks his stepfather with a knife, in his mother's defense. When he was ten, Gorky entered the employ of a crafty shoemaker, a dishonest man surrounded by equally dishonest helpers. Gorky retained his scruples. Later Gorky worked on a Volga steamer, was an apprentice to an icon-maker, then to a baker, served as a janitor, worked in fisheries and on the railroad, sold *kvas*, and tramped through the countryside: "My wandering through Russia was prompted not by a lust for tramping but by a desire to see the land I was living in and the people around me." In 1898 Gorky, influenced by Korolenko, turned to writing, publishing in that year two volumes of stories. Tolstoy and Chekhov noticed him. Gorky became interested in the revolt against the Czar. Constantly in trouble with the officials, he was the first proletarian writer to serve the socialist movement in Russia. Gorky later visited the United States, where he wrote his novel, *Mother*.

AUTOBIOGRAPHY (1873), by John Stuart Mill. John Stuart Mill's *Autobiography*, while an important and self-revealing document of the life and intellectual evolution of one of England's most ingratiating thinkers, is primarily an account of the social history of England in the first three-quarters of the nineteenth century. It is the personal, yet objective, story of the conflict of an integrated mind with ideas and with the affairs of men. In his work Mill relates, step by step, the development of his views. As the son of James Mill, who together with Jeremy Bentham, founded the Utilitarian movement, he dedicated himself to the utilitarian increase of the greatest good for the greatest number. He was already looked upon as a leader of thought when, in his twenty-first year, a mental crisis occurred. This was a consequence of the physical and mental strain to which he, a child prodigy, had been subjected by his two tormenting mentors, his doting father and Bentham, both of whom saw in the boy the potentialities of great leadership for their utilitarian cause. He tells us that he was "in a dull state of nerves." The objects in life for which he had been trained and for which he had worked lost their charm. He then asked himself the following question: " 'Suppose that all your objects in life were realized; that all the changes in institutions and opinions which you are looking forward to could be completely effected at this very instant—would this be a great joy and happiness to you?' and an irrepressible self-consciousness distinctly answered *No!* At this my heart sank within me. The whole foundation on which my life was constructed fell down." This mental crisis led him materially to change his views. He adopted what he later found was Carlyle's anti-self-consciousness theory of happiness, not as an end, but to be attained only by having another aim, such as the happiness of others. He came also finally to change his social views to a position where he could say of himself and his wife: "Our ideal of ultimate improvement went far beyond democracy, and would class us decidedly under the general name of Socialists. . . . The social problem of the future we considered to be, how to unite the greatest liberty of action with a common ownership in the raw materials of the globe, and an equal participation of all combined labor."

AUTOBIOGRAPHY (1931), by Lincoln Steffens. The story of Steffens' life is a history of social and economic progress in the United States, and of the author's evolution of a theory of government. The country's most impassioned and untiring debunker, Steffens' long newspaper career was devoted to exposing corruption, espousing "lost causes," and correcting injustices to the weak. He was frankly a radical, and toward the end of life a Communist, but his social crusades won for him the respect of all classes of people. The *Autobiography* contains valuable eyewitness information about America's labor struggles, and the celebrated civil liberties cases at the turn of the century. It is a self-portrait of an exceptional human spirit.

AUTOBIOGRAPHY (1924), by Mark Twain. See LIFE ON THE MISSISSIPPI, by Mark Twain.

AUTOBIOGRAPHY OF ALICE B. TOKLAS, THE (1933), by Gertrude Stein. With her characteristic whimsicality, Gertrude Stein presents her autobiography as the work of her secretary and companion. "Alice B. Toklas," with tongue in cheek, records the original life, pranks, opinions and memorable conversations of her dear friend. The book is a revealing study of a now moribund Parisian Bohemia. The reader is taken into the abstractionist fastnesses of artists' studios, cafés, and Montmartre salons. Introduced "in bedroom slippers" are such personages as Picasso, Braque, Cocteau. In the center, however, is always the egotistic, irrepressible American expatriate.

Lectures in America (1935) explain Miss Stein's controversial literary technique—a presentation by repetition, rhythm and free association. Her most comprehensible work is *Three Lives*, privately printed in 1909. Consisting of three novelettes, the book is unified by the fact that the three principal characters are domestics of Bridgepoint, Connecticut. "The Good Anna" is a devoted servant whose life and death in the service of Miss Mathilda are poignantly delineated. The second story, by far the longest, has for its heroine Melanctha Herbert, a Negro girl whose unhappy love affair is recounted. "The Gentle Lena" is a submissive German maid who marries a tailor and patiently endures an unhappy life.

AUTOBIOGRAPHY OF AN EX-COLORED MAN, THE (1912), by James Weldon Johnson. In this novel concerning the social, emotional and psychological problems which a Negro must face, the question of miscegenation is thoroughly and candidly discussed. Prejudice against the young, unnamed hero forces him into a painful self-consciousness. He marries a white woman, but his evolution as a mature man has awakened him to the necessity and pride of asserting without fear or apology his membership in the Negro race. The *Autobiography* helps to illuminate in a profound way an important problem.

AUTOBIOGRAPHY OF BENJAMIN FRANKLIN, THE (1868), by Benjamin Franklin. This famous work, written in the form of a letter to his son, was never completed past an account of the year 1757; and was not published completely in English until 1868. It is the story of a self-made man, free from pose, anxious to establish the truth about his life. Without any apologies, Franklin reveals the difficulties of his career, describes his early struggles as an apprentice, journeyman, and finally master printer; and tells of achieving at last wealth and the affection of his acquaintances. The style is plain, but the contents rich with quaint wisdom and the worldliness for which the author was renowned. One of the earliest significant works written in this form, it influenced subsequent autobiographers, notably Jean Jacques Rousseau.

Franklin was early a journalist, later contributing to *The Pennsylvania Gazette,* which was printed by his own press. *Poor Richard's Almanack* (1733–1758), a best-seller in America and Europe, contained provocative maxims and adages which revealed the author as an optimistic pedagogue.

Franklin also wrote scientific reports, political dissertations, and unimportant items for the amusement of his friends.

AUTOCRAT OF THE BREAKFAST-TABLE, THE (1858), by Oliver Wendell Holmes. These conversation pieces, written in Holmes' inimitably learned and witty style, began to appear for the first time in the November 1857 issue of *The Atlantic Monthly* (which Holmes named). The author was society's most irrepressible talker at the time, and his merry intellectual soliloquies helped create the New England "Brahmin" tradition. *The Autocrat* is filled with rapidly shifting themes expounded with a philosophical, whimsical humor. Holmes was a liberal, and his papers breathe this spirit from first to last. A number of his many poems are included in the first volume: "The Chambered Nautilus" is an encouraging allegory of human progress, and "The Deacon's Masterpiece" ("The Wonderful One-Hoss Shay") is a veiled attack on Holmes' Unitarian fathers. The leading personages in the papers are the landlady, her daughter, the poor relation, the divinity student, and the schoolmistress. Later series of the papers include *The Professor at the Breakfast-Table* (1860), *The Poet at the Breakfast-Table* (1872), and *Over the Teacups* (1891).

Elsie Venner (1861), one of Holmes' three novels, is an entertaining essay on heredity in fictional form, and an informative guide to pre-Civil War New England. The heroine herself scarcely ever speaks during the two volumes.

AUTUMN OF MANHOOD, THE (1653), by Baltasar Gracián. See CRITICK, THE, by Baltasar Gracián.

AVERROES (1126–1198). Averroes, the famous Arabian philosopher and theologian, was known as the "Commentator," because of his interpretations of Aristotle. These, denying the Creation and immortality, propounding psychological and moral determinism, and declaring the "double truth" of philosophy and religion—what was true for one was not necessarily true for the other—were so subversive to the Christian faith that Thomas Aquinas and Albertus Magnus were called upon to refute them. His commentaries were written in three lengths: long ones, quoting and discoursing on each paragraph; shorter ones, or digests; and brief paraphrases. Averroes was also a master of law, mathematics, and medicine. His treatises on these subjects, and also on grammar and astronomy, still exist, though many are untranslated.

AWAKE AND SING! (1935), by Clifford Odets. See WAITING FOR LEFTY, by Clifford Odets.

AWAKENING (1920), by John Galsworthy. See FORSYTE SAGA, THE, by John Galsworthy.

AWAKENING OF SPRING (1906), by Frank Wedekind. This drama, by one of the forerunners of the expressionistic movement in Germany, shocked the public at its initial presentation in 1906. In dealing with the problems concerning the newly-felt sex urge of the adolescent, the playwright throws light upon a vicious school system, and the ineptitude of parents to give sympathetic explanations on sex. Wendla Bergmann, a girl of 14, is misled by her mother into believing that childbirth results from fervent love and thus allows herself to be seduced by Melchior Gabor, a young schoolboy. Melchior is expelled from school for being responsible for several pages of sexual explanations which he had given to a curious schoolmate, Moritz Stiefel, who later committed suicide over failure in schoolwork. Wendla takes ill and her mother realizes that her daughter is to bear a child. The young girl soon is in her grave—the victim of abortives. Melchior's parents send him to an institution from which he escapes and comes upon the cemetery, where he meets the headless ghost of Moritz. The play ends with Melchior's insanity, as he is pictured being carried off over the graves by a phantom masked-man.

Among Wedekind's other plays available in English, and marked by a wooden, stylized speech and symbolical type characterization, are *Earth Spirit* and *Pandora's Box*.

AWKWARD AGE, THE (1899), by Henry James. See TURN OF THE SCREW, THE, by Henry James.

AXE OF WANDSBECK, THE (1947), by Arnold Zweig. See CASE OF SERGEANT GRISCHA, by Arnold Zweig.

AXEL'S CASTLE (1931), by Edmund Wilson. This is a selective critical study of the world's imaginative literature from 1870 to 1930. Wilson interprets the works of eight writers whom he describes as belonging to the Symbolist school: William Butler Yeats, Paul Valéry, T. S. Eliot, Marcel Proust, James Joyce, Gertrude Stein, Villiers de L'Isle-Adam, and Rimbaud. With the possible exception of Gertrude Stein, Wilson has an enthusiastic admiration for all. His portraits and biographies chronicle their writings, philosophies and aesthetic canons. He regards them as having achieved historical importance because they broke away from the established routine of literature practiced since the Renaissance.

The Triple Thinkers (1938) contains ten literary essays. *Memoirs of Hecate County* (1946) are six frank short stories designed to investigate the personalities and lives of wealthy, intellectual New York suburbanites.

BABBITT (1922), by Sinclair Lewis. With the character of Babbitt, Lewis satirically defined a certain middle-class attitude. The central character typifies the American go-getter, and his name has since been widely used to describe such a person. George F. Babbitt is a well-to-do realtor in Zenith, a midwestern boom city. A high-powered salesman, he is aggressive and knows how to take advantage of every person and opportunity that comes his way. His home life, however, is devoid of any beauty, although he lives in lovely surroundings in a standardized residential section. Babbitt dimly realizes the emptiness of his life, and attempts, at the age of forty-six, to rebel. With his friend, the dreamer Paul Rieseling, he takes a short vacation in Maine; but this is unsuccessful, and shortly thereafter Paul is jailed for the murder of his wife Zilla. George, now more rebellious, alienates his friends by espousing a radical cause and by engaging in a short affair with his client, Mrs. Tanis Judique. But he fears ostracism above all, and finally sinks back to his Good Citizens' League life, and domestic conventionality. When his son Ted leaves school suddenly and elopes, however, Babbitt encourages him.

Lewis wrote two other novels about American businessmen, *Dodsworth* (q.v.); and *Work of Art* (1934), a sympathetic story of hotelman Myron Weagle, and his ideals, which flourish despite all disillusion.

BABBITT, IRVING (1865–1933). Irving Babbitt, a leader with Paul Elmer More (q.v.) of the New Humanist movement, wrote his most inclusive attack on romanticism and its champion Rousseau in *Rousseau and Romanticism* (1919). This book condemns emotional naturalism as a philosophical basis for life, and extols discipline as a better law for man. The individualist who challenges ethical standards just because they are traditional is dangerous to society, the author declares. Babbitt criticizes particularly the romantic concept of nature, which excludes man.

The New Laokoön (1910) attempts to solve the confusion of mixed artistic genres, inaugurated by romanticism. It challenges the romantic theory of anti-intellectual "spontaneity" of production, program music as epitomized by the emotional unrestraint of Hector Berlioz, and the sensuous word painting of the nineteenth century. Babbitt considered this question of the proper boundaries of the arts not only as an aesthetic consideration, but as a basic attitude toward life.

BACCHAE, THE (ca. 405 B.C.), by Euripides. The play was written after Euripides' self-imposed exile in Macedonia, and produced at Athens only after his death. It is named after the devotees of Bacchus or Dionysus. The scene is Thebes and the time, the reign of Pentheus, who has replaced his aged grandfather Cadmus on the throne. The people of Thebes, especially the women, have been caught up in a frenzy of religious enthusiasm for the new and mystic wine god, Dionysus. Dressed in fawn skins and fondling serpents, they abandon their homes and follow the god himself in ecstatic rapture as he leads them in his orgiastic dances over the wooded hills. As the play opens, Cadmus and Tirsias enter dressed as votaries of the god. They are soon joined by Pentheus who has, in stern sobriety and contempt for the new religion, confined the votaries, forbidden the rites, and now orders the seizure and imprisonment of the god in whose divinity he does not believe. These orders are duly accomplished, but the god is miraculously freed as the earth quakes and the palace rocks. Meanwhile the Bacchae have also been set free from their confinement, and Pentheus now orders his men to hunt them down. Here the god lays his trap and, working on Pentheus' real desire to witness the orgies, persuades the King to spy upon the women in woman's guise himself. Completely under the god's spell, Pentheus yields, but in the midst of his spying he is discovered by the women who, led by Agave, the King's mother, rend his body limb from limb in their religious frenzy. Agave herself, in one of the most tragic scenes of Greek tragedy, bears in the head of her son under the ghastly delusion that it is that of a lion which she has slain, and wishes her son might share her triumph. Cadmus sorrowfully brings Agave to her senses, and here the play ends for us, since a page or more was lost from the archetype of our manuscript. The real significance of the play is a baffling riddle, but it is obviously Euripides' last word on mystic forces of religion and the inadequacy of mere human reason and strength to oppose their course.

BACCHYLIDES (ca. 505–450 B.C.). This poet, famed as the "Cean Nightingale," was the rival of Pindar as a lyric poet and composer of odes in honor of victors at the Greek games. Until 1896, only brief quotations from his poems were known, but in that year thirteen of these odes and six of his other poems were recovered from an Egyptian papyrus. From these new poems, we come to know a brilliant and facile poet. His poetic imagery, while not so bold as that of Pindar, is vivid and yet unobtrusive. The richness of his poetic vocabulary is indicated by the fact that the new poems contained many words hitherto unknown in Greek, mostly his own coinage. His narrative style is fluent and almost epic. The most beautiful and perhaps the most interesting of these poems is a "Paean" to Apollo entitled "The Youths" or "Theseus," which tells the myth of how the hero, to prove his divine parentage, plunged overboard from the ship on which he and his companions were being carried away to Crete, and brought back from his father Poseidon's palace at the bottom of the sea the ring of his challenger, Minos.

BACK TO METHUSELAH (1921), by George Bernard Shaw. This long play, divided into five parts, treats of creative evolution. In the first part, called *In the Beginning,* Lilith tears herself in two to create Adam and Eve. To Eve is imparted the secret of creation and Adam's share in it. These two invent birth and death, and Cain invents murder and war.

In the second part, *Gospel of the Brothers Barnabas,* Conrad Barnabas, a noted biologist, has written a book adjusting the lifespan to three hundred years, for, as he tells his brother, it takes that length of time for the human race to mature. Burge and Lubin, two rival politicians who have seen England through a devastating war, come to ask Conrad's support in a coming election. He goes into a biological explanation of the immaturity of mankind in handling the problems of government and expounds his longevity theory, which is nothing but the will to live.

In the third part, *The Thing Happens,* Archbishop Haslam in the year 2170 is two hundred and eighty-three, but looks only fifty; Mrs. Lutestring, Conrad's former parlor-maid, is two hundred and seventy-four, and is now acting as Domestic Minister. Both regard the present generation as adolescent. England is governed by Chinese (Confucius is Chief Secretary), and African women. Burge-Lubin, the President, can talk to his secretaries visually, by means of a special switchboard.

Part four, *Tragedy of an Elderly Gentleman,* takes place in the year A.D. 3000. People are now classified as primaries, secondaries and tertiaries, according to the number of centuries they have lived. The Elderly Gentleman, an unfortunate "short-liver," is destroyed by the glance of the Oracle, a secondary.

In the fifth part, *As Far As Thought Can Reach,* human life in the year A.D. 31,920 is depicted. The race now produces offspring which hatch from eggs at the age of seventeen; pass through a four-year adolescent period, when they love, dance, play games, and enjoy the arts; then mature and become Ancients, bald and sexless, devoted to intellectual study.

In an Epilogue, Adam, Eve, Cain and Lilith judge the future state of man. Adam is puzzled, Eve is glad cleverness prevails, Cain is sorry war is not permitted, and Lilith waits for the day when man shall completely overcome matter.

BALL OF TALLOW (1880), by Guy de Maupassant. See BOULE DE SUIF AND OTHER TALES, by Guy de Maupassant.

BALLAD OF READING GAOL (1898), by Oscar Wilde. Like Wilde's *De Profundis,* this simple but profound poem is a result of his imprisonment. The *Ballad* lacks the decadent sophistication of his earlier work. The theme that "each man kills the thing he loves" runs throughout the story of the author's mental suffering for a fellow prisoner who must hang for murder. The poem is a moving portrayal and bitter denunciation of a system in which the "vilest deeds, like poison weeds, bloom well in prison air." It is his most celebrated piece of verse, still enjoying wide popularity on the Continent as well as in English-speaking countries. His other poems are less likely to endure, with the exception of that other sincere piece, "Requiescat," in memory of his young sister.

BALLAD OF THE BROWN GIRL (1924), by Countee Cullen. See CULLEN, COUNTEE.

BALLADS AND OTHER POEMS (1842), by Henry Wadsworth Longfellow. See LONGFELLOW, HENRY WADSWORTH.

BALLADS, ENGLISH AND SCOTTISH POPULAR (1882–1898), edited by Francis James Child. This famous and definitive collection of old ballads gathered from oral tradition was published in five volumes. It contains 305 ballads in over a thousand versions. A ballad is a song that tells a story in four-line stanzas usually rhyming abcb, the first and third lines being iambic tetrameter, the second and fourth iambic trimeter. Most of the ballads in the Child collection go back to the fifteenth century and before. There are, first, ballads of the supernatural, involving fairies, elves, water-sprites, demons, and ghosts. "The Wife of Usher's Well" is an example; her three dead sons pay her a visit one night, but must leave at cock-crow. The ballads of the greenwood feature Robin Hood, e.g., "Robin Hood and Guy of Gisborne" (q.v.). "Sir Patrick Spens" (q.v.) is a specimen of the possibly historical ballad. "Chevy Chase" tells of a border fight in which

Percy the Englishman and doughty Douglas, the Scotchman, are killed. There are ballads of domestic tragedy, such as "Edward," whose brand drips with his father's blood, and "The Twa Sisters," the elder of whom drowns the other in a fit of jealousy. Border feuds and forays form another class. "Bonnie James Campbell" rides off on one of these campaigns, and is never seen again. But there is a non-tragic class too. Witness "Get up and Bar the Door," with its humorous contention between man and wife as to who will speak first and so make himself the one to bar the door.

The great predecessor of Child's collection was Thomas Percy's *Reliques of Ancient English Poetry* (1765).

BALZAC (1944), by Stefan Zweig. See ZWEIG, STEFAN.

BAMBI (1929), by Felix Salten. *Bambi* is a simple poetic tale of animal life in the woods. The animals act, talk, think and feel like human beings. The story has a folk quality and is full of rapture for the mysterious beauty of forest life; it progresses at a quiet pace. The hero is Bambi, and his destiny is traced from tiny fawn to mature stag. He has relations, friends and acquaintances. There are Bambi's loving mother, his cousin Ava, and her two little fawns, Gobo and Faline. Then there are Prince Ronno and Karus the young deer; also Bambi's friends, the hare, the squirrel, the old stag, the woodpecker, the screech-owl, the magpie, the crow, the doe Marena, and the wicked fox who meets his just ends from He. Now *He* is the only human little animal in the forest. He is diabolically clever and seems to be everywhere. With a little stick in his hand that makes a loud report, he deals death. He kills young Gobo that way. Toward the end of the story, he even shoots Bambi in the leg. But the young stag recovers, falls in love with Faline, marries her and has children by her.

Bambi, originally published in 1929 in German, has become a favorite with children in many countries; the book has been immortalized again by the animated cartoons of Walt Disney in this country.

BAMETZAR (1921), by Zalman Shneiur. See SHNEIUR, ZALMAN.

BAR SINISTER, THE (1903), by Richard Harding Davis. See DAVIS, RICHARD HARDING.

BARBARIC ODES (1877–1887), by Giosue' Carducci. See CARDUCCI, GIOSUE'.

BARBER OF SEVILLE, THE (1775), by Pierre Augustin Caron de Beaumarchais. *The Barber of Seville* is, in essence, a gentle and innocent comedy, in the *commedia dell' arte* vein. The wily and light-hearted barber, Figaro, a pure buffo-comedy type, enables Count Almaviva to woo and win Rosine from her close-fisted, severe guardian, Barthols, who has intended to marry her himself and claim her fortune. The device adopted for this *coup* is the stock trick of the suitor posing as the elderly and crotchety music teacher, while Figaro, barber and general town factotum, carries out distracting maneuvers with the guardian. The significance of the play, not immediately visible in its plot, lies in the subtle shadings of characterization and dialogue by which the folly of the noble and wealthy characters is contrasted with the simpler, cleverer and more honest persons of no rank. The play, as such, has dropped out of usage, but remains very much alive in the operatic version by Rossini. The author is the same political liberal who procured arms for the Colonials in the American Revolution, and then narrowly escaped the guillotine after helping start the Revolution in France.

BARCHESTER TOWERS (1857), by Anthony Trollope. This is the second novel in the Barsetshire series, a sequel to *The Warden* (q.v.). Upon the death of the Archbishop, Archdeacon Grantly desires to succeed his father, but a governmental shift blocks his aspirations and brings to the Deacon's Palace Dr. Proudie—and, hardly to be overlooked, Mrs. Proudie. The Proudies give the people of Barchester a party containing one of Trollope's most famous episodes. During the stir caused by the appearance of Canon Stanhope's lovely invalid daughter, his son Bertie attempts to free Mrs. Proudie's train from the castor of a sofa, and the haughty woman utters her deathless phrase, "Unhand me, sir." The Stanhopes have arrived from Italy, seeking a match for Bertie with Dr. Harding's widowed daughter, Eleanor Bold. The latter, however, prefers Rev. Arabin. The villainous Obediah Slope, Mrs. Proudie's protégé, courts both Eleanor and Canon Stanhope's daughter—a bit of boldness for which the angry Mrs. Proudie forces him from his sinecure as Bishop's Chaplain. Neither is Dr. Harding reinstated at the Hospital; the post goes to Rev. Quiverful, who has fourteen children.

BARD, THE (1806), by Vincenzo Monti. See MONTI, VINCENZO.

BARD, THE (1840), by Taras Shevchenko. See KOBZAR, by Taras Shevchenko.

BARLEY FIELDS, THE (1926), by Robert Nathan. See NATHAN, ROBERT.

BARNABY RUDGE (1841), by Charles Dickens. This is an historical novel of the anti-Catholic riots of 1780. Led by Lord George Gordon, the rioters used "No Popery!" for their motto. The novel is notable for its vivid descriptions of the mobs, who destroy and pilfer the churches, and burn Newgate Prison. Among Gordon's followers are Hugh; Ned Dennis, the hangman; and Samuel Tappertit, captain of the "Prentice Knights." Barnaby Rudge is the idiot son of a murderer. He is unwittingly among the rioters, and is consequently jailed. He is pardoned on the scaffold. Among the many characters are: Sir John Chester, father of Hugh and of Edward, the latter in love with Emma; Gashford, Gordon's secretary; Geoffrey Haredale, and his niece, Emma; blind Stagg; Gabriel Varden, locksmith, and his daughter Dolly; Miss Miggs, Varden's treacherous servant; John Willet, host of the Maypole Inn, and Joe, his son. Barnaby's father is the murderer of Geoffrey Haredale's brother, Reuben, and is himself found dead after he blackmails his wife, the unfortunate Mrs. Rudge.

BARON MÜNCHHAUSEN (1785), by Rudolph Erich Raspe. See MÜNCHHAUSEN.

BARRACK-ROOM BALLADS AND OTHER VERSES (1892), by Rudyard Kipling. This volume of poetry is divided into two sections: the ballads, serious in tone, written in conventional English, with many themes taken from ancient legends and sea tales; and the barrack-room ballads in cockney dialect, which deal with the varied experiences of the British common soldier throughout the empire. The latter echo with colorful slang and native expressions. One reason for their enormous popularity is that because of their strong rhythms, catchy refrains, and energetic style, they have an appeal even to people who do not usually read poetry. The subject matter of the poems has a wide range. Some of the best-known are "Gunga Din," about the heroic water-boy who died for his men, "Fuzzy Wuzzy," the "first-class fightin' man," "Danny Deever," who was hanged, and what became especially popular when set to music, "Mandalay." The imperialism shown in some of Kipling's earlier writings he effectively took back in his later poem, "Recessional," written on the sixtieth anniversary of the reign of Queen Victoria (1897). His most popular moral poem is "If—." His most famous humorous line occurs in "The Betrothed," in the collection of light verse called *Departmental Ditties* (1886): "And a woman is only a woman, but a good Cigar is a Smoke."

BARREN GROUND (1925), by Ellen Glasgow. This novel is the story of Dorinda Oakley, daughter of a poor tenant farmer of Virginia. Life on the land, which is not their own, is bleak; they make their living out of barren ground. Into the humdrum pattern of the twenty-year-old's existence, love enters. The object of her passion is Jason Greylock, an irresponsible son of the village doctor. He is at length forced to leave her and marry a former fiancée, on the very eve of their ceremony. Dorinda travels to New York and becomes a nurse. She refuses an offer of marriage, vaguely seeking something else in life. Finally, she returns to the land, with a new knowledge of scientific agriculture, and makes the farm fruitful. She marries the colorless, middle-aged Nathan Pedlar, to provide a home for his children, but mourns for him without grief when he dies. All her passion has been transferred to the ground. Her bitterness gone, she is later able to lend a helping hand to the unfaithful lover of her youth.

Ellen Glasgow's many novels have concerned themselves with the social history of the South, and with woman's place in society. *In This Our Life* (q.v.) was awarded a Pulitzer Prize. *Vein of Iron* (q.v.) is another rural study of the same region. Miss Glasgow also wrote several satirical novels of manners, such as *The Romantic Comedians* (1926), which relates the amorous experiments of the sixty-five year old Judge Gamaliel Bland Honeywell.

BARRIE, SIR JAMES MATTHEW (1860–1937). Besides the world-famous play and story *Peter Pan* and the novels *The Little Minister* and *Sentimental Tommy* (qq.v.), three other plays by this Scotch master of sentiment and ironic romanticism should be singled out, as well as his biography of his mother, *Margaret Ogilvy* (1896). In the latter book, he is humorous and free of Victorian reticence, and yet worshipful about this dominating influence on his personality and life. She was a dour but likeable Scotswoman with a great reservoir of inner strength. *The Admirable Crichton* (1902) tells of the butler of a radical peer, who saves Lord Loam's whole party from perishing when his lordship's yacht is wrecked on a desert isle in the Pacific. Crichton, unlike his master, is a reactionary, a believer in class distinctions, is the practical leader in the emergency, while Lord Loam becomes the handyman. But no sooner is the party rescued than the original status quickly resumes, and Crichton is a butler again, renouncing with magnificent consistency of conviction his short-lived majesty. *What Every Woman Knows* (1908) shows that it is the woman who makes or breaks the man. Maggie is the heroine, in the background of John Shand's every success. In *Dear Brutus* (1917) to the problem of whether people would behave differently if they had a chance to live their lives over, Barrie answers no. The scene is an enchanted forest where the unhappy characters are given, in vain, their second chance. *Quality Street* (1902) and *A Kiss for Cinderella* (1916) are other popular plays.

BAR-ROOM BALLADS (1940), by Robert W. Service. See SERVICE, ROBERT W.

BARRY, PHILIP (1896–). Philip Barry, who wrote his first play at the age of thirteen, has a number of popular successes to his credit. *Paris Bound* (1927) is a sophisticated comedy on the theme of the modern approach to marriage. Jim and Mary Hutton have agreed that each shall have the freedom to take other lovers. Mary's realization that Jim has done so, however, almost wrecks the marriage.

Holiday (1928) is a sympathetic play about children's revolt against parental morality. John Chase, a young lawyer, has an easy-going way of life which is dubiously regarded by haughty Julia Seton, his fiancée, and her pompous father. Not so Julia's older sister Linda, who goes off with Johnny in the end.

Hotel Universe (1930) is a mystical play in which old Stephen Field, before his death, gets in touch with the supersensory world. He points out to his daughter Ann and her weekend guests the errors of their early lives which have caused their present unhappiness. With this knowledge, the young people relieve their frustrations and face life with confidence.

Tomorrow and Tomorrow (1931) also shows Barry's interest in psychological character analysis. The play concerns Eve Redman, whose son Christian is treated by the psychoanalyst Nicholas Hay, actually the youth's father. Eve refuses to leave her husband Gail, realizing how important to him is the love of his wife and child.

The Animal Kingdom (1932) deals with modern family life. Wealthy Tom Collier leaves his mistress Daisy Sage to marry Cecelia Henry; but, finding her less sympathetic to his personality, at length returns to Daisy.

The Philadelphia Story (1939) concerns Tracy Lord, prudish young woman from the Main Line, who is accidentally compromised by a roving reporter, and through the sympathetic understanding of her first husband—whom she remarries—learns to understand herself better.

BARTHOLOMEW FAIR (1614), by Ben Jonson. This rollicking, bawdy comedy is a satire on the hypocrisy of the Puritans, and the general licentiousness of London. Littlewit desires to go to the Fair, and begs his wife, Win, to pretend a longing for roast pig so that they can persuade her mother, Dame Purecraft, and the latter's suitor, Zeal-of-the-Land Busy, to go too. Busy decides the longing is justified, and they eat their pig in the booth of Ursula, the pig-woman. Littlewit wants to see more of the Fair, so he contrives to have Busy put in the stocks, and Dame Purecraft follows him. Justice Overdo, in disguise, is the innocent tool whereby Cokes, a genteel nitwit, has his purse snatched by Edgeworth and is accused of having snatched the purse himself. Winwife, who is courting Dame Purecraft, and his friend, Quarlous, are spectators too, and have several adventures. Winwife wins Grace Wellborn, Overdo's ward, away from Cokes, to whom she is betrothed. Quarlous, masquerading as a madman, wins Dame Purecraft, who is looking for a mad husband because of a fortune teller's prediction.

BASE YEAR, THE (1922), by Boris Pilnyak. See PILNYAK, BORIS.

BATTLE OF KOSOVO (ca. 1389). A cycle. See MARKO, THE KING'S SON.

BATTLE OF MALDON, THE (after 991). This is one of the finest poems in Old English, though only a fragment without beginning or ending. It commemorates a battle between the Danes and the English where the magnificent ealdorman Bryhtnoth, the friend of Aelfric, fell on the bank of the Panta, or Blackwater, in Essex. He angrily rejects the messenger who comes from the enemy demanding tribute as the price of peace. He will defend against the heathen "the home of Aethelred, my prince, the people and the ground." After ebb-tide the Vikings can rush to the attack. Bryhtnoth is hewn down, along with Aelfnoth and Wulfmaer. Godric, the son of Odda, flees, coward that he is, but another Godric, the son of Aethelgar, and Offa and other valiant Englishmen stand and exhort their men. The words of the aged Bryhtnoth are famous: "Thought shall be the harder, heart the keener, courage the greater, as our might lessens."

BATTLE OF THE BOOKS, THE (written 1697; published 1704), by Jonathan Swift. Inspired by his patron, Sir William Temple, who had defended ancient over modern learning in a contemporary literary squabble, Swift brilliantly satirizes the controversy in prose, bringing into the fray Dryden and Richard Bentley, prominent exponents of the greater value of modern works, as well as Descartes, Milton, Hobbes, and others. In an imaginary, allegorical battle between Ancient and Modern books staged in St. James's library, the Bee, representing the Ancients, who rely upon Nature for their honey, is entangled in the web of the Spider, who, like the Moderns, spins knowledge entirely out of himself. The Ancients, led by such worthies as Homer, Aristotle, Euclid and Plato have the advantage, but the issue is ultimately left undecided.

Swift's *Journal to Stella* (written 1710–1713) consists of letters addressed from London to Esther "Stella" Johnson and her older companion Rebecca Dingley. This was the period of Swift's greatest political activity in England, and there are many intimate and casual pictures of the life of the time, with comments on eminent personalities. The vein is often jocular.

BAY PSALM BOOK, THE (1640), by Richard Mather, Thomas Welde, and John Eliot. One of the first books to be printed in English in North America, this book was adopted at once by almost every congregation in the

Massachusetts Bay Colony, from which it derived its name. The psalms had been apportioned for metrical translation to all the principal clergymen of the colonies, particularly to Richard Mather of Dorchester and to Thomas Welde and John Eliot of Roxbury. Their English style is generally regarded as clumsy, and their Hebrew scholarship as inferior. The translators confessed that they had "attended Conscience rather than Elegance." The makeshift psalm book went through twenty-seven editions between 1640 and 1752, however, before being replaced by another volume.

BEARD, CHARLES A. (1874–1948). Charles Beard, after establishing Ruskin College for labor leaders at Oxford, returned to America as professor of political science at Columbia University. His first historical volumes were texts on European history. *The Development of Modern Europe,* written with J. H. Robinson (1907–1908), is a standard work. Thereafter, he turned his attention to the American scene. A champion of economic interpretation of history, Beard's liberalism caused him to leave academic life. He devoted himself after 1917 to history writing and democratic activities. *The Rise of American Civilization,* written with his wife Mary R. Beard (1927), is an exposition of democracy's evolution and bright future; and *America in Midpassage* (1939) is an examination of American social and economic institutions. Shortly before his death he completed *American Foreign Policy in the Making: 1932–1940* (1946), in which his political beliefs are quite different from those in his earlier works.

BEATRIJS (14th c.), Anonymous. This Flemish epic tells of a noble nun, fighting with Satan to kill the love which she felt for many years for one of her former friends. Finally she allows herself to be abducted from the nunnery by him, but not before she has fulfilled her duties as sacristan, as faithfully as possible. She deposits her nun's dress at the foot of the image of Mary. She knows that she will feel remorse for her flight, yet she goes and lives in opulence with her lover for seven years. Then the lean years come; the man abandons Beatrijs and the two children she bore him. Necessity forces her to lead an impure life. After seven years, the loathing over her sins causes her to break with her past, and with her two children she goes through the land begging, until she arrives in the vicinity of her former nunnery. She finds lodging with an old woman, from whom she draws information about conditions in the nunnery. She hears that no nun has ever escaped and that the sacristan has fulfilled her task faithfully. At night three voices call to Beatrijs. They order her to leave her children and to return to the nunnery. In the dark she finds the orchard's gate opened. In the chapel, before the image of Mary, lie her shoes, cowl and veil, in the same place she put them fourteen years ago. No one has missed Beatrijs, for the Mother of God has performed the sacred duties in Beatrijs' likeness. By its simple narration and realistic portrayal, but above all through pure humaneness, this poem is one of the most beautiful creations of the Middle Ages. In 1908, P. C. Boutens gave it modern story form; in 1923, Herman Teirlinck used it as the basis for his drama *Ik dien.*

It was reprinted by Pantheon Books, New York, 1944, with an introduction by Jan-Albert Goris.

BEAUCHAMP'S CAREER (1876), by George Meredith. See ORDEAL OF RICHARD FEVEREL, THE, by George Meredith.

BEAUTIFUL MAGELONE, THE (1797), by Ludwig Tieck. See TIECK, LUDWIG.

BEAUTIFUL PLAY OF LANCELOT OF DENMARK, A (1923), translated by P. Geyl (1923). See MEDIEVAL FLEMISH PLAYS.

BEAUTY AND LOVE (1778), by Sheyh Galib. This long poem written by Sheyh (1757–1799), the head of the Whirling Dervishes of Pera, is in the traditional form of Turkish epic poems in which the two halves of each verse rhyme. It is an allegory of the universe. A girl, Beauty, symbolizing the Divine Beauty, is wooed by Love, who represents the human soul with all of its aspirations. In the beginning Beauty loves Love and finally through the force of the Divine, Love recognizes this fact and reciprocates. He then starts out through the world in search of something that is worthy to be presented to his beloved. After many experiences, he is led to the conclusion that Love is Beauty, and Beauty is Love, and finally passes within the veil of Beauty. The language of the poem is filled with the Arab and Persian words that were the stock in trade of the Turkish of the period, but the poem itself expresses some of the higher thoughts and aspirations of the religion of Islam in a figurative form.

BEAUX' STRATAGEM, THE (1707), by George Farquhar. This gay and lively comedy is Farquhar's best-known play and has enjoyed a long life on the stage. The author was influenced by Milton's tracts on marriage and divorce, and derived some of the ethical ideas in this play from them. Aimwell and Archer, two gentlemen of broken fortunes, journey to an inn near Litchfield in hope of mending them. Aimwell poses as master, with Archer as his servant. Boniface, the landlord, harbors a highwayman, Gibbet, and he suspects them of belonging to the brotherhood of the road. Therefore he sets his pretty daughter, Cherry, to spying on Archer. Aimwell is captivated by Lady Bountiful's daughter, Dorinda. Dorinda has a brother, Sullen, a boorish country squire, who has married a sophisticated London lady. Scrub, Sullen's servant, invites Archer to drink beer with him in the servant's hall, and Archer meets Mrs. Sullen, who is attracted to him and realizes he is not a servant. Aimwell feigns illness, thus requiring the administration of Lady Bountiful, and by this artifice manages to propose to Dorinda. Count Bellair, a Frenchman, is attentive to Mrs. Sullen and she encourages him while her husband is listening, hoping to arouse his jealousy. Archer discovers from Scrub an intrigue to hide the Count in Mrs. Sullen's closet, and he forces Foigard, an impostor and the Count's friend, to let him take Bellair's place. In the meantime, Gibbet and two accomplices break into Sullen's house. Cherry warns Aimwell, who goes to rescue Lady Bountiful and Dorinda. Sir Charles Freeman, Mrs. Sullen's brother, arrives and assists her in freeing herself from her husband. Sir Charles tells Aimwell he has come into a fortune through the death of his older brother, so Dorinda and Aimwell are happily united. Mrs. Sullen is free to marry Archer.

BED OF FRAGRANCE, by Moses Ibn Ezra. See IBN EZRA, MOSES.

BEDFORD VILLAGE (1944), by Hervey Allen. See ANTHONY AD-VERSE, by Hervey Allen.

BEFORE ADAM (1906), by Jack London. See LONDON, JACK.

BEFORE DAWN (1889), by Gerhart Hauptmann. See HAUPTMANN, GERHART.

BEGGAR ON HORSEBACK (1924), by Marc Connelly. See GREEN PASTURES, THE, by Marc Connelly.

BEGGAR'S OPERA, THE (1728), by John Gay. Lawyers, ladies, marriage, trade—all are satirized in this famous musical play. Macheath, a handsome highwayman, is loved by two girls: Polly Peachum, daughter of an innkeeper who receives stolen goods, and Lucy Lockit, daughter of a warden at Newgate Prison. Mrs. Peachum is furious when she discovers Polly has actually married Macheath, and she and some of her female friends surround him and have him arrested. In Newgate Macheath sees Lucy, who asks him to marry her. He promises, although Lucy suspects he is already married to Polly. The latter visits him while he is in prison, and Peachum comes to take her from Macheath by force. Lucy helps him escape, though she knows he may return to Polly. Macheath is captured again, and Polly again visits him at Newgate. Both Polly and Lucy decide they have been too fond of the highwayman, and Macheath, in a dilemma with his two loves, resigns himself to hanging, but is saved by the mock intervention of a beggar and a player. Macheath's execution is called off, the highwayman and Polly are reunited and the play ends in a general dance. The opera is filled with lively lyrics and gay music. It forms the basis of Bertholdt Brecht's modern musical play, *The Three-Penny Opera,* with music by Kurt Weil.

BEHIND THE CURTAIN (1949), by John Gunther. See INSIDE EUROPE, by John Gunther.

BEHRMAN, S. N. (1893–   ). S. N. Behrman became a successful American playwright with the production, in 1927, of his comedy *The Second Man.* Clark Storey is a third-rate writer whose intelligence has turned to cynicism and superficial sophistication. He is personally charming, and has proved irresistible to Mrs. Kendall Frayne, a wealthy widow. Storey is also irresistible to young Monica Grey, and in spite of himself has admitted that he loves her. He will not permit himself to marry a poor girl, however, and has been trying to promote a match between her and his rich friend Austin Lowe, a scientist, who idolizes Monica. The impetuous young girl cannot bear the thought of Storey's "loveless marriage" to Kendall, so although she has accepted Austin's proposal, she suddenly announces the false news that Storey is the father of her unborn child. Kendall and Austin are shocked: the former plans to go abroad; the latter makes an unsuccessful attempt to kill Storey. At last Monica realizes the invincibility of Storey's "second man," who looks on, dispassionate, amused, and won't permit the writer to be really decent. She gives up, decides to marry the kindly Austin. And Kendall, who does understand Storey and his "second man," will marry him.

In *Biography* (1932) Marion Froude, a mediocre portrait painter, but a sympathetic personality, wishes to publish her autobiography, but at length destroys the manuscript because of the concern of Leander Nolan, her childhood sweetheart, who fears the revelations will injure his political career. The young editor Richard Kurt, who has been fired because of the pressure of Nolan, wishes to marry her; but Marion realizes she is not his type of girl, and refuses.

Other plays by Behrman include *Brief Moment* (1931), describing the difficult marriage of a nightclub singer and a member of society; and *No Time for Comedy* (1939), about a successful comedy playwright who aspires to do serious work.

BEL-AMI (1885), by Guy de Maupassant. See PIERRE AND JEAN, by Guy de Maupassant.

BELFRY OF BRUGES AND OTHER POEMS, THE (1845), by Henry Wadsworth Longfellow. See LONGFELLOW, HENRY WADSWORTH.

BELLY OF PARIS, THE (1873), by Emile Zola. See ROUGON-MACQUART, THE, by Emile Zola.

BELOVED RETURNS, THE (1939), by Thomas Mann. See MANN, THOMAS.

BENCHLEY, ROBERT (1889–1945). The humor of life's complexities and the struggles of the ordinary man faced by the preposterous problems of everyday life is Benchley's forte. His incomparable essays and stories appear in many volumes, often illustrated by Gluyas Williams, such as *Of All Things* (1921) and *The Treasurer's Report* (1930). The last books were *Inside Benchley* (1942) and *Benchley Beside Himself* (1943).

BENÉT, WILLIAM ROSE (1886–   ). Although Benét attended the Sheffield Scientific School at Yale, he early determined to be a poet. Beginning in 1911 as a reader for a magazine, he has remained prominent in editorial work; he is a co-founder of *The Saturday Review of Literature*. Benét prefers narrative verse, and has written poetry ranging from Oriental fantasy to western American ballad. *Man Possessed* (1927) is the selected verse of the author. He has also writen two verse novels: *Rip Tide* (1932); and the Pulitzer Prize winner, *The Dust Which Is God* (1941), an autobiographical work.

BEN-HUR (1880), by Lew Wallace. *Ben-Hur* is a tale set in Jerusalem, during the early Christian era. The hero, Judah Ben-Hur, head of a rich Jewish family, is sentenced to life at the galleys, after being accused by his former friend Messala of attempting to assassinate the new Governor of Jerusalem. His fortune is confiscated; his mother and young sister Tirzah are walled up in a forgotten prison cell, where they contract leprosy. The novel concerns Ben-Hur's escape, his revenge during an exciting chariot race, his search for his mother and sister and their miraculous cure by Christ, who (with His followers) is an important character. The family is converted to Christianity, and the crucifixion on Calvary is graphically described.

General Wallace, whose own life was most exciting, also wrote the popular *The Fair God* (1873). This concerns Cortés' invasion of the Aztec empire and his defeat by Guatamozin, the nephew of Montezuma, who killed the vacillating leader to save his country. It is a chronicle of the fierce fighting, the massacre of the patriotic Aztecs, and the ruthlessness of the Spanish. The book is written in realistic style, with close attention to Aztec archaeology, religion and art. *The Prince of India* (1893) presents the capture of Constantinople by the Turks, describing in detail the reduction of the city by the infidel artillery, the first such instance in military annals.

BENT SHALL BECOME STRAIGHT, THE (1909), by Samuel Joseph Agnon. See BRIDAL CANOPY, THE, by Samuel Joseph Agnon.

BENT TWIG, THE (1915), by Dorothy Canfield. See CANFIELD, DOROTHY.

BEOWULF (ca. 700). This is the oldest epic poem in any modern European language, and the "beginning" of English literature. Of unknown authorship, most of the material was circulated orally, then written down by two unidentified tenth-century scribes. That the Beowulf epic may have been a development of older sagas is apparent in its Scandinavian background and structural form. Hrothgar, King of the Danes, builds a palace, Heorot, which is visited nightly by the monster, Grendel, who devours Hrothgar's thanes and haunts the palace for twelve years. Beowulf, nephew of Higelac, King of the Geats (a tribe in southern Sweden), arrives with fourteen companions to get rid of Grendel. As they are sleeping in the hall of Heorot, Grendel breaks in and devours Hondscio, one of Beowulf's men. Beowulf struggles with the monster, who loses an arm and flees to his cavern beneath a lake, to die. As Hrothgar and his men celebrate, Grendel's mother enters the hall to avenge her son's death. She carries off Aeschere, one of Hrothgar's followers, and Beowulf pursues her to her lair. Using an enchanted sword, Beowulf cuts off the witch's head and also Grendel's, and returns to Hrothgar with his prizes. After the deaths of Hrothgar and his son, Heardred, Beowulf succeeds to the throne and reigns for fifty peaceful years. Then a dragon devastates the kingdom, and Beowulf, with eleven companions, searches for him. Deserted by all his men except Wiglaf, Beowulf kills the dragon but is mortally wounded in the struggle. His body is burned on a funeral pyre with his armor and the dragon's treasure. Many details of Germanic court life are included in the sage. Christian spirit pervades the work; yet the background material is derived from ancient pagan legends.

BÉRÉNICE (1670), by Jean Baptiste Racine. See ANDROMAQUE, by Jean Baptiste Racine.

BERG DER DROOMEN, DE (1913), by Arthur van Schendel. See SCHENDEL, ARTHUR VAN.

BERG VAN LICHT, DE (1906), by Louis Couperus. See COUPERUS, LOUIS.

BERMANNUS (ca. 1530), by Georgius Agricola. See DE RE METAL-
LICA, by Georgius Agricola.

BERNARD CLARE (1946), by James T. Farrell. See STUDS LONI-
GAN, by James T. Farrell.

BERRETTO A SONAGLI, IL (1916), by Luigi Pirandello. See PI-
RANDELLO, LUIGI.

BETROTHED, THE (1825), by Alessandro Manzoni. *I Promessi Sposi*
(*The Betrothed*), the greatest Italian novel of modern times, holds the place
in Italian literature that Tolstoy's *War and Peace* (q.v.) does in Russian. Although historical in its conception, *The Betrothed* transcends the limits of
history and can be considered a capital work of literature for the beauty of
its style and the greatness of its conception. The scene is laid in Lombardy
under the Spanish rule, in the seventeenth century. The marriage of two
peasant lovers, Renzo and Lucia, is thwarted by the infamous plans of a
local Signore, Don Rodrigo, and by the cowardice of the village priest, Don
Abbondio. A series of adventures presents lofty as well as petty characters.
Among the former is Fra' Cristoforo, a courageous monk whose life, formerly
corrupt, is now devoted entirely to piety and assisting the needy; Cardinal
Borromeo, who in Manzoni's eyes represents the highest and purest interpretation of Catholic doctrine and practice; and the "Unknown," a most powerful Signore of Lombardy who, inspired by the sufferings and sincerity of
Lucia whom he has imprisoned in his castle to be handed to his dissipated
friend, Don Rodrigo, turns gradually to goodness and faith, frees Lucia and
is instrumental in the happy ending of the book, which concludes with the
marriage of the couple. Among the many remarkable scenes of the book
is that describing the plague in Milan.

BETTER THINK TWICE ABOUT IT (1916), by Luigi Pirandello.
See PIRANDELLO, LUIGI.

BETWEEN TWO WORLDS (1941), by Upton Sinclair. See JUNGLE,
THE, by Upton Sinclair.

BEYOND GOOD AND EVIL (1885), by Friedrich Nietzsche. See
NIETZSCHE, FRIEDRICH.

BEYOND HUMAN POWER (1883), by Björnstjerne Björnson. In
this poetic and moving play, Hanna Roberts returns to Norway, after a long
absence in America, to see her sister, Clara. The latter is married to Pastor
Adolph Sang, who has a mission church in a remote and desolate spot in the
far north. He is a deeply spiritual man and has a strange power of healing
with prayer. Hanna finds her sister paralyzed, and Clara tells her that she
has sacrificed everything for her husband, even her health. She had sent
the children, Elias and Rachael, away to be educated and they have returned
on the same steamer with their aunt. Their once complete faith in their
father has been shaken by contacts with the outside world, and Sang feels
their doubts and goes into the church to pray for their mother. A landslide
turns aside, miraculously, avoiding the church and the house, and when
Clara falls into a deep, peaceful sleep, Rachael and Elias feel their faith re-

vived. People come from all over the surrounding country and kneel outside the church to pray; and Sang can be heard singing. The Bishop and ministers, who were on board the mission ship, hear of the miracle Sang has performed and come to investigate, holding counsel in his house. Suddenly Clara rises and walks into the room, and Sang, who had sensed her cure, rushes into the house, radiant, and takes her in his arms. But the effort has been too much for her, and she dies. Sang is so stunned that he is overcome, also, and dies from strain and shock. To a mortal—who should spend his energies in the development of natural gifts—the cost of the miracle is supreme sacrifice.

BEYOND THE HORIZON (1920), by Eugene O'Neill. Rob Mayo, a sensitive young man ill equipped for the farm life to which he was born, is about to embark on a sea voyage on the ship of his uncle, Captain Scott. On the eve of departure he confesses his love to Ruth Atkins, his brother's girl. Ruth, carried away by his sensitivity and eloquence, believes herself in love with him. As a consequence, in a shake-up that rocks the Mayo family, it is Andrew, the genuine farmer, who, in his· disappointment, embarks on the sea voyage, and Rob who marries Ruth and stays behind to run the farm. Rob is no good in his misfit profession. After his father's death, the farm deteriorates swiftly. Ruth becomes embittered and realizes her rash mistake. This strikes her cruelly when Andrew, on his first return trip, assures her that he has got over "that silly nonsense." The marriage is a sordid, hostile affair. At the end Rob, still dreaming of something ahead, "beyond the horizon," dies of tuberculosis. His last vain hope for Ruth is that she may yet find happiness with Andrew.

BEYOND TRAGEDY (1932), by Reinhold Niebuhr. See NIEBUHR, REINHOLD.

BEZONNEN VERZEN (1931), by Pieter Cornelis Boutens. See BOUTENS, PIETER CORNELIS.

BHAGAVAD-GITA, THE. The *Bhagavad-Gita* occupies the same exalted position in Hindu as the Gospels in Christian literature. It is described in Sanskrit as "the teaching given in song by the Supreme Exalted One," who is Krishna, the incarnate form of the only and eternal God of the Universe, believed to be an ever-present help to those who call upon Him. The *Bhagavad-Gita* is imbedded in the vast, ancient epic, the *Mahabharata* (q.v.). It recounts in dramatic dialogue the great fratricidal battle between the Kauravas and the Pandavas. Krishna, siding with the righteous Pandavas, attempts to induce the warlike Kauravas to make peace, but their general, Duryodhana (The Unconquerable), is bellicose and unappeasable. Krishna points out to Arjuna, the hero of the Pandavas, that each man has his particular duty and calling; as he is a warrior, it is his duty to fight; but he must do it not out of hatred for his enemy nor in hope of any gain for himself, but for the welfare of the world and as service to his God. If in the battle he should be destroyed, there is no such thing as death for one who has found his life in God: "My servant will come to Me." Arjuna, who is accompanied by the disguised Krishna as the driver of his chariot, is overcome with horror and pity as he regards the soldiers on both sides. He becomes weak and dejected, not so much because he is in doubt of being victorious, but by the thought that he would be obliged to kill "those who are my own people," and because the bloody strife would be a sin against the sacred laws of brotherhood.

Krishna first comforts Arjuna and reveals to him his "supreme utterance" that what was happening was not the work of man, nor proceeded from the human will, but was the will of the eternal God of Destiny Himself, who decides and ordains all things. Chastened, Arjuna's pacifist resistance is finally broken, and he acknowledges his readiness to enter into battle.

The *Bhagavad-Gita* was translated by Sir Charles Wilkins in 1785.

BIALIK, HAYYIM NAHMAN (1873–1934). The most skilled and best loved Hebrew poet of modern times was born in Volhynia, Russia; was eulogized by world Jewry on his sixtieth birthday in 1933; and died in Tel Aviv on July 4, 1934. He appeared at a time when long-suffering and pogromized Israel had turned from hope of some miraculous redemption to active efforts toward regaining the land of their fathers, reviving the Hebrew tongue, and resuscitating the battered Jewish spirit. He was seven when his father died; circumstances then subjected him to the influences of poverty, devout learning, and communion with nature. Later he read medieval philosophy and mysticism, stories, poems, essays, all in Hebrew; and at the famed rabbinical academy of Voloshin he received a deep grounding in the *Talmud* (q.v.). His first poem was published in Odessa in 1892. He was a teacher, among other occupations, but kept writing steadily, and in 1900 helped to establish a publishing house. To escape Bolshevism he went to Berlin in 1922, and to Tel Aviv in 1924. He visited the United States in 1926. Bialik's early poems were mainly concerned with the dark plight of his people in Russia. The outstanding long poem of this period was "The Talmud Student," glorifying the youthful day-and-night readers of that great body of literature. Other verses sang of Zion. Perhaps the most moving of his elegiac poems is "The City of Slaughter," based on the horrors of the Kishineff massacre of 1903. Often he decried the helplessness and futility of his people in the face of persecution. But he was able to write light songs for children, folk songs, legends in verse, and prose works on Jewish legendry, published in Tel Aviv. Many of these poems have been ably translated into English; and Volume I of Bialik's complete poetic works in English was published in New York in 1948.

BIBLE (ca. 1000 B.C.–A.D. 150). The *Bible* is not a homogeneous volume but a collection of books, as indicated by the meaning of its Greek name, *Ta Biblia,* The Books. Thirty-nine of them, written mostly in Hebrew from the eleventh to the second centuries B.C., form the Old Testament, or Scripture of the Synagogue. Twenty-seven others, written in Greek from 40 A.D. to 150, constitute the New Testament which, together with the Old Testament, is the Scripture of the Christian church.

No literary monument has exercised a more decisive and continuous influence upon Western civilization in general and English-speaking culture in particular. By its style alone, the *Bible* has molded the tongue of countless poets and writers, from Chaucer to Lincoln, from Luther to Mann, from Chrestien de Troyes to Gide. Its legal and ethical precepts have influenced the codes and customs of the Occidental world. Its lucid realism with regard to the motives of human nature and the tragedy of man's destiny still challenges modern psychologists. In part or in whole, it inspires and controls the faith of all forms of Jewry and Christendom. When Sir Walter Scott on his death-bed called for "the Book" and Lockhardt queried, "Which one?" the dying man replied, "Need you ask? There is only one." Many people today reject the uniqueness of the *Bible* as authority for individual and social conduct, but few would deny that it occupies a singular place in mankind's heritage.

The Books of the Old Testament

The Hebrew Scripture is divided into three parts: A. The Law or Pentateuch; B. The Prophets; C. The Hagiographa or Writings.

THE LAW OR PENTATEUCH

The Pentateuch, whose name derives from two Greek words meaning "five scrolls," includes the first five Books of the *Bible,* which are Genesis, Exodus, Leviticus, Numbers and Deuteronomy. Traditionally held as the work of Moses, it is now generally recognized as a composite document resulting from the conflation of four main groups of oral traditions which were written down respectively in the eleventh, eighth, seventh, and sixth centuries B.C. It contains a mass of heterogeneous materials, such as mythological poems, tribal sagas, genealogies, historical legends, liturgical hymns, secular songs, etiological tales, aphorisms and fables, legal decisions, ritual and moral precepts, civil and criminal codes.

From this literary hodgepodge, however, one large theme unfolds itself— that of man's nature and destiny in the face of God, the creator of the universe. The Pentateuch is not a textbook of physical and historical sciences, but essentially a religious treatise. It describes primarily, neither the creation of the world nor the origin of man and evil, but the tragedy of a broken relationship between man and his creator (Genesis 1-11) and the inception of a "grand design" for the salvation of mankind through the election of the people of Israel (Genesis 12-Deuteronomy 34).

Using archaic myths as a mode of theological expression, the writers situate man carefully in his relation to nature on the one hand and to the deity on the other. Man is created in the image of God and receives dominion over a world which is "very good indeed." Yet this same *Adam* (not a proper name, but "man," a representative of mankind) is extracted from the dust of the *Adamah* (ground). The story of the garden shows that the pathos of man's existence lies in his attempts to doubt the motives of his creator and to assert himself as an autonomous being. It is through a lack of faith that he becomes estranged from his God—paradoxically enough, at the precise moment when he tries to bridge the distance which separates him from the divine realm.

Cain's murder of Abel and the erection of a tower to ascend heaven constitute other manifestations of an evil which vitiates "every impulse of the thoughts of man's heart" (Genesis 6:5). Such a pessimistic view of human nature renders the gracious aspect of the deity's concern the more remarkable.

Abraham and his posterity are chosen for the healing of all the nations. The memory of this ancient promise, together with the leadership of Moses, is one of the factors which bring Israel into national consciousness (fourteenth century B.C.). Yesterday slaves in Egypt, now free but destitute in the wilderness, they accept solemnly the terms of a covenant which binds them one to another and all of them to their God. Alone among those of the ancient world, their religion is inserted in history. The name of the deity they worship is Yahweh (misread into Jehovah) which means probably, "He that causes to be," and underlines the historical emphasis of the Hebrew faith.

The sons of Israel know that if they keep the covenant and obey the voice of their God, they shall be forever, Yahweh's own possession, a "peculiar treasure from among all peoples, a kingdom of priests and a holy nation" (Exodus 19:5). The Decalogue in its succinct form of ten "words" without elaboration (Exodus 20:2-17 and Deuteronomy 5:6-21) may have been part of the terms of the covenant. The ritual laws (mainly in Leviticus) appear to represent posterior legislation. The Hebrew word for "covenant" was translated into Latin *"testamentum,"* hence the use of the word "testament" for describing the books which are associated with Hebrew religion.

THE PROPHETS

The Books which follow the Pentateuch are called in the Hebrew text "The Earlier Prophets," while in the English versions the same are commonly known as "Historical Books." They are Joshua, Judges, Samuel and Kings, and they describe the entry of the Hebrews into Canaan, the conquest of the land, the rise of the monarchy under David and Solomon, the schism between the two kingdoms of Israel and Judah, their decline and their respective falls in 722 and 586 B.C. These books were edited in the sixth and fifth centuries.

"The Later Prophets" include three of the so-called "major prophets," Isaiah, Jeremiah and Ezekiel, as well as the twelve "minor prophets." This distinction refers not to their comparative importance, but to the length of their books. They should be read in their chronological order:

Amos (ca. 751 B.C.). In a time of material prosperity, Amos announces the doom of the kingdom of Israel. Speaking through the prophet's mouth, Yahweh declares to a self-righteous people, "You alone have I known among all the families of the earth, therefore I shall visit upon you all your iniquities." (3:2)

Hosea (ca. 745 B.C.). Hosea preaches in the same vein as Amos but he deepens the concept of divine justice, and reveals a God whose volition is torn between judgment and grace and who asks, "How can I give thee up, Ephraim?" (11:8)

Isaiah (738–696 B.C.). With his motto, "No faith, no staith," (7:9) Isaiah of Jerusalem lays the corner-stone of prophetism. When he sings that "unto us a child is born," (9:6) he initiates the messianic hope. He announces the advent of a kingdom of peace in which "the wolf shall dwell with the lamb" (11:6). By his concept of the conversion of a remnant within the dying nation, he prepares the sociological miracle of Judaism and Christianity and makes way for a community which transcends the limitations of political nationalism, a spiritual congregation which will survive the annihilation of a state.

Micah (ca. 700 B.C.). Micah of Moresheth in Judah speaks on the behalf of the oppressed poor, and, a generation later, an annotator of his book summarizes the teaching of the eighth-century prophets in a formula which appears to separate religion from ritualistic legalism:

> It has been revealed to thee, O man,
> What good is and what Yahweh seeks from thee:
> Nothing at all, except to act justly, to love mercy,
> And to be humble in walking with thy God! (6:8)

Zephaniah, Nahum, Habakkuk (626–ca. 600 B.C.). Zephaniah (626) and Nahum (612) hold fast to their faith in the God of judgment, while Habakkuk (ca. 600) expresses a quasi-philosophical perplexity at the spectacle of injustice in history. He concludes that "the righteous shall live by his faith" (2:4).

Jeremiah (626–ca. 580 B.C.). Jeremiah announces and witnesses the long agony and death of Jerusalem (597–586). His passion concerning man's inability to do good makes him ask, "Can the Ethiopian change his skin or the leopard his spots?" (13:23) and prepares him to apprehend the mystery of a new covenant by which God will write his law in the heart of men (31:31).

Ezekiel (593–571 B.C.). In order to keep up the spirit of the Judean exiles in Babylonia, Ezekiel proclaims that the sons are no longer responsible for the guilt of their fathers. He announces that Yahweh will restore his nation, not for her sake, but for the sake of his holy name, so that "the nations shall know that I am Yahweh, when I shall be sanctified in you before their eyes." (36:23)

Second Isaiah (ca. 545 B.C.). When Cyrus of Persia begins his military conquests, an anonymous Jew, now called Second Isaiah because his poems have been preserved in the book of Isaiah (40-66), interprets the events of history as a mighty act of the Lord of all nations. "Comfort ye, comfort ye, my people!" (40:1ff.) His anthology contains several excerpts from the "Songs of the Suffering Servant," in which Israel appears to be personified as a slave making atonement for the guilt of the pagans.

Post-exilic Prophets. After a handful of "Zionists" return to Palestine, Haggai (520 B.C.) and Zephaniah (520–518 B.C.) move them to rebuild the temple of Jerusalem. Malachi (ca. 460 B.C.) and Joel (ca. 400 B.C.) attempt to reform the religion and ethics of the community. The story of Jonah (ca. 400–350 B.C.) stands out as a plea for racial tolerance and religious universalism.

THE HAGIOGRAPHA OR WRITINGS

The third part of the Hebrew *Bible* is a collection of late writings which were not considered sacred when the books of the Prophets were declared authoritative.

The Psalms. Although it includes many hymns and prayers of earlier times, the Psalter is the hymnal of the post-exilic temple. In it is reflected the whole history of Hebrew worship. The Psalmists sing Israel's praise for God the creator, sorrow for national guilt and trials, joy over salvation, assurance in God's ultimate rule in history. More than any classic of devotional literature, the Psalter belongs to the spirituality of the whole Western world.

Job (ca. 500–400 B.C.). The poem of Job is a discussion of the meaning of true religion. "Does Job fear God for nought?" is a question more important for the poet than the tragedy of undeserved suffering. Through his ordeal, the hero learns how to forfeit pride in his moral righteousness and to confide only in the gratuitous mercy of his creator.

Proverbs (ca. 300 B.C.). The sayings of the Hebrew wise throughout eight centuries or more have been collected in the book of Proverbs. Hebrew wisdom stresses neither ritual nor covenant but insists on the religious roots of a practical philosophy of life and discovers its beginning in "the fear of Yahweh."

The Megilloth or Scrolls (ca. 400–200 B.C.). Five short books are set aside for reading at the five main festivals of Judaism. They include Ruth, the Song of Songs, Ecclesiastes (Qoheleth), Lamentations, and Esther.

Daniel (165–164 B.C.). The book of Daniel is an apocalypse or "revelation" concerning the end of history. It proclaims, during the Maccabean revolt against Hellenistic oppression, the proximity of national salvation as well as the resurrection of many of the dead, "some to everlasting life and some to shame and everlasting abhorrence." (12:2)

Chronicles, Ezra-Nehemiah (ca. 300 B.C.). The last three books of the Hebrew *Bible* relate, from a priestly point of view, the history of Israel and of the Jerusalem community after the exile.

The Formation and Transmission of the Old Testament

The Pentateuch became authoritative or "canonical" (from the Greek word *kanón*, rule) soon after the Babylonian exile. The Prophets were set aside as sacred some time in the third century B.C., while the Hagiographa were not recognized before the end of the first century A.D. The Hebrew text and vocalic pronunciation of the Old Testament were fixed from the sixth to the ninth century A.D. by Jewish scholars, especially those called the Masoretes (from the Hebrew word *masorah*, tradition). The Masoretic text is the basis of modern editions of the Hebrew *Bible* (see *Biblia Hebraica*, third edition, by R. Kittel, Stuttgart, 1937).

The Greek Version and the Apocrypha of the Old Testament

The Hebrew *Bible* was translated into Greek from the third to the first century B.C. for the benefit of the Greek-speaking Jews of Alexandria. Known as the Septuagint, the Greek *Bible* includes not only the books of the Hebrew *Bible,* but also fourteen other books and additions which are now called the Apocrypha ("hidden" from public use); the most important of them are Tobit (200 B.C.), Ecclesiasticus or the Wisdom of Jesus ben Sirach (180 B.C.), Judith (150 B.C.), First and Second Maccabees (100 B.C), and the Wisdom of Solomon (50 B.C.).

The Books of the New Testament

Soon after the crucifixion of Jesus "under Pontius Pilate" (A.D. 29), a handful of his disciples waited for his triumphant return and the advent of God's kingdom. While waiting, they unwittingly founded the Christian Church. The witnesses of the risen Christ spread in a few years beyond Palestine and reached the larger cities of the Roman Empire. They repeated the sayings of Jesus, they told stories of His life, death, and resurrection, they meditated on the meaning of His work and person, and they transmitted to the next generation an oral tradition which was then transformed into written "gospels."

At about the same time traveling missionaries like Paul of Tarsus wrote various letters to the communities they had founded or hoped to visit. These documents were copied for the sake of diffusion and preservation. Some of them, together with the "gospels," formed the nucleus of a library heralding the "new covenant" or "new testament" granted by God to mankind. The collection of the New Testament contains four sections: A. The Gospels and the Acts of the Apostles; B. The Epistles of Paul; C. The Pastoral and General Epistles; D. The Book of Revelation.

The Gospels and the Acts of the Apostles

The four Gospels describe the life, death and resurrection of Jesus. They do not belong to the historiographic type of literature, for the explicit purpose of their composition is to preach the "good news" (*euangelion* or gospel) so that men "may believe that Jesus is the Christ, the son of God, and believing, [they] may have life through his name." (John 20:31)

The first three Gospels, traditionally attached to the names of Matthew, Mark and Luke, are called "synoptic" because they may be printed on three parallel columns for the purpose of study (*syn-opsis,* view-together).

Mark (ca. 65). The second Gospel is the earliest of the three. It begins, not with the birth of Jesus, but with a short notice on John the Baptist, and proceeds immediately to the public career of the Galilean preacher. It shows Jesus announcing the good news of the coming of God's kingdom and then traveling in foreign territory after having been hailed by his disciples as the Messiah (*mashiach* means "anointed," which in Greek is translated by *christos*). The book then presents its hero going to Jerusalem in order to be tried by Jewish and Roman authorities and to be executed as a criminal. The Gospel ends, however, not with the death, but with the resurrection of Jesus.

In this book are preserved several details of a concrete and picturesque nature which suggest the testimony of an eyewitness (see the "pillow" in 4:38 and the "green grass" in 6:39). The plan is a masterly conception, not only as the unfolding of an historical drama, but also as the conjunction of psychological forces. The Marcan Gospel emphasizes the human aspect of Jesus, who refuses to be called "good" (10:18) and displays neither omniscience (9:33) nor omnipotence (6:4-6); yet it conveys the numinous element of His character (4:41) and shows a lay teacher who heals the sick, spurs the patriotism of the crowds, and then refuses to associate himself with the political ideologies of a nationalistic messianism, but intends to "give his life as a ransom for many." (10:45) The evangelist succeeds in sketching a figure who is at all times the master of His own life and deliberately provokes the knotting and denouement of His own "tragedy."

Matthew and Luke (ca. 75–85). The first and third Gospels appear to be independent revisions of Mark's, and they include substantial additions dealing mainly with the birth and the teaching of Jesus (Sermon on the Mount, parables). While the Matthean writer lays stress on the Jewishness of the teacher from Nazareth and pictures him as the supreme Law-giver, the Lucan evangelist, on the contrary, emphasizes racial tolerance (parable of the good Samaritan), social concern (sayings on the poor, women and children) and especially the gratuitous love of God (parable of the prodigal son and his elder brother). From the third Gospel have come the most remarkable hymns of the Christian liturgy ("Magnificat," "Benedictus," "Ave Maria," "Gloria in Excelsis," "Nunc Dimittis").

John (ca. 95). The fourth Gospel differs greatly from the Synoptics and is on the whole a meditation on the ever-living Christ. It spiritualizes to a considerable extent the teaching of Jesus on judgment and kingdom, and it explains salvation as the present possession of eternal life in perfect unity with Christ (allegory of the vine and branches).

The Acts of the Apostles (ca. 85). This book presents itself as a sequel to the Lucan Gospel and appears to come from the same editor. It tells the story of the early church in Jerusalem, the preaching of Peter, Stephen and Philip, the conversion of Saul of Tarsus, and it traces some of the Christian expansion throughout Asia Minor and Greece toward Rome. While dominated by an irenic spirit (it ignores the rift which occurred between Peter and Paul), it tends to show that Christianity is not a Jewish sect and that it is not dangerous to the imperial administration, although world-wide in its goal.

THE EPISTLES OF PAUL

Most of the letters written by "the apostle of the pagans" are examples of circumstantial epistolary writing and do not constitute formal treatises of theology.

First and Second Thessalonians (50–51). These two letters are probably the earliest written documents of the New Testament. The Christians of Thessalonica, who are feverishly hoping for the end of the world, are exhorted to wait patiently in holy conduct and brotherly love, and continuously to work on this earth.

Galatians (53–55). Some Jewish Christians having persuaded new converts in Galatia to accept the rite of circumcision as a prerequisite for salvation, Paul states earnestly his views on the Old Testament Law and Christian freedom. For him, obedience to the outward requirements of a cultic law does not necessarily bind the inward personality, and it creates a self-righteousness incompatible with the grace of God. In order to become a Christian, one must be radically transformed and become "a new creature" by identification with the death and rebirth of Christ. "I have been crucified with Christ: if I live, then, it is not I who live any longer but Christ who lives in me."

(2:20) If righteousness can be obtained by obedience to a law, then the grace of God is superfluous and Christ has died in vain (2:15-21). The Law is only a "tutor" or a "guardian" whose purpose is to lead men to Christ. When these are "clothed in him as in a mantle," they become the true descendants of Abraham (3:21-25; 4:1-7). The author draws a series of conclusions which have become the basis of Christian ethics. All men in Christ are equal (3:28), free (5:1-13), and brothers (5:14-26). Thus the democratic motto of "liberty, equality, and fraternity" is grounded in the mystery of spiritual death and rebirth and may not be grasped outside of a life crucified in Christ. Few books of the New Testament have had an influence comparable to that of Galatians, which has been called the *Magna Charta* of Christianity.

First and Second Corinthians (55–56). The two letters to the Corinthians give advice on matters of community life, and they reveal the passionate temper as well as the self-giving personality of their author. Paul wrote at least four times to the Christians of Corinth. The first letter is now lost (see First Corinthians 5:9); the second letter is now First Corinthians; the third is preserved in Second Corinthians 10 to 16, and the fourth, or part thereof, is found in First Corinthians 1 to 9.

Romans (56). The epistle to the Christians of Rome is not dictated by conflicts and cares of the moment. The apostle writes to people with whom he is not yet acquainted, instead of visiting them as he had planned. These circumstances of composition may explain the breadth of the letter's outlook, the tranquillity of its tone, and the harmony of its structure. Paul attempts to translate in intellectual terms the mystical experience of crucifixion and resurrection of the self with Christ, and he describes the Christian awareness of sin, grace and faith. The contemplation of man's inner drama, with his inability to carry out his will to do good, leads him to despair and to the consciousness of his condemnation (7). Only in this moment of self-loss is he ready to recognize the compelling character of God's love manifested in Christ. Possessed by the life-giving spirit, the Christian becomes certain of his adoption as "a child of God," of his predestination from all eternity to receive such a grace, and of the hope of his glorification (8).

The exponent of racial universalism does not forget his Hebrew origins, and in the second part of his letter he reflects on the destiny of Israel. "I have in my heart a perpetual sorrow. I wish I were myself anathema and separated from Christ for the sake of my brothers, my kinsmen by race, the Jews!" (9:1-5) He finally expresses assurance of their salvation (11-12).

Philippians (ca. 61–64). Now in Rome awaiting trial before the emperor, Paul thanks the Philippians for their generosity toward him. His only desire is now to go and live with his Lord. "For to me to live is Christ and to die is gain." (1:21)

Philemon, Colossians (64). In a delightful note to Philemon of Colossae, Paul requests a Christian master to take back as brother a runaway slave now converted to Christianity. He writes at the same time to the Colossians and shares with them some of his reflections on the mystery of the person of Christ and of the Church, the body of Christ.

THE PASTORAL AND GENERAL EPISTLES

Ephesians, First and Second Timothy, Titus (ca. 70–80). These epistles are traditionally ascribed to Pauline authorship and may contain fragments of personal messages written by the apostle himself.

Hebrews, James, First and Second Peter; First, Second, and Third John (ca. 80–150). Other letters of the second and third generations are homilies on the meaning of faith and Christian living. The anonymous letter to the Hebrews describes the ministry of Christ by the use of Old Testament allegory.

THE BOOK OF REVELATION (CA. 90–95)

The Apocalypse or Revelation of John the Divine differs in style and content from any other book of the New Testament. Influenced by the imagery of Daniel and other Jewish Apocalypses, the author relates a number of visions concerning the proximate end of the world and especially the last judgment, with the defeat of Satan. In a time of persecution, he believes that God will create a new heaven and a new earth where "death shall be no more." (21:4) Like Hebrew religion, Christianity is oriented toward the future. It is significant that the *Bible* which began with the words "In the beginning God" finishes at the close of the Apocalypse with the prayer, "Come, Lord Jesus!"

The Formation and Transmission of the New Testament

The early church had no scripture besides that of Judaism, mostly through its Greek version of the Septuagint. The idea of a Christian "canon" arose in the second century A.D., but the present list of twenty-seven books did not appear before 367.

Some of the more important manuscripts of the Greek text of the New Testament are the *Sinaiticus,* the *Alexandrinus* (both in the British Museum) and the *Vaticanus* (in the Vatican Library). Modern editions of the Greek New Testament are based on a careful comparison of all the extant manuscripts (see *Novum Testamentum Graece,* ed. by D. E. Nestle, 18th edition, Stuttgart, 1948).

The English Versions of the Bible

The Middle Ages knew the *Bible* mainly through the Latin translation of Jerome (390–404), which became known as the Vulgate and received official recognition by the Roman Catholic Church. An English version appeared as early as the fourteenth century (Wyclif) and many other translations were published during the sixteenth century (Tyndale's New Testament and parts of the Old Testament, *Coverdale's Bible, Matthew's Bible,* the *Great Bible,* the *Geneva Bible,* the *Bishop's Bible,* the *Douai Bible*). The *King James Version* (1611) has won world-wide acclaim, and in spite of archaisms, obscurities and some errors, it remains the most popular translation, with an unsurpassed literary value.

A New Translation by James Moffat (1922) and *An American Translation* edited by J. M. P. Smith and E. J. Goodspeed (1939) present in an attractive vernacular the results of scholarly criticism and textual reconstruction. The *English Revised Version* (1881–1885), the *American Standard Version* (1901), and the forthcoming (American) *Revised Standard Version* (New Testament, 1946) aim at modernizing the language of the *King James Version* and attempt to offer an accurate rendering of the original text.

The Significance of the Bible for Christians

Christians consider the *Bible* as the only authoritative record of God's intentions toward mankind. Most of them have abandoned a belief in the literal inspiration of the Bible, but they maintain that members of the universal church, when moved by the inner testimony of the Holy Spirit, find in Scripture "the Word of God." They recognize that Israel and the church stand at once, by virtue of their respective covenants, under the rigor of judgment and the grace of election.

Although the *Bible* does not offer them a rational solution for the mystery of life and evil, they cling to its witness and thereby renounce man-made schemes of salvation. While history is moving toward its appointed end, Scripture makes them place their destiny at the mercy of the God of Moses and of Jesus Christ, and it bids them share with other men the assurance of their faith.

BIBLE IN SPAIN, THE (1843), by George Borrow. Borrow was sent to Spain by an English religious society as a missionary and distributor of Bibles. With a healthy instinct for empirical knowledge, he sought out the common people of the country. He also visited Portugal, and the book describes his adventures in both countries. Its character has little to do with religion of the *Bible*. Borrow, the passionate gypsy and gay lover of life, is etched in all three volumes of his memoirs. He records the Spain of wonder and mystery that he has come to know after a sojourn of five exciting years: the Spain of muleteers, peasants and shepherds.

BIBLE TRANSLATION, by Martin Luther. See LUTHER, MARTIN.

BIBLE'S TEACHINGS ABOUT CHRIST, THE (1862), by Viktor Rydberg. See LAST ATHENIAN, THE, by Viktor Rydberg.

BIBLIOTHECA MEDICA (1771–1777), by Albrecht von Haller. See ELEMENTA PHYSIOLOGIAE CORPORIS HUMANI, by Albrecht von Haller.

BIERCE, AMBROSE (1842–1914?). Ambrose Bierce, between the appearance of *Tales of Soldiers and Civilians* (1891) and his own disappearance in Mexico in 1913, was a powerful literary figure.

The first stories, retitled *In the Midst of Life* (1892; revised, 1898) are a panoramic impression of the physical and psychological sensations of soldiers in battle. They reveal also Bierce's predilection for tales of terror, generally written with a sardonic humor and a surprise ending. "An Occurrence at Owl Creek Bridge" describes the rapid series of hallucinations which passes through the mind of a Southerner who is being hanged by Union soldiers.

Can Such Things Be? (1893) is another volume of stories concerning the

Civil War and the western frontier. Such tales as "My Favorite Murder" continue the strain of perverse humor.

Another mark left on American fiction by the sometime journalist, hackwriter, essayist and poet, was *The Devil's Dictionary* (1911), originally titled *The Cynic's Word Book* (1906). This is a collection of definitions editorially tinged with bitterness, skepticism, pessimism and social comment. "Piracy," remarks Bierce, is "commerce without its folly-swaddles, just as God made it."

BIG MONEY, THE (1936), by John Dos Passos. See U.S.A., by John Dos Passos.

BIGLOW PAPERS, THE (1848, 1867), by James Russell Lowell. See LOWELL, JAMES RUSSELL.

BILLY BUDD (published 1924), by Herman Melville. See MOBY-DICK, by Herman Melville.

BIOGRAPHIA LITERARIA (1817), by Samuel Taylor Coleridge. This is an elaborate extension of Coleridge's projected paper: "Autobiographia Literaria: Sketches of My Literary Life and Opinions." That Coleridge was a great, if rambling, critic, is beyond dispute. His digressions upon all occasions are brilliant, and he casually displays an astonishing variety of learning. In the *Biographia* he claims that poetry is the ideal medium of literary creation, and that the end of poetry is pleasure. He states that the "ultimate end of criticism is much more to establish the principles of writing than to furnish rules on how to pass judgment upon what has been written by others." To achieve this end, he examines English poetry from Chaucer to his own day. He also discusses the philosophical ideas of Descartes, Spinoza, Leibnitz, Kant, Fichte and Schelling, and the outmoded psychology of David Hartley, insofar as they affect creative literature and literary criticism. Chapters fourteen to twenty deal with Wordsworth's theory and practice, and the inconsistency between them. Somewhat whimsical narrative enters the book with three letters written while Coleridge was in Germany.

BIOGRAPHY (1932), by S. N. Behrman. See BEHRMAN, S. N.

BIRD OF TIME, THE (1912), by Sarojin Naidu. See NAIDU, SAROJIN.

BIRDS, THE (414 B.C.), by Aristophanes. This delightful comedy was produced when the Athenian expedition against Sicily was in progress, and mirrors the wild political speculations then rampant in Athens. Two elderly Athenians, Euelpides and Pisthetaerus, tired of conditions in their native city, set out to consult Tereus, who had been changed into a bird, the Epops, to see if he can tell them of some ideal spot where they may live. Epops suggests a number of places, but they are rejected by Euelpides. Pisthetaerus then reveals a grandiose scheme whereby the supreme power of the universe could be put in the hands of the birds. Epops is enchanted with the idea and summons all the birds. These support the plan with enthusiasm, and the two Athenians follow Epops into the thicket to procure wings and work out the details of the scheme. The Chorus of Birds recounts the early history of the world, as conceived by them, in a beautiful and poetic passage, interspersed with bird calls. The Athenians return, equipped with wings, and start to organize the new city which is to be called "Cloud-cuckoo-land" and which will shut out the gods. Envoys from Athens are ignored by the builders until Iris arrives, bearing a message from Zeus, who desires peace with the human race. A peace is concluded between the gods and the new city of the birds, and the latter are granted all their old rights. The comedy ends with the marriage of Pisthetaerus and Basileia, a daughter of Zeus.

BIRDS OF AMERICA (1827–1838), by John James Audubon. The 435 colored plates of 489 species of American birds, comprising this book, are magnificently drawn and colored, marvelous in detail and fidelity. There is equal accuracy in depiction of flowers and animals. *Birds of America* was designed to be seen, primarily. William MacGillivray collaborated in the writing of the text. The paintings are the products of years of observation in the American wilderness. The book was termed by the naturalist, Cuvier, "The most magnificent monument yet raised by art to science."
In 1848 the *Journals* of the naturalist were published by Maria R. Audubon.

BISHOP'S WIFE, THE (1928), by Robert Nathan. See NATHAN, ROBERT.

BLACK ARMOUR (1923), by Elinor Wylie. See WYLIE, ELINOR.

BLACK BEAUTY (1877), by Anna Sewell. This story of a horse, told in human terms, has long been a children's favorite. The gentle thoroughbred "Black Beauty" is carefully raised and considerately treated until a vicious groom injures him. Then he is sold to various masters at whose hands he experiences unkindness. At length Mr. Thoroughgood nurses him back to health; and he spends his final days happily with a family of ladies and their friendly coachman.

BLACK BOY (1945), by Richard Wright. See NATIVE SON, by Richard Wright.

BLACK CLOUDS (1930), by Han Yong-woon. See MEDITATIONS OF THE LOVER, by Han Yong-woon.

BLACK OXEN (1923), by Gertrude Atherton. See ATHERTON, GERTRUDE.

BLACK RIDERS, THE (1895), by Stephen Crane. See RED BADGE OF COURAGE, THE, by Stephen Crane.

BLACKSTONE'S COMMENTARIES. See COMMENTARIES ON THE LAWS OF ENGLAND, by Sir William Blackstone.

BLEAK HOUSE (1853), by Charles Dickens. The novel contains sharp criticism of the courts of chancery through its story of the involved case of Jarndyce vs. Jarndyce. As in similar cases, the litigants spend years trying to conclude the proceedings, during which time the estate is consumed by court costs. The two suitors in Jarndyce vs. Jarndyce are Richard Carstone and his pretty cousin, Ada Clare. The two young people are kindly treated by John Jarndyce, an older relative. He takes them to his home, Bleak House, to live.

Richard and Ada secretly marry, and Richard slowly allows nervous anxiety and deferred hope over the expected fortune, still "in chancery," to ruin his health. Continually excited about his prospects, he is unable to settle down to any serious work. Finally, sunk in misery, he dies. Shortly thereafter, news is received that the case is finished, but that the money has been dissipated. With Ada at Bleak House is Esther Summerson, one of the narrators of the story. Esther believes herself to be an orphan; she is a person of great common sense, sweetness, and generosity.

Lady Dedlock, adored wife of Sir Leicester Dedlock, appears to be a bored and indifferent member of society. However, she has a guilty past which she is anxious to conceal. In her youth she had been engaged to a Captain Rawdon. As a result of their affair, a daughter was born to her shortly after Rawdon's reported death at sea. She believes her child is dead, too. Rawdon, in fact, is not dead but has returned, a poverty-stricken scrivener. In the presence of her crafty and malicious lawyer, Mr. Tulkinghorn, Lady Dedlock glimpses Rawdon's handwriting on a legal paper and starts violently. Tulkinghorn takes note of her reaction and is determined to find the cause. Lady Dedlock tries to find Rawdon, and finally, with the help of Jo, a pathetic little street-sweeper, she locates his newly-covered grave in a pauper's field. From Jo's unwitting information, Tulkinghorn immediately proceeds to unravel all the facts about Lady Dedlock. He threatens to expose her to her husband, but is murdered by a former maidservant of Lady Dedlock's before he can do so. Bucket, a policeman, then tells Sir Leicester the truth about his wife. Lady Dedlock, discovering that her husband knows her secret after all, escapes from the house. Her husband and Esther, who now knows that Lady Dedlock is her mother, search for her, but are too late to save her. She is found dead near Rawdon's grave.

Esther, while living at Bleak House, has succumbed to smallpox and is afraid her good looks have vanished. She and her physician, young Dr. Woodcourt, have fallen in love. Mr. Jarndyce also loves her and asks her to marry him, and she, grateful for his unfailing kindness and trust, feels she must accept. But when Mr. Jarndyce learns that she really loves the young doctor, he withdraws his suit.

Dickens' gallery of characters includes Mrs. Jellyby, whose family suffers from neglect because of her foolish philanthropic activities; Miss Flite, the pathetic and crazed little woman who was driven out of her mind by a chancery case; Krook, the dealer in rags who dies spectacularly and horribly of "spontaneous combustion"; Jo, the slum-child, one of Dickens' most pitiful and heart-rending characters; and Mr. Chadband, the pious hypocrite. Leigh Hunt is said to have been the model for the debonair Mr. Skimpole.

BLESSED DAMOZEL, THE (1847), by Dante Gabriel Rossetti. Inspired by Poe's "The Raven," which Rossetti regarded as the perfect utterance of the grief of the earthly lover, this poem tells of the yearning of the loved one in heaven. She muses over the joyful day when her lover shall be brought to her there. They will stand together before the Virgin Mary, who will bring them to Christ. Of Him they will ask to live together in heaven forever. Her musing ceases; she weeps. *Jenny* (1870) caused a sensation when it appeared, it being a rather sentimental reverie over a prostitute. *The House of Life* (1870, 1881) is a sequence of one hundred and two sonnets tracing the poet's affection for his deceased wife, in quiet, mystical vein.

BLIND, THE (1890), by Maurice Maeterlinck. This play is an allegory in declamatory poetic prose, defeatist in philosophy and disenchanted with all moral and religious values. The characters are six men and six women, all blind, who represent mankind, wandering blindly in a faithless, hopeless world, led only by dead and useless ideals. Their guide is a priest, an old man returned from the dead, who finally abandons them in the forest. The setting itself is weird and uncanny. The blind grope along in an attempt to return to their refuge, but only lose themselves further. Alone and helpless, they wait for death.

BLOND ECKBERT (1797), by Ludwig Tieck. See TIECK, LUDWIG.

BLOOD, SWEAT AND TEARS (1941), by Winston Churchill. A collection of the speeches made by Winston Churchill from May, 1938, to February 9, 1941; it unfolds step by step the tragedy of the making of World War II. Churchill begins his warning to the English people in his speech of May 9, 1938, in Manchester when his topic is "The Choice of Europe." "We must gather round the joint strength of Britain and France and under the authority of the League all countries prepared to resist, and if possible to prevent acts of violent aggression. There is the path to safety." A little more than two weeks later, when the news of the Nazi massing of troops for the invasion of Czechoslovakia began to alarm the English people, Churchill addressed the House on the air defenses of Britain and appealed for greater activity in this direction: "At the present time the attitude of the Government is clearly that all may be carried on safely upon the existing methods." The clash between Churchill and Prime Minister Chamberlain began to sharpen with the former's speech on "The Munich Agreement." "What I find unendurable is the sense of our country falling into the power, into the orbit and influence of Nazi Germany, and of our existence becoming dependent upon their good will or pleasure." The speeches which follow illustrate the developing Nazi menace: The Case for a Ministry of Supply (Nov. 17, 1938); The Fruits of Munich; The Strength of the Navy (Mar. 16, 1939); The Invasion of Albania (April 13, 1939); Hitler Speaks (April 28, 1939); The New Army: Three Months of Tension (June 28, 1939); The Summer Adjournment (Aug. 2, 1939); Europe in Suspense (Aug. 8, 1939); War (Sept. 3, 1939); The First Month of War (Oct. 1, 1939); The Loss of the *Royal Oak* and the War at Sea (Nov. 8, 1939); Ten Weeks of War (Nov. 12, 1939); Traffic at Sea (Dec. 6, 1939); The Battle of the Plate (Dec. 18, 1939); A House of Many Mansions; A Time to Dare and Endure (Jan. 27, 1940); A Sterner War (Mar. 30, 1940); Norway; Prime Minister; Be Ye Men of Valor; The Capitulation of King Leopold (May 28, 1940); Dunkirk; The Fall of France; The Tragedy of the French Fleet; The War Situation (Aug. 20, 1940); We Will Never Cease to Strike (Nov. 9, 1940); To the People of Italy (Dec. 23, 1940); United States Cooperation (Jan. 9, 1941); Put Your Confidence in Us (Feb. 9, 1941). The title *Blood, Sweat and Tears* is taken from one of his famous speeches as England's wartime Prime Minister, an indication of the sacrifices required for survival and ultimate triumph.

BLOT IN THE 'SCUTCHEON, A (1843), by Robert Browning. Simple and forthright in its effects, Browning's famous verse-play treats of the snobbish narrowness of Thorold, Earl of Tresham. He has one all-absorbing interest in life—to maintain the family honor. But a blot in the ancestral escutcheon is brought about by the clandestine love affair between his sister Mildred and Henry, Earl Mertoun, whose estates border his own. Informed by his hawk-eyed retainer, Gerald, of the illicit affair, Thorold lies in ambush at night in the garden and intercepts the luckless lover as he is about to ascend to Mildred's room. They draw swords, and Henry is killed. Thereupon, Thorold takes poison, leaving his sister to die of a broken heart.

BLUE ANGEL, THE (1904), by Heinrich Mann. See MANN, HEINRICH.

BLUE BIRD, THE (1909), by Maurice Maeterlinck. On Christmas Eve Tyltyl and Mytyl, the children of a poor wood-cutter, are watching a Christmas party in a rich child's house. The Fairy Bérylune appears and sends them to search for the Blue Bird of Happiness. Aided by a magic diamond that releases the souls of animals and inanimate objects, the children set off on their journey accompanied by the Dog, who is fanatically loyal to his "little gods" and the Cat, a smooth fellow, who is the villain of the piece. Fire, Bread, Milk and Light also form part of the company, a timid and cautious crew with the exception of Light, who is a beautiful and fearless young girl and guides the children on their difficult and adventurous journey. From the palace of the Fairy Bérylune they visit the Land of Memory, and the Palace of Night. They find numerous Blue Birds in a moonlit garden, but none survives the light of day. The Cat organizes the Trees and Animals against the children in a scene in the Forest, where Tyltyl has to be rescued by the faithful Dog. In the Kingdom of the Future, among the souls of the children about to be born, they meet their little brother who will be born and die. But nowhere do they find the Blue Bird until they return home and discover that the Blue Bird has been in their cage all the time. When Tyltyl gives it to a neighbor's little girl, who has been ill, the bird escapes and flies away. The implication is that happiness lies in the search, not in the possession, and, though sought for in distant places, it is usually found close by, and is the result of unselfish acts. With *Pelleas and Melisande* (1892) and *The Blind* (q.v.), this play is the basis of Maeterlinck's fame as a symbolic dramatist.

BLUE VOYAGE (1927), by Conrad Aiken. See AIKEN, CONRAD.

BOEKEN DER KLEINE ZIELEN, DE (1901–1903), by Louis Couperus. See COUPERUS, LOUIS.

BOERENPSALM (1935), by Felix Timmermans. See TIMMERMANS, FELIX.

BOKE NAMED THE GOVERNOUR, THE (1531), by Sir Thomas Elyot. Elyot was not a university man. Educated at home, he early learned

Latin, Greek and Italian. This is his first and best known book. It is a long and exhaustive treatise on education for those who govern. It starts with a dissertation on various forms of government, approving monarchy as the best. This calls for gentlemen in official posts. A gentleman's education begins at birth. His nurse trains him until he is seven, when a selected tutor takes over. Elyot enumerates the books to be read, the physical exercise to be practiced—wrestling, hunting, swimming and, above all, dancing. Tennis and shooting with the cross-bow are also necessary. Next are proposed the lofty ideals which should inspire those who govern. The whole book is filled with references to classical antiquity, and it describes, in Book I, the very education which Italian patricians had been having for a century. Elyot emphasized high moral ideals in the later books, following a plan which was claimed by Erasmus' friend, Wilibald Pirkheimer, as his own. However, Elyot popularized the classical renascence and brought it to the mass of people who could not be reached by learned Latin treatises.

BOLTS OF MELODY (1945), by Emily Dickinson. See DICKINSON, EMILY.

BONDS OF INTEREST, THE (1907), by Jacinto Benavente. Crispín, a seasoned adventurer, comes to a city with his younger and less cynical companion, Leandro, who is weary of poverty and sham. Crispín goes to an inn and shouts for the servants to come out, and when the Landlord appears, tells him that his master, Leandro, is so great a personage that he cannot divulge his name. The Landlord, impressed, gives them the best rooms in the inn. The Captain, an impecunious soldier, and Arlequín, a hungry poet, make their acquaintance and are treated to a magnificent meal. Crispín continues to spread rumors about his master until the whole town is talking about the mysterious visitor. Crispín calls, in Leandro's name, on Colombina, Arlequín's mistress, who, with Doña Sirena, is giving a fete. He foots the bills and promises Doña Sirena a handsome purse if she will help Leandro win the hand of Silvia, daughter of rich Polichinela. Polichinela, a scoundrel who has amassed his fortune in shady ways and who knows Crispín, objects to the marriage. Silvia, madly in love with Leandro, runs away to Doña Sirena's house and threatens not to return unless she becomes Leandro's wife. Since Crispín has established so many "bonds of interest," having incurred so many debts and made so many promises, his creditors and friends see to it that Polichinela relents. And thus the wedding of Leandro and Silvia, the most honest and lovable persons in the play, comes to pass.

BOOK OF DISCUSSION AND REMEMBRANCE, by Moses Ibn Ezra. See Ibn Ezra, Moses.

BOOK OF DIVINE LOVE, THE (1330), by Juan Ruiz. Little is known about Juan Ruiz (1283–1350) except that he was Archpriest of the town of Hita, that he was deprived of his post on charges of licentiousness and that, while in prison, he wrote one of Spain's outstanding literary masterpieces: the *Libro de Buen Amor* (1330). By "buen amor" (good love) he meant the love of God and righteousness as opposed to "loco amor" (sensual love), but in spite of himself, the sinning Archpriest seems to be chiefly interested in "loco amor." Filled with the joy of living, this brother of Rabelais, Chaucer and Boccaccio pursued wine, women and song. The *Libro de Buen Amor* is a poetical miscellany: a picaresque novel in rhyme set in a grand lyrical pageant. This magnificent hodgepodge opens with a quaint prayer; a sermon in prose, quite reminiscent of *The Canterbury Tales* (q.v.); and two charming poems on "The Joys of the Holy Mary." After the eminently religious preliminaries, the Archpriest plunges with sinful delight into a picaresque detailing of his love affairs: the first one, with Cruz, the baker-girl, who preferred his go-between, Ferrand García, to him. Laughing at his own expense, the Arch-priest now employs a more efficient go-between, the wily old hag Trotacon-ventos, who serves him in a number of wooings, most of which prove to be fiascos. Amid the various philanderings, there are apologues, versified tales, bitter-sweet pastorals, fables ("The City Mouse and the Country Mouse," "The Frogs Who Wanted a King," etc.), a dramatic interlude ("Battle between Lent and Meat"), short poems (the famous "Praise of Little Women," "A Christian's Armour," and wonderful satire on the influence and corruption of money), and a hymn to Our Lord. With such a conglomerate of themes and leitmotifs, the Archpriest carries out a wide variety of metrical experimenta-tions, mixing the comic with the tragic, imbuing life into a vast assortment of characters. Though his exuberant individualism belongs to the Renaissance, very often a medieval anguish (the world as a vale of tears, etc.) permeates the complex texture of his work. He is sensual and devout, has a keen eye for essential details, is vivid, piquant, and often cynical. His lyrical vein reflects with subtle spiritual depth and profound psychological understand-ing a material world fraught with irresistible joyousness.

BOOK OF HOURS, THE (1906), by Rainer Maria Rilke. See RILKE, RAINER MARIA.

BOOK OF INTERPRETATIONS OF THE GOSPEL FOR THE WHOLE YEAR (1441), by Peter Chelčicky. See NET OF THE TRUE FAITH, THE, by Peter Chelčicky.

BOOK OF KINGS (10th c.), by Firdusi. See SHAH-NAMEH, by Firdusi.

BOOK OF MARTYRS, or ACTS AND MONUMENTS OF THESE LATTER PERILOUS TIMES . . . (Latin 1559, English 1563), by John Foxe. The work, a survey of the Christian Church, includes detailed accounts of many martyrs, beginning with the first, St. Stephen, and dwelling most on the Protestant martyrs who died at the stake during the reign of the Catholic queen, "Bloody" Mary. Recent martyrs are apt to be unpopular, and it was with great difficulty and personal risk that Foxe managed to gather his stories. Violently prejudiced against everything that smacked of papistry, Foxe allowed his strong bias to permeate his accounts. Devoid of literary orna-mentation, even monotonous in its presentation of each martyr meeting his death in the same manner, the book achieves great power and pathos through its very starkness. The fortitude of the martyrs and the grimly realistic description of the actual business of execution combine to make certain passages unforgettably vivid. Popular with the masses, this book was in-fluential in furthering the cause of Protestantism in England.

BOOK OF MIRACLES, A (1939), by Ben Hecht. See HECHT, BEN.

BOOK OF MORMON, THE (1830), by Joseph Smith. Based on golden plates which Joseph Smith claimed were revealed to him, and which he unearthed from Cumorah Hill, New York, this book is roughly similar in structure to the *Bible* (q.v.). The sacred book of the Mormon religion is subdivided as follows: The First Book of Nephi; The Second Book of Nephi; Book of Jacob, The Brother of Nephi; Book of Jarom; Book of Omni; The Words of Mormon; Book of Mosiah; Book of Alma; Book of Halaman; Book of Mormon; Book of Esther; Book of Moroni. The Mormons revere this volume as the "Fulness of the Gospel of Jesus Christ . . . The history of the ancient inhabitants of America, who were a branch of the House of Israel, or the Tribe of Joseph, of whom the Indians are still a remnant." Emphasized are the doctrines of pre-existence, perfection, the after-life, and Christ's second coming.

This book has had an annual American sale of some 20,000 copies for well over a century.

BOOK OF PICTURES (1902), by Rainer Maria Rilke. See RILKE, RAINER MARIA.

BOOK OF SMALL SOULS, THE (1901–1903), by Louis Couperus. See COUPERUS, LOUIS.

BOOK OF SONGS (1827), by Heinrich Heine. See HEINE, HEINRICH.

BOOK OF THE DEAD, THE (2500 B.C.). *The Book of the Dead* contains ancient prayers and hymns which had been learned by heart and recited from memory long before the emergence of historical writing in Egypt. They prove conclusively that not only the worship of Isis and Osiris, but all of the mythological philosophy connected with it, were accepted more than five thousand years ago. They form one of the oldest and most complete documents of primitive belief concerning man's hopes and fears of the world beyond the grave. The work is essentially mythological, and assumes the reader's thorough knowledge of the myths and legends of ancient Egypt. It was considered by Egyptians to be an inspired work. It is the god Thoth himself who speaks, revealing to man the will of the gods and the mysterious nature of divine things. Portions of the book are expressly stated to have been written by the very finger of Thoth himself.

The Book of the Dead has neither beginning nor end—the chapters were thrown together without method, and the parts have no organic connection. It includes a description of the judgment and a list of the sins of which the deceased must be able to declare himself innocent, as well as prayers and incantations. Texts from it were written upon coffins and inscribed upon the walls of tombs or laid, in papyrus form, in the grave for the departed to carry with him as a passport and an aid to slipping memory. For it was believed necessary to sing hymns of praise in the other world as well as in this one. The right word could ward off demons and hostile beasts, open gates, procure food and drink, justify a man's life before the dread god Osiris and the forty-two judges, and secure for him the status and privileges of a god. As with all other scriptural writings handed down from father to son, in the course of time exegetical commentaries were required to clarify, reconcile and explain away inconsistencies.

It was not given final form as an authoritative canon until about the seventh century B.C. The English translation was done by E. A. Wallis Budge.

BOOK OF THE DUCHESS, THE (1369), by Geoffrey Chaucer. This is an allegorical poem in octosyllabic couplets, lamenting the death of Blanche of Lancaster. Having read in a romance that the gods can bring sleep and significant dreams, the poet falls into a slumber and dreams he leaves a sunny chamber to join a hunting party of the Emperor Octavius. In the woods he meets a man in black who is mourning the loss of his lady. Encouraged by Chaucer, this knight tells in detail of his lady's loveliness, of their courtship, and of his present sadness. Asked why he is sad, he declares that the lady Whyte is dead. The hunting party returns to the castle, a bell strikes, and Chaucer awakes, still holding the romance over which he had fallen asleep.

The interpretation of a later allegorical poem of Chaucer's, "The Parliament of Fowls," is in dispute. The poet has been reading the *Somnium Scipionis* when he himself falls asleep and has a dream. Guided by Africanus, he sees first the temple of Venus and then a hill, where all the birds are assembled before the goddess of Nature on Saint Valentine's Day. They have come to choose their mates. Three tercel eagles dispute for a formel eagle on the goddess's hand, but decision is postponed.

A third allegory, "The House of Fame," is unfinished. Chaucer in a dream leaves the temple of Venus and is carried up to the House of Fame by an eagle, who explains that Jupiter has allowed the poet this privilege as a reward for his studies and his verses. The castle is filled with men seeking the favor of the Lady Fame, who disposes of their pleas arbitrarily, ordering them to be dismissed by Aeolus by the trumpet of fame or of slander. The poet next visits the whirling House of Rumor. Here are people telling news, both false and true, all of which goes to Lady Fame.

BOOKS OF THE POLISH PILGRIMAGE, THE (1832), by Adam Mickiewicz. See MICKIEWICZ, ADAM.

BOORISH YEARS (1804–1805), by Johann Paul Richter. See RICHTER, JOHANN PAUL.

BORIS GODUNOV (1825), by Alexander Pushkin. Irritated with the shallowness of contemporary drama, Pushkin turned to Shakespeare for inspiration, and to history for his theme. He kept in mind *Macbeth* and *Richard III* as he wrote *Boris,* and the result was one of the greatest plays of the early nineteeth century, full of the fury and dark passion from which emerged that complex historic figure. Spanning the years 1598–1605, the play deals with the reign of Boris and his fatal struggle against the false Dimitrí, the pretended son of Ivan the Terrible. Boris had caused the murder of the Czarevitch and had then seized the throne for himself. When the play opens, he is thinking of retiring to a monastery, and the nobles are restless and dissatisfied. He is powerfully portrayed as a murderer tormented by conscience, as a sly politician, and as an affectionate father. Dimitrí is an unscrupulous, ambitious young monk whose lust for power is so compelling that, in order to achieve his ends, he is ready to betray his country to the Polish enemy by instigating a war of annihilation against it. Momentarily diverted from his purpose by the vaguely-drawn Mariana, for whom he cultivates a romantic attachment, he is able to ignore her threat to reveal to the world his base origin and his unfounded pretensions to the throne of the Czar. In Moscow, Czar Boris calls a council of the Boyars and the Patriarch, tightens his rule on the people, and appoints Basamanov, an ambitious, self-made man, to command the army. The Czar is suddenly taken ill and sends for his son Feodor, to bid him farewell. The people condemn the dying Boris as an interloper against dynastic traditions and supplant him with Dimitrí, because they regard him as a scion of the old line. After the Czar's death, Feodor and his mother commit suicide in prison. The composer, Moussorgsky, wrote a powerful opera based upon the theme, also under the title of *Boris Godunov*.

BOSTON (1928), by Upton Sinclair. See JUNGLE, THE, by Upton Sinclair.

BOSTONIANS, THE (1886), by Henry James. See JAMES, HENRY.

BOTH YOUR HOUSES (1933), by Maxwell Anderson. See WINTERSET, by Maxwell Anderson.

BOTKIN, BENJAMIN A. (1901–   ). Ben Botkin, who edited the first important collections of American folk and regional writings in a book whose title word he coined, *Folk-Say, A Regional Miscellany* (1929–1932), has been Folklore Editor of the Federal Writers' Project, Fellow of the Library of Congress in Folklore, and president of the American Folklore Society. *A Treasury of American Folklore* (1944) is an encyclopedic volume of legendary characters, stories and songs from all parts of the United States. *A Treasury of New England Folklore* (1947) and *A Treasury of Southern Folklore* (1949) have followed.

BOTYOV, KHRISTO (1848–1876). Khristo Botyov was the leading poet of the Bulgarians before their liberation. He received much of his education in Russia, where he became the friend of many of the Russian radical leaders of the sixties. He then moved to Braila, and became active in the preparation of a revolution in Bulgaria. With about 200 friends, he seized a Danube steamship and invaded the country. The attempt was a failure, and in the first battle Botyov was killed. His body was never recovered.

He left twenty-two short poems, such as "Hadji Dimitur," "To My First Love," etc. They are purely subjective flashes of a romantic tendency, but they sum up the spirit of the times and are still the favorite poems of the Bulgarians. In sharp, quick strokes, they reveal the entire nature of the poet and of his search for liberty and freedom for his people. There may be doubts as to the nature of his ideals, but there can be none as to the beauty and vigor of his works, which were dashed off on the impulse of the moment. They express the full content of the soul of this romantic revolutionist who threw away his life at the age of twenty-eight, and did more by that act to kindle the flames of the revolt than by all of his previous efforts.

BOULE DE SUIF AND OTHER TALES (1880), by Guy de Maupassant. *Boule de Suif* is an episode of the Franco-Prussian war. During German occupation, a *diligence* leaves Rouen, with a few travelers who are an image and a summary of contemporary society: aristocrats, bourgeois, one loud democrat, nuns, and Boule de Suif, a prostitute. Because of her profession, Boule de Suif is, at first, scorned by her companions. But the *diligence* has to stop; the travelers get hungry; good-hearted Boule de Suif shares her provisions and becomes less unpopular. Then a German officer refuses to let the coach proceed unless Boule de Suif gives in to his will. Egged on by her traveling companions, she finally acquiesces, in order to help them. Then the coach can go on. But the travelers, having no more use for Boule de Suif, look down on her, and she weeps silently in her corner. The story was first printed in *Les Soirées de Médan,* a collection written by Emile Zola and four young admirers. Maupassant's eye for sharp realism, and his gift for the brief, frequently bitter tale, make him supreme in this sort of literature.

BOURGEOIS GENTILHOMME, LE (1670), by Molière. Monsieur Jourdain, wealthy bourgeois whose father made a fortune selling cloth, wants to ape the nobility. He becomes a protector of the arts, hires masters of fencing, philosophy, dancing and music, and even composes (with help) a serenade for the noble lady he thinks he loves. His vanity makes him easy prey to flatterers and cynical hangers-on, but also makes him hard to live with; he will let his daughter, Lucille, marry no one but a noble. She loves a commoner, Cleante. Here Cleante's valet, Covielle, comes to the rescue just when the hour is darkest by disguising his master and presenting him to Jourdain as the son of the Grand Turk. Jourdain consents to the marriage and, in a fantastic ceremony, is raised by the Turk to the imaginary rank of *Mamamouchi*—a word still current in French to designate the self-satisfied holder of an empty dignity.

Molière called his play a comedy-ballet. Music for it was by Lulli.

BOUTENS, PIETER CORNELIS (1870–1944). For years Boutens was the leading figure in modern Dutch poetry. Beginning with a very individual style of extreme precision, he turned in 1910 to a clearer and simpler choice of words; then he found for his sonorous verses a form of classic beauty and equilibrium. Strongly influenced by Plato's philosophy, he sings in *Stemmen* (1907), *Vergeten liedjes* (1909), *Carmina* (1912), of earthly beauty, conceived as a reflection of a perfect world of pure harmony, which shall be revealed to man after his death. His influence on today's generation of poets in Holland is immeasurably great. Notwithstanding the somewhat involved character of his poetry, it has found resonance in the broad social layers of the people. No poet since Vondel has felt so deeply the beauty of Holland's nature, has felt himself so deeply to be Dutch. This appears clearly in the poetry of his advanced years: *Bezonnen Verzen* (1931) and *Hollandsche Kwatrijnen* (1932). Superb are his translations of Homer, Aeschylus, Plato and Sophocles; from the English, he translated Rossetti and Wilde.

Some of his poems were translated by Sir Herbert Grierson in *Two Dutch Poets* (Clarendon Press, Oxford, 1936).

BOY'S MAGIC HORN, THE (1806–1808), by Achim von Arnim and Clemens Maria Brentano. See KNABEN WUNDERHORN, by Achim von Arnim and Clemens Maria Brentano.

BOY'S WILL, A (1913), by Robert Frost. See FROST, ROBERT.

BRACEBRIDGE HALL (1822), by Washington Irving. See SKETCH BOOK, THE, by Washington Irving.

BRAND (1866), by Henrik Ibsen. First written as an epic poem, *Brand* was not intended for the stage. After being recast in the dramatic form, it was produced in Stockholm in 1885. The action takes place in Norway where Brand, a serious young priest, is struggling to answer the call of duty in a distant town. He has a soul to save, and continues along the icy mountain fields at the risk of his life. Brand is contemptuous of the compromising religion practiced by his countrymen, and believes that "all or nothing" should be the principle of faith. He rigidly practices this principle although it costs him the lives of his wife, Agnes, and their son, Alf. His parish rebels against his strict beliefs and, turning against him, drives Brand out into the snow, to perish under an avalanche. His last appeal to God is answered by the cry, "He is the God of Love." Other characters include Einar, an old schoolmate of Brand's; Gerd, a wild girl of fifteen who follows Brand to the end; and Brand's mother, a covetous old woman who thinks more of money than she does of God.

BRASS CHECK, THE (1919), by Upton Sinclair. See JUNGLE, THE, by Upton Sinclair.

BRAVE NEW WORLD (1932), by Aldous Huxley. In the "brave new world," reproduction is a standard laboratory matter, turning out people systematically conditioned for the several strata of life. Sex and all other sensory matters are exploited contentment media. Production and consumption are the purposes of life; the commonplace is apotheosized. Literature, art, philosophy are suppressed; and a variety of pacifying sensory gratifications, all standardized, are substituted. Ford (sometimes called Freud), legendary father of standardization, has been deified. Workers are content because they are so conditioned, possessing no aspiration beyond the sops of drugs. Near this environment is reared a "savage," on an Indian reservation kept as a scientific museum.

Meanwhile, even in Utopia, there is some dissatisfaction. In the Psychological Bureau, Bernard Marx feels socially isolated because of slight physical deficiencies—and the resultant insecurity makes him cynical. His Alpha Plus friend, Helmholtz Watson, feels a vague creative restlessness and isolation caused by his very superiority. With Lenina Crowne (who is proud that men think her "pneumatic") Bernard is disgusted, and Helmholtz bored.

When Bernard brings John, the savage, into the new world, there are immediate repercussions. Helmholtz, hearing the youth recite Shakespeare, first questions his own long-conditioned set of artificial values. He and Bernard join John in an abortive demonstration against the use of "soma," the universal drug; the three are summoned before Mustapha Mond, the Resident World Controller for Western Europe.

The Controller is an understanding man. A radical in his youth, he had accepted a governmental position and "conventionality" rather than exile—that he might further his dearest interest, pure science. Bernard and Helmholtz, however, now choose differently. The latter welcomes exile, the stimulation of physical hardship and mental freedom; the cowardly Bernard must be drugged and dragged away. John is maddened by the soulless horror of the new world. Retained as the subject of scientific experimentation, and trapped by the ambivalence of a physical attraction to and mental repulsion from Lenina, he commits suicide.

The harshly ironic fantasy of *Brave New World* has gained in impact with the years rather than diminished.

BRAVO, THE (1831), by James Fenimore Cooper. See SPY, THE, by James Fenimore Cooper.

BREAD AND WINE (1937), by Ignazio Silone. In *Bread and Wine* Silone depicts the peasants, workers, intellectuals and revolutionaries of Italy struggling to achieve their freedom from Mussolini. The hero, Pietro Spina, an exile from fascist Italy, after many years abroad returns to his native Abruzzi to engage in underground revolutionary activities against Mussolini's regime of terror. He wanders through Italy, disguised as an itinerant priest, and finds all the people frightened to death; the peasants are resigned like sheep; the workers in Rome are crushed; the intellectuals are bribed by fat jobs in the bureaucratic machine of Il Duce. Among others, Spina meets a young student who, he thinks, is ready for revolutionary work. But Spina eventually finds that the student, succumbing to the Ethiopian war psychosis, has betrayed him to the authorities. He takes precipitate flight from certain persecution. Other characters of significance in the story are: Cristina, saintlike and religious, who represents the quieting effects of religion; and the liberal priest, Don Bernedetto, who believes in active virtue and who himself falls a victim of the brutal oppression. The sacramental wine he drinks as he celebrates mass is poisoned. The title takes on a mystical meaning, apparently the only solution the disillusioned Silone can offer: the bread and wine of that sacramental love which impelled Jesus to offer himself as a sacrifice for erring men.

Ignazio Silone achieved an international reputation with his anti-fascist story *Fontamara* (1933).

BRECHT, BERTOLT (1898–   ). One of the strangest writers of the twentieth century is the German, Bertolt Brecht, whose pioneering contribution to modern drama is not yet generally recognized. In debt to Wedekind and somewhat associated with the Expressionistic movement in his younger days, he stands nevertheless as alone in our days as Georg Büchner a century ago. (cf. *Danton's Death*). He is the foremost protagonist of the so-called "epic drama" today. Brecht achieved his only popular success with an adaptation of John Gay's *Beggar's Opera* (music by Kurt Weill) under the title *Three Penny Opera* (1928). A lifelong foe of fascism, he spent the years after 1933 in exile, and fought Hitler with sharp ballads, satires and plays, including *Private Life of the Master Race* (1944). His historical *Galilei* was performed in New York in 1947. Partly inaccessible at present, Brecht's literary work may be more highly valued in the decades to come.

BREWSTER'S MILLIONS (1902), by George Barr McCutcheon. This fantasy concerns young Monty Brewster, who inherits a million dollars, but learns that another inheritance, from an uncle, of seven million dollars, is to be his only if he is penniless at his next birthday. Monty desperately spends his first million, only to discover that the uncle's legacy is a hoax.

BRIDAL CANOPY, THE (1937), by Samuel Joseph Agnon. The hero of the story, the simple pious Jewish scholar, Reb Yudel, lives and goes through adventures in a manner that makes him a Jewish prototype of Don Quixote. He journeys over the full extent of the world he knew under his Kaiser, for the purpose of discovering bridegrooms for his three languishing daughters. He possesses a team of horses and the services of a contemplative wagoner. The verbal exchanges with the driver and various wayfarers are extraordinary contributions to Jewish and general folklore. There are irony and gaiety in every page, but no concealment of the general cruelty shown itinerant Israelites. When Yudel at length discovers a groom for his eldest child, he is compelled to set out once more to obtain a dowry for the girl—he has been mistaken for a man of wealth. But Reb Yudel, living in the spirit of the beliefs and sanctities of the Pentateuch, and pervaded with the joyful faith of the Jewish sect of *Hassidim,* remains forever trustful of God's goodness—and all ends well. Agnon, who has long been a resident of Palestine, is the foremost Hebrew novelist. Among his books in Hebrew are: *Forsaken Wives* (1907); *The Bent Shall Become Straight* (1909); *The Sandy Hill,* a story of modern Palestine (1919); a series of love stories (1923); *The Outcast,* on the struggles of Hassidism (1926); *Poland* (1926); six volumes of short stories; and *Days of Awe* (1938; American edition, 1948), which gathers and expounds the copious folklore and sayings clustering about the Jewish high holidays.

BRIDE OF LAMMERMOOR, THE (1819), by Sir Walter Scott. This gloomy but popular novel was transformed into an opera by Donizetti, *Lucia di Lammermoor.* Lucy, the tragic heroine, is a sweet and loyal soul, but with no will of her own. Her father, unscrupulous Sir William Ashton, and her haughty mother, Lady Ashton, dominate her completely. Sir William is a lawyer and an ambitious parvenu who has amassed a fortune and has achieved high public office by dishonest means. He has built his success on the ruin of Lord Ravenswood's estate, which ruin he himself brought about by legal trickery. Despite the fact that Ravenswood's son, Edgar, has vowed vengeance for this deed, the young man finds himself in love with Lucy. The two become secretly betrothed. At first, the designing Sir William encourages the suit, but his arrogant wife, who has other plans for her daughter, drives Edgar away. Edgar goes abroad on a mission for a kinsman. While he is away, Lady Ashton forces Lucy into a marriage with Frank Hayston, Laird of Bucklaw, a dissolute, unattractive person. On her wedding night, Lucy, overcome with grief, goes out of her mind. In her deranged state, she stabs and critically wounds her husband. She dies the following day. Edgar, thinking Lucy has forgotten him, is engulfed by quicksand while on his way to fight a duel with young Ashton, Lucy's brother. This somber novel is enlightened by the character of Caleb Balderstone, Ravenswood's devoted retainer, who is determined to conceal the poverty-stricken condition of the family by any lies or ingenious devices that occur to him.

BRIDE OF MESSINA, THE (1803), by Friedrich von Schiller. See SCHILLER, FRIEDRICH VON.

BRIDGE, THE (1930), by Hart Crane. See CRANE, HART.

BRIDGE OF SAN LUIS REY, THE (1927), by Thornton Wilder. On a July day in 1714, the finest bridge in Peru breaks and plunges to their deaths five persons who were on it. Brother Juniper, a Franciscan missionary, views the accident as the judgment of God, and probes into the lives of the victims to bear out his belief. The book thereupon surveys in brief the stories of the Marquesa de Montemayor, who had devoted her life to her brilliant but selfish daughter Clara; Pepita, her Indian maid; Esteban, whose love for his twin Manuel had been tormented by the presence of the actress La Périchole; Uncle Pio, La Périchole's coachman; and Jaimé, her small son. The threads of these mysteriously linked lives are finally drawn together on a mystical note, their deaths having occurred at a significant moment of their human dramas. Mr. Wilder's book was awarded the Pulitzer Prize, best-seller recognition, and motion picture treatment.

The Ides of March (1948) is a historical novel which re-creates the life of Rome during Caesar's time, by means of letters supposedly written by several contemporary figures and circulated among them. Among the author's plays is the famous Pulitzer Prize winner, *Our Town* (q.v.).

BRIDGES (1912), by Zalman Shneiur. See SHNEIUR, ZALMAN.

BRIEF MOMENT (1931), by S. N. Behrman. See BEHRMAN, S. N.

BRIMMING CUP, THE (1921), by Dorothy Canfield. See CANFIELD, DOROTHY.

BRING! BRING! (1925), by Conrad Aiken. See AIKEN, CONRAD.

BRITANNICUS (1669), by Jean-Baptiste Racine. See ANDROMAQUE, by Jean-Baptiste Racine.

BROKEN JUG, THE (1808), by Heinrich von Kleist. See KLEIST, HEINRICH VON.

BROKEN WING, THE (1915–1916), by Sarojin Naidu. See NAIDU, SAROJIN.

BROOK EVANS (1928), by Susan Glaspell. See GLASPELL, SUSAN.

BROOKE, RUPERT (1887–1915). A late romantic, yet perhaps the earliest twentieth-century poet to be influenced by Donne, Brooke wrote immortal lyrics before he joined the British Mediterranean Expeditionary Force in the Dardanelles Campaign and died of blood-poisoning at Scyros in the Aegean at twenty-seven. His best-known work is the short sonnet-sequence "1914" and particularly the fifth sonnet, "The Soldier":

> If I should die, think only this of me;
> That there's some corner of a foreign field
> That is for ever England. There shall be
> In that rich earth a richer dust concealed . . .

In "The Great Lover" he zestfully catalogues the things he has loved, while "The Hill," "Kindliness," "Libido," "Jealousy," "The Busy Heart" are love poems in the usual sense: sensual, vexed, conversational. Donne's "metaphysical" school has affected the two octosyllabic poems, "Dining-Room Tea" and "The Old Vicarage, Grantchester," in the latter of which an Englishman has playful home-thoughts from abroad. The *Collected Poems* appeared in 1915.

BROTHERS ASHKENAZI, THE (Eng. tr. 1936), by Israel Joshua Singer. Translated from the Yiddish and published in the United States in 1936, this novel by Singer (1893–1944) is not only the most popular, but also the most dramatic of his fictional writings. It tells the story of the cultural and industrial rise and decline of the Russian city of Lodz, through the characters of antithetical twin brothers, Max and Yakob Ashkenazi. Max, the older, is ambitious, brilliant, ruthless, indifferent to others; he dreams of completely ruling the city's extensive weaving industry. Yakob is a lover of life, greedy for experience, lacking Max's drive and ambition, gifted only in his personality, and rising by sheer accident while his brother succeeds through hard effort. Neither understands the rising proletariat labor movement, regarding their schoolmate Nissan, harassed labor leader, as a lunatic. During and after the World War, they discover how tenuous is their hold on their riches and the community, when anti-Semitism spreads. Yakob is killed in cold blood before Max by a brutal officer; Max dies of heart failure soon thereafter. All of Lodz assembles at the funeral: "They saw in the death of Max Ashkenazi the death of the city, and his funeral was that of Lodz." Singer attained world notice with publication of his short stories, *Pearl* (1923). The play *Yoshe Kalb*, called in English *The Sinners*, was produced in New York in Yiddish in 1932, and printed in an English rendering the next year. Later works translated into English are the short story volume *The River Breaks Up* (1938), and *East of Eden* (1939). There are a half dozen more popular novels, only one of which has been translated.

BROTHERS KARAMAZOV, THE (1880), by Feodor Dostoevsky. Regarded as his outstanding work, this psychological novel is Dostoevsky's final judgment on modern times, on a humanity succumbing to what he calls "socialist materialism," on individuals abandoning true Christianity. A deeply religious work, obsessed with man's search for faith, it is also a sordid story of crime, and an account of the struggle within the soul of man for truth and virtue. The tragedy is dominated by the patriarchal Father Zossima, who has achieved holiness by renouncing his reason and will. The elder Karamazov is a roué and sot who has sunk into a swamp of corruption and has dragged his young mistress, Grushenka, with him. A cunning old reprobate, he is intelligent enough to understand the deeper motives of his behavior, and suffers maudlin pangs of conscience. The struggle between him and his eldest son, Dmitrí, for the carnal love of Grushenka, is the pivotal motive for the crime that ensues. Under the sly promptings of another son, Ivan, the old man's epileptic, illegitimate son, Smerdyakov, murders his father. Dmitrí is suspected, and is sentenced to die for the crime on the grounds of circumstantial evidence.

All three legitimate sons of Karamazov, Dmitrí, Ivan and Alyosha, are tainted in varying degrees with the Karamazov hereditary weakness of character. It is most pronounced in Dmitrí. He is a fine, simple soul, tormented by inner conflicts, and in his quest for ideal values, treads the sorrowful way of the blundering heart. At his trial, overwhelmed by the spectacle of crime and spiritual confusion, he at last finds God and inner peace. He publicly flays his soul for its shortcomings. He admits with gratitude that in order to see the light, it is first necessary to undergo purgation by tragedy: "I accept the torture of accusation, and my public shame. I want to suffer, and by suffering I shall purify myself . . . But listen, for the last time, I am not guilty of my father's blood." Dostoevsky argues that it was really Ivan who was the murderer of his father, rather than the weak-minded Smerdyakov who actually committed the crime, or the brooding Dmitrí who vicariously suffered for it. It was Ivan who planted the seed of evil in Smerdyakov's mind. Everyone shared in the crime, for the whole world must be held responsible for all the evil that passes under the sun. In the questioning, doubting Ivan, Dostoevsky wished to castigate the rationalism of his time, which he saw as bereft of feeling and faith, and which would turn into a demoniacal force if let loose. Ivan, too, had the Karamazov taint in him, but it was intellectual rather than sensual. The youngest Karamazov, Alyosha, as a novice in a monastery, seeks spiritual rapture, guided by Father Zossima. He too bears the Karamazov rot in his otherwise pure young soul. He, like his brothers, wrestles with the Evil One, but emerges triumphant: "He longed to forgive everyone and for everything, and to beg forgiveness. Oh, not for himself, but for all men, for all and for everything."

It is this novel that contains the famous story of "The Grand Inquisitor," so much anthologized, and it is in the equally famous chapter preceding this —"Ivan Karamazov's Confession of Faith"—that Ivan utters the celebrated and oft-quoted phrase: "It is not God that I don't accept, Alyosha, only I most respectfully return Him the ticket."

BROTHERS OF SERAPION, THE (1819–1821), by E. T. A. Hoffmann. See HOFFMANN, E. T. A.

BROWNING, ROBERT (1812–1889). Besides such long poems as *The Ring and the Book, Paracelsus, A Blot in the 'Scutcheon,* and *Pippa Passes,* and the briefer *Pied Piper of Hamelin* (qq.v.), Browning wrote comparatively short dramatic monologues that are among the most famous poems in the language. There are, first, those showing his interest in Italian stories and settings, such as "My Last Duchess" (1842), a concentrated study of a nobleman of Ferrara who broke his first wife by his pride and his jealousy and by treating her as just another of his possessions—and who is now bargaining for a new duchess. Three years later Browning published a lesser known sequel, "The Flight of the Duchess," long and fantastic. "Fra Lippo Lippi" (1855), "Pictor Ignotus" (1855) and "Andrea del Sarto" (1855) introduce great painters of the Renaissance, each of them in rebellion—the unknown painter against the soiling world outside his cloister, Fra Lippo Lippi against the stifling asceticism within it, and Andrea del Sarto against his betrayal of his own genius on account of his greedy, unfaithful wife. "A Grammarian's Funeral" (1855) portrays with compassionate irony the scholar's quest for knowledge. "Love among the Ruins" (1855) is nameless in its setting, as is the puzzling but provocative ballad "Childe Roland to the Dark Tower Came" (1855). "The Bishop Orders His Tomb at St. Praxed's Church" (1845) shows sly worldliness among the old clergy, while "Soliloquy of the Spanish Cloister" (1842) presents a ritualistic villain. Love leading to murder is the subject of "Porphyria's Lover," who strangles his beloved with her own hair ("And yet God has not said a word!"), and of "The Laboratory," where a diminutive female fiend watches eagerly the preparation of the poison she plans to use at the ball. Frustrated love enters into "The Statue and the Bust" (1855) and "Evelyn Hope" (1855) and "The Last Ride Together" (1855). More philosophical, not simply romantic, are "Prospice" (1864), where the poet faces death, and "Rabbi Ben Ezra" (1864), where he faces old age. In still other keys are "Memorabilia" (1855) in honor of Shelley, "De Gustibus—" (1855), with its dispute over English versus Italian scenery continued from "Home-Thoughts from Abroad" and "From the Sea" (both 1845), the childhood favorite "Incident of the French Camp" (1842), the rousing "Cavalier Tunes" (1842) and the galloping "How They Brought the Good News from Ghent to Aix" (1845). The poet's genius, mainly dramatic, though never expressed in plays intended for production, poured itself into many subjects, several periods of history—he translated Euripides' *Alcestis* (q.v.) in "Balaustion's Adventure" (1871)—and many verse forms, yet with a consistency of attitude perhaps best expressed by his Andrea del Sarto:

> Ah, but a man's reach should exceed his grasp,
> Or what's a Heaven for?

BRUNO, GIORDANO (1548–1600). Bruno's philosophic writing was the product of many of the forces that developed during the Renaissance. Influenced by Platonic mysticism, Aristotelianism, pantheism, naturalism, and the new natural science, he came to be skeptical of all forms of Christianity. He developed a secular philosophy, but one in which God played an important part. He conceived of God as one with the universe. The universe is a diversity in unity in which all the diverse parts themselves exhibit unity. There is intelligence and life in everything, and the human soul is God's greatest achievement. These views, in conflict with established authority, led to his being burned at the stake.

BRUT, THE (ca. 1205), by Layamon. A chronicle, in more than 32,000 alliterative lines, of the history of Britain from the destruction of Troy to the year 689, Layamon's *Brut* is one of the earliest and most important writings in the vernacular. His chief aim was to tell the noble thoughts of Englishmen in their own tongue. Especially interesting is his contribution to the legend of King Arthur, though he adds little to the Arthurian material already supplied by his predecessors, Geoffrey of Monmouth (who wrote, however, in Latin), and Wace (whose work was in French). Layamon mentions for the first time in English the stories of Lear and Cymbeline, that Shakespeare later made immortal. The title, *Brut,* derives from the legend that Brutus, a descendant of Aeneas, was the founder of Britain.

BUCOLICS (ca. 37 B.C.), by Vergil. See ECLOGUES, by Vergil.

BUDDENBROOKS (1900), by Thomas Mann. This first novel by Thomas Mann, written when he was twenty-five years old, is the story of the decline of a German bourgeois family through four generations. When the book opens in 1835, Johann Buddenbrook, an important grain merchant, rules over his little world in feudal splendor. The skeptical and genial accumulator of wealth is serious and pious, but this does not prevent him from being a hard-headed businessman. His family, his friends, his surroundings, are drawn with meticulous care for realistic detail. When Johann's son Thomas succeeds him as the head of the firm, the process of decay is beginning to present itself. Commerce is only a matter of family duty to him; he is diverted by literary and philosophical interests. While his brother Christian is distinctly psychopathic and his sister Toni is driven from one broken marriage to the next domestic failure by a kind of brainless vitality, Thomas suffers from world-weariness and is plagued by nervousness. He dies from a stroke. The final stage in the decline of the Buddenbrook family is reached with little Hanno, a delicate and refined musical prodigy. He dies of typhus, thus extinguishing the family name and completing the author's thesis.

The decadence of the *fin de siècle* and the overpowering influence of Schopenhauer are extraordinarily recaptured in this novel which introduces Richard Wagner's "Leitmotif" into German literature: the characterization by means of standard phrases which serve to identify the figures of the book in the reader's mind. *Buddenbrooks* was widely translated, and sold in Germany alone more than one and one half million copies before Hitler.

BULFINCH'S MYTHOLOGY (1855–1863), by Thomas Bulfinch. This work is divided into three parts:

The Age of Fable, or, *Stories of Gods and Heroes; The Age of Chivalry,* containing *King Arthur and His Knights, The Mabinogion,* and *The Knights of English History;* and *Legends of Charlemagne.*

"Mythology," declares Bulfinch, "is the handmaid of literature . . . Without a knowledge of mythology much of the elegant literature of our own language cannot be understood and appreciated." The author undertook to make the bewildering mythological allusions in ancient literature, and in English and American poetry, amusing to the reader. A pleasurable, rather than solemn study, was his aim. He followed closely the original classical, Scandinavian, Celtic, and Oriental fables and myths; and although he was honest enough to say, "Our book is not for the learned . . . but for the reader of English literature," he strove for accuracy throughout. Most of the information on Greek and Roman antiquity he drew from the poets Ovid and Vergil. The mythos of the north he drew from Mallet's *Northern Antiquities.*

BULKYO YUSHINLON (1928), by Han Yong-woon. See MEDITATIONS OF THE LOVER, by Han Yong-woon.

BULWARK, THE (1946), by Theodore Dreiser. See AMERICAN TRAGEDY, AN, by Theodore Dreiser.

BUNNER, HENRY CUYLER (1855–1896). Henry Cuyler Bunner, while editor of *Puck,* contributed much of the light humor which made that weekly magazine popular. The first of his six volumes of short stories, *Short Sixes,* appeared in 1891. These bold portrayals of big city life were precursors of O. Henry's work, and deft character sketches which once permitted the author successfully to represent a piece of his own as a Maupassant adaptation. "Col. Brereton's Aunty" describes an impetuous young Southerner in a New York small town, whose old Negro servingwoman keeps him on his good behavior by frequent spankings. "Zenobia's Infidelity" concerns the sentimental behavior of a drunken elephant. "The Love-Letters of Smith" recounts the shy romance of a retired seaman and a seamstress he has never seen, by means of letters passed between windows.

The Midge (1886) is a novel set in Greenwich Village. Dr. Evert Peters discovers, when his French ward reaches eighteen, that he loves her. This is a little too late, however, for young Paul Hathaway has already claimed her affections. *The Story of a New York House* (1887) is a chronicle of three generations in two New York families.

BURLADOR DE SEVILLA, EL (1630), by Tirso de Molina. See LOVE ROGUE, by Tirso de Molina.

BUSCÓN, EL (1626) by Francisco de Quevedo. See PABLO DE SEGOVIA, THE SPANISH SHARPER, by Francisco de Quevedo.

BUTTERFIELD 8 (1935), by John O'Hara. See APPOINTMENT IN SAMARRA, by John O'Hara.

BURY THE DEAD (1936), by Irwin Shaw. See SHAW, IRWIN.

CABBAGES AND KINGS (1904), by William Sydney Porter. See PORTER, WILLIAM SYDNEY.

CABBALAH (ca. 1200). The Jewish mystical philosophy devised in the Middle Ages called *Cabbalah* (doctrines "received" by oral tradition) is noteworthy for its subsequent influence on Christian as well as Jewish theological and exegetical literature. Christian cabbalists through the fifteenth century sought confirmation of such doctrines as the trinity and incarnation in these purely Jewish mystical writings. The speculative and attenuated structure of *Cabbalah* doctrines lent themselves to all manner of theological elaborations. Reputed to have arisen in Spain about 1200, it rapidly spread to Palestine and other Mediterranean lands, as a protest against the too cerebral and logical Jewish philosophy. Instead of philosophic speculation and mere religious living, it was taught that union with God could best be attained through contemplation of and concentration on certain secret aboriginal traditions of mankind. Thus, God—the En Sof or "Endless One" (Eternal)—created the world through intermediate spiritual emanations, and not directly. There are ten Spheres through which God renders Himself visible to His creatures. The prayers, commandments, ceremonies and biblical books are all to be understood on the basis of the Spheres, and the interaction through them between

God and Israel. All souls were created with the world itself; transmigration and reward and punishment are inherent in that concept. The Messiah was the last soul created, and he will appear when all souls are perfected and clothed in flesh. The book that forms the basis of *Cabbalah*, ascribed to an early mystic, Rabbi Simeon ben Yohai, but actually written in the thirteenth century, is known as the *Zohar* ("Splendor"; q.v.). Isaac ben Solomon Luria, Palestinian mystic of the sixteenth century, developed the "practical" or wonder-working elements of *Cabbalah*. These were made evident in the movement called Hassidism, instituted by Israel ben Eliezer (Baal Shem Tob) of the Ukraine (1700–1760). In Hassidism the rabbis were credited with miracles on earth and in heaven; and emotional and other-worldly ecstasy marked the devotees' religious observance. Interest in *Cabbalah* is still maintained today by the remnants of the pious and ecstatic Hassidic movement.

CAESAR AND CLEOPATRA (1898), by George Bernard Shaw. This play presents a very perspicacious and unromantic Caesar and a very young, kittenish Cleopatra. She has just awakened from sleeping between the paws of the Sphinx when they first meet, and she does not learn his frightening name until he has reinstalled her on her throne and the Roman soldiers salute him. The Queen is far from imperial, since her nurse Ftatateeta still dominates her, and she is older only than her brother, the boy-king Ptolemy. She has a childish longing for power and revenge, and plays such pranks as coming to Caesar during a siege rolled up in a rug, to the horror of the respectable Britannus, who says she cannot stay without the companionship of some matron. Caesar tries in vain to hasten her maturity, and at the end almost forgets to say good-bye to her. She is sad, but consoled by Caesar's promise to send her a younger man—Antony.

CAIUS GRACCUS (1800), by Vincenzo Monti. See MONTI, VINCENZO.

CALEB WILLIAMS, THE ADVENTURES OF (1794), by William Godwin. In a psychological novel of one man's strange hold upon another, mingled with adventures, imprisonments and escapes in England in the late eighteenth century, Caleb Williams tells the story of his admiration for his master, Ferdinando Falkland, a man of high repute whom he discovers to have been the murderer of the scoundrel, Barnabas Tyrrel, and consequently of two laboring men erroneously convicted of the crime. Caleb tries to leave the man he both loves and hates, but Falkland is fearful the boy will disclose the secret, and has him imprisoned for theft. Caleb escapes from jail, changes his name, and becomes a wanderer. Hunted and harassed by Falkland, Caleb in desperation finally publicly accuses him. Falkland is tried, confesses, and dies three days later. Caleb, still under his spell, never throws off the remorse of having been the instrument of the man's undoing. The book was made into a play, *The Iron Chest*.

CALL OF THE WILD, THE (1903), by Jack London. This is the story of the dog Buck, half St. Bernard and half Scotch shepherd, who strives to adapt himself to a hostile Klondike environment, struggling against cruel elements and crueler men. Buck is taught to draw a sledge, and is glad to serve his new master, John Thornton; but when Thornton is murdered, Buck escapes and becomes the leader of a wolf pack. The Darwinian theme of this most famous of dog stories is that adaptation to environment is the sole means of survival in a ruthless world governed by "the law of claw and fang."

CALLING OF DAN MATTHEWS (1909), by Harold Bell Wright. See WINNING OF BARBARA WORTH, THE, by Harold Bell Wright.

CAMBRIDGE HISTORY OF AMERICAN LITERATURE, THE (1917–1920), edited by Carl Van Doren. See VAN DOREN, CARL.

CAMERA OBSCURA (collected 1839), by Hildebrand (Nicolaas Beets). These sketches from life made by Hildebrand (1814–1903) as a student were collected by him in 1839. The title reminds one of the periscopic instruments, used before Daguerre, to make sketches from nature. The enormous popularity of this work until the present day is reflected in the unveiling at Amsterdam of a large and complex Hildebrand statue, done by Ronne, on which are sculptured the various characters depicted in this book. Neither the composition nor the events related are the cause of the popularity of the book, but the sharp observations about and personifications of the middle class in the small towns of Holland. With humor, love and some sentimental feeling, Hildebrand depicted his types, sometimes looking down on them, but ever honest in his sympathy. They remain recognizable until this very day. "De Familie Stastok" sketches the small town life of a retired tradesman, spasmodically attached to tradition and shaking his head about the godless trends of modern times. Hildebrand, as guest, enlivens the scene with his student spirit; but, when he departs by omnibus, after a week's visit, life no doubt will go on as unruffled as the surface of the quiet canals of the old town. "De Familie Kegge" analyzes the difficulties of a West Indian newly rich, who, settled in the decorous city of R———, attempts to arouse the envy of the upper class by ostentatiously showing off his riches. The supercritical type is etched in "Een onaangenaam mensch in de Haarlemmer Hout." The writer exhibits his social compassion in short intermezzos, such as the story of the semi-senile little man, inmate of an old men's home, who has to live from cradle to grave in charitable institutions and fights desperately for one thing for himself: his shroud. This social consciousness is shown sharply, but still humorously, in the sketch "De Schippersknecht." Burgomaster Dikkerdak has to economize, and decides therefore to discharge his man-servant, who has served him devotedly for many years. The burgomaster "promotes" him, with the connivance of the town's government, against his will, to be assistant on a ferry boat, but he does not get the opportunity to protest, and has to appear to be grateful in the bargain. In the more dramatic stories, such as "Teun de Jager," the modern reader is annoyed by a too large degree of romantic sentimentality.

Dramatization of these sketches is very popular among theatrical companies and amateurs in the Netherlands and Flanders.

CAMILLE (1852), by Alexandre Dumas, fils. Margherita Gauthier, clever, fashionable and easy, has found her way into the most sophisticated Parisian society, and had wretched affairs with two roués, de Giray and de Varville, but has never known real love. She finds it when she meets Armando Duval at an evening party. For a brief while, Margherita and Armando find true happiness in a quiet country house near Paris. When his money is exhausted, she readily sells her jewels and horses. Moved by her selflessness, Armando goes to Paris in order to sign over to her his share in his mother's estate. But while he is away, his father, Collector-General Duval, persuades Margherita to give up Armando in order to save his career. She returns to her circle of dissolute men and women, and when Armando comes to look for her, she gives him the impression that she has once more become de Varville's mistress. Indignant with her cynicism and infidelity, Armando insults her and then leaves on a long journey. Margherita breaks down. Armando's father, impressed by her nobility, is contrite over what he has done. He consents to accept her as his daughter-in-law and assures her he will bring Armando back to her. Armando does hurry to her, but he finds her dying.

CAN SUCH THINGS BE? (1893), by Ambrose Bierce. See BIERCE, AMBROSE.

CANBY, HENRY SEIDEL (1878–   ). Henry Seidel Canby's long career as a literary critic includes editorships of the *Yale Review* and the *Saturday Review of Literature,* both of which he helped to found. His quietly-written autobiographical commentaries on American life in the 90's, *The Age of Confidence* (1934) and *Alma Mater* (1936) are carried into the 40's by *American Memoir* (1947). Besides these volumes, and a genealogical survey of his family, Canby has written one novel, much academic material (including textbooks), and distinguished criticism. Into this latter category fall his two biographies, *Thoreau* (1939) and *Whitman* (1943).

CANCIONERO DE ROMANCES (1550), Anonymous. See ROMANCERO, THE, Anonymous.

CANCIONERO GENERAL (1511), Anonymous. See ROMANCERO, THE, Anonymous.

CANDIDA (produced 1895), by George Bernard Shaw. In one of his most popular comedies, Shaw pits the worth of the penetrating, visionary and poetic genius of Marchbanks against that of the bold, but ultimately conventional Christian Socialism of Morell. Morell is a popular clergyman in a poor district of London, who owes much of his success to his brilliant wife, Candida. When the play opens, Candida, who has been away with their children, returns accompanied by Marchbanks, a young poet. Morell offends Marchbanks, who is in love with Candida, by speaking smugly of his happy marriage. He informs the minister that Candida is worthy of more than her husband's complacency. Morell's vanity is injured, and he orders the poet to leave but, at that moment, Candida enters, treats Marchbanks kindly and invites him to stay. The minister is for the first time uncertain of himself. He looks old and worn, and Candida worries about his overworking. Morell courageously decides to leave Candida and Marchbanks alone together while he is speaking at a meeting. By the time he returns, the poet is calling her by her first name. The men quarrel and finally ask Candida to choose between them. Candida takes her husband, who is the weaker of the two and needs her more.

CANDIDE (1758), by Voltaire. In Westphalia, where the story starts, the preternaturally earnest and simple Candide is very happy. He has just learned the joys of love from Cunegunde, daughter of the Baron of Thunder-ten-Tronckh, and the Leibnitzian doctrine that "all is for the best in this best of possible worlds" from the philosopher Pangloss. But the Baron kicks Candide off his estate, and when war breaks out, Candide is pressed into the army. Cunegunde becomes booty of war. Misfortune follows all three characters in their attempts to find each other. Pangloss survives illness, shipwreck, earthquake and the torture of the Inquisition; Cunegunde is raped by soldiers, made the mistress of an Inquisitor, mutilated by pirates. In the best of possible worlds they see an auto-da-fé, the Lisbon disaster, the shooting of Admiral Byng for losing a battle, Huguenots sent to the galleys, missionaries exploiting the natives in South America—in fact, every kind of intolerance and injustice. The one happy land they find is El Dorado, which of course does not exist. Old and worn, Candide and Cunegunde end in Constantinople, where they settle down to "cultivate their garden." Voltaire gave this tale the subtitle "—or Optimism."

Others of his philosophical tales are *Zadig* (1747), a series of episodes in which a wise man of Bagdad learns that Providence, if it exists, is entirely inscrutable; *Micromegas* (1752, but probably written some fifteen or twenty years earlier), a Swiftian story of a visit to the Earth by giants from other planets who find humans and their concerns to be of microscopic importance; and *The Huron* (1767), the story of a simple Indian who visits Europe and finds its alleged civilization frequently offensive to common sense.

CANFIELD, DOROTHY (Dorothy Canfield Fisher; 1879–   ). Dorothy Canfield has done her writing in Vermont, where she is prominent in cultural affairs. Besides such translations as Papini's *Life of Christ* (1923), studies in education, and literary essays, the author has written many novels and collections of short stories.

The Bent Twig (1915) is a social-psychological study of American middle-class family life, in a midwestern university town. Sylvia Marshall has been raised by genial, easy-going parents. When she enters college, she is slighted socially because of the contempt in which they are held by the conventionally-minded. The Marshalls are regarded as "peculiar," their home a rendezvous for all the college "freaks" or intellectuals. Sylvia, an impetuous young lady, becomes involved with a gay, popular man. Then, tiring of him, she falls in love with Austin Fling, a serious-minded radical determined to improve the conditions of the miners. The "bent twig" is finally straightened out.

The Brimming Cup (1921) concerns the struggle of a woman between love for husband and family, and passion for another man.

The Deepening Stream (1930) describes the maturing of a woman born in the West, who later lives in France.

Hillsboro People (1915), one of her volumes of short stories, contains twenty-five pieces written over a period of ten years, which reveal the profundities of superficially uninteresting people. "Petunias" is a satirical story about a girl who returns to the family farm after college and a European trip, contemptuous of the simple folk, and ignorant that they regard her with pathos. "The Portrait of a Philosopher" is a tale in the manner of Balzac in which a portrait artist completes a canvas of an ascetic New England college professor, revealing in the expression the suppressed hereditary passions of the man. "The Red Quilt" sketches a woman, held in contempt by her family, who exhibits her handiwork at the village fair and sits in front of it to drink in the admiration of all.

CANNERY BOAT, THE (1933), by Takiji Kobayashi and others. See CONTEMPORARY JAPANESE LITERATURE.

CANON OF MEDICINE (ca. 1012), by Avicenna (Abu Ali al-Husain ibn Abdallah ibn Sina). The *Canon* is an enormous encyclopedia of medicine comprising about a million words. It is divided into five books, the first and second on physiology, the third and fourth on methods of treating disease, and the fifth on the composition and preparation of remedies. Some idea of the scope of the work can be obtained by noting the fact that the materia medica includes some 760 drugs. Classification is one of Ibn Sina's strong points: he distinguishes, for example, among fifteen different qualities of pain. The author of the *Canon* borrows heavily from the learning of the ancients, notably Galen, Hippocrates and Aristotle. A typical instance of this is his introduction into medicine of the Aristotelian four causes. He also includes the Muslim knowledge of medical matters. Ibn Sina's own personal observations, sound and careful, are overshadowed by his skill as an encyclopedist. The excellence of his systematization accounts in part for the extraordinary reputation of the *Canon*. It superseded the works of his predecessors—Rhazes, Ali ibn al-Abbas, Avenzoar, and even Galen—and reigned supreme in the West from the twelfth to the seventeenth century. Translated into Latin by Gerard of Cremona (ca. 1114–1187), the *Canon* became the chief textbook in European universities and continued in use at the Universities of Montpellier and Louvain as late as 1650. Gerard of Cremona's translation was published at Milan in 1473, and served as the basis for approximately thirty Latin editions. Ibn Sina (or Avicenna, as he was known in the West) also wrote treatises on all the Arabian sciences, mathematics, physics, music, astronomy, theology and philology. He lived from 980 to 1037. In Islam he retains his reputation as "Prince of all learning," and to this day his *Canon* is used and published in the East.

CANTERBURY TALES, THE (1387–1400), by Geoffrey Chaucer. This is Chaucer's greatest work. It is almost entirely in heroic couplets, approximately 17,000 lines in length. In the Prologue, Chaucer tells of meeting a company of twenty-nine persons at the Tabard Inn in Southwark. All are embarking on a pilgrimage to Thomas à Becket's shrine at Canterbury. (There are actually thirty-one persons in the group, including Chaucer himself, and not counting the Canon's Yeoman, whom they meet on the way; apparently Chaucer changed his mind about the number of persons but left his work unrevised.) Following is the list of personages from the contemporary life which Chaucer so vividly portrays: Knight, Squire, Yeoman, Prioress, Nun, Three Priests, Monk, Friar, Merchant, Clerk of Oxford, Sergeant of Law, Franklin, Haberdasher, Carpenter, Weaver, Dyer, Tapestry Maker, Cook, Shipman, Doctor of Physic, Wife of Bath, Parson, Plowman, Miller, Manciple (steward), Reeve (bailiff), Summoner (official of the ecclesiastical court), Pardoner (seller of indulgences), Host, and Chaucer himself.

The company approves the Host's suggestion that each pilgrim tell two stories on the sixty-mile ride to Canterbury and two on the way back. The best raconteur is to be rewarded upon their return by a dinner at the others' expense. The poem was not completed, and we have only twenty finished tales, two unfinished, and two interrupted, instead of the one hundred and twenty called for by the ambitious scheme.

"The Knight's Tale," a version of Boccaccio's *Teseide,* is of the royal cousins, Palamon and Arcite, who as prisoners of Duke Theseus fall in love with Emelye, sister of Queen Ypolita, and contend for her possession in a tournament. Arcite, the winner and a favorite of Mars, is fatally thrown from his horse through the intervention of Venus and Saturn. Emelye weds Palamon after a long period of mourning.

"The Miller's Tale" recounts how a jolly clerk, Nicholas, cuckolds a rich carpenter at Oxford and plays a lewd trick on Absalom, a parish clerk, who also loves the carpenter's wife, Alison.

"The Reeve's Tale," a retort to the Miller since the Reeve had once been a carpenter, is about two clerks who are robbed of a part of a meal by a miller. They take their revenge on the miller's wife and daughter. It is drawn from a French fabliau, *De Gombert et ses deux Clers,* and from Boccaccio's *Decameron* (q.v.), D. ix, N. 6.

"The Cook's Tale" is another ribald story, unfinished, and omitted in some manuscripts. Some manuscripts include "The Cook's Tale of Gamelyn," about a younger brother, robbed of his inheritance, who becomes an outlaw and eventually defeats his wicked eldest brother: it is probably not by Chaucer, however.

"The Man of Law's Tale" is drawn from Gower's *Confesio Amantis,* B. ii, and tells of the harrowing adventures of Constance, an emperor's daughter, twice married and twice set adrift in the sea by wicked mothers-in-law, but finally reunited with her second husband.

"The Wife of Bath's Tale" is preceded by a lusty prologue in which she condemns celibacy, herself having outlasted five husbands. Her tale recounts the story of a knight who must answer correctly within a year, under pain of execution, the question, what do women most love. An old witch gives him the answer, which is "sovereignty," with the provision that he marry her. He carries out his promise reluctantly, and the witch is turned to a beautiful young girl. This tale is similar to the story of Florent in Gower's *Confesio Amantis,* B. i.

"The Friar's Tale," maliciously directed against the Summoner, tells of the wickedness of a summoner at the instigation of the devil dressed as a bailiff. When the summoner tries to cheat a widow, she consigns him to the devil, whereupon that personage appears and conducts him to hell.

"The Summoner's Tale" in retaliation insults the Friar with a vulgar story of a grasping friar's humiliation.

"The Clerk's Tale," which comes from Petrarch via Boccaccio's *Decameron,* tells how the Marquis of Saluces marries the lowly, patient Griselda and subjects her to all manner of indignities to try her virtue and patience.

"The Merchant's Tale" is about a young wife married to an old man; the husband becomes blind. The young woman and her lover make love in a pear tree in his presence, whereupon Pluto suddenly restores his sight. However, through the help of Proserpine, the wife and the lover are able to deceive the old man.

"The Squire's Tale" is of Canace, daughter of Cambuscan, King of Tartary, who receives a ring from the king of Arabia which enables her to understand the language of birds. She hears a story of desertion from a female falcon. The story is incomplete. This tale is referred to in Spenser's *Faerie Queene* (q.v.) and in Milton's *Il Penseroso.*

"The Franklin's Tale" is about Dorigen, wife of Arveragus, who, to be rid of her lover, Aurelius, promises to be his only if he will remove all the rocks from the coast of Brittany. This impossible task is performed through the aid of a magician, but Aurelius generously releases Dorigen from her promise. Versions of this appear in Boccaccio's *Filocopo,* B. v., and in the *Decameron,* D. x, N. 5.

"The Second Nun's Tale" describes the life and miracles of the Roman Cecilia and her ultimate martyrdom with her husband, Valerian. This is from the Golden Legend of Jacobus à Voragine.

"The Canon's Yeoman's Tale" is an indictment of the charlatanism of alchemists.

"The Doctor's Tale" is about the wicked judge, Apius, who wants to possess Virginia. The latter begs her father to kill her rather than allow her to suffer this fate, and this her father does. A version of this is to be found in the *Roman de la Rose,* although Chaucer attributes the tale to Livy.

"The Pardoner's Tale" begins with a splendid invective against gluttony and swearing. It tells of three rioters who would slay the old man, Death. Finding gold under a tree, they send one of their number after provisions. He arranges to poison the other two. When he returns, they treacherously slay him and unknowingly drink the poisoned wine; thus all three meet Death. This story was also used by Hans Sachs, and is similar to one in the Italian *Cento Novelle Antiche.*

"The Shipman's Tale," similar to one in the *Decameron,* D. viii, N. i, is of the beautiful wife of a rich but grasping merchant. Her desire for clothes induces her to ask a priest for a loan. The priest borrows money from the merchant and turns it over to the wife, who decks herself out, after repaying the priest with her virtue. When the merchant demands his money from the priest, he is told that it has already been handed over to his wife. She, unable to deny receiving it, must suffer the consequences.

"The Prioress's Tale" is in rhyme royal, and it recounts how a little boy was murdered by the Jews for singing "Alma Redemptoris Mater," and how his singing it on after death brings his murderers to justice.

Chaucer contributes two tales himself. The first, "Tale of Sir Thopas," ridicules the romances of knight-errantry by contemporary writers. This is interrupted, and he turns to the "Tale of Meliboeus," a prose translation of a French romance, which concerns a long debate between Meliboeus and his wife, Prudence, on the best way to deal with enemies.

"The Monk's Tale" is made up of a number of tales of persons fallen from high estate, and is modeled after Boccaccio's *De Casibus Virorum Illustrium*.

"The Nun's Priest's Tale" is of a vainglorious cock, Chauntecleer, whose dreams of portending danger from a fox are ridiculed by his favorite wife, Pertelote. Later, Chauntecleer is seized by a fox, but saves himself by a ruse. This may have been drawn from the French tales of Reynard the Fox.

"The Manciple's Tale" describes a white crow who reveals to his owner, Phebus, the infidelity of his wife. Phebus kills his wife in anger, and then, in a fit of remorse, deprives the crow of his power to speak and plucks out his feathers—which explains why crows are black.

"The Parson's Tale" discusses penitence, the various sins and their appropriate remedies. It is a sermon rather than a story.

CANTI (first complete collection 1845), by Giacomo Leopardi. Giacomo Leopardi (1798–1827), one of the greatest Italian poets of the nineteenth century, can be considered both a Romantic, for the melancholy and sadness of his inspiration, and a Classicist for the concise beauty of his form and the vigor of his concepts. Among the most celebrated of Leopardi poems—collected and published under the title *Canti*—are: "To Sylvia," where the poet expresses his love and sympathy for a girl to whom untimely death denied the few worthwhile joys of life; "La Ginestra," an ode to the humble broom-plant flourishing on the lava-fields of Mount Vesuvius; the "Son of a Shepherd Wandering through Asia," where the futility of human life is expressed; the "Lonely Sparrow" and "Evening of a Festive Day," deeply permeated with the poet's constant feeling of death and pessimism; "Quietness after the Storm," where nature itself seems to be part of the general futility and senseless reality of the world. Three patriotic odes, "To Italy," "On the Florentine Monument to Dante" and "To Angelo Mai" express Leopardi's great love for his country, but at the same time his despair for the condition of Italy. Leopardi's untimely death, in Naples, deprived Italy of one of her greatest poets. His influence on Italian and foreign culture, and especially on intellectual youth, has been tremendous.

CANTICLE OF THE SUN (1234), by St. Francis of Assisi. The son of a rich textile merchant, Francis of Assisi was able to see very clearly the great disproportions existing in his time between the immense poverty of the people and the huge fortunes of the few wealthy families. When he reached the age of twenty-five, tired of his dissipated life, Francis turned to religious mysticism and founded the Franciscan order, which had as its rule poverty, sacrifice and pure love. Two years before he died, Francis—so at least the legend says— dictated to one of his disciples his wonderful *Canticle of the Sun*. There he expressed the idea that all things which exist are brothers and sisters, not only the human beings, but also the animals and the inanimate things; brother is the sun, brother is the wind; sisters are the water, the earth, the moon; sister is also Death, given us by God—Death which no one can escape. The *Canticle* *of the Sun,* for its mystical deepness and its sincere inspiration, is considered one of the finest compositions of Italian literature. Its simplicity and unpretentiousness, however, clearly reveal that the *Canticle* was written or dictated without any literary intention, rather as a spontaneous expression of candor and faith.

CÁNTICO ESPIRITUAL ENTRE EL ALMA Y EL ESPOSO (1627), by San Juan de la Cruz. See SPIRITUAL SONG BETWEEN THE SOUL AND THE HUSBAND, by San Juan de la Cruz.

CANTOS (1925–), by Ezra Pound. See POUND, EZRA.

CANTOS DE VIDA Y ESPERANZO (1905), by Rubén Darío. See SONGS OF LIFE AND HOPE, by Rubén Darío.

CANZONIERE, IL, by Francesco Petrarch (1304–1374). Francesco Petrarch, perhaps the most learned man of the fourteenth century and one of the great humanists, owes his main inspiration as a poet to his lifelong love for a Laura whose real identity has never been firmly established. In *Il Canzoniere* Petrarch expresses, through a series of sonnets and canzoni, the manifold aspects of his passion. The book is divided into two parts: the first, *In Vita di Madonna Laura,* written when Laura was still living, recounts the various episodes of his love and the sentiments which inspired it since, on the night of Holy Friday, 1327, he saw her for the first time and fell in love with her. Laura appears as the ethereal ideal of all womanhood. The poet feels ennobled by his profound feeling. But Laura, alive, causes constant conflict between the senses and reason, flesh and spirit. Often the poet turns to God in despair, in the attempt to resolve his inner conflict. Death did resolve it: the same happy and fatal night of Holy Friday, in 1343, supposedly at the very same hour of their first encounter, Laura died. Her passing inspires the second book, *In Morte di Madonna Laura.* The poems comprising the second book express either the poet's lament for the loss of his beloved, or consolation derived from her spiritual presence on earth or in heaven. Laura, who has now become only a dream, attracts the poet in a more tranquil mood of sadness. He misses her deeply, but his spirit is no longer perturbed by the desires of the flesh.

CAPTAIN CAUTION (1934), by Kenneth Roberts. See NORTHWEST PASSAGE, by Kenneth Roberts.

CAPTAIN CRAIG (1902), by Edwin Arlington Robinson. See ROBINSON, EDWIN ARLINGTON.

CAPTAIN'S DAUGHTER, THE (1832), by Alexander Pushkin. This bears the same relationship to Pushkin's prose that *Eugène Onegin* (q.v.) does to his verse. The story is historical, and centers around the Pugachev uprising during the reign of the Empress Catherine. Tolstoy considered it Pushkin's greatest work. Indeed it has some of the qualities of *War and Peace* (q.v.) and contains the author's best character drawing. Young Grinyev is sent by his father to join the army, and eventually finds himself fighting the Pretender, Pugachev, who claims to be the rightful Czar and has a considerable following among disloyal Cossacks. The war, bloody and cruel, is vividly described. When the story opens, Grinyev has been sent to the fortress of Byelogorsk, where he is befriended by Captain Mironoff and his wife, Vasilisa. Marya, their daughter, and Grinyev fall in love. She is pursued by another suitor, Schvabin, who is with Pugachev. Pugachev eventually takes the fort, and the captain and his wife are killed. Grinyev escapes with his life because of a favor he had once done for Pugachev, but is forced to leave the fort. Marya is persecuted by Schvabin, but finally rescued by Grinyev. Schvabin tries to have Grinyev sent to Siberia as a spy, but Marya obtains a pardon from the Empress for him. Pugachev is finally defeated and hanged.

CAPTAINS COURAGEOUS (1897), by Rudyard Kipling. Harvey Cheyne, a spoiled American boy, falls, while seasick, from an ocean liner into the Atlantic. He is rescued by some Gloucester fishermen from the schooner *We're Here,* on which he is required to stay and work—for ten dollars a month —until the fishing season is over. Harvey objects strenuously, often referring to his father's wealth and position, but the skipper, Disko Troop, is unmoved. Gradually the boy fits into the rough-and-tumble life on the schooner. He learns to do hard work and to obey orders, to control himself, and to be self-reliant. He grows rugged and hardy under the discipline of sea life. When, at the end of the season, he and his father are reunited. Mr. Cheyne is delighted with Harvey's regeneration but puzzled about how to repay Troop, who would be offended at the offer of a monetary reward. The problem is solved when Cheyne diplomatically gets Troop to agree to let his son Dan, from whom Harvey learned many of his valuable lessons, ship as a seaman on the *San José,* one of the merchant vessels owned by Mr. Cheyne. The final chapters deal with conversations between Harvey and his father, in which Harvey adds to his newly-acquired practical learning a knowledge of business principles.

The Light That Failed (1890), Kipling's first novel, is noteworthy for the character of Maisie, the boyhood sweetheart of the artist Dick Heldar. He struggles with blindness alone, trying desperately to finish his masterpiece before all is blacked out. When Maisie learns of his trouble, she declines to stand by him, and Heldar goes back to Egypt, deliberately exposes himself to the enemy, and is killed.

CAPTIVE, THE (1923), by Marcel Proust. See REMEMBRANCE OF THINGS PAST, by Marcel Proust.

CARDUCCI, GIOSUE' (1835–1907). Giosue' Carducci, one of the greatest Italian poets of the nineteenth century, reflects in his inspiration the political passion for liberty and the disappointment that the patriots of the "Risorgimento" felt when Italy, after a long struggle, at last found her unity. Rightly, Carducci was called the first and most outstanding poet of the young Italian nation. The lyrics of Carducci's first period are collected in the volumes entitled *Juvenilia* (1850–1860), *Levia Gravia* (1861–1871), *Decennale* (1860–1870), *Giambi ed Epodi* (1867–1879) and *Rime Nuove* (1897). A furor was aroused in 1865 by the publication of his *Hymn to Satan,* in which the poet strongly opposed the insidious machinations of the Papacy, tending to undermine Italy's hard-won political unity. In this *Hymn* Carducci reveals himself to be deeply pagan in his conception, and in opposition to all kinds of mysticism. But his anti-Christian feeling is not sectarian and vulgar; his "red-haired Galilean" is not the Christ of the Gospels, but the medieval Christ, the Christ of asceticism, whom Carducci considers a barbaric import. In his *Barbaric Odes,* composed between 1877 and 1887, Carducci tried, as he himself said, "so far as it was possible in a lyric poem, to resume the history of pantheistic naturalism and of revolt against the oppression of dogma and a bland submission to Greek and Roman tradition." History contributes much to Carducci's poetry. It is mainly through history that he sees, in its manifold aspects, lights and shadows of the Latin spirit, from Rome, through the Middle Ages and Renaissance, up to modern times.

CARMEN (1847), by Prosper Mérimée. While traveling in Spain, the narrator meets a highway robber known as José Navarro. The two men have the opportunity of helping each other, and separate on good terms. Later, José, in the prison where he awaits death by garroting, is visited by the narrator and tells him his life story. He had come from the Basque country and his real name was Don José Lizzarrabengoa. As a corporal in a cavalry regiment, he was stationed in Seville, and there first met Carmen, an attractive, voluptuous gypsy. He was to take her to prison because she had assaulted a girl in the cigar factory where she worked, but had let her go instead. He saw her again, became infatuated with her, killed a man because of her, deserted from the army, and started on a career of robbery and smuggling. He had also killed Carmen's *rom,* or husband. But Carmen was a coquette and a liar, and even though she had once loved him, she liked her freedom better. She refused to change her life and go with him to America. Incensed by Carmen's independence and coquetry, Don José, in a fit of passion, killed his girl and gave himself up to the authorities.

Mérimée's hard, sharp prose and eye for local color have long been admired. His work falls in a special category, longer than the ordinary short story, but shorter than the full-blown novel. The familiar opera is based on this story.

CARMINA (1912), by Pieter Cornelis Boutens. See BOUTENS, PIETER CORNELIS.

CAROLING DUSK (1927), by Countee Cullen. See CULLEN, COUNTEE.

CARPET OF LIFE, THE (1899), by Stefan George. See GEORGE, STEFAN.

CASE BOOK OF SHERLOCK HOLMES, THE (1927), by Sir Arthur Conan Doyle. See SHERLOCK HOLMES, by Sir Arthur Conan Doyle.

CASE OF SERGEANT GRISCHA, THE (1928), by Arnold Zweig. Sergeant Grischa is an amiable, warm-hearted and thoroughly simple-minded Russian who escapes from a German camp for prisoners of war during World War I. He finds himself in a forest and meets Babka, whose lover he becomes. Not knowing who he is, she gives him the clothes of the spy Bjuscheff, who had been killed some time before. When Grischa falls into the hands of the Germans, he is consequently implicated as a spy, too. The cynicism of Prussian militarism is mercilessly laid bare when Grischa's proof of his innocence is im patiently brushed aside. He is sentenced, and dies with the childlike wonder and gentleness of the good.

The Case of Sergeant Grischa reverses the usual concept of the war as a destroyer of men en masse to project the miseries of the helpless individual caught by the forces of blind hatred. Meant by its author to stir consciences everywhere into wakefulness to safeguard the value of the individual, the novel, published in 1928, met with tremendous international acclaim. Arnold Zweig, who became one of the most distinguished prose writers of the Weimar Republic, went into exile after Hitler's rise to power. His *The Axe of Wandsbeck* (1947), deals with the life of a "simple" Nazi in Germany.

CASES OF CONSCIENCE CONCERNING EVIL SPIRITS (1693), by Increase Mather. See MATHER, COTTON.

CASPAR HAUSER (1908), by Jakob Wassermann. This story of a foundling who appeared in 1828 in the City of Nuremberg and was later assassinated, is based on historical fact. Jakob Wassermann, whose own grandfather still remembered having seen Caspar Hauser, planned to write the life of the unhappy foundling. Aided by considerable research and inspired by a treatise of the famous German criminalist Feuerbach, the author published his account, the novel *Caspar Hauser*, in 1908. Without going into the legal aspects of Hauser's claim to the throne of one of the South-German states, Wassermann leaves no doubt that he does not consider the youth an impostor. It is the psychological angle of the unusual case that interests the novelist: the clash between a social outcast, a human being cheated out of his childhood, and an indifferent and cruel society. Having spent the first sixteen years of his life in the utter and almost inconceivable desolation of dark and solitary confinement, Hauser is suddenly thrown into the world, confronted with experiences he has never known. Hardly able to walk, he must learn to speak and to read and to master the whole scale of human relations. Undergoing a belated development of his mind and senses, the young man passes from one tutor and guardian to another until he is murdered by an assassin, who has been hired by dynastic interests. Although the novel focuses entirely around the strangely pure and touching figure of the foundling, there are a number of sharply portrayed guardians through whose hands he passes, the most notable of whom is Feuerbach.

Jakob Wassermann was born in a small Bavarian town in 1873, experienced extreme poverty and hunger before he succeeded as a writer and moved to Austria in 1898, where he remained until his death in 1934. He became one of the most successful European novelists, whose books were translated into many languages. Banned during the Hitler regime, Wassermann's books are being reissued in Germany today. Among his most famous novels are *The World's Illusion* (q.v.) and *The Maurizius Case* (1928).

CASS TIMBERLANE (1945), by Sinclair Lewis. See ARROWSMITH, by Sinclair Lewis.

CASTING AWAY OF MRS. LECKS AND MRS. ALESHINE, THE (1886), by Frank R. Stockton. See LADY OR THE TIGER? THE, by Frank R. Stockton.

CASTLE, THE (1926), by Franz Kafka. See TRIAL, THE, by Franz Kafka.

CASTLE OF INDOLENCE, THE (1748), by James Thomson. This poem is in the allegorical manner of Spenser and employs the Spenserian stanza. It tells of "a pleasing land of drowsyhead" where the wizard Indolence dwells and lures weary pilgrims with his siren-song of idleness and ease. The inmates after a time become diseased and loathsome. But in Canto II the Knight of Art and Industry frees them from their dungeon. The fifteen-hundred-line poem, with its obvious moralizing, took about fifteen years to complete.

CASTLE OF OTRANTO, THE (1764), by Horace Walpole. In this romantic and melodramatic novel, the first of the type which was to be called "Gothic," the tyrannical villain is Manfred, the prince of Otranto, grandson of a usurper of the realm who had poisoned Alfonso, the rightful ruler. It had been prophesied that the usurping line would rule as long as the castle was big enough to hold the rightful owner. Manfred has plotted to marry his only son Conrad, to Isabella, daughter of the Marquis of Vicenza. When Conrad is crushed by a gigantic plumed helmet, Manfred is determined to marry Isabella himself; for though his wife is still alive, she is not likely to present him with another heir, whom Manfred needs in order to keep control of the realm. Isabella repulses him and, helped by Theodore, a handsome peasant youth, escapes to Friar Jerome's chapel. Manfred, momentarily interrupted by an interview with his grandfather's portrait, which has come to life, orders Theodore executed, but he is forced to spare the boy when his true lineage is revealed. Frederick, Isabella's father, appears with a powerful company to claim Otranto. In accordance with the prophecy, the ghost of Alfonso, having grown too large for the building, tears down the castle, forcing Manfred to reveal that he is not the rightful ruler. Alfonso rises from the rubble and proclaims Theodore, Isabella's rescuer and future husband, as the true heir.

CASTLE RACKRENT (1801), by Maria Edgeworth. This novel by Miss Edgeworth, who was noted for her unparalleled pictures of Irish character, depicts the riotous living and reckless spending of some Irish landlords in the eighteenth century. By squeezing their tenants, the landlords were able to live in luxury, but were eventually brought to ruin by their own foolhardiness. Thady Quirk, a steward who works for the Rackrent family, tells their story in a vivid fashion. Sir Patrick was a true and hospitable Irishman, hard-drinking and jovial, and when he dies, his funeral is one of the finest ever beheld. Sir Murtagh, the lawyer, oppresses his tenants without mercy, while his wife, a member of the Skinflint family, holds a charity school at which the pupils are forced to spin for her ladyship. Sir Kit, the next landlord, marries a rich Jew and keeps her locked in her room for seven years because she refuses to part with her jewels. Sir Condy Rackrent spends the remaining bit of the family wealth and dies from drinking. Thady's son, Jason, a lawyer, finally purchases the debt-ridden hall and its lands.

CATHER, WILLA (1876–1947). Willa Cather's youth was spent among the pioneers of Nebraska, and several of her popular novels have this background. These include *O Pioneers!*, *My Antonia*, and *A Lost Lady* (qq.v.), novels of the struggles of women in this environment. Two other works tell of the escape of young people into other worlds: *The Song of the Lark* (1915) concerns Thea Kronborg, whose aspirations are satisfied by a singing career, and not personal happiness; *One of Ours* (1922), a Pulitzer Prize novel, concerns a young man whose fulfillment comes through duty as a soldier in France during World War I. *Lucy Gayheart* (1935) relates the tale of a midwestern girl whose musical career takes her out of her environment. This novel has a tragic ending, however; Lucy is deserted by a lover, and meets an accidental death.

Willa Cather's interest in New Mexico is shown chiefly by her novel *Death Comes for the Archbishop* (q.v.), but is indicated in *The Professor's House* (1925). This novel concerns Professor Godfrey St. Peter, whose middle age in a university town in the 1920's is made interesting by completion of a work on Spanish explorers in America. Another theme is the Professor's gradual adjustment to personal loneliness. His wife Lillian has bought a new house, but he prefers to work in his old study; his daughters have married; his favorite student, Tom Outland (who had explored an old New Mexican cliff city) has died in the first World War. Rosamond and her husband Louie Marsellus are wealthy from a patent willed to her by Tom, her former fiancé. Kathleen is married to Scott McGregor, a writer who makes money by producing commercial pieces. One summer the Professor is about to commit suicide when the friendship and sympathy of old Augusta, a sewing woman, give him courage to face life again.

Sapphira and the Slave Girl (1940) is based on a Virginia story which Willa Cather heard as a child. Henry Colbert was a fine soul who in 1856 took his wife Sapphira with him to a Virginia frontier town and ran a mill. The once energetic wife became an invalid, and the tension between the couple had its morbid consequences. Sapphira was tormented by jealousy of the mulatto slave girl Nancy Till. Nancy was sent to Canada, and returning to the town twenty-five years later, impressed everyone with an assurance gained by her life as a housekeeper.

Willa Cather also wrote literary essays, and a volume of stories, *Youth and the Bright Medusa* (1920), dealing with artists' careers.

CATO (1713), by Joseph Addison. This poetic drama, which is actually a political polemic, referring symbolically to the unrest prevailing in England during Queen Anne's illness, raises the question of the succession. Marcus Porcius Cato, the philosopher, the center of the tragedy, retires to the little republic of Utica in Africa out of disgust with Caesar's tyrannical rule of Rome. But Caesar reaches out his vengeful arm to crush the little republic. Cato is aided by Juba, a Numidian prince who loves Cato's daughter, Marcia. However, defeat is inevitable, and Cato, after aiding his friends to escape, kills himself with his sword. A famous scene in this drama is that of Cato's final soliloquy when, holding Plato's treatise on the immortality of the soul in one hand and a drawn sword in the other, the unhappy and virtuous man bids farewell to life, saying, "Cato shall open to himself a passage."

CATRIONA (1893), by Robert Louis Stevenson. See DAVID BALFOUR, by Robert Louis Stevenson.

CATULLUS (Gaius Valerius Catullus, 84–54? B.C.). The hundred-odd poems of Catullus make a volume as slight as their author's life was brief. His short life was filled with friendships, loves, enthusiasms, disillusionments and sorrows, which translated themselves into poetry of the highest order. The collection as we have it apparently was not made by Catullus himself. The first group (1-61) contains short lyrics in various meters on a wide range of topics, from bridal songs written for the weddings of friends at the one extreme to the most personal love poems at the other. The latter are addressed to Lesbia, a name which is but a slight disguise for that of Clodia, the most courted and faithless beauty of her day in Rome. In these poems we can trace the uneven course of the love of the impecunious poet for the great lady, beginning with tender and insouciant devotion and ending with utter bitterness and disgust. The most famous of these is his imitation of Sappho's "Ode to Anactoria." The second group (62-68) comprises longer and less inspired poems, experiments in the Alexandrian manner, which are elegant in finish but allow little opportunity for the personality of the poet to express itself. The third and last group (69-116) are all in elegiac couplets and are distinguished by their epigrammatic brevity. Here too there are some of the Lesbia poems, but most distinctive of the group are those bitter invectives and lampoons in which he poured out the bitterness of his spleen against any, including the great Caesar, who offended him. His acerbity often expresses itself in language so foul as to defy translation into printable English.

CAUSERIES DE LUNDI (1851–1862), by Charles Augustin Sainte-Beuve. This brilliant collection of essays in criticism covers an enormous range of literary subjects. Sainte-Beuve's interests were catholic, his taste only slightly less so. Generally he preferred to interpret, explain and describe, rather than to judge. Later critics have sometimes complained that he "lacked standards" and was "too much the relativist." And when he did judge, he frequently went wrong, particularly in his estimates of his contemporaries, Flaubert, Stendhal, Baudelaire and Balzac. But where his historical method could be used freely, he was and remains supreme. His great attainment was the revitalizing of older literature.

Sainte-Beuve stands with Hugo and Balzac among the great producers of the nineteenth century. The *Causeries* were long newspaper articles, turned out with great regularity. He had begun his career as an apologist for Hugo's Romantic group, written poetry and a novel, been a professor at Lausanne and at Liége, and written a long history of Jansenism, his *Port Royal* (1840–1859). After 1848 he wanted to settle down. The *Causeries,* continued in a second series, were written for a less specialized public than his earlier work, and remain today the most impressive of nineteenth century critical achievements.

CAUTIONARY TALES (1613), by Miguel de Cervantes. The *Novelas Ejemplares* comprise twelve cautionary tales, i.e., stories resembling moral exempla and therefore quite different in intent from the pornographic Italian *novelle* so much in vogue in those days. Cervantes' diapason is rich and varied: some of his *novelas,* such as "El amante liberal" ("The Liberal Lover") and "La espanola inglesa" ("The Spanish Englishwoman"), are adventure stories in which the interest lies in the extraordinary events which take place. In others, on the contrary, the action is insignificant: the "Coloquio de los perros" ("The Dogs' Colloquy"), for instance, is an exceedingly witty dialogue in which two dogs, having been granted for one day the gift of speech, satirize the behavior of men. Then again, some of the *novelas* tend to be more realistic, depicting the world of rogues ("Rinconete y Cortadillo") or that of gypsies ("La gitanilla" —"The Little Gypsy Girl") or that of kitchen-wenches ("La ilustre fregona"— "The Illustrious Kitchen-wench"). "El licenciado vidriera" ("Licenciate Glass") is pure fantasy and is often considered a forerunner of *Don Quixote*. It is the story of a law student who believes he is made of glass and in constant danger of being broken. At the same time he preserves, like Don Quixote, an extraordinary intellectual lucidity. People come to listen to him, and are amazed at the soundness of his reasoning. Later on, however, he is cured by a holy monk and enabled to practice his profession as a lawyer. As soon as people perceive him to be of sound mind, however, they abandon him and leave him to starve, whereupon he enlists as a soldier.

CAVALLERIA RUSTICANA (1884), by Giovanni Verga. See MASTRO DON GESUALDO, by Giovanni Verga.

CAWDOR (1928), by Robinson Jeffers. See JEFFERS, ROBINSON.

CELEBRATED JUMPING FROG OF CALAVERAS COUNTY, THE (1867), by Mark Twain. See LIFE ON THE MISSISSIPPI, by Mark Twain.

CELESTIAL MECHANICS (1799), by Pierre Simon Laplace. See MÉCANIQUE CÉLESTE, by Pierre Simon Laplace.

CELESTINA (1499), by Fernando de Rojas. To the end of the fifteenth century has been ascribed a novel in play form generally known as *La Celestina*, a short title for *La Tragicomedia de Calixto y Melibea*. Although originally published anonymously, it is assumed that its author was a converted Jew named Fernando de Rojas, who was born in the province of Toledo about 1475 and died after 1537. In the first edition (1499) the work contained sixteen acts, but later five acts were inserted (XV-XIX), probably by a different writer. The descriptive "Tragicomedia" notwithstanding, *La Celestina* is a novel and not an acting drama: its length, as well as the slowness of its action, precludes representation on the stage.

The scene is laid in what is probably Toledo. When the handsome young aristocrat Calixto, "with many graceful qualities richly endowed," enters beautiful Melibea's garden to retrieve his stray hawk, he experiences love at first sight. The virtuous Melibea coldly rejects his pleas. However, following the advice of a servant, he enlists the services of Celestina, a clever procuress, well versed in the art of witchcraft. Posing as a peddler of materials for needlework, Celestina gains entrance to Melibea's house, works upon her feelings, and gradually awakens her pity. The lovers meet at night, and Melibea responds to Calixto's passion. However, upon leaving her room, he falls from a ladder and is killed. Distraught and now completely in love with him, Melibea commits suicide by hurling herself from the tower of her house. Celestina, who had promised to share with some servants (her collaborators) the gifts Calixto had lavished upon her, falls victim to her avarice, and she is killed by them; they, in turn, are slain by the agents of justice.

The novel is a fugue of vice and virtue, of crass materialism and supreme idealism. The aristocratic world of the lovers is lofty, Petrarchian, imbued with the colors of the Renaissance; the plebeian world of Celestina and the servants, steeped and hardened in vice, is base, with an aura of medieval superstitions and witchcraft. So always the high-flown rhetoric of the lovers seems to find a counterpoint in the earthy slang of the lower depths. The dominating and ubiquitous Celestina, a masterpiece of characterization, bridges the gap, for she is equally conversant with the seraphic tongue of the good angels and the demonic language of the slums. More than for the tragic idyll of Calixto and Melibea, precursor to that of *Romeo and Juliet* (q.v.) and of all romantic tragedies, it is perhaps for the creation of Celestina, a portrait which surpasses in depth Chaucer's Wife of Bath, Juan Ruiz' Trataconventos and Rabelais' Panurge, that Rojas will be remembered in literary history.

CELLULAR PATHOLOGY (1858), by Rudolf Virchow. The great German pathologist Rudolf Virchow presented his views on cellular pathology in a course of lectures at the Pathological Institute of the University of Berlin in 1858. The effect of these lectures, based upon his findings in physiological and pathological histology, was to revolutionize the theory of the nature of disease. Virchow's object was "to furnish a clear and connected explanation of those facts upon which, according to my ideas, the theory of life must now be based, and out of which also the science of pathology has now to be constructed." He also aimed to offer a view of the cellular nature of all vital processes, both physiological and pathological, animal as well as vegetable, in order to demonstrate the unity of life in all organized forms. This, wrote Virchow, he attempted to do "in opposition to the one-sided humoral and neuristical (solidistic) tendencies which have been transmitted from the mythical days of antiquity to our own times, and at the same time to contrast with the equally one-sided interpretations of a grossly mechanical and chemical bias—the more delicate mechanism and chemistry of the cell."

According to the prevailing scientific medical view in the eighteen-fifties, there were in the bodies of men and animals a group of tissues nearly destitute of cells. Virchow, however, proved the presence of cells in the bones and cartilage, as well as in the connective tissues. He thus dealt a heavy blow to the theory of the free-cell formation. By the numerous tests he made of the constitution and behavior of diseased tissues, he showed that the action of disease consists in the alteration of cells, and that the life of an individual depends upon the life of his cells.

Aided by all the medical investigations which had been stimulated by his experimental school of thought, Virchow continued to build up his pathology upon the foundations which his discoveries in cellular pathology laid. The cellular principle was the basis of the greatest advances of the nineteenth century in that field. In fact, the whole modern science of biology is built upon Virchow's law of the cell succession. Also to his immense credit is his epoch-making pioneer work ahead of Koch in the field of bacteriology, which is explicit in his theory of the nature of disease.

CENCI, THE (1819), by Percy Bysshe Shelley. Shelley's best known poetic tragedy was not produced until 1886 in London, when it raised a storm of comment because of its subject matter. In a preface Shelley describes the source of his material as a manuscript copied from the archives of the old Cenci Palace in Rome. Count Francesco Cenci, an old libertine, kept the coffers of Pope Clement VIII well lined by buying pardons for his numerous crimes. He bids his wife, Lucretia, and his daughter, Beatrice, attend a feast, and then announces it is to celebrate the death of two of his sons in Spain. Beatrice pleads with Cardinal Camillo and other nobles to protect her and Lucretia from her unnatural father. Also she sends a petition to the Pope by the crafty Orsino. Cenci ravishes Beatrice, and in desperation she and Lucretia and other conspirators plot his death. The murder is discovered, and they are taken to Rome and tried. All are sentenced to death. They hope vainly for a pardon from the Pope which is denied them.

The central theme and situation in *The Cenci*, heroic resistance to tyranny, was of all subjects the most kindling to Shelley. Ranking with Greek and Elizabethan drama, this is one of the finest poetical plays in the English language.

CENT NOUVELLES NOUVELLES, LES (ca. 15th c.), Anonymous. This collection of prose tales, salty and often shrewdly critical of human follies, is sometimes attributed to a courtier named Antoine de la Salle. Many of the tales are borrowed from Italian sources, but the general down-to-earth realism identifies them as belonging to the vein of bourgeois *gallis* literature which goes back to the *fabliaux* and has persisted down a long line of great French story tellers, including Rabelais, Voltaire and Anatole France.

CENTURY OF THE CHILD, THE (1900), by Ellen Key. See KEY, ELLEN.

CÉSAR BIROTTEAU (1837), by Honoré de Balzac. See HUMAN COMEDY, THE, by Honoré de Balzac.

CHAINBEARER, THE (1845), by James Fenimore Cooper. See SPY, THE, by James Fenimore Cooper.

CHAMBERS' ENCYCLOPEDIA (1859–1868), by Robert Chambers. See VESTIGES OF THE NATURAL HISTORY OF CREATION, by Robert Chambers.

CHAMPION FROM FAR AWAY, THE (1931), by Ben Hecht. See HECHT, BEN.

CHANCE ACQUAINTANCE, A (1873), by William Dean Howells. See RISE OF SILAS LAPHAM, THE, by William Dean Howells.

CHANTECLER (1910), by Edmond Rostand. See L'AIGLON, by Edmond Rostand.

CHAPMAN'S HOMER (1598–1616), by George Chapman. Chapman's verse translations of the *Iliad* (q.v.) and the *Odyssey* (q.v.) and minor poems no longer attributed to Homer, were the first complete translation of Homer in English, and some, such as John Keats in his famous sonnet "On First Looking into Chapman's Homer," have thought it the best. Though Chapman strays far from the original, turning Homer into an Elizabethan full of quaint conceits, he is a poet in his own right, quotable for the swing of his meter and his vigorous, if now antiquated, language. For the *Iliad,* which he did first, and some books of which may have served Shakespeare as a source, he used rhyming "fourteeners." The *Odyssey* is in heroic couplets.

CHARACTERS (1614), by Sir Thomas Overbury. These are short sketches in imitation of the *Characters* of Theophrastus (q.v.): "Many witty characters, and conceited Newes, written by himselfe, and other learned Gentlemen his friends." It is not known how many were written by Overbury. The original edition contained twenty-two *Characters* and was added to the second edition of his poem "A Wife." Additional *Characters* were written and added until the last publication contained eighty-three. They are witty, satirical and epigrammatic. The first were of the upper and professional classes; later the lower classes were included. Some are direct attacks on individuals. Among the titles are: "A Good Woman," "A Flatterer," "An Amorist," "An Old Man," "My Taylor," and, most famous, "A Fair and Happy Milkmaid." This genre developed in the seventeenth century under such other writers as Nicholas Breton, John Earle, and Thomas Fuller, and often the *Characters* are so vivid that they seem to be looking for a story, and even toward the novel.

CHARACTERS, by Theophrastus (d. 287 b.c.). Theophrastus of Eresus in Lesbos was a pupil of Plato, and the disciple and successor of Aristotle as head of the Peripatetic school. Of his voluminous writings, only four are preserved. The *Characters* are thirty neatly and vividly drawn sketches of type characters such as "the flatterer" and "the superstitious man." This concern with character is an outgrowth of Aristotle's analysis of the virtues and vices in his *Ethics,* and had its influence in turn on such representatives of Greek New Comedy as Menander, a friend of Theophrastus, who made extensive use of stock comic characters.

CHARLES MEN, THE (1897–1898), by Verner von Heidenstam. This is a large, significant tragic epos in memory of Charles XII and his soldiers. Technically, it is a novel; but it has no continuous narrative in the usual sense. It is a composite of thirty-four separate aesthetic units, all bound together for a common purpose by the incomprehensible, outwardly imperturbable personality of a king who shared all—poverty, suffering, starvation, cold, humiliation and death—with his men. The author, a Nobel laureate, was primarily a poet and a painter; so his work—really a poem in prose—is an artist's conception of isolated tales and panoramic canvases, which in our imaginative minds become a historic mosaic unity. We can follow, now dimly, now realistically, certain characteristic phases of the life of the tragic hero—so often dubbed a fool—from the cradle to his grave, not through his victories but through his adversities in exile—in Poland, Turkey, and finally at Fredrikshald in Norway, where a bullet ended his sense of duty and public responsibilities. It is a motley array of gallant, orderly, but often ragged, desperate, borrowing Swedes who pass in review, and who maintained among themselves a state, even in captivity. As for Charles XII, what an enigma in the history of character and military commanders! A genius in the field, when he had anything to work with, his death was eventually desired by many of his own impoverished countrymen; yet he was feared, respected, and even loved by those who knew him, and seldom, if ever, hated. In him circumstances had bred fanaticism and perhaps a blind, distorted sense of justice and public welfare. . . . A more unified, organic historical novel is *The Tree of the Folkungs* (1905–1907), which is localized in the period of the early Scandinavian sagas.

CHARLES O'MALLEY, THE IRISH DRAGOON (1840), by Charles James Lever. Charles O'Malley tells his own adventurous story. The incidents occur during the first part of the nineteenth century. Nephew of Godfrey, of O'Malley Castle in Galway, Ireland, Charles is destined to become an Irish country gentleman. Instead, he leaves Trinity College to take the rank of Captain in the Fourteenth Light Dragoons, and fights in the Napoleonic Wars under the Duke of Wellington. Mickey Free, O'Malley's faithful valet, shares his experiences. Duels, wars, soldier life, are colorfully described. When Napoleon is defeated, O'Malley marries Lucy Dashwood, the girl he has loved since his youth. He returns home with "fame and fortune, to dwell among his own people in the home of his father."

CHARLEY'S AUNT (1892), by Brandon Thomas. This is one of the most popular farces in the English language. The action takes place in Oxford, where Jack Chesney and Charley Wykeham wish to ask their girls, Amy Spettigue and Kitty Verdun, to lunch in order to propose marriage before the girls' guardian, Mr. Spettigue, hustles them off to Scotland. Charley's aunt, Dona Lucia d'Alvadores, from Brazil, is coming to visit him; they think she would be a suitable chaperon. When she wires she cannot come, the boys are desperate and press Lord Fancourt Babberly, who has been practicing amateur theatricals, into service as Charley's aunt. He acts a very robust aunt and flirts outrageously with Amy and Kitty, who think him a dear old lady. When the real Dona Lucia turns up with Lord Fancourt's girl, Ela Delahay, the complications increase rapidly, but there is a happy ending.

CHARTERHOUSE OF PARMA, THE (1839), by Stendhal. The hero of this novel, a young Italian named Fabrice del Dongo, learns that Napoleon has returned from Elba, and sets off to join the forces of his idol. He arrives in Belgium just in time for the battle of Waterloo, which he sees as a member of Marshal Ney's escort, but does not understand at all. He is wounded, and manages to get home to the little state of Parma months later. There he finds that he has been denounced as a conspirator against the state, and barely escapes prison. Deciding, as did Julien Sorel (cf. *The Red and the Black*), that with Napoleon gone the army no longer promises a career, he plunges into local intrigue. His doting and scheming aunt, the Countess Sanseverina, aided by Count Mosca, the Prince's minister, sets out to make Fabrice an archbishop, but he has the misfortune to kill a man in a duel and is finally imprisoned. Here he falls in love with Clelia, daughter of General Conti, his warder. With his aunt, she engineers his escape. After many adventures, he is finally pardoned by the new Prince, and subsequently becomes a vicar, general and a great preacher. Clelia, in the meantime, has married another man. After her death, Fabrice renounces the world and enters the local monastery of the Carthusian monks—whence the story's title.

Many admirers of Stendhal consider this novel superior even to *The Red and the Black* (q.v.), ranking it well above his other works like *Lucien Leuven* (published 1894) and *Armance* (1827).

CHEKHOV, ANTON PAVLOVICH (1860–1904). Anton Chekhov vies with Maupassant in the art of the short story. He wrote hundreds of pieces, ranging from the slight humorous sketches of his twenties to the unforgettably beautiful tales of men and women of his maturity, who were always getting enmeshed in irrational situations out of which they always managed to draw the greatest suffering.

Perhaps the most famous of his stories is "The Darling," in which a woman who flourished on men's love changed her interest in life with every succeeding lover. Did Chekhov intend to ridicule this woman? Tolstoy said of this story that when Chekhov came to write it, "he, like Balaam, intended to curse, but the god of poetry forbade him, and commanded him to bless." Other famous stories are "The Black Monk," "The Steppe," "Ward Number 6," "The Kiss," "The Two Volôdyas" and "In Exile."

Never bitter, never cynical, Chekhov related the everyday life and activities of the little man, the cornered peasant, the teacher, the government clerk, the student, the down-at-the-heel intellectual—for the most part the gray, hopeless, superfluous, maladjusted people. He universalized commonplaces and lent the dignity of pathos to the most ludicrous personalities. He loved people and laughed with them, rather than at them. Nemirovich-Danchenko called Chekhov the poet of the bourgeoisie, which may account for the fact that the Soviets have little use for him. He exercised considerable influence on English writers, especially during the 'twenties, both with his stories and his plays (qq.v.).

CHEMICAL HISTORY OF A CANDLE (1861), by Michael Faraday. See EXPERIMENTAL RESEARCHES IN ELECTRICITY, by Michael Faraday.

CHERRY ORCHARD, THE (1904), by Anton Chekhov. The story is laid in the 1890's and treats of the triumph of industrialization over the old aristocratic order. The play opens with the return of Madame Ranevsky to her estate after an absence of nearly six years in Paris. The famous cherry orchard is in bloom, but the estate has fallen into decay. Madame Ranevsky had left after her husband's death and the tragic drowning of her little boy. In France, she had taken a lover who was selfish and demanding, and who had preyed on her financially. In the meantime, her adopted daughter, Varya, had remained at home, trying her best to manage the depleting finances of the estate. Madame Ranevsky's party includes Anya, her daughter, a young girl of seventeen; the governess, Charlotte; a young man-servant, Yasha. Lopakhin, a successful business man and son of a former serf on the estate, advises Madame Ranevsky to pay off her debts by selling the estate for a suburban development, though it would mean cutting down the cherry orchard. She refuses Lopakhin's proposition, and drifts on aimlessly, hoping for some miracle that will save her land and her beloved orchard. Her brother Gayev thinks of nothing but playing billiards. Anya falls in love with Trofimov, a young university student, and Yasha flirts with Dunyasha, the maid. The family talks interminably about getting money to save their land, but nothing positive is done, and in the end they are forced to sell. It is bought by Lopakhin; Madame Ranevsky weeps when she gives up the keys. She decides to return to Paris, and during her preparations to leave she can hear the sound of chopping coming from the cherry orchard. The fall of the cherry orchard symbolizes the disintegration and disappearance of the aristocracy.

CHESTERTON, GILBERT KEITH (1874–1936). G. K. Chesterton's writings embrace many fields, including poetry, criticism and the short story. Prominent among his novels is *The Man Who Was Thursday* (1908), a fantastic spy story with religious and political overtones. His essays are stamped with strong individuality. *Heretics* (1905) deals with a number of his contemporaries, generally considered extremists. Chesterton, himself a traditionalist and a conservative, admired sound dissenters; he wrote appreciations, for example, of G. B. Shaw.

The essays in *Orthodoxy* (1908) deal with orthodox Christianity, the author's progressive understanding of it, and the fallacious thinking of its various opponents.

CHILD FROM FIVE TO TEN, THE (1946), by Arnold L. Gesell. See GESELL, ARNOLD L.

CHILD'S GARDEN OF VERSES (1885), by Robert Louis Stevenson. This slender volume of verses has delighted both children and grown-ups from the time that it was written. The poems are uniquely written for children as if by a contemporary, rather than about children for the reminiscent pleasure of adults. And yet there is much for the adult to smile about as he is taken back in memory to his childhood. An oft-quoted example of the collection is the two-line poem, "Happy Thought":

> The world is so full of a number of things,
> I'm sure we should all be as happy as kings.

"My Shadow" and "The Lamplighter" are particular favorites.

CHILDE HAROLD'S PILGRIMAGE (Cantos I and II, 1812; III, 1816; IV, 1818), by George Gordon, Lord Byron. In Spenserian stanzas, the various parts of this travel poem were a huge success, and in 1812 Byron "awoke and found himself famous." Jaded English taste was stimulated by the novelty of this pilgrim seeking surcease from the pain of disappointed love, by the vivid descriptions of Spanish bullfights, of minarets and muezzin call, of Turkish mosque and the sound of revelry by night before the dread battle cannon of Waterloo. Later come splendid descriptions of the Alps, of the falls of Terni, of the sea and mountains which the hero sought in mystic communion, all in the romantic tradition. Rousseau is appropriately mentioned. Italian cities and notables fill the fourth canto. The human interest of the poem was aided by the public's identification of Byron himself with the wandering hero. In fact, in the fourth canto the poet speaks frankly in his own person.

CHILDREN AND HOUSEHOLD TALES (1812–1815), by Jacob and Wilhelm Grimm. See FAIRY TALES, by Jacob and Wilhelm Grimm.

CHILDREN'S HOUR, THE (1932), by Lillian Hellman. See HELL-MAN, LILLIAN.

CHIN P'ING MEI (1580), by Hsu Wei. *Chin P'ing Mei (The Adventurous History of Hsi Men and His Six Wives)* was written by Hsu Wei, a politician and playwright. It is a novel with realistic detail of the comic and tragic situations in domestic life. Because of its frank treatment of sex, it was considered forbidden literature in China. However, many words and phrases are capable of two interpretations: one for the puritan Confucian, the other for the more vulgar-minded.

Tradition says that a Confucian scholar named Wang Shih Cheng (1526–1593) wrote this novel of some 1600 pages, painting into it the picture of the hero Hsi Men, borrowed from another novel called *Shui-hu Chuan*. According to popular legend, it is supposed to be a bitter satire on the private life of his enemy Yen Shih-fan, but this is without scholarly foundation.

There is a German translation which has been retranslated into English by Bernard Miall and Franz Kuhn (1940) with an Introduction by Arthur Waley.

CHINESE CLASSICS, THE (24th–4th c. B.C.). *The Chinese Classics* are not sacred books in the sense that they are believed to be the word of God Himself, but they are venerated as the accumulated wisdom of China's long past. The collection is divided into two groups, called the Five Classics (Wu Ching) and The Four Books (Ssu Shu). The Five Classics are selections from the literature of China's "golden age," supposedly compiled by Confucius, who "never tired of studying the ancients." They are concerned with history, government, ceremonials and poetry. The Four Books give the ethics and philosophy of Confucius: his own words, incidents about him, and writings of some of his distinguished followers.

Confucius (551–478 B.C.) spent most of his life in informal teaching of young men, with whom he talked of literature, history, government, and life. He believed that the universe is governed by moral forces; that rulers are under obligation to follow the Way and the Will of Heaven; that leaders must study "the ancients" and set an example of right living, for men are by nature good and evil is the result of ignorance. Confucius combined aristocracy with democracy, for the truly princely man is such by his own nature and self-mastery, not by birth or wealth. If a ruler does not prove worthy, the right of revolution always rests with the people.

The Classics teach that the fundamental virtues are propriety and reciprocity. Propriety is a sense of the fitness of things, a fine respect for all persons and for nature itself. Reciprocity is benevolence, wishing for others what one wishes for oneself. The family is the central unit of social life; reverence for parents and consideration for brothers are the foundation of all goodness.

The Five Classics (Wu Ching)

SHU CHING (The Book of History) covers a period from the twenty-fourth to the eighth century B.C., giving us glimpses of the time before Confucius. This is the most ancient record of the annals of the Chinese Empire. Some documents are protests against luxury and ill-treatment of the people:

> The people should be cherished,
> And not looked down upon.
> The people are the root of a country;
> The root firm, the country is tranquil. . . .
> When the palace is wild of lust,
> And the country is wild for hunting;
> When spirits are liked, and music is the delight;
> When there are lofty roofs and carved walls;—
> The existence of any one of these things
> Has never been but the prelude to ruin.

SHIH CHING (The Book of Songs) is a selection of 311 out of 3,000 songs collected from all over the country. Confucius arranged these songs according to their music. They include folk-songs by the people, musical songs by the government officials, and eulogies by rulers and statesmen. Each song is classified either as *fu* (description), *hsing* (inspiration or allusion), or *pi* (metaphor). These songs are very valuable as an index to Chinese life in the early Chou period; they deal with warfare, marriage, feasting, parties, joy rides after country fairs, and separation of wives and husbands.

YI CHING (The Book of Change) consists of separate chapters, written by different authors at different times (ca. 1500 B.C.). *Yi* means change in any form, the predominant characteristic of all activities, and according to Chinese thought, caused by the interaction of *Yin* (female) and *Yang* (male) principles in the universe. All change arises from motion, which is produced by the pushing of that which is active against that which is passive. Activity is known as "the easy" and passivity as "the simple." It is from the "simple" and the "easy" that all complexity and multiplicity of life and change have arisen. "In all conduct and affairs, the most perilous is always known from that which is easy. . . . In all conduct and affairs, that which is confronted with the greatest obstacle is always known from the simplest."

LICHI (The Record of Rites) contains the Chinese standard of good behavior. *Li* means order, a positive force, in contrast to negative law, or *fa*. Ideally, Chinese institutions are under the encouragement of *li*. *Li* shows us what should be done toward the habit of right practice; law only warns against the wrong. Law punishes the evil that has been done; *li* prevents crime in advance. *Li* is the principle of refinement in all activities. "No matter how sincere the thought of a man may be, if it is not acted upon by *li*, he is no more than a wild man." The theory of the three stages of social progress is also found in this book: a world of disorder, small tranquillity, and great unity.

CH'UN CH'IU (Spring and Autumn) is a chronicle of Lu, the native state of Confucius, covering a period of 242 years (722–480 B.C.). It has linguistic importance, but it tends to a mechanical and pedantic view of literature. As to its deeper significance, Mencius says: "The world had fallen into decay and right principles had dwindled. Perverse doctrines and violent deeds had arisen. Ministers murdered their kings, sons murdered their fathers. Confucius was afraid and wrote Ch'un Ch'iu."

Besides these five classics, there was a sixth, the Yueh (Music). There are two schools of traditional scholarship concerning the relation of Confucius to these classics. One says Confucius wrote all these books. The other maintains Confucius was the author of Ch'un Ch'iu, the commentator of the Yi Ching, the reformer of the Li Chi and the Yueh, and the compiler of the Shih Ching and Shu Ching. But some modern scholars believe Confucius had nothing to do either with writing, editing or commenting on any of the classics.

The Four Books (Ssu Shu)

LUN YU (The Analects) consists of 20 chapters, compiled by his disciples, chiefly of the views and sayings of Confucius, who formulated the golden rule, "What you would not others should do unto you, do not unto them." The principle of *Jen,* or human relationship, is emphasized. Confucius tried to teach his pupils to be useful to state and society. He was "a transmitter and not an originator." He was concerned for the achievement of good government, and held that this would be brought about by a return to the teachings of the great sages of the past. He set himself and his followers to the study and observance of the ancient ritual and to the cultivation of uprightness.

TA HSUOH (The Great Learning) is a book of about 1750 words of unknown authorship, devoted to a discussion of the main principles of Confucian teaching and the seven related acts. These are: to investigate things in order to extend knowledge; to be sincere in thought; to rectify the mind; to cultivate the person; to regulate the family; to order well the state; to make tranquil and happy the world. The whole philosophy of modern China, from the eleventh century to the present day, has centered on the interpretation of this book.

CHUNG YUNG (Doctrine of the Mean) deals with the *Tao* or the Way. "Tao is the natural way. What heaven has conferred is called nature. Accordance with this nature is called *Tao.*" All laws, social customs, and religious beliefs should move according to this natural way. According to tradition, this book was written by Tzu-ssu, the grandson of Confucius, but a large part of it may have been written later. "When a nation is about to flourish, there are sure to be happy omens; when it is about to perish, there are sure to be unlucky omens."

MENG TZU (Mencius) contains seven books, consisting mostly of the sayings and doings of Mencius (372-289 B.C.) himself; although a follower of Confucius, he was more original, vigorous and independent than his master. According to him, human nature is good. There are four principles of goodness: benevolence, righteousness, propriety and knowledge. Man's nature must be educated, an environment made favorable by good will, by music, by art, and by the good care of the rulers. He would justify as heaven's will rebellion against hopelessly corrupt rulers.

These books were translated by James Legge as *The Chinese Classics* in 1871.

CHINESE NIGHTINGALE, THE (1917), by Vachel Lindsay. See LINDSAY, VACHEL.

CHITA: A MEMORY OF LAST ISLAND (1889), by Lafcadio Hearn. See HEARN, LAFCADIO.

CHOICE OF PEARLS, by Solomon Ibn Gabirol. See IBN GABIROL, SOLOMON.

CHOONGAMJIP, by Kim Chung. See SHIJO-YUCHIP.

CHOSEN DOKLIP WOONDONG KAMSANG (1933), by Han Yong-woon. See MEDITATIONS OF THE LOVER, by Han Yong-woon.

CHRISTABEL (I, 1797; II, 1800; published 1816), by Samuel Taylor Coleridge. In this unfinished poem, the metrical principle is four accents to a line; however, the number of syllables varies. Coleridge calls for "a willing suspension of disbelief" for a supernatural tale. Christabel, lovely daughter of Sir Leoline, meets at midnight a lady who calls herself Geraldine and pretends to be in distress. Christabel offers her the sharing of her bed for the night, but the indications mount that the lady, alleged daughter of Sir Leoline's former friend, Lord Roland de Vaux of Tryermaine, is a malignant spirit. The innocent maid faints next morning at the sight of the guest's serpent eye. Sir Leoline sends Bracy the bard to renew the friendship with Lord Roland de Vaux and tell him his daughter Geraldine is safe. Here the incomparably magic poem breaks off.

CHRISTIAN YEAR, THE (1827), by John Keble. This was an enormously popular book, and had a great influence. There is an anecdote that Wordsworth, who admired it, said that it was so good that if it were his he would rewrite it. These are pious poems, for poetry, in its essence, was to Keble simply religion. On every page one feels that here is a saint and a scholar, who has found quietness and confidence and love of nature, by way of faith.

CHRISTMAS CAROL, A (1843), by Charles Dickens. This Christmas story of nineteenth century England has delighted young and old for generations. In it, a miser, Scrooge, through a series of dreams, finds the true Christmas spirit. Ebenezer Scrooge had scoffed at Christmas and turned his back on his needy clerk, Bob Cratchit. He is visited by the chained ghost of his dead partner, Jacob Marley, who warns him that three spirits will visit him, to offer him a last chance to escape the dismal eternal punishment of avarice. At the stroke of midnight, the Ghost of Christmas Past arrives, and Scrooge sees his boyhood. The Ghost of Christmas Present takes him to the homes of his nephew and Bob Cratchit, where Scrooge sees himself, through their eyes, as an ugly miser. The Ghost of Christmas Yet to Come shows Scrooge his own death, and he hears people's comments of disrespect for the "old miser." Scrooge awakens on Christmas Day, a changed man. He opens his heart to those against whom he had hardened it. The story ends with the much-quoted cry of Tiny Tim, the crippled son of Bob Cratchit, whom Scrooge now aids: "God bless us, every one!"

CHRISTOPHER COLUMBUS (1921), by Johannes V. Jensen. See LONG JOURNEY, THE, by Johannes V. Jensen.

CHRONICLE OF SPARROW STREET (1857), by Wilhelm Raabe. See RAABE, WILHELM.

CHRONICLES (completed ca. 1400; appeared in France ca. 1490), by John Froissart. The content and intention of Froissart are clear from the full title of the work: *Chronicles of England, France, Spain and the Adjoining Countries, from the latter part of the reign of Edward II to the coronation of Henry IV.* Froissart began his work in 1357 and ended it in 1400, collecting his material by traveling around and interviewing personally many types of people, from peasant to knight. No historian in the modern sense, he appears as a gifted and highly observant recorder of feudal life and manners. In his own time, and even centuries later, Froissart's work was considered an authority. In our day, it still presents a record of battles and sieges, marches and warriors, tournaments and tilts, loves and wassailings, and a valuable and colorful picture of the Crusade of 1390. The *Chronicles* is divided into four books.

CHRONICLES OF DENMARK, THE (ca. 1208), by Saxo Grammaticus. On the advice of Archbishop Absalon of Denmark, Saxo, surnamed Grammaticus because of his excellent "grammatical" Latin style, began about 1185 to write this history of the Danes. It was founded in part on information furnished by the Archbishop, but mostly upon oral tradition and old Scandinavian, particularly Danish, songs, which he translated freely into elegant Latin. It proved to be the greatest Danish intellectual effort of the Middle Ages, and as soon as it had become generally known, won European admiration. The first edition of it appeared in Paris, 1514, and a Danish version, by A. S. Vedel, in 1575. The work is composed of sixteen "books," of which the first nine deal with the semi-legendary kings and heroes down to about 950. Among these is the shrewd and active, realistic, wide-awake Prince Amblet or Hamlet, who, in the original, dies on the field of battle and differs considerably from Shakespeare's melancholy, brooding Dane. But Saxo, directly or indirectly, was his source. In the tenth and eleventh parts, historical truth and legend wrestle with each other for supremacy, but from the twelfth on, we have more authentic records. While it is now to be regretted—praiseworthy as the Latin version may be—that Saxo did not write down his findings in the vernacular, it made the author and his country known to other Latin writers of Europe, and Erasmus of Rotterdam, for example, praised the rich, sublime style of the *Chronicles,* its vivid, ardent spirit and elegance of diction, as well as its "sound principles and remarkable variety of imagery."

Saxo's work has long been available in English, but the version is antiquated, and a new definitive translation of it is now being prepared.

CHRONICLES OF ENGLAND, SCOTLAND AND IRELAND (1577), edited by Raphael Holinshed. This important and still readable source book begins with Noah and the flood. The *History of England,* written by Holinshed himself, continues up to the time of publication. The *Description of England* is by William Harrison, who made the translation for that of *Scotland* besides. Ireland was covered by the Jesuit writers Richard Stanyhurst and Edmund Campion, and by a translation of Giraldus Cambrensis. The work, though done by many hands, preserves a uniformity of character and is not lacking in a simple eloquence. It has always been known by the name of its editor. "Master Holinshed hath much furthered and advantaged me," said Edmund Spenser; and it is well known that Shakespeare went to Holinshed for the "facts" in his historical plays.

CHUNGSUNGJIP, by Sung Taejung. See SHIJO-YUCHIP.

CHUNHYANG CHUN (18th c.), Anonymous. There are some thirty versions of *Chunhyang Chun* (*The Fragrance of Spring*), the most popular story of Korea. One of the best-known was written by Shin Zaehyo (Shin Owichang, b. 1812). The location of the novel is the city of Namwon, in the province of Chulla Namdo, South Korea. The hero, Mongyong, is the handsome, brilliant and dutiful son of the Prefect Li Fusa. The story treats of the love of Mongyong (Toryung) for the beautiful Chunhyang, whom he marries secretly. She is the daughter of a *kisang* (dancing girl). The lovers endure many difficulties, chiefly caused by a dishonest magistrate who covets Chunhyang. The hero triumphs in the end, when a certain poem composed by him and forming an important motif in the novel represents the drinking and banqueting of the corrupt official as a feast of the flesh and blood of thousands of people.

Chunhyang Chun often has been set to music, and sung by some of the greatest singers in Korea. The effect of the music is an integral part of the novel and has delighted the people of Korea for generations.

CHUNTOKYO KYOCHI (1921), by Choi Jewu, Choi Siyung, Son Pyunghi, etc. This book (*Doctrine of the Heavenly Way*) concerns Chuntokyo, a religion of Korea created in 1864. The prime object was preserving all Eastern customs and ideals and opposing the rapid adoption of Christianity. Its forms are those of Confucianism, its spirit and voice are those of Buddhism and Taoism. The founder, Choi Jewu (1824–1864) was a great classical scholar, with originality in ethical thought. Choi's belief was that man is a god, that he must keep his god-given qualities, and develop them by emancipating body, mind and soul. Each morning Chuntoists pray and offer pure water, as the symbol of the blood of the sage, Choi, who was accused of heresy and executed. Choi Siyung (1827–1899) preached the teaching of his master and established churches throughout Korea. He too was executed. Son Pyunghi (1861–1922) became his successor, leading the Tonghal Rebellion. He signed the Declaration of Independence in 1919, and was put in jail by the Japanese, where he died. The Chuntoists circulate thousands of books voicing popular demands for reforms, and support many schools.

CICERO (M. Tullius Cicero, *Orations*, 81–43 B.C.) In Republican Rome one's effectiveness as a statesman depended on one's ability as a public speaker, and education was aimed at attaining that end. The courts, the senate, and public assemblies were constantly the scenes of desperate but none the less artistic duels of wits and words. In an age of brilliant orators, Cicero far surpassed all contenders for the crown of eloquence, and established a style and standard of speaking which were to be an object of emulation and a cause of desperation to speakers and writers for centuries to come. Of his orations we still have fifty-eight covering the full length of his career. One of the earliest is the plea for Roscius, in which the rising young advocate dared to risk the displeasure of the powerful Sulla. With his speeches delivered in the prosecution of Verres, he made his reputation as an incorruptible castigator of corruption in high places by winning a conviction against the defense of the most eminent criminal lawyers of the day. In 66 B.C. he launched himself on his public career with a speech in favor of the command of Pompey against the Cilician pirates, thus aligning himself with the great man of the moment and with the people's party. In 63 he was elected consul, and during his tenure of this highest office had to meet an extreme emergency, the Catilinarian conspiracy. His four speeches delivered at various stages in the suppression of this revolution are masterpieces of the orator's dramatic art and well deserve the place they have enjoyed as a school classic. For his service to the state, Cicero was hailed as father of his country. A few years later we find him entering a brilliant plea in behalf of his friend, the Greek poet Archias, wherein he delivers one of the most glowing encomia of literature as an exaltation of the human spirit ever to be pronounced. But soon his political career was eclipsed by the rising star of the triumvirate. He was even exiled, and we have a series of querulous speeches dealing with this indignity, followed by a number of defenses of individuals, capped by that for Milo, which he was prevented from delivering by threats of physical violence, but which he published nevertheless. The civil war again interrupted his activity. Although, as a conservative, he now chose the losing side, he was not slow to make his peace with Caesar, and after 46 there are several speeches known as *Caesarian,* since they fall in line with the wishes and policies of the great dictator. After the Ides of March in 43, the old champion of senatorial rule once more entered the lists in bitter opposition to the ascendancy of Mark Antony. This final burst of eloquence is embodied in his fourteen *Philippics,* some of which were circulated as pamphlets rather than being actually delivered. Cicero himself gave them this name because of the crusading spirit which inspired them as it had the speeches of Demosthenes against Philip of Macedon. It is difficult to say whether Cicero's oratorical prose is more to be admired for its skillful playing upon the emotions or for its rolling and musical periods. Certain it is that every word, every phrase, and every majestic sentence was carefully chosen, selected and constructed with a deliberate calculation of its effect. Cicero was not only an artist in the persuasive use of words, but also a theoretician of rhetoric, and we have seven treatises by his hand covering all phases of the history, theory and technique of oratory.

CID, THE (1636), by Pierre Corneille. Rodrique, a young Spanish nobleman, is in love with and is loved by Chimène, daughter of a prominent family. The course of their love runs smoothly until the Spanish code of honor complicates matters. Chimène's father quarrels with Rodrique's father and strikes the older man. Rodrique, honor bound, challenges Chimène's father to a duel and kills him. The Spanish code called for Chimène to take vengeance by demanding his death. Rodrique, overcome by the hopelessness of the situation, is inclined to commit suicide. His father persuades him to seek the more honorable course of dying in battle. At the head of a small force, he repels a Moorish invasion, and instead of dying, becomes the hero of Spain. Though Chimène still loves him, she continues to seek vengeance for her father. The King tells her to appoint a champion and arranges a duel, with Chimène the prize. Rodrique is willing to permit himself to be defeated, but Chimène, unable to hold out any longer, admits her love and begs him to win. He does so and they are united.

Since Corneille was trying to conform to the classic unities of time, place and action, of which the French had just become conscious, this action takes place in twenty-four crowded hours. Modern audiences are still able to detect a certain sublimity in the sentiments of hero and heroine, but otherwise the main effect is of stiltedness. The play remains in the repertory of the Comédie Française as a landmark. It opened the period of the French drama which culminated in the tragedy of Racine and the comedies of Molière. Corneille wrote many other plays, best known among which are *Cinna* (1640), *Horace* (1640), and *Polyeucte* (1643).

CIMARRON (1930), by Edna Ferber. See SHOW BOAT, by Edna Ferber.

CINNA (1640), by Pierre Corneille. See CID, THE, by Pierre Corneille.

CINQ-MARS (1826), by Alfred de Vigny. *Cinq-Mars,* the best and most widely known novel of the Romantic poet Alfred de Vigny, is an historical romance of the French seventeenth century. It tells the story of the conspiracy of young Marquis de Cinq-Mars and his friend De Thou against Prime Minister Cardinal de Richelieu. The Cardinal, having discovered the plot, asks the King for the two young men's heads. Louis XIII, who is very fond of Cinq-Mars and resents Richelieu's authority, dismisses his minister. But he realizes quickly that he cannot reign alone: the burden of government is too heavy. He recalls the Cardinal and abandons his favorite. Cinq-Mars and de Thou will be executed.

More exacting than Walter Scott, Vigny borrows from history the background, the actors, the data of his works. But, while he respects the general outlines of history, he sometimes alters the meaning of events and the real character of men. *Cinq-Mars* helped start the tremendous vogue of historical novels in France.

CIOPW (1931), by E. E. Cummings. See ENORMOUS ROOM, THE, by E. E. Cummings.

CIRCLE, THE (1921), by W. Somerset Maugham. Arnold Champion-Cheney's pretty wife, Elizabeth, has invited his mother, Lady Catherine Champion-Cheney, and Lord Porteous, with whom Lady Catherine had run away when Arnold was a baby, to visit them. As Arnold's father and Lady Porteous would not divorce their respective mates, marriage for the lovers had been impossible. Elizabeth thinks it pathetic that Arnold does not remember his mother; and she volunteers to question his father, C. C., who lives near by. The latter tells her that she resembles his wife, a beautiful young woman, and that Lord Porteous had been about to be Prime Minister when the couple ran away.

Lady Kitty (Catherine) turns out to be a faded beauty, frivolous and flighty, and Lord Porteous is a grumpy, complaining old man. C. C. resumes friendly relations with his wife, much to her lover's annoyance. Teddie Luton, a young colonial planter, who is a house guest, has been courting Elizabeth. She decides to go off with him in spite of the depressing example of Lady Kitty. Strictly honorable, she tells Arnold she loves Teddie and asks for a divorce, which he refuses to grant.

Lady Kitty warns Elizabeth, "You don't know what it is to have a man tied to you only by his honor. When married people don't get on, they can separate, but if they're not married it's impossible. It's a tie only death can sever." But Elizabeth, young and independent, thinks otherwise. Arnold, acting on his father's advice, tells her that he loves her so much that he will give her a divorce and an allowance, and the ruse nearly works, for overcome by his generosity, she is about to give up Teddie. When he tells her that if she came to him with any such proposition he would give her a black eye, she is carried away; and the lovers go off in Lord Porteous' car with the old couple wishing them good luck. This is one of the best known and most popular of Maugham's plays.

CIRCUS IN THE ATTIC, THE (1948), by Robert Penn Warren. See WARREN, ROBERT PENN.

CITIES OF THE PLAIN (1921–1922), by Marcel Proust. See REMEMBRANCE OF THINGS PAST, by Marcel Proust.

CITIZEN OF THE WORLD, THE (1762), by Oliver Goldsmith. These "letters from a Chinese philosopher residing in London, to his friends in the East" satirically describe the evils of English society and its hypocrisies, its desecration of beauty through absurd fashions, and the shallow thought of the time. The imaginary Lien Chi Altangi probes even deeper into the heart of England, foreseeing the results of her American colonial policies, and exposing the sham of her society. He cuts at abuses prevalent during the eighteenth century in church and in government, and ridicules her theater-going beaux.

CITIZEN TOM PAINE (1943), by Howard Fast. This novelized biography of Thomas Paine reveals the Revolutionary pamphleteer from many angles: Paine the fool, Paine the inept politician, but always Paine who felt and understood the meaning of America, who knew the inevitability of his times.

The Last Frontier (1941) is the 1878 epic of American Indians' struggle for freedom against a country bent on enslaving or annihilating them. Dull Knife and Chief Little Wolf lead a band from a Northern Cheyenne reservation, in an escape from the White Men's cruelty. Captain Murray of the cavalry troops (the book's sole purely fictional character) leads a punitive expedition which captures and massacres Dull Knife's band. Little Wolf's group is permitted by the government to settle in the Powder River country, and Murray, disgusted at what he has done, resigns.

Freedom Road (1944) tells the story of a Negro who becomes a member of Congress, against a background of the South during its Reconstruction period.

The American (1946) is the story of John Peter Altgeld, the German-born liberal lawyer who became governor of Illinois, but was defeated for re-election because of his "radical" sympathies in the Haymarket Riot and the Pullman Strike.

CITIZEN TURNED GENTLEMAN, THE (1670), by Molière. See BOURGEOIS GENTILHOMME, LE, by Molière.

CITIZEN WHO APES THE NOBLEMAN, THE (1670), by Molière
See BOURGEOIS GENTILHOMME, LE, by Molière.

CITIZENS OF CALAIS, THE (1913), by Georg Kaiser. See GAS, by
Georg Kaiser.

CITY OF DREADFUL NIGHT, THE (1874), by James Thomson. A
poem without hope, without a concept of God, called blasphemous on its first
appearance, a poem filled with a passionate faith in pessimism as the sole
philosophy—this stands unique among works that have attained fame. It is
at the opposite pole from the optimistic Browning, whom Thomson admired.
Thomson was a man of genius, but weak-willed and sickly. Love for a girl
who died young, insomnia, poverty, ill-health, dipsomania haunted him. As
he says in his famous poem:

> If any cares for the weak words here written,
> It must be someone desolate, Fate-smitten,
> Whose faith and hope are dead, and who would die.

The city is in some of the descriptions London, at other times allegorical—
human life without goodness in it. Several visions give it the quality of a
nightmare.

CITY OF GOD, THE (426), by St. Augustine (Aurelius Augustinus).
Not until the appearance of the *Summa Theologica* (q.v.) of Thomas Aquinas
in the thirteenth century was St. Augustine's *City of God* rivaled in the universal esteem of Christendom. For one thousand years it reigned as the most
influential apologia for Christianity. Augustine was one of the most cultured
and profound of the church fathers, and one of the most genuinely pious. A
teacher of rhetoric and a man of broad learning, he brought eloquence and
loftiness to Patristic writings. *The City of God* was evoked by the chaos of
the times in which Augustine lived. The sack of Rome by the Goths under
Alaric in 410 stirred the imagination of all thinking men as a sign of the disintegration of the Roman Empire. Defeatism poisoned the atmosphere. Men's
hearts, wrote Augustine, were "failing them for fear and for looking after those
things that were coming on the earth." Moral and intellectual confusion accompanied the imperial downfall of the "Eternal City." Augustine at last saw
his opportunity to win over, by marshaling historical proof and eloquence, the
multitudes of cultivated pagans who could no longer find çomfort and assurance
in the pagan pantheon. Augustine divided his work into twenty-two books.
Books I-V present a refutation of the belief of the pagan masses that polytheism
was necessary to mortal happiness. Books VI-X meet the assertion of the philosophers that the worship of the gods was advantageous in view of the prospect
of life after death The latter part of the work concerns itself with the presentation of a constructive philosophy of life to take the place of pagan worship.
Books XI-XIV contain "the origin of the two cities, the City of God and the
city of the world." Books XV to XVIII contain "their process or progress."
Books XIX-XXII reveal their "appointed ends." Augustine finds much wretchedness in the city of the world in contrast to the splendor of the City of God.
He finds there is one commonwealth for all Christian men: "That heavenly city
which has Truth for its King, Love for its Law, and Eternity for its Measure ..."

CITY OF TREMBLING LEAVES, THE (1945), by Walter Van Tilburg Clark. See OX-BOW INCIDENT, THE, by Walter Van Tilburg Clark.

CIVIL DISOBEDIENCE (1849), by Henry David Thoreau. See WALDEN, by Henry David Thoreau.

CLARISSA HARLOWE, or THE HISTORY OF A YOUNG LADY (1748), by Samuel Richardson. Richardson is credited with introducing the novel of character, and this, which many consider his masterpiece, has surprisingly few incidents considering that, first published in seven volumes, it is the longest novel in the English language. It presents the story, in protracted detail, of the ruin of an almost perfect woman through no clear fault of her own, but through the tyranny of her parents and the crafty persistence of the profligate Robert Lovelace, who, after surrounding her with false friends, finally drugs her. Clarissa's parents, egged on by her haughty brother and ill-natured sister, try to force on her as a husband the odious Mr. Solmes. They imprison her in her room and accuse her of fondness for the dashing, disreputable Lovelace. Finally she is tricked into putting herself under his protection, and would perhaps—had he pressed her and shown some signs of reforming—have consented to marry him, but he is bent on having her on other terms. After his nefarious schemes have come to their climax, Clarissa, her reputation gone, breaks away from him and pines to death from shame and her family's scorn. Her cousin, Colonel Morden, kills Lovelace in a duel. In contrast to Pamela (q.v.), Richardson's earlier creation, Clarissa is well born, well educated, essentially delicate and keenly sensitive. Thus her humiliation is augmented by an exaggerated consciousness of self-betrayal. The story is told through letters, mainly between the heroine and her confidant, Miss Howe, and between Lovelace and his friend Belford.

CLASS REUNION (1930), by Franz Werfel. See FORTY DAYS OF MUSA DAGH, THE, by Franz Werfel.

CLASSICAL POETRY OF JAPAN (Eng. tr. 1880). See MANYOSHIU, THE.

CLAYHANGER TRILOGY, THE (1910–1911, 1915), by Arnold Bennett. Realistic and sometimes satiric in tone, the action of these novels takes place in a drab potters' region in Staffordshire, England. The works comprising the trilogy are: *Clayhanger* (1910), *Hilda Lessways* (1911), and *These Twain* (1915). The historical and social elements are never subordinated to the psychological conflicts and characterizations, but enhance them and bring them into clearer relief.

The first volume, *Clayhanger,* is a depressing chronicle of young Edwin Clayhanger's maladjustment in an unsympathetic home. The most desperate emotional warfare is forced upon him by his ruthless, unimaginative father, Darius. Edwin has striking artistic talent. However, his plans frustrated by Darius, he is doomed to waste himself in a provincial town, stifled by its Wesleyan bigotry and disheartened by the potters' sordid struggle with poverty. But in 1880 Edwin, at twenty-three, meets Hilda Lessways at the home of his friends, Charles and Janet Orgreave. At first his inexperience with women and his repressed puritanical nature stand in the way of their friendship. She is self-possessed and masculinely aggressive. He is at first repelled by her, but after further acquaintance impressed by her strong character and bold intelligence. A year later, when she again visits with the Orgreaves, she secretly becomes engaged to Edwin. But when Janet Orgreave informs him shortly thereafter that Hilda has suddenly wedded George Cannon, Edwin begins to hate her. Ten years later, after the death of his father, he discovers her in a destitute condition as the landlady of a rooming-house in Brighton. Her husband has been jailed for bigamy, her marriage had been declared invalid, and her little boy deprived of legitimacy. Despite all that has passed, Edwin is still in love with her.

Hilda Lessways goes back to 1878 to tell Hilda's story from her point of view. It shows her bored and restless life with her widowed mother, and the slow growth of an intimacy with the solicitor Cannon. Hilda will master Edwin, but here she is herself mastered. At the end she feels no less a sinner than Florrie, her seduced maid.

These Twain is an account of the marital misfortunes of Edwin and Hilda, their lives already complicated by their tortured past. They quarrel over the most trifling matters. Edwin becomes a successful man, enters politics, buys a country house, and, in order to insure peace, permits himself at last to be dominated by the neurotic, masculine Hilda.

CLEANNESS (ca. 1370), Anonymous. See PEARL.

CLOAK, THE (1842), by Nikolay Vasilyevich Gogol. This famous long short story, which had a marked influence on Russian fiction, has also been translated as *The Greatcoat* and *The Overcoat*. The first piece of Russian realism as we understand it today, Dostoevsky said of it that "we've all issued from *The Cloak*." It tells the story of a poor governmental clerk who, the humblest of his kind and the butt of his colleagues, manages to subsist on his tiny salary, nursing the single ambition of saving enough for a new overcoat, to replace the old tattered one. After excessive privation, he saves enough to get the overcoat, only to be deprived of it by thieves on the first evening he goes out. The story is full of that humanity and pathos which were to become the distinguishing mark of much Russian fiction that followed; Dostoevsky was inspired by it to write his first novel, *Poor Folk,* which won immediate fame. The distinguishing trait of *The Cloak* is a kind of humor, both gentle and satiric, of which Gogol was a master.

CLOISTER AND THE HEARTH, THE (1861), by Charles Reade. This historical novel, depicting life in the fifteenth century, was declared by Walter Besant to be the greatest historical novel in the English language. It is the story of Gerard, an artist of Holland and the father of Erasmus. Gerard plans to study for the priesthood, but falls in love with Margaret Brandt, the daughter of a humble scholar. Against the will of Elias, his father, Gerard and Margaret are betrothed. His father and his two brothers, with the aid of the burgomaster, imprison him. He manages to escape to Margaret, but is finally forced to flee the country. After many colorful adventures in Germany and Burgundy, he reaches Italy. There Gerard receives, through the deliberate cruelty of his enemies, false news of Margaret's death. He attempts suicide, is saved, and, after a period of wild living, he enters the Dominican order.

Margaret, in the meantime, gives birth to Gerard's son and awaits his return. As the months become years, she begins to despair of seeing him again. However, Gerard finally does return to Holland, where he is amazed to find Margaret alive and to learn that he has a son. Bound by his vows, he realizes that he and Margaret must live apart. The author derides the celibacy of priests by dramatically depicting the tragic separation of the lovers. Gerard does, however, settle near Margaret. She is struck by the plague and dies, and Gerard soon follows her, dying of a broken heart.

Peg Woffington (1853) is a pleasant little novel about a famous Irish actress, who helps a painter friend against his critics by sticking her head in a frame and so fooling them.

CLOUD DREAM OF THE NINE, THE (1689), by Kim Manchung. See KUWUNMONG, by Kim Manchung.

CLOUDS, THE (423 B.C.) by Aristophanes. This comedy is a brilliant piece of personal caricature as well as a biting attack on the new intellectualism of the Sophists. Strepsiades, an old man who is overwhelmed by debt, seeks out Socrates, foremost of the philosophers, desiring to be taught the art of false reasoning so that he may evade the payment of his debts by hoodwinking the judges in court. The old man is rejected by Socrates as too old and dull to learn. In his place he sends his wastrel son, Phidippides. He learns his lesson so well that he enables his father to put his creditors to rout without further ado. But then Phidippides turns on Strepsiades, gives him a sound drubbing, and proves with his new-found logic that it is just for a son to beat his father. Strepsiades has had enough and goes to burn down Socrates' "logic shop." In the comedy Socrates is unmercifully caricatured and appears like a *deus ex machina* swinging in a basket and proclaiming that he treads on air and holds converse with the clouds. Tradition has it that Socrates was in the audience when the play was presented and rose for a good-natured bow. The identification of Socrates with sophistic argumentation was completely unjustified, but helped form a popular prejudice which, as Plato makes him complain, was in the long run partly responsible for the verdict that condemned him to death.

CLOWN AND HIS DAUGHTER, THE (1936), by Xālide Edib Adivar. Xālide Edib Adivar (better known as Halide Edib; b. 1883) is the most widely known modern Turkish author. She has played an important part in the evolution of her country; because of her activities, she was exiled for almost fifteen years, living mostly in England and the United States. Hence this novel (*Sinekli Bakkal*) appeared in English a year before publication in the original Turkish.

The story takes its name from the poor section of Istanbul, Sinekli Bakkal, and reflects the conflicts of individuals in a rapidly modernized country. Kiz Tevfik, a jester and puppet player, marries Emine, daughter of the Imam of the region; the couple have one daughter, Rabia, who becomes a talented musician and interpreter of both the old and the new music. Rabia and her music teacher husband, Peregrini, have a son. Kiz Tevfik is banished by the Sultan for his outspoken jests at the regime; he is later pardoned and returns to his family. But he again falls into disfavor, and can return safely only after the Revolution of 1908 and the fall of Sultan Abdul Hamid. But he is no longer interested in politics. His major plan involves the addition of a child character to his puppet show, in honor of his grandson.

In 1942 the novel received the first prize offered by the Turkish government for modern literature. It is an excellent picture of the manners and customs of Turks during the stifling regime of the ever-suspicious Abdul Hamid. Xālide Edib Adivar is also known for her *Memoirs* (1926), the *Turkish Ordeal* (1928), and other volumes on the history of modern Turkey and the emancipation of Turkish women.

CODE OF HAMMURABI (ca. 2067 B.C.), by Hammurabi. In all Oriental research no event can compare in importance with the chance discovery of the *Code of Hammurabi* in 1902, on the site of the Acropolis of Susa which was the capital of ancient Elam in Persia. The zenith of Babylonian civilization was reached during the time of Hammurabi, who reigned supreme for 43 years (2067-2025 B.C.) over a united and highly centralized Babylonian Empire. He was a model Oriental despot with strongly benevolent inclinations toward his subjects, as can be seen in his *Code* which consists of 282 paragraphs, preceded by a Prologue and concluded by an Epilogue. His object in promulgating the *Code,* he tells us, is to insure "that the strong oppress not the weak, that the orphan and widow be protected."

The outstanding merit of the *Code* as an historical document is that it affords a contemporary insight into the cultural and social life of Babylonians some 4,000 years ago. The laws do not resolve themselves into general principles of jurisprudence; they have practical application to human conduct, social and economic relations. They deal with witchcraft, legal evidence, duties and privileges of royal servants, tenure, rents and cultivated lands, trade and commerce, deposit and prosecution for debt, family law, marriage settlements, divorce, inheritance, adoption, criminal law, slavery, care of canals and wages of architects, surgeons and boatmen.

It is to be assumed that Hammurabi did not start with a clean legal slate. He grafted his new concepts on the old, deriving from the civic institutions that had hitherto shaped people's lives. His *Code* was an adaptation, as well as the amalgam, of several systems of ancient ethics.

COLLECTED ESSAYS (1894), by Thomas Henry Huxley. See EVOLUTION AND ETHICS, by Thomas Henry Huxley.

COLLECTED POEMS (1915), by Rupert Brooke. See BROOKE, RUPERT.

COLLECTED POEMS (1933), by Hart Crane. See CRANE, HART.

COLLECTED POEMS (1938), by E. E. Cummings. See ENORMOUS ROOM, THE, by E. E. Cummings.

COLLECTED POEMS (1936), by T. S. Eliot. See ELIOT, THOMAS STEARNS.

COLLECTED POEMS (1939), by Mark Van Doren. See VAN DOREN, MARK.

COLLECTED WRITINGS (1909), by Zalman Shneiur. See SHNEIUR, ZALMAN.

COLLECTION OF TEN THOUSAND LEAVES (750). See MAN-YOSHIU, THE.

COLLEGE WIDOW, THE (1904), by George Ade. See ADE, GEORGE.

COLORED STONES (1852), by Adalbert Stifter. See LATE SUMMER, THE, by Adalbert Stifter.

COMEDY OF ERRORS, THE (1594), by William Shakespeare. This is one of Shakespeare's earliest and most rollicking comedies. Aegeon, a merchant of Syracuse, lands in Ephesus. According to the laws of that city, anyone from Syracuse is condemned to death unless he can raise a large ransom. He is looking for his son, Antipholus, and his servant, Dromio, from whom he had parted in Syracuse seven years before, when the pair went in search of their twin brothers of the same names, from whom they had been separated in infancy by shipwreck. The missing Antipholus and Dromio live in Ephesus, where the former is a most respected citizen, and married to Adriana. Both pairs of brothers are identical twins.

Antipholus and Dromio of Syracuse arrive in Ephesus, and warned by a merchant, the master says that he comes from Epidamnum, and sends his servant to the inn with money. Dromio of Ephesus is looking for his master, and, meeting Antipholus of Syracuse, tells him to come home to dinner, that his mistress is waiting. Adriana, searching for her husband, encounters Antipholus and Dromio of Syracuse, and insists on their returning to dinner. Luciana, Adriana's sister, pleads with Antipholus to be less cold to his wife, and he makes love to Luciana. Antipholus of Ephesus had ordered a gold chain for his wife, from Angelo, the goldsmith, and brings him home to dinner, only to find himself shut out by Dromio of Syracuse. Angry, he dines with a courtezan, and promises her the chain, for which she gives him a ring. Angelo gives the chain to Antipholus of Syracuse, and has Antipholus of Ephesus arrested, for refusing to pay for what he has not got. The latter sends Dromio of Ephesus to Adriana to get the money for his bail. But he delivers it to Antipholus of Syracuse.

The confusion continues until at length Antipholus and Dromio of Ephesus are bound and put in a dark cellar, and the other pair take refuge in a priory. Finally all four appear together. Aegeon, who is being led to execution, recognizes his sons. The lady abbess of the convent turns out to be Aegeon's wife, Aemilia, who had been separated from her husband and children in the shipwreck.

The plot comes from the *Menaechmi* (q.v.) of Plautus, with borrowings also from his *Amphitrio*.

COMING OF AGE IN SAMOA (1928), by Margaret Mead. See FROM THE SOUTH SEAS, by Margaret Mead.

COMMENTARIES (ca. 58–44 B.C.), by Gaius Julius Caesar. The *Commentaries on the Gallic War* are a crisp, straightforward and nontechnical third person narrative of the campaigns of the years from 58 B.C. on, in which Caesar subjugated Gaul and made it a permanent part of the Roman Empire. This general, who never lost a campaign and never left the field before an organized enemy, had little reason to exaggerate or misrepresent, except perhaps in his justification of the war. The commentary was not regarded as a polished literary form, but even Caesar's bitter enemy, Cicero, says of those *Commentaries* that, rather than providing the future historian with new material, they robbed him of all opportunity to deal with the events. Each of the first seven books covers the activities of a single year.

Book I (58 B.C.): The campaign against the Helvetii and Ariovistus. Book II (57 B.C.): Campaigns against the Belgae and maritime tribes of Normandy and Brittany. Book III (56 B.C.): Subjugation of the Veneti and submission of Aquitania. Book IV (55 B.C.): Punitive operations against the Usipetes and Tencteri; crossing of the Rhine and display of strength in Germany; first expedition to Britain. Book V (54 B.C.): Second expedition to Britain; rebellion of the Belgae. Book VI (53 B.C.): Suppression of the rebellion of the Belgae; second crossing of the Rhine. Book VII (52 B.C.): General insurrection of the Gauls under Vercingetorix; siege and capture of Alesia and consequent suppression of the rebellion. Book VIII (51–50 B.C.) was written by Aulus Histius, a staff officer, after Caesar's death. It recounts the stamping out of the remnants of the rebellion and the beginnings of Caesar's trouble with political enemies in the senate at Rome which led to the civil war.

The *Commentaries on the Civil War* between Caesar and Pompey in two books are also by Caesar's hand, but lack the finish of those on the Gallic War. They plead the justification of Caesar in taking up arms against his enemies in the state.

Book I (49 B.C.): The invasion of Italy from the crossing of the Rubicon to Pompey's abandonment of Brindisi; the defeat of Pompey's forces in Spain. Book II (48 B.C.): The campaign against Pompey in Greece and victory at Pharsalus; pursuit and death of Pompey; Alexandrian campaign and restoration of Cleopatra to the throne of Egypt.

The three *Commentaries* on the Alexandrine, African and Spanish wars are by other contemporary hands.

COMMENTARIES ON THE LAWS OF ENGLAND (1765–1769), by Sir William Blackstone. Blackstone's monumental four-volume work is a milestone in English and American jurisprudence. It contains the substance of a course of lectures which the author gave at Oxford. In it the vast mass of details which makes up the common and statute law is brought together and presented as an organic structure. The meaning of each provision is clarified and emphasized; the relations of the various parts are indicated and illustrated so that the whole body of the law appears as a living organic thing, animated by purpose, a triumph of human reason and ingenuity.

Blackstone's style is clear, eloquent and ceremonious. Jeremy Bentham, who had attended Blackstone's Oxford lectures, remarked about him that he, "first of all institutional writers, has taught jurisprudence to speak the language of the scholar and the gentleman." Perhaps this is not exactly a compliment in the evaluation of the modern reader who has democratic and idealistic notions about the philosophy of law; however, Blackstone did depart from the narrow professional Inns of Court attitude toward legal education. As a humanist, he saw the correlation of law and history, philosophy and politics. It was he who introduced into university law schools the systematic study of theoretical law as a unified, continuous and rational science. There is little doubt that in his philosophy of law he expressed the interests and ideals of the English aristocracy. He was a Tory of Tories, fully satisfied with the superior virtue of English law over all others. Bentham was very bitter about his smugness and reactionary tendencies. It may be said that this stimulated Bentham's movement for utilitarian legal reform.

In the United States, as in England, Blackstone's *Commentaries* have exercised a profound influence on law. It had a significant historical effect on the course of events following the Declaration of Independence. The radicals, led by Thomas Jefferson, wanted to adopt French laws, but the conservatives, under the political whip of Alexander Hamilton, fell back on Blackstone's toryism and won the battle. However, under the pressure of the American people's will, the evolution of our laws has been progressive and democratic, slowly departing from Blackstone's upper-class jurisprudence.

COMMENTARIOLUS (ca. 1529), by Nicolaus Copernicus. See DE REVOLUTIONIBUS ORBIUM COELESTIUM, by Nicolaus Copernicus.

COMMENTARY ON THE MISHNAH (1168), by Maimonides. See GUIDE FOR THE PERPLEXED, THE, by Maimonides.

COMMODORE'S DAUGHTERS, THE (1886), by Jonas Lie. This is one of the best known works of Jonas Lie, the founder of the modern Norwegian novel. The Commodore, an old sea dog, is an enemy of convention. Fru Jutta, his frivolous wife, idolizes their foppish son Karsten, a naval lieutenant. She neglects her charming daughters, Cecilie and Martha, whose misadventures in love form the story of the novel. Cecilie, beautiful and confiding, wins the love of Lieutenant Fasting, a worthy young man. Her reprobate brother, however, casts suspicion upon the motives of his fellow officer. Cecilie, easily frightened, avoids Fasting, although she still loves him. Fasting, bewildered by her apparently coquettish conduct, ceases his attentions. Cecilie finally realizes her mistake, but is unsuccessful in winning back Fasting, who marries one of her friends, breaking Cecilie's heart. Martha loves her cousin Jan, a poor relation who lives with her family. Fru Jutta disapproves of their affection, and forces Jan to leave on a long journey. Martha bears his child, and when Fru Jutta learns of her daughter's condition, she sends her to Germany in order to avoid scandal. There Martha's child is born, and there she leaves him to be reared by a foster-mother. Back in Norway, she receives news of her baby only once in every three months. Not until Martha is dying does Fru Jutta send for the child, Jan. Martha bequeaths her son to Cecilie in hope that the bleak emptiness of her sister's life may be somewhat relieved by the love of the child.

Some critics regard *The Family at Gilje* (1883) as Lie's outstanding novel. It is a strong tale of tragic parental practicality, drunkenness, disappointed love, and resignation.

COMMON SENSE (1776), by Thomas Paine. This celebrated treatise, the first complete defense for political independence of the colonies, electrified its readers. The pamphlet, which sold the then amazing number of 120,000 copies in three months, was viewed by Washington, Jefferson, and other leaders of the American cause as an indispensable aid in the forging of independence. *Common Sense* attacks the institution of monarchy, denies the adaptability of the English constitution to conditions prevailing in the American colonies, and extols the economic advantages for the American people inherent in independence. It laid the foundation for The Declaration of Independence (q.v.), which appeared six months later. The pamphlet is divided into four arguments: "Of the Origin and Design of Government in General," "Of Monarchy and Hereditary Succession," "Thoughts on the Present State of American Affairs," and "Of the Present Ability of America, with some Miscellaneous Reflections."

Paine, the son of an English corsetmaker, dismissed exciseman and bankrupt, was aided by Benjamin Franklin to start fresh in Philadelphia. *Common Sense* made his fame. As a Continental soldier, he wrote *The American Crisis* (1776–1783), a sixteen-pamphlet sequence defending the Revolution. "These are the times that try men's souls," began Paine, during a gloomy period of the fight. Washington had the inspiring work read before all his men. It was an influence on the Trenton and Princeton victories, boosted morale, and militated against compromise.

The Rights of Man (1791–1792) was Thomas Paine's response to Edmund Burke's aristocratic fulminations against democracy. It led to his conviction by England for treason, and to a new British law against seditious writing. Dedicated to Washington, it affirms that power is granted by an ever-changing majority vote, that the goal of the state is freedom for the individual, and that happiness is the natural right of all men.

The Age of Reason (1794–1795) is a deistic work, although it brought upon its author the charge of atheism. Its writing was interrupted by a prison sentence in France. *The Age of Reason* proves the existence of God by philosophical arguments, but brands the *Bible* (q.v.) and religious institutions as enslaving devices. Religious man's goal is to imitate the beneficent God who exists everywhere in the world. But beyond mere good will, Paine pointed out, positive social action is a citizen's obligation.

COMMON SENSE BOOK OF BABY AND CHILD CARE, THE (1945), by Benjamin Spock. See SPOCK, BENJAMIN.

COMMUNIST MANIFESTO, THE (1848), by Karl Marx and Friedrich Engels. As a document the *Manifesto* is the most concise and influential statement of Marxism. It is written with epigrammatic force and literary skill. Published on the eve of the epidemic of social revolutions in Europe in 1848, it was designed as a program for the Communist League, a workers' organization, which, although German at first, soon achieved international scope. The *Manifesto* embodied the materialistic conception of history evolved by its authors. It states its thesis with the directness of a challenge: "The history of all hitherto existing societies is the history of class struggles." It then attempts to array all historical proof for such a theory, finally bringing it down to nineteenth century capitalistic Europe, arguing that even as the bourgeois revolution destroyed feudalism, so in its turn capitalism would be displaced by a workers' society. This, the authors stated, was an historical inevitability: "The proletarian movement is the self-conscious, independent movement of the immense majority, in the interest of the immense majority." According to the *Manifesto,* the Communists were the most advanced and determined section of all working class parties, "that section which pushes forward all others." Their aim was the "abolition of private property." Just as the first step of the bourgeois revolution was the overthrow of the feudal power, so the later proletarian revolution would strive "to raise the proletariat to the position of ruling class, to win the battle of democracy." Most dramatic is the *Manifesto*'s introductory sentence: "A spectre is haunting Europe," and equally apocalyptic are its concluding words: "The workers have nothing to lose but their chains; they have a whole world to gain. Workers of all countries, unite." *The Communist Manifesto* has gone through countless editions, and has been translated into almost all languages.

COMPLEAT ANGLER, THE (1653), by Izaak Walton. Walton was sixty years old when he published his *Compleat Angler.* Although it is ostensibly a guide for gentlemen fishermen, written in the form of a dialogue, in reality it is a quaint, whimsical, meditative book about Walton. "The whole discourse is a kind of picture of my own disposition, at least of my disposition in such days and times as I allow myself when honest Nat and R. R. and I go a-fishing together." He begins with a debate between an angler, a falconer and a hunter, on the relative merits of their recreations. He characteristically ends with St. Paul's advice, "Study to be quiet." In 1676 Charles Cotton added a supplement on trout fishing.

Charles Lamb recommended the work enthusiastically to Coleridge: ". . . it breathes the very spirit of innocence, purity, and simplicity of heart; . . . it would sweeten a man's temper at any time to read it; it would Christianise every angry, discordant passion. . . ." It is not hard to explain why, through several centuries, schoolboys and scholars, poets and philosophers alike, have read Walton's unique work.

"I write not for money, but for pleasure," declared the amiable author. Accordingly, *The Compleat Angler* is replete with delightful extravaganzas and whimsical fancies. Walton believed, or so he pretended, that fish could hear; if they do, their vocabulary must be hideous with awful curses of impatient anglers. "God is said to have spoken to a fish, but never to a beast," he proudly declares. Logically then, he comes to the conclusions that anglers are superior people and that their pastime "is somewhat like poetry: men are to be born so."

Walton's "practical" advice to anglers is not of much worth. It is rather as a unique literary personality that he is cherished today, as an erudite, benevolent old soul who loved philosophy and poetry as much as he loved fish, and who, whenever he went fishing, took a book along with him.

COMPOTUS (composed ca. 1232 or 1244; printed ca. 1538) by Joannes de Sacrobosco. See SPHAERA MUNDI, by Joannes de Sacrobosco.

COMUS (1634), by John Milton. A masque, presented at Ludlow Castle in honor of John Egerton, Earl of Bridgewater, it first introduces the Attendant Spirit, whose duty it is to watch over the offspring of that noble peer. Hearing footsteps, he steps aside, invisible, to watch the dance of Comus and his rout of monsters. The dance breaks off when the Lady approaches; the monsters slip away. The Lady tells Comus, disguised as a villager, that she has been separated from her brothers. He promises to lead her to them, and she goes with him. The brothers then appear, searching, the Second Brother pessimistic, the Elder Brother philosophical, and are met by the Attendant Spirit, now disguised as Thyrsis, their father's shepherd. He tells them of their sister's abduction by Comus. They start after him, first receiving instruction from Thyrsis about breaking magic spells. They find their enchanted sister eloquently resisting Comus, and rush upon him, but he escapes. Thyrsis calls up the Nymph Sabrina, who breaks the charm Comus has placed on the Lady. The children are then presented to their parents, and the Spirit epilogizes to the effect that Virtue alone is free and strong, but that Heaven would help her even if she were feeble.

Lawes wrote the music and acted the Attendant Spirit. The story was supplied partly by Peele's *Old Wives Tale* and partly by Milton's own imagination embroidering the Circle myth. It is a splendid poem, and there are some who consider it, for length and poetical quality together, as fine as anything Milton ever wrote.

Among Milton's best-known shorter poems "L'Allegro" and "Il Penseroso" (published 1645) contrast two ways of life, or two moods. After the opening lines beginning respectively, "Hence, loathed Melancholy" and "Hence, vain deluding joys," the poems are in tetrameter couplets. As *the cheerful man* Milton enjoys country scenes and folk pastimes in the day and "tow'red cities" at night, where a play of Jonson's or Shakespeare's may be given. As *the contemplative man* he likes the time after curfew for reading. In the daytime he seeks the shade, and in old age hopes for a "peaceful hermitage."

Milton wrote occasional sonnets, of which three are outstanding. "When I consider how my light is spent" seeks consolation for his blindness. "On the Late Massacre in Piedmont" carries the thunder of the poet's indignation, while "Methought I saw my late espoused Saint" is tender over the phantom of his deceased wife.

CONCEPT OF NATURE, THE (1920), by A. N. Whitehead. See WHITEHEAD, ALFRED NORTH.

CONCERNING METALS (1556), by Georgius Agricola. See DE RE METALLICA, by Georgius Agricola.

CONDE LUCANOR, EL (1335), by Juan Manuel. See COUNT LUCANOR, by Juan Manuel.

CONDEMNED FOR MISTRUSTFULNESS (1635), by Tirso de Molina (Gabriel Téllez). This has been called "the most perfect theological play ever written." It is, indeed, one of the first "thesis plays" of modern times, illustrating the conflict between free will and predestination: "that a single mortal sin of which the sinner refuses to repent entails eternal damnation, but a single act of sincere contrition effaces all sins and wins salvation."

For ten years the hermit Paulo has lived in penance in the fastnesses of the mountains, resisting all temptations except that of pride. He feels that because of the rigor and purity of his life he deserves eternal salvation. On one occasion the devil appears to him in the guise of an angel, and tells him that he will have the same fate as a certain Enrico, who lives in Naples. Certain that this Enrico is a paragon of saintliness, Paulo goes immediately to Naples. However, upon finding that Enrico is a wicked man, guilty of all crimes, Paulo distrusts divine justice, loses all hope of being saved, and takes to a bandit's life. An angel in the guise of a shepherd visits him, advising him to repent and to trust God. To no avail. Whereas Enrico repents before his death, confesses all his sins and is saved, Paulo, mortally wounded in battle, loses his soul as he dies bereft of faith, refusing, in his pride, to confess his sins.

CONDENADO POR DISCONFIADO (1635), by Tirso de Molina. See CONDEMNED FOR MISTRUSTFULNESS, by Tirso de Molina.

CONDITION OF MAN, THE (1944), by Lewis Mumford. See TECHNICS AND CIVILIZATION, by Lewis Mumford.

CONDUCT OF LIFE, THE (1860), by Ralph Waldo Emerson. See ESSAYS, by Ralph Waldo Emerson.

CONFESSIO AMANTIS (1386–1393), by John Gower. There are more than a hundred stories of various lengths included in this poem of 33,000 lines. The seven sins—Pride, Envy, Wrath, Sloth, Avarice, Gluttony and Lechery—make the divisions, with an additional book between the latter two. Gower's purity of English style and graceful fluency of expression exerted a marked influence on the development of the English language. He was also the author of Latin and French poems. Sidney, in his *Apology for Poetry,* ranked Gower as equal with Chaucer, but he is important today mainly for historical reasons.

CONFESSION, A (1879), by Count Leo Tolstoy. This, the most important of Tolstoy's autobiographical writings, is conceded by critics to be a confessional masterpiece which will bear comparison with the most famous ever penned. Beginning with the sentence, "I was baptized and brought up in the Orthodox Christian faith," the author proceeds to give some account of his own life, his early moral and religious training, and how he came to lapse from the faith in which he had been trained. The chief cause, he explains, was in the fact that what was taught him was at complete variance with practice. Members of his own family, he says, winked and even approved of departures from the moral code; indeed, such departures were generally accepted in his social circle. He recalls those years with "horror, loathing, and heartache," years in which "I killed men in war, and challenged men to duels in order to kill them; I lost money at cards, consumed the labour of the peasants, sentenced them to punishments, lived loosely and deceived people." There was no crime he did not commit—he mentions "lying, adultery of all kinds, drunkenness, violence, murder"—and for all that, he claims, people praised his conduct and considered him "a comparatively moral man." He proceeds to describe his gradual awakening from this, the realization of the wrongness of his life, and his quest of the truth.

This book gains importance from the fact that Tolstoy widens his inquiry by passing from himself to the world in general; and he finds that it is all one problem, that it involves all, and that there is no solution but in living up to the Christian moral laws. The Jesus that Tolstoy has in mind and whose law he invokes, is human rather than divine. Tolstoy's *Confession* speaks, with the voice of a prophet and in the language of a great artist, of the ills of our age

In *What I Believe* (1884) Tolstoy has written a sequel to *A Confession*. It is on a less personal plane, and is more of a sermon than a work of art. The author examines the teaching of the Gospel, the command of non-resistance, the law of God and the law of man, misunderstanding of Christ's teaching, Jesus and the Mosaic law. He criticizes the Church, which he declares dead, and exhorts men to follow the teaching of Christ. "I believe," he writes, "that my welfare in the world will only be possible when all men fulfill Christ's teaching, and practice non-resistance."

CONFESSION OF A FOOL, THE (1887–1888), by August Strindberg. *The Confession of a Fool* is the record of Strindberg's jealousy mania. It chronicles the course of his first marriage, to Siri von Essen, a relationship which endured precariously from 1877 to 1892. Strindberg wrote this book out of malice and exhibitionism. The last words in *The Confession* are: "This book, Beloved, is my revenge." He even wrote a little jingle about it:

> There hangs in the book-store window,
> A thin-clad little book.
> It is a torn heart bleeding
> Which dangles on its hook.

When his friends upbraided him for his callousness, Strindberg confessed: "This is a terrible book. I fully admit it, for I regret that I ever wrote it. How did I write it? Because I felt under a powerful and justifiable compulsion to wash my corpse before it was laid in the coffin forever." *The Confession* bristles with suspicions of infidelity, plots and counter-plots, all products of the author's imagination. Even during his courtship of his wife, he suspected that she was unfaithful to him. After his marriage, his love gradually began to contend against a loathing for her which he could not conceal. He was facile in building up a rationale for this transformation of his feelings. He found the most biased and the most bizarre proofs to confirm his suspicions. He stopped at nothing: he became an eavesdropper, secretly read his wife's correspondence, and finally turned detective to track down her alleged infidelities. The climax to this nightmarish story came when he tried to strangle her and drown her and their children "like kittens." Siri, according to her husband's accusation, went far beyond her original objective: to make a wretched cuckold of him. She plotted to draw his friends away from him by all sorts of diabolical machinations, and finally he began to suspect that she was planning to have him committed to an insane asylum. Strindberg had a clear idea of what was happening inside his sick brain: "She triumphed. I was on the verge of insanity, and the first symptoms of persecution mania showed themselves. Mania? Did I say mania? I was being persecuted; there was nothing irrational in the thought."

CONFESSIONS (ca. 400), by St. Augustine (Aurelius Augustinus). "Confession of sin all know," declared St. Augustine, "but confession of praise few attend to. . . . The former but showeth the wound to the physician, the latter giveth thanks for health." This, in brief, expresses the aim of Augustine in writing his *Confessions*. It treats of his deep religious experiences against a background of personal unhappiness and moral conflict. The work created a new literary genre: the confessional autobiography. Its main object, however, was a defense of the Latin Church against the heretical sects of his day. The author had in mind the Roman intellectuals whom he was eager to win over from paganism. He also wished that his book might serve as a source of spiritual edification to his brethren in their evangelical labors. He commented ruefully upon the onesidedness and aridity of contemporary intellectualism: "Men desire to learn the rules of learning, but neglect the eternal rules of everlasting salvation." The early chapters of the *Confessions* are extraordinarily moving. Augustine was a great man who could expose his weaknesses and errors without attempting to justify them. He had a sensitive, probing mind, a philosophical passion for objective truth. His work breathes a devotional and penitential mood. In his early years he had fallen into licentious habits. Although he had an avid desire for learning, and even wrote Latin treatises on the arts and on the *Categories* of Aristotle in his twenties, he had lacked a unifying world view. His love of pleasure, which had manifested itself since his boyhood, was constantly opposed to his guilty conscience, which craved a spiritual reality. After stubbornly resisting the preaching of St. Ambrose, Augustine finally accepted Christian baptism at his hands in his thirty-second year. The rest of the *Confessions* (Books X–XIII) is an apologia for the Roman Church. He examines and illuminates the Scriptural texts with the dialectical skill and learning he had formerly lavished on his Aristotelian commentaries. He attempts to expose the contradictions and untenable doctrines of the Christian sects regarded by the Latin Church as heretical. The *Confessions* is one of the foundation stones of Catholicism.

CONFESSIONS (1781–1788), by Jean Jacques Rousseau. Rousseau's *Confessions* inaugurated a new school of autobiographic literature based on an attempt at scrupulously honest self-analysis. Whether he succeeded in being candid in this work is open to question. Sometimes he is over-facile in justifying his "misdeeds." The very fact that he, Rousseau, a great and wise man, should fearlessly lay his soul bare regardless of the consequences, fills him with childish pride: "I undertake an unexampled enterprise, the execution of which can never be imitated." Regardless of the motive, Rousseau's *Confessions* is an extraordinary portrait of a genius who was not a fraction as lovable or as noble as he fondly thought he was, but a vain, jealous, calculating individual. To his credit it must be remembered that this is only one aspect of his baffling, contradictory character—that he also struggled for a free world, championed intellectual freedom and social responsibility and justice. The *Confessions* was written when Rousseau was already middle-aged, some parts going back to his childhood forty years before, and his memory was not trustworthy. He was sick, and possibly a little insane. His *Confessions* frequently document his philosophical works, furnish a fascinating view of people he loved or hated—Hume, Voltaire, Diderot, Grimm, Mme. d'Houditot, etc.—and contain passages of great lyric beauty; they are more readable than many novels.

CONFESSIONS OF AN ENGLISH OPIUM EATER (1822), by Thomas De Quincey. Starvation as a youth in Wales and London brought on a gastric ailment from which De Quincey suffered great physical pain. First neuralgia, then this, led him to take opium in large doses. He describes his nightmare experiences while under the influence of the drug, and his tremendous struggle to conquer the habit when he realized it threatened his life. The gradual reduction of his dosage was in itself a torture, but he was finally successful in freeing himself from the habit. He felt superior, in this respect, to Coleridge. Part I is straight autobiography, dealing with a runaway youth's struggles, and ending with his poignant story of the prostitute Ann, the dear friend he won and lost in London. Part II is entitled "The Pleasures of Opium"; Part III, "The Pains of Opium." De Quincey is a superb if feverish stylist here, without rival in the English language as a describer of fantastic dreams. He was, in other writings, a great critic and a leader in the Romantic movement.

CONGO, THE (1914), by Vachel Lindsay. See LINDSAY, VACHEL.

CONICS (ca. 225 B.C.), by Apollonius of Perga. See TREATISE ON CONIC SECTIONS, by Apollonius of Perga.

CONISTON (1906), by Winston Churchill. See RICHARD CARVEL, by Winston Churchill.

CONNECTICUT YANKEE IN KING ARTHUR'S COURT, A (1889), by Mark Twain. See INNOCENTS ABROAD, THE, by Mark Twain.

CONQUEROR, THE (1902), by Gertrude Atherton. See ATHERTON, GERTRUDE.

CONQUERORS, THE (1928), by André Malraux. See MAN'S FATE, by André Malraux.

CONQUESTS OF XERXES, THE (Eng. tr. 1930), by Louis Couperus. See COUPERUS, LOUIS.

CONQUISTADOR (1932), by Archibald MacLeish. See MACLEISH, ARCHIBALD.

CONSCIOUS LOVERS, THE (produced 1722), by Richard Steele. Steele's last play is a well-known "sentimental comedy." As he did in many of the *Tatler* and *Spectator* essays, Steele here satirizes dueling, cold-blooded marriage compacts, and foolish family pride. Sir John wishes his son, Bevil, to marry Lucinda, the daughter of Sealand, a wealthy Indian merchant. Lucinda is loved by Myrtle, a friend of Bevil's, and Bevil's affections are engaged by Indiana, a poor girl whom he has rescued from want, and who depends on his bounty. Mrs. Sealand is anxious to have her daughter marry Cimberton, a coxcomb. To please his father, Bevil promises to marry Lucinda, but plots to avoid it. He finally tells Lucinda he is averse to marrying her, and Myrtle, misunderstanding his motives, challenges him to a duel. Bevil refuses, and in his speech on this occasion Steele is able to express his own thoughts on dueling. Indiana turns out to be Sealand's daughter by his first wife. When this is discovered Sealand is happy to marry her to Bevil. Cimberton abandons his suit when Lucinda's dowry is shared by Indiana, and Myrtle and Lucinda are united.

CONSERVATION OF FORCE, ON THE (1847), by Hermann Helmholtz. The nineteenth century often is characterized in the history of science as the "century of correlation." Of the numerous correlating theories—the cellular theory, the germ theory of disease, the theory of evolution, and others—perhaps none had more far-reaching significance than the law of the conservation of energy, enunciated in full generality by Helmholtz in his *Conservation of Force*. Helmholtz was not the original discoverer of the law. Conservation theorems are perhaps as old as science itself, and "nihil ex nihilo" was one of the assumptions underlying Greek thought. Descartes in 1644 asserted the quantitative invariance of motion in the universe; Galileo in 1638 explained the principles of the pendulum and inclined plane in terms of the conservation of kinetic energy under elastic impact; and Daniel Bernoulli in 1738 asserted that this principle was valid for all situations, terrestrial and celestial. The difficulty at the time with all general theorems of conservation was that they were justified only by faith in the unity of nature, not by experimental evidence. On numerous occasions it had been suggested that heat was a form of motion, but only in 1798 was a rough mechanical equivalent of heat calculated by Count Rumford. More accurate estimates of the interconvertibility of heat and work were made by half a dozen men in the crucial decade from 1837 to 1847. Mohr, Grove, Séguin, Colding and Mayer did their work from 1837 to 1842. Mayer was the first person to publish a clear-cut statement that heat and work are qualitatively different forms of something—Helmholtz called it force, but now it is known as energy—which is quantitatively invariant, and to give a reasonably accurate value of the mechanical equivalent of heat derived from experimental data. Independent and more accurate determinations were made from 1843 to 1847 by Joule, but the principle neverthless failed to carry conviction until Helmholtz published *Conservation of Force*. Helmholtz was a physiologist who wished to banish from biology the concept of "vital force," and hence he sought to measure the heat produced in muscles during chemical changes. From such studies, he was first led to the conservation of energy. However, the many-sided Helmholtz was also a physicist and mathematician, and so he sought to establish the law upon a sound postulational basis. He found the necessary first principles in the impossibility of perpetual motion and Newton's third law of motion. Through an elaborated mathematical discussion, he showed that all the known cases of the transformation of energy could be traced back to these principles, and from them Helmholtz deduced the law which he called "The Conservation of Force." It thus was his classic treatise which made the conservation of energy scientifically acceptable.

CONSOLATIONS OF PHILOSOPHY, THE (ca. 523), by Amicius Manlius Severinus Boëthius. Boëthius lived at a transitional point between two historical epochs—the ancient and the medieval. He was a great scholar, and a reverent student of Greek philosophy. He is best remembered for his *Consolations*, which he wrote in the prison at Pavia while awaiting his execution at the hands of Theodoric. Its five books have been characterized as "the last work of Roman literature." Book I tells of a vision the philosopher had. A woman appeared before him, holding a book in one hand and a scepter in the other. She offers him the promise of solace. He recognizes her; she is his lifelong companion—

Philosophy. He pours out to her his tale of woe, and she listens with sympathy. In Book II Philosophy upbraids Boëthius for his foolish ambition to achieve eminence as a statesman and philosopher, showing that greatness has no enduring value. In Book III there is a discussion of the Supreme Good. The conclusion is that it does not consist of riches, power or pleasure, but that it resides in God. In Book IV the problems of evil and the freedom of the will come under scrutiny. The subject of the freedom of the will is further pursued in the fifth and final book, and is reconciled with predestination. In the ninth century Alfred the Great translated the book into Anglo-Saxon. Chaucer made an English translation which was published by Caxton in 1480.

CONSTANT NYMPH, THE (1924), by Margaret Kennedy. This is the story of a family of sensitive, freedom-loving children and their defeat by conventional society. Albert Sanger, a musician, has seven children: Kate, Caryl, Antonia, Teresa, Paulina, Sebastian, and Susan. They have all inherited his brilliant, erratic spirit. His death ends their bohemian life in the Tyrol, and they are separated by guardians. An English composer, Lewis Dodd, an Austrian millionaire, and some wealthy English cousins attempt to fit the children to their own patterns of life. The story centers on Tessa, a sensitive girl of fourteen who finds herself unable to adapt herself to the restrictions of an English boarding school, or to forget her love for Lewis, who has married her English cousin, Florence Churchill. Lewis, a sensitive musician, soon finds his life with the conventional Florence unbearable, and discovers too late that he really loves Tessa. The two elope to Brussels, but Tessa suffers a heart attack on the way and dies shortly after they arrive. Her death in a poor and ugly room in a lonely town is symbolic of the tragedy of their futile escape.

CONSTITUTION OF ATHENS (ca. 329 B.C.), by Aristotle. In preparing to write his *Politics* (q.v.), Aristotle made a study of the constitutions of some 158 Greek city-states. The *Constitution of Athens* is one of the by-products of this study. The first forty-one chapters are a concise sketch of the constitutional and political history of the Athenian state down to Aristotle's own time. The remaining twenty-eight chapters give a detailed account of the constitution as it was operative in the fourth century B.C. There was, of course, no written constitution of Athens, and what Aristotle describes are the executive, legislative and judicial institutions through which and under which Athenian democracy functioned. In the historical section he describes the evolution of these institutions from the time of the legislation of Draco. This work was known only by title and through a condensation until 1891, when the full text was published from a papyrus found in Egypt. Even so, the beginning and end of the work are still missing. It is unquestionably the most important document on Greek history discovered in modern times.

CONTE DEL GRAAL (12th c.), by Chrétien de Troyes. Chrétien's version of the quest for the Grail is the story of the youth and knighthood of Perceval, sheltered son of a widowed mother. One day he sees some knights and wants to follow them. Fearing the dangers he must run, his mother first resists, and then lets him off only after she has outfitted him in ludicrous leather and linen, in hopes that the ridicule he will meet will discourage his ardor. But the boy gradually learns the ways of knighthood and at last achieves his heart's desire: he is knighted and instructed in charity and piety. New adventures teach him true love—he rescues a distressed damsel—and eventually take him to the castle of the Fisher King. There he sees pass in procession a wonderful sword, a lance dripping blood, a ten-branched candelabrum, and at last, carried by a maiden, the mysterious Grail itself.

Chrétien veils the Grail in mystery, fills his poem with symbols and hidden meanings, imbues everything with chivalric idealism. He died without finishing this work, but poets from Gaucher de Denain to Richard Wagner have tried their hands at completing it. Written in Champenois French by a very skilled and sophisticated court poet, Chrétien's Grail story ranks with his version of the Tristram tale as the best treatment in French of the Arthurian materials.

CONTEMPORARIES (1885–1889; additional volume 1918), by Jules Lemaître. Lemaître, one of the eminent French literary critics and dramatists at the turn of the century, possessed an oblique satirical manner which won for him a horde of friends and no few enemies. His eight volumes of literary portraits, *Contemporaries,* built up the permanent reputation of many French writers and destroyed that of others. He was unorthodox, and passionately attached to modern literature. Particularly important are his studies of Anatole France, Renan, Huysmans, Maupassant, Leconte de Lisle, Alphonse Daudet, the Goncourt brothers, Gaston Paris, Paul Bourget, Mérimée, Verlaine and Mallarmé. His adversaries, however, argued that Lemaître was a "mere impressionist," whose judgments were unsupported by solid critical standards. His theatrical criticisms, less permanent in value but immensely influential in their time, have been collected in *Theatrical Impressions.*

CONTEMPORARY AMERICAN NOVELISTS, 1900–1920 (1922), by Carl Van Doren. See Van Doren, Carl.

CONTEMPORARY JAPANESE LITERATURE (1939). This book, published in Tokyo, includes eighty-four selections by sixty-nine modern Japanese writers, the most important of whom are Natsume Soseki (1866–   ), represented by "Botchan" (Young Scions of the Wealthy Intelligentsia), and Akutagawa Ryunosuke (1892–1927), with his "Hokyonin no Shi" (Death of a Christian). Japan's war era began early in the 1930's. One of the first conscious elaborations of the martial spirit was the novel, *Japan Arises,* by Nooki Misoko, published in 1932. During the war years, Japanese readers were given mostly this sort of propaganda literature. Other writers in the collection are: Kinikida Doppo, "Shuchu Nikki" (Wine-Soaked Diary); Takahama Kyoshi, "Furyu Seppo" (Romantic Confession); Mori Ogai, "Kamen" (Mask); Iwano Homei, "Tandeki" (Indulgence); Nagatsuka Takashi, "Tsuchi" (Earth); Kikuchi Kan, "Chichi Kaeru" (The Father's Return); Uno Koji, "Kura no Naka" (In a Storehouse); Chikamatsu Shuko, "Korokami" (Black Hair); Tsubota Joji, "Obake no Sokai" (The World of Ghosts); Uni Chiyo, "Io Zange" (Love Confession); Shimaki Kensaku, "Rai" (Leprosy); Yamamoto Yuzo, "Onna no Issho" (Life of a Woman); Tanikaki Jun Inhiro, "Tade Ku Mushi" (Tastes Will Differ).

A discussion of these writers can be found in *Tomorrow* magazine, May, 1945: "The Japanese Mind Is Sick," by Younghill Kang. A few of the writers have been published in English in *The Cannery Boat,* by Takiji Kobayashi and others (1933).

CONTES, by Jean de La Fontaine. See FABLES IN VERSE, by Jean de La Fontaine.

CONVERSATION (1940), by Conrad Aiken. See AIKEN, CONRAD.

COPLAS POR LAS MUERTE DE SU PADRE (1476), by Jorge Manrique. See STANZAS UPON THE DEATH OF HIS FATHER, by Jorge Manrique.

CORINNE (1807), by Madame de Staël. See DELPHINE, by Madame de Staël.

CORIOLANUS (probably 1608), by William Shakespeare. Shakespeare took his material from the life of Coriolanus in Plutarch. The action covers a period of about four years. The main scene is Rome, where the hungry people have revolted, and are asking for corn. Menenius Agrippa, a patrician, pacifies them, but Caius Marcius, a soldier, who despises the rabble, addresses them scornfully. Two tribunes are elected by the people to speak for them, Sicinius Velutus and Junius Brutus. The Volscians are in arms, and Caius Marcius is one of the generals sent against them. Both tribunes dislike Marcius and think his pride will be his undoing. Tullus Aufidius, General of the Volscians, and an old enemy of Marcius, holds the city of Corioles. Marcius captures it, covering himself with glory. He returns to Rome triumphant, and is given the surname of Coriolanus. The Senate proposes to make him Consul, but first he must show himself to the citizens in the Forum, humbly dressed, exhibit his wounds, and ask for their voices. He stirs up resentment by his haughty, overbearing manner, and reluctance to comply with this custom. Sicinius and Brutus inflame the people against him, saying that if he is elected Consul he will take away their liberty. Coriolanus, who is incapable of flattery or compromise, is finally banished. He goes to Corioles in disguise and offers his services to Aufidius, who receives him as a friend, giving him a joint command in his army. They march on Rome and sweep everything before them, but Aufidius becomes jealous of Coriolanus.

Emissaries come to Coriolanus from Rome, begging him not to sack the city, but he is deaf to them all, even his old friend, Menenius. As a last resort his mother, Volumnia, his wife, Virgilia, and their son come, dressed in mourning. He listens to Volumnia's entreaties and agrees to make peace between Rome and the Volscians. He returns triumphant to the Volscian city of Antium, but Aufidius has plotted his downfall. Aufidius accuses him of being a traitor, and of having made a disgraceful peace with Rome. Finally he incites the Volscians to rise against Coriolanus, and they, remembering him as a former enemy, fall upon him and kill him.

CORNET CHRISTOPHER RILKE, TALE OF LOVE AND DEATH OF (1906), by Rainer Maria Rilke. See RILKE, RAINER MARIA.

CORVO, IL (1761), by Carlo Gozzi. See GOZZI, CARLO.

COSMOS (1845–1858), by Alexander von Humboldt. See KOSMOS, by Alexander von Humboldt.

COSSACKS, THE (1852–1853), by Count Leo Tolstoy. Such an informed and discerning critic as D. D. Mirsky considers *The Cossacks* to be Tolstoy's masterpiece before *War and Peace* (q.v.). Though written in the years 1852–1853, it was not actually published until 1863, to enable its author to pay some gambling debts. It is probable that the cultured nobleman Olenin, a volunteer in the army, who lives in a Cossack village and observes the life of its inhabitants, is something of a self-portrait. The free, natural lives of the villagers are contrasted with the cultivated self-conscious personality of Olenin, to the latter's disadvantage. They do all the things which are condemned as sins in a civilized community—without a guilty conscience. The portraits are wholly objective, and, apart from their indubitable artistic quality, are interesting as a record of Cossack life in the Caucasus in the middle of the nineteenth century.

COSTUMES BY EROS (1928), by Conrad Aiken. See AIKEN, CONRAD.

COTTER'S SATURDAY NIGHT, THE (1785), by Robert Burns. The poem, in Spenserian stanzas, among the most beloved in the English language, presents an idyllic picture of family life in rural Scotland. Writing partly in English and partly in Scots, the poet says in his salutation:

> "To you I sing in simple Scottish lays,
> The lowly train in life's sequester'd scene;
> The native feelings strong, the guileless ways."

The family is described as living in perfect harmony, with emphasis on the genuine human values as contrasted with wealth and social rank. These are the pure affections of the youth:

> "O happy love! where love like this is found!"

Finally the family becomes the occasion for a patriotic hymn to Scotland:

> "O Scotia! my dear, my native soil!
> For whom my warmest wish to Heaven is sent!
> Long may thy hardy sons of rustic toil
> Be blest with health, and peace, and sweet content!"

COUNT LUCANOR (1335), by Juan Manuel. The masterpiece of medieval Spanish prose is a collection of apologues or moral tales, *El Conde Lucanor* by Juan Manuel (1282–1349), a nephew of the learned King Alfonso X. Conversant with the Arabic language and literature, Juan Manuel in his *El Conde Lucanor* imitated a typical "framing tale," so common among the Arabs, which holds together numerous short stories within one general narrative. The young Count Lucanor seeks advice from his old counselor Patronio, who inevitably remembers a tale or a fable, which he thereupon relates, and derives a moral applicable to the situation. Some of the fables derive from Aesop or Phaedrus; some of the tales from the *Arabian Nights* or remote Oriental sources; others come from the folklore of Europe at large or from Spanish history. *El Conde Lucanor* has been widely read since the fourteenth century, and a great many of its tales are widely known under different guises in some of the world's classics. For instance, Example 32, "Wherein is told what happened to a King with the weavers who wove the cloth" reads like a primitive version of Hans Christian

Andersen's "The Emperor's New Clothes"; Example 35, "Wherein is told what happened to a young man who married a very strong and very wrathful woman," contains the gist of *The Taming of the Shrew* (q.v.) and at least four examples (2, 5, 6 and 7) are quite familiar to the reader of La Fontaine as "The Miller, His Son and the Ass," "The Crow and the Fox," "The Lark and Her Young," and "The Milk-Maid and Her Pail." Despite the awkwardness of the framework and the crudity of certain stories, *El Conde Lucanor* is an engaging, vivacious work, quite reminiscent of *The Decameron* (q.v.), though it must be remembered that Juan Manuel compiled his collection in 1323–1335, some thirteen to twenty years before Boccaccio.

COUNT OF MONTE CRISTO, THE (1845), by Alexandre Dumas, *père*. *The Count of Monte Cristo,* one of the most popular romances of the fertile Dumas *père,* is also the only one of his stories to be placed in modern times. Edmond Dantès, a young sailor unjustly accused of helping the exiled Napoleon in 1815, has been arrested and imprisoned in the Chateau d'If, near Marseille. After fifteen years, he finally escapes by taking the place of his dead companion, the Abbé Faria; enclosed in a sack, he is thrown into the sea. He cuts the sack with his knife, swims to safety, is taken to Italy on a fisherman's boat. From Genoa, he goes to the cavern of Monte Cristo and digs up the fabulous treasures of which the dying Faria had told. He then uses the money to punish his enemies and reward his friends.

COUNTERFEITERS, THE (1926), by André Gide. This book, Gide's only attempt at a full-length novel, centers upon the character of Edouard, who represents the author. Edouard is writing a novel, and his search for knowledge, particularly in a group of his own adolescent relatives, is an artificial arrangement for displaying the effects upon society of youth's corruption of traditional standards. The collapse of morality is illustrated in Edouard's nephew Vincent, who has deserted his lover Laura, a married woman, and become the victim of Count Robert de Passavant, a pervert. Vincent runs away with the Count's mistress, Lillian, Lady Griffiths, but later murders her and goes insane. Laura's love for Edouard is unrequited, for he and Olivier, another nephew, maintain a homosexual relationship. A subplot concerns George, Olivier's younger brother, whose fascination by Ghéridanisol, a counterfeiter, ends only when that bully's degrading criminality causes a murder. The three themes—the problem of morals, the problem of the literary artist, and the problem of society—have been treated elsewhere in his work and *The Counterfeiters* should be read in the light not only of the *Journal* (q.v.) but of fictional works like *The Immoralist* (1902), *Strait Is the Gate* (1909), and *The Vatican Swindle* (1914), and with an awareness that Gide is fully as capable of irony as of deep seriousness, and delights in being elusive. His novel has shocked many, especially in middle-class France, and fascinated many others. In the latter group should be counted Aldous Huxley, who imitated it in *Point Counter Point* (q.v.).

COUNTRY DOCTOR, A (1884), by Sarah Orne Jewett. See COUNTRY OF THE POINTED FIRS, THE, by Sarah Orne Jewett.

COUNTRY OF THE POINTED FIRS, THE (1896), by Sarah Orne Jewett. These stories of a Maine seaport town are told through the gossip of

Mrs. Almira Todd. There are local color and character sketches in abundance. Old Captain Littlepage relates a story of the Arctic, where he claims to have discovered Purgatory. Mrs. Fosdick tells of her childhood on shipboard. Joanna, Mrs. Todd's cousin, now lives alone on an island, after an unhappy romantic experience. Abby Martin is interested in Queen Victoria, who was born at exactly the same time as she. At length, Mrs. Todd's shy brother William, who has been courting Esther Hight, a shepherdess, for forty years, is accepted by her.

Deephaven (1877), which established the author's reputation, is another series of sketches of Maine life. Kate Lancaster and Helen Denis, two Boston girls, go to spend a summer in the half-deserted seaport town of Deephaven. Helen writes of their life in the decaying old town, portraying housewives, old fishermen, and sea captains living in their memories of bygone days. Memorable are the sketches of Mrs. Kew, methodical wife of the lighthouse keeper; and lonely Miss Chauncey, a remnant of the old aristocracy. The people of the ancient community keep to their old ways, cling to class lines, and abhor the innovations of modern times.

Other novels include: *A Country Doctor* (1884), about Dr. Leslie, whose adopted daughter Nan chooses to follow the medical profession instead of marrying George Gerry; and *A Marsh Island* (1885), the love story of a New England girl and a planter.

Sarah Orne Jewett wrote several books of short stories, a volume of poetry, and pieces for children.

COUNTRY WIFE, THE (1675), by William Wycherley. This is a witty Restoration comedy from which Sheridan later took his idea for *The School for Scandal* (q.v.). Horner, a rake, returns to London from France and has a rumor spread that disease has made him a eunuch. This permits him greater freedom with ladies who have jealous husbands. Pinchwife, an overly jealous man, has married an innocent country girl. He brings her to London for the wedding of Alithea, his sister, who is engaged to a wit, Sparkish. Pinchwife, fearing his wife will receive too much attention, dresses her in boy's clothes when he takes her out, and introduces her as his brother-in-law. They meet Horner, who invites them to supper, where he makes love to the country girl. Pinchwife forces his wife to write Horner a letter, saying that he had insulted her. She, however, substitutes another and her husband delivers it. It develops that Pinchwife has led his wife into an affair through his excessive jealousy. Sparkish, on the other hand, loses Alithea to Harcourt, another suitor, through too great a belief in her fidelity.

COUPERUS, LOUIS (1863-1923). Consciousness of the menacing fatality behind all sensuous beauty is the fundamental motif of the works of Couperus. In his first period, he wrote principally in a deterministic mood. At the publication of his novel *Eline Vere* in 1889, the born storyteller and keen observer became famous at once. Enjoying *fin-de-siècle* opulence, he analyzed at the same time mercilessly the decadence of the period, as revealed in the psychic dissolution and downfall of the young woman, Eline Vere. A similar disintegration, this time of a whole generation, he outlined in a series of four novels, *De Boeken der Kleine Zielen* (1901-1903) (the last three were translated by Alexander Teixeira de Mattos: *The Later Life, The Twilight of the Souls, Dr. Adriaan*).

The same process is pictured in *Langs Lijnen van Geleidelijkheid* (1900; translated by Teixeira as *The Law Inevitable*). The writer exhibits in all of his works a mighty mastery of language and a very uncommon power of imagery.

He turned, in an escape from realism, to the symbolic fairy-tale (e.g., *Psyche*, translated by B. S. Barrington), a type of writing which reached its richest flowering during the few years he lived in Italy. His re-creations of decadent imperial Rome in *De Berg van Licht* (1906), of the antique life of the stage in *De Komedianten* (1917; translated by J. Menzies Wilson), of ancient Egypt in *Antiek Toerisme* (1911; translated by Teixeira), and the urge of expansion of the Persians in *Xerxes* (1919; translated as *The Conquests of Xerxes*, 1930) form a mighty series, which finally found its culmination in the biography of Alexander the Great, *Iskander* (1920). In the latter work the author depicts how the virile conqueror, through contact with Oriental culture, is estranged from the semi-barbarian country of his forefathers; slowly but inevitably, he is deprived of his virility and poisoned by the mystic decadence of ancient Persia.

COURTIER, THE (1518), by Baldassare Castiglione. Castiglione, one of the most accomplished courtiers and diplomats of his time (Emperor Charles the Fifth called him "one of the best knights in the world"), served the Duke of Urbino, and typified Italian refinement at the English court, where he was sent to receive the Garter for his sovereign. When he wrote *The Courtier* Castiglione was the Duke's ambassador to the splendid court of Pope Leo X and an intimate friend of the most cultured men and women of his age. The book is a report of dialogues presumably held at the court of Urbino among the distinguished guests who visited the Duke on various occasions and spent short or long periods of time in his magnificent palace. Through the dialogues, the author conveys the idea of what a perfect courtier, a very accomplished and refined gentleman, must be; what habits he has to follow, and how he has to profess courtesy and civility. But, although this is the main theme of the book, often the conversation deals with important social and political problems of the time, such as the best form of government, the condition of women, etc. The dialogues are also interspersed with pleasant stories which give a fascinating picture of Italian court life.

COURTSHIP OF MILES STANDISH (1858), by Henry Wadsworth Longfellow. See LONGFELLOW, HENRY WADSWORTH.

COUSIN BETTY (1847), by Honoré de Balzac. See HUMAN COMEDY, THE, by Honoré de Balzac.

COUSIN PONS (1847), by Honoré de Balzac. See HUMAN COMEDY, THE, by Honoré de Balzac.

COWPERWOOD NOVELS, THE (1912, 1914, 1947), by Theodore Dreiser. *The Financier* (1912) traces the growth from youth to maturity of Frank Cowperwood, a pre-Civil War Philadelphia bank clerk. When war arrives, the forceful young man, now married to Lillian Semple, an older widow, is a successful note-broker. He is a financial and social success, but, ambitious, becomes involved with the politically influential Edward Butler. He establishes a liaison with Butler's attractive daughter Aileen. At the peak of his career he is caught in the panic of 1871. Butler refuses to aid him, and he is imprisoned, his father ruined, and his family life destroyed. Later, he is released. When Butler dies, Lillian divorces him, he marries Aileen, regains a fortune in trading, and leaves for Chicago.

The Titan (1914) traces Frank's rise to power in Chicago. The Cowperwoods are not accepted socially, however. Frank seeks the company of other women; Aileen suffers personal degeneration, and accepts several lovers. At length, in New York, Frank discovers the young, beautiful Berenice Fleming, daughter of a former brothel-keeper. When Chicago business competitors ruin Frank, he goes to Europe with her.

The Stoic (1947) tells of the lovers in London. Aileen discovers the affair; and at last Frank's health, strained for so long, breaks. He returns to America, spurned by Aileen, and dies with Berenice. After his death, his fortune disappears in legal maneuvering; Aileen dies penniless. Berenice, after a trip to the Orient, devotes herself to the reform of materialistic American society.

CRAIG'S WIFE (1925), by George Kelly. This Pulitzer Prize play is a penetrating character study. Harriet Craig intends to use marriage as "a way toward emancipation." She is jealous of everyone, however, including her husband's friends. Craig's aunt, Miss Austen, warns him of the consequences, but he does not listen. The Craigs become involved, due to Harriet's curiosity, in the mysterious deaths of the Passmores, Craig's friends. Finally disillusioned by Harriet's selfish conduct during this difficulty, Craig leaves her. He is followed by the servants, Miss Austen, and Harriet's niece Ethel, whom she had tried to separate from her fiancé. Craig's wife is left alone in the empty house.

George Kelly has written many one-act plays. His other famous longer piece is *The Show-Off* (1924). This comedy tells of the braggart Aubrey Piper. His wife Amy is much impressed by the back-slapping idea man, and after Amy's brother Frank Hyland is forced to save Aubrey from several scrapes, Aubrey does indeed talk a company into doubling their offer for an invention that Joe, another brother-in-law, has made.

CRANE, HART (1899–1932). With only two books of verse published before his suicide, Ohio-born Hart Crane established himself as a strong influence on a number of young American poets. *White Buildings* (1926) is a collection of lyric verse pertaining to his experience with his American background; *The Bridge* (1930), an uncompleted epic poem on America, uses familiar symbols such as Columbus, Rip Van Winkle, the Brooklyn Bridge, the subway, as well as other abstract and mystical images, to show the unity of past and present through man's creative spirit. *Collected Poems* (1933) includes previously unpublished pieces.

CRANFORD (1853), by Elizabeth Cleghorn Stevenson Gaskell. These sixteen interrelated sketches of early Victorian life in England were first published in *Household Words* (1851–1853). Mary Smith, the narrator, visits the little village of Cranford and relates tales of the villagers, who are mostly spinsters and widows living in genteel poverty. There are tea parties, robberies, quarrels, and gossip. The characters include: Captain Brown (killed by a train) and his two daughters, Mary and Jessie; Betsy Barker and her cow; Miss Pole; the Misses Deborah and Matilda (Matty) Jenkyns; Lady Glenmire; Mrs. Jamieson; Mrs. Forrester. When Deborah Jenkyns dies, Matty sets up a shop in the parlor. Their long-lost brother, Peter, returns from India and brings new life to Cranford. Some of the sketches include old letters and love affairs: between Jessie and Major Gordon; Lady Glenmire and Mr. Hoggins; Matty and Thomas Holbrook. The stories are not as important as the pictures of the people and customs of the day, charmingly presented.

CREAM OF THE JEST, THE (1917), by James Branch Cabell. See JURGEN, by James Branch Cabell.

CREATIVE EVOLUTION (1907), by Henri Bergson. Basing his theory on the hypothesis that the evolution of consciousness is just as real as the material evolution of the species, and, moreover, that both are not static but dynamic in the creative sense, Henri Bergson advances the existence of a vital impulse (*élan vital*) in man which impels him to improve himself and his environment. Instinct and intelligence are the foundation stones of man's drive to universal harmony. The philosopher reaches the conclusion that the highest degree of the vital impulse is achieved by "the moral man" whose own purposeful action can kindle in others the generous impulse for self-improvement and the need to follow spiritual goals. Because of this *élan* man does not remain isolated in humanity, nor is humanity isolated from Nature. "All hold together and all yield to the same push." God is the radiating force of life, action and freedom. There are therefore no limitations to man's capacity for achieving personal worth and greater social good.

CRESCENT MOON, THE (1914), by Rabindranath Tagore. See TAGORE, RABINDRANATH.

CRICKET ON THE HEARTH, THE (1845), by Charles Dickens. In this short Christmas fairy tale of a happy English home, the cricket chirps when all is well, and is silent when sorrow enters. Mr. and Mrs. Perrybingle (John and Dot) give refuge to an old stranger, Edward Plummer. John sees the stranger, as a young man, without his disguise, put his arm around Dot. The cricket takes the form of a fairy and counsels him. John does not judge his young wife and is ready to forgive her. However, Edward bursts in with his bride, May Fielding, and explains everything. He had come to discover if May really loved the man she was to marry, Tackleton, the toy merchant. Everyone is happy again, and Edward is reunited with his father, Caleb, and his blind sister, Bertha.

CRIME AND PUNISHMENT (1866), by Feodor Dostoevsky. One of the great psychological crime novels, this book has probably never been surpassed in its field. Raskolnikov, a student, is suffering severely from poverty and ill-health. His life seems thwarted and crushed. As a last straw comes word that his sister is contemplating an obviously distasteful marriage in the hope of bringing some financial benefit to her mother and brother. In a morbid state approaching delirium, he plans the murder of a repellent, aged woman pawnbroker who preys, harpy-like, upon such poor students as he. He rationalizes himself into believing that it is his right to kill the old woman on the ground that she is a parasite, in fact a positive evil in society, and that she hoards means which could be used to further his own progress in some constructive career. After elaborate preparations he commits the crime. Utter panic overwhelms him, and the neat structure of his plan crumbles. The pawnbroker's sister returns unexpectedly and he kills her as well. He fails to find the money chest and at last flees with merely a purse and a handful of trinkets, almost being detected in his escape. He hides his trifling haul under a stone and never touches it again.

The book follows the course of his slow breakdown under the pressure of remorse. He begins to indulge in cryptic, suspicion-arousing eccentricities. In the course of time he enters into a prolonged intellectual game of cat-and-mouse with Inspector Porfiry Petrovitch, with whom he is first thrown into contact socially. No account can do credit to the suspense and terror of this subtle conflict, known only to the two men involved. Inevitably Raskolnikov is tracked down. He confesses to Sonya, an unfortunate girl whose family he has aided. She urges him to give himself up. At last Porfiry extracts a tacit acknowledgment from him, but withholds arrest, advising voluntary surrender. Raskolnikov accepts this course and purges his soul. He is sentenced to eight years in Siberia where, with Sonya's love and loyalty, he struggles to remake himself spiritually.

CRIME OF SYLVESTRE BONNARD, THE (1891), by Anatole France. Sylvestre Bonnard, a kind old scholar, meets Jeanne, a poor girl, and discovers she is the daughter of his first and only love. He wins her affection, decides to dower her and after many difficulties succeeds in doing so. He has to commit the "crime" of abducting a minor, to save his protégée from a cruel guardian. He escapes prosecution because the guardian has left Paris with the money of his clients. Later, Bonnard sells his library to secure the girl's dowry; his last years are brightened by the presence of Jeanne, and after her marriage, of her child. *Le Crime de Sylvestre Bonnard* is noteworthy for the grace of its style, humor and irony, and for its essential kindliness. It was France's first successful novel.

CRIMEAN SONNETS (1825), by Adam Mickiewicz. See MICKIEWICZ, ADAM.

CRISIS, THE (1901), by Winston Churchill. See RICHARD CARVEL, by Winston Churchill.

CRITIC, THE (1651, 1653, 1657), by Baltasar Gracián. The Jesuit Baltasar Gracián, who was so profoundly admired by Arthur Schopenhauer, wrote in his maturity his masterpiece, *El Criticón* (*The. Critic*), in three parts (*The Spring of Childhood,* 1651; *The Autumn of Manhood,* 1653; and *The Winter of Old Age,* 1657). It is an allegory of human life. The wise and noble Critilo, wrecked on the desert island of Santa Elena, meets there its only inhabitant, a savage who is unable to speak any language. Critilo teaches him Spanish and gives him the name of Andrenio. In Part I Andrenio tells of his life in a cave among wild beasts and of his impressions on discovering the sea, the rivers, the stars. Parts II and III depict the experiences of Critilo and Andrenio after they have been rescued from Santa Elena. Together they make a tour of Europe. As cicerone, Critilo points out to Andrenio the various customs and institutions of the civilized world. Their discussions and observations form a sort of inventory of man's follies. The frequent intercourse with allegorical personages reminds the reader of *Pilgrim's Progress* (q.v.). *The*

Critic is a work of panoramic sweep, of interest to moralist, scholar and statesman. It is infected, however, by the baroque extravagances so much in vogue in Spain during the latter half of the seventeenth century.

CRITICAL, HISTORICAL AND MISCELLANEOUS ESSAYS (1825–1844), by Thomas Babington Macaulay. Macaulay's *Essays* are among the most illustrious in the English language. He was a great liberal, defending the French Revolution against his Tory contemporaries, although himself a lord. He warmly advocated Italian freedom and praised Milton for his heroic and steadfast fight against despotism, and for conscience and free thought. He could not understand Dr. Johnson's strictures on Milton. It was Macaulay's brilliant enthusiasm for Bacon which resurrected the fame of that great man for his countrymen. It was characteristic of the reading public of the first half of the nineteenth century that it required from its authors pleasure as well as instruction. Macaulay furnished both. He had learning and wit and a charm of eloquence which made the sober prose of Bacon and other formidable early English writers take on new life under his analyses.

CRITIQUE OF PRACTICAL REASON (1788), by Immanuel Kant. Kant's ethical views were first suggested by his *Critique of Pure Reason* (q.v.) and were first stated in his *Metaphysics of Morals* (1785). In the *Critique of Pure Reason* Kant had shown the limits of scientific knowledge as well as its presuppositions. In the *Critique of Practical Reason,* he attempts to do the same thing for morals and moral knowledge. The metaphysical framework is the same. Morality presupposes a thing-in-itself, a moral personality underlying our empirical selves. He believes that it is possible to find absolute moral principles, and the fundamental and most famous of them are: *always act so that you treat every individual, yourself included, as an end and never as a means only,* and *always act as if the principle of your action were to become a universal law of nature.* The basic concept of morals for Kant is duty, which is obedience to law for its own sake. He rejects pleasure and happiness as the ends of human life, though he shows their relation to true morality. Belief in God, freedom and immortality, which he showed to be possible in his *Critique of Pure Reason,* are the presuppositions he considers to be necessary for a moral life.

CRITIQUE OF PURE REASON (1781), by Immanuel Kant. The title itself suggests Kant's objective, i.e., to discover the scope as well as the limitations of the rational power. He concluded from his investigation that reason had transcended its own sphere and was the source of speculative error and mental confusion. The *Critique* was written to remedy this condition. The philosopher's motive may be said to have been ethical in the beginning. He was perturbed by contemporary philosophical skepticism which corroded belief in God, in immortality and in freedom. This he regarded as speculative chaos and falsehood. He finally concluded that reason is only a limited faculty and that it cannot serve as a means by which we may demonstrate those ideas upon which life is based. If critically used, however, it can be an effective instrument. The outcome of this critical inquiry, says Kant, is to destroy knowledge and substitute belief for it. Reflection by itself cannot produce conviction. By dogmatic objections the religious faith of people is destroyed. By disproving these objections people will be able to follow their higher spiritual instincts, and to believe in the practical implications of life without any need of philosophical demonstration. Kant described his philosophy as *critical* philosophy, distinct from the philosophy that preceded his, which he called empirical as well as dogmatic. The empiricism of Locke had reached a nihilistic development in David Hume. Locke based his philosophy on experience; Hume demonstrated that when the mind remains passive, experience itself is only a disappearing phantasm which makes all knowledge impossible. Kant said that Hume aroused him out of his dogmatism. He found a new instrument of inquiry: the critical mind. He attempted to show that all scientific knowledge is of *phenomena* and that this knowledge is a product of sense perception (its material) and thought (its order and system). The nature of the world independent of mind can never be discovered by science.

CRITO, THE (427–347 B.C.), by Plato. That this and other works of Plato dealing with the last days and death of Socrates were written after Socrates' death in 399 B.C. is certain, but exact dates are uncertain. *The Crito's* aim appears to be to establish for all time the integrity of Socrates. His character in one light only is touched on here, that of the good citizen. He has been unjustly condemned, but he will give up his life because such is the law of the land. Crito visits Socrates with a plan of escape from the prison where the latter awaits execution; the argument ensues. All consideration of loss of personal reputation or injury to his children, Socrates dismisses. His only desire is to discover what is right and then do the right. Probably Plato invented this incident in order to put his master in a good light. Shelley, who is of the opinion that Socrates did well to die rather than escape, does not like the "sophistical" reasons put in his mouth by Plato in *The Crito*. But it is improbable that Plato intended to answer the question of casuistry. More likely, he only desired to show that in the face of imminent death Socrates adhered to the opinions he had professed all his life. This he succeeds in doing in this famous dialogue.

CROCE, BENEDETTO (1866–   ). Croce is the foremost Italian philosopher of the twentieth century. His system is often called Hegelian, though it seems to have independent sources in the Italian tradition. Central in his conception is the notion of history as providing both the context for human life and thought and as suggesting the method for dealing with human problems. His theory of artistic creation is important in contemporary aesthetics.

CROCK OF GOLD, THE (1912), by James Stephens. This wise and aphoristic fairy tale for adults tells of the two philosophers who lived in the pine wood Coilla Doraca, of their quarrelsome old wives, of their respective offspring Seumas Beg and Brigid Beg, and of the strange consequences of a feud with the leprechauns. One philosopher and his wife spin themselves to death, and the surviving philosopher is accused of murder. The two children are kidnaped for a while by the leprechauns, who in turn suffer by having their crock of gold, which leprechauns always keep by them in case they need it for ransom, hidden under a thorn bush. Meehawl MacMurrachu's daughter meets Pan and later the beautiful god Angus Óg, with both of whom the

Philosopher also has conversations before being imprisoned. At last there is reconciliation, the crock of gold is restored to the leprechauns, and the divine allies of the country rescue the Philosopher, or the Intellect of Man, from the city.

CROSS CREEK (1942), by Marjorie Kinnan Rawlings. See YEARLING, THE, by Marjorie Kinnan Rawlings.

CROSSING, THE (1904), by Winston Churchill. See RICHARD CARVEL, by Winston Churchill.

CROTCHET CASTLE (1831), by Thomas Love Peacock. A collection of prose, dialogue in play form, and poetry of the doings and sayings of a group of English dilettanti of the early nineteenth century, this is a novel with little plot. Ebenezer MacCrotchet, a widower of Scotch and Hebrew descent, buys a castle and coat-of-arms. He and his two children, young Crotchet and Lemma, live at Crotchet Castle and entertain innumerable guests: Rev. Dr. Folliott, Susannah Touchandgo, MacQuedy, Lady.Clarinda, Mr. Chainmail, and others. They discuss life, literature, art and philosophy.

Headlong Hall (1816) is another set of conversations and humorous incidents, the discovery of "the skull of Cadwallader" being the principal event.

CRUSADERS, THE (1900), by Henry Sienkiewicz. See WITH FIRE AND SWORD, by Henry Sienkiewicz.

CULLEN, COUNTEE (1903–1946). Countee Cullen, by the time he had earned his master's degree at Harvard University, had seen his poetic works published in many magazines, and received several prizes and honors, one awarded in 1924 for *The Ballad of the Brown Girl.* Teacher and editor, Cullen also edited an anthology of Negro verse, *Caroling Dusk* (1927); wrote a novel, *One Way to Heaven* (1932), and music for some of his verses. Cullen, who was influenced by Keats, and whose lyricism is not marked by a racial feeling either in content or rhythm, believed that Negro art, like any other, should be considered only within the critical standards of pure aesthetics.

CULTURE AND ANARCHY (1869), by Matthew Arnold. This book-length essay won for Arnold the questionable descriptive "sweetness and light," introducing a new expression into the language. The poet-essayist, religious and conservative, took the intellectual-aristocratic attitude of aloofness to the political-social ferment of mid-Victorian England. He wished to defend culture against "the philistines" (another expression Arnold introduced), and believed he had found in it a secure base for the faith of modern man. Impartially, he attacked conservatives, liberals and radicals, calling for knowledge and clear ideas, before acting on the problems of life. "We [Arnold], indeed, pretend to educate no one, for we are still engaged in trying to clear and educate ourselves." In short, he wished "to recommend culture as the great help out of our present difficulties."

CULTURE OF CITIES, THE (1938), by Lewis Mumford. See TECHNICS AND CIVILIZATION, by Lewis Mumford.

CURÉ OF TOURS, THE (1832), by Honoré de Balzac. See HUMAN COMEDY, THE, by Honoré de Balzac.

CURSOR MUNDI (ca. 1300), Anonymous. In his prologue to this vast Northumbrian poem the author, a cleric, declares:

This is the best book of all,
"The Course of the World" men do it call.

The work is a storehouse of medieval legends, mostly religious. In the preface the poet points to the popularity of romances about Alexander and Julius Caesar, the Trojan War, King Arthur and the knights of the Round Table, Charlemagne and Roland. He proposes to honor the best lady of all, the Virgin Mary. He launches into the Biblical history of the world, beginning with the creation, the war in Heaven, Eve's fall, and ending with Doomsday.

CYMBELINE (ca. 1610), by William Shakespeare. The story is laid principally in Britain, and opens with the banishment of Posthumus Leonatus, an adopted son of Cymbeline, King of Britain, for having married the King's daughter, Imogen. The King puts her under the guardianship of her stepmother, the Queen. Cloten, the Queen's son by a former marriage, wishes to marry her. Posthumus arrives in Rome, where a gentleman, Iachimo, admires a ring Imogen had given him. Posthumus says she is as virtuous as she is beautiful. Iachimo makes a wager that he will go to Britain, and prove her unfaithful. If he succeeds, he is to have the ring. Imogen receives Iachimo as her husband's friend, but he manages to hide in her room and steal a bracelet; Posthumus believes his story, gives him the ring and writes his servant, Pisanio, to kill Imogen. Pisanio shows her Posthumus' letter and advises her to disguise herself in boy's clothes, and seek service as a page with Caius Lucius, a Roman General. The Romans are invading Britain, as Cymbeline had refused to pay tribute to Caesar. Imogen, in disguise, is taken by Belarius, and his two adopted sons, Guiderius and Arviragus, who live in a cave. Cloten, dressed as Posthumus, is killed and beheaded by Guiderius while seeking Imogen. Imogen thinks the headless corpse is her husband. Roman troops led by Caius find her, and he takes her into his service. Posthumus has arrived in England, and joins the Britons. He and Belarius and his two sons turn the tide of the battle; the Romans are defeated, and their leaders taken prisoner. Imogen's reputation is finally cleared, and she is united with her husband and father.

The historical elements in this play were compiled from Holinshed's *Chronicles* (q.v.). The story of Imogen was derived from Boccaccio's *Decameron* (q.v.). In this play are the two well known songs, "Hark, hark! the lark at heaven's gate," and "Fear no more the heat of the sun."

CYNIC'S WORD BOOK, THE (1906), by Ambrose Bierce. See BIERCE, AMBROSE.

CYNTHIA'S REVELS (1601), by Ben Jonson. See JONSON, BEN.

CYRANO DE BERGERAC (1897), by Edmond Rostand. Cyrano, a gallant, poetic Gascon soldier with a gigantic nose, dominates the play. The opening scene is in the hall used for theatrical purposes in the Hotel de Bourgogne in Paris; the date is 1640. Various characters are introduced to the audience, till Cyrano enters, stops the play and sends the audience home. He is insulted by a gallant, Valvert, and challenges him to a duel. While they fight, Cyrano composes a ballade, and on the last line, wounds his opponent. Roxane, Cyrano's cousin, witnessing the duel from a box, is much impressed by her cousin's valor, and sends her duenna with a request for him to meet her the next day at Ragueneau's, a shop famous for pastry and as a gathering place of poets. Cyrano, who worships Roxane, is greatly elated. He stuffs the duenna with sweets, and sends her outdoors to consume them. Roxane confesses to her old childhood friend that she is in love with Christian, one of the young cadets in his company. The disappointed Gascon promises to aid the lovers, and, taking young Christian under his wing, composes his love letters, and in a famous scene impersonates Christian under Roxane's balcony, pouring out his own romantic love for her. He outwits her guardian, De Guiche, and holds him up with an amusing nonsensical harangue while the young couple are being married. But the cadets leave for the front, and Christian is parted from his bride.

In the fourth act, during the siege of Arras, Christian is killed, and Cyrano revenges his death in an heroic counter-attack. Fifteen years pass, and Roxane, mourning Christian's memory, has retired to a convent near Paris. Cyrano, now aging and poor, comes daily to see her. But he has been too outspoken, and made powerful enemies who now contrive his death. Fatally wounded, he still manages to come and see Roxane at the appointed hour. He reads aloud some old letters of Christian's, and she recognizes the impassioned voice she heard under the balcony. Cyrano dies happy in the knowledge that she realizes her love for him.

Cyrano is the prime example of swashbuckling romantic theater.

DAISY MILLER (1878), by Henry James. This study of an ingenuous young American girl tells of the nouveau-riche Mrs. Miller, who is visiting Switzerland with her daughter Daisy. Frederick Winterbourne, an American expatriate, is amazed at Daisy's naive enthusiasms and lack of concern at being seen alone with him. Later at Rome, however, Winterbourne is upset to discover that this uncontinental behavior has caused the girl to be ostracized. He sees her one night in the Colosseum, accompanied by Giovanelli, an Italian not highly regarded by society; Daisy declares that she is not engaged to him. A few days later Daisy contracts malaria, and dies. Giovanelli, at the funeral, tells Winterbourne that he had indeed hoped to marry her, but doubts that the beautiful young innocent would have accepted him.

D'ALEMBERT'S DREAM (1830), by Denis Diderot. See DIDEROT, DENIS.

DAMAGED GOODS (1902), by Eugène Brieux. Georges Dupont, a young Frenchman, discovers that he has contracted syphilis. An eminent specialist tells him this immediately before he is to be married to his cousin, Henriette. The doctor warns him that he must put off his wedding for three or four years. Dupont, however, places himself in the hands of a quack, and, considering himself cured after six months' treatment, marries Henriette. A child is born to them with the mark of the disease. Henriette discovers the truth, and returns to her father with the child. The play ends with the doctor denouncing the prejudices of society which keep young people ignorant of the dangerous consequences of a widespread disease.

Damaged Goods is one of the more successful thesis-plays, a dramatic type once—but no longer—very popular in France.

DAME CARE (1888), by Hermann Sudermann. Old Max Meyerhofer is a thriftless farmer who loses his land by speculation. His youngest son, Paul, at whose cradle Dame Care seemed to preside, assumes the burden of the family. His mother teaches him to respect adversity and to practice self-sacrifice as a sacred obligation. Her influence induces in him a morbid humility which leads him to renounce the pure love of Elsbeth Douglas and to toil like a plow-horse for his twin sisters, Katie and Greta. Finally, in an excess of neurotic scruple, he sets fire to the farm buildings which he has himself built in order that he might prevent his insane father from burning down a neighbor's house. He is sent to prison for arson, and here finds ample leisure to re-examine the course of his past life. He determines to salvage as much joy as possible, and it is intimated that he will marry Elsbeth and that Dame Care will leave his side.

Sudermann's novel is a picture of country life in Germany, written in a sentimental yet realistic style. Its author, who has fashioned a number of once very popular novels, is better known to the world as a second-rate but successful playwright.

DAMNATION OF THERON WARE, THE (1896), by Harold Frederic. In the late nineteenth century a young Methodist minister, Theron Ware, is assigned to a small, predominantly Irish Catholic town, Octavius, New York. Theron is fired with ambition to write a great book on Abraham. His contacts with the town's life lead him to become friendly with the Catholic priest, Father Forbes, and through him, Dr. Ledsmar and Celia Madden. In their society he comes to realize his own ignorance and naivete. Father Forbes shows him another religious world; the agnostic doctor puts doubts into his mind; Celia arouses his senses. Theron is finally denounced by all three when they discover that he mistakenly suspects Father Forbes and Celia of a liaison. Sick and hurt, he leaves the ministry to go west with his wife, there to start a new life.

DANCE OF LIFE, THE (1923), by Havelock Ellis. The famous English psychologist indulges here in a philosophical discussion of the contention that all life is art and, in its highest form, resembles most nearly the art of dancing. There are five chapters on the arts of dancing, thinking, writing, religion and morals. The conclusion is concerned with civilization as an art, and presents man as an artist and as an aesthetician. As the former he is an actor, as the latter a contemplator. The book ends with the hope that the aesthetic instinct, which gives man the power of enjoying things without the necessity of possessing them, may answer the needs of the modern world.

DANTON'S DEATH (1835), by Georg Büchner. One of the most talented playwrights of the nineteenth century German theater was the gifted young revolutionary, Georg Büchner, who died at the age of twenty-four in 1837. When he was only twenty-one, he wrote his most notable dramatic work, *Danton's Death*. The play is essentially a mass drama, but its central figure is an impressive portrait of a liberal horrified by the villainy and bloodshed of the French Revolution which he had labored to launch. Danton, once the die is cast and the heads begin to fall, proves too mild to satisfy the aroused people and the fanatical Robespierre. He is engulfed in the tide and swept to his death.

Another drama, *Wozzeck* (pub. 1879), is marked by a strange blend of realistic and expressionistic elements that in the twentieth century focused new interest on the playwright's work. Alban Berg based his opera *Wozzeck* on Büchner's play; and *Danton's Death* was produced in this country by both Max Reinhardt and Orson Welles.

DAPHNIS AND CHLOË (2nd c.), by Longus (?). Nature in all its candid beauty is the setting for this charming Greek romance of the shepherd children, Daphnis and Chloë. It is a prose pastoral tale after the manner of Theocritus, and, unlike the romances of Heliodorus, contains few literary extravagances. The settings are the island scenes of Lesbos, with its groves, mountains and forests. An amorous mood pervades the story, the author assuring the reader: "Never was there and never will there be a man able to resist love, so long as beauty exists in the world and there are eyes to behold it." The story has as its aim the consolation of those who have already loved, and the instruction of those who have never experienced love. In this aim it succeeds, for *Daphnis and Chloë* is a naïve and uninhibited history of the erotic impulse, its awakening and its fulfillment.

DARING YOUNG MAN ON THE FLYING TRAPEZE, THE (1934). by William Saroyan. See TIME OF YOUR LIFE, THE, by William Saroyan.

DARK LAUGHTER (1925), by Sherwood Anderson. See WINESBURG, OHIO, by Sherwood Anderson.

DAS GRASDACH (1931), by Younghill Kang. See GRASS ROOF, THE, by Younghill Kang.

DAUGHTER, THE (1413), by Jan Hus. See HUS, JAN.

DAUGHTER OF JORIO, THE (Eng. tr. 1907), by Gabriele D'Annunzio. D'Annunzio, a man of letters, lover, bankrupt, adventurer, Condottiero and mystic, is one of the most discussed figures of contemporary Italian literature—either extolled to the sky or vilified in the extreme. *The Daughter of Jorio,* one of the most famous of D'Annunzio's tragedies, can be defined a baroque eclogue. While in the house of Candia della Leonessa, benedictions are being bestowed upon her son Aligi, a shepherd, and his prospective bride Vienda, Mila di Cadrio (Jorio's daughter), a sorceress, rushes in panting, pursued by a mob of frenzied harvesters who want to possess her. Young Aligi succeeds in keeping the lust-maddened men out of the home. The second act shows Aligi and Mila living together in a cave of the mountain, in the fervor of their love. They know they are sought. Mila feels that Aligi must return to his home and that she alone must pay for their sin. Lazaro, Aligi's father, discovers them, and Aligi is carried away by his servants. In the third act, again in the house of Candia della Leonessa, Aligi drinks a poison that leaves him unconscious. Mila is led to the stake and dies in the ecstasy of her self-sacrifice. In *The Daughter of Jorio,* as in most of his literary productions, D'Annunzio gives vent to the sense of luxury which was predominant in his life and which made him confess: "I was ill with the disease called 'women.' Had I been received in a monastic order, I must have confessed that my soul lay under the yoke of concupiscence."

DAUGHTER OF SLAVA, THE (1824), by Jan Kollár. Jan Kollár (1793–1852) was a Slovak Lutheran writing in Czech. While a student in Jena, his enthusiasm for a united Germany was aroused; and at the same time he fell in love with a young girl whom he married many years later. While they were parted, he came to imagine her as a descendant of a Slav race which had disappeared, and in her honor he composed this series of sonnets which was later divided into three cantos—the "Saale," the "Elbe" and the "Danube," the three rivers which at one time were the centers of the Slav lands. Later he added two more cantos, "Lethe" and "Acheron," but it was with the version of 1824 that his reputation was made. The sonnets are a powerful plea for the unity of the Slav peoples—and, with a striking prologue and epilogue, review the history of the Slavs as Kollár saw it. The work almost became the bible of the Slav revival at the beginning of the nineteenth century, and represented the finest aspirations of a sincere man who thus felt that he was contributing to the welfare of the human race. His appeal to halt the absorption of the Slavs was echoed by every Slav people; for the next quarter of a century, all Slav work was under the influence of this poem.

DAUGHTER OF THE MIDDLE BORDER, A (1921), by Hamlin Garland. See SON OF THE MIDDLE BORDER, A, by Hamlin Garland.

DAVID BALFOUR (1893), by Robert Louis Stevenson. This novel is a sequel to *Kidnapped* (q.v.). Having come into his rightful estate, David wishes to help the Jacobite Alan Breck Stewart escape from Scotland, and also to testify to the innocence of Alan's kinsman, James Stewart, who is awaiting trial for murder. Accordingly, David goes to Prestongrange, the Lord Advocate, and gives him an eyewitness account of the murder, though he realizes that he may be hanged as an accomplice. The affair being a political contest between the Stewarts and the Campbells, Prestongrange tries eloquently but vainly to dissuade David from testifying. Finally, he has David kidnapped and held on an island until James's trial is over. Although he fails to save James's life, David is more successful in helping Alan escape to France. After his return from the island, David stays for several months in the home of Prestongrange, whose daughter, Barbara Grant, supervises his lessons in manners and dress, and helps to prepare him for the University of Leyden. In the meantime, David has fallen in love with Catriona Drummond, the daughter of James More Drummond, an unscrupulous rogue. When David leaves Scotland for Holland, he finds that Miss Grant has arranged for Catriona to sail on the same boat to join her father. On their arrival, they are unable to find Drummond, and David is forced to assume charge of Catriona. They live together as brother and sister until Drummond appears. Catriona refuses to marry

David, thinking that her father is forcing the match. Later David and Alan visit her in France. Discovering that Drummond has plotted Alan's capture, they escape, taking Catriona with them. Catriona and David are married in Paris, returning later to Scotland to live at David's ancestral Shaws, where they settle down to rear a happy family and forget a turbulent but interesting past.

DAVID COPPERFIELD, THE PERSONAL HISTORY OF (1850), by Charles Dickens. In one of the most beloved books in English literature, David Copperfield tells his own story, beginning with his birth and ending with his middle years, when he is a happily married and successful man. Much of the book relates his sad experiences as a youth, his school days, and his struggles in London to make a living. There are many characters and minor plots.

Mrs. Clara Copperfield is a widow of six months when David is born. When she marries villainous Edward Murdstone, the boy's struggles begin. Through all of his unhappiness, he finds help and friendship from the Peggotty family: Clara, his nurse, who marries Barkis, Dan'l, Ham, and Little Emily. David is called home from school at the death of his mother and newborn stepbrother, but he runs away from the Murdstone household. His aunt, Miss Betsey Trotwood, becomes his guardian. He is happy in her home, shared with poor, good-natured, feeble-minded Mr. Dick, whose literary attempts are frustrated by an obsession with King Charles's head.

Two more tragedies occur; handsome James Steerforth, David's school friend, seduces Little Emily and she disappears, later to die with her lover in a shipwreck, while faithful Ham Peggotty drowns trying to save her. Dora Spenlow, David's pretty but rattlebrained child-wife, dies. He had married her, blind to the deep devotion harbored for him by Agnes Wickfield. In search of peace and happiness, which literary success has not brought him, David goes to the continent. On his return, he realizes that he has always loved Agnes Wickfield. She is enmeshed in the toils of the unctuous scoundrel, Uriah Heep, who has gained financial hold over her father. Heep, one of the most famous characters in fiction, is foiled, with the help of Mr. Micawber, another famous fictional personage. David marries Agnes and finally finds happiness and success as a writer.

The last two chapters relate what has happened to the many characters: Miss Mowcher, the dwarf; Mr. Mell; Tommy Traddles; Dr. Strong; "lone and 'lorn" Mrs. Gummidge; the family of the bungling, hopeful, indigent Micawber, who is continually expecting something to turn up; Mr. Creakle; and Jane Murdstone.

This was Dickens' own favorite among his novels, perhaps because it was partly autobiographical. A fine motion picture was based on it in 1935.

DAVID HARUM (1898), by Edward Noyes Westcott. This simply-written story of a country banker who is a humorous but shrewd character, was a best seller in American fiction. David Harum, though well-to-do, lives unpretentiously in Homeville, Freeland County. His elderly stepsister Polly Bixbee keeps house for him, supplies him generously with several helpings of turkey at Christmas time, and listens to a great deal of philosophizing. Romance enters the book with John Knox Lenox, son of a New York stock broker, and David's assistant at the bank. A romantic idealist, John remains faithful to the memory of Mary Blake, the girl to whom he had been engaged. They have been separated by a misunderstanding, but eventually marry, settle in Homeville, and name their son after David.

DAVIS, RICHARD HARDING (1864–1916). Davis was the leading reporter and correspondent of his time. He covered several wars, including World War I, and published his international observations. Gifted with dramatic ability, he was also well known as a short-story writer, and published in 1891 *Gallegher and Other Stories.*

The title piece concerns a slangy, young Irish newsboy, Gallegher, who becomes fascinated by the murder of the wealthy lawyer, Richard F. Burrbank. The youth begins to trace clues, and is instrumental in helping a reporter and a detective locate the criminal finally on the occasion of a popular prize fight. Thereupon, Gallegher exerts all his ingenuity to achieve the journalist's goal of rushing his "scoop" to the office first.

This volume is one of a dozen collections of short stories, in all of which Davis' facility is shown. *Van Bibber and Others* (1892) presents Mr. Cortland Van Bibber, a charming young aristocratic Robin Hood of the New York '90's. Van Bibber dresses in splendid clothes, attends the opera, visits the dressing rooms of glamorous actresses, eats at Delmonico's, leads cotillions among the "400." Van Bibber became an American ideal and a social fashion setter. *Episodes in Van Bibber's Life* appeared in 1899.

Among the novels is *Soldiers of Fortune* (1899), a story about Robert Clay, an adventurous engineer working in South America. Clay had admired from afar Alice Langham, daughter of his employer, but eventually falls in love with her sister Hope, during a revolution in which he plays a part.

Davis wrote twenty-five plays, of which the most popular is *The Dictator* (1904). Brooke Travers is fleeing New York under the impression that he killed a man during a street fight. Before arriving at a Central American capital, Colonel John Bowie of the same boat discovers that there has been a revolution subsequent to the one which installed him as dictator; and he sends the unknowing Travers to take his place. Travers and his valet Simpson plan a counter-revolution which culminates when Hynes, a wireless operator, accidentally summons a battleship. The military coup succeeds, and Travers discovers that the man in New York did not die after all.

In *The Bar Sinister* (1903), Davis revealed a certain superficiality of content, but wrote a novel which has long retained its sentimental hold upon readers. It is a tale, told in the first person, of a mongrel who becomes a champion fighting dog, and whose eventual reunion with his mother refutes slurs cast upon his genealogy.

DAY, THE (1763), by Giuseppe Parini. In his poem *The Day* Giuseppe Parini (1729–1799) sharply ridicules the aristocrats of his time for their stupid and unproductive life and, implicitly, defends the ideas which later found expression in the French Revolution and in the subsequent liberal movements throughout Europe. *The Day* is divided into four parts, Morning, Noon, Evening and Night. A tutor gives satirical instructions to a young nobleman, guiding him through the several occupations which are supposed to fill his day. In the morning hours the "Giovin Signore" has to sing, to dance, to play the violin, to learn French, the fashionable language of the time. Then, properly dressed, he goes out in his coach, gossiping with some lady of his own class. Later in the day, it is his duty to join his dissolute friends. After dinner, the young man is supposed to gamble. At nightfall the Signore's beautiful palace receives its master, who takes with him a lady-love with whom he will spend most of the night. In the poem the moral degradation of the rich is contrasted with the simple, healthier and happier life of the laborers and farmers. The corrupt atmosphere of the city is compared to the natural and enchanting beauty of the country.

DAY OF THE LOCUST, THE (1939), by Nathanael West. See MISS LONELYHEARTS, by Nathanael West.

DAYS AND NIGHTS (1945), by Konstantine Simonov. In this novel, Konstantine Simonov, a Russian journalist with considerable first-hand experience on the Russian war fronts in World War II, has written the story of the last part of the siege of Stalingrad, following such models as *Sevastopol* and some of Tolstoy's other early works. A mood of suspense dominates the story throughout, from the moment that strong Captain Saburov sets out for the besieged city, beyond which "is the naked steppe, east of the Volga, the edge of the world, the line beyond which there could be no more retreating." It is here that we see the cold and hungry defenders dominated by the idea that they must take their stand to the death. There is something epic about the resolution of the Russians and about the fighting itself by day and night. The fierceness of the night attacks by the Germans and the counter-attacks under terrific fire are described with a realism which carries conviction. There is no respite for either attacker or defender; not a moment of the story but is consumed with action. In a scene of triumphant emotion, when Russian artillery approaches to relieve the city, we have a penetrating psychological study of Captain Saburov, given with the characteristic simplicity for which Russian writers are famous. The most impressive thing about this novel is the sense of reality it conveys. Its men and women are palpably alive, whether heroic or not. Anya, the heroine, is the incarnation of youth; the love between her and Saburov is both tender and exultant.

DAYS OF AWE (1938; Eng. tr. 1948), by Samuel Joseph Agnon. See BRIDAL CANOPY, THE, by Samuel Joseph Agnon.

DAYS OF WRATH (1935), by André Malraux. See MAN'S FATE, by André Malraux.

D'AZEGLIO, MASSIMO (1798–1866). Massimo d'Azeglio was not only a writer and a painter, but also an outstanding political figure of the Italian Risorgimento. A man of straightforward character and high moral integrity, he was bitterly disappointed at the political compromises that took place during the various phases of the struggle for Italian independence and unity. A Prime Minister in 1849, he soon resigned his position and devoted himself to literary work. Outstanding are his two historical novels, *Nicolò dei Lapi* (1841), in which he describes the siege of Florence in 1530; and *La Disfida di Barletta* (1883), where, among many other historical facts of the time, the battle between French and Italians in 1503 is vividly and imaginatively depicted. But D'Azeglio's main work is considered *I Miei Ricordi* (1867, *My Memoirs*), an autobiography which he wrote with the intention of educating the Italians by the example of a strong and uncompromising character.

DE AMICITIA (44 B.C.), by Cicero. See ON FRIENDSHIP, by Cicero.

DE ANIMALIBUS (printed 1651), by Albertus Magnus. See OPERA OMNIA, by Albertus Magnus.

DE ARTE COMBINATORIA (1666), by Gottfried Wilhelm Leibnitz. See MATHEMATISCHE SCHRIFTEN, by Gottfried Wilhelm Leibnitz.

DE AUGMENTIS SCIENTIARUM (1623), by Francis Bacon. See ADVANCEMENT OF LEARNING, by Francis Bacon.

DE DIVINATIONE, by Cicero. See PHILOSOPHICAL ESSAYS, by Cicero.

DE FATO, by Cicero. See PHILOSOPHICAL ESSAYS, by Cicero.

DE FINIBUS, by Cicero. See PHILOSOPHICAL ESSAYS, by Cicero.

DE HUMANI CORPORIS FABRICA (1543), by Andreas Vesalius. This book is one of two famous treatises which are taken to mark the beginnings of modern science, the other being the *De Revolutionibus* (q.v.) of Copernicus, published in the same year. Both works break sharply with previous tradition, the one in anatomy, the other in astronomy. The *De Fabrica,* a cornerstone in modern biology, opens with a description, based upon the works of Galen, of man's skeletal structure. In this, races and individuals are classified according to cranial measurements. The author's study of the muscles is noteworthy for the excellence of the anatomical figures; but it is Vesalius' account of the heart which marks the revolutionary nature of the book. Anatomists from the time of Galen had assumed the existence of pores in the septum of the heart separating the ventricles through which blood passed. Vesalius, after examining the septum carefully, dared to question the authority of the "Prince of Physicians," and to suggest that Galen had been wrong. Many other hoary errors were likewise questioned or repudiated. The age of reliance upon bookish tradition was giving way to the spirit of observation and direct inquiry into the facts of nature. Vesalius performed dissections with great care, studying comparative anatomy and the functions of the various organs. In his lectures on anatomy before the students at Padua, he did not follow the usual practice of leaving the demonstrations to unskilled barber-surgeons; he himself laid bare the parts of the human body. Similarly, one of the most original parts of the *De Fabrica* is the last chapter in which he describes his method of dissection. For these reasons, Vesalius generally is regarded as the founder of modern anatomy.

To present-day readers, the *De Fabrica* appears to be far from revolutionary, and much too close to the physiology of Galen. Nevertheless, the book met with a storm of opposition from orthodox Galenists, and Vesalius burned his notes and left Padua to become court physician to the emperor, Charles V. However, the tradition he had set at Padua was continued through a line of brilliant successors—Servetus, Columbus, Fallopius, and Fabricus. It was at Padua under Fabricius that William Harvey laid the foundation for his discovery of the circulation of the blood, so that his work may be regarded as a direct outcome of Vesalius' teaching.

DE MAGNETE (1600), by William Gilbert. This famous book, by the personal physician to Queen Elizabeth, marks the beginning of the science of magnetism and electricity as a science. It is significant not only for the new discoveries which it contains, but also for the clear statement of modern scientific method. Gilbert emphasized the importance of careful observation, followed by the drawing of proper inferences. Nevertheless, his theory of electric attraction was heavily indebted to medieval and Aristotelian ideas of form and matter. The book begins by reviewing previous works on the subject, and refuting the old wives' tales which circulated at the time. Then, in the main body of the volume, he describes his own experimental work on magnetism, in which he made use of a large spherical lodestone which he called a *terrella* (a miniature earth). He determined the poles by using a minute compass needle. He increased the effectiveness of lodestones by "arming" them with iron caps. Through the study of terrestrial magnetism, Gilbert was led to favor the Copernican astronomical hypothesis, justifying the earth's motion on teleological grounds and attributing it vaguely to magnetic virtue. Here he seems to have been influenced by Bruno and Kepler.

Most of Gilbert's volume is devoted to magnetism, but Book II of the work is given over to phenomena of electrical attraction, which Gilbert first distinguished from magnetic attraction. The chief contribution here was the disclosure that the attractive power of amber, when rubbed, is by no means an isolated phenomenon, for Gilbert listed more than a score of substances with similar properties. These he called "electrics," the name from which our word "electricity" is derived. Gilbert's electrics are what now would be called non-conductors of electricity.

De Magnete was the only work published by Gilbert during his lifetime (he died in 1603, the same year as his queen); but in 1651 there appeared posthumously a book, *On Our Sublunary World,* in which he expounds a cosmology along the lines of that of Bruno.

DE MOTU CORDIS ET SANGUINIS (published 1628), by William Harvey. This work is one of the greatest and most famous contributions to physiology, for it introduced into biology the doctrine of the complete circulation of the blood. Partial anticipations of Harvey's great discovery go back to the thirteenth century, when the pulmonary or lesser circulation was proposed by Ibn-an-Nafis. In 1553, Servetus said that blood flows from the heart to the lungs, and that here it mixes with air to form the arterial blood which flows back to the heart. Between 1570 and 1590, Cesalpino suggested, in controversy with Galenists, that the movement of the blood was more like a circulation than an oscillation; but his views lack clarity. In 1603, Fabricius of Acquapendente published a work clearly describing the valves in the veins and showing that they hinder the flow of blood away from the heart. From 1597 to 1602, Harvey had studied at Padua, and he made a careful study of the heart and the movement of the blood. By 1616, he was presenting in lectures his case for the circulation of the blood, but it was not until 1628 that he published it in his classical work, *De Motu Cordis et Sanguinis*. This book is important both for the discovery of the complete circulation and for the experimental, quantitative and mechanistic methodology which Harvey introduced. He looked upon the heart, not as a mystical seat of the spirit and faculties, but as a pump analyzable along mechanical lines; and he measured the amount of blood which it sent out to the body. He observed that with each beat two ounces of blood leave the heart; so that with 72 heart-beats per minute, the heart throws into the system 540 pounds of blood every hour! Where could all this blood come from? The answer seems to be that it is the same blood that is always returning. Moreover, the one-way valves in the heart, like those in the veins, indicate that, following the pulmonary circulation, the blood goes out to all parts of the body through the arteries and returns by way of the veins. The blood thus makes a complete closed circuit. As Harvey expressed it, "There must be a motion, as it were, in a circle." There was, however, one stage in the circulation which Harvey was not able to see—that in which the veins and arteries lose themselves by subdivision into the tiny capillary vessels. It was in 1660, three years after Harvey's death, that Malpighi saw the blood moving in the capillary vessels of the frog's lung, and thus supplied the missing link in Harvey's proof of the circulation of the blood.

DE NATURA DEORUM, by Cicero. See PHILOSOPHICAL ESSAYS, by Cicero.

DE OFFICIIS, by Cicero. See PHILOSOPHICAL ESSAYS, by Cicero.

DE ORTU ET CAUSIS SUBTERRANEORUM (1544), by Georgius Agricola. See DE RE METALLICA, by Georgius Agricola.

DE PROFUNDIS (published 1905), by Oscar Wilde. *De Profundis* was written in prison by the English wit and playwright, Oscar Wilde, in the form of a letter to his friend, Lord Alfred Douglas. It is a bitter confession of suffering, humility, and the belief that the secret of life is revealed through sorrow. He describes his past life and success, his fall into sensual ease, and his final disgrace. In prison he has learned that external things are of no importance and that sorrow is the highest emotion of which man is capable. There is a long passage on Christ, considered as the supreme romantic type. *De Profundis* ends on a note of hope, expressing the conviction that the author has become a deeper and wiser man. The refuge that Society denies he will find in Nature.

DE RE METALLICA (1556), by Georgius Agricola (Georg Bauer). This book, the greatest treatise on technological chemistry of early modern times, gives a detailed account of mining geology and engineering in Germany in the fifteenth and sixteenth centuries. It is profusely illustrated with woodcuts of tools and processes, and it includes full descriptions of the assaying and analysis of ores and alloys. The work is divided into a dozen books, of which the first two are general and historical. The next four books deal with mining operations and their administration. The seventh book is on methods of assaying ores, and the eighth on the preparation of ores for smelting. Book nine is devoted to the processes and machinery used in smelting, and book ten to the mineral acids used in assaying and in the separation of gold and silver from various ores. The eleventh book describes the "liquation" process of separating silver from copper, and the last book deals with the soluble salts.

Agricola, a physician who practiced in the mining districts of Joachimstal and Chemnitz, published other works on mineralogy—*Bermannus* (ca. 1530), *De ortu et causis subterraneorum* (1544), *De veteribus et novis metallis* (1546), etc.—but his reputation rests mainly on his *De re metallica,* which appeared at about the time of his death (1555). This folio work of some 600 pages reappeared in a second Latin edition (1561), and in German (1557) and Italian (1563) translations. In 1912 it was issued in a scholarly English translation by Mr. and Mrs. Herbert C. Hoover. For more than a century after its first publication, the book was unsurpassed in its field; and it is with justification that Agricola is known as "the father of mineralogy."

DE REVOLUTIONIBUS ORBIUM COELESTIUM (1543), by Nicolaus Copernicus. Copernicus was born in 1473 at Thorn, on the Vistula, and after attending schools there and at Cracow, he studied at universities in Italy. At Bologna he was in close touch with Domenico di Novara, a professor of astronomy who was strongly neo-Pythagorean in viewpoint. With him Copernicus discussed the errors in Ptolemy's *Almagest* (q.v.) and the possibility of improving upon the Ptolemaic system. He became familiar with various ancient astronomical schemes including the heliocentric system of Aristarchus. He also studied law, and after his return to Poland he became canon of the cathedral at Frauenberg. Here he spent the last thirty years of his life, much of his time devoted to administrative affairs. But it was in this period that Copernicus worked out the details of his astronomical scheme which was to be decisive in showing that the earth moved about the sun. About 1529 he circulated among his friends a manuscript, entitled *Commentariolus,* in which he presented his system with the calculations omitted. About ten years later a young astronomer named Rheticus visited Copernicus and published an account of the system in a book entitled *Narratio Prima* (1540). To Rheticus the old and ailing Copernicus committed for publication the manuscript of his great work, the *De Revolutionibus.* The printed book appeared in 1543, and the story goes that the first copy was placed in the hands of Copernicus a few hours before he died. In the dedicatory apologia, addressed to Pope Paul III, Copernicus states: "I too began to reflect on the earth's capacity for motion. And though the idea appeared absurd, yet I knew that others before me had been allowed freedom to imagine what circles they pleased in order to represent the phenomena of the heavenly bodies. I therefore deemed that it would readily be granted to me also to try whether, by assuming the earth to have a certain motion, representations more valid than those of others could be found for the revolution of the heavenly spheres." The body of this work falls into six books. In Book I Copernicus sets forth his general arguments for believing in the mobility of the earth, and for substituting the heliocentric for the geocentric point of view. He sketches the heliocentric arrangement of the solar system in broad outline and gives the modern explanation of the seasons. Book II deals with spherical astronomy and treats of the problems connected with the rising and setting of the sun. In Book III Copernicus treats of the earth's several motions and the elements of its orbit. Book IV deals with the theory of the moon's motions and the determination of the distances of the sun and moon. Books V and VI, in which Copernicus investigates the motions of the five planets and the sizes of their orbits in relation to that of the earth, are the most significant part of the work.

Rheticus, to whom Copernicus entrusted the printing of his book, was unable to see the whole work through the press, and he left the supervision to Osiander, a Lutheran clergyman. Osiander, afraid that the Copernican doctrine would offend philosophers and churchmen, undertook to insert in the preface a statement that the whole work was to be regarded as a device of computation rather than as a statement of physical truth. Not until long afterward was it discovered that this interpolation had been made against the expressed wishes of Copernicus. This disarming passage probably accounts for the fact that the book was not immediately banned. The Catholic Church, for example, tolerated Copernican astronomy until the days of Galileo. The new astronomy spread slowly at first, for the evidence at hand made a decision between this and Ptolemaic astronomy difficult. The chief advantage of the Copernican scheme was, at that time, a greater degree of mathematical harmony and simplicity. Only when the calculations of Kepler and the telescopic observations of Galileo came to its support did the preponderance of evidence very clearly favor the heliocentric system. By that time, moreover, the elaborate scheme of circles which Copernicus proposed was giving way to the far simpler Keplerian system of ellipses. Nevertheless, with the possible exception of Ptolemy's *Almagest* (q.v.) and Newton's *Principia* (q.v.) the *De Revolutionibus* represents the most important single treatise in the history of astronomy.

DE SENECTUTE (44 B.C.), by Cicero. See ON OLD AGE, by Cicero.

DE SUBTILITATE RERUM (1551), by Jerome Cardan. See ARS MAGNA, by Jerome Cardan.

DE VARIETATE RERUM (1557), by Jerome Cardan. See ARS MAGNA, by Jerome Cardan.

DE VEGETALIBUS (1651), by Albertus Magnus. See OPERA OMNIA, by Albertus Magnus.

DE VETERIBUS ET NOVIS METALLIS (1546), by Georgius Agricola. See DE RE METALLICA, by Georgius Agricola.

DEAD END (1935), by Sidney Kingsley. This grimly realistic play contrasts the glittering vanities of a rich East River apartment house with the poverty of adjacent slums, where tough boys are conditioned inevitably toward delinquency. The author interweaves several stories. Gimpty, a crippled young architect self-raised from the slums, loves Kay, mistress of the millionaire, Jack Hilton. When he receives a sum of money for informing against the killer Babyface Martin, however, Kay refuses to cast in her lot with him. In her bitter wisdom, she knows their happiness would not last, and decides to marry Hilton. We see the killer, Martin, seeking out his mother, who repudiates him, and his first sweetheart, who has become a whore. We see Drina, an earnest, struggling girl fighting to save her young brother Tommy from drifting into the channels of crime. Gimpty gives his reward money for Tommy's defense, when he is arrested.

Beside this popular play, Kingsley wrote the Pulitzer Prize play *Men in White* (1933). George Ferguson, a young surgeon, plans to combine a honeymoon and post-graduate work in Vienna. His wealthy fiancée, Laura Hudson, uses her father's influence to obtain him an associateship at the hospital. Dr. Hochberg, with whom George has been working, thinks him too immature for the job, and George himself realizes that his professional need is study. George has had an affair with Barbara Dennin, a nurse. As a result of pregnancy, Barbara is brought to the hospital for a serious operation. Laura breaks with George, who plans to marry Barbara although he does not love her. Barbara dies, however, and Laura, her understanding broadened by Hochberg, sends George to Vienna alone, promising to share his problems on his return.

DEAD SOULS (1846), by Nicolay Vasilyevich Gogol. Admired as the greatest humorous novel in the Russian language, this was written in the same satirical *genre* as *Don Quixote* (q.v.), *Pickwick Papers* (q.v.) and *Gil Blas,* which inspired him. In the days of serfdom in Russia, serfs were referred to as "souls," and a man's wealth was measured by the number of "souls" he possessed. The absurd hero of this book is the redoubtable Chichikov. He is a petty official, bursting with ambition to be a success in the world. He is obese, lazy and crafty, with a strong acquisitive hunger. Chichikov hits upon the ingenious plan of buying up the souls of those serfs who have died since the last official census, and are therefore not officially dead. By pawning these souls, he expects to raise enough money to buy himself an estate. His quest leads him all through Russia, and in the course of his voyage he meets many odd and droll characters, representative of Russian life. Chichikov's machinations with "dead souls" create around him a fantastic legend. One good-natured owner, Manilov, donates his deceased serfs free of charge. The greedy woman Korobotchka manages to drive a bargain at fifteen rubles per soul. The boorish Sobakevitch demands a hundred rubles, but in the end is content with two and a half rubles per soul. Another, Plushkin, disposes of a hundred and twenty souls on condition that Chichikov give the assurance that he will pay the tax on them. Having thus acquired a host of fictitious "souls," he proceeds to register them with officials whose acquaintance he had taken the trouble to make previously. He passes for a wealthy landowner, since one is judged by the number of "souls" he possesses; and since he is also a bachelor, he becomes a great favorite with the ladies. It is, of course, now possible for him to raise capital on his "dead souls," but just as he is on the way to making a success of his venture, the talkative Korobotchka and the malicious Nozdrev —the latter has refused to make a deal for "souls"—upset the apple-cart by making known the kind of wares he had been buying. The growing rumors and gossip finally reach the Vice-Governor's ear, and the hero finds himself in a peck of trouble. Gogol never completed this work, his masterpiece.

It is when Chichikov attempts to fly from justice in his fast troika that one of the most famous passages in Russian literature occurs, in which Russia herself is compared to a speeding troika which none could stop.

DEAR BRUTUS (1917), by Sir James M. Barrie. See BARRIE, SIR JAMES MATTHEW.

DEATH, A (1909), by Zalman Shneiur. See SHNEIUR, ZALMAN.

DEATH AND THE FOOL (1893), by Hugo von Hofmannsthal. At the opening of this short verse play, Claudio sits by the window in his luxurious home, ruminating on the meaningless nature of his existence. A frightened servant enters and tells him of the presence of eerie beings in the garden. Then Claudio hears the haunting sweet tone of a violin. Death, the musician, appears. Claudio, who feels that he has never lived, does not want to die. Death calls up the shades of Claudio's mother, of the woman he loved and left, and of his friend betrayed by him. Claudio awakens to the realization that he had never appreciated his mother, had mistreated his love, and had been disloyal to the friend of his youth. But illumination comes only at the brink of death, and in dying Claudio cries out:

> . . . so I in feeling to excess
> Wake up from life's dream in the
> Wake of death.

The beautiful playlet by the eighteen-year-old Austrian is one of the most characteristic examples of neo-romantic tendencies in German literature, of which Hofmannsthal was the undisputed leader.

DEATH AND THE LOVER (1930), by Hermann Hesse. See HESSE, HERMANN.

DEATH COMES FOR THE ARCHBISHOP (1927), by Willa Cather. This novel concerns the Catholic Church and its missionary work in the New Mexico desert country. The book is a collection of episodes turning about the personality and the priestly existence of Jean Latour, Archbishop of Santa Fé, and his vicar Father Joseph Vaillant. Latour, an intellectual skeptic, had come to the wilderness in 1848 with his seminary friend Vaillant, a man never beset by doubts, to convert the Indians. Aided by Kit Carson and the Indian guide Jacinto, a diocesan empire is carved out of chaos; but there is incessant contention with the fanaticism and avariciousness of the Spanish priests Padre Martinez and Padre Lucero. The spiritual loneliness of the Archbishop increases, but after forty years his apostolic mission is complete, and he faces death with serenity, convinced that he is on the threshold of a new revelation.

Also about Catholicism, *Shadows on the Rock* (1931) recounts the last days of Le Comte de Frontenac, Governor of Quebec, that "rock" in the St. Lawrence. The romantic plot is seen through the eyes of little Cécile Auclair, who at the end of the story marries Pierre Charron, a colorful fur-trader.

DEATH IN THE AFTERNOON (1932), by Ernest Hemingway. See SUN ALSO RISES, THE, by Ernest Hemingway.

DEATH IN VENICE (1911), by Thomas Mann. See MANN, THOMAS.

DEATH OF A HERO (1929), by Richard Aldington. This is as bitter a book as the First World War produced. It is an expression of the despair of one section of British society. George Winterbourne, brought up in a neurotic environment, reaches the threshold of maturity only to find himself drafted and sent to the trenches in France. Mr. Aldington, who says this was a work of "atonement," had a reputation as a poet long before its publication. This first novel is an addition to the literature of the realistic and debunking school. If written in a warped and frenzied state of mind, as the author insinuates, this did not impede the craftsmanship. The book contains many fine passages, excellent characterization, implicit and explicit criticism of society, its moral and spiritual deficits. But above all, it is a novel of modern warfare and its psychological impact on the young "heroes," the English equivalent of *All Quiet on the Western Front* (q.v.).

DEATH OF A SALESMAN (1949), by Arthur Miller. Willy Loman is a salesman whose escapist tendencies have blinded him to his real mediocrity. At sixty-three, the company which has employed him for thirty-four years takes him off salary; and on commission only, the financial distress of the family, which has always purchased on the installment plan, becomes even more acute. His son Happy is a moderate business success, but lonely. Biff, whom Willy has educated to consider the world a jungle, has tried many jobs, but at thirty-four is antagonistic toward Willy, who by his belief that success and happiness depend on deceit and ruthlessness, has warped the lives of his wife Linda and the two boys. Final attempts are futile, as Willy is fired and Biff cannot get a good job. Biff believes himself a failure, but finally tells Willy that he is to blame also. Willy, whose mind is failing, commits suicide to give the family insurance money. He leaves Linda, who has just made the last payment on the house after twenty-five years, confused and lonely, and Happy infected with the fatal success compulsion.

DEATH OF EMPEDOCLES, THE, by Friedrich Hölderlin. See HÖL-DERLIN, FRIEDRICH.

DEATH OF IVAN ILYITCH, THE (1886), by Count Leo Tolstoy. This, probably the most impressive of the shorter tales by the great Russian realist, describes the lonely, pathetic journey of a man through the developing stages of cancer and into the valley of death. The progress of the disease that attacks Ivan Ilyitch is noted with clinical fidelity, like the painstaking report of a doctor, but the emphasis is on the moral struggle of the unfortunate man, with his fear of death. Ivan Ilyitch Golovin was a member of a provincial Court of Appeals. He led an easy, comfortable, but empty life. His marriage was a failure from the outset, for his wife Praskovia Feodorovna, who came from the nobility, despised him for being a bourgeois nonentity. After one year, they established a cool formal relation. Ivan found consolation in his judicial office, with its dignity and power. With the onset of his illness, he grew irritable. He and his wife quarreled ceaselessly. Ivan began to visit numerous doctors, trying to deceive himself into feeling better. Everyone knew he was doomed. His family found the spectacle of his disintegration so painful that they turned from him. Only his old servant, Gerasim, took pity on him and it was Gerasim who made him see the meaning of faith and love, by tending him to the end. When he died, his former friends and colleagues felt relieved, rather than sorrowful.

A short novel written around a similar theme is *Master and Man* (1895). The story relates how the rich merchant Vasily Andreyevich faces approaching death by exposure in a snow storm. Master and man warm each other with their bodies, and the master suddenly grasps meaning from this brotherly contact with a fellow man; for in the final analysis there is no difference between master and man in the eyes of God.

DEBIT AND CREDIT (1855), by Gustav Freytag. Of the numerous works by the prolific and once very popular writer Gustav Freytag, *Debit and Credit* is his best. Extolling business, thrift and work as national ideals, this novel points out to German youth the unlimited possibilities for advancement that awaited those in Germany who would take advantage of them. The chief characters are Anton Wohlfahrt, son of an accountant, and the young nobleman Fritz von Fink. The first is energetic, wholesome and productive; the latter has not yet learned to stop wasting his energy. The novel, divided into six books, narrates the metamorphosis in outlook and activity that takes place in the young nobleman, who finally comes to the conclusion that the feudal tradition of parasitism deserves to be submerged by the vigorous mercantile class.

Freytag's slight little comedy *The Journalists* (1852), dealing with the rivalry of two newspapers at an election, ranks among the handful of dramatic works in a lighter vein that have maintained their place in the German repertory.

DECAMERON, THE (ca. 1350), by Giovanni Boccaccio. Boccaccio's epoch-making *Decameron* is composed of a hundred stories told by seven young women and three young men in ten successive days. They all gather in the country outside the city of Florence, to escape the Great Plague. Boccaccio takes the originals of his stories from traditional folklore, or French fabliaux, or Oriental tales. The ten stories of the first day are freely chosen by the party; those of the second day tell of adversities finally overcome, with a happy ending for each story. On the third day, the reader encounters people realizing their dreams through their ingenuity; on the fourth, unhappy lovers; on the fifth, lovers able to achieve their desires. The sixth day describes dangerous events cunningly avoided with the help of brilliant ideas and solutions; on the seventh day, unfaithful wives are portrayed; on the eighth, unfaithful husbands. The ninth day is again left free to the narrator's will, and the tenth recounts liberal deeds of illustrious knights and liberal-minded men.

Boccaccio's greatness as a master of narrative has made his *Decameron* one of the most popular books of all times, and for many centuries the supreme model for many storytellers.

DECENNALE (1860–1870), by Giosue' Carducci. See CARDUCCI, GIOSUE'.

DECLARATION OF INDEPENDENCE, THE (1776), by Thomas Jefferson. A charter of human liberty, this document, adopted by the Continental Congress on July 4, 1776, articulated the social and political aspirations of the American patriots during their struggle for independence. It boldly states that natural law prescribes the full equality of all men, who have a sovereign right to "life, liberty, and the pursuit of happiness." It further states that the moral validity of any government can be derived only from the free will and consent of the governed, who have the right to change it, if it ceases to represent them. The declaration recites all the instances of George III's despotism. It concludes with the solemn statement that by the authority of the governed (the people of the united colonies) all political connections with Great Britain are dissolved, and that the colonies are the free and independent United States of America. The brief manifesto had its antecedents in the works of Locke and the eighteenth century French philosophers. It was penned by Jefferson, and reworked by Franklin, Adams, and the Congress.

DECLINE AND FALL OF THE ROMAN EMPIRE, THE HISTORY OF THE (1776–1788), by Edward Gibbon. Gibbon's *History,* although it was written almost a century and three-quarters ago, in many ways remains today an unequaled historical study of ancient Roman society. Gibbon epitomizes his subject with the tart bold epigram: "I have described the triumph of barbarism and religion." He held that human progress entered into its decline with the advent of Christianity, which he treats (notably in Chapter XV) with a stately irony that has been repeatedly resented by believing Christians as slanderous and "wicked," and, conversely, has been defended with an equal amount of warmth by the nonreligious. Gibbon's views of society and the universe were shaped by the liberal French thought of the day, which was anticlerical, antifeudal and democratic. In the outmoded tradition of eighteenth century historical writing, Gibbon's fine historical balance was frequently tipped by his didactic air, his satirical analyses and his soliloquies. He was very erudite, and his work is still regarded as substantially accurate. His historical method was quite novel to England, whatever the influence on him of such French writers as Voltaire and Montesquieu.

The Decline and Fall is in seven volumes, and it runs in continuous unity from the time of the Antonines (180) to the fall of Constantinople in 1453. Gibbon was an enthusiast for Roman civilization at its best: "In the second century of the Christian era, the empire of Rome comprehended the fairest part of the earth, and the most civilized portion of mankind. The frontiers of that extensive monarchy were guarded by ancient renown and disciplined valour. The gentle but powerful influence of laws and manners had gradually cemented the union of the provinces. Their peaceful inhabitants enjoyed and abused the advantages of wealth and luxury. The image of a free constitution was preserved with decent reverence." Gibbon saw the forces of disintegration as setting in upon the death of Marcus Aurelius. However, he was not a particularly profound student of Roman life. He had an unfortunate tendency to romanticize the Roman rulers and their administrators as starkly good or bad, without giving enough emphasis to the social decay around them. But his work is an unrivaled monument in the grand style; it stands in the forefront of both history and literature.

DECLINE OF THE WEST, THE (1918), by Oswald Spengler. Spengler attempted to combine information from many fields (mathematics, natural sciences, the arts, history) into a systematic philosophy of history. In his conception, cultures are similar to living things that are born, grow to maturity, decline, and die. He studied a variety of cultures, tried to plot their life courses, and found many interesting parallels from one to another. As the title of his book indicates, he believed that western civilization was in the declining phase of its life-cycle, and was to be replaced by a new and more vigorous culture.

DEEPENING STREAM, THE (1930), by Dorothy Canfield. See CANFIELD, DOROTHY.

DEEPHAVEN (1877), by Sarah Orne Jewett. See COUNTRY OF THE POINTED FIRS, THE, by Sarah Orne Jewett.

DEERSLAYER, THE (1841), by James Fenimore Cooper. See LEATHERSTOCKING TALES, by James Fenimore Cooper.

DEFENCE AND ILLUSTRATION OF THE FRENCH LANGUAGE (1549), by Joachim du Bellay (?). See DU BELLAY, JOACHIM.

DEFENCE OF POETRY, A (written 1821; published 1840), by Percy Bysshe Shelley. In addition to Coleridge's criticism, especially *Biographia Literaria,* the Romantic poets' theory of poetry is best expressed in Wordsworth's *Observations Prefixed to the Second Edition of Lyrical Ballads* (1800), and, more philosophically, in this essay by Shelley. Wordsworth's declared aim had been "fitting to metrical arrangement a selection of the real language of men in a state of vivid sensation." He had called poetry "the spontaneous overflow of powerful feelings," taking "its origin from emotion recollected in tranquillity: the emotion is contemplated till, by a species of reaction, the tranquillity gradually disappears, and an emotion, kindred to that which was before the subject of contemplation, is gradually produced, and does itself actually exist in the mind." He found poets different from other men, not in kind, but only in degree, and, as Shelley was to do, separated the knowledge of the poet from that of the man of science. "Poetry is the breath and finer spirit of all knowledge." Like Shelley too, and in reaction to eighteenth century practice, he put emphasis on the primitive.

Shelley separates reason and imagination. "Reason respects the differences, and imagination the similitudes of things." Poetry is not confined to meter: Plato is a poet, even Francis Bacon, and certainly the great religious leaders. "Poetry is the record of the best and happiest moments of the happiest and best minds." Particular cases are considered, and Shelley characteristically finds the rebellious Satan the hero of *Paradise Lost* (q.v.). After some historical review and much Platonic eloquence, the essay ends with the famous statement: "Poets are the unacknowledged legislators of the world."

DEIRDRE (1907), by William Butler Yeats. See YEATS, WILLIAM BUTLER.

DEIRDRE OF THE SORROWS (1909), by John Millington Synge. See YEATS, WILLIAM BUTLER.

DELIVERANCE (1907), by Herman Heijermans. See OP HOOP VAN ZEGEN, by Herman Heijermans.

DELPHINE (1802), by Madame de Staël. Delphine d'Albermar, heroine of this autobiographical novel, is a feminist resolved to live her own life the way she thinks best, in defiance of convention and social prejudice. She possesses the virtues of wealth, beauty, goodness and intelligence. Her charms win Léonce, a persecuted Jacobin soldier and conspirator. Unfortunately, he is an over-dutiful son, and to please his mother, he marries another woman. Later, he regrets this step, but is so bound by convention that he refuses to get a divorce. He proposes, instead, that he and Delphine elope to a foreign land, but this is prevented when he is arrested, falsely accused of being an enemy of the Revolution, and shot. This novel, written in the form of letters, is full of thinly disguised historical characters. Delphine is Madame de Staël herself; the interfering mother is Talleyrand. Napoleon was so incensed by the book that he banished the author. Her other novel is *Corinne,* published in 1807.

DELUGE (1891), by Henry Sienkiewicz. See WITH FIRE AND SWORD, by Henry Sienkiewicz.

DEMIAN (1919), by Hermann Hesse. See HESSE, HERMANN.

DEMOCRACY IN AMERICA (1835–1840), by Alexis de Tocqueville. Tocqueville, a young French aristocrat, and his friend Beaumont came to the United States in the 1830's with a commission from their government to study the prison systems of this country. While traveling here, Tocqueville made extensive observations of all phases of American life—economic, political, social, religious and intellectual. *Democracy in America* is his report to the French on how democracy was faring on the other side of the Atlantic. He was neither a violent critic nor a rabid supporter of the American way of life. His standards of evaluation enabled him to see virtues and defects, and to present a balanced estimate. In the course of his analysis of American institutions, Tocqueville indicated the outlines of his general philosophy of history. He felt that Western society showed a providential trend toward democracy, which for him meant equalitarianism. In itself, this was neither good nor evil. If the tendency of democracy to create a tyranny of the majority was not curbed, the consequences would be disastrous for society. If this tendency was curbed, and Tocqueville felt that this was possible, then the future of democracy was indeed bright. This sociological and historical study, perhaps the best ever written on this country, was ignored for many years after its appearance, but it has been recently revived and is now studied by social scientists with renewed interest. This is partly explained by the accuracy of many of Tocqueville's predictions.

DEMOCRATIC VISTAS (1871), by Walt Whitman. See LEAVES OF GRASS, by Walt Whitman.

DEPARTMENTAL DITTIES (1886), by Rudyard Kipling. See BARRACK-ROOM BALLADS, by Rudyard Kipling.

DERUGA TRIAL, THE (1917), by Ricarda Huch. See HUCH, RICARDA.

DESCENT OF MAN (1871), by Charles Darwin. See ON THE ORIGIN OF SPECIES, by Charles Darwin.

DESCRIPTION OF THE ADMIRABLE TABLE OF LOGARITHMS, A (Eng. tr. 1616), by John Napier, Baron of Merchiston. See MIRIFICI

LOGARITHMORUM CANONIS DISCRIPTIO, by John Napier, Baron of Merchiston.

DESCRIPTION OF THE WONDERFUL RULE OF LOGARITHMS (1614), by John Napier, Baron of Merchiston. See MIRIFICI LOGARITHMORUM CANONIS DESCRIPTIO, by John Napier, Baron of Merchiston.

DESDÉN CON EL DESDÉN, EL (1654), by Augustín Moreto y Cavana. See DISDAIN MET WITH DISDAIN, by Augustín Moreto y Cavana.

DESERTED VILLAGE, THE (1770), by Oliver Goldsmith. In this best-known of Goldsmith's poems, the poet revisits Auburn, the village of his early childhood. Finding it depopulated, he deplores the national economy that permits rich men to buy the land, thereby driving the inhabitants to a choice between industrial slavery in the cities or emigration to foreign lands. He pictures the hopelessness of the peasant's life in the city, where he is surrounded by "profusion that he must not share"; the homeless maiden betrayed; and "the various terrors of that horrid shore" to which the people must go. The poet writes of the evils of a society where "wealth accumulates and men decay." Although the poem is didactic and rather sentimental, the pentameter couplets have a flowing rhythm that is natural and easy. Finding Auburn in ruins brings back to the poet memories of its earlier and happier days. He describes the games on the village green, the inn, the schoolhouse, the summer evenings, the simple joys of the country folk. His personalities are clear-cut and charming. The two most vivid characters are the village parson, "passing rich on forty pounds a year," who is drawn from Goldsmith's father; and the schoolmaster, stern ruler of his little school, about whom the rustics marvel "that one small head could carry all he knew." Oliver Goldsmith was also the author of one of the earliest English novels, *The Vicar of Wakefield* (q.v.).

DESIRE UNDER THE ELMS (1924), by Eugene O'Neill. The locale of this play is New England in 1850. Seventy-five-year-old Ephraim Cabot marries young Abbie Putnam, his third wife. His two elder sons depart for California, but Eben, the youngest, who feels that the farm is rightfully his, remains. Abbie's cupidity is blocked by Eben, but she is strongly attracted to him. After seducing him, she persuades Ephraim to sign over the property to her heir, making her husband believe he is to be the father. After the child is born, Eben tells his father the truth, and learning about the inheritance, wishes the child were dead. Abbie, who now loves Eben, strangles the baby to prove her devotion. Eben is horrified and goes for the sheriff, but realizes that he cannot live without Abbie, and insists on going to jail with her.

DEVELOPMENT OF MODERN EUROPE, THE (1907–1908), by Charles A. Beard and J. H. Robinson. See BEARD, CHARLES A.

DEVIL, THE (Eng. tr. 1908), by Ferenc Molnar. See LILIOM, by Ferenc Molnar.

DEVIL AND DANIEL WEBSTER, THE (1939), by Stephen Vincent Benét. See JOHN BROWN'S BODY, by Stephen Vincent Benét.

DEVIL'S DICTIONARY, THE (1911), by Ambrose Bierce. See BIERCE, AMBROSE.

DEVIL'S DISCIPLE, THE (produced 1897), by George Bernard Shaw. This is one of the plays in the collection entitled *Three Plays for Puritans* (1901). "The Devil's Disciple" is among the most popular and amusing of Shaw's works. It has an American setting and was given its world première in this country by the actor-manager, Richard Mansfield. The play maintains, in effect, that those who are considered wicked by the standards of rigid morality are often pure and noble spirits. Dick Dudgeon is regarded by the Puritan community of colonial New England as a depraved, free-thinking soul, who is little short of being in league with the devil. His mother, a hard-bitten, self-righteous woman, casts him out. Yet Dudgeon is the one person who shelters and protects Essie, the orphan girl who lives in his mother's harsh household. Moreover, although Judith, the wife of Parson Anderson, is repelled by his supposed wickedness, she is greatly shaken when Dick allows himself to be taken captive mistakenly by the British, in place of her husband who is Captain of the rebels. Dudgeon carries his masquerade to the foot of the gallows, when he is rescued by Anderson who arrives in the nick of time. Mrs. Anderson reveals her conventional misconception of human conduct by assuming that Dudgeon's gallantry must stem from an improper attraction for her, and is taken aback when he refuses to accept any reward from her. The play contains the military trial of Dick Dudgeon, conducted in the presence of British General "Gentleman Johnny" Burgoyne, and presented in a masterly satiric vein. One of the author's purposes, as avowed in the provocative preface, was to write a popular play in which love is not the primary motivation—hence, a play "for Puritans."

DEVIL'S ELIXIR, THE (1815), by E. T. A. Hoffmann. See HOFFMANN, E. T. A.

DEVOTIONS UPON EMERGENT OCCASIONS (1624), by John Donne. See DONNE, JOHN.

DeVOTO, BERNARD (1897–   ). Born of a pioneer background in Ogden, Utah, DeVoto became impatient with local political attitudes and finished his education at Harvard and Cambridge. Then he returned to the West, and began to write about it. Always a facile writer, with a businesslike approach toward the marketing of his work, he soon became known. In 1932, *Mark Twain's America* established his reputation as a critic. *Mark Twain's America* is not a mere critical monograph; it is a social history. DeVoto does not attempt to interpret the author's intentions, or to fit literary phenomena into a scheme of facts in his own mind; he expounds the product of Mark Twain as it was meaningful to Mark Twain's contemporary readers. Thus, DeVoto is more an American historian than a literary historian.

A similar work of Americana was *The Year of Decision: 1846* (1943), an analysis of forces at work within the country at that time. *Across the Wide Missouri* (1947) is a chronicle of the Rocky Mountain fur trade.

DeVoto has written novels, and *The Literary Fallacy* (1914), which urges authors to accept his own credo of active participation in life, to validate interpretation.

DEWEY, JOHN (1859–   ). This many-sided and gifted thinker is probably the most influential American philosopher. A prolific writer, he has produced important books on all aspects of philosophy as well as on psychology and education. In general, he represents a naturalistic and empirical point of view. His own name for his approach is "instrumentalism." This philosophy was influenced by Peirce, James, British empiricism, and Hegelianism, which was Dewey's starting-point. He begins by asking for a new orientation for philosophy, a new understanding of the function of thought. Thought is instrumental in human action, and action consists in the solution of the problems with which man is continually faced. Thus man is conceived of as a problem-solving creature, and thought has no other function than to aid in this practical work. This version of pragmatism was severely critical of the traditional philosophic view of thought as the highest function of man and hence an end in itself. In his *The Quest for Certainty* (1929), Dewey attempts to show that this old view stems from man's failure to cope with the problems of this world. He searches for absolute knowledge as a refuge in thought from the pressing problems of social and physical existence. In Dewey's view, the modern development of scientific method has made it possible for man to face his problems and solve them through the use of organized intelligence. This means that the scientific, hypothetical, experimental method should replace all forms of absolutism, authoritarianism and dogmatism. The essential condition necessary for the social use of this method is freedom of inquiry, discussion and criticism.

In his social philosophy, Dewey is a democratic liberal who rejects all *a priori* solutions whether of the right, left or middle. He advocates the experimental approach to politics, rather than suggesting some blueprint for the future. In *Liberalism and Social Action* (1935) and *Freedom and Culture* (1939), he states his position in terms of immediate problems, and in the latter book severely criticizes Marxist dogmatism and abdication of science.

In his philosophy in general, he has attempted to avoid speculative metaphysics. He conceives of the function of philosophy as the critique of culture, that is, the re-evaluation of the basic conceptions and ideals of culture in the light of ever-new experience, as a means for eliminating intellectual deadwood and liberating the mind for the scientific approach to man's problems. The philosophic basis for this approach is given in his *Experience and Nature* (1925) and *Logic: The Theory of Inquiry* (1939). In his *Art as Experience* (1933) he develops an empirical theory of artistic creativity and aesthetic appreciation. Perhaps the best introduction to his thought is to be found in the series of lectures he gave in Japan published under the title *Reconstruction in Philosophy* (1920).

Some critics assert that in his attempt to make philosophy a functionally integrated part of man's life in society, Dewey has neglected certain ultimate problems. This criticism does not seem to have concerned him.

DIALOGUE CONCERNING THE TWO CHIEF SYSTEMS OF THE WORLD, THE PTOLEMAIC AND THE COPERNICAN (1632), by Galileo Galilei. Copernicus in 1543 had published the heliocentric theory in his *De Revolutionibus* (q.v.), but the system had gained adherents so slowly that the formal opposition of the Church was long delayed. With the astronomical observations and writings of Galileo, however, the situation changed so rapidly that one may reasonably speak of the "Galilean revolution." Having heard of the discovery in Holland of the telescope, Galileo in 1609 constructed one and used it for the first time as a scientific instrument. With it he saw the mountains and valleys on the moon, four satellites of Jupiter, the phases of Venus, and the nature of the Milky Way. In 1613 he published his *Letters on the Solar Spots,* which clearly marked him as Copernican in view. He was accused of heresy, all books teaching the doctrine of the earth's motion were banned, and Galileo in 1616 was warned specifically by Pope Paul V not to "hold, teach, or defend" the Copernican theory. Galileo remained silent until after the election of a new pope, Urban VIII. Then in 1632, believing circumstances to be favorable, he published (in Italian) his epoch-making treatise, *Dialogues Concerning the Two Chief Systems.* The book had been passed by the censor, but a storm broke out over it. The work is written in the form of dialogues between two Copernicans, Salviati and Sagredo, and a simple-minded Ptolemaist and defender of tradition called Simplicio; and it is said that the Pope was persuaded that Simplicio was intended as a caricature of himself. At all events, the book was banned and the author was summoned to Rome by the Inquisition. There in 1633 Galileo was threatened with torture and recanted. After several months of detention he was allowed to live in seclusion near Florence, where he devoted himself especially to the science of mechanics. The *Dialogue* and other "Copernican" works remained on the Index until 1822.

The *Dialogue* consists of four comprehensive parts or "days." It opens with a point of great importance for science—an attack on the Aristotelian doctrine that other celestial bodies are different in nature and composition from the earth, and that they are perfect and indestructible. The lunar mountains and solar spots are cited in opposition. The rotation of the earth on its axis is compared with the alternative motion of the fixed stars about the earth at a fantastic speed. The Copernican system is defended upon the grounds of its greater simplicity in the explanation of astronomical phenomena. The *Dialogue* also answered the two chief objections to the heliocentric scheme: the lack of stellar parallax is attributed to the enormous distances of the stars; and the fact that an object thrown directly upward is not displaced from its vertical position by the earth's rotation is explained by the principle of inertia. In the clarity of its argument and in the influence it exerted, the *Dialogue* is entitled to rank, along with the *De Revolutionibus* of Copernicus and the *Principia* (q.v.) of Newton, as one of the three greatest masterpieces in the history of astronomy.

DIALOGUES (ca. 150–170), by Lucian. The greatest of all the Sophists of the second century was Lucian of Samosata (ca. 120–180), a Syrian-Greek of sparkling wit. He cuts deep with the impatient scalpel of his skeptic ridicule into all the weaknesses and pretensions of his age. There are some 130 pieces bearing his name, many of them in dialogue form. Some of these are on literary subjects, a notable example being the "Lexiphanes," a riotous attack on the stilted Atticists who overloaded their own writings with polysyllabic, obsolete words. Another type of dialogue is the quasi-philosophic treatise, in which

Lucian himself sometimes appears as Luciscus. In this class belong his re-nowned "Dialogues of the Dead," little dramatic sketches lampooning wealth and pride, pedantry and moral posturing. Lucian had a dislike for the rich and pretentious. In "Charon" and in "Descent into Hades" he shows a whole boatload of them crossing the Styx and tells of the undignified reception they receive in Hades. Another famous dialogue is "Philosophers for Sale," in which he makes sport of the rival schools and their pretensions. Lucian satirized the deities in the "Dialogues of the Gods." His "Dialogue of the Courtesans," "Against an Ignorant Book-Collector" and "Concerning Hired Companions" give realistic pictures of the life and manners of the age and are as fresh and alive today as they were seventeen hundred years ago. Lucian's device has been employed in part in Fontenelle's *Dialogues of the Dead* and Landor's *Imaginary Conversations*.

DIALOGUES (399-347 B.C.), by Plato. There are extant today forty-one dialogues ascribed to Plato (ca. 428–347), but fourteen of them are certainly for-geries or imitations and the authenticity of three others is doubtful. Of all the dialogues deemed genuine, it is not possible to affix a definite date of composition for a single one; consequently only a few can be read in any time-sequence. The dialogues represent no rigid philosophic system, being rather an effort at the apprehension of wisdom, virtue, truth and beauty. In a large measure they are not original, as Plato himself testified in his *Seventh Epistle:* "The opinions called by the name of Plato are those of Socrates in his days of youthful vigor and glory." The profound spell the oral teachings of Socrates cast on Plato during his youthful years endured throughout his life and is fully revealed in the dialogues. Socrates not only appears as the protagonist in many of them but the Socratic outlook on life, the Socratic moral and intellectual aims, are stamped on all of them. Furthermore, the famed Socratic dialectical method is uniformly used by Plato. Although Plato was deeply disheartened by the execution of his master and took little active part in public life because of it, the precepts and example of Socrates inspired his life and philosophy. It is, however, possible to observe a progression toward a higher degree of dog-matism evidenced and accompanied by a diminished importance of Socrates' role in the dialogues and his final disappearance, as in the *Laws*. The dialogue as a vehicle for the expression of philosophic ideas was not Plato's invention. He probably selected it because it was so well adapted to Socrates' customary manner of discussion. His artistic mastery of the form is unsurpassed. He chooses the most homely and unpretentious incidents or remarks upon which to build his speculations on the nature of wisdom, virtue and knowledge. Many of the characters that people his dialogues are his friends, relatives, pupils, and fellow-philosophers. Plato was an earnest searcher after the eternal truths. Like Socrates he believed virtue is synonymous with knowl-edge. Constantly he dwells upon man's capacity for good derived from his ability to discriminate and reason. The best-known English translations of the *Dialogues* are those by Jowett, Bury, and I. A. Richards. The following are the dialogues of Plato about whose authenticity there is no doubt: *Euthyphro, Apology* (q.v.), *Crito* (q.v.), *Phaedo* (q.v.), *Cratylus, Theaetetus, Sophist, Statesman, Parmenides. Philebus, Symposium* (q.v.), *Phaedrus, Charmides,*

Laches, Lysis, Euthydemus, Protagoras, Gorgias, Meno, Ion, Republic, Timaeus (q.v.), *Critias, Laws.*

DIALOGUES OF THE DEAD (1683), by Bernard le Bovier de Fontenelle. These contain the best examples of Fontenelle's brilliant paradoxes. Faustina, for example, tries to convince Brutus that her thousand infidelities to Marcus Aurelius were as disinterested and high-minded as his murder of Caesar: "And if I should tell you that I wished to terrify likewise all husbands, so that no man should dare to be a husband after the example I made of Aurelius . . ." When she goes on to attack the double moral standard, Brutus rebukes her for her revolt against a masculine world. She slyly retorts: "I am a Roman and I have a Roman feeling for liberty." In the dialogue between Socrates and Montaigne, the Greek philosopher informs the Frenchman that he need have no illusions about the classic Golden Age, for there were just as many fools and knaves then as there are in Paris. The pieces quoted possess the characteristics of most of Fontenelle's dialogues. Although devoted to the proposition that reason and truth are the best instruments for happiness, he is a thoroughgoing skeptic.

DIALOGUES ON NATURAL RELIGION (1779), by David Hume. See TREATISE ON HUMAN NATURE, by David Hume.

DIANA OF THE CROSSWAYS (1885), by George Meredith. Beautiful and orphaned Diana Merion enters early nineteenth century English society under the sponsorship of her beloved Lady Emma Dunstane. After a brief flight, she suddenly marries Augustus Warwick, who has leased her ancestral home, Crossways; but this marriage comes to grief over her innocent friendship with influential Lord Dannisburgh. Courageously, Diana returns to society, separated from Warwick, after her vindication at a trial, to become a successful novelist and one of London's wittiest hostesses. She comes to love Percy Dacier, nephew of Lord Dannisburgh and a rising politician. Prevented once from running away with him only by the illness of Lady Emma, Diana finally loses him when she thoughtlessly sells his important political secret in her desperate need for money. Broken-hearted for a time, she finally recognizes the worth of her long-faithful admirer, Thomas Redworth, and marries him after Warwick's death. Diana, in this, one of Meredith's most popular novels, was said by him to be modeled after Lady Caroline Norton, with the novelist's license to embellish and invent.

DIARY (1641–1706; first published 1818), by John Evelyn. Aside from Samuel Pepys, John Evelyn was the greatest of the English seventeenth century diarists. His diary was written in part during a three-year sojourn in Italy. Less personal than Pepys', it is full of interesting anecdotes; there are also some curious notes on scientific research, which in Evelyn's time was pursued by aristocratic dilettantes, as well as by serious scientists, because of the lack of organized public support. Evelyn personally knew Charles II and James II and many of the royal ministers and eminent men of his day. Parts of his *Diary* contain comment on these persons and their affairs. One of the founders of the Royal Society, Evelyn displays himself in his diary as a patron of men of science and the fine arts.

DIARY (1660–1669), by Samuel Pepys. The great diarist, son of a tailor and a domestic, wrote of the years 1660–1669 in one of the most entertaining and revealing personal narratives in the English language. Its artlessness, good humor, slyness and *joie de vivre* have endeared it to many generations of American and English readers. It is valuable as a record of well-to-do English family life of the seventeenth century, and is written without pretense or inhibition. It remained unpublished for a hundred and sixty years. Written in beautiful shorthand, it consisted of six leather-bound octavo volumes accidentally found in Pepys' library. The deciphering took three arduous years; the work appeared in 1825. The virtually complete text (with some expurgations) had to wait for the Wheatley edition, first published in 1893–1899 in ten volumes. Pepys was a realist, free from cant and supernaturalism. He wrote with the honesty of a man writing for himself, with no eye to posterity's applause or his own dignity. He was twenty-seven years old when he began his diary; thirty-six when he discontinued it because of his poor eyesight. He delineated himself, his conduct on various occasions, and his motives, with ingratiating honesty. Living in an age in which virtue was a handicap to any man aiming at a public career, he exposes all the devices by which he attained the high offices of Secretary to the Admiralty and President of the Royal Society. He had a passion for fine music and pretty girls, and would often steal kisses from the latter. His characterizations of the great personages of his day are full of unconscious humor, and his eyewitness account of the great London fire remains a literary masterpiece.

DIARY OF SAMUEL SEWALL, THE (1652–1730), by Samuel Sewall. Sewall, New England divine, businessman, councilor, and Puritan judge, kept a diary for more than fifty-five years. It has been compared with the work of Pepys as a re-creation of an era and an individual character. It is less witty and worldly, but as a record of colonial New England under the harsh domination of a dying Puritanism, it is unique in contemporary Americana. It is rich in historical minutiae, unrecorded by more pretentious chronicles, which helps to animate the daily lives and problems of the early colonists. Although frequently uncouth, coarse, and blunt, the *Diary* is refreshingly honest and confidential. Sewall was not a great man, or at all times a good man; he represented all the vices and virtues of his milieu. A contradiction of his pleasant nature was the savage part he played in the Salem witch persecutions. His records of the murders have a nightmarish ring. He later publicly recanted.

DICKINSON, EMILY (1830–1886). Emily Dickinson led, quite by choice, a most secluded life in Amherst, Mass. During her last twenty-five years she saw only her most intimate friends—often men with whom she enjoyed stimulating intellectual companionships. Withdrawn from society, she devoted herself to poetry. She authorized none of her pieces to be published during her lifetime, and posthumous publications have often been unsystematic, undiscriminating collections. It is clear now, however, that she was a poet of great importance, a precursor of the Imagist school, and a strong influence on the women poets of the 1920's.

The Single Hound (1914) is an example of the small delights of her perception, motivated by natural phenomena, or inward speculation. There are metaphysical meditations, fantasies on nature, warm lyrics addressed to individuals. Her style is delicate, but often her ideas are expressed in daring metaphors and paradoxes.

Bolts of Melody (1945) is a more carefully edited selection of poems previously suppressed by the family.

DICTATOR, THE (1904), by Richard Harding Davis. See DAVIS, RICHARD HARDING.

DIDACTICA, THE (1631), by Comenius. Jan Amos Komensky, better known under his Latin name of Comenius (1592–1670), last bishop of the Czech Church of the Unitas Fratrum, has been called the father of modern education. During his long and difficult life (as an émigré from his native land during the Thirty Years War), he worked out his philosophy of education in nearly all the countries of Europe and at one time was even invited to become the President of Harvard University.

In his *Didactica,* Comenius sharply challenged most of the principles of medieval education; he continued in a second edition in the *Great Didactica* of 1638, which was literally a volume to describe the means of educating almost everyone. He demanded that education be made universal, without regard to age, country or sex. It was to be based upon instruction in the student's native language; memorizing of rules was to be replaced by object lessons and general practical experience. He developed his theories in many other books; in 1657 many were reprinted in one collection. Among them were such works in Latin and Czech as: *Janua linguarum reserata* (The Gate of Languages Opened); *Orbis Pictus,* the first illustrated textbook; the *Schola Pansophica* and the *Schola Ludus,* both plays for children.

Apart from these are *Labyrinth of the World and the Paradise of the Heart* (1625), an allegory somewhat on the style of *Pilgrim's Progress* (q.v.); and the *Testament of the Dying Mother* (1650), which contained the key to the later Czech revival. The ideas of Comenius have been extraordinarily fruitful, even though they seemed to have fallen on sterile soil. They have passed into contemporary life though the books themselves have gone unread, except by scholars, for many years.

DIDEROT, DENIS (1713–1784). As editor of the famous French *Encyclopédie,* Diderot exercised great influence on European thought in the eighteenth century. This compendium of knowledge was revolutionary in that it emphasized science and practical arts to the detriment of theology and speculative knowledge. Diderot himself was a naturalist and a pantheist whose main interest was in the progress of the sciences. In his *Thoughts on the Interpretation of Nature,* he formulated some of the fundamental principles of scientific method. A follower of Bacon, he overestimated experiment and underestimated the importance of mathematics. Much of his other writing was considered too subversive to print and was known to contemporaries only in clandestinely circulated manuscript. His drama, in which he tried to work outside the French classical tradition, with bourgeois characters and hypermoral, sentimental plots, has not survived, but three novels—*La Religieuse* (1796), *Rameau's Nephew* (1821; complete ms. 1891) and *Jacques the Fatalist*

(1796)—are still widely read. He also excelled in a sort of ironical, frequently paradoxical, philosophic dialogue of which his *D'Alembert's Dream* (1830) is perhaps the best example.

DIE GRUNDLAGEN DER ALLGEMEINEN RELATIVITÄTS-THEORIE (1916), by Albert Einstein. See RELATIVITY, by Albert Einstein.

DIE JUDENBUCHE (1842), by Annette von Droste-Hülshoff. See DROSTE-HÜLSHOFF, ANNETTE VON.

DINNER AT EIGHT (1932), by George S. Kaufman and Edna Ferber. See OF THEE I SING, by George S. Kaufman and Morrie Ryskind.

DISCOURSE ON METHOD (1637), by René Descartes. The *Discourse* is divided into six parts and touches upon various matters concerning the sciences: the principal rules of Descartes' method, the rules of morality deduced from this method, proof of the existence of God and the soul, investigations in the field of physics, conclusions concerning the motion of the heart and other anatomical problems, and finally, a program for the further investigation of nature. Descartes stresses constantly the fundamental importance of method: "For to be possessed of a vigorous mind is not enough; the prime requisite is rightly to apply it." As a mathematician, Descartes was concerned to discover the method which enabled him to make his discoveries. He proceeded as follows: he started by attempting to doubt everything, and finds grounds for doubting the evidence of the senses, nature in general, and even mathematics. What he cannot doubt, in the very process of his doubting, is the fact that he is thinking. From this he derives his basic philosophical principle, "I think, therefore I am." Upon this basis, using a rigorous mathematical method, Descartes builds his philosophy. This philosophy is dualistic in character; mind and body are conceived of as distinct. The movement of bodies is mechanical and can be described by mathematical laws. Mind is independent of this mechanical system, but through reason can grasp its structure. The problem of the relation of mind to matter was Descartes' legacy to modern philosophers. When he comes to summarize his method, Descartes lists four principles: 1) accept only that which is clear and distinct as true; 2) divide each difficulty into as many parts as possible; 3) start with the simplest elements and move by an orderly procedure to the more complex; and 4) make complete enumerations and reviews to make certain that nothing was omitted. The philosophical implications of these principles were further elaborated by Descartes in his *Meditations* (1642).

DISCOURSES (ca. 60-140), by Epictetus. Epictetus was a slave owned for a time by Nero's secretary, who permitted him to study under Musonius Rufus, the great Stoic teacher. Like Socrates he did not commit his thoughts to writing. These have survived because of his good fortune in having as pupil the historian, Flavius Arrian, who recorded his discourses as they were delivered during informal conversations. They give a comprehensive picture of the old philosopher, his gentle character, lively and temperamental method of discussion, and his lofty moral outlook. His teachings were principally concerned with practical morality on which he is not always in agreement with orthodox Stoicism. Devoutly religious, he believed that the universe is governed by an all-wise, divine Providence. Sorrow, pain, and persecution are the will of God, part of His universal plan, and therefore, from the point of view of the whole, are good. Man is duty-bound to reconcile his own will to the will of God and to accept the doctrine of necessity as God's will and grace. Only by doing this may he achieve happiness. The *Discourses* originally consisted of eight books, but only four have survived the ravages of time.

DISCOURSES (1769–1791), by Sir Joshua Reynolds. These consist of fifteen lectures which the eminent English painter of the eighteenth century delivered before the students of the Royal Academy between 1769 and 1790. Addressed principally to students, they give a philosophy of art, besides being also a technical manual for the practitioner. In the last *Discourse*, devoted to his idol Michelangelo, Reynolds explains his qualifications for electing himself a guide to art students in their pursuit of beauty: "I had seen much, and I had thought much upon what I had seen; I had something of a habit of investigation, and a disposition to reduce all that I had observed and felt in my own mind to method and system." Reynolds possessed objectivity and critical judgment to a degree unusual for a creative artist. Portrait painting, the only field of art in which he showed distinction, he placed low in rank among the various genres of the art of painting, urging his students to paint in the grand manner of the Renaissance masters, Michelangelo and Raphael. The *Discourses* received universal approbation except for one sour note sounded by William Blake, England's most original artist as well as poet. In the light of present knowledge of the psychology of the artistic personality, Blake stood on firm ground in his criticism. He charged that "Reynolds' opinion was that genius may be taught, and all pretence to inspiration is a lie or deceit, to say the least of it. If it is deceit, the whole Bible is madness."

DISCOURSES ON THE FIRST TEN BOOKS OF TITUS LIVIUS (1513), by Niccolò Machiavelli. Machiavelli is usually thought of first as the author of *The Prince* (q.v.). His *Discourses* written at about the same time gives a more comprehensive and adequate picture of his views on the most desirable form of political organization. Incomplete as it stands, the *Discourses* is a series of loosely connected and not too well organized *pensées* mostly devoted to a consideration of the practical problems involved in constituting, maintaining and expanding a republican government. Machiavelli takes as his point of departure Livy's account of the Roman Republic, and uses Livy's material to draw out principles which apply to all republics at all times, man being essentially the same in all ages. This procedure limits Machiavelli to a discussion of the city-state type of republic which Rome was and which existed in his own time. Within this area he discusses such problems as the role of leadership in a republic, how the leader should treat the people, the motives and character of the people individually and collectively, the relation of a military establishment to a republic, the place of a national religion in a republic, how unity of the state is to be achieved, and the relative merits of a republic and a princely government. On the last-mentioned point, he seems to defend republican government, but not on the basis of a set of universal moral principles or abstract rights of man, but rather in view of practical considerations of strength, unity, and possibility of expansion (this last being the basic test of the success of any state). Less well known than *The Prince,* the *Discourses* has had a more thoroughgoing and lasting influence on later political theorists.

DISCOURSES ON TWO NEW SCIENCES (pub. 1638), by Galileo Galilei. The best-known work of Galileo is the *Dialogue Concerning the Two Chief Systems* (q.v.), in which his defense of Copernican astronomy brought him in conflict with the Inquisition. This book, however, is also of great importance. It was written in Italian and completed in 1636 while he was under surveillance; but it was published two years later in Holland because his works were banned in Italy. Throughout his life Galileo had been occupied with problems in mechanics, and he concentrated upon these after his conflict with the Church in matters of astronomy. His epoch-making contributions here lay mainly in the field of dynamics, in which he discovered the laws of falling bodies, the principle of the pendulum, and the path of projectiles.

In antiquity Archimedes had laid the foundations of statics, but he avoided questions in dynamics. Aristotle's omnivorous curiosity included the problem of motion, but he drew hasty conclusions and asserted that objects fall with speeds which are proportional to their weights. During the medieval period this error persisted, but the Schoolmen improved upon the Peripatetic doctrines by introducing the idea of inertia and by suggesting that objects fall freely with uniform acceleration. A systematic mathematical theory of dynamics, however, was lacking until the appearance of Galileo's *Discourses.* The purported demonstration by Galileo that large and small weights fall from the Leaning Tower of Pisa in the same time and with equal speeds—thus correcting the Aristotelian error—was not new, if authentic; but his laws of motion were essentially novel. He clarified the medieval notions of inertia and acceleration, and he derived for the first time the law that the distance covered by a falling body varies as the square of the time elapsed. He verified this law by first showing that it held also for inclined planes and then actually measuring times and distances along these. His discovery of the isochronism of the simple pendulum is widely cited, but this was less important than his law that the square of the period is inversely proportional to the length of the pendulum. Possibly the most striking part of the *Discourses,* however, is the demonstration of the parabolic path of a projectile.

The "two new sciences" referred to in the *Discourses* are one, cohesion and resistance to fracture, and two, dynamics. It is in connection with the first of these that Galileo combats the notion that "nature abhors a vacuum" in explaining the operation of hydraulic pumps, but he missed the idea of atmospheric pressure which his pupil Torricelli discovered. The *Discourses* include notes on a wide variety of topics in physical science; but none of these compares, in lasting value, with the sections devoted to motion. It is for this reason that Galileo frequently is referred to as "the founder of modern dynamics."

DISDAIN MET WITH DISDAIN (1654), by Augustín Moreto y Cavana. Diana, the daughter of the Count of Barcelona, laughs at love and refuses to marry under any circumstance. Her father induces the most illustrious gentlemen to come to his court and engage in tournaments and sports in order to win her favor, but the haughty beauty treats them with equal coldness and even disdain, until at last Carlos, Count of Argel, cleverer than the other aspirants, comes upon an original and efficacious plan: to administer her a dose of her own medicine, to meet disdain with disdain. Thus, concealing his deep passion for her, he treats Diana with such contempt that gradually she begins to admire him and finally declares her desperate love and consents to marry him. This play was adopted from four separate plays by Lope de Vega, and later imitated by Molière in *La Princesse d'Élide*.

DISFIDA DI BARLETTA, LA (1883), by Massimo d'Azeglio. See D'AZEGLIO, MASSIMO.

DISQUISITIONES ARITHMETICAE (published 1801), by Karl Friedrich Gauss. The three greatest mathematicians of all time, it is universally agreed, were Archimedes, Newton, and Gauss. The first of these emphasized pure mathematics; Newton stressed the applications to science. Gauss excelled in both pure and applied mathematics. In a famous statement, he called mathematics the queen of the sciences and arithmetic the queen of mathematics. Gauss contributed to almost all fields of mathematics then known—complex numbers, infinite series, statistics, algebra, calculus, non-Euclidean geometry, differential geometry, elliptic functions, astronomy, geodesy, electromagnetism. He was extraordinarily precocious as a boy and his unusual ability remained with him through a long life (1777–1855). It has been said that he was the last person to cover the whole field of mathematics. Yet of all branches there was one which was his favorite—arithmetic or the theory of numbers. His mathematical diary is replete with discoveries of recondite theorems. One of 1796 was that every positive integer is the sum of three triangular numbers. Even then, at the age of nineteen, Gauss was planning his masterpiece, the *Disquisitiones Arithmeticae,* and this great work was completed two years later. A publisher's difficulties held it up until 1801, and Gauss meanwhile had printed his doctoral dissertation—the first satisfactory proof of the fundamental theorem of algebra—in 1799. The *Disquisitiones Arithmeticae* is in seven sections, of which the first three treat of the theory of congruences. The fourth is on the theory of quadratic residues, the fifth on binary quadratic forms, and the last two are on special topics in Diophantine analysis, including the construction of regular polygons. The work has been called "a book of seven seals," for it is difficult even for experts to read. It is a work of art, having flawless perfection; and it exerted an immediate influence upon mathematics, raising higher arithmetic to a place on a par with algebra, analysis and geometry. Gauss had hoped to publish a second volume on arithmetic, but in 1801 his interest was turned toward applied mathematics through the discovery of the planetoid Ceres. He became director of the Göttingen Observatory, and astronomical problems preoccupied him for some time. His results were published in 1809 in a masterly treatise, *Theoria et Motus Corporum Coelestium,* in which he made use of his method of least squares. Through astronomy Gauss was led to questions of geodesy and terrestrial magnetism, on which he published important memoirs from 1833 to 1846. He laid the foundation of the mathematical theory of electro-magnetism, and constructed an electric telegraph. Gauss continued to contribute to mathematics but he never returned whole-heartedly to his first love, arithmetic, to complete the *Disquisitiones Arithmeticae.* Nevertheless, this work remains the greatest of all works on the theory of numbers—the masterpiece of the "Prince of Mathematicians."

DIVAN, THE (14th c.), by Hafiz, Shame-Ed-Din Muhammud. Hafiz, the Persian, is the immortal singer of Shiraz, and *The Divan,* a collection of exquisite odes, is undoubtedly the best known of his works. He emerged as a poet and philosophical mystic out of the culture dominated by the dissident Mohammedan sect, the Sufi, during the twelfth century in Persia. The poets produced by this movement were not professionals. Every cultured man strove to be a poet; Hafiz, Omar Khayyam, Sadi, Jami, Nizami and Khwaju of Kerman represent the flowering of the poetry of Persia in this period. Their verses are characterized by perfect symmetry, an indescribable delicacy of feeling, subtle use of imagery, and sensuous delight in the beauty of the earthly life, as well as an undertone of melancholy and world-weariness. *The Divan* contains these elements to as great extent as any of Hafiz' contemporaries' verses. Through it he achieved great fame during his lifetime. He sings chiefly of joyous things: of lovely women, youth, the rose, the nightingale, and scented wine. As a mystic and an Oriental, Hafiz sometimes treats these things as allegorical, pointing to deeper meanings. Nevertheless, he remains a poet of simple passion.

DIVINE COMEDY, THE (1314–1321), by Dante Alighieri. *The Divine Comedy* is a grandiose monument of the Middle Ages, symbolizing the allegory of the human soul which from error and ignorance can reach the highest degree of perfection—contemplation of God.

The *Comedy* is divided into three Canticas: Hell, Purgatory and Paradise. Each Cantica consists of thirty-three Cantos. Another Canto, preceding the whole poem as an introduction, makes a total of a hundred, a number which for Dante is symbolic of true perfection. In the introduction Dante explains that he finds himself in a dark, tangled forest (symbolizing error). At its edge there is an illuminated hill, but a leopard, a lion and a wolf oppose the poet's ascent. Virgil, the great Roman poet, for whom Dante had the deepest admiration, and whom he selects as his guide through the voyage in Hell, appears. He guides Dante to the entrance of the Inferno, which is the figure of a gigantic inverted cone having its top at the center of the earth.

Inferno: In the outer court of Hell, Dante sees countless legions of spirits bitten by wasps until their blood mingles with their tears. They are the cowards and the undecided. In the First Circle are the virtuous who died unbaptized, and good heathens, such as Homer, Horace, Ovid and Lucan. Hell actually begins in the Second Circle of the descending cone, where a whirlwind blows the spirits of those who sinned with carnal lust, among whom Dante finds the unhappy lovers Paolo and Francesca da Rimini. In the Third Circle Dante encounters the gourmands who lie in the mud watched by the fierce Cerberus; in the Fourth, misers and spendthrifts collide, as they push huge rocks forward.

Virgil then leads Dante into the swamp of Styx which constitutes the Fifth Circle. Here the ill-tempered dwell in mud and filth. The Sixth Circle is a strange city, the City of Dis. Thousands of devils prevent the two poets from entering until an angel sent by God breaks their resistance. As they proceed, Dante and Virgil see a vast graveyard in which heretics and teachers of errors, with their disciples, lie in red-hot tombs. Dante recognizes Farinatadegli Uberti, a great Florentine patriot, and Cavalcante Cavalcanti, the father of his intimate friend and fellow-poet Guido Cavalcanti. In the Seventh Circle tyrants and murderers are doused in a stream of boiling blood. The Eighth is inhabited by deceivers, a category comprising seducers, flatterers, simoniacs, soothsayers, barrators, hypocrites, thieves, evil counselors, schismatics and falsifiers. In the Ninth Circle the most grievous of all crimes, treachery, is expiated. There are traitors to their kindred, traitors to their country, traitors to their friends and traitors to their lords and benefactors. Especially impressive for its poetical beauty, among the encounters of Dante with traitors, is the episode of Count Ugolino, who died of starvation with his children in the tower of Pisa. Now, in the Inferno, he rabidly devours the head of his fatal enemy, Archbishop Ruggero. At the very end of Inferno—the top of the inverted cone—is the giant Lucifer who champs with his teeth Brutus, Cassius and Judas Iscariot, the three arch-sinners.

Purgatory: Purgatory has the shape of a mountain divided into seven terraces. At the peak is the divine forest of earthly Paradise. Outside the gate of Purgatory Dante finds four classes of negligents waiting to be admitted into the place of penance and purification. On the seven terraces are punished the Deadly Sins: Pride, Envy, Anger, Sloth, Avarice and Prodigality, Gluttony, Lust. On the stairs leading to the gate of Purgatory stands an angel who, with the point of his sword, traces on Dante's forehead seven P's—the initial of the Latin word *peccata,* sins. Dante is bidden to wash the seven letters off, one by one, in the seven circles of Purgatory. During the ascent, as Dante wanders from one circle to another, an angelic choir sings the Beatitudes in contrast to the Seven Deadly Sins. When Dante reaches the Seventh Circle, where the sins of carnal lust are cleansed, he is moved by the sight of penitents moving in flame and singing the hymn of divine clemency. On the other side of the flame stands the angel of chastity who, with the cry "Blessed are the pure in heart" bids the poet to go through the fire. He is now purged of all sins and the last P has been erased from his brow. Dante and Virgil have now reached the mountain summit and they enter the forest of earthly Paradise. Beatrice, the woman whom Dante most loved in his life and who represents in his eyes the embodiment of human perfection, appears adorned with heavenly beauty. He then is immersed in the waters of Lethe and thus purified is ready for his flight to Paradise. Beatrice now replaces Virgil as Dante's guide.

Paradise: Dante's Paradise consists of nine Heavens all surrounded by the Empyrean Sphere where dwells the Divine Presence. The earth, with its Inferno and Purgatory, is the center around which they revolve. Led now by the spirit of Beatrice, Dante is flooded by an ocean of light. His inner hearing is opened to receive the celestial harmonies of the Spheres. Beatrice informs him that now he is in Heaven, borne there by the longing of his purified soul for the presence of God. As they journey from Sphere to Sphere, Beatrice's beauty grows ever more radiant. In the First Sphere, that of the Moon, Beatrice discourses learnedly on the mystic powers of the moon and the stars. The first of the blessed souls appears. In the Second Sphere, the Sphere of Mercury, Dante is joyfully surrounded by the blessed spirits who, seeing that he is blessed by God, wish to increase their love through him. As they soar to the Third Sphere, Beatrice imparts to him all the secrets of the Redemption, which are hidden from all except those who have been purified by the flames of love. In the Fourth Sphere, that of the Sun, reside the great teachers of the Church: Albertus Magnus, Thomas Aquinas, Peter Lombard, King Solomon, Boethius, Isidore of Seville and the Venerable Bede. St. Thomas then proceeds to instruct the poet in the manner of the risen body of saints. In the Sphere of Mars, the Fifth Heaven, and surrounding the Cross, appear the spirits of those who have borne arms in the service of the Lord. Dante meets Joshua, Judas Maccabeus, Charlemagne and Roland. In the Sixth Heaven, of Jupiter, appear the blessed spirits of upright monarchs. In the next, the Sphere of Saturn, appear the saints of the contemplative life. In the Eighth Heaven, that of the fixed stars, Dante beholds in awe the splendor of Christ, surrounded by the Virgin Mother and the Apostles. When he finally rises to the Ninth or crystalline Heaven, Dante can behold its glories only through the pure eyes of Beatrice. He sees the nine choirs of angels moving in concentric circles around the throne of God. He receives instructions on the various hierarchies of angels and on their creation and fall. Then Beatrice leads him to the Empyrean where he gazes on the seat of God and the blessed who surround him. In the heavenly zone Beatrice bids him farewell and takes her place among the blessed. St. Bernard de Clairvaux assumes the role of guide and reveals to Dante the final aim of man. St. Bernard utters a prayer of intercession to the Virgin for him. Dante then obtains, in an outburst of ecstasy, the grace to plunge himself into the contemplation of God, the highest, the supreme goal of man. The poet ends on a lofty note: "But now my desire and my will were revolved, like a wheel which is moved evenly, by the Love which moves the sun and the other stars."

Dante's immortal poem reveals, in their highest form and essence, the religion, philosophy and morality of the Middle Ages. It is like a gigantic cathedral, built on the spacious road of human history, to indicate that a whole epoch is finished and another begins. But it is not to these qualities, no matter how important, that *The Divine Comedy* owes its immortal fame. Dante the philosopher, Dante the theologian and Dante the political theorist are all surpassed by an even greater Dante—the poet. Throughout the marvelous voyage, in its dramatic encounters with the damned, the spirits in penance or the blessed, Dante gives vent to his individual passions and feelings, revealing a vehemence hardly equaled, never surpassed, both in hatred and love. His artistic capacity to translate this passionate feeling into beauty makes of Dante one of the outstanding poets of all time.

DIWAN, by Moses Ibn Ezra. See IBN EZRA, MOSES.

DR. ADRIAAN (1901–1903), by Louis Couperus. See COUPERUS, LOUIS.

DR. DOLITTLE TALES (1920–1928), by Hugh Lofting. The best known of the Dr. Dolittle nonsense stories for children are: *The Story of Dr.*

Dolittle (1920); *The Voyage of Dr. Dolittle* (1922); *Dr. Dolittle's Circus* (1924); *Dr. Dolittle's Zoo* (1925); *Dr. Dolittle's Caravan* (1926); *Dr. Dolittle's Garden* (1927); and *Dr. Dolittle in the Moon* (1928). *The Story of Dr. Dolittle* tells of the eccentric man's love for animals. He harbors queer pets and alarms his unsuspecting patients. His passion for animals makes him abandon his medical practice and become a veterinarian. In time he learns the languages of birds and animals, being taught by Polynesia, the wise old parrot. Then he proceeds to Africa to find a cure for a disease ravaging the monkeys of the dark continent. *The Voyages of Dr. Dolittle* recounts the quaint and merry adventures of the ex-medico and Tommy, the cobbler's son, when they go off to hunt for jabizri beetles on Spidermonkey Island. *Dr. Dolittle's Zoo* is a lively description of the good doctor's animal friends who so love him that when his life is in danger they rush to his rescue.

DOCTOR FAUSTUS (1947), by Thomas Mann. This novel in biography form is inspired by the old German folkbook of the magician and charlatan Faustus who made a pact with the devil in order to receive knowledge and worldly treasures. Serenus Zeitblom, a retired high school teacher of classical languages, starts in 1943 to record the life story of his best friend, the composer Adrian Leverkuehn who had died in 1940. Interspersed with the faithful professor's notes on the contemporary scene, based on diaries, letters and personal recollections, Leverkuehn's tragic and lonely life emerges: the story of a creative genius who renounced human love for the sake of inspiration. The composer, as a young student, had contracted syphilis; the last decade of his life he had lingered on as an insane wreck. To Leverkuehn himself, his affliction had been an arrogant and self-imposed act, confirmed by the devil with whom he had once carried on an imaginary conversation about it. While Zeitblom finishes his friend's biography, the Allies approach his little Bavarian retreat. Thus, Leverkuehn's end coincides with Germany's doom.

Thomas Mann's latest novel is symbolic of the fate and aspirations of Germany and an allegorical treatment of his life-long controversy: artist versus bourgecis. It is a new variation of the Faust theme, which links the magician of the folkbook and Goethe's hero with the spirit of music, the disease of romanticism, and the resonance of Nietzsche, whose life is in parts the model for Leverkuehn. Mann's description of music never actually composed is one of the most daring innovations of modern fiction. In the last analysis, *Doctor Faustus* concerns the creative individual ir our time.

DR. FAUSTUS, THE TRAGICAL HISTORY OF (1589), by Christopher Marlowe. The Faust legend, in one form or another, goes back to the Middle Ages. The earliest of its famous and still current forms is the play by Christopher Marlowe, Shakespeare's brilliant contemporary and near-equal. In form it is infinitely simpler than the huge two-part structure which Goethe erected from the same materials. Of Elizabethan plays other than Shakespeare's, it is one of the most effective to read, though difficult to produce.

The over-ambitious scholar Faustus, tempted by his craving for universal knowledge and worldly power, contemplates selling his soul to the devil in return for these prizes. His learning in the dread art of black magic has taught him how he may effect this transaction. Alone in a grove, he performs mystic incantations within a ring of smoke and fire. First a dragon appears in the air above him, then comes Mephistophilis in so horrible a guise that Faustus cannot endure him. With his magic spell he orders Mephistophilis to go and return, ironically enough, in the garb of a Franciscan friar.

After much deliberation Faustus commits himself to the fateful decision and signs with his own blood a contract providing that Mephistophilis shall serve him absolutely for twenty-four years, at the end of which time his body and soul shall be delivered over to Lucifer.

Throughout his twenty-four years Faustus journeys over the world and gratifies his every wish for wealth, power, wisdom and pleasure, even to summoning up Helen of Troy, "the face that launched a thousand ships." But at the expiration of the contracted time, strangely dissatisfied, he faces the hour in which he must fulfill his part of the bargain, by surrendering his soul. He is overcome with terror. Encouraged by his friends, he hopes he may save himself by an eleventh hour repentance. But nothing avails. The clock strikes twelve and Mephistophilis appears with a horde of devils to carry off his screaming victim. Thus it ends; the story of the man who gained the whole world at the loss of his own soul. The play contains many sweeping passages of blank verse, clearly demonstrating the power of what has been called "Marlowe's mighty line."

DR. JEKYLL AND MR. HYDE, THE STRANGE CASE OF (1886), by Robert Louis Stevenson. The theme of this powerful psychological allegory is the duality of man's nature, with its alternation of good and evil impulses. Having often expressed an interest in this problem, Stevenson is said to have hit upon a proper vehicle for its expression one night in a feverish dream. The story has remained a classic in stage and film dramatization. Dr. Jekyll is a highly respected London physician, a good and kindly man, who in his youth had showed inclinations toward evil which, however, he succeeded in suppressing. Interested in drugs, the doctor now chances upon one which enables him to change his external form to that of a repulsive dwarf, the very embodiment of evil, whom he calls Mr. Hyde. A similar dose permits him to return to the form and personality of the benevolent doctor. Many times the doctor becomes Mr. Hyde, thereby giving this side of his nature more and more power. Jekyll finds it increasingly difficult to regain his virtuous entity and also finds himself occasionally becoming Hyde without the use of the drug. Hyde brutally murders Sir Danvers Carew, then, when the drug will no longer resummon the person of Jekyll, prepares a will leaving all Jekyll's possessions to Hyde. Through the investigations of Jekyll's attorney, Utterson, and an early confidence Jekyll had made about his discovery to Dr. Lanyon, the truth is discovered. Hyde kills himself.

DOCTOR THORNE (1858), by Anthony Trollope. This, the third novel in the famous Barsetshire series, follows *Barchester Towers* (q.v.). The opening chapters provide the description of a great English country house, Greshambury, where the Greshamburys have lived and been squires for centuries. Dr. Thorne arrives with his niece Mary and opens a practice. He becomes a good friend of the Squire of Greshambury, who comes to the doctor with his troubles. Mary is educated with the daughters at the big house and all goes well until Frank, the only son and heir, falls in love with Mary who is penniless and, worse still, illegitimate. Mary has a hasty temper and is proud, but no prouder than the Squire's wife, who is a De Courcy, daughter of an Earl. Only a daughter-in-law with money can save the broad acres of Greshambury, so heavy is the mortgage. Two nouveaux riches figure in this novel: Miss Dunstable and Sir Roger Scatcherd, who is a vulgar drunkard and only learns that Mary Thorne is his sister's child on the eve of his death. Then a peculiar run of circumstances and the death of the Scatcherd heir makes Mary heiress to such a fortune as East Barsetshire can scarcely imagine. Thus all the lovers' troubles are ended—for even the De Courcys bow to Midas. Like all of the Barset novels this is made up of the intimate details of the lives of the people, so intimate and so minutely observed by Trollope as to give a verisimilitude rarely found in novelists of his day. People are actual people, not personifications of some odd trait. Good and bad are mixed as they are in life.

DOCTOR'S DILEMMA, THE (1906), by George Bernard Shaw. This play is satire on some aspects of the medical profession. Sir Colenso Ridgeon, just knighted for the discovery of a new treatment for tuberculosis, receives the congratulations of Sir Patrick Cullen, retired, who believes no discoveries are new; Walpole, a surgeon, who thinks all illnesses can be cured by removing the nuciform sac; and Sir Ralph Bloomfield Bonington, who has used Ridgeon's opsonin treatment for typhoid fever and cured little Prince Henry, which is the real reason Ridgeon had been knighted. Beautiful Jennifer Dubedat comes to plead with Ridgeon to save her husband. Ridgeon demurs, but invites Jennifer to bring her husband to a dinner that he is giving for his colleagues.

Louis Dubedat is a young genius and a brilliant rascal; he borrows money from everybody, including Blenkinsop, a poor practitioner, also tubercular, and a friend of Ridgeon. After he leaves, the maid proves Dubedat is her husband. At his studio, when the doctors come for a consultation, he blandly admits to bigamy. The doctors abandon him, with the exception of Bonington. Ridgeon, forced to choose between saving Blenkinsop or Dubedat, decides to save Blenkinsop. Jennifer pleads with him unsuccessfully. Bonington misapplies Ridgeon's treatment, stimulates the disease, and Dubedat becomes fatally ill. His death scene is moving and tender in contrast to what we have previously seen of his character. A year later Ridgeon meets Jennifer at a one-man show of her husband's pictures and she remarks that she has seen Blenkinsop looking well and happy. Ridgeon confesses that he had permitted Dubedat's death because he wanted to marry Jennifer himself. She tells him she has already married again in fulfillment of Dubedat's wish for her happiness.

DOCTRINE OF THE HEAVENLY WAY (1921), by Choi Jewu, Choi Siyung, Son Pyunghi. See CHUNTOKYO KYOCHI, by Choi Jewu, Choi Siyung, Son Pyunghi.

DODSWORTH (1929), by Sinclair Lewis. Samuel Dodsworth is president of the Revelation Motor Company in this famous novel. A sincere, intelligent, likable fellow, he is restless; he consents, at the urging of his wife Fran, to a trip to Europe. This trip brings about, gradually, the separation of the Dodsworths. Fran is an intolerable snob, bored with Sam, sick of America, and grimly determined to become a complete European. Sam is patient and pathetically loyal during a trying period in which his wife involves herself with a series of unpleasant people, beginning with the Englishman Major Clyde Lockert. The worst influence is the Parisian Renée de Pénable, through whom Fran has an affair with Arnold Israel. Another affair, with the young, impoverished Baron Kurt von Obersdorf, is intended to terminate in marriage. Fran begins divorce proceedings. Sam, hurt and lonely, finds a rewarding companionship in Italy with Edith Cortwright. His peace is threatened when Fran, jilted by her new lover, tries to reclaim him. But he finally manages to free himself from her and approaches the task of building a new life.

DOG OF FLANDERS, A (1872), by Ouida (Louise de la Ramée). Nello, who wants to be an artist, and his faithful dog, Petrasche, live in the Flemish town of Antwerp with Jehan Daas, Nello's grandfather. Alois Cogez, daughter of a wealthy miller, is loved by Nello, but her father, Baas, is cruel to the boy. The thoughtless actions of Baas towards Nello are imitated by the townspeople. Jehan dies, and Nello is left penniless and homeless. His hopes of winning an art scholarship are defeated. As he wanders about in the snow, he finds a purse full of money belonging to Baas. In spite of his destitute condition, he returns it and leaves his hungry dog with the family. He then wanders to the church to look at Ruben's Christ, and is followed by Petrasche who refuses to be parted from his master. Both die of hunger and cold. The townspeople repent their harshness, and, as a last bit of irony, an artist who had found in Nello's painting a rare touch of genius, offers—too late—to teach the boy.

Although not valued by the sophisticated, this sentimental novel appears to survive changes of literary taste and finds new readers in each generation.

DOLL'S HOUSE, A (1879), by Henrik Ibsen. One of the best known of Ibsen's plays and one of the most widely discussed, it raised a furor at the time it was first produced, as it dealt with the question of woman's social position and was far in advance of its day. An almost perfect example of a realistic three-act drama, the action takes place at Christmastide in Christiania in the space of three days. Torvald Helmer, a vain but conscientious lawyer, has just received a promotion at the bank, and his wife, Nora, pretty, lighthearted and seemingly frivolous, feels that they can squander a little money on Christmas festivities. Helmer, who treats her like a child and calls her his "little lark," warns her that she must be more careful, as money always slips through her fingers, and she is continually asking him for more. Mrs. Linden, an old widowed friend of Nora's, calls and admits that she had heard of Helmer's improved position and had hoped that maybe Nora could find her a place in her husband's bank. Nora proudly tells her friend that she has been earning money too. Helmer was very ill the first year of their marriage and to save his life it was necessary to take him to Italy. Nora borrowed the necessary money, but told Helmer that she had received a small legacy from her father. She has managed to pay the interest out of her clothes allowance, and sometimes found work unknown to her husband. But now the debt is almost paid off. Helmer agrees to employ Mrs. Linden and gives her the position in the bank held by Nils Krogstad, a lawyer of shady character who had been convicted of forgery. Krogstad is the man from whom Nora had borrowed the money and he threatens to reveal the loan to her husband if he loses his job. He points out that her father, who was supposed to have signed the paper for the loan, was dead at the time. Nora finally admits that she forged her father's signature. She tries to coax her husband to keep Krogstad, who is trying to regain his position in society, but Helmer says the former was a forger and insists on replacing him. Mrs. Linden, an old friend of Krogstad's, promises to appeal to him in Nora's behalf, but discovers that he has gone out of town. In the meantime Krogstad has written Helmer a letter telling him the story, and Nora is desperate. She sees the letter in the letter-box, but cannot remove it as her husband has the key. She does everything to prevent his reading it. They go to a fancy dress party in the apartment above with a friend, Dr. Rank, who knows he is dying, and is hopelessly in love with Nora. She wears an Italian costume and dances the tarantella, trying to keep her husband diverted by her feverish gaiety. In a despairing mood she plans to slip out and commit suicide at the moment Helmer discovers the letter. When he reads it he accuses her of having committed a serious crime which will ruin him, and tells her she is not fit to associate with their children. His self-righteousness exceeds even her anticipation. Krogstad sends back the promissory note, and Helmer cries that he is saved. But Nora has been too deeply shocked to return to her husband, and in a dramatic scene leaves him to support herself, and learn to do her own thinking. She gives him a ray of hope that if a miracle should occur perhaps they can be reunited.

DOM CASMURRO (1900), by Joaquim Maria Machado de Assis. In *Dom Casmurro*, which is one of Machado de Assis' most popular works, the weak and unhappy hero discovers that his wife has betrayed him. He is quite distressed and above all, puzzled, for he and his wife have known each other from childhood. Much of the novel is devoted, therefore, to an analysis of the hero, who ponders whether she was a hypocrite or the victim of her impulses. Machado de Assis is Brazil's outstanding novelist and one of America's truly great writers as evidenced by some of his magnificent productions: *Tales* (1870–), *Resurrection* ('872), *Helena* (1876), *Iaia Garcia* (1878), *Posthumous Memoirs of Braz Cubas* (1881), *Quincas Borba* (1892), and *Memorial de Aires* (1908). In Machado de Assis may be discerned that mixture of romanticism and realism which is associated with the French master Flaubert, but in his psychological penetration he goes almost as far as Stendhal and Proust.

DOMBEY AND SON (1848), by Charles Dickens. Dombey, a proud and wealthy man, loses his wife, children and fortune, but through the love of his daughter, Florence, finds happiness again. The story opens with the birth of a son and heir, Paul Dombey, and the death of Mrs. Dombey. The frail boy does not live long. His father, bitter at losing what he most wanted, neglects his daughter, Florence. She is a lonely child, forever trying to win her father's love. Dombey's second wife, Edith Granger, is kind to the girl. This arouses her husband's jealousy, which complicates matters for Florence. She becomes friendly with kind Walter Gay, a young man employed by Dombey. Edith had married for money and position but dislike for her harsh, cold husband finally forces her to leave. She goes to Paris with crafty Mr. Carker, business manager for Dombey and Son. Mr. Dombey follows and Carker is accidentally killed while trying to escape. Florence turns to Captain Cuttle, a friend of Walter's.

It is believed that Walter is lost at sea, but he unexpectedly returns and marries Florence. The firm of Dombey fails; Dombey finds himself alone and miserable. He regrets the loss of his daughter; her sweet face and kind words haunt him. Florence returns and once more begs for his love, which he is more than willing to give now. With his grandchildren, Dombey tries to make retribution for the past.

DOME OF MANY-COLORED GLASS, A (1912), by Amy Lowell. See LOWELL, AMY.

DON CARLOS (1787), by Friedrich von Schiller. See SCHILLER, FRIEDRICH VON.

DON JUAN (1819–1824), by George Gordon, Lord Byron. This is a sixteen-canto epic satire in ottava rima. Don Juan is a young Spanish grandee who, having been seduced by a married woman, flees the vengeance of her husband. Shipwrecked on an Aegean island he is saved by the lovely Haidée, a Greek girl. The two fall in love and decide to marry. At the height of the wedding festivities, Haidée's father, Lambro the pirate, who has been given up for dead, makes his appearance. He disarms the groom and carries him off to Constantinople where he sells him as a slave to the Sultana Gulbayez. Haidée, heartbroken, dies. Later Juan escapes from the jealous Sultana and participates in the assault on Ismail by the Russians. He so distinguishes himself on the battlefield that he is dispatched to St. Petersburg with the glad tidings as special courier to the Empress Catherine II, who makes Juan her lover and sends him as ambassador to the Court of England. Byron uses this epic as a vehicle in which he satirizes English life and customs, manners and morals.

DON JUAN TENORIO (1844), by José Zorrilla. The most popular work of the modern Spanish theater is unquestionably Zorrilla's *Don Juan*. This seven-act play in verse is performed throughout the Spanish-speaking nations during the first week of November. A reworking of the Don Juan legend, the striking departure of Zorrilla's version is that the wicked rake and cynical sensualist is in the end saved from the fires of hell by falling in love with the pure Doña Inés. Don Juan repents of his sins and prays to God for forgiveness but what really effects his salvation is Doña Inés' prayers on his behalf. In addition to its lofty moral and religious conception, the play is intense and fast moving, depicts life with animation and color and shows remarkable spontaneity and richness of versification.

DON QUIXOTE OF LA MANCHA (1605, 1615), by Miguel de Cervantes. An elderly country gentleman of La Mancha becomes so utterly mad reading romances of chivalry that he finally believes them to be true and, considering himself a knight-errant, goes forth into the world to defend the oppressed and to undo wrongs. Since knights-errant cannot exist without lady-loves, he chooses as the lady of his thoughts a peasant girl he had known in former years and gives her the name of Dulcinea. After his first sortie, in which he is knighted, he urges an ignorant and credulous but good-natured middle-aged peasant of his village, by name Sancho Panza, to follow him as esquire. Knight and esquire sally forth in search of adventures and there is no dearth of them, thanks to the imagination of the Don, who forever transforms the common into the extraordinary: windmills become giants; inns, castles; galley-slaves, oppressed gentlemen. The esquire's more pedestrian perception of the truth forms a contrast to the illusions of his masters, but both suffer the most excruciating discomfitures and are brought home somewhat crushed in body and spirit.

Ten years later, spurred by the appearance of a spurious *Don Quixote*, Cervantes published the second part of his novel. This is perhaps superior to Part I, showing more invention, vigor and richer material: Don Quixote's dream in the cave of Montesinos, the puppet show of Maese Pedro, the adventures at the castle of the Duke, Sancho as governor of his island, the scenes with the Robin Hood Roque Guinart, and the final defeat of Don Quixote. By the time of the death of the Knight, Sancho Panza has become an altogether lovable, quixotic character, so that the reader parts from them and their exciting world of marvels with deeply felt regret. The novel which obviously had for its genesis the satire of romances of chivalry, gradually grew into a vast panorama of Spanish life and into a most entertaining work of fiction, the first modern novel, read and admired to this day as one of the world's great literary achievements.

DON SEGUNDO SOMBRA (1926), by Ricardo Güiraldes. At the death of a wealthy rancher, his illegitimate son is sent to town to be brought up by his spinster aunts. Discontented with his lot, the orphan becomes lazy and incorrigible. But he has aspirations, and one day they are crystallized when an old gaucho, Don Segundo Sombra, comes riding into town. The lad runs off with Don Segundo who initiates him into the life of the herder. Thenceforth the novel is a story of wanderings and adventures and fleeting love-affairs; there are stirring horse races, cockfights, cattle driving, bronco busting, all spiced with Don Segundo's tall and subtly philosophical yarns. After several colorful and exciting years, just as the waif has won his spurs, he is called back to inherit the property of the family. He leaves with deep regret.

DOÑA BÁRBARA (1929), by Rómulo Gallegos. After completing his law studies in Caracas, the youthful Santos Luzardo returns to his ranch in the isolated inland delta lying between the Apure and the Upper Orinoco. The last of an old Venezuelan family decimated by an ancient feud, he finds his estate in a rundown condition: its overseers have been weaklings in the hands of Doña Bárbara. But who is Doña Bárbara? As a child she had been kept on a pirogue (river boat) that plied the waters of the Orinoco. Surviving the rough treatment of the crew, she had developed into a beautiful mestizo woman. Hasdrubal the vagabond had won her love, but since the captain of the pirogue wanted her for himself, he was soon put out of the way. Embittered, subject to daily punishment by the captain, Bárbara became a bloodthirsty maenad. With her beauty and her knowledge of witchcraft she avenges herself on men, seducing or destroying them. In her fight against the honest Santos, however, she meets her Waterloo. He finally marries her illegitimate daughter. Masterfully apprehended, the landscape of the Venezuelan llanos remains from the opening pages of this novel a living presence, organically related to the windswept saga.

DOÑA PERFECTA (1876), by Benito Pérez Galdós. The young engineer Pepe Rey comes to visit his aunt, Doña Perfecta, a kind and just woman, but a religious bigot, who lives on her country estate in the provincial town of Orbajosa. His father and Doña Perfecta have arranged for his betrothal to his cousin Rosario. Upon meeting, the young people fall in love with each other. At first Doña Perfecta encourages the match, but her confessor, Don Inocencio, the Canon of the cathedral, is determined that his lawyer-nephew, Jacintito, should marry Rosario for her wealth, and he engages in a conspiracy to drive Pepe away. He undermines Pepe's position by exposing him to his aunt as an atheist and blasphemer, and in time Doña Perfecta, who notices that her nephew despises her beloved town and its customs, begins to hate him and plots to do away with him. She, Don Inocencio, and the latter's sister, María Remedios, persuade the swaggering Caballuco to murder Pepe. When the latter comes to Doña Perfecta's house to elope with Rosario, the assassin lies in wait for him and shoots him. Rosario then goes out of her mind. Thus Pérez Galdós, illustrating the havoc wrought by bigotry, dramatized his anti-clerical thesis.

DONNE, JOHN (1572–1631). The years following World War I saw a great rediscovery of Donne under the critical leadership of T. S. Eliot. Modern readers have found this troubled and paradoxical poet and preacher a witty, fascinating and oddly familiar voice. He is of the present era in his struggle with disillusion, with the new science, in his close psychological analyses, his concern with sex, the very colloquialism and experimental looseness of his verse. Essays began to pour out in appreciation of his quality of felt thought, and the newest poets stole tricks from him. He was at once recognizable and novel, and he was enviable in having at last quieted his own flame by merging it in the light of faith. Having, before he was twenty-five, written so passionately and cleverly about his mistress, he turned, in his *Divine Poems* to writing no less passionately and cleverly about God. The posthumously published *Songs and Sonnets* (1633) contain such now famous poems as the "Song" ("Go and catch a falling star"); "The Flea," a good example of the far-fetched comparisons of the "metaphysicals," where the parasite that has bitten lover and mistress serves as an argument for the final yielding of the mistress; "The Canonization," beginning "For God's sake hold your tongue and let me love"; his "Song" on parting from his wife, "Sweetest love, I do not go"; "A Valediction Forbidding Mourning," with its famous comparison of the compasses; "The Relique," with its great all-summing line, "A bracelet of bright hair about the bone." But the poem into which Donne put most of his secular philosophy is "The Ecstasy," with its subtle exploration of the body-soul equilibrium. There are no true sonnets in this part of the volume: they come, after Donne took orders, with the *Divine Poems*, and two stand out, "At the round earth's imagined corners, blow" and "Death be not proud, though some have called thee." Also notable is "A Hymn to God the Father," where Donne puns on his name:

> And, having done that, Thou hast done,
> I fear no more.

After the erstwhile cynic and sower of wild oats gave himself to the church and became Dean of St. Paul's in London, he preached great sermons, some of which are still read. There are several modern selections from *LXXX Sermons* (1640), *Fifty Sermons* (1649), and *XXVI Sermons* (1660). Most famous is "Death's Duel," Donne's last sermon, which he rose from his deathbed to preach and which is full of unforgettable images of decay and dissolution, death being in fact a subject that stirred him to great heights in prose and verse. Some attention has also been paid his *Devotions* (1624), written during a serious illness. The full title reads: "Devotions upon emergent occasions and several steps in my sickness digested into: 1. Meditations upon our human condition. 2. Expostulations and debatements with God. 3. Prayers upon the several occasions to Him." The seventeenth Meditation provided Ernest Hemingway with the title for his novel *For Whom the Bell Tolls* (q.v.).

DOUBLE MAN, THE (1941), by Wystan Hugh Auden. See AUDEN, WYSTAN HUGH.

DOUBTFUL MAN, THE (1619), by Juan Ruiz de Alarcón. Don Garcia, the hero of the play, is a young gentleman of lofty birth, wealthy, amiable, handsome, but with one great defect: his habit of lying. On his arrival in Madrid from Salamanca, at whose University he had been studying, he meets the beautiful Jacinta, whose name—through a series of errors—he takes to be Lucrecia, that of her best friend. He courts her, unnecessarily pretending to be a rich Indiano, i.e., a Spaniard returned from the Indies. When his father wants to marry him to Jacinta, precisely the girl he loves under a different name, he declines, claiming that for honor's sake he had married a lady in Salamanca. Enmeshed in the web of his own lies, Don Garcia is shamed and disgraced and finally compelled to marry some other lady.

Corneille took material for his *Menteur* from Ruiz de Alarcón's play and with it gave the French theater its first great comedy of manners.

DOWNFALL, THE (1892), by Emile Zola. See ROUGON-MAC-QUART, THE, by Emile Zola.

DOWNSTREAM (1920), by Sigfrid Siwertz. This is a long, powerful novel of personal and social degeneracy, by a member of the Swedish Academy, rightly acclaimed an "accomplished stylist," in "plastic and colorful prose." It is a tale of incredible greed and egotism, by five members of the Selamb family, the eldest son of which develops into a classic personification of the selfishness of wealth, a selfishness which survives even the principal instrument of it— "Peter the Boss." He is a profiteer who cheats everybody, including his brothers and sisters, all through life, but keeps out of jail. He is ever amassing money. His grandfather had been a rascal, so what could you expect? At the end, through a shrewdly constructed will, made just before his death, Peter leaves his entire fortune to his illegitimate son, without legally acknowledging him as such, not in order to ease his conscience but to die with the satisfaction that the three surviving members of the family—one brother had committed suicide in the meantime—will not get it. The fortune is too much for the young son, and he soon enters a drunkard's grave. The brother and two sisters have some pride, but are almost as ruthless as their scheming brother, with ever-recurring evidences of indolence, intrigue, debts, wealthy marriages to pay those debts, morbid sex inhibitions, and "violent primitivism." The novel is not pleasant reading, but grips and holds interest as the action moves on, irresistibly, relentlessly, toward the inevitable finale of boredom, unhappiness, and a vague sense of lives misspent. But there is a bright spot: in America lives a young engineer, the only Selamb heir, who had early understood the circumstances at home and escaped at sixteen from his divorced but remarried mother. Some day perhaps, through him, the Selamb millions will be of some use to society.

DRACULA (1897), by Bram Stoker. In this, perhaps the most blood-curdling book-length story in the English language, the chief figure is the king of vampires, Count Dracula. The narrative takes the form of journals or letters by various characters. Jonathan Harker has to go on business to the castle of Count Dracula, where three beautiful women, kept as vampires, seek to conquer him. Harker is at last able to escape and lies with brain fever in Budapest, where he marries his old friend from England, Mina Murray, who came to nurse him. Meanwhile Mina's friend Lucy Westenra in England gets a mysterious disease and dies under terrible circumstances, bloodless, a mark on her throat. After her death she too becomes a vampire. Her fiancé Lord Godalming and her two admirers, Dr. Seward, who has an insane asylum near by, and Quincey Morris, seek to revenge their friend with the help of the famous Dutch scientist Van Helsing. First they free Lucy by driving a stake through her heart and cutting her head off. Mina is also showing the dread symptoms. Renfield, a patient in the asylum who seeks to prolong his life by eating flies and spiders, is killed when he tries to help. After many adventures and Morris' death, the surviving allies bring the vampirism in Transylvania to an end.

DRAGON HARVEST (1945), by Upton Sinclair. See JUNGLE, THE, by Upton Sinclair.

DRAGON'S TEETH (1942), by Upton Sinclair. See JUNGLE, THE, by Upton Sinclair.

DRAM SHOP, THE (1877), by Emile Zola. See ROUGON-MAC-QUART, THE, by Emile Zola.

DRAMA NUEVO, UN (1867), by Manuel Tamayo y Baus. See NEW DRAMA, A, by Manuel Tamayo y Baus.

DRAYMAN HENSCHEL (1898), by Gerhart Hauptmann. See HAUPTMANN, GERHART.

DREAM OF THE RED CHAMBER (1754), by Tsao Hsueh-Chin. See HUNG LOU MENG, by Tsao Hsueh-Chin.

DREAM OF THE ROOD, THE (ca. 10th c.?), Anonymous. In this, the most beautiful of Old English religious poems, the dreamer sees a tree surrounded by bright light. It becomes a brilliant shining cross, the beacon of Christ—a jeweled cross, exquisitely wrought. The cross is speaking of its own sorrows when Christ appears and mounts the rood. Here the style of the poem changes. No longer is it leisurely; a new urgency has come. The horror of the tree rises steadily, but Christ is swift, He must play out His part. The cross and Christ are vividly presented. The dreamer worships the cross, and hope is born anew.

DRED, A TALE OF THE DISMAL SWAMP (1856), by Harriet Beecher Stowe. See UNCLE TOM'S CABIN, by Harriet Beecher Stowe.

DRIEKONINGENTRYPTIEK (1923), by Felix Timmermans. See TIMMERMANS, FELIX.

DROGON (1896), by Arthur van Schendel. See SCHENDEL, ARTHUR VAN.

DROLL PETER (Eng. tr. 1930), by Felix Timmermans. See TIMMERMANS, FELIX.

DROLL TALES (1832–1833), by Honoré de Balzac. See HUMAN COMEDY, THE, by Honoré de Balzac.

DROSTE-HÜLSHOFF, ANNETTE ELISABETH VON (1797–1848). One of the most important German poets of the nineteenth century, Annette von Droste-Hülshoff was possessed of a pious nature which served to cover an intensity of emotional conflict. This is reflected in her *The Spiritual Year* (published 1852), a collection of deeply religious poems, and *Gedichte* (1844), another poetry collection. In her lyrics and ballads, which exhibit a sharp observation and an earnest feeling for a many-faceted nature-atmosphere, she skillfully sings of home and folk and of the common life of her native homeland. Characterized by a realistic preoccupation with detail, the firmness of her poetic art often affords a masculine touch, in contrast to the womanly element which expresses a quiet, unpropagandistic protest at the limitations of feminine life. Although previously influenced by an older Romanticism, her later work shows, besides the realistic touch, a genuine modest humor—this placing her outside the Romanticists. Her novelle (long short-story) *Die Judenbuche* (The Jew's Beech Tree; 1842) is a tale of a conscience-stricken murderer of a Jew who returns to hang himself on the beech tree where he had committed the deed. The story ranks among the masterpieces of short prose fiction.

DRUMS ALONG THE MOHAWK (1936), by Walter D. Edmonds. This novel tells of a Mohawk Valley farm during the Indian fighting of the American Revolution. Gilbert Martin and his wife, Magdelana, settle in Deerfield in 1776, but are forced to leave and seek shelter with Mrs. McKlennar. Gil joins the fight, and after the war returns to take Lana and the children back to Deerfield. Subplots tell of John Wolff, who is tried for treason and committed to Newgate Prison; and Nancy Schuyler, who accepts the protection of the Indian Gahota for her fatherless child, later marrying him. This novel gives the farmer's point of view of the Revolutionary War: his struggle without government help, his suffering from the depredations of land which take place while he is fighting, his brave perseverance.

Mr. Edmonds had previously made his mark as a New York historian with the novel *Rome Haul* (1929). This is the story of Dan'l Harrow, a young farmer who spends a year on the Erie Canal. He becomes the owner of a boat, the "Sarsey Sal," and falls in love with Molly Larkins, a true daughter of the "canawlers." Gotham Klore, Molly's former lover, vows vengeance and the men fight a terrific battle. Dan wins, but decides to give up his drifting life. Molly, knowing that their happiness together had been founded in the life of the canal, sends him back alone to the farmland.

DRYDEN, JOHN (1631–1700). Quite apart from his work in the drama, such as *All for Love* and *Marriage à la Mode* (qq.v.), there has been in recent years a return to appreciation of Dryden as an artful poet of statement, as a complete master of the heroic couplet, and as one of the few great satirists in English verse. Moreover he is the first great English critic. His various prefaces and essays are monuments both to his sound judgment and his remarkably modern, flexible prose, as can be seen notably in his *Essay of Dramatick Poesie* (q.v.).

Unquestionably his small masterpiece in satire is *MacFlecknoe, or A Satyr upon the True-Blew-Protestant Poet, T.S.* (1682), of which the butt is Thomas Shadwell, who had answered Dryden's *The Medall, A Satyre against Sedition* (1682) with *The Medal of John Bayes,* and who superseded Dryden as poet laureate after the revolution of 1688. Richard Flecknoe, who was an obscure Irish priest and poet, is pictured as yielding the throne of Dulness to his truest son:

> Shadwell alone of all my sons is he
> Who stands confirm'd in full stupidity.
> The rest to some faint meaning make pretence,
> But Shadwell never deviates into sense.

On a larger scale is *Absalom and Achitophel* (Part I, 1681), a clever allegory about the rebellion of the Duke of Monmouth (Absalom), the natural son of Charles II (David). The principal villain is the scheming Earl of Shaftesbury (Achitophel), and the object of the poem was to quiet the uprising before it attained serious proportions. Dryden shows himself a tactful monarchist and a belittler of anxieties over a future Roman Catholic king in the king's brother, the Duke of York. Part II (1682) was mostly written by Nahum Tate, but contains two hundred brilliant lines by Dryden against Shadwell and another minor poet, Elkanah Settle. Dryden, himself a convert to the Roman church, defended it in another allegory, *The Hind and the Panther* (1687), where the "milk-white hind" of Catholicism is pursued by the spotted panther of the Church of England. The poet, notoriously a turncoat, at least until the Glorious Revolution, had espoused the opposite cause in *Religio Laici* (1682).

Convincing proof that this poet was not confined to the heroic couplet is provided by two favorites of anthologists, "A Song for St. Cecelia's Day" (1687) and "Alexander's Feast; or the Power of Musique" (1697), besides the striking narrative poem "Annus Mirabilis" (1667), dealing with the previous year, when the Dutch fleet was defeated and the plague was succeeded by the great fire of London, which is presented as a monster in stride. There are 304 quatrains.

DU BELLAY, JOACHIM (ca. 1525–1562). Poet and theorist, Du Bellay was the nephew of the Cardinal of the same name, whom Rabelais may have served as personal physician. In Rome, where he was a head steward in his uncle's household, Du Bellay learned much from the poets of the Italian renaissance, and experienced the homesickness which inspires so much of his best verse, *The Antiquities of Rome* and *The Regrets* (both 1558).

> Happy who like Ulysses or that sage
> Who raped the fleece . . .

Earlier he had been better known as a Petrarchist who wrote poems to a lady named Olive, as a sporadic translator, and as a satellite of Ronsard (q.v.).

As theorist he is generally credited with the *Defence and Illustration of the French Language,* but his role at this point seems to have been that of collaborator with Ronsard, and in any case scholars have demonstrated that this work is largely derived from an Italian model. Apart from his own poetry, Du Bellay's contribution to the development of the French poetic tradition consisted in what he did to bring the literatures of France and Italy closer together.

DUBLINERS (1914), by James Joyce. This collection contains fifteen short stories: "The Sisters," "An Encounter," "Araby," "Eveline," "After the Race," "Two Gallants," "The Boarding House," "A Little Cloud," "Counterparts," "Clay," "A Painful Case," "Ivy Day in the Committee Room," "A Mother," "Grace," "The Dead." They are vivid, clear sketches of life in Dublin, stories of death, love, school life, social life. "The Sisters" is a story of a boy's impression of a priest's death. "Eveline" is a woman afraid to love. "A Mother" is the ambitious woman who will ruin her daughter. "A Painful Case" is the story of a celibate who refuses love to the woman who loves him, and at her death finds he is alone.

DUCHESS OF MALFI, THE (published 1623), by John Webster. This Italianate play exemplifies the Senecan tragedy of blood and the heaping up of horrors. The Duchess, a young widow, has two brothers, Ferdinand of Calabria, and the Cardinal, who do not wish her to marry again. The Cardinal orders Bosola, his tool and a former slave, to spy on her. She secretly marries Antonio, her faithful steward, and has several children by him. Eventually Bosola betrays her marriage to Ferdinand, and she and Antonio are banished from Malfi. At Ferdinand's orders Bosola captures the Duchess, tortures her mentally, and finally strangles her and her children. Bosola is then stricken with remorse and slays the Cardinal after killing Antonio whom he mistakes for the Cardinal. He in turn is killed by Ferdinand who goes mad.

DUEL, THE (1905), by Alexander Ivanovich Kuprin. Famous as a writer of short stories, Kuprin achieved his first great literary success with this novel. This was partly due to its singular timeliness, for it appeared shortly after the military and naval disasters of Mukden and Tsushima. Though an indictment of the Russian military bureaucracy, its author actually had been at work on this novel before these debacles. There is excellent characterization of individuals of the military, of which the book is a severe criticism. Both the hero, Second Lieutenant Romashov, and the heroine, Shurochka, the wife of a lieutenant, are portrayed with exceptionally skillful realism.

Another book which achieved a certain popularity in translation is *Yama* (*The Pit;* 1912), which describes minutely life in a house of prostitution. As a piece of literature this novel is negligible.

DUINESE ELEGIES (1922) by Rainer Maria Rilke. See RILKE, RAINER MARIA.

DULCY (1921), by George S. Kaufman and Marc Connelly. See OF THEE I SING, by George S. Kaufman and Morrie Ryskind.

DUN CHON, by Li Jip. See SHIJO-YUCHIP.

DUNBAR, PAUL LAURENCE (1872–1906). Paul Dunbar is a poet who uses the idiom of his people to create fine lyricism in the pathos and humor of Negro folk material. *Lyrics of Lowly Life* (1896), *Lyrics of the Hearthside* (1899), and *Lyrics of Love and Laughter* (1903), illustrate his musically graceful and sincere works. They reveal, too, the poet's bitterness against the oppression of his people, whom he defends and loves passionately. *Lyrics of Sunshine and Shadow* (1905) are more derivative and sentimentalized pieces, often in dialect.

The poet also wrote novels, the most popular *The Sport of the Gods* (1902).

DUNCIAD, THE (Anonymously, 3 books, 1728; "New Dunciad," 1742; Complete work, 1743), by Alexander Pope. This is an audacious verse satire, in heroic couplets, on Grub Street scribblers, poetasters, dullards and literary hacks. It began as an attack on Theobald in answer to his criticisms of Pope's edition of Shakespeare. In the early editions, Theobald was the central character, but later Colley Cibber was substituted. Book I: The rule of Dulness is depicted; Cibber is anointed King of the Dunces, ruling the Empires of Emptiness and Dulness. Book II: The coronation is celebrated with games and contests. The critics are to decide which of the poets' works is the best, but cannot keep awake through their reading. Book III: Cibber in a dream is carried to the Elysian Fields and there Elkanah Settle, bombastic city poet and rival of Dryden, shows him how Dulness has prevailed in the past and how it shall triumph in the future. Book IV: Settle's prophecies come to pass; corruption rules in the universities and Dulness reigns supreme. Pope takes this occasion to lampoon publishers exclusively intent on profits, and hacks and slanderers of the weekly journals.

DUSANTES, THE (1888), by Frank R. Stockton. See LADY OR THE TIGER? THE, by Frank R. Stockton.

DUST WHICH IS GOD, THE (1941), by William Rose Benét. See BENÉT, WILLIAM ROSE.

DUTIES OF MAN (1840), by Giuseppe Mazzini. The great libertarian fighter addresses his work to the Italian working class in hopes that it will fulfill "a mission of republican progress for all." When Mazzini speaks of duties he refers to God, Humanity, Fatherland and Family. He praises the inculcation of virtue, moral improvement and the education of the masses. "Men are creatures of education," he insists. Anti-rational and anti-materialistic, he remained a conservative liberal, although a revolutionary. He preached the evangel of world religion of humanity which was to supersede all modern obsolete faiths and thus unite all mankind. Opposed to the Socialists of his day his creed is expressed in the following words: "The origin of your duties is in God. The definition of your duties is in His law." He is chiefly remembered for his fusion of the liberal and nationalistic traditions. After 1848, his influence waned and nationalism aligned itself with militarism and autocracy.

DUTIES OF THE HEART, THE (1040), by Bakhya Ibn Pakuda. The first Jewish attempt at the systematic exposition of ethics, *Duties of the Heart* was originally written in Arabic, translated into Hebrew more than a hundred years later. Its author was remarkably erudite, having mastered the scientific and philosophical literature of the age as well as Jewish rabbinic literature. Bakhya said that the seeker after spiritual and moral truth must not spurn natural science, mathematics, anthropology, zoology, history, etc., as means for achieving his goal. Man's duty is to accept "learning from everybody, no matter to what race or creed he may belong." He holds that the outward act of man is of no moral significance unless it is a manifestation of an inner intention. Not religious formalism but ethical motivation should be the gauge of human conduct. Bakhya's ethics are non-theological; they do not base themselves on Scriptures, or the will of God, or the authority of the rabbis. He claims to deal with the problems of absolute being by the aid of reason and by observation of the material world. It is reason alone which is the final arbiter of whether man's acts are ethical or unethical. The duties of the heart are controlled by purposeful intelligence.

DYNASTS, THE (Part I, 1904; Part II, 1906; Part III, 1908), by Thomas Hardy. This immense, panoramic poetic drama of the Napoleonic wars ranks among Hardy's finest work. Written in three parts, each is a play in itself; he planned it for "mental performance" rather than production on the stage. Four groups of Phantom Intelligences preside over the destinies of mankind, "The Ancient Spirit of the Years," "The Spirit of the Pities," "Spirits Sinister and Ironic," and "The Spirit of Rumour." These spirits act in the capacity of a Greek chorus, though sometimes, like Greek gods, they take on human form and mingle with the multitude.

The story begins in March, 1805. George III, through his ministers, has replied to a friendly letter of Napoleon's offering peace, that he must consult the other Continental Powers. We see Pitt debating the Defense Bill with Sheridan in the House of Commons, while across the Channel Napoleon reviews his troops, waiting for invasion; and in May is crowned in Milan Cathedral in a second coronation. Pitt is ill and tired, but King George will not let him give up. Napoleon defeats General Mack at Ulm. Nelson defeats Villeneuve, the French admiral, at Trafalgar. He dies of wounds and his body is brought back to England for burial. Napoleon wins Austerlitz. Part I ends with the death of Pitt.

Part II begins with Fox as Secretary of State, and the episode of Guillet de Gevrillière's offer to assassinate Napoleon. The French invade Spain through the Pyrenees, and the English back the dethroned Bourbons. Napoleon tells Josephine he is thinking of divorcing her. Sir John Moore is killed at Coruña. Napoleon defeats the Austrians at Wagram. He divorces Josephine to marry Marie Louise of Austria. George III's health fails, and the Prince Regent entertains in London.

Part III begins with the invasion of Russia, while Wellington is fighting in Spain. The Grand Army retreats from Moscow, and Napoleon deserts them, and rushes back to Paris. He abdicates and is sent to Elba, escapes and comes back to be defeated at Waterloo by Wellington.

DZIADY (1823, 1832), by Adam Mickiewicz. See MICKIEWICZ, ADAM.

EARLY AUTUMN (1926), by Louis Bromfield. See GREEN BAY TREE, THE, by Louis Bromfield.

EARTH IS OURS, THE (1935–1939; Eng. tr. 1940), by Vilhelm Moberg. This powerful realistic trilogy in novel form, localized in the author's native province of Smaland, in south-central Sweden, scored on its appearance a literary triumph of great magnitude. Partly autobiographical, the work deals with Knut Toring, who has left his country home for the city, where he has found material success, but is forced by an inner compulsion to return to the scenes of his boyhood. As the novel progresses it concerns itself more and more with the social, political, and economic problems of the day, and the third volume, written just before World War II, registers a forceful protest against totalitarianism.

EARTH SPIRIT (1895) by Frank Wedekind. See AWAKENING OF SPRING, by Frank Wedekind.

EARTHLY PARADISE, THE (1868–1870), by William Morris. This is a series of twenty-four tales in verse, two for each month of the year. They appeared in three volumes. In imitation of Chaucer, they are bound together by the Prologue. A great pestilence spread over Europe in the fourteenth century and drove a group of Scandinavians from their homes. "Shriveled, bent and grey" they wander long after an "earthly paradise" only to reach at last an island in a distant sea where a Hellenic city has been preserved intact. Here they rest, and twice a month they and their hosts meet and tell a story.

The twelve stories told by the Greek elders are of classical origin; the twelve told by the Scandinavian wanderers are from French, Latin and Icelandic medieval romances with some pilfering from the *Arabian Nights* (q.v.) and Mandeville. There are ten-syllable and short couplets, with short lyrics interspersed, and varying other metres as needed. Morris often embellished various stories during his life. "The Life and Death of Jason," which contains "I know a little garden-close," and the Christmas Carol in "The Land East of the Sun and West of the Moon" are among the loveliest lyrics Morris wrote.

News from Nowhere (1891) is a serious prose attempt at a Utopia, a Socialist utopia that returns to the ideals of craftsmanship of the Middle Ages, where men live together harmoniously and simply, moved by love and beauty.

EAST GOES WEST (1937), by Younghill Kang. See GRASS ROOF, THE, by Younghill Kang.

EAST OF EDEN (1939), by Israel Joshua Singer. See BROTHERS ASHKENAZI, THE, by Israel Joshua Singer.

EAST RIVER (1946), by Sholem Asch. See NAZARENE, THE, by Sholem Asch.

EASTWARD HO (1605), by Ben Jonson, George Chapman, John Marston. The name of this comedy is taken from Eastward-Westward Ho cries of the wherry-men on the Thames. Touchstone, a goldsmith, has two apprentices, Golding and Quicksilver. The latter is as gay and dissipated as the former is steady and sober. He has also two-daughters, Gertrude and Mildred. The former is engaged to a knight, Sir Petronel Flash; her main ambition is to be a lady and drive in her coach. Sir Petronel, by arrangement with Quicksilver, sells his wife's property to Security, an old usurer with a pretty young wife, Winnifred, with whom Sir Petronel plans to elope to Virginia, on his wife's fortune. They are wrecked at the outset by a storm, and land near Greenwich. Golding, who has married Mildred with her father's approval, is already an alderman and a deputy. He intercedes for Quicksilver and Sir Petronel after Touchstone has them cast into prison, convinces the latter of Quicksilver's sincere repentance, and gains their release.

ECCLESIASTICAL HISTORY OF THE ENGLISH NATION, THE (731), by Bede. Precious both as history and as literature, this work was written in Latin at the monastery of Jarrow, and its author is often referred to as the Venerable Bede. Divided into five books, it begins, after a dedication, with a physical description of Britain, mentions briefly the early Roman conquerors and persecutors, becomes detailed with the beginning of the fourth century, and proceeds very closely from the year 596 when Pope Gregory the Great sent Augustine to King Ethelbert's court to introduce Christianity. The story of the gradual conversion of the English is continued until within four years of Bede's death. It is in many ways a pagan story of violence and invasion, of relapses into idolatry, of abject superstition. But the faith gradually spreads, aided, apparently, by many visions and miracles, such as the wonders wrought before and after death by St. Cuthbert. One of King Edwin's counselors, when Paulinus comes before them, compares the life of man "to the swift flight of a sparrow through the room wherein you sit at supper in winter," while the hearth is burning and outside there is a storm. Also memorable is the anecdote about the sudden power of song given the ignorant herdsman Caedmon, the first poet in English literature whose name we know.

ECLOGUES (ca. 37 B.C.), by Virgil (Publius Vergilius Maro). These ten poems of Virgil's youth are also known as the *Bucolics* or *Pastorals*. When published at Rome they made an immediate impression on the literary world, thanks in part perhaps to Virgil's patron, Maecenas, the friend and confidant of Octavian. In external form they are a frank imitation of the *Sicilian Idyls* of Theocritus, with shepherds and rustics for characters. Virgil also follows his model in inserting himself and his friends and contemporaries into the poems in the guise of shepherds. At times this convention verges on allegory, as in the fourth or so-called Messianic Eclogue. In this poem he makes a graceful and elaborate compliment to his friend Pollio that the birth of his child will usher in a new Golden Age. The reference is sufficiently veiled that it was possible later for Christians to maintain the poem was a pagan prediction of the birth of Christ. What the poems lacked in originality of conception they made up in beauty of verse, for they were more polished than any Roman hexameter that had then been written.

EDGAR ALLAN POE (1926), by Joseph Wood Krutch. See KRUTCH, JOSEPH WOOD.

EDWARD II (1593), by Christopher Marlowe. Marlowe's most finished tragedy, though not so rich in description as *Tamburlaine* or *Faustus,* is the last he completed. Edward II, upon succeeding to the English throne, sends for his favorite, Gaveston, to return from exile in Paris. The nobles, led by the two Mortimers, oppose Gaveston, whom the King loads with honors, and for whom he neglects his Queen, Isabella. Edward is forced to banish his favorite, but the Queen, to win back her husband's love, pleads for Gaveston's pardon with Mortimer, who consents, as he thinks it will lead to the King's overthrow. Edward arranges a marriage for Gaveston, with the Duke of Gloucester's daughter, and Spenser, one of the Duke's followers, becomes another favorite. When the king refuses to ransom the elder Mortimer, a prisoner in Scotland, the nobles, jealous of the lavish gifts showered on Gaveston, rise. The latter flees but is captured by Warwick and Pembroke. Edward requests one last interview with his favorite, which is granted by Pembroke. Warwick has Gaveston murdered.

The rebels are defeated and Warwick and Lancaster beheaded, but young Mortimer manages to escape from prison. He joins Isabella and her son, Edward, at the court of her brother, the French King. She leaves France to go to Hainault where she prepares to return to England to make war on her husband. Edward and Spenser flee to Ireland, but their ship is wrecked on the English coast. They are captured at the Abbey near Neath by Leicester. Edward parts regretfully from his friends Spenser and Baldock, mourns for Gaveston, his dear friend, for whose sake he has drowned his kingdom in blood. He is obliged to resign his crown. Mortimer is made protector for young King Edward III. Mortimer and the Queen do not feel safe while Edward II is alive. The Protector keeps changing the latter's prison, causing him to be treated with cruelty and great indignity; at last he has Edward murdered. The young Edward III, hearing of his father's murder, goes over to the Lords. He then avenges his father by beheading Mortimer and confining his mother in the Tower.

EDUCATION OF HENRY ADAMS, THE (1907), by Henry Adams. Looking backward upon his own life, Adams' thesis in this distinguished book is that he had been equipped with an eighteenth century education to cope with a twentieth century life—a paradox which he points out applies to all lives prepared by the study of humanities at our universities. The significant corollary to this idea is that our moral progress has not kept pace with the accelerated advance of science, and that sooner or later this conflict will bring about a world catastrophe.

The author employs the symbols of the Virgin and the electrical dynamo to illustrate our changing emphasis from religion to mechanization. He pities the child born at the start of our century. Toward the end of his life, "all that the historian won was a vehement wish to escape. He saw his education complete, and was sorry that he ever began it. As a matter of taste, he greatly preferred his eighteenth century education when God was a father and nature a mother, and all was for the best in a scientific universe. He repudiated all share in the world as it was to be, and yet he could not detect where his responsibility began or ended."

As an autobiography, this pessimistic, urbane work is incomplete, but there are complete views of his affiliations with Harvard, diplomatic developments of the Civil War, Darwin's theories, and the dynamic theory of history.

The *Education* is a complementary work to *Mont-Saint-Michel and Chartres* (1905), in which thirteenth century Europe is viewed as a grand era in world culture. Contrasted with twentieth century multiplicity, this period was a unification of Man and society, best expressed by the Cathedral of Amiens and the works of Aquinas, Abélard, Mary of Champagne. The work is in part a valuable document of medieval art and architecture, a study of the times which produced it, and an analysis of the spiritual reasons for its flowering.

EDWIN DROOD, THE MYSTERY OF (1870), by Charles Dickens. This novel Dickens left unfinished at his death. The striking opening scene shows John Jasper, precentor of Cloisterham cathedral, in an opium den. He is the uncle of Edwin Drood, and persecutes with his evil passion Rosa Bud, to whom Drood is betrothed by an arrangement made by the late respective fathers of the two orphans. Actually Edwin is cool to Rosa, and it is another orphan, Neville Landless, who is attracted to her. The sinister Jasper foments a quarrel between Edwin and Neville, not knowing that the engagement has already been broken off. The same night Edwin disappears, and there is circumstantial evidence pointing to Neville as his murderer. The latter is arrested, but as no body has been found, is released. There turns up in the neighborhood a white-haired stranger who calls himself Datchery and acts like a detective on the trail of Jasper. Here the story breaks off with no indication as to how it would have ended, though many guesses have been made and several "completions" of it have been published.

EEN KLEIN HELDENDICHT (1906), by Herman Gorter. See MEI, by Herman Gorter.

EEN ZERVER VERLIEFD (1904), by Arthur van Schendel. See SCHENDEL, ARTHUR VAN.

EFFIE BRIEST (1895), by Theodor Fontane. The German Fontane wrote *Effie Briest* in his old age in a style markedly apart from his earlier tendencies while he was a journalist—influenced by the French naturalistic writers of his day. Effie marries a former suitor of her mother. She suffers from lack of sympathy and understanding at the hands of the stiffly formal old man. She drifts, in due time, into the arms of a much younger, more romantic man. She is always in fear of discovery; her guilt comes to light after several years and her lover falls in a duel. Alone and broken-hearted, Effie finally returns to her girlhood home. The novel exhibits Fontane's coldness to the confusion engendered by sentimentality and dreamy romanticism. His *Irrungen, Wirrungen* (1888; translated as *Trials and Tribulations*) deals with the conflict between love and honor. In 1892 there appeared the book *Mrs. Jenny Treibel,* a psychological, analytic study of Berlin society, and in 1899 *The Stechlin,* which deals with the life of the nobility. As a critic, Fontane recognized the significance of democracy and industrialism in his day and was among the first to acknowledge the naturalistic movement. His style of realism approaching naturalism had considerable influence on contemporary and succeeding German novelists.

EGIL'S SAGA (late 13th c.). See NJÁL SAGA, THE.

EGMONT (1787), by Johann Wolfgang von Goethe. See GOETHE, JOHANN WOLFGANG VON.

EGOIST, THE (1879), by George Meredith. This is one of Meredith's finest novels. When Sir Willoughby Patterne of Patterne Hall is jilted by Constantia Durham, shocked gossips hope that he will marry Laetitia Dale, accomplished daughter of his invalid pensioner. But Sir Willoughby falls in love with beautiful Clara Middleton. Through a whirlwind campaign for her hand and heart, he gains her consent to marriage after a six months' reprieve to be spent with her father at Patterne Hall. There she meets Vernon Whitford, Willoughby's scholarly cousin and secretary, whose ideas about the education of Crossjay, Sir Willoughby's twelve-year-old ward, Clara shares. Many incidents, revealing Sir Willoughby's ingenuous inability to see himself at fault, convince Clara that she has made a mistake. Horrified by the thought of a second jilting, Sir Willoughby persuades himself that Clara is jealous of Laetitia, then that she is infatuated with De Craye, his charming but untrustworthy friend; to save face he proposes to Laetitia, whose former devotion has turned to amused contempt. Her refusal is overheard and revealed by Crossjay, who adores Clara. The humiliated Sir Willoughby, thinking at least to keep Clara from De Craye, releases her on condition that she marry Whitford, to which condition Whitford and Clara, deeply in love, gladly agree. Laetitia is prevailed upon to marry the man she considers "vindictive and an incorrigible egotist."

EICHENDORFF, JOSEPH VON (1788–1857). One of the most imaginative and original minds of late German Romanticism, Eichendorff is especially recognized for his superior lyric poetry. As revealed in his collection of poems, Eichendorff is essentially a poet of nature—admiring and capturing its moods and interpreting the music within it. Ordinary experience, simple love and the life of the wanderer are expressed in his unpretentious, singable verse. Far removed from the poetic art which is derived principally from thought and intellect, Eichendorff's poetry finds its basis in the realm of feeling and "Gemüt"—permeated by a sighing longing for that which lies beyond the things of this world. As a prose writer his best-known work is *From the Life of a Good-For-Nothing* (1826) which portrays the life of a wandering musician. In addition to dramas, narrative poems and critical works, Eichendorff translated several religious plays from the Spanish of Calderón.

EIMI (1933), by E. E. Cummings. See ENORMOUS ROOM, THE, by E. E. Cummings.

EITHER MINE OR NOBODY'S (1929), by Luigi Pirandello. See PIRANDELLO, LUIGI.

ELCKERLIJC (ca. end 15th c.), by Peter Dorland (van Diest). See MEDIEVAL FLEMISH PLAYS.

ELECTIVE AFFINITIES (1809), by Johann Wolfgang von Goethe. See GOETHE, JOHANN WOLFGANG VON.

ELECTRA (414 B.C.), by Euripides. This play tells the story of the vengeance Electra and her brother took upon their mother for the murder of their father, as described by Aeschylus in the *Choephoroe* and by Sophocles in his *Electra* (q.v.) The action takes place before a hut on a desolate mountainside. In the prologue a peasant describes how Agamemnon had been murdered at the hands of Aegisthus and Clytaemnestra and how Electra had then been forced by the former to wed him, a mere peasant, in order that her children might be baseborn and so unfit to take revenge on the noble Aegisthus. He says he has respected Electra's rank and their marriage has never been consummated. Thus she awaits hopefully the coming of her brother, Orestes, from retreat in Phocis. Soon Orestes arrives with his boon companion, Pylades. An old man, a former servant of Agamemnon, brings about the mutual recognition of the long separated brother and sister, and tells them Aegisthus is, even now, in a nearby forest making sacrifice to the wood nymphs. As a matter of courtesy he will be forced to ask Orestes and Pylades, whom he will not recognize, to join the feast, thus giving Orestes the opportunity to avenge his father's murder. The old man is sent to Clytaemnestra with a false report that Electra has just borne a child. Orestes and his friend set out and soon return with the dead body of Aegisthus which is borne into the hut at Electra's bidding. Hereupon Clytaemnestra arrives and goes with Electra into the hut to make sacrifice for the birth of a child. Her cries for mercy are soon heard from within. The doors open and Orestes and Electra come forth, stained with their mother's blood and followed by attendants bearing the bodies of Clytaemestra and Aegisthus. Brother and sister are both overcome with remorse and Electra covers her mother's body. The gods Castor and Polydeuces, brothers of Clytaemnestra, appear and pronounce judgment on the matricides. Electra is to be given in marriage to Pylades, and Orestes is to wander over Hellas until finally at Athens he will be forgiven his sin and find peace. Electra is a remarkable character in this play, shamefully maltreated, but bitterly vengeful and strong-willed where her brother is humanly weak, until in the fullness of vengeance her strength is dissipated.

ELECTRA (ca. 410 B.C.?), by Sophocles. This play, like that of the same name by Euripides, deals with the vengeance taken by Electra and her brother, Orestes, on their mother Clytaemnestra, who, with the aid of her paramour, Aegisthus, had murdered her husband, Agamemnon, the King of Mycenae, upon his victorious return from Troy. As the play opens in Mycenae, Electra is held a virtual prisoner in the palace by Aegisthus and lives only in hope of the return of Orestes, whom she had given as a child for safe-keeping into the hands of an old retainer of Agamemnon. This old man appears with Orestes and his friend, Pylades. Their plan for vengeance involves the announcement that Orestes has been killed in a chariot race at the Pythian games. Orestes and Pylades are to pose as Phocians bearing Orestes' funeral urn. As they leave the scene, Electra appears from the palace bitterly lamenting her fate and praying for the return of her brother. She is soon followed by her sister, Chrysothemis, a foil to her intransigeance, who has resigned herself to life in the household of her father's murderers. As she leaves to lay an offering from the conscience-stricken Clytaemnestra on Agamemnon's tomb, the mother herself enters and defends the murder of her husband on the ground that he had unhumanly sacrificed their daughter, Iphigenia, to placate Artemis. This dialogue is interrupted by the entrance of the old retainer who announces Orestes' death and is welcomed to the palace by Clytaemnestra, leaving Electra desolate. Chrysothemis returns excitedly with word that she has found tokens of Orestes' presence at the tomb, but is brusquely dismissed by Electra who is convinced of her brother's death. Orestes and Pylades then arrive with the funeral urn and Orestes reveals his identity to his grieving sister. The joy of their reunion is interrupted by the reappearance of the old retainer who recalls them to their purpose. Orestes enters the palace with the urn and Clytaemnestra's cries for mercy are soon heard. Orestes appears with hands dripping blood but re-enters the palace as the return of Aegisthus is announced. Aegisthus' joy at the rumored death of Orestes is turned to craven terror at the discovery that the body within the palace is that of Clytaemnestra. The play ends with the completion of Electra's vengeance assured as Orestes forces Aegisthus to enter the palace at sword's point.

ELEGY WRITTEN IN A COUNTRY CHURCHYARD (1751), by Thomas Gray. Within the thirty-two stanzas of this enormously popular poem are expressed practically all the reflections and emotions common to man in the presence of death. The pentameter quatrains seem perfectly fitted to lend an air of dreaminess and unreality to the fading landscape. Scarcely a stanza fails to include at least one line so pertinent that it is widely quoted. The sweet melancholy, the polished and musical verse, and the democratic sentiment make the *Elegy* memorable. It is one of the best-known poems in English literature.

ELEKTRA (1903), by Hugo von Hofmannsthal. See HOFMANNS-THAL, HUGO VON.

ELEMENTA CHEMIAE (1732), by Hermann Boerhaave. Boerhaave has been called "perhaps the most celebrated physician that ever existed, if we except Hippocrates." In 1702 he was appointed professor of medicine at Leyden, and later he also was awarded chairs in botany and chemistry. Through his great reputation many students were attracted to the university, raising it to a position of eminence in medicine and science. Boerhaave's lectures on chemistry were extraordinarily popular, and an unauthorized edition of them was published in 1724 under the title *Institutiones et Experimenta Chemiae,* and again in English translation in 1727. This work was so full of errors that Boerhaave repudiated it and in 1732 published his own *Elementa Chemiae,* a two volume work on the history, theory, and applications of chemistry. The *Elementa* soon became the most popular chemical treatise of the time, more than a dozen editions in several languages appearing within a generation.

The *Elements of Chemistry* is a comprehensive collection of chemical facts and processes then known. The material is presented in a lucid and sober manner, with none of the mysticism and allegory frequently encumbering chemical works of that day. It was written expressly for students and the book was widely adopted in schools. Boerhaave carried out extensive experimental researches, although he made no discovery generally regarded as epoch-making. He discredited the lingering pretensions of the alchemists by showing that mercury can not be obtained from lead by transmutation. He held that chemical agents are ultimately reducible to a few simple categories, and he believed that vital processes are expressible in chemical terms. He made studies on the conservation of mass under chemical changes, and he suggested to Fahrenheit an investigation of the thermal capacities of water and mercury.

As a physician Boerhaave adopted no one system of medicine. His *Institutiones Medicae* (1708) was a rival in popularity and significance of his *Elementa Chemiae*. The former work introduced the term "physiology" in the modern sense and established the subject as a part of the medical curriculum. Both books exerted a strong and favorable influence on the first half of the eighteenth century, but the *Elementa* declined in popularity with the rise of the speculative phlogistic theory. When the "chemical revolution" disproved the existence of phlogiston and chemists returned to views more akin to those of Boerhaave, the famous *Traité Élémentaire de Chimie* (q.v.) of Lavoisier filled the place once occupied by Boerhaave's textbook. Nevertheless, the *Elementa Chemiae* remains a classic treatise of the transition period from Boyle to Lavoisier.

ELEMENTA PHYSIOLOGIAE CORPORIS HUMANI (1757–1765), by Albrecht von Haller. Haller undoubtedly was the greatest physiologist between William Harvey in the seventeenth century and Claude Bernard and Johannes Müller in the nineteenth century. He was an infant prodigy who had learned Greek and Hebrew by the age of ten. He was attracted to Leyden by Boerhaave and obtained his medical degree at nineteen. He traveled widely and studied in many fields, from botany to mathematics. In 1730 he began to practice medicine at Berne, but he devoted much of his time to anatomy and physiology. He achieved a wide reputation through his research and publications, and a chair in anatomy, botany, medicine and surgery was created for him at the newly-founded University of Göttingen. After seventeen active years there, he returned to Berne, where he continued his literary and scientific work until his death in 1777 at the age of seventy.

The physiological contributions of Haller were numerous. He made notable observations on the embryology of the chick, on the mechanics of respiration, and on bone formation; but his best-known discovery was on the response of muscles to stimulation. He established the fact that the organs of the body are partly irritable, partly non-irritable, and that irritability (or contractibility) is to be distinguished from sensibility. Haller thus contributed to science through experimentation; but it is as an expositor of science that he is most often recalled. He produced an enormous quantity of literary and scientific work, but his compendia on physiology rank as the greatest. In his *Elements of Physiology* he combined the facts and theories of the subject into a unified whole, making physiology an independent branch of science instead of a mere adjunct of medicine. The first volume of this monumental work was published in 1757, and the eighth and last volume appeared in 1765. It is a trustworthy account of physiological knowledge of the time.

Haller's publications cover a wide range, from philosophical romances to pathological surgery. In his poetry he is regarded as having discovered the beauty of the Alps, and his *Gedichte* (1732) appeared in at least a dozen editions. His prodigious energy enabled him to complete the botanical, anatomical, and surgical parts of an ambitious project entitled *Bibliotheca Medica* (1771–1777). He wrote also against the biological taxonomy of Linnaeus, whose reputation he seems to have envied. But of all Haller's numerous works, none exceeds in greatness the *Elementa Physiologiae*. Of this many-volumed treatise Sir Michael Foster has said that it marks "the dividing line between modern physiology and all that went before."

ELEMENTARY TREATISE OF CHEMISTRY (1789), by Antoine Laurent Lavoisier. See TRAITÉ ÉLÉMENTAIRE DE CHIMIE, by Antoine Laurent Lavoisier.

ELEMENTS OF GEOLOGY (1838), by Sir Charles Lyell. See ANTIQUITY OF MAN, by Sir Charles Lyell.

ELEMENTS OF GEOMETRY (3rd c.), by Euclid. The author of these thirteen books taught and founded a school at Alexandria, where his fame as a geometer drew many students from all parts of the Hellenic world. The famous mathematician De Morgan wrote in 1848: "There never has been, and till we see it we never shall believe that there can be, a system of geometry worthy of the name, which has any material departures from the plan laid down by Euclid." Geometry did not originate wholly with Euclid but reached its highest development in his mathematical genius. His early Greek editor Proclus states that Euclid "put together the *Elements,* collecting many of Eudoxus' theorems, perfecting many of Theaetetus; and also bringing to irrefragable demonstration the things which were only somewhat loosely proved by his predecessors." When King Ptolemy of Alexandria asked Euclid if there was in geometry any shorter cut than that of his *Elements,* the mathematician replied, "There is no royal road to geometry." The first six books of the *Elements* were long used as a modern introductory text to geometry and in England it was customary to speak of studying Euclid, rather than geometry.

The first two books of the *Elements* are on the geometry of the straight line, much of the material probably being derived from the Pythagoreans. Books three and four, on the circle, may have been due largely to Hippocrates of Chios; and books five and six, on the theory of proportion, probably were based on the methods of Eudoxus. One thinks of the *Elements* as exclusively devoted to geometry, but books seven to nine summarize the knowledge in Euclid's day on the theory of numbers, including the well-known "Euclidean algorithm" and a proof that the number of primes is infinite. Book ten, on incommensurable magnitudes, is one of the most finished and remarkable of the thirteen. The last three books are devoted to solid geometry, and the *Elements* closes with the proof that there are five, and only five, regular solids. Some editions of the *Elements* include two further books—a fourteenth and fifteenth—but these are later interpolations. Euclid, the "Elementator," was the author of a number of other mathematical works, including one on the conic sections and another on optics; but most of these have been lost.

The *Elements* of Euclid is without any doubt the best-known mathematical work. It is the oldest of the ancient Greek treatises on mathematics which have survived; and it was widely used by the Arabs and by medieval Latin scholars. It was one of the earliest books on mathematics to be printed, appearing in an edition of 1482. Since then it has been published in over a thousand editions—more, probably, than can be boasted by any book with the exception of the *Bible* (q.v.).

ELENE (8th c.), by Cynewulf. This is undoubtedly Cynewulf's masterpiece. The legend also occurs in the "Legenda Aurea"; whether it reached England in Latin or earlier Greek form is not known. It is the story of the discovery of the true cross by Helena, the mother of Constantine. As a result of his famous vision of the cross, described here in Canto I, the Emperor was converted and the course of history changed. As early as 701 the festival celebrating Constantine's conversion was established in the western church. In Cynewulf's poem there are fifteen cantos. The imaginative and descriptive narrative is of great beauty. We read of the glamour of war, of ships proud in their pomp, of gorgeous jewels of women and men. After Constantine's vision, the symbol of ignominy became for mankind a symbol of eternal glory. It is to convey this important fact that Cynewulf wrote; his poem is permeated with the seriousness of his mission.

Cynewulf also wrote *Crist,* which some think is the most interesting from a literary point of view of all his poems. It is divided into three parts: Christ's life and search; His ascension; His second coming. *Juliana,* about a Christian martyr in the days of Maximilian, and *Andreas,* are also attributed to him.

ELINE VERE (1889), by Louis Couperus. See COUPERUS, LOUIS.

ELIOT, THOMAS STEARNS (1888–   ). Considered the outstanding poet and critic writing in English today, Eliot received the Nobel Prize for Literature in 1948. Born in St. Louis and educated at Harvard, he has lived in England since 1914 and is a British citizen. Both as poet and as critic he has been extremely sensitive to the French *Symbolistes* and to the literature of seventeenth century England; the major contemporary influence on him was Ezra Pound.

Eliot's longest and most important poem is *The Waste Land* (1922), which at least one post-war generation found the perfect echo of its disillusion and despair. Within the symbolic framework of the medieval Grail legend and certain still older fertility rites, the sordidness and sterility of modern life are set forth. Many different kinds of verse are employed in the five divisions of the poem. "The Burial of the Dead" deals with the coming of spring in a land that has been barren. "A Game of Chess" juxtaposes past glory and present squalor, and the latter is emphasized in "The Fire Sermon," with the introduction of Tiresias, whom Eliot in his appended notes calls the most important personage in the poem, as a spectator. The brief "Death by Water" shows the happier fate of a drowned Phoenician sailor, who at least is not dying, like the moderns, by thirst in a land of drouth. The decay of modern Europe is symbolically conveyed in "What the Thunder Said." The poem ends in a medley of quotations from several literatures; indeed, erudite or otherwise obscure allusions are a favorite device with Eliot. *The Waste Land,* in the course of its four hundred and thirty-three lines, contains references to or echoes of no less than thirty-five different writers, and six languages are directly introduced, including Sanskrit.

The title poem of *Prufrock and Other Observations* (1917) is an ironic study of a timid and aging sentimentalist. *Poems* (1920) contains "The Hippopotamus," an allegory on the true church derived from Gautier, "Mr. Eliot's Sunday Morning Service," where a Renaissance painting of the baptism of Christ is contrasted with Eliot's gross recurring modern character, Sweeney, who appears most notably in "Sweeney Among the Nightingales," to be plotted against in some disreputable coffee-house and compared to the slain king Agamemnon. *Ash Wednesday* (1930) won Eliot staunch admirers of an orthodox sort he had not had before, with its theme of salvation and its religious symbols, its echoes of the Gospels and of the Litany. For the erstwhile rebel had by now proclaimed himself a "classicist in literature, royalist in politics, and Anglo-Catholic in religion." This was a not altogether surprising evolution from the despair of *The Hollow Men* (1925), who died with a whimper. The *Collected Poems* (1936) included "Burnt Norton," which became the first of the *Four Quartets* (1943), where the resonant lines justify the analogy with music and where the themes are the effort for discipline and the desire to glimpse timeless reality in the world of time.

The Rock (1934) is a pageant about the Church triumphant. The play *Murder in the Cathedral* (1935) was produced in both New York and London, and is occasionally revived. It tells of the struggle between Thomas à Becket, Archbishop of Canterbury, and King Henry II, and the murder of the former in 1170. The play is in both rhymed and unrhymed verse. Most memorable is the interlude of a Neo-Thomist sermon Thomas delivered at the Cathedral on Christmas Day four days before his death. *The Family Reunion* (1939), another verse drama, is a pathological study of a curse on a house.

Eliot's principal volumes of criticism have been *The Sacred Wood* (1920), *Homage to John Dryden* (1924), *For Lancelot Andrewes* (1928), *Selected Essays* (1932), *The Use of Poetry and the Use of Criticism* (1933), and *After Strange Gods* (1934), the latter two consisting of lectures delivered respectively at Harvard and at the University of Virginia. There is an acknowledged connection between Eliot the poet and Eliot the critic, for as a critic he has liked the poets and dramatists who have influenced his poetry, such as Donne and the "metaphysical" school and the dramatists Middleton and Webster; he has scorned those temperamentally alien, such as the Victorians, who seemed to him only to ruminate, and Shelley. In his famous essay on *The Metaphysical Poets* (1921), he declared that since the seventeenth century English poetry had taken a turn for the worse through a loss of unified sensibility and a consequent powerlessness to fuse thought and feeling. As recently as 1936 he found Milton responsible for much bad poetry in later English literature. But in recent years Eliot has been reversing his earlier judgments, even as his own poetry changed. He quoted from *Samson Agonistes* (q.v.) in *Four Quartets,* and in a lecture published in 1948 found that the time had come to praise Milton. Similarly between 1922 and 1936 he revised his opinion of Tennyson. But these are but two examples of development rather than whimsical contradiction in one of the greatest and most stimulating critics the world has known, who has been in our time, the evidence abounds, a virtual literary dictator.

ELIZABETH AND ESSEX (1928), by Lytton Strachey. Strachey subtitles this "A Tragic History," into which he looks with a novelist's insight.

It is the story of the turbulent relationship between Queen Elizabeth in her old age and the last and most brilliant of the courtiers with whom she flirted, the young and impetuous Robert Devereux, Earl of Essex, who died a traitor's death in 1601. A dashing general, a poet, a patron of Francis and Anthony Bacon, the hero of Cadiz—in fact always ready to embark against the Spaniards, Essex rose to a popularity that at last undid him, leading to his abortive rebellion after his final fall from favor when the Queen found him inefficient and insubordinate in the campaign against the Irish. But the volatile Essex (who some think may have served as the model for Hamlet) and the temperamental Queen were always incompatible, though the last two years of her reign were mournful without him. "Robin" had succeeded his stepfather, that other "Robin," Leicester, in the Queen's favor, and was even more widely known than Sir Philip Sidney had been as the beau ideal of an age that all saw was passing.

ELIZABETH THE QUEEN (1930), by Maxwell Anderson. See WHAT PRICE GLORY, by Maxwell Anderson and Laurence Stallings.

ELLEN TERRY AND BERNARD SHAW, A CORRESPOND-ENCE (1931), edited by Christopher St. John. The letters exchanged between the Irish playwright and the English actress in the course of four decades of friendship possess two particular characteristics. They reveal the celebrated wit and the most famous English actress of her time in an intimate manner as personalities. They also throw much light upon the inside history of the London stage at the turn of the century. Not having been written with any thought of publication in mind, the letters are distinguished by an off-the-record frankness unique in theatrical correspondence. Many famous names of the last generation—playwrights, directors, producers, actors, actresses and others in public life —are familiarly discussed, and much material, ordinarily not included in conventional biographies, is presented here. There are about two hundred letters by Ellen Terry and a lesser number by Shaw. The playwright has furnished an introduction to the published *Correspondence*.

ELMER GANTRY (1927), by Sinclair Lewis. See ARROWSMITH, by Sinclair Lewis.

ELOISA TO ABELARD (1717), by Alexander Pope. See ESSAY ON MAN, by Alexander Pope.

ELSIE, THE STRANGE MAIDEN (1850), by Jeremias Gotthelf. See GOTTHELF, JEREMIAS.

ELSIE VENNER (1861), by Oliver Wendell Holmes. See AUTOCRAT OF THE BREAKFAST-TABLE, THE, by Oliver Wendell Holmes.

EMBASSY TO GAIUS, THE, by Philo Judaeus. See PHILO JUDAEUS.

ÉMILE (1762), by Jean Jacques Rousseau. This description of the education of Émile and Sophie presents Rousseau's views on the fundamental principles of education so necessary for producing the morally noble individuals required by a free society. In general Rousseau's views on this subject would today be called "progressive." He is against discipline, formal training, and restriction in general. Since the child is born morally good, our aim should be to prevent civilization from corrupting him. His only discipline should be natural punishment. His natural tendencies should be allowed free development. This book was influential on later philosophers of education—Pestalozzi, Froebel, and others.

EMILIA GALOTTI (1772), by Gotthold Ephraim Lessing. See NA-THAN THE WISE, by Gotthold Ephraim Lessing.

EMINENT AUTHORS OF THE NINETEENTH CENTURY (1882), by Georg Brandes. Brandes once said of himself: "I am not a philosopher; for that I am too small. I am not a critic; for that I am too big." This was a very apt intellectual self-portrait and is verified by his work, *Eminent Authors of the Nineteenth Century,* which consists of nine literary portraits: Paul Heyse, Hans Christian Andersen, John Stuart Mill, Ernest Renan, Esaias Tegnér, Gustave Flaubert, Frederik Paludan-Müller, Björnstjerne Björnson, and Henrik Ibsen. Brandes was largely responsible for the fact that Ibsen took a firm stand for those ideals that revealed him as the master craftsman in dramatic art. The essays on Ibsen and Björnson did much to insure their appreciation by the public. Except for Tegnér, Brandes was personally acquainted with all his subjects. He wrote about them with penetrating insight and sympathy. About Andersen, the greatest teller of fables, he wrote: "In the 'Ugly Duckling,' one of his most exquisite stories, there is the quintessence of Andersen's entire life—melancholy, humor, martyrdom, triumph—and of his whole nature; the gift of observation and the sparkling intellect which he used to avenge himself upon folly and wickedness, the varied faculties which constituted his genius." The mode of treatment in these nine essays is greatly diversified. In some of them the individuality of the author portrayed is represented as exhaustively as possible; in others, Brandes attempted to present the man in his actual person. Some of the biographical monographs are treated purely from a psychological standpoint, others from the aesthetic. In all of them the characteristics of the individual are so chosen as to bring out the most important features of the author's life and works. The men portrayed belong to six nationalities. Common to all of them is that they are *modern* authors, modern in the sense that they represent the modern style of mind, which is concerned with the essentials of man's life, with his problems and trials and his effort to free himself from the tyranny of prejudice and superstition.

EMINENT VICTORIANS (1918), by Lytton Strachey. The four biographical portraits are of Cardinal Manning, Florence Nightingale, Dr. Thomas Arnold and General Charles Gordon. The author treats them as candidly as Dr. Johnson portrayed the eminent Carolines and Jacobeans. In other words, he mercilessly dissects them, inspects all the fissures, warpings and growths in their characters with as much enjoyable malice as devotion to truth. To cite Dr. Johnson's method of biographical analysis: concerning Dr. Sprat's *Life of Cowley* he approvingly commented that it was "a funeral oration rather than a history." Strachey, with one eye fixed on Dr. Johnson, chats conversationally about his subjects as if he had actually been on intimate terms with them. His style is unconventional, chatty, knowing, devoid of objectivity; he likes and dislikes with open partiality. He is a natural controversialist and enjoys exposing pedantry or intellectual vanity.

He states his thesis in *Eminent Victorians* with a certain bravado: "Je n'impose rien; je ne propose rien; j'expose." The choice of these four figures for scrutiny was a special piece of audacity. Sainted characters all, he stripped them of their legendary aura; he "exposed" them. Florence Nightingale, the "Lady of the Lamp," he drew as a prig and a bully; Dr. Arnold was done up brown in the tradition of English upperclass snobbishness; the saintly Cardinal Manning stood out as an intriguing church politician; the intrepid General Gordon was nothing but a lump of putty in the hands of the British Government officials. The book achieved great notoriety because it came just at the time when "Victorian" had become a term of abuse among Englishmen and debunking was in fashion. It had constructive uses, pointing the way toward more honest biographical studies.

EMINESCU, MIHAIL (1850–1889). Mihail Eminescu (the pen name of Mihail Iminovici) was undoubtedly Romania's greatest poet. He was not prolific, and was early prevented by insanity from working. His poems, such as "Venus and the Madonna," the "Epigony," etc., show the delicately sensitive and pessimistic nature of the man. His disappointments drove him to the pessimism of the *fin de siècle* and he found himself attracted by many of the aspects of Indian thought. Yet there is a wide range in his themes, and a beauty in all that he wrote that puts him on a par with the best Romantic poets of other countries.

EMMA (1816), by Jane Austen. *Emma* stands only below *Pride and Prejudice* (q.v.) in popularity among Jane Austen's novels. Here are present in their perfection the qualities peculiarly characteristic of the author. Life in this small English town is a settled affair; nothing ever happens. Miss Woodhouse, after the marriage of her companion, is left alone with her widowed father; Emma has a restless personality; her chief pleasure is in arranging the lives of her friends. She takes up with a simple country girl, Harriet Smith, and tries to make her out a paragon; when she attempts to marry her to the local clergyman she fails. Rev. Mr. Elton brings a bride from elsewhere; this gives the author a chance for a witty study of vulgarity. Emma's interference between Jane Fairfax and Frank Churchill is equally infelicitous, although it is with her protégée, Harriet, that her fingers are most severely scorched. Poor simple Harriet has been convinced by Emma that she is quite superior. In her new-found satisfaction Harriet is bemused enough to fancy that John Knightley desires to marry her, though nothing is further from this haughty man's intention. As is forecast in the first chapter, Emma finally succumbs and marries John Knightley, while Harriet marries the simple farmer, Robert Martin, whom she had fancied before she fell under Emma's spell.

EMPEROR JONES, THE (1920), by Eugene O'Neill. Brutus Jones, swashbuckling Negro ex-Pullman porter and fugitive from justice, establishes himself by shrewdness and brutality as emperor of a small island in the West Indies, ruling the natives with an iron hand, and dominating the craven white trader, Smithers. He has accumulated a considerable fortune for himself. But as the play opens, the natives, unable further to endure his tyranny, have fled to the hills to stir up a revolt. There begins the throbbing of their voodoo drums, symbolical presence of Jones's antagonist, which never stops until the end of the drama. Jones, contemptuous, has foreseen the revolt, and sets out for the forest which lies between his palace and the coast. When he arrives at the edge of it, night has fallen. Confident, and familiar with his path at first, he is unnerved by a succession of terrifying night scenes. The brush assumes weird forms; the pounding drum rhythm becomes more menacing. Slowly, Jones reverts to the savage. Superstitious fears grip him, and he loses his way. At length his course brings him around in a circle, his revolver emptied even of the final silver bullet intended for himself. The natives kill him. The distinguished play has been made into an American opera by Louis Gruenberg, and is an American cinema classic.

Outstanding among O'Neill's other expressionistic plays is *The Hairy Ape* (1922). Yank, a stoker, takes pride in his sense of belonging to the world of the machine. When a bored society girl, Mildred Douglas, visits the hold of the ship and shows her revulsion, Yank's resentment and class consciousness are aroused. In a series of scenes, O'Neill depicts his search for something else to which he can belong. Arrested for molesting Fifth Avenue strollers, Yank hears of the I.W.W., and hopes to revenge himself on society through them. They throw him out, however. In the end, Yank visits the zoo and liberates a gorilla, which crushes him in its arms and thrusts him into the vacant cage.

EMPIRE, THE (1878), by Hippolyte Taine. See ORIGINS OF CONTEMPORARY FRANCE, THE, by Hippolyte Taine.

ENCYCLOPÉDIE (1751–1777), edited by Denis Diderot. See DIDEROT, DENIS.

END IS NOT YET, THE (1947), by Fritz von Unruh. See UNRUH, FRITZ VON.

ENDYMION (1818), by John Keats. This poem whose opening line is so familiar, "A thing of beauty is a joy forever," was composed between April and November, 1817. It has a loose style and is weak in narrative content; and is so replete with color and music, with such enchanted atmosphere and scenery, that it often amazes by its lack of reticence. Yet here are strokes of pure beauty no cautious artistry could achieve. There is sheer magic in this story of Endymion and the moon, and the former's wanderings over the earth and under it, and in the sea and through the air, with no sharp line between what happens and what is dreamt. More than any other poem, perhaps, it shows Keats, whatever his drab surroundings, as the sensuous lover of all loveliness. Whether he digresses to legends of Cybele, Glaucus and Scylla, or Alpheus and Arethusa, in no way related, does not seem to matter. The "Hymn to Pan" (Book I) and the roundelay to Bacchus, "O sorrow" (Book IV), mark the heights of the poem, and are familiar by inclusion in anthologies. Keats himself told his critics that he recognized in *Endymion* "a feverish attempt rather than a deed accomplished."

ENDYMION, THE MAN IN THE MOON (performed ca. 1587; printed 1591), by John Lyly. This play in prose, presented before the Queen at Greenwich, is, like most of Lyly's plays, apparently an allegory of the court, with a mythological basis. Cynthia undoubtedly stands for Queen Elizabeth, but what courtier Endymion stands for has been a matter of controversy, with Lyly's patron, the Earl of Oxford, as the likeliest guess. Endymion turns from his former mistress Tellus (Latin for Earth) to Cynthia the Moon, who, however, seems hopelessly cold. Tellus seeks revenge through the witch Dipsas, who puts Endymion to sleep for forty years. The spell is broken only by a kiss from Cynthia. There is a comic subplot featuring the braggart Sir Tophas.

ENEMY OF THE PEOPLE, AN (1882), by Henrik Ibsen. In this play Ibsen attacks the compact, complacent majority. Dr. Stockmann, a poor physician, has seen his dream of establishing municipal baths in his native town come true. The town is now a thriving health resort. He is appointed medical officer of the baths, and for the first time his family is in comfortable circumstances. He discovers, however, that the baths are contaminated by nearby tanneries and capable of spreading typhoid fever. He was about to publish in the liberal "People's Messenger" a glowing account of the benefits of the baths, but he informs Hovstad, the editor, of his discovery and also sends a detailed report to his brother, Peter Stockmann, who is mayor of the town and chairman of the baths. The doctor is in a pleasant glow over the service he is doing his town. Hovstad, who is against the group of officials headed by the mayor who control the town, promises the doctor the support of his paper and the House-owners' Association, as well as that of Aslaksen, the printer, who is prominent in the Temperance Society. In the meantime, the mayor makes a private investigation and finds that alterations on the baths would cost twenty thousand pounds. He therefore asks his brother to take back some of the assertions he has made. The doctor refuses, and the mayor then threatens to have him dismissed from his post of medical officer. Hovstad also withdraws his support when he learns that the town will have to pay the bill and that the work will take at least two years. Dr. Stockmann angrily declares that he will carry the truth to the people, but can find no hall in which to hold a meeting. Captain Horster, a friend, offers him a large room in his house. The mayor, Hovstad, and Aslaksen attend the meeting and Aslaksen is elected chairman. Dr. Stockmann tries to tell the people that their "medicinal baths are standing on pestiferous soil," but he is shouted down. He then attacks the town, saying "the whole fabric of our civil community is founded on the pestiferous soil of falsehood." The meeting finally ends in a riot, and the doctor is called the "enemy of the people." His clothes are torn, his windows broken; his daughter loses her position as schoolteacher. The mayor accuses his brother of collaborating on the story of the baths' pollution with Morten Kiil, the doctor's father-in-law, who owns one of the tanneries and who has willed his daughter, the doctor's wife, a considerable sum of money. Shortly thereafter Morten Kiil himself enters and shows the doctor stock in the baths he has been buying with the money he intended to leave his daughter. He threatens to give the money to charity unless the physician will retract his story about the baths. Hovstad and Aslaksen also attempt to bribe him to retract, but Stockmann chases them out. In the end he is left alone with his loyal family to face the town.

ENNEADS, by Plotinus (204-270). In these treatises Plotinus gives the classical exposition of Neo-Platonism. This product of the union of Platonic metaphysical thought with the mysticism of the East had its origin at Alexandria where Plotinus studied under Ammonius, the founder of the school. The central concern of Plotinus' doctrine is with the nature of the soul, the conception of which is based on Plato's theory of *ideas*. Thus the highest reality is God, from whom we descend by various stages or emanations to the human soul and the world of phenomena. The soul is defiled by contact with phenomenal existence and must return to its source by the practice of virtue, asceticism, and ecstatic contemplation of the one and infinite source of all existence. The Greek title *Ennead* means "group of nine," and was given to Plotinus' works as they were arranged for publication, probably by his follower, Porphyry, in six groups of nine treatises each.

ENOCH ARDEN (1864), by Alfred Tennyson. This narrative poem relates the story of Enoch Arden, Philip Ray, and Annie Lee, who grow up together in a little seaside town. Both boys love Annie, but it is Enoch who wins her. They are happy together until bad luck forces Enoch to ship out on a merchantman. When shipwrecked, he is given up for dead. After ten years, Annie, poverty-stricken, marries Philip, who has loved her faithfully throughout the years. Enoch, rescued, returns to witness unseen the happiness of his wife and children. He leaves broken-hearted, but resolved that Annie shall never know of his return until his death.

ENORMOUS ROOM, THE (1922), by Edward Estlin Cummings. Although this best known of E. E. Cummings' books is referred to as a novel, it is more truly nonfiction. Cummings was a driver in the Norton-Harjes Ambulance Corps in France during World War I. His friend, *B*, was seized by the French government on a false charge of treason. Because of their intimacy, Cummings was also arrested. The book recounts how they were apprehended and committed to La Ferté Macé, a concentration camp, in Orne, France. "The enormous room" is the great barracks in which they and a variegated crowd of prisoners were confined, except for walks in a narrow courtyard and adjournments to the mess hall. The relations of Cummings and *B* to the bewildered people about them range from·the poignant to the grotesque and comical. Unforgettable are such characters as Mexique, the Gypsy Wanderer, the Zulu, Surplice, and the simple giant, Jean Le Nègre. All in the prison suffer at the hands of the jailers, but manage to retain their individuality, which the author praises as the highest of human values.

Cummings is also known as a lyric poet of cynically realistic verse which depends partly upon unusual punctuation, odd juxtapositions of words, and typographical eccentricities to provoke the reader into a study of the author's meaning.

Other books by Cummings include: *him* (1927); *Eimi* (1933), a bitter denunciation of regimentation in Soviet Russia; *Tom* (1935); *CIOPW* (1931), a collection of drawings and paintings; *Santa Claus* (1946), a play; and *Collected Poems* (1938).

ENRICO IV (1922), by Luigi Pirandello. See PIRANDELLO, LUIGI.

EPHEMERA (1915), by Rabindranath Tagore. See TAGORE, RABINDRANATH.

EPIC OF AMERICA, THE (1931), by James Truslow Adams. The author of this unconventional history of America is concerned with an attempt to discover how Americans came to be what they are. He is interested primarily in origins, tracing the evolution of various concepts, ideas, and slogans that may be characterized as American. In his opinion, the nation's greatest contribution to the world has been its unceasing aspiration to bring a fuller, richer, and happier life to the common man; an aspiration which was breathed first during America's beginnings, and which has been growing with the years. The *Epic* begins with explorations of the various parts of America, the development of its varied and virile civilization, the emergence of a new nation, the struggles for liberty and equality in our several wars, the ideals and disappearance of the frontier, the rise of finance, capital and industrialization with their new problems. Adams finds the prospects for our democracy today discouraging but not hopeless. He believes that the common man's faith will bring about the American dream.

The work which won Adams a Pulitzer Prize and fame as an American historian was *The Founding of New England* (1921), a work based upon original records. This work discounts the popular conception of American origins determined by freedom-loving Pilgrim Fathers, and proposes the thesis that the struggle in New England between a bigoted theocracy and landed gentry on the one hand, and the poor masses on the other, had a much more profound influence on the origins of American democracy than our war against England.

EPIGRAMS (80–104), by Martial (Marcus Valerius Martialis). All of Martial's writings are gathered under the collective title of *Epigrams*. These consist of fifteen books of verse and contain about sixteen hundred poems varying in length from one to somewhat over twenty lines. *The Book of the Games* consists of occasional pieces written at the time of the dedication of the great Colosseum in Rome under the Emperor Titus. The books entitled *Friendly Gifts* and *Favors* are made up of couplets and include comprehensive inventories of Flavian dietetics, costumes, furniture and bric-a-brac. The former were written to accompany gifts and the latter favors at dinner parties. The remaining twelve volumes contain epigrams of the type usually recognized by that name. According to a famous Latin distich:

> Three things must epigrams, like bees have all:
> A sting, and honey, and a body small.

Lessing remarks that before Martial there were poets who composed epigrams, but before Martial there was no epigrammatist. Martial's epigrams reveal a remarkable versatility and scope, both in subject matter and meter. Diverse subjects receive diverse treatment. Martial was, like all sophisticates, inclined toward cruelty in exposing pitiful human weaknesses. He was the Roman counterpart of our modern candid-camera journalistic photographer, taking devastating snapshots of Roman life and manners. He overlooked nothing and spared none; his observations were canny and graphically descriptive. The Latin language with its essential conciseness made it possible for Martial to concentrate the point of his epigrams in a few terse words. The English translation will sometimes make one of his epigrams three times as long as the original.

EPILOGUE TO 1849 (1850), by Alexander Ivanovitch Herzen. See HERZEN, ALEXANDER IVANOVITCH.

EPIPSYCHIDION (1821), by Percy Bysshe Shelley. See SHELLEY, PERCY BYSSHE.

EPISODES IN VAN BIBBER'S LIFE (1889), by Richard Harding Davis. See DAVIS, RICHARD HARDING.

EPISTLES (20–13 B.C.), by Horace (Quintus Horatius Flaccus). The two books of Horace's *Epistles* are the first example of a collection of poetic letters. Like his *Satires* (q.v.) they are in dactylic hexameter; and he himself thought of them as belonging in the category of satire. A personal address and tone is often the only feature that justifies the name Epistle. The collection as a whole is dedicated to his friend and patron, Maecenas. In the first Epistle the poet laureate renounces the writing of light and lyric verse and promises to devote himself to philosophy. The Epistles which are not strictly personal in character are indeed devoted to exhortation to the Stoic virtues, with a mild and mellow temperament that only Horace could read into that stern way of life. The last Epistle is the longest and certainly the best known. It is also distinguished from the others by its subject matter, and is often known as the *De Arte Poetica*. Next to Aristotle's *Poetics* (q.v.) it is the most important ancient work on literary theory and criticism.

EPITHALAMION (1594), by Edmund Spenser. This noblest espousal—along with *Prothalamion* (q.v.)—of English hymns, will forever be associated with Spenser's adopted country, Ireland. It was written for his own marriage in 1594. While it breathes the same heroic Platonism as his "Hymnes to Love and Beautie," he here carries the lyrical style first attempted in *The Shepheards Calender* (q.v.) to an unexcelled height of harmony, splendor and enthusiasm. It was a chance reading of *Epithalamion* about 1812 that first turned the mind of seventeen-year-old Keats to poetry.

EPITOME ASTRONOMIAE COPERNICANAE (1618–1621), by Johann Kepler. See ASTRONOMIA NOVA, by Johann Kepler.

ÉPOQUES DE LA NATURE (1779), by Georges Louis Leclerc, Comte de Buffon. See HISTOIRE NATURELLE, by Georges Louis Leclerc, Comte de Buffon.

ERASMUS MONTANUS (1731), by Ludvig Holberg. This farcical five-act comedy ridicules academic pedantry and the "vapid formalism of logic," as once taught at the University of Copenhagen. Rasmus Berg, a student at the University, saturated with logic, Latin and metaphysics, returns to the home of his proud parents as Erasmus Montanus. He is very learned indeed, and ready at all times to dispute, in Latin, with anybody on any subject. Even the local deacon and bailiff are properly impressed. But there is one serious obstacle to his coveted success and happiness: he comes back from Copenhagen full of revolutionary ideas, maintaining, for example, that the world is round, whereas everyone in town, including his prospective father-in-law, the wealthy Jeronimus, knew perfectly well that the earth was as "flat as a pancake." There is great confusion and argument, the latter well spiced with Latin. His betrothed, Lisbed, to whom the shape of the earth is of small consequence, urges Erasmus, for her and his own sake, to say it is flat; and since he does not have faith enough in himself and his convictions to stand up against "the Philistines," and since a lieutenant has tricked him by threatening to keep him in the army as a simple soldier, he finally gives in to his father-in-law, who has influence with the lieutenant, asserts that the world is really flat, and marries the daughter. Much is won, and nothing serious is lost. Because of the human interest in the characters of this play, the farce has become almost classic drama, a "Danish culture-comedy of universal significance." Of twenty-six comedies by the author, most of them successfully performed, this is one of the three best.

The others are: *Jeppe of the Hill* (1722), the tale of a drunken peasant who through a trick wakes up in a baron's bed and believes himself in Paradise and gets into difficulties; and *The Political Tinker* (1722–1731), a satire on those who sit about criticizing the local mayor and council members without comprehending their duties. Holberg first won international fame by *Niels Klim's Subterranean Journey* (1741), written in Latin to evade Danish censorship, which tells of a visit to strange nations at the center of the earth. It is a biting satire on the customs of contemporary society.

EREWHON (1872), by Samuel Butler. By projecting his satirical imagination into a land peopled by extraordinary creatures with exasperating ideas, Butler attempted to lampoon English society, its customs and manners. The hero, George Higgs, seeks his fortune abroad. On a sheep farm, apparently in New Zealand, he meets with a native, who tells him about Erewhon ("nowhere" spelled backward), a fabulous country where monsters dwell, and leads him there. Higgs finds the citizens of Erewhon principally preoccupied with keeping healthy and pretty. To catch a cold was regarded as treasonable, whereas an act against the moral code was treated as an illness. A man accused of consumption was condemned to life-long imprisonment (in a sanitarium). A man who made more than £20,000 per annum was worshiped as a genius and was exempt from paying taxes. Visiting the College of Unreason, the School of Inconsistency, and the School of Evasion, he discovers that "consistency is a vice which degrades human nature, and levels man with the brute." Higgs escapes from Erewhon to England in a balloon with a girl of the country whom he loves.

EREWHON REVISITED (1901), by Samuel Butler. As a sequel to *Erewhon* (q.v.) this work brings George Higgs back to the land of the strange people after an absence of twenty years. He finds Erewhon has undergone a remarkable transformation. The aborigine Chowbock who first led him there has changed his name; he is now Bishop Kahabuka, head of the Christian missionaries. To his amazement Higgs is told that a cathedral has been named after him to celebrate his miraculous ascent in the balloon. The natives, taking him for a child of the Sun-God, had established a new religion which they called Sunchildism. The Church Fathers are Professors Hanky and Panky and Dr. Downie, all three experts in complicating the simple and in juggling theological hocus-pocus. Higgs is appalled at this misinterpretation but his attempt at dissipating the myth is thwarted. Eventually he is removed secretly from the country.

ERIK DORN (1921), by Ben Hecht. See HECHT, BEN.

EROS INVINCIBLE (1893), by Ricarda Huch. See HUCH, RICARDA.

ESCAPE (1924–1927), by Louis Bromfield. See GREEN BAY TREE, THE, by Louis Bromfield.

ESMOREIT (ca. 15th c.), Anonymous. See MEDIEVAL FLEMISH PLAYS.

ESSAY CONCERNING HUMAN UNDERSTANDING (1690), by John Locke. The purpose of this essay was "to inquire into the origin, certainty, and extent of *human knowledge,* together with the grounds and degrees of *belief, opinion,* and *assent."* Locke argues against the doctrine of innate ideas, that is, knowledge preceding experience. He starts by assuming that at birth the mind is blank, like a sheet of white paper, and attempts to show how all our knowledge is engraved upon it by experience. In working out this empiricist theory, Locke develops a dualistic metaphysics. He conceives of the universe as made up of particles of matter in motion. There are certain qualities which these bodies possess in themselves—the primary qualities: solidity, extension, figure, motion or rest, and number. When we perceive the world, these qualities are imprinted on the mind together with other qualities which exist for the perceiver only and do not reside in the bodies. These latter are the secondary qualities: color, sound, size, etc., which exist only where there is a proper organ to perceive them. This distinction between primary and secondary qualities, which proved to be unsatisfactory to later philosophers, served as the philosophic foundation for the Newtonian world view, and rationalized the investigations of physical scientists. Locke never did make clear his view as to the exact nature of knowledge. Sometimes he held that it consisted in the agreement of ideas with one another. At other times he seemed to believe that it consisted in the agreement between ideas and things. This latter view is difficult to understand, since, according to Locke, all we can ever know is the ideas in our own minds. This ambiguity gave rise to two subsequent traditions in philosophy. The French followers of Locke, emphasizing the primary qualities, developed in the direction of mechanical materialism. His English followers, accepting his view that ideas exist only in the mind, rejected the distinction between primary and secondary qualities, and turned toward subjective idealism (Berkeley) and phenomenalism (Hume). Locke may be said to be a philosopher of common sense; many of his postulates and principles are credible, but their philosophic implications lead to perplexing difficulties.

ESSAY OF DRAMATICK POESIE, AN (1668), by John Dryden. In reply to Sir Robert Howard's Preface to his *Foure New Plays* (1665) in which the use of the rhymed couplet in the drama was disparaged, Dryden wrote in remarkably modern prose an apology in classical dialogue form. He wished to vindicate the literary innovations of the English writers against such Francophiles' as Howard. His views are clearly expressed in one of his triplets:

The Unities of Action, Place and Time,
The Scenes unbroken, and a mingled chime,
Of Jonson's manner and Corneille's rhyme

Dryden, through the instrumentality of four imaginary characters, bearing the Greek names of Crites (Sir Robert Howard), Lisideius (Sir Charles Sedley), Eugenius (the Earl of Dorset) and Neander (Dryden), discuss the Greek and Latin poets and dramatists, also Ben Jonson, Corneille, Fletcher, Shakespeare and Molière. He concludes with the reflection: "I think him (Jonson) the most learned and judicious writer which any theatre ever had."

ESSAY ON CRITICISM, AN (1711), by Alexander Pope. Written when Pope was only twenty-one years old, this didactic poem in heroic couplets discusses good taste in poetry, the principles of verse structure, and the laws of criticism. Pope lays down the rules which critics should observe and gives examples of what can be approved and what cannot. He does not neglect all those common causes of literary quarrels in which he himself was soon to get embroiled. Throughout he is borrowing precepts from the ancients, putting platitudes memorably, and in Part III he gives a brief history of criticism.

ESSAY ON MAN (1732–1734), by Alexander Pope. This philosophical poem contains six hundred heroic couplets divided into four epistles. The aim is to prove the wisdom of the universal scheme of things, and to show that man is unable to see this wisdom because of his finite vision. Man should not try to find his place in God's plan but should be content and submissive. He should confine his study to mankind. The four epistles deal respectively with man and his relation to the universe, to himself, to society, and to happiness. The poem abounds in widely-quoted lines, including "Whatever is, is right" and "Hope springs eternal in the human breast."

Eloisa to Abelard (1717) is rare as showing Pope attempting to deal with the tender passion, and was based on a French version of the famous Latin correspondence. Eloisa is represented as being unable to keep her thoughts from her lover, to "make my soul quit Abelard for God." There is much rhetorical passion in a melancholy setting in this heroic epistle.

ESSAY ON RIME (1944), by Karl J. Shapiro. See SHAPIRO, KARL J.

ESSAY ON THE PRINCIPLE OF POPULATION, THE (1798), by Thomas Robert Malthus. Malthusianism may be described as a theory, first broached by numerous writers such as Montesquieu and Benjamin Franklin, but popularized by Malthus: that population has a tendency to multiply faster than subsistence, and that some people must necessarily go hungry unless society adopts measures to prevent the natural increase of the population. In short, Malthus proposed to cure poverty by race suicide through sexual abstinence and prohibition of marriage among the poor. Malthus' "humanitarianism" had, for a clergyman, the unsentimental aspect of wholesale extermination by "natural processes." Socialist writers took Malthus to task by pointing out that it is not lack of subsistence or overpopulation that is the cause of poverty but inequalities in distribution and in buying power resulting from the lopsided profit system. Malthus' thesis was in part an attack on ~hilanthropy, particularly on the Poor Law Bill sponsored by William Pitt in '96, which aimed to ameliorate the misery among the English masses at-ndant upon the rise of industrialism. Also, it was provoked by the writings the Utopian socialists, such as Godwin, the poet Shelley's father-in-law.

ESSAYS (1841 and 1844), by Ralph Waldo Emerson. Until the publication of the first series of his *Essays* in 1841, Emerson had been known chiefly as a lyceum lecturer to the inner circles of New England culture. The *Essays,* originally delivered as lectures, might be described as elegant table talks, full of ripe wisdom, German transcendentalism, and poetic mysticism. Emerson was a clergyman, and moral issues sometimes draw attention from the limpid quality of his prose. "The Over-Soul," a Platonic concept, is one of his basic ideas. It is the theory of one basic force animating all mankind, a divine omnipresence whose intimations furnish man with all revelations of truth and beauty. "Compensation" describes a dualism implicit in man's personality. By divine justice any act, good or bad, rewards or punishes itself. "Circles" is a reconciliation of pantheistic law with the principle of human progress. "Self-Reliance" is a plea for courageous individualism. Emerson urges everyone to consider the dignity of his own mind, not social pressure, tradition or authority. The second series of *Essays,* in 1844, deals with more practical concerns, such as "Politics" and "Manners," and further ethical problems, such as "Character."

Emerson's addresses were famous, and his 1837 oration, *The American Scholar,* is considered one of the masterpieces of New England literature— "our intellectual Declaration of Independence." It was delivered before the Phi Beta Kappa Society of Harvard at its anniversary meeting. Decrying dependence upon European cultural patterns, Emerson made an appeal for leadership of American society by American thinkers, to be developed through contact with creative work of the past and through contact with nature and their fellow men. The Scholar is Man Thinking, guided by the mottos "Know Thyself" and "Study Nature." He must act as well as think. He must be an individual.

Society and Solitude (1870) is a series of essays which iterate the idea that since it is man's moral obligation to serve his fellow men, he must blend personal self-sufficiency and social usefulness. *The Conduct of Life* (1860) includes nine chatty, philosophical essays reflecting on the powers of fate, power, wealth, culture, behavior, worship, beauty and illusions. *Representative Men* (1850) proposes that it is the aim of civilization to produce great men, and considers six geniuses which represent as types the philosopher, mystic, skeptic, poet, man of the world and writer.

Emerson wrote poetry of an intellectual and metaphysical nature, and was a prolific letter-writer and journalist.

ESSAYS (1825–1844), by Thomas Babington Macaulay. See CRITICAL, HISTORICAL AND MISCELLANEOUS ESSAYS, by Thomas Babington Macaulay.

ESSAYS (1580, 1588, 1595), by Michel de Montaigne. Rich, scholarly in a desultory way, and saddened by the death of a close friend, Montaigne retired to his estate near Bordeaux to read quietly and annotate his books. Shortly the notes overflowed the margins. Eventually he found that he had written a book of his own, about himself and the things that interested him most; chatty and wise, in a style which followed the twisted contours of his thought, "simple and unaffected, the same in writing as on the tongue." He explored his own character in great detail, and would, if it had been possible, "have painted himself naked." The result is an extraordinarily complete portrait of a human being, diverse, sometimes inconstant, but always interesting. But in spite of what Montaigne says of his subject, most of the essays are not about Montaigne, as the titles, though often untrustworthy, themselves suggest: "Of Sadness," "Of Liars," "Of Pedantry," "Of Friendship," "Of the Inequality That Is Amongst Us," "Of the Vanity of Words," "Of Smells," "Of Democritus and Heraclitus," "Of Conscience." Particularly recommended are "On Some Verses of Virgil" and the letter to Countess Diana of Foix, "On the Education of Children." As age increased his wisdom, and the pain of his kidney stones taught him new lessons and sent him traveling about Europe in search of relief, he retouched the essays, modifying a statement here, adding a line or paragraph there. His philosophy changes, becomes less stoic, goes through a period of skepticism, finally takes a more Epicurean or naturalistic tinge. Enlightened, liberal, tolerant, undogmatic in a time when religious wars had put such things out of fashion, his combination of wisdom with humor and of sad reflectiveness with zest for life has interested readers as different in temperament as Shakespeare and Emerson.

ESSAYS, COUNSELS, CIVIL AND MORAL, THE (1597, 1612, 1625), by Francis Bacon. With its epigrammatic, balanced sentences, chiseled and exquisite, each one virtually a paragraph in content, the *Essays,* in the words of Bacon, "handle those things . . . whereof a man shall find much in experience but little in books." They reveal the author one of the founding fathers of modern science, as a man of universal knowledge, genius and taste. His lines are filled with reflection, ideas and advice on how to spend a good and useful life. The 1625 and final edition contained fifty-eight essays on such characteristic themes as "Religion," "Death," "Cunning," "Love," "Friendship," "Riches," "Ambition," "Deformity," "Truth," "Vain Glory," "Envy," "Gardens," "Travel," "Seditions and Troubles," and "Vicissitude of Things." The compressed style is equaled only by parts of the King James version of the *Bible* (q.v.). These are not familiar essays, like Lamb's, for Bacon reveals himself only indirectly. But he makes up in brightness for what he lacks in warmth.

ESSAYS IN CRITICISM (First Series 1865; Second Series 1888), by Matthew Arnold. The function of literature, averred Matthew Arnold, is "a criticism of life." These *Essays,* therefore, are as much a commentary on life and society as on writing. As a poet and critic, Arnold was an evangelist, pointing moral lessons. The function of criticism he defined as follows: "A disinterested endeavor to learn and propagate the best that is known and thought in the world." His didacticism is closely akin to the social-consciousness school of contemporary literature. Arnold was a cosmopolite culturally, although in his moral judgments he was incorrigibly a mid-Victorian. He sought great variety of subject matter for his essays. In this he resembled Carlyle and Pater. He wrote critiques on Heine, Joubert, the two de Guérins, Spinoza, Tolstoy, Amiel, Marcus Aurelius, Pagan and Medieval Religious Sentiment, Milton, Byron, Shelley, Keats, Wordsworth and Gray. In *The Study of Poetry* (q.v.) he advocated the use of great short passages of poetry—touchstones—for measuring all other poetry, but omitted Chaucer as lacking "high seriousness." The *Essays* are a mirror of the personality and ideals of Arnold. In the field of criticism they occupy the rank of a major classic. Although scholarly and stiff in style, a little somber, perhaps even pontifical, they are, nevertheless, a reflection of the sprightliness of the universal interests on the part of their author.

ESSAYS OF ELIA (1823), by Charles Lamb. The *Essays of Elia* are readable and interesting examples of the informal, friendly essay. Filled with gentle, whimsical humor, they are, as someone has said, "a great prophylactic against priggery." Although Lamb has other rights to literary fame, it is for his essays that he is chiefly remembered. Most of them he wrote during his spare time as a clerk, and took a former clerk's name as a pseudonym. They are almost all thinly disguised autobiographical accounts of his experiences and thoughts. The people in his essays are his family, friends, and relatives. He also wrote about places that he loved. Almost every phase of his life forms the background for an essay. Lamb is never didactic; he takes sides on no question, tries to prove nothing. His power lies in his charm, indefinable but perfectly apparent even to the most casual reader. Nor does he attempt to conceal his weaknesses. Some of the essays are melancholy; some, humorous; some are reminiscent; others, visionary. All are intensely human and touch upon the deepest emotions and truths. In most, sentiment and humor are happily combined. Some of the most famous of the essays are: "Dream Children," "The Praise of Chimney Sweepers," "Dissertation on Roast Pig," "The Superannuated Man," and "Old China."

ESSAYS ON HEREDITY (1889), by August Weismann. In this collection of essays on heredity and other biological problems, Weismann advances his original germ-plasm theory of heredity and denies that acquired characteristics are transmissible. His contention that there had to be a reduction-division of the chromosome was found years later to be correct. The orthodox Darwinists opposed his views, but with time even they had to bow before altered and extended knowledge of the subject. The essays in the chronological order of their composition are: "The Duration of Life" (1881); "On Heredity" (1883); "Life and Death" (1883); "The Continuity of the Germ-Plasm as the Foundation of a Theory of Heredity" (1885); "The Significance of Sexual Reproduction in the Theory of Natural Selection" (1886); "On the Number of Polar Bodies and Their Significance in Heredity" (1887); "On the Supposed Botanical Proofs of the Transmission of Acquired Characteristics" (1888); "The Supposed Transmission of Mutilations" (1888); "Retrogressive Development in Nature" (1888); "Thoughts Upon the Musical Sense in Animals and Man" (1889); "Remarks on Certain Problems of the

Day" (1890); "Amphimixis, or, The Essential Meaning of Conjugation and Sexual Reproduction" (1891).

ESTHER (1689), by Jean Racine. See ANDROMACHE, by Jean Racine.

ESTHER WATERS (1894), by George Moore. Esther, daughter of a drunken father, is forced to leave home and seek employment. She is a deeply religious girl and a Plymouth Sister. She enters service at the Barfield house, where everyone is interested in gambling on races. She is kindly treated by Mrs. Barfield, a Plymouth Sister like herself. When she is twenty, she meets William Latch, who seduces her, then deserts her. Esther's place is lost. After a period of wretched poverty the girl enters the hospital, where her child is born. From here she is forced to go to the workhouse and endure all sorts of humiliating situations, but in all vicissitudes she fights bravely to rear her child. Again she meets William, and after he obtains a divorce they are married. He is good to her, but her security is short-lived. He gets in trouble with the authorities, then dies from an illness caught by exposure at the race-track. Esther, again penniless, finally returns to live with Mrs. Barfield, who is now alone and poor. In her house she finds contentment. Jackie, her son, grows up and enlists in the army. Esther feels she is rewarded in having accomplished her woman's work of rearing the child.

ESTRELLA DE SEVILLA (1617?), by Lope de Vega. See STAR OF SEVILLE, THE, by Lope de Vega.

ESTUDIANTE DE SALAMANCA, EL (1840), by José de Espronceda. See STUDENT OF SALAMANCA, THE, by José de Espronceda.

ETERNAL HUSBAND, THE (1870), by Feodor Dostoevsky. In theme and texture, this novel is one of Dostoevsky's lighter works, though the element of cruelty enters into it as it does in most of his writings. It tells of the death of a woman who has been described as a sort of "Russian Madame Bovary." She has left letters which for the first time reveal to her duped, innocent husband Pavel Pavlovich Trusotsky that she had conferred favors on a large number of lovers. *The Eternal Husband* tells of the relations which followed between the husband and one of the lovers, Velchaninov, presumably the father of the child who has passed as Trusotsky's. It turns on the theme of the unforgivable injury inflicted on the husband and his consequent loss of dignity, and on the husband's subtle revenge, which is double-edged since it injures him as well as the wrongdoer. The same theme treated tragically in some of Dostoevsky's other works is dealt with here more in terms of comedy. Incidents borrowed from *The Idiot* (q.v.) find new expression in a new setting. The husband and the lover emulate in some ways the psychological tactics of Rogozhin and Myshkin, even to the final episode when the rivals sleep side by side on divans, and the same kind of murder is attempted, on this occasion a razor being used. The tension of Dostoevsky's great novels is absent, yet the basic Dostoevskian elements are all here: dramatic dreams in profusion, the madness of human lives, situations aroused by the subconscious, superb complications, the duality of personality, intellectual conceptions stated emotionally. The final situation in which "the eternal husband" is being bullied by his new wife and is forced to make a silent plea that Velchaninov refrain from cuckolding him again is one of the most entertaining and touching in fiction. This has been called Dostoevsky's one Western novel.

ETHAN FROME (1911), by Edith Wharton. New England life in an old farmhouse, near Lenox in the Berkshires, is the setting for Mrs. Wharton's chronicle of anguish and frustration. Ethan, a gaunt, silent man, is prompted by his own loneliness as well as by pity for Zenobia (Zeena), an invalid and hypochondriac seven years older than himself, to marry her. In time she obtains a cruel, selfish hold on him. When Zeena's homeless young cousin, Mattie Silver, comes to live with them he turns to her for warmth. Zeena, driven to extremities by fear and jealousy of her cousin, begins to persecute her. Ethan, who sees everything that is going on, is constrained by pity as well as by his poverty from deserting her and going away with Mattie to start life anew. Instead he and Mattie enter into a suicide pact: they go sledding and deliberately crash into an elm tree. But the consequences are different from what they had expected; Ethan is hopelessly crippled and Mattie's spine is broken. Ironically it is the grasping Zeena who, although an invalid herself, now undertakes to care for Ethan and Mattie. This is considered Mrs. Wharton's masterpiece, and was her acknowledged favorite.

ETHICS (1662–1665), by Benedict de Spinoza. For the lay reader the *Ethics* is somewhat forbidding because of its highly abstruse and technical form. Spinoza employed the geometric method to establish his ethics on a tested, scientific basis. The reason for his choice of this method was his contention that, since Nature is governed by eternal and immutable laws, man, being a part of Nature, also must be studied scientifically, i.e., geometrically.

The central idea in the *Ethics* is that all things in Nature are determined by necessity. God is identical with the universe; and far from being outside and above it, He too acts according to necessary laws. Whatever is, is one. Therefore, Spinoza constructed a philosophic system based on a universal determinism. But it is a common error to suppose that his determinism was a form of fatalism. Spinoza sought to establish that all events and men's actions are *determined* by their proper causes and are not just accidental or providential. This is a scientific concept that was far in advance of Spinoza's time and for which he was to pay dearly in his lifetime. He was an austere realist, albeit moved by a profound sympathy for human hungers and failings. He stated: ". . . it must be among our chief ethical rules to see that we build the lofty structure of human society on the sure and simple foundations of man's organism." Furthermore, reason instructs that the surest way to human happiness is by co-operative and not competitive activity, i.e., the *desideratum* of a highly self-conscious social organization. Reason and knowledge are the tools of insight and understanding with which to regulate life in a harmonious way; therefore, the highest blessedness of man resides in his intellectual love of God or universal Nature, which, in an ethical sense, really means man. The *Ethics* is arranged in five parts, each fully buttressed with definitions, axioms and postulates. The titles are indicative of their content: Part I, "Of God"; Part II, "Of the Nature and Origin of the Mind"; Part III, "Of the Origin and Nature of the Emotions"; Part IV, "Of Human Bondage," or "Of the Strength of the Emotions"; Part V, "Of the Power of the Intellect," or "Of Human

Liberty." The moral reasonableness of the *Ethics* is shown by that proposition which runs counter to accepted religious concepts of the Reward of Virtue: "He who loves God cannot desire God's love in return, for, so desiring, he would desire that God should not be God."

ÉTUDES SUR LA BIÈRE (1876), by Louis Pasteur. See OEUVRES, by Louis Pasteur.

ÉTUDES SUR LA MALADIE DES VERS À SOIE (1870), by Louis Pasteur. See OEUVRES, by Louis Pasteui.

ÉTUDES SUR LE VIN (1866), by Louis Pasteur. See OEUVRES, by Louis Pasteur.

EUGÈNE ONEGIN (1825–1833), by Alexander Pushkin. *Eugène Onegin*, the dramatic poem on which Tschaikowsky composed his opera of the same name, is regarded by many critics as the greatest of Pushkin's works. This poet, part Russian, part Negro, rivals Byron in celebrity as a romantic poet. He worked on the poem for nine years. What distinguishes it from other European romantic-dramatic poems is its Russian national character. This was in keeping with Pushkin's strong nationalist spirit; he felt indignant and abashed at the feeling of inferiority that made Russians slavishly copy foreign models.

The subject is slight indeed. It sprawls over seven thousand excessively embellished lines. For the sake of solitude Onegin has retired to the country. There he meets the simple-hearted Tatiana, who artlessly gives him her love. Onegin, feeling superior as a cultivated man of the world, scorns her love. Being a man of formal honor, he arranges a meeting with her and in the most sententious manner informs her that he is not the man for her. They part, Tatiana grieving and humiliated, and Onegin not a bit pleased with himself and his exemplary conduct. Several years later he meets her again, this time under reversed circumstances. Tatiana is a great lady now—a princess. She is married to a gouty old husband and is the idol of a band of adorers. This time it is he who confesses his love to her. She replies coldly: "I cannot give myself to you. I have loved you. I love you still. But I am married. I will keep my faith."

It has been remarked that Eugène Onegin could not have existed outside of Russia. Moody, capricious, alternating between joy and grief, arrogance and humility, cruelty and the most abject of consciences, he has no particular justification for living, and goes through life cutting idiotic capers and making himself generally obnoxious, although, had he but had a moral basis for living, he might have wound up as a good man instead of a superfluous one. A famous Russian critic calls *Eugène Onegin* "an encyclopedia of Russian life."

EUGÉNIE GRANDET (1833), by Honoré de Balzac. See HUMAN COMEDY, THE, by Honoré de Balzac.

EUNUCH, THE (161 B.C.), by Terence (Publius Terentius Afer). Phaedria, a young Athenian gentleman, is in love with Thais, a courtesan, whom he keeps. She is also courted by Thraso, a bragging, pretentious captain, who has promised to present her with a young girl who had been brought up with her as her sister and then sold into slavery, and whom he has bought, but now that he knows Phaedria also enjoys Thais' favors, he is loath to keep his promise. Thais asks Phaedria to leave town for a few days and leave the way clear for the captain so that he will fulfill his promise. Phaedria has also promised Thais a eunuch as a gift and he leaves his servant, Parmeno, in charge of delivering him. Gnatho, a parasite, has charge of delivering the girl, Pamphila, and Chaerea, Phaedria's younger brother, chances to see her in the street and falls in love with her on the spot. He meets Parmeno in front of Thais' house just as Pamphila has vanished within. Parmeno recognizes her from Chaerea's description and tells him she has been presented to his brother's mistress. Chaerea decides to disguise himself as the eunuch and thus gain admittance to Thais' house in order to be close to Pamphila. Thais tells her maid, Pythias, to put the new eunuch in charge of the girl, and Chaerea takes full advantage of his opportunity. He then comes out, meets a friend and goes off. Phaedria returns and hears that his eunuch has raped Pamphila and run off. He sends for the real eunuch, Dorus, and discovers the trick his brother has played. After much plotting and counterplotting, in which Pythias takes her revenge on Parmeno and Pamphila turns out to be the sister of Chremes, another young Athenian gentleman who arranges a marriage between his sister and Chaerea, the comedy ends to the satisfaction of everyone but the braggart captain. The play was adapted by Terence from a Greek work of Menander by the same name.

EUPHUES (1579–1580), by John Lyly. This prose romance is often described as a manual of courtly culture. Lyly was a humanist in whom upperclass interests, loyalties, and taste for elegant worldliness predominated. He addressed himself to educated and well-bred young men, and more particularly young women, for Lyly said: "*Euphues* had rather lie shut in a lady's casket than open in a scholar's study." *Euphues* may be described as a "Book of Courtesy."

The work is divided into two parts: *The Anatomy of Wit* (1579) and *Euphues and His England* (1580). The aim of the novel is intensely nationalistic: to rally English scholarship and culture against the Italianate influences which were predominant throughout Europe at the time. However, it was not the content that interested English ladies and gentlemen of Elizabeth's day; they were delighted with the elegant and artful style, since termed "euphuistic." A near contemporary, Edmund Blount, wrote in 1632: "that beautie in court which could not parley Euphuism was as little regarded as she which nowe there speakes not French." *Euphues* made Lyly the most popular writer of the gentry of England.

In the unimportant and artificial plot, Euphues, the hero, goes on an extended tour of the continent. In Naples he falls in love with the Governor's flirtatious daughter, Lucilla. But she is already committed to his friend, Philautus. Consumed by his passion, Euphues forgets his loyalty to his friend and steals the affections of the young lady. In turn, however, Lucilla throws him over for another. Cured of his infatuation, repentant of his disloyalty, Euphues returns to London, where he virtuously devotes himself to the pursuit of knowledge. In Book II Philautus and Euphues are in London. The book is concerned mainly with the love affairs of Philautus. Eventually Euphues goes to Greece, whence he writes to the European ladies concerning English life and institutions. The book closes with a letter of advice to Philautus.

EUROPEANS, THE (1878), by Henry James. See AMBASSADORS, THE, by Henry James.

EVANGELINE (1847), by Henry Wadsworth Longfellow. See LONG-FELLOW, HENRY WADSWORTH.

EVE OF ST. AGNES, THE (1819), by John Keats. Amidst "argent revelry" lovely Madeline determines to retire, in the hope that, according to the legend of St. Agnes' Eve, she may have midnight visions of her true love. While she lingers, Porphyro, youthful scion of an enemy house, secretly observes her dancing. Enamored, he persuades her ancient, palsied nurse, Angela, to conceal him in Madeline's chamber. Waking her at midnight, he woos her with music. Her heart is wholly his; together they flee into the storm. Spenserian stanzas, masterfully used to create the haunting, luxurious atmosphere of medieval romance, embellish the slight narrative. The poem's sensuousness is also Spenserian.

EVELINA (1778), by Frances Burney. Evelina Anville had a hard-hearted father who deserted his wife when he discovered she possessed no fortune. Evelina was brought up by the Reverend Arthur Villars, a friend of her grandfather, who taught her to live by principle. At seventeen, with his benign approbation, she journeys to London to live with his friend, Lady Howard. Evelina now enters the fashionable, gay world of English society. She meets handsome Lord Orville, whose conversation she found "really delightful." At the same time, the foppish Sir Clement Willoughby begins his courtship of her, but Evelina has enough worldliness to recognize that he is a philanderer and rake. Following Willoughby's unsuccessful attempt to abduct her after the opera she begins to value Lord Orville more than ever. Evelina's "low-born" grandmother, Madame Duval, supplies the comedy for the tale, with her vulgar parvenu antics which are a source of embarrassment to Evelina. Sir John Belmont, Evelina's father, has been duped into believing that the child of a servant he has reared from infancy is his own daughter. The true Evelina is eventually recognized by him. She marries Lord Orville.

EVERY MAN IN HIS HUMOUR (1598), by Ben Jonson. This is the first play written in its entirety by Jonson; it created a new type of comedy. By caricaturing the individual foibles of his characters, he shows how ridiculous is the indulgence in one quirk of character, or "humour," as he calls it. Knowell, an old gentleman whose "humour" is worrying about his son's behavior, becomes so suspicious of him that he finally determines to set a spy on him. Edward, his son, has a friend in Wellbred, who is lodging in the city with his brother-in-law, Kitely, whose "humour" is jealousy. He fears that his pretty wife will flirt with the young university students that frequent the house. Edward has a mischievous servant, Brainworm, who plays a trick on his master by disguising himself as an old soldier returned from the wars, forced to beg for a living. Knowell employs the pretended soldier to spy on his son. Brainworm, by a number of different impersonations, tangles up the characters. His antics bring about the meeting of Kitely and his wife under circumstances in which each thinks the other is being unfaithful. Such a snarl occurs that it takes the aid of kindly Justice Clement to straighten them out. The element of romance is supplied by the love affair between Bridget, Kitely's sister, who is a willing and pretty young lady, and Edward. One of Jonson's best characters, Captain Bobadill, a boastful braggart who consorts with the young men, appears in this play. Another interesting character is Master Matthew, a stupid and pretentious writer of dull verses.

EVERYMAN (15th c.), Anonymous. At the opening of this morality play, God, discouraged by Mankind's neglect of spiritual matters, determines to demand a reckoning of Everyman. He sends Death forth with a summons. Everyman is taken by surprise. He is dismayed when Death identifies himself and orders him to prepare for the long journey. He pleads for more time, which Death refuses him. When Death will give him no stay, Everyman next asks for the right to ask his friends to accompany him. This request Death grants, saying that he may have the companionship of anyone who will venture forth with him.

Everyman approaches Good Fellowship, who, seeing him cast down, offers to do him any service even to laying down his life. But when Everyman explains the nature of his journey and begs his company, Good Fellowship flatly refuses. Everyman then has the same experience with Kindred and Goods, who abandon him. In despair Everyman looks for Good Deeds, but Good Deeds cannot rise from the ground; he is weak, weighted down helplessly by Everyman's sins. Good Deeds would go with him but cannot. Knowledge enters, bringing Confession. By their advice, through penance, Good Deeds is allowed to rise to accompany Everyman. They are joined by Strength, Discretion and Five Wits; after Everyman has gone to a priest for the last rites, they set out upon the journey.

When they come in sight of the grave, Strength, Discretion and Five Wits desert. Knowledge says that he can go no farther than the grave's edge, although he has no fear. Only Good Deeds can go the whole way. Thus Everyman, realizing how misguided he has been in not loving Good Deeds most through all his life, enters the grave with this true companion, with his book of reckoning in order, certain of being saved.

Everyman is the work of an unknown author, in all probability a priest. It antedates the reign of Henry VIII. It is the perfect type of the morality play, the most famous of its kind. It is still alive in the theatre and has had a number of modern American productions, one of the most interesting of which was performed in the Cathedral of St. John the Divine in New York City in 1938.

For all its archaic phrasing and moralistic content, *Everyman* is astonishingly moving and human. This is because it is rooted in one of the profound and basic experiences common to all men, or to "every man": the final reckoning with Death and the mystery of the hereafter.

EVERYMAN (ca. end 15th c.), by Peter Dorland. See MEDIEVAL FLEMISH PLAYS.

EVERYMAN (1912), by Hugo von Hofmannsthal. See HOFMANNS-THAL, HUGO VON.

EVIDENCES AS TO MAN'S PLACE IN NATURE (1863), by Thomas Henry Huxley. See EVOLUTION AND ETHICS, by Thomas Henry Huxley.

EVOLUTION AND ETHICS (1893), by Thomas Henry Huxley. T. H. Huxley was a distinguished zoologist and an ardent advocate of evolution. "Darwin's bulldog" he was called because of his stubborn defense of the *Origin of Species* (q.v.). He had collected material on evolution for many years, and in 1863 he published a series of lectures entitled *Evidences as to Man's Place in Nature,* in which one finds the first clear statement that man was descended from an ape-like ancestor. Huxley's rule of morality was always to speak the truth, and he did not evade issues. In 1870 he published a collection of essays, *Lay Sermons, Addresses, and Reviews,* a number of which again are courageous defenses of Darwinism. One of the reviews is on "agnosticism," a word coined by Huxley to describe his own philosophical position. Huxley expressed himself with energy and audacity, styling himself an "agent for the promulgation of damnable heresies." He was much in demand as a speaker, and the volume on *Evolution and Ethics* includes lectures delivered in the same year, 1893. Here he presents his scientific interpretation of right and wrong, contrasting the moral order with the cosmic order. Similar ideas run through two other volumes of essays also published in 1893: *Science and Hebrew Tradition* and *Science and Christian Tradition.* In 1894 Huxley gathered a representative set of his popular writings in the *Collected Essays.*

EXCURSION, THE (1814), by William Wordsworth. Wordsworth's poem in nine books of blank verse contains his most mature reflections on God, nature and man. Loosely constructed, the poem has passages of great beauty and wisdom. Concerned mainly with discourses by the Wanderer, who travels with the poet, on subjects ranging from despondency and its correction, to society and government, the poem also contains moving stories of peasant life. The moving story of Margaret, left to die alone in her ruined cottage, is contained in Book I. Other characters are the Pastor, who discourses on the virtuous life, and the Solitary, an unhappy man.

EXPERIENCE AND NATURE (1925), by John Dewey. See DEWEY, JOHN.

EXPERIMENTAL RESEARCHES IN ELECTRICITY (1831–1855), by Michael Faraday. The life of Faraday reads like a romantic fairy tale of a poor boy who achieved world-wide fame. First permitted by Sir Humphry Davy to do chores about the laboratory, Faraday before long undertook research of his own, and became the greatest discoverer in the field of electromagnetism and electrochemistry. It was from his work that the development of the electric dynamo and motor resulted. Faraday's earliest studies were in the chemistry of gases, following in the footsteps of Davy and Dalton; but these were soon overshadowed by his electrical discoveries. Oersted in 1820 had observed the deflection of the needle of a compass near a wire carrying an electric current, and Faraday's first notable contribution was the production in 1821 of a continuous rotation about each other of magnets and wires conducting electricity—the first primitive electric motor. Faraday here was accused of appropriating the discoveries of others; but it is quite clear that, although Oersted, Wollaston, Ampère, and others had suspected the possibility of such a continuous motion, Faraday was the first one to achieve success. It was ten years later that Faraday made possible his greatest discovery, the induction of an electric current in a wire by means of a magnet or by a current in another wire. This made possible the electric dynamo and the transformer. In this same year Faraday presented to the Royal Society the first of a long series of papers entitled *Experimental Researches in Electricity*. These were published in the *Philosophical Transactions* between 1831 and 1854, and they were collected in the famous three-volume work of the same title which appeared from 1844 to 1855. If the present period in history sometimes is referred to as "the electrical age," this is primarily due to the profound discoveries presented in this classic treatise by Faraday.

The researches of Faraday from 1821 to 1841 were concerned primarily with electromagnetism, but in 1845 he began a second great period of research, this time concentrating upon electrochemistry and photoelectricity. In 1845 he discovered the rotation of the plane of polarization of light through magnetism. This was one of the first hints of the electromagnetic nature of light. In his study of the electrolytic action of a current passing through a solution, Faraday in 1834 had formulated the quantitative laws of electrolysis known by his name; and in the second period of his experimental activity he continued his work on electrolytic dissociation. These results also appeared in the *Experimental Researches in Electricity* and in his *Experimental Researches in Chemistry and Physics* (1859). Faraday published several lesser works, including a popular *Chemical History of a Candle* (1861); but his fame rests chiefly upon his papers and three-volume treatise on electricity.

EXPERIMENTAL RESEARCHES IN CHEMISTRY AND PHYSICS (1859), by Michael Faraday. See EXPERIMENTAL RESEARCHES IN ELECTRICITY, by Michael Faraday.

EXPERIMENTS AND OBSERVATIONS OF DIFFERENT KINDS OF AIR (1774–1786), by Joseph Priestley. The ancients recognized four classes of substances which they named respectively: earth, water, air, and fire. Gases were not distinguished from ordinary air until in 1644 van Helmont coined this word to indicate the existence of various aeriform substances. In 1727 Stephen Hales devised the "pneumatic trough" for collecting gases, and in 1756 Joseph Black published a work describing what he called "fixed air" (carbon dioxide). The eccentric philosopher Henry Cavendish in 1766 presented to the Royal Society a paper "On Factitious Airs"—i.e., on gases produced artificially, as distinct from ordinary air—in which he described the production of "inflammable air" (hydrogen) by the action of acids on certain metals. It was at this point that the study of gases was taken up by the Unitarian minister, Joseph Priestley. So greatly did he develop and improve the preparation, manipulation and study of gases that he has been called "the father of pneumatic chemistry." He showed that green plants give off a respirable gas, and he prepared and studied ammonia, hydrogen chloride, sulphur dioxide, nitric oxide, nitrous oxide (laughing gas), and nitrogen peroxide. These gases he referred to as "different kinds of air." But his greatest discovery was the recognition and isolation in 1774 of "dephlogisticated air." This he obtained by heating red oxide of mercury and other substances under a bell jar over mercury, using a large "burning glass." A few months after making this discovery, Priestley communicated his results to Lavoisier; and the latter gave the new gas its modern name, oxygen, and made it a cornerstone in his new chemical theory of combustion.

In 1775 Priestley presented his work to the Royal Society and published it in Volume II of *Experiments and Observations*. He did not realize that in Sweden the chemist Scheele also had discovered oxygen at about the same time. Priestley was exceptionally skillful in planning and executing experiments, and these are fully described in the six volumes of his best-known work, *Experiments and Observations on Different Kinds of Air*, a revised and condensed edition of which appeared in three volumes in 1784. His election to the Royal Society, however, had resulted from the publication of another widely read volume—*History and Present State of Electricity, With Original Experiments* (1767). A few years later he did for optics what he had done for electricity, publishing a comprehensive *History and Present State of Discoveries Relating to Vision, Light and Colours* (1772). It is upon these three books that his scientific reputation rests; although he published numerous other works on political, educational and theological topics.

EXPERIMENTS AND OBSERVATIONS ON ELECTRICITY

(1751), by Benjamin Franklin. Gilbert's *De Magnete* (q.v.) in 1600 had awakened scientists to the importance of electrical phenomena, but progress for the next century and a half had been slow. The two most important contributions in this period had been the invention of the electrostatic machine by von Guericke in 1660 and the discovery of the Leyden jar (condenser) by Musschenbroek in 1746. It was the latter event which motivated Franklin, when he was forty years old, to undertake experimentation in electricity. During the next half dozen years he discovered the importance of points in drawing off charges, identified lightning as an electrical phenomenon, proposed the single-fluid theory of electricity, and observed a number of properties of condensers: that the charges reside in the glass and not in the metal coatings; that these charges are equal but opposite; and that the efficacy does not depend upon the shape. Franklin's scientific writing took the form of letters addressed to Peter Collinson and others in England, and they eventually found their way into the *Philosophical Transactions* of the Royal Society of London. In 1751 the letters (about two dozen in number) were collected and published in England in a volume with the title *Experiments and Observations on Electricity*. This work has reappeared in numerous editions and several foreign languages. Of it Priestley, in his *History and Present State of Electricity*, wrote: "Nothing was ever written upon the subject of electricity which was more generally read and admired in all parts of Europe than these letters."

EXPERIMENTS IN PLANT-HYBRIDIZATION (1865), by Gregor

Mendel. Few publications have so enduringly influenced the course of science as has this work by the Austrian Augustinian monk, Gregor Mendel. Although it lay forgotten for decades, the rising interest in the study of heredity

was the impetus for its rediscovery in 1900, and his views, known as Mendelism, are now a focal point in biological research. The monograph in which
these views were presented was the product of eight years of experimentation
in hybridization in which Mendel employed an original approach. Where
formerly botanists had taken a summary view of a whole generation of plants,
he confined himself to studying separately and closely the effects of hybridization upon each individual plant. Large numbers of crosses were made between
peas differing from each other in one specific characteristic. Mendel found
that in each case the offspring of the cross exhibited, in almost undiminished
intensity, the characteristic of one of the parents. In the case of each pair of
"characters" there is thus one which in the first cross prevails to the exclusion
of the other. This prevailing character (yellow or round, for example) Mendel
calls the *dominant* character, the other (green or wrinkled) being designated
as the *recessive* character. He next allowed the hybrids to fertilize themselves
and produce a new generation. In the latter he discovered that the numerical
proportion of dominants to recessives is approximately constant, being about
three to one. Again self-fertilized, the offspring of the recessives now remained *pure recessive*. In subsequent generations they never produced the
dominant again. Mendel's law of dominance has been discovered to apply to
animals as well as plants, and consequently it is a fundamental law of biology.
It asserted a proposition absolutely at variance with previously formulated
laws of ancestral heredity. It implied that the cross-breeding of parents need
not diminish the purity of their germ cells or, consequently, the purity of their
offspring, for Mendel introduced a particulate view of inheritance. It has
been a matter of much speculation for biologists what course the philosophy of
evolution might have taken had Darwin known about Mendel's investigations.
As it was, however, the work of Mendel was overlooked until at the turn of
the century it was rediscovered simultaneously by three distinguished botanists:
de Vries, Correns and Tschermak. Thenceforward Mendelism gained ground
steadily, and has come to rival Darwinism in the importance of its influence
upon biological science.

EXPLANATION OF THE TEN COMMANDMENTS (1412), by Jan
Hus. See HUS, JAN.

EXPOSITION DU SYSTÈME DU MONDE (1796), by Pierre Simon
Laplace. See MÉCANIQUE CÉLESTE, by Pierre Simon Laplace.

EYVIND OF THE HILLS (1911; Icelandic edition, 1912), by Jóhann
Sigurjónsson. This tragedy, written by an Icelander in Danish, with its
"seriousness, rugged force, and strong feeling," was acclaimed by Georg
Brandes as manifesting "poetic talent of high order." It is in prose, a stern
drama of life in the wilderness dealing with an outlaw who had been led by
hunger and circumstances to become a thief. He had fled to the mountains,
but longed for human companionship, and descended into a valley where he
was unknown and took service with a rich widow, Halla, who fell in love
with him. She knew his history, but because of her great love insisted on
sharing his lot. They escaped to his old haunt in the mountains; had two

·children, which she later was obliged to sacrifice; trials multiplied; and they fled farther away. "The last act finds the outlaw and his wife facing each other in a lonely hut, in the midst of a snowstorm which has shut off every avenue of resistance. Although the beautiful reality of love is there, they are tormented by hunger and utter need into doubts and mutual reproaches, and at last seek death in the snow." On the stage the tragedy has a powerful appeal.

According to the historical facts on which the action is based, the lives of the outlaws were saved in the last moment by a stray horse which suddenly appeared before the hut of the starving couple. The dramatist used this happy ending in a version rewritten for the Copenhagen stage, changing the last scenes and concluding the play with the exclamation by Halla: "So there is then a God!" We can take our choice of endings. (Cf. Introduction to *Modern Icelandic Plays,* New York, 1916.)

EZO VIKOLINSKY (1890), by Hviezdoslav. See HVIEZDOSLAV.

FABLE FOR CRITICS, A (1848), by James Russell Lowell. See LOWELL, JAMES RUSSELL.

FABLES, by Aesop. The *Fables of Aesop,* or, better, *Aesopic Fables,* so familiar to all in English translations and adaptations, are based directly or indirectly upon Greek tradition. The extant collection of *Aesopic Fables* in Greek prose is of late date, but we have the earlier versified renderings of Babrius in Greek and of Phaedrus and Avianus in Latin. In fact, we are told that Socrates, while in prison awaiting execution in 399 B.C., whiled away his time turning Aesop into verse. According to Herodotus, Aesop was a slave who lived about 550 B.C., and it would seem that he came from Sardis in Asia Minor. In all probability he was not a Greek. The ancient biographies are entirely apocryphal. The type of moralized beast tale current under his name is common the world over and is certainly no invention of his. It is to be found in Greek poetry as early as the seventh century B.C., and in the oldest portions of the Old Testament. Yet whatever the origin of the fable and whatever the historicity of Aesop, the fable as we know it is that type which became familiar to the Greek world under Aesop's name.

FABLES (1810–1820), by Ivan Andreevich Krylov. The greatest of all Russian fablers was, like all fablers, influenced by La Fontaine, whose work he had translated. His *Fables* met with an enthusiastic reception when they first appeared. A master of language, he wrote simply and colloquially, even racily, so that the most ordinary person could understand him. His prose is singularly alive. Written in simple rhyme, his *Fables* have been for generations memorized by all classes of people. They have attained the anonymity of popular folk art. There is a common sense quality in them which is generally associated with proverbs. They satirized, with a considerable measure of ridicule, the fashionable world of shams, snobbery and stupidity. The best available translation in English is that by Sir Bernard Pares, who has caught something of the spirit of the original in an English idiom. Here follow the first few lines of his translation of *A Quartet,* typical of Krylov's style:

The tricksome little monkey,
The goat with tangled hair,
The donkey,
And the clumsy-fingered bear
A great quartet had planned to start;
They got the notes, viola, fiddles, bass,
And sat beneath a lime-tree, on the grass,
To charm creation with their art. . . .

FABLES AND STORIES (1746), by Christian Fürchtegott Gellert. See GELLERT, CHRISTIAN FÜRCHTEGOTT.

FABLES IN SLANG (1899), by George Ade. See ADE, GEORGE.

FABLES IN VERSE (1668), by Jean de La Fontaine. Like his contemporaries Racine and Molière, La Fontaine excelled in making new art out of old materials. On the surface, the *Fables* repeat in French verse the animal fables familiar since antiquity, with such stock characters as the Lion, the Fox, and the Ass appearing in traditional roles. The language is racy, the verse neat, the narration effortless. But the interest is no longer in the moral of the tale. La Fontaine revives the spirit of the old *fabliaux* and the animal epics; the *Fables* constitute a broad criticism of human nature in general, with here and there a reflection on the organization of society. In the animals surrounding the Lion the seventeenth-century reader could, if inclined, watch the behavior of a royal court, and the arbitrary behavior of the Lion might even be interpreted as a comment on the ways of Louis XIV. In structure, many of the *Fables* were dramatic, complete with setting, dialogue, and denouement—for example, "The Grasshopper and the Ant," and "The Fox and the Cheese"— comedies in miniature. Others express a serious philosophy, much closer to the classical Stoics than to the Christianity of La Fontaine's time.

A second part was added to the *Fables* in 1679 and a third in 1693. Less well known, but fully as interesting, are his *Contes,* prose tales of the sort made famous by Boccaccio and Marguerite de Navarre.

FABLES OF BIDPAI. See ARABIAN NIGHTS' ENTERTAINMENTS.

FACTORY OF THE ABSOLUTE, THE (1927), by Karel Čapek. See R.U.R., by Karel Čapek.

FACUNDO, O LA CIVILIZACION Y LA BARBARIE (1845), by Domingo Faustino Sarmiento. See LIFE IN THE ARGENTINE REPUBLIC IN THE DAYS OF THE TYRANTS, OR CIVILIZATION AND BARBARISM, by Domingo Faustino Sarmiento.

FAERIE QUEENE, THE (1589–1596), by Edmund Spenser. In the tradition of the great Renaissance narrative poets of Italy, particularly Ariosto, this tremendous allegorical poem is at once a chivalric romance, a handbook of morals and manners, and a national epic. Spenser completed six of the twelve books, twelve cantos each, planned to celebrate a twelve-day feast held by Gloriana, Queen of Fairyland (Queen Elizabeth). On each day a knight, embodying one of Aristotle's twelve virtues, is chivalrously employed in adventures. All virtues are combined in the central figure of Prince Arthur (Magnificence).

Book I tells how St. George, the Red Cross Knight (Holiness), accompanies Una (Truth), slays the Dragon (Error or Sin) which besieges the castle of Una's parents, and is rescued from the giant (Orgoglio) by Prince Arthur, who overcomes Duessa (False Faith). In Book II Sir Guyon (Temperance) spurns the worldly temptations of Mammon's cave, destroys the Bower of Bliss, abode of the enchantress Acrasia (Intemperance), and is saved from Cymochles and Pyrochles by Prince Arthur, who delivers Alma (the Soul). In Book III Britomart (Chastity, sometimes Queen Elizabeth), a feminine knight, rescues Amoret (Wifely Devotion) from Busirane (Unlawful Love). Book IV develops the virtue of friendship by narrating the legend of Cambell and Triamond, with separate episodes showing contrasting vices. Book V reveals the nature of justice in the actions of Sir Artegal (Lord Grey), lover of Britomart. In Book VI Sir Calidore (Courtesy) finally overtakes and temporarily chains the Blatant Beast (Slander).

The allegory is far more complex than an outline can indicate. Queen Elizabeth, when Spenser desires, becomes Belphoebe or Britomart; Duessa is False Faith, Mary Queen of Scots, or the Papacy. It is impossible to give any idea of the profusion of material or the gorgeous richness of the varied allegory. Lacking the depth of Dante, Spenser has exalted ethical designs. The "verray parfit, gentil knyght" of Chaucer could no longer be quite believed in and was soon to become a subject for satire; Spenser's object was to fashion "a gentleman or noble person in vertuous and gentle discipline" in the person of Arthur. Spenser, dealing with an antique time, did not attempt to portray allegory in action. We do find the chivalrous spirit, such as Sidney, personified; but it was to the patriot Queen that Spenser linked all the romance he had learned from Geoffrey of Monmouth and the *Morte d'Arthur* (q.v.). It is not until the fifth book that contemporary politics play much part.

In the last two fully completed books the Christian spiritual sense is more apparent, the allegory is less evident and adventures more frequent. The picturesque pastoral and antiquarian descriptions of the earlier books give way to a new sublimity. There is nothing finer in the apotheosis of Christian allegory than the fragmentary legend, at the end, of Constancy, of the Titaness Mutability (the moon):

> Thence to the circle of the Moone she clambe,
> Where Cynthia raignes in everlasting glory,
> To whose bright shining palace straight she came,
> All fairely deckt with heavens goodly storie;
> Whose silver gates (by which there sat an hory
> Old aged Sire with hower-glasse in hand,
> Hight Time) she entred, were he liefe or sory;
> Ne staide till she the highest stage had scand,
> Where Cynthia did sit, that never still did stand.

This is the Spenserian stanza, named after its inventor, and used in long poems by Thomson, Byron, Keats, Shelley and others.

FAILURES, THE (1920), by Henry René Lenormand. A young play-wright and his wife, an actress, bring themselves to ruin by abandoning their ideals for the expediency of loose morality. When the play opens, Montredon, the manager of an unsuccessful theater, has promised to produce the young man's play about incest. However, he cannot find the proper actors. The couple lose touch with Montredon for two years, during which time they have been going steadily down hill. Montredon offers the wife a contract to tour the prov-inces which she is glad to accept. Her husband does not want to remain alone in Paris and so comes with her. Her salary does not prove adequate for the two of them, and to contribute to their support she begins meeting men after the theater. He follows other women and starts drinking excessively. They quarrel and make up, but finally in a fit of drunken jealousy he kills her and shoots himself.

FAIR GOD, THE (1873), by Lew Wallace. See BEN HUR, by Lew Wallace.

FAIRY TALES (1835), by Hans Christian Andersen. Hans Christian Andersen loved children and understood them well. Moreover, he possessed a remarkably lively and poetic imagination, which, together with his elfin wit, gaiety and pedagogic skill, made possible what is perhaps the most enchanting series of fairy tales ever written. Andersen, fully aware of the child's sensitiv-ity, not only to nature but to every inanimate object, makes use of everything in his stories—fancy and reality form a perfect synthesis under his imaginative handling. A cat, a plant, a bird, a doll, a sunbeam, a cloud, the wind, the sea-sons, a "leap-frog made out of the breastbone of a goose," and even household furniture, enter into his dramatis personae. Folklore tales abound in Ander-sen's works, such as "The Shepherdess and the Chimney-Sweep," "The Tinder-Box," "Little Claus and Big Claus," "The Little Match Girl," and others. Whether of the nursery class or of the didactic category, the tales contain many lyrical passages, full of sweetness and sentiment, and sometimes of great sadness. Andersen had a profound compassion for the unfortunate and the suffering, and he possessed the genius with which to stir the child's heart and mind. Un-derneath this gravity, however, flows the tranquil stream of his sunny make-believe which has charmed and will continue to charm countless generations of children.

FAIRY TALES (1812–1815), by Jacob and Wilhelm Grimm. It took the brothers Grimm thirteen years to collect their imperishable "Kinder- und Haus-märchen" (Children and Household Tales). They went about from village to village, from town to town, in the districts of Hesse and Hanau which they knew best, and transcribed the folk and fairy tales directly from the lips of the common people. These tales, transmuted by the Grimms' poetic feeling and love for children, include such everlasting favorites as "Hänsel and Gretel," "Cinderella," "Little Red Ridinghood," "Snow White," and "Rumpelstiltskin." The principle on which the Grimms worked in collecting their stories was truth and exactness. They added nothing of their own, embellished no incident, but faithfully presented their material as they received it. However, the mode of presentation, the poetic feeling, the details were conspicuously the two collaborators' contribution. The *Fairy Tales* of the Grimm Brothers, like those of Hans Christian Andersen, will remain everlasting literary masterpieces.

FAITHFUL SHEPHERDESS, THE (ca. 1609), by John Fletcher. In this pastoral tragicomedy, in rhymed and unrhymed verse which had a strong influence on Milton's *Comus* (q.v.), there are love affairs ranging from the gross to the ethereal. Clorin, the faithful shepherdess, lives beside her lover's grave, culling magic herbs. She is admired for her constancy by Thenot. Perigot loves Amoret and is in turn wooed by Amarillis, who arranges with her wooer, the Sullen Shepherd, a transformation whereby Amarillis takes on the shape of Amoret and shocks Perigot by her unchaste conduct. He wounds the real Amoret when next he sees her. This tangle is straightened out by Clorin and the Satyr who is her attendant spirit. The wantonness of Cloe is also exposed, she having pursued in quick succession Thenot, Daphnis, and Alexis.

FALL OF THE CITY, THE (1937), by Archibald MacLeish. See MacLEISH, ARCHIBALD.

FALLING INTO TROUBLE, by Chu Yuan. See LI SAO, by Chu Yuan.

FAMILY AT GILJE, THE (1883), by Jonas Lie. See COMMODORE'S DAUGHTERS, THE, by Jonas Lie.

FAMILY CHRONICLE, A (1846–1858), by Sergei Timofevich Aksakov. Aksakov's famous *Chronicle* consists of three separate books: *A Russian Gentleman* (sometimes called *A Family Chronicle*), *Years of Childhood* and *A Russian Schoolboy*. Perhaps the best of these is *Years of Childhood*. It has little episodic content. The story of a peaceful and uneventful childhood, it is exceptional in that it describes in beautiful prose the extreme sensibility of a child, a sensibility stimulated by a fitting education. It has been called Proustian, but it is wholly free from perverse and morbid elements. The work presents perceptively the continuity of life, without resort to the unusual or the dramatic. The sensitivity to nature is extraordinary, and the book contains some of the most famous descriptive passages of nature in literature. It is all on so quiet and uneventful a plan that it is almost impossible to synopsize it.

On the other hand, *A Family Chronicle* is very episodic, highlighted with character drama and entertainment. Highly objective, it deals with Aksakov's parents and grandparents prior to the author's own birth. We have a narrative of a serf-owner's life in the age of Catherine the Great. It describes vividly a patriarchal household, with the landlord owing no allegiance except to God and the Czar. Such is Stepan Mikhailovich Bagrov, a sturdy patriarch who, though kind and generous and just, exacts the rights of a feudal lord. Another kind of serf-owner is Kuraselov, wicked and tyrannical. He marries Bagrov's cousin, and is eventually brought back to sane ways by Bagrov.

The book's later pages have a tremendously interesting and entertaining picture of the wooing by Aksakov's father of Sophie Zubova, a truly remarkable figure—done in simple, primitive, heroic colors, reminiscent of Homer. Aksakov's father himself was, on the whole, an ordinary man, but the portrait in this book presents him as singularly vivid and, in a way, picturesque—to the Western eye, at least. The influence of Gogol in Aksakov's work is clearly discernible.

FAMILY REUNION, THE (1939), by T. S. Eliot. See ELIOT, THOMAS STEARNS.

FANTASTIC PIECES IN CALLOT'S MANNER (1814–1815), by E. T. A. Hoffmann. See HOFFMANN, ERNST THEODOR AMADEUS.

FAR AWAY PRINCESS, THE (1895), by Edmond Rostand. See L'AIGLON, by Edmond Rostand.

FAR FROM THE MADDING CROWD (1874), by Thomas Hardy. This pastoral novel is one of Hardy's greatest. It is concerned with the comedies and tragedies of life among people in humble circumstances. The farm activities, including the lambings, are described with faithful attention to details. The central story concerns Bathsheba Everdene, a country girl impatient of rustic ideas concerning marriage, and her three lovers, Gabriel Oak, Boldwood, and Troy. Comedy is sustained throughout the book in rustic characterizations of the peasants, who are shrewd in their judgments, simple, and richly humorous. Hardy's philosophy of pessimism is apparent but less intense than in *The Return of the Native* (q.v.).

Gabriel Oak, well on his way to becoming a small farmer in his own right, proposes to Bathsheba, a penniless girl. However, he frightens her away with the prospect that every time she looks up, he will be there, and when he looks up, she will be there. Bathsheba's imagination supplies a boring picture of married life. Shortly after this incident, Oak loses everything through an accident. Forced into humble circumstances, he wanders away in search of work. He again meets Bathsheba when he saves her crop from fire. Now, through the death of her uncle, she is a small farmer herself. She hires him as her shepherd and later as her bailiff, but the changed circumstances prevent him from pursuing his suit. Farmer Boldwood also falls in love with Bathsheba because of a valentine she sends him as a joke. But both Oak and Boldwood are discarded in favor of dashing Sergeant Troy, whom Bathsheba marries.

The fact that Troy has been the cause of the ruin and death of Fanny Robin leads to his desertion. Reports of his death are received, and Boldwood renews his hope of winning Bathsheba. Troy returns, however, and is killed by Boldwood, in a fit of rage at Troy's cruel treatment of Bathsheba. Her unfortunate marriage and the fact that the faithful Oak has stood by her through everything makes Bathsheba realize that she really loves him.

FAREWELL TO ARMS, A (1929), by Ernest Hemingway. Frederic Henry is a lieutenant in the Ambulance Corps of the Italian Army during World War I. He meets Catherine Barkley, an English nurse, with whom he contemplates a casual affair. Henry sustains a severe wound. Nursed in the hospital by Catherine, he perceives a new meaning to their relationship: they find themselves very much in love. By the time he returns to active service, she is pregnant. The Italian Army disintegrates in the course of a retreat from Caporetto. Soured by the war, like his depressed Italian friend Rinaldi, and seeing no point to remaining with the shattered and impotent army, Henry deserts and escapes to Switzerland with Catherine. They live an idyllic life for a few months until their child is due. Both Catherine and the child die in childbirth. Henry is left stunned by the completeness of the disaster.

FASTI, by Ovid (Publius Ovidius Naso, 43 B.C.–ca. A.D. 18). This versified Roman calendar or almanac covers in its six books the first six months of the year. The six books for the second half of the year were apparently never written. The *Fasti* recite in elegiac verse all the numerous religious holidays and anniversaries of the Roman calendar. Ovid drew upon excellent sources to explain the origin of the various festivals and gave full rein to his unmatched genius for storytelling in explaining the practices associated with each. The explanations involve myth, legend, folklore, religion and astronomy as well as history. For example, the 4th of April was the festival of the Great Mother of the gods and Ovid tells the oriental myth of Attis; for the 9th he records the setting of the constellation Orion; for the 14th he mentions the victory of Octavian at Mutina in 43 B.C.; and for the 25th he describes the rites in honor of the old indigenous Roman goddess, Mildew.

FATAL INTERVIEW (1931), by Edna St. Vincent Millay. See MILLAY, EDNA ST. VINCENT.

FATE, by Cicero. See PHILOSOPHICAL ESSAYS, by Cicero.

FATHER, THE (1887), by August Strindberg. This, one of Strindberg's best known and most powerful plays, was written at the height of his career and translated into French almost as soon as it appeared in Swedish. Strindberg's hatred of women is given vent in the picture of the pitiless housewife who dominates this play. The action takes place in the Captain's house in the country. He wishes to send his daughter, Bertha, to school in town. His wife is determined to keep her at home where she can control her. To accomplish her purpose, Laura, the wife, a cruel and strong-willed woman, hints that perhaps her husband is not the father of the child. She keeps up her insinuations until the Captain, always a nervous person, actually becomes ill. The heartless woman, who wants to control her household and her child alone, then intimates that her husband is probably insane and shows him a letter he had written declaring he was going crazy. She threatens to have him confined to an asylum. Finally, driven to a frenzy, he attacks her and attempts to leave. However, he is detained by a wily old nurse and confined to a strait jacket in his own home. His wife reigns supreme in the house. He becomes desperate, and ultimately so violently excited that he dies of a stroke.

FATHER AND SON (1940), by James T. Farrell. See STUDS LONIGAN, by James T. Farrell.

FATHER BROWN, THE INNOCENCE OF (1911), by Gilbert Keith Chesterton. The Father Brown stories—*The Innocence of Father Brown* (1911); *The Wisdom of Father Brown* (1914); *The Incredulity of Father Brown* (1926); *The Secret of Father Brown* (1927)—are now definitely a part of the history of distinguished detective fiction, on which they have conferred added stature. Father Brown, who had "a face as round as a Norfolk dumpling . . . eyes as empty as the North Sea," and who carried about brown paper parcels and a large, shabby umbrella which constantly fell to the floor, was drawn from an actual character, a Catholic priest to whom Chesterton had taken a liking. Father Brown, in his role of detective, gave but little attention to the minutiae of detection of which other writers have made so much. Father Brown himself says in one of his stories: "I try to get inside the murderer. Indeed, it's much more than that, don't you see? I *am* inside the man. I am always inside the man, moving his arms and legs; but I wait till I know I am inside a murderer, thinking his thoughts, wrestling with his passions . . . and when I am quite sure that I feel exactly like the murderer myself, of course I know who he is." There is a whimsical humor about the Father Brown stories, and not a little sagacity and an inexhaustible ingenuity. They serve incidentally as a vehicle for Catholic propaganda, but it is all accomplished with so much charm and literary skill that it is not taken amiss by his thousands of non-Catholic readers. It would be hard to compare Father Brown to any other fiction detective; he is unique. One does not have to be a detective-story fan to enjoy these stories.

FATHERS AND SONS (1861), by Ivan Sergevich Turgenev. This, the most important of Turgenev's novels, was the cause of considerable unhappiness to him because of the unusual critical response with which it met. It was at once both a success and a *cause célèbre*. Ironically, it was acclaimed and glorified by his enemies and repudiated by his friends. This curious result was unexpected and unjust. There had appeared in the 1860's in Russia a movement of skepticism and iconoclasm among Russian youth, which was to become known, largely through the christening by Turgenev, as Nihilism. It is this phenomenon which Turgenev is minutely scrutinizing in his novel in the person of its central character, Bazarov. Turgenev views his hero with a kindly objectivity, not glossing over the undeniably offensive aspects of his character. As was more or less inevitable, with such partisan feelings extant, the young generation considered the book an attack upon it, as did the reactionaries—to their satisfaction.

The novel is simple and leisurely in pace. Arkady Kirsanov, a student, returns to the home of his father, Nikolay Petrovitch, bringing with him his friend, the medical student Bazarov. The young men call themselves Nihilists. By Arkady's definition, "A Nihilist is a man who does not bow down before any authority, who does not take any principle on faith, whatever reverence that principle may be enshrined in."

The views of the brash young men bring them into conflict with the gentle, romantic Nikolay Petrovitch and his brother, the courtly, old-world Pavel Petrovitch. The second sequence carries the two youths through a prolonged stay at the country home of the charming widow, Madame Odintsov. The rest of the book carries the two youths to the home of Bazarov's parents, back to Madame Odintsov, and back again to Arkady's home, where the friction between Bazarov and Pavel culminates in a duel, harmless in consequence, and superbly comic in its effect. The book closes with a tragedy. Young Bazarov contracts surgical poisoning and dies at the home of his parents, his cynical skepticism finding its fullest justification in his own end. The rather ineffectual Arkady, always the disciple of his forceful friend, happily marries the young sister of Madame Odintsov. Bazarov, however cocky, however offensive at times, is a fully-rounded character, compelling both our respect and our involuntary affection. The book pulses with life and movement; although it is, in a large measure, an intellectual novel in that it gives voice to ideas and to the clash of ideas.

FAULKNER, WILLIAM (1897–   ). Faulkner, born of a prominent Southern family, returned from World War I with a taste for poetry acquired while in England. While working at various odd jobs, he began to write newspaper pieces on literature. His novels were not popular until *Sanctuary* (q.v.), originally written and rejected as a pot-boiler horror tale, was published in its revised form.

Soldier's Pay (1926) concerns Donald Mahon, a wounded aviator of World War I and his homecoming in Georgia. His family and friends misunderstand the compassion of his nurse, the attractive young widow Margaret Powers; and by the time Donald dies his ordeal has revealed the lives of many characters, and changed some.

Sartoris (1929) was the first of his novels which constitute a bitter panorama of the decadent Sartoris and Compson families of Jefferson, Mississippi. The genteel society of the old Civil War South decays, during three generations, and is replaced during the post-World War I period of disillusion, by such families as the unscrupulous Snopes, protagonists of *The Hamlet* (1940).

The Sound and the Fury (1929) is devoted to the Compsons. Partly narrated by thirty-three-year-old idiot Benjy, it describes his neurotic parents, his nymphomaniac sister Caddy and his brother Quentin, who commits suicide tormented by incestuous feelings. Following these reminiscences, there is the further tragedy of the child's displaying her mother's perverted traits, robbing Benjy's brother Jason, and eloping with a circus performer.

As I Lay Dying (1930) is a stream-of-consciousness novel which investigates the psychology of another subnormal Southern family. When Addie Bundren dies, her family prepare to honor her last wish, that she be buried in her native town. Son Cash is crippled rescuing a horse which is washed away while crossing a ford, and later traded by Anse. Idiot son Darl sets fire to a barn, burning his brother Jewel, and eventually being arrested. Daughter Dewy Dell, who is pregnant, pays for a quack medication by giving herself to the drug clerk, and is robbed by her father, Anse, who needs the money for a set of false teeth. And Anse returns from the trip with a new wife.

Light in August (q.v.) is a somewhat more balanced novel. Among short-story collections is *The Unvanquished* (1938), pieces about the Sartoris family.

FAUST (1870), by Estanislao del Campo. This witty poem, written in the gaucho vernacular, is a little gem, and for decades has retained its popularity throughout Latin America. An Argentine cowboy goes to Buenos Aires, and on seeing a queue near the box office of the Teatro Colón goes in and sees a performance of Gounod's *Faust*. He believes that everything that takes place on the stage is literally happening. On his way home he meets a friend and retells, in his superbly picaresque way, the story of *Faust*.

FAUST (Part I, 1808; Part II, 1831), by Johann Wolfgang von Goethe. This epic drama is truly the lifework of the versatile poet, dramatist, novelist, philosopher, statesman, scientist, art critic and theater manager Goethe. Notwithstanding the preoccupations of so diversified a career, the writing of *Faust* was begun in his youth and the finishing touches were put to the second part just before his death in 1832 at the age of 82. Part I begins like a mystery play with the celebrated prologue in Heaven, essentially a paraphrase of the first part of the Book of Job. The same bargain is struck, in both cases. The Lord, at Satan's challenge, gives him permission to make a test of the integrity of God's servant, Faust. Mephistopheles makes a bargain with the aged Faust. If Faust is granted one moment of complete contentment, he loses his soul. Faust regains his youth, and with Mephistopheles he travels about enjoying every form of earthly pleasure. He has a love affair with a simple girl, Margaret, whom he betrays and for whose downfall and death he is responsible. Mephistopheles thinks he will capture the soul of Margaret, but the purity of her betrayed love for Faust and her refusal to be rescued from death by Mephistopheles cause her to be saved. As the first part of the play ends, Faust has not yet found, in the world of desire and passion, that wonderful moment of existence to which he could really wish to cling. The second part of *Faust*, that of the world of public life and aesthetic beauty, is a profound philosophical poem, less of a familiar drama than the first. In it Faust tastes every form of intellectual and worldly power, but still fails to find the moment for which he so eagerly seeks, even in the love of Helen of Troy. Mephistopheles has almost despaired of his bargain. At last, once again an old man, the weary, sated Faust takes an interest in a project to reclaim land from the sea, a project which will mean little to him personally, but which will bring untold good to countless numbers of people. Here to his astonishment, in this disinterested and socially constructive occupation, Faust finds truly profound happiness. So noble is this impulse that Mephistopheles at the end is deprived of the soul of Faust, who, like the unfortunate Margaret of the first part, is redeemed.

Faust is a monument that will stand as long as literature endures. It is not of great importance on the actual stage, for its difficulties of production are enormous. Primarily it is a literary-poetic work. However, on rare occasions, both parts have been performed in careful adaptations. The first part, by itself, has received fairly frequent performances, and is the basis of Gounod's popular opera *Faust*, also of the opera *Mefistofele* by Boito, and the *Damnation of Faust* by Berlioz.

The semi-legendary figure of the magician and charlatan Faustus has not only attracted many poets (Marlowe, Lessing), but the adjective "Faustian" has become synonymous (since Oswald Spengler's use of it) for the striving quality of modern Western civilization. The latest prose variation of the theme is Thomas Mann's novel *Doctor Faustus* (q.v.).

FAUST (1836), by Nikolaus von Lenau. See LENAU, NIKOLAUS VON.

FEDERALIST, THE (1787–1788), by Alexander Hamilton, John Jay and James Madison. This work consists of a series of letters written to the New York press in support of the Federal Constitution agreed upon by the Federal Convention on September 17, 1787. It is considered to be the classic document in American political theory. Its background is the government set up in America after the Revolution, the government under the Articles of Confederation. This Confederation of sovereign states was too loose and weak a union to work effectively. After a few years a constitutional convention was called in Philadelphia to write a new constitution. Hamilton, Jay and Madison participated, and the resulting constitution is the one defended in this work. The need for a stronger union is eloquently argued on the grounds of common defense and prosperity. The fundamental principles are discussed and clarified. At the time of its presentation, there were many objections to the new constitution. These came mostly from people who were concerned lest the new federal government encroach on the rights of the states. The arrangement of the Constitution was defended in two ways: 1) the powers given the central government were essential to the performance of its functions, and 2) these powers were clearly limited and all remaining powers were left to the states. Various other objections are considered, both general and specific. The various branches of the government are described in some detail, the method of selection of their officers, their powers and the limitations on their powers, and their relations to other branches is made clear. This persuasive document not only did much to spread an understanding of the Constitution, but has served as a basic American political text ever since.

FEELING A DOG'S PULSE (1664), by Robert Boyle. See SCEPTICAL CHYMIST, THE, by Robert Boyle.

FERREX AND PORREX (1562), by Thomas Sackville and Thomas Norton. See GORBODUC, by Thomas Sackville and Thomas Norton.

FEUCHTWANGER, LION (1884–   ). A successful playwright in the Germany of the Weimar Republic, Lion Feuchtwanger is better known to the world at large as the author of many intelligent historical novels. On the Nazi death list for his devastating portrayal of Hitler and his Munich putsch in *Success* (1930), he fled to France in 1933, and is now an American citizen. His historical novel *Power* (1925) is still his most famous achievement.

FIDELITY (1915), by Susan Glaspell. See GLASPELL, SUSAN.

FIFTH COLUMN AND THE FIRST FORTY-NINE STORIES, THE (1938), by Ernest Hemingway. See SUN ALSO RISES, THE, by Ernest Hemingway.

FIHRIST (987). See ARABIAN NIGHTS' ENTERTAINMENTS.

FINANCIER, THE (1912), by Theodore Dreiser. See COWPERWOOD NOVELS, THE, by Theodore Dreiser.

FINGAL, AN ANCIENT EPIC POEM, IN SIX BOOKS (1762), by James Macpherson. See OSSIAN'S POEMS, by James Macpherson.

FINNEGANS WAKE (1939), by James Joyce. This, Joyce's final and most puzzling literary experiment, had occupied him for seventeen years, and parts of it had appeared as *Work in Progress*. *Ulysses* (q.v.) dealt with the conscious; *Finnegans Wake* is supplementary in treating of the unconscious or the half-conscious. The earlier novel carried a group of Dubliners through a single summer's day. *Finnegans Wake* carries a single character through a summer Saturday night's sleep. It has all the mystifications of a dream—the hero's fantasies, forbidden desires, dim memories, half-conscious sensations. The dreamer is Humphrey Chimpden Earwicker, of Scandinavian descent, keeper of a public-house in Dublin. He has lost interest in his wife Maggie (who sleeps beside him), but is physically drawn toward his grown daughter, Isobel, and one of his twin boys, Jerry. In the background is the ballad about the Irishman who fell off a scaffold and was taken for dead, but came to life when the word "whiskey" (which etymologically means "water of life") was mentioned. In the background too is the cyclical view of history promulgated by Giambattista Vico, as well as Giordano Bruno's dialectical concept of nature. "Finnegan" is the "end-(French *fin*)again"; the book comes round full cycle, starting with the latter part of a sentence which is begun at the end of the book, and toward the end Earwicker, like the ballad hero, partially wakes up from dream-death, even as a man is partially renewed in his children. Fortunately before he died Joyce gave certain disciples clues to his meaning, and careful additional study has clarified a good deal of the dream symbolism and the free-association language. (W. Y. Tindall has observed that with Joyce "the pun is mightier than the word.") In addition to the experimental language, or as part of it, the book is enormously learned, abounding in polylingual puns, in allusions, myths, history (the siege of Sevastopol in the Crimean war is of detailed importance at one stage), and in Freudian disguises and Jungian drawings on the racial unconscious. Earwicker poses as Tristram in love with Iseult la Belle, a disguise for Isobel, and more at large loves Anna Livia Plurabelle, a river (ana—upper— Liffey, near where the public-house is) standing for the feminine principle, even as the Hill of Howth (H.C.E.—Howth Castle and Environs), another local landmark, is the masculine principle. In various phases the dreamer is Adam, Oliver Cromwell and other invaders, and Jonathan Swift. Besides being himself an individual troubled with incestuous and homosexual fantasies, he is universal man, part of all history and myth and biological experience, his name alliterating with Here Comes Everybody and Haveth Childers Everywhere.

FIRST FIVE YEARS OF LIFE, THE (1940), by Arnold L. Gesell. See GESELL, ARNOLD L.

FIRST WIFE, THE (1933), by Pearl Buck. See GOOD EARTH, THE, by Pearl Buck.

FISH, THE (1870), by Mendele Mocher Sefarim. See MENDELE MOCHER SEFARIM.

FISHER, DOROTHY CANFIELD. See CANFIELD, DOROTHY.

FIVE MASTERS (1930), by Joseph Wood Krutch. See KRUTCH, JOSEPH WOOD.

FLORA AND BELLONA (1918), by Erik Axel Karlfeldt. See KARLFELDT, ERIK AXEL.

FLORA AND POMONA (1906), by Erik Axel Karlfeldt. See KARLFELDT, ERIK AXEL.

FLOWERS OF EVIL, THE (1857), by Charles Baudelaire. These poems are credited with being the model of most recent French poetry. In their time they had few admirers, created scandal, and on publication landed their author in court for corrupting public morals. Immensely sensitive, inclined toward mysticism, and endowed with an unparalleled musical ear, Baudelaire was also sickly, chronically on the outs with his family, eternally in debt and generally unhappy. His central theme was the evil inherent in the human heart. The first poem of the *Flowers* makes it clear that he means the human heart in general, including the heart of the reader. Subsequent poems explore the various possibilities of vice, depravity and sin with a thoroughness which makes a comparison with the Dante of the *Inferno* inevitable. Yet occasionally, particularly in some of his love poems, Baudelaire achieves a kind of somber beauty which was—and still is—something new in poetry. Technical experts regard him as a great creator of metaphor.

Many of the themes of *The Flowers of Evil* are treated again in his less famous *Little Poems in Prose* (1869). Baudelaire was also a sensitive though unprolific critic of art, music and literature and a gifted translator. His translation of Poe, from whose aesthetic theories he learned much, is still standard.

FLOWERING JUDAS (1930), by Katherine Anne Porter. See PORTER, KATHERINE ANNE.

FLOWERING OF NEW ENGLAND, THE (1936), by Van Wyck Brooks. A minute and understanding study of that brilliant flowering of culture and learning which occurred in New England between 1815 and 1865. Brooks wrote, "My subject is the New England mind, as it has found expression in the lives and works of writers." Accordingly, with a rare ability to evoke the mood and spirit of the period, he conducts us along the main highroads and a number of by-paths of his New England. He describes the growth of Harvard College, and introduces many of its notable professors, such as George Ticknor, Longfellow, and Agassiz. We meet the New England historians, Sparks, Bancroft, Prescott, Motley; and come to know Longfellow the youthful romantic, rather than the bearded, venerable poet. The strange but appealing figure of Hawthorne and his somber Salem background are presented. Emerson and Thoreau, Lowell, Holmes, Dana, Melville, Margaret Fuller, and Bronson Alcott are also portrayed.

The literary history has been continued in *New England: Indian Summer* (1940), to 1915; in *The World of Washington Irving* (1944), the first two decades of the 1800's outside New England; and in *The Times of Melville and Whitman* (1947).

America's Coming-of-Age (1915) develops the idea that our Puritan background smothered aesthetic expression and fostered materialism.

The Pilgrimage of Henry James (1925) is a distinguished literary biography. *The Ordeal of Mark Twain* (1920) is an enthusiastic study which reveals the injustice that has been done in pigeonholing that author as a whimsical entertainer. Brooks had objective, even documentary proof for his strictures on Twain's "self-betrayal." Twain led a counterfeit life because of the excessive influence of two persons—his mother, who preferred seeing him good to seeing him great, and his wife, whose ambition was to see her husband "a gentleman." The unfortunate clown, muses Brooks, despised himself; for he possessed an acute and honest intelligence. This interpretation of Mark Twain's character has been challenged by Bernard DeVoto and other literary critics.

FLUTE OF THE KING (1910), by Kostes Palamas. See PALAMAS, KOSTES.

FLYING DUTCHMAN, THE (1843), by Richard Wagner. See WAGNER, RICHARD.

FOLKLORE OF CAPITALISM, THE (1937), by Thurman Arnold. A variety of legal and economic principles generally considered as fundamental to this capitalistic society are examined on a semantic basis. The author deals with confusions of meaning arising from the use of indefinite and emotional words to describe social facts, from the personification of corporations, misconceptions of the ideas and purposes of taxation, etc., in an attempt to expose the myths underlying supposedly "logical" attitudes toward modern American culture. He concludes with a set of principles for Political Dynamics, which are to serve as guides, rather than authoritarian standards, toward intelligent changes and adjustment of government in a period of social stress.

FOLK-SAY, A REGIONAL MISCELLANY (1929–1932), by Benjamin A. Botkin. See BOTKIN, BENJAMIN A.

FOLLOWING THE EQUATOR (1897), by Mark Twain. See INNOCENTS ABROAD, THE, by Mark Twain.

FOMA GORDEYEV (1899), by Maxim Gorky. See GORKY, MAXIM.

FONS VITAE, by Solomon Ibn Gabirol. See IBN GABIROL, SOLOMON.

FONTAMARA (1933), by Ignazio Silone. See BREAD AND WINE, by Ignazio Silone.

FOOL IN CHRIST, EMANUEL QUINT (1910), by Gerhart Hauptmann. See HAUPTMANN, GERHART.

FOOL OF FAITH, A (1931; Eng. tr. 1935), by Jarl Hemmer. The original title of this powerful Finnish novel, written in Swedish, means, literally, "A Man and His Conscience," and portrays in psychological manner the frantic search by a priest for faith through the direction of his own conscience. It is the story of one believing clergyman who begins to doubt, and of another, the hero, a doubter and once self-confessed notorious sinner, who finds faith and ultimately peace through the voluntary supreme self-sacrifice for a fellow-prisoner with wife and children. Johan Samuel Strang becomes the Finnish Sydney Carton. There is no plot in the usual sense; but we have a series of vital, gripping pictures of hideous suffering during the Finnish Revolution of 1917–1918, interspersed with profound discussions of the problems of the universe. Are there any answers to the questions in which mankind is most interested? If there is a God, why all the evil, hopelessness, and tragedy in the world? But at the end even the cynical prison physician, Dr. Ceder, begins to waver in what he believed to be his absolute convictions. He had vowed that he would never attend the funeral of Bro (as Strang is called when officiating as chaplain in the prisoner's camp), if the latter took the insane step of mingling with the prisoners as one of them and dying as a criminal with them; but we know from the last line of the book that he changed his mind.

FOR LANCELOT ANDREWES (1928), by T. S. Eliot. See ELIOT, THOMAS STEARNS.

FOR WHOM THE BELL TOLLS (1940), by Ernest Hemingway. Robert Jordan is an American fighting in the International Brigade on behalf of the Spanish Loyalists; he is motivated by a love of Spain and of freedom. During a period of four days he prepares for the vital task of blowing up a strategically located bridge near Segovia. This is to be timed with the opening of a Loyalist offensive, though Communist bureaucracy and suspicion make matters delicate. He enlists the aid of a band of peasant guerrillas, and has the co-operation of all except the surly and untrustworthy Pablo, erstwhile leader. Pablo's woman Pilar, a strong-minded and warm-hearted person, is the real leader of the group. Interwoven with the main plot is Jordan's love affair with Maria, who has suffered at the hands of the Loyalists, and whose desire to live he restores. In a tense climax, Jordan's mission is successfully fulfilled, at the expense of his life, though it has been discovered that the objective is lost. Hemingway attempts to demonstrate here that freedom unites the peoples of the world in a cause transcending all local struggles.

FOREFATHER'S EVE (1823), by Adam Mickiewicz. See MICKIE-WICZ, ADAM.

FOREST AND THE FORT, THE (1943), by Hervey Allen. See ANTHONY ADVERSE, by Hervey Allen.

FOREST LOVERS, THE (1898), by Maurice Hewlett. This medieval romance, in the mysterious setting of the Forest of Morgraunt, describes the numerous exciting, dangerous and romantic experiences of Prosper le Gai. Prosper, seeking adventure but not romance, marries a poor little girl to save her from being hanged for witchcraft. He feels only pity for her, but she loves him and almost sacrifices her life for him. Gradually Prosper's feeling changes from pity to interest, then to genuine love at last. His wife is discovered to be Isoult la Désirée, long before given up as lost or dead. She is the daughter of Isabel, Countess of Hauterive and Lady of Morgraunt.

FORGOTTEN MELODIES (1909), by Pieter Cornelis Boutens. See BOUTENS, PIETER CORNELIS.

FORSAKEN WIVES (1907), by Samuel Joseph Agnon. See BRIDAL CANOPY, THE, by Samuel Joseph Agnon.

FORSYTE SAGA, THE (1906–1921), by John Galsworthy. This chronicle of three generations of the Forsyte family consists of three novels, with two connecting "interludes." *The Man of Property* (1906) opens with a gathering of the prosperous tribe at the home of old Jolyon Forsyte on June 15, 1886, to celebrate the engagement of his granddaughter June to Philip Bosinney, architect. He is young and unconventional, and the clan have their doubts about him, especially as there has already been one renegade in the family in June's father, young Jolyon, who abandoned his wife, now dead, to run away with a foreign governess to whom he has been married for six years. They have returned to England to bring up their two children, Holly and Jolly, but naturally do not appear at this tea. "The man of property" is Soames Forsyte, son of James, who has married the incompatible and at last rebellious Irene, whose "Beauty impinging on a possessive world" is the theme of all three novels to a large extent. Soames engages Bosinney to build him a house in the country. Bosinney and the unhappily married Irene fall in love. June gradually learns that she has lost her fiancé. But Soames makes the same discovery, insists on his husband's rights, and deliberately bankrupts Bosinney by getting a court to declare that the architect has spent hundreds of pounds more than was contracted for on the house. Bosinney, with the mark of doom on him, is run over in the London fog.

The first interlude, *Indian Summer of a Forsyte* (1918), shows the effect of Irene's beauty on old Jolyon in the last weeks of his life. He has bought the house that Bosinney built, and she, having left her husband and begun to support herself by music lessons, wanders onto the grounds for memory's sake. Old Jolyon dies while excitedly awaiting another of her visits.

In Chancery (1920) leaps ahead twelve years, when Soames, desirous of a son to inherit his property, seeks a reconciliation with Irene and drives her to find protection and at last love in Jolyon, whose children, Holly and Jolly, are now grown. Holly's cousin Val makes love to her before going off with Jolly to the Boer War, where Val is wounded and Jolly dies of a fever. After his divorce Soames marries a French girl, Annette, and gets some sense of property and consolation even though only a girl, Fleur, is born to them.

The second interlude, *Awakening* (1920), tells of little Jon waiting for his father and mother, Jolyon and Irene Forsyte, to come home from a vacation. Irene, at thirty-eight, enchants him; he awakens to her beauty.

To Let (1921) has a kind of Romeo-and-Juliet theme in that the love of Fleur and Jon is shadowed by the family feud, and Jon finally abides by his mother, whom he worships. Fleur marries Michael Mont, son of a baronet.

Less read are Galsworthy's later Forsyte stories, which include *A Modern Comedy* (1929), a trilogy consisting of *The White Monkey* (1924), *The Silver Spoon* (1926), and *Swan Song* (1928), and a collection of "apocryphal Forsyte tales," *On Forsyte-Change* (1930).

FORTUNE AND FALL OF KING OTTOKAR (1825), by Franz Grillparzer. See GOLDEN FLEECE, by Franz Grillparzer.

FORTUNES OF RICHARD MAHONY, THE (1930), by Henry Handel Richardson (pseudonym of Henrietta Richardson). This trilogy is the story of a man's struggle to conquer impending madness. Realistically written, it is a tragic tale of a proud man and his loving wife.

In this tale of Australia in the 1850's (*Australia Felix*, 1917), Dr. Richard Townshend-Mahony comes from Ireland during the gold rush to find that he has to open a store to make a living. He marries sixteen-year-old Mary (Polly) Turnham. Encouraged by her, he starts to practice medicine. With money from shares he buys from Tom Ocock, and a rising practice, he buys a fine house and becomes moderately successful. Mary's relatives are always with them: brother John, and his children; sister Sarah (Zara). Mahony shows early signs of physical and mental weakness; at forty-five becomes so restless and irritable that he insists on returning to England to start a new life.

In the late 1860's (*The Way Home*, 1925), Mahony starts a practice in Leicester, England, becomes discouraged and goes to Buddlecombe. When notified that stocks he has in the Australia Felix Mining Company are paying dividends, he and Mary hurry back to Australia. Mahony decides to live a leisurely life. He builds a new house, Ultima Thule, and stocks his library with books. Three children are born: Cuthbert Hamilton (Cuffy), and twin girls, Lucie and Lallie. Still dissatisfied, Mahony sells his house and takes his family back to England. They travel on the continent, but Richard enjoys none of it. In Venice he receives word that he may be ruined financially. He takes the next boat home; Mary and the children follow six months later. Her only desire is to keep her family together. She is not aware of her husband's weakness, but he fights to stay the madness that he knows is coming.

Richard is forty-nine years old in 1870 (*Ultima Thule*, 1929). In Australia once more, he finds he has no money, so he again starts a practice in the north country—Barambogie. His daughter, Lallie, dies. Mary takes the two remaining children for a vacation, leaving Richard to fight the oncoming madness alone. He receives messages from his dead child; walks the country alone, feeling that if he can keep back a scream, he will be all right. Mary returns at his request to find that all the patients have left, because of their fear of the "old doctor" who talks to a ghost. Accused of not setting a boy's leg correctly, Dr. Mahony takes his family and flees to a town near the sea. This last incident is too much for the doctor. At last the scream bursts from his throat and his reason leaves him. Mary puts Richard in an insane asylum, and takes a position as postmistress. Later she brings him home. He is now a helpless insane invalid. Mary's love never wavers. Sanity returns for a moment at Mahony's death. He thanks Mary for being a "dear wife," her reward for a lifetime of unwearied sacrifice.

FORTY DAYS OF MUSA DAGH, THE (1934), by Franz Werfel. This is a heroic epic of the desperate stand of the Armenian people against a Turkish campaign of annihilation during World War I. Faced with the threat of extermination, the Armenians of the village of Yoghonoluk retreat to the mountain of Musa Dagh and fortify themselves for a desperate defense. Their leader is a Parisian-bred Armenian named Gabriel Bagradian who organizes the frightened and unmilitant band of people into an able and dauntless fighting unit with the help of the Armenian priest Ter Haigasun. Inadequately armed, with the most meager supplies and with no hope for relief, the Armenians repel every advance of the well-armed Turks for a forty-day siege. At the end the survivors of the heroic colony are rescued by the French navy, except Bagradian, who is overlooked by a tragic error after he has wearily fallen asleep following the successful completion of the evacuation. He dies by a Turkish bullet upon the rude grave of his young son. The book possesses tragic stature, and Werfel has recorded the stirring events with an artistry and passion worthy of the material. The two leaders are unforgettable characterizations, and in the portrayal of lesser figures the book is no less rich. The novel is generally considered his best work.

Franz Werfel was born in Prague in 1890 and died as a refugee from Nazism in California in 1945. In his younger days he was one of the chief lyrical spokesmen of Expressionism in Germany and published a number of very influential verse volumes during and after World War I. Of his many plays the political comedy *Jakobowsky and the Colonel* (1942) is probably best known in the United States. His world-wide fame rests on his reputation as a prolific novelist. His most distinguished novels are *Verdi* (1920), *Class Reunion* (1930), and *The Song of Bernadette* (1943).

42ND PARALLEL, THE (1930), by John Dos Passos. See U.S.A., by John Dos Passos.

FOUNDING OF NEW ENGLAND, THE (1921), by James Truslow Adams. See EPIC OF AMERICA, by James Truslow Adams.

FOUR HORSEMEN OF THE APOCALYPSE, THE (1916), by Vincente Blasco Ibáñez. The Desnoyer family's chronicle begins with the elder, Don Marcelo, as he flees France, the country of his birth, to avoid military service in the war of 1870. Chance carries him to Argentina, where he falls in with a wealthy eccentric, builds a tremendous fortune and marries the daughter of his patron. The depiction of life in the Argentine pampas in this long introductory section is a splendid achievement. After rearing two children, Julio and Chichi, Don Marcelo and his wife succumb to the current fashion and return to the continent, re-establishing themselves on French soil. At the same time Don Marcelo's sister-in-law returns to the native land of her husband, Germany, bringing with her three sons. The war finds one sister's family pitted against the other's in a struggle to the death, with the young son of the Desnoyers against the three sons of the Hartrott family. The soldiers in the German branch of the family are exterminated, as is Julio, and the parents are left to the contemplation of the Four Horsemen of the Apocalypse: War, Famine, Disease and Death.

FOUR PP, THE (1544), by John Heywood. See RALPH ROISTER DOISTER, by Nicholas Udall.

FOUR QUARTETS (1943), by T. S. Eliot. See ELIOT, THOMAS STEARNS.

FOURE NEW PLAYS (1665), by John Dryden. See ESSAY OF DRAMATICK POESIE, AN, by John Dryden.

FRAGRANCE OF SPRING, THE (18th c.), Anonymous. See CHUN-HYANG CHUN, Anonymous.

FRANCIAD, THE (1572–1578), by Pierre de Ronsard. See RONSARD, PIERRE DE.

FRANKENSTEIN, OR THE MODERN PROMETHEUS (1818), by Mary Wollstonecraft Shelley. This is one of the world's favorite terror stories, yet its stature is greater than such a classification implies. It is a highly imaginative, poetic novel. In the summer of 1816, the Shelleys and Byron were in Switzerland. For want of something more diverting to do they entered into a friendly ghost-story competition. Mary claimed that she had dreamed her story of *Frankenstein*. The plot is developed in the course of a series of letters from the Arctic by Robert Walton to his sister, Margaret.

Upon coming into his inheritance, Walton goes off to the North Pole on an expedition of exploration. One night he encounters a remarkably big man on a dogsled. The latter comes on board Walton's ship, on being told that the expedition is Pole-bound. This stranger is Frankenstein, a Swiss. Frankenstein tells Walton that he is the son of a nobleman and has dabbled in the mystic sciences of the medieval Paracelsus, Cornelius Agrippa and Albertus Magnus. His principal obsession was to discover the elixir of life. By means of his knowledge of the esoteric, he has actually created a living man. Horrified by the sight of this huge and revolting creature, Frankenstein flees from it. Later he receives word from his father that his little brother, William, has been found murdered. Hurrying home, he catches his monster lurking in the woods. Frankenstein realizes in a flash that his creature was the murderer, not the accused maidservant, Justine. But, as he is certain that no one will believe him, he does nothing about it. At Chamonix on the *mer de glace* Frankenstein comes face to face with the monster. He wants to kill him, but the creature restrains him with the words: "All men hate the wretched." As his creator, argues the monster, Frankenstein has a responsibility which he cannot evade. He promises to leave him in peace provided he creates for him a wife, for he wishes to be like other men. He feels frustrated and rejected, which is the cause of his bestiality.

Frankenstein accordingly sets about making a wife, for he is moved by the story of the monster. But, at the very moment of breathing life into her, he recoils from the thought that he is creating the possibility of a race of monsters which might yet destroy mankind. In revenge, the monster kills Frankenstein's best friend and his bride. Horrified and maddened with hatred, Frankenstein seeks him in the frozen North. But in the end Walton finds the monster standing grief-stricken over Frankenstein, whom he has murdered.

FRÄULEIN ELSE (1925), by Arthur Schnitzler. See SCHNITZLER, ARTHUR.

FREE WHEELING (1931), by Ogden Nash. See NASH, OGDEN.

FREEDOM AND CULTURE (1939), by John Dewey. See DEWEY, JOHN.

FREEDOM ROAD (1944), by Howard Fast. See CITIZEN TOM PAINE, by Howard Fast.

FRENCH REVOLUTION, THE (1837), by Thomas Carlyle. Carlyle had long been attracted by the phenomenon of the French Revolution and its drama. He was an ardent republican. Despite the bloody events that accompanied the social convulsion in feudal France in 1789–1795, he was convinced that the results were well worth while. Democracy, in the modern sense, was born. There is little doubt that his espousal of the cause of the Revolution in France, with all that it implied, favorably affected the intellectual attitude toward it. *The French Revolution,* besides being a vivid narrative, is also an interpretation. Carlyle was a man of deep insight, although he was full of prejudices and frequently unreasonable. His partiality for mystical intuitions, in the German philosophic sense, frequently led him astray; his judgments were rarely tempered with restraint. If this work can no longer be regarded as an altogether reliable history of that remarkable event, it remains one of the most original and powerful literary works of the nineteenth century.

FRESCOES FOR MR. ROCKEFELLER'S CITY (1933), by Archibald MacLeish. See MacLEISH, ARCHIBALD.

FREUD, SIGMUND (1856–1939). Freud was the founder of that school of psychiatry known as psychoanalysis. Led to his investigations through observations on the use of hypnosis in the cure of hysteria, Freud eventually abandoned hypnosis as a method and replaced it with "free association." In this method, a patient suffering from a nervous disorder thinks aloud before a trained analyst, who attempts to discover the pattern of his thought. If the analyst is successful in tracing the present disorder back to the original situation (usually in childhood) which gave rise to it, he can then, according to this theory, explain the matter to the patient, who will be relieved of his burden and cured. In developing this approach, Freud formulated a theory of the mind which had several distinctive features. He postulated the existence of an unconscious level in the mind which influenced conscious thought and behavior. The view that the sexual instinct is the basic one in the human personality led Freud to discover and describe the presence of sexual behavior even in infants. He developed the theory that there are various forces in the personality, "ego," "id," "super-ego," and that mental disorders come about through conflicts that arise among these forces, or through the repression of one by another. Freud had great influence on medicine, psychology, philosophy, social thought, and especially on literature. The most easily accessible of his books for the general public is *Psychopathology of Everyday Life* (1904; Eng. tr. 1914). A large school of analysts grew up around him, including Adler, Jung, Jones and others, most of whom differed from the master in more or less important respects.

FRIAR BACON AND FRIAR BUNGAY (1594), by Robert Greene. Some of the material for this play was derived from *The Famous Historie of Friar Bacon,* a prose pamphlet, and was probably suggested by Marlowe's *Faust* (q.v.) which preceded it by about a year. It tells the story of how Friar Bacon, reputedly a famous magician, and Friar Bungay constructed a brass head. The Devil, called forth by Bacon, promises that the head will speak within a month. Bacon watches ceaselessly for three weeks, then, succumbing to drowsiness, tells his serving boy, Miles, to stand guard, giving him orders to wake him should the head speak. Miles watches, and finally the head utters two words, "Time is." Miles thinks this is not enough to warrant waking the Friar. The head again speaks: "Time was." Then with "Time is past," it falls and breaks. Bacon wakes and berates poor Miles angrily. A minor plot tells of Edward, Prince of Wales, who, while hunting, saw and fell in love with Margaret of Fressingfield, the keeper's daughter. At the suggestion of his fool he sends his friend, Lacy, Earl of Lincoln, to woo her for him. He and his courtiers then go to Oxford to consult the great scholar, Friar Bacon, who shows them in a magic glass Margaret being wooed by Lacy. Edward rides to Fressingfield to confront the two who have fallen in love, but ends by forgiving them. The Emperor of Germany, the King of Castile, and many other notables come to England to arrange a match between Eleanor of Castile and Prince Edward. With them comes Jaques Vandermast, a German scholar, and accompanied by King Henry of England, they all journey to Oxford to watch Vandermast in an amusing contest against Bacon, the latter coming out victorious.

FRIDOLIN'S SONGS (1898), by Erik Axel Karlfeldt. See KARLFELDT, ERIK AXEL.

FRIENDLY ARCTIC, THE (1921), by Vilhjálmur Stefánsson. See STEFÁNSSON, VILHJÁLMUR.

FRITHIOF'S SAGA (1825), by Esaias Tegnér. This romantic epic is a modernization and idealization of the fictional Norwegian pagan saga of Frithiof the Bold, and is composed of twenty-four poems or songs, each in a different meter, with one of three meter forms. It was translated in part by Longfellow—who had translated the author's "The Children of the Lord's Supper"—and edited by Bayard Taylor. There are fifteen complete translations of it in English and about thirty in German, and it was the first purely literary Swedish work to become well known abroad. Many of its songs have been set to music, and the *Saga* as a whole has been made into an opera at least once. The *Saga* tells the story of Frithiof's presumptuous love for a king's daughter, his foster-sister Ingeborg, who returns his love. But her royal brothers have other plans, and ultimately marry her off to the aged King Ring. Before this happens, however, the lovers had met secretly in Balder's Grove, which was a desecration of the pagan sanctuary. As punishment Frithiof is sent on a dangerous expedition to collect tribute for his royal master, a venture from which he is not expected to return. But he does, with the tribute, and in his anger and triumph at a meeting of all concerned inadvertently causes the burning of Balder's sacred temple. Thereupon he goes into exile as a Viking, but eventually returns; appears in disguise before Ingeborg, now the Queen of King Ring, who soon dies; and after rebuilding the temple, as an act of atonement (and when other, lesser obstacles are removed), he is united to Ingeborg. The *Saga* shows definite Christian influence—the author was a Lutheran bishop—and because of its romance, setting, thrilling narrative, lyricism, pathos, irony and general philosophy of life is still popular in the North.

FRÖDING, GUSTAV (1860–1911). This Swedish author, loved and respected by readers of all classes, is probably the greatest poetic genius that Sweden has produced. Both in content and form he is a creator. Against a background of sadness and melancholy, but with a realistic idealism—faith in the inner goodness of man—he is one of Sweden's, if not the world's, most original humorists. He wrote *On Humor* (1890), and in his attacks on Naturalism advocated art as an end in itself. His first collection of poems, *Guitar and Concertina* (1891), inaugurated a new domain in poetry, the description of inimitable types of Värmland characters from his own native province, whose humor was brilliant and contagious. The picture of the lieutenant with the white waistcoat; the parson's old manservant and his horse, Jonte and Brunte; and "They Danced by the Roadside," will not soon be forgotten. Here was artistry and musical virtuosity in abundance in rhythm and rhyme. *New Poems* (1894) and *Splashes and Rags* (1896) contained perhaps even greater masterpieces: the rhythmically unique "Mountain Troll"; "The Prayer Meeting," which shows that human nature is much the same everywhere, in any group, even in a pious assemblage; and the symbolic "The Way of the World," a dark, powerful vision of a ship that sails on without paying any attention to a man overboard. Later collections of verse revealed traces of the inherited insanity which plagued the latter part of his life. Himself a master of verse melody, many of his poems have been set to music. In the history of Swedish verse, he is the pioneer who restored faith in the possibilities of poetic form.

FROGS, THE (405 B.C.), by Aristophanes. This comedy, one of its author's best, is a literary satire. It was written and performed shortly after the death of Euripides, last of the great tragic dramatists, and is a bitter lampoon of him. Dionysus, patron god of the drama, hungers for the verse of Euripides, recently departed to Hades. He determines to follow him to the nether depths in order to bring him back to Athens and hear more of his tragedies. With his servant, Xanthias, he makes the journey. In Hades a controversy is raging. Euripides has brashly tried to depose Aeschylus from the seat of the mightiest of dramatists. The older playwright defends his position. A trial is held, with Dionysus as judge, in which the two dramatists criticize and attack one another's work on grounds ranging from professional skill to social, political and moral philosophy. Finally they resort to flinging phrases from their works upon the scales of a balance to determine whose style is the weightier. At last the decision is awarded to Aeschylus, and Dionysus plans to take him back to earth again. The victor insists that in his absence Sophocles and not Euripides shall occupy the seat of honor. One of the notable features of this comedy is the celebrated chorus of frogs greeting the descent of Dionysus to Hades: "Brekekekex, koax, koax." To understand the play we have to realize the position of the men involved. Euripides was a free thinker and an iconoclast strongly sympathetic with the most advanced thought of his day as represented by Socrates and the Sophists. Aristophanes, on the other hand, was instinctively conservative. Artistically, he was capable of appreciating Euripides, although he did not approve of all of his technical innovations, but morally he sympathized with the sterner and more conventional virtues portrayed by Aeschylus.

FROM MORN TO MIDNIGHT (1916), by Georg Kaiser. See GAS, by Georg Kaiser.

FROM THE LIFE OF A GOOD-FOR-NOTHING (1826), by Joseph von Eichendorff. See EICHENDORFF, JOSEPH VON.

FROM THE OTHER SHORE (1850), by Alexander Ivanovitch Herzen. See HERZEN, ALEXANDER IVANOVITCH.

FROM THE SOUTH SEAS (1939), by Margaret Mead. *From the South Seas* is a single-volume publication of Margaret Mead's three famous sociological-anthropological works written after an eight-year study of the primitive peoples of the South Seas. They form an investigation of how the human character is molded by cultural environment.

Coming of Age in Samoa (1928) focuses on the adolescent girl, and explains her household, community, maturation, education.

Growing Up in New Guinea (1930) concerns the girl of preadolescent age among the Manus of the Admiralty Islands.

Sex and Temperament in Three Primitive Societies (1935) treats the co-operative society of the mountain-dwelling Arapesh, the cannibalistic river-dwelling Mundugumors, and the lake-dwelling Tchambulis.

FROM THE STREET OF TRIUMPH (1902), by Ricarda Huch. See HUCH, RICARDA.

FRONT PAGE, THE (1928), by Ben Hecht and Charles MacArthur. This play is a comedy melodrama about newspapermen. Hildy Johnson, a glib reporter, conceals in a desk Earl Williams, escaped murderer of a Negro policeman. Johnson becomes involved in the case, one of the many which have delayed his wedding with Peggy Grant. While he and his editor, Walter Burns, are contriving a sensational newspaper treatment of their potential "scoop," the governor sends a reprieve. Sheriff Hartman and the mayor have delayed this for political purposes. Hildy does break the story, and leaves with Peggy on a honeymoon, but Burns, to keep his star reporter on the job, orders his arrest at the railroad station, for the "theft" of a watch which was his wedding present.

FRONTIER IN AMERICAN HISTORY, THE (1920), by Frederick Jackson Turner. See TURNER, FREDERICK JACKSON.

FROST, ROBERT (1875–   ). Robert Frost was early interested in poetry, but his apprenticeship was one of varying occupations and slow recognition. In 1912 he moved to England, where *A Boy's Will* (1913), *North Boston* (1914), and *Mountain Interval* (1916) were published. The advent of World War I brought the poet, now well-known and beloved, back to America. He settled in New England, and has pursued an independent, unhurried literary career, which has three times been honored by Pulitzer Prizes.

A Boy's Will breathes the characteristic New England flavor which is Frost's trademark. The verses are full of controlled emotion, having as their main themes isolation, misunderstanding, and the understanding of oneself. *North of Boston* uses the dry Yankee idiom, which nevertheless "begins with a lump in the throat," as Frost defines poetry. The pieces are keen character studies, for instance "Servant to Servants," a blank-verse monologue describing a lonely farm wife whose longings for beauty and love are suppressed by a routine of menial tasks.

The title piece of *New Hampshire* (1923) extols the poet's adopted state, and a philosophy of the simple life. Other selections are genial lyrics, monologues and vernacular verses about informal matters.

Editions of the collected poems of Frost appeared in 1930 (receiving the Pulitzer Prize in 1931), 1939, and 1949. These maintain the same balance of New England local color, character study and humor. In *A Witness Tree* (1942), also a Pulitzer Prize winner, epigrams rather than fresh dramatic monologue are emphasized.

FUENTE OVEJUNA (1619), by Lope de Vega. See SHEEP WALL, THE, by Lope de Vega.

FUNDAMENTA BOTANICA (1736), by Carolus Linnaeus (Carl von Linné). See SYSTEMA NATURAE, by Carolus Linnaeus.

GABOR VIKOLINSKY (1899), by Hviezdoslav. See HVIEZDOSLAV

GALILEI (1947), by Bertolt Brecht. See BRECHT, BERTOLT.

GALLEGHER AND OTHER STORIES (1891), by Richard Harding Davis. See DAVIS, RICHARD HARDING.

GAMBLER, THE (1866), by Feodor Dostoevsky. This, one of the shorter of Dostoevsky's novels, is unmistakably autobiographical. Alexey Ivanovitch, the hero, speaks of the true Russian's antipathy to "the German method of amassing riches by honest toil," and contends that since the Russian needs money like anyone else, it is perfectly logical that he should resort to the roulette wheel. Nonetheless, it is fairly certain that Dostoevsky did not indulge in gaming for mere profit—he lost more often than he won —but to satisfy an inner craving amounting to an abnormal passion. This, indeed, is the theme of his story, which is an extraordinary revelation of the gambling fever that can possess a man, as it possessed the author. Incidentally, his portrait of the heroine Polina Alexandrovna is also taken from life; Polina is Suslova, his mistress at the time. She is pictured as a woman who, giving happiness to her lover, regrets her generosity and reacts to it by punishing her lover as well as herself. "Man is by nature a despot," says Alexey to Polina, "and loves to torture; you love it terribly." This theme is repeated in other novels by Dostoevsky.

GAME, THE (1905), by Jack London. See LONDON, JACK.

GAMMER GURTON'S NEEDLE (printed 1575), by William Stevenson (?) or John Bridges (?). The play follows *Ralph Roister Doister* (q.v.) as the second English comedy in verse. Gammer Gurton has lost her precious needle while mending the breeches of Hodge, her servant. Her entire household is thrown into an uproar by this misfortune. Tib, her maid, and Cook, her serving boy, join in the search. Hodge tells Diccon the Bedlam, a kind of wandering fool, about the mishap. Diccon, to have some sport, suggests that Dame Chat, Gammer Gurton's gossip, has taken the needle; he arouses the ire of Dame Chat by telling her that Gammer Gurton has accused her of stealing her cock. Gammer, accompanied by Hodge, calls on Dame Chat and demands the needle. Dame Chat answers by beating her and Hodge. By this time the whole village has joined in the fray. Gammer sends for Doctor Rat, the curate. Diccon offers to show him a back way into Dame Chat's house where he can spy on her. In the meantime, he tells Chat that Hodge is going to steal her chickens and warns her to be on the watch for him Thus, Doctor Rat gets the beating Dame Chat intended for Hodge. The indignant curate goes to Bayly, the clerk, who calls them all together. It is soon discovered that Diccon has instigated the brawl. Finally Diccon beats Hodge with the flat of his hand, and poor Hodge soon becomes conscious of the fact that the needle is in the seat of his breeches.

GARDEN OF ALLAH, THE (1904), by Robert Hichens. A wealthy, beautiful English lady, Domini Enfilden, is traveling with her maid in the Sahara Desert. Unmarried at thirty-two, Domini has turned for solace to religion. At a desert resort, she meets Boris Androvsky, a strange, uncouth man, who interests Domini because he is apparently suffering from some great sorrow. They fall in love and are married. In the desert Boris, unable to bear his secret longer, confesses that he is a Trappist monk who has broken his vows. Heartbroken, Domini decides that reparation for sin requires his return to the monastery. After they part, Domini's loneliness is lessened by the birth of her son.

GARDEN OF ROSES (ca. 1240), by Sa'di. See GULISTAN, THE, by Sa'di.

GARDEN PARTY, THE (1922), by Katherine Mansfield. "At the Bay," "The Garden Party," "The Daughters of the Late Colonel," "Mr. and Mrs. Dove," "The Young Girl," "Life of Ma Parker," "Marriage à la Mode," "The Voyage," "Miss Brill," "Her First Ball," "The Singing Lesson," "The Stranger," "Bank Holiday," "An Ideal Family," "The Lady's-Maid," all stories of Miss Mansfield's native New Zealand and England in the twenties are included in this book. In each is a portentous note hidden deftly in an incident, thought or word. For example, in the title piece, the happy Sheridan family is planning a garden party. Laura is gay and expectant. At the start of the party, word comes that a man living nearby has been killed. Laura takes a basket of food to the bereaved family, and is suddenly struck by her lack of understanding of her feelings concerning life, death and the future. Katherine Mansfield's husband, the critic Middleton Murry, did not exaggerate when he called her "the most remarkable short-story writer of her generation in England."

GARDENER, THE (1913), by Rabindranath Tagore. See TAGORE, RABINDRANATH.

GARGANTUA AND PANTAGRUEL (1532–1564), by François Rabelais. Rabelais' great novel was published in five parts, the Fifth Book, which appeared after his death, having perhaps been written by another hand from his notes. The First Book tells of the birth, education and farcical adventures of Gargantua, son of Grandgousier and Gargamelle. With Friar Jean des Entommeures, Gargantua takes part in the war waged by his father against his neighbor Picrochole. As a reward for his aid, Grandgousier and Gargantua build for Jean des Entommeures the Abbey of Thélème, the rules of which are contained in those words: "Fais ce que voudras" (Do what you please). In Book II, Pantagruel is born, the son of Gargantua and Badebec. As a youth he visits the most famous universities of Europe. His father sends him a letter, embodying some of Rabelais' ideas on what an encyclopedic education should be. Pantagruel makes the acquaintance of Panurge, and takes part with him in the war against the Dipsodes and the giants. In Book III, Panurge, now the inseparable friend of the hero, deliberates whether or not he will marry. He consults the Sybille of Panzoust, the poet Raminagrobis, the magician Herr Trippe, Doctor Rondibilis, the philosopher Trouillogan and mad Triboulet—who finally advises him to go and ask the oracle of the Divine Bottle. In Book IV, Panurge, Friar Jean, Pantagruel and a few friends embark on a sea voyage and visit various fantastic countries such as the islands of Chicanous, Tapinois, Farouche, Papefigues (Protestants), Papimanes (papists), Messire Gaster (the Epicureans' country), etc. Book V takes our heroes to the country of Lanternois, residence of the oracle of the Divine Bottle, and there they receive the enigmatic answer of the priestess: "Drink."

The story, such as it is, serves largely as an excuse for Rabelais' unrestrained hilarity. Much of his book is sheer buffoonery, full of high spirits and the joy of living. His giants eat, drink and are very merry indeed

They are frequently obscene and always funny. He parodies heroic literature; lampoons schoolmen, lawyers, monks, theologians, overbearing rulers, stuffed shirts in general; makes mock of everything which is opposed to naturalness and human nature's most human qualities. Here and there he turns serious and seems to be arguing for life according to the ways of nature as opposed to life according to the religious ideals of the Middle Ages. But his liberalism stops "this side of the faggots." Try to tie him down to a set philosophy and he eludes you with shouts of laughter, advising you to open another bottle and try a good laugh yourself: "For laughter is the proper occupation of man."

GARIBALDI AND THE NEW ITALY (1906), by Ricarda Huch. See HUCH, RICARDA.

GAS (1918 and 1920), by Georg Kaiser. The play is a part of a trilogy which includes *Coral* (1917), *Gas I* and *Gas II*. *Gas I* reveals the Billionaire's Son as the owner of the gas works which supply the vital gas upon which the city depends for its life. The production of the gas soon gets out of hand, and an explosion results in which many are killed and maimed. Despite the warnings and entreaties of the Billionaire's Son for the workers to return to a simple, unaffected life without the gas works, they overrule him and rebuild the plant. In *Gas II* the rebuilt works are now in the hands of the women and infirm, since the men are away at war. In the face of the enemy's occupation of the city, the Billionaire's Son pleads for peace but to no avail, since the Engineer announces the discovery of poison gas. One character preaches passive resistance for the people, and upon seeing the futility of his attempts, destroys them with a cloud of poison gas. The New Man, born to the sister of the Billionaire's Son, remains.

As one of the leading playwrights of the Expressionistic movement, Kaiser employs symbolism in his allegorical works to represent the mechanized world and its effect on humanity. Personality of character vanishes in favor of abstracted types which become automatons in *Gas II*. The intensity of expression gives rise to a clipped, telegraphic style of speech—characteristic of the Expressionists' attempt to vanquish externals and symbolize an inner, more permanent reality. Among Kaiser's other plays are *The Citizens of Calais* (1913) and *From Morn to Midnight* (1916).

GATE OF LANGUAGES OPENED, THE (collected 1657), by Comenius. See DIDACTICA, THE, by Comenius.

GATHERING STORM, THE (1948), by Winston Spencer Churchill. This is the first in a series of volumes by Great Britain's wartime Prime Minister to be known collectively as *The Second World War*. It is obvious that no one else was so well qualified both by the supreme position he held and by his literary gifts as a professional author and one of the greatest orators the world has known (see *Blood, Sweat, and Tears*) to write the history of the war from the British point of view. The first volume tells "how the English-speaking peoples through their unwisdom, carelessness, and good nature allowed the wicked to re-arm." It is divided into two books, the first covering the period between wars, 1919–1939. This is a review of various "follies" on the part of the victors in World War I whereby Germany was allowed to grow both in rancor and in strength, and how an unworkable system of reparations and loans led to world-wide depression, into which vacuum Fascism, "the shadow or ugly child of Communism," was able to make portentous strides. Though he was out of office for most of the period, Churchill published warnings which he can quote to show what a deadly accurate prophet he was. His moment of greatest gloom came on February 20, 1938, with the news that Anthony Eden, opponent of Chamberlain's policy of appeasement, had resigned as Foreign Secretary. There followed "the rape of Austria," the seizure of Czechoslovakia, "the tragedy of Munich," and the German-Soviet neutrality pact. Book Two describes "The Twilight War," September 3, 1939, to May 10, 1940, when, with the invasion of Holland and Belgium the Chamberlain government fell and Mr. Churchill became Prime Minister. At the beginning of the war the author had been called into the War Cabinet and to his old post of a quarter of a century before, First Lord of the Admiralty; the Fleet was signaled the heartening news, "Winston is back." But it was at first a dark time for the British Navy, with the U-boat war and the loss of capital ships such as the *Royal Oak*. Meanwhile Poland was overrun, and Scandinavia, with Finland, made joint victims of aggression. *The Gathering Storm* naturally contains many intimate revelations and quotations from once highly secret documents, including the beginning of that correspondence with President Roosevelt which was to continue until the President's death. This correspondence plays a conspicuous part in the next volume in the series, *Their Finest Hour* (1949), which deals with the period when Britain bore the brunt of war alone.

GAWAIN AND THE GREEN KNIGHT (ca. 1370). One of the best of the alliterative English verse romances, this opens in King Arthur's court on New Year's Day. A huge green knight rides a green horse into the hall and challenges any of Arthur's knights to give him a blow with the axe he bears, the Green Knight to return the blow a year later. Accepting the challenge, Gawain strikes off the knight's head. The knight picks it up and rides away. As the end of the ensuing year approaches, Gawain makes his perilous way to search for the Green Chapel. He stops at a splendid castle on Christmas Eve and is cordially received by its lord, whose wife tests Gawain's chastity each of the three days he is there. Having agreed to accept from the lord the trophies of the lord's daily hunts in return for whatever he, Gawain, has received, he gives the lord the kisses he got from the lady but not the magic girdle she also gave him on the third day. Then he meets the Green Knight at the chapel nearby. Gawain flinches under the axe once; the knight feints once; then the blow is harmlessly delivered. The Green Knight, Bercilar de Hautdesert, is the lord of the castle in disguise; the whole affair was a test of the hero.

GEDICHTE (1844), by Annette Elisabeth von Droste-Hülshoff. See DROSTE-HÜLSHOFF, ANNETTE ELISABETH VON.

GEDICHTE (1732), by Albrecht von Haller. See ELEMENTA PHYSIOLOGIAE CORPORIS HUMANI, by Albrecht von Haller.

GELLERT, CHRISTIAN FÜRCHTEGOTT (1716–1769). Gellert enjoyed tremendous popularity during his lifetime, chiefly for his *Fables and*

Stories (1746). Despite a mediocre poetic ability, a skillful blend of genuine humor and broadmindedness on the one hand and didacticism and moralization on the other won for him an enthusiastic public drawn from all classes of society. Gellert by inclination was a man of the people who intended his writings to be appreciated by them. The sympathetic portrayals and genuine satire paved the way into the average German home for his *Fables.*

Among Gellert's other works are the social novel *Life of the Swedish Countess von G——* (1747–1748) and a collection of letters which long exerted influence on the letter-writing style of his time.

GENEALOGY OF MORALS (1887), by Friedrich Nietzsche. See NIETZSCHE, FRIEDRICH.

GENERAL WILLIAM BOOTH ENTERS INTO HEAVEN (1913), by Vachel Lindsay. See LINDSAY, VACHEL.

GENIUS, THE (1915), by Theodore Dreiser. See AMERICAN TRAGEDY, AN, by Theodore Dreiser.

GENIUS OF CHRISTIANITY, THE (1802), by François René, Vicomte de Chateaubriand. This is an apologia for Christianity. Chateaubriand had been an agnostic. His conversion took place after a series of tragedies which overtook his aristocratic family during the Revolution and which culminated in the death of his mother. "My conviction came from the heart," he writes, "I wept and I believed." The thesis of his book is that Christianity has been more productive of literature and art, and thus more culturally fruitful, than was classical antiquity. The limitations of Christian culture he blames on three kinds of enemies: heretics, sophists and cynics. High on the list of these he places the eighteenth-century figures of Voltaire, Condorcet and Diderot. Much of his effort is devoted to demonstrating the great beauty of Catholicism. Written at a time when Napoleon was trying to reconcile the Catholic Church with the State, the book was an overwhelming public success. Later critics, less enthusiastic, have often accused Chateaubriand of "confusing the beauty of holiness with the holiness of beauty."

GENJI MONOGATARI (10th c.), by Murasaki Shikibu. See TALE OF GENJI, THE, by Murasaki Shikibu.

GENTLE GRAFTER, THE (1908), by William Sydney Porter. See PORTER, WILLIAM SYDNEY.

GENTLEMAN DANCING-MASTER, THE (1673), by William Wycherley. Wycherley borrowed the incident on which the play turns from Calderon's comedy, *El Maestro de Danzar.* The action takes place in London. Don Diego, really Mr. James Formal, a man who affects the Spanish mode, betroths his daughter, Hippolita, to his Frenchified, affected nephew, who calls himself Monsieur de Paris. Hippolita, to escape her marriage, invents a story that Gerrard, a young man about town, has been courting her through the window. She dares Monsieur to give him a message that she is to be married the next day unless he comes to forbid the banns. Monsieur, thinking it an excellent joke, tells Gerrard, who keeps the appointment and climbs in at

Hippolita's window. They are caught by her father and her aunt, Mrs. Caution, but Hippolita passes Gerrard off as her dancing-master, sent by Monsieur. They have difficulty in keeping up the deception, as Gerrard cannot dance or sing. They let Monsieur in on the situation. Thinking it very amusing, he helps them along, till he finds Gerrard has married Hippolita. Don Diego forgives the young couple.

GENTLEMAN FROM INDIANA, THE (1899), by Booth Tarkington. See TARKINGTON, BOOTH.

GENTLEMAN FROM SAN FRANCISCO, THE (1916), by Ivan Bunin. This long short story is commonly considered Bunin's masterpiece. It belongs to the same genre as Tolstoy's *Ivan Ilyich,* and has the same meaning: the vanity of civilization and the presence of death as the only reality. It is, in its way, a very simple tale; the author does not rely for his effect on psychology, but rather on straightforward, terse narrative, which carries its own implications. The chief character, who gives the story its title, remains nameless throughout, as do also his wife and daughter, who accompany him on the fatal journey to southern Italy, where he meets an undramatic sudden death in the hotel reading room, before he has had time to relish the pleasures he had promised himself, among other things "the love of young Neapolitan women, conferred—let us admit—not with wholly disinterested motives," the Carnival in Nice, Monte Carlo, "toward which the most select society gravitated at this season—that society upon which all the blessings of civilization depend: not alone the cut of the smoking jacket, but also the stability of thrones, and the declaration of wars, and the welfare of hotels. . . ." The pleasures of the financial nabob on the immense luxury liner are wonderfully described, and the portrait of the "gentleman from San Francisco" is meticulously presented, as well as the anticipations which, unbeknown to him, were so soon to come to naught.

Among other well-known works of Bunin, who won the Nobel Prize in 1933, are *The Village* (Eng. tr. 1923), *Mitya's Love* (Eng. tr. 1926), *The Grammar of Love* (1934), and *The Well of Days* (Eng. tr. 1933); the last named is an autobiographical novel.

GEOGRAPHY (ca. 150), by Claudius Ptolemy of Alexandria. The *Geography* of Ptolemy is the most famous work in that field of science coming down to us from antiquity. The Alexandrian Greek author of this study towered head and shoulders above his contemporaries at a time when the Graeco-Roman culture was in its decline, a circumstance that won for him a celebrity he hardly deserved as a scientist. The truth of the matter is that Ptolemy's computations of distances were very faulty, inasmuch as he relied for this information on travelers and navigators known to him. In his measurement of the earth's circumference, moreover, he accepted Posidonius' erroneous estimate which fell short of the truth by one-sixth. The mere fact that Ptolemy organized his geography into a complete system and enhanced its authority with carefully drawn maps gave it prestige and the reputation for a definitiveness which it did not in reality possess.

The work is divided into eight books, of which the first treats of the principles of mathematical geography and of the projection of maps, together with a discussion of the length and breadth of the habitable world. The six books that follow contain tables which give the names of the places marked on the maps of the separate countries, together with the latitude and longitude of each. There are, in addition, notices of the boundaries of the countries. In ancient times these tables proved extremely valuable for purposes of reference. They enabled the student who did not possess the author's maps to reconstruct them for himself. The eighth and last book of the *Geography* was written more from the standpoint of astronomy than of geography. From the most important positions which he had already determined on his maps, he deduced from their latitudes and longitudes such results as the length of the longest day at each, and, for tropical places, the course of the sun with respect to them.

While an examination of Ptolemy's map of the world will reveal that he had corrected a number of gross mistakes made by his cartographical predecessors, he, in turn, introduced a number of serious errors of his own. All in all, he took great pains to be exact, and it is astonishing that he managed in his map of the coastline of England to approximate the actual reality. With his pioneer labors he left his indelible marks on this science.

GEOGRAPHY (25), by Strabo. The greatness of this work is its encyclopedic comprehensiveness. Strabo's aim was to bring together, and to exhibit in a readable form for the practical use of educated men, all that was important to know about the different countries of the known world and their inhabitants. The first two books are introductory, III-X are devoted to Europe, XI-XVI to Asia, and XVII, of which we have only a brief summary, to Egypt and Libya. He described the conformation of the ground in each district, the nature of the products, the character and condition of the inhabitants, and similar topics. Historical geography was his principal interest, and he excelled in it. Side by side with the geography of a country he presented its history, and tried to demonstrate the close connection existing between the two. Striking is the way in which he traces the influence of the climate, natural resources and topography of a land on the character and history of its inhabitants. This historic and economic geography is far different from the severely scientific treatise of Ptolemy.

GEOGRAPHY (printed 1462), by Ptolemy of Alexandria. See ALMAGEST, by Ptolemy of Alexandria.

GEORGICS (37–29 B.C.), by Virgil. Landscape gardening, the love of nature, domestic animal breeding, agriculture and the hunt are the subjects in which the Latin poet (70–19 B.C.) attempts to instruct his reader. The verses are elegant, yet full of practical knowledge. They are didactic and ardent, and were modeled after Hesiod's *Works and Days* (q.v.). In teaching the prospective farmer, Virgil employs the form of personal address. It is patent that his aim is to inspire a love of the soil of Italy and of the virtuous life encouraged by rustic surroundings. He makes plain that man can wrest his livelihood and peace from Nature by labor, patience and the propitiation of the gods by prayer and piety. While he exalts toil, he does not elevate it as an end in itself but as a duty demanded by life, the price to be paid for serenity, abundance and happiness. The *Georgics* are in four books. Book I treats of religious and mythological ideas as well as "what makes the cornfields happy . . . the care of cattle . . . the management of flocks . . . the knowledge you need for keeping frugal bees." Book II has for its theme:

Now it's the turn of wine, and with it the trees that crowd
In woody copse, and the produce of the gradual-growing olive.

Book III:

You too, great goddess of sheepfolds, I'm going to sing, and you,
Apollo, a shepherd once, and the woods and streams of Arcady.

Book IV:

Next I come to the manna, the heavenly gift of honey.

Virgil drew upon the works of all the Greek and Latin authorities on agriculture, including those of Democritus, Xenophon, Cato, and Varro.

GÉOMÉTRIE, LA (1637), by René Descartes. In 1637 Descartes published his celebrated *Discourse on the Method of Seeking Truth in the Sciences* (q.v.). This treatise is a landmark in the history of philosophy, and the fame its author achieved in that field often has obscured the part he has played in the beginnings of modern mathematics. The *Discourse on Method* contained three appendices—one on the rainbow, another on the law of refraction, and a third on geometry. The last of these three treatises, entitled *La Géométrie*, is by far the most important, for it marks the first publication of "analytic geometry," one of the essential steps in the development of mathematics which made the calculus possible. Ancient geometry had been closely related to the study of various special cases of figures and constructions. It was not aided by general algebraic methods, and it had a rigidity of form which, while logically flawless, had little heuristic value. The *Elements* of Euclid is a typical example of the ancient synthetic point of view. The characteristic form of Greek geometry made it difficult for Greeks to develop a theory of curves, not half a dozen different curve types being known in antiquity. The lack of a general method of approach made the study of problems involving loci difficult also. Descartes was much impressed by the power of mathematical reasoning, but he formed a low opinion of ancient methodology. He himself had emphasized generality, with respect to which the Greeks had been weak because they lacked an adequate algebra. This latter aspect of mathematics had later been developed by the Arabs, and Descartes was familiar with their methods. He therefore hit upon the device of referring geometric figures to a system of coordinates by which the properties of a curve would be expressible in algebraic terminology. That is, he discovered that, with respect to a coordinate system, every curve corresponds to an equation, and conversely. In this way he reduced difficult geometric problems to simple algebraic calculations. His method, he boasted in *La Géométrie,* is to that of the ancients as the rhetoric of Cicero is to the a, b, c's of children. *La Géométrie* is not a systematic elementary exposition of analytic or algebraic geometry, but it contains all the essentials of the subject as applied to certain difficult problems involving higher plane curves and loci. The work is divided into three books, of which the first relates the arithmetic operations to geometric constructions; the second is on curves, loci, tangents, and normals; and the last deals mainly with the construction of the roots of algebraic equations.

It should be noted that analytic geometry was discovered independently by another French mathematician, Pierre de Fermat, before *La Géométrie* appeared in 1637. The work of Fermat was more systematic and more elementary than that of Descartes, but it did not appear in print until 1679. Priority, both of discovery and of publication, belongs to Descartes; and it is not without justification that analytic or coordinate geometry frequently is referred to as "Cartesian geometry," for it was from *La Géométrie* that the world learned of this powerful method.

GEORGE, STEFAN   Writing in an exclusive style of unconventional punctuation and syntax and of abundance of elliptical expression, George represents a serious search for definite form. He gathered about him an influential literary cult, which, in expressing its aristocratic individualism, glorified the artist as a leader of mankind. Under the influence of Nietzsche, he sought a hierarchy of poetic values which was to correspond with nothing in the conventional society of rationalistic materialism. In submitting to a rigid intellectual discipline, George's poetry was supposed to have required a complete lack of earthly motivations and the arrival at a point beyond the personal to a state of spiritualization, before it could be put into words.

The George Circle's periodical, *Leaves of Art,* included unsigned works of its members. Among George's poetry are the short volumes, *The Carpet of Life* (1899), a dialogue between a lonely man and his soul, *The Seventh Ring* (1907) and *The Star of the Covenant* (1914). Exploiting linguistic sound and rhythm, George attempted to create an atmosphere divorced from all common reality.

GERMANIA (98), by Publius Cornelius Tacitus. At the time this work was written, interest in Germany and its people had been stimulated by Domitian's recent wars against them and by Trajan's defensive stand on the frontiers of the Rhine and the Danube. The *Germania* is outwardly an ethnological treatise in which the habits, customs, laws, institutions and life of the northern peoples are described in detail. As one reads the treatise, however, he is more and more impressed with the fact that, although Tacitus is apparently preoccupied with his presentation of the mores of the Germans, his underlying motive is something quite different. In speaking effusively of German womanhood and its virtue he is implicitly condemning the immorality of Roman womanhood and the decadence of Roman society. Still it would be a mistake to regard the *Germania* as an appeal to return to nature. Tacitus is a moralist in all his works, and this one falls into its proper place when regarded as a by-product of the writing of his *Histories.*

GERMANY (1813), by Madame de Staël. This book revealed to the French the existence of a German culture, and introduced them to the works and ideas of Goethe, Schiller, Lessing, Wieland, Klopstock, Kant, Schelling and Fichte. German Romanticism was in full flower. Madame de Staël described it as a kind of poetry which combines the spirit of chivalry with Christian ethics. Her view was instrumental in broadening that of a whole generation of French writers and in paving the way for the Romantic revolt of 1825-1830. Her admiration for Germany led her to protest against the political subjugation of the country. She also praised the French Revolution wholeheartedly, and left no doubt of her dislike for the no longer revolutionary Napoleon. In 1810, when Madame de Staël finished her book, the Emperor suppressed it; his troops were occupying the German provinces. Madame de Staël had long irked him. It was 1813 before *Germany* reached its public.

GERMINAL (1883), by Emile Zola. See ROUGON-MACQUART, THE, by Emile Zola.

GERMINIE LACERTEUX (1865), by Edmond and Jules de Goncourt. See JOURNALS, by Edmond and Jules de Goncourt.

GESELL, ARNOLD L. (1880–   ). Dr. Gesell's work with the Yale Clinic of Child Development has made him a leading authority on infant and child care. Among his volumes are *The First Five Years of Life* (1940); and *The Child from Five to Ten* (1946), with Frances L. Ilg, in collaboration with Louise Bates Ames and Glenna E. Bullis. *Infant and Child in the Culture of Today* (1943) is also written with Frances L. Ilg.

GESHARIM (1912), by Zalman Shneiur. See SHNEIUR, ZALMAN.

GESTA DANORUM (ca. 1208), by Saxo Grammaticus. See CHRON ICLES OF DENMARK, by Saxo Grammaticus.

GESTA ROMANORUM (compiled ca. 1350; printed ca. 1472). The *Gesta Romanorum* was as widely read for several centuries as the *Arabian Nights* (q.v.) or the *Morte d'Arthur* (q.v.). It has been a treasury of entertainment and moral education for all kinds of readers. Its full title, *Gesta Romanorum moralizata*, indicates its compiler's didactic purpose. The work was an inexhaustible source that furnished the raw material for great literature from Boccaccio and Chaucer to Schiller and Rossetti. It was fathered by monks. The tales were allegedly derived from Roman history but are in truth merely legends. At a later stage the moral aspect became secondary; the collection was prized chiefly as a book of entertainment. Oriental allegoric influences are clearly indicated, as for instance the fables of Bidpai and the *Arabian Nights*. The method of teaching by the parabolic art was widely employed in ancient times among all peoples and civilizations. The general illiteracy of the masses during the Middle Ages prompted the monks to use entertaining, didactic fables to illustrate their preaching in order to make a more incisive impression. The authorities cited for classical allusions are the minor luminaries of Roman antiquity: Valerius Maximus, Macrobius, Aulus Gellius, Pliny, Seneca, Boëthius and occasionally Ovid.

The *Gesta Romanorum* was considered a thesaurus for preachers. The story "Of Rebukes to Princes" is characteristic: "Augustine tells us in his book *De Civitate Dei* that Diomedes, in a piratical galley, for a long time infested the sea, plundering and sinking many ships. Being captured by command of Alexander, before whom he was brought, the king enquired how he dared molest the seas. 'How darest *thou*,' replied he, 'molest the earth? Because I am master only of a single galley, I am termed a robber; but you, who oppress the world with huge squadrons, are called a king and a conqueror. Would my fortune change, I might become better; but as you are the more fortunate, so much are you the worse.' 'I will change thy fortune,' said Alexander, 'lest fortune should be blamed by thy malignity.' Thus he became rich; and from a robber was made a prince and a dispenser of justice." The moral application appended to this cynical little tale by its author as a guide for preachers has an incredible twist: "My beloved, the pirate in his galley is a sinner in the world; Alexander is a prelate."

GETTYSBURG ADDRESS, THE (1863), by Abraham Lincoln. Delivered at the dedication of a national cemetery during the Civil War, this speech was ignored by Lincoln's contemporaries, but is now considered one of the noblest expressions of democracy ever spoken:

"Fourscore and seven years ago our fathers brought forth on this continent a new nation, conceived in liberty, and dedicated to the proposition that all men are created equal.

"Now we are engaged in a great civil war, testing whether that nation, or any nation so conceived and so dedicated, can long endure. We are met on a great battlefield of that war. We have come to dedicate a portion of that field as a final resting-place for those who here gave their lives that that nation might live. It is altogether fitting and proper that we should do this.

"But, in a larger sense, we cannot dedicate—we cannot consecrate—we cannot hallow—this ground. The brave men, living and dead, who struggled here, have consecrated it far above our poor power to add or detract. The world will little note nor long remember what we say here, but it can never forget what they did here. It is for us, the living, rather, to be dedicated here to the unfinished work which they who fought here have thus far so nobly advanced. It is rather for us to be here dedicated to the great task remaining before us—that from these honored dead we take increased devotion to that cause for which they gave the last full measure of devotion; that we here highly resolve that these dead shall not have died in vain; that this nation, under God, shall have a new birth of freedom, and that government of the people, by the people, for the people shall not perish from the earth."

Another of Lincoln's public addresses was his *Second Inaugural* (1864) which gave hope, with victory in sight, for a humane rebuilding of the nation. The President ended:

"With malice toward none; with charity for all; with firmness in the right, as God gives us to see the right, let us strive on to finish the work we are in, to bind up the nation's wounds; to care for him who shall have borne the battle, and for his widow, and his orphan—to do all which may achieve a just and lasting peace among ourselves, and with all nations."

GEZELLE, GUIDO (1830–1899). The priest Gezelle is the most excellent singer of Flemish modern poetry. Like a mediaeval pious man, he enjoys nature as a reflection of God's greatness and grace. His descriptions of nature are in essence nothing but adoration. Infatuated as he was with the beautiful sounds of softly flowing Flemish, he selected from all dialects the loveliest words and used them in his simple, pure poems, which straightway penetrated to the heart of the people. Through this, the poetry of Gezelle has been of priceless value in the bitter struggle which the Flemish people in Belgium had to wage for the equal rights of Flemish with French, acknowledged by the government as the official language. Gezelle's flourishing period occurred after his sixtieth year. The collections *Tijdkrans* (1893) and

Rijmsnoer om en om het Jaar (1897) are like breviaries, arranged according to the year's seasons, and glorifying therein the beauty of Flanders' lands in continuous adoration of the Creator. Young, refreshing and virile his poetry remained to the last. He translated Longfellow's *Song of Hiawatha* into Flemish verse.

GHOSTS (1881), by Henrik Ibsen. *Ghosts* was written the year after *The Doll's House* (q.v.) in answer to the critics who had interpreted the latter play as an argument for free love, according to H. L. Mencken. The two plays are probably the best known and the most often produced of Ibsen's dramas. Duse, Mrs. Fiske, and Nazimova included *Ghosts* in their repertory. In *Ghosts,* a powerful play on heredity, Ibsen advanced a step further in the technique he had set up in *The Doll's House,* revolutionizing the well-made play of that period. The scene is laid in Mrs. Alving's house on one of the fjords in western Norway. She has built an orphanage to her husband's memory, and it is to be dedicated on the tenth anniversary of his death. Pastor Manders, an old friend and her clergyman, comes to perform the ceremony, and go over the business details. Manders, cautious and worldly wise, thinks it wiser not to insure the buildings, as the public might doubt their belief in divine protection. Oswald, Mrs. Alving's only son, a talented artist, has returned from Paris in time for the dedication. Manders rebukes Mrs. Alving for reading liberal books, and for having kept her son so much away from home. She refers to the time in her early married life when she had run away from her home and sought refuge with him, and he had sent her back to her dissolute husband. She tells him she had been her husband's drinking companion, and had covered up his dissipation for Oswald's sake. She had sent the boy away so that he would not be disillusioned about his father. Regina, her maid, is Alving's illegitimate daughter and Oswald's half-sister, though she passes for the daughter of Engstrand, a hypocritical carpenter. She and Manders overhear Oswald flirting with Regina in the dining-room, and Mrs. Alving feels they are ghosts of her husband and Regina's mother. She plans to get Regina out of the house. A fire breaks out in the new orphanage and it is burned to the ground. Oswald returns from the fire very tired and tells his mother that he is ill, threatened with a terrible disease. If it were inherited he would not mind so much, but he feels he has brought it on by his own indiscretions. He wishes to marry Regina; he needs her joy of living. Mrs. Alving tells him about his father, eases his conscience about himself, and explains that he cannot marry Regina, as she is his half-sister. Oswald asks the latter to stay on as his sister, but, disgusted, she leaves the house to join on a departing steamer Pastor Manders and her father, who is planning to open a seamen's tavern. Oswald, in a dramatic scene, tells his mother that his brain is softening, that he will probably become an imbecile, and asks her when the attack occurs to give him some morphine tablets. Mrs. Alving shrinks in horror from the idea, but finally promises to do so if necessary. The disease suddenly overtakes Oswald. Mrs. Alving gives him the overdose and allows him to die.

GIAMBI ED EPODI (1867–1879), by Giosue' Carducci. See CAR- DUCCI, GIOSUE'.

GIANTS IN THE EARTH (1927), by Ole E. Rolvaag. This novel is a story of the life and vicissitudes of Norwegian settlers in the South Dakota plains. Per Hansa, a viking transplanted from the sea to the earth, struggles with the unyielding soil of his farm in the New World. He and his family live in a sod hut and raise crops for trade as well as food. Per is a natural pioneer, passionately devoted to the land. Unfortunately, his weak-willed wife, Beret, loathes the solitude and hardship of frontier life. She is desperately nostalgic for the refined comforts and charm of the Norwegian town she has left. Per's peace is ruined by her lamentations, but he stubbornly clings to his chosen path, hoping that in time she will become reconciled to their life. Beret's new-born son, Peder Victorious, at first gives her no joy. She is afraid he is a lost soul because there is no minister to christen him. Finally a minister does stop to visit with them, and Beret's state of mind improves. Religion comes to be her solace and eventually her obsession. When a friend, Hans Olsa, lies dying she insists that Per get the minister, who lives at some distance. The weather is stormy and Per is reluctant to go. Finally yielding to her insistence, he leaves in the blizzard and never returns.

GIDEON PLANISH (1934), by Sinclair Lewis. See ARROWSMITH, by Sinclair Lewis.

GIJSBREGHT VAN AEMSTEL (1637), by Joost van den Vondel. See VONDEL, JOOST VAN DEN.

GIL BLAS (1715), by Alain René Le Sage. Gil Blas, a student, has no sooner set off for what he thinks will be a quiet life of study than he is fleeced by a swindler and then carried off by brigands. This begins a long series of adventures, in the course of which he has to deal with all the social classes, meet members of all the professions, and win his way as best he can by his agile wits. Versatile and ingenious, he serves as assistant to a famous— and murderous—surgeon, as secretary to a churchman, as administrator of a rich man's estate; he rescues beautiful ladies, aids lovers in distress, and contracts two marriages himself. This is a novel of the road; both the form and the episodes are taken over from the stock materials of the Spanish picaresque tale. But the people whom Gil Blas meets and abuses—or is abused by—live on the page. Le Sage's fame comes from his ability to make his yarn an oblique commentary on the manners of the Europe of his time, and for his shrewdly satirical portraits of familiar social types.

GILDED AGE, THE (1873), by Mark Twain and Charles Dudley Warner. See INNOCENTS ABROAD, THE, by Mark Twain.

GIRL OF THE GOLDEN WEST, THE (1905), by David Belasco. See RETURN OF PETER GRIMM, THE (1911), by David Belasco.

GITANJALI (1914), by Rabindranath Tagore. See TAGORE, RABIN-DRANATH.

GIVE YOUR HEART TO THE HAWKS (1933), by Robinson Jeffers. See JEFFERS, ROBINSON.

GLACIER, THE (1909), by Johannes V. Jensen. See LONG JOUR-NEY, THE, by Johannes V. Jensen.

GLASPEARLGAME, THE (1943), by Hermann Hesse. See HESSE, HERMANN.

GLASPELL, SUSAN (1882–1948). Susan Glaspell, one of the organizers of the famous Provincetown Players, has written many works for the stage.

Suppressed Desires (1914) is a one-act satire of psychoanalysis. Henrietta Brewster, a progressive young woman, insists that her husband Steve and her sister Mabel be psychoanalyzed. When diagnoses indicate that Steve's desire is to be free of Henrietta, and Mabel's is to have Steve, she drops the idea.

The Inheritors (1921) is a longer play about the Morton and Fejevary families whose third generations clash in a university matter because of a difference in political ideologies.

Alison's House (1930) is a Pulitzer Prize play believed to be based on the life of Emily Dickinson. The Stanhopes are breaking up the old family home, where Alison Stanhope, a famous poet, had lived before her death eighteen years before, with her sister Agatha, now an old woman. Just before she dies, Agatha gives her niece, Elsa, a little portfolio of Alison's. Jennie, an old servant, tells Elsa that Agatha had wished the portfolio burned. The Stanhopes find it contains some of Alison's best work, and reveals that she had loved a married man but given him up. Influenced by her aunt's poems, Elsa decides not to return to her own lover, a married man; and the Stanhopes decide to preserve Alison's work.

Susan Glaspell wrote short stories, a biography of her husband, and several novels. These include *Fidelity* (1915), about a girl's romance with a married man; *Brook Evans* (1928); *Norma Ashe* (1942), about the lives of several college students in the thirty years following graduation; and *Judd Rankin's Daughter* (1945), the family story of a homely American philosopher.

GLASS MENAGERIE, THE (1945), by Tennessee Williams. The Wingfields live in a St. Louis tenement apartment. The only characters in this play are Amanda, the querulous mother, whose main comfort is the memory of days as a southern belle before she met her ne'er-do-well husband; Tom, her son, a warehouse worker who supports the family, but whose poetic soul cannot tolerate the meanness of their life; twenty-three-year-old Laura, his shy, crippled sister, and James O'Connor. Amanda's domination of her children creates an atmosphere of despair and futility. Her obsession is that Laura entertain "gentlemen callers." In truth, Laura's sense of inferiority has caused her to withdraw entirely from the world since high school days, and spend all her time with ancient phonograph records and a collection of glass animals. In obedience to Amanda's nagging, Tom brings home his friend, James O'Connor, a shipping clerk, who has been Laura's secret love since they were in the same class. Tom, an extrovert, is attracted to Laura, and encourages her when he discovers how shy she is. But, not realizing her deep devotion to him, he steps out of her life without bringing matters to any conclusion. Tom leaves to join the Merchant Marine, but is forever haunted by the memory of Laura.

Tennessee Williams' reputation was enhanced by the production of his hit play, *A Streetcar Named Desire* (1947), which takes place in the French Quarter of New Orleans. Blanche Du Bois, a sensitive young southern girl, is haunted by the memory of a tragic marriage which warped her life. She comes to visit her sister Stella, but the lusty bohemian life of Stella and her husband, Stanley Kowalsky, is shocking to Blanche. After a series of forceful episodes, including a violent card party and Stanley's brutal rape of Blanche while his wife is in the hospital having a baby, Blanche's mind fails, and she is taken to a mental hospital.

GLIMPSES OF UNFAMILIAR JAPAN (1894), by Lafcadio Hearn. See HEARN, LAFCADIO.

GLOBE, THE (before 1241), by Snorri Sturlson. See HEIMSKRINGLA, by Snorri Sturlson.

GLORIANT (ca. 15th c.), Anonymous. See MEDIEVAL FLEMISH PLAYS.

GOD OF VENGEANCE (1918), by Sholem Asch. See NAZARENE, THE, by Sholem Asch.

GOD'S LITTLE ACRE (1933), by Erskine Caldwell. See TOBACCO ROAD, by Erskine Caldwell.

GOETHE, JOHANN WOLFGANG VON (1749–1832). Johann Wolfgang Goethe, the greatest man of German letters, was born on August 28, 1749, and died on March 22, 1832. Carrying the classical concept of humanistic self-development to unsurpassed heights, and anticipating the nineteenth century in the realms of technology, science, and social ideas, the German author was not only a poet, dramatist, biographer and essayist, but a statesman, lawyer, administrator, cabinet member, theater manager, director, actor, art collector and scientist. The scion of a patrician Frankfurt home, he studied at the universities of Leipzig and Strasbourg, practiced law in his home town, and was already a world famous author at the age of twenty-five when he followed an invitation to the little mid-German Court of Weimar, where he assumed the post of privy councilor and president of the chamber for more than a decade. It was here that the classical age of German literature came into being and finally ripened into its golden maturity, with Schiller, Wieland and Herder occupying prominent positions, and with Goethe holding the limelight as the unchallenged master.

Goethe's universality of interests and activities, which also includes an almost endless row of richly rewarding and deeply inspiring love affairs, makes it difficult to separate his literary work from his life. His poems, plays and novels are always radiations of the individual stages of his life experiences, or, as he himself expressed it, "just fragments of a great confession." It seems still possible, however, to consider the Italian trip he undertook from 1786 to 1788 as the most important event that divided his literary production into two more or less distinct phases. It is mainly as the leader of the "Storm and Stress" movement that the young Goethe ranks in the history of German literature. The young student in Strasbourg received great stimulation from Herder, who opened his eyes to the beauties of Gothic architecture and the greatness of Shakespeare; and under the influence of a new and genuine love for a country girl (Friederike Brion) his true poetic gifts were awakened. Two of the most precious lyric gems may be named as examples: "Welcome and Departure" and the "May-song." In 1773 he published his Shakespeare-inspired historical drama of the Reformation period, *Götz von Berlichingen*. The loosely constructed play, not hampered by any dramatic "unities," with its restless changes of scene and its many sharply drawn characters, was widely acclaimed, and made the young author the undisputed head of the "Storm and Stress" movement. It was, however, the novel in letter form, *The Sorrows of Werther* (q.v.) that spread Goethe's fame all over Europe. Based on an unhappy love for the bride of a friend, Charlotte Buff, and prompted by the suicide of a young acquaintance, the over-emotional slender book became a literary sensation in an age known for its sentimentalism. Among the many literary projects of Goethe's earlier years, including several plays, dramatic satires, fragments (*Faust* in its initial stages), the drama *Egmont* may finally be mentioned; it was not completed before 1787 but is essentially a youthful work. Immortalized by Beethoven's music, the play deals with the struggle of the Netherlands against Spanish rule. Unlike the historical Egmont, Goethe's hero is a joyful, amiable leader of the people who turns to Clärchen, a simple girl, and is finally led, through his own carelessness, into a trap set for him by the Duke of Alba. He is imprisoned and finally executed. Deficient in dramatic structure, the drama owes its popularity to the tender love scenes between Egmont and Clärchen.

The second phase of Goethe's writing comprises the years after the trip to Italy, where he found his search for a higher ideal of beauty and art realized. A new conception of classical harmony, a shift from the individual toward the typical, characterizes his literary work after his return to Weimar. The most perfect example of the new style is perhaps *Iphigenie auf Tauris,* based on Euripides, which Goethe rewrote in iambic pentameters in Italy and published in 1787. Also changed from the original prose version to verse was *Torquato Tasso* (1789), a dramatic character study of the Italian poet, whose life at the Court of Ferrara bears some similarity to Goethe's own position in Weimar. The new and intimate friendship with Schiller during the decade from 1795 until 1805 marks the most productive period of the mature Goethe. Both men collaborated on a number of periodicals, and some of Goethe's best known works profited from Schiller's keen and sympathetic criticism, notably *Wilhelm Meister's Apprenticeship* (q.v.), the classical German novel of education. A year later, 1797, the short verse epic *Hermann and Dorothea* (q.v.) was published. It was also in those years that he wrote some of his finest ballads. At the age of sixty he published *The Elective Affinities* (1809), a strangely modern psychological but somewhat pale novel about the relations of two marriage partners each of whom is attracted by another person. As is often the case with great creative artists, the last two decades of Goethe's life were largely devoted to reaping the harvest of a life's work, bringing to a conclusion projects that had occupied him over the course of many years. His charming autobiography, *Poetry and Truth* (1811–1833), ranking with Rousseau's *Confessions* (q.v.), which breaks off at the departure to Weimar, was written and partly published; the second volume of Meister, *Wilhelm Meister's Travels,* was finished in 1829, and finally, his "chief business" as he used to call it, *Faust* (q.v.), of which the first part had appeared in 1808, was completed a few months before his death.

Goethe is not only the greatest author of German literature, but he is the most universal human phenomenon of the Western World to appear in the last two centuries. One of the finest lyrical poets of all times, he is also a social thinker, philosopher and scientist of amazing stature whose modernity has not even been fully realized two hundred years after his birth. He transcends national boundaries as well as fields of interest and movements of thought.

GOLDEN ASS, THE (before 124), by Apuleius of Madaura. The tale of *The Golden Ass* is narrated in the first person by a licentious young man, Lucius, who is devoured by an overpowering curiosity about things and people. On a trip to Thessaly he induces the maid of his sorceress hostess to steal for him a magic salve by means of which he would be able to metamorphose himself into an owl. But the maid gives him another salve by mistake, and so Lucius turns into an ass. In this inconvenient form he wanders through Greece, experiencing strange adventures as he passes from the hands of one owner to another. At last he is restored to his human shape through the help of the goddess Isis after eating the petals of roses. Interspersed in the course of the main narrative are many romantic, salacious and comic stories. The book is full of gay intrigues, ravished brides, hair-raising scenes of witchcraft, and secret raids. The hero-ass wanders over hill and dale, visits strange towns and listens to macabre or romantic tales in robber-caves or village inns. The famous story of Cupid and Psyche, e.g., fills two of the eleven books of the work.

Ever since its appearance during the first half of the second century *The Golden Ass* of Apuleius has enjoyed a continuous popularity rarely equaled. This was particularly true during the pleasure-loving Renaissance centuries when gay and racy *novelle* were read with great enthusiasm. The work left an indelible imprint on such writers as Cervantes, Boccaccio and Rabelais, who did not hesitate to borrow from Apuleius, who, in his own turn, had derived his plot and tales from Greek literary predecessors.

GOLDEN BOUGH, THE (1890; 1907-1915), by James G. Frazer. In many respects this is a unique work in the field of anthropology. The author's purpose is to give an extended description and explanation of magic, religion, cults and folk-lore. An indefatigable collector of information on ancient and "primitive" beliefs, practices and social institutions, Frazer attempted to weave this data into a series of integrated pictures of various cultures. His sympathetic approach and his talented pen made the book a work of art as much as a treatise in anthropology. Prefatory to and lying behind all of Frazer's accounts is a conceptual framework that has not stood up under the critical scrutiny of later and more analytic anthropologists. Thus Frazer is valued most today for his uncanny insight and imaginative re-creation of other cultures, rather than for any theoretical contributions he may have made. His book is still used as a source book by other students, and has been used by specialists outside his own field. Freud went to it for data to support his psychological theories, though Frazer rejected psychoanalysis. Originally a two-volume work, *The Golden Bough* was gradually expanded to twelve volumes. In 1922 a one-volume abridgment which has proved to be very popular appeared under the same title.

GOLDEN BOWL, THE (1904), by Henry James. The last complete novel of James is a long, elaborate work. Maggie Verver, an intelligent, cultured American girl, marries Roman Prince Amerigo in London. Later, her widowed father Adam marries her friend Charlotte Stant. It is then revealed that the Prince had been Charlotte's lover, but lack of money had caused them to part. A golden bowl, of almost flawless craftsmanship, becomes symbolic of the personality of the Prince during this delicate situation. When Maggie learns that her husband has again become Charlotte's lover, she begins to seek a solution to the problem. And her sympathy causes Adam to return to America with Charlotte, and the Prince to appreciate fully his wife.

GOLDEN BOY (1937), by Clifford Odets. Joe Bonaparte, twenty-two years old, is a talented violinist and loves music. In spite of the pressure of his old father, who wants Joe to have a musical career, the youth's ambition for wealth and fame induce him to brazen his way into the prize ring. The intense pugilist shows promise, and eventually rises to the top, at the sacrifice of his hands. One night, he kills another fighter in the ring, by accident. The whole emptiness of his career overcomes him. He drives off recklessly with his sweetheart Lorna, the mistress of his manager; and both are killed in a crash.

GOLDEN FLEECE (1820), by Franz Grillparzer. The trilogy, written in verse, consists of *The Guest Friend, The Argonauts* and *Medea,* the last of which enjoys the greatest popularity. *The Guest Friend,* a short prologue, relates how King Aëtus treacherously gains possession of the Golden Fleece, which carries a curse for him and his daughter, Medea. In *The Argonauts,* Medea the Amazon, touched by love for the stranger Jason, aids him in making off with the Fleece. He, in turn, takes her with him as his wife. *Medea,* written in a somber classic style, reveals the plight and humiliation of Jason in his native Greece, since his wife is a sorceress and a barbarian. To no avail is her willingness to renounce her magical powers and to adapt herself to the ways of the new land. Jason finds it impossible to be true to Médea and turns to Creusa, a childhood friend. With all this confronting Medea, her barbaric passions break forth once more. She kills her two children, and in a trail of destruction, leaves Jason, taking the Fleece with her.

Also notable among Grillparzer's works is the play *The Fortune and Fall of King Ottokar* (1825), where the author turns to the history of his native Austria at the beginning of the Hapsburg dynasty. *Woe unto the Liar* (1838) tells how a servant ventures among the barbarians to rescue his master's nephew. He is successful with truth as his weapon, since he has been forbidden to tell a single lie. The fine skill and thoroughgoing humor which Grillparzer lavished upon the play earn for it a position among the greatest comedies in the German language.

Grillparzer's artistic grandeur has rarely been denied. He combined consistent excellence in style with a deep insight into human motivation.

GOLDEN THRESHOLD, THE (1905), by Sarojin Naidu. See NAIDU, SAROJIN.

GOLDEN TREASURY, THE 1861). See PALBRAVE'S GOLDEN TREASURY.

GOLOVLYOV FAMILY, THE (1872–1876), by M. E. Shchedrin. M. E. Shchedrin is the pseudonym of Michael Evgrafovich Saltykov. Half novelist and half journalist, he won recognition and became one of the accepted classical writers of Russia. Any reader who becomes acquainted with the Golovlyovs is not likely ever to forget them. This serf-owning family, as a Russian critic has said, exemplifies the reign of brute matter over human life, which "has never been portrayed with greater force."

The most important character is Iudushka, "little Judas," whose formal name is Porfiro Golovlyov. This unctuous hypocrite has a tongue which flows on and on like Tennyson's brook. His empty mechanical mind is dehumanized by the endless effort to talk and talk. Not that any of the family is an improvement on "little Judas." On the contrary; they are all spiteful, greedy, with such evil-ridden and gloomy souls that happiness is impossible.

In the simplest manner possible the author presents these characters to us; the inevitable misery, the unalloyed gloom lies in the family itself. Even Iudushka is not a conscious hypocrite, which may be why he has been called the Russian Tartuffe. Anninka and Lubinka, provincial actresses, are two minor characters of importance, but it is Stephen, Anna and Pavel with their mother, Arina Petrovna, and Iudushka's son, Petenka, who make up the famous Golovlyov family.

This is probably the gloomiest novel of Russia. The atmosphere of dumb darkness is achieved with great skill; the author never resorts to melodrama.

GONE WITH THE WIND (1936), by Margaret Mitchell. Young, high-tempered Scarlett O'Hara marries Charles Hamilton, piqued that his sister Melanie, and not she, is to be the bride of her neighbor Ashley Wilkes. When Charles dies in the Civil War, and Atlanta is seized by the Northerners, Scarlett is poverty-stricken. She is forced to struggle for her family, and also the aristocratic Ashley, who has not been trained to work with his hands, but determines to keep Tara, her father's plantation. She does manual labor, marries her sister's fiancé Frank Kennedy for his money; and after his death in a duel to avenge her honor marries Rhett Butler, an unscrupulous profiteer. Because of her lasting love for Ashley, however, Rhett deserts Scarlett. She realizes at last, after the death of Melanie and the indifference of Ashley, that Rhett, similar in spirit to her, was her real love.

This popular historical romance was the 1937 Pulitzer Prize winner.

GOOD-BYE, MR. CHIPS (1934), by James Hilton. This short novel of the memories of the gentle, kindly schoolmaster, Mr. Chipping, or "Chips," opens in 1933 when he is eighty years old, retired since the armistice and living at Mrs. Wickett's, across the street from his beloved Brookfield school in England. As he looks back on the years, his story unfolds: his arrival in Brookfield in 1870; his marriage to Katherine Bridges in 1896; her death two years later; his growing popularity and sense of humor; retirement; return as head during World War I; final retirement in 1918. A new boy, Linford, comes to visit; when he leaves he calls, "Good-bye, Mr. Chips." The beloved schoolmaster dies the following night, hearing the names of his thousands of boys in a final chorus.

GOOD COMPANIONS, THE (1929), by John Boynton Priestley. Three performers leave homes and settled lives to join a troupe of traveling players or 'pierrots' (Good Companions) in England during the 1920's. Jesiah Oakroyd, Yorkshire laborer, becomes handy man; Elizabeth Trant, a maiden lady, becomes manager; and Inigo Jollifant, a school teacher, who composes music and writes essays, becomes the piano player. They have a gay, adventurous time. The book opens with the three leading characters at home. They join the company one by one. Their experiences are described in great detail, by letters written home. The book ends with the break-up of the company, which includes: Jimmy Nunn, Jerry Jerningham, Elsie Longstaff, and Susie Dean. An epilogue relates the subsequent experiences of each one. Elizabeth Dean (Inigo's sweetheart) continues with her career; Inigo is mildly successful as a writer; Oakroyd goes to Canada; Elizabeth Trant marries Dr. Hugh McFarlane, an old friend.

GOOD EARTH, THE (1931), by Pearl Buck. The book opens in China in the late 1920's, with the poor peasant Wang Lung going to the House of Hwang for a wife. O-Lan, a kitchen slave, is chosen for him. The couple work side by side, bound by common reverence for husbandry and the land, and parting only during the birth of O-Lan's children. They are moderately prosperous, but there is a famine, during which kindhearted Wang Lung is unable to kill their ox for food; O-Lan, the strong one, does it. They are later forced to travel south, begging for food, Wang Lung carrying his old father.

Strange talk of revolution is abroad, and on the night a rich man's house is stormed, Wang Lung follows and finds gold. With jewels O-Lan has found, the couple buy more land and hire a neighbor to work with them. Three sons and two daughters are born during their continuing good fortune. Wang Lung dresses like a rich man. O-Lan, plain, tired, and ill, becomes unpleasant in her husband's eyes. He finds Lotus, a former prostitute, and acquires her as a second wife, later taking Lotus' beautiful slave as a concubine.

His two elder sons marry and bring home their wives. But the youngest becomes a revolutionary leader, and Wang Lung learns when he is dying that the other two do not love the land, but plan to sell it and move to the city.

This fine tableau of the Chinese farmer, his family life, religion, and love for the earth, was a Pulitzer Prize novel. Its sequels are *Sons* (1932) and *A House Divided* (1935). Pearl Buck has written many other novels, biographies of her parents, children's books, and essays about China.

Among her volumes of short stories is *The First Wife* (1933). In this, three groups of short stories describe the conflict between the old and the new in the lives of contemporary China. The title piece deals with the impasse between a western-educated Chinese husband and his wife, who is steeped in ancient tradition. She finally commits suicide.

GOOD HOPE, THE (Eng. tr. 1912), by Herman Heijermans. See OP HOOP VAN ZEGEN, by Herman Heijermans.

GOOD SOLDIER SCHWEIK, THE (1920–1923; Eng. tr. 1930), by Jaroslav Hašek (1883–1923). The full title, *The Fate of the Good Soldier Svejk in the World War,* summarizes the contents of a book which became popular not only in Czechoslovakia but in many other countries. Hašek, a journalist and novelist, was for a while a member of the Czechoslovak Legion in Russia, and later a free-lance journalist in Prague.

His great character Schweik has been dubbed a Czech Sancho Panza. Schweik was an ordinary dogcatcher in Prague when World War I began; a man with an extraordinary capacity for playing dumb, and a complete lack of interest in the affairs of the world. He seems a ridiculous figure, one meant to be ordered around and laughed at, but there is a shrewd, peasant wisdom about him which enables him to get out of the scrapes into which he has plunged or been plunged. He is arrested by the Austrians for a supposed insult to the Emperor, and is drafted; this gives the author a splendid opportunity to poke fun at the stupidity of the Austrian government, which was no more clever than Schweik himself. In a Russian uniform, he lands in a Russian prisoner of war camp in Austria. Later as a Russian prisoner he passes through the Russian Revolution. In everything he does, Schweik is a comical character who can be used, often in a coarse way, to point out the folly of those who think they are intelligent.

GOOD WOMAN, A (1927), by Louis Bromfield. See GREEN BAY TREE, THE, by Louis Bromfield.

GORBODUC (1562), by Thomas Norton and Thomas Sackville. This tragedy is the first in English, and the first play in blank verse. The authors resorted to dumb show to explain their piece. A chorus of four ancient Britons ends every act except the last. All the numerous murders are offstage, narrated by the characters. The material was drawn from the old Chronicles. Gorboduc, a legendary king of Britain, divides his realm in his lifetime between his two sons, Ferrex and Porrex. Ferrex is jealous of his younger brother. They war on each other, and Porrex kills his brother. Videna, the queen, their mother, slays Porrex to avenge Ferrex. The people rise in rebellion, kill the king and queen; civil war follows. The first three acts are the work of Norton; the last two, of Sackville.

GORKY, MAXIM (1868–1936). Gorky (Alexey Maximovich Peshkov) came as a reaction to Chekhov. Chekhov painted the Russian bourgeoisie, the "grey people" who came into existence with the introduction of industrialism. Gorky, though he had a respect for Chekhov as a writer and a man, was at war with the world of petty people he portrayed. His own people are romantic, colorful, in revolt against society. His characters were disillusioned tramps, hand-to-mouth vagrants, down-at-the-heel philosophers, ex-jailbirds, virile young men who wanted to force life to give them what they considered was their due, and spirited women who had a fondness for "supermen." Such characters reappear in his novels, plays and short stories.

A typical example of Gorky's fiction is his early novel, *Foma Gordeyev* (1899), an absorbing study of the effort of a man born into the bourgeois class to find his soul. The story moves slowly, and the plot rambles, but this only serves to enhance the forcefulness of Foma's inevitable outburst. Foma, the son of Ignat Gordeyev, a ruthless merchant who operated a fleet of trading vessels on the Volga, spent his early years at the home of his godfather, Mayakin, also a merchant. His mother had died when he was young. Ignat adored his son, whom he finally brought home and placed in the care of his old sister, Anfisa. Ignat had risen from the status of day laborer and hoped to leave his son a fortune, and early tried to indoctrinate Foma with his own harsh business doctrines. Foma, idealistic but uneducated, inherited his father's vitality, and on his first trip on the Volga proclaimed himself master of the expedition. When his father died, he found himself in possession of a thriving business and considerable wealth. Dissatisfied with himself and his ignorance, Foma plunged into reckless dissipation. His godfather tried to check his extravagance, but Foma felt that if he were rid of his money he could be free. When Mayakin refused to take over the business for him so that he might study, he plunged into further excesses. During a bout of dissipation he met Yozhov, an old friend who was now a clever but half-starved journalist. Foma finally returned to his home, but found himself in disfavor with his friends. At Mayakin's suggestion, he went on a trial trip of a new steamer built by Kononov, a rich merchant. In the midst of a gay celebration, Foma denounced the wealthy merchants as thieves, liars, cheats and hypocrites. He was bound and declared a madman and sent to an insane asylum; and emerged after three years only to take to drink.

To Gorky's later period belongs *Yegor Bulitchev and Others* (1932). The action takes place during World War I. Yegor Bulitchev, a wealthy merchant, is ill. His family, consisting of his wife Xenia, his daughter Varvara, her husband Zontzov, and Yegor's illegitimate child, Shura, is waiting for him to die in order to claim his money. His sister-in-law, an abbess, visits him so that she can withdraw her money from his business; his priest, Father Palvin, is most attentive. Bulitchev, cynically amused, sees through them all. He tries various healers, among them a trumpeter, a sorceress, and a prophet. Finally when Shura leads him to the window to hear the singing of the revolutionists, he realizes he will lose his possessions and drops dead.

Of Gorky's short stories the most famous are "Varenka Olesova" (which in the English translation bears the name of "A Naughty Girl"; 1897), a story of the educated classes; "Twenty-Six Men and a Girl" (1899), whose scene is a cellar bakery where twenty-six men employees idolize a girl until one of them seduces her on a wager; "Chelkash" (1895); "Malva" (1897); "Creatures That Were Once Men" (1897).

GÖSTA BERLING'S SAGA (1891), by Selma Lagerlöf. *Gösta Berling's Saga,* a prose epic, is a masterly composite based on local tales about life in Värmland, a province of Central Sweden. Gösta himself, a minister of the early part of the last century, is young, strong, beautiful, full of the joy of life. Women find him irresistibly attractive. He possesses all the qualities and virtues of the romantic hero. He can dance and hunt; he is a moving speaker and an inspired poet. Moreover, he is a brave, adventuresome young man. As a consequence of a prank played by one of his friends on the Bishop, Gösta abandons his career in the ministry and gives himself to a life of dissipation. He finally is rescued from this by the mistress of Ekeby Hall, who owns seven great mines. She keeps twelve cavalier pensioners who are supplied with bed and board through her bounty. Gösta becomes one of these.

The story, full of gaiety and romance and written in a fairy-tale style, falls into three parts, each consisting of twelve chapters. Part I recounts the three love adventures of Gösta and terminates with his dismissal by the Countess Elizabeth, a beautiful and virtuous young married woman. Part II deals with the misfortunes and contumely that follow the Countess Elizabeth because of her luckless and innocent love for Gösta. She is thrown out of her home by her jealous mother-in-law, and her husband finally annuls their marriage. Part III tells of the storming of Ekeby Hall by the *canaille* (modeled after the Reign of Terror during the French Revolution). The mistress of Ekeby dies, the cavaliers are humbled, and Gösta goes forth with Elizabeth, her love at last rewarded by her becoming the wife of Gösta. Together they plan to build up the ruined estates and devote themselves to their fellow men.

Gösta Berling's Saga has been translated into more than thirty languages. The *Saga* and subsequent works won for Lagerlöf the Nobel Prize in Literature and a membership in the Swedish Academy, of which she was the first woman member.

GOTTHELF, JEREMIAS (1797–1854). The Swiss clergyman, Albert Bitzius, used the pseudonym, Jeremias Gotthelf, which he made more well-known than his real name. Gotthelf's novels are didactic in nature; and he employs a straightforwardness which sometimes reaches the level of coarseness to describe contemporary peasant life. His reputation as a writer of fiction for the people has won acclaim for him as one of the foremost novelists of modern peasant life. He also paved the way for another Swiss writer in the field of realistic prose, Gottfried Keller. Among Gotthelf's novels written in the Swiss dialect are *Uli the Serf* (1841), *Uli the Tenant Farmer* (1846), and *Elsie, the Strange Maiden* (1850).

GÖTZ VON BERLICHINGEN (1773), by Johann Wolfgang von Goethe. See GOETHE, JOHANN WOLFGANG VON.

GOZZI, CARLO (1720–1806). The personality and literary stature of the Venetian playwright Carlo Gozzi can be understood only when compared to those of his lifelong rival, Carlo Goldoni. Both men are a typical expression of Venetian life in the eighteenth century, the last period of its splendor. But, while Goldoni devoted all his efforts to the renewal of the conventional forms of the theater and to the creation of a new, original and more natural comedy, Gozzi tried desperately to revive the old conception of the Commedia dell' Arte and of the four traditional Italian masks (Brighella, Pantalone, Arlecchino and Colombina). Among Gozzi's outstanding *fiabe* and plays are *The Love of the Three Oranges* (1761), *Little Green Bird* (1765), *The Raven* (1761), *King Stag* (1762), and *Turandot* (1762). Gozzi's rabid envy of Goldoni led to his misfortune. His melancholia shattered his nerves and his imagination became erratic. He had frequent fits and hallucinations. His autobiographical book *Useless Memories* (1797) narrates his tormented existence up to 1795.

GRACE ABOUNDING (1666), by John Bunyan. This autobiography, dealing with Bunyan's spiritual struggles, recounts with almost painful delicacy of conscience the events that led to his wrestling with sin, his temptations, and his conversion. Although at times he despaired of God's mercy, he nonetheless was delivered from guilt and fear through the compassionate mediation of Christ. His first wife brought him two pious books that set him on the right path. The course of his non-Conformist martyrdom, self-elected and stoically borne, is then related. His call to the ministry, his tribulations as well as raptures in it, and his experiences during his long imprisonment in Bedford Jail, highlight the last part of the book. The whole of the title reads *Grace Abounding to the Chief of Sinners, or the brief Relation of the exceeding Mercy of God in Christ to his poor Servant John Bunyan.*

GRAINS (1936), by Rabindranath Tagore. See TAGORE, RABIN-DRANATH.

GRAMMAR OF LOVE, THE (1934), by Ivan Bunin. See GENTLE-MAN FROM SAN FRANCISCO, THE, by Ivan Bunin.

GRAN GALEOTO, EL (1881), by José Echegaray. See GREAT GALEOTO, THE, by José Echegaray.

GRANDMOTHERS, THE (1927), by Glenway Wescott. This novel is told through the reminiscences of Alwyn Tower. The youth has removed himself from an unfriendly American midwestern background, and gone to Europe. Nostalgic, he leafs through a book of family portraits, and from the faces of his ancestors, of pioneer stock, he reconstructs their lives—sad, frustrated, and full of loneliness.

Apartment in Athens (1945) deals with the 1943 Nazi occupation of Greece. A family of Greeks silently analyze the character of a German officer lodged among them; and in the end the mother determines that her children shall participate in the secret resistance movement.

GRANTH, THE (16th c.). *The Granth,* the sacred book of the Sikhs of India, was compiled by Arjun, the fifth Guru, in the late sixteenth century. It includes verses of Kabir, a deeply spiritual religious teacher and gifted poet; of Nanak, his disciple; and of other Gurus and writers. The tenth Guru made additions to *The Granth,* then declared he was the last Guru, or sage; hereafter *The Granth* was to be the only teacher.

The chief point of doctrine is the unity of a Supreme Being. The work is divided into thirty-one sections, or *Rags,* containing the teachings of the Gurus. All dwell on the vanity of misspent lives devoted to meaningless ends and, conversely, on the desirability of virtue and thoughtfulness. Kabir asks: "Why do men cling to covetousness and waste the jewel of their lives?" He regarded the earthly life as a torment and a vanity: "The life in the world is like a dream. Considering it as true, we make friendship with it, abandoning the treasure of virtue." The liturgical poet remarks on the emptiness of formal religion. "Within his heart is filthiness, though he bathe at a Tirtha. . . . What then is true piety?" "If by immersion in the water salvation be obtained, know that the frogs bathe continually."

Nanak, wishing to do away with the superstitions and abuses of the Hindu religion, taught that there is only one God, who may be worshiped by all men, regardless of race or caste. He stressed the virtues of truthfulness and kindness to the poor. Connected to the Temple at Amritsar is a soup kitchen, to make clear that loyalty to the one God of all men carries with it care for the needy.

A copy of *The Granth* is the center of worship in every Sikh house of prayer; services are very simple, consisting of reading the scriptures and prayers. At their most holy temple, Amritsar, *The Granth* is read continuously.

GRAPES OF WRATH, THE (1939), by John Steinbeck. This realistic novel traces the Joad family, one of many Oklahoma dust-bowl dwellers driven from the land by poverty and drought. Enticed by leaflets advertising employment in California, they make the long trek in a dilapidated car, only to find a more oppressive economic system. The book, rich in character portrayal, contains numerous tragic stories. Tom Joad becomes involved in a murder, and determines to carry on the labor-organizing work of Casey, an ex-preacher who was killed by vigilantes. Dull-witted Noah and weak-willed Connie desert the caravan, the latter leaving his wife Rose of Sharon to give birth to a stillborn child. Lusty old Grampa and weary, religious Granma die. But Ma, brave and tenacious, articulates the determination of the jobless to keep on fighting. The bitterness and indignation of this contemporary classic permeated social thinking and had an influence on legislation.

Tortilla Flat (1935) is an epic of the *paisanos* of the Spanish section of California. The ne'er-do-well Danny inherits two small houses, and numerous picturesque friends. This group of superstitious, amoral, pleasure-loving yet stoic personages dissipates after his death.

Of Mice and Men (1937) is a tragedy set in motion by three itinerant workers' dreams of a house of their own. George Milton is the self-appointed guardian of the simple-witted giant Lennie Small. On a Salinas Valley ranch the two meet Candy, a broken old man whose meager savings seem enough to secure a piece of land for the three. Unfortunately, Lennie murders the promiscuous wife of Curley, the boss's son, accidentally using his enormous strength when she tricks him into embracing her. George kills his friend to save him from lynchers' vengeance.

The Long Valley (1938) is a volume of short stories. It contains two previously published pieces: "The Red Pony," episodes in the maturing personality of Jody Tiflin, whose first knowledge of tragedy is the death of his beloved pony; and "Saint Katy the Virgin," an ironic parable narrating the medieval conversion of a pig.

Many of Steinbeck's later novels have been symbolic social statements. *The Pearl* (1948) tells of a Mexican fisherman whose great wealth, suddenly acquired by finding a large pearl, brings unhappiness upon his people.

GRASS ROOF, THE (1931), by Younghill Kang. The opening of this story has the quality of an idyl, for it tells of a little boy's life in Song-Dune-Chi, a lovely Korean valley where the most respected man was the poet and the philosopher. As the tale goes on, the idyl is broken—the passions of greed and hatred enter into the land with the Japanese, and the end is a tragic drama. Han Chung-pa's account of his own life describes the members of his family:

his old grandmother, his happy-go-lucky uncle, his poet uncle, his playmates. The boy, it was thought, would be a poet, but the seizure of the land by the Japanese changed his ambition, though it involved rebellion against those he loved most. He ran away to Seoul—his journey there on foot was full of incident and color—to gain Western learning. He then went to other Eastern countries; then realized that he must leave the East to learn the West, and so made his way to America. It is an adventurous tale, told with the utmost sensibility, of the struggle for life, truth, and beauty.

The story continues in another book, *East Goes West: The Making of an Oriental Yankee* (1937). Han Chung-pa broke forever with his placid Korean homeland and the unhurried life of scholarly ancestors to start a new existence in New York. The transplanting process was one filled with struggle, misunderstandings, near tragedy, and a vast amount of humor.

The Grass Roof has been translated into several languages: *Tsodang* is the Oriental title; *Au Pays du Matin Calme,* French; *Das Grasdach,* German.

GRAUWE VOGELS (1937), by Arthur van Schendel. See SCHENDEL, ARTHUR VAN.

GREAT CIRCLE (1933), by Conrad Aiken. See AIKEN, CONRAD.

GREAT EXPECTATIONS (1861), by Charles Dickens. Philip Pirrip (Pip), as a boy, has great expectations of becoming a gentleman. His dreams are realized, but he finds they were shallow. Through a series of fateful circumstances, he changes from a boy of false standards to a man of character. Pip is an orphan living with his sister (twenty years older than himself) and brother-in-law, Mr. and Mrs. Joe Gargery. In his youth, he is influenced by eccentric Miss Havisham, who was jilted by her lover on her wedding night; and her adopted niece, Estella, who has been brought up to hate and torture men. Pip's great expectations are realized when he is given a fortune by an unknown benefactor. He forsakes his humbler friends, moves to London and proceeds to become a gentleman. Later, he learns that a convict, Abel Magwitch, alias Provis, whom he had helped years earlier, is his benefactor and is also the father of Estella. Pip's dreams fade with this knowledge. When he is about to be arrested for bad debts, kind-hearted Joe Gargery saves him. Pip returns home, turns to honest work, and changes his ways. He is reunited with Estella, his early love, when her husband, Bentley Drummle, dies. Other characters are: Biddy, who becomes Joe's second wife; the Pocket family; Matthew, Sarah, and Herbert (Pip's good friend); Uncle Pumblechook; Dolge Orlick, the murderer of Pip's sister; and Mr. Jaggers. According to Dickens' biographer, John Forster, the happy ending was contrived on the advice of Bulwer-Lytton. The novel was made into a successful film in 1948.

GREAT GALEOTO, THE (1881), by José Echegaray. This three-act melodrama in verse popularized the name of Echegaray so far and wide that it was largely responsible for bringing him the Nobel Prize. It is the dramatization of gossip. When middle-aged Don Julian, married to young Teodora, brings into his distinguished and blissful household his protégé, the young Ernesto, people soon begin to voice innuendoes and pointed jibes. As a result Ernesto, who is extremely grateful to the couple, becomes embroiled in quarrels and even in a duel with a certain viscount. In trying to prevent it, Teodora commits certain indiscretions and adds fuel to the flaming gossip. Don Julian challenges the viscount, and dies as a result of wounds received in the duel. Teodora's relatives want to drive Ernesto from the house, but he takes care of her and ends by marrying her.

GREAT GATSBY, THE (1925), by Francis Scott Fitzgerald. Jay Gatsby lives mysteriously in an expensive Long Island colony in 1922, playing lavish host to hundreds of people. He is rumored to be everything from ex-German spy to murderer. Nick Carraway lives next to Gatsby, and Nick's cousin Daisy, with her husband, the wealthy but crude Tom Buchanan, live nearby. To Nick, Gatsby discloses part of his story: Daisy's marriage to Tom had followed a brief love affair between Gatsby and her before the war. Gatsby persuades Nick to bring them together, and their former love seems still to exist. Slowly the whole structure of Gatsby's life becomes clear. Born James Gatz, of poor midwestern background, his wealth·has come from sinister transactions. Gatsby's dream of regaining Daisy is frustrated when Tom wins her back. Then Daisy, driving Gatsby's car, fatally injures Tom's mistress Myrtle Wilson, never learning her identity. The car is traced. Gatsby, remaining silent to shield Daisy, is ambushed and shot by the dead woman's husband. Gatsby's fair-weather friends disappear. At his funeral there are only Nick, Gatsby's aged father, and one strange frequenter of the former Gatsby entertainments.

GREAT GOD BROWN, THE (1926), by Eugene O'Neill. See MOURNING BECOMES ELECTRA, by Eugene O'Neill.

GREAT HUNGER, THE (1916), by Johan Bojer. The story of Peer Holm, in this novel by the distinguished Norwegian novelist, is the quest of a man for his soul. Bojer is a devoutly religious man, and his hero is a composite of Prometheus, Job, and St. Francis. Like Prometheus he must suffer for his virtue, like Job he must face his trials with meekness and unswerving faith, like St. Francis he must return good for evil, bread for stones. The tale concerns Peer Holm, a man brought up in poverty. After much struggle and privation, during which he turns from God, he has succeeded in acquiring an education, in becoming a great engineer. He acquires culture, wealth, power and love. Yet somehow he is dissatisfied with himself, knowing full well that he has not achieved what he wishes most; and what this is mysteriously eludes him. He at last loses health, wealth and power and becomes a broken, disillusioned man. The poverty he knew as a child again sucks him in. Only in the midst of sorrow does he at last realize what he has been seeking, and he then reads the riddle of human existence. It is very simple: Christian love. He reaches truth in the lightning flash of revelation that comes with a crisis. His dearly beloved child is killed by a fiendish dog belonging to the feuding neighbor on the adjoining farm. Instead of seeking justice or vengeance, he sees the meaning of the Golden Rule. Although he and his family will have to go without food themselves, he realizes that his brutal neighbors are starving, and he secretly brings them his produce which he has put aside for the spring sowing.

GREAT MEADOW, THE (1930), by Elizabeth Madox Roberts. See TIME OF MAN, THE, by Elizabeth Madox Roberts.

GREAT RECONSTRUCTION, by Francis Bacon. See NOVUM ORGANUM, by Francis Bacon.

GREAT SYNTAXIS (ca. 125–150), by Ptolemy of Alexandria. See ALMAGEST, by Ptolemy of Alexandria.

GREAT WAR, THE (1912–1913), by Ricarda Huch. See HUCH, RICARDA.

GREAT WRATH, THE (1906), by Olof Högberg. This Swedish historical novel pictures Norrland, the vast forest country between the Dale River in Sweden and the Finnish border, at the end of Sweden's period of greatness, the reign of Charles XI (ending 1697) and that of Charles XII (1718). It is a work of epic proportions, in which tales, legends and myths abound, with supernatural powers represented by the mystical Gray Hunter of the Ångerman country, who constantly intervenes in the destinies of people. The plot of the book is the essentially democratic struggle between the inherited pagan culture of the district and the civilization coming from the South; or "between the great common people on one side and the officials and clergy on the other." Its central idea is wholly modern, and its interest far beyond the purely literary. Written by a thinker of lowly origin who understood the peasant's mode of thought, the work reveals both the imagination of the poet and the insight of the scholar. Furthermore, the novel is a rich source for students of folklore, both local and variants of Norwegian and Russian traditions that traveled over the region. Ethnographic and cultural-historical, it describes the breaking up of an age-old society. The value of *The Great Wrath* is enhanced by its archaic style of unusual expressions and constructions which faithfully reproduce the bold, simple speech of the people and the elegant, pompous language of the officials. The novel is the masterpiece of a creative writer. (Cp. Topsöe-Jensen in *Scandinavian Literature.*)

GREATCOAT, THE (1842), by Nikolay Vasilyevich Gogol. See CLOAK, THE, by Nikolay Vasilyevich Gogol.

GREEK ANTHOLOGY, THE (10th c). This collection, known also as the *Palatine Anthology,* was made in the tenth century, and includes in its fifteen books some 4500 poems by nearly 300 poets, representing over 1000 years of Greek poetry. The original basis of the collection was the much smaller compilation made about 60 B.C. by the accomplished Hellenic poet Meleager, who had been born in the Judean town of Gadara. This original anthology Meleager called the *Garland;* in his own poetic introduction to it he says:

> Whereunto many blooms brought Anyte,
> Wild flags; and Maero many—lilies white;
> And Sappho few, but roses.

Included are 131 of his own poems, some of the most sensitive and whimsical of the erotic epigrams. About the *Garland* as a core various additions were subsequently made until the *Anthology* reached its present proportions. There are relatively few poems by the earlier poets, such as Simonides, who is represented by his epitaphs on the Greeks who fell fighting the Persians. The Alexandrine poets who developed the epigram more nearly are done justice. Probably of greatest general interest are the amatory epigrams of Book V. The whole has had a tremendous influence on modern European poetry.

GREEN BAY TREE, THE (1924), by Louis Bromfield. John Shane built a steel plant in the Midwest, amassing a fortune and creating an industrial empire. In the heart of it, he erected a pretentious house. Upon his death, the family begins to disintegrate; but his widow, the proud and shrewd Julia, persists in maintaining the elegance of "Shane's Castle." Two neurotic daughters, Lily and Irene, will have none of it: Lily finds escape in pleasure, Irene wishes to become a nun but is forbidden. The novel principally concerns the beautiful Lily and her Bohemian amours. The governor of the state is in love with her. Although she is pregnant, she refuses his proposal of marriage, and goes to Paris, where her son is born. Upon Julia's death, she returns, to find the mill workers on strike, aided by Irene. Lily is attracted by the leader, Stepan Krylenko, but when the strike fails, he moves on to other mills. Lily returns to Paris, and, after World War I, marries a cabinet minister to secure companionship during her remaining years. Irene enters a convent.

This novel, Bromfield's first, was dramatized in 1927 as *The House of Women*.

Bromfield followed *The Green Bay Tree* with three other novels concerning the same characters, *Possession* (1925), *Early Autumn* (1926), and *A Good Woman* (1927). *Early Autumn,* the Pulitzer Prize winner of the tetralogy (*Escape*), concerns Olivia, of the Chicago McDonnells, who marries without love into the blue-blooded Pentland family, of Massachusetts. Her husband Anson is a pedantic bore. There are two children; Jack, an invalid, and an eighteen-year-old, Sybil. John Pentland is a bitter man. Mrs. Pentland is insane, and he is in love with Mrs. Soames, an elderly neighbor. He despises his son Anson, and spitefully controls the family fortune. Olivia falls in love with Michael O'Hare, a Boston politician. After her son's death, she decides to wait only until Sybil's marriage, before escaping with him. But her father-in-law successfully thwarts her intentions, and she is forced to give up her lover and remain with the Pentlands, who, it develops, are not in fact of distinguished lineage at all.

GREEN COCKATOO, THE (1899), by Arthur Schnitzler. See SCHNITZLER, ARTHUR.

GREEN HENRY (1854–1855; revised in 1880), by Gottfried Keller. In the long row of the typically Teutonic "Bildungsroman" (educational novel) *Green Henry* is the most outstanding link between Goethe's *Wilhelm Meister* (q.v.) and Thomas Mann's *Magic Mountain* (q.v.). The long novel, in four volumes, is the story of a young man searching for his call, his real self. The action moves slowly from Henry's childhood in his native Switzerland, stormy school years, artistic apprenticeship in Zürich, desultory university studies and unsuccessful attempts at painting in Munich, despair and starving, to final return to his native town as a sedate official. Somewhat formless in construction, the novel is rich in charming episodes, striking character portraits, chaste and moving love scenes. The picture of the hero's mother, a sturdy Swiss woman, is no less a masterpiece than the delicate pastel of the country teacher's ethereal daughter Ann or the contrasting picture of the deft, full-blooded and mature Judith, both women reciprocating Henry's feelings. Long after childlike Ann's premature death, Judith's tender, amorous friendship cheers the lonely life of the bachelor, who, after realizing his failure as a painter, succeeds in securing through strenuous efforts a respected place in a well-ordered community.

The life and tribulations of Henry are autobiographical of Keller's own youthful efforts to become a painter in Munich; and just as the aging Henry returned to "respectability" in Switzerland, so his creator, after having met with moderate literary success in Berlin, went back to his native Zürich and held for fifteen years a minor bureaucratic position as a city clerk. It is mainly as the undisputed master of the novelette that Gottfried Keller holds his eminent position in German letters. Poetic invention, wealth and depth of ideas, subtle humor, and a crystalline, melodious, highly original prose style characterize the two volumes of Keller's long short stories, published under the title *The People of Seldwyla* (1856 and 1874).

GREEN HILLS OF AFRICA, THE (1935), by Ernest Hemingway. See SUN ALSO RISES, THE, by Ernest Hemingway.

GREEN MANSIONS (1904), by William Henry Hudson. The plot of *Green Mansions* concerns itself principally with the story of Rima, a child of Nature, who is discovered in her Guiana jungle solitude by Abel, a sophisticated Venezuelan vagabond from Caracas. She is unspoiled and wild, like the animals, a sort of feminine equivalent of Tarzan. She knows neither the evil nor guile common to all civilized humans. This gives her supernatural stature in the eyes of the worldly Abel, who falls passionately in love with her. Toward the end Rima is burned to death by hostile and corrupt Indian tribesmen, whom, to protect her beloved birds and animals, she had driven from their hunting ground by preying upon their superstitious fears. Abel's dream bursts like a soap bubble. The book's qualities are of a striking and original sort. It has enchantment; its pages are haunted by an unearthly perception of beauty and a wonderment that stir the imagination. *Green Mansions* is the work of a great naturalist and a poet in prose. In Kensington Garden, London, there is a statue of Rima, by the sculptor Jacob Epstein, erected as a memorial to W. H. Hudson.

GREEN PASTURES, THE (1930), by Marc Connelly. Opening in the Louisiana Sunday School of the Reverend Deshee, *The Green Pastures* narrates the highlights of Old Testament stories as conceived in simple Negro folklore —the Creation, Adam and Eve, Noah, Moses, and the later Babylonian captivity. A rich, but always reverent humor pervades the play. Outstanding is the characterization of "de Lawd God Jehovah." This subtle study of His transition from a God of Wrath to a God of Mercy attains, against the naïveté of the play as a whole, a larger theology of a God compelled to change at the need and demand of Man.

The play is based on Roark Bradford's *Ol' Man Adam an' His Chillun* stories (1928). Among Connelly's other productions is *Beggar on Horseback*

(1924) written with George Kaufman, a play which satirizes society's repression of the artist, through the story of the composer Neil McRae.

GREENLAND (1942), by Vilhjálmur Stefánsson. See STEFÁNSSON, VILHJÁLMUR.

GRENADIERS, THE (1819), by Heinrich Heine. See HEINE, HEINRICH.

GRETTIS SAGA (late 13th c.). See NJÁL SAGA, THE.

GREY BIRDS (Eng. tr. 1939), by Arthur van Schendel. See SCHENDEL, ARTHUR VAN.

GROWTH OF THE SOIL (1917; Eng. tr. 1920), by Knut Hamsun. The hero, Isak, personifies the primitive man, vital and persevering. In the author's words: "The man is strong and coarse, he has a red, wiry beard, and scars show in his face and on his hands—these disfigurements, do they tell of toil or fight?" Isak knows what he is after. He wants a place on which to establish a home. He finds himself a strip of land in the wilderness. At first he sleeps like an animal under an overhanging rock. Then he goes to work and breaks ground. He makes birch shingles and carries them to the distant village and brings back with him victuals and a few tools and kitchen utensils. Finally he acquires three goats. This rouses him to the necessity of building a sod hut, which he shares with the goats. From the possession of a house and three goats to his need of a woman to help him and bear him children is a logical step. One day in the spring, a strong, coarse-faced young woman, disfigured by a harelip, chances to pass by. Her name is Inger. Isak invites her in, and she stays, for she too is lonely. Tragedy finally mars the primitive home. The third child of Inger and Isak, a girl, is born with a harelip in consequence of a curse put on Inger by a jealous old woman of the village. Recalling her own wretchedness because of this deformity, Inger kills the child immediately after its birth. Her deed is discovered, and she is sentenced to eight years in prison, but pardoned before her time is up. She returns changed and citified, her harelip removed by surgical skill. She is no longer fit for primitive life and falls into loose ways. The rest of the story tells of Isak's growing prosperity and of his decline as a primitive man. *The Growth of the Soil* was an instantaneous success and won for its author the Nobel Prize for Literature in 1920.

GRUNDTVIG, NICOLAI FREDERICK SEVERIN (1783–1872). Founder of the religious antidogma movement which bears his name, Grundtvig was to the general public undoubtedly the most influential spiritual and intellectual Danish personality of the first half of the nineteenth century. His fellow-countryman Sören Kierkegaard's influence came later. Opposed alike to rationalism and apostolic or post-apostolic doctrines of the Church, he preached the "living word," and a "joyful Christianity," with a personal faith in Christ as the central figure in the world's development. He wrote over a hundred volumes in all branches of literature, in which, however, content and thought were the all-important factors: form counted little. He published a work on Norse mythology; he translated Saxo's *Chronicles of Denmark* (q.v.)

from the Latin; did Snorri Sturluson's *Heimskringla* (q.v.) and the Anglo-Saxon *Beowulf* (q.v.) into Danish; and in general called attention to the earliest English literature. Today Grundtvig is best known as the founder of the Scandinavian folk high school, a peculiarly Northern type of a popular institution for adults, which was to represent a "fusion of national and Christian elements." The folk high schools, for common, nonacademic citizens are now numerous in Scandinavia, especially in Denmark, and in several other countries. Grundtvig strengthened national feeling, furthered the cause of the people, and revived religious life in Denmark. For a time he was forbidden to preach in Denmark, but he died a bishop.

GUARD OF HONOR (1948), by James Gould Cozzens. See LAST ADAM, THE, by James Gould Cozzens.

GUARDSMAN, THE (Eng. tr. 1924), by Ferenc Molnar. See LILIOM, by Ferenc Molnar.

GUERMANTES WAY, THE (1920), by Marcel Proust. See REMEMBRANCE OF THINGS PAST, by Marcel Proust.

GUEST, EDGAR A. (1881–   ). The philosophical newspaper poet is famous for his homely verse, collected in such books as *Just Folks* (1917). His simple morality and fondness for the ordinary aspects of life are revealed in such pieces as "The Pup," "The Old Time Family," and "The Little Church."

GUEST FRIEND, THE (1820), by Franz Grillparzer. See GOLDEN FLEECE, by Franz Grillparzer.

GUIDE FOR THE PERPLEXED, THE (1190), by Maimonides (Rabbi Moses ben Maimon). This work is an effort by one of the greatest and most famous Jewish minds in all history to resolve the doubts of learned and pious men bewildered by "the ambiguous and figurative expressions in the holy writings." The author, born in Cordova in 1135, as a youth studied rabbinism, science, mathematics, astronomy, philosophy, metaphysics and medicine. Though his family was forced out of Cordova in 1148 by a fanatical Mohammedan sect, to settle ultimately near Cairo in 1165, the youth forgot no part of his learning, and continued preparation for the important works that bear his name. In Egypt he became court physician for Saladin, refusing a similar position offered him by the English Richard Coeur de Lion. In one of his letters that have come down to us, he bemoans his constant attendance on the ill of the court and the populace which renders his application to scholarship so brief and difficult. When he died, in 1204, he was acclaimed as the most distinguished son of Israel since the first biblical Moses.

The works of Maimonides include a *Treatise on the Jewish Calendar* (1158); a book on logic (1158); the extraordinary *Letter on Apostasy,* which permitted a Jew to pretend to accept another faith if necessary to save his life, except if he were compelled thereby to commit murder, incest, or idol-worship; the *Commentary on the Mishnah* (1168), containing his syncretization of Hellenism and Hebraism, and the "Thirteen Creeds" found in the synagogue ritual; the *Mishnah Torah* (1180), a tremendous fourteen-book compendium and codification of Jewish law and religion; a *Treatise on Resurrection*—asserting his belief therein (1191); the *Letter to the Rabbis of Marseilles,* denouncing superstition (1194); many medical, scientific, and rabbinic treatises; and the famed *Guide,* written first in Arabic, translated by an admirer into Hebrew, and then given its Hebrew name, *Moreh Nebuchim.*

The Guide for the Perplexed is an effort to demonstrate the oneness of reason and faith, to prove Judaism in harmony with philosophy, and to reconcile the philosophy of Aristotle, who was the writer's model of perfection in reasoning, with everything in the *Bible* and the *Talmud.* To this end Maimonides takes up every problem of law and wording in the *Bible,* and covers all matters of contemporary philosophic and theologic discussion. That the scientific and rational spirit thus introduced into the study of Judaism was to bear extensive fruit is attested by the vast influence exercised by Maimonides on such Christian theologians as Thomas Aquinas and Albertus Magnus, and on Benedict Spinoza.

Above all, Maimonides is to be remembered for a liberalism extraordinary in his period, and especially for a member of the most persecuted of races. He refused to permit his coreligionists to call either Christianity or Mohammedanism unworthy faiths, with any touch of idolatry; on the contrary, he declared that the teachings both of Jesus and Mohammed "help to bring mankind to perfection."

GUITAR AND CONCERTINA (1891), by Gustav Fröding. See FRÖDING, GUSTAV.

GULISTĀN, THE (ca. 1240), by Saʻdī (Sheik Muslih-uddīn). Saʻdī, like Hafiz, was a native of Shīrāz, and was also intellectually and artistically a product of its refined culture during the twelfth century. By whatever yardstick we measure his genius, Saʻdī remains one of the world's great poets. Written in a curious verse and prose combination, *The Gulistān,* also called the *Garden of Roses,* consists of short tales and anecdotes, divided into eight sections. These are: the morals of kings; the morals of dervishes; the excellence of contentment; the advantages of taciturnity; love and youth; imbecility and old age; the effects of education; and rules for the conduct of life. The fact that this work is still being read with veneration in China as well as in Islamic Africa eight hundred years after his death, is a tribute to his universal appeal. A great traveler, Saʻdī had spent years roaming the three continents, seeking knowledge and truth. It is believed that for some time he was a captive of the Christians then crusading in the Middle East.

GULLIVER'S TRAVELS (1726), by Jonathan Swift. Swift started working on this book apparently around 1720, when the idea was advanced in the Scriblerus Club, of which he was a member. It was to have been incorporated in the "Memoirs of Scriblerus." It has the advantage of being a book of interest to adults because of its satire on man and his institutions, and to children because of its fantasy. It is divided into four parts, told in the first person.

Part I: On May 4, 1699, Lemuel Gulliver, a ship's surgeon, sails from Bristol. After a shipwreck, he swims ashore to find himself on the island of Lilliput, whose inhabitants are no more than six inches high. Here Swift satirizes the meanness of human beings by showing how ridiculous are wars waged by these little people, who take part in them with all seriousness. Political parties are attacked, too. In Lilliput the parties are known by the height of their heels; their greatest controversy involves a vigorous argument about on which end an egg should be broken.

Part II: Gulliver finds himself in Brobdingnag, the natives of which are as tall in proportion to him as the Lilliputians were short. Here, in discussions with the king, England in particular and humanity in general are again attacked. The huge king cannot understand the enormous pretensions and vanities of the little people about whom Gulliver tells him. He denounces them as "the most pernicious race of little odious vermin that nature ever suffered to crawl upon the surface of the earth."

Part III: In this book Gulliver makes sport of the vain endeavors of scientists and philosophers by telling about Laputa, where men forget all common sense and concern themselves in speculative philosophy. In Lagado, the flying island, he sees scientists engaged in all sorts of foolish pursuits, one being the extraction of sunbeams from cucumbers.

Part IV: This contains the most vicious satire of all, and tells of Gulliver's visit to the land of the Houyhnhnms, a race of intelligent horses who are served by a despised, filthy, and degenerate human race known as Yahoos. In the end, Gulliver returns to his wife and family, but finds them unbearable after associating with the Houyhnhnms.

GUY MANNERING (1815), by Sir Walter Scott. The action takes place in Scotland in the middle of the eighteenth century. Guy Mannering, a young Englishman journeying through the country, stops at the home of the Laird of Ellangowan. A son is born to the Laird that night. A student of astrology, Guy forecasts the child's future. He reluctantly reveals that there are two crises impending, one in the child's fifth year and another in his twenty-first. Mannering then goes on his way. The Laird falls into financial difficulties, and is further oppressed by the disappearance of his son at the age of five. His wife dies of shock and he outlives her by only a few years. His daughter, Lucy, is left in the care of Dominie Sampson, an honest old teacher and friend of the family. Mannering, returned to England after years of military service in India, invites Lucy and Dominie to live with him and his daughter, Julia. He is followed to England by Captain Brown, who had served under him. Mannering erroneously suspects Brown of being in love with his wife. In India he had dueled with the Captain on this account, had wounded him and left him for dead. In reality Brown is in love with Julia. Brown is ignorant of the fact that his real name is Harry Bertram, and that he is the son of the Laird of Ellangowan. He had been kidnaped by Glossin, an evil lawyer, who hoped to acquire the Ellangowan estate when there was no heir. This he had accomplished after the death of the Laird. Brown is recognized by the gypsy, Meg Merrilies, who loves the Ellangowan family. She is determined to see Brown restored to his rightful inheritance. Glossin tries to effect a second kidnaping of Brown, but is prevented by Meg and her farmer friend, Dandy Dinmont. Glossin and his accomplice, Hatteraick, are captured and imprisoned. Brown regains his true name and with it the friendship of Mannering. He and Julia are married.

GUYS AND DOLLS (1932), by Damon Runyon. See RUNYON, DAMON.

GUZMÁN DE ALFARACHE (1599, 1604), by Mateo Alemán. Forty-five years after the appearance of *Lazarillo de Tormes* (1554; q.v.), the second, and perhaps second best, picaresque novel of Spanish literature, *Guzmán de Alfarache,* was published by a Sevillian named Mateo Alemán. The immediate success of Part I (1599) brought forth a spurious continuation which stimulated Alemán to write a Part II (1604). Like all picaresque novels, *Guzmán* assumes the form of an autobiography. As a boy, Guzmán escapes from his mother, after the ruin and death of his father, a disreputable Genoese merchant established at Seville. Guzmán finds his way to Madrid, where, first as a kitchen boy and then as an errand boy he learns the ways of a cruel world and is hardened in iniquity. Seizing a good opportunity, he steals a large sum of money with which he is entrusted and runs off to Toledo. There he plays the dandy and gentleman. Tricked out of his money, he enlists for the Italian wars. In Barcelona he again turns sharper and thief, and in desperation turns beggar in Genoa. In Rome a cardinal makes him his page. But Guzmán returns to his tricks and frauds. After losing heavily at cards he leaves. Part I closes with Guzmán servant in the house of the French Ambassador.

In the opening section of Part II Guzmán seems to be thriving as pimp in the utterly degrading atmosphere of the Ambassador's palace. However, his own follies force him to flee. After a tour through Milan, Bologna and Genoa, he is robbed and cheated by one Sayavedra (Alemán's enemy, author of the spurious *Guzmán*). In Madrid Guzmán becomes a merchant and cheats his creditors by a fraudulent bankruptcy. He marries, but his wife dies shortly thereafter, and he studies for the priesthood, only to marry, however, for the second time. Just as he is getting rich, thanks to the beauty of his wife, she deserts him in Seville and elopes with a lover to Italy. Reduced to abject poverty, Guzmán becomes major-domo to a rich widow, fleeces her, and is sent to the galleys, where, in forced retirement, he writes his autobiography. In the end he reveals a conspiracy and is rewarded with his freedom and a full pardon.

At first Alemán thought of calling his book *A Beacon Light of Life,* a most appropriate title for a basically moral book which, in addition, is entertaining, displays profound knowledge of human beings and mirrors faithfully the customs and manners of his times.

GYGES AND HIS RING (1855), by Christian Friedrich Hebbel. In this verse drama, based upon a story by Herodotus, King Kandanles of Lydia is proud of the attractiveness of his wife, Queen Rhodope, as he is of his other possessions. The King invites the young Gyges to view her unclothed beauty, since Gyges possesses a magic ring which renders him invisible in the bedchamber. The Queen, however, learns of the affront, demands of Gyges that King Kandanles die by his hand, after which he is to become her husband. He carries out the plot, but the Queen takes her own life after the marriage. The entire action is permeated by an overpowering sense of conflict, and exhibits Hebbel's preoccupation with the complications of psychological motivations.

Maria Magdalena (1846) shows Hebbel's deep understanding of the tragic. Klara, a simple girl, fearing that a scandal will result after the man whom she loves has left her, gives herself to a second man. He deceives her, and out of a passionate sense of her own and her father's honor, she puts an end to her existence by drowning. She is a helpless victim of ruthlessness and is judged by an exacting moral code. *Herod and Mariamne* (1850) depicts the passions and hatreds of the two characters against an impressive background of Oriental splendor. The trilogy, *The Nibelungs* (1862) is an artistic, dramatic recasting of the old Germanic epic, *The Nibelungenlied* (q.v.). Hebbel's diaries (published 1885–1887) afford a means of delving into both the personality of the author and the philosophical substance of his works.

HAKON JARL (1807), by Adam Gottlob Oehlenschläger. See ALADDIN, by Adam Gottlob Oehlenschläger.

HALEVI, JUDAH BEN SAMUEL (1086–1141). Probably the greatest devotional poet of the Middle Ages, Judah Halevi (the Levite), was born in Toledo, Spain, in 1086, and died, reputedly under the hoofs of an Arab's horse, before the walls of his beloved Jerusalem in 1141. He wrote light lyrics on love, paeans to his Maker, and above all, passionate expressions of Israel's devotion to the Holy Land. More than 300 of his poems have been incorporated in the Hebrew books of prayer. In his day Christians and Mohammedans were engaged in a struggle for the mastery of Spain, with the Jews expecting only to be ground down by both sides. The Crusades seemed the final assurance of Israel's doom. It was the love and optimism of Judah's verses that sustained the waning spirit of his people. Many of his poems have been translated by Heine, Zangwill, and other writers in various tongues. The versatile poet earned his livelihood as a physician, but he was renowned for his Talmudic and general learning and for a notable philosophic and theological work, called *Kitab al-Khazari* in Arabic and *Ha-Kuzari* in Hebrew. This treatise, in five dialogues, is framed in the dramatic story of the King of the Khazars, who after long deliberation became a convert to Judaism. Though it contains much abstruse and technical material, it is essentially poetic in its effort to prove that Israel is the heart of mankind. Judaism is favorably contrasted with Christianity and Mohammedanism. This book, which is to be found today in complete English translation, has taken its place among the contributions to medieval philosophy. But the author is best remembered as the greatest Hebrew poet following the prophets and singers of the Old Testament.

HAMBURG DRAMATURGY (1767–1768), by Gotthold Ephraim Lessing. See NATHAN THE WISE, by Gotthold Ephraim Lessing.

HAMLET (1603), by William Shakespeare. *Hamlet* was published in 1603 in quarto and again in 1604, but had been acted before these dates. The story was known to Elizabethans through François de Belleforest's *Histoires Tragiques* and Saxo Grammaticus. An earlier, now lost, play about Hamlet had been written by 1589, possibly by Thomas Kyd. Shakespeare's *Hamlet* is the most famous play of the modern world.

The story is laid in Denmark. Hamlet, the royal Prince, is mourning the death of his father, and the hasty marriage of his mother, Gertrude, to Claudius; her husband's brother, now king. The former king's ghost has appeared to sentinels on the battlements of the castle at Elsinore. They report this to Hamlet, who waits to verify their statements. He meets the ghost and learns that his suspicions about his uncle's bad character are true: Claudius had killed his brother while he was sleeping in an orchard so that he could marry the queen and seize the kingdom. Hamlet makes his friend, Horatio, and the officer, Marcellus, swear to secrecy regarding the appearance of the ghost. The ghost demands revenge and Hamlet swears he will execute it. However, his brooding and his melancholy, together with his soul searching, and his stated fear that the ghost may be a devil, prevent him from immediate action. Hamlet feigns madness. The court takes this to be caused by his love for Ophelia, daughter of the chancellor, Polonius.

Hamlet hears that players have come to the castle, and asks them to give a drama, re-enacting the murder of his father, before the king and queen. Claudius, as he watches the play unfold, is tormented by his conscience. Hamlet, observing him closely, is now sure he is guilty. The king leaves the play hastily and is followed by the queen, who asks for an interview with her son. The king, now angry and suspicious, arranges for Hamlet to be sent to England. He plans to have him executed there. When Hamlet visits the queen, she begins the interview by upbraiding him. He turns on her and accuses her of falsity to the memory of her dead husband. Polonius, always meddlesome, is hiding behind the arras in the queen's chamber. Hamlet, detecting his presence and mistaking him for Claudius, stabs him to death. He departs for England with two courtiers, Rosencrantz and Guildenstern.

Ophelia, in the meantime, goes mad, overwhelmed by the death of her father, Hamlet's strange actions toward her, and her brother's long-continued absence in France. Her brother, Laertes, returns, incensed over the murder of his father and vowing revenge. Claudius puts the blame on Hamlet. To her brother's grief, Ophelia drowns herself. Hamlet's ship, in the meantime, is attacked by pirates, who send him back to Denmark. When he arrives he witnesses Ophelia's funeral procession. He and Laertes, both frantic with sorrow, leap into her grave and fight over which shall be chief mourner. Claudius, knowing Laertes' desire for revenge, suggests that he challenge Hamlet to a fencing match. Not suspecting that the king has had Laertes' sword tip poisoned, Hamlet accepts.

In the match, the queen, to do her son honor, drinks to him from a poisoned cup the king had prepared for Hamlet. Laertes wounds Hamlet, and in the scuffle they exchange swords and Hamlet wounds Laertes. The queen dies; Laertes falls, and, dying, confesses Claudius is to blame and asks Hamlet's forgiveness. Hamlet stabs the king and bids Horatio tell Fortinbras, Prince of Norway, whose martial music is heard in the distance, that he has his dying voice for his election as next king. Fortinbras arrives after the death of the young prince and promises to give him a soldier's funeral.

Sir Laurence Olivier's film version of *Hamlet* is one of the most masterful dramatizations of this tragedy.

HAMLET OF A. MACLEISH, THE (1928), by Archibald MacLeish. See MacLEISH, ARCHIBALD.

HAND-MADE FABLES (1920), by George Ade. See ADE, GEORGE.

HANNELE (1893), by Gerhart Hauptmann. This short play marks the author's transition from Naturalism to neo-Romanticism: poetic imagination and verse are blended with realistic description of social environment. Hannele, a young girl whose mother has died, is so brutally beaten by her stepfather Mattern that she tries to drown herself in an icy pond. Brought to the village almshouse by her teacher Gottwald, she is put to bed in the same room with a turbulent crew of paupers. The scenery fades and the spectator is presented with the girl's feverish hallucinations. In her delirium Hannele imagines her mother has come from heaven, angels enter and sing, and the schoolmaster finally appears as Christ. Suddenly the stage darkens and the reality of the almshouse returns. Hannele is dead. That Hauptmann had outgrown the extreme Naturalism of his earlier days when he wrote the play, can clearly be seen from the fact that he originally conceived a third act which was supposed to occur in heaven, but was never published.

HANS BRINKER or, **THE SILVER SKATES** (1865), by Mary Mapes Dodge. In a little Dutch village on the Zuyder Zee lives the modest family Brinker. Father Raff Brinker is employed on the dykes, and during a threatened inundation he falls from the scaffolding. After that he never works again; his mind and memory are gone, and he becomes a strange, silent man. The Brinkers, however, if poor in worldly goods, are blessed with two splendid, unspoiled children—Hans, who is fifteen, and Gretel, who is twelve. On the occasion of a gala skating match held on the birthday of Mevrouw van Gleck, wife of the burgomaster of the town, the prize is to be a pair of silver skates with silver bells and buckles. The Brinker children have no skates with which to enter the competition, although they are the best skaters in the town. Encouraged by kindly little Hilda van Gleck, Hans and Gretel invest in ice skates; it is Gretel who wins the silver skates. A subsidiary story tells of the cure effected by the famous Dr. Boekman on Raff Brinker. Happy results ensue: Mynherr Brinker recalls the spot where he had buried 1,000 guilders before he lost his memory. He also helps Dr. Boekman find his long-lost son.

HAPPY PRINCE AND OTHER FAIRY TALES, THE (1888; 1891), by Oscar Wilde. Written between 1882 and 1891 as a distraction from Wilde's more serious writing, these stories were first conceived vocally as he wove them out of his fancy for the entertainment of his small children. When they were published they were immediately acclaimed as the most beautifully written stories ever penned for children. For more than fifty years English-speaking people, grown-ups as well as children, have been delighted with the delicate, poetic charm of "The Happy Prince," "The Nightingale and the Rose," "The Selfish Giant," "The Devoted Friend," "The Remarkable Rocket," "The Young King," "The Birthday of the Infanta," "The Fisherman and His Soul," and "The Star-Child," the last four forming the second collection, published as *A House of Pomegranates*. The stories, ostensibly for children, are really for adults, and for literary adults at that. Who else would be able to grasp the brittle irony, the cloying beauty, the undertone of wistfulness and regret over life's cruelties and inexplicabilities? An artful artlessness lingers in their superb musical cadences and faultless imagery. A hothouse quality of unreality, of a vapory combination of Fragonard, Rossetti and Wordsworth, of studied ingenuousness, pervades all these stories. There is also the unmistakable influence of Pre-Raphaelite painting in them, and of Walter Pater's escapist erudition. One's attention is fascinated by the glitter of precious stones, the sheen of metals, the scents of exotic flowers, the pungency of rare spices and the ravishment of beautiful brocades and silks. And, to heighten the antique effect, Wilde evokes the pastoral simplicity of Biblical language. All words are treated musically. A striking device, taken from poetry, the repetition of particular phrases, conjures up soft harmonies and a sensuous languor.

HARD TIMES (1854), by Charles Dickens. This novel is a protest against educators who think only of material things. "Facts, facts, facts," is Thomas Gradgrind's motto. His children, Louisa and Thomas, suffer from his materialistic teachings. Acting on her father's principles, in order to help her weak brother Tom, whom she loves dearly, Louisa enters into a loveless marriage with Josiah Bounderby, an elderly and extremely practical banker. Tom, who is in the employ of the banker, robs him. He casts suspicion on an innocent weaver, Stephen Blackpool. James Harthouse, a heartless young politician, loves Louisa. To escape an affair with him, she goes to her father, who, shocked by the results of his teaching, protects her. She separates permanently from Bounderby. Tom flees the country; Blackpool is cleared of all accusations. Other characters are: M'Choakumchild, the exacting schoolmaster; Mr. Sleary of the circus; Sissy Jupe, daughter of one of the circus performers; Mrs. Sparsit, Bounderby's housekeeper.

HARMONICES MUNDI (1619), by Johann Kepler. See ASTRONOMIA NOVA, by Johann Kepler.

HARP-WEAVER, AND OTHER POEMS, THE (1923), by Edna St. Vincent Millay. See MILLAY, EDNA ST. VINCENT.

HARTZ JOURNEY, THE (1824), by Heinrich Heine. See HEINE, HEINRICH.

HAUPTMANN, GERHARDT (1862–1946). Born in the Silesian mountains, Gerhardt Hauptmann went to the Art Academy in Breslau, later became acquainted with biology and related subjects at the University of Jena, settled in Rome for a while, married early, and finally began writing in one of the northern suburbs of Berlin, where he achieved a rousing success with his first drama, *Before Dawn,* in 1889. The provoking realism of the plot, in which the excesses of the *nouveaux riches,* hereditary alcoholism and lasciviousness, are contrasted with the idealistic hero's high-flown theories of eugenic purity, made the twenty-seven-year-old playwright the undisputed leader of German naturalism. Three years later, in 1892, he reached the peak of the revolutionary new style with his social mass drama *The Weavers* (q.v.), which established him as the leading dramatist on the European continent. Hauptmann's transition to the new romantic trend of the time is first noticeable in *Hannele* (q.v.), the dream vision of an abused dying girl. Three years later he achieved his greatest popular success with his most obviously neo-Romantic play, *The Sunken Bell* (1886), a typical "Künstler drama." The founder Heinrich, after failing to create a great bell, tries to reach his productive aims, aided by the beautiful elf Rautendelein, after he has left wife and children. Autobiographical and romantic elements are equally interwoven in this rather confused symbolic drama, which owes its international success to the beauty of language and the possibilities of elaborate staging. It may be said that after vacillating between the two poles of extreme Naturalism and neo-Romanticism Hauptmann became the master of a more mature realism, less concerned with social problems than with the fate of man. Some of his most effective and lasting plays belong to this phase of his writing. *Drayman Henschel* (1898), a character study of a good-natured, simple-minded man driven to suicide by his evil second wife; and *Rose Berndt* (1903), a modern version of the old familiar Storm-and-Stress theme of the child-murderess.

Besides being Germany's foremost modern dramatist, Hauptmann was a formidable writer of prose and verse epics. Of particular interest to Americans is perhaps the novel *Atlantis* (1912), based on the crisis of his first marriage and the resulting trip to the United States and describing in amazing detail the disaster of the *Titanic* two years before it actually happened. His most important novel is *Fool in Christ, Emanuel Quint* (1910), an effort to retell the story of Christ in modern setting. The hero, Emanuel Quint, the illegitimate son of a cabinetmaker, relives the action of Jesus' life, wandering through the villages of Silesia until, after conflicts with the worldly authorities, he disappears in the distance. Nowhere are the author's deep roots in Silesian mysticism more apparent than in this novel.

Awarded the Nobel Prize for Literature in 1912, Gerhardt Hauptmann has secured a prominent place in the history of modern drama. Hailed as "poet of pity" all over the world, he was the only important man of letters to remain in Germany after Hitler had proclaimed lack of pity as the official policy of that country. Whatever the moral judgment of future historians will be, the uncontested fact is that Hauptmann's plays have been and still are in the standard repertory of the German theater.

HAVELOK THE DANE, THE LAY OF (ca. 1300). In this romance in verse, Havelok, the son of Birkabeyn, King of Denmark, and Goldborough, daughter of Aethelwold, King of England, are mistreated by the men in whose charge their dying fathers left them. Havelok, given to Grim to be drowned, is saved when Grim and his wife recognize him, by the flame from his mouth and a mark on his shoulder, as of royal blood. They take him to England. Working at menial tasks, Havelok wins renown for his diligence and prowess. Godrich, having promised Goldborough's father to carry her to the best man in the realm, marries her to Havelok to degrade her. She also sees the flame from Havelok's mouth and recognizes its import; besides, an angel tells her that she and Havelok will rule England and Denmark. The lovers go to Denmark with Grim, where Ubbe, a Danish earl, sees the flame, knights Havelok, and gives him an army with whose help Havelok becomes king. Godard, who had murdered Havelok's sisters and ordered him drowned, is killed. Overcoming Godrich, Havelok becomes King of England too. He has Godrich burned at the stake. Grim is rewarded by the noble marriages arranged for his daughters. Grimsby, in England, is so named because Grim is said to have landed there.

HAZARD OF NEW FORTUNES, A (1890), by William Dean Howells. Dryfoos, a farmer who has become a rich capitalist, backs a magazine in order to help his son Conrad achieve business experience. When the editor, Basil March, hires the socialist Lindau, Dryfoos orders March to discharge him; March refuses. Then during a strike Conrad and Lindau are killed while trying to maintain order. Grief-stricken, Dryfoos pays for Lindau's funeral, then sells the magazine to March. In this novel, Howells began to train his delicate realistic fiction on social problems. Now a socialist, he turned from portrayals of the "everyday things of life" to the issue of capitalistic exploitation versus social democracy. Not a strong enough writer to meet head-on the theme of class conflict, Howells expressed social criticism in two Utopian romances, *A Traveler from Altruria* (1894), which reveals the ruthless difference between democratic ideals and realities, and *Through the Eye of the Needle* (1907), a sequel which describes the Ethiopian Altruria.

In *The Landlord at Lion's Head* (1897) Howells tells the story of a new, nonethical type of American businessman, Jeff Duggin, proprietor of a New England farm turned fashionable resort. *The Son of Royal Langbirth* (1904) concerns the second generation of this new sort of person. A robber baron's son struggles with the decision of exposing the private misdeeds of his father, a public benefactor.

The Kentons (1902) was Howells' late reaffirmation of simple, small-town American life.

HE WHO GETS SLAPPED (1922), by Leonid Andreyev. This play is outwardly a melodrama showing the gay, swift-moving life of the circus into which comes *He*, a gentleman whose wife and friend have been false to him, and who hopes to escape from life and lose his identity beneath the make-up of a clown. The inner action of the play is symbolic. *He* is really Andreyev; Consuelo, his love, is a pagan fancy of his that he would keep pure at any cost. And Life is the *Gentleman* who has robbed him of all that makes existence worth while. The scene is laid in Briquet's circus. While the clowns are practicing *He* comes and offers his services as a clown to Briquet. Jackson, one of the clowns, gives him the title of *He who gets slapped*, and after that *He* goes by that name. Only Zinida, the lion tamer, Briquet's wife, knows who *He* is. Consuelo, a beautiful bareback rider, believes she is the daughter of Mancini, who calls himself a Count. He is an unscrupulous gambler, and does not hesitate to use her youth and beauty for his own benefit. He plans to marry her to Baron Regnard, an elderly roué. Alfred Benzano, another bareback rider, is in love with Consuelo, but lacks the courage to carry her off. *He* makes love to her, only to be slapped as a clown, but *He* makes a last appeal to Benzano to save Consuelo, urging him to kill the Baron, if necessary. Benzano takes his suggestion in the wrong spirit. At Consuelo's benefit performance *He* has champagne sent in, and while they are drinking toasts poisons Consuelo to save her from the Baron, and then drinks poison himself. The Baron, overcome by Consuelo's death, shoots himself. The play ends with *He* saying that the Baron had loved her so much that he was getting ahead of him even there. But in the hereafter they would know whose she was to be forever.

HEADLONG HALL (1816), by Thomas Love Peacock. See CROTCHET CASTLE, by Thomas Love Peacock.

HEADSMAN, THE (1833), by James Fenimore Cooper. See SPY, THE, by James Fenimore Cooper.

HEARN, LAFCADIO (1850–1904). This Irish-Greek author with an international education found nothing but unhappiness in the United States. He struggled all his life against poverty, ill health, a pathological shyness, and the opprobrium caused by his unorthodox way of living. Always fascinated by Eastern literature, Hearn turned his sensitive perception upon Japan, and wrote many sketches, translations, stories, and observations of his adopted people. *Glimpses of Unfamiliar Japan* (1894) consists of twenty-seven travelogues interpreting the life and customs of "a world of strangeness." The people are seen through the eyes of a nineteenth century exotic who had de-Occidentalized himself.

Chita: A Memory of Last Island (1889) is a vivid description of the destruction by a tidal wave of a Caribbean island.

HEART OF DARKNESS (1902), by Joseph Conrad. The seaman Marlow tells of his harrowing experiences while captain of a little steamer that forged its way up and down the Congo visiting trading posts ot a company that dealt in ivory. The greed and sickness and degeneration of the white agents, the hunger and death and virtual slavery of the natives are incidental background to the particular story of Mr. Kurtz, a kind of genius who in strange ways got more ivory than any of his competitors, and whom some of the tribes and more than one white person adored. He has reveled in forbidden power, but when Marlow meets him is little more than a voice, shrunken in his last tropical illness. He dies on board the steamboat, murmuring, "The horror! the horror!" Marlow takes a packet of letters to the girl back home who mourns him, and in the presence of her pathetic delusions about Kurtz restrains his own opinion. He feels obliged to tell her that the last word her fiancé spoke was her name.

HEART OF MIDLOTHIAN, THE (1818), by Sir Walter Scott. By many considered the finest of Scott's novels, this has fewer characters and less description than usual. The title refers to Tolbooth, the city jail in Edinburgh, the "stony heart" of Midlothian, where Effie Deans is confined on a charge of having murdered her illegitimate baby. Her half-sister, Jeanie, cannot bring herself at the trial to tell the slight lie that will save Effie, but she does go on the long journey to London to get Queen Caroline's pardon. Moreover she is enabled to marry the Presbyterian pastor Reuben Butler. Meanwhile Effie has managed to elope with her seducer, George Staunton, the son of a nobleman. Years later, known as Lady Staunton, she learns that her husband has been shot by a young lad, one of a group of vagabonds, who was actually her lost son, not murdered after all by Meg Murdockson, the midwife, but stolen away by Madge Wildfire, Meg's crazy daughter. The widowed sister now uses her influence at court to help the children of Jeanie. The early chapters of the novel are laid against the background of the Porteous riots; the main plot itself was founded on an actual case.

HEART OF THE WEST (1907), by William Sydney Porter. See PORTER, WILLIAM SYDNEY.

HEARTBREAK HOUSE (1917), by George Bernard Shaw. *Heartbreak House* is one of the most significant and impressive of all Shaw's works. It has already established its lasting qualities. Due to its profound searching of human character, it is no doubt destined to live on every vital stage for years to come. With characters ranging from the upper to the lower classes, representing virtually every walk of life, Shaw contrived a brilliant conversation piece in which the frustrations, distortions, and bewilderments of each are laid bare. Sardonically he did not end the play by any turn of plot, but in the tumult of a droning, thundering air raid, unannounced and undiscussed at any time in the play. This is the only thing which serves to galvanize its characters into true awareness of life. Aged Captain Shotover, one of the most extraordinary characters ever set upon any stage by any dramatist, sounds the warning: "Do you think the laws of God will be suspended in favor of England because you were born in it?"

The other characters of the play are equally adrift. Captain Shotover seeks the seventh degree of concentration in a rum-sustained dotage. Hesione Hushabye, one of the Captain's daughters, dominates her husband and the other men who come under her spell. Hector Hushabye battens his ego by weaving fantastic tales of heroism around him. Lady Utterword, the Captain's other daughter, enjoys her husband's position as a Colonial administrator. Boss Mangan, the great industrialist, is a helpless, overgrown child when the bubble of his vanity and his financial empire is pricked. Mazzini Dunn's passionate and naïve idealism has kept him a victim of exploitation all his life. Ellie Dunn's spectacular revolt is the product of exposure to her father's policy of futility.

HEAVENLY ARCANA (1749–1756), by Emanuel Swedenborg. This principal theological work of the Swedish mystic was finished in 1756, thirteen years after its author, a talented scientist, abandoned science for theology following a supposed personal revelation of God in a London tavern. In his Introduction to the *Arcana,* Swedenborg states his thesis and program with his characteristic forthrightness: ". . . of the Lord's Divine mercy, it has been granted me, now for several years, to be constantly and uninterruptedly in company with spirits and angels, hearing them converse with each other, and conversing with them. Hence it has been permitted me to hear and see things in another life which are astonishing, and which have never before come to the knowledge of any man, nor entered into his imagination. I have there been instructed concerning different kinds of spirits, and the state of souls after death—concerning Hell, or the lamentable state of the faithful—and particularly concerning the doctrine of faith which is acknowledged throughout all Heaven: on which subjects, by the Divine mercy of the Lord, more will be said in the following pages." The mystic then presents, in more than seven thousand pages, his own account of the spiritual significance of creation and an esoteric doctrine of the "spiritual sense." Its most striking parts are those discussing the nature and process of death, the conscious entrance into the interior life, the nature of the soul, Heaven and its joys, Hell and its torments, the harmonious organization of Heaven, the correspondence of the numerous heavenly societies with the different body organs and the senses. Also, he treats of the spirits that inhabit the starry spheres. All these subjects he tries to relate to a true understanding of the Divine Word. This extraordinary personality, comparable in his success as the creator of new religious doctrines to Mary Baker Eddy and Joseph Smith, numbered among his many converts such literary luminaries as Balzac, William Blake, Emerson, Strindberg and Selma Lagerlöf, and so homely a figure as the celebrated Johnny Appleseed, who preached his doctrines in the cabins of frontiersmen.

HECHT, BEN (1894–   ). This literary phenomenon, later the highest-paid motion picture writer of his time, was a jack-of-all-trades after refusing to attend college. Hecht became a well-known Bohemian, iconoclastic writer in post-World War I Chicago, and came into his own with the novel *Erik Dorn* (1921). Erik Dorn, a brilliant but cynical Chicago journalist, has left his devoted wife Anna and taken up with the young artist Rachel Laskin. Rachel deserts him for other admirers, including the radical Emil Tesla, Frank Brander, and prudish George Hazlitt, a lawyer. Dorn goes to Germany and becomes a noted historian, then joins the Marxist, Baron von Stinnes, in a revolutionary moment, just for the excitement. He takes another mistress. Later he meets Hazlitt and kills him in self-defense. Von Stinnes quixotically takes the blame, and commits suicide. Dorn returns to Chicago, to find that Anna has no use for him, and has secured a divorce.

Ben Hecht is a master of the cynical-romantic short story, collected in such volumes as *The Champion from Far Away* (1931) and *A Book of Miracles* (1939). He is author (with Charles MacArthur) of the popular play, *The Front Page* (q.v.).

HEDDA GABLER (1890), by Henrik Ibsen. Critics still debate whether Hedda Gabler is a frustrated woman seeking power or a complete introvert. Aristocratic, the beautiful daughter of a general, she has married George Tessman, a middle-class, plodding professor. She mistakenly believes he has a brilliant future and a large income. When the play opens they have just returned from a six months' honeymoon abroad, during which he has done research work for a book he is planning on medieval history. During their courtship, Hedda had expressed a desire for a particular villa, and Tessman has borrowed the money from Judge Brack to buy it for her. His aunts have mortgaged their annuity to pay for the furniture. Hedda has luxurious tastes and finds herself bored to death, as she confides to her friend and admirer, elderly Judge Brack. Tessman had counted on meeting his increased expenses by obtaining a government appointment which had been promised him, but the Judge tells him that he has a likely rival in Eilert Lövborg. The latter, once a dissipated genius and an admirer of Hedda's, has stopped drinking, reformed, and just published a highly successful book. Thea Elvsted, an old schoolmate of Hedda's, had employed Lövborg to tutor her stepchildren. She is responsible for his reform and has helped him write his book. She confides to Hedda that she has left her home forever to be with Lövborg. Hedda has had an intimate friendship with Lövborg, but when he became too demanding she had threatened him with a pistol and they had separated. Now she is jealous of Thea's interest in him, and when he comes to call on her husband about a second book he is writing she urges them to attend Brack's bachelor party together. Thea is horrified at the thought that Lövborg might succumb to his old craving for alcohol, and would like him to stay away from the party. By a turn of events, Hedda comes into possession of Lövborg's manuscript for his new book. He believes it is lost, and she conceals the fact that she has it. In searching for it he becomes involved in a drunken row with a low woman whom he accuses of its theft. Lövborg, terribly wrought up, tells Thea that he has destroyed the manuscript. He reveals to Hedda that he cannot bear to reveal to Thea the truth that it has been lost in a drunken brawl. Despairing, he contemplates suicide, and Hedda, giving him one of her father's pistols, tells him to do it beautifully. She then deliberately burns his book. To her husband she makes the excuse that she feared Lövborg was trying to undermine his position. In the meantime, Judge Brack discovers that Lövborg has killed himself with one of the general's pistols. He threatens Hedda with this fact, and she, afraid of the consequences if the truth should be made generally known, shoots herself, while Thea and Tessman are planning to reconstruct Lövborg's book from Thea's notes.

HEIDENMAUER, THE (1832), by James Fenimore Cooper. See SPY, THE, by James Fenimore Cooper.

HEIMSKRINGLA (before 1241), by Snorri Sturluson. This is the most important of all the sagas that deal with the kings of Norway. Beginning with legendary times, this work relates in Old Icelandic (Old Norse) the history of the Norwegian kings down to 1177—one interpreter says 1184. It is undoubtedly Snorri's greatest literary achievement, exhibiting, as it does, sound critical judgment, scientific accuracy, and a mastery of style. It describes the careers of royal heroes "on the throne, in Eastern courts and camps, or on forays in distant lands, from the earliest time to the reign of Sverrir" (Brodeur). The sources were: oral tradition, written genealogical records, old songs or narrative lays, poems of court poets, and especially songs sung "before the chiefs themselves or the sons of them; and we hold that true," says Snorri, "which is found in these songs concerning their wayfarings and their battles." The prose sources of Ari the Learned had also been consulted. Snorri's task was the ambitious one of uniting disjointed biographical monographs on Norwegian monarchs into an organically continuous history, with courses of life determined by cause and effect, the deeds of one generation following logically upon those of the preceding one. The *Heimskringla* has been called by Eiríkr Magnússon the "first pragmatic history ever penned in any Teutonic vernacular." It is a curious irony of fate that the author, having incurred the royal displeasure of King Haakon of Norway for failing to bring Iceland under Norwegian rule, was at the latter's order murdered in Iceland in 1241.

HEINE, HEINRICH (1797–1856). One of the greatest lyric poets of Germany, Heine, born into the Jewish faith and later baptized for expediency, scorned law and business to devote himself to writing. In his writings, despair and bitterness constitute a noticeable undercurrent. As a Romantic, his works are filled with irony which often reaches an unrelenting cynicism. Although not considered one of the leaders of his day in the world of ideas, he was a Republican and was associated with the pro-French Young Germany Movement. Continually mocking himself, society, God and man, and then in turn praising a previously vilified institution or custom, he has been accused of superficiality and incongruity. Heine is best known for his *Book of Songs* (1827) in which he is misleadingly simple to hide his sharp wit. In 1844 appeared his *New Poems*. *Atta Troll* (1847) is a highly romantic quasi-epic poem dealing with a dancing bear, in which the true intention is political. Alternately prose and verse, *The Hartz Journey* (1824) satirizes German philistinism and smugness in his typically caustic, flaying style. The most famous of his ballads, "The Grenadiers" (1819), and his "Lorelei" are continual favorites, up to the present day. Despite the inconsistency and complexity of his thought, much of his poetry contains the elements of typical folk lyric. Some poems gained such popularity that·they are today considered to be folk songs by the German people.

HEINRICH VON OFTERDINGEN, by Novalis. See NOVALIS.

HELENA (1876), by Joaquim Maria Machado de Assis. See DOM CASMURRO, by Joaquim Maria Machado de Assis.

HELIOGABALUS (1920), by George Jean Nathan. See NATHAN, GEORGE JEAN.

HELLENICA (after 362 B.C.), by Xenophon. This Greek history covers the period 411 to 362 B.C. in seven books, and tells of the victory of Sparta in the Peloponnesian War, her subsequent fall and the rise of Thebes to the hegemony of Greece. The work falls into three parts: the conclusion of the Peloponnesian War (411–409 B.C.), events to the Peace of Antalcidas (404–387 B.C.) and events to the battle of Mantinea (387–362 B.C.). The work was obviously conceived as a continuation of the history of Thucydides, for it begins, without even any introduction, with reference to the situation as Thucydides had left it. Therefore Xenophon has invited comparison of his work with that of his immeasurably greater predecessor. It must be admitted that he had strong prejudices, is frequently inconsistent and uneven in his treatment of events. On the other hand, he is honest and clear-sighted, without a single demonstrable misstatement of fact to his discredit for the whole period of his history. He writes in a clear and simple style, of events with which he himself was familiar, and is the best authority we have for this period of Greek history. The *Hellenica* is a good if not a great history.

HELLMAN, LILLIAN (1905–   ). Lillian Hellman has produced a succession of popular and effective plays.

The Children's Hour (1932). In the private school for girls of Karen Wright and Martha Dobie is the irresponsible, neurotic Mary Tilford. The child flees deserved punishment, spreading a rumor of Lesbian relationship between Karen and Martha, which has entered her mind from surreptitious reading. Before this malicious lie can be exposed, it results in a lawsuit, the destruction of the school, the ruining of the relationship between Karen and her fiancé, and the suicide of Martha, who realizes that she was guilty in thought, though not in deed.

The Little Foxes (1939). This is a serious social study of a Southern family who try to retain power despite internecine quarrels. Horace Giddens, critically ill of heart disease, is brought home by his wife Regina, to discover that she only wants his money for an industrial venture. His nephew Leo Hubbard has taken some of Horace's bonds from the bank. Regina is denied the money by Horace, who makes a will leaving her only the stolen bonds. She deliberately permits her husband to die, and blackmails Leo and his brother; but finds herself completely alone, repulsed even by her daughter. *Another Part of the Forest* (1947) concerns the same family group, and narrates the events leading up to the earlier play; particularly the acquisition of control by Horace's thankless children, from him, by blackmailing him about an occasion when he gave information to the Union Army.

Watch on the Rhine (1941). Old Fanny Farrelly of Washington, D.C., welcomes home her daughter Sara and her anti-Nazi German husband Kurt. Teck de Brancovis, a royal house·guest, spends most of his time gambling at the German embassy, while his wife Marthe has an affair with Fanny's son David. Teck tries to blackmail Kurt. Fanny and David bargain with him; but in the end Kurt catches him off guard and murders him. "Die Wacht am Rhein" is an anthem to which old Germans remember their soldiers marching, three separate times.

HÉLOÏSE AND ABÉLARD (1921), by George Moore. This fictionalized version of the classic love affair of the twelfth century opens in Paris. Ten-year-old Héloïse, at the death of both parents (Philippe and Jeanne), is put under the guardianship of her uncle, Canon Fulbert of Notre Dame. At the age of sixteen, she returns from convent schooling, meets and loves Abélard, the most brilliant philosopher of his day, who has been engaged as her tutor. Héloïse and Abélard flee from Paris with Madelon, the serving woman of Fulbert; their son, Astrolabe, is born; they return to be married. Both go back to the religious life, and Fulbert, thinking Abélard is untrue to his niece, causes him to be set upon and emasculated. The story ends just before the famous letters were written, when the lovers say a last farewell, Héloïse to return to the convent as Abbess, and Abélard to the monastery as Abbot.

HENRY, KING OF FRANCE (1938), by Heinrich Mann. See MANN, HEINRICH.

HENRY IV (1922), by Luigi Pirandello. See PIRANDELLO, LUIGI.

HENRY IV, KING: PART I (1598), by William Shakespeare. The main source of this play, as of most histories of the author, is Holinshed's *Chronicles* (q.v.), but as usual Shakespeare modifies history to suit his purpose. King Henry would have been in his thirties, but he makes him middle-aged, while he makes Hotspur younger by ten years or so, that he may be a foil to Prince Hal; the projected crusade is also antedated by about ten years. The action takes place from the summer of 1402 to the summer of 1403. This Part is usually considered, together with Part II, as the "flower of Shakespeare's second period and the crown of his achievements in historical drama." Falstaff is his greatest comic figure.

The play opens at the palace in London, with the King, his younger son, John of Lancaster, Earl of Westmoreland, Sir Walter Blunt, etc., who discuss the civil war. After a glimpse of Hal and Falstaff, we again find the King in serious discussion; this time Northumberland, Hotspur and Worcester are present. Among the barons later there is hot argument as to whether the late King Richard named Mortimer his heir—Northumberland declares he heard him do so. It develops that Hotspur may join the plot against Henry, led by his father, Earl of Northumberland. The meeting at the Archdeacon's House in Bangor with Mortimer and Glendower sees the plot well advanced. Meanwhile Prince Hal romps with his companions of the alehouses. The Boar's Head Tavern in Eastcheap is the scene of much hilarity in the play. Glendower, the doughty, half-mad Welshman, is a figure as memorable as any historic creation of Shakespeare's.

The famous battle of Shrewsbury is the climax of Part I. The Earl of Douglas kills Sir Walter Blunt, and Hotspur challenges Hal: "If I mistake not, thou art Harry Monmouth . . . the hour is come to end the one of us. . . ." They fight. Douglas fights Falstaff, who drops and pretends to be dead. Percy (Hotspur) dies, and Hal soliloquizes about ambition and its dire outcome. King Henry has won; Prince Hal is a hero. Worcester and Vernon are prisoners, but the war is not ended. The barons are still in rebellion. John of Lancaster and the Earl of Westmoreland leave for York to meet Northumberland and the Archbishop, Scroop; the King and Harry post to Wales to meet Glendower and the Earl of March. Women play but small parts in this martial bid for dynastic power; Lady Percy, Lady Mortimer and Mistress Quickly appear but briefly.

HENRY IV, KING: PART II (1598), by William Shakespeare. As in Part I Shakespeare drew on *The Famous Victories of Henry V,* and on Holinshed. The play begins just after the battle of Shrewsbury, when messengers come to the Duke of Northumberland telling him of his son's death, and the defeat of the latter's army. In the meantime Falstaff has arrived in London triumphant, with a page to bear his sword and buckler. He is on his way to York to join Prince John of Lancaster. Mistress Quickly, Hostess of the Inn at Eastcheap, has taken action to have Falstaff arrested for debt. He and his follower, Bardolph, are about to draw on the sheriff when the Lord Chief Justice appears. He remembers Falstaff from the robbery at Gadshill, and orders him to pay his debt. But Falstaff wheedles Mistress Quickly into letting him have ten pounds, and she arranges to have Doll Tearsheet meet him for supper.

News comes to the Chief Justice that Northumberland and the Archbishop of York have marched against Lancaster. Poins and the Prince are in London. They discover from Falstaff's page and Bardolph that he is supping with Doll, and plan to wait on him as drawers at the inn. Pistol and Bardolph drop in as Falstaff is quaffing sack with Doll, and provoke him so that he draws his sword and drives them out. The Prince and Poins enter, disguised, and watch the old knight as he kisses Doll. Peto and Bardolph bring word that a dozen captains are waiting for him, and he swaggers out. On his way north he goes to Justice Shallow's in Gloucestershire. Shallow, who had known him in his youth, has some recruits for Falstaff, who lines them up for questioning. The most courageous is a tailor. Bardolph finds two are able to buy themselves off, and Falstaff selects the worst of the lot.

The rebels under York and Mowbray are in Gaultree Forest when Westmoreland comes to them from the Duke of Lancaster. He offers to make peace with the understanding that both armies are to be dismissed. As soon as he hears the rebels have dispersed, he arrests the leaders. Falstaff, arriving late as usual, meets a fleeing rebel knight and pretends he took him prisoner. King Henry becomes very ill and summons the Prince, who, watching by his father's bedside, tries on the crown. The King wakes and misses it. He sends for his son, who relieves his anxiety by promising to maintain it. Falstaff is at Justice Shallow's when he hears that his old friend, Prince Hal, is now Henry V. He posts to London with high hopes for himself and Prince Hal. The King banishes Falstaff, but gives him a pension to keep him out of mischief.

HENRY V, KING (1599), by William Shakespeare. Containing some of his finest poetry, this is one of Shakespeare's most moving historical plays. He took the leading incidents of his *Henry IV* and *Henry V* from an anonymous play, *Famous Victories of Henry V,* written about 1588, but he drew his historical materials mainly from Holinshed's *Chronicles* (q.v.). When the story opens the young King Henry has changed greatly from the merry, irresponsible Prince Hal. He has shed his boon companions and is keenly aware of his dignity and responsibilities as a monarch. He has made claim to certain dukedoms in France, and receives the French ambassador, who brings sarcastic answer from the Dauphin, a treasure chest of tennis balls. Henry prepares to invade France. Before he sails he discovers a plot against his life and deals promptly with the conspirators.

Pistol, Nym and Bardolph appear again in this play. They prepare to join the army. The hostess, Mistress Quickly, now married to Pistol, gives a description of Falstaff's death. Henry lands in France, besieges and takes Harfleur. The French underestimate his ability as a leader, but greatly outnumber him. Nym, Pistol, and Bardolph turn up on the battlefield and continue their rogueries. At Agincourt the opposing armies camp very close together. Henry is a noble, conscientious man at heart. He is anxious the night before the battle, as the French troops are fresh, and his men are weary. Dressed simply, he wanders about the camp unrecognized, talking to the soldiers, encouraging them, and leading them on to express their opinions. To Williams, a soldier, he says a king is but a man with emotions like other men. But when Williams criticizes the King, he agrees to wear Williams' glove, and gives him his own. If they survive the battle, they will make a quarrel of it. Then, in a famous soliloquy, he ponders on the responsibilities of a king, who must keep vigil while the peasant sleeps. Sir Thomas Erpingham comes for him as the nobles are waiting anxiously in his tent.

The next morning Henry exhorts his army in a heroic speech. He tells them that anyone who does not wish to fight may leave. But he reminds them how they will show their wounds in pride that they fought at Agincourt on St. Crispin's Day. The French herald comes once more, when the battle begins. York is killed and Henry mourns his death. The French herald comes again; humbly he cedes victory to the British. The battle over, Henry can be light-hearted again. He meets Fluellen, a Welsh captain, and gives him Williams' glove to wear in his helmet, telling him he took it from a Frenchman. He sends Warwick and Exeter after the Welshman to see that no real harm comes of his little joke. Williams, recognizing the glove, promptly strikes down Fluellen, then Henry comes forward and tells Williams who he really is. Peace is made. At the end Henry woos Katherine, the vivacious daughter of the French king, in a lively scene.

In technicolor, with Sir Laurence Olivier as Henry V, this play has been made into one of the finest English language films.

HENRY VI, KING: PART I (1592), by William Shakespeare. Based on materials found in Holinshed's *Chronicles* (q.v.), the first part of this trilogy about a very troubled reign begins just after the death of Henry V. The Duke of Bedford, uncle to King Henry VI, is Regent of France. Messengers arrive telling of the defeat of the English armies in that country and the capture of their leader Lord Talbot. Feuds exist among the English barons. The Bishop of Winchester, great-uncle to the King, and the Duke of Gloucester, his uncle, and the Protector are rivals for power. In France Joan of Arc, called La Pucelle, is helping the Dauphin Charles drive out the English.

In London, in the Temple-Garden, the Earl of Somerset and Richard Plantagenet ask the Earl of Warwick to settle a dispute. He refuses and Plantagenet plucks a white rose. He asks the gentlemen who agree with him to do likewise. Somerset plucks a red rose, and his followers take it as their emblem. The King patches up the quarrel between Gloucester and Winchester. He names Plantagenet Duke of York. In France, La Pucelle enters Rouen, and crosses swords with Talbot, who had been exchanged for another prisoner. She persuades the Duke of Burgundy to desert the English and join the French. King Henry goes to France to be crowned, with Somerset and York in his train.

In settling a dispute between two of their followers, the King assumes the red rose of Somerset, and orders both him and York to help Talbot, who is besieging Bordeaux. Somerset and York, jealous of each other, fail to cooperate. Talbot's forces are outnumbered, and he is killed in battle. La Pucelle is captured and burned as a witch. Margaret, the daughter of Reignier, Duke of Anjou, and titular King of Naples, is captured by Suffolk, who is so impressed with her beauty that he suggests her as bride for King Henry; the latter favors the idea, and drops an alliance which his uncle, the Bishop of Winchester, now Cardinal Beaufort, had planned for him.

HENRY VI, KING: PART II (ca. 1592), by William Shakespeare. With Holinshed's *Chronicles* (q.v.) as the base, the second part of the trilogy opens with the arrival of Queen Margaret in England. The English barons resent a dowerless queen, and the gift of the King to her father, the King of Naples, of the provinces of Anjou and Maine, for which the English had fought so gallantly. The Queen despises Henry as a weakling, while she admires Suffolk, who had wooed her for the King. She dislikes the Duke and Duchess of York, particularly the latter. The Duke is next in line to the throne; Suffolk plays on his wife's credulity and ambition. Led on by his man, Hume, the Duchess consults a witch, Margery Jourdain, as to the probable fate of the King, the Duke of Somerset, and Suffolk. The conspirators are arrested and tried. The Duchess is publicly disgraced and banished.

Henry ends Gloucester's protectorship, taking over the kingdom. The

Queen and Suffolk want Gloucester out of the way, so Suffolk arrests him on a false charge of treason. While he is awaiting trial, he is murdered. A rebellion occurs in Ireland; York is sent to crush it. Suffolk, suspected of Gloucester's death, is exiled; later he is captured by pirates and beheaded. York is concerned in the uprising of a Kentish ruffian, Jack Cade, who calls himself Lord Mortimer, and claims descent from the Duke of Clarence. He claims he is rightful heir to the throne, and enters London followed by a rabble, but is finally routed. York had formerly claimed that he had a better right to the throne than Henry; now he returns from Ireland with a strong force and proclaims his old enemy, Somerset, a traitor. Henry sends Buckingham to appease York, and tells him Somerset will be put in the Tower. York discovers the King has not kept his word. He declares open war. He puts the King and Queen to flight, then he and his followers march on London.

HENRY VI, KING: PART III (ca. 1592), by William Shakespeare. The third part of this trilogy opens in London with York attempting to seize the throne. Henry agrees that York shall succeed him. Queen Margaret upbraids him bitterly for disinheriting his own son. She and the young Prince leave the king, and join Northumberland and other northern lords. With his two sons, Edward and Richard, York is planning to seize the throne, when Queen Margaret arrives with a large force to besiege Sandal Castle. York is taken prisoner. She and Clifford taunt and deride him, before Clifford finally stabs him, and places his head on the gates of York. The Queen persuades King Henry to revoke his oath to York about the succession. Warwick backs young Edward, now Duke of York, and they proclaim him King in the towns as they advance.

In the battle near Towton, Clifford is killed by York; the Queen and Henry flee. Edward, as king, names his brother George, Duke of Clarence, and Richard, Duke of Gloucester. Henry, who had fled to Scotland, returns in disguise, and is captured. Warwick goes as Edward's ambassador to France, where Margaret and her son had taken refuge, to ask King Louis for the hand of his sister-in-law, Lady Bona. Word comes from England that Edward has married Lady Grey, an English widow. Furious and humiliated, Warwick throws in his lot with Margaret and her son. Aided by the French they land in England. Edward is taken prisoner, and Henry re-established on the throne. Guarded by his brother, Clarence, who has deserted to Warwick, Edward escapes with the help of Gloucester. He wins the next battle; Warwick is killed, Henry taken prisoner. Margaret and her son are both captured. Gloucester stabs the young Prince; then stabs Henry. Margaret is sent back to France.

HENRY VIII, KING (1613), by William Shakespeare and John Fletcher. The collaborators took their material from Holinshed, and Foxe's *Book of Martyrs,* modifying chronology for dramatic convenience. The scene opens in London just after King Henry's return from the famous meeting with Francis I, at the Field of the Cloth of Gold. The Duke of Buckingham suspects Cardinal Wolsey of being ready to stir up trouble between France and England, and of plotting with Charles V. Wolsey has Buckingham arrested, tried on a charge of high treason, and beheaded. Queen Katherine and the

Cardinal are antagonistic. He tries to persuade the King to divorce her. Henry had begun to doubt the legality of his marriage, because Katherine had been his brother's wife.

Wolsey favors an alliance with a French princess. In the meantime Henry has fallen in love with Anne Bullen, the Queen's maid of honor, whom he named Marchioness of Pembroke. Cardinal Campeius arrives from Rome for the Queen's trial. She makes her famous plea to Henry beginning, "Sir, I desire you do me right and justice." Katherine declares that Wolsey is her enemy. She challenges him as her judge, appeals her case to the Pope, and leaves the court. Henry, feeling the Cardinals are trifling with him, sends Cranmer, Archbishop of Canterbury, to Rome. Katherine is sad; to cheer her one of the ladies sings the well-known song, "Orpheus with his lute made trees." Wolsey and Campeius offer her their services and counsel. Katherine replies that she is alone and unfriended in England, that no Englishman would dare give her counsel, if he wished to remain a subject. She ends by listening to Wolsey. Cranmer returns from Rome and declares the divorce legal.

Henry marries Anne privately. There are rumors of plans for her coming coronation; Katherine is called the Princess Dowager. Letters from Wolsey to the Pope, in which the Cardinal asks His Holiness to stay judgment on the divorce as Henry is entangled with Anne Bullen, fall into Henry's hands. The latter also finds among state papers an inventory of Wolsey's treasure, showing his great wealth. Furious, the monarch gives back the papers to the Cardinal, including the letter to the Pope. He sends for the great seal, which Wolsey refuses to deliver. Realizing he is doomed, Wolsey utters the famous soliloquy beginning, "Farewell, a long farewell, to all my greatness!" and tells his assistant, Cromwell, to serve the King faithfully. Katherine, ill, is living in retirement at Kimbolton. Griffith, her gentleman usher tells her of Wolsey's humiliation and death; finally Katherine is able to forgive her enemy. Cranmer is to be tried by the council on certain charges, King Henry warns him. He gives him his ring in case he needs help. The King, concealed, listens to the trial. Coming forward at the critical moment, he clears Cranmer. The play ends with the christening of the newly arrived Princess Elizabeth.

HENRY ESMOND (1852), by William Makepeace Thackeray. Although Thackeray himself regarded *Vanity Fair* as his *chef d'oeuvre,* he sometimes inclined to the opinion that his reputation as a novelist would best rest on *Henry Esmond.* To which the eminent critic George Saintsbury fully assented: "A greater novel than *Henry Esmond* I do not know; and I do not know many greater books."

The setting is the England of Queen Anne, with style to match. Great historical personages are woven into the story of the career of Henry Esmond: General John Webb, Marlborough, Richard Steele, Addison, Swift, the Pretender James Edward, and others. All these characters Thackeray has brilliantly reanimated. Esmond tells the story of his youth in retrospect. Out of the subconscious whirlpool, isolated experiences emerge, significant in the hero's life. Thackeray narrates these in a tender, poetic mood with classic clarity. Esmond is first seen as the supposedly illegitimate dependent of the house of Castlewood. The tragedy of his birth pursues him throughout, scarring his spirit. He reveres Rachel, Lady Castlewood, who is unhappily wed. Lord Mohun enters the scene, a dissipated philanderer who kills the jealous Lord Castlewood in a duel. Esmond, because he acted as Castlewood's second, is jailed for one year, and later goes to fight in the War of the Spanish Succession. His hopeless love for Beatrix, the coquettish daughter of Lady Castlewood, gradually turns to dislike when she is instrumental in preventing the Jacobite Restoration plot. He eventually marries Lady Castlewood, and they emigrate to Virginia.

HENRY THE EIGHTH (1929), by Francis Hackett. This biographical study of the English ruler attempts a "psyche history." The author frankly states that he applies to his work "imagination and intuition," his purpose being to put life into the researches of scholars. To achieve this end, he uses the so-called fictionalized method, employing direct speech freely. He claims to have invented none of the dialogue, although it is apparent that it is transposed freely from one situation to another.

HEPTAMERON, THE (1558), by Marguerite de Navarre. This collection of tales follows the model of Boccaccio. Some ladies and gentlemen, detained by bad weather in the Pyrenees, turn to story-telling for amusement. The subjects are somewhat similar to those of the *Decameron* (q.v.), the social level of the characters distinctly higher. A strange combination of concern with religion and refined voluptuousness, complicated by occasional ventures into freethinking and even licentiousness, gives the book a marked Renaissance flavor. Although the work is customarily attributed to Marguerite de Navarre, its general sparkle and literary grace have made scholars suspect that various of the trained writers whom she befriended, possibly the poet Marot or the novelist Bonaventure des Périers, had more than a small share in the writing.

HERCULES ON OETA, by Seneca. See TRAGEDIES, by Seneca.

HERDER, JOHANN GOTTFRIED VON (1744–1803). Born in East Prussia in 1744, Johann Gottfried von Herder studied at the University of Königsberg, where he was influenced by the philosophers Kant and Hamann. He travelled extensively and held several temporary theological positions, and wrote a number of critical and historical-philosophical works. In 1770 he met Goethe in Strasbourg and became his intellectual mentor, introducing the young genius and leader of the "Storm and Stress" movement to Shakespeare, Ossian and the folksong. After several years as pastor in a small mid-German town he followed a call to Weimar, which had become the Athens of the time under Goethe's influence. Here Herder held the post of Court Chaplain and continued to write, while his relations with the younger and more famous poets Goethe and Schiller became strained. In 1803 Herder died, a bitter and querulous old man.

Herder has sometimes been called the gatekeeper of the nineteenth century, and indeed, he anticipated, developed and stimulated many of the conceptions that are called "modern" today, especially in the realms of historic evolution and literary understanding. He does not rank high as a maker of German literature because his creative output is of a strangely fragmentary nature, but he was an intellectual pioneer and stimulating force of rare strength. His collection of popular songs and ballads of many nations, published under the title

Voices of the Nations (1778–1779), was based on his teacher Hamann's concept that "poetry is the mother-tongue of the human race." Modern research in folksong and comparative literature, even anthropology, owes much to Herder's insight. His most important book, however, was *Ideas about the Philosophy of History of Mankind,* which was published in four parts between 1748 and 1791. With this work Herder proved himself a forerunner of Hegel, Spengler and Toynbee. History was viewed here under the aspect of evolution for the first time. Among the great philosophers of history Herder will always maintain an esteemed position.

HERE LIES (1939), by Dorothy Parker. See PARKER, DOROTHY.

HEREDITARY GENIUS, ITS LAWS AND CONSEQUENCES (1869), by Francis Galton. Galton, the founding father of eugenics, laid the basis for his movement to improve the race biologically with his *Hereditary Genius*. A cousin of Charles Darwin, the evolutionist, Galton deduced his eugenic notions from Darwinian principles. He aimed at utilizing the Darwinian theory for the amelioration of man's estate. "It is," he wrote, "now practically certain . . . that the physical characters of all living beings . . . are subject approximately to the same hereditary laws." A man's natural abilities, states Galton, are "derived from inheritance" under exactly the same limitations as are the form and physical features of the whole organic world. Just as it is easy to produce by careful selection a permanent breed of dogs or horses gifted with peculiar powers of running or doing anything else, so it would be quite practicable to produce a highly gifted race of men by judicious mating during the course of several consecutive generations. During the next score of years Galton published several other books on eugenics, as well as memoirs on anthropometry and other subjects. His works appeared later than Mendel's overlooked *Experiments in Plant-Hybridization* (q.v.), but they make no reference to the Mendelian laws or to the particulate nature of inheritance.

HERINNERINGEN VAN EEN DOMMEN JONGEN (1935), by Arthur van Schendel. See SCHENDEL, ARTHUR VAN.

HERMANN AND DOROTHEA (1797), by Johann Wolfgang von Goethe. This is one of Goethe's best known and most charming narrative poems. Written in classical hexameters and divided into nine cántos, the short epic tells the story of Hermann, the son of a prosperous village innkeeper, and Dorothea, a refugee maiden. When the pastoral opens, Hermann has driven off with his splendid stallions, the carriage well filled with supplies to meet the exiles who have left their homes fleeing from the victorious French. The young man meets one of the refugee girls driving an oxcart. She begs him to help her neighbor who has just given birth to a child. Hermann gives her the linen and supplies, and returns home very much in love. To quiet his father's objections he takes the pastor and the apothecary with him to an adjacent village where Dorothea is stopping. At first she thinks Hermann is asking her to return as a servant to his father's inn. However, she soon learns his real intentions, and the two are married.

HERO AND LEANDER (published 1598), by Christopher Marlowe and George Chapman. Of this poem, modeled on Musaeus' *Hero and Leander,*

Marlowe lived to write two sestiads, to which Chapman added four. The heroic couplets tell the classic story of the two lovers who drowned in the Hellespont. Hero, a priestess of Venus, dwelt at Sestos, where the beautiful Leander of Abydos saw her and was kindled at the sight. "Whoever lov'd, that lov'd not at first sight?" is the famous line that Shakespeare quoted in *As You Like It.* The first night's meeting is sensuously described, Leander swimming the Hellespont each way. Here Marlowe's part ends. Chapman's portion is much less pagan, and characteristically full of metaphysical obscurities. He tells of Hero's inward struggle, of the portents that reach her, of the storm that blows up as Leander is swimming for another meeting with his beloved, of Hero's seeing his bruised body at dawn from her tower and falling on top of him to die.

HERO OF OUR TIMES, A (1840), by Mikhail Yurevich Lermontov. This book was immediately successful upon publication. Indeed, Russian critical opinion puts it ahead of its author's famous poetry. It is a romantic novel *par excellence*, consisting of five parts. In the first, Bela tells of the meeting of the hero, Petchorin, and Captain Maxim Maximych, on the Tiflis road. The latter tells the story of Petchorin's love affair with a Caucasian girl. In the second part, it is told how Maximych came to possess Petchorin's diary, from which the last three books are taken. The first of these is *Taman,* which relates an incident with smugglers. *The Fatalist* and *Princess Mary* follow. The first is akin to Pushkin's prose; the other is a long short story which can stand independently. It concerns itself with a young cadet, Grushnitsky, who uses a crutch because of an injured foot. He falls madly in love with the young Princess Mary. He and Petchorin quarrel about her and fight a duel. A wildly romantic young girl, she loves Petchorin, or imagines she does. Grushnitsky can't fire when he wins the first shot. Petchorin, after repeatedly demanding a retraction of the slander Grushnitsky has circulated about him and a full apology, on being refused kills the man in calm disdain. He then goes to Princess Ligovsky, Mary's mother, who assures him that her daughter is in love with him. In an unusually telling scene the two meet. He does his best to disillusion the young Princess. A second story runs through this part; it concerns Vera, who loves Petchorin madly, and who is married to an older man. She is dying of consumption.

The whole is in the full bloom of the romantic tradition. Petchorin is the strong silent man with a noble bearing, shy, contemptuous of the common herd, and even more of the aristocratic herd. He has a poetic soul, but assumes the mask of a bully and acts the snob. Not only was Petchorin a great literary hero in Russia, but he exercised a social influence as well; for he was imitated in life no less than in fiction.

HEROD AND MARIAMNE (1850), by Christian Friedrich Hebbel. See GYGES AND HIS RING, by Christian Friedrich Hebbel.

HERODES AND HERODIAS (1909), by Hviezdoslav. See HVIEZDOSLAV.

HERZEN, ALEXANDER IVANOVICH (1812–1870). Herzen, who, though a moderate, exercised considerable influence on Russian revolutionary thought, fled Russia in 1847, and spent the rest of his life in Europe, chiefly in London. Not even after the death of the despotic Nicholas I and the accession of the liberal Czar Alexander II could he have returned to Russia, because of his revolutionary writings.

One of his most impressive books is *My Past and Thoughts* (1852–1855), a voluminous autobiography, a singularly spontaneous and sincere work, free from rhetoric and giving the effect of good conversation. It has value both as history and as a series of portraits of great contemporaries. Herzen describes the development of Russia and Europe, and attempts to establish the relation between them. There is a disarming charm in his narrative of the events of his time. So great is his frankness that he does not hesitate to speak of his wife's love affair with the famous German romantic poet Herwegh.

Though *My Past and Thoughts* is regarded as the more significant and attractive by a majority of readers, there are others who are inclined to consider *From the Other Shore* (1850) as Herzen's most important contribution to literature. It expresses his violent disillusion with revolution. For the Russian edition of this work he wrote the *Epilogue to 1849*, which opens with the words: "A curse upon thee, year of blood and madness, year of victorious stupidity, brutality and dullness. A curse upon thee!" For Herzen regarded the failure of 1848 as a bitter comment on the prospects of the revolutionary and socialist Europe he had hoped to see. The work is by no means propaganda, but a cry against the idealistic optimism of revolutionaries who spoiled their own cause. It was Herzen's intent to replace the empty if fanatical zeal of revolutionaries and socialists with a carefully directed will. It is in this book, which consists of eight essays, three of them in dialogue, that he sees history as a creative process, by no means working toward a preordained and inevitable end.

HESPERIDES (1648), by Robert Herrick. A collection of over a thousand short and generally faultless secular poems, *Hesperides* shows the interest of its witty and urbane author, often called the typical courtier, in country festivals, attractive ladies, Devonshire superstitions, books, and flowers. The best-known lyrics in the volume are probably "To the Virgins, to Make Much of Time," "The Night-Piece to Julia," "Cherry-Ripe," "Corinna's Going A-Maying," and "Upon Julia's Clothes." Herrick, for most of his life a country clergyman, writes in "The Argument of His Book,"

> I write of hell; I sing, and ever shall,
> Of heaven, and hope to have it after all.

As if to make amends for his pagan outbursts, he added a "divine" section of pious poems, which he called "Noble Numbers."

HESSE, HERMANN (1877–   ). The German-Swiss author and poet Hermann Hesse, born in South Germany in 1877, moved to Switzerland for permanent residence in 1912. In deep disagreement with aggressive nationalism and militarism, he became a stern critic of German politics as early as 1914, although he never ceased to consider himself a German poet who primarily wrote for German readers. A prolific author of some forty books, comprising novels, short stories, essays and poetry, he was awarded the Nobel Prize for Literature in 1946 and the Goethe prize of the city of Frankfurt in 1947. Widely known in many parts of the world and translated into many languages, Hesse met with little response in America, though leading contemporary authors like

Thomas Mann and André Gide have long ago acclaimed him as one of the truly great writers of our time.

With many Germans, Hesse shared a total disregard for political reality in the prosperous years preceding World War I. The heroes of his novels were usually sensitive outsiders of the bourgeois world who clashed with the rude forces of ordinary society. It was not until the war in 1914 that Hesse's world was completely shattered. The anonymously published novel *Demian* (1919) may be named as an outstanding example of the author's new development. In this book Hesse tries to show the typical conflicts confronting the modern German Protestant youth. The novel (reissued in the United States in 1948) had a tremendous influence on the younger generation of Germans after 1918, to whom it meant almost as much as Goethe's *Werther* (q.v.) had meant around 1775. The next major novel, *Steppenwolf* (q.v.), is an indictment of the chaotic postwar period in Germany. The book reads almost like the case history of a psychoneurotic, and is one of the most striking examples of Freud's influence upon modern German literature. The hopeless dualism of man is still the subject of Hesse's next novel, *Death and the Lover* (1930). Two basic human types are here confronted: the man of the spirit and the protagonist of the senses. In his last great work, *The Glaspearlgame* (1943), Hesse resolves the conflict of modern man's dualistic nature in favor of the mind, the reason, the spirit. Written in the objective form of a biography, the book tells the short life story of one Joseph Knecht, who occupies a high position in the order of the glaspearl game players in some imaginary future. The human mind works similarly to a player who moves pearls of different size and color on a row of strings. The mind needs both meditation, which Hesse has learned from oriental heritage, and training, which the glaspearl game provides. Viewed from the perspective of German literary history, the work is the most outstanding "Bildungsroman" between Mann's *Magic Mountain* (q.v.) and *Doctor Faustus*. (q.v.).

In stressing Hesse's prose work, one should not overlook his lyrical production and his critical essays. His verse volumes have enjoyed large circulations; the poems are simple and musical, reminiscent of the folksong and of the poets of German Romanticism. His essays and book reviews are many, and his erudition is hardly surpassed by any living man of letters.

HET FREGATSCHIP JOHANNA MARIA (1930), by Arthur van Schendel. See SCHENDEL, ARTHUR VAN.

HEZAR AFSANE, by Princess Homai. See ARABIAN NIGHTS' ENTERTAINMENTS.

HEZIONOT (1921), by Zalman Shneiur. See SHNEIUR, ZALMAN.

HIAWATHA (1855), by Henry Wadsworth Longfellow. See LONGFELLOW, HENRY WADSWORTH.

HIGH TOR (1937), by Maxwell Anderson. See WINTERSET, by Maxwell Anderson.

HILDA LESSWAYS (1911), by Arnold Bennett. See CLAYHANGER TRILOGY, by Arnold Bennett.

HILDEBRANDSLIED (ca. 800). Extant in a sixty-nine-line fragment of a copy made by two monks, the *Hildebrandslied* is one of the most valuable remains of the earliest German literature. Written in divided alliterative verse, the story tells of Hildebrand, who, while at the head of his master's army, comes upon a strange army headed by Hadubrand, who soon turns out to be his son. Despite Hildebrand's attempt to avert a clash, Hadubrand provokes the duel before he realizes that it is his father who opposes him. At this point, the story breaks off without any definite conclusion. The presumption is, however, that the end is tragic, with the death of Hadubrand at the point of his father's sword.

HILLSBORO PEOPLE (1915), by Dorothy Canfield. See CANFIELD, DOROTHY.

him (1927), by E. E. Cummings. See ENORMOUS ROOM, THE, by E. E. Cummings.

HIND AND THE PANTHER, THE (1687), by John Dryden. See DRYDEN, JOHN.

HIPPOLYTUS, THE (428 B.C.), by Euripides. The theme of this play is the same as the story of Potiphar's wife. Theseus, king of Athens, had in his youth wed the Amazon queen, Hippolyte, by whom he had a son, Hippolytus. Then he had put aside Hippolyte and taken the Cretan princess, Phaedra, to wife. At first sight of Hippolytus Phaedra had been smitten with secret love for him. Then Theseus had slain a kinsman and been forced to go into exile to Trozen, where Hippolytus was living under the guardianship of his grandfather. In the prologue to the play Aphrodite explains that Hippolytus scorns her power, glories in his virginity, and is over-devoted to the virgin goddess, Artemis. For this he must be punished, and his punishment is the love of Phaedra. Phaedra struggles valiantly against her passion, but is betrayed by her overfond nurse, who worms the secret out of her. In Theseus' absence the nurse, after swearing Hippolytus to secrecy, discloses Phaedra's secret passion and begs him to have mercy on her mistress. Hippolytus is outraged to the depths of his virgin soul by such an unholy proposal and rebuffs the nurse. He would even denounce her perfidy to Theseus if he were not reminded of his oath. When Phaedra learns of her nurse's ill-advised efforts on her behalf, her outraged modesty drives her to try to rescue her reputation at all costs. She takes her own life, and leaves a note to Theseus accusing Hippolytus of improper advances. When Theseus returns and reads the accusation of the note, against which Hippolytus cannot defend himself without breaking his oath, he curses the self-righteous youth. The curse is immediately fulfilled, for it embodies a wish, and Poseidon had promised to fulfill three wishes for Theseus. As Hippolytus drives off along the seashore, his horses are stampeded by a monster appearing from the sea and drag their master to his death. The mangled but still breathing body of Hippolytus is brought back to his father, and Artemis appears to tell Theseus the truth of his son's purity and honor, thus revealing the full measure of Aphrodite's vengeance. Euripides had previously written another version of this tragedy in which Phaedra was made a far less virtuous woman; it was this version which Seneca imitated and Racine after him in their plays named after Phaedra (q.v.).

HIS LAST BOW (1917), by Sir Arthur Conan Doyle. See SHERLOCK HOLMES, by Sir Arthur Conan Doyle.

HISTOIRE NATURELLE (1749–1804), by Georges Louis Leclerc, Comte de Buffon. Among eighteenth century naturalists Buffon occupies a place of pre-eminence. His contemporaries, notably Linnaeus, Réaumur and Ray, made significant history through the classification of animals and plants into logical categories, species and varieties, and Buffon complemented their work by giving descriptions of their nature, habits, uses and properties. He was a brilliant writer, and one of the ablest of scientific popularizers. His great *Natural History,* appearing in forty-four volumes over a period of fifty-five years, sought to cover the whole area of natural knowledge. The superb anatomical drawings of mammals are a notable feature of the work.

Included in the first volume was his "theory of the earth," sharply criticized in his day by the religious for its materialistic treatment of nature. Buffon essayed also an investigation "of the internal structure of the globe, its composition, form, and manner of existence." He critically examined the hypothesis of the English astronomer Whiston that every event which happens on the earth is determined by the motions of the stars. Next he demolished the theologian Burnet, "whose brain was so heated with poetical visions, that he imagined he had seen the creation of the universe." The third victim of his objectively scientific scalpel was the naturalist Woodward, who explained the appearance of the globe by stating that an immense abyss yawned in the bowels of the earth, and that the outer rim of the earth was but a thin crust that served as a covering to the fluid it enclosed.

Buffon, on the basis of observations of geological phenomena and of marine life, came to the interesting theory "that the waters of the sea at some period covered, and remained for ages upon, that part of the globe which is now known to be dry land; and consequently the whole continents of Asia, Europe, Africa, and America were then the bottom of an ocean abounding with productions similar to those which the sea at present contains." One of the best known of the many volumes of the *Natural History* is that entitled *Époques de la Nature* (1779). In this Buffon conceived that the earth (and other planets) arose from the collision of a comet with the sun. Thus arose a molten spheroid, the history of which Buffon divided into seven epochs, in the sixth of which man appeared.

In other volumes of the *Natural History* Buffon presents remarkably detailed studies of birds, fish, insects, reptiles, animals, and, finally, of man. The latter he treats as an animal—an outrage to religious sensibilities of the time—and he goes into ethnological descriptions and analyses of the various races and peoples of the earth. On the question of the fixity of species Buffon did not express himself categorically, but he generally supported, against Linnaeus, the idea of transformation. He noted that animals have organs with no apparent function, and to explain this he concluded that some species are degenerate forms of others. The ape, for example, is a degraded man, and in the alteration of form, some of the original features have been retained. Buffon in some respects was primitive in his knowledge; but he had a fully mature mind, and he treated natural phenomena with a genuinely scientific attitude. His *Natural History,* the first work to present the vast field of general science in a popular and generally intelligible form, appeared in several editions and languages, and it exerted a wide influence.

HISTORIA DANICA (ca. 1208), by Saxo Grammaticus. See CHRONICLES OF DENMARK, by Saxo Grammaticus.

HISTORIA NATURALIS (77), by Pliny the Elder. See NATURAL HISTORY, by Pliny the Elder.

HISTORIA REGUM BRITANNIAE (ca. 1136), by Geoffrey of Monmouth. See HISTORY OF THE KINGS OF ENGLAND, by Geoffrey of Monmouth.

HISTORY (ca. 390), by Ammianus Marcellinus. Such authorities as Gibbon rank Ammianus as one of the great historians of all time. He was a Greek, native of Antioch in Syria, and served as an officer in the Roman army under the Emperor Julian. In his later years he devoted himself to the writing of his *History,* which was conceived as a continuation of the *Histories* of Tacitus, whom he admired and emulated. The thirty-one books of his work began with the accession of Nerva (96) and continued through the battle of Adrianople (378). Only the last eight books, beginning with the reign of Constantius II (353), are preserved, but these are the most valuable, since Ammianus speaks as an eyewitness for most of the period, and from personal experience and observation on the reign of Julian. Ammianus' critical historical judgment is excellent, but his style is inferior, partly because the Latin in which he wrote was not his native tongue.

HISTORY AND PRESENT STATE OF DISCOVERIES RELATING TO VISION, LIGHT AND COLOURS (1772), by Joseph Priestley. See EXPERIMENTS AND OBSERVATIONS ON DIFFERENT KINDS OF AIR, by Joseph Priestley.

HISTORY AND PRESENT STATE OF ELECTRICITY, WITH ORIGINAL EXPERIMENTS (1767), by Joseph Priestley. See EXPERIMENTS AND OBSERVATIONS ON DIFFERENT KINDS OF AIR, by Joseph Priestley.

HISTORY OF AGATHON (1767), by Christoph Martin Wieland. See WIELAND, CHRISTOPH MARTIN.

HISTORY OF CRITICISM AND LITERARY TASTE IN EUROPE, A (1900–1904), by George Saintsbury. Saintsbury, the most eminent of modern English literary critics, established his reputation with his *A History of Criticism and Literary Taste in Europe* in three volumes. It is a work full of solid scholarship, so remarkably well organized that it has served as a textbook on the history of literary criticism for a number of decades in the universities of English-speaking countries. Saintsbury avoids any long discussion of what he described as slightly abstruse subjects, i.e., transcendental aesthetics, theories of beauty, and any psychological analysis of "artistic pleasure." He avoids generalizations and tries, so far as it is possible, to confine his analysis to the particular and the actual, stating his theory of criticism with brevity: "The criticism of literature is first of all the criticism of expression as regards the writer, of impression as regards the reader."

Some literary critics, particularly Georg Brandes, have taken exception to this strictly objective method of criticism, inasmuch as it results in an absence of "insight," which, they aver, can be achieved only by the subjective method. For instance, when Saintsbury discusses Aristotle, he writes from the viewpoint of an "outsider," consciously avoiding identifying himself with the Greek point of view and feeling.

HISTORY OF CIVILIZATION IN ENGLAND (Vol. I, 1857; Vol. II, 1861), by Henry Thomas Buckle. Treating history from the scientific point of view, Buckle's famous work traces the influences of climate, food and soil on English national characters and events. He states categorically that human progress is mainly due to the advance and diffusion of knowledge. He paints a very broad canvas and presents a great many generalizations and theses, largely concerning the impersonal laws that govern the arrest or progress of civilization, claiming that reverence for ancient beliefs and customs has slowed up the advance of civilization and that healthy skepticism, on the other hand, speeds its progress. This book caused a great deal of bitter controversy, coming as it did on the heels of Darwin's new theory of evolution.

HISTORY OF EGYPT, A (1905), by James H. Breasted. This general history of Egypt from the earliest times to the Persian Conquest is conventional in conception, planned for the student. The work is divided into eight books. Book I presents a preliminary survey of the earliest known facts. Book II traces the Old Kingdom down to the Sixth Dynasty. Book III describes the feudal age of the Middle Kingdom. Book IV chronicles the rise of the empire of the Hyksos. Book V tells of the first period of the Empire, to the fall of Ikhnaton. Book VI tells of the second period, to the time of Rameses III. Book VII reveals the decadence culminating in the triumph of Assyria. Book VIII charts the restoration and the final struggles with Babylon and Persia.

This oriental archaeologist and historian also collaborated with J. H. Robinson to write the standard *History of Europe, Ancient and Medieval* (1920).

HISTORY OF ENGLAND (1848–1861), by Thomas Babington Macaulay. Macaulay had begun to write his five-volume *History of England* in March, 1839; the fifth volume was published posthumously in 1861. The work instantly achieved a world-wide celebrity equaled only, in the annals of English letters, by the works of Byron and Sir Walter Scott. Its success was largely due to the author's Victorian-gentleman's philosophy of "Britannia Rules the Waves" and to his polyphonic English rhetoric, which greatly appealed to that age. Macaulay produced better romance than history. As one critic wrote: "The tale, as we proceed, flows on faster and faster. Page after page vanishes under the entranced eye of the reader; and, whether we will or no, we are forced to follow as he leads—so light, and gay, and agreeable does the pathway appear."

Macaulay stated the intended scope of his work in the very first sentences of the *History:* "I purpose to write the history of England from the accession of King James the Second down to a time which is within the memory of men still living." But he did not get past the reign of William III, whom he regarded as the greatest hero of the English people. He frequently reveals brilliant insight into character, in, for instance, his description of Charles I: "Faithlessness was the chief cause of his disasters, and is the chief stain on his memory. . . . There is reason to believe he was perfidious, not only from constitution and from habit, but on principle. He seems to have learned from the theologians whom he most esteemed that between him and his subjects there could be nothing of the nature of a mutual contract; that he could not, even if he would, divest himself of his despotic authority, and that in every promise which he made there was an implied reservation that such promise might be broken in case of necessity, and that of the necessity he was the sole judge." Chapter III, particularly the description of the coffee houses where the wits assembled, is the most famous.

HISTORY OF EUROPE, ANCIENT AND MEDIEVAL (1920), by James H. Breasted. See HISTORY OF ·EGYPT, A, by James H. Breasted.

HISTORY OF EUROPEAN MORALS FROM AUGUSTUS TO CHARLEMAGNE (1869), by William Edward Hartpole Lecky. Of the five chapters the first, entitled "The Natural History of Morals," describes "the rival claims of intuition and utility to be regarded as the supreme regulator of moral distinctions" and supports the former. Bentham and his utilitarian school set "the greatest happiness for the greatest number" as the supreme aim and tried to show that anything conducive to this end was virtue. But this position is found low and selfish; it leads to paradoxes and incongruities and goes against the common language and feelings of men. Lecky argues rather for the view that there has always been in men an intuitive perception that certain parts of our nature are higher or better than others, though actual moral practice varies sharply with different stages of civilization and other special circumstances. Chapter Two deals with the Roman Empire in its pagan phase, showing how Stoicism was modified by a gentler and more cosmopolitan spirit coming from Greece. Actually the people remained corrupt, amid sensuality, slavery, and gladiatorial shows. The last philosophic influence, that of the Pythagorean and Neoplatonic schools, prepared, however, for Christianity by inculcating humility, prayerfulness, purity of thought, and association of moral ideals with deity rather than with man. Chapter Three, "The Conversion of Rome," is an account of the early changes, including the persecutions. Chapter Four, "From Constantine to Charlemagne," demonstrates that the first consequences of Christianity were a new sense of the sanctity of human life and absorption of the doctrine of universal brotherhood. But there is also a "mournful history" of corruption to tell, of asceticism and intolerance, of transformations and retrogressions, as the Christian Empire decayed and barbarian kingdoms replaced it, and feudalism arose. The last chapter goes back to a subject often incidentally mentioned before, "The Position of Women." In Greece wives were kept hidden in the inner apartments, while such prominence and public influence as there were for the sex went to the courtesans. The Romans kept their wives in subjection too, but had higher ideals. Christianity brought various strictnesses, including asceticism and eventual celibacy for the clergy, but there came in its wake scandalous deviations from the lofty ideals

HISTORY OF FERDINAND AND ISABELLA, by William Hickling Prescott. See HISTORY OF THE CONQUEST OF MEXICO, by William Hickling Prescott.

HISTORY OF GREECE, A (1900; revised 1913), by John B. Bury. This has become the standard one-volume work in the field for both the general reader and the student. Beginning, in the revised edition, with a long and brilliant chapter on the Aegean civilization of the second millennium which archeologists had just unearthed, the history shows the early expansion of Greece, as settled by obscure migrant tribes long unable to write, until it became a Mediterranean power and a cultural force that still endures. The Persian threat to the West was repelled, only to be succeeded by an exhausting civil war between the victors, the oligarchic land power of Sparta and the imperialistic naval power of Athens. At the end both sides were ripe for conquest by Macedonia. The *History* comes to a close with the death of Alexander (323 B.C.) and of Aristotle (322 B.C.).

HISTORY OF ENGLISH LITERATURE (1863–1864), by Hippolyte Taine. Taine wrote his history to demonstrate his theory that genius may be explained by its causes, which he classified as heredity, environment and time. The introduction is probably Taine's best statement of his philosophy and methods of literary criticism. In Book I he goes to the source of English literature and studies the writings of the Saxons and Normans and the emergence of England's first poet, Chaucer. Book II treats of the Pagan Renaissance, Spenser, Burton, Browne and Francis Bacon; of the Elizabethan theater, Ben Jonson and Shakespeare; of the Christian Renaissance and Milton. Book III analyzes the writers of the Restoration, Dryden, Addison, Swift, Fielding, Smollett, Defoe, Richardson, Sterne, Goldsmith, Dr. Johnson, Hogarth and Pope. Book IV evaluates Burns, Cowper, Wordsworth, Shelley, and Byron. Book V is devoted to Dickens, Thackeray, Macaulay, Carlyle, John Stuart Mill and Tennyson. Taine's method, largely inspired by current ideas in the biological sciences, is no longer accorded the absolute validity he claimed for it, but few critics since his time have dared neglect the special circumstances in which works of art are produced. His influence may be traced down a long line of influential writers and interpreters of literature, from Paul Bourget and Zola to Vernon Louis Parrington.

HISTORY OF FRANCE (final edition: 1867), by Jules Michelet. This is a history inspired by an intense passion for democracy, freedom and social justice, written with great eloquence in the Romantic style. Anticlerical, Socialist and strongly proletarian in his sympathies, Michelet interpreted the history of his country as the triumph of his own convictions, through a, kind of unconscious spiritual progress. He was anything but a "scientific" and objective historian, but his work survives as few histories do, for the sheer imaginative power of his re-creation of the past.

HISTORY OF ITALIAN LITERATURE (1870), by Francesco de Sanctis. Francesco de Sanctis can be considered the most outstanding literary critic of Italy in modern times. His main work, *History of Italian Literature,* although published in 1870, was the result of many years of experience and profound study of Italy's life, virtues, faults and political and spiritual vicissitudes. First a professor in Naples, then an exile in Turin and Zurich, de Sanctis carried with him wherever he went the inner vision of Italian history and literature as a whole, an organic body impossible to understand unless its fundamental sense of unity is constantly kept in mind. The *History* is a notable literary and critical expression of this principle of unity. The book begins with an examination of the beginnings of Italian literature, with a chapter illustrating the Sicilian School. Other chapters, following progressively, are on the Tuscans, Dante's lyrics, early prose, the Mysteries and Visions, the Trecento, the *Divine Comedy,* the *Canzoniere,* the *Decameron,* the last of the Trecentisti, the Stanze, the Cinquecento, the *Orlando Furioso,* the Maccaronea, Machiavelli, Pietro Aretino, Torquato Tasso, Marino, the New Science, and the New Literature. De Sanctis' *History of Italian Literature* constituted a real revolution in the conception of aesthetics. Arbitrary judgments that had measured the value of art and literature by fixed rules and models were alien to the conception of de Sanctis, for whom, as an outstanding disciple of de Sanctis—Benedetto Croce—points out, "poetry and literature, being products of the human spirit, were judged as expressions of the social life of a people and as such were put into continual relation to its moral, social and political history."

HISTORY OF MR. POLLY, THE (1910), by H. G. Wells. This is a novel concerning the English lower middle class and the struggle of a human soul to escape its stultifying influence. Mr. Polly starts as a draper's apprentice at the age of fourteen, spends fifteen years as the unsuccessful proprietor of a small shop and the husband of a small-minded woman who tricked him into marriage. In desperation he attempts suicide and fails, burns down his shop and leaves his wife. Mr. Polly becomes a tramp and ends up as handy man at a small country inn. When he returns five years later to see how his wife is getting along, he discovers that she had believed him drowned and set herself up in a tea shop with the insurance money. She is as horrified as he at the idea of taking up their marriage again, and Mr. Polly returns happily to anonymity and his pleasant country existence. Mr. Polly's drab life with its moral and physical indigestion, his hunger for experience and beauty and his final escape, is described with Wells' inimitable pathos and humor.

HISTORY OF ROME, by Livy (Titus Livius; 59 B.C.–A.D. 17). Livy's *History* draws an elaborate picture of the past of his people as he sees it, and, being a moralist, he extracts lessons from it to guide his own day. He states this intention quite frankly: "This is the most wholesome and most fruitful outcome of historical knowledge, to have before one's eyes conspicuous and authentic examples of every type of conduct, whence the student may choose models for his own imitation and that of his country, and be warned against things ill begun which have likewise ended ill." The work originally covered all of Roman history, from the myth of Romulus to contemporary events. His aim is "neither to affirm nor to refute" legendary material. Originally the *History* consisted of 142 books. About one-quarter survived the Middle Ages, but summaries of the entire work have come down from the fourth century. Books 1-5 tell of the founding of Rome by Romulus to its rebuilding after the disaster in Gaul (389 B.C.). Books 6-10 extend to the triumph of

Carvilius over the Samnites (294 B.C.). Books 11-20 are lost but, according to the surviving summary, cover the ground up to the eve of the Second Punic War. Books 21-30 describe the events of the Second Punic War (219-201 B.C.). Then follow the Macedonian Wars and concomitant events. Book 40 ends with the death of Philip of Macedonia. Book 45, the last preserved, concludes with the triumph of L. Aemilius Paulus over Perseus, the last Macedonian king.

HISTORY OF ST. LOUIS, THE (1310), by Jean, Sire de Joinville. De Joinville, seneschal to St. Louis, King of France, completed his *History* in 1310 at the age of ninety. He had accompanied his royal master on a crusade to the Holy Land in 1248 and his chronicle contains an account of his adventures during six years of fighting and traveling. Book I of the work describes the saintly character, precepts and sayings of Louis IX. Book II in its first twenty chapters continues to present the virtues of the King, and also contains the account of the feudal history of Champagne. The remainder of the book concerns itself with the adventures of Joinville and the King on their crusade. Generally speaking, the work is more a memoir than a history, full of personal reminiscence and gossip, of picturesque detail and of sincere adulation of the King.

Modern historians regard Joinville's *History* as an invaluable source of information, not so much about the important happenings during the thirteenth century as about the subjective outlook and the values of the individual feudal lord, reared in piety and living according to the code of knightly chivalry.

HISTORY OF THE CONQUEST OF MEXICO (1843), by William Hickling Prescott. Originally published in three volumes, this comprehensive history is organized in seven parts: Book I, Introduction; View of Aztec Civilization; Book II, Discovery of Mexico; Book III, March to Mexico; Book IV, Residence in Mexico; Book V, Expulsion from Mexico; Book VI, Siege and Surrender of Mexico; Book VII, Conclusion; Subsequent Career of Cortés. The broad canvas of the *History,* in this hitherto unexplored field, involves studies ranging from the Spain of Charles V to the fabulous empire and court of the great Montezuma, to the heroic figure of Hernando Cortés. The ancient, shadowy story of the Aztecs, their society, military organizations, and religion, is traced in a manner both scholarly and glamorous. The *History* is actually a documented tragedy. Prescott is the embodiment of the finest aspects of the now defunct school of Romantic history, sound research combined with narrative sweep and bravura.

The *History of the Conquest of Peru* (1847) is a companion volume about the sequel to that wave of Spanish exploration. The characterizations of the Pizarro brothers and their cohorts, and of the young Inca Atahualpa, are vivid; but the background is less comprehensive. The earlier *History of Ferdinand and Isabella* (1838), which took the author eight years of preliminary reading and six years of writing, and enjoyed a success never before seen or heard of in the country, had encouraged him to undertake the subsequent projects.

HISTORY OF THE CONQUEST OF PERU (1847), by William Hickling Prescott. See HISTORY OF THE CONQUEST OF MEXICO, by William Hickling Prescott.

HISTORY OF THE CONSULATE AND THE EMPIRE (1845–1862), by Louis Adolphe Thiers. This history rehearses at great length the familiar story of the young Corsican officer and how he became a general of the Revolution, reorganized France after the anarchy of the *Directoire,* created a strong and centralized state and then failed in a grandiose attempt to build, through military conquest and the liberation of nationalities, a new order in Europe. It emphasizes the military successes at the expense of the history of literature, the arts, economic progress and culture in general, and glosses lightly over the harm caused by Napoleon's ambition. Much of the work's success may be explained by the facts that most of the twenty volumes appeared during the Second Empire of Napoleon III and that the legend· of Napoleon himself was especially precious to the French.

HISTORY OF THE KINGS OF ENGLAND (ca. 1136), by Geoffrey of Monmouth. The importance to literature of Geoffrey of Monmouth's *History of the Kings of England* is well known to students of medieval, especially Arthurian romance. Geoffrey has preserved for posterity many native Welsh and Breton traditions which he gathered at a time when they were still current among the common people. The source of his information, he says, was a "most ancient book" written in the Welsh tongue, but this has been doubted. In some respects Geoffrey's *History* is a prose romance; in its Arthurian portions, it is a deliberate excursion into fiction, founded on legend and folklore. The *History* first appeared in Latin under the title: *Historia Regum Britanniae.* Geoffrey's innovation on the accepted version of British history in his day was his insertion of the "histories" of the intermediate British kings, among them King Leir, from which account Shakespeare derived his tragedy of *King Lear* (q.v.). The legends and stories of the *History* stimulated the literature of France and England for eight hundred years.

HISTORY OF THE PELOPONNESIAN WAR, by Thucydides (ca. 455–399 B.C.) Thucydides was the first truly critical historian with an adequate conception of historical causation. His famous narrative analyzes with surgical incisiveness the long and bloody struggle between the Athenians and the ·Peloponnesians to the year 411 B.C. When the war first broke out, Thucydides, grasping its great historical importance, began to take notes of all events with singular objectivity. "I have described nothing," he wrote, "but what I either saw myself or learned from others of whom I made the most careful and particular inquiry." The history is largely a study of the downfall of the imperialistic Athenian state, which, by its arrogance and tyranny, brought upon itself the bitter opposition of the conservative Spartans fighting to assert their hegemony among the Greeks. As Thucydides puts it, "The real, though unavowed cause, I believe to have been the growth of the Athenian power, which terrified the Lacedaemonians [Spartans] and forced them into war." Although Thucydides' aim was to record the events of the war from its beginning in 431 B.C. to the fall of Athens in 404 B.C., his narrative breaks off abruptly without explanation at the end of the twenty-first year of hostilities. The whole work is arranged in eight books. Books 1-4 and part of 5 bring the chronicle down to the Peace of Nicias in 421 B.C. The rest of Books 5, 6 and 7 cover the six years of the truce, which actually was no truce at all, since it was devoted to diplomatic maneuvers on both sides; the Athenians encouraging Argos to attack Sparta in order further to weaken her. Book 8 opens on the third phase of the war, when, the truce being terminated, the two enemies were again at each other's throats. An interesting feature of the history is the introduction of speeches attributed to the various actors in this real tragedy. Thucydides writes: "As to the speeches which were made either before or during the war, it was hard for me, and for others who reported them to me, to recollect the exact words. I have therefore put into the mouth of each speaker the sentiments proper to the occasion, expressed as I thought he would be likely to express them." Thus these speeches serve as Thucydides' interpretation of the motive forces at work behind events. Probably the most famous of all these speeches is the funeral oration (Book 1) of Pericles over the Athenians who died in the first campaign. Proud of Athens' greatness and scorning the enemy, he said: "For we have compelled every land and every sea to open a path for our valor, and have everywhere planted eternal memorials of our friendship and our enmity." Powerful scenes are drawn everywhere, particularly in Book 2, which carries a description of the plague that struck Athens; in Book 5, which details the alleged treachery of Alcibiades; and in Book 7, which gives a breathless account of the naval engagement between the Athenian and Syracusan fleets with both contending armies watching anxiously from opposite shores.

HISTORY OF THE PERSIAN WARS, by Herodotus (ca. 490–425 B.C.). Herodotus well deserves his title, the "Father of History." His nine books are the earliest extant Greek prose, and in them he lifts himself from the level of his predecessors, who were still retailing myth for history, to the eminence of that title. The work that we have is his history of the conflict between the Persians and Greeks culminating in the great battles of Thermopylae and Salamis. To make this conflict understandable he goes back to the beginnings of oriental aggression and traces the growth of the Persian empire. The first six books are devoted to this background, while the last three narrate the actual expedition and invasion of Greece under Xerxes. Herodotus was the first man anywhere to write history in our sense of the word, sifting reports, searching for the truth and thereby exalting man's intelligence. Perhaps his greatest accomplishment lies in the very conception of the events he narrates as a historic unit. But Herodotus is much more than a historian, or rather his history is much more than an arid chronicle of events; he is an enthusiastic and fascinating storyteller. The customs and traditions of strange and distant peoples such as the Egyptians and Scythians, some of which he knew from his own extensive travels, always intrigued him. Thus he gives us such stories as that of Rhampsinitus in Book II, a story to match anything from the *Arabian Nights,* but remarks with a saving grace, "It is my business to tell what was told me, but not necessarily to believe it." The familiar motto of the Post Office Department, "Not snow, nor rain, nor heat, nor gloom of night stays these couriers from the swift completion of their appointed rounds" is taken from Herodotus' description of the courier system of the Persian king Darius.

HISTORY OF THE RENAISSANCE IN ITALY (1875–1886), by John Addington Symonds. This, the greatest work in English on the Renaissance in Italy, appeared in seven volumes, beginning with *The Age of the*

Despots in 1875. Symonds was a brilliant stylist. Having lived and studied for many years in Italy and absorbed its wonderful works of art into his aesthetic consciousness, he was ideally suited for the monumental task.

The other volumes in Symond's studies on the Renaissance are: *The Revival of Learning, The Fine Arts, Italian Literature* (in two volumes) and *The Catholic Reaction* (in two volumes). All are replete with those minor details which collectively give one an intimate view of a bygone civilization. Symonds sees the influences of the Renaissance permeating modern thought and culture in a vital and expansive manner. In this historical continuity he perceives the hope for mankind.

HISTORY OF THE SKY (edited 1666), by Tycho Brahe. The astronomical observations of Tycho Brahe (1546–1601), the Danish scientist, were edited in 1666 by the learned Jesuit, Albertus Curtius, under the title of *History of the Sky*. But his edition is faulty and has been superseded by a definitive edition in fifteen volumes of Brahe's astronomical writings (*Opera Omnia*) completed in 1929.

Tycho Brahe began to observe the planets in 1563 when he was only seventeen, and he continued ardently in this pursuit until his death in 1601. He rejected both the geocentric planetary system of Ptolemy and the heliocentric scheme of Copernicus, proposing instead a geo-heliocentric arrangement. In the Tychonic universe Venus and Mercury moved in circular orbits about the earth, while the earth and the remaining planets revolved around the sun. This plan won many supporters in the succeeding half-century. Nevertheless, the work of Tycho Brahe is far more significant for the accuracy of his observations than for his theoretical contributions; there are few important astronomical constants which he failed to determine with greater preciseness than had his predecessors. He greatly improved the instruments of his science. He proved, by showing the lack of sensible parallax, that the distance of a comet from the earth was much greater than that of the moon, that it was a body moving through interstellar space. This was a revolutionary idea which overthrew the old doctrine of crystalline celestial spheres.

Brahe's observations of the moon were the most accurate since Ptolemy. He discovered the "variation" and the "annual equation," the third and fourth inequalities in the moon's motion in longitude, the variability of the inclination of the moon's orbit to that of the earth, and the irregularity in the motion of the nodes from east to west.

Kepler, his mathematical assistant, had such faith in the accuracy of Brahe's observations that he persisted in his attempt to reconcile the Copernican system with them; when he failed, he abandoned the Copernican circles for elliptical orbits. The *Opera Omnia* of Brahe thus forms an important link in the chain of astronomical works from the *De Revolutionibus* (q.v.) of Copernicus to the *Principia* (q.v.) of Newton. Had Brahe not lived, Kepler would not have been the "Legislator of the Heavens," and Newton would not have deduced the law of gravitation from Kepler's laws.

HISTORY OF THE VARIATIONS OF THE PROTESTANT RELIGION (1688), by Jacques Bénigne Bossuet. Six of the sixteen chapters of the *History* are largely given over to an attack on Luther. It goes on to excoriate Melanchthon, Calvin, Erasmus, and a number of other leaders of the Reformation. Bossuet himself saw the value of his book as polemical; this was the last word on the subject of "the Protestant controversy." Recent readers have tended to assign more importance to the highly informative studies of such things as the Albigensian and Waldensian revolts. Otherwise Bossuet, Bishop of Meaux, erstwhile tutor to the Dauphin, and famed preacher of rhetorically impeccable sermons, appears in this book to be distinguished largely by his great zeal.

HISTORY OF THE WARS, THE (ca. 490–575), by Procopius of Caesarea. Procopius of Caesarea was one of the foremost historians of Constantinople at the time of Justinian. He served as the adviser to Belisarius, the great general, travelling with him on most of his campaigns. This afforded an opportunity to be familiar with the actual course of events connected with the reign of Justinian, and Procopius took advantage of his position to record the details not only of the wars but of the most important events in the entire empire. *The History of the Wars* is in eight books. The first two describe the campaigns of Belisarius against the Persians; the next two deal with the conquest of the Vandals in Africa; and the fifth, sixth and seventh cover the Byzantine campaigns for the recovery of Italy. The eighth book carries the general story down to 554. Procopius was influenced by Herodotus and Thucydides.

He later published two other works, the *Anecdota* or *Secret History,* which is a bitter attack upon the policies of Justinian and a scathing denunciation of the Empress Theodora; and *On the Public Buildings,* a formal description, with considerable flattery of the Emperor, of the buildings erected by Justinian.

HISTORY OF THE WORLD (1614), by Sir Walter Raleigh. Written during Raleigh's imprisonment in the Tower of London, this book, now of little value as history, is a monumental work, important for its style and as a repository of legends. Divided into five parts, it traces historical events and developments from the Creation to Abraham, from Abraham to the destroying of Solomon's temple, from the destruction of Jerusalem to Philip of Macedonia, from Philip to the death of Pyrrhus, and from Antigone to the overthrowing of Macedonia and Asia by the Roman conquerors. This book is an example of the author's erudition. The apostrophe to death is especially quotable: "O eloquent, just, and mighty Death! whom none could advise, thou hast persuaded; what none hath dared, thou hast done: and whom all the world hath flattered, thou only hast cast out of the world and despised: thou hast drawn together all the far-stretched greatness, all the pride, cruelty, and ambition of man, and covered it all over with these two narrow words, *Hic jacet* [Here lies]."

HISTORY OF THREE KINGDOMS, by Kim Pusik. See SHIJO-YUCHIP.

H. M. PULHAM, ESQ. (1941), by John P. Marquand. See LATE GEORGE APLEY, THE, by John P. Marquand.

HOFFMANN, ERNST THEODOR WILHELM (1776–1822). Besides being outstanding in the field of German romantic prose fiction, Hoffmann was an artist and musician in his own right. Among other musical compositions he wrote the opera *Undine* (1816). Music played an important role in many of his writings. In the literary realm, he is marked by a predilection for the fantastic and supernatural. *Fantastic Pieces in Collot's Manner* (1814–1815), a four-volume collection of tales, established his fame. Among this group of stories, "The Golden Pot" is the most outstanding. In 1815, he brought forth *The Devil's Elixir,* a psychological short story (novella) which describes the consequences which follow when a monk sips of the drink, and how he is redeemed. *Little Zaches* (1819) draws upon German folklore for its central figure, a devilish mandrake. Among the series of tales entitled *The Brothers of Serapion* (4 vols.; 1819–1821) are found the clever and imaginative pieces, "Master Martin," "Fräulein von Scudery" and "Doge and Dogaressa." His *Tomcat Murr's Views of Life* (1820–1822) depicts, by means of the fictitious musician, Kreisler, his personal aspirations and feelings.

Hoffmann's popularity may be ascribed to his deft way of producing a skillful blend of real life scenes and an extreme of grotesque imagination to the point where the atmosphere becomes a credible reality. Coupled with a wealth of imagination and creative power is a tendency to accentuate the bizarre and morbid spirit. Despite a definite element of the unhealthy, his works exerted considerable influence upon succeeding Romantics in music and literature, notably in France.

HOFMANNSTHAL, HUGO VON (1874–1929). At the age of seventeen young "Loris," as he was called by his writer friends, was regarded the greatest lyrical genius of German literature since Goethe. Indeed, the beauty and musicality of Hofmannsthal's verse has hardly any counterpart in German letters, either before or since Goethe. Although few in number, his poems are rare gems of word music. Starting as a precocious follower of the literary masters, the young Austrian poet wrote a number of short verse dramas that became models for the new anti-Naturalistic writers at the turn of the century. Influenced by the symbolism of Maeterlinck, he became the most important neo-Romantic dramatist of German literature. As a born aesthete and connoisseur of world literature, he adapted already existing works rather than invented new plots. In *Elektra* (1903) he gave an emotionally distorted, romantic version of the Greek legend, and his modern adaptation of an English morality play, *Everyman* (1912), became one of the most successful repertory pieces of the Salzburg Festivals, which he helped found with his friend, Max Reinhardt. To the English-speaking world Hofmannsthal is mainly known as the librettist of Richard Strauss' operas, especially of *Rosenkavalier* (1911) and *Ariadne of Naxos* (1912).

HÖLDERLIN, FRIEDRICH (1770–1843). Neither connected with German Classicism nor associated with the Romantics, the Swabian poet Hölderlin signifies the purest amalgamation of Greek and Teutonic spirit. The first part of his life was an unbroken chain of unhappiness, failure, frustration and loneliness, and tragic insanity wrapped his consciousness and made him linger on as a senile child during his last thirty-five years. A protégé of Schiller, he was filled with a fervent passion for classical Greece; and he succeeded completely in adopting the German language to the rigid pattern of ancient strophes and meters. Many of his odes belong to the greatest poetry ever written in German. Not primarily a dramatist, he nevertheless left an unfinished tragedy, *The Death of Empedocles,* which many playwrights have since tried to complete, among them Bertold Brecht. Hölderlin's most famous work is an epistolary novel in rapturous prose, *Hyperion* (1797–1799). The book relates with little coherence the experiences of a young Greek, who takes part in the unhappy struggle of his people against the Turks in 1770. In the center is Hyperion's friendship to Alabanda and his love for Diotima, both relationships ending tragically, with the hero finally going into voluntary exile in Germany. It is the dream-world re-creation of a Hellas that the poet never saw, and the power of a dithyrambic prose not surpassed until Nietzsche, which make Hölderlin's novel a unique achievement of German letters.

HOLIDAY (1928), by Philip Barry. See BARRY, PHILIP.

HOLLANDSCHE KWATRIGNEN (1932), by Pieter Cornelis Boutens. See BOUTENS, PIETER CORNELIS.

HOLLOW MEN, THE (1925), by T. S. Eliot. See ELIOT, THOMAS STEARNS.

HOLY DESIRE OF THE SOUL, THE (1652), by Angelus Silesius. See SILESIUS, ANGELUS.

HOMAGE TO JOHN DRYDEN (1924), by T. S. Eliot. See ELIOT, THOMAS STEARNS.

HOME TOWN (1940), by Sherwood Anderson. See WINESBURG, OHIO, by Sherwood Anderson.

HOMERIC HYMNS, THE (8th-5th c. b.c.?) These thirty-three hymns, although Homeric in style, are certainly not by the poet of the *Iliad* (q.v.) nor by any one author. Neither are they hymns in our sense of the word. They are dactylic poems ranging in length from 3 to 580 lines and addressed to some one of the Greek gods. They all end with a transitional formula such as, "of thee shall I be mindful and of another lay," from which it is clear that they were written and used as ceremonial prologues to the recitation of epic lays such as the *Iliad* and *Odyssey* (q.v.). The shorter hymns are only a brief praise of the god in question, but those of greater length expand this praise into a narrative of the god's birth, career, or benefits to man. The most celebrated is the Hymn to Demeter, which tells in touching and dignified style of the Rape of Persephone, of Demeter's grief and suffering until she was restored, and how the cult at Eleusis was established in honor of them. The Hymns to Apollo, to Hermes, and to Aphrodite are also of considerable length. The collection was made perhaps as late as Alexandrine times, but the original poems seem to range in date from the 8th to perhaps the 5th century.

HONG KILDONG (1600), by Huh Kyun. *Hong Kildong,* a famous Korean novel, takes place during the Sejong period (1419–1451). Minister Hong had two sons by his wife and one, Kildong, by his concubine. Kildong was handsome and wise, and a great student of literature. Because he was his father's favorite son, he was despised and abused by his father's first wife. Disillusioned by the unjust treatment of society to a concubine's son, Kildong became the leader of a band of thieves who robbed corrupt priests and government officials, only to give their loot away to the oppressed in the most approved Robin Hood fashion. The government tried without success to capture Kildong and his followers. Finally, Kildong left the country to become a king in a Utopian state somewhere in China.

Huh Kyun was the author of many other works. His brother and sister were famous poets. Huh Kyun and four friends of his were executed August 24, 1618, because of his frank criticism of the government.

HONOR (1889), by Hermann Sudermann. See MAGDA, by Hermann Sudermann.

HOPPLA! WE LIVE (1928), by Ernst Toller. See MAN AND MASSES, by Ernst Toller.

HORACE (1640), by Pierre Corneille. See CID, THE, by Pierre Corneille.

HORATIUS AT THE BRIDGE (1842), by Thomas Babington Macaulay. See LAYS OF ANCIENT ROME, by Thomas Babington Macaulay.

HORNEY, KAREN (1885–). With the publication of Dr. Horney's *The Neurotic Personality of Our Time* (1937), there came into prominence a new, independent thinker whose special contribution to contemporary psychological thinking was the importance of the impact of cultural and social environment on neurosis.

New Ways in Psychoanalysis (1939) makes her challenge to the central principles of Sigmund Freud's theory more explicit. She sets forth, side by side, their divergent views on such basic topics as the Oedipus Complex, the death instinct, the emphasis on childhood experience, anxiety, and neurotic guilt feelings.

Other volumes have developed and extended Karen Horney's theories. *Self Analysis* (1942) considers the origins of neuroses and the ordinary psychoanalytic process—a cooperation between analyst and patient—and outlines the feasibility of self analysis, with its spirit, rules, resistances to be overcome, and limits.

A still later volume is *Our Inner Conflicts* (1945). In this volume, the author expounds a "constructive theory of neurosis," as caused by people's reactions, "moving toward," "moving against," and "moving away from" one another. Neurosis can not be cured by simple means, Dr. Horney points out, but skillful treatment succeeds in making patients progressively better adjusted, and happier. Dr. Horney founded and is at present dean of the American Institute for Psychoanalysis.

HOTEL UNIVERSE (1930), by Philip Barry. See BARRY, PHILIP.

HOUND OF HEAVEN, THE (1893), by Francis Thompson. This is one of the most famous religious poems in the English language. It embodies the mystical idea of God as the Hound of Heaven pursuing the stray soul here below that mistakenly tries to flee and happily cannot succeed. "I fled Him, down the nights and down the days." The form is that of an irregular Pindaric in the seventeenth century mode; and one critic called Thompson "Crashaw born again, but born greater." The swift, swirling stanzas are familiar in all the anthologies. No one is likely to forget the Voice which "beat more instant than the feet" and says, "Rise, clasp My hand, and come!"

HOUND OF THE BASKERVILLES, THE (1902), by Sir Arthur Conan Doyle. See SHERLOCK HOLMES, by Sir Arthur Conan Doyle.

HOUSE AT POOH CORNER, THE (1928), by A. A. Milne. See WINNIE-THE-POOH, by A. A. Milne.

HOUSE DIVIDED, A (1935), by Pearl Buck. See GOOD EARTH, THE, by Pearl Buck.

HOUSE OF CONNELLY (1932), by Paul Green. See IN ABRAHAM'S BOSOM, by Paul Green.

HOUSE OF FAME, THE (ca. 1370), by Geoffrey Chaucer. See BOOK OF THE DUCHESS, by Geoffrey Chaucer.

HOUSE OF LIFE, THE (1870; 1881), by Dante Gabriel Rossetti. See BLESSED DAMOZEL, THE, by Dante Gabriel Rossetti.

HOUSE OF MIRTH, THE (1905), by Edith Wharton. The title of this novel, which began Mrs. Wharton's literary career, is taken from *Ecclesiastes* 7:4: "The heart of fools is in the house of mirth." The intention is to reveal "high society" in all its shoddiness, vulgarity and selfishness. Lily Bart is a minor edition of Becky Sharp; beautiful, clever, intelligent, she loves luxury and will stop at nothing to secure it. An orphan, she lives with her aunt, Mrs. Peniston, who gives her an allowance she considers insufficient. Yet while visiting her rich friends, the Trenors, she loses heavily at cards and permits her host Gus to pay off her debts. Gus offers to invest her small capital for her, and she does not realize that his subsequent checks are from his own pocket—until she repulses his advances. Greatly distressed, she promises to pay back every cent. Lily can marry Simon Rosedale, a rich Jew, but is not in love with him; and Laurence Selden, whom she does love, has not the money. While considering her problem, she goes on a yachting trip and becomes involved in a scandalous affair with George Dorset. She is innocent in fact, but all her wealthy connections drop her. Her aunt dies, and leaves her only a tiny legacy.

Now Lily decides to marry Rosedale, but he no longer wants her. The poverty-stricken girl lodges in a cheap boarding house and takes up millinery. Ill and discouraged, she visits Selden and tells him how much he has meant to her, then returns and takes poison. Selden, on his way to her to propose, hears of her death. She has left her legacy to Gus, and her debt is paid.

HOUSE OF POMEGRANATES (1891), by Oscar Wilde. See HAPPY PRINCE, THE, by Oscar Wilde.

HOUSE OF THE SEVEN GABLES, THE (1851), by Nathaniel Hawthorne. In this study of the dark, gothic corners of Salem life, the great seven-gabled Pyncheon house is blighted by a curse given when old Colonel Pyncheon of early Salem had obtained the property by falsely convicting of witchcraft its rightful owner, Wizard Maule. Present inhabitants are old Miss Hepzibah Pyncheon, her weak-minded brother Clifford, their country cousin Phoebe, and young Holgrave, a lodger. Poverty forces Hepzibah into petty shopkeeping. The only rich member of the clan is hypocritical cousin Judge Pyncheon, who had previously railroaded Clifford to jail, and now is attempting to have him declared insane, because he believes Clifford to be withholding the secret of concealed family wealth. The judge's hand is stayed by death, and his wealth reverts to his intended victims. Phoebe marries Holgrave, Maule's descendant, the long inheritance of fraud is broken, and joy returns to the house of the seven gables.

Beside Hawthorne's other great novel, *The Scarlet Letter* (q.v.), there is *The Marble Faun* (1860), an Italianate romance about the amoral Count Donatello, whose murder of a mysterious man almost blights the love of Hilda and Kenyon, two Americans.

Hawthorne was a master of the short story, and produced many popular volumes. *Twice Told Tales* (1837) deals with the life, history, and legends of New England, and with the strange emotions and secrets of the heart. *Mosses from an Old Manse* (1846) contains other supernatural pieces, such as "Rappacini's Daughter," a tale of science and mysticism; satirical pieces, such as "The Celestial Railroad," about a modern mode of travel over the route of the *Pilgrim's Progress* (q.v.); and historical pieces, such as "Roger Malvin's Burial," about the escape of two survivors of Lovewell's flight during the eighteenth century Indian massacre. *Tanglewood Tales* (1853) contains stories for children.

HOW BEAUTIFUL WITH SHOES (1935), by Wilbur Daniel Steele. See STEELE, WILBUR DANIEL.

HOW I FOUND LIVINGSTONE (1872), by Sir Henry Morton Stanley. James Gordon Bennett, then the young editor of the *New York Herald,* believed that David Livingstone, the Scottish explorer, who was given up for lost in the jungles of Central Africa, was still alive. Accordingly, in 1869 he commissioned a reporter, English-born Sir Henry M. Stanley, to lead an expedition of search for him under the auspices of the *Herald.* The hardships endured by the party, the dangers they encountered on the way, the remarkable sights and adventures they experienced are all chronicled here. The imagination of the entire world was stirred by Stanley's wanderings through mysterious and unknown parts of Africa. In Ujiji he found and greeted the lost explorer with the celebrated words: "Dr. Livingstone, I presume?" The book contributed to the American conception of "Darkest Africa," but it remained for later men, such as Carl Akeley, to project a clearer view of the "Dark Continent," which periodically fires the imaginations of authors and readers.

HOW THE OTHER HALF LIVES (1890), by Jacob A. Riis. See MAKING OF AN AMERICAN, THE (1901), by Jacob A. Riis.

HOW TO WRITE SHORT STORIES (1924), by Ring Lardner. See LARDNER, RING.

HRAFNKEL'S SAGA FREYSGODA (late 13th c.). See NJÁL SAGA, THE.

HSI HSIANG CHI (13th c.), by Wang Shih-fu. One of the most popular plays of China, *Hsi Hsiang Chi* is considered the finest example of the Chinese drama extant. The play opens with Madame Cheng, the wife of the Prime Minister, her serving maid Hung Niang, and her daughter, Ying Ying, arriving at a monastery in the spring of the year. Here scholar Ch'ang stops on his way to the capital, where he expects to take official examinations., He sees the beautiful Ying Ying, and falls in love with her at once. The serving maid, Hung Niang, is the true heroine of the play. It is she who carries messages to and fro, but so secretly that it is only at the end of the play that the reader sees she had aided the two lovers to close the gulf Madame Cheng opened between them.

Ying Ying's letters bear a double meaning, so if they should fall into the wrong hands the information would not be harmful. The messages of the lovers are full of sparkling wit and poetry, but, involving as they do much play upon words, are very difficult to translate into Western languages.

An English translation of *Hsi Hsiang Chi,* called *The West Chamber* (1936), was made by Henry H. Hart.

HSI YU KI (16th c.), by Wu Ch'eng-en. *Hsi Yu Ki* or *The Pilgrimage to the West* is an enormous Chinese novel written by Wu Ch'eng-en (ca. 1505–1580). It is divided into three sections, 100 chapters in all. The first part describes the creation of the world by the pure essence of Heaven and the five savors of the earth. A rock magically becomes pregnant, giving birth to a stone monkey, who wishes to study esoteric doctrine. The second part describes the monkey's journey to India with Hsuang Tsang. Historically, Hsuang Tsang, a Buddhist monk, really made pilgrimage to India by order of the Chinese Emperor in the seventh century with instructions to bring the Buddhistic scriptures into China. On the way the monkey subdues dragons, ogres, and demons by his wit and his magic, including a cudgel which he could reduce to the size of a needle and carry behind his ear. The monkey finally becomes a Buddhist saint himself, in the third part of the book. The novel is famous for its combination of beauty with absurdity, of profundity with nonsense. It is satire aimed at the so-called saints.

Arthur Waley translated parts of *Hsi Yu Ki* under the title *Monkey.*

HUCH, RICARDA (1864–1947). The foremost representative of a large number of German women writers, Ricarda Huch was born into an old patrician family and was one of the first women to secure a German Ph. D. Despite her tendency to spread a romantic veil over all that is unpleasant, she employs a technique that contains definite realism and a frank and analytic approach. Exhibiting a vigorous style and a profound understanding of the subject, she wrote in various forms. Her two-volume work *Romanticism* (1899–1902) is a stylized literary study. A writer also of lyric poetry (*De Profundis*), her overshadowing prose works reflect her intense scholarly interest in the past. *The Great War* (1912–1913) is a prose study of the Thirty Years' War. A remarkable picture of moral and physical degradation is found in a series of sketches of an Italian town, *From the Street of Triumph* (1902). The novels *Eros Invincible* (1893; Eng. trans. 1931) written in the form of a family chronicle, *Vita Somnium Breve,* later *Michael Unger*

(1902) exhibit her clear and delicate artistic skill and beauty of language. Also available in English translation are the psychological crime novel, *The Deruga Trial* (1917), and the biography, *Garibaldi and the New Italy* (1906).

HUCKLEBERRY FINN, THE ADVENTURES OF (1884), by Mark Twain. A sequel to the picaresque *Adventures of Tom Sawyer* (q.v.), this book is a more adult local color treatment of the Mississippi River region. Huck himself narrates his experiences, which begin with his residence with the Widow Douglas. His mean father, seeking the boy's fortune, kidnaps him, but Huck escapes and starts down the river on a raft with Jim, a runaway slave. Picking up two eloquent rogues en route, Huck witnesses a murder and helps settle a false claim for a legacy. Jim has been sold to Tom Sawyer's Aunt Sally, and in an abortive rescue attempt Tom is wounded. It is revealed, however, that Jim's owner has died, freeing the slave in her will. Huck's fortune is safe also, but he plans to continue his vagabond life to escape adoption and education by Aunt Sally. John Galsworthy described this story as "the perfect example of the familiar spirit permeating both the book and its characters." The "immorality" of Huck's decision that he would rather go to hell himself than be the means of sending Nigger Jim back into slavery is what caused the book to be banned from the public libraries of Concord, Mass., and Brooklyn, Omaha, and Denver. But it sold at the rate of 40,000 copies before publication.

HUDIBRAS (Part I, 1663; II, 1664; III, 1678), by Samuel Butler. The author of this burlesque-heroic poem is of course to be distinguished from the nineteenth century author of *The Way of All Flesh* (q.v.). Butler wrote this politico-religious satire in jogging octosyllabic couplets, getting his general and some of his particular inspiration from Cervantes' *Don Quixote* (q.v.). Sir Hudibras, a Presbyterian justice in the Commonwealth, a learned dunce, pot-bellied and humpbacked, sets out on a quest attended by his squire Ralpho, who is an Independent in politics and religion. Their heated discussions on the way satirize the sectarian strife still prevalent in Restoration days. Sir Hudibras and Ralpho have many adventures, mostly mishaps, including encounters with Crowdero, the bear-baiter, and Sidrophel, the astrologer. They try to reform English society by suppressing everything pleasurable in Puritan fashion. The meddling knight falls in love with a widow, and goes to ridiculous and unsuccessful lengths to win her.

HUGHES, LANGSTON (1902–   ). Langston Hughes, descendant of Negroes set free· before the Emancipation, traveled in America during his youth, and worked his way through Europe with an initial capital of seven dollars. His poetic talents were recognized early by critics and vindicated in 1926 by the publication of *The Weary Blues*. These poems are objective and free in form. In content, Hughes's work is often rather sardonic. Good use is made of the Negro folk idiom and sensitivity to jazz rhythms. Hughes has written plays, a novel, a volume of short stories, and an autobiography.

HUGH SELWYN (1920), by Ezra Pound. See POUND, EZRA.

HUGH WYNNE, FREE QUAKER (1897), by S. Weir Mitchell. A descendant of a long line of Welsh squires, Hugh Wynne is a Quaker who possesses a firm loyal character. He is the narrator of the story, supplementing it with extracts from the diary of his friend Jack Warder. He tells about his boyhood and schooldays in pre-Revolutionary Philadelphia, his upbringing by his stern Quaker father and warm-hearted Aunt Gainor. As a youth he was a rich idler, gambling and drinking with the British officers in the tavern. But as the rebellion agitation grew he became thoughtful, for his sympathies lay with the patriot cause. When a Tory cousin, Captain Arthur Wynne, insulted his mother he knocked him down and precipitated a bitter feud. Aggravating their relations further was their rivalry for the love of Darthea Peniston. The course of the Revolution is followed with descriptions of the Meschianza Ball given by the Tories in honor of Gen. William Howe, the victorious British commander, the siege of Yorktown, André's execution, and the Battle of Germantown, during which Hugh is taken prisoner. Hugh's escape from the Walnut Street jail in Philadelphia and his happy reunion with Darthea end the tale.

Mitchell, whose first writings were papers and popular books on science, wrote poetry, short stories, novelettes, and several other novels. The most popular was *Roland Blake* (1886), a story of the Civil War, important for its treatment of personality and character under the stress of dramatic circumstances.

HUH SAING CHUN (18th c.), by Park Jiwon. The *Huh Saing Chun* is a Korean novel based on the theme of the scholar's contempt for worldly goods. The hero, Huh Saing, left Seoul to become a great writer. He planned to study for ten years in a mountain solitude. But after seven years his wife complained of her poverty. Borrowing a large sum of money from a rich man by the name of Pyun, Huh Saing went to a faraway island and devoted himself to business. He made so much money that he paid back Pyun twofold. He gave some of his money to poor people, some to sea pirates, and some he threw into the sea. Pyun, amazed by the mystery of Huh Saing, followed him to the South Mountain and found the humble cottage in which he had hidden himself, but could not find Huh Saing. Li, a high government official, also became interested, after hearing Pyun's account of Huh Saing, and made the pilgrimage himself. He found Huh Saing, but when asked to answer the three most difficult questions of the day, Li could not do so. He pretended that he needed time, but when he returned for another interview with the sage, Huh Saing could not be found.

Park Jiwon's pen name was Yunam (Swallow Rock). In his youth he too went to a South Mountain solitude, where, it is said, he studied so hard that at 25 years of age his beard and hair had turned gray. At 29 he visited the famous Diamond Mountain to study and write. When he was 43 he went to Peking, and finding the Chinese emperor was in Yulha, followed him there, where he wrote his novel *Yulha Ilki*. *Huh Saing Chun* was published in a revised version in 1924.

HUKPOONG (1930), by Han Yong-woon. See MEDITATIONS OF THE LOVER, by Han Yong-woon.

HUMAN BEAST, THE (1890), by Émile Zola. See ROUGON-MACQUART, THE, by Émile Zola.

HUMAN COMEDY, THE (1829–1850), by Honoré de Balzac. Under this title Balzac put together the long series of novels which established him in first place among realistic novelists. During a long apprenticeship he had written reams of romantic claptrap. At last he had found his vein in novels which dealt with the life of his own century. It has been said that after God and Shakespeare there has been no greater creator of human beings. Gradually he saw that his books were forming a complete picture of French life. Repeatedly, as new possibilities dawned on him, he altered and enlarged his plan. There would be pictures of Paris, of life in the provinces, country life, life as lived in the professions and trades. The more he wrote, the more he saw to do. A person of expensive tastes and many debts, he wore out his tremendous physique writing day and night, keeping awake on coffee, starting a new novel as soon as the last was completed and sometimes with the plans of three different ones boiling in his head at once. His novels were so full of people characterized in such minute detail, with their surroundings so carefully described, that for years Balzac passed for a genius at observation. Today we realize that his work is a triumph of imagination—observation would have required more time than he could spare from his writing. He died with his *Comedy* unfinished. Among the best known of the novels are:

César Birotteau (1837), a novel about shopkeepers and bourgeois life in Paris during the Restoration. César Birotteau, wearing peasant sabots, comes from his native Vendée to Paris. He works his way up, becomes the owner of a perfume shop. He is rich, a knight of the Legion of Honor. But this distinction goes to his head. He dreams of enlarging his shop and of pushing himself into society. He speculates and loses everything. He takes a little job in an office, and in misfortune becomes a noble figure. Finally he dies, having regained his self-respect and overcome with joy at his rehabilitation.

Eugénie Grandet (1833), one of the "Scenes of Provincial Life," is set in the town of Saumur. Grandet, a rich miser, has an only child, Eugénie. She falls in love with her charming but spoiled young cousin Charles. When she learns he is financially ruined, she lends him her savings. But her father will never consent to her marrying a bankrupt's son. Charles goes to the West Indies, secretly engaged to marry Eugénie on his return. Years go by. Grandet dies and Eugénie becomes an heiress. But Charles, ignorant of her wealth, writes her to ask for his freedom: he wants to marry a rich girl. Eugénie releases him, pays his father's debts, and marries without love an old friend of the family.

Old Goriot (1834), another of the "Scenes of Parisian Life," is a story of Parisian society under the Restoration and of a man whom Balzac calls "a *Father,* as a saint, a martyr, is a *Christian.*" Goriot, a retired manufacturer of vermicelli, is a good man and a weak father. He has given away his money in order to ensure the marriage of his two daughters, Anastasie and Delphine. Because of his love for them, he has to accept all kinds of humiliations from his sons-in-law, one a *gentilhomme,* M. de Restaud, and the other a financier, M. de Nucingen. Both young women are ungrateful. They gradually abandon him. He dies without seeing them at his bedside, cared for only by young Rastignac, a law student who lives at the same boarding house, the pension Vauquer.

Other Balzac novels, fully as well known, are *Cousin Pons* (1847), the story of an amiable victim of a mania for collections; *The Curé of Tours* (1832), which is about an old priest whose life is ruined when he loses his room in a comfortable boarding house; and *Cousin Betty* (1847), a tale of how a rich family goes to seed because its head becomes pathologically obsessed by women. One reason for the success of *The Human Comedy* is Balzac's device of having familiar characters, like Rastignac—young, ambitious, out to grasp the main chance—and Vautrin—picturesque criminal and Rastignac's advisor—turn up in several novels.

Ironically, Balzac's *Droll Tales* (1832–1833), a collection of Rabelaisian tales and hardly more than a pot-boiler, is perhaps more often read in America than is his serious work.

HUMAN COMEDY, THE (1943), by William Saroyan. See TIME OF YOUR LIFE, THE, by William Saroyan.

HUMAN MIND, THE (1930), by Karl A. Menninger. This is a systematic interpretation of the personality, with emphasis not on the "normal," but the average—the new psychiatric viewpoint. Menninger describes life as a process of meeting problems. Unless complete success (adjustment) is gained in overcoming them, there can be three kinds of results: broken personality (mental disorder); broken situation, or incorrect solution of problem (crime); or compromise (compensation in other fields). There is a listing of seven personality types, with case histories and historical examples to prove that no single one is irrevocably doomed to failure in society. Menninger goes on to describe symptoms of stress (deficiencies, excesses and distortions), personality motives as censored and changed by the unconscious, treatment of disorders by prevention beforehand, or diagnosis and medical care afterward, and finally applications of psychiatric aid at critical points in society—school, industry, the law, the church, and the medical profession.

HUMPHREY CLINKER, THE EXPEDITION OF (1771), by Tobias Smollett. Sometimes called the greatest of epistolary novels, this disjointed work reveals Smollett at his mellow and mature best. The story is unraveled through a series of letters which include some of the most humorous in the language, particularly those of Winifred Jenkins, the maid to the Bramble family, whose spelling is magnificently confusing. Of merit are Smollett's revelations of contemporary manners and peculiarities; for example, the curious picture of Scottish idiosyncrasies, and the gently mocking take-off on the frivolities and absurdities of Hot Wells, a fashionable watering place and health resort. Matthew Bramble is an eccentric and somewhat valetudinarian bachelor, a little soured with age and ill health, a little disenchanted, and sensitive to "the dirt, the stench, the chilling blasts, and perpetual rains," that render "intolerable" to him the same Hot Wells that his niece, Lydia, finds rapturously charming. His humors are complemented by those of his sister, Tabitha, a cross old maid.

The story involves a journey begun at Gloucester, where Lydia, at boarding school, has been corresponding with a handsome young actor, Wilson, whom Lydia's brother, Jerry Melford, a Cambridge student, almost meets in a duel. En route Mr. Bramble accepts into service as his coachman, Humphrey Clinker, a poor, ragged ostler, who later turns Methodist preacher and is imprisoned on a false charge of robbery. Clinker proves to be Brambles son, and he and Winifred are united.

At Durham the party is joined by a cantankerous and whimsical Scottish soldier, Lieutenant Obadiah Lismahago, who tells horrific tales of his sufferings at the hands of his Indian captors, and wins the favor of Tabitha Bramble. Lydia's erstwhile suitor, Wilson, crops up in various disguises at different stages of the journey. He is really George Dennison, a gentleman of rank and wealth, his acting career merely an escape from a marriage dictated by his parents. He weds Lydia.

HUNDRED VERSES FROM OLD JAPAN, A (1253; Eng. tr. 1909). See HYAKU-NIN ISSHU.

HUNG LOU MENG (1754), by Tsao Hsueh-chin. *Hung Lou Meng* by Tso Hsueh-chin (1719–1764) is considered one of the greatest Chinese novels. It has 421 characters: 232 men and 189 women. The author was the extremely gifted son of a wealthy scholarly family, but his failure in his official literary examinations barred him from any real advancement.

The novel tells of the love of Ling Tai Yu (Black Jade) for the heroine Chia Pao Yu (Precious Jade), and how she returned that love; it tells, too, of a whole series of family plans and intrigues whereby Precious Jade was tricked into marrying Hsueh Paoyu (Precious Virtue), cousin of Black Jade; and finally, of how Black Jade died tragically. Precious Jade also vanished in a mysterious disappearance that the reader can interpret only as death.

The *Hung Lou Meng* is original and effective as a love story. As a novel on the Chinese social life, it has no rival. C. C. Wang translated part of the novel as *Dream of the Red Chamber*.

HUNGARIAN NABOB, A (1853–1854), by Maurus Jókai. Maurus Jókai (1825–1904) was one of the most prolific and popular writers of Hungary; during his long life he published over three hundred novels, thirty plays, and a number of other works which filled one hundred volumes in an incomplete edition. A realist and romanticist, he possessed a fertile imagination, and drew his subjects not only from all periods of Hungarian life, but from scientific fantasy and an overpowering imagination.

A Hungarian Nabob (Eng. tr. 1898) was based upon a real incident which Jókai transformed into a novel. It is the story of one of the richest landowners in Hungary, John Karpathy, an eccentric, kindly fellow whom his neighbors call Master Jock. One day his greedy nephew and heir, Abbelino Karpathy, appears. This disagreeable young man speaks affected French rather than honest Hungarian. To spite him and thwart his efforts, Master Jock marries a pretty milliner, Fanny Meyer, who is the object of Abbelino's unwelcome attentions. Maddened by this, the nephew suggestively sends his uncle a coffin for a birthday present. There is a complication in the story when Fanny falls in love with an idealistic young nobleman, Rudolf Szentormay, who is madly devoted to his wife, Countess Flora, Fanny's bosom friend. Rudolf, blind to what is happening, discovers Fanny's secret love when it is too late, and the two part forever. Fanny dies in childbirth, and when Karpathy dies soon after, he leaves his infant son in the guardianship of Rudolf.

HUNGER (1890; Eng. tr. 1899), by Knut Hamsun. Dealing with the psychopathology of starvation in a highly sensitive and introspective personality, *Hunger* is a distinguished example of its genre. The hero is an unsuccessful author, sick physically and mentally. The pangs of devouring hunger induce in him grotesque and fearful hallucinations. The victim of this torture records his states of consciousness with harrowing fidelity. There is no plot in the conventional sense. It is a searing chronicle in which only fleeting moments of hope and inspiration give relief to monotonous days of despair and hunger. What goes on inside the delirious mind of the unnamed protagonist is the whole story.

HUNGER-PASTOR, THE (1864), by Wilhelm Raabe. See RAABE, WILHELM.

HURON, THE (1767), by Volaire. See CANDIDE, by Voltaire.

HURRICANE, THE (1936), by James Norman Hall and Charles Bernard Nordhoff. See MUTINY ON THE BOUNTY, by James Norman Hall and Charles Bernard Nordhoff.

HUS, JAN (ca. 1373–1415). Jan Hus was the leader of a complicated religious and nationalist movement in the medieval kingdom of Bohemia. For a while he was rector of the University of Prague. Then, with his interests concentrated more and more on national and religious themes, he became a leading antagonist of German influence and of the position of the Pope. A popular preacher and teacher, he anticipated by a century most of the teachings of Protestantism, and was finally burned at the stake at the Council of Constance. He is better known for his leadership and death than for his writings, and yet these left an indelible mark upon the future history of his country. They consist largely of doctrinal books written in Latin and Czech and including *Postila (Sermons;* 1412–1413), *Explanation of the Ten Commandments* (1412), and *The Daughter or The Knowledge of the Right Way for Salvation* (1413). There are many of these tracts in both Latin and Czech.

He wrote his *Letters from Constance* (1414–1415), where he was awaiting execution, to encourage his friends and supporters. They are among his most attractive works. He wrote to almost all of his close friends in a natural Czech, and in a system of orthography of his own devising. These letters, like his sermons, have contributed to the outstanding character of Czech literature.

HÜSNÜ ASHK (1778), by Sheyh Galib. See BEAUTY AND LOVE, by Sheyh Galib.

HUTTEN'S LAST DAYS (1871), by Conrad Ferdinand Meyer. See MEYER, CONRAD FERDINAND.

HVIEZDOSLAV (1849–1921). Hviezdoslav (the pen name of Pavol Országh) was the foremost poet of Slovakia. He followed Romantic ideals and methods in his early work, but he later wrote epic poems—like the "Gamekeeper's Wife," the story of a simple woman who, after killing the son of her master when he forces his attentions upon her, becomes temporarily insane; and the two related epics of *Ežo Vikolinsky* (1890) and *Gabor Vikolin-*

sky (1899), which describe the regeneration of a decadent noble family through the intermixture of healthy peasant blood. Hviezdoslav also drew extensively upon Biblical subjects for *Herodes and Herodias* (1909), a drama; and two poems, *Agar* (1883) and *Rachel* (1891). He was a translator of Shakespeare, Madach, Goethe, and Pushkin, but his great works, like the "Bloody Sonnets" after World War I, reflect the aspirations and hopes of the Slovak people in their efforts for liberation. He outlined the future role of his people and adapted their language to the higher purposes of poetry.

HYAKU-NIN ISSHU (1235). *Hyaku-nin Isshu* is a collection of Japanese poems made in 1235 by a court noble named Sedaiye. It contains short songs from the seventh to the thirteenth century, and is the best known of all Japanese anthologies. All these poems are used in card games.

This anthology was translated as *Japanese Odes* by F. V. Dickins in 1866 and as *A Hundred Verses from Old Japan* by William N. Porter in 1909.

HYDRIOTAPHIA (1658), by Sir Thomas Browne. The discovery of Roman burial urns at Norwich is the starting point of this somber yet fancifully written discourse. The author proceeds to comment upon modes of burial throughout man's history; his real purpose seems to be to point out that time mocks men's dreams of earthly immortality or lasting fame. The futility of pyramids, arches, and obelisks is shown; there is no such thing as a lasting monument. Man should be content simply to have existed. As this great English stylist sonorously says, "the iniquity of oblivion blindly scattereth her poppy."

HYMN TO SATAN (1865), by Giosue' Carducci. See CARDUCCI, GIOSUE'.

HYMN TO THE RISING SUN (1936), by Paul Green. See IN ABRAHAM'S BOSOM, by Paul Green.

HYMNS TO THE NIGHT (1800), by Novalis. See NOVALIS.

HYPATIA (1853), by Charles Kingsley. Printed first in *Fraser's Magazine* in 1851, this historical novel gives an account of the conflict between Greek philosophy and Christianity in the old city of Alexandria in the fifth century. The decadent city is in the last throes of its brilliant civilization. To Alexandria comes a young Christian monk, Philammon, who hopes to save mankind from destruction for its sins. He is fascinated and turned from his faith by the pagan Greek philosopher, Hypatia, a beautiful and noble woman. Even as he is drawn to Hypatia by the saneness and purity of her doctrines, he is disgusted and sickened by the fanaticism of the Alexandrian monks, led by the aggressive, vicious patriarch, Cyril. The city is kept under inadequate control by the legionnaires of the cynical prefect Orestes, who is unable or unwilling to attempt to curb its turbulent elements. Hypatia is attacked in her lecture room and torn to pieces by the Christians, who are enraged at her teachings. After this violence, Philammon returns to the desert, having learned the lesson of tolerance. The Hypatia of history was a Neoplatonic philosopher who died in the same manner as the Hypatia of Kingsley's novel. Her death was a symbol of the final decay of a once great city.

HYPERION (1797–1799), by Friedrich Hölderlin. See HÖLDERLIN, FRIEDRICH.

HYPERION (1839), by Henry Wadsworth Longfellow. See LONG-FELLOW, HENRY WADSWORTH.

HYPERION, A FRAGMENT (1818–1819), by John Keats. Miltonic in tone and in projected scope, this epic was intended apparently to cover the concluding phase of the war of the Titans, led by Cronus (Saturn) against victorious Zeus and his brothers; Hyperion (the Sun) alone of the Titans has not been deposed when the action begins. In Book I Coelus (the Sky) urges him to resist his foes. In Book II, which pictures the fallen Titans brooding over their fate, Oceanus, as Keats' mouthpiece, recommends acquiescence to eternal law. Book III represents Apollo, symbolizing the spirit of poetry, preparing to supersede through greater perfection the splendid though crass Hyperion. Incomplete, it remains the greatest achievement of one of England's finest poets. Keats maintains that only with imagery and symbolism through pain can beauty be won. Poetry, he held at this time, was incomplete if it left unexpressed "the agonies, the strife of human hearts." The sustained splendor of this poem shows what Keats might have done on a large scale if he had lived. An inferior version, *The Fall of Hyperion*, also survives.

HYPNDEI CHOSUN MOONHAK (1938). This collection in six volumes contains some of the best modern Korean writing in poetry, drama, the novel, and essays. Many Korean writers today are in a rebellious mood against conventional morality. They are hungry for new patterns and meanings in life, and feel growing repugnance toward the old classical tradition which has held them back so many centuries and not fortified them against the shock of Western civilization. At present, an intellectual and artistic ferment goes on in Korea. It is probably sharper and more desperate and more vital here than in either China or Japan, because Korea is in the throes of a death-birth.

Some of the best-known writers in this collection: Li Kwangsoo (1892– , author of some 20 novels); Liang Chudong (1903– , poet and critic); Kim Dong Whan (1903–); Li Eunsang (1903–); Chung Jiyng (1903–); Park Palyang (1904–); Yim Wha (1908–); Park Chongwha (1901–); Kim Dongmyung (1901–); Li Teichoon (1904–); Park Teiwon (1909–); Chang Duckcho (1915–); Kim Dongin (1900–); Chang Hyungchu (1905–); Chun Yungteik (1892–); Han Sulya (1902–); Li Shang (1911–1937); Li Sunhi (1911–); Kang Kyungai (1908–); Choi Chunghi (1910–); Yu Chino (1906–); An Jeihong (1891–); Sul Chungsik (1911–); Kim Dongsuk (1907–); Kim Namchun (1909–); Chu Soowon (1910–); Lim Haksoo (1911–); Li Changhi (1902–1929).

I MIEI RICORDI (1867), by Massimo D'Azeglio. See D'AZEGLIO, MASSIMO.

I PROMESSI SPOSI (1825), by Alessandro Manzoni. See BETROTHED, THE, by Alessandro Manzoni.

IAIA GARCIA (1878), by Joaquim Maria Machado de Assis. See DOM CASMURRO, by Joaquim Maria Machado de Assis.

IBN EZRA, MOSES (ca. 1070–1138?). Born in Granada, and not heard of after 1138, Moses ben Jacob ibn Ezra was a member of a distinguished family of scholars and poets. We know that he was a rabbinic scholar, philosopher, and linguist, studying assiduously despite a life of ease and luxury. The disillusionment and bitterness that mark so many of his stanzas, and his predilection for composing penitential prayers, are generally ascribed to an unrequited love for his niece, but may more probably be due to personal misfortunes following a political overturn in his home city. Little is known of his life beyond his works. These include a book on God, nature, and the intellect (*Bed of Fragrance*); a treatise on rhetoric and poetry (*Book of Discussion and Remembrance*); *Tarshish,* largely secular poetry; and the *Diwan,* secular poems, with many encomia and elegies, and penitential poems. The last are to be found throughout the Jewish liturgy for the New Year-Atonement period. Moses ibn Ezra, though recognizing that poesy must be inspired, laid stress on the art of poetry; he accepted the Arab laws of poetics as conformable to the spirit of the Hebrew language. He provided biographical and critical data concerning previous Hebrew poets of Spain, and wrote extensively on the rules of verse structure. Frequently philosophical, his poems are marked by fine imagery, grace, and power. He had remarkable skill in interpolating scriptural verses within his own compositions. Part of Ibn Ezra's distinction lies in the fact that he was among the earliest Jewish poets to extend his prosodizing to worldly matters, such as physical pleasures, wine, love, and riddles.

IBN GABIROL, SOLOMON (1021–ca. 1058). An outstanding poet and philosopher of medieval Spain, Solomon ibn Gabirol was born in Malaga late in 1021; he died in Valencia about 1058. Early orphaned, he was taken to Saragossa, center of Jewish culture, where he displayed his precocity in rapidly amassing all the learning of his age. The larger portion of his literary work has not come down to us, but we know that it can be divided into Biblical exegesis, grammar, philosophy and ethics, and poetry. Nor have we any knowledge of the dates on which his books appeared. Much of his religious hymnody has been included in Jewish liturgy. He wrote *Choice of Pearls,* a collection of Arabic maxims; and an ethical treatise, *The Improvement of the Moral Qualities,* unique for its odd arrangement of the virtues and vices in relation to the senses. In a day when versification was not limited to so-called poetic themes, but could be employed as a vehicle for law, science, and mathematics, Ibn Gabirol composed a long poem on Hebrew grammar. More than a score of philosophical essays, of which we have no trace today, were written by him in Arabic; and by an error in reading the word meaning "The Malagan," they were recorded as by "King Solomon the Jew" instead of by Solomon ibn Gabirol. Through an even more unusual error his major philosophical work was for centuries ascribed to one "Avicebron," corrupted in several stages from the author's name. This book, *Fons Vitae* (Latinized from the Hebrew *Meḳor Hayyim*), is a neo-Platonic treatise which fortuitously quotes no Biblical or Talmudic verse. This dialogue between master and disciple, which posits matter and form as the basis of existence and the source of all life, was accepted as a good Christian classic by the Franciscans (Alexander of Hales, Duns Scotus) and rejected by the Dominicans (Thomas Aquinas). The error which permitted many scholastics and later Christians to employ a Jewish theological work as a document of their faith was not discovered until the 1840's.

ICELAND: THE FIRST AMERICAN REPUBLIC (1939), by Vilhjálmur Stefánsson. See STEFÁNSSON, VILHJÁLMUR.

ICELAND FISHERMAN, THE (1886), by Pierre Loti. This is an extremely simple, poetic story about a brave Breton fisherman and his girl. Yann and Gaud love each other, overcome their bashfulness enough to admit the fact, and are married only six days before the fishing fleet leaves for the Iceland Banks. There is a storm at sea, and she never sees him again. Meanwhile a secondary interest is furnished by the story of Sylvestre, another Breton lad who ships with the Navy, is wounded in China, and dies on the voyage home. The book abounds in pictures of life at sea and of sentimental vignettes of the women left waiting ashore in Brittany.

Loti exploited the same sadness and simplicity in a long series of novels, many of which were based on his own experiences in the Navy.

ICEMAN COMETH, THE (1946), by Eugene O'Neill. See MOURNING BECOMES ELECTRA, by Eugene O'Neill.

ICONOCLASTS (1905), by James Gibbons Huneker. See IVORY APES AND PEACOCKS, by James Gibbons Huneker.

IDEA OF A UNIVERSITY, THE (1852–1873), by John Henry (Cardinal) Newman. In opposition to the growing power of Brougham and the utilitarians who wanted to put scientific research in the forefront of university teaching, Newman wrote this book to set out his own contrary ideas. It was as a prologue to the formal opening of Dublin University, where he was installed as the first president, that he delivered much of the matter contained in this book.

He asserts the chief role of a university is to teach, to stimulate the latent intelligence, to instil habits of accurate thought. He attacked the prevailing idea of separating education from religion and asserted that all knowledge is one and knowledge of God cannot be cast out without injuring all that remains. He justifies the ancient university systems and the tutorial supervision. He thought it was for the church to fashion and mold. He wanted both science and literature to occupy their proper places, but he heartily disapproved of the dissemination of "useful knowledge" in smatterings, for "nutshell views for the breakfast table." Newman's is the most eloquent defense of a liberal education extant.

IDEA OF COMEDY AND THE USES OF THE COMIC SPIRIT, THE (1877), by George Meredith. Meredith explains why the comic poet has been a rare apparition. He needs a highly cultivated society, subtle-minded. Neither Puritans, who do not laugh at all, nor Bacchanalians, who laugh too much and in too animal a way, will appreciate him. The Sentimentalists, especially women, are also his foes. The French are shown to be superior to the English in depicting that relation to society wherein comedy lies. Molière, the best example, is contrasted with Congreve. The comic is an aid against folly and dullness and toward improvement (e.g., Aristophanes) of society. The English excel in satire and humor, which are different. "The test of true comedy is that it shall awaken thoughtful laughter." The laughter of the comic spirit is wholly beneficial.

IDEAS ABOUT THE PHILOSOPHY OF THE HISTORY OF MANKIND (1784–1791), by Johann Gottfried Herder. See HERDER, JOHANN GOTTFRIED.

IDEAS OF GOOD AND EVIL (1903), by William Butler Yeats. See YEATS, WILLIAM BUTLER.

IDEËN (1862–1877), by Multatuli. See MAX HAVELAAR, by Multatuli.

IDES OF MARCH, THE (1948), by Thornton Wilder. See BRIDGE OF SAN LUIS REY, THE, by Thornton Wilder.

IDIOT, THE (1868), by Feodor Dostoevsky. Like the other major novels of Dostoevsky, *The Idiot* plumbs the profound depths of the human spirit. The hero, Prince Myshkin, is a nobleman belonging to an ancient Russian house. From his early youth he has suffered epileptic fits, which have affected his physical and mental health. He has no worldly faults and possesses an exceptionally simple, sincere and lovable character. Two women with diametrically different backgrounds, characters and motives fall in love with him. One is the young daughter of General Epanchin, and the other is a neurotic lady of easy virtue who had been discarded by a wealthy merchant. The first, Aglaia, the highly principled Myshkin won't marry because he deems himself unworthy of her and mentally too ill to hope that he will ever bring her happiness; the other, Nastasia, he finally wishes to make his wife, motivated by the spirit of Christian self-sacrifice. Myshkin's will to martyrdom is irrepressible. However, the highly complicated Nastasia, moved by a selfless desire to spare him his sacrifice for her, runs off in the end with a brutish suitor, Rogozhin, who, maddened by jealousy, murders her. The unforgettable last scene shows Myshkin and the repentant murderer talking gravely, in an inspired mood, over the corpse of the murdered woman. In the death of Nastasia they cross the barriers of love and hate, good and evil, fear and the courage that is more enduring than death. However, Myshkin's sensitive spirit cannot bear the shock of Nastasia's murder, and he becomes truly what he has often been accused of being, an "idiot."

IDIOT'S DELIGHT (1936), by Robert Sherwood. See ABE LINCOLN IN ILLINOIS, by Robert Sherwood.

IDYLS (ca. 270 b.c.), by Theocritus. These poems are typical of the artificiality and refinement of Alexandrian court poetry. Theocritus, a Syracusan, wrote in his native Doric dialect usually on pastoral or bucolic themes. The characters of the *Idyls* are shepherds, fishermen and farm girls, though these may be but a slight disguise for the poet's learned friends, as in the seventh Idyl. The situation described or presented dramatically may be mythical or simply imaginary, but usually presents a compact genre scene such as those popular in Alexandrine art, whence the name Idyl, meaning "little scene." Theocritus is credited with originating this type of poetry, which has had many distinguished imitators from Virgil to the poets of the ninteenth century, but much of the charm of his poetry lies in the simple and seemingly unaffected character and language of his shepherds.

IDYLLS OF THE KING, THE (1842–1885), by Alfred, Lord Tennyson. The *Idylls* are composed of twelve allegorical, narrative poems in blank verse, which form the continuing story of the legendary Arthur from his supernatural birth to his supernatural death. It tells of his ideals in the establishment of a Round Table of perfect knights and ladies. We read a chronicle of his noble deeds and those of his knights, of the many events of his reign, the gradual breakdown of the noble plan through the corruption of the court, and the destruction of his kingdom. The materials which Tennyson used were Malory's *Morte d'Arthur* (q.v.), Geoffrey's *History* (q.v.), the Welsh *Mabinogion* (q.v.), and Layamon's *Brut* (q.v.). He did not, however, follow any of these accounts very closely, though he used Malory the most. The component parts of the *Idylls* are:

The Coming of Arthur (1869). Arthur, crowned king of Britain with the aid of Merlin, the magician, falls in love with Guinevere, daughter of Leodogran of Cameliard. He conquers his own rebellious lords and restores Leodogran's kingdom. Leodogran hears the story of Arthur's mysterious birth from Bellicent, wife of Lot of Orkney, and consents to the marriage.

Gareth and Lynette (1872). Lynette seeks a knight to rescue her sister Lyonors, held captive by four knights. Gareth takes the quest, much to Lynette's disgust, since she believes him to be a kitchen knave. Bearing her insults with humility, Gareth overcomes his opponents and wins her love. The court is at that time united loyal to Arthur and his ideals.

Enid. Later divided into *The Marriage of Geraint* and *Geraint and Enid* (1859). Fearing that Guinevere will corrupt his beautiful young wife Enid, Geraint returns to his land. Suspecting Enid of disloyalty, Geraint subjects her to undeserved tests of loyalty which she bears nobly and heroically. She later convinces him of her innocence and regains his love.

Balin and Balan (1885). Balin is so angered by vicious reports about the queen he adores that he mutilates his shield bearing her crown. His brother, Balan, mistakes Balin for a demon; both brothers are killed in the ensuing duel.

Merlin and Vivien (1859). Vivien, who hates Arthur, comes to his court to spread suspicion. She enchants the magician Merlin, learns his secrets, and uses one of them to shut him up in a tree forever.

Lancelot and Elaine (1859). The guilty love of Lancelot and Guinevere is beginning to bring retribution. Lancelot refuses the love of Elaine, who dies, leaving Lancelot remorseful.

The Holy Grail (1869). The knights search for the grail. Only a few, among them Sir Galahad, have the spiritual power to see it. The court has begun to disintegrate. Lancelot is denied even the vision because of his sin with Guinevere.

Pelleas and Ettarre (1869). Young and artless, Pelleas discovers that not only Ettarre, whom he loves, is faithless, but most of the others at the court. The shadow of impending tragedy is plainly apparent.

The Last Tournament (1871). Tristram wins the tournament, and, unfaithful to his own wife, takes the prize to Mark's wife. Mark discovers and kills him. Arthur returns to find that Guinevere has fled. The disintegration of the Round Table is almost complete.

Guinevere (1859). Guinevere, conscience-stricken and fearful, meets Lancelot for the last time. They are spied upon by Modred. Guinevere flees to a nunnery, is visited by Arthur, who upbraids, then forgives her. Guinevere remains at the convent, where she dies three years later.

The Passing of Arthur (1869). The final idyl describes Arthur's last battle with the rebel Modred, whom he slays after being mortally wounded by him. The poem concludes with Arthur's return to the supernatural world.

IK EN MIJN SPEELMAN (1927), by Aart van der Leeuw. The youthful nobleman Claude de Lindres turns his back on the frivolous life of the eighteenth century French court to escape a marriage being forced on him with an unknown lady. Fascinated by the playing of the hunchback violinist Valentijn, he follows him. Stripped by bandits, he has to learn from Valentijn how to make a living. Valentijn becomes his benevolent guiding spirit, teaches him to play the clarinet, reveals him to himself, and makes him appreciate the simple life. In a tavern, they meet the girl Madeleen, who henceforth wanders with them. She has fled from her family for the same reasons as Claude. They fall in love, and when they marry, discover that they are the bride and bridegroom who had fled one from the other. "A humoristic novel of adventure, which in final analysis touches what lives deepest in my heart: the contrast between Babylon and the New Jerusalem," i.e., the hollow worldly existence against the worshiping joy over the beauty of the earth.

Of Aart van der Leeuw's (1876–1931) other stories and novels, which are all written with wise humor, *De Kleine Rudolf* (1930) had an enormous success. It is the story of the poetic dreamer Rudolf, who through profound self-denial and the misery of many disappointments attains complete victory over himself, in such measure that the social Rudolf and the poetic dreamer are capable of living together in the same person. Through its simple narration and colorful, light touch, this book became a sublime testimony to the joyful acceptance of life, rooted in wisdom.

ILIAD OF HOMER, THE (1870), translated by William Cullen Bryant. See THANATOPSIS, by William Cullen Bryant.

ILIAD (9th c. B.C.?), by Homer. This magnificent Greek epic is one of the unquestionably great poems of all time, ranking in literary importance and influence with the *Bible* (q.v.) and Shakespeare. Its origin remains obscure despite the devoted efforts of generations of scholars. It is the earliest extant literature, and in fact the first written record of Western civilization. From its very perfection it must have had a long tradition of predecessors, and was almost certainly preserved by oral tradition before it was ever reduced to writing. Herodotus believed that Homer lived about 850 B.C., and that may not be far from the actual date of the poem. The incidents, however, of the

Trojan war which it describes, and which have been made to seem far more substantial and real by archaeological discoveries of the last century both at Troy and in Greece, belong apparently to the twelfth century B.C.

The materials for the epic were drawn from the Trojan legend which told how the barbarian city of Troy, or Ilium, was besieged for ten years by an army of Greeks and finally captured and sacked to regain Helen and avenge her abduction from King Menelaus by the Trojan prince, Paris. The story unfolded by the *Iliad* is but an incident, lasting some seven weeks, in the tenth year of the war. The unifying theme is the wrath of the Greek hero, Achilles, and throughout the twenty-four books of the poem we see its cause and effects. Agamemnon, the commander of the Greek force, injures the sensitive pride of Achilles by demanding from him a captive handmaiden, his share of the spoils of war. Achilles is forced by the gods to comply, but in his heroic wrath he swears to withdraw himself and his Myrmidons from further combat until Agamemnon sorely feels the need of him. Through the interference of the gods the Greek army is brought to dire extremities by the Trojans under the leadership of Hector. Agamemnon humbles himself so far as to send an embassy imploring Achilles to return to the battle but cannot bend his will. Achilles does consent reluctantly to the importunate pleas of his bosom companion, Patroclus, and permits him to join the conflict. Heedless of warnings Patroclus involves himself in conflict with Hector and is slain. As the Greeks are now truly humbled, Achilles rejoins the fray, defeats and kills Hector. The spirit of Patroclus is appeased by an elaborate burial; and the epic ends on a chivalrous note of reconciliation with the ransoming of the corpse of Hector to Priam, his aged father.

The pace of the poem is stately and majestic. The heroes are made to speak dramatically for themselves and the poet never obtrudes himself upon one's consciousness. He presents the Trojans with as great if not greater sympathy than he does the Greeks. Hector becomes at times, indeed, as in the famous scene of his parting from his wife and infant son, the most humanly moving character in the epic. The lasting popularity of the *Iliad* is evidenced by the frequency with which it has been translated. Chapman's translation, which inspired Keats' sonnet, is hardly read today. Among the poetic versions may be mentioned those of Alexander Pope and William Cullen Bryant. The prose rendering in English which is preferred by many who do not read Greek is that of Lang, Leaf and Myer's, who followed the suggestion laid down by Matthew Arnold. A. T. Murray has made a scholarly translation for the Loeb Classical Library with the original Greek and English on facing pages—this is excellent for the reader who knows a little Greek.

IMAGINARY CONVERSATIONS (1824–1853), by Walter Savage Landor. These essays did not begin to appear until Landor was past the middle of his unusually long life. Their subjects are varied, ranging from Greek to contemporary figures. Comedy and tragedy, imagination and history, sentiment and scenery, all enhance the attractions of the collection. The *Imaginary Conversations* have been compared with Fontenelle's *Dialogues of the Dead* (q.v.), which he wrote in avowed imitation of Lucian. Swinburne was an enthusiastic admirer of Landor: "He has won for himself such a double-crown of glory in verse and in prose as has been won by no other

Englishman but Milton." This is his most renowned prose work; he has used every device of color and rhythm, sound and word effect. No one who knows and loves the English language can escape their appeal. The beauty of his cadence and modulation, its tender grace and restrained strength will be found on every page. In emotional prose which never overreaches itself, Landor is one of the complete masters in English. We read of Xerxes and Artabamus, Alexander and the Priest, Epicurus, Leontion and Ternissa, Lucullus and Caesar, Wallace and Edward I, Fra Filippo Lippi and Pope Eugenius IV, Dante and Beatrice, Cromwell and Walter Noble, Louis XIV and Father La Chaise, Catherine of Russia and Princess Dashkof, Rhadamistus and Zenobia, John of Gaunt and Joanna of Kent, Melanchthon and Calvin, Bossuet and the Duchess de Fontanges.

IMAGINARY INVALID, THE (1673), by Molière. See MALADE, IMAGINAIRE, LE, by Molière.

IMITATION OF CHRIST (1415), by Thomas à Kempis. The *Imitation of Christ* by Thomas à Kempis (Thomas from Kempen) is the most famous devotional book in Christian literature. The French eighteenth century philosopher Fontenelle referred to it as "the finest work that has proceeded from the pen of man, the Gospel being of divine origin." The work was first published in English by the Dean of Canterbury in 1696.

Thomas à Kempis, who was a contemplative German Augustinian monk, wrote simply and from the heart. He went straight to the point in the opening sentence: " 'He that followeth me, shall not walk in darkness, but shall have the light of life,' says Christ, who declares Himself 'the light of the world.' The true importance and design of which words is doubtless to instruct us that the way to be truly enlightened, and to deliver ourselves from a blindness of heart, is to make His holy life the object of our imitation, and to form our dispositions and actions upon the perfect model of that bright example."

The *Imitation* had a profound influence on John Wesley, and, consequently, on the rise of Methodism. Wesley himself published an English translation of it under the title: *The Christian's Pattern*. Upon the death of Thomas à Kempis a long and acrimonious dispute arose between the Canons Regular of the Augustinians and the Benedictines, the first claiming their brother Thomas à Kempis as the author of the *Imitation* and the latter claiming that it was the work of the Benedictine theologian John Gerson, the chancellor of the University of Paris. This argument has raged incessantly for some 500 years, and there have been published enough articles, pamphlets and books on the controversy to fill a library.

Like Meister Eckart, Thomas à Kempis believed that God was all and man nothing: "Where can man find that which is truly good, and which enduringly satisfies? Not in the multitude of things which distract, but in the *One* which collects and unites. For the One does not proceed from the many but the many from the One. That One is the one thing needful, the chief good, and nothing better and higher either exists or can even be conceived. Compared with Him the creature is nothing, and only becomes anything when in fellowship with Him. Whatever is not God is nothing, and should be counted as nothing." The soul should devote itself to union with God, and Thomas traces the progress which leads to that union.

IMMENSEE (1852), by Theodor Storm. This short story of scarcely 40 pages, flashing back from an old bachelor's solitary life to his childhood love and later resignation, is devoid of an actual plot. Its loosely connected scenes, endowed with the melancholy charm of romantic music and enhanced by beautiful lyrical poems, have endeared *Immensee* to the German public and won a world-wide fame for the author. This story of recollection captures the reader by indirection and the intense though unspoken passion of the frustrated lovers. The symbolic white water lily which the nightly swimmer cannot reach in spite of his desperate efforts still haunts the twilight reminiscence of the old man.

Storm has written many masterful novelettes besides *Immensee,* and one volume of poems. He is one of the finest representatives of bourgeois realism in Germany, has had a great popularity, and even influenced Thomas Mann in his younger days.

IMMORALIST, THE (1902), by André Gide. See COUNTERFEITERS, THE, by André Gide.

IMPERIALISM (1917), by Nikolay Lenin. This work, subtitled *The Highest State of Capitalism,* is the elaboration of the implications of Marxism, as Lenin saw them, for the twentieth century. Capitalism, having run its course, is in a process of contraction, and in desperation capitalistic nations are in a life and death struggle for control of the few remaining undeveloped areas in the world. The consequence of these economic conflicts is military conflict, which is to be the death throes of capitalism and the opportunity for the proletariat to take command of the state as anticipated by Marx.

IMPORTANCE OF BEING EARNEST, THE (1895), by Oscar Wilde. In this "Trivial Comedy for Serious People," the scene opens in Algernon Moncrieff's rooms in Half Moon Street. He is expecting his aunt, Lady Bracknell, and her daughter, Gwendolen. Jack Worthing, who is courting Gwendolen, arrives first. Algy discovers that Jack has a ward, Cecily, and has told her he has a younger brother Earnest. In fact, Jack calls himself Earnest in town and Jack in the country. Jack and Gwendolen become engaged, but Lady Bracknell will not hear of it, when Jack admits he was found in a handbag in a railroad station. Algy goes to Jack's house in the country, and introduces himself to Cecily as her cousin Earnest; they become engaged. Jack arrives in deep mourning, having decided to kill off Earnest. Gwendolen appears, and for a few minutes both girls think they are engaged to the same Earnest. Lady Bracknell follows Gwendolen, and recognizes Miss Prism, Cecily's governess, as the woman who disappeared with a baby, and left a novel in his pram. Jack turns out to be the baby, whom Miss Prism had put in her handbag instead of the novel. And his name really is Earnest.

IMPRESSIONS OF KOREAN INDEPENDENCE, THE (1933), by Han Yong-woon. See MEDITATIONS OF THE LOVER, by Han Yong-woon.

IMPROVEMENT OF THE MORAL QUALITIES, THE, by Solomon Ibn Gabirol. See IBN GABIROL, SOLOMON.

IN ABRAHAM'S BOSOM (1927), by Paul Green. This long Pulitzer Prize play of Negro life is Paul Green's most famous work, and includes two earlier one-act plays. Abraham McCranie is resentful of circumstances which made him the child of a plantation master and a colored woman. Rebelliously active, he attempts to found a school for Negroes, but is persecuted by them as well as by whites; and finds himself at length at the mercy of Lonnie, his sadistic white half-brother. He marries Goldie McAllister, but is unhappy with her, and with his son Douglas. He spends several years of itinerant existence, eventually gravitating to the original plantation, where his aspirations of founding a school are revived. Douglas, just out of prison, discloses Abraham's aspirations, and causes him to be brutally attacked by a band of masked men. When Lonnie informs him that his farm crop is about to be appropriated, Abraham murders him in a rage; but he is in turn shot down by a mob.

The House of Connelly (1932) is a play about the personal degeneration of a group of southern planters. When Patsy Tate, daughter of a new tenant farmer, marries weak Will Connelly, she rouses him from his lethargy, and sets about restoring the land and the family.

Hymn to the Rising Sun (1936) is a one-act play about life in a prison camp.

IN CHANCERY (1920), by John Galsworthy. See FORSYTE SAGA, THE, by John Galsworthy.

IN DISTRESS (1921), by Zalman Shneiur. See SHNEIUR, ZALMAN.

IN MEMORIAM (1850), by Alfred, Lord Tennyson. This great elegy consists of a prologue, epilogue, and 131 short lyrics, held together through a logical development of a single idea. The theme is the death of Arthur Halam, Tennyson's best friend, and the stages of grief and consolation the poet went through. Begun at the height of his grief, the poem was written over a period of seventeen years. The stanzas are all written in iambic tetrameter quatrains rhyming abba. The poems form a cycle, beginning with Tennyson's complete despair, going through periods of recollection of past times, doubts, and reassurances, to a calm faith in the immortality of the soul.

IN MORTE DI MADONNA LAURA, by Francesco Petrarch. See CANZONIERE, THE, by Francesco Petrarch.

IN OUR CONVENT DAYS (1905), by Agnes Repplier. See REPPLIER, AGNES.

IN THE MIDST OF LIFE (1892), by Ambrose Bierce. See BIERCE, AMBROSE.

IN THE WORLD (1917), by Maxim Gorky. See AUTOBIOGRAPHY, by Maxim Gorky.

IN THIS OUR LIFE (1941), by Ellen Glasgow. See BARREN GROUND, by Ellen Glasgow.

IN VITA DI MADONNA LAURA, by Francesco Petrarch.   See CANZONIERE, THE, by Francesco Petrarch.

IN WAR TIME AND OTHER POEMS (1864), by John Greenleaf Whittier.   See SNOW-BOUND, by John Greenleaf Whittier.

INN KEEPER, THE (1752), by Carlo Goldoni.   As a playwright Carlo Goldoni (1707–1793) had in mind the well-defined purpose of emancipating the Italian comedy from its artificial and conventional character and giving it a new source of spontaneity and charm.   *The Inn Keeper* is an outstanding example of Goldoni's efforts in that direction.   The very plot of the comedy reveals the author's sense of ridicule for the aristocratic class, and, at the same time, his respect and sympathy for the middle class and for common people earning their living by useful and honest work.   Mirandolina is the charming keeper of an inn, guests of which are Chevalier Ripafratta, Marquis of Forlimpopoli, and Count of Alba Fiorita.   Both the Marquis and the Count are fond of Mirandolina and so is Fabrizio, the waiter of the inn.   Only Chevalier Ripafratta, a woman-hater, seems to be indifferent to the charms of the lovely girl.   Soon, however, conquered by Mirandolina's tactful strategy, he joins the others in their ardent and manifold professions of love.   Mirandolina, who likes to play, but who is fundamentally a most virtuous girl, constantly keeps the situation in hand with perfect common sense and balance. She manages to refuse the guests' offers of love without hurting their feelings. At the end she decides to marry Fabrizio, the waiter, since she feels he is the only one who really loves her sincerely and honestly.   The others were infatuated and moved rather by pride and their class-superiority complex than by a genuine sentiment.

INCREDULITY OF FATHER BROWN, THE (1926), by Gilbert Keith Chesterton.   See FATHER BROWN, THE INNOCENCE OF, by Gilbert Keith Chesterton.

INDIAN SUMMER OF A FORSYTE (1918), by John Galsworthy.   See FORSYTE SAGA, THE, by John Galsworthy.

INFANT AND CHILD IN THE CULTURE OF TODAY (1943), by Arnold L. Gesell.   See GESELL, ARNOLD L.

INFANT JESUS IN FLANDERS, THE (1918), by Felix Timmermans. See TIMMERMANS, FELIX.

INHERITORS, THE (1921), by Susan Glaspell.   See GLASPELL, SUSAN.

INNOCENCE OF FATHER BROWN, THE (1911), by Gilbert Keith Chesterton.   See FATHER BROWN, THE INNOCENCE OF, by Gilbert Keith Chesterton.

INNOCENTS ABROAD, THE (1869), by Mark Twain (Samuel L. Clemens).   The most famous American travel book of its generation, this book, subtitled *The New Pilgrim's Progress,* resulted from the author's voyage to Europe on the *Quaker City.*   Its popularity was partly due to the fact that it flattered the self-esteem of Americans, who had until then been taught to admire all things foreign, and scorn things native. Mark Twain attacked this prejudice, somewhat unfairly.

He described the revered European culture as pretentious, European society as decayed, Europeans as petty persons without dignity or love of liberty. By contrast, he found Americans uncorrupted and generous, if a little rough. The author was disappointed in the famous continental art treasures and historic scenes. Wandering among the ancient palaces and ruins, he gave free rein to his Western American humor.

Roughing It (1872) continues this tradition of travel reportage, spicing the journalism with humorous stories and tall tales. The author recalls his years of Western prospecting, and describes graphically local sights such as the pony express, a buffalo hunt, and the coyote.

A Connecticut Yankee in King Arthur's Court (1889) is a rather extraordinary flight into fantasy—for Mark Twain—combined with his characteristic idiomatic realism. A Bridgeport shop foreman is translated *backward* thirteen and half centuries into King Arthur's England. He finds himself surrounded by all the Knights of the Round Table, Arthur, Guenever, Merlin and Morgan le Fay. He trains an apt pupil, Clarence, to help him; and after Alisande escorts him on his required damsel-rescuing expedition, goes through a series of hair-raising adventures to expose the "fol-de-rol" of knight-errantry and the bitter injustice of sixth century English laws. This is the real purpose of the book, as its brief but stinging preface shows. Some of the biggest and most typical Mark Twain situations are the eclipse of the sun, the stopped-up well, the bicycle squad, the expedition with the King, the sewing machine hitched up to St. Simeon Stylites, the tournament which "the Boss" wins with lasso and revolver against all the knights of England, and finally their wire-fence electrocution in one colossal holocause. The story has been filmed twice, once with Will Rogers, to the delight of millions of theater-goers.

INQUIRY CONCERNING THE HUMAN UNDERSTANDING (1749), by David Hume. See TREATISE ON HUMAN NATURE, by David Hume.

INQUIRY CONCERNING THE PRINCIPLES OF MORALS (1751), by David Hume. See TREATISE ON HUMAN NATURE, by David Hume.

INSECT COMEDY, THE (Eng. tr. 1923), by Joseph and Karel Čapek. See R.U.R., by Karel Čapek.

INSIDE BENCHLEY (1942), by Robert Benchley. See BENCHLEY, ROBERT.

INSIDE EUROPE (1936), by John Gunther. *Inside Europe* is a foreign correspondent's report on the various countries of the continent during a most critical period of their history. The political-sociological reports are provocative and accurate within the limits of careful research and personal survey. The first volume was followed by *Inside Asia* (1939), *Inside Latin America* (1941), *Inside U.S.A.* (1947), and *Behind the Curtain* (1949).

INSIDE OF THE CUP, THE (1913), by Winston Churchill. See RICHARD CARVEL, by Winston Churchill.

INSPECTOR GENERAL, THE (1836), by Nikolay Gogol. Gogol satirizes the political corruption in provincial Russia. A little town has been rotting peacefully when the Mayor receives word from an old friend in St. Petersburg that an Inspector General is being sent, probably incognito, to look into the town's affairs. The Mayor calls his officials together and tells Hospital Commissioner Artemy Fillipovitch to wash the nightcaps on some of the patients and to conceal the German doctor, who cannot speak a word of Russian to his patients. The courthouse also needs cleaning, since the porters raise poultry in the courtroom, and the halls are filthy and full of feathers. Bobchinsky and Dobchinsky, two local landowners, bring word that there is a young man staying at the inn who has demanded everything, and not paid his bill for two weeks. The Mayor and his officials conclude he must be the inspector, and decide to wait on him in person. Khlestakov, an impecunious young gentleman who has been threatened with arrest if he does not pay his bill, thinks at first that the Mayor and his delegation have come to take him to jail, but when he finds how the wind blows he promptly takes advantage of the situation and accepts the Mayor's invitation to stay at his house. Khlestakov makes love to the Mayor's wife and daughter, and engages himself to the latter, Marya. He finally drives off in great style to St. Petersburg, promising to return shortly and marry her. The whole family is enchanted with the prospect of such a brilliant match and are receiving the congratulations of their friends when the Postmaster, who opens letters, arrives with one Khlestakov has written to a friend telling him of the hoax he has played on the town. In the midst of their grief and consternation the real Inspector General arrives.

INSTITUTES, THE (533), by a legal commission under the Emperor Justinian. The code of Justinian, known as the *Corpus Iuris Civilis,* is the most influential legal document the world has known. Justinian, a Slav born in Illyria in 493, deserves great credit for the vision and executive ability displayed in the formation of his code. On his accession to the throne of the eastern Roman Empire in 528 he initiated work by the appointment of successive commissions who collected and revised all previous imperial constitutions (*Codex Constitutionum*) and condensed all previous laws, decrees, and opinions into one comprehensive treatise (*Digestæ* or *Pandectæ*). These works being far too vast, technical and cumbrous for any but the learned and expert jurists, Justinian ordered an elementary abridgment so simplified that it would be adapted to the use of beginning students of law. This elementary work was accordingly prepared by the eminent jurists Tribonian, Theophilus, and Dorotheus on the basis of an earlier work by Gaius and given the force of law as part of the *Corpus* under the title of *Institutes.* It begins with general observations on the nature, the divisions and the sources of law. Then it proceeds to treat, first of persons, then of things, of successions to deceased persons, of obligations, and finally of actions. The work is still used as an introductory text to the study of Roman law.

INSTITUTES OF THE CHRISTIAN RELIGION, THE (1536), by John Calvin. In the realm of Protestant doctrinal literature the *Institutes* of Calvin occupy a position similar to that of the *Summa Theologiae* of Aquinas in Catholic dogma. It is authoritarian, systematic and comprehensive. First published in 1536, when Calvin was only 26, as merely a sketch of the enlarged form of later years, it has gone through innumerable editions in all countries of the world. The emphasis in the *Institutes* is on God's will, His holiness, and His majesty, unrelieved by the traditional conception of Christian love or mercy. Man's function in life is to serve his God in the manner prescribed by the *Bible,* eschew pleasure and happiness, and fulfill faithfully and unquestion-ingly the role "divine providence" assigns to him. The central doctrine enunciated in the *Institutes* is that of absolute predestination, which is the foundation stone of Calvinism. Anticipating criticism from theologians, Calvin denies that his doctrine of predestination makes God the author of sin, since He leaves mankind helpless without free will: "Their [sinners'] perdition depends on the divine predestination in such a manner that the *cause* and *matter* of it are found in themselves. For the first man fell because the Lord had de-termined it should so happen." The *Institutes* is written with elegant simplicity and its meanings are very lucid. Calvin's literary, philosophical and legal training were of a very high order and endowed all his writings with a clarity and readability unexcelled in his day. The work is a distinguished one purely on literary grounds. Undoubtedly he was one of the great molding forces of modern times. He was to Western Europe what Luther was to Germany. His influence on American civilization and religious life was ef-fected through the New England Puritans and the Scotch Presbyterians, who interpreted his doctrine of obedience to God's will as a justification for re-sistance to earthly tyrants.

INSTITUTIO ORATORIA (ca. 70), by Quintilian. Of Quintilian (40–ca. 100) and his widely renowned *Institutio Oratoria* the epigrammatist, Martial, for once discarded his mocking tone and wrote:

> Quintilian, sovereign guide of wayward youth,
> Quintilian, glory of the Roman gown.

Quintilian kept an academy for budding orators. The *Institutes,* a work in twelve volumes, was the result of twenty years of teaching. Book I treats of preschool education from infancy; Book II of the initial training under a professor of rhetoric. Quintilian here defines rhetoric, in which the important elements are the right subject matter and the use of the right style. Five books (III-VII) are devoted to choosing the right subject matter and to its allied art, that of proper arrangement. Books VIII-XI are assigned to style and its allied subjects, memorizing of a speech and its delivery. Book XII is the culmination point of the *Institutes,* and portrays the author's ideal conception of an orator. However, it is Book I which reveals Quintilian for the superb educator that he was, a man full of novel and progressive ideas, remaining sound and imbued with common sense all the while in his recommendations. The *Insti-tutes* is therefore more than a mere textbook for orators; it is a mirror of Roman culture, and gives a unified view of the educated "gentlemen's" out-look on life, of which oratory, an essential of all public life, was an integral part. For oratory reflected character, initiation into the liberal arts, and a well of information about everything from philosophy to politics. Quintilian over-looked nothing: the speech of the child's nurse, the example of the parents, the manners of the slaves, the early teaching methods, etc. He recommends that education should at first bear the form of amusement to hold the flagging interest of the untrained child. School is preferred to the home because under the healthy stimulation of other contacts and group life the child develops a healthy ambition, about which Quintilian remarks: "Ambition may be a vice, but it is often the root of virtues."

INSTITUTIONES MEDICAE (1708), by Hermann Boerhaave. See ELEMENTA CHEMIAE, by Hermann Boerhaave.

INTERESES CREADOS, LOS (1907), by Jacinto Benavente. See BONDS OF INTEREST, THE, by Jacinto Benavente.

INTIMATE JOURNALS (1921), by Paul Gauguin. See NOA NOA, by Paul Gauguin.

INTRIGUE AND LOVE (1784), by Friedrich von Schiller. See SCHILLER, FRIEDRICH VON.

INTRODUCTION TO THE PRINCIPLES OF MORALS AND LEGISLATION (1789), by Jeremy Bentham. This incomplete work by the founding father of English Utilitarianism was meant to serve as a basis for a complete legal system, civil and criminal. Bentham sought to reorganize legal principles on a rational basis. The fundamental principle is that of *utility*. Mankind is conceived of as governed by two masters, pleasure and pain. Utility is the capacity of an act to promote pleasure and avoid pain. All men act in accordance with these principles whether aware of the fact or not. Bentham advocates that these principles be recognized and used by rulers or parliaments as the basic criteria in determining suitable legislation. He develops an elaborate system by which the pleasurable and painful consequences of proposed acts can be measured and compared so that resulting legislation will tend to promote the "greatest happiness of the greatest number." Bentham was a supremely confident genius who somewhat oversimplified the problem, but was nevertheless extremely influential because of the clarity and persuasiveness of his views. Much English legal, social, and political reform of the nineteenth century can be traced back to him.

IPHIGENIA IN AULIS (ca. 406 B.C.), by Euripides. Euripides opens his play when the Greek fleet, waiting to sail to Troy, is becalmed in Aulis. Calchas, the prophet, has told Agamemnon that favorable winds will blow if he sacrifices his daughter, Iphigenia, to Artemis, whose stag Agamemnon has killed. The latter has asked his wife, Clytaemnestra, to bring Iphigenia to Aulis on the pretext that she is to be married to Achilles before the army departs. He has sent a second message to his wife telling her not to come, but it is intercepted by his brother, Menelaus, husband of Helen, for whose recovery from Troy the expedition is being made. In the meantime, a messenger arrives with the news that Clytaemnestra, Iphigenia and the young Orestes have arrived and are on their way to Agamemnon's tent. Iphigenia and Clytaemnestra are full of excitement at the thought of the marriage. Agamemnon greets his daughter gravely, trying to hide his sadness, and puts off his wife's questions about the marriage ceremony and her daughter's prospective husband, Achilles. The latter comes to Agamemnon's tent and Clytaemnestra greets him as her future son-in-law, much to his bewilderment, as he had never heard of the marriage. The true situation is explained to them by an old servant, and Achilles, deeply moved by Clytaemnestra's distress, promises to rescue Iphigenia. Agamemnon announces that all is ready for the marriage ceremony. Clytaemnestra calls out her weeping daughter and the child, Orestes, and tells Agamemnon she hates him. She asks why Menelaus does not sacrifice his own daughter, Hermione, and begs him to give up this murder. Iphigenia, too, pleads with her father for her life. "What have I to do with Helen's love?" she asks, and then, turning to Orestes, begs even him to plead for her. Agamemnon replies by pointing to the ships, saying that they cannot sail unless he makes the sacrifice, and concludes that he is no slave to Menelaus but bows to Hellas. Weeping, Iphigenia flings herself in her mother's arms. Achilles returns with the bad news that the whole camp is clamoring for the sacrifice, and, led by Odysseus, they are coming for the maiden, ten thousand strong. He offers to make a last attempt to rescue her from the altar. Iphigenia speaks now with great composure and dignity, choosing death of her own free will. She is ready to die for Greece, and, begging her mother not to mourn for her, she goes out to the sacrifice. Artemis, however, rescues the girl and substitutes a deer for the sacrifice. This is one of the most melodramatic tragedies of Euripides and perhaps his last. It was probably not finished by Euripides before his death, and the last scene in which the substitution of the deer is announced is almost certainly not by his hand.

IPHIGENIA IN TAURIS (ca. 412 B.C.), by Euripides. The plot of this tragedy is a sequel to that of the *Iphigenia in Aulis* (q.v.) although the play was written some six years earlier. The scene is laid in the land of the Taurians, the present Crimea, whither Iphigenia had been spirited away by Artemis after being rescued from the sacrificial knife in the hands of her father. Here she serves as priestess of Artemis, and upon her falls the barbaric duty of sacrificing all strangers who reach this shore. As the play opens, she has had a dream that her brother Orestes, her only hope of rescue, is dead, and she goes into the temple to prepare sacrifice for him. Orestes, fleeing the avenging Furies of his murdered mother, enters accompanied by his friend, Pylades. Apollo's oracle has promised that if he succeeds in carrying off the image of Artemis from this temple and in bringing it back to Athens, he will be cleansed of his sin and find peace. The two friends consult and decide to hide until nightfall, when they may hope to escape capture and hope to remove the image. As they leave, Iphigenia re-enters from the temple, and a herdsman brings word that the two strangers have been captured and bids her to prepare for their sacrifice. The captives arrive in bonds; long and devious questioning on the part of Iphigenia effects a mutual recognition. Thus aware of their plight they plot escape with the image. When Thoas, King of the Taurians, arrives for the expected sacrifice, Iphigenia tells him the divine image has been polluted by the presence of Orestes, a murderer, and must be purified along with him in sea water. Permission is granted, and the three depart with only a few of the King's attendants. Presently a messenger returns to tell how they had come to the hidden ship of Orestes, how the attendants had been overpowered, and how Iphigenia had escaped with the image aboard Orestes' ship. Thoas issues orders for pursuit but is halted by the appearance of the goddess Athena, who forbids the pursuit and foretells the safe arrival of brother and sister in Greece. This play, like the *Iphigenia in Aulis,* is more melodramatic than tragic and is rich in the element of suspense. Less tragic themes seem to have been favored by Euripides during the last years of the long and exhausting Peloponnesian War, perhaps as something of an escape mechanism.

IRON HEEL, THE (1907), by Jack London. See LONDON, JACK.

IRRUNGEN, WIRRUNGEN (1888), by Theodor Fontane. See EFFIE BRIEST, by Theodor Fontane.

IS SEX NECESSARY? (1929), by James Thurber and E. B. White. See THURBER, JAMES.

ISABELLA or THE POT OF BASIL (written 1818; published 1820), by John Keats. This narrative poem in sixty-three *ottava rima* stanzas adapts a story from Boccaccio's *Decameron,* D. IV, N. 5. The scene is Florence, where Isabel's two proud brothers discover her love for Lorenzo and take their revenge by murdering him in a forest. The crime is revealed to Isabel by the ghost of Lorenzo. She goes to the forest and digs up his head and plants it in a pot of basil and keeps it by her, watering it with her tears. The brothers discover her grisly secret and flee Florence. Isabel, her pot of basil stolen, pines and dies.

ISKANDER (1920), by Louis Couperus. See COUPERUS, LOUIS.

ISRAFEL (1926), by Hervey Allen. See ANTHONY ADVERSE, by Hervey Allen.

IT CAN'T HAPPEN HERE (1935), by Sinclair Lewis. See ARROW-SMITH, by Sinclair Lewis.

ITCHING PARROT, THE (1816; complete in four volumes 1830), by José Joaquín Fernández de Lizardi. This picaresque story by the Mexican writer was the first novel written and printed in Latin America. However, its lasting popularity—it has sold over 100,000,000 copies—cannot be attributed to its historic importance but rather to its verve and vitality. Forced by the turbulent conditions of colonial Mexico to live the dangerous life of a rogue, Periquillo is in turn barber, quack doctor, cleric, grave-robber, thief, gambler, soldier and merchant, and in the course of these transformations, which bring him joys and indignities, a lively chronicle of Mexican life is unfolded. Despite the heavy moralizings, for Lizardi was a profoundly ethical writer, this Mexican work bears comparison to *Gil Blas* (q.v.), *Tom Jones* (q.v.), and all the other outstanding novels of roguery.

ITINERARY FROM PARIS TO JERUSALEM (1811), by François René de Chateaubriand. See ATALA, by François René de Chateaubriand.

IVANHOE (1819), by Sir Walter Scott. This romantic adventure story, set in the days of chivalry, serves as a rewarding introduction to the feudal period. The fictitious romance is woven with actual events of the times to form a colorful, exciting picture of twelfth century England with its two contrasting groups: the dispossessed Saxons, sturdy, rather commonplace; and the Norman conquerers, brilliant, haughty, tyrannical, but knightly. The scenes also include the forest where Robin Hood leads his lawless but kindly life. The principal historical event concerns the return of Richard the Lionhearted from the Crusades, to find that his brother, John, has usurped the throne. Richard retrieves the throne, restoring justice and finally winning even the Saxon loyalty. The fictional story is about Ivanhoe, who has also just returned from Palestine, where he has won honor and become a favorite of King Richard.

Ivanhoe is disinherited because he loves Rowena, a Saxon heiress and a ward of Cedric, his father. Cedric is trying to arrange the marriage of Rowena to Athelstane, a descendant of Edward the Confessor, hoping through this match to reunite the Saxon factions and restore the older monarchy. Ivanhoe, disguised, enters the tourney at Ashby, is wounded, but crowned the victor by Rowena. He is cared for by a friend, Isaac of York, a wealthy and persecuted Jew, and his daughter Rebecca. Rowena is captured and imprisoned by De Bracy, who tries to force her to marry him. After her release and through the efforts of Richard, Rowena and Ivanhoe are married. Dignified, beautiful, and gentle, Rowena is probably a less interesting character than is Rebecca, who is generous, gifted, attractive, and wholly unselfish in her love for Ivanhoe. He champions her when she is convicted of sorcery and saves her life, after which she leaves England with her father. Other important characters include: Ulrica, a half-mad Saxon who sets fire to Torquilstone Castle; Robin Hood, who besieges the castle; Girth, the swineherd; and Wamba, Cedric's jester.

IVORY APES AND PEACOCKS (1915), by James Gibbons Huneker. A miscellany of essays by Huneker, collated from various sources and having no recognizable unity. As in the case of his other essays, these show vast and variegated learning, an anecdotal wit, an iconoclastic verve, and a lively literary style. He is discursive on such subjects as: the genius of Joseph Conrad; the musical "primitive," Moussorgsky; the masters of hallucination, Kubin, Munch, and Gauguin; Lafcadio Hearn.

In *Iconoclasts* (1905) Huneker writes of ten bold European dramatists: Ibsen, Strindberg, Becque, Hauptmann, Sudermann, Hervieu, Gorky, D'Annunzio, Maeterlinck, and Shaw.

Huneker's earliest books are about music and musicians, but his later works encompass more general fields. *Painted Veils* (1920) is a novel reveling in the exotic atmosphere of New York Bohemians and dilettantes. *Steeplejack* (1920) is a gossipy autobiography which also traces music, literature, art, and life in Philadelphia, New York and New Orleans, for three decades.

JACKPOT (1940), by Erskine Caldwell. See TOBACCO ROAD, by Erskine Caldwell.

JACOB'S ROOM (1922), by Virginia Woolf. This short novel tells the simple story of a young middle-class Englishman named Jacob Flanders—his boyhood at Cornwall with his two brothers and widowed mother, Betty Flanders; his undergraduate days at Cambridge; his independent life in

London; his early love affairs; his tour through Italy, France and Greece; and his untimely death in World War I. The character, tastes, and disposition of Jacob are brought out by the impressions he makes on such people as Bonamy, his best friend and exact opposite; conventional Clara Durrant; frivolous Florinda; Fanny Elmer, the artist's model; and sophisticated Sandra Williams; by his reactions to the different people with whom he comes in contact; and by the pleasures, doubts, and longings he experiences in his various surroundings. The book is filled with word pictures, brief character sketches, and reflections of the author on many topics ranging from letters and loneliness to the fluidity of time.

JACQUES THE FATALIST (pub. 1796), by Denis Diderot. See DIDEROT, DENIS.

JAKOBOWSKY AND THE COLONEL (1942), by Franz Werfel. See FORTY DAYS OF MUSA DAGH, THE, by Franz Werfel.

JAMBS AND EPODES (1867–1879), by Giosue' Carducci. See CARDUCCI, GIOSUE'.

JAMES, HENRY (1843–1916). Henry James was an exponent of intellectualized, self-conscious artistry in writing. He influenced the history of the novel by emphasizing psychological character analysis, complicated formal structure, and polished prose styling.

James' first novel was *Roderick Hudson* (1876), set in Rome. Wealthy old Rowland Mallet has brought Roderick, a promising sculptor, to develop his genius by European study. The youth has a romance with the beautiful Christina Light, neglecting his fiancée Mary Garland, and disillusioning Mallet. Torn between passion and remorse, he falls to his death from an Alpine cliff.

Another novel concerning art and the tragedy of mean passions is *The Spoils of Poynton* (1897). Owen Gareth, heir to the great house at Poynton, spurns his mother's favorite, Fleda Vetch, to marry Mona Brigstock. Old Mrs. Gareth thereupon removes the art treasures from Poynton. Owen was in fact in love with Fleda, and offers her any object she may desire at Poynton, but suddenly the house is ruined by an accidental fire, which ruins the spoils that have warped so many lives.

Among several satirical novels is *The Bostonians* (1886), involving New England philanthropists. Olive Chancellor is a radical feminist, and Miss Birdseye an altruistic worker for lost causes. Basil Ransome at length wins the beautiful Varena Tarrant away from the influence of these two.

Novels based on character analysis include *The Ambassadors* (q.v.), *The American*, and *The European; The Portrait of a Lady, The Wings of the Dove, Daisy Miller*, and *The Golden Bowl* (qq.v.)—all concerning American and continental characters. *The Turn of the Screw* (q.v.) is one of the novels that reveal James' sensitive treatment of children; while his production in any one of his other genres—short stories, lectures, essays, plays, autobiography—would have been sufficient alone to have established a literary reputation.

JAMES, WILLIAM (1842–1910). The best known figure in American pragmatic philosophy, William James started as a medical man and psychologist and later in life turned to more general philosophic problems. In his *Principles of Psychology* (1890), which was in many respects a pioneering work, he laid the foundation for the modern empirical science of psychology. It was here that he developed his stream of consciousness theory of mind and made his initial analysis of perception and concepts. In his later work, he developed and popularized "pragmatism," a philosophic approach he owed to C. S. Peirce. In *Pragmatism* (1907) he presented an approach which, he claimed, would make possible the solution of the age-old problems of philosophy. The pragmatic theory of meaning asserts that the meaning of a concept or proposition is the difference that its being true makes for our anticipation of future experience. If the anticipation is fulfilled, the idea becomes true. Taking the traditional conflicting schools of philosophy, he asks, what difference does it make if one rather than the other is true? If none, then the problem is no real problem. If there is a difference, only future action and observation will enable one to judge between them. In his *Will to Believe* (1897) James anticipates some of these ideas and uses them to justify religious belief. In his later works he draws what he considers to be the metaphysical implications of these views, though most pragmatists do not go along with him on these enterprises.

JANE EYRE (1847), by Charlotte Brontë. The story is told by Jane, a plain-faced, strong-willed girl who has had an unhappy childhood, many struggles and tragedies, but who finds happiness with the man she loves, Mr. Rochester. As an orphan, Jane lives with the Reeds, her dead uncle's wife and children, Eliza, John, and Georgiana. They dislike her, and at the age of ten she is sent away to Lowood school. At eighteen she takes a post at Thornfield as governess to Mr. Rochester's ward, Adele Varens. Jane loves her employer and consents to marry him. On their wedding day, a Mr. Mason accuses Rochester of having a wife. He admits his guilt and shows Jane the woman he married, Bertha Antoinetta Mason, a madwoman who is confined in the upper part of the house, tended by Grace Poole. Jane is broken-hearted and leaves. She is befriended by the Rivers family, St. John, Diana, and Mary, who, she discovers later, are her cousins. Jane rejects St. John's proposal of marriage, and inherits a fortune. She returns to Thornfield and finds it has been destroyed by fire through the wild actions of Mrs. Rochester, who had jumped from the burning house to her death. Mr. Rochester is now blind. Jane goes to him and they are happily married.

In *Villette* (1853) another poor girl, Lucy Snowe, makes her way by teaching, as she watches unhappily John Bretton's infatuation for the flirt Ginevra Fanshawe, then falls in love herself with and transforms the professor, Monsieur Paul Emanuel.

JANUA LINGUARUM RESERATA (collected 1657), by Comenius. See DIDACTICA, THE, by Comenius.

JAPANESE ODES (1235; Eng. tr. 1866). See HYAKU-NIN ISSHU.

JAPANESE POETRY (905; Eng. tr. 1911). See KOKIN-SHIU.

JAVA HEAD (1919), by Joseph Hergesheimer. Java Head (meaning quiet harbor) is the Salem, Massachusetts, home of Jeremy Ammidon, ship-owner. His son Gerrit returns from a voyage to the Orient with a high-born Chinese wife, Taou Yuen. In Salem she is received only by Rhoda, the wife of Gerrit's brother William. The degenerate Edward Dunsack becomes infatuated with Taou Yuen, who commits suicide. Jeremy dies of apoplexy when he discovers that his ships are in the opium trade. Gerrit marries Nettie Vollar, Dunsack's niece, whom he has long loved, but whom the family disliked.

The Three Black Pennys (1917) is a three-part novel describing the rise and decline of a Pennsylvania iron family, each generation with one "black" individual, a rebellious, passionate throwback to the Welsh strain of the aristocratic English family.

Linda Condon (1919) is the romantic character study of an aloof girl who succeeds in finding a passion outside herself at last in the masterpiece of her sculptor cousin.

JEFFERS, ROBINSON (1887–   ). Robinson Jeffers has spent most of his life in seclusion with his family; and although he has maintained an independent attitude toward the world of letters, has had a great effect on modern American verse.

Tamar and Other Poems (1924): "Tamar" adapts the Biblical story to modern life, by telling the tragedy of the incestuous Cauldwell family, California farmers. "The Tower beyond Tragedy" is a poetic treatment of the story of Electra, with mystic overtones. Typical of the lyric pieces is "Night," a free-verse hymn to night as it falls on the California coast. "Roan Stallion," added to the collection in the 1924 edition, is the story of Johnny's half-breed wife California. California loathes her brutal farmer husband, and aids in his killing by a stallion which has fascinated her, in a half-mystical, half-passionate way. Then, motivated by a vague impulse, she shoots the stallion.

The Women at Point Sur (1927) is the story of Dr. Barclay, a California preacher, whose acceptance of a mysterious new spiritual freedom sets in motion a train of savage tragedies of passion. *Cawdor* (1928) is another tragedy of passion concerning the beautiful Fera Martial and her blind father. *Thurso's Landing* (1932) is the story of Rick Armstrong, whose guilty, reciprocated love for Helen, Reave Thurso's beautiful wife, causes the deaths of all three. *Give Your Heart to the Hawks* (1933) is another verse melodrama of lust, obsession and madness. *Such Counsels You Gave to Me* (1937), also a drama of neurosis and incest, is the Scottish ballad *Edward, Edward* told in modern dress.

In the poetry of Jeffers, there is usually a realistic background of California coast nature; the melodramas are allegorical, and the theme of illicit love is an expression of evil as it results from man's excessive concern with himself.

JENNIE GERHARDT (1911), by Theodore Dreiser. Jennie Gerhardt is a poor midwestern girl working as a servant in the home of the wealthy Kanes of Cleveland. She becomes the mistress of young Lester. Eventually he learns that Jennie has a daughter, Vesta, whose father, Senator Brander, had died before he could marry Jennie. Somewhat disenchanted with his mistress, he resumes a former affair with Letty Gerald, of his own social position. Jennie discovers, moreover, that her affair with Lester is keeping his legacy from him. She persuades Lester to terminate it, and he marries Letty. Later when Lester is fatally ill, however, he summons Jennie; and the two realize that their love was the true one.

JENNIFER DORN (1923), by Elinor Wylie. See WYLIE, ELINOR.

JENNY TREIBEL (1892), by Theodor Fontane. See EFFIE BRIEST, **by** Theodor Fontane.

JEPPE OF THE HILL (1722), by Ludvig Holberg. See ERASMUS MONTANUS, by Ludvig Holberg.

JERUSALEM DELIVERED (1575), by Torquato Tasso. In his great poem, *Jerusalem Delivered,* Torquato Tasso (1544–1595) celebrates in twenty-four canti the epic of the medieval Crusades and the liberation of Jerusalem from the Saracens. Idraote, king of Damascus, instigated by the devil, sends the beautiful Armida to the Christian camp under the walls of Jerusalem. A series of adventures develop, in which the main warriors of both sides, as well as charming young ladies like Armida, Clorinda and Erminia, are involved. The warrior Rinaldo leads an attack against the Saracens to liberate the Holy City. Tancred, the noble hero of the poem, kills the mighty Argante; Rinaldo kills his opponent Solimano, and Raimond kills ferocious Aladino. Following these victories Jerusalem is taken and the infidel armies are utterly defeated. Although the poem in celebration of such a great event had to be, in Tasso's mind, what Homer's *Iliad* (q.v.) and Virgil's *Aeneid* (q.v.) had been for the pagan world, *Jerusalem Delivered* is permeated with a new characteristic which was alien to those ancient poems and which makes Tasso's work something quite different: a melancholy and a soft melody, which flow through the whole poem, making its spirit more lyric than epic.

JESTER'S CAP, THE (1916), by Luigi Pirandello. See PIRANDELLO, LUIGI.

JEU D'ADAM, LE (12th c.), Anonymous. See ADAM, Anonymous.

JEW OF MALTA, THE (ca. 1592; published 1633), by Christopher Marlowe. The Island of Malta is threatened by the Turks, who want ten years' back tribute money. The Governor, Ferneze, calls on the Jews to provide it by taking half their fortunes. Barabas protests. All his wealth is seized, including his house, which is turned into a nunnery. To revenge himself on Ferneze he orders his daughter, Abigail, to betroth herself to the Governor's son Lodowick, and also to Mathias, a gentleman, her true love. He plays on the jealousies of the two young men, forges challenges which his rascally slave, Ithamore, delivers. Both her lovers are killed in the duel which follows. Ithamore tells the grief-stricken Abigail that her father is responsible. She retires into the nunnery. Barabas is enraged at his daughter. He decides to poison her with a dish of rice, which kills all the nuns. Abigail, dying, confesses to Father Bernardine that her father was responsible for the deaths of Mathias and Lodowick, and begs the Father to save him. Friar Jacomo and Friar Bernardine both try to convert the Jew and get his money for their order. Barabas, afraid of Father Bernardine, strangles him with Ithamore's help, and makes it appear that Friar Jacomo committed the murder. The latter is hanged. Ithamore, now Barabas' heir, falls under the influence of Bellamira, a courtesan. He brags how he and the Jew were responsible for the death of the Governor's son, and she reports it to Ferneze. Barabas admits the Turks to the City of Malta, which they are besieging, and dies by falling into a cauldron of boiling water with which he had intended to kill Calymath, the Turkish leader.

JEW'S BEECH TREE (1842), by Annette Elisabeth von Droste-Hülshoff. See DROSTE-HÜLSHOFF, ANNETTE ELISABETH VON.

JEWISH WAR, THE (ca. 79), by Flavius Josephus. This history gives our most complete and detailed account of the war in which the Jews were defeated and subjected to the rule of the Roman Empire; it is written by a Jew, a Pharisee of priestly family, who had commanded against the Romans. The first two books review the history of the Jews from the capture of Jerusalem by Antiochus Epiphanes to the beginning of the war with Rome in 67. Much space is devoted to the dynastic squabbles in which the Romans from the time of Pompey were invited to intercede until Judea was finally constituted as a Roman imperial province under Augustus. The remaining five books describe the war as prosecuted by the Emperors Vespasian and Titus from 67 to 73 and as witnessed and participated in by Josephus himself. He was captured at the siege of Jotapata in the first year of the war, succeeded in ingratiating himself with Vespasian, and after Vespasian became emperor remained with Titus and served as an intermediary with the Jews. After the war he lived as a pensioner of Rome, where he did much of his writing. He has been quite justifiably regarded by the Jews as a renegade. *The Jewish War* was written first in Aramaic and then translated into the Greek form in which we have it. His express purpose in writing was to arouse the interest of the Graeco-Roman world in the history and character of his despised people.

"JOHANNA MARIA," THE (Eng. tr. 1935), by Arthur van Schendel. See SCHENDEL, ARTHUR VAN.

JOHN BARLEYCORN (1913), by Jack London. See LONDON, JACK.

JOHN BROWN (1929), by Robert Penn Warren. See WARREN, ROBERT PENN.

JOHN BROWN'S BODY (1928), by Stephen Vincent Benét. This Pulitzer Prize winner is a long narrative novel in verse. The story begins with Brown's audacious raid on Harper's Ferry. The fervent idealism of "Ossawatomie" Brown and his martyrdom in the cause of liberation are the keynotes. The fictional protagonists are Jack Ellyat, a Northerner, and Clay Wingate, a Southerner. The canvas also includes contemporary cabinet members, army officers, other leading figures, and battles. Prefaced by a slave ship episode symbolizing North-South antagonism, events are narrated up to 1865, when the dream of an aristocratic America was ended. It is the goodness of common people that Benét extols. He portrays the American tradition of liberty and justice as a reality in their daily lives. His verse is rich with the music and rhythm of folk songs and folklore.

Western Star (1943) is an uncompleted epic poem of America's westward migration. Benét wrote several novels, and librettos for two operas.

One opera is from the play *The Devil and Daniel Webster* (1939). In this now famous bit of American folklore, Jabez Stone, an unlucky New Hampshire farmer, sells his soul to the Devil for a period of prosperity. When the latter calls to collect, however, Jabez refuses to surrender, and Daniel Webster, the peerless tribune, is called as advocate to defend him against a jury composed of America's most notorious traitors. The virtuous orator wins, and the Devil is routed.

This drama appeared as a short story in the 1937 volume, *Thirteen O'Clock*.

JOHN GILPIN, THE DIVERTING HISTORY OF (1783), by William Cowper. This ballad, supposed to have some basis in fact, tells how the linen draper John Gilpin borrows a horse to follow after his wife on their twentieth wedding anniversary, but, when mounted, finds it easier to start than to stop. The horse carries him at a mad pace through several towns until it reaches the owner's house, whereupon it turns and runs right back. The citizens think that John is riding a race.

JOHN HALIFAX, GENTLEMAN (1856), by Dinah (Mulock) Craik. The life of John Halifax is told by Phineas Fletcher, invalid son of a rich tanner, Abel Fletcher, a Quaker. It points the moral that gentlemen are made, not born. The hero, a poor orphan, rises through his hard work and nobility of character to wealth and happiness.

In the year 1800, a "year of war, famine, and tumult," a riotous, hungry mob storms Abel Fletcher's mill. Angered and intent on teaching them a lesson, Abel throws the bags of wheat into the river. John Halifax, whom Abel has hired as an apprentice, hides Abel. With the help of Phineas he quells the mob. Then he opens Fletcher's house to the crowd. All the food in the place is put before them.

The hero marries the beautiful and good Ursula March whom he loves devotedly, after she has prevented his migration to America. This causes Ursula's cousin and legal guardian, Mr. Brithwood, to disown her. When Abel Fletcher dies Phineas lives with the Halifax family as brother and uncle. Five children are born: Muriel Joy, blind at birth, Guy, Edwin, Walter and Maud. Ursula inherits the Brithwood fortune after all, and the family rise socially. John is now a factory owner. He retains his democratic ideas, assists the workers, aids ejected tenants of Lord Luxmore.

From this point the story revolves around the Halifax children. Blind Muriel dies. Guy loses the woman he loves to his brother Edwin and leaves for America. Maud is courted by Lord Ravenel, son of Lord Luxmore, but John Halifax refuses his consent to the marriage until Lord Ravenel rights the wrongs done by his father. He becomes a changed man under John Halifax's tutelage and returns titleless to Maud Halifax. Guy returns from America. The family again achieves great happiness. John Halifax dies "on the eve of the great Reform Bill of 1832, which represents to him the fulfillment of his dreams." He has spent his long life like a true Christian gentleman, helping the needy. So in spite of various calamities, all of which he has surmounted by moral force and personal integrity, he dies a happy and successful gentleman. This is an excellent picture of English country life.

JOHN INGLESANT (1881), by Joseph Henry Shorthouse. This historical novel deals with the England of Charles the First and the Italy of a somewhat spent Renaissance. John Inglesant, as pure and honorable a gentleman as can be found in fiction, had been trained from his earliest childhood for a diplomatic career at court. His tutor was the Jesuit St. Clare, who planned that the dreamy, sensitive John should act as an intermediary between the Catholics and Protestants. John is introduced at the English court, and begins a dramatic career continued later in Italy, where he seeks his twin brother's murderer. It is characteristic of Inglesant that, when he has the murderer at his mercy, he turns him over to God for His retribution. The book gives a complete and sympathetic picture of the complexity of the religious life of the time. It is also filled with unusual descriptions of seventeenth-century life with all its spectacles and excesses.

JOHN KEATS (1925), by Amy Lowell. See LOWELL, AMY.

JONATHAN WILD (1743), by Henry Fielding. So discerning a critic as V. S. Pritchett considers *Jonathan Wild* to be the diamond among all of Fielding's novels, "the most dazzling piece of sustained satirical writing in our language." The object of Fielding's satire is "the great man," the man held up as a hero simply because of his bold and clever exploits. It might be the "greatness" of Alexander, Caesar, or Napoleon that he is writing about. Actually, Jonathan is an arrant thief and a scoundrel, a man who uses his overweening ambition in aggrandizing himself by means of whatever victims come to hand. To be sure, his way leads to Newgate and the gallows, meeting "a death as glorious as his life had been," a reflection which leads the author to liken Jonathan's fate to that of other "heroes" of history. As a foil to Jonathan we have the character of Heartfree, the simple, good man heartlessly victimized by the evil man whom the author satirically makes his hero. Miss Laetitia Snap, who becomes Mrs. Jonathan Wild, is another foil for Fielding's humor.

JONSON, BEN (1572–1637). Besides his dramas Jonson is famous for his lyrics, about half of which were published during his lifetime in the first volume of his *Works* (1616) under the headings *Epigrams* and *The Forest*. A third group, called *Underwoods*, appeared in the second volume of the *Works* of 1641. Other lyrics are scattered through his plays and masques, notably "Queen and huntress, chaste and fair," from *Cynthia's Revels* (1601) and "Come, my Celia, let us prove," from *Volpone* (q.v., 1607). His famous apostrophe "To the memory of my beloved The Author, Mr. William Shakespeare: And what he hath left us" appeared in the First Folio Shakespeare (1623). This is his most important critical tribute in verse, where, though noting that Shakespeare had "small Latin and less Greek," he perceives that "He was not of an age, but for all time!" Everyone knows the "Song, to Celia," beginning "Drink to me only with thine eyes," though many do not know that the classical-minded poet was here paraphrasing from the Greek prose of Philostratus. Similarly in some of his epigrams and epitaphs he looked back to Martial and Catullus and the *Greek Anthology* (q.v.), just as his philosophy is often paganly *carpe diem* in his love poems, whether the mistress be Celia or Charis. On the one hand he can be exquisite in brief:

> Underneath this stone doth lie
> As much beauty as could die.

On the other hand he can write such sensuous descriptive poetry as "To Penshurst," celebrating the estate of the Sidney family in Kent. His range goes from humorous poems about himself or scurrilous epigrams about others to Pindaric odes, and hymns such as "An Hymn to God the Father," with its short, groaning lines.

JOSEPH AND HIS BROTHERS (1933–1943), by Thomas Mann. One of the most gigantic literary undertakings of our time, this prose epic is a modern version of the Biblical tale of Joseph, Jacob's son, who was sold by his jealous brothers into Egypt, where he rose to high honors as Egyptian food administrator. What was a narration of some twenty pages in the Old Testament, grew under Thomas Mann's pen into a tetralogy of more than 2000 pages: *Joseph and His Brothers, Young Joseph, Joseph in Egypt, Joseph the Provider*. Probably caused by some etchings and drawings to which Mann was asked to provide a preface, and possibly stimulated by an autobiographical reference of Goethe's to an abandoned epic about Joseph, the novel was conceived in Munich in 1925 and completed in California in 1943. As usual, there are strong autobiographical elements noticeable, particularly in the third volume, where the hero's Egyptian exile gives the German author an opportunity to reflect on his own refugee years in Switzerland and America. Critics were quick to point to the obvious parallel between Joseph's agrarian reforms, his rationing and taxation, his regulation of business and socialization of property, and the ideas of the New Deal in the last volume. It is also possible to see in Mann's story of the gifted, artistic, sensitive, "intellectual" Joseph another of his lifelong variations of the artist-bourgeois theme. More than anything, however, the epic probes into the origin and character of mythology, monotheistic religion, moral law, and the birth of the individual ego. The way from Canaan to Egypt is the road from the primitive and canonical to the sophisticated and individual; thus Mann's work is essentially a symbol of humanity.

JOSEPH ANDREWS AND HIS FRIEND MR. ABRAHAM ADAMS, THE HISTORY OF THE ADVENTURES OF (1742), by Henry Fielding. The sentimentality which swept over England as a result of Richardson's *Pamela* (q.v.) induced Fielding to pen this satire in reply. It takes its name from young Joseph, "brother of the illustrious Pamela, whose virtue is at present so famous," who, when he is only seventeen, is footboy to the licentious Lady Booby, of whom we scarcely hear a thing after Chapter X, though she causes enough trouble for an entire book while she is active on the scene. Joseph is discharged after Lady Booby makes an unsuccessful attempt on his virtue. Fanny Goodwill, with whom he is in love, is also dismissed. Fanny sets out for London, and is saved from a fate worse than death by the redoubtable Parson Adams, who is the real hero of the story. Parson Adams is a kindly, simple-hearted old man, drawn directly from William Young, a clergyman of Gillingham (Dorset). He is one of the most famous characters in fiction, often compared with the Vicar of Wakefield. Joseph soon joins Fanny and Parson Adams, but the vengeful Lady Booby has the young people arrested for theft. Fanny is constantly preyed upon and rescued in diverting fashion. Matters, however, become really distressing when it looks as if Fanny is Joseph's sister; in the end, however, Joseph discovers he is the son of the fine country gentleman, Mr. Wilson. But before this amazing news reaches him he has many strange and entertaining adventures on the road and at inns with his friend, Parson Adams. Fielding himself said he wrote this "in imitation of the manner of Cervantes." His book, however, has long been regarded on its own merits as a milestone in the development of the English novel, for it ceases to be a mere burlesque after the early chapters.

JOSEPH IN DOTHAN (1640), by Joost van den Vondel. See VONDEL, JOOST VAN DEN.

JOSEPH IN EGYPT (1936), by Thomas Mann. See JOSEPH AND HIS BROTHERS, by Thomas Mann.

JOSEPH THE PROVIDER (1943), by Thomas Mann. See JOSEPH AND HIS BROTHERS, by Thomas Mann.

JOURNAL (1882), by Henri Frédéric Amiel. See AMIEL'S JOURNAL.

JOURNAL (1947, 1948, 1949), by André Gide. The first volume covers the years 1889–1913; the second, 1914–1927; the third, 1928 to the present. The volumes provide a running account of Gide's spiritual self-probings, of contemporary occurrences and of his opinions on them, of his attitudes on social problems, homosexuality, the Jewish question, etc. They contain his judgments of Shakespeare, Baudelaire, Nietzsche, Freud, Dickens, as well as of many living writers whom he has known personally. Since the entries are by nature fragmentary, desultory notations upon hundreds of subjects, some of them scant and factual indeed, it is too early to estimate the permanent importance of the *Journal* except as a record of the time, made from a very personal angle of vision. Close students of Gide, however, believe that the *Journal* will eventually appear to be the greatest work of a man who, by his personal influence as much as by what he has written, has been most instrumental in shaping the course of the French literature of this century. Dates given above are for the three-volume American translation. No definite edition yet exists in the original language.

JOURNAL OF EUGÈNE DELACROIX, THE (published 1893–1895). Delacroix kept this journal from 1822, when he was 24, until his death in 1863. It provides an intimate portrait of one of the most fascinating personalities of the Romantic movement, gives a running account of the author's participation in the movement to free modern painting from an honorable but somewhat musty tradition, and furnishes much first-hand information about many of the artist's great contemporaries. Especially interesting are the accounts of Delacroix's search for new subjects, a search which involved much travel. The *Journal* presents probably the best available opportunity for modern readers to see the world and life through the artist's eye.

JOURNAL OF THE PLAGUE YEAR, A (1722), by Daniel Defoe. The subject of this alleged journal is expressed pithily in verse:

> A dreadful plague in London was,
> In the year sixty-five,
> Which swept an hundred thousand souls
> Away; yet I alive!

Contemporaries of Defoe thought the *Journal* was authentic; it gave such persuasive details of the London plague. However, it was instead a clever hoax.

The *Journal* contains precise descriptions of how the frightened citizens fled to the country for safety, how they hid in caves and lived in makeshift huts. To add to the verisimilitude of the tale, Defoe mentions names, dates and places. He tells, for instance, of Dr. Heath, who remained behind to treat the stricken and to study the pestilence. He gives a minute account of John Haywood, the under sexton, who accompanied the dead cart with a bell. He even exposes the medical quacks and belittles the vicious rumor that the nurses were murdering their patients. In an episodic, reportorial style, Defoe wrote of events which had occurred during his early childhood; and left us an account of the plague which, if fictionalized, is nevertheless of great historical interest.

JOURNAL TO STELLA (written 1710–1713), by Jonathan Swift. See BATTLE OF THE BOOKS, by Jonathan Swift.

JOURNALS (published 1848), by John James Audubon. See BIRDS OF AMERICA, by John James Audubon.

JOURNALS (1887–1896), by Edmond and Jules de Goncourt. In their studies of art and history, the Goncourt brothers had found very useful source material in contemporary, day-by-day accounts such as the *Memoirs* of Bachaumont. With the idea of providing a similar document of their own time they started their own *Journal* on December 2, 1851. It continued until the death of Edmond, in 1892. Wealthy, sociable, artistic and insatiably curious, the brothers went everywhere in Paris, knew everyone, saw everything. Their accounts of the weekly "Magny" dinners, which were attended by Gautier, Flaubert, Sainte-Beuve, Renan, Taine, Turgeniev and many lesser lights, are especially interesting. Although "incapable of general ideas"—as one of their friends remarked—the Goncourts were shrewd observers. Nine volumes of the *Journal* have been printed; material for as many more remains in manuscript.

The novels of the Goncourts reveal the same talent for observation. *Germinie Lacerteux* (1865) studies a case of female hysteria through its successive stages. *Manette Salomon* (1867) reports on the life of artists. *Renée Mauperin* (1864) is a document of the wealthy middle class. Written in a style much influenced by contemporary painting, the novels combine a great concern for good writing with a subject matter which prefigures Zola and Naturalism.

JOURNALISTS, THE (1852), by Gustav Freytag. See DEBIT AND CREDIT, by Gustav Freytag.

JUDD RANKIN'S DAUGHTER (1945), by Susan Glaspell. See GLASPELL, SUSAN.

JUDE THE OBSCURE (1895), by Thomas Hardy. This last novel by the famous English novelist is the tragic story of a sensitive, ambitious young man thwarted by nature and the social system under which he lives. Jude Fawley, who teaches himself Latin and Greek while he works as a stonecutter's apprentice, has set his heart on going to Christminster and becoming a scholar. First he is tricked into marriage with a vulgar, sordid woman, Arabella. When that fails and he at last gets to Christminster where he is hoping to enter the university, he falls passionately in love with his cousin Sue. She is an intellectual, cold and unbalanced. When she discovers that Jude is married she marries Mr. Phillotson, an elderly schoolmaster, out of spite. Later she and Jude both get divorces and live together, though as a result of their former matrimonial experiences they cannot bring themselves to become man and wife legally.

Jude is pushed further and further from the realization of his dreams. They are miserably poor and socially shunned; after the tragic death of their children Sue becomes neurotically religious. She returns to the schoolmaster as expiation for her sins, and Jude, alone and tubercular, is again tricked into marrying Arabella. The book ends with Jude's lonely death in Christminster, the city of his dreams, while his sluttish wife is enjoying herself at the boat races.

The novel is an excellent example of Hardy's preoccupation with the theme of the cruelty of nature and the artificiality of the social system, both of which combine to destroy man's finer aspirations and lead him to ruin. The bigotry of the university officials, which prevents Jude's entrance because he is an obscure and poor young man, and his own natural impulses which lead him into disastrous relationships with the two women in his life, are responsible for the defeat and death of a man with great potentialities.

JUDENBUCHE, DIE (1842), by Annette Elisabeth von Droste-Hülshoff. See DROSTE-HÜLSHOFF, ANNETTE ELISABETH VON.

JUDGMENT DAY (1935), by James T. Farrell. See STUDS LONIGAN, by James T. Farrell.

JUGURTHINE WAR, THE, by Sallust (Gaius Sallustius Crispus; 86–ca. 35 B.C.). Sallust is the earliest extant Roman historian. *The Jugurthine War*, however, is hardly history but rather a historical essay written to demonstrate the corruptness of the Roman nobility after the end of the Punic Wars. This position Sallust took as a loyal supporter of Caesar and the popular party at Rome. The work tells how Jugurtha, the shrewd and ruthless warrior king of Numidia, in his lust for power took full advantage of the weakness of Rome, which resulted from the incompetence and greed of her nobility. He thus defied the might of Rome's armies for years (111–105 B.C.) by corrupting their generals. When Marius was chosen as commander by an incensed Roman populace, Jugurtha was quickly defeated. He was then surrendered by his father-in-law, Bocchus, King of Mauretania, to whom he had fled, and was finally put to death in the prison at Rome. Sallust writes in a terse and vigorous style that owes much to Thucydides. Perhaps the most notable feature of this style, aside from a flavor of archaism in comparison with Cicero, is the use of speeches which are put in the mouths of his characters and subtly create the impression the author wishes to convey. Sallust exerted a strong influence on Tacitus, and has been much admired by such modern stylists as Nietzsche.

JULIUS CAESAR (ca. 1599; First Folio 1623), by William Shakespeare. This is one of Shakespeare's best known tragedies. The author found his material in Plutarch's lives of Caesar, Antony, and Brutus. Julius Caesar has returned from the foreign wars and is cheered in the streets by the Roman citizens. A soothsayer calls out to Caesar to beware of the Ides of March. Cassius and Brutus listen to the shouts of the crowd, as Caesar three times refuses a crown offered to him by Mark Antony. Cassius is jealous of Caesar. Casca joins them, and their discontent with Caesar grows until finally a group of conspirators meet at Brutus's house and determine to kill the man whose ambition they fear.

Calpurnia, Caesar's wife, dreams of his murder and begs him not to go out that day, but he is persuaded to go to the Senate by Decius Brutus, one of the conspirators. Before the Capitol he meets the soothsayer, who warns him the Ides of March have safely come, but not gone. In the Senate he is stabbed first by Casca, then by the other conspirators, and last by Brutus, when Caesar makes the famous remark, "Et tu, Brute? Then fall Caesar!" Antony, afraid of Brutus and Cassius, has fled. Cassius had wanted to kill him too, but Brutus had insisted on sparing him.

Antony makes advances to Brutus, who sends word to come to him. Antony shakes hands with all the conspirators, and asks leave to speak at Caesar's funeral. Cassius warns Brutus to be careful. Brutus plans to speak first, and tells Antony he can say all the good he can of Caesar, and with their permission. Antony makes the famous speech, "I come to bury Caesar, not to praise him." The crowd who had been with Brutus are now swayed in the opposite direction. Antony tells them of Caesar's will, and shows them his mantle where the daggers of the conspirators had pierced it. The citizens are now thoroughly roused, but Antony holds them still longer and stirs their emotions, describing the arbors and newly-planted orchards Caesar has left them for their recreation.

Caesar Octavius arrives in Rome, and he and Antony and Lepidus form a triumvirate, and plan to revenge Caesar's death. Brutus and Cassius lead the opposing faction; they quarrel over money and are reconciled. Brutus' conscience troubles him. Both armies are converging toward Philippi. Caesar's ghost appears to Brutus and tells him, "Thou shalt see me at Philippi." The two armies meet; Brutus feels that he is doomed. Cassius causes himself to be killed by his servant Pindarus; Brutus runs on his sword and dies. The triumvirate are victorious and Caesar is avenged.

JUNG, CARL (1875–   ). A disciple of Freud, Jung developed his own school, which he called analytic psychology. He is known for his classification of human personality types as "introverted" and "extroverted." His understanding of the unconscious differs from Freud's, and the sexual element in human personality does not play so important a part as in Freud's view. Jung postulates a creative urge. He also develops a theory of the collective unconscious of the human race which influenced literary artists including, among others, James Joyce.

JUNGLE, THE (1906), by Upton Sinclair. This is the story of Lithuanian and Polish immigrant workers in the slaughterhouses and stockyards of Chicago. It follows the epic struggle of Jurgis Rudkus, a powerful young Lithuanian, who comes with his family and his betrothed to seek the wealth for the working man which America has been represented as holding out to him. He finds himself swindled from the outset, and flung into the hideous abyss which is the meat-packing industry. Before the jungle has finished with him it has broken him in body, killed his children, driven into prostitution and at last killed his wife, and has likewise killed or demoralized all the little group who had accompanied him. This harrowing story is the vehicle with which Sinclair launched a merciless and searching probe into the economic, moral, and hygienic horrors of the meat-packing industry. It is a saga of corruption, greed and criminal wholesaling of poisoned and refuse-ridden foodstuffs. The sensation created by the book resulted in Congressional revision of the federal meat inspection laws.

King Coal (1917) is a similar treatment of the Colorado coal-mining camps. The leading character is Hal Warner, an investigator who discovers the tragic facts of labor conditions. Hal falls in love with "Red Mary" Burke, a spirited Irish girl fighting for reform, and works with her. *Oil!* (1927) is based on the Southern California oil scandals of the Harding administration. The protagonist is Bunny Ross, an oil mogul's son. Bunny discovers the seething discontent of the industry's workers, and eventually espouses socialism. Other matters as diverse as World War I, "flapper morals," and religious revivals, are discussed. *The Brass Check* (1919) is a tract attacking American journalists and showing particular resentment for the Associated Press. The first part describes the author's twenty-year feud with the press; the second cites eminent witnesses to journalistic crimes; the third proposes as remedy a practical program including the establishment of a sincere truth-telling weekly. *Boston* (1928), based on the Sacco-Vanzetti case, is an indictment of Boston tradition and privilege. The novel, a vast pageant of the crime, is the story of Cornelia Thornwell, wife of a former governor, who leaves her life of ease to take a job in a factory. She befriends the two Italian workmen, witnesses the trials and the appeal, and works vainly to save them.

A ten-volume literary phenomenon is Upton Sinclair's Lanny Budd series. The ten-thousand-page manuscript with its three million words and vast panorama of characters—real and fictitious—is a heroic effort to seize thirty-three years of history's most significant events and give them a new clarity in printed form. Sinclair uses the device of a single protagonist, Lanny Budd, to chronicle the sequence of dramas. *World's End* (1940) begins in World War I Europe. *Between Two Worlds* (1941) progresses from Versailles to the great crash of 1929. *Dragon's Teeth* (1942) tells of Germany through the 1934 purges. *Wide Is the Gate* (1943) continues to 1938 Hitler's Germany and also Franco's Spain. *Presidential Agent* (1944) tells of the appeasement tragedy of 1938. *Dragon Harvest* (1945) finds Lanny a secret agent in the period from Munich to the fall of Paris. *A World to Win* (1946) embraces Vichy France and Stalin's Russia of 1942. *Presidential Mission* (1947) brings pre-invasion Africa and the Orient into the picture. *One Clear Call* (1948) concerns the invasions of Italy and Normandy, and continues up to the Battle of the Bulge with the American Army. *O Shepherd, Speak!* (1949) concludes the series.

JUNGLE BOOKS, THE (1894–1895), by Rudyard Kipling. These two volumes of stories were intended for children but are also read widely by adults. They are far more interesting than most animal stories, because Kipling's animals think, act, and speak as beasts of their own kind, not as human beings in the guise of animals. Mowgli, an infant boy, loses himself in a forest, where he is nurtured by a mother wolf and accepted by the wolf pack and the other jungle animals after some difficulty. When Mowgli returns to civilization, he is wise in the ways of the jungle. He has learned from Baloo, the brown bear, the justice of the jungle laws, which are far more fair and equitable than are human laws. The reader also meets Shere Khan, the boastful, proud Bengal tiger; Shere Khan's servant, the jackal, Tabaqui; the python, Kaa; Bagheera, the panther; and the chattering monkeys, who steal Mowgli and from whom he is rescued by Baloo and others. The incidents in these stories are romantic and picturesque. The accounts of the personal, social, and political life of the wolf pack are highly diverting.

JUNO AND THE PAYCOCK (1924), by Sean O'Casey. One of O'Casey's strongest plays, this is a penetrating study of a Dublin family during the struggle between the Free Staters and the Republicans. The Boyles live in a tenement in a poor district of Dublin. Juno, an understanding, middle-aged woman, is the backbone of her family. Her husband, "Captain" Jack, is a bragging, worthless drunkard, who develops pains in his legs whenever there is work to be done. He spends most of his time in bars with his crony, "Joxer." Johnny, the only son, had lost an arm during the battle of Easter Week, and is nervous and self-pitying. His sister, Mary, an attractive girl, had been going with Jerry Devine, a young labor leader, but has left him for Charlie Bentham, an intellectual schoolteacher. The latter tells Boyle that he has inherited a considerable sum of money from his cousin, and that he, Bentham, had written out the will. The family, overjoyed with the good news, borrow money from their friends on the expected inheritance, buy furniture, a gramophone, and other luxuries, and invite the neighbors in. They are in the midst of their celebration when Mrs. Tancred, who lives upstairs, comes in on the way to the funeral of her only son who had been killed in a fight between the Free Staters and the Republicans. Johnny had been his friend at one time, and is in the same battalion. Boyle asks why should they care what happens, when it's the government's business. Juno replies that it's very much their business, and mentions the number of women in the house who had lost relatives on both sides. The expected inheritance does not materialize, leaving the Boyles deeply in debt. They cannot pay the installments on their furniture. The neighbors are resentful over the grand way in which Boyle has spent their money. Bentham has gone to England, and Juno, thinking Mary looks bad, takes her to a doctor and learns that she is pregnant. When Juno breaks the news to him, Boyle disowns his daughter. Two "Irregulars" come for Johnny, and take him away, for having betrayed Tancred to the Free Staters. Mrs. Boyle hears her son is dead in the hospital. She thinks of Mrs. Tancred, as she and Mary leave Boyle forever, to start a new life together.

JURGEN (1919), by James Branch Cabell. Jurgen, a fifty-year-old, prosaic pawnbroker, enters a cave on Amneran Heath in search of garrulous Dame Lisa, his wife, who has been carried off by Satan. Meeting the centaur Nessus, he is carried to the garden between dawn and sunrise. Here he finds his lost love, and is permitted by divine dispensation to relive a year of his youth. His adventures are part of the folklore of Poictesme, Cabell's mythical medieval world. Jurgen's adventures are merry, impudent, cynical and fantastic. Among the merry episodes are many improbable characters and situations: Jurgen meets his grandmother's God in Heaven; has adventures in Hell; and encounters Guinevere. There are Queen Sylvia Teriu who vanishes at cock's crow; voluptuous Anaïtis in Cocaigne; the dimpled Hamadryad; the cruel but lovely Dolores of Philistia; and Florimel, who dispatches unchristened children in the sea of blood.

This novel won Mr. Cabell a reputation partly because it was declared obscene and suppression was attempted. Of the author's many novels, the last of the Poictesme series, in sequence of action, is *The Cream of the Jest* (1917). In this book it is the author Felix Kennaston who returns to a mythical land, Storisende, and seeks the ageless beauty Ettarre. Returning to his own life, he discovers in his wife the object of his search.

JUST FOLKS (1917), by Edgar A. Guest. See GUEST, EDGAR A.

JUST OUT OF COLLEGE (1905), by George Ade. See ADE, GEORGE.

JUSTICE (1910), by John Galsworthy. This well-known drama deals with the injustice of justice. Falder is a junior clerk in the respectable law firm of James and Walter How. He is in love with Ruth Honeywell, a pretty woman who is married to a brutal husband. Falder plans to take her and her children out of the country; in order to do so he commits forgery. He is discovered and James How decides to prosecute. At the trial, Falder's advocate, Frome, puts up a plea of temporary insanity in view of the fact that Ruth had come to Falder the morning the check had been altered to tell him her husband had nearly strangled her. Frome pleads that Falder is a young man of hitherto excellent character and that imprisonment will ruin him. The jury, however, finds him guilty; he is given three years' penal servitude. Ensuing scenes show the governor refusing to grant Falder the right to work in the shops or in the yards with the other prisoners, since it is against regulations, and a view of Falder, lonely and desperate in his cell. After two years he is released on probation. He and Ruth ask Cokeson, the managing clerk at How's firm and Falder's advocate to the governor, to beg How to give him another chance. How agrees on the condition that Falder give up Ruth. This he refuses to do. A detective approaches Falder to arrest him for failure to report, but the young man commits suicide by jumping out the window. This he chooses rather than return to prison even for a few months.

JUVENILA (1850–1860), by Giosue' Carducci. See CARDUCCI, GIOSUE'.

KALEVALA (published 1822). The *Kalevala,* or *The Land of the Heroes,* which is its literal English translation, is the national epic of Finland. It consists of a considerable number of narrative ballads, the first collection of which was published in 1822 by Zacharias Topelius, and completed by Elias Lonnrot. The religion of the poem is largely that of primitive magic and animism, with only a thin veneer of Christianity—thus testifying to its predominantly pagan origin. In the course of the centuries it underwent an evolution of marked religious changes which were really only superficial. It is a triumph of the art of poetic narrative. Longfellow, who read the German and probably the Swedish translation of the poem, was so impressed with both its metre and material that he applied both to his writing of "Hiawatha." An English translation was made by John Martin Crawford in 1889.

The *Kalevala* is a storehouse of information regarding the period covered by the stories. Written in Finnish, it clearly belongs to prehistoric times except for its later Christian portions. It relates the history of four heroes: Vainamoinen, "wise and truthful," who is the son of the wind and a great patriarchal bard whose genius for music gives him godlike stature; his brother Ilmarinen, a great smith and craftsman, and a hero in conflict; Lemminkainen a jolly, mischievous fellow who always gets into trouble and barely escapes destruction; and finally, Kullervo, a wicked, bullying giant. All four are learned in the black arts of magic.

The most stirring runes or cantos concern the exploits of Vainamoinen in quest of truth and virtue in a world full of strife and enchantment, ever contending with evil spirits, ogres and treacherous men. The Finnish composer Jean Sibelius has masterfully evoked the sombre music of the ancient minstrel in his "Swan of Tuonela." The last picture we have in the *Kalevala* is of the patriarchal Vainamoinen, with his great gray beard floating in the breeze, sailing away in his copper boat toward that "bourn from which no traveller returns," not angry or resentful, but a little sad as he looks for the last time on the loveliness of mountain and forest and sea, that loveliness which he had helped to create with the music he had drawn from his golden harp.

KAPITAL, DAS (1867–1885), by Karl Marx. This theoretical work on which modern socialism is based is perhaps the most epoch-making study in the literature of economic theory. It has been the cornerstone, with important variations, of all the Marxist Socialist movements in the world. Labor alone, says Marx, creates value. The value of a commodity is determined by the work which normally goes into its production. The price of a commodity, which is its money form, is actually expressed in *imagined* money, the value of which is purely ideational. In tracing the development of capital, Marx begins with the obvious fact that capitalists turn their capital to account by exchange; they buy raw materials for their money, and afterwards sell manufactured goods for more money. This "profit," which Marx calls "surplus value," is created by the workers. It is to the interest of the capitalist to make working hours as many as possible in order to get more "surplus value" from his labor. The struggle over working hours, i.e., for surplus value between capital and labor, is as old as the first free workers that appeared. The wages actually paid a worker he earns in a small number of hours; the rest of his work day he spends to increase the profits of his employer. Marx contends that the social injustices and irrationalities of capitalism are the weapons for its own self-destruction: i.e., it is committing economic, social and political suicide. A socialist society and economy are inevitable, he claims.

Das Kapital treats of the following subjects: commodities and money; the process of commodity exchange; money, or the circulation of commodities; the transformation of money into capital; the buying and selling of labor power; the production of absolute surplus value; the labor process and the process of producing surplus value; constant and variable capital; the rate of surplus value; the working day; rate and mass of surplus value; division of labor and manufacture; machinery and large scale industry; appropriation of labor power by machinery; the worker's struggle against the factory system and machinery;

machinery and surplus value; law of value and rate of profit; and the stock exchange.

KARLFELDT, ERIK AXEL (1861–1931). This Swedish lyricist is the singer of his native Dalecarlia, one of Sweden's most beautiful districts, whose proud inhabitants had played a major role in the history of the kingdom. With humor, pathos, and peasant wisdom, the poet describes the scenery of the region, and the life and traditions of its people. According to a native authority, he is, as a portrayer of landscapes, "perhaps the greatest of the Swedish poets." He has an intense feeling for nature. His production is not large but weighty. Among the six volumes of his verse are: *Fridolin's Songs* (1898), *Flora and Pomona* (1906), and *Flora and Bellona* (1918). Karlfeldt was offered the Nobel Prize in Literature in 1920, but refused it, probably because he was the Secretary of the Swedish Academy which awarded it. The honor was, however, given to him posthumously in 1931.

KAROLINERNA (1897–1898), by Verner von Heidinstam. See CHARLES MEN, THE, by Verner von Heidinstam.

KENILWORTH (1821), by Sir Walter Scott. The events of this story take place during Elizabeth's reign. Leicester, the Queen's favorite, has married Amy Robsart, daughter of Sir Hugh Robsart, secretly, to avoid incurring Elizabeth's wrath. He shuts Amy away in lonely Cumnor Place under the care of Tony Foster and his daughter, Janet. Edmund Tressilian, a kindly Cornish gentleman, formerly betrothed to Amy, finds her, and, believing her to be the mistress of Varney, Leicester's villainous ally, tries to convince her that she should leave. Failing in his plea, he goes to Elizabeth with his story. Varney saves Leicester by asserting that Amy is his own wife. Elizabeth orders him to bring Amy to Kenilworth, Leicester's estate, where the entire court is to assemble for pageants. Refusing to appear for even an hour as Varney's wife, Amy escapes her guardians and goes to Kenilworth alone and forces Leicester to acknowledge her, thus bringing down the anger of the Queen. Varney convinces Elizabeth that Amy is mad. He is ordered to take her home and care for her. He also succeeds in making Leicester suspicious of Amy's relationship with Tressilian; through this ruse he gets Leicester's signet ring, empowering him to act for the Earl. Varney removes Amy quickly to Cumnor Place and murders her, only a few minutes before Sir Walter Raleigh and Tressilian arrive. Leicester, having discovered the falseness of Varney's accusation, has confessed the entire affair to the Queen. Extremely angry and hurt at first, she later recalls Leicester to court and favor.

KENTONS, THE (1902), by William Dean Howells. See HAZARD OF NEW FORTUNES, A, by William Dean Howells.

KEY, ELLEN (1849–1926). It is difficult to determine which of the thirty volumes of essays by this distinguished feminist is the most vital. Many of them have been translated into English, French, German, Italian, and other languages. With her sincerity, courage, personality, persuasive force, and characteristic style, Miss Key has won many admirers in many lands, whether the details of her provocative social program are accepted or rejected, for her love of humanity is undisputed. She has written numerous works on distinctive literary figures like Elizabeth and Robert Browning, and on *War, Peace, and the Future* (1914; Eng. tr. 1916), but her most consequential writings are probably: *Misused Feminine Power* (1896), which criticizes exaggerated feminism and emphasizes the natural function of the mother; *The Century of the Child* (1900; Eng. tr. 1909), which focuses attention upon the home as the "primary moral and educational institution"; and *Love and Marriage* (1909; Eng. tr. 1911), where the author expresses her own modern ideas on those subjects. Because of the vigor and earnestness of her campaign for moral reforms her influence will, in many countries, last for a long time.

KEY LARGO (1939), by Maxwell Anderson. See WHAT PRICE GLORY, by Maxwell Anderson and Laurence Stallings.

KEY TO UNCLE TOM'S CABIN, A (1853), by Harriet Beecher Stowe. See UNCLE TOM'S CABIN, by Harriet Beecher Stowe.

KIDDUSH HASHEM (1926), by Sholem Asch. See NAZARENE, THE, by Sholem Asch.

KIDNAPPED (1886), by Robert Louis Stevenson. Stevenson describes the contents of *Kidnapped* as "Memoirs of the adventures of David Balfour in the year 1751; how he was kidnapped and cast away; his sufferings in a desert isle; his journey in the wild highlands; his acquaintance with Alan Breck Stewart and other notorious highland Jacobites; with all that he suffered at the hands of his uncle, Ebenezer Balfour of Shaws, falsely so called." David Balfour, after his father's death, went to his uncle's house near Edinburgh. His uncle, a mean and extremely stingy man, was a thoroughgoing scoundrel, who, after an unsuccessful attempt to murder his nephew, plotted to sell him into slavery in America. Accordingly, he had David kidnapped and shipped aboard the brig *Covenant* to prevent his discovering that the Shaws estate was rightfully his. On board ship he met the daring, spirited Jacobite, Alan Breck, one of Stevenson's most fascinating and best-drawn characters. Together, Alan and David defeated the entire crew of the *Covenant* and had many other exciting experiences which are vividly related. The *Covenant* struck a reef and was sunk. David, barely escaping with his life by swimming to shore, underwent a series of unhappy adventures. He met Alan again, and together, under suspicion of murder, they crossed through hostile territory under perilous conditions. The book is brought to a rather abrupt close with David's return to Shaws, where, with the aid of Alan and the lawyer, Rankeillor, he recovers his rightful inheritance.

The story was not finished because the author fell ill, but a sequel, *David Balfour* (q.v.) was published in 1893.

KIERKEGAARD, SÖREN (1813–1855). Kierkegaard, a Danish philosopher and theologian, was long unknown in this country. Revived and translated into English in the last few years, his works seem to suit the temper of the times and have commanded much attention. The existentialist movement coming out of Germany and France during and after World War II has intensified this interest, since Kierkegaard is claimed as one of the early existentialists. In general his position is an affirmation of an austere, individualistic, and irrational Christianity against the easygoing religion of his time. His special opponent was Hegel, whose rationalistic view of human life, society and religion was felt to be a distortion of man's true situation in the universe. Kierkegaard's religion emphasizes eternity, otherworldliness, and sin, and despairs of man's prospects in this world.

KIM (1901), by Rudyard Kipling. *Kim*, one of the English writer's best novels, deals with the adventures of an Irish orphan who grows up in the native quarter of Lahore. He meets a Tibetan lama and joins him in his search through India for the River of Immortality. Kim is finally picked up by the English and sent to a Catholic college in Lucknow, where he is groomed for the British Secret Service. His first assignment is successful when he captures the papers of a Russian spy in the Himalayas. The atmosphere of India, its bazaars and its teeming millions, the inner workings of the British Secret Service, and the charming character of Kim, all combine to make this novel an outstanding adventure story.

KINDEKEN JEZUS IN VLAANDEREN (1918), by Felix Timmermans. See TIMMERMANS, FELIX.

KING COAL (1917), by Upton Sinclair. See JUNGLE, THE, by Upton Sinclair.

KING COFFIN (1935), by Conrad Aiken. See AIKEN, CONRAD.

KING JASPER (1935), by Edwin Arlington Robinson. See ROBINSON, EDWIN ARLINGTON.

KING JOHN (ca. 1598; printed 1623), by William Shakespeare. This tragedy is founded on an old play, *The Troublesome Raigne of King John of England*. Shakespeare improved greatly on the older play. The story opens with the arrival of the French ambassador, claiming the crown of England for Arthur, Duke of Bretagne, nephew of King John, and son of his elder brother Geoffrey. John takes with him to France Philip Faulconbridge, a bastard son of Richard I, who acts the part of chorus throughout the play. Constance, Arthur's mother, is with the French King; Philip, his son Lewis, with their army, are camped before Angiers. The English under King John arrive. Both kings lay claim to the city. The citizens stay neutral while the French and English fight it out. The battle ends in a tie. Both decide to besiege the city. When the spokesman for Angiers suggests that John should marry his niece, Blanch of Spain, to the Dauphin, Lewis, John agrees and promises her a handsome dowry. King Philip, seeking the advantageous alliance, drops Constance's quarrel. The match is made. Constance withdraws in anger. Cardinal Pandulph, the Pope's legate, comes to John and threatens him with excommunication if he continues to defy the church. John replies that the Pope usurps his authority. Pandulph puts the curse of Rome on John, and forbids France to be friendly with him. King Philip breaks his alliance with John. Arthur is captured in the battle which follows. John puts him in charge of his follower Hubert, who knows he wishes the boy out of the way. Pandulph suggests to Lewis that he lay claim to the English crown through his wife if anything should happen to Arthur. Hubert has an order from John to put out Arthur's eyes. The boy pleads so effectively he has not the heart to do it, but tells John the boy is dead. Salisbury and Pembroke, who had been asking John for his release from prison, are horrified when they hear he is dead. In the meantime Arthur, trying to escape, falls from the ramparts and is killed.

King John receives word that the French under the Dauphin have landed in England. Pembroke, Salisbury, and other nobles join the enemy. Pandulph arrives in England, John having made peace with the Pope. The King asks him to go to the French and see what terms he can make with them. The Dauphin, however, is determined to carry on the war and lay claim to the English crown. The battle goes against the English, and the King, ill, goes to the abbey at Swinstead. The French lose one of their leaders, Count Melun; the English barons drop away. Pandulph arranges a peace. John has been poisoned by a monk at the abbey and dies. His son, Prince Henry, succeeds him.

KING LEAR (ca. 1605), by William Shakespeare. In many ways the most powerful of Shakespeare's tragedies, *King Lear* has been criticized for being obscure of plot and arbitrary in motivation, and Charles Lamb thought it burst the bounds of the theater. Yet it is without question one of the greatest plays. The story of Lear and his daughters is found in Geoffrey of Monmouth's *History* (q.v.), in Holinshed, and in an older play. King Lear determines to give over to his daughters and their husbands all the wealth and powers of his rank, retaining only his title. He proposes to retire and live with his various daughters in rotation. As a guide to division of his kingdom he demands an expression of their love. Regan and Goneril hypocritically protest great love and are richly rewarded. Honest Cordelia, apple of his eye, says plainly that she loves him "according to my bond; no more nor less." Infuriated, Lear disinherits her and bestows her dower on the other two. Cordelia is wedded, dowerless, by the King of France, who perceives her fine qualities. The rest of the play traces Lear's swift mental deterioration as he is betrayed and cast out by first one and then the other of his unnatural daughters. He goes mad while shelterless in a storm. In a parallel sub-plot the Earl of Gloucester, almost the only still faithful follower the old king has, has done injustice to his true son Edgar in favor of his villainous bastard son Edmund. All these unfortunates, Lear, Gloucester, whose eyes have been put out, the disinherited Edgar pretending to be mad, and Lear's fool form a pathetic party whose wrongs are righted too late. At last the King of France, together with a handful of Lear's loyal adherents, crushes the forces of villainy. Regan, Goneril, and Edmund are justly dead. Cordelia has been slain. Lear, utterly demented, dies of grief.

KING OF THE GOLDEN RIVER, THE (1851), by John Ruskin. This fairy tale is the story of three brothers, Hans, Schwartz and Gluck, who own Treasure Valley; it tells what happened when they met the strange little king of the Golden River. It describes the separate journeys of the three to the Golden River at the top of the mountain which they believe can be changed into real gold by three drops of holy water. Hans and Schwartz are turned into black rocks by the king because of their cruelty, while little Gluck, who gives away his last drop of water, is rewarded. This book has remained a classic for years, not only because of its beautiful descriptive style but because of the simple moral it points concerning kindness and selfishness.

KING'S HENCHMAN, THE (1927), by Edna St. Vincent Millay. See MILLAY, EDNA ST. VINCENT.

KING, THE GREATEST MAYOR, THE (1616?), by Lope de Vega. A young shepherd named Sancho, humbly poor but of good stock, loves Elvira, daughter of the wealthy farmer, Nuño. He seeks Nuño's blessing on their marriage and receives it cordially. But Nuño urges the young man to obey the formal custom of the country and secure permission of Don Tello de Neira, a young feudal lord of the region. Don Tello and his sister are very gracious; he gives his consent to the match and offers twenty cows and a hundred sheep as a wedding gift, paying him the further honor of promising that he and his sister will themselves attend the wedding that very evening.

When Don Tello arrives for the wedding he sees Elvira for the first time, and is so overcome by her beauty that he determines to have her for himself. Abruptly he orders the postponement of the wedding, and that night has Elvira abducted and carried off to his castle. Sancho and Nuño come to the castle to demand Elvira's release, but, though his sister pleads with him to come to his senses, Don Tello angrily has the two men whipped out of the castle.

Sancho, in desperation, goes to the King, renowned for his sense of justice and his interest in the welfare of the common people. He is so angry at the injustice done to Sancho that he writes an order for Elvira's release. Armed with this, Sancho returns to Don Tello's castle. The young lord meanwhile has been spurned by Elvira. When Sancho brings him the King's order he is filled with blind rage and once again ejects him from the castle.

There is nothing for Sancho to do but return to the King with an account of his failure. Sancho begs for a strong alcalde who will bring the rebellious Don Tello to obedience, and the King himself, "el mejor alcalde" (the best judge), goes to Galicia incognito to administer justice. After being met at first with insolence by Don Tello, the King reveals his identity. Don Tello is humbled. The King ignores his pleas for mercy, and sentences him to death, ordering that first he must make the wronged Elvira his wife. Then, says the King, when Don Tello has been beheaded, Sancho shall marry Elvira and have half of Don Tello's lands for himself.

Regarded as one of Lope de Vega's most important plays, this tragedy is based on an anecdote attributed to King Alfonso VII (1126–1157), which illustrated the insubordination of petty tyrants like Don Tello, and the generous, democratic spirit of the monarch. Using the past, Lope de Vega in fact reflected the struggle being waged in his own day between the forces of the relatively progressive idea of centralized monarchy as against the local tyranny of feudal lords.

KINGSBLOOD ROYAL (1947), by Sinclair Lewis. See ARROWSMITH, by Sinclair Lewis.

KISS FOR CINDERELLA, A (1916), by Sir James M. Barrie. See BARRIE, SIR JAMES MATTHEW.

KITAB AL-KHAZARI, by Judah Halevi. See HALEVI, JUDAH.

KITTY FOYLE (1939), by Christopher Morley. See MORLEY, CHRIS-TOPHER.

KLEINE RUDOLF, DE (1930), by Aart van der Leeuw. See LEEUW, AART VAN DER.

KLEIST, HEINRICH VON (1777–1811). Although usually classed with the Romantics, the writings of Kleist also contain definite elements of classicism and realism. Born in Prussia, Kleist led a bitter life, so devoid of recognition that he committed suicide. Continually driving toward basic truth and toward a capturing of pure emotional feeling, his work reflects an overflowing restlessness. Thoroughly preoccupied with the questions of fate and character, he seeks to find their place in the realm of phenomena. In the tragedy *Penthesilea* (1808) the queen of the husband-slaying Amazons, in conflict with Achilles, is overcome by him. She finally kills him, and according to the true form of queens, wills her own death. In *Prince of Homburg* (1810) the powerful character study of the Prince reveals a similarity to Kleist's own disposition. The Prince, against orders, leads a successful attack, only to be condemned to death for insubordination. He rises above personal concern until he finally merits pardon. One of the few great German comedies is *The Broken Jug* (1808), which sharply portrays a lecherous small-town magistrate. In a humorous court scene, where the accused is charged with breaking into a girl's room, the magistrate incriminates himself and is revealed as the culprit.

Michael Kohlhaas (1810), a novella (long short story), is set in the times of Luther. Kohlhaas, a historical figure, mistreated by the nobility, goes to the extreme of sacrificing his life to incite revolt against the bald travesties of justice to which he was subjected. Realistic in style and powerful in effect, it is considered one of the outstanding works in German prose fiction.

KNABEN WUNDERHORN (1806–1808), by Achim von Arnim and Clemens Maria Brentano. *Knaben Wunderhorn* (The Boy's Magic Horn) is the product of two members of the later German school of Romanticism, Clemens Maria Brentano (1778–1842) and Achim von Arnim (1781–1831). It is a collection of folk songs and ballads intended not to present a scholarly work but rather to draw attention to the richness of the popular literary heritage. Varied in form, simple and direct in expression, the poems cover a wide variety of subjects, including tales of love and sentimentality, ballads of humor, supernaturalism and adventure. This collection, marked by the typical desire for spontaneity of the later Romanticists, reflects the manifold moods of this popular disposition. Later German writers were to derive stimulation for their own literary activity from *Knaben Wunderhorn* through the interest it awakened in the German past and in the plain German folk.

KNICKERBOCKER'S HISTORY OF NEW YORK (1809), by Washington Irving. See SKETCH BOOK, THE, by Washington Irving.

KNIGHT OF THE BURNING PESTLE, THE (printed 1613), by Francis Beaumont and John Fletcher. Tales of knight-errantry, such as

Amadis de Gaul, were beginning to appear ridiculous to the sophisticates of the Elizabethan age. Beaumont and Fletcher's play, like *Don Quixote* by Cervantes (q.v.), attempted to burlesque the excesses of this chivalric nonsense. The heroine, Luce, is in love with Jasper, the poor apprentice lad of her merchant-father. The latter, however, has set his mind on the rich Humphrey for his son-in-law. With great cunning, Luce invites her elderly suitor to elope with her. He is flattered:

> I am resolv'd to venture life and limb
> For one so young, so fair, so kind, so trim

but just as the marriage is about to take place, Jasper appears and gives Humphrey a beating. As he carries Luce off, the vixen teases the luckless dolt:

> Farewell, my pretty nump; I am very sorry
> I cannot bear thee company.

Luce is finally caught by her father and locked up. Feigning death, Jasper is brought to his mistress in a coffin. He then frightens her father by pretending to be his own ghost, whereupon the reluctant merchant gives his consent to the marriage. This is a play-within-a-play, the other plot involving the burlesque escapes of the apprentice Ralph, the Knight of the Burning Pestle.

KNIGHTS, THE (424 B.C.), by Aristophanes. Dramatically *The Knights* is of little interest but it is one of the most violent political lampoons on record. It is an attack upon Cleon, a popular leader, and was produced on the stage at Athens and won first prize in competition at a time when Cleon had just achieved a most brilliant political and military triumph for which he had received the highest honors that could be paid an Athenian citizen. The plot is extremely simple. Nicias and Demosthenes, the two generals upon whose planning and execution Cleon had opportunistically capitalized to achieve his triumph, here presented as slaves of Demus, a personification of the Athenian people, consider how they may get their master out of the clutches of their fellow slave, the rascally and thieving Cleon. Their decision is to fight fire with fire. They incite Agoracritus, the sausage-seller, an even greater rogue than Cleon, to attack Cleon and displace him in the affections of Demus. The major portion of the comedy is devoted to the rival efforts of Cleon and Agoracritus, in which the latter is, of course, eventually successful. He is ably seconded by the chorus of Knights, representing the conservative class of citizenry. Demus himself is represented as a lazy and indifferent master, open to cajolery but fundamentally decent. He is finally restored to his senses and repudiates all such rascally servants.

KNOWLEDGE OF THE RIGHT WAY FOR SALVATION, THE (1413), by Jan Hus. See HUS, JAN.

KOBZAR (1840), by Taras Shevchenko. Taras Shevchenko (1814–1861), the greatest Ukrainian poet, deserves to be ranked with Pushkin and Mickiewicz. Born a serf, he won his liberty with his artistic ability, when the great painter Bryulov sold for this purpose a portrait of the Russian poet Zhukovsky in 1837. Later, he was condemned for his anti-Russian sentiments, and served ten years in a Russian penal battalion in central Asia. His best known collection was the *Kobzar* (1840). It is a collection of poems, largely in the Romantic style, bewailing the poet's separation from his beloved Ukraine, and also the passing of the old Ukrainian spirit. Then, after poems describing the exploits of the Zaporozhian Kozaks in the past, he concludes the series with "Katerina," the verse tale of a Ukrainian girl seduced and abandoned by a Russian lover. The *Kobzar* at once was recognized as the work of a master of the Ukrainian language. Shevchenko followed it with the "Haydamaki," a story of the Ukrainian uprising against Poland in 1768, and with a long series of other stories like the allegorical "Great Grave," which mourned the loss of Ukrainian liberty. The *Kobzar* has been translated several times into English, most recently by C. A. Manning in *Selected Poems* (1945). It requires but a slight acquaintance with the poet's work to note how he passes from the full height of Romanticism to the emphasis upon the sufferings of the people in a fully realistic manner.

KOKIN-SHIU (905). *Kokin-Shiu* is a Japanese anthology of poems compiled in the early tenth century, chiefly by Ki no Tsurayuki (883–946), the author of *Tosa Nikki*. There are 1111 poems. The chief poets in this collection are Ariwara no Narihara (825–880) and Ono no Komachi (834–880). There are only five *naga-uta,* or long poems, the rest being *tanka,* or short songs. The arrangement of the poems shows the Seasons, Greeting, Joy, Sorrow, Departure, etc. The introduction, in Chinese, reads like that of the Chinese Book of Songs, often word for word. The form of *tanka* is the same as that in *Manyoshiu* (q.v.).

These songs were translated by Basil Hall Chamberlain as *Japanese Poetry* (1911).

KOMEDIANTEN, DE (1917), by Louis Couperus. See COUPERUS, LOUIS.

KONRAD WALLENROD (1828), by Adam Mickiewicz. See MICKIEWICZ, ADAM.

KORAN (ca. 660), by Mohammed. The *Koran,* meaning "that which is recited," is the production of Mohammed as set down by his scribes, among them the devoted Abu Bakr, who collected "from palm-leaves, skins, bladebones" fragments which various hearers had copied. The *Koran* is the sacred book of Islam, believed to be the word of God, dictated to Mohammed by Gabriel, the Angel of Revelation in both Persian and later Jewish and Christian thought. Mohammed was afflicted with epilepsy, which was regarded until modern times as supernatural evidence of sanctity or demon possession.

Written in the purest Arabic, the *Koran* consists of 114 *suras,* varying in length from 4 to 285 verses, and abounding in repetitions of ideas, personal experiences, dire warnings by Mohammed to his enemies, and exhortations to his followers. To the believer, the *Koran* is a miraculous work containing the utterances of God. The orthodox think that it should never be translated into another language. One may not touch the *Koran* without previous bodily purification; it is forbidden to hold it below the waist. Many buildings and decorative objects are blazoned with quotations from the *suras.*

Two dominant ideas stand out in the *Koran:* the certainty of a Day of

Judgment, when good and bad will be separated; and the unity and majesty of one God. The *Koran* prescribes the forms of prayer, five times a day; the month of fasting; the pilgrimage to Mecca; and almsgiving; all of which have given the Moslems, widespread as they are among many races and in many lands, a sense of community and a civil and moral code permeating their entire society. Disjointed, crude as the *Koran* may sound to the modern ear, it is nonetheless the only one of the great religious scriptures to be the creation of one man, given to his followers within the brief period of twenty years. It is the source of truth and wisdom for some 400,000,000 people; and proclaims the equality and brotherhood of man.

KOSMOS (1845–1858), by Alexander von Humboldt. The world-wide fame of Humboldt's gigantic work, called by him *Kosmos* to include in a single name the sidereal and the terrestrial phenomena of the universe, rests on the first two volumes. The subsequent volumes of 1850 and 1858, and a fifth with fragmentary remains published posthumously in 1862, only supplemented specific details of the physical sciences treated, without adding to the sweeping synthesis of the former portions. Humboldt was a man of 78 years when he astounded the literary and scientific world through the crowning achievement of his fruitful life. The unique quality of *Cosmos: Sketch of a Physical Description of the Universe* lies in a combination of the broad philosophical ideas of the eighteenth century with the scientific exactness of the nineteenth. Humboldt has fully achieved what he set as his aim in the Preface: "The principal impulse by which I was directed, was the earnest endeavor to comprehend the phenomena of physical objects in their connection, and to represent nature as one great whole, moved and animated by internal forces"; and he has also fulfilled his promise "to give due prominence to the consideration of the existence of one common bond encircling the whole of the organic world, of the control of eternal laws and of the causal connection." The fact that the natural sciences have immensely progressed since Humboldt's day cannot detract from the pleasure and information conveyed to the reader by the famous introductory essay, "Reflections on the Different Degrees of Enjoyment presented to us by the Aspects of Nature." The first part of *Kosmos* is a collection of facts —astronomical, geological, and biological—covering comets, volcanoes, climate, physical geography, evolution, and the beauty of nature. The second part is on the history of science; and in this Humboldt discusses with profound knowledge and deep understanding "the difference of feeling excited by the contemplation of nature at different epochs," analyzing descriptive poetry from the ancient Greeks to Goethe. He then proceeds to the contemplation of landscape painting and the cultivation of tropical plants, everything envisaged with a wide command of facts and with keen insight. An important part of the work is that devoted to the interrelation between the progress of discovery of new lands and the development of civilization.

Kosmos is as much a literary as a scientific achievement, and Humboldt's prose style has become a model for later German travelogues. Physical geography, especially as taught in German universities and high schools, owes much to the publication of *Kosmos*.

KRAKATIT (Eng. tr. 1925), by Karel Čapek. See R.U.R., by Karel Čapek.

KREUTZER SONATA (1889), by Count Leo Tolstoy. This is one of the so-called "sexual" stories of Count Tolstoy. Actually it is a study of jealousy. A diatribe against the prevailing sexual education, it has been read as widely as many of Tolstoy's more important works. It is an arresting book even today, sixty years after its first publication. No masterpiece, unless a masterpiece of propaganda, this story of adultery and murder works out to its inevitable end. Pozdnishev is a man of intellect, a psychologist of sorts; he tells of the life he had when young, how he wooed and won his wife, of his marriage and his growing hatred of his wife. He goes on to relate how the lover came on the scene, his suspicions, his certainty, the murder. It is the recital of a supreme egoist. Tolstoy writes passionately; he calls for reform. He shows the outcome of a loveless marriage which offers no possibility of divorce. Pozdnishev is inhuman; hence, Tolstoy's argument is less effective than it might otherwise be. His foolish sister-in-law begs Vasa at the end to go to his wife Liza, who only stares at him in horror and exclaims: "I hate you!" He had killed Trukhatehevsky, the man she loved. Such is the outcome of marriages based on physical attraction, Tolstoy warns. Passion of any sort destroys, he contends with conviction in this lurid tale.

KRISTIN LAVRANSDATTER (1920–1922; Eng. tr. 1923–1927), by Sigrid Undset. This novel-trilogy of medieval Scandinavia is largely a demonstration of the author's distaste for the liberalism of modern life which made her turn to the past when authority determined all of man's activity. It was her conservatism and stern moralistic outlook which induced Sigrid Undset to renounce Protestantism and enter the Catholic Church. *The Bridal Wreath,* the first volume of the trilogy, relates the tempestuous love story of Erlend Nikulaussön and Kristin Lavransdatter and ends with their marriage. *The Mistress of Husaby* tells about their fifteen years of troubled happiness on the great estate of Husaby. In order to possess each other they have wronged others. They pay in full for their selfishness, although, truth to tell, they have been just as much sinned against as sinning. Nemesis catches up with them when Erlend gets involved in a political intrigue. He is imprisoned and cruelly tortured. At the last moment he is rescued from a terrible death by the intervention of Simon Andressön, to whom Kristin had been betrothed before she met Erlend. *The Cross,* the last part of the trilogy, describes the new mode of life Kristin, Erlend, and their seven sons are obliged to enter into. Because of Erlend's political intrigues, the estates of Husaby have been taken from them. They live on Kristin's father's lands, which at his death fell to Kristin. The couple keenly feel that they have been declassed, being no longer members of the great land-owning gentry. This situation they meet in different ways and according to their characters. Kristin toils incessantly to salvage whatever she can out of their broken fortunes; she is anxious to leave some inheritance for her children. The proud and pleasure-loving Erlend cannot resign himself to his downfall. Kristin chides him for not sharing her responsibility, and he finally runs away to live in his mountain lodge, the only piece of property he owns in his own right. Kristin visits him and begs him to return; a son is born of this meeting. She is openly accused of adultery with Ulf, her faithful steward, but Erlend comes from his retreat to protect her name. In protecting her, he is killed. Kristin eventually retires to a convent, and dies while helping the sick during the Black Plague.

Kristin Lavransdatter is one of the great historical novels. Undset is superior to other novelists in her use of history and in her employment of psychology. Her characters are warmly and humanly drawn, three-dimensional, credible beings. One must agree with the Nobel Prize Committee that she is one of the great fiction masters of our time.

KRUTCH, JOSEPH WOOD (1893–). Joseph Wood Krutch, student, teacher, and critic, is author of the popular *The Modern Temper* (1929). This is an analysis of modern society, by an intellectual who pessimistically declares that science has blasted his concept of a happy cosmos, and psychology his concept of the dignity achievable by man. Only curiosity and the search for knowledge are valid motivations for life.

Samuel Johnson (1944) is an inclusive book for the general reader, a running account of the good doctor's life, character, and work, as they appeared to contemporary knowledge and judgment. Beginning with the casual undergraduate who quit Oxford at the age of twenty-six, married a widow twenty years his senior, and began a career of literary hackwork, Johnson is followed through the period of his pension (£300 a year, awarded somewhat by chance), his friendship with Boswell, his twenty years of work on the subscription edition of Shakespeare, his political writings, and late failing health. It is an account of Johnson more objective than Boswell's work, yet more human than works which merely trace his famous productions, such as the *Dictionary,* or *Lives of the Poets* (q.v.).

Other literary studies include *Edgar Allan Poe* (1926), a psychoanalytic biography; *Five Masters* (1930), an examination of the lives, times, and writings of Boccaccio, Cervantes, Richardson, Stendhal, and Proust; and *Henry David Thoreau* (1948).

KUBLA KHAN (1798), by Samuel Taylor Coleridge. This magic fragment of a poem in fifty-four lines actually came to the poet in a dream, after he had been reading *Purchas his Pilgrimes.* The poem tells of the building of "a stately pleasure-dome" by the great Mongolian conqueror, and more particularly describes the surrounding park. The few wonderful lines break off with the vision of the Abyssinian maid playing on her dulcimer. It is one of Coleridge's three great poems, and one of the greatest in all romantic literature.

KUPONGJIP, by Song Ikpil. See SHIJO-YUCHIP.

KUWUNMONG (1689), by Kim Manchung. *Kuwunmong* or *The Cloud Dream of the Nine* is perhaps the most idyllic romance of polygamy in existence. The time of the story is the Chinese T'ang dynasty about 840. The hero, Songjin, young and handsome, one of the 600 disciples of a Buddhist monastery on Lotus Peak, is sent by his spiritual master with a greeting to the Dragon King, who then deceives him with wine. Returning, he encounters eight fairy maidens in the service of the Queen of the Genii, now a Taoist by divine command and settled on a mountain near Lotus Peak. For their light actions, Songjin and the eight fairies are sentenced by the King of Hell to an earthly existence. All are born into different families, and as human beings know nothing of their former existence. Songjin becomes Master Yang, the only child of a poor hermit. He rises from obscurity to fame and from poverty to wealth; one by one the eight fairies become part of his household as the story unfolds the love-drama of nine. No shadow of jealousy mars their perfect affinity. In the end, the aged priest from Lotus Peak appears to summon Yang, who becomes again Songjin, the acolyte, as his earthly power and his eight wives vanish as a dream. All nine are restored to a spiritual paradise.

Kim Manchung wrote the book while he was in exile in 1689, as a means to cheer and comfort his mother. On his death, the state erected a Gate of Honor for his filial piety. Confucian, Taoistic and Buddhistic ideas mingle in this joyous Korean novel, which has been popular both for its picture of earthly paradise and its all-enveloping mysticism.

There is an English translation by James S. Gale.

LABYRINTH OF THE WORLD AND THE PARADISE OF THE HEART (1625), by Comenius. See DIDACTICA, THE, by Comenius.

LADY CHATTERLEY'S LOVER (1928), by D. H. Lawrence. The novel has appeared in three versions. The earliest, *The First Lady Chatterley*, was published here in 1944. The unexpurgated version, banned in England and the United States, circulates privately in copies printed in Florence and in France. The abridged version is itself a very clear hymn to physical love as embodying all that is meaningful to the human spirit. To Lady Chatterley her husband, who has come back from the war a permanent invalid, paralyzed from the waist down, becomes the hated symbol of all that is sterile and joyless, including class consciousness. The gamekeeper Mellors is not her first lover, but their instinct for each other is instantaneous, and she deliberately seeks him, and soon, in the midst of quadrangular scandal, faces her husband with the announcement of whose child she is soon to bear. Hatred breaks out in two great scenes, as does love in the many others—solemn, peace-bringing love, to Lawrence a veritable religion.

LADY INTO FOX (1922), by David Garnett. This short, fantastic novelette is laid in England in 1880. Silvia Fox Tebrick is transformed into a fox. Her husband, Richard, a country gentleman, does his best to keep up appearances. He shoots his dogs, discharges his servants, and tries to keep their usual way of life, playing cards with his fox-wife, dressing her in clothes, etc. She, however, is truly a fox; soon she expresses her newly acquired instincts. Richard takes his wife to the cottage of Mrs. Cork (Nanny) and her children, Simon and Polly. There, Silvia discards her clothes and runs wild. She disappears and returns one day with five cubs. Richard, at first jealous, relents and christens them Sorel, Kasper, Selwyn, Esther and Angelica. People of the countryside think he is mad, including Silvia's uncle, Rev. Canon Fox. Mrs. Tebrick is finally attacked by hounds and dies in her husband's arms. "For a long time his life was despaired of, but at last he rallied, and in the end he recovered his reason and lived to a great age."

LADY OF THE AROOSTOOK, THE (1879), by William Dean Howells. See RISE OF SILAS LAPHAM, THE, by William Dean Howells.

LADY OF THE LAKE, THE (1810), by Sir Walter Scott. This poem in six cantos, the narrative parts in octosyllabics with interpolated songs and introduced by one or more Spenserian stanzas, tells of the suitors of Ellen Douglas, the lady of Loch Katrine. The first of these, a stranger, calls himself James Fitz-James, after she has met him while he was hunting. Roderick Dhu, the Border chieftain, is their host, and when war with the King of Scotland is imminent, Fitz-James proposes to Ellen and offers to bear her away to safety. But she loves Malcolm Graeme. Another suitor, Roderick himself, is later wounded in a fight with Fitz-James. Ellen had been given a ring by the latter that he said would procure for her from the King any boon she asks. She brings the signet to court, asks pardon for her outlawed father, Lord James of Douglas, and finds that Fitz-James is the King. Roderick dies and Ellen marries Graeme. The poem contains the famous boat song, "Hail to the Chief" and the dirge, "Soldier, rest! thy warfare o'er."

LADY OR THE TIGER?, THE (1884), by Frank R. Stockton. In a certain town, it is the King's fancy to punish crimes by placing the offenders in an arena with two doors. Behind one of them is a hungry tiger; behind the other, a lovely maiden. Each hapless culprit takes his chance, and is devoured or wed.

Enraged at surprising a young man wooing the Princess, the King sentences him to the test. The distracted Princess succeeds in learning the secret of the doors, but is torn between compassion for her lover and jealousy that he should marry another. At the final moment the prisoner glances at her and observes a slight signal indicating one of the doors. Without hesitation, he opens it. Then the story ends, with the question, "Which came out of the open door—the lady or the tiger?"

This tour de force took the country by storm. Countless tricks were used to plague Stockton into committing himself about the outcome, but the author steadfastly refused to give the answer to his question, which has remained famous in American fiction.

Frank Stockton wrote the whimsical fantasy, *Rudder Grange,* in 1879. The title is the name of a houseboat, the home of Euphemia and her husband. Pomona, their highly original housemaid, lives according to the romances which she has read. After many humorous adventures, Pomona is married by Jonas, a young farmer, who tempers her imagination.

Among his later books is the amusing *The Casting Away of Mrs. Lecks and Mrs. Aleshine* (1886). This novel tells of two middle-aged women, and Mr. Craig, who are shipwrecked in the Pacific Ocean, paddle to an island, and set up housekeeping. Ruth Enderton, a missionary's daughter, arrives with her father and three sailors, and at length marries Craig. Before returning to civilization, they leave a note for the Dusantes, owners of the house they have lived in. *The Dusantes* (1888) continues the tale. The party has returned to America, and under exciting circumstances meets the Dusantes. Back in Pennsylvania, Mrs. Aleshine's son marries the Dusantes' daughter, the sailors become farmers, and they settle down to live together.

LADY WINDERMERE'S FAN (1892), by Oscar Wilde. Wilde's most brilliant social comedy shows Lady Windermere, an orphan, about to celebrate her twenty-first birthday by giving a ball. She learns that her husband has been seen with a Mrs. Erlynne, and it is said that he is spending large sums of money on her. Lord Windermere asks his wife to trust him; he wishes to invite Mrs. Erlynne to the party. Indignant, Lady Windermere refuses. However, Mrs. Erlynne comes on Lord Windermere's invitation, enraging Lady Windermere. She decides to leave her husband, and go off with an admirer, Lord Darlington. Mrs. Erlynne is really Lady Windermere's divorced mother, and Lord Windermere is trying to keep her without revealing her identity to his wife. She discovers where Lady Windermere has gone, and, her maternal instincts roused, follows her to Lord Darlington's rooms. She has just persuaded her to leave when he comes in with some friends, Lord Windermere among them. He recognizes his wife's fan. Mrs. Erlynne claims the fan as hers, saying she had picked it up by mistake; Lady Windermere escapes unseen. The next day Mrs. Erlynne, who has sacrificed her own reputation to save her daughter's, returns the fan to a grateful Lady Windermere. Mrs. Erlynne is forced to leave for the Continent.

L'AIGLON (1900), by Edmond Rostand. At the opening curtain of the play, Metternich is holding the young Duke of Reichstadt, Napoleon's son, a captive at the court of Austria so that the *Aiglon* will not attempt to imitate and avenge the old Eagle. Bonapartist conspirators plot to restore him to the throne and plan the escape for a night when Metternich is giving a masked ball. While his cousin, Countess Camerata, impersonates him at the masquerade, the Eaglet makes his escape. He gets as far as the battlefield at Wagram and there, worried about what may happen to his cousin, loses his nerve. While he hesitates, Austrian soldiers overtake him and he returns penitently to captivity. At the last curtain, he is dying of consumption.

Written as a vehicle for Sarah Bernhardt, this play is typical of Rostand's semi-operatic theatre, less popular than his *Cyrano de Bergerac* (1897; q.v.), but more durable than his *Chantecler* (1910) and *The Faraway Princess* (1895).

LALLA ROOKH (1817), by Thomas Moore. This is a combination of highly descriptive prose and poetry that has been translated into many languages, sung all over the world, and dramatized at the German Court. The story of Lalla Rookh is related in prose; the songs by the poet, Feramorz, are in poetic form. Lalla Rookh, daughter of the Emperor of Arabia, is betrothed to Aliris, King of Lesser Bucharia. On her journey to Cashmere, where the wedding is to take place, she falls in love with the Cashmerian poet, Feramorz. He sings "The Veiled Prophet of Khorassan," "Paradise and the Peri," "The Fire-Worshippers," and "The Light of the Harem," which is the story of the Feast of Roses at Cashmere. Lalla decides to try to forget Feramorz and marry the King she has never seen. She discovers Feramorz is actually the King of Bucharia.

Moore is well known also as the author of the three songs: "Believe Me, If All Those Endearing Young Charms," "The Harp That Once Through Tara's Halls!" and "The Last Rose of Summer."

LAMIA (1819), by John Keats. In heroic couplets, revealing Dryden's influence on Keats, this allegorical poem concerns a beautiful serpent-woman, or lamia, who bribes Hermes to restore her woman's form and transport her to Corinth, where lives Lycius, a godlike and scholarly youth whom she loves. She woos and wins him. As the lovers pass hand-in-hand through Corinth, Lycius avoids Apollonius, his sage mentor. In the palace of Lycius the two enjoy their love until Lycius determines to invite friends to their wedding. Apollonius, whom Lamia fears, appears unbidden; recognizing in Lamia no mortal woman, and thinking her evil, he fixes upon her the withering eye of "cold philosophy." She vanishes forever; Lycius dies.

LAMIA, ISABELLA, THE EVE OF ST. AGNES, AND OTHER POEMS (1820), by John Keats. See ODES, by John Keats.

LANCELOT (1920), by Edwin Arlington Robinson. See ROBINSON, EDWIN ARLINGTON.

LAND OF HEART'S DESIRE, THE (1894), by William Butler Yeats. See YEATS, WILLIAM BUTLER.

LAND OF HEROES, THE (published 1822). See KALEVALA.

LANDLORD AT LION'S HEAD, THE (1897), by William Dean Howells. See HAZARD OF NEW FORTUNES, A, by William Dean Howells.

LANGS LIJNEN VAN GELEIDELIJKHEID (1900), by Louis Couperus. See COUPERUS, LOUIS.

LANIER, SIDNEY (1842–1881). As a youth, Sidney Lanier's musical studies were interrupted by the Civil War. After service, he returned from imprisonment in Maryland, his health undermined. *Tiger-Lilies* (1867), a novel of war experience, encouraged him to turn to literature. *Poems* appeared in 1877, and resulted in a lecturing tour. He was a professional flutist, and it was his theory, articulated in *The Science of English Verse* (1880), that the physical laws of poetry and music were identical. He emphasized ballad and lyric forms in his own verse, and used strange rhythms and conceits. His results were uneven, but include many meritorious pieces.

The Song of the Chattahoochee (1883) is a verse epic of a river's inevitable flow to the main, with its obedience to "duties" such as turning mill wheels. *The Symphony* (1875) is an onomatopoetic exposition of the orchestral instruments, which discuss in turn the problems of industrialism and aesthetics. "The Marshes of Glynn" (1878) is a lyrical hymn to the sea marshes of Georgia. It was one of three written, of a projected series of six. In his fine ode "Psalm of the West" he uses the sonnet form for narrative purposes in a rare and masterly fashion. His "A Ballad of Trees and the Master" is one of the most powerfully moving of religious poems.

LANSELOET (ca. 15th c.), Anonymous. See MEDIEVAL FLEMISH PLAYS.

LARDNER, RING (1885–1933). Ring Lardner, in spite of his parents' wishes that he study for the ministry or engineering, became a newspaper man and sports writer. His first volume of stories, *You Know Me, Al* (1916) employs the idiom of athletes, and narrates the life of a young professional baseball player. Lardner was soon recognized as a serious writer.

How to Write Short Stories (1924) is a collection which the author slyly presents as examples of his admittedly nonexistent literary theories. Using American vernacular, Lardner attacks by implication certain native foibles. "Alibi Ike" tells of a star baseball player who finds it necessary to make excuses for his every action. "The Golden Honeymoon" chronicles the dullness and irritations in the lives of a superficially happy old couple. "Champion" is an exposé of the mean, seamy side of a professional pugilist's career.

His facile style and pessimistic views appear in later collections, such as *The Love Nest* (1926). The title story reveals the crudities and frustrations in the life of the wife of a boastful motion-picture magnate, "Who Dealt?" discloses, in the frivolous chatter of a bridge player, the tragic story of her husband's previous romance.

LAST ADAM, THE (1933), by James Gould Cozzens. Dr. George Bull, town physician of New Winton, Connecticut, is a coarse, ignorant man possessed of inexhaustible vitality. Despite his failings, he continues to browbeat the entire township. When, due to his dereliction of duty as health inspector, a typhoid epidemic strikes New Winton, he faces disgrace. The community holds an indignation meeting. But Dr. Bull seems destined to overcome all obstacles and retain his influence in the town.

S.S. San Pedro (1931) was based on the facts of the sinking of the *Vestris*. It describes the sailing of the freighter from Hoboken, loaded with one million dollars in gold for Montevideo, freight, and 172 passengers. Captain John Clendenning, old and infirm, is too confused to issue abandon ship orders when the badly listing vessel founders in a storm. Anthony Bredell, second senior officer, is badly injured, and taken off in a boat at last by Miro, the Brazilian quartermaster. The sinking of the boat climaxes an atmosphere of mystery begun when the ominous figure of Dr. Percival made a presailing tour of inspection.

Guard of Honor (1948) is a Pulitzer Prize novel about the nature of human conflict. "Bus" Beal, young Major General in the Army Air Forces, takes command of the base at Ocanara, Florida. During the next three days, the mounting tension of personal interrelationships, scandal, racial discrimination, politics among the top brass, reaches a climax unparalleled even during Ira Beal's combat career.

LAST ATHENIAN, THE (1859), by Viktor Rydberg. This classical Swedish novel, localized in and near Athens in the fourth century, is an ardent plea for freedom of thought and religious toleration. It is, in substance, a glorification of Hellenic ideals of truth, wisdom, reason, beauty, harmony, and philosophy, none of which should be discarded in the study of the history and interpretation of moral and religious thinking. The novel is directed not against the basic principles of Christianity but at all, and especially the contemporary, bigoted, cruel, intolerant leaders of it. The hero, Krysanteus, is a rich, noble, intellectual "arch-pagan," the first citizen of Athens, revered by most Athenians but hated and feared by the intriguing Christian rascal, Bishop

Petros, who covets Krysanteus' wealth for himself and his Church, and in whom the hero eventually recognizes his former slave. The Bishop's shrewd and terrifying persecution strikes not only nonbelievers but all Christians who in any way differ with his own interpretation of the Scriptures. He ultimately incites and helps lead a military campaign against the "heretics" and their friends, among whom are some pagans, including Krysanteus. There is plenty of action in the novel, many good minor characters, and several tragic romances: the love of the hero's daughter Hermione for Karmides (who is stabbed on his wedding night by Rabbi Jonas for having previously seduced a Jewish maiden, Rachel); the suicide by drowning of Rachel, holding her infant son in her arms, after she had been cast out by her father; and Hermione's self-destruction in the great temple after a forced baptism. It is well-constructed propaganda for democracy in fiction form. Krysanteus represents idealized humanity, both ancient and modern.

Other notable works by the same author are: *Singoalla* (1858), a romantic story of pure artistry which tells of a knight's love for a gypsy girl; *The Armorer* (1891), a historical novel from the period of the Reformation, where the hero represents culture and mature experience as against the religious intolerance of Magister Lars; and *The Bible's Teachings about Christ* (1862), a plea for freedom of research.

LAST CHRONICLE OF BARSET, THE (1867), by Anthony Trollope. This two-volume story completes the famous Barsetshire series. Readers are so reluctant to come to an end of their happy friendships with the people of Barchester (probably based on the cathedral city of Winchester) and the shire, that not long ago the clever and erudite Father Ronald Knox of Oxford carried their stories almost up to date to the amusement and pleasure of Trollope enthusiasts. The Crawleys, whom we came to know slightly in earlier books and somewhat better when Lucy Robarts nursed the children and Mrs. Crawley through an illness, just before she accepted Lord Lufton's proposal of marriage, hold the center of the stage in this last novel. The story is built around the presumed theft by Rev. Josiah Crawley of twenty pounds.

Trollope considered this the best novel he had written, and many readers agree with him. Mrs. Proudie returns to the scene with her old assurance; she demands that Crawley be prevented from preaching in his village church and sends her curate to preach in his place. But Josiah Crawley proves such a match for the redoubtable Mrs. Proudie that he actually causes her death from apoplexy, leaving the henpecked Bishop disconsolate but relieved. Josiah might have his head in the clouds, but he was certain he had never taken a cent that he did not have a full right to take. But how explain the mistake? That he could not do. He was summoned to appear before the magistrates and before his Bishop.

Meanwhile Archdeacon Grantly had been brought into the outskirts of the unfortunate affair by his younger son's determination to marry Grace Crawley, who has gone to stay with Lily Dale in Allington. The Luftons try to help Mr. Crawley, who, it turns out, had the check quite in proper fashion from Mrs. Arabin who (years before when Eleanor Harding had married Dr. Bold and soon been widowed) had gone directly to Italy, so had heard nothing of the horrible affair. The Archdeacon actually discovers that he is human; he is enchanted with Grace Crawley. Where he went to censure, he returns to praise, to the innermost delight of his wife, who is a worthy child of Dr. Harding as well as a worthy wife of the Archdeacon. Dr. Harding dies, sainted and very old. The children of the first books are ready for marriage now. It is this intimate family quality in these tales which makes them perennial favorites.

Trollope did not confine himself to the Barset novels; he turned out an immense number of novels of all sorts. There is a political series in which, however, he cannot compare with Disraeli (in one of them, in Mr. Dabney, he draws his own picture of the great Prime Minister).

LAST DAYS OF POMPEII, THE (1834), by Lord Edward Bulwer-Lytton. This novel of first century Pompeii begins a few days before the eruption of Vesuvius (A.D. 79) and ends with the disaster. It is filled with descriptions of the life and manners of Roman society. The Christian era is just beginning. Glaucus, the brilliant and charming hero, loves Ione, a good and beautiful Greek girl. Arbaces, an Egyptian, is also in love with her; she is his ward. He murders Ione's brother, and accuses Glaucus of the crime. In the amphitheater, Glaucus faces a lion, and death. Nydia, his blind slave, rescues him just as Vesuvius erupts. After guiding Glaucus and Ione to safety, and wishing to escape her love for Glaucus, Nydia throws herself into the sea.

LAST FRONTIER, THE (1941), by Howard Fast. See CITIZEN TOM PAINE, by Howard Fast.

LAST OF THE MOHICANS, THE (1826), by James Fenimore Cooper. See LEATHERSTOCKING TALES, by James Fenimore Cooper.

LAST PURITAN, THE (1935), by George Santayana. Consisting largely of philosophical ruminations made by its chief character, the Connecticut Puritan Oliver Alden, this novel attempts the dissection of the New England Brahmin type which disappeared from the scene at the advent of World War I. Oliver, born into a cold, loveless puritanical home, turns out to be an inhibited, frightened intellectual. His father, Peter, commits suicide, frustrated in a search for happiness. Oliver befriends the opportunistic Jim Darnley, and falls in love with Jim's sister Rose. Rose is in love with Oliver's hedonistic cousin Mario, but Mario is unaware of this. Meanwhile, Oliver finds life intolerable, for all his impulses are arrested by austere thoughts. He proposes to Rose, that she may inherit his fortune. She rejects him, and he leaves to join the army, later being killed overseas.

This is the author's only novel. He is famous for *The Sense of Beauty* (q.v.), a treatise on aesthetics; *The Life of Reason* (q.v.), a work on society, religion, science and art; and two volumes of memoirs, *Persons and Places* (1943) and *The Middle Span* (1945).

Soliloquies in England (1922) is an examination of Anglo-Saxon characteristics. Fifty-five discursive essays philosophize about such "eternal verities" as "Hamlet's Question," "English Architecture," "Dickens," and "The Irony of Liberalism."

LAST TIME I SAW PARIS, THE (1942), by Elliot Paul. See LIFE AND DEATH OF A SPANISH TOWN, THE, by Elliot Paul.

LATE GEORGE APLEY, THE (1937), by John P. Marquand. A novel ostensibly written by Horatio Willing, official biographer of eminent Bostonians of good Plymouth Rock heritage, this concerns one George Apley, a wealthy citizen who died in 1933, at the age of sixty-six. From Apley's memoirs and letters the biographer pieces together the life of this pillar of society, a Puritan with a solid façade, but a slightly soft heart. Conventional, hedged in by habits, repressions and traditions, he is a pathetic symbol upon whom the author turns his ironic regard, contrasting him with his seventeenth century Puritan ancestors, who at least lived courageously by their convictions. In the story, old Apley is shocked when his son marries a divorced woman, and his daughter falls in love with a Midwesterner.

The Late George Apley won the Pulitzer Prize for 1938, and was made into a play and a motion picture.

H. M. Pulham, Esq. (1941) is another novel satirizing the standards of a New Englander. Henry Moulton Pulham is a wealthy, Harvard-educated Massachusetts blue-blood. After World War I he moves to New York, where he meets and falls in love with a young business girl; awakened to the responsibilities of his Brahmin caste, however, he abandons her for Kay, a girl of his own set. Ironically, Kay has married Henry on the rebound from a love affair with a New York advertising man. Twenty years later, Henry meets his New York love again. They decide to go away together, but at the last minute reconsider. Coincidentally, Kay meets her former lover; they, too, think of running away but decide not to. All settle down to the life which class tradition has prescribed for them.

LATE SUMMER, THE (1857), by Adalbert Stifter. This novel by the Bohemian-born Stifter deals with the educational development of a central figure. Published at a time when literary realism was at its height, the novel centers on the steady, uninterrupted striving toward the ideal by the main character, Heinrich Drendorf. It is a typically romantic attempt to carry the reader beyond the materialism of this world toward the fulfillment of the longing for peace and harmony. Peculiarly devoid of personal passions but filled with symbolism, the book describes the attainment of the concept of the Utopian ideal upon which Stifter had touched in his earlier works. Autobiographical in nature are both the account of the educational effect of science and art on Heinrich and the synthesis of the two, as symbolized by the far-off House of Roses. *The Late Summer* is the key to the mind and writings of Stifter. His other works include the historical novel *Witiko* (1864–1867), which deals with twelfth-century Bohemia and its relations to the Holy Roman Empire, and the collections of stories *Studies* (1844–1850) and *Colored Stones* (1852).

LATER LIFE, THE (1901–1903), by Louis Couperus. See COUPERUS, LOUIS.

LAUGHING BOY (1929), by Oliver Hazard Perry La Farge. One of the few realistic novels of American Indian life, concerned with its moral and social problems in relation to its white setting, this Pulitzer Prize novel centers on the personalities and psychological reactions of two Navajo Indians. The incorruptible Laughing Boy marries Slim Girl, an intelligent idealist. She accepts Christianity, only to discover that white people give it mere lip service. Smarting under the deception, she vows to avenge herself on the white oppressors of her people. She makes a white man fall in love with her and then forces him to enrich her and Laughing Boy, thus enabling them to rise above the condescending whites. Her plan ends in tragedy when Laughing Boy discovers her with the lover and shoots them both. The wounds are not fatal, and the Indian couple have a reconciliation. Matured, they begin a trip back to their people. Red Man, a jealous Indian, ambushes them and kills Slim Girl. Laughing Boy is grief-stricken and wishes for revenge at first; but after the funeral he returns to his tribe.

LAVENGRO, THE SCHOLAR—THE GYPSY—THE PRIEST (1851), by George Borrow. This celebrated romanticized autobiography consists of picaresque sketches. It was published in two volumes: *The Romany Rye* (1857) as the sequel to *Lavengro*. They tell of Borrow's earliest dreams and sentiments, his relations with his family, his astounding curiosity about people, his interest in gypsies. Upon the death of his father he went to London, where he starved as a hack translator of verse for reviews and magazines. His passion for experience finally led him to explore the "low" classes of England, "chiefly to gratify the curiosity of a scholar." He was bent upon a career of roving adventure, becoming tinker, gypsy, postilion and hostler, combining this interest with a loving pursuit of philology from Irish to Chinese. "Lavengro" means "philologist" in the gypsy tongue. His cronies were an old applewoman on London Bridge and an old man who knew Chinese "but could not tell what was o'clock." The most admired episode in the autobiography is Lavengro's (Borrow's) meeting with Belle Berners, the beautiful blonde giantess. She is journeying with a knight of the road, the "Flaming Tinman"; Lavengro is traveling in his pony-cart, tinkering on the way. The two men fight for her and the athletic scholar downs the tinman. Belle has had an unfortunate life, having been born in a workhouse. She has become a lady-errant of the road. Lavengro cares for her but her past stands like a wall between them. Afraid that he might want to marry her and knowing he would regret it, she leaves him and goes to America.

LAW INEVITABLE, THE (1900; Eng. tr. 1921), by Louis Couperus. See COUPERUS, LOUIS.

LAWS OF ECCLESIASTICAL POLITY, THE (1594–1597), by Richard Hooker. The ideas of social contract and government under law which usually served revolutionary causes were used by Richard Hooker to defend the Elizabethan monarchy. Writing primarily about church government, he recognized that all government rests on the same principles. Hence his principles are generally applicable. In attempting to refute the Puritan criticism of the established church, Hooker presented the last important statement of political theory in the medieval tradition. All men acknowledge rules of reason. Men form societies because of their native sociability. Society must have a government, and government rests on tacit consent. Political obligations rest ing on consent are perpetually binding. The ecclesiastical laws of England are as binding on all citizens as any other laws. Thus his theory was a blend of mediaeval and nationalist elements, and he managed to compromise theories which tore England apart in the seventeenth century. John Locke, who referred to him as "the judicious Hooker," learned much from him.

LAWS OF MANU, THE (ca. 200 B.C.). *The Laws of Manu* is one of the best known in Occidental countries of sacred Buddhist writings. It is written in epic meter and resembles the versified forms of the ritual *Sutras*.

The Laws of Manu belong to the second class of Sanskrit law books; that is, they were intended to popularize the earlier laws and to be put into practical use in the courts of India. They consist of some 2,685 regulations (verses). The text of this work has been consulted by the English courts of India and even by the Privy Council in England on matters pertaining to litigation between Hindus of different caste membership.

The intention of the work is made immediately clear with the first statement: "The great Seers having approached Manu, seated intent, having reverenced him, duly spoke this speech: 'Lord! Deign to tell us truly in order the rules of all the castes, and of all the castes that arise between them. For thou, Lord, alone knowest the true sense of the objects of this universal, self-existent system, unattainable by simple reason, not to be reasoned out.' " Manu answers in a discourse on cosmogony, for the Buddhists saw an interconnection between the material, the spiritual and the social world of man. A divine causality arranged both the stars and the hierarchy of the various castes and caste-relationships in India.

The second lecture is on the first condition of life for a Brahmin; the third on marriage and its duties; the fourth on private morals; the fifth on ceremonial purification for burial and the duties of women. The sixth lecture is on the third and fourth forms of life; the seventh treats of the duties of a king —also of the second caste. The eighth lecture discusses civil and criminal law; the ninth is on the third and fourth castes. The remaining three lectures cover the mixed castes and classes; procedure in time of need; penance, expiation, etc.; and conclude with the exposition of philosophical principles whose sole object is the achievement of final happiness. All these lectures contain subject matter which is an odd mixture of aboriginal tabus, religious superstitions, and sound, practical sense about human relationships derived from thousands of years of experience. Prejudices, plain stupidity and cruelty are also treated.

LAXDAELA SAGA (late 13th c.). See NJÁL SAGA, THE.

LAY OF THE LAST MINSTREL, THE (1805), by Sir Walter Scott. This long romantic poem came as a natural result of Scott's ballad studies. It is divided into six cantos, sung or recited by the old minstrel to the Duchess of Buccleuch in the state room of Newark Castle. This permits a delightful simplicity throughout. Scott was indebted to Coleridge for the elastic metrical form, but the *Lay,* except for its meter, has little in common with *Christabel.* The story tells of two lovers separated by a family feud. Lord Cranstoun finally wins Margaret of Branksome Hall through fighting for her little brother, who has been kidnaped and who will be the prize for whoever defeats Sir

Richard Musgrave in single combat. Outstanding is the poem beginning, "Breathes there the man, with soul so dead . . ."

LAY SERMONS, ADDRESSES, AND REVIEWS (1870), by Thomas Henry Huxley. See EVOLUTION AND ETHICS, by Thomas Henry Huxley.

LAYS OF ANCIENT ROME (1842), by Thomas Babington Macaulay. This is the volume famous for containing "Horatius," the story of how Rome was saved by the three who stood and held off the Tuscan enemy until the bridge across the Tiber could be cut down. Horatius, after his two companions have crossed the bridge just before it collapsed, swims across despite his wounds and his armor, while both sides stand amazed. The other ballads are "The Battle of Lake Regillus," "Virginia," and "The Prophecy of Capys," which are likewise dedicated to the firm Roman virtues. Macaulay branched into Renaissance history when he added in 1848 "The Battle of Ivry" and a fragment, "The Armada."

LAZARILLO DE TORMES (published 1554), Anonymous. Lázaro was born in a mill on the banks of the Tormes, near Salamanca, of a not very honest miller and a base and brutal woman who, to get rid of him, places Lázaro in the employment of an extremely astute blind man. During the beggar's peregrinations, Lázaro (now called Lazarillo, i.e., blind man's guide) learns from him the fine and slippery art of mendicancy and roguery. Unable to stand the blind man's stinginess and rough treatment, Lazarillo runs away and enters the service of a clergyman who is an even worse miser. To keep alive Lazarillo has to use a key to steal his food from the chest where the clergyman hoards it. Finally caught by the clergyman, he is soundly trounced and dismissed. Lazarillo's new master is a vain squire, extremely proud of his nobility but heavily in debt and in the direst poverty, so that in the end Lazarillo is forced to support him by begging. This whole section dealing with the impoverished squire is a masterly portrait worthy of the Russian realists, especially Gogol. Thereafter Lazarillo serves in rapid succession a mendicant monk, a great enemy of "psalm-singing" who delights in fun and frolic; a nimble seller of papal bulls and indulgences; and a chaplain who makes a water vendor of him. After four years of this hard life Lazarillo leaves his job to marry an archpriest's servant girl, but she, devoted amorously to her holy master, artfully deceives Lazarillo, who is obtusely unaware of his cuckoldry.

Written probably after 1539, but published in 1554, *Lazarillo de Tormes* is the earliest and also the best picaresque novel. Reacting against the artificial world of the then popular chivalric romances, the picaresque novel dealt with "picaros" or rascals who had to live by their wits in a Spain undergoing a most disastrous economic crisis. By having one main character running through a series of loosely connected episodes, the novel can depict with audacious truth and directness the various social strata.

LAZARUS LAUGHED (1927), by Eugene O'Neill. See MOURNING BECOMES ELECTRA, by Eugene O'Neill.

LEATHERSTOCKING TALES (1823–1841), by James Fenimore Cooper. These five novels of frontier life were not written in a sequence chronological with the life of the hero, Natty Bumppo, a brave woodsman who lived and fought among the Indians and early settlers of America.

The Deerslayer (1841) is a record of Natty Bumppo's early days as a young hunter brought up among the Delaware Indians, engaged in warfare against the Hurons. He helps defend the family of Tom Hutter, a settler, from attack. Judith, who is really not Tom's daughter, but a girl of noble birth, loves Natty Bumppo and begs him not to return to the Iroquois, who have released him on parole from capture. Bumppo does return, but is rescued by the intervention of Judith, who thereafter disappears, and the Delaware Chief Chingachgook, who remains a lifelong friend.

The Last of the Mohicans (1826) presents Chingachgook and his son Uncas as the last of the Iroquois aristocracy. Natty Bumppo, the scout Hawkeye, is in the prime of his career in the campaign of Fort William Henry on Lake George under attack by the French and Indians. The commander's daughters, Cora and Alice Munro, with the latter's fiancé Major Duncan Heyward, are captured by a traitorous Indian but rescued and conveyed to the fort by Hawkeye. Later Munro surrenders to Montcalm, and the girls are seized again by Indians. Uncas and Cora are killed, and the others return to civilization.

The Pathfinder (1840) finds Natty Bumppo at the age of forty. A small outpost on Lake Ontario is under attack. Mabel Dunham helps in the defense, and with the aid of Pathfinder, Chingachgook, and Jasper Western, a young sailor, the Iroquois are routed. Lieutenant Muir, who had proposed to Mabel, has been captured by the Indians and is now freed. He arrests Jasper as a traitor, but when Muir is revealed as the guilty one, he is killed by Arrowhead, a Tuscarora Indian. Jasper wins the love of Mabel.

The Pioneers (1823) tells of Bumppo the veteran frontiersman as he retreats across the Alleghenies from advancing civilization. His companions are young Oliver Edwards and John Mohegan (old Chief Chingachgook). Judge Marmaduke Temple, a post-Revolution New York landowner, accidentally shoots Edwards, later befriending him—as does his daughter Elizabeth, though she scorns the friendship of Chingachgook. Bumppo rescues Chingachgook from a forest fire, but the old Indian dies. Edwards rescues Elizabeth and falls in love with her. Edwards turns out to be the grandson of Edward Effingham, an old Loyalist friend of Temple's, and Bumppo a former family employee.

The Prairie (1827) tells of Bumppo in 1804, nearly 90, but still a frontiersman. In an emigrant party led by Ishmael Bush and Abiram White, there are a woman captive, Ellen Wade, and her lover, Paul Hover. Bumppo helps guide the party, and is joined by a soldier, Duncan Uncas Middleton (descendant of Duncan Heyward, *Last of the Mohicans*). When he learns Ishmael's captive is his kidnaped fiancée, he and Bumppo free her. With Paul and Ellen they subsequently escape the Sioux, a fire, and a buffalo stampede, but are captured by Ishmael. He accuses Bumppo of a crime, but Abiram is found to be guilty. Middleton's soldiers provide safety for all. At last the aged Bumppo dies, surrounded by both white and Indian friends.

LEAVES OF GRASS (1855–1891), by Walt Whitman. *Leaves of Grass* first appeared in 1855, a collection of twelve poems which received little attention. The work reflected influences of Emerson and transcendentalism, Utopian socialism, Greek paganism, the German philosophers, and contemporary science. A preface, later omitted, delineated the ideal poet, a lover of the universe and of America, and a stylist whose simplicity seeks to represent the organic growth of the verses.

During the next thirty-six years, successive enlarged editions met a progressively enthusiastic audience. The 1891 volume contained all the poetical works of the author. The most popular are as follows:

"Song of Myself," untitled introduction to the first edition, states the equalitarian doctrine that "a leaf of grass" is as important as the grandest cosmic design. Whitman's philosophy, discounting the contradictions of his enthusiasms, is a mystical pantheism.

"Song of the Broad-Axe" praises that weapon taken from the earth, used by American pioneers, and symbolic of freedom.

"Out of the Cradle Endlessly Rocking" describes the plaintive cry of a lonely sea bird, and symbolizes love, death, and poetic creation.

"Calamus" is a sequence of forty-five poems defending Whitman's non-conformist individuality and praising the spiritual love of mankind. "Children of Adam" is a complementary sequence of sixteen pieces concerning physical love.

"Drum-Taps" and "Sequel to Drum-Taps" are a record of the Civil War, considered a literary monument to the greatness of a nation in crisis. There are martial poems, and elegiacs on the death of Lincoln, such as "When Lilacs Last in the Door Yard Bloom'd," and "O Captain! My Captain!"

"A Backward Glance O'er Travel'd Roads" is a prose epilogue intended to reveal the personality of the poet, and naming the Civil War as a greater force in his career than all purely artistic influences.

This poet, whose desire to portray the average man was articulated by a unique personality and literary ability, wrote also *Specimen Days and Collect* (1882), containing reminiscences of early New York days, journal jottings of Washington during the Civil War days, and nature notes. *Democratic Vistas* (1871) is a prose invocation to the free man in a just society. A glowing tribute to democracy, it is also an endorsement of individualism, which was Whitman's hope for a vigorous, prosperous post-Civil War era.

LECTURES IN AMERICA (1935), by Gertrude Stein. See AUTOBIOGRAPHY OF ALICE B. TOKLAS, THE, by Gertrude Stein.

LECTURES ON THE PRINCIPLES OF POLITICAL OBLIGATION (delivered in 1879), by Thomas Hill Green. After a survey of the contributions to political theory of Spinoza, Hobbes, Locke, and Rousseau, Green outlines a political philosophy which is Kantian, idealistic, and anti-utilitarian in character. Rejecting the atomistic theory of the Utilitarians, he develops an organic theory of the state. The responsibility of the state is to provide the conditions for the moral self-realization of individuals. This is positive freedom as distinguished from the negative freedom (absence of restraint) emphasized by the classical liberals. Thus this view can be seen to be an attempt to synthesize the valuable elements of the English liberal tradition with the insights of Rousseau and the classical German tradition.

LEE'S LIEUTENANTS (1942–1944), by Douglas Southall Freeman. See R. E. LEE, by Douglas Southall Freeman.

LEGEND OF GOOD WOMEN, THE (ca. 1384–1386), by Geoffrey Chaucer. On the first of May the poet goes into a field where he finds and honors a daisy. That evening he dreams of his Queen, Alceste, who is somehow connected with the daisy, and of the God of Love, who chides him for writing about faithless women. The Queen defends him, mentioning his works which are favorable to the fair sex, but directs him to write in future of women who were true lovers. He is to begin with Cleopatra. The stories completed by the poet—in new heroic couplets—are those of Cleopatra, Thisbe, Dido, Hypsipyle and Medea, Lucretia, Ariadne, Philomela, Phyllis, and Hypermnestra.

LEIBNITZ, GOTTFRIED WILHELM (1646–1716). A universal mind with a very wide range of interests, Leibnitz made his mark in the practical world as well as in scientific and philosophical thought. As a diplomat, he traveled widely and became acquainted with the great intellects of his time, Newton, Malebranch, Huyghens, and others. He wrote on mathematics, logic, physics, politics, diplomacy, international law, civil law, philosophy, and theology; he discovered the differential calculus independently of Newton; and he applied the techniques of mathematics to logic. This latter discovery represents the first contribution to the science of symbolic logic, which was to develop and flourish in the nineteenth and twentieth centuries. In philosophy, he was a critic of the dualism that was explicit in the views of Descartes and implicit in those of Spinoza. He attempted to develop a monistic view of the universe in which he made force the basic category. The universe, for him, was made up of ultimate centers of force, which he called "monads." Leibnitz offered proofs of the existence of God, and believed that He had established a harmony of the monads. This view was an optimistic one which can be summarized in the formula, "All is for the best in the best of all possible worlds." These theories are elaborated in his *New Essays on Human Understanding* (1701), *Theodicy* (1710), *Monadology* (1714), and in other writings.

LENAU, NIKOLAUS VON (1802–1850). Possessed of an unhappy nature, the Austro-Hungarian Lenau wrote lyric poetry far removed from the political preoccupations of his contemporary fellow poets. His work, dominated by Romantic tradition, is suggestive of sadness and death—the tragic having a particular fascination for him. His poetry exhibits a deep and melodious feeling for nature, and he is devoted to an "eternal autumn" of gentle melancholy. Heightened disappointment and despair finally resulted in his insanity. Devoid of humor, his works include the epic drama *Faust* (1836), *Poems* (1832), and *New Poems* (1838–1840). The last especially is permeated with a cynical pessimism and bitterness which left an indelible stamp upon the poetic atmosphere of succeeding years.

LESSER ASTRONOMY, by Ptolemy of Alexandria. See ALMAGEST, by Ptolemy of Alexandria.

LET YOUR MIND ALONE (1937), by James Thurber. See THURBER, JAMES.

LETTER ON APOSTASY (ca.1158–1168), by Maimonides. See GUIDE FOR THE PERPLEXED, THE, by Maimonides.

LETTER TO THE RABBIS OF MARSEILLES, THE (1194), by Maimonides. See GUIDE FOR THE PERPLEXED, THE, by Maimonides.

LETTERS (ca. 1130), by Abélard and Héloïse. Abélard, young, handsome and brilliant French philosopher, was one of the great thinkers and popular teachers of his century. For a time he went to live at the house of Canon Fulbert of the Cathedral of Notre Dame. There he met the Canon's beautiful and talented seventeen-year-old niece, Héloïse. The Canon made Abélard Héloïse's tutor. They fell in love. In his own confession, Abélard says: "And so, our books lying open before us, more words of love rose to our lips than of literature, kisses more frequent than speech. Oftener went our hands to each other's bosom than to the pages; love turned our eyes more frequently to itself than it directed them to the study of the texts." The culprits were discovered by the Canon and Abélard was punished by emasculation. The mutilated philosopher became a monk, and at his request Héloïse entered the convent at Argenteuil. To the very end they remained devoted to each other. The tender faithfulness of their love has fascinated poets from Villon to the present time.

LETTERS (1537), by Pietro Aretino. This book is a collection of letters addressed by one of the most profligate men of the Renaissance to princes, artists, prelates and writers, and constitutes an important document of that period of history. There are six volumes of Aretino's *Letters,* many of them full of wit and charm. Aretino broke many a lance against the pedantry and stuffiness of contemporary Italian literature, which was based almost exclusively on the classic patterns. But many of his other letters reveal the author as a literary blackmailer whose brilliant pen was employed to extort money or power from the great men of his age. No one illustrated the character and personality of Aretino, as revealed by his *Letters,* better than the critic F. De Sanctis when he said, "the centre of his world was himself—he thought that the world existed to serve him . . . and the rest of the world was rather like him; many would gladly have copied him, but they had not his brains, nor his diligence, nor his penetration, nor his versatility, nor his wit. So they admired him."

LETTERS (1810–1824), by George Noel Gordon, Lord Byron. The two most romantic figures in the nineteenth century were perhaps Napoleon and Lord Byron. In Byron's letters we come to know and understand him intimately. They are always witty and amusing, but above all their author is alive in them, burning with a fiery personality. Theirs is an outstanding perfection. To defend himself against the charge of sentimentality he forged an ironic, pungent humor. His early letters are to his mother, his half-sister, his lawyer, the charming Elizabeth Pigot and her brother, John Scrope Davies, a likable companion, the sedate Hobhouse, and the clergyman, Hodgson. After the publication of, *Childe Harold* (q.v.) and his rise to fame they are to Tom Moore, R. C. Dallas, John Murray, his publisher, Kinnaird, his banker and friend. The women who loved him are here; letters to Caroline Lamb, Lady Frances Webster, Lady

Oxford and Anne Isabella Milbanke, whom at first meeting he christens the Princess of Parallelograms.

Lady Melbourne is the most remarkable of his women correspondents. Byron preferred her cynicism to Lady Caroline's sentimentalism. For two years Lady Melbourne and Augusta Leigh were the very center of his life. But soon enter the Shelleys, Claire Clairmont who bore his child, Medwin, Treadway, the Williamses and Leigh Hunt. Teresa Guiccioli and her amazing husband, her brother Gamba and those who took part with him in the Greek adventure in which Byron lost his life: Stanhope, Prince Mavrocordates, Samuel Banff, etc. Perhaps the most charming of all is the letter to Tom Moore about the Carnival in Venice; there is one to Caroline Lamb that bristles with his dislike of scribblers. Uniform is the combination of wit, art and vigor.

LETTERS (ca. 1867), by Fyodor Dostoevsky. A man with a full share of human failing, Dostoevsky was a gambler by nature. His letters more often than not deal with his constant desperate need of money. One of the most well-known contains a virulent attack on Turgenev, whom he met in 1867. The letters describe his gambling in Baden and how his wife pawned her last and most precious possessions; he even lost her wedding ring in gambling. Goncharov keeps talking to him of Turgenev, which moves Dostoevsky to see the latter; but he picks a fight with him and vows never to cross his threshold again. Like all his letters, this tirade ends with a request for a loan. It is the human element of these letters that provides the chief interest. It is unlikely that they were written with any idea of future publication.

LETTERS (1815–1820), by John Keats. Keats's mind was so imbued with beauty that bits of it punctuate even his most routine letters. At his best they are so full of intuitions of beauty and wisdom as to be most unusual; they also are unrivaled for zest, whim and fancy. They breathe the very spirit of generous English youth. His love letters to Fanny Brawne alone have disappointed some. Matthew Arnold thought he discerned the shadow of failing health here; Keats certainly was near his death. Middleton Murry, on the contrary, maintains that only by understanding the love letters can we understand the poetry of their author, for both "spring from a single source."

His trip to Scotland and the resulting letters are among the most charming in the language; in many he dashes off magnificent poetry, and flashes of penetrating literary criticism. Addressed to Reynolds, George Keats, Bailey, Fanny and Thomas Keats, they show the poet's youth bubbling over. Later ones are addressed to John Taylor, George and Georgianna Keats, and Fanny Brawne. Those to the latter reveal a sometimes painful, sometimes frolicsome passion. From Rome he writes to Charles Brown in his last letter: "I have an habitual feeling of my real life having passed, and that I am leading a posthumous existence." Although Dr. Clark tried to encourage him, at twenty-five Keats knew he was dying.

LETTERS (1697), by Madame de Sévigné. Madame de Sévigné's *Letters,* mostly addressed to her daughter, Madame de Grignan, who was living in the provinces, were widely read in manuscript during the author's lifetime, but were published only after her death. They are a precious chronicle of contemporary events—the marriage of the Grande Mademoiselle, the suicide of Vatel, the execution of the Marquise de Brinvilliers, the Fouquet case, the death of Turenne, the intrigues at the court of Louis XIV, etc.   But they survive for the picture they offer of the devotion of a gifted, witty and extremely alert woman to a daughter who seems to have possessed none of these qualities and was never sensitive to the value of what appeared to her a routine correspondence.

LETTERS (1732–1797), by Horace Walpole. The more than thirty-five hundred letters of this witty and civilized man are among the most brilliant of all time.   The men and women of fashion whom the Earl of Orford honored with these masterpieces of correspondence were treated to his observations on a great variety of subjects, mostly inconsequential but nevertheless delightful. He gossiped about the personalities of the times, told jokes, talked about his hobbies, described the latest fashions and his opinions of them; praised or criticized both great and little things, as suited his fancy of the moment.   His life and observations cover the greater part of the eighteenth century and reflect it to the generations which followed him.   Besides affairs in Europe, Walpole demonstrated considerable interest in developments in America.   To Horace Mann in 1774 Walpole expressed his ideas on the New World as follows: "The next Augustan age will dawn on the other side of the Atlantic.   There will perhaps be a Thucydides at Boston, a Xenophon at New York, in time a Vergil at Mexico, and a Newton at Peru."   Again, philosophically, he wrote, "The world is a comedy to those that think, a tragedy to those who feel."

LETTERS BY JACOPO ORTIS (1798), by Ugo Foscolo. See SEPULCHRES, THE, by Ugo Foscolo.

LETTERS FROM A FARMER IN PENNSYLVANIA (1768), by John Dickinson. This pamphlet of letters first published serially during 1767–1768 is a logical argument against England's arbitrary taxation. Dickinson points out that since the government is committed to the protection of property, the external levy is illegal and contrary to principle. The author is philosophical in his arguments, but forceful in his advice to resist, by peaceable methods first, then arms. A leader of the conservatives in the Pennsylvania legislature, and a member of both Continental Congresses, Dickinson hoped always for the success of peaceable methods, and voted against the Declaration of Independence.

LETTERS FROM AN AMERICAN FARMER (1782), by Michel-Guillaume Jean de Crèvecoeur. These *Letters* record Crèvecoeur's impressions of his travels in the nascent United States. The description of American ideals and practices which they contain was intended to influence the course of events both in France and elsewhere in insurgent Europe. A warm sympathizer with the doctrines which were shortly to be the slogans of the French Revolution, Crèvecoeur found much in America which he liked and recommended—and at the same time was violently repelled by the institution of slavery in the American South. His book, which appeared over the signature "Hector St.-John, a Farmer of Pennsylvania," was widely read and reprinted in Europe, and in America was esteemed by Washington, Franklin, Jefferson, Madison, etc.

LETTERS FROM CONSTANCE (1414–1415), by Jan Hus. See HUS, JAN.

LETTERS FROM MY MILL (1869), by Alphonse Daudet. See LETTRES DE MON MOULIN, by Alphonse Daudet.

LETTERS FROM PRISON (1928), by Nicola Sacco and Bartolomeo Vanzetti. Written during the seven years of their imprisonment, beginning at the time of their arrest in 1920 for the murder of a payroll agent, these letters constitute a remarkable and moving document. The spirits of the condemned men, one barely literate, transcend their vocabularies. The imprisonment and death of the shoemaker and fish-peddler precipitated one of the classic questions of justice in all American judicial annals; and figured in many literary works, such as Maxwell Anderson's *Winterset* (q.v.), Upton Sinclair's *Boston* (v. *The Journal*), and Edna St. Vincent Millay's "Two Sonnets in Memory."

LETTERS OF CICERO (66–43 B.C.), by Cicero (Marcus Tullius Cicero). Of all Cicero's voluminous works his published correspondence is next in bulk to the *Orations,* and still we have only about half of what was once available. These 864 letters cover the major portion of his active political career, and help to make the first half of the first century B.C. the best documented period of Roman history. They were not published by Cicero but probably by his secretary and friend, Tiro, after his death. The collection includes letters of all sorts, from the most personal and the most trivial to the most formal and important. Many certainly are not those the great man would have chosen to publish revealing his reflections, uncertainties and regrets in an unsparing light. The result is a wealth of biographical detail such as is not available for any other individual from antiquity. Sixteen books of the letters are those which he wrote to his lifelong friend and confidant, Atticus, who remained aloof from politics himself but supplied Cicero with valuable information, lent a receptive ear and offered able advice. Another sixteen books are addressed to various persons ranging from his son at school and his wife at home to the most important men of his time, such as Caesar and Pompey. These, unlike those to Atticus, also contain some replies. There are also three books of his correspondence with his brother Quintus and two of that with Marcus Brutus. But few of the letters are written in a formal style. In most of them the language and tone is far different from the formidable and rolling prose of the *Orations.* The statesman unbends, drops into friendly colloquialism, jokes and indulges his weakness for puns.

LETTERS OF JUNIUS, THE (1772), by "Junius." This series of letters was published in the London *Public Advertiser* from 1769 to 1771. Many men have been named as the author, but the real author—as he said he would—took his secret to the grave. The letters are addressed to the printer, the Duke of Grafton, Rev. M. Horne, Lord Mansfield and others. They are criticisms of the existing administration and its men, written from the viewpoint of the Whig party. Filled as they are with exposés of private lives and political actions, they have some historical value, besides being masterpieces of vituperative and cutting irony.

LETTERS OF PLINY (ca. 97–113), by Gaius Plinius Caecilius Secundus. The younger Pliny, nephew of a prominent and scholarly uncle, was born to and lived the life of a polished gentleman in the highly cultured if oversophisticated and artificial Roman society of his time. This society is reflected in his letters as in a mirror. The ten books of his correspondence were carefully written, selected and published by the author with a calculating eye to presenting himself in the light in which it was his fondest hope that posterity would view him. His models were the classic epistles of Cicero, but the result is something fresh and new, stamped with Pliny's own very human personality. Among his addressees are prominent literary personages of the day, such as Suetonius and Tacitus. To the latter are addressed two long letters describing vividly the eruption of Vesuvius of 79 as he had witnessed it. The main interest, however, is not historical but personal. He writes of his houses, his slaves, his philanthropies, his friends and his enemies, and leaves an impression of an able and genial man who had risen to eminence as an advocate and public servant through a combination of inherited position and natural worth, basking in the sun of prominence and indulging his inclination to pomposity and self-importance. The tenth book, all letters written by Pliny as governor of Bithynia to the Emperor Trajan, is of peculiar interest as containing replies from the Emperor. The ninety-sixth of these discusses the Christians and the special problems they were raising within the Roman state. It is one of the most important documents on the early history of the church.

LETTERS ON THE SOLAR SPOTS (1613), by Galileo Galilei. See DIALOGUE CONCERNING THE TWO CHIEF SYSTEMS OF THE WORLD, by Galileo Galilei.

LETTERS TO HIS BROTHER THEO (1872–1886), by Vincent Van Gogh. These are letters from the great Flemish painter to his brother, written from 1872 to 1886. They reveal a rare passion for beauty and an even deeper compulsion to serve his fellow men. Van Gogh might be described best as a Christian Socialist. He was foredoomed to suffer misunderstanding, physical privation, abuse and martyrdom at the hands of an unsympathetic world. The *Letters* reveal Van Gogh in his successive phases as day-dreaming youth, as ardent preacher of the Gospels in London "in imitation of Christ," as young art student seeking God in beauty, as struggling artist in the garrets of Paris, as missionary to the miners in Le Borinage, as devoted friend of Gauguin, as despised lover, as the husband of a former streetwalker, and, above all, as a superior man with a vision of beauty, truth and humanity. Unable to cope with a life of which he expected so much, Van Gogh finally went insane and shot himself. His letters are the record of a tragic life of a pathologically sensitive man, who carried to the extreme the familiar hostility of the modern artist for a world manifestly unconcerned with his welfare.

LETTERS TO HIS SON (1774), by Philip Dormer Stanhope, Fourth Earl of Chesterfield. It is ironic that Lord Chesterfield, who had achieved great fame in English intellectual and public life, should be remembered in our time only for the letters he had written to his natural son. There are a thousand of these letters covering a wide range of subject matter, abounding in an intensely worldly wisdom and wit. Characteristic of the sophistication and moral cynicism of his advice is his tongue-in-cheek counsel: "Make your court particularly and show distinguished attention to such men and women as are best at court, highest in the fashion, and in the opinion of the public; speak advantageously of them behind their backs, in companies, who, you have reason to believe, will tell them again." Despite their advocated hypocrisy, the *Letters* make delightful reading. They crackle with wit, mockery and gaiety, and give a remarkable insight into the life, thought, manners and character of aristocratic eighteenth century England. Chesterfield also wrote many letters in the same vein to Philip Stanhope, his godson.

LETTERS WRITTEN BY A TURKISH SPY (1687–1694), by Giovanni Paolo Marana. The author, supposedly Mahmut the Arabian, is a spy serving the Turkish Sultan Ibrahim. He writes his reports on Christian courts to the Divan at Constantinople, addressing them variously to the Vizier, the Chief Mufti, Court ministers, functionaries, physicians, Jews and savants. Supposedly Mahmut has resided undiscovered in Paris for forty-five years and during that time has developed extraordinary facility in political and other espionage. He is the eyewitness to many great changes in the affairs of France, including its Court intrigues during the years 1637–1682. He describes the Catalonian Revolution, and the revolutions in the kingdoms of Naples, Portugal and England. Some of the leading contemporary figures of Europe are presented: Cardinals Richelieu and Mazarin, Prince de Condé, Gustavus of Sweden, the Duke de Rohan, Cardinal de Valette, King Casimir of Poland and the philosopher Descartes. With astonishing erudition the spy discourses on ancient literature, the ten tribes of Israel, and a vast number of unrelated subjects to fill eight volumes of observations.

This work was the progenitor of the pseudo-foreign report since employed by many writers to criticize and reform various aspects of their countries.

LETTRES DE MON MOULIN (1869), by Alphonse Daudet. The substance of the *Letters* is light: a miller who goes on milling imaginary wheat in his old mill, a papal mule that gives her tormentor a delayed but beautiful kick, a goat who wants to be free and is eaten by a wolf, etc. The tales are charmingly told, are good-humored and poetically fanciful. Daudet wrote them during a stay in southern France, where he had been sent for his health.

LEVIA GRAVIA (1861–1871), by Giosue' Carducci. See CARDUCCI, GIOSUE'.

LEVIATHAN (1651), by Thomas Hobbes. Subtitled *The Matter, Forme, and Power of a Commonwealth, Ecclesiasticall and Civill,* this book, divided into four parts, treats respectively: Of Man, Of Commonwealth, Of a Christian Commonwealth, and Of the Kingdom of Darkness. In the first part Hobbes presents a mechanistic theory of human nature and describes man's natural state as one in which all men strive to acquire as much as they can with no government to keep them at peace. This is the war of all against all. Through man's power of reason he learns that the first law of nature is to seek peace and follow it; and from this emerges the second law, that, for the sake of peace, a man should be willing to lay down his right to all things when other men are also willing to do so. In the second part, Hobbes discusses the ways in which commonwealths are instituted. Central is the doctrine of the social contract in accordance with which men confer all their power and strength on one man or one assembly (the Sovereign) so that with absolute power that Sovereign may preserve order among men. There is no peace among men unless there is a supreme power to keep them all in awe. In the third and fourth parts of the *Leviathan*, Hobbes outlines the principles which should govern the relation be tween the state and church, and attacks the universal claims of the Roman Cath, olic Church. Hobbes' writings on political theory were extremely influential and served as the basis for modern realistic political theory and political science.

LI-PO (705–762). Li-Po was one of the two greatest poets of China; he has had no equal since the eighth century when he lived. After a long period of obscurity he is considered today, even through the unsatisfactory medium of translation, as one of the world's greatest lyrists. In Chinese literature he is described as "A Banished Immortal From Heaven," which, in its Occidental equivalent, means a genius. His ideas and sentiments are untrammeled by convention. His spirit is untamed, different from the common run of men. As with Lord Byron, we find many extremes in his character. He is a lover of beauty, nonetheless he is an incorrigible drunkard and wastrel. He seeks the solitude of nature, yet he loves the pleasures of city life and gay roistering. He is a misanthrope when in the quiet of the forest glade, yet he is a man of fine feeling and sympathetic turn of mind. Proud and valorous at times, he often cries like a baby. He is a pessimist, hating the society of his fellow men, yet he looks eagerly for friendship. Moreover, although he grieves over the brevity of life he is always ready to unsheathe his long sword and die defend- ing his friends and the wronged.

Li-Po's complex personality is startlingly reflected in his verses. He sings of the delicate moods and beauty in Nature. He praises beautiful women and he is ecstatic over the raptures of winebibbing. He laments the sweet sorrow of parting and of mutual pining between separated lovers, husband and wife, and friends. Some critics say that Li-Po's poetical range is narrow and that his subjects are trivial, including wine, women, parting and longing. This is unjust. Though Li-Po wrote much about these matters, he also dealt with friendship, nature, history, traditions, and philosophical meditations—in all of which his exquisite genius is made manifest. Luckily, Amy Lowell's transla- tions of Li-Po's poems are competent and easily available.

LI SAO (4th c. B.C.), by Chu Yuan. The *Li Sao* (*Falling into Trouble*), written by the poet-statesman Chu Yuan (332–296 B.C.) is the most famous elegy of ancient China. It is said in China that the Dragon Boat festival originated from the search for the body of the author, who is said to have drowned himself in 296 B.C. in despair over the failure of his prince to take his advice against the schemes of the astute Chang I.

Liu Hsieh, writing in the sixth century, says: "When he speaks of his suffering, we are pierced to the heart, and when he describes mountains and streams, we hear their sounds and see them before our eyes, and when he talks of times and seasons, as we unroll the poem, we see the times and seasons. . . ."

All over China and Korea his songs are remembered on the fifth day of the fifth month—the day of his suicide in the Milo River.

LIBERALISM AND SOCIAL ACTION (1935), by John Dewey. See DEWEY, JOHN.

LIBRO DE BUEN AMOR (1330), by Juan Ruiz. See BOOK OF DIVINE LOVE, THE, by Juan Ruiz.

LIEUTENANT GUSTL (1901), by Arthur Schnitzler. See SCHNITZLER, ARTHUR.

LIFE AND DEATH OF A SPANISH TOWN, THE (1937), by Elliot Paul. In 1931 the author and his wife went to live in the small town of Santa Eulalia, situated on an idyllic Balearic island off Spain. The islanders were simple folk who wished for nothing more than to live in tranquillity. When the Spanish Fascists under Franco started their rebellion, they remained calm. They knew the disposition of their people; the Fascists were not numerous and the rebellion would be suppressed. They did not count on Franco's military aid from Nazi Germany and Fascist Italy. Incredulity gave way to despair when the Fascists triumphed and their remote little town was sucked into the conflict, its serenity shattered forever. The Elliot Pauls fled Santa Eulalia. The next day, troops set up a Fascist administration on the island.

The Last Time I Saw Paris (1942) is a friendly account of Parisians and expatriates of a lost generation.

LIFE AND DEATH OF MR. BADMAN, THE (1680), by John Bunyan. This allegory, didactic and edifying in style, is told in a dialogue between Mr. Wiseman and Mr. Attentive. It is about Mr. Badman, who lives an evil life and dies unrepentant. From early childhood he was addicted to lying, stealing, and "greatly given also to swearing and cursing." Bunyan gives him every opportunity to reform, surrounding him with good influences, to no avail. Mr. Badman's father made him an apprentice but he chose to idle. Later the father set his son up in trade, but Mr. Badman preferred to feather his nest with other men's goods. He amassed a fortune by dishonest means, yet he remained an unrepentant wretch "to the very day of his death and the moment in which he died."

LIFE I GAVE YOU, THE (1923), by Luigi Pirandello. See PIRANDELLO, LUIGI.

LIFE IN THE ARGENTINE REPUBLIC IN THE DAYS OF THE TYRANTS, OR CIVILIZATION AND BARBARISM (1845), by Domingo Faustino Sarmiento. The great democratic leader and educator who became President of the Argentine Republic endeavored to demonstrate in his *Facundo* that the geography of Argentina, especially the pampa with its gauchos, was responsible for the emergence of such dictators as Rosas, supreme exemplar of caudillism. At the time he wrote *Facundo*, Sarmiento had travelled but little, so that his physical description of Argentina was derived more from hearsay than observation. Nevertheless it is to his credit that *Facundo* remains to this day one of the most penetrating essays in human geography ever written. Basing his analysis on the influence of geography and history upon the social and political life of Argentina, Sarmiento put his finger on one of the chief causes of his country's malady. By showing how tyranny (Rosas) was engendered by anarchy (of the gauchos), he predicted the downfall of Rosas and charted the way for organic reconstruction. Even though Sarmiento's work is predominantly social and political, the first part, with its emphasis on human geography, is an important contribution to gaucho literature, one that left a profound mark upon its development.

LIFE IS A DREAM (1635), by Pedro Calderón de la Barca. The mother of Segismundo, only son of the King of Poland, dies in giving him birth. Having read in the stars that the Prince is destined to be a monster of cruelty and impiety, the King sacrifices his fatherly love to the welfare of the nation, and, announcing that Segismundo was born dead, locks him up in a tower in the fastnesses of the mountains. With only a guard to take care of him, Segismundo grows up in captivity, a mixture of man and beast. In a monologue of great lyrical beauty he envies the freedom of the animals of the fields. Realizing that he had taken the prediction of the stars too literally, the King, who has aged considerably and needs a successor, has his son drugged and brought back to his palace. Segismundo awakes in the royal suite and is dazzled by the splendor. He is instinctively opposed to the ostentation of his new surroundings. Informed of his birth and lineage, he is outraged, and in his fury attempts to kill one of his father's henchmen and to run off with the beautiful princess Estrella. Rebellious against his father because of the cruel oppression he had inflicted upon him, he claims the throne and is about to seize it when the masked soldiers of the King arrest him and lock him up in the tower again. A revolt by a company of soldiers results in his release. He is proclaimed King, marries Estrella, and imprisons his father in the tower. Segismundo refuses to believe that all this happiness is true and insists that life is still a dream, that he may awake on the morrow to cruel reality. Thus Calderón portrayed the conflict of fate and free will and gave the Spanish theater of the Golden Age its philosophical masterpiece.

LIFE OF AGRICOLA, THE (97), by Tacitus (Gaius Cornelius Tacitus). Agricola was the father-in-law of Tacitus, the Roman historian. Tacitus admired him for his straightforward character and his upright administration of Britain as Roman governor, and therefore in a spirit of filial piety he honored his father-in-law's memory with a biography which he completed in 97. The work is a minor masterpiece in its sympathetic portraiture, in its account of the country and people of ancient Britain and in its record of the progress of Roman domination in the island. In its extremely terse and epigrammtic style Tacitus' memorial study of his father-in-law remains a unique work in Latin literature. It stands out in strong contrast to the stereotyped biographical form of such a writer as Suetonius.

LIFE OF CHRIST (1921), by Giovanni Papini. Translated (1923) by Dorothy Canfield. See CANFIELD, DOROTHY.

LIFE OF DR. JOHN DONNE (1640), by Izaak Walton. See LIVES, by Izaak Walton.

LIFE OF DR. SANDERSON, LATE BISHOP OF LINCOLN (1678), by Izaak Walton. See LIVES, by Izaak Walton.

LIFE OF JEANNE D'ARC (1908), by Anatole France. See REVOLT OF THE ANGELS, THE, by Anatole France.

LIFE OF JESUS, THE (1863), by Ernest Renan. *The Life of Jesus* is the first of Renan's seven-volume study on the origins of Christianity, a moral and psychological inquiry into the character and teachings of Christ, based on available historical documents. His conception of Jesus was that he was "the creator of the eternal religion of mankind" and an "incomparable man." In his estimation, although Christ was not the Son of God, He was transcendently greater than other leaders, such as Moses, Buddha or Mohammed. "Christianity," states Renan, "has become almost the synonym of religion; all that is attempted outside its great and fertile tradition is doomed to sterility." Based on German philosophy, Renan's method is relativistic: Jesus is the product of a given moment and a given environment, and Renan studies him in relation to these special circumstances, almost as Balzac studies the characters in his novels. Balzac's admirer, Taine, in fact called *The Life of Jesus* a great historical novel. Scholars have found many flaws in the vast erudition of Renan's book. Its greatness as poetry is unchallenged.

LIFE OF MR. GEORGE HERBERT (1670), by Izaak Walton. See LIVES, by Izaak Walton.

LIFE OF MR. RICHARD HOOKER (1655), by Izaak Walton. See LIVES, by Izaak Walton.

LIFE OF NELSON (1813), by Robert Southey. This life story of Horatio Nelson, the English naval hero, was intended by the author as a manual of inspiration to sailors. In it Southey traced Nelson's career, describing his early start in the navy and his role in the numerous engagements—ending with the famous battle of Trafalgar—which helped materially to crush Napoleon as well as to establish British naval supremacy. In addition to Nelson's professional accomplishments and skill, great emphasis is placed on his fine personal traits—his kindness, self-sacrifice, patriotism, and courage—which gained him the love of his men and the English people as a whole.

LIFE OF QUINTUS FIXLEIN, THE (1796), by Johann Paul Richter. See RICHTER, JOHANN PAUL.

LIFE OF REASON, THE (1905–1906), by George Santayana. In this five-volume study, which is more of a philosophico-literary work than a systematic presentation of a philosophical system, Santayana describes the life of reason as "a name for all practical thought and all action justified by its fruits in consciousness." He in turn examines and repudiates as aids to reason modern philosophy, scientific positivism, and Christian thought, and then finds his ideal in the ancient Greeks, particularly in Heraclitus, Democritus, Socrates, Plato, and Aristotle in the field of nature and morals. Volume I of *The Life of Reason* consists of "Reason in Common Sense"; Volume II, "Reason in Society"; Volume III, "Reason in Religion"; Volume IV, "Reason in Art"; and Volume V, "Reason in Science."

LIFE OF SAMUEL JOHNSON, LL.D., THE (1791), by James Boswell. The principal virtue of Boswell's work is that it is a remarkably vivid portrait of one of the most elusive and complicated characters in literary history. Dr. Johnson resembled Socrates in that he largely spurred others on to engage in literary labors. He lived literature more than he created it. It was this untamed, original man of unrivaled learning and common sense whom Boswell chose as both the object of his affections and the subject for his great literary work, after meeting him in 1763. By a self-invented system of shorthand the faithful and ubiquitous biographer noted down all the conversations, monologues, experiences and opinions of Dr. Johnson, cherishing the minutest detail. He would frequently draw Johnson out to display his qualities. The product is a great work of art, abounding in wit, wisdom, truth and color, for Johnson possessed all these attributes. But a great deal of praise for the astounding portrait presented belongs to its perceptive author. It is one of the most complete and satisfactory biographies ever written, the greatest in the English language, by common consent.

LIFE OF SIR HENRY WOTTON (1651), by Izaak Walton. See LIVES, by Izaak Walton.

LIFE OF SIR WALTER SCOTT, THE (1838), by J. G. Lockhart. This outstanding biography has been favorably compared with Boswell's *Johnson* (q.v.) not only because of the author's first-hand knowledge of Scott, but also because of his literary style. Lockhart describes sympathetically and completely Scott's life and personality as a clerk and sheriff, editor, and reviewer; his early successes as an author; his long and prolific writing career; his unfortunate business ventures; and his efforts, which broke his health, to work off the great debt thus acquired. Scott's journals and letters provide much of the material.

LIFE OF WASHINGTON (1855–1859), by Washington Irving. See SKETCH BOOK, THE, by Washington Irving.

LIFE OF WESLEY (1820), by Robert Southey. In conjunction with the life and career of John Wesley, Southey here traces and comments on the rise and progress of Methodism, of which Wesley was the founder. The part played by Whitefield, the Moravians and Calvinists, its growth in various countries, its lay and spiritual coadjutors, its doctrines, opinions, manners, and effects are described. Southey acknowledges Wesley's contribution of awakening a zealous spirit in the Church, but sees him as ambitious and domineering. The author accuses him, moreover, of encouraging enthusiasm and extravagances, of being too amenable to false propositions, spreading superstition as well as piety, and causing a wide-spreading schism in Protestantism.

LIFE ON THE MISSISSIPPI (1883), by Mark Twain (Samuel L. Clemens). This book is at once autobiographical reminiscence, regional epic, and storehouse of Mark Twain anecdotes.

In 1882, twenty-one years after he had worked on the Mississippi as a pilot, Mark Twain revisited the river with a nostalgic feeling for his happy youth. He traveled down from St. Louis to New Orleans and up again to St. Paul. One phenomenon that interested him was a change that had taken place in the traffic. A fierce competition had sprung up between the monopolistic rail-roads financed by Eastern manipulators, and the individual towing fleets still operated by "small fry." The author saw with regret the deteriorated status of the river pilot.

Worse yet, life in the bank towns and villages had disintegrated rapidly. Mark Twain had come home to find dying a world of the past he had known and loved. *Life on the Mississippi* recalls these sad impressions; but it also includes recollections of his own career as pilot, and is gay and humorous in its documentation. The book remains a vivid account of the heroic post-Civil War steamboat age.

The Tragedy of Pudd'nhead Wilson (1894) is a melodramatic novel of violence on the Mississippi, concerning slave-owner Percy Driscoll's son Tom, and Chambers, the son of his slave Roxy. When Percy dies, his brother adopts Chambers, believing him to be Tom. Chambers is a bad youth, eventually committing a murder and causing the blame to fall upon a pair of Italian twins. David Wilson, a lawyer whose lack of success has inspired the townspeople to nickname him "Pudd'nhead," at last vindicates the twins and convicts Chambers. Tom regains his position.

Twain dictated an authorized account of his life to his secretary, and the *Autobiography* appeared in 1924. Many critics consider Twain's main contribution to American literature a summing up of western humor and realism, which are perhaps best shown in his short stories, *The Celebrated Jumping Frog of Calaveras County and Other Sketches* (1867).

LIFE UNSHAKABLE (Eng. tr. 1921, 1923), by Kostes Palamas. See PALAMAS, KOSTES.

LIFE WITH FATHER (1935), by Clarence Day. In this autobiographical book Clarence Day celebrates the eccentric character of his father, a product of the gaslight civilization of New York City in the '90's. Through various scenes showing his father as a business man, a gourmet, an unwilling equestrian, a violent opponent of the telephone, a reluctant host, and others, he reveals him as a high-and-mighty gentleman of the upper middle class, self-righteous in his ideas, bursting with self-esteem and ruling over his household with pompous authority. Beneath it all, however, the son finds a deep substratum of sentimentality, gruff kindness, and touching human weaknesses. This work was dramatized both for the stage and films.

LIGHT IN AUGUST (1932), by William Faulkner. Behind the bare facts of the murder of forty-one-year-old Joanna Burden by the Negro Joe Christmas, his capture, escape, and brutal death at the hands of Percy Grimm of the state National Guard, there is the cruel, dark story of his tragic life. The novel begins with the pregnant orphan Lena Grove walking from Alabama in search of her lover, Lucas Burch. She is misdirected to Byron Bunch, at a Jefferson sawmill, and he falls in love with her. Burch, using the name of Joe Brown, is working at the same mill. He is living in a small shack with Joe Christmas, and knows that the latter visits Miss Burden, a white spinster, at night. When she is murdered, he informs on Christmas to gain the reward, but flees when Lena sees him. Christmas is captured. His grandfather, Eupheus Hines, a religious fanatic, arrives in town hoping to help lynch him. We learn the various facts about Joe's birth (child of Hines's daughter Milly and a circus worker), youth (adopted by Simon McEachern, whom he later kills in a fight over a woman) and struggles. After Christmas' death, Lena accepts the proposal of Byron Bunch, and the two—with Lena's baby—start walking homeward.

LIGHT THAT FAILED, THE (1890), by Rudyard Kipling. See CAPTAINS COURAGEOUS, by Rudyard Kipling.

LILIOM (1909), by Ferenc Molnar. Ferenc Molnar (b. 1878) early acquired an international reputation for his plays, which reveal a sense of dramatic composition and an ability to summarize and present certain unexpected attributes of human nature. Among these plays is *Liliom*. Liliom is the pseudonym of a successful barker in a Budapest carrousel. He is fundamentally a coarse and vulgar loafer interested in living with the least possible effort. He loses his job and marries a poor servant girl, Julie, by whom he is to have a child. Though he treats her badly, beats her, and scarcely supports her, she is deeply in love with him and idealizes him. He goes out with a friend to hold up a bank clerk, Linzman, who is supposed to be carrying a lot of money. Linzman has already delivered the cash, and to make matters worse, he overcomes the would-be bandits. In this crisis, Liliom commits suicide to escape arrest. The heavenly police bring him before the authorities, and since the judge gets little satisfaction, he sends Liliom back to earth for one day sixteen years later to see if he can do one good deed. He finds his wife and daughter still in poverty, but the mother has brought the daughter up to idealize her father. Confronted with this situation, Liliom, in the guise of a beggar, tells the girl the truth about himself and gives her a resounding slap, much to the annoyance of the heavenly police who are accompanying him. Yet the girl declares that the slap feels like love.

Liliom has easily been one of the most successful of Molnar's plays, many others of which, like *The Devil* (Eng. tr. 1908), *The Guardsman* (Eng. tr. 1924), have attracted attention in all countries.

LINDA CONDON (1919), by Joseph Hergesheimer. See JAVA HEAD, by Joseph Hergesheimer.

LINDSAY, VACHEL (1879–1931). A windfall for the unsuccessful artist and itinerant reformer Vachel Lindsay was the publication in 1913 of *General William Booth Enters into Heaven*. The title piece's unsophisticated version of the apotheosis of the Salvation Army leader echoes the bass-drum booms and the cymbal clashes of a religious revival. It is a syncopated utterance of the devotional reflections of a Midwestern American.

The Congo (1914) brought Lindsay the leadership of the "new poetry" movement. The title piece, an epic of the black race, is deliberately primitive, recapturing by means of sensational musical effects their folk music and verses. Its characteristics are a naïve realism, an unrestrained passion, and a grotesque imagery. The various pieces are arranged for chanting, recitation, and acting. Among other poems is "Abraham Lincoln Walks at Midnight," a vision of the mourning president walking through Springfield, sleepless because of the bitterness abroad on the eve of World War I.

The Chinese Nightingale (1917) is a delicate evocation of ancient China; and "The Ghost of the Buffaloes" is a subtle, melodic picture of the romantic plains before white civilization.

Johnny Appleseed, title piece of a later poetry collection (1923), is a verse epic of Lindsay's favorite pioneer hero crossing the mountains with the seeds of fruit trees.

LITERARY FALLACY, THE (1944), by Bernard DeVoto. See De-VOTO, BERNARD.

LITTLE CLAY CART, THE (ca. 900 B.C.), by Shudraka. It is generally believed by scholars that *The Little Clay Cart* has been attributed to King Shudraka in the same complimentary way *The Song of Songs, The Book of Ecclesiastes,* and *The Wisdom of Solomon* have been designated as the compositions of the Jewish king. A modest and far from royal author must have lurked in the background, for *The Little Clay Cart* has a simple, unaffected style most singular in a Sanskrit play. There is great variety of invention and considerable skill of characterization as well as an infectious humor. *The Little Clay Cart* in its original Sanskrit text consists of ten acts, a staggering number for non-Orientals.

Act I: "The Gems Are Left Behind." Charudatta is conversing within his house with his friend Maitreya, deploring his poverty. Outside on the street the courtesan Vasantasena is being pursued by Sansthanaka, who makes her offensive offers which she indignantly rejects. Vasantasena runs into Charudatta's house for refuge. She leaves a casket of gems for safekeeping and returns to her home.

Act II: "The Shampooer Who Gambled." Vasantasena confesses to her maid that she is in love with Charudatta. Then a shampooer appears in the streets pursued by a gambling master and a gambler, who demand that he pay them ten gold pieces which they won from him. When Vansantasena learns that the shampooer had once served Charudatta she pays his debt. The penitent wretch then resolves to turn Buddhist monk.

Act III: "The Hole in the Wall." Sharvilaka, who is in love with Madanika, the maid of Vasantasena, is resolved to steal the casket of gems with which to buy his lady love's freedom. He makes a hole in the wall of the house, enters, and steals the gems.

Act IV: "Madanika and Sharvilaka." The thief comes to purchase the maid Madanika's freedom, which Vasantasena grants, although she overhears the facts concerning the theft. Maitreya arrives with a pearl necklace from Charudatta to repay for the stolen gems.

Act V: "The Storm." During a storm Charudatta receives Vasantasena in his garden. She explains to him how she again came into possession of the gem casket. The storm growing in violence, she is compelled to spend the night in Charudatta's house.

Act VI: "The Swapping of the Bullock Carts." The following morning she meets her host's little son Rohasena, who complains that he can now have only a little clay cart to play with instead of finer toys. Vasantasena gives him her gems to buy a toy cart of gold. Charudatta's servant rides up in his master's bullock cart to take Vasantasena to the park to meet him. In the meantime, Aryaka, an escaped prisoner, hides in Charudatta's cart.

Act VII: "Aryaka's Escape." Charudatta discovers Aryaka in his cart and, giving it to him, helps him to escape.

Act III: "The Strangling of Vasantasena." Sansthanaka, discovering Vasantasena in the cart, repeats his indecent proposals to her. Repulsed, he strangles her. The Buddhist monk, formerly the shampooer, revives her and conducts her to a monastery.

Act IX: "The Trial." Sansthanaka accuses Charudatta of murdering Vasantasena for her gems. Charudatta is condemned to death.

Act X: "The End." As Charudatta is about to be hanged Vasantasena and the Buddhist monk appear. The truth is revealed. Aryaka, who has become King, rewards Vasantasena for her kind heart by issuing an edict freeing her from her courtesan status. Charudatta shows magnanimity and pleads for the pardon of his wicked accuser.

The play ends with a Hindu epilogue with virtuous overtones.

LITTLE DEMON, THE (1907), by Feodor Sologub (Feodor Kuzmich Teternikov). The publication of this novel made the author's reputation in Russia and brought him universal fame, enabling him to live on his literary income and give up teaching. It has been called the "most perfect novel since the death of Dostoevsky." Realistic but at the same time symbolical, it transcends realism. The mysterious demon, Nedotykomka, might be explained away as an hallucination of Peredonov's, were it not Sologub's obvious intention to paint the evil of life as God has created it. The petty life of a small town is described in satirical terms bordering on the grotesque, but it is not without poetry. Peredonov is the embodiment of the joyless evils of life, while the idyllic love of the young Sasha Pylnikov and Liudmila Rustilova has subtle if sensuous elements. Even this pure beauty bears a taint, the author seems to insist. "Peredonovism" is now a word in the Russian language meaning "sullen evil." Peredonov knows no joy and resents anyone else experiencing it. He is filled with sullen hatred and believes all life is against him. Logically, he commits murder in a fit of insanity while possessed of ideas of persecution. The author worked on the book from 1892 to 1902, and for several years could not find a publisher. In 1905 parts appeared in magazines.

LITTLE DORRIT (1857), by Charles Dickens. In prison for debt, William Dorrit lives with his children, Edward, Fanny, and Amy (who is Little Dorrit) at Marshalsea. Little Dorrit was born at the prison and lives most of her life there; there she finally chooses to be married. William's children struggle to make a living outside the prison gates, returning every night with their earnings. Little Dorrit does sewing for Mrs. Clennam and meets her son Arthur, who helps free Mr. Dorrit. The Dorrit family attains sudden affluence, and becomes as arrogant and despicable as it had been pitiable. Little Dorrit is the only one who does not change, retaining her sweet, self-sacrificing disposition to the end. She is in love with her middle-aged benefactor, Arthur, who has recently returned from India to find his mother enmeshed in religious fanaticism, a prey to a villain named Blandois. In Arthur's struggle with the civil service, Dickens levels an attack on the "Circumlocution Office," a satirization of complicated governmental procedures.

Arthur is eventually incarcerated in debtor's prison, where Little Dorrit bends her efforts to help him. Their love ends happily, and they are married at the old prison church. A vein of mystery runs through the story in connection with Mrs. Clennam. It is finally revealed that she is not Arthur's mother, and that she has been influential in keeping the Dorrit family from their rightful inheritance. The many characters include the soft-hearted Meagles family; the incompetent, bungling Barnacles; love-lorn John Chivery; the collector, Mr. Pancks, and his deceitful employer, Casby; Flora Casby and her fabulous aunt; the poor but worthy Plornishes; and many other lesser characters. Dickens' father was himself imprisoned at Marshalsea.

LITTLE FOXES, THE (1939), by Lillian Hellman. See Hellman, Lillian.

LITTLE GREEN BIRD, THE (1765), by Carlo Gozzi. See GOZZI, CARLO.

LITTLE JEW, THE (1875), by Mendele Mocher Sefarim. See MENDELE MOCHER SEFARIM.

LITTLE LORD FAUNTLEROY (1886), by Frances Hodgson Burnett. This popular children's book tells of little Cedric Errol, son of an American mother and the deceased Captain Errol, whose father, the Earl of Dorincourt, had disowned him for marrying out of his class. The old Earl sends his lawyer, Havisham, as emissary to New York to announce that Ceddie has become heir to title and fortune. The lad thereupon sets out for Dorincourt. At first, his grandfather refuses to meet the American mother, who is forced to live a little distance away. Another claimant to the title appears, moreover, but is proved false by Dick the bootblack, one of Cedric's American friends. The Earl finally gives his approval to Cedric's mother, and all three settle at Dorincourt.

LITTLE MAN, THE (1864), by Mendele Mocher Sefarim. See MENDELE MOCHER SEFARIM.

LITTLE MEN (1871), by Louisa May Alcott. See LITTLE WOMEN, by Louisa May Alcott.

LITTLE MINISTER, THE (1891), by James M. Barrie. The first long novel Barrie wrote has its setting in the weaving village of Thrums, a town much resembling the author's birthplace in Scotland.

Gavin Dishart, a new Presbyterian minister, has come to town. He is young, inexperienced, and as perpetually hungry as the weavers to whom he preaches. Driven to despair by a reduction in wages, the weavers, under militant Chartist leaders, riot. The gypsy Babbie comes to warn the workers that Lord Rintoul, the great local landowner, has summoned the soldiers to arrest them. The Battle of the Market Square of Thrums ensues. Gavin rescues Babbie from the soldiers. The two fall in love. Gavin never suspects that she is a lady of quality, in fact the elderly Lord Rintoul's betrothed. The townspeople are scandalized by Gavin's association with the gypsy girl, so Babbie finally renounces him. On the eve of her marriage to Rintoul she and Gavin are unexpectedly reunited. They decide to marry hastily and in gypsy fashion. However, the marriage is exposed to Lord Rintoul, and a flood breaks up the proceedings. It is not until much later that the lovers are reunited. Gavin by that time is again in favor with his community.

LITTLE POEMS IN PROSE, (1869), by Charles Baudelaire. See FLOWERS OF EVIL, THE, by Charles Baudelaire.

LITTLE REGIMENT, THE (1896), by Stephen Crane. See RED BADGE OF COURAGE, THE, by Stephen Crane.

LITTLE SHEPHERD OF KINGDOM COME, THE (1902), by John Fox, Jr. See TRAIL OF THE LONESOME PINE, THE, by John Fox, Jr.

LITTLE WOMEN (1868), by Louisa May Alcott. This popular girls' story is founded on the author's experiences. It tells of events in the lives of the Marches of New England: Mrs. March, the cheerful housewife; her husband, a Civil War chaplain; and four girls—ungainly Jo, who wants to be an author; Meg, who wants to be a real lady; delicate Beth, the musician; and the beautiful Amy. The girls attend school, work to earn money for the family, and make friends with their neighbors, the Laurences. Meg marries John Brooke, the Laurences' tutor. Laurie, the Laurences' grandson, is refused by Jo; he goes to Europe, meets Amy, and marries her. Beth dies. Jo, whose first plays were acted at home, finally becomes a writer. In New York, she meets Professor Fritz Bhaer and marries him.

Among the author's similar books are *An Old-Fashioned Girl* (1870), about Polly Milton and her sophisticated city friends the Shaws; and *Little Men* (1871), about Jo and Fritz Bhaer, who successfully rear their own children and conduct a school for boys.

LITTLE ZACHES (1819), by E. T. A. Hoffmann. See HOFFMANN, E. T. A.

LIVES (1640–1678), by Izaak Walton. These five short biographies form a production marvelously different from *The Compleat Angler* (q.v.). The *Life of Dr. John Donne* (1640) tells with some intimacy, though also with some reserve, the story of the poet's struggle with poverty and a hostile father-in-law, and of his conversion from early worldly excesses and Catholicism to the Church of England and the high position of Dean of St. Paul's. It is the later Donne, the Donne of the sermons, that is emphasized, and his last illness is lingered over, including his insistence on being painted in his shroud. The *Life of Sir Henry Wotton* (1651) traces the career of the provost of Eton, who was sent abroad as an ambassador "to lie for the good of his country." The *Life of Mr. Richard Hooker* (1655), the only one of his subjects Walton did not personally know, gives a picture of sweet reasonableness in the author of *Of the Laws of Ecclesiastical Polity* (q.v.) and corresponding domination by his wife, who saw to it that the great scholar tended sheep on occasion or rocked the cradle. The *Life of Mr. George Herbert* (1670) treats of another successful struggle against worldliness. Herbert could have had a brilliant secular career, but he found peace as the rector of Bemerton and poet of God. Least important, both as subject and as biography, is the *Life of Dr. Sanderson, Late Bishop of Lincoln* (1678).

LIVES OF ITALIAN PAINTERS, SCULPTORS AND ARCHI-TECTS, by Giorgio Vasari (1511–1574). Of the many biographies written in the sixteenth century, the *Lives* by Giorgio Vasari is among the most important. Vasari, himself an excellent painter and architect, wrote the biographies of over two hundred Italian artists, from Cimabue to his (Vasari's) contemporaries. Vasari's book is not only important from the literary viewpoint, but also because through its pages one can see and determine the evolution and development of Italian art. The author makes good use of his own experience as an artist. Living at a time when picturesque stories and anecdotes about artists were in great demand, Vasari is generous with both, to the joy of his readers. In his *Lives* Vasari shows a great admiration for the early and contemporary Tuscan School, but his information about the important Schools of Venice and Lombardy is imperfect. However, modern readers are indebted to him for his good taste in art and in literature, and especially for the mass of particulars about outstanding artists.

LIVES OF THE CAESARS (119–121), by Suetonius (Gaius Suetonius Tranquillus). These biographies include those of Julius Caesar and of the Roman Emperors from Augustus to Domitian, in eight books. They are written according to a stereotyped pattern, for a public which was more eager for scandalous anecdote than for balanced historical judgment. The pattern proceeds from an account of the emperor's ancestry and family to his early life and education, and, after a detailed enumeration of the stages and events of his career, terminates with a sketch of his character and disposition. Suetonius was a cloistered research scholar with a flair for the sensational, rather than a thinker or man of letters. As an imperial secretary he had access to imperial archives not available to such contemporaries as Tacitus. These he used frequently, but even more frequently he gives greater prominence to gossip and scandal. The style is simple and readable but not dramatic. The historical significance of the work lies in its coverage of events not touched by Tacitus and in the superiority of Suetonius' sources.

LIVES OF THE ENGLISH POETS, THE (1779–1781), by Samuel Johnson. This book, or set of books, arose out of a business venture. The author was approached by publishers who wanted to drive a Scottish reprint of English poets out of the market. Johnson accepted before May, 1777, when he wrote to Boswell of the contract. Fifty-two poets are covered, from Cowley and Waller to Collins and Gray. The work is an equipoise of criticism and biography, the biographical facts coming first, colored frequently with moralistic, typically Johnsonian comment. The criticism is uneven, a monument of Johnson's prejudices. He found Milton's *Lycidas* (q.v.) a failure, a poem without sincerity: "the diction is harsh, the rhymes uncertain, and the numbers unpleasing." As a Tory he could not stomach Milton's republicanism. In treating of Cowley he lashes at the metaphysical poets, Donne and his school, so popular today. We also find him overappreciative of Pope, while he omits Marvell altogether. But the ideas of a generally great critic are here, in his famous style; moreover, though the work has in most cases been superseded by individual biographies of greater length and interest, it remains the source for many facts and anecdotes.

LIVES OF THE PHILOSOPHERS (ca. 275), by Diogenes Laertius. Little is known of the author of this ten-book work on Greek philosophers, but he is one of the most important of our sources of information on the history of Greek philosophy. In the biographies he discusses the lives, doctrines and sayings of the philosophers in anecdotal style. He was certainly no philosopher himself and had very little true insight into his subject. His division of the philosophers into the Ionian and Italian schools is perverse and misleading. It is, in fact, the lack of better authorities which gives Diogenes' work its importance. The tenth book, however, occupies a peculiar position, since it quotes in full three long letters of Epicurus which give a very fair picture of that philosopher's system. As literature the *Lives of the Philosophers* is also inferior, but it is a mine of anecdote and repartee.

LOGIC: THE THEORY OF INQUIRY (1939), by John Dewey. See DEWEY, JOHN.

LOHENGRIN (1850), by Richard Wagner. See WAGNER, RICHARD.

LONDON, JACK (1876–1916). Jack London, of obscure parentage, itinerant family, meager education, and varying, elemental occupations, spent the latter part of his short life in extreme popularity. His productiveness was enormous.

Distressed by the inequalities of London society, London wrote the descriptive *People of the Abyss* (1903). Making the wretched slums a proving ground for social research, he lived for a while in the East End rookeries. From the precariousness of this "other half's" existence, he drew a political-economic indictment. *John Barleycorn* (1913) relates the progressive deterioration of a drunkard. Thought to be semi-autobiographical, the work is frankly temperance propaganda.

Martin Eden (1909), also semi-autobiographical, is a novel that examines the problems of a writer. The hero's fiancée, Ruth Morse, had broken off an engagement when Martin was unsuccessful, then attempted to resume it when he became famous. When his friend Russ Brissendon commits suicide, Martin also loses his will to live.

The Iron Heel (1907) is a "prophetic" novel of 1912–1918, narrating the advent of a great capitalistic, fascist dictatorship, with its treacherous liquidation of the middle class and the power of labor. The hero is Ernest Everhard, a socialist revolutionary of the group which finally overthrows "The Iron Heel."

In spite of these and other socially oriented novels, London's fame rests largely on his work typified by *The Call of the Wild* (q.v.); novels inspired by a concept of the brute which underlies the social behavior of men and animals. Some of these are as follows:

The Sea-Wolf (1904). Wolf Larson, ruthless captain of the tramp steamer *Ghost,* receives as unexpected passenger on the high seas Humphrey Van Weyden, a wealthy ne'er-do-well. In spite of his selfish brutality, Larsen becomes an instrument for good. The treatment he gives to the dilettante Van Weyden teaches the latter to stand on his own legs. He and the poet Maude Brewster, whom the "Sea-Wolf" loves also, escape to an island as the *Ghost* sinks and Larsen, mortally sick, is deserted. The lovers later return to civilization. *The*

Game (1905) is a novel about the pugilist Joe Fleming, whose fiancée Genevieve is jealous of his career. To explain to Genevieve the fascination of the prize ring, Joe has her watch his fight with the brutal John Ponta. During the fight, Joe is accidentally killed. *Before Adam* (1906) is a sentimentalized version of prehistoric life. The characters are Big Tooth and his mate Swift One, their enemies the Fire People, and the fierce beasts of the mid-Pleistocene era. *White Fang* (1906) is about a dog, a cross-breed, sold to Beauty Smith. This owner tortures the dog to increase his ferocity and value as a fighter. A new owner, Weedon Scott, brings the dog to California, and, by kind treatment, domesticates him. White Fang later sacrifices his life to save Scott.

LONELY WAY, THE (1904), by Arthur Schnitzler. Seee SCHNITZLER, ARTHUR.

LONG JOURNEY, THE (1909–1922), by Johannes V. Jensen. It was probably this ambitious, monumental work which more than any other won for its author the Nobel Prize in Literature in 1944. It was the gigantic task of tracing the development of man from his survival as a brute superanthropoid, with a gradually awakening intelligence, down to his modern status, or more precisely, to the discovery of America, when man had emerged as a builder, discoverer, and inventor. It is a stupendous combination of Darwinian science, imagination, humor, history, and beauty. It is a racial epic in prose in six novels,—yet not novels in the usual sense—which in order of their contents are: *The Glacier* (1909); *The Lost Land* (1919); *Norn Guest* (1919); *The Trek of the Cimbri* (1922); *The Ship* (1912); *and Christopher Columbus* (1921). An English translation of all parts, with the above title, appeared in three volumes, 1922–24. By traveling in the Orient, Europe, and America, Jensen obtained first-hand information about the physical aspects of glaciers, volcanoes, and modern inventions and industry; and he had pondered profoundly such influences of environment as the climate of Scandinavia. Through the development of a certain racial theory he traced a connection between the ancient Cimbri of his native Jutland and the Anglo-Saxons. *The Long Journey* is, then, a fictional yet historical survey of the Northern race from the preglacial tropical age down to Columbus. Jensen is not always correct in his scientific deductions, but the grandeur of conception and power of imagination of the work had never before been achieved in Danish and "rarely in any literature."

LONG, LONG AGO (1943), by Alexander Woollcott. See WOOLLCOTT, ALEXANDER.

LONG VALLEY, THE (1938), by John Steinbeck. See GRAPES OF WRATH, THE, by John Steinbeck.

LONGFELLOW, HENRY WADSWORTH (1807–1882). Henry Wadsworth Longfellow, after college and foreign study, settled down to teaching at Harvard and founding a poetic career applauded throughout America and Europe. He introduced into American college curricula the study of modern foreign languages, and was one of the most successful teachers of his time.

Hyperion (1839) is a prose romance, actually semi-autobiographical. Paul

Flemming's wandering in Switzerland is interspersed with philosophical digressions, literary criticism, and translations from German romantic poetry.

Various pieces in subsequent volumes have become well known. Thus, in *Ballads and Other Poems* (1842) there are: "The Village Blacksmith," in which the industrious smithy represents the good life; and "The Wreck of the Hesperus," in which the skipper lashes his daughter to the mast when the ship goes down. In *The Belfry of Bruges and other Poems* (1845) there are: "The Arsenal at Springfield," a poem recounting the horrors of war and prophesying an era of peace; and the title piece, recalling that city's ancient glory.

Longfellow's longer works were instantly successful. *Evangeline* (1847) is a narrative romance about Nova Scotia farmers deported from Acadia during the French and Indian wars. Evangeline Bellefontaine wanders through Louisiana and Michigan, searching for Gabriel Lajeunesse, who had been her fiancé. The lovers almost meet several times; but it is not until Evangeline has become a Sister of Mercy in Philadelphia that she finally discovers Gabriel, an epidemic victim. The two die and are buried together.

Hiawatha (1855) is an Indian epic. Hiawatha is an Ojibwa reared by old Nokomis, daughter of the Moon. He grows wise in nature lore, revenges a wrong done to his mother Wenonah by his father the West Wind, and becomes the leader of his people. He teaches them the ways of civilization, but later his wife Minnehaha is taken by sickness, and the youth departs to rule the land of the Northwest Wind, urging his people to accept the religion and guidance of the advancing white men.

In 1854 Longfellow retired to devote himself entirely to literature. *The Courtship of Miles Standish* (1858) narrates the apocryphal wooing of Priscilla by the Plymouth Colony captain, through the emissary John Alden. Priscilla prefers John, and when Standish is reported killed in war, the lovers prepare to marry. On the evening of the ceremony, Standish returns, but is reconciled with the couple.

Tales of a Wayside Inn (1886) is a collection of narrative poems grouped like the *Canterbury Tales* (q.v.). The twenty-one stories are episodes of many lands. The first one, however, is the popular "Paul Revere's Ride," a romanticized account of how the news of advancing redcoats was spread from Charlestown to Lexington and Concord.

LOOK HOMEWARD, ANGEL (1929), by Thomas Wolfe. This autobiographical first novel is a bitter portrayal of life in a small Southern town, and of the family of stonecutter Oliver Gant. Eugene, the baby of the family, is tormented because of his sensitiveness, by the atmosphere of bickering and squalor. Eliza, his shrewish mother, finally leaves her husband. The other children are the corrupt Steve, shy Daisy, high-strung Helen, quiet Ben, and exuberant Luke. Eugene attends the university, and awakes from adolescence into a gradual adjustment to the realities of life. After certain emotional shocks—his love for Laura, Ben's death—Eugene breaks with the family and sets out to make a vague pilgrimage in life.

Of Time and the River (1935) is a sequel describing Eugene's work at Harvard and his friendship with the affected Francis Starwick, the terrible death of his father, and finally the companions of his New York period. After several love affairs, Eugene travels to Paris with Starwick. Appalled at the romantic complications which ensue, and the discovery that Starwick is a homosexual, Eugene breaks away to tour Europe alone, until his money runs out.

The Web and the Rock (1939) is an overlapping sequel in which the struggling writer George Weber—an early version of Eugene Gant—returns from Europe and has an affair with Esther Jack. Weber finds a publisher for his book, tears himself away from Esther, and goes to Europe again, still restless.

You Can't Go Home Again (1940) continues the story of Weber, as a successful novelist, an unsuccessful lover, and a friend of several dynamic literary personalities. Weber makes an attempt to return to Old Catawba, but during the 1920's the small town has degenerated morally and the writer is repelled. Weber is disillusioned also in the corruption of romantic Germany, and of individuals in all society, but continues to believe in the future of America.

These four main books of Wolfe, the last two posthumous, are generally considered to be one passionate autobiographical document.

LOOKING BACKWARD: 2000–1887 (1888), by Edward Bellamy. Julian West, a wealthy Bostonian, after spending the evening with his fiancée Edith Bartlett, finds that he cannot fall asleep. Hypnotized by Dr. Pillsbury, he awakens to find that it is 113 years later. Still retaining the vigor and appearance of his youth in 2000 A.D., he falls in love with another Edith, the great-granddaughter of his first fiancée. She guides him on a tour of the co-operative commonwealth which has come into existence. Labor is the cornerstone of society; all work and share alike. The State is the Great Trust. Economic security and a healthy moral environment have reduced crime. The cultural level has risen. Julian dreams that he is again in the old society, which now appals him as ruthless, greedy, and unjust. To his relief, however, he awakens and finds himself still in the new Utopia.

This best-selling novel led to the birth of the Nationalist Party. Bellamy also founded *The New Nation* and made a career of social reform until his early death.

LORD JIM (1900), by Joseph Conrad. Conrad's most admired novel. *Lord Jim,* has for its dark psychologic theme the frustration of a man who dreams of heroic acts but who is tragically tormented by secret fears. Lord Jim, the son of a clergyman, serves as an officer on the pilgrim ship *Patha.* One night in the Red Sea the vessel begins to sink. Before the eight hundred pilgrims know what is happening, the captain of the ship and his officers, including Lord Jim, lower the only lifeboat and rescue themselves. The consciousness of this monstrous crime and the attendant disgrace forever torment Lord Jim, in spite of the fact that all the pilgrims were saved. Lord Jim becomes a wanderer in far-off places, finding reminders of his moral lapse wherever he goes. Doramin, chief of a wild tribe in Pafusan, makes him his trusted adviser, and here he finds peace. But when a crew of bloodthirsty pirates is caught and Lord Jim intercedes on their behalf, he works his own undoing. Doramin permits them to march back to their ship, but on the way they murder his son and a number of other resting warriors. In expiation Lord Jim goes to the grieving father and allows himself to be shot. Only in death could he find remission of his sins.

LORNA DOONE (1869), by Richard Doddridge Blackmore. The hero-narrator of this romantic novel is John Ridd, a yeoman farmer living in Exmoor during the reign of Charles II. He lives with his mother and sister, tilling the soil and pursuing a virtuous life. The shadow of a tragedy, however, constantly rests upon them. Seven years before, John's father had been murdered by the Doones, a band of outlaws living in Glen Doone. It happened that in one of their forays the wild Doones had captured a little girl whom they adopted and named Lorna. One day, venturing into Glen Doone, John meets Lorna and falls in love with her. Learning of John's love for Lorna, Carver Doone declares war on him. Lorna escapes and goes to live with the Ridds. Later she journeys to London, inherits her title and lands, becoming Lady Dugal, the mistress of vast estates. In the meantime, John has gone to war and is knighted by King James II. After killing the murderous Carver, he marries Lorna.

LOST HORIZON (1933), by James Hilton. This is a fanciful story of an ageless existence in a perfect place. Three English citizens and one American are kidnaped in a plane and taken by Chang to Shangri-La. Rutherford tells Hugh Conway's story. Roberta Brinklow, missionary, Henry Barnard, American, and Conway are satisfied to remain in the paradise of the Valley of the Blue Moon in Tibet, but Captain Charles Mallison is discontented. The High Lama tells Conway the history of Shangri-La and the agelessness of its lamas. Perrault, a Capuchin, built it in 1734 at the age of fifty-three, discovered the secret of longevity, and is now the High Lama. Just before his death, he appoints Conway as his successor. However, Mallison is anxious to leave with Lo-Tsen, so Conway leads the way. Hugh disappears and the reader is left wondering whether he will find his way back. The only evidence to prove Rutherford's tale is the fact that Lo-Tsen lost her youth when she left the valley.

LOST LADY, A (1923), by Willa Cather. The story of Marian Forrester is told by Niel Herbert, a Midwestern youth. Married to rugged old empire-builder Captain Forrester, Marian's graciousness sets her much above her commonplace neighbors. She becomes the lover of his friend, Frank Ellinger, however; and after the Captain's death due to a stroke, the lover of Ivy Peters, the man who acquires her home. Peters marries, and the impoverished Marian returns to the West, a "lost lady" in the eyes of her youthful admirer, Niel. He later hears that Marian, married to a wealthy Englishman, won the respect and admiration of all in her new surroundings.

LOST LAND, THE (1919), by Johannes V. Jensen. See LONG JOURNEY, THE, by Johannes V. Jensen.

LOVE AND MARRIAGE (1909), by Ellen Key. See KEY, ELLEN.

LOVE FOR LOVE (1695), by William Congreve. Congreve's play is a satirical indictment of the shallowness and promiscuity of seventeenth century

England, written with striking realism. The hero of the story is the philandering Valentine. His father, Sir Samson Legend, tired of his son's debts and extravagances, wants him to sign a bond making over his inheritance to his brother, Ben. Valentine's immediate reward for this will be four thousand pounds. Enmeshed in debt, he does sign the bond. Ben, who is away at sea, has a marriage arranged for him by his father, to Miss Prue, a countrified young girl who is being instructed in the art of love by Tattle, a fop. Miss Prue's father, Foresight, advertises himself as being a great seer. Valentine, fearing ruin by the loss of his fortune, pretends to have gone out of his mind in order to avoid the final signing away of his estate and to win the sympathy of the charming Angelica, the heiress, with whom he is in love. Angelica then wins Sir Sampson over. He falls in love with her and proposes marriage. In feigning acceptance she is able to secure Valentine's bond. He, in the meantime unhappy because Angelica is to marry his father, offers to sign the final papers. But she tells him of her scheme and destroys the bond.

LOVE IS THE BEST DOCTOR, (1665), by Molière. See PHYSICIAN IN SPITE OF HIMSELF, THE, by Molière.

LOVE NEST, THE (1926), by Ring Lardner. See LARDNER, RING.

LOVE OF THE THREE ORANGES, THE (1761), by Carlo Gozzi. See GOZZI, CARLO.

LOVE ROGUE (1630), by Tirso de Molina (pseud. of Gabriel Téllez). This play gave world literature one of its most popular and extraordinary characters, Don Juan. From its very first scene, the world of love and intrigue opens up as this dissolute young noble, gambler, rake and blasphemer, goes from one adventure to another. First Don Juan enters the bedroom of the Duchess Isabella under the guise of her fiancé, Octavio. In his flight from the consequences, he is shipwrecked on the Tarragona coast. He is carried to the house of the fisherwoman Tisbea, whom he deceives with the promise of marriage and then abandons. In Seville he enters the house of Doña Ana, daughter of the Comendador Don Gonzalo de Ulloa, by means of an intercepted letter which had been directed to Doña Ana's lover, inviting him to her bedroom. When Doña Ana discovers the deception, she screams, and her father hurries to her aid. In the ensuing struggle Don Juan kills the Comendador and flees. His journey carries him next to the town of Dos Hermanas, where he comes upon the prenuptial celebration of two peasants. By flattering the bride, and promising her father great wealth, he cheats the hapless bridegroom of his intended, and leaves behind him one more deceived and unhappy woman. Don Juan then returns to Seville. In the church where the Comendador lies buried, he sees a stone statue of his victim. In a burst of bravado he pulls his beard and invites him to dine with him. At midnight, while Don Juan is making merry with his friends, there is a knock at the door. The statue enters. Unabashed and with utter aplomb, Don Juan entertains his guest. The dinner over, the statue offers to reciprocate Don Juan's courtesy and invites him to dinner at his tomb the following night. Undaunted as ever, Don Juan presents himself at the appointed time, and grasping the statue's hand, is consumed by hellfire.

LOVE'S LABOUR 'S LOST (ca. 1594; quarto 1598), by William Shakespeare. This youthful comedy suffers from thinness of plot and a multitude of topical allusions about which scholars are still arguing today. The style, whether blank verse or rhymed, or Euphuistic prose, is often fantastic, and sometimes seems to be a deliberate parody. The last song ("When daisies pied and violets blue") is, however, one of Shakespeare's best. King Ferdinand of Navarre, with three of his attendant lords, Biron of Berowne, Longaville, and Dumain, bind themselves mutually to forswear all worldly and social delights, devoting themselves to sober study and meditation for the space of three years. Most urgent of their vows is that renouncing the companionship of women. At this inopportune time the Princess of France arrives on business of state. With her are Rosaline, Maria, and Katherine. The graces of the four women severally break down the resolutions of the four men. One by one they woo, and finally win. The father of the Princess dies. This occasion of grief is turned, by the ladies, to an occasion of discipline. They condition their surrender by the test of a year's fidelity of purpose. If their suitors, at the termination of this time, still press their pleas, then will the ladies grant their hands.

LOWELL, AMY (1874–1925). Amy Lowell, after a careful childhood education, and travels to various parts of the world, returned to Boston. There in the heart of her distinguished New England family she settled down and interested herself in library work. About 1902 she decided to devote herself to creative literature. Accordingly, she read much, traveled in a literary set, and in 1912 published *A Dome of Many-Colored Glass*. This volume contains traditional pieces. It was after she had met European members of Ezra Pound's Imagist School that she began to work with their colloquialism, freedom of expression, and concentrated aestheticism; and with polyphonic prose, a rhythmic writing which sacrifices formal meter for a continuity by mood. *Sword Blades and Poppy Seeds* (1914) was her embracing of the "new poetry," with which she experimented for about three years thereafter. These pieces are noted for an emphasis on visual, sensual images.

Patterns (1916) is a free-verse monologue dramatizing the struggle between desire and decorum in an eighteenth century woman's mind.

John Keats (1925), a two-volume biography, is a zestful, if sometimes undiscriminating, prose study.

LOWELL, JAMES RUSSELL (1819–1891). James Russell Lowell published in 1848 the most important works which established him as poet, critic, humorist and social commentator.

A Fable for Critics is a whimsical literary criticism of pre-Civil War America. In a mythological formula, he lampoons a collection of contemporary giants such as Emerson, Longfellow, Holmes—and himself.

The Vision of Sir Launfal is a narrative poem of the Holy Grail legend, in which the knight at last discovers that Christ's presence is even in a leprous beggar, whom he had spurned at the beginning of his adventure. Service to mankind is Launfal's resolution, and the poem's didactic message.

The Biglow Papers, first series, are humorous verses in Yankee dialect, written in opposition to the Mexican War. The three main characters are

Hosea Biglow, a farmer; Homer Wilbur, a pastor; and Birdofredum Sawin, a Massachusetts private who at length is converted to the Confederate cause. The second series (collected in 1867) is a support of the North in the Civil War. There are views on Reconstruction, and an idealized contemplation of the expected peace. The most amusing sequence is "The Courtin'," letters which maliciously burlesque speeches of Jefferson Davis and contemporaries. Lowell's later work was largely literary criticism.

LOWER DEPTHS, THE (1903), by Maxim Gorky. See NIGHT'S LODGING, A, by Maxim Gorky.

L'UCCELLINO AZZURO (1765), by Carlo Gozzi. See GOZZI, CARLO.

LUCIEN LEUVEN (1894), by Stendhal. See CHARTERHOUSE OF PARMA, THE, by Stendhal.

LUCIFER (1654), by Joost van den Vondel. See VONDEL, JOOST VAN DEN.

LUCK AND PLUCK (1869 ff.), by Horatio Alger, Jr. See ALGER, HORATIO, JR.

LUCK OF ROARING CAMP AND OTHER SKETCHES, THE (1870), by Bret Harte. With this volume of short stories which he had been publishing in his *Overland Monthly,* Bret Harte became famous throughout the country. Soon after, the quality of his production waned; but he had left his mark on American literary history. The background of the stories is California during the 1849 gold rush; the emphasis is on local color and a "realistic" morality which was startlingly original at the time. The title story concerns a prostitute, Cherokee Sal, whose baby, christened Thomas Luck after her death, has a mellowing effect upon the lawless miners, one of whom is subsequently drowned trying vainly to save him.

"The Outcasts of Poker Flat" tells of the eloping Tom Simpson and Piney, who fall in with a group of questionable exiles from a California mining town. Snow traps the group. Mother Shipton, a prostitute, starves herself to save food for Piney, but the latter dies, in the protective embrace of the Duchess, another prostitute. John Oakhurst the gambler kills himself to provide Tom with a chance for life.

"Tennessee's Partner" concerns a miner of dubious reputation who retains the friendship of his partner even after running off with his wife. When Tennessee is hanged as a highway robber, the sad partner touches the hearts of the crowd by claiming the body and performing a rude funeral service.

"Miggles" deals with a former prostitute, and "Brown of Calaveras" with a professional gambler. The "Idyll of Red Gulch" is the love affair of a prim school teacher and a drunken vagabond.

Plain Language from Truthful James (1870) is a humorous ballad about Truthful James and Bill Nye, who plan to cheat the Chinese Ah Sin in a card game, but by "ways that are dark" are always outwitted by "the Heathen Chinee."

LUCKY PER (1898-1904), by Henrik Pontoppidan. Published originally in eight volumes, and finally in three (1907), this long novel by Denmark's most important creative writer of the naturalistic vein, is a continuation of the critical, antisocial writing by the author already exhibited in his shorter prose works and in the large cycle of novels, *The Promised Land* (1891–1895; Eng. tr. 1896). The title is ironic. The hero, Per Sidenius, is, like the author, the son of a clergyman, who rebels against his home and family and fails to realize his great engineering plans, because—the novelist would have us believe—of his racial inheritance that continuously hampers his powers of action at the crucial moment. It is the old story of heredity versus environment. So he fails to conquer the world, as he had intended, and ultimately returns to the ideals taught him from childhood. The book included realistic scenes from contemporary Copenhagen, with portraits of several prominent characters of the Danish capital, such as the Jewish Dr. Nathan, who represents Dr. (Georg) Brandes. One of the best features of the work is the contrast of the Lutheran atmosphere of the Sidenius family with the "completely worldly Jewish money aristocracy" represented by Per's fiancée, Jakobe. In 1917 Pontoppidan shared the Nobel Prize in Literature with his countryman Karl Gjellerup.

LUCKY SAM McCARVER (1925), by Sidney Howard. See THEY KNEW WHAT THEY WANTED, by Sidney Howard.

LUCY GAYHEART (1935), by Willa Cather. See CATHER, WILLA.

LUMIE DI SICILIA (1913), by Luigi Pirandello. See PIRANDELLO, LUIGI.

L'UOMO, LA BESTIA E LA VIRTU' (1919), by Luigi Pirandello. See PIRANDELLO, LUIGI.

LUSIAD, THE (1572), by Luis de Camões. *Os Lusíadas* is the literary masterpiece of Portugal. The subject of this epic poem in ten cantos is actually the praise of Portugal, whose glory, during the reign of King Henry, was enhanced by its navigators, who sailed all the seven seas in search of India. The main action is centered on Vasco de Gama's expedition, but the exploits of other heroes of the Golden Age of Discovery and empire building are recounted in heroic meter. Camões, strongly impressed by the epics of Greece and Rome, wove into his contemporary tale the myths of pagan antiquity. Into all this he poured his own Portuguese passion and patriotism. His elegance of style and his ability to draw a glowing narrative to a noble climax lend a classic purity to his epic.

LUTHER, MARTIN (1483–1546). Martin Luther was a central figure in that period of religious, political, economic, and intellectual ferment known as the Reformation. Born in Germany, Luther became a Catholic priest in 1507. He made a trip to Rome and was revolted by the corruption and luxury of the Church. This feeling was intensified in 1517 when a Dominican, John Tetzel, traveled through Germany selling indulgences, which, it was claimed, would release the soul of a departed relative from Purgatory. Luther wrote his famous *Ninety-five Theses* (1517), which he posted on the door of the church in Wittenberg, and offered to defend them against all comers. Luther advocated a return to an earlier and simpler form of Christianity, opposed the power of the Roman Catholic hierarchy, and defended the secular rulers in their conflict with the Pope. He was forced by circumstances to justify greater and greater power for kings and princes, and this, together with the rejection of the authority of the Pope, led to his excommunication. His view prevailed in much of northern Europe, and resulted in the establishment of national churches. Among other works, his *Letters* and *Sermons,* his extraordinary translation of the Greek New Testament (1522), and *De Servo Arbitrio* (1525) in debate with Erasmus, are well-known.

LYCIDAS (written 1637; published 1638), by John Milton. *Lycidas,* one of the great pastoral elegies in the English language, has been called "the high-watermark of English poetry." The monody mourns the death of Edward King, a fellow student but probably not a close friend of Milton's, who was drowned in August, 1637. The conventions of the Greek and Latin pastoral elegies, especially those of Theocritus, Bion, and Virgil, are adopted by Milton, who makes his poem serve as a vehicle for his noble thoughts concerning earthly fame and heavenly judgment. An attack on the corrupt and selfish Anglican clergymen of Milton's time breaks into the elegy, forecasting some of Milton's later controversial prose. The poem then calms again; the famous roll call of the flowers is given, followed by the traditional reversal— in which the poet turns from mourning Lycidas' death to rejoicing that he has been received into Heaven. Henceforth Lycidas will be the guardian spirit for all those who wander over the sea.

LYRICAL BALLADS (1798), by William Wordsworth and Samuel Taylor Coleridge. In his preface to the first edition of the *Lyrical Ballads,* which also included Coleridge's *The Rime of the Ancyent Marinere* (q.v.), Wordsworth remarked: "The majority of the following poems are to be considered as experiments. They were written chiefly with a view to ascertain how far the language of conversation in the middle and lower classes of society is adapted to the purposes of poetic pleasure." Actually these poems were semipolitical "experiments" as well, for at the time both Wordsworth and Coleridge had radical sympathies. Wordsworth, being a mystic, glorified rustic speech also because of its romantic associations with nature. Among the twenty-three poems in the collection are such well-known poems as: "We Are Seven," "Goody Blake and Harry Gill," and "Lines Written a Few Miles Above Tintern Abbey" (q.v.). The little volume was the manifesto of the Romantic movement in English literature.

LYRICS OF LOVE AND LAUGHTER (1903), by Paul Laurence Dunbar. See DUNBAR, PAUL LAURENCE.

LYRICS OF SUNSHINE AND SHADOW (1905), by Paul Laurence Dunbar. See DUNBAR, PAUL LAURENCE.

LYRICS OF THE LOWLY LIFE (1896), by Paul Laurence Dunbar. See DUNBAR, PAUL LAURENCE.

LYSISTRATA (411 B.C.), by Aristophanes. The *Lysistrata* was produced on the stage toward the end of the Peloponnesian War. It makes its appeal for peace to men of common sense. The plot is simple. The women of Athens, who normally lead a cloistered life, seize the Acropolis and open negotiations with the women of Sparta, the enemy state. The scheme of the Athenian women's leader, Lysistrata, calls for a boycott on all marital relations until their husbands make peace. The original difficulty of persuading the women to take so drastic a course is overcome, and the seizure of the Acropolis freezes the treasury with its funds for the prosecution of the war. Lysistrata's embassy to Sparta meets with some delay, and the women's resolution begins to totter. But the forces of nature are at work and the men are in an equally sad plight. The return of the embassy with assurances of solidarity on the part of Sparta's women is soon followed by a herald from Sparta empowered by his desperate fellow countrymen to make peace. The terms are soon struck, and the comedy ends with general reconciliation and jubilation. As low comedy the play is unsurpassed among Aristophanes' works. The frankness and earthy character of its language have made it less popular than many of the others, but its appeal to the universal love of peace on understandable human terms raises it above time and place.

MABINOGION, THE (ca. 10th–15th centuries). *The Red Book of Hergest,* which is included in Lady Charlotte Guest's translation of *The Mabinogion,* was compiled in the fifteenth century. The correct title for the four Welsh tales in which Arthur does not appear would probably be "the four branches of the Mabinogi"; separately the tales are known as: "Pwyll, Prince of Dyved," "Branwen, daughter of Llyr"; "Manawyddan, son of Llyr" and "son of Mathonwy." Then come "The Dream of Maxen Wledig" and "Dud and Lleyelys," probably somewhat later in date. In none of these tales does Arthur figure.

In the remaining five stories Arthur plays his part. These form a distinct group. "Kulhwch and Olwen" and "The Dream of Rhonabwy" appear to be of British origin. The three tales in the second and better known group are "The Lady of the Fountain," "Geraint, son of Erbin" and "Peredur, son of Evrawc"; these are of French origin.

As a whole the collection is artistic and delightful. It is probably the most interesting extant example of early Celtic genius. Miracles are everyday affairs. There is delicacy and tenderness and a love of nature which is wholly unlike the French equivalents. These stories were probably composed by professionals, but they retain a naïveté of which Renan has said: "We have the simple recital of a child, unwitting of any distinction between the noble and the common. . . . The skillful Chrétien de Troyes, himself, remains in this respect far below the Welsh story-tellers."

MACBETH (1606? Folio, 1623), by William Shakespeare. Shakespeare drew his material from Holinshed's *Chronicles* (q.v.). The play was written in honor of James I. It is one of the most popular and powerful of Shakespeare's tragedies, closely knit in structure, direct and concentrated in impact.

Macbeth, victorious Scottish warrior and Thane of Glamis, is confronted on a heath by three witches. They prophesy that he will become Thane of Cawdor, then King of Scotland. It is also said that the sons of his friend, Banquo, shall enjoy the subsequent succession to the throne.

Immediately thereafter Macbeth does acquire the title, Thane of Cawdor. He becomes obsessed with fulfilling the prophecy that he will be King. Lady Macbeth becomes inflamed with the same lust for power. When Macbeth's spirit quails before the consequences of his ambition, she fiercely impels him onward. Together they murder King Duncan as he sleeps, a guest in their own castle.

Macbeth is now launched upon a bloody course. His fears and suspicions drive him to a series of murders. Banquo is slain in an attempt by Macbeth to frustrate the witches' prophecy that his own line shall not inherit the throne, but Banquo's son Fleance escapes. Macbeth cruelly slays the wife and and son of Macduff, one of his mortal foes.

He takes comfort in the assurance of the witches that he will not be overthrown "till Birnam wood do come to Dunsinane," and that he cannot be slain by man born of woman. But catastrophe follows. Lady Macbeth, tortured by guilt, slays herself. His enemies advance upon Dunsinane under the camouflage of boughs torn from Birnam wood. Finally he is slain in combat by Macduff, who "was from his mother's womb untimely ripp'd."

The philosophical content of the play is of great interest. Both Macbeth and Lady Macbeth, contrary to their superficial ruthlessness, are complex studies of disintegration of the will under the pressure of remorse. Lady Macbeth's famous sleepwalking scene, and the growing realization of Macbeth that the game has not been worth the candle, testify to this.

Shakespeare further presents a fascinating pattern in the symbolic figures of the witches, who betray men to folly by cryptic half-truths, treacherous to him who counts upon them.

Of great significance is the subtle snare into which Macbeth falls by gambling on presumptive fate and seeking foolishly to avert part of the same prophecy, that Banquo's sons shall be the kingly line.

On these counts the play is susceptible to varied and stimulating interpretations. But so universal are its motivations, and so vividly alive in all eras are the phenomena of the ruthless will to power, that the vigor of the play remains unabated.

MacFLECKNOE (1682), by John Dryden. See DRYDEN, JOHN.

MACHINE-WRECKERS (1923), by Ernst Toller. See MAN AND MASSES, by Ernst Toller.

MacLEISH, ARCHIBALD (1892). Archibald MacLeish's poetry has passed through several stages. As an expatriate, a postwar pessimist, and a poetic modernist, he wrote subjective works. *The Hamlet of A. MacLeish* (1928) is a reinterpretation of that play in the light of the author's own negativistic feelings. Like Laertes, he resigns himself to chance, in a scheme of things where science and philosophy are meaningless. *The Pot of Earth* (1925) is a reinterpretation of a fertility legend from *The Golden Bough* (q.v.). The sensuous verse narrative ends with the death of the heroine, after her still-born child.

Following these pieces, MacLeish returned to the United States, and began to produce works concerning its cultural and social traditions. *Frescoes for Mr. Rockefeller's City* (1933) are six poems of America, many of them satirizing the labor-industrialist contrast. The poet mocks the American expatriate who ostentatiously turns to Europe for artistic inspiration. He depicts modern industrialism as unworthy of such early efforts as the Lewis and Clark expedition. He burlesques the foreign-born, in striking contrast to the matured liberalism of his later work.

Of this period, too, is *Conquistador* (1932), in which the reflections of Bernal Díaz tell the epic conquest of Mexico. There are the struggles of Cortés against the new land, the Indians, and his rival, Governor Velásquez. The climax is the *noche triste* when Montezuma's men expel the Spaniards from the capital.

After these works, MacLeish began to concentrate on particular social questions. *Panic* (1935) is a verse play describing the collapse of banker McGafferty during the 1933 financial panic. Despite the love of his mistress Ione, McGafferty's confidence is shattered by the pessimism of Immelman, his assistant. Soon the helpless people in the street learn that McGafferty has killed himself. *The Fall of the City* (1937) is a radio play symbolizing the march of Fascism. The omen-ridden, vacillating populace throw themselves on the mercy of the helmeted conqueror. Prostrate, they do not see that his opened visor reveals emptiness.

MAD HERCULES, by Seneca. See TRAGEDIES, by Seneca.

MADAME BOVARY (1865), by Gustave Flaubert. Emma Rouault, the convent-bred daughter of a Norman farmer, marries a dull and uninteresting young doctor, Charles Bovary. Naturally the marriage fails to give Emma the exalted happiness which she has read and dreamed about. Discontented with her small-town surroundings and tedious family life, she rushes from one folly to another, dallying first with a timid law clerk named Leon, then embarking on a genuine affair with the cynical, wealthy Rodolphe. Jilted by Rodolphe, she again turns to Leon, but the latter, after the first thrill of their liaison, becomes frightened of Emma's desperate enthusiasm. Morally bankrupt and hopelessly involved in debt, blackmailed by the cunning merchant L'Heureux, who has encouraged her extravagant gifts to her lovers, Emma takes arsenic. Charles, never truly knowing what it is all about, dies shortly thereafter, leaving their hapless child adrift on the same ocean of bourgeois mediocrity which has swallowed up her parents.

The book's power comes from Flaubert's masterly, savage picture of the mediocrity of his time—of which Emma is at once an example and a victim. The one character who emerges from the story successful and honored, the pharmacist Homais, is the most bombastically mediocre of all.

Flaubert was obsessed by style, and *Madame Bovary,* which took him more than five years to write, is called his artistic triumph. Many prefer it to his other works: *Salammbô* (q.v.), *The Temptation of Saint-Anthony* (q.v.), *The Sentimental Education* (q.v.), *Three Tales* (q.v.) and *Bouvard and Pecuchet* (1881).

MADAME SANS-GÊNE (1893), by Victorien Sardou and Emile Moreau. One of Sardou's most famous plays, this was popular with actresses in the nineteenth century. It opens in Paris on the 10th of August, 1792, when the Swiss Guards fire on the people and the King and Queen are taken from the Tuileries. Catherine Hubscher, a jolly girl who runs a laundry, is affianced to a sergeant of the citizen army. Among her customers are Fouché and Napoleon. She shelters the fleeing Count de Neipperg, an Austrian, and helps him escape. The sergeant becomes a Marshal in Napoleon's armies and his wife (nicknamed Madame Sans-Gêne) retains her former free and easy manners and fears nobody, not even the Emperor himself. When the latter suggests to her husband that he divorce her she faces him down, and presents an unpaid laundry bill to His Majesty, and even straightens out the difficulties of her old friend de Neipperg, who had returned to France with the Empress Marie Louise.

MADEMOISELLE DE MAUPIN (1835), by Théophile Gautier. The heroine of this novel, Mademoiselle de Maupin, is an adventurous girl who has disguised herself as a man in order to move about more freely and to be able to study the men she meets. For most of them she has only contempt, but she does come to respect, if not love, young d'Albert, an aesthete who is very fond of "gold, marble and royal purple." He sees through the disguise and falls in love with Madelaine. His mistress, deceived by the disguise, falls in love with her also. Eventually Madelaine gives herself to d'Albert for one night and then leaves him forever.

Much admired by poets and artists, including Swinburne, *Mademoiselle de Maupin* created no small scandal among ordinary readers. Today it is interesting largely as a manifesto of the amoralist, Art-for-Art's-Sake school.

MAGDA (1893), by Hermann Sudermann. A German provincial town is in the throes of preparing for a music festival in which a famous Italian opera singer is to appear. The artist turns out to be Magda, the daughter of Lieutenant-Colonel Schwartze, who once ordered her out of the house because she refused to marry Hefterdingt, the local pastor. At first Schwartze refuses to see Magda, but is finally persuaded to receive her. The family insists on Magda's staying with them instead of at the hotel, to which she agrees on condition that they do not inquire into her past life. Soon the household is in a furor with a corps of foreign servants entering and the local ladies calling on Magda. Among the visitors is Dr. von Keller, Magda's lover in the old days in Berlin, now living a correct and pious life after deserting her. She tells him how she has "labored and starved to bring up their son," that his desertion really started her on her career. Schwartze eventually learns the truth about his daughter's illegitimate child and orders Magda to accept Keller's formal marriage proposal. She refuses when Keller, for the sake of his career, does not want to acknowledge his son. The struggle between father and daughter becomes intense. At last the old man, who had threatened to shoot Magda, dies of a stroke. *Magda* is one of Sudermann's best known plays. The richly dramatic role of the heroine has made it an international favorite with many great actresses, including Duse and Bernhardt. After the meteoric success of *Honor* (1889) Hermann Sudermann was considered second to Gerhardt Hauptmann as a dramatist before World War I; grossly underrated and often ridiculed in his later years, the playwright also achieved considerable fame as a novelist.

MAGGIE: A GIRL OF THE STREETS (1896), by Stephen Crane. See RED BADGE OF COURAGE, THE, by Stephen Crane.

MAGIC MOUNTAIN, THE (1924), by Thomas Mann. This tremendously long and celebrated novel is almost entirely devoid of plot in the established sense. Hans Castorp, a young North German engineer, comes to visit his cousin Joachim Ziemssen in a tuberculosis sanatorium high in the Swiss mountains near Davos. Instead of staying a few weeks as he had planned, he is fascinated by the spectacle of decay, drugged by a sense of timelessness and helplessly caught by the "magic" life on the mountain. He discovers symptoms of the dread disease, and stays on for seven years until the outbreak of World War I. The theme of the book is Castorp's education and self-development. Not endowed with intellectual brilliance but of rather average mind and talents, the young man is slowly exposed to the issues, trends and ideas of Europe. Among his most notable teachers are the Italian liberal and humanist Settembrini; the medievalist, neo-Thomist Jesuit Naptha; the powerful realist Mynheer Peeperkorn. It is, however, the capricious and charming Russian lady, Clavdia Chauchat, who holds the greatest sway over Hans throughout his stay on the Magic Mountain. Thomas Mann's novel is a symbolic and philosophical treatment of modern man's problems on the highest level. After Goethe's *Wilhelm Meister* (q.v.) the book is the most outstanding example of the educational novel ("Bildungsroman") in the German tradition. Touching upon almost all ideas and issues of the twentieth century, from psychoanalysis to relativity, from Eastern dogmatism to Western liberalism, *The Magic Mountain* is one of the most gigantic works of modern world literature.

MÁGICO PRODIGIOSO, EL (1637), by Pedro Calderón de la Barca. See WONDER WORKING MAGICIAN, THE, by Pedro Calderón de la Barca.

MAGNALIA CHRISTI AMERICANA (1702), by Cotton Mather. See MATHER, COTTON.

MAGNIFICENT AMBERSONS, THE (1918), by Booth Tarkington. See TARKINGTON, BOOTH.

MAGNIFICENT OBSESSION (1929), by Lloyd C. Douglas. See ROBE, THE, by Lloyd C. Douglas.

MAHABHARATA, THE (ca. 200 B.C.). The *Mahabharata* has for its subject the great war that is supposed to have taken place about 1400 B.C. in India. There is no doubt that its narrative songs were conceived by bards and minstrels who sang of the glories of their people's heroes as Homer sang of the exploits of his nation's heroes in the *Iliad* (q.v.). Much that is legendary beclouds the historical truth of this epic. It is largely the imaginative remembrance of India's great past which the bards wove freely from oral tradition and the folklore of India. The work is of a composite nature, many of its verses arbitrarily incorporated through the centuries. It has a companion in the *Ramayana* (q.v.), another epic of the same period of composition.

The *Mahabharata* has ninety thousand couplets; it is seven times as long as the *Odyssey* (q.v.) and the *Iliad* combined. Exclusive of its numerous episodic inclusions, the leading narrative of the epic forms only one-fourth of the work. The war of the *Mahabharata* consisted of the eighteen battles fought on eighteen consecutive days. The one characteristic feature which distinguished this poem from all other Sanskrit literature is its simplicity. It is almost bare of simile and ornamentation. Its heroes, godlike in their heroism and virtue, are invariably well characterized and stand out in relief in the collective frieze.

The scene of the *Mahabharata* is the ancient kingdom of the Kurus on the shores of the upper Ganges. Its narrative covers the war which is fought between the Kurus and a neighboring people, the Panchalas. The rivalry between the heroes Arjun and Karna is the leading thread of the epic.

MAID OF ORLEANS (1801), by Friedrich von Schiller. See SCHILLER, FRIEDRICH VON.

MAID'S TRAGEDY, THE (1619), by Francis Beaumont and John Fletcher. Amintor, in love with Aspatia, is a submissive vassal to his liege lord, the King. He abandons Aspatia at the King's behest and marries Evadne. In the bridal chamber Evadne confesses that she has been the King's mistress and denies herself to Amintor. Amintor is too loyal to his King to reveal his position, but it is discovered by Melantius, his friend, who is Evadne's brother. Melantius forces his sister to murder the King; he himself takes possession of the palace. Meanwhile, Aspatia, grief-stricken at the loss of her lover, disguises herself as her brother and provokes Amintor to a duel, in which she is killed. Evadne does not get the pardon she expected from her husband, so she kills herself. Amintor cannot survive the death of his true love, Aspatia.

Edmund Waller rewrote the last act of the play to give it a happy ending.

MAIN CURRENTS IN AMERICAN THOUGHT (1927–1930), by Vernon Louis Parrington. This work in three volumes (the last one unfinished) is a history of American ideas as revealed by literary production. Parrington, a liberal, evaluated American writing by an economic and social interpretation. His critical sweep of the scene has distinction, originality and accuracy. The first two volumes received the Pulitzer Prize for 1928.

MAIN CURRENTS IN NINETEENTH CENTURY LITERATURE (1872–1890), by Georg Brandes. The greatest champion of "freedom of inquiry and freedom of thought" in the last quarter of the nineteenth century was Georg Brandes, the most influential literary critic since Taine. He was much more than a critic—he was a missionary who wished to tear away the blinders of Romanticism from the eyes of his generation and bring them down to the sober realities of life. In opposition to the romantic tendency he maintained that a literature is proven to be alive by its ability and willingness to discuss problems. A work of art was to be evaluated less from the æsthetic point of view and more from its ideological and social preoccupation. This conception of art is the yardstick he employs in his most famous work, the monumental six-volume *Main Currents in Nineteenth Century Literature*. Brandes found European literature shackled by prejudices, insulated from the realities of the world. In his crusade against such prejudice he found brothers-in-arms in Taine, Sainte-Beuve, John Stuart Mill and Rénan, in Ibsen and in Strindberg. His lectures on *Main Currents in Nineteenth Century Literature* were nothing less than a declaration of war against the existing state of things. He was boldly a partisan of French revolutionary ideals. He traced gloomily the victory of escape Romanticism over the social ideals of the Revolution. But he gloried in the renascence of that dynamic spirit with Byron and Shelley in England, with Hugo, Flaubert and Zola in France, with Turgenev, Dostoevsky and Tolstoy in Russia, with Ibsen, Strindberg and Björnson in Scandinavian countries, with Heine and Börne in "Young Germany."

The Main Currents consists of the following separate studies: *The Literature of the French Emigrés* (1872); *The Romantic School in Germany* (1873); *Reaction in France* (1874); *Naturalism in England* (1875); *The Romantic School in France* (1882); *Young Germany* (1890). In all of these works Brandes is critic, polemicist and apologist. He proclaims a new philosophy, the Positivism of Comte (which in later years he was to change for Socialism), the Utilitarianism of his friend John Stuart Mill, and the aesthetics of Taine's Naturalism. Life, not dreams, should be the objective of literature, he wrote.

Brandes' influence on writers the world over was tremendous. He transcended the conventional role of the literary critic as a judge of books to become a critic of the literature of life instead.

MAIN STREET (1920), by Sinclair Lewis. *Main Street* is the story of Gopher Prairie, Minnesota, which has a population of 3,000 smug, dull people, interested only in getting on in life and preventing others from doing the same. Whatever is progressive is despised. There is opposition to civic reform, culture and education. The honored citizens are bankers. . . . There is not much conventional plot; it is a documentary compilation of episodes, caricatures, and satirical tintypes. The central character is Carol Milford, a college-educated librarian. She marries Dr. Will Kennicott and goes to live with him in his home town of Gopher Prairie, entering into a long struggle to adjust herself to its stagnant life. Unable to do this, she tries to change it—raise its cultural level. She organizes a little theater, but the response is chilling; the villagers despise her for her superiority. Carol begins to lose her affection for Will, and turns to Erik Valborg, a kindred spirit. At length she leaves town and lives for two years in Washington, D. C., where she is a government clerk. But unable to establish her own life, she returns to Gopher Prairie, this time bringing a greater understanding of the forces which shape Main Street.

MAIN-TRAVELLED ROADS (1891), by Hamlin Garland. See SON OF THE MIDDLE BORDER, A, by Hamlin Garland.

MAJOR BARBARA (1905), by George Bernard Shaw. This is a satire on the social conditions that breed poverty, and on organized charity. Lady Britomart has left her husband, Undershaft, a munitions manufacturer, because of the firm's policy of adopting foundlings to place in business. She feels that this lessens the chances of their son, Stephen. When her daughters are about to be married she sends for their father, since she feels they need his financial help. Sarah is engaged to Charles Lomax, a harmless young man, and Barbara, who feels that the capitalistic system is the cause of poverty and social evils, and who is a major in the Salvation Army, is engaged to Adolphus Cusins, a professor of Greek. He has joined the Army on Barbara's account. Barbara invites Undershaft to visit her shelter; this he promises to do if she will come to his factory. When her father adds five thousand pounds to the gift of a whiskey baron in order to keep the shelter open, Barbara resigns from the Army, realizing that capitalism supports the charities thus remedying its own evils. The next day she goes with Undershaft to his factory. They inspect the works and the up-to-date town connected with them. His workers are well paid and contented. Undershaft and Cusins like each other, and they discover that since Cusins is a foundling he is eligible to go into the munitions business. Barbara finds that she still wants to marry him. She has swung around to her father's viewpoint on capitalism, and begins to think that the degradation that accompanies poverty causes all evil of itself.

MAKING OF AN AMERICAN, THE (1901), by Jacob A. Riis. This autobiography of the Danish-American journalist is a book of genial reminiscence. The author recounts adventures of his boyhood, his early jobs as factory worker and ship laborer—and his jobless, vagrant days—and then his successful newspaper career. The rest of the volume concerns Riis's efforts in connection with the slum areas of New York City, which he had written about in *How the Other Half Lives* (1890). This earlier work was a crusade to call attention to the economic evils and social waste among the underprivileged. It discussed the genesis of the tenement, and the formation of racial minority groups in the slums.

MAKROPOULOS SECRET, THE (1925), by Karel Čapek. See R.U.R., by Karel Čapek.

MALADE IMAGINAIRE, LE (1673), by Molière. In *The Imaginary Invalid*, as in *The Physician in Spite of Himself* (q.v.), Molière vigorously attacks quackery in medicine. Argan, a wealthy hypochondriac, enjoys ill health, employs doctors and apothecaries, and doses himself with all sorts of nostrums— much to the disgust of the amusing and vigorous servant, Toinette, who is the backbone of the family. His pretty second wife, Béline, caters to his whims because she is interested in his money. She wants him to put both his daughters in a convent. But Argan decides to marry the eldest, Angélique, to the nephew of Monsieur Purgon, his doctor, so that he will always have a doctor in the family. The nephew, Thomas Diafoirus, is pompous and ridiculous, an echo of his father, Monsieur Diafoirus, also a doctor. But Angélique has met a young man, Cléante; when Argan first mentions the subject of matrimony she is most agreeable—until she discovers her father's intentions. In the meantime Béline has Argan draw up a will in her own favor. Thomas calls to ask for Angélique's hand, recites long, flowery, carefully prepared speeches, and presents Angélique with his thesis on the circulation of the blood. To save the situation Toinette disguises herself as a famous new doctor and prescribes cutting off Argan's arm and ear; this leaves him doubtful of the judgment of doctors. Then, when Argan puts wife and elder daughter to the test, the motives of each become clear, even to him, and Argan consents to the marriage of Cléante and Angélique.

MALE ANIMAL, THE (1940), by James Thurber and Elliot Nugent. See THURBER, JAMES.

MALQUERIDA, LA (1913), by Jacinto Benavente y Martínez. See PASSION FLOWER, THE, by Jacinto Martínez.

MAMBA'S DAUGHTERS (1929), by DuBose Heyward. See PORGY, by DuBose Heyward.

MAN AND MASSES (1921), by Ernst Toller. *Man and Masses* is the most distinguished of the revolutionary dramas by the late Ernst Toller, in his lifetime one of the most brilliant of political exiles from Nazi Germany. The play is an expression of Toller's views on the violence and ironic ruthlessness of revolution. A liberal woman is an active leader in the revolt of the workers against a war being waged for imperialistic ends by the State. The success of the rebellion is such that the workers, seeing a greater victory easily in their grasp, wish to pursue their struggle into an outright violent revolution. The woman leader will no longer stand with them in this expansion of their original purpose. She is cast into prison, refuses to accept deliverance by force, and when the revolution is crushed, ironically dies at the hand of the State as its instigator. *Man and Masses* was produced in this country by the Theatre Guild in the 1920's. Other plays by Toller, in the same expressionistic vein, were *Machine-Wreckers* (1923) and *Hoppla! We Live* (1928). While imprisoned in 1923 because of his part in the abortive Bavarian Revolution after World War I, Ernst Toller wrote a series of poems, published under the title *The Swallow-book* (1924).

MAN AND SUPERMAN (1903), by George Bernard Shaw. Shaw has taken his idea of the Superman from Nietzsche and has made use of the character of Don Juan, but has made him a revolutionist in love with a moral. Ann Whitefield's father has made a will naming as her guardian, at her own request, John Tanner, a young revolutionist. Ann, who is a pretty English girl, is in love with John and wants to marry him. Extremely determined, Ann usually gets her own way but manages to hide her obstinacy. Tanner, however, is not fooled, and is furious when he hears he is her guardian. He has a bachelor's fear of marriage. When he realizes that Ann is after him, he decides to fly to Spain. While there, he has a dream in which he becomes Don Juan. In hell he meets Doña Ana of Mozart's opera, who resembles Ann, and the Statue, Doña Ana's father, who has come down from heaven because of its dullness. Doña Ana is furious at finding herself in hell, but Don Juan advises her that it is the true haven of seekers after happiness. He has a long argument with the Devil on war and marriage. He expounds on the Life Force which will draw two strangers into each other's arms. It is the Life Force which urges man to discover Truth, and impelled by the Life Force he finds his way to heaven and reality. Tanner is awakened by the arrival of a motor party. Ann has followed him to Spain. She announces that her mother wishes her to marry him. This her mother denies, and Tanner rejects her. However, Ann and the Life Force win out as the play ends.

MAN IN THE IRON MASK, THE (1847), by Alexandre Dumas, *père*. See THREE MUSKETEERS, THE, by Alexandre Dumas, *père*.

MAN OF FEELING, THE (1771), by Henry Mackenzie. Harley journeys to London to lease the property adjacent to his neighbor, Walton, whose daughter Harley loves. His many experiences along the route include being swindled by gamblers; visiting the horrible Bedlam Hospital for the insane; and dining with a misanthrope who airs the ills of the world. He rescues Miss Atkins from a brothel and takes her home. He also exposes the East India Company's cruel treatment of its people. On returning home, he is stricken ill by the report that Miss Walton is engaged to marry another. Even her profession of love fails to save his life. His motives are well directed, but he is the victim of too keen a "sensibility," an emotion which was greatly in vogue at the time this novel was written.

MAN OF MODE, THE (1676), by Sir George Etherege. The theme of this comedy of manners is pungently expressed by the cynical Dorimant: "Next to the coming to a good understanding with a new Mistress, I love a quarrel with an old one." Dorimant is a well-mannered, witty, heartless man of the world. His preoccupation with his mistresses absorbs his working and leisure hours. First he has the burdensome Mrs. Loveit for his bachelor companionship, but meeting the gay Bellinda he decides to jilt the former. To her successor the deposed mistress remarks bitterly: "There's nothing but falsehood and impertinence in this world, all men are villains or fools; take example from my misfortune, Bellinda; if thou wouldst be happy, give thyself wholly up to goodness." Bellinda's fortunes also decline when Dorimant meets the sharp-tongued heiress, Harriet. The latter is hard to win, but Doriman unscrupulously succeeds. There is considerable farce introduced into the action by Sir Fopling Flutter, the Frenchified Englishman who struts and attitudinizes.

MAN OF PROPERTY, THE (1906), by John Galsworthy. See FORSYTE SAGA, THE, by John Galsworthy.

MAN POSSESSED (1927), by William Rose Benét. See BENÉT, WILLIAM ROSE.

MAN, THE BEAST AND VIRTUE, THE (1919), by Luigi Pirandello. See PIRANDELLO, LUIGI.

MAN WHO CAME TO DINNER, THE (1939), by Moss Hart and George Kaufman. See WOOLLCOTT, ALEXANDER.

MAN WHO DIED TWICE, THE (1924), by Edwin Arlington Robinson. See ROBINSON, EDWIN ARLINGTON.

MAN WHO MADE FRIENDS WITH HIMSELF, THE (1949), by Christopher Morley. See MORLEY, CHRISTOPHER.

MAN WITHOUT A COUNTRY, THE (1863), by Edward Everett Hale. This long short-story concerns Philip Nolan, a young officer of the United States Army who is tried for the Aaron Burr conspiracy. During the court-martial he exclaims, "Damn the United States! I wish I may never hear of the United States again!" The court thereupon sentences him to live out his life on a naval vessel, and never hear news of the United States. The story recounts the mental torments of the countryless prisoner, who after fifty-seven years finally learns that his nation is thriving, and dies happy. Although this tale is fictitious, Hale, who is remembered principally for it, also wrote the complementary novelette, *Philip Nolan's Friends* (1867), a true account.

A satirical fantasy in strong contrast to these patriotic pieces is *My Double and How He Undid Me* (1868). This take-off on the contemporary preoccupation with dual personality concerns the lazy Reverend Frederic Ingham, who has his impersonator do all his chores. Unfortunately, the double confuses everything.

MAN'S FATE (1933), by André Malraux. This tense and violent novel is based on the actual Communist uprising in Shanghai in 1927. Under the leadership of men like the half-breed Kyo and the Russian Katov, local Communists seize a shipload of arms, take over the police stations, precipitate a general strike, and seem on the point of making the city a Communist stronghold. But the International, for reasons of long-range policy, refuses to support the revolt and orders a compromise with Chiang Kai-shek's Nationalists, who are strongly backed by European business interests represented by the tycoon Ferral. For the local leaders this means tragedy; the cause to which they are committed has sacrificed them to its own inscrutable purposes. The individualist Ch'en revolts against party discipline and dies in an effort to murder Chiang Kai-shek. Kyo and Katov feel that they have no choice but to make their deaths an example of the human dignity to which—because they believe that only revolution can give it to the masses of Asia—they have dedicated their lives; the nature of their dilemma and the manner in which they accept their destiny give them something of the stature of tragic heroes. Surviving at the end of the story are Clappique, the absurd character who engineered the seizure of the arms at the beginning of the revolt but who has proved too reckless to be otherwise useful; Hemmelrich, who, ironically, has always wanted to die for the cause; and such nonbelligerents as Kyo's father and the "intellectual" Gisors.

This story, which has been variously interpreted according to the political complexion of the critics, is the best known of a series which includes *The Conquerors* (1928), *The Royal Way* (1930), *Days of Wrath* (1935), *Man's Hope* (1936), and the still untranslated *Noyers de l'Altenburg* (1943), all deeply influenced by Nietzsche and Dostoevsky and preoccupied with finding a new meaning in human life.

MAN'S HOPE (1937), by André Malraux. See MAN'S FATE, by André Malraux.

MANETTE SALOMON (1867), by Edmond and Jules de Goncourt. See JOURNALS, by Edmond and Jules de Goncourt.

MANFRED (1817), by George Gordon, Lord Byron. This dramatic poem in rhymed and unrhymed verse owes something to the Faust legend. The scene is the Alps, where Manfred summons up spirits to help him forget some blot in his past. They can do nothing for him, and in desperation he tries to jump from a cliff, but is restrained by a chamois hunter. The Witch of the Alps hears his incoherent confession. In the Hall of Arimanes evil spirits bring to him the phantom of Astarte, whom he has wronged, and she prophesies an end of his earthly ills on the morrow. At the appointed time spirits come for him, but he dismisses them and dies.

MANHATTAN TRANSFER (1925), by John Dos Passos. See U.S.A., by John Dos Passos.

MANN, HEINRICH (1871–   ). The influence of Heinrich Mann on the younger German writers of the Weimar Republic was for a while almost greater than the literary impact of his more celebrated younger brother Thomas. A relentless foe of militarism and Fascism, Heinrich Mann was the last president of the Writers' Section of the Prussian Academy; he fled Hitler in 1933, continued his fight against Nazism in French exile, and now lives in America. The most powerful social satirist of the Kaiser's Germany and one of the sharpest pamphleteers in German, he has always been an international-minded left-wing protagonist of a new European humanism. His novel *Small Town Tyrant* (1904), which served as the model for Marlene Dietrich's celebrated motion picture vehicle "The Blue Angel," is a merciless exposure of high school life in imperial Germany. The hero of *The Patrioteer* (1918), the manufacturer Diederich Hessling, is an ironically reduced satirical portrait of Wilhelm II. In addition to Mann's many other books, there are two historical novels about Henry IV, written in exile: *Young Henry of Navarre* (1935) and *Henry, King of France* (1938). In addition to being a satirist, Heinrich Mann is a brilliant essayist and one of the master stylists of the German language.

MANN, THOMAS (1875–   ). Born in Lübeck on the Baltic Sea, the son of a North German city senator and wholesale merchant and of a partly Portuguese mother, young Thomas Mann left high school at sixteen and after the death of his father followed his family to Munich, where he remained for many years. After a brief interlude as a business clerk he devoted himself to literature, became an editorial staff member of *Simplicissimus,* Germany's most famous satirical-political weekly under the Kaiser, spent a year in Italy with his older writer brother Heinrich, and published in 1901 his first novel, *Buddenbrooks* (q.v.), which established him at once as an important author. The romantic theme of artist versus bourgeois occupied Thomas Mann until World War I. Always strongly autobiographical, the young, happily married family man dealt with the problem of the non-bourgeois outsider and ordinary society in his next novel, *Royal Highness* (1909), the romantic love story of the lonely crippled German prince Klaus Heinrich and the American millionaire's daughter Imma Spoelman. Other famous prose works of the same period were *Tonio Kröger* (1903) and *Death in Venice* (1911), both masterful examples of the modern German novella—the short novel—and both reflections of the same conflict: art and beauty against ordinary and normal life.

In his next great novel, *The Magic Mountain* (q.v.), Thomas Mann reached the climax of a development that had transformed the bourgeois conservative German prose writer into one of the leading European humanists. Mann's development toward Western democracy is reflected in the leading position he assumed in the German Republic after 1918. Next to Hauptmann he was the most honored and representative German author until 1933. In 1929 he received the Nobel Prize in Literature. Sensing the approaching danger of Fascism, he publicly opposed Hitler as early as 1930 in his famous Berlin speech, "Appeal to Reason." The advent of Nazism found him on a vacation trip to Switzerland, from which he never returned to Germany. He is now an American citizen.

The fruit of Mann's first decade of exile is the gigantic tetralogy *Joseph and His Brothers* (q.v.), a cycle of four novels centering in the Biblical Joseph of the Old Testament. Feeling the need of a rest after the third volume, the author worked on a novel about the aging Goethe, which was published under the title *The Beloved Returns* (1939) in America. The plot concerns the visit of Charlotte Kestner of *Werther* fame to the city of Weimar, the residence of the highly honored old Privy Counsellor Goethe. Much that Thomas Mann had to say about literature and Germany he pronounced here through the mouth of the German master, for whom he had felt a special affinity ever since the relation of artist and citizen became one of the major problems of his own existence. It is not surprising, therefore, that the shadow of Goethe is still to be seen in the title of Mann's latest published novel, *Doctor Faustus* (q.v.).

MANON LESCAUT (1731), by Abbé Prévost. Manon is a young harlot with whom the Chevalier des Grieux falls madly in love. He gives up his studies to follow her. They elope. Manon shortly proves faithless. The rest of the story details Manon's infidelities and des Grieux' inability to give her up. In a way Manon loves him, but not as much as she loves the luxuries other lovers provide. When finally she is arrested as a common prostitute and transported to the colony of Louisiana, des Grieux, who has already given up fortune, family and friends, goes with her. He almost commits murder for her sake. After her death he is unable to pick up the pieces of a ruined life. The story, told in the first person after Manon's death, is a masterpiece of pathos, and has enjoyed remarkable longevity both as a novel and as a well-known opera.

MANSFIELD PARK (1814), by Jane Austen. See NORTHANGER ABBEY, by Jane Austen.

MANYOSHIU, THE (750). An anthology of Japanese poems. The *Manyoshiu* (Collection of Ten Thousand Leaves), compiled during the Nara (710–794) is considered the greatest literary monument of the famous eighth century, the Golden Age of Japanese poetry. The form is known as *tanka*, or short song, consisting of five lines, 31 syllables in all, arranged: 5,7,5,7,7. There is no rhyme or accent; each line must end in one of the five vowels or n. The following is a typical *tanka*:

"Na wo to wa wo	"Men have dissevered
Hito zo saku naru	You and me, you and me!
Ide wagimi	O come, my lover!
Hito no naka goto	The meddling words of men
Kiki kosu na yume"	Dream not of hearing!"

In contrast to the *tanka*, there are *naga-uta* or long songs which originated in imitation of Chinese and Korean poems. There are only 324 *naga-uta* in this collection, and 4173 *tanka*. The *naga-uta* form, in which 5- and 7-syllable lines alternate, was found to be not successful. Therefore most of the Japanese poets practice the *tanka* form. Although a few of these songs may have been written in the fourth or fifth centuries, most of them are from the period 670 to 759. The major poets of this collection are Kakinimoto no Hitomaro and Yamabe no Akahito.

Kamo Mabuchi, a well-known Japanese critic, writing in 1770, says of this anthology that it may be considered as "a real record of the feelings of the men and women who wrote its songs, and thus throws a valuable light on that period."

The Manyoshiu was translated by Basil Hall Chamberlain in 1880 as *Classical Poetry of Japan*.

MARBLE FAUN, THE (1860), by Nathaniel Hawthorne. See HOUSE OF THE SEVEN GABLES, THE, by Nathaniel Hawthorne.

"MARCO MILLIONS" (1927), by Eugene O'Neill. See MOURNING BECOMES ELECTRA, by Eugene O'Neill.

MARDI (1849), by Herman Melville. See MOBY-DICK, by Herman Melville.

MARGARET OGILVY (1896), by Sir James M. Barrie. See BARRIE, SIR JAMES MATTHEW.

MARIA MAGDALENA (1846), by Christian Friedrich Hebbel. See GYGES AND HIS RING, by Christian Friedrich Hebbel.

MARIE ANTOINETTE (1932), by Stefan Zweig. See ZWEIG, STEFAN.

MARIE GRUBBE, A LADY OF THE SEVENTEENTH CENTURY (1876), by Jens Peter Jacobsen. Based on objective research, this Danish historical novel is the author's chief work, the background of which is a rich, accurate, colorful description of the baroque period in Denmark and elsewhere. Even dialect is employed. It is, in masterly prose, a super-realistic product, where inborn characteristics, upbringing, and milieu are even more important than the characters themselves. The central figure is a nobleman's daughter, an historical person, who after the death of her first love married first Ulrik Frederick Gyldenlöve, a King's son; second, a middle-class official; and, finally, after an affair with Sti Hög, a humble ferryman, Soren. Her life is predominantly sad and tempestuous, but she possesses natural instincts of real love, and finds some happiness as the wife of Soren. He beats her occasionally, but he had once tried to commit murder to prove his love for Marie, and she can never forget that.

Another work by Jacobsen that is famous in European literature is *Niels Lyhne* (1880), "the so-called Bible of atheism," a problem novel.

MARIEKEN OF NIEUMEGHEN (ca. end 15th c.), Anonymous. See MEDIAEVAL FLEMISH PLAYS.

MARIUS THE EPICUREAN (1885), by Walter Pater. Depicting Roman life in the second century, under the rule of Marcus Aurelius, this philosophical work is the story of Marius, from his school life in Pisa, his search for a philosophy, his Epicureanism, to his death as virtually a Christian martyr. Manners of the day and social and political life are portrayed. Much of the book describes the philosophies of the times: Cynicism, Epicureanism (Cyrenaicism), Stoicism, and the philosophies of Plato and Socrates. Marius meets Cornelius; they travel to Rome, where the boy discovers Christianity and is impressed by the mass he hears in the home of Cecilia. Cornelius and Marius are arrested. Marius arranges for his friend's escape. On a long march the Roman soldiers force him to make, Marius contracts a fever and dies, tended by Christians.

MARJORIE DAW AND OTHER STORIES (1873), by Thomas Bailey Aldrich. See STORY OF A BAD BOY, THE, by Thomas Bailey Aldrich.

MARK TWAIN'S AMERICA (1932), by Bernard DeVoto. See DeVOTO, BERNARD.

MARKO THE KING'S SON (ca. 1389), a cycle. The two cycles of *Marko the King's Son (of Prilep)* and the *Battle of Kosovo* in 1389 are two of the finest of the cycles of Serb epic poetry, although they have never been organized into long epics and have remained as series of individual songs. The cycle of *Kosovo* describes how Tsar Lazar preferred a heavenly to an earthly kingdom, and fought and died with his cavalry at Kosovo. The cycle of *Marko,* which is even more widely popular throughout the Balkans, describes the exploits of the son of King Vukashin. The real Marko was killed in 1393, but in legend he has been transformed into a splendid hero without fear or reproach. Mounted on his wonder horse Sharats (Dapple), he moves around the Balkans as the defender of the abused and enslaved Christians. Both cycles picture the culture of the Balkans in the fourteenth century, and show the Serb genius at its best. There is hardly any other epic poetry which has so consistently been purged by its oral custodians of all traces of barbarism and savagery. Marko has become the embodiment of unselfish service to his fellow men, and with his wife, Helen, and his mother, Evrosine, he is brought into contact with those leaders of the Balkan peoples like Sibinjanin Yanko (Hunyadi Janos) who were struggling to form a coalition which would check the triumphant advance of Islam into Europe. Both cycles have often been translated into English (as by Noyes and Bacon, *Heroic Ballads of Servia,* 1913, and D. H. Low, 1922). They are among the best examples of an art which has won the commendation of the greatest modern poets—among them Goethe, who was amazed at the revelation of the artistry and idealism of the Serb bards.

MARMION, A TALE OF FLODDEN FIELD (1808), by Sir Walter Scott. Scott's forte in this poem is description, and the final battle in which the hero-villain is killed is unrivaled in his other poems. Constance de Beverley has broken her vows as a nun in order to follow Lord Marmion, whom she loves, disguised as a page. But she is betrayed to her convent and doomed to be walled up alive. Meanwhile Marmion seeks to win the wealthy Lady Clare, having left his rival Sir Ralph de Wilton for dead in the lists. Wilton survives, and dressed as a palmer uncovers the machinations of Marmion, and fights on the English side at Flodden Field, where Marmion dies a heroic death. Wilton and Clare are wed. One interlude in this poem is the famous song "Lochinvar."

MARRIAGE À LA MODE (1673), by John Dryden. After a five-year absence from the Court of Sicily at Palermo, Palamede returns and meets Doralice, the wife of his dearest friend, Rhodophil. Palamede falls in love with the lady, not knowing her true identity. Rhodophil later confesses to his friend that he has been unhappily married for two years, and has taken the affected coquette, Melantha, as his mistress. By dramatic coincidence, the latter has been promised to Palamede by her father. Palamede cannot endure her brassy, shallow pretensions, just as Rhodophil cannot tolerate Doralice's sophisticated, chattering ways. The two gentlemen at last grow jealous of each other, thinking their respective mates must possess some hitherto unnoticed attraction. In the final act of this comedy, they finally decide to stick by their lawful loves and so abandon their conquests without rancor.

MARRIAGE OF FIGARO, THE (1784), by Pierre Augustin Caron de Beaumarchais. This sequel to *The Barber of Seville* manifests a profound change in the attitude and intention of Beaumarchais. He has reversed the relationships of his characters, turning a one-time romantic hero into a villain. Count Almaviva here becomes a contemptible figure. Figaro, his loyal henchman of a former day, is about to marry a maid-in-waiting of the Countess. Almaviva, through a series of unscrupulous tricks, attempts to prevent the marriage and secure the girl as his mistress. After a hard battle of wits, the wily Figaro once more triumphs and the play ends happily.

The revolutionary significance, which may seem slight and obscure at this long range, was very real in the circumstances, and lay in the thoroughgoing exposure of the extreme corruption of the aristocracy contrasted to the virtues of the lower classes. The first performance caused riots, and the play was promptly suppressed by the tottering government of Louis XVI.

MARRIAGE OF HEAVEN AND HELL, THE (ca. 1793), by William Blake. Mystical and revolutionary in nature, magnificently illustrated by the poet himself, this work is an attempt to plumb the depths of the mystery of Good and Evil. Blake states his philosophy explicitly: "Without Contraries is no progression. Attraction and Repulsion, Reason and Energy, Love and Hate, are necessary to Human existence. From these Contraries spring what the religious call Good and Evil. Good is the passive that obeys Reason, Evil is the active springing from Energy. Good is Heaven. Evil is Hell." This theme, explained by arguments, proverbs and aphorisms, is continued in five related prose compositions, each called *A Memorable Fancy*.

MARSH ISLAND, A (1885), by Sarah Orne Jewett. See COUNTRY OF THE POINTED FIRS, THE, by Sarah Orne Jewett.

MARSMAN, HENDRIK (1899–1940). Of the modern generation of poets, Marsman has found more than anyone else the ear and the heart of the people of the Netherlands. The struggle for existence, interpreted in his poems, is the reflection of a typical Dutch conflict: the contradiction between the worthlessness of sinful man, as accepted by Calvinist tradition, and the beauty and glory of the pagan, earthly life, everlastingly discovered anew by the individual. The titles of Marsman's collections of his poems are sufficiently characteristic: *Paradise Regained* (1927) and *Tempel en Kruis* (1940); of the latter, the cycle of poems "De Zodiac" was translated by A. J. Barnouw in *The Sewanee Review,* April, 1947, and his last poem "The Sea," by E. Prins and C. M. MacInnes in *War Poetry from Occupied Holland* (Bristol, 1945). Again and again the desperation over the sins of the mortal body and the fear of death as punishment are repeated in his fiercely molded poetry (as expressed in his epic poems "Breeroo" and "Don Juan"); again and again he rises out of despondency into a jubilation over the glorious beauty of the universe, enjoyed by all the senses: "De Toren van Babel," "De Wijnpers," "Paestum," and "De Boot van Dionysos." As essayist, he has striven to make this fierce acceptance of life (so-called "vitalism") into the foundation and direction of his own younger generation. He was conscious of the dangers inherent in it, after the rise of Fascism, which he resisted with loathing and vehemence.

MARTA OF THE LOWLANDS (1897), by Angel Guimerá. When this Catalan play was first staged in an English translation by Mrs. Fiske in New York (1903) it created a sensation. It is a powerful rural tragedy, and has no equal in the history of the theater of Catalonia.

Marta, an orphan peasant girl, while yet a child is forced to become the mistress of the villainous landlord Sebastian. Sebastian, desirous of acquiring additional wealth, schemes to marry a wealthy woman. He is still in love with Marta, however, and formulates a plan whereby he can keep her as his mistress and still marry. To expedite matters, he arranges for a brutish yet simple goatherd, Manelich, to marry Marta. She at first refuses, but is forced into submission. In time she realizes that Manelich is not only an earthy, kind fellow, but is deeply in love with her. Marta falls in love with Manelich and confesses to her husband the reason for their marriage. Enraged, Manelich revolts against Sebastian, and plans to flee to the mountains with Marta. Sebastian, however, has Manelich driven off the land and then attempts to take Marta for himself. Manelich returns in time to save Marta. He kills Sebastian and escapes with his wife to the mountains.

MARTIN CHUZZLEWIT, THE LIFE AND ADVENTURES OF (1844), by Charles Dickens. In this novel, wealthy old Martin Chuzzlewit, young Martin's grandfather; the old man's brother, Anthony; Anthony's son, the villain, Jonas; crafty Seth Pecksniff, architect; Seth's daughters, Charity and Mercy; and Mary Graham, an orphan raised by old Mr. Chuzzlewit, are the central characters. Young Martin loves Mary, but Mr. Chuzzlewit, embittered by the greed and selfishness of his family and suspecting that he detects similar traits in Martin, has the boy turned, almost penniless, out of his position as pupil to Mr. Pecksniff, who is Martin's hypocritical cousin. Martin and his loyal friend, Mark Tapley, travel to America, where Martin becomes architect for the Eden Land Corporation. In this fraudulent enterprise he loses everything. He contracts a fever of which he almost dies (this section of Dickens' narrative was highly distasteful to his American public). Martin returns home, cured by his hardships of the incipient selfishness his grandfather had recognized in him. In the meantime, Mr. Chuzzlewit and Mary have gone to live with Mr. Pecksniff, who reveals his true character by trying to force Mary to marry him. Mr. Chuzzlewit denounces him and accepts Martin once more. Martin and Mary are finally joined. Another plot deals with the unscrupulous, cruel Jonas. He bullies his wife, Mercy; virtually murders his own father; kills a man who has threatened and blackmailed him; and finally, fearing exposure, commits suicide. The nurse, Mrs. Sarah Gamp, with her umbrella and her imaginary friend Mrs. Harris, is one of Dickens' most unforgettable creations.

MARTIN EDEN (1909), by Jack London. See LONDON, JACK.

MARTÍN FIERRO (1872, 1879), by Jose Hernández. With *Martín Fierro* the gauchesque tradition of Argentine poetry reached its apogee. Hernández knew intimately the pampas and its gauchos and became their staunchest defender. In his masterpiece he dramatizes the plight of a good gaucho, Martín Fierro, who is taken away from his family and treated abominably by army officers. He is given no pay, no food, and is finally thrown against the cruel Indians. After years of indescribable anguish and misery Martín deserts the army, and becomes a gaucho *matrero* (wicked), getting into brawls, murdering two men, and, as a last resort, joining the Indians. Thus ends Part I, which was published in 1872 and had a phenomenal success, finding its way to a wide audience comprising gauchos as well as men of letters. The condition of the gauchos did improve, and no small credit should be ascribed to *Martín Fierro*. Encouraged by the reception and its results, Hernández wrote a second part in 1879, in which Martín returns to his pago, meets his two sons, young men now, and begins life anew.

Martín Fierro remains one of the outstanding literary achievements of Latin American literature and one that illustrates its socially minded trend. Rooted in the American soil, it exhibits a genuine, deeply felt milieu and a profound knowledge of its inhabitants.

MARTYRS, THE (1809), by François René de Chateaubriand. See ATALA, by François René de Chateaubriand.

MARTYRDOM OF ALI, THE. Analogous to the Christian Passion of Christ is the Shi'ite Persian Passion of Hasan and Husain. In dramaturgical form this Mohammed sectarian tragedy, rejected by the orthodox Mussulmans of Turkey and Arab countries, is centered in the slaying of Husain and Hasan, the grandsons of Mohammed the Prophet of Allah, in the Massacre of Karbala in 680. In this terrible incident of bestial vengeance, the favorite grandchildren of the Prophet of Islam were butchered, together with all the other adult males of their household. Their father, Caliph Ali, had been slain by his enemies nineteen years before. The death of Ali and his two sons, in the estimation of the Shi'ites, was a deliberate sacrifice for the salvation of their co-religionists, a vicarious atonement for their sins. Accordingly, *The Martyrdom of Ali*, which is only one section of *The Miracle Play of Hasan and Husain*, has exalted ritual significance for the Persian Moslems. The anniversary of the Massacre of Karbala is commemorated with the performance of many of the fifty-two pageants that round out the early struggles of Mohammed and his kin to establish the new religion in a hostile world. *The Martydom of Ali* is one of the most popular of these dramatic works. It is played with convincing sincerity by the pious believers just as the Passion of Christ is performed to this very day in Italy and Spain by devout peasants.

The continuous performance of the fifty-two pageants takes ten days. The performers and audience alike are moved to tears and angry outcries. The women wail and beat their breasts, crying: "Ya Ali! Ya Hasan! Ai Husain, Husain Shah!" The performances are preceded by processions through the streets during which many of the worshippers expiate symbolically with self-inflicted wounds for their failure to come to the aid of Ali, Husain and Hasan. Holy water is handed out to the spectators in symbolism of the martyrs' terrible thirst.

The first scene of *The Martyrdom of Ali* describes the poverty in which the Prophet of Allah and his family lived during the first years of his divine mission. Most Arabs still bitterly oppose him and the glory of Allah languishes. Scene two presents the death of Mohammed and Omar's violent efforts to force the devoted Ali to surrender to him his right to the caliphate. The last scene, poignantly expressive, depicts the stubborn refusal of Ali to cede his mandate given him by the Prophet, and his inevitable martydom. The miracle happens when Ali is joyously received by Mohammed in Heaven, and, as a reward for his uncompromising fidelity, is appointed to be forevermore the holy intercessor with God for the sins of his brethren in Islam.

MARVELOUS HISTORY OF MARY OF NIJMEGEN, A (15th c.), Anonymous. Translated by Professor Harry Morgan Ayres. See MEDIAEVAL FLEMISH PLAYS.

MARY OF SCOTLAND (1933), by Maxwell Anderson. See WHAT PRICE GLORY, by Maxwell Anderson and Laurence Stallings.

MARY STUART (1800), by Friedrich von Schiller. See SCHILLER, FRIEDRICH VON.

MASTER AND MAN (1895), by Count Leo Tolstoy. See DEATH OF IVAN ILYITCH, THE, by Count Leo Tolstoy.

MASTER BUILDER, THE (1892), by Henrik Ibsen. Solness, a prominent architect, has fought his way to the top ruthlessly. He now employs Brovik, an old architect who had given him his start. Brovik's son Ragnar is his draughtsman and Ragnar's fiancée is his bookkeeper. Solness, fearful of Ragnar's ability, has won the heart of his fiancée. Aline, the wife of Solness, has been ailing since her house burned down, the conflagration killing her two boys. Solness guiltily realizes that the burning of the house had been providential in the fostering of his success. He knew of a flaw in the chimney, and had long hoped the place would burn. His conduct toward the Broviks also causes him uneasy moments. Hilda, a girl who represents the younger generation, enters his life at this point. She inspires him to change his attitude toward the Broviks. His new house has just been completed. Solness has a great fear of heights, but urged on by Hilda he carries a dedicatory wreath to a high tower of the house. On the tower, he loses his balance and falls to his death.

MASTER BUILDERS (1935), by Stefan Zweig. See ZWEIG, STEFAN.

MASTER OF BALLANTRAE, THE (1889), by Robert Louis Stevenson. This is the tragic story of enmity between two brothers, as narrated by John Mackellar, steward of Ballantrae. When Prince Charlie lands in 1745, the Master, James Durie, enlists on the side of the Stuarts, while Henry rides for King George. After Culloden the Master is reported dead, and Henry marries Alison Graeme, a kinswoman who had been destined for the Master, largely to replenish the estate with her fortune. But an Irish soldier Burke reports that actually the Master had escaped to sea, and soon those at home get letters from him demanding money. For seven years Henry drains the estate to satisfy the Master, until Mrs. Durie, who does not yet realize that she still loves James, learns of the secret and stops further outlays. The Master thereupon returns and insults his brother. They duel, and Henry leaves him for dead, but James has a charmed life and the "corpse" vanishes. When yet again the Master pays a visit, the persecuted family sail for New York, only to be trailed by their enemy into the wilderness. Henry's brain has been affected by these troubles, and it was rumored that he tried for a last time to have his brother killed. But an Indian servant buries the Master alive, meaning to save him afterward through an Oriental trick of suspended animation. Henry's party arrives on the scene as James's body is being lifted from the grave. The eyelids flutter, and Henry drops dead at the movement. But James has also died. The fraternal enemies are buried side by side.

Weir of Hermiston (written 1894) was left unfinished by Stevenson at his death, but contains some of his best writing. It tells of Archie Weir and his love for Christina. Archie has been banished by his stern father, the judge, to the solitude of the village of Hermiston, where the two lovers meet.

MASTER PATHELIN (ca. 1464), Anonymous. Master Pathelin, a dishonest small-town lawyer, cheats his draper out of a piece of cloth by pretending that he is sick whenever the bill is presented. The draper now turns about, and to even accounts cheats a shepherd, Thibault Aignelet by name, out of a sheep. Thibault, no man to give up easily, has the draper into court and engages the wily Pathelin to take his case. Pathelin has Thibault feign stupidity and reply to all questions with the "baa" of a sheep. They win their case, but Pathelin meets his match. When he presents his bill to Thibault, the shepherd merely replies with the same sheeplike noise.

Thoroughly immoral, but distinguished by careful characterization and its use of what have since become the stock devices of dramatic farce, *Master Pathelin* is considered the first masterpiece of the French comic tradition.

MASTERSINGERS OF NUREMBERG, THE (1868), by Richard Wagner. See WAGNER, RICHARD.

MASTRO DON GESUALDO (1892), by Giovanni Verga. Giovanni Verga (1840–1922) owes his fame as a novelist to his descriptions of Sicilian life and characters, and the conspicuous place he gives to womanhood. *Mastro Don Gesualdo* describes the devotion of a pastoral woman, Diodata, to the man she loves with all obedience and blind passion, Don Gesualdo. The master, however, has for Diodata only an infatuation. After having possessed her, Don Gesualdo wants to marry instead a noble-born Signora of the town. Diodata is to be satisfied to become the wife of a lout who will act as a father for the master's children. Diodata makes this sacrifice only because Mastro Don Gesualdo desires it. Her devotion to him continues unlimited. When sickness reduces her beloved to solitude, Diodata is back at his bedside, giving the dying man the last signs of her affection. Another famous novel by Giovanni Verga, *Cavalleria Rusticana* (1884), was used by Mascagni as the subject for his opera of the same title.

MATHEMATICAL PRINCIPLES OF NATURAL PHILOSOPHY (1687), by Sir Isaac Newton. See PHILOSOPHIAE NATURALIS PRINCIPIA, by Sir Isaac Newton.

MATHEMATICAL WORKS (published 1849–1863), by Gottfried Wilhelm Leibnitz. See MATHEMATISCHE SCHRIFTEN, by Gottfried Wilhelm Leibnitz.

MATHEMATISCHE SCHRIFTEN (1849–1863) by Gottfried Wilhelm Leibnitz (1646–1716). The fame of Leibnitz as a philosopher has often obscured the fact that he was the greatest German mathematician before the time of Gauss. Mathematics in Germany had reached a very low point when he entered the University of Leipzig; yet Leibnitz, a youthful genius, in 1666 published a short treatise, *De Arte Combinatoria,* in which he anticipated the ideas of Boole (1854) on the formal laws of logic and algebra. After meeting Huygens at Paris in 1672, Leibnitz undertook the study of higher mathematics, and in the study of Cartesian geometry he was attracted by the problem of finding the tangent to a curve. It was only a year later that he saw the connection between problems of tangency and the determination of the areas of curved figures, a discovery which makes him one of the two founders of the calculus. Newton had invented the method of fluxions some years earlier; but the work of Leibnitz has been recognized, following a bitter quarrel over priority, as independent of that of Newton. The first published account of Newton's calculus appeared in the *Principia* (q.v.) of 1687; but Leibnitz in 1684 and 1686 had anticipated this by the publication of two papers on the calculus in the *Acta Eruditorium.* Leibnitz intended to write a complete treatise on the subject of infinitesimal analysis, but this project was not carried out. Most of his contributions to mathematics are therefore to be found in short articles published in learned periodicals and in his voluminous correspondence. Leibnitz had many enthusiastic mathematical disciples who spread his methods throughout the continent. During the eighteenth century his notations were not used in England; but ultimately the superiority of the Leibnitzian terminology was recognized, and now it has been universally adopted.

The mathematical correspondence of Leibnitz was collected and edited by C. I. Gerhardt under the title *Mathematische Schriften.* This seven-volume work, published in 1849–1863, constitutes series II of *Leibnizens Gesammelte Werke,* edited by H. Pertz. The first volume includes correspondence with the British scientists Collins, Oldenburg, and Newton; the second contains letters exchanged with Huygens and L'Hopital, the latter being the author of the first published textbook on the calculus. Volume III, comprising almost a thousand pages, covers the correspondence of Leibnitz with the Bernoullis; and volume IV includes letters exchanged with Wallis in England, Varignon in France, Grandi in Italy, Hermann in Switzerland, and Tschirnhaus in Germany. The final three volumes contain Leibnitz' mathematical studies, the last one including also a supplement to his correspondence with Christian Wolf. Probably no other mathematician can boast a correspondence as wide and influential as that found in the *Mathematische Schriften* of Leibnitz.

MATHER, COTTON (1663–1728). Cotton Mather entered Harvard at twelve, became minister of the Second Church in Boston, and interested himself in political affairs. He believed that his heritage fitted him for Massachusetts leadership in the spirit of his nonprogressive forefathers. But Cotton Mather's conservatism during a period of progress caused the frustration of his aspirations.

He wrote prolifically. During the Salem witchcraft trials, which he endorsed, he published *Memorable Providences, Relating to Witchcrafts and Possessions* (1689), the study of a victim; *The Wonders of the Invisible World*

(1693), trial narratives and observations about devils; and *Magnalia Christi Americana* (1702), which objected, at least, to methods employed in the notorious trials. Punctuating his works on science, history and philosophy—for he was one of the greatest of contemporary scholars—were many pieces of extreme religious zeal. He also left an enormous diary.

Increase Mather (1639–1723), Cotton's father, also a Harvard-educated teacher in the Second Church in Boston, and intellectual leader of the colony, wrote about the Salem trials in *Cases of Conscience Concerning Evil Spirits* (1693). His disapproval was mainly for the use of supernatural evidence. Somewhat bigoted, Increase Mather was a rationalist; his books plumb the sacred and secular questions of the day.

MAURIZIUS CASE, THE (1928), by Jakob Wassermann. See CASPAR HAUSER, by Jakob Wassermann.

MAUVE DECADE, THE (1926), by Thomas Beer. *The Mauve Decade* is a fanciful canvas of American life at the close of the nineteenth century. A series of urbane and cynical anecdotes, involving famous personages from Oscar Wilde to Theodore Roosevelt, in illustrative incidents, reveal the foibles of the time—the theme being Whistler's jest, 'Mauve is just pink trying to be purple.'

Typical of Beer's early novels is *Sandoval* (1924), a romance of New York in 1870. *Stephen Crane* (1923) is a novelized biography of the author, whose fame the book aided substantially.

Thomas Beer also wrote a number of amusing short stories, collected in the popular *Mrs. Egg and Other Barbarians* (1933). Mrs. Egg, of the title story, is a lovable lady whose chief pleasures are eating and philosophizing.

MAX HAVELAAR (1860), by Multatuli (Edward Douwes Dekker). With this book, published in 1860, Multatuli (1820–1887) aroused storms of enthusiasm and indignation. His purpose was twofold: first, a protest against the oppression of the Javanese population by its native princes and against the inertia of the Netherlands government in relation to these abuses; second, to justify his own conduct as an official of that government, which had disowned him when he wanted to set bounds to the arbitrariness of these Indonesian princes in the region administered by him. According to his view, the weak policy of the government was a direct consequence of the innermost nature of the Netherlands people, that showed interest in the Indies only when it could profit financially. Therefore, first and foremost, Multatuli attacks in his book the vulgar, materialistic merchant, for whom counting money and making more money is the highest vocation and virtue. With biting sarcasm he has characterized this narrow-minded, self-conscious section of the human race in the coffee broker Droogstoppel; the incomparably clever delineation of this super-respectable "business-is-business" man gives to the book its enduring value, even after the main issues have been outlived.

Multatuli tells how Droogstoppel meets an old schoolmate, who had become a writer and who delivers a large bundle of manuscripts at his home. In this collection the broker finds the story of Max Havelaar: how he, as Assistant-

Resident had been assigned to the Javanese region of Lebak and how he had attempted to persuade the native princes to co-operate with him to increase the welfare and prosperity of the native population—only to be broken by the corrupt native princes and his superior colonial officers.

Many of Multatuli's other literary creations are found in *Ideën* (1862–1877). These "ideas" appeared in installments, at irregular times. Among much that is unripe, they contain brilliant conceptions and scintillating thoughts. In this series appears *Vorstenschool* (1872; School for Princes), a drama in blank verse, often staged, and *Woutertje Pieterse* (1890), the auto-biography of Multatuli's youth in a petty middle class environment. Through his unabated struggle against a middle-class society, devoid of ideals, his attacks on bourgeois liberalism and its doctrines, and his clear-cut exposure of the causes of poverty, Multatuli has exerted great influence on the working class in the years of nascent socialism.

Translations: *Max Havelaar or the Coffee Auctions of the Dutch Trading Company,* translated from the original manuscript by Alphonse Nahuys (London, Hamilton, Adams and Co., 1868). *Max Havelaar or the Coffee Sales of the Netherlands Trading Company,* translated from the Dutch by W. Siebenhaar, with an introduction by D. H. Lawrence (New York and London, Alfred A. Knopf, 1927).

MAXIMS, THE (1665), by François, Duc de la Rochefoucauld. These 504 epigrams reveal an embittered man—and a great deal of truth about human nature. The Duke of La Rochefoucauld had been disappointed in politics and severely wounded in the *Fronde,* when the nobles of France revolted against the King. He was tired, with nothing to do and no future. Humanity was motivated, he could see, by self-interest; behind the most noble gestures were the most sordid motives. And since he had time to polish his style endlessly, he said so in a French which for sheer brilliance stands by itself.

MAYOR OF CASTERBRIDGE, THE (1886), by Thomas Hardy. This Victorian novel, typical of Hardy's pessimistic philosophy, in which "happiness was but the occasional episode in a general drama of pain," is set in Wessex, England, shortly before 1830. Young Michael Henchard, seeking work as a hay-trusser in Weydon-Priors, when the Fair is in full sway, stops to eat frumenty with his wife, Susan, and baby, Elizabeth-Jane. Despondent, and presently a little drunk, he auctions off his wife and child to a sailor, asserting they are only a drag on him. His wife warns him she will accept the results of the auction, and too stubborn to back down, he wakes in the morning to find his family gone. Unable to ascertain the sailor's name, he loses all trace of them. The falsely reported death of the sailor, Richard Newson, seventeen years later, brings Henchard's family in search of him. They find him mayor of Casterbridge. Elizabeth-Jane, sent by Susan to tell Henchard of their arrival, watches Henchard persuade clever young Donald Farfrae, passing through Casterbridge on his way to America, to stay as manager of his grain business. Henchard decides to remarry Susan, although he had been plan-ning to marry a woman in a neighboring town, who had been for some time his mistress. The remarriage brought comfort to Henchard and his family until the death of Susan within the same year. Meanwhile, Henchard, jealous of Farfrae's popularity and business acumen, has quarreled with him and stopped his courting of Elizabeth-Jane.

His wife's death reveals to Henchard that Elizabeth-Jane is really Newson's daughter, his own baby having died. Hurt by Henchard's sudden coldness, Elizabeth-Jane becomes a companion to Lucetta Templeman, Henchard's former mistress. Henchard begins to court Lucetta again. But it is Farfrae, again his rival, who wins her hand in marriage. Likewise Farfrae prospers in a business venture in which Henchard loses much of his money. For revenge Henchard reads to Farfrae many of Lucetta's old letters, only withholding her name. But the story becomes known that Henchard and Lucetta were once lovers; Lucetta, distraught by the disgrace and public ridicule of some local mummery, dies in childbirth.

Elizabeth-Jane, ignorant of the scandal and of Henchard's repentant attempt to bring Farfrae back to his dying wife, leaves him. She has discovered her real father Newson. She marries Farfrae, unable even on her wedding day to forgive Henchard his former deceit. When, remorseful, she seeks out Henchard a month later, she finds he has died in misery and poverty a half hour before her arrival.

MAYOR OF ZALAMEA, THE (1651), by Pedro Calderón de la Barca. The Spanish forces are moving westward to the conquest of Portugal (1578) when Captain Don Alvaro, a typical arrogant and licentious army man, finds lodgings in the house of the rich peasant Pedro Crespo. During the army's sojourn in Zalamea Crespo orders his daughter Isabel to remain in retirement in the upper rooms of the house. Curious to see the beautiful girl, Don Alvaro breaks into her room, but Crespo intervenes in the nick of time. He is about to punish Don Alvaro's daring when General Lope de Figueroa comes in and becomes enraged at a simple peasant taking justice in his own hands. The ensuing discussion between the gouty old General and the self-respecting peasant is admirable for its verve and vivacity; the two have much in common psychologically and become friends, and the General takes to Crespo's son, deciding to take him under his wing. However, when the Spanish army moves away, Don Alvaro takes Isabel by force, and after dishonoring her, leaves her in the forest. Crespo, who has just been appointed judge and mayor of Zalamea, arrests him. In vain he asks the Captain to repair his daughter's dishonor by marrying her. Although the General claims the prisoner as being under his jurisdiction, Crespo forces the Captain to marry his daughter and then condemns him to be hanged. King Philip not only absolves Crespo but makes him permanent mayor of Zalamea.

El Alcalde de Zalamea has been considered the "most perfect and best known among tragic plays." The sentiment of honor ("punto de honor"), so cherished by Spanish tradition, finds here vivid dramatization.

McTEAGUE (1899), by Frank Norris. *McTeague* is a naturalistic novel of contemporary middle and lower-class life in California, in which heredity and environment unleash a series of disasters. McTeague is the son of a mine boss and an ignorant but ambitious woman. After an apprenticeship with a quack, he opens a dental parlor in San Francisco, leading a coarse but not vicious life. He marries Trina Sieppe. When she wins $5,000 in a lottery, Marcus Schouler, a former suitor, exposes McTeague's malpractice out of jealous spite. McTeague is banned, and his household begins to deteriorate. He treats Trina, who has become miserly, with brutality, finally murdering her for her money. Escaping to Death Valley, he is followed by Schouler, who is killed after handcuffing himself to McTeague. McTeague then dies from thirst under the blazing sun.

MEASURE FOR MEASURE (ca. 1604; Folio, 1623), by William Shakespeare. The material for this play is drawn from Cinthio.

Measure for Measure is probably the most unjustly neglected of all the plays of Shakespeare. For years it has been relatively little read and seldom performed, yet it is one of the most quoted of the plays. This is possibly due to the fact that the implications of the play spread out in ever-widening circles, ultimately bringing under question many of the most established political and moral attitudes of our society. The play is what the Victorians would unquestionably have called "unsavory." We can readily understand why it is rarely produced.

The Duke of Vienna leaves the city, delegating chief authority in his absence to Angelo, a rigorously righteous man. The Duke's secret purpose is the hope that the stern Angelo will bring again into enforcement many laws which have been neglected under his own lenient rule and which he cannot with good grace enforce. This presents the issue of the evasion of political responsibility.

Invoking an old statute, Angelo throws Claudio into prison for getting a young woman with child. For this, with unprecedented severity, Claudio is sentenced to death. His sister Isabella, who had been about to take holy orders, comes to Angelo to implore mercy for her brother. Angelo at first remains adamant, but the passion and persistence of Isabella's pleading arouses his lust. He surrenders to his impulse and offers to pardon Claudio if she will yield herself to him.

Claudio, when he learns of this, begs Isabella to save him. She is repelled and is in despair. But the Duke has returned in the guise of a friar to observe his experiment. He now intercedes. Under his instruction Isabella makes a clandestine appointment with Angelo. The appointment is kept by Mariana, the former fiancée of Angelo who had been spurned by him. Believing the bargain to be fulfilled, Angelo nevertheless treacherously orders Claudio's execution. The Duke forestalls this and Angelo at last is exposed. At Isabella's intercession he is pardoned and weds Mariana. The Duke, in turn, asks Isabella's hand.

Technically the play is a comedy. But the ramifications of its plot raise problems of the responsibility of authority, the invoking of obsolete laws as a device of tyranny, corruption in office, and the value of chastity.

MEASUREMENT OF A CIRCLE, by Archimedes. See ARCHIMEDES.

MEAT TAX, THE (1869), by Mendele Mocher Sefarim. See MENDELE MOCHER SEFARIM.

MÉCANIQUE CÉLESTE (1799–1825), by Pierre Simon Laplace. In 1687 Newton had published his famous *Principia* (q.v.), in which the law of gravitation was first presented. For a century thereafter astronomers tested the law against celestial motions. Laplace in particular published memoirs from 1773 to 1786 in which he established the stability of the system of the universe in accordance with Newtonian principles. In 1796 Laplace published his *Exposition du Système du Monde* (2 vols.), in which he gave a general account of the origin and motions of the planets. This popular book quickly went through half a dozen editions. However, Laplace is better known for his greatest treatise on mathematical astronomy, the five-volume *Mécanique Céleste*. The first two volumes of this latter work appeared in 1799, and the other three volumes were published successively in 1802, 1815, and 1825. In this impressive treatise, which has been termed a "second edition of the *Principia*," Laplace dispelled the last doubts as to the sufficiency of the doctrine of universal gravitation to explain all cosmical phenomena. The author himself described the object of the work as the treatment of astronomy "as a great problem of mechanics, from which it is important to banish as much as possible all empiricism,"—i.e., to reduce all the known phenomena of the system of the world to strict mathematical principles. He wished to complete the investigations of the motions of the planets, satellites and comets begun by Newton and "to present a connected view of these theories." The work is divided into two parts. In the first he furnishes the necessary methods and formulas, including the well-known "Laplace equation" and potential theory, derived from advanced mathematics; and in the second he applies these to determine the motions of the then known members of the solar system. He concludes the work with an historical account of earlier contributions and with an examination of some fundamental questions relating to the universe. The *Mécanique Céleste* was the first comprehensive elaboration of what Voltaire had called "Newtonianism." Laplace is to be remembered also for his classical treatise, *Théorie Analytique des Probabilités* (1812), which, like the *Mécanique Céleste,* unified all previous work on the subject.

MEDEA (431 B.C.), by Euripides. Medea, in the myth of Jason and the quest of the Golden Fleece, typifies the impetuous and passionate barbarian in contrast to the measured self-control of the Hellene. For love of Jason she had betrayed her father and murdered her brother, had left home and country to follow Jason back to Greece, had even employed her magic arts to give him vengeance on his enemies, and had borne him two sons. In this masterpiece of Euripidean tragedy the character of Medea is exploited to measure the lengths to which a woman may pursue hatred. The scene is laid in Corinth, where Jason has found favor at the court of Creon. Jason is prepared to take the princess Glauce as his lawful wedded wife to win position and security. Medea's old nurse fears what Medea may do in her injured rage. Fuel is added to the fire of this rage by the report that Medea and her children will be banished from the land by Creon. As Medea pours forth her bitterness to the chorus, Creon comes to order her to depart. By an impassioned plea she gains a stay of twenty-four hours. Before Jason appears with his sickening banality to try to mollify her wrath, Medea's tortured mind has formulated a plan for revenge against both him and Creon. Still to make revenge complete she must extricate herself also; the arrival of an old friend, Aegeus, king of Athens, who promises her refuge in his land, offers the necessary escape. Then she moves with barbaric ruthlessness toward her goal. She feigns a change of heart, recalls Jason, and, in token of reconciliation, sends the children back with him to bear a splendid robe as bridal gift for Glauce. The robe is smeared with poison to consume the flesh of whoever wears it, and soon after the return of the children word is brought of the agonized death of Glauce, and of Creon, who has tried to save her. Medea retires with the children, and soon the stunned Jason appears to beat upon her door. But Medea within has murdered her own beloved children to punish their father and rescue them from bastardy. Her last words are spoken to Jason from a chariot borne aloft by winged steeds who will take her to the safety of Athens. She denies Jason the burial of his sons and prophesies for him an ignominious death. The character of Medea is humanized by her love for her children, but that of Jason is left weak and selfish. He is made to personify the smugness of Hellenic virtue, of which Euripides was a most disquieting critic.

MEDEA (1820), by Franz Grillparzer. See GOLDEN FLEECE, by Franz Grillparzer.

MEDEA, by Seneca. See TRAGEDIES, by Seneca.

MEDIEVAL FLEMISH PLAYS. Of the "artful plays" (which are perhaps written by the same anonymous poet), *Esmoreit, Lanseloet,* and *Gloriant* are regularly performed in the Netherlands and Flanders. The second one is rightfully the most admired.

The knight Lanseloet is in love with one of the ladies-in-waiting of his mother, who considers the beautiful Sanderijn below his station. To cure him of his infatuation, the old woman leads Sanderijn into the arms of Lanseloet, under the condition that he says to the girl after a night of love: "I have had so much of thee, as if I had eaten seven pounds of bacon." This he does. Deeply insulted, Sanderijn leaves the castle and departs for a faraway country, where another ardent noble suitor takes her as his bride and wife. But the love of Lanseloet is not dead. He discovers where Sanderijn is living, and is prepared to risk all to get her back. Sanderijn lets him know through a symbolic message that her love for him is dead. Lanseloet is no longer able to commit deeds of violence, and dies of remorse and desire. (Translated in 1923 by Dr. P. Geyl as *A Beautiful Play of Lancelot of Denmark.*)

Toward the end of the fifteenth century another unknown author wrote the miracle play *Marieken of Nieumeghen,* a drama of a female Faust. The beautiful orphan Marieken is sent by her uncle and guardian to do some errands in the city of Nijmegen. As evening falls, she tries to lodge with an aunt, but she is turned away with shameful curses by the old woman, who is enraged because her political party has been defeated. Totally upset, Marieken wanders around and finds consolation with Moenen—the devil—who offers her everything her heart desires, under the condition that she surrender to him completely. The next acts picture the scandalous life she lives with him for seven years. They return one fine day to Nijmegen, where in the market place a spiritual play is performed about the grace of God. Overpowered by repentance, Marieken tears herself away from the devil, who, seeing his prey escape, tries to break her neck by dragging her with him high in the air and letting her fall on the market place. Marieken survives. She goes from one priest to another to have her sins forgiven; but only the Pope can give her absolution, for she has been the mistress of the devil. Her penance is fixed: to be shackled on neck and arms and to lead a life of penance; when her shackles fall off by themselves, only then God will have forgiven her. This happens after many years. The play has remained very popular with the modern theatergoing public in the Netherlands and Flanders because of its colorful realism and deep humanity. Soon after its creation the play was both put into prose and printed by Jan van Doesborgh at Antwerp. A facsimile was produced by the Harvard University Press in 1932. It was translated by Prof. Harry Morgan Ayres as *A Marvelous History of Mary of Nijmegen* (The Hague).

At probably about the same time Peter Dorland (also called "van Diest") wrote the morality play *Elckerlijc,* that soon thereafter was translated into English as *Everyman* (see Prof. Dr. R. W. Zantvoort: *English Studies,* February 1 and April 2, 1941). God charges Death to call "Elckerlijc" to account. No one wants to join him on this pilgrimage. Only Virtue remains true, but she is for the time being too weak through his neglect of her. Knowledge leads him to confession, and through self-castigation he makes Virtue strong again. In the cloth of penance and sustained by Virtue, Elckerlijc commences his journey to the grave alone. Before he descends, he receives Holy Communion. He dies in consolation and his soul is carried into Heaven. As an open-air play, the drama is performed regularly in the Netherlands.

MEDICI, THE (1910), by G. F. Young. This is the classic study of one of the great banking families of the late Middle Ages. In the two branches there were two Popes of Rome (Leo X and Clement VII) and two Queens of France, one married to Henry II and one to Henry of Navarre. When Giovanni di Bicci died in 1428 he left immense fortunes to his two sons, Cosimo and Lorenzo. It is Cosimo's branch which contains all the greater Medici and which stamped for hundreds of years their name on Florence, and adorned this Italian city with works of art which have made her immortal. Lorenzo, Il Magnifico, was the grandson of Cosimo. He was the leading figure of the Renaissance; to his table and employ came not only Michelangelo, Botticelli and dozens of other artists, but Pico della Mirandola, the golden-haired youth who spoke twenty-two languages and was the leading literary figure of his century, Politian, another talented man, and many others, who revived classical learning in the West. These Grand Dukes brought to Florence such distinguished women as Eleanor of Toledo, the lovely Madeleine de la Tour d'Auvergne, as their wives, and their blood runs in others farther afield, as Francis II, who married Mary, Queen of Scots; Elizabetta the wife of Philip II of Spain, etc. The last true Medici was Anna Maria Ludovica, the wife of William, Elector of Palatine. She died in 1743 and left her possessions to the city of Florence to remain there forever. Since the day of this art-loving family Florence has been the Mecca of all who love the plastic arts, whether painting, sculpture, or architecture.

MEDITATIONS (ca. 170–180), by Marcus Aurelius Antoninus. This is a rare work of its kind, a book of philosophical meditations written in Greek by a Roman Emperor while commanding his legions on the distant and barbaric borders of his empire. Marcus Aurelius was thoroughly steeped in later Stoic moral philosophy as represented by Epictetus, and his *Meditations* are, as the name suggests, his reflections along Stoic lines on ethical problems. Typical both of the personal tone and of the benevolent character of the work is one of his thoughts on the brotherhood of man: "My nature is rational and social, and my city and my country, so far as I am Antoninus, is Rome; but so far as I am a man, it is the world." Neither Marcus Aurelius nor the world was ready for the practical application of what has always remained an ideal, and he cannot justly be censured for his persecution of the Christians, which fell within his duty as head of the Roman state.

MEDITATIONS (1642), by René Descartes. See DISCOURSE ON METHOD, by René Descartes.

MEDITATIONS OF THE LOVER (1925), by Han Yong-woon. *Meditations of the Lover* (*Nim-e Chimmuk*) by a Korean poet, Han Yong-woon (1878–1944), was published after his release from a Japanese prison. These quiet poems present some remarkable concepts drawn from transitional Far Eastern thought, but raised to new levels of perception. It is the kind of poetry in which the artist transforms personal fantasy into myth. It has been translated by Frances Keely and Younghill Kang. In Korea today he is widely read and highly regarded, as part of the awakening consciousness and spiritual ferment of that country.

Han Yong-woon has also written: *Bulkyo Yushinlon* (*Renovation of Buddhism*, 1928), *Yusimlon* (*The Mind Alone Exists*, 1929), *Chosun Doklip Woondong Kamsang* (*The Impressions of Korean Independence*, 1933), and one novel, *Hukpoong* (*Black Clouds*, 1930).

MEEK HERITAGE (1919), by Frans E. Sillanpää. Frans Eemil Sillanpää (b. 1888) is modern Finland's most distinguished author. His range of subjects is rather narrow, for he writes almost exclusively about the simple peasants of his native region in the western part of the country. Yet within this narrow range his keen eye and his lyrical sense find abundant material for picturing life. In 1939 he received the Nobel Prize for his novel, *Meek Heritage*, which had appeared in English in 1938. It is a stark, naturalistic study of the peasant Jussi Toivola from his birth in 1857 to his death in the Bolshevik Revolution of 1917. He is born out of wedlock to the lecherous and drunken Benjamin, the owner of a farm at Nicila. Though his father later marries his mother, Maja, as his third wife, it does not prevent him from bringing in as his mistress still another dissolute creature. The children, Eva, Marko and Jussi, are aware of this situation, and become morally depraved. When drink at last brings about the eviction of Benjamin from his farm, Jussi and his mother go to live with her brother. Here they are treated harshly and finally driven out. Jussi, always anxious about his future, takes to drink and marries a stupid servant girl, Rina. Their life is so hard that when she dies he feels relieved. Then he sends his thirteen-year-old daughter, Hilda, into service in town, and the frightened girl drowns herself. This drives him to a passionate hatred for the master class, and makes him susceptible to the arguments of his friend, Kalle, who fans this smoldering resentment: "You ought to join the battle with us, seeing that you are a worker, and cast off the yoke of capitalism." Jussi takes his advice and dies before a firing squad, a fate that brings him a spiritual release from a tragic, suffering life.

MEI (1889), by Herman Gorter. Gorter (1864–1925) published this lyric epic in three cantos, in 1889. The uncommon power of imagery of the poem aroused admiration and respect in all strata of the population of the Netherlands and Flanders. The first canto is considered excellent in every respect. Gorter depicts May (the personification of the flowering month) as a young Greek goddess, who, emerging from the sea, sojourns to Holland and marches through the country, everywhere decorating the fields, canal banks and villages with flowers. Before long she meets the poet, an encounter which reveals that May is for Gorter more than the symbol of the month. How he conceives her as the personification of mortal, earthly beauty becomes clearer in the second canto, which sings about a region of Norse mythology. After she has once beheld the poet-god Balder and heard him sing, she searches through all the palaces of the gods and through all the heavenly meadows, until she finally finds again the blind god, wandering in exile. But he, the very symbol of eternal beauty, not bound to material existence, refuses her: a union of these two is unthinkable. May flees back to earth, and in the third canto rediscovers the earthly poet, who is able to console her because in him she recognizes at least something of Balder. The lamentation "about the eternal transitions of existence and non-existence, which wraps itself around the earth as a haze" dominates this last canto, which finishes with May's inevitable death on the beach of the sea from which she had emerged.

After a period of extremely sensitive poetry, Gorter (who had translated Spinoza's *Ethica* into Dutch) arrived at a form of philosophical art in his *School der Poëzie* (1897). Soon thereafter he turned to Marxism. He wrote about a new communal life in *Een Klein Heldendicht* (1906) and *Pan* (1916). These epics did not receive the general attention accorded to *Mei*.

Gorter's works have not been translated into English.

MEJOR ALCALDE, EL REY, EL (1616?), by Lope de Vega. See KING, THE GREATEST MAYOR, THE, by Lope de Vega.

MEKOR HAYYIM, by Solomon Ibn Gabirol. See IBN GABIROL, SOLOMON.

MEMOIRS (1926), by Xālide Edib Adivar. See CLOWN AND HIS DAUGHTER, THE, by Xālide Edib Adivar.

MEMOIRS (1828), by Giacomo Casanova. Of Casanova, whose international reputation as a delightful and successful rogue has made his name a synonym of licentious adventure, the Inquisition of his native Venice said, in a secret memorandum in the year 1775: "He is said to be a man of letters, but to have an intelligence rich in cabals. It is reported that he . . . has gained inexcusable advantages at the cost of knights and ladies, for it has ever been his way to live at others' expenses, and to get the better of the credulous." Casanova wrote his *Memoirs* toward the end of his tumultuous life. Although not too rich in literary merit, the long book is especially recommended as a document of Venetian and European life in the second half of the eighteenth century. The author devotes particular attention to his battles of love, in most of which he claims to have been the victor. But descriptions of political or social events are not missing. Especially interesting is the description of the author's escape from the dreadful Piombi prison, in Venice.

MEMOIRS (1717), by Paul de Gondi, Cardinal de Retz. These *Memoirs* of the seventeenth century churchman reveal a startlingly picturesque and unecclesiastical character. Retz had entered the priesthood because his parents wanted to keep the office of Archbishop of Paris in the family. Ambition made him want to be the King's Minister. An eloquent and generous priest, he ingratiated himself with the people of Paris, became Coadjutor to the Cardinal Archbishop his uncle, and, in 1651, a Cardinal himself. But in his intrigues he had thrown his lot with the rebellious nobles who had stirred the civil disturbance of the *Fronde*. The *Fronde* collapsed; and in 1652 Retz was imprisoned. In 1653, still in prison, he inherited the Archbishopric. Subsequently he escaped, went into exile, succeeded in bargaining with the King and obtaining very rich concessions in return for resigning his office, so that he lived out his declining years in grace and dignity. His memoirs are a justification, sometimes at the expense of truth, of his career but not of himself. The character which emerges from them is allowed to appear unscrupulous and uninhibited, and entirely fascinating. Readers have long admired the literary portraits which crowd the pages.

MEMOIRS (published 1830), by Saint-Simon. This Duke and peer of the realm, one-time soldier, later Counsellor of the Regency and, very briefly, Ambassador of France to Spain, had been taking notes since he was eighteen. After his retirement at the end of the Regency, annoyed by the obsequiousness of available accounts, he began putting together his version of the last twenty years of the reign of Louis XIV. At great length (the original edition is in twenty volumes) he put down what he had seen and what he knew and sometimes also what he suspected. Prejudiced, socially snobbish, frequently undependable as a historical document, his report is obviously the work of a very limited but highly observant individual. He had disliked the King and the King had disliked him. His pride had often been ruffled. And the *Memoirs* are thus slanted. No student of French history and culture dares either trust or neglect them. Written toward the middle of the eighteenth century, Saint-Simon's work was not published until 1830.

MEMOIRS AND LETTERS (1848), by Hector Berlioz. This extraordinary document sheds light on an astonishing character, reveals the interior workings of a man of genius, and reconstructs the artistic and intellectual life of the first half of the nineteenth century with great vividness. The work encompasses the period from 1821 to 1868, since to the original *Memoirs* have been added letters from the later period of the composer's life. Berlioz is extremely blunt; he makes no secret of how he feels about people like Cherubini, Goethe, Kreutzer; his accounts of the Academy and of the competitions for the *prix de Rome* are uproarious. He made a host of enemies, but on the other hand his friendships with men like Liszt, Chopin and Heine were durable indeed. The character which emerges from these personal papers is unstable. Berlioz was exaggeratedly tender and violent by turns. His nature was volcanic—and it is small wonder that his life was a perpetual struggle against parental opposition, hunger and illness, and complicated by fierce personal antagonisms and fabulously tangled love affairs.

MEMOIRS FROM THE HOUSE OF THE DEAD (1861–1862), by Feodor Dostoevsky. This book, written shortly after the author's return from his four years' Siberian exile, provides a rich record of the life of a Russian convict in a Siberian prison in the middle of the nineteenth century. Its detail is remarkable. We learn the conditions under which the convicts lived, what they did, and how they amused themselves. We learn of the nature of their quarrels, how they managed to move about and dress while weighed by their fetters, how they behaved under the cruelty of the guards, who were also sometimes known to be kind. Again, we are made to witness the terrible floggings, and how men conducted themselves before and after, all described with the unfaltering realism of a novelist famous for his qualities of observation, and with psychological asides which make the work memorable. The passage in the book describing the convicts in the bathhouse was called Dantesque by Turgenev, but on the other hand because of its straightforward narrative and description it has been called by Edward Hallett Carr the least Dostoevskian of all Dostoevsky's work. Despite the horrors of the prison life and its terrible victims, Dostoevsky found something human about them, and the book's ultimate message is one of faith in human nature under the most degraded circumstances.

MEMOIRS FROM UNDERGROUND (1864), by Feodor Dostoevsky. Sometimes translated *Notes from Underground,* this is, chronologically, the first book that expresses the essential Dostoevsky after his return from Siberia. It is a cruel, bitter book, and is said to reflect the personal misery he endured during a winter of misfortune. Its importance derives from the fact that it is even more an exposition of the author's philosophy than a work of fiction. The first part has been called an explanation of the philosophy of malice; the second relates a series of incidents from the life of the narrator, the malicious man. The work contains a picture of the duality for which his characters, as well as the author himself, were famous. The keynote is struck in the first lines: "I am a sick man. I am a malicious man. I am an unprepossessing man. I think I have a disease of the spleen . . . I refuse remedies out of malice." This book is, in a sense, an introduction to his great novels. It is rich in that prophetic gift which marks his best work. A typical sentence, which follows, might apply with truth to Hitler (to mention a single example): "I shall not be a bit surprised if in the midst of this Universal Reason that is to be there will appear, all of a sudden and unexpectedly, some commonfaced, or rather cynical and sneering gentleman who with his arms akimbo will say to us: 'Now then, you fellows, what about smashing all this Reason to bits, sending their logarithms to the devil, and living as we like according to our own silly will.' " In this book Dostoevsky seems to have foreseen modern psychology. He reveals the irrational in human nature, today accepted as a commonplace but not in his day. Critics see in it the spiritual crisis of our own time. The work is full of paradoxes. The story itself consists of a single episode. The hero, the spiteful man, strikes up an acquaintance with Liza, a young woman of easy virtue. He talks with her at great length, tormenting her cruelly. He awakens her sympathy, however, and she is ready to help him with her love. But he refuses her kindness, and torments himself in fits of self-laceration. He is sadistic and masochistic by turns; and his paradoxical nature subjects him to the ups and downs of good and evil impulses and emotions.

MEMOIRS OF A REVOLUTIONIST (1898–1899), by Peter Kropotkin. First published serially in the *Atlantic Monthly*, this work is one of the most impressive and stirring autobiographies in literature. The *Memoirs* begin with Kropotkin's sheltered and idyllic childhood and youth. There are masterly portraits of his mother, sisters, teachers and the old trusted servants. He describes with graphic skill the various scenes of the patriarchal life they led in this house of the royal descendant of Rurik the Red. The sensitive boy was painfully aware of a corresponding hell to his heaven, a hell in which thousands of serfs toiled and suffered hopelessly to make life sweet for the Kropotkins. Thus the ardent idealist and social revolutionary was born; thus the Czar's proud cousin and page, Prince Kropotkin, was transformed into a persecuted, impecunious radical, Peter Kropotkin, who spent his life in exile after his long and crushing imprisonment in the Peter and Paul Fortress. Concurrently we have the history of the labor and socialist movements in Europe during the second half of the nineteenth century. Kropotkin became a convert to the social philosophy of Michael Bakunin, the communist-anarchist, during his maturity, after he had already achieved world fame as geographer and geologist. He had gradually arrived at the conclusion that the pursuit of science was of no use in the unethical society in which the principle of dog-eat-dog prevailed. Living in poverty, and in social usefulness, he confessed, he found greater peace and *raison d'être* than as a foolish prince.

MEMOIRS OF HECATE COUNTY (1946), by Edmund Wilson. See AXEL'S CASTLE, by Edmund Wilson.

MEMOIRS OF SHERLOCK HOLMES (1894), by Sir Arthur Conan Doyle. See SHERLOCK HOLMES, by Sir Arthur Conan Doyle.

MEMORABILIA, by Xenophon (ca. 430–359 B.C.). As a young man Xenophon had been an interested follower of Socrates, but later joined the expedition against the Persian king, which he describes in the *Anabasis* (q.v.), and Socrates had been put to death before he returned to Greece. The four books of the *Memorabilia* or *Recollections of Socrates* is the principal of his so-called Socratic works. In it Xenophon recalls various conversations of Socrates with many different persons, all calculated to disprove the contention upon which he was tried, namely that he was a pernicious influence. The impression of Socrates which results from these conversations is rather different from that given by Plato and somewhat less inspiring. It may be used as a corrective of Plato's attribution of his own ideas to Socrates, but must be used with caution, since Xenophon apparently failed to comprehend the true inwardness of much of the master's thought. The organization of the material in the *Memorabilia* follows no logical or systematic scheme, and therefore the work is more pleasant as occasional reading than as a steady diet. The other Socratic works are the *Apology of Socrates,* which is an account of Socrates' trial rather than his purported plea before the court, the *Symposium* or *Banquet,* a dinner conversation of Socrates at the house of a wealthy friend, and the *Oeconomicus,* a discussion of household management which Socrates is made to report as having heard from a friend. The latter is especially interesting for the picture it gives of Athenian domestic life; and all these works are full of charming details of the everyday life of Athens of the period.

MEMORABLE PROVIDENCES, RELATING TO WITCHCRAFTS AND POSSESSIONS (1689), by Cotton Mather. See MATHER, COTTON.

MEMORIAL DE AIRES (1908), by Joaquim Maria Machado de Assis. See DOM CASMURRO, by Joaquim Maria Machado de Assis.

MEMORIE INUTILI (1797), by Carlo Gozzi. See GOZZI, CARLO.

MEMORIES FROM BEYOND THE TOMB (1811–1846), by François René de Chateaubriand. See ATALA, by François René de Chateaubriand.

MEN AGAINST THE SEA (1934), by James Norman Hall and Charles Bernard Nordhoff. See MUTINY ON THE BOUNTY, by James Norman Hall and Charles Bernard Nordhoff.

MEN IN WHITE (1933), by Sidney Kingsley. See DEAD END, by Sidney Kingsley.

MEN WITHOUT WOMEN (1927), by Ernest Hemingway. See SUN ALSO RISES, THE, by Ernest Hemingway.

MENAECHMI, THE, by Plautus (Titus Maccius Plautus; 254–184 B.C.). *The Menaechmi* was derived from a Greek original of unknown authorship. The story, in a slightly different form, is familiar to all readers, since Shakespeare based his famous *Comedy of Errors* (q.v.) on this Latin farce. The English comedy is usually considered inferior to the Latin model. The complex situation is sketched in a prologue. A merchant of Syracuse had identical twins, and took one of them with him on a voyage. At Tarentum the little boy was separated from his father in a crowd, and taken home by a rich merchant from Epidamnus, who adopted him and made him his heir. The father, unable to locate his missing son, eventually died of despair. The news of his death and the disappearance of the twin finally reached Syracuse, and the grandfather gave the remaining twin his brother's name of Menaechmus. When he reaches manhood Menaechmus II sets out with his slave, Messenio, to find his lost brother. After years of wandering he arrives at Epidamnus, where he is immediately taken for his brother, Menaechmus I, by the latter's courtesan, Erotium, his wife, and his parasite, Sponge. The substance of the play is an exploitation of this confusion. The Menaechni are not a very moral pair. Menaechmus I steals a dress from his wife for Erotium, and Menaechmus II is not above taking advantage of Erotium's mistaking his identity, accepts her invitation to dinner, and intends to make off with the dress which she asks him to take to the embroiderer's. Finally Messenio meets his master's brother, unravels the tangled skein of identity and enlightens the less sharp-witted brothers.

MENCKEN CHRESTOMATHY (1949), by H. L. Mencken. See AMERICAN LANGUAGE, THE, by H. L. Mencken.

MENDELE MOCHER SEFARIM (1836–1917). "Mendel the Bookseller" is actually Shalom Jacob Abramowitsch, famed as the "grandfather" of modern Yiddish literature. He was born in Lithuania, and died in Odessa. He was a precocious student, who, after his father's death when he was fourteen, studied in distant rabbinical academies, took up for a period with a beggar, and, after being aided financially and educationally by a literary patron, became a teacher in a government school in 1856. It was Mendele who in 1864 determined to make the despised Yiddish tongue his full medium of expression. He adopted the pseudonymical device of "bookseller" because these traveling purveyors were close to the masses and had their respect. His sympathetic portrayal of the ghetto world in all its aspects provided a revolutionary impetus to succeeding Yiddish literature, giving the "jargon" standing in the literary world. Two early works satirized the oppressive officialdom of the day: *The Little Man* (1864) and *The Meat Tax* (1869). Then came *The Fish* (1870); *The Old Mare* (1873), a satire on Jewish history; *The Little Jew* (1875); *Sabbath Songs* (1875); *The Travels of Benjamin III* (1878), the tour of the town fool and a companion, two noble innocents, to see the world, ending in their conscription; *The Wishing Ring* (1879), historical story of the period; many works, both light and scholarly, in Hebrew; and the final venture of a Yiddish translation of Genesis (1913). Little of Mendele's work has been translated from Yiddish, although historians of Yiddish literature give him all credit for founding what has become a literature of great power and significance. In 1949 there appeared an English translation of *The Travels of Benjamin III*, which offers an appropriate sampling of Mendele's style and aptitudes.

MENSCHENHATER, DE (1941), by Arthur van Schendel. See SCHENDEL, ARTHUR VAN.

MENTAL HEALERS (1931), by Stefan Zweig. See ZWEIG, STEFAN.

MERCHANT OF VENICE, THE (1596?; Quarto, 1600), by William Shakespeare. A remarkable example of literary metamorphosis is to be found in *The Merchant of Venice*. In the Elizabethan theater it was written and received as a comedy, which technically it is. For many years now, however, it has been regarded as a serious drama dominated by the character who had originally been its butt. Shylock has become transformed, through changing social perspectives, from a villainous buffoon to a dignified tragic figure. Shakespeare drew his material from Giovanni Fiorentino's *Il Pecorone* and from the *Gesta Romanorum* (q.v.).

In Shakespeare's day a Jew was the natural and inevitable victim of buffoonery. Shylock's villainy required little demonstration. It was fitting and proper, to the Elizabethan audience, that he should deal harshly and be dealt with more harshly.

The superior genius of Shakespeare is demonstrated in the pains he took to probe into and motivate, even to justify, this character, who would have been readily accepted in a single dimension. It is well established that Shakespeare was partly inspired by Marlowe's *The Jew of Malta* (q.v.), a play which, although vigorous, presents Barabas, the counterpart of Shylock, as a psychopathic fiend in contrast to Shakespeare's temperate creation. The true artist and humanist appeared in the shaping of Shylock. Yet Shakespeare allotted to Shylock no more than his due place in this otherwise conventional comedy. He appears not at all in the last act.

Bassanio, a Venetian gentleman who wishes funds with which to go a-wooing, seeks to borrow from his friend, the merchant Antonio. Antonio has all his money invested in cargoes at sea, but his credit is good in Venice. Accordingly he borrows, for Bassanio, from Shylock the usurer. Shylock has often smarted under insults from Antonio, and upbraids him on this point; then, to prove that a Jew is not incapable of generosity, offers to lend the sum at no interest, on the jesting forfeiture of a pound of flesh in the event of failure to repay.

Meanwhile, Bassanio goes to court the noble Portia, a wealthy heiress. Her father's will had specified that whosoever sought to wed her must choose one of three caskets, of gold, silver and lead respectively, each bearing a cryptic legend. The one containing Portia's picture would yield the triumph. After many have failed Bassanio chooses correctly and wins her hand.

Word comes, in the meantime, that Antonio's ships have been sunk. The bond falls due. Shylock is filled with a bitter malice against all Christians, for during this interval his daughter Jessica has eloped with the Christian, Lorenzo. Shylock determines, implacably, to exact his pound of flesh. Bassanio, with his newly-wedded wealth, offers to pay thrice the bond, but Shylock will not yield. There seems no escape for the unfortunate Antonio.

Portia, disguised as a young lawyer, appears at the trial. She examines the bond and confirms that the forfeit must be paid. But as Shylock triumphantly whets his knife she cautions him that he must shed no drop of Antonio's blood, at forfeit of his life, for the bond gives him rights to nothing but flesh. In dismay Shylock tries to claim the previously offered triple payment, then merely the principal, but the court holds these to be forfeited. Portia then countercharges Shylock with an indirect intent to murder. For this, half his wealth is given over to Antonio, the other half is made over to Jessica as an inheritance. He is further enjoined to become a Christian.

After this stern reckoning with Shylock, a final moonlit act winds up the threads of the love story, bringing Portia and Bassanio together and revealing her role in the trial.

MERLIN (1917), by Edwin Arlington Robinson. See ROBINSON, EDWIN ARLINGTON.

MERRY WIVES OF WINDSOR, THE (1600–1601?; Quarto 1602), by William Shakespeare. This play is a sequel, partaking of all the weaknesses supposedly common to sequels. There is a tradition that Queen Elizabeth, delighted with the Falstaff of the two parts of *Henry IV* (q.v.), requested Shakespeare to show her Falstaff in love. Presumably this comedy represents the command performance of the fat knight. That the play is a hack job is quite clear. Falstaff, one of the playwright's immortal characters, is here only the shadow of himself, coming vigorously alive only in momentary flashes, marching through the mazes of a feeble plot, flanked by inferior characterizations in tedious sub-plots. He is not the match of the sublime braggart who "rose and fought a long hour by Shrewsbury clock."

The main body of the play deals with the attempt of Sir John Falstaff to enter into affairs with Mistress Ford and Mistress Page, as much tempted by the purses of their husbands as by their own charms. He writes identical letters to them, which the two women immediately compare. Indignantly, they decide to make a butt of the lecherous knight by making appointments with him and planning tricks and harassments for his undoing.

At the same time, a disgruntled henchman of Falstaff betrays the knight's purpose to Page and to Ford. Page laughs at the matter but the jealous Ford broods upon it. He visits Falstaff, who has never seen him, calls himself Brook, and ascertains his purposes by offering him money to corrupt the wife of Ford that he himself may hope to win her. It happens, therefore, that Ford learns from Falstaff of each of the assignations made with him by Mistress Ford. He is not aware of the motive behind these and is consumed with jealousy.

As Falstaff keeps his appointments Ford attempts to apprehend him. The knight escapes once in a laundry basket, being later dumped in the Thames, and once in the guise of an old woman. Finally, when Ford has been taken into the conspiracy, Falstaff is lured to the woods by night and trapped by the conspirators. When his humiliation has been achieved all is forgiven and the play closes in a spirit of revelry.

This, one of the poorer of Shakespeare's plays, has been turned into a superb opera, *Falstaff,* by Giuseppe Verdi.

MERTON OF THE MOVIES (1915), by Harry Leon Wilson. See RUGGLES OF RED GAP, by Harry Leon Wilson.

MESSER MARCO POLO (1921), by Donn Byrne. The story is narrated by an imaginative old Irishman, Malachi Campbell of Long Glen. He tells of young Marco Polo's youth in the Venice of the Middle Ages, how he listened to the yarns of a Chinese sea captain and heard from him an entrancing account of Golden Bells, daughter of the Khan. Marco falls in love with the beautiful Chinese, sight unseen, and dreams of her constantly. It so happens that Marco's father Nicolo and his uncle Matthew trade with China, and are obliged to undertake several dangerous expeditions to that far-off country ruled by the legendary Kubla Khan. The latter, having his interest aroused in the Christian religion, commissions the elder Polos to send him a Christian teacher. Upon their return to Venice Marco induces them to send him as a messenger to Kubla Khan. In the court of the great emperor he meets Golden Bells. He finds her even more entrancing than the account the Chinese captain gave of her. He converts her to Christianity and makes her his wife. After three years she dies, but Marco remains on for seventeen years, the bravest warrior of the Khan. When the old Khan lies dying, Golden Bells returns to Marco in a vision and commands him to return to Venice, since the Khan's jealous warriors may harm him after the ruler dies.

MESSIAH, THE (1748–1773), by Friedrich Gottlieb Klopstock. *The Messiah* sings in twenty cantos Christ's Passion, the Redemption, and the

Saviour's Ascension. The rhymeless verses are hexameters. It took the poet a quarter of a century to complete his gigantic undertaking. The first three cantos, published anonymously in 1748 when Klopstock was twenty-four years old, aroused immense enthusiasm. They inaugurated a new era in German literature. Deepfelt emotions, waves of religious feeling, a new conception of human dignity, were released by Klopstock's highly musical poetry and the lofty grandeur and religious sweep of his epic. Cantos 4 and 5 were published in 1751, cantos 6 to 10 followed four years later. These first 10 cantos of *The Messiah* gave the German youth of that time an intoxication comparable to that which Romantic music conveyed to the nineteenth century. However, this enthusiasm slackened with the publication of the last two volumes in 1768 and 1773. A new generation had grown up, and asked for the gifts which Herder, Goethe, and their fellow writers had to offer. In our time the 20,000 lines of *The Messiah* are no longer read, but they have become an object of scholarly study. Klopstock's epic has not attained the durability of his great model, Milton's *Paradise Lost* (q.v.).

METAMORPHOSES (ca. 8), by Ovid (Publius Ovidius Naso). This is Ovid's masterpiece of storytelling. The poem in fifteen books relates in epic style all the remarkable transformations of mythology, from the Creation to Caesar's appearance as a star after his death. The myths, drawn largely from Greek sources, are not items of faith or belief for the sophisticated Ovid or his audience. They were chosen rather for the manifold opportunities they afford for the exercise of narrative art. Among some of the best known are those of Deucalion and Pyrrha, Apollo and Daphne, Arachne, Midas, and Pyramus and Thisbe. Greek myths generally have been better known to modern readers through Ovid than through any other ancient source. These stories he retells without great depth of feeling but with a brilliant whimsicality that he had learned from the Greek poets of Alexandria. The individual stories are told with a fine eye for their dramatic possibilities, and are linked together by a variety of unobtrusive devices so that the whole flows on with a continuity hardly to be expected in such a medley of unrelated tales.

METAMORPHOSIS (1916), by Franz Kafka. See TRIAL, THE, by Franz Kafka.

METAPHYSICAL POETS, THE (1921), by T. S. Eliot. See ELIOT, THOMAS STEARNS.

METAPHYSICS, by Aristotle (384–322 B.C.). This important work of Aristotle deals with what he himself referred to as first or primary philosophy, that is, all which lies beyond natural philosophy (physics) and would be called theology from the religious point of view. The name *Metaphysics* is not apparently of the author's choosing. It means *what comes after the Physics,* and was probably a designation used by the followers of Aristotle to indicate the position of the treatise in the body of Aristotle's published works. The *Metaphysics,* in thirteen books, is not attractive in style and bristles with technical phrases. It is quite possible that it represents something like lecture notes for the treatment of the subject in the Lyceum, Aristotle's "school." Much space is devoted to criticism of Aristotle's predecessors and their theories

Plato's theory of ideas, e.g., is discussed, and rejected in favor of a more materialistic conception of reality. The meat of the *Metaphysics* is the discussion of reality or existence (ontology). The problem is attacked from all conceivable angles, and neither the arguments nor the conclusions admit of brief summary. He does not deny the reality of ideas but associates them closely with actual phenomena as the fulfillment of potentiality. One of the most important aspects of Aristotle's reasoning here is his treatment of the progression from potentiality to actuality, from acorn to oak, from builder to building. The discussion of substance and essence is fundamental to this reasoning, and it is carried on in terms of Aristotle's four causal categories: material, efficient, formal and final. Still the fundamental dichotomy between substance and essence, real and ideal, remains. It is bridged by Aristotle's god, who is pure existence without substance, and, though himself unchanged, effects all change in the universe, not by any action but by serving as a guiding end and ideal toward which everything strives.

METAPHYSICS, by Avicenna. See AVICENNA.

METAPHYSICS OF MORALS (1785), by Immanuel Kant. See CRITIQUE OF PRACTICAL REASON, by Immanuel Kant.

METHOD FOR THE EASY COMPREHENSION OF HISTORY (1566), by Jean Bodin. This book, Bodin's first major work, is one of the most important contributions of that transitional period between the medieval and the modern age, when superstition and rationalism coexisted in some of the best minds.

Bodin's philosophy of history is partly authoritarian and supranatural, partly natural and scientific. He does not completely reject the theory of a providential determination of history, and classes among natural causes the influence of numbers and of heavenly bodies propelled by the Prime Mover. But he introduces variables not immediately derived from the Prime Mover, and devotes an entire chapter of his book to the theory that the course of events is determined by popular traits and these in turn by climate.

The most original part of *Methodus* deals with the proper method to be followed by historians. Bodin stresses the importance of a correct organization of knowledge, of a critical appraisal of all material, and, above all, of a non-prejudiced, objective attitude. He himself, however, is not exempt from prejudice: his patriotism and his religious sense of eternity prevent him from following too closely the main currents of his philosophy.

Bodin's views were widely quoted in his lifetime, and many later writers, such as Montesquieu, borrowed from him at least his conception of the influence of geography on the shaping of human nature.

MEYER, CONRAD FERDINAND (1825–1883). A native of Switzerland, Meyer is regarded as a towering master of form, who wrote with infinite care and great objectivity. The themes of his works are rooted in the past, with a predilection for the age of the Renaissance. The vivid imagery and plasticity of expression are never complicated by subjective questions nor directed toward the sentimental tastes of his day—Meyer being an aristocrat in background and practice. His poems and ballads, although not suitable for singing, are dramatic and reflective in character, never the direct outpouring of emotions. They are considered to be among the finest since Goethe. His works include the epic in monologue form, *Hutten's Last Days,* and *The Saint* (1880), a novel on Thomas à Becket. His fame mainly rests upon his long short stories. Among these are *The Monk's Marriage* (1884) and *The Sorrows of a Boy* (1883). Meyer sought symbols of universal experience and truth. A stylistically strange mixture of realism, classicism and Romanticism makes it difficult to include him in any particular school.

MICHAEL KOHLHAAS (1810), by Heinrich von Kleist. See KLEIST, HEINRICH VON.

MICHAEL UNGER (1902), by Ricarda Huch. See HUCH, RICARDA.

MICKIEWICZ, ADAM (1798–1855). Adam Mickiewicz, the greatest poet of Poland, was born in the north and educated in Wilno, where he moved in the university circles that were bitterly anti-Russian. For this he was removed to Russia in 1824, where he remained until he went abroad in 1828. From then on he lived chiefly in Paris, until, at the outbreak of the Crimean War, he went to Constantinople to secure aid in raising a Polish Legion to fight Russia; it was there that he died soon after.

The poems of Mickiewicz fall into distinct categories. During his early life he was the definite founder of Romanticism in Poland, and with his romances and his ballads he covered almost the entire range of Polish and Lithuanian history. Then, during his stay in Russia, he wrote the *Crimean Sonnets* (1825), with all of their splendid and luxurious imagery. Later he wrote *Konrad Wallenrod* (1828), a forceful story of the defeat of the Teutonic Knights by the Lithuanians, and the third part of his *Forefather's Eve* (1923), in which he outlines the evils done to Poland by Russian control. At the same time the prose *Books of the Polish Pilgrimage* (1832) outline the poet's faith in the Messianic mission of Poland, which had suffered innocently at the hands of its neighbors. In poetry he produced *Pan Tadeusz* (q.v.), the Polish national epic, and the *Dziady (Forefather's Eve)*, dealing with the fate of Poland and its relation to divine justice. Part III was written in 1823; Parts II and V in 1832; Part I was never written.

Mickiewicz ranks with the Russian Pushkin and the Ukrainian Shevchenko as a great poet. His works have been translated by George Rapall Noyes and many other writers. For the Poles he still remains not only the superb master of the language but the inspirer, the teacher and the glorifier of the national traditions in verse of incomparable beauty.

MICROBE HUNTERS (1926), by Paul de Kruif. This book is a series of chronicles of the lives and adventures of scientific pioneers. Beginning with Anton van Leeuwenhoek, the seventeenth century Dutchman who fashioned the first microscope and looked into the world of tiny organisms, de Kruif charts the exciting and difficult battles which brought new truths to medical science. There are the stories of Louis Pasteur, whose great contribution was the proof that microbes cause sickness, Walter Reed and his heroic efforts to stamp out yellow fever, Paul Ehrlich and his "magic bullet" against syphilis, and many others.

MICROMEGAS (1752), by Voltaire. See CANDIDE, by Voltaire.

MIDDLE SPAN, THE (1945), by George Santayana. See LAST PURI-TAN, THE, by George Santayana.

MIDDLE-AGED MAN ON THE FLYING TRAPEZE, THE (1935), by James Thurber. See THURBER, JAMES.

MIDDLEMARCH (1872), by George Eliot. There are two complicated stories intertwined in this novel. One is that of Dorothea Brooke and her two marriages. The other is about Dr. Ludgate and the Vincy family.

Dorothea and her sister Celia, orphans, live with their uncle on his estate near Middlemarch. Dorothea is an idealist, and dreams of finding some social outlet for her energy. A young neighbor, Sir James Chettam, is courting her, but she is attracted by the elderly pedantic Rev. Casaubon, who, she thinks, has a great soul. She marries him, only to discover her mistake. When she meets his nephew, the charming, artistic Will Ladislaw, they are mutually attracted. Her husband becomes jealous. When he dies he leaves his fortune to Dorothea, but with the stipulation that if she marries his nephew she forfeits the money.

A new situation is created with the appearance on the scene of Dr. Lydgate, a young radical doctor, anxious to reform the practice of medicine. He is in love with beautiful Rosamond Vincy, the Mayor's daughter, and marries her. She is shallow and scheming. The two live beyond their means. When they get into financial difficulties and an ensuing scandal, Rosamond shows her true colors. The only one to come to Dr. Lydgate's aid is the widowed Dorothea. She gives him money to clear himself from criminal charges.

With the years Dorothea's love for Ladislaw becomes more compelling. When she meets him again she renounces her fortune in order to marry him. As for Dr. Lydgate, he muddles along not too happily with Rosamond. Her way of living forces him to give up his scientific research, to look for rich patients, and develop a good bedside manner. Disappointed in life, he dies young.

MIDDLETOWN (1929), by Robert S. and Helen M. Lynd. This study in contemporary American culture was made by a staff of researchers who merged themselves for a year into the total life of a city (Muncie, Indiana) and studied it objectively. "Middletown," a representative city of about thirty thousand, was studied with regard to the following general activities: earning a living, making a home, training the young, using leisure time, engaging in religious practices, and participating in group activity. A most comprehensive approach to the project was employed, and material analyzed ranged from his-torical data to industrial statistics to folk talk and typical conversation.

The sociologist and his wife have also written the sequel, *Middletown in Transition* (1937).

MIDGE, THE (1886), by Henry Cuyler Bunner. See BUNNER, HENRY CUYLER.

MIDSUMMER NIGHT'S DREAM, A (1595–1596?; Quarto 1600), by William Shakespeare. Three threads are woven into the fabric of this ever popular comedy, this fable of lovers and fairy revels in the woods of Athens. The first of these concerns the pending marriage of Theseus, Duke of Athens, to Hippolyta, Queen of the Amazons. To the Duke comes Egeus, desiring that his daughter Hermia be compelled to marry Demetrius instead of Lysander, the suitor of her choice. Also involved in this affair is Hermia's friend Helena, who loves Demetrius. Theseus, upholding parental authority, orders Hermia to marry Demetrius or choose between death and the life of a nun.

The second thread deals with the efforts of a group of Athenian tradesmen, Bottom the weaver, Quince the carpenter, Snug the joiner, and others, to prepare a play for presentation at the celebration of the Duke's nuptials.

The final thread treats of a dispute between Oberon, King of the Fairies, and Titania, his Queen. These three aspects of the plot are brought together when Hermia and Lysander appoint a tryst in the woods, to escape from the Athenian law. Demetrius and Helena, separately, follow them. At the same time the tradesmen meet in the woods to rehearse their play. Oberon, and his servant, the prankish Puck, weave spells and enchantments about these mortals. After many farcical complexities all is resolved, as a result of the spritely intercessions. Demetrius is caused to love Helena, clearing the obstacle from the path of Hermia and Lysander. The couples are forgiven by Theseus and Egeus. Oberon and Titania are reconciled. The nuptials of Hippolyta and the Duke and the two other couples are celebrated with merriment, and the tradesmen produce their play, "Pyramus and Thisbe."

This masque-like play is enhanced in charm by the lyric qualities of its verse and the deftness of its management. It has a perennial popularity on the stage. An elaborate film version of the play was made by the director Max Reinhardt.

MIJNHEER OBERON EN MEVROUW (1940), by Arthur van Schendel. See SCHENDEL, ARTHUR VAN.

MILL ON THE FLOSS, THE (1860), by George Eliot. This is the story of the Tulliver family of Dorlcote Mill, on the River Floss, in England. Tom and Maggie, affectionate brother and sister, come to odds but are reunited in death. Tulliver loses his mill through a lawyer, Makem, and dies of a stroke. Maggie and Wakem's son, Philip, fall in love but are separated because of Tom's hatred for the son of the man who ruined his father. Stephen Guest, fiancé of Lucy Deane, who is a cousin of the Tullivers, loves Maggie and compromises her. Tom buys back the mill and denounces his sister, as do the rest of the townspeople. Philip, Lucy, and Mrs. Tulliver remain loyal to Maggie. Dr. Kenn is also a kind friend and adviser. During a flood, Maggie takes a boat and goes to rescue Tom. Seeing they are lost, they embrace and go to their death. On their gravestone is inscribed, "In their death they were not divided."

MILLAY, EDNA ST. VINCENT (1892–   ). Edna St. Vincent Millay became well-known upon publication of her first volume of poetry, *Renascence and Other Poems* (1917). The title piece is a rapturous expression, in symbolic yet poetically simple terms, of an individual's acceptance of and identity with the divine scheme of things. For a period, the poet's works showed a certain flip cynicism. *Aria da Capo* (1919) is a one-act fantasy with antiwar intentions. Pierrot is a sophisticated, intellectual New Yorker; Columbine is a shallow post-World War I flapper. In the midst of their amorous dallying, the stage manager presents two primitive shepherds who burlesque capitalism and nationalism, and end by killing each other. Then Pierrot and Columbine reappear and continue their imperturbable love-making.

Although the author maintained her interest in social themes, her lyricism took on an increased maturity in subsequent poetry, such as *The Harp. Weaver and other Poems* (1923) and the Elizabethan sonnet cycle, *Fatal Interview* (1931).

She wrote a libretto for an opera, *The King's Henchman* (1927), which was extremely popular. This Anglo-Saxon story concerns Aelfrida, the mistress of assassinated King Cynewulf. She marries the knightly hero Aethelwold and makes him victim of her evil enchantments, revenging herself for Aethelwold's deception of King Eadgar which prevented her from becoming queen.

MIND ALONE EXISTS, THE (1929), by Han Yong-woon. See MEDITATIONS OF THE LOVER, by Han Yong-woon.

MIND OF PRIMITIVE MAN, THE, (1911), by Franz Boas. This book consists of a course of lectures given at the Lowell Institute in Boston (1910–1911) in which the author, the outstanding anthropologist in this country at the time, summarizes the results of research into such fields as the influence of environment and heredity on man's bodily form, thought processes, and behavior. It was a landmark in the systematic study of these subjects. A rewritten and revised edition appeared in 1938, bringing it up to date. In 1940, the author's selections of his most important papers was published under the title of *Race, Language, and Culture*.

MINGO (1884), by Joel Chandler Harris. See UNCLE REMUS, by Joel Chandler Harris.

MINNA VON BARNHELM (1767), by Gotthold Ephraim Lessing. Of Lessing's plays *Minna von Barnhelm* has been the most popular. Major von Tellheim, a discharged officer, gives up his apartment at an inn in Berlin to a lady and her maid who have come to town. The lady is the beautiful Minna von Barnhelm, an heiress from Saxony, who, with her maid Franziska, is searching for Major von Tellheim. Tellheim, who is hard up, gives his valet Just his engagement ring to pawn. Just pledges it to the landlord, who shows it to Minna, and she redeems it. When Tellheim learns about Minna's presence, he is overjoyed and greets her affectionately, but soon stiffens and becomes formal. Being wounded and poor and with his honor under a cloud, he is no match for a great heiress. So he tears himself away and sends her a letter. Minna, determined to win her major back, pretends to be poor, too; and after complications that involve the pawned ring and a seemingly dishonorable financial action by Tellheim, which is being cleared up with the help of Minna's uncle, all conflicts are resolved. Not only have the couple been reconciled, but Tellheim's former Sergeant, Werner, has fallen in love with Minna's Franziska. *Minna von Barnhelm* was first produced in Hamburg in 1767 and met with little success. After the Berlin performance of the following year, however, the play became very popular. In the meager repertory of German comedies the amusing love struggle of the honor-stricken and stubborn Prussian with the charming and clever girl from Saxony has maintained a cherished place.

MIRACLE PLAY OF HASAN AND HUSAIN, THE. See MARTYRDOM OF ALI, THE.

MIRIFICI LOGARITHMORUM CANONIS DESCRIPTIO (1614), by John Napier, Baron of Merchiston. Hume, the historian, regarded Napier as the greatest man Scotland had produced; and this claim to fame rests primarily upon his invention of logarithms. The problem of simplifying calculations through the conversion of products to sums had long occupied the thoughts of mathematicians. In particular, trigonometric formulas for writing products of sines and cosines in terms of sums or differences of sines and cosines had been in use at the observatory of Tycho Brahe in Denmark in the method known as prosthaphaeresis. When James VI of Scotland (later James I of England) visited Tycho, he heard of this method and it was reported back to Scotland. Napier was thus encouraged to work on the question; and he developed a method which not only had far wider applicability as a tool of calculation, but which later became an important part of the theory of functions. Napier worked on the perfection of logarithms (the name was coined by him) for at least twenty years before publishing an account of his discovery in the famous *Descriptio* of 1614. This work was printed two years later in English translation as *A Description of the Admirable Table of Logarithms*. It is curious that the invention of logarithms preceded the use of exponents, so that Napier's line of thought differed from the modern point of view. He based his tables upon a comparison of the positions of two points which move along a straight line, one with uniform speed and the other with a speed which decreased in proportion to its distance from a fixed point which it was approaching. In the *Descriptio* he applied his invention only to the logarithms of trigonometric functions, using a base closely allied to that of the "natural" or "Napierian" system, and giving a table of logarithms of sines of a quadrant for every minute.

Napier died in 1617, but two years later there appeared posthumously his second work on logarithms, the *Mirifici Logarithmorum Canonis Constructio*, in which he explained the manner in which the tables of logarithms were constructed. Napier wrote a number of other works, including one on the *Revelation of Saint John* (1593) and another on *Rabdologia* (pub. 1617). The latter is on methods of calculation, and includes the device known as "Napier's bones" (or rods); and in its day it was highly regarded. Today, however, Napier's reputation is secured by his two treatises on logarithms. The invention of logarithms is generally regarded as one of the three greatest aids to calculation, the others being the Hindu-Arabic numerals and the decimal fractions. For this reason Napier's *Descriptio* is a landmark in the history of mathematics and science.

MIRROR FOR MAGISTRATES, A (1563), by Thomas Sackville and others. The first folio edition of *A Mirror for Magistrates* appeared in 1559. The scheme, with its device of an interlocutor, was taken from Lydgate's adaptation of *De Casibus Virorum* by Boccaccio; in fact it is a continuation, and was intended to be bound in one volume with *The Falls of Princes*. The book was a collection of poems, tragic legends of early monarchs and noblemen, and the contributions were by important men of the period. Sackville's famous "Induction," considered the finest poem between Chaucer and Spenser, is included in the 1563 edition, and also his "Henry, Duke of Buckingham." The "Induction," written in a seven-line stanza, describes approaching winter, and with the rising of the moon—Cynthia—a lone, woeful figure appears— Sorrow—who has come from Pluto's kingdom of Hades. She takes Sackville back with her, and shows him Remorse, Dread, Revenge, Old Age, Malady, War, symbolic figures like the medieval allegories. He sees the ancient battle-fields, and Caesar, Pompey, and Hector. The Duke of Buckingham enters, and prefaces his tragic connection with King Richard, and the murder of the Princes in the Tower.

It was immensely popular all through the sixteenth century. Many imitations appeared. Had Sackville's poetical work been more extensive he might have been included with the masters of the grand style.

MISANTHROPE, THE, (1666), by Molière. One of the more famous of the comedies of Molière, this play contains less action and complexity of plot than such a work as, for example, *The School for Wives* (q.v.). The *Misanthrope* reveals more fully the intellectual-satirical aspect of Molière's talent. Alceste, a gentleman, is so obsessed with the ideal of basic honesty that he has become completely maladjusted to his surroundings and society. In spite of the advice of his best friend, Philinte, he insists upon speaking to everyone about everything with such utter candor that he alienates all his associates, involves himself in unfortunate litigation, and brings down a score of troubles upon his head. To add to his woes, he is madly in love with Célimène, who embodies all the worst and most frivolous defects of the times. He tries to reform her by upbraiding her constantly. Finally, in despair, he begs her to retire from the world with him. Célimène, however, does not want to give up society. Alceste decides to leave the city alone, and when the play ends Philinte and Philinte's fiancée, Eliante, are trying to persuade him to remain.

MISÉRABLES, LES (1862), by Victor Hugo. This is Hugo's best known novel, partly a historical tale, partly a social and humanitarian treatise. The central figure of the book is Jean Valjean, an honest, simple peasant who steals a loaf of bread to feed his sister's starving children. Condemned to five years of hard labor, he tries to escape, is caught, and has to serve nineteen years in the galleys. On his release, he begs in vain, becomes hardened, steals again. But Bishop Myriel, a kind old man whom Jean Valjean has robbed, tells the police that he has freely given Valjean the stolen silver. Valjean is deeply moved by the Bishop's true Christian spirit, and is converted. Working hard, he takes another name and becomes a rich manufacturer and philanthropist, but he is recognized by Javert, an implacable policeman, is arrested again and returns to the galleys. He escapes and rescues Cosette, the daughter of Fantine, another victim of society. Later, he arranges the marriage of Cosette with a worthy young man, Marius, and provides for her future.

Best known in France as a lyric poet, Hugo is familiar to the non-French world largely as a novelist. Among his other novels the most successful are *Notre Dame de Paris* (q.v.), *Toilers of the Sea* (1866), which critics have compared to *Moby-Dick* (q.v.), and *Ninety-Three* (1873), a tale of the French Revolution.

MISFORTUNE OF BEING CLEVER, THE (1822–1823), by Alexander Sergeyevich Griboyedov. Sometimes translated as *Woe from Wit,* this work, the first important Russian play, is classical in temper, in the tradition of Molière. It is distinguished for its characterization, and though written in verse, is realistic. The sense of real conversation is here in spite of the rhymes. It owes no little of its quality to its well-portrayed individuals.

The scene of this satire is laid in the town house of Famusov, rich landowner and government official. The selfish, corrupt, artificial society of the time is held up to ridicule. The leading male character, Chatsky, is in revolt against this society, its Frenchified ways, and its contention that nothing good could come out of Russia.

In the beginning it is evident that Famusov's daughter Sophia is greatly taken with Molchalin, his secretary. Having much to gain from her infatuation, Molchalin pretends that her feelings are reciprocated, though much of his time is occupied with flirting with Sophia's maid, Eliza. Famuso discovers Sophia and his secretary keeping a tryst, but Sophia manages to mollify him. Chatsky, in love with Sophia, endangers his own prospects by his sharp tongue. She resents his criticism of her other suitors, and spreads the rumor that Chatsky is not quite right in his wits, a report which is accepted seriously.

Molchalin is caught by Sophia and Chatsky making love to Liza, whereupon Sophia interrupts the scene and repulses Molchalin when he grovels at her feet. Then Famusov, accompanied by several servants, comes on the scene, and gives them all a scolding. He threatens to use his influence against Chatsky, who, aiming his sarcasm against both father and daughter and against Russian society, declares that he intends to leave Moscow for good in any case. At the end Famusov is left worrying as to what people will say about him and his family.

MISHNEH TORAH (1180), by Maimonides. See GUIDE FOR THE PERPLEXED, THE, by Maimonides.

MISS JULIE (1888), by August Strindberg. This, one of Strindberg's most important tragedies, has often been compared to Ibsen's *Ghosts* (q.v.). Striving for naturalism, the author has written the drama in one long act, and like Shaw has added a preface explaining the characters and their motives. The action takes place in the kitchen of the count's country house on Midsummer Eve. Jean, a good-looking young valet, is pursued by Miss Julie, the count's daughter, a romantic, willful young woman. At first he repels her advances, but finally his behavior changes from that of a menial to one of complete mastery of her. Julie realizes that she cannot stay on the estate, and Jean suggests that they go to Lake Como and open a hotel. She rifles her father's chiffonier for the money for the journey, and suggests to Christine, the cook, with whom Jean had been keeping company, that she join them. The count's unexpected return brings matters to a crisis. Julie is unable to face her father or to run away, and influenced by Jean's suggestion, to save her honor and her father's name, goes out with Jean's razor to commit suicide.

MISS LONELYHEARTS (1933), by Nathanael West. "Miss Lonelyhearts" is a newspaper man on the New York Post Dispatch, who writes a column of advice to the lovelorn. His cynical attitude and amusement at the problems of those who address him at length change to sympathy and depression. Throughout the book, there is an ambivalence of comedy and tragedy, as in the affair of Mrs. Fay Doyle. The thirty-two-year-old woman requests an interview with "Miss Lonelyhearts," and pours out her problem—marriage to an older, infirm man after her affair with Tony Bonelli, who is the father of her child Lucie, loneliness, etc. In his bachelor apartment the newspaper man listens morosely to the stout Mrs. Doyle's familiar complaints, and does his best, by rather personal overtures of sympathy, to diminish her sorrows.

The Day of the Locust (1939) concerns a group of diverse Hollywood personalities whose aspirations lead them in the end to violence. Presented from the viewpoint of Tod Hackett, a young artist, the colorful tableau includes a portrait a dwarf who believes himself a Casanova. The novel is an indictment of a society which neglects spiritual values in a frenzy of self-gratification.

MISS SARA SAMPSON (1755), by Gotthold Ephraim Lessing. See NATHAN THE WISE, by Gotthold Ephraim Lessing.

MISS THOMPSON (1921), by W. Somerset Maugham. Steamer passengers, forced into quarantine on Pago Pago in the Samoas, suffer physical discomforts and, worse, the never-ceasing rain. The prostitute, Miss Sadie Thompson, relieves the monotony by carrying on her trade with the garrison soldiers only to run afoul of her fellow passengers, the fanatical missionaries, Mr. and Mrs. Davidson. Using every weapon—prayer, sermons, his powerful personality—Davidson finally resorts to threatening her with deportation. Faced with prison in the States, Sadie gives in. Triumphant at saving a human soul, Davidson leads her to accept prison, as a penance, and prays with her day and night. Dr. Macphail watches in amazement. On the morning the ship docks in San Francisco he is mystified to learn of Davidson's suicide, and shocked to find Sadie arrayed in her finery. But at his remonstrance, when she spits in reply, "You men. . . . You're all the same. . . . Pigs!" he understands.

First published in *The Trembling of a Leaf,* this famous story has had several theatrical productions as *Rain,* and was done again as *Sadie Thompson* in 1944.

MISUSED FEMININE POWER (1896), by Ellen Key. See KEY, ELLEN.

MITYA'S LOVE (Eng. tr., 1926), by Ivan Bunin. See GENTLEMAN FROM SAN FRANCISCO, THE, by Ivan Bunin.

MOBY-DICK (1851), by Herman Melville. Ishmael ships as a whaler on the *Pequod* out of Nantucket. The *Pequod's* master is Captain Ahab, a stern-visaged man with an ivory leg. It becomes at once apparent that this is no ordinary whaling cruise. Ahab's leg had been bitten off by a white whale of legendary cunning and ferocity, known as Moby Dick. It is Ahab's insanely obsessive purpose to hunt down Moby Dick and avenge himself. The *Pequod* cruises across the length and breadth of the Pacific in search of Ahab's prey, pursuing, meanwhile, some of its normal business of whale hunting. But Ahab's preoccupation never abates. At last Moby Dick, the adversary, is sighted. For three days Ahab pursues the whale. In each attack the wily Moby Dick eludes the harpoon and smashes the boats, bringing death and destruction. On the third day Ahab is caught about the neck by the flying whale line and whipped out of the boat to his death, pinioned to the whale. Moby Dick then batters the *Pequod* until its timbers are shattered. It sinks and all are lost but Ishmael, who clings to an empty coffin until rescued by another ship, the *Rachel*.

The novel is larded with chapters on the natural history of the whale, marveling rhapsodically upon its fearful and wonderful attributes. Melville in *Moby-Dick* strove to synthesize all the turbulent and painful torments of his inner spirit. The book, which stands as one of the epic adventure stories of the sea, is equally a ponderous, impressive allegory of man's struggle against the malignant and imponderable forces of the universe, typified in the white whale.

Melville's popularity had already been established by his first five books, semi-autobiographical adventure novels. *Typee* (1846) and *Omoo* (1847) deal with Tom and Toby, who live among South Sea cannibals, escape, and ship on an Australian whaler on a trip off Japan. *Mardi* (1849) is an allegorical romance, with satirical portraits of various countries. *Redburn* (1849) is the distressing narrative of a youth unfitted for command of a ship. *White Jacket* (1850) is an account of the inhumane conditions of life on a United States frigate. *Pierre* (1852) damaged Melville's popularity. The protagonist, Pierre Glendinning, tortured by the ambiguities of good and evil, becomes involved in a love affair with Isabel, his illegitimate half-sister. There follows a series of tragic deaths, climaxed by the lovers' suicides. The book is philosophical and iconoclastic in tone.

Melville also wrote poetry; and short fiction, such as *The Piazza Tales* (1856). The title piece describes Melville's Massachusetts farmhouse. "Bartleby, the Scrivener" is an allegorical tale of a copyist who works, is arrested, and dies in mysterious silence. "The Encantadas" are sketches of the uninhabited Pacific Galápagos Islands. "Beneto Cereno" is an account of mutiny on a slave ship. Another short novel is *Billy Budd,* which narrates the hatred of petty officer Claggart for Billy, handsome Spanish sailor. Billy strikes and kills Claggart, and is condemned by Captain Vere even though the latter senses Billy's spiritual innocence.

MOCK DOCTOR, THE (1666), by Molière. See PHYSICIAN IN SPITE OF HIMSELF, THE, by Molière.

MODERN CHINESE LITERATURE (1933). This collection, published in Shanghai, contains much of the most important contemporary Chinese writing. Everything included is written in the "plain language," and hence is accessible to more than the small educated class who read literary

Chinese. All the items are realistic. The literary revolution known as the *Pei Wha* (Plain Language) began with Hu Shih and Chen Tusiu, but the actual creator of the new literature is Lu Hsun (1881–1936), the most important short-story writer. The poet Hsu Tchimou tried to utilize Western poetic forms through the New Moon Society.

Some of the most important writers in this collection are: Mao Tun (1896–   ); Chang T'ien-i (1907–   ); Jou Shih (1901–1931); T'ien Chun (1908–   ); Kuo Mojo (1892–   ); Sha Ting (1904–   ); Ting Ling (1907–   ); Hsu Tchimou (1895–   ); Ho Chifang (1911–   ); Ch'en Mengchia (1911–   ); Chou Tsojen (1885–   ); Li Kwangt'ien (1906–   ); Lin Keng (1910–   ); Pien Chihlin (1910–   ); Shen Ts'ungwen (1902–   ); Sun Tayu (1905–   ); Wen Yituo (1898–   ); Yu Ping-p'o (1899–   ); Mao Tsetung (1893–   ); Yu Minchuan (1915–   ); Feng Chih (1905–   ); Lin Yutang (1895–   ); Pa Chin (1896–   ); Shao Hsunmei and Tien Ch'ien.

Some of these writers have been translated in the following books: *Living China* (1935), edited by Edgar Snow; *Modern Chinese Poetry* (1945), edited by Harold Acton; *Contemporary Chinese Short Stories* (1939), translated by C. C. Wang; *The Quest of Love of Lao Lee* (1948), and *Rickshaw Boy* (1945), by Lau Shaw; *Village in August* (1942), by T'ien Chun.

MODERN COMEDY, A (1929), by John Galsworthy. See FORSYTE SAGA, THE, by John Galsworthy.

MODERN INSTANCE, A, (1881), by William Dean Howells. See RISE OF SILAS LAPHAM, THE, by William Dean Howells.

MODERN KOREAN LITERATURE (1938). See HYUNDEI CHO. SUN MOONHAK.

MODERN LOVE (1862), by George Meredith. In a series of fifty sixteen-line sonnet-like stanzas, a husband reflects on the death of love in his marriage. His wife's mental infidelity has disillusioned him, though they present to society a seemingly happy marriage. Bitter, he sees love now as an animal passion. He determines to try to find at least some pleasure in another woman, because husband and wife cannot come to an understanding even when they wish. With his "Lady," his new mistress, he is "content to play the game of Sentiment," but finds that "something more than earth I cry for still." His Lady and Madam, his wife, exchange pleasantries while he stands amazed at their hypocrisy. Later he is reconciled for a moment with his wife, but again they separate. He realizes that "in tragic life, God wot, no villain need be! Passions spin the plot." The couple are reconciled only upon the wife's death, by poison, apparently ("Lethe had passed those lips"). He concludes that the soul gets but a "dusty answer" when it seeks "certainties in this our life."

MODERN PAINTERS (1843–1860), by John Ruskin. Although the first volume of the three-volume work *Modern Painters,* by John Ruskin, was published when he was only twenty-three and still a student at the university, it influenced British art enormously, particularly that of the rising Pre-Raphaelite brotherhood. The purpose of this critical study is announced by the author himself in his first preface: "The work now laid before the public originated in indignation at the shallow and false criticism of periodicals of the day on the works of the great living artists to whom it principally refers. . . ." There is little question that Ruskin made an important contribution to the philosophical field of aesthetic theory. Like Keats he accepted the artistic canons of the Greeks: there could be no beauty without truth: "The moment ideas of truth are grouped together, so as to give rise to an idea of imitation, they change their very nature—lose their essence as ideas of truth—and are corrupted and degraded." The first volume of *Modern Painters* treats of the nature of ideas and general truths. The second volume analyzes various ideas of beauty, discusses the theoretic faculty and the imagination. The third volume, written ten years later, treats "of many things" in art, each of the eighteen chapters being devoted to a different subject. Some of these subjects are: style, realization, ideal, novelty and landscape. Ruskin remarks ruefully that he had given ten years of his life to the "single purpose of enabling myself to judge rightly of art." The fourth and fifth volumes treat of landscape painting, first theoretically and technically, then historically.

MODERN REGIME, THE (1891), by Hippolyte Taine. See ORIGINS OF CONTEMPORARY FRANCE, THE, by Hippolyte Taine.

MODERN TEMPER, THE (1929), by Joseph Wood Krutch. See KRUTCH, JOSEPH WOOD.

MODEST PROPOSAL FOR PREVENTING THE CHILDREN OF POOR PEOPLE FROM BEING A BURDEN TO THEIR PARENTS OR THE COUNTRY AND FOR MAKING THEM BENEFICIAL TO THE PUBLIC, A (1729), by Jonathan Swift. This essay, first issued as a pamphlet, is filled with Swift's savage irony, covering his indignation over the desperate state of Ireland. In a matter-of-fact style he tells of the destitution and famine of the country caused by English laws. His proposal is to sell 100,000 one-year-old children (out of 120,000) for ten shillings apiece and to use them for food. He gives recipes. Six principal advantages are listed. The humor is as horrible as the cause for its writing. Swift used this means of satire to expose conditions of starvation among his countrymen.

MOKMINSIMSOO, by Chung Yakyong. See SHIJO-YUCHIP.

MOLL FLANDERS (1722), by Daniel Defoe. Probably the first social novel of modern times, *Moll Flanders* has for its theme the conviction that "poverty is the worst of all snares." Moll's beginning was somberly inauspicious: she was born in Newgate Prison. Upon her release, Moll's mother was shipped to a penal colony in America. Moll herself became a public charge: the parish provided for her upbringing.

When Moll grew up she discovered she was beautiful and that men were drawn to her. She desired a life of ease; as she had been educated in a good home, she did not regard her humble origin as too much of a handicap. In love with the elder son of the house, she nonetheless was forced by her cruel protectors to marry the younger. He died soon after, leaving her penniless with two children.

From this point on, driven by necessity and a chronic dislike for work, Moll flitted from one man to another. First she married a gentleman draper. He ran away because of business difficulties. Next she married a rich American planter and followed him to America. She had three children by him only to discover he was her brother. Horrified, she returned to England, and took up with a wealthy man, to whom she bore a son. Then he decided he did not want her any more. Her dire need drove her into a liaison with a banker. Next she got involved with an Irish highwayman, although she was ignorant of his profession. She bore him a son too. (Her total for the book is twelve births.) Finally she went back to her banker and married him. They lived happily until she was forty-eight, when he died. Poverty drove her to theft. She became an expert in the art and grew rich. Then the cycle of her fateful life completed itself: she was caught and sent to Newgate. There she met again her highwayman. Both were remorseful. They resolved henceforth, if they escaped the noose, to live a life of respectability. They were condemned to be transported to Virginia, where they settled down to an honest living.

MOLL PITCHER (1832), by John Greenleaf Whittier. See SNOW-BOUND, by John Greenleaf Whittier.

MONADOLOGY (1714), by Gottfried Wilhelm Leibnitz. See LEIB-NITZ, GOTTFRIED WILHELM.

MONDAY CHATS (1851–1862), by Charles Augustin Sainte-Beuve. See CAUSERIES DE LUNDI, by Charles Augustin Sainte-Beuve.

MONEY (1891), by Émile Zola. See ROUGON-MACQUART, THE, by Émile Zola.

MONGWAJIP, by Kim Changjip. See SHIJO-YUCHIP.

MONISH (1887), by Isaac Loeb Peretz. See PERETZ, ISAAC LOEB.

MONK, THE (1796), by Matthew Gregory Lewis. Laid in eighteenth century Madrid, this story is of a type popularized at the time by Horace Walpole's *Castle of Otranto* (q.v.) and Mrs. Radcliffe's *Mysteries of Udolpho*. Full of the most obvious melodramatic devices, the novel enjoyed wide acclaim. It was highly praised by Scott. The author earned for himself the nickname of "Monk" Lewis. The story tells of a holy man, Ambrosio, who tempts Satan's interest by his delight in his own worthiness. He succumbs eventually to the vision of a woman sent by the Evil One. This downfall leads to other and more horrible crimes, until Ambrosio finds himself so enmeshed in sin that he sells his soul to the Devil. Upon this plot the author builds every conceivable horror.

MONK'S MARRIAGE, THE (1884), by Conrad Ferdinand Meyer. See MEYER, CONRAD FERDINAND.

MONKEY (16th c.), by Wu Ch'eng-en. See HSI YU KI, by Wu Ch'-eng-en.

MONSIEUR BEAUCAIRE (1900), by Booth Tarkington. See TARK-INGTON, BOOTH.

MONT SAINT MICHEL AND CHARTRES (1905), by Henry Adams. See EDUCATION OF HENRY ADAMS, by Henry Adams.

MONTI, VINCENZO (1754–1828). Vincenzo Monti was one of the most celebrated poets of his time. Later criticism, however, reduced his literary stature to more modest proportions—which does not mean that Monti does not deserve his place among the Italian poets of the tempestuous European period that culminated in the French Revolution and its Napoleonic aftermath. Military ardor, admiration of Bonaparte, hatred for the Revolution, despair, terror, cowardice, are expressed by Monti in terse verses, magnificent in their formal beauty, but poor in real content and inspiration. Monti's poetry is a direct offspring of his character, mild and benevolent, but at the same time cowardly, ready to use flattery, to follow the trend and to imitate others.

Celebrated among the Napoleonic poems are *Prometeo* (1797), *Bardo* (1806), *La Spada di Federico* (1806) and *Palingenesi Politica* (1809). On the other hand, in the "Basvilliana" the invectives against the French Revolution reveal in Monti what was perhaps his truest nature—a profound inclination to political reaction. Monti owes most of his fame to his tragedies, among which *Aristodemo* (1786) and *Caio Gracco* (1800) are outstanding. His Italian translation of Homer's *Iliad* (q.v.) also deserves mention as a literary work of high quality.

MOON AND SIXPENCE, THE (1919), by W. Somerset Maugham. This novel is based on the life of the French painter, Paul Gauguin. The author calls his hero, who is apparently an ordinary broker, Charles Strickland. At the age of forty, his urge to paint causes him to leave his wife and child to go to Paris. There he is helped by Dirk Stroeve, a Dutch painter. Strickland seduces Madame Stroeve, deserts her; she commits suicide. Strickland wants nothing of love; he only wishes to be left alone to paint. He goes to Marseilles, then to Tahiti, where he lives with a native woman, Ata, and their children. His genius is not recognized until his death. Contracting leprosy, he paints the walls of his hut with his last masterpiece. Dr. Coutras and Ata bury him. Ata fulfills his last wish and burns the hut—his last act of contempt against society.

MOONSTONE, THE (1868), by Wilkie Collins. This story has been called by T. S. Eliot "the first, the longest, and the best of modern English detective novels." He adds: "We may even say that everything that is good and effective in the modern story can be found in *The Moonstone*." The author constructs his story by using the convenient device of documents written by the various characters. The moonstone was originally fixed in the forehead of an idol in a Buddhist temple. After the capture of Seringapatam by the British, an English officer, Herncastle, wrests the stone from the priests, who place a curse on all who possess it, and brings it back to England as his personal loot. When he dies, he bequeaths the priceless gem to his niece; soon after it disappears. Three intrepid Brahmins have traveled from India to England to retrieve the stolen jewel and return it to the temple. Disaster and tragedy accompany the disappearance of the stone, and the adventures of Herncastle's niece and her friends make up the body of the story. Sergeant Cuff is a genuine realistic creation, brilliant but not infallible. The terrible scenes on the shivering sands, like many others in the book, remind the reader of Dickens (compare the shipwreck of Steerforth in *David Copperfield* [*q.v.*]). The author was a great friend of Dickens.

MOORE, MARIANNE (1887–   ). By the time *Selected Poems* appeared (1935), with an introduction by T. S. Eliot, Marianne Moore's work had become less and less direct. It represents the more elusive school of modern verse; incise and original thoughts proposed with a cerebral and difficult style. "England" is a series of provocative observations on various countries—arbitrarily clipped off into verse and metre. "The Fish" is a dazzling arrangement of rhymes and brief phrases whose lines are indented in a pattern describing a wavy sea motif.

MORAL ESSAYS (1st c.), by Lucius Annaeus Seneca. Seneca (ca. 4 B.C.– A.D. 65), the Stoic and moralist, was the tutor of the young Nero. He can hardly be blamed for his failure to make any lasting impression upon such an unlikely pupil, but his lofty moral precepts are sometimes in strange contrast with the life of luxury and ease he lived as an imperial retainer. He was the leading literary light of his time, and his great accomplishment lay in his popularization of Stoic philosophy in a form more palatable to the upper classes of Rome in his day. Although Stoicism is the fundamental element in this philosophy, it is shot through with features drawn from other sources which make of Stoicism a milder and more beneficent way of life, containing so much in common with Christianity that Seneca was long thought to have been secretly Christian. His voluminous moral or ethical works form a large and heterogeneous collection. There are the so-called dialogues on Providence, Constancy, Anger, the Happy Life, Leisure, Peace of Mind, Shortness of Life, Consolation (3). To these are added the larger works on Benefits and Clemency and the twenty books of Moral Epistles addressed to his young friend Lucilius.

MORAL MAN IN IMMORAL SOCIETY (1932), by Reinhold Niebuhr. See NIEBUHR, REINHOLD.

MORE, PAUL ELMER (1864–1937). More was a leader with Irving Babbitt (q.v.) in the movement known as the New Humanism. This philosophy, current during the 1920's, endorsed the basically ethical nature of man's personality, and criticized the romantic stress of the supernatural elements of life. It embraced Hellenism, as it expounded a doctrine of reason, but attempted to transcend the temporary aesthetic or moral codes of any particular group or age.

More's *Shelburne Essays* (1904–1935) develop the thesis, and reveal the author's broad scholastic background. Treating literature, philosophy, and religion, the pieces urge a return to the classical standards of life.

MOREH NEBUCHIM (1190), by Maimonides. See GUIDE FOR THE PERPLEXED, THE, by Maimonides.

MÖRIKE, EDUARD (1804–1875). Influenced by Goethe and the romantics, the Swabian Mörike is one of the most genuine and unpretentious lyrical artists in German literature. His collected *Poems* (1838) are melodious, simple, and close to the folk song. Of his stories the most famous one is "Mozart on the Way to Prague" (1855), based on an episode in the castle of a count during the composer's trip to the première of *Don Giovanni*.

MORLEY, CHRISTOPHER (1890–   ). Since Christopher Morley's contributions to his college paper, in the first decade of the century, he has produced a vast amount of literary material. Poetry, both sentimental and humorous, short stories, plays, travel literature, essays, children's books and novels have flowed from his prolific pen. From 1924 to 1940 he contributed a column to the *Saturday Review of Literature.*

Where the Blue Begins appeared in 1922; and its success encouraged the author to write further novels. This book is a fantasy about Mr. Gissing, a dog who takes a brief, unsatisfying flier into the human world and is glad to return to the canine state. *Thunder on the Left* (1925) is also a fantasy, concerning the children of the Richmond family. Ten-year-old Martin and his little sister Bunny, and several other children, spy on their parents to discover if adults have fun. The author projects the lives of the children twenty years into the future, to demonstrate the changes that time works in human personality.

Kitty Foyle (1939) is Morley's popular novel about a white-collar girl of the lower middle class. Written in the first person, it chronicles Kitty's life from childhood to the age of twenty-eight. Kitty is the daughter of "Pop" Tom Foyle, Londonderry Irishman, who is a Philadelphia night watchman. At eighteen she is in love with Wynn Strafford, scion of a leading Main Line family; she dreams of going to college and improving herself. Pop's sickness and death end her social ambitions, for Wynn is not strong enough to desert his social class for the robust Irish girl.

The Man Who Made Friends with Himself (1949), which its publishers call a "novel," is a characteristically Morleyan potpourri of puns, wisecracks and clever literary allusions. It is Richard Tolman's posthumous, rambling reminiscences of his adventures as an "author's representative." Tolman equals "tout le monde"—everybody.

MORTE D'ARTHUR, LE (ca. 1470; printed 1485), by Sir Thomas Malory. Besides being the best English prose of its century, this compilation from unknown French sources has served such poets as Spenser and Tennyson as the definitive account of the Arthurian legends. Caxton divided the work into twenty-one books. The story begins with Merlin's contrivance by which Uther Pendragon and Igraine become the parents of Arthur. In due time Arthur draws the sword from the stone and is crowned king, begins his victorious campaigns, sees the questing beast, and gets his sword Excalibur from the Lady of the Lake. Gradually other characters are introduced—Balin and Balan, the brothers who slew each other; Guenever, with whom comes the Round Table; Sir Gawaine; the damsel who fatally deceives Merlin; Sir Accolon of Gaul, sent by the evil Queen Morgan le Fay; Lucius, defeated Emperor of Rome. Book VI is given to the exploits of Sir Launcelot du Lake, Book VII to the exploits of Beaumains or Sir Gareth, who leaves the kitchen and proves to the scornful Lady Linet his prowess. Books VIII-X tell of Sir Tristram and King Mark and La Beale Isoud. Book XI recounts how Sir Launcelot was tricked into becoming the father of Galahad. The way is thereby paved for "the noble table of the Sangreal," which is not achieved until Book XVII. The sin of Launcelot and Guenever is recounted and the lovely tale of the Maid of Astolat, who grieves to death for Launcelot and is carried afterward on a barge to within sight of the court, is a premonition of numerous tragedies to come. Queen Guenever is tried for treason and rescued by her lover. Sir Mordred stirs up war between Launcelot and Arthur, and in their absence usurps the throne. In the battle that follows at Dover Arthur slays Mordred, only to be himself mortally wounded by him. Borne away in a magic barge, he may yet come again. Guenever dies a nun, and Launcelot leaves his hermitage to bury her at Glastonbury, and shortly thereafter dies himself.

MOSES (1905), by Ivan Franko. Ivan Franko (1856–1916), the foremost Ukrainian author, came from Western Ukraine, the old Austrian Eastern Galicia. He lived the life of a hard-working journalist, yet became a master of nearly all forms of literature. By the time of his death, he was recognized as a cultural leader of his people. In addition to his novels and dramas, which treated of various aspects of Ukrainian life under Austria-Hungary, he was also a poet of no mean stature.

In *Moses* we have a reworking of the Biblical story, but with specific allusions to Franko's own life and the experiences of his people. The poem takes place in the desert, where the children of Israel have lost all hope of reaching the Promised Land. Rebel leaders like Dathan and Abiram have persuaded the people that if anyone dares to call himself a prophet of Jehovah he is to be stoned. Moses defies them, but he is wearied by the years of struggle and apparent failure, and plans to leave them and go on alone. He withdraws from the camp, and then on Mount Nebo, Azazel, the dark spirit of the wilderness, tempts him with the idea that he is not working for the good of the people, but is trying to reshape them in his own image for his own pride. Moses for a moment gives way and curses God. Yet Moses has no sooner vanished than his teachings take effect, and the younger people under the leadership of Joshua rise up, condemn the rebels, and push on to victory.

The last section has been well translated by Percival Cundy (1948), but the entire work has appeared several times in inadequate translations.

MOSSES FROM AN OLD MANSE (1846), by Nathaniel Hawthorne. See HOUSE OF THE SEVEN GABLES, THE, by Nathaniel Hawthorne.

MOTHER (1907–1908; Eng. tr. 1907), by Maxim Gorky. See AUTO-BIOGRAPHY, by Maxim Gorky.

MOTHER, THE (1930), by Sholem Asch. See NAZARENE, THE, by Sholem Asch.

MOTHER, THE (1924), by Grazia Deledda. Grazia Deledda belongs to a group of modern Italian writers—like Verga, Fogazzaro, De Marchi—who emphasize the character of one or another particular region of Italy. The scene of *The Mother*—the best known novel by Deledda and the one which won her the Nobel Prize in Literature in 1926—is laid in a remote village of Sardinia, the author's native island. Its theme is the struggle between the mother and a pretty widow, Annessa, for the body and soul of the young priest Paolo. Annessa, the lady of the village manor, threatens to denounce Paolo from the altar as an adulterous priest unless he runs away with her. Stiffened in his resolution by his saintly mother, Paolo defies her virtuously. As the young woman makes her way to the altar to reveal Paolo's secret shame, a power from heaven grips her. Overwhelmed, she falls on her knees and prays for divine forgiveness, only to discover, as she steals out of the church, that Paolo's mother lies dead in her pew.

MOTIVES OF PROTEUS (1909), by José Enrique Rodó. In this long essay in two volumes, the Uruguayan thinker shows in an elaborately eloquent prose the boundless possibilities of man's spiritual growth. His message, inspired by Bergson's "creative evolution" (although at times reminiscent of an incongruous ideological combination: Emerson and Dale Carnegie), emphasizes the renewal of self. A man must never admit defeat. Life has no impassable barriers. Try, and if you fail, try again. Perseverance, mixed with dynamic flexibility, is a requirement for victory. To illustrate his thesis of self-renewal, Rodó binds together biographical sketches, anecdotes, parables and poems in prose which is strikingly beautiful and convincing.

MOTLEY, JOHN LOTHROP (1814–1877). Motley, a young Boston aristocrat, spent ten years in preliminary study for an historical work on the Netherlands. *The Rise of the Dutch Republic* (3. vols.) made its striking appearance on the literary scene in 1856. Motley was inclined to minimize politics and sociology; he charted instead the sweeping advance of Protestantism under William of Orange over Catholic autocracy, represented by Philip II, which to him epitomized the progress of modern history. The first two volumes of his sequel, *History of the United Netherlands,* appeared in 1860, the last two in 1867. This material covers the period after William's death, and ends with the truce of 1609. *The Life and Death of John of Barneveld* (1874; 2 vols.), is a study of the Thirty Years' War. Motley left uncompleted a fourth section, which was to treat of the war's conclusion and events up to 1648.

MOUNTAIN WREATH, THE (1847), by Petar Petrovich Nyegosh. Petar Petrovich Nyegosh (1811–1851), the last Prince-Bishop of Montenegro, is undoubtedly the greatest South Slavonic poet. He was also a successful military commander, a bishop, a poet, a philosopher, and an educator. Nyegosh summed up the life and culture of his people just at the time when the Balkans were beginning to be freed from Mohammedan control. *The Mountain Wreath* is his greatest work. It is a form of poetic drama, a succession of scenes describing, after a dedication to the liberator of the Serbs, Karageorge, the efforts of the Montenegrins in the beginning of the eighteenth century to wipe out those renegades who had accepted Mohammedanism and who were menacing the integrity of the Montenegrin Christians. Nyegosh describes all the different types of his mountain people. There is Bishop Danilo, more a man of thought than of action, the aged and blind monk Stephen with his wisdom of experience, the various heads of the different clans, and in contrast to them the representatives of the Mohammedan Montenegrins and the Turkish vizier. Yet it is far more than the tale of a mountain feud culminating in a Christian victory, for Nyegosh knew how to merge it in a truly Shakespearean sense with the highest aspirations and thoughts of humanity.

In addition to this and his shorter poems, Nyegosh wrote the *Rays of the Microcosm* (1845), a free and independent version of Milton's *Paradise Lost* (q.v.), which he knew from a Russian translation; and while this is not so great as *The Mountain Wreath*, it is easily the finest philosophical poem in South

Slavic. The achievements of the poet are the more remarkable when we remember his short and busy life. *The Mountain Wreath* was translated into English by James W. Wiles (1930), and it has been translated into nearly all the languages of Europe.

MOUNTAINS OF CALIFORNIA, THE (1894), by John Muir. This is a standard work on the California mountains, although written a half century ago. The eminent American naturalist describes in vivid style the Sierra Nevada range, its glaciers, slopes, lakes, and meadows; and the mountain forests. He gives a detailed description of the trees, wild sheep, bee pastures. The geological history and appreciation of natural beauty is colored by personal narratives and the author's drawings. "A Wind Storm in the Forests" is considered one of our finest nature descriptions.

MOURNING BECOMES ELECTRA (1931), by Eugene O'Neill. This modern trilogy, based on Greek legend, consists of *Homecoming, The Hunted,* and *The Haunted.* The scene is laid at the close of the Civil War.

Part I. The Mannons are the most important family in town. Their large mansion was built by Ezra Mannon's father. Lavinia, Ezra's daughter, hates her mother Christine, a beautiful, sensual woman. She discovers that her mother has been having an affair with Adam Brant, a sea captain. She herself cares for Brant, who is revealed to be the son of her Uncle David, disowned by the family. Brant had made advances to Christine to revenge himself on the Mannons, but is now in love with her. Lavinia, who worships her father, has written him and her brother Orin, both still in the Army, rousing their suspicions of Brant. Knowing Ezra will soon be home, she tells her mother she must not see Brant again. Christine decides to poison Ezra on his return, then join Brant. On the night of Ezra's death Lavinia discovers the pills and suspects her mother.

Part II. Orin comes home for his father's funeral. Gentler than the other Mannnons, he has always been Christine's favorite. Realizing now that she has neglected him for Brant, he is jealous. His mother urges him to marry Hazel Niles, a neighbor. Orin and Lavinia follow their mother to Brant's ship, and overhear the guilty conversation. In a rage, Orin shoots Brant. Overcome, Christine commits suicide.

Part III. Lavinia takes Orin away on a long South Sea voyage. When they return a year later, she has blossomed into a beautiful woman, resembling her mother. Orin, feeling morose and guilty, has become a typical Mannon. He threatens to expose the murder if Lavinia marries Peter Niles, Hazel's brother; makes incestuous overtures to her; and finally shoots himself. Lavinia, frightening away Peter with the impetuousness of her love, shuts herself in the old Mannon mansion, to live in solitude.

Strange Interlude (1928) was an earlier experimental play, composed of nine acts told in stream-of-consciousness technique. Nina Leeds, a confused neurotic, marries ineffectual Sam Evans, on the advice of Dr. Edmund Darrell, an admirer. When Sam's mother reveals that there is insanity in the family, the experiment of having a child by another man is decided upon. Darrell, who thinks that passion can be regulated like a scientific matter, is the choice. The child is born, and Sam, believing himself the father, becomes a successful personality. Eleven years later, the boy, Gordon, prefers Sam to Darrell. Nina has lost her lover, her husband (Sam dies suddenly), and her son (Gordon goes off with Madeline Arnold in spite of her disapproval). Hopelessly, she marries the novelist Charles Marsden, who has always loved Nina, although he was excessively attached to his mother. Darrell returns to his neglected career.

The Great God Brown (1926), also experimental in technique—multiple masks are worn to symbolize the characters' changing personalities—is by intention a condemnation of modern materialism. Super-realistic is O'Neill's long, depressing *The Iceman Cometh* (1946), a negativistic tragedy set in Harry Hope's New York waterfront dive. Hickey, a salesman respected by the various characters, arrives with the suggestion that they all do the things they have been delaying. When Hickey is arrested for murder, however, the characters hopelessly sink back into their former apathy. *Lazarus Laughed* (1927) is, by contrast, an affirmation of life. The parable of Lazarus' resurrection dramatizes the power of love.

Between the experimentation of *The Great God Brown* and the stark naturalism of *The Iceman Cometh*, may be classified a play which is also an indirect attack on modern life. *Marco Millions* (1927) dramatizes the story of Marco Polo, showing him as a soulless, acquisitive person with a vulgar disregard for life's true values.

MOZART ON THE WAY TO PRAGUE (1855), by Eduard Mörike. See MÖRIKE, EDUARD.

MR. CREWE'S CAREER (1908), by Winston Churchill. See RICHARD CARVEL, by Winston Churchill.

MR. DOOLEY (1898–1919), by Finley Peter Dunne. Mr. Dooley, one of the sagest of folk philosophers and wits created by American humor, is an Irish saloonkeeper on Archey Road in Chicago. He is a bachelor, sedulously cultivating his Roscommon brogue and blarney. His aphorisms and *mots* are often touched with pathos. His discourses cover such subjects as the ironies of life experienced on Archey Road, an absurd newspaper item, or a tall story. A typical humorous anecdote is the account of the strange workings of universal suffrage in St. Louis—how the opposition ballots are fed to a hungry goat. Frequently Mr. Dooley vigorously enters the lists to flay public callousness to the helpless and the poor. The best known Dooley books cover the period 1898–1919.

MR. HODGE AND MR. HAZARD (1928), by Elinor Wylie. See WYLIE, ELINOR.

MR. MIDSHIPMAN EASY (1836), by Frederick Marryat. This adventurous sea story of the early nineteenth century is based on the author's personal experiences. Jack, the son of an English philosopher, Nicodemus Easy, who has instilled into his son the idea that all men are equal, goes to sea at sixteen on the ship *Harpy* under Captain Wilson. There he finds all kinds of adventures: war, mutiny, duels, shore adventures with his colored friend, Mesty. He sails through the Mediterranean, and falls in love with a Sicilian girl. At his mother's death Jack returns home to his father, who is now insane. After his death Jack goes back to Sicily for his sweetheart. They marry and return to England.

MR. PIM PASSES BY (1919), by A. A. Milne.   George Marden, a conservative country gentleman, has married Olivia, the pretty, tactful widow of a fraudulent Australian promoter, Telworthy.   Mr. Pim, a vague, elderly gentleman from Australia, calls with a letter of introduction to George.   Dinah, the latter's voluble niece, tells him of her engagement to Brian, a young artist with Socialistic ideas, and mentions that her aunt's name had been Telworthy.   Mr. Pim thinks he recollects a man by that name on the boat coming home.   It looks as if Olivia had committed innocent bigamy.   George, conscientious, cannot bear the idea of their living in sin.   He takes the view of his reactionary Aunt Julia that the marriage should be annulled.   Brian sticks up hotly for Olivia.   Fortunately Mr. Pim remembers the man died in Marseilles from swallowing a herring bone, so Olivia is again a widow.   She makes George propose all over again, and keeps him guessing till he consents to Dinah's engagement.   After all this Mr. Pim remembers the gentleman's name was Polmittle.

MRS. DALLOWAY (1925), by Virginia Woolf.   All the outward incidents in this novel occur on a June day in 1923 in London.   There is no plot: the characters' emotions of the moment and their memories of past years are what count.   Perhaps it can be said that there is a subplot, however, in the story of Septimus Smith, which comes to an end that day.   A veteran of the war, in which he had lost a friend, he has had a nervous breakdown and is on the brink of insanity and suicide, because of the general practitioner, Holmes, whose bullying normalcy he has come to loathe; Holmes does not grasp the situation.   Though the eminent psychiatrist Sir William Bradshaw, consulted that afternoon, has prescribed a rest home, Smith, on returning to his room with his Italian wife Lucrezia, seems his old self again for the first time since his trouble.   But terror seizes him when the hearty Holmes forces his way in upon him, and he plunges from the window to his death.   At the end of the book the news of this stranger's death, casually let out by Bradshaw, a guest at Mrs. Dalloway's party that night, casts a shadow over the prosperous festivities at this home of a member of Parliament. Clarissa Dalloway, fifty-two, is first seen going to the store that morning for flowers. Peter Walsh, whom she rejected some thirty years before to marry Richard, comes unexpectedly back from India.   The once reckless and still exuberant Sally Seton, now the mother of five sons, also turns up at the party.   The theme is what time has and has not done to the several characters and what they think of each other.   Mrs. Dalloway is herself a mother; the most unpleasant character she comes in contact with during the day is Miss Kalman, the indigent, frustrated religious fanatic who is trying to win away her daughter Elizabeth.

MRS. WARREN'S PROFESSION (1898), by George Bernard Shaw.   This play, thought shocking, caused a great sensation when it was first produced.   Vivie Warren, a mathematics student fresh from Cambridge, comes for a holiday to her mother's cottage in Surrey.   She tells Praed, an old friend of her mother's, that she wants a business career.   Vivie is ignorant of the fact that her mother operates a chain of brothels on the continent.   Mrs. Warren brings home a friend, Sir George Crofts, an unattractive older man.   Frank Gardner, worthless but agreeable suitor of Vivie's, is the son of the Reverend Samuel Gardner, rector of the parish.   Crofts falls in love with the girl, but fears she might be his own daughter. When he discovers that Frank's father was also an old lover of Mrs. Warren's, he breaks up the match between the young people by telling them they are half-brother and sister. Mrs. Warren admits the truth of her life to her daughter, who forgives her. She leaves to join a friend in London, determined to make her own living. Frank, who loves Vivie, does not believe Crofts' story but when he learns the details of Mrs. Warren's business he feels he cannot marry Vivie, though he tries to prevent the parting interview between Vivie and her mother.

MUCH ADO ABOUT NOTHING (1598–1599?; Quarto 1600), by William Shakespeare. This pleasant comedy is extremely ingratiating in style, and burgeons with some of the most amusing, most telling, and most familiar passages in Shakespeare. The main plot revolves around the love of Claudio for Hero, daughter of the Governor of Messina. Don Pedro, Claudio's patron, helps him to make the match. But Pedro's malicious bastard brother, desiring to make trouble, contrives to create the false impression that Hero is unchaste. The marriage is halted by this blight. Fortunately, however, the villainy is discovered, and in the end Hero is vindicated and the lovers are reunited. A subordinate plot tells the story of Beatrice and Benedick, a pair of caustic wits who are virtually tricked, by their friends, into acknowledging their love. These two are singularly like the hard-boiled, wise-cracking lovers whose rudeness is tenderness, so much in vogue on our stage and screen today and supposedly so modern. There are many charming characters in the play, not the least of whom is Dogberry, a masculine precursor of Mrs. Malaprop.

MÜNCHAUSEN. The remarkable tales of adventure ascribed to Baron Münchausen belong in that category of imaginary travels and adventure which includes *Gulliver* (q.v.) and *Robinson Crusoe* (q.v.). Strictly speaking, the tales of Baron Münchausen were designed as a caricature of the exaggerated reports of travelers returning from foreign lands. They introduced a new literary genre: that of lies and incredible stories told with tongue in cheek. The original of the hero was Baron Karl Friedrich Hieronymus von Münchhausen, a cheery and expansive aristocrat of Göttingen, who entertained his guests with outrageously improbable tales narrated with a straight face and a puckish humor. The first German author to be attracted by the famous liar was Rudolph Erich Raspe, whose *Baron Münchhausen* appeared in 1785. Two generations later Karl Immermann followed him with his long novel *Münchhausen* in 1839. The last known version was written by Carl Haensel in the 1920's.

MÜNCHAUSEN (1839), by Karl Immermann. See MÜNCHAUSEN.

MURDER IN THE CATHEDRAL (1935), by T. S. Eliot. See ELIOT, THOMAS STEARNS.

MUTINY ON THE BOUNTY (1932), by James Norman Hall and Charles Bernard Nordhoff. This novel is based on the mutiny which the crew of the British war vessel, the *Bounty*, successfully carried out in 1787 against her cruel commander, William Bligh. The story is begun by the elderly Captain Roger Byam, who in retrospect unfolds the drama of the incident, during which he was serving aboard that ill-fated vessel as a midshipman. Roger Byam, in a sympathetic desire to do justice to the members of the crew, explains the origins of the revolt, the deep-seated grievances of the men led by Acting-Mate Fletcher Christian, and the ruthlessness of Captain Bligh. He traces the course of events which inexorably followed the mutiny: the incarceration of the mutineers, the court martial, and the hanging of three leaders from the yard-arm of the *Brunswick* before the eyes of the entire royal fleet of England.

The book is part of a trilogy: *Men Against the Sea* (1934), and *Pitcairn's Island* (1934), which tells how Captain Bligh and seventeen followers left the *Bounty* in the hands of the mutineers, and rowed to a tiny island. After twenty years of Utopian existence—and murders—the native women at last put their children into an open cutter and set out for Tahiti, 1200 miles away. *The Hurricane* (1936) portrays the Polynesian natives of Tuamotu. Terangi is an upright character who recoils from the unprincipled conduct of the island's French rulers. He is unjustly imprisoned, and the events which follow this act culminate in a dramatic hurricane.

MY ANTONIA (1918), by Willa Cather. Antonia Shimerda is the daughter of Bohemian immigrants to the Nebraska frontier. Her life and trials are narrated by her childhood friend, Jim Burden, son of earlier arrivals to America. His friendship endures through the difficult years when the Shimerdas, tricked into buying poor land, struggle unsuccessfully. Antonia is a fine girl with generous impulses. When her father, frustrated in his farm work, commits suicide, she bravely takes over. Later, she has a menial job in town. There she is deceived by the philandering Larry Donovan, who abandons her with a child. She returns to the farm of her brother and marries Anton Cuzak, her pioneer spirit a sustaining strength for them. When Jim next sees her, she is surrounded by a large, happy family, having achieved from the healthy soil well-being and peace.

MY CHILDHOOD (1913), by Maxim Gorky. See AUTOBIOGRAPHY, by Maxim Gorky.

MY DAYS OF ANGER (1943), by James T. Farrell. See STUDS LONIGAN, by James T. Farrell.

MY DOUBLE AND HOW HE UNDID ME (1868), by Edward Everett Hale. See MAN WITHOUT A COUNTRY, THE, by Edward Everett Hale.

MY HEART AND MY FLESH (1927), by Elizabeth Madox Roberts. See TIME OF MAN, THE, by Elizabeth Madox Roberts.

MY LIFE AND HARD TIMES (1933), by James Thurber. See THURBER, JAMES.

MY LIFE WITH THE ESKIMO (1913), by Vilhjálmur Stefánsson. See STEFÁNSSON, VILHJÁLMUR.

MY MEMOIRS (1867), by Massimo D'Azeglio. See D'AZEGLIO, MASSIMO.

MY PAST AND THOUGHTS (1852–1855), by Alexander Ivanovich Herzen. See HERZEN, ALEXANDER IVANOVICH.

MY UNIVERSITIES (1923), by Maxim Gorky. See AUTOBIOGRAPHY, by Maxim Gorky.

MY WIFE ETHEL (1940), by Damon Runyon. See RUNYON, DAMON.

MYSTERIES OF UDOLPHO, THE (1794), by Ann Radcliffe. This book, by an Englishwoman, represents the highest development of the Gothic novel in the eighteenth century. It concerns Emily de St. Aubert, a beautiful orphan, and her adventures with ghosts, bandits and various villains, until all the complications are unfolded and she is united to her lover, Velancourt. There are numerous ghost scenes in the gloomy castle of Udolpho and in the haunted chateau of the De Villeforts, and many descriptions of the wild and melancholy aspects of nature.

MYSTERIOUS UNIVERSE, THE (1930), by Sir James Jeans. Sir James Jeans, the distinguished English physicist, wrote *The Mysterious Universe* as an answer to the widespread conviction "that the new teachings of astronomy and physical science are destined to produce an immense change in our outlook on the universe as a whole, and in our views as to the significance of human life." While he sees the issue as belonging in the domain of philosophic discussion, Jeans believes that the philosophers' cosmic speculations should be based upon all the ascertainable scientific facts and provisional hypotheses. *The Mysterious Universe* supplies this fundamental knowledge.

Jeans states that, as a result of an accident to the sun some two thousand million years ago, the earth came into existence. Mankind has always questioned its origin, and speculations about this have never ceased. Primitive man regarded simple things as obviously regular, while complex things were apparently capricious. In the course of the ages greater attention to complex phenomena brought them increasingly from the category of caprice to that of regularity. Ultimately scientists began to regard the universe as a machine. In recent years the machine concept of the universe has been breaking down.

The Mysterious Universe is an excellent and remarkably lucid account of the recent developments in physics for the lay reader. Its contents are: "The Dying Sun," "The New World of Modern Physics, Matter and Radiation," "Relativity and the Ether," and "Into the Deep Waters," the latter a summing up. Jeans attempts to give a comprehensive, although benumbing, picture of the mysterious universe in terms of general knowledge: "A few stars are known which are hardly bigger than the earth, but the majority are so large that hundreds of thousands of earths could be packed inside each and leave room to spare; here and there we come upon a giant star large enough to contain millions of millions of earths. And the total number of stars in the universe is probably something like the total number of grains of sand on all the seashores of the world. Such is the littleness of our home in space when measured up against the total substance of the universe."

Controversy has raged among scientists ever since *The Mysterious Universe* appeared, because of Jeans' emphatic view that the sun of our system is dying and that with its death will come the extinction of our earth and of mankind. He declares that not only astronomy but physics as well, through the second law of thermodynamics, predicts the "heat-death" of our universe. "It matters little," says Jeans with frightening calm, "by what particular road this final state is reached; all roads lead to Rome, and the end of the journey cannot be other than universal death." However, the sun will still remain warm enough for human survival another million years.

NAIDU, SAROJINI (1879–). Many Hindus refer to the contemporary Hindu woman poet Sarojini Naidu as "the nightingale of India." Poetry came naturally to her. "One day," she writes, "when I was eleven, I was sighing over a sum of algebra. It wouldn't come right; but instead, a white poem came to me suddenly. I wrote it down. From that day my poetic career began." Edmund Gosse, the eminent Victorian critic, was the discoverer of Sarojini Naidu as a poet writing in English, but her countrymen had already become acquainted with her verse in Hindustani. Arthur Symons, in his introduction to Mrs. Naidu's first work, *The Golden Threshold* (1905), describes her poems in glowing praise: "They hint, in a delicately evasive way, at a rare temperament, the temperament of a woman of the East." But the English critic has understated the Hindu poet's scope. She is more than a temperament; she is a fiery champion of Indian independence. As a leader of the Nationalist Indian Congress she was jailed repeatedly for her patriotic efforts on behalf of her homeland.

Like all poets of India Mrs. Naidu has a fascinating musical instinct which is always unerring in beat, subtle rhythm, lyrical line and suggestiveness of smell, touch and hearing. She writes either in the nineteenth century English style or in the manner of the ancient Hindu poets.

There are three volumes of Sarojini Naidu's published works in English: *The Golden Threshold, The Bird of Time* (1912), and *The Broken Wing* (1915–1916).

NAKED AND THE DEAD, THE (1948), by Norman Mailer. This big novel chronicles the adventures of an Army reconnaissance patrol during the assault on the Japanese-held island of Anopopei, in the Pacific. There is a series of close-ups of the various G.I. types in the operation, from commander of the American forces to lowliest infantry malcontent. Flash-back biographical sections reveal the elements which have formed the characters of the various men: Major General Edward Cummings, son of the richest man in a New England town, who has used military life as a device to satisfy his fierce lust for power; Lt. Robert Hearn, scion of Midwestern aristocracy, whose neuroses disgusted him with prewar literary life in New York and whose assignment to the platoon brings him into a strange conflict with Cummings; Platoon Sergeant Sam Croft, the egocentric Texan with a secret love of violence; Julio Martinez, the scout, who joined to escape anti-Mexican discrimination in Texas; Woodrow Wilson, the Southerner, whose main interests are women and liquor. The climax of the advance is a tortuous ascent of Mount Anaka—actually unnecessary since the island has fallen—during which the interior dramas of the men emerge into the external conflict of the war story. This book was one of the first novels about World War II to gain wide recognition.

NAKED YEAR, THE, by Boris Pilnyak. See PILNYAK, BORIS.

NANA (1880), by Émile Zola. See ROUGON-MACQUART, THE, by Émile Zola.

NARRATIO PRIMA (1540), by Rheticus. See DE REVOLUTIO-NIBUS ORBIUM COELESTIUM, by Nicolaus Copernicus.

NARRATIVE POEMS (1923), by Rabindranath Tagore. See TAGORE, RABINDRANATH.

NASH, OGDEN (1902–   ). Ogden Nash's poetry is light verse, often satirical, with a style he has invented: metrical and rhyme foibles sometimes ingeniously precise, sometimes perversely distorted. The sophisticated yet popular Nash pieces have been appearing every few years since *Free Wheeling* (1931). The latest volume is *Versus* (1949).

NASR-ED-DIN, THE TALES OF. Many of the humorous stories told by the Turkish people are connected with the name of Nasr-ed-Din. He seems to have been an historical person, but he has become the subject of so many tales that his real personality and history have disappeared and his fame has spread far beyond the narrow boundaries of Turkey to all the Turkic peoples and their neighbors. He is represented as a simple but cunning individual who disdains all the obvious advantages of a settled life and who travels around evading responsibility and yet succeeding in accomplishing a great deal of good for himself and for his fellow men. He extricates himself and his friends from the most difficult situations; he does all with perfect good humor and a keen tongue which leave most of his enemies discomfited. His stories have been told in part by H. D. Barnham (*Tales of Nasr-ed-Din Khoja,* 1923) and Alice G. Kelsey (*Once the Hodja,* 1943).

NATCHEZ, THE (1826), by François René de Chateaubriand. See ATALA, by François René de Chateaubriand.

NATHAN, GEORGE JEAN (1882–   ). Mr. Nathan, as the complement of Henry Mencken, the realistic satirist, was the ivory-tower sophisticate of his era. The two critical arbiters collaborated on several original works. Mr. Nathan's own works include plays, such as the satirical *Heliogabalus* (1920); essays such as *The World in Falseface* (1923), which reveals his hedonistic and art-for-art's-sake attitude; collections of his reviews; and *Since Ibsen* (1900), a statistical historical outline of the popular theater since 1900.

NATHAN, ROBERT (1894–   ). Robert Nathan is a versatile creator; author, musician, and artist. His many short novels include many works of satirical fantasy such as *One More Spring* (1933). This parable of charity concerns Jared Otkar, an unemployed antiquarian, and Morris Rosenberg, a concert violinist. The homeless artists set up a ménage in Central Park with Elizabeth, a homeless prostitute, and a banker who attempted to commit suicide. Otkar and Elizabeth go off to the South, while the banker and Rosenberg remain, talking vaguely of a recital.

Mr. Nathan's delicate prose is well revealed in *They Went On Together* (1941), a serious novel about the Nazi invasion, revealing the barbarities inflicted on the weak through the story of Paul and his sister Marie Rose, who are fleeing with their mother before the enemy bombers.

Five of his other novels are known as *The Barley Fields.* These include *The Woodcutter's House* (1927), about a mountain girl; *The Bishop's Wife* (1928), about an angel posing as an archdeacon, who becomes personally involved with the people he is trying to help; and *There Is Another Heaven* (1929), about a converted Jew in a Calvinist heaven.

NATHAN THE WISE (1779), by Gotthold Ephraim Lessing. The story of *Nathan the Wise* takes place in Jerusalem during the Third Crusade. Saladin, the great commander of the Saracens, has his palace there. Nathan, called the Wise, is a wealthy and benevolent Jew of the city. A young Templar, a German soldier captured by the Saracens, saves the life of Recha, Nathan's adopted daughter. When Nathan is told of this by Daya, her Christian companion, he seeks out the Templar to thank him. The Knight, however, is so scornful of the Jew that he does not wish his thanks. Nathan's passionate plea for tolerance mollifies him somwehat.

In the meantime, Saladin summons Nathan and asks of him which is the true religion, that of the Christian, Mohammedan or Jew. Nathan answers with the parable of the Ring. The ring, supposedly endowed with magic powers, has passed from favorite son to favorite son throughout many generations of a family. One father, loving his three sons equally, has two replicas made and bestows a ring upon each. The original ring can never be identified. But, says Nathan, the virtue of each ring must now be equal, as the father's love had bestowed each upon each impartially.

Meanwhile the Templar has learned that Nathan's foster-daughter was a Christian orphan, whom Nathan has reared as a Jewess. Believing that he must save her soul, the Templar reports the matter to the Christian patriarch of Jerusalem. The penalty for such an offense is death. The threatening web woven around Nathan is broken when he reveals a strange complication which had been brought about in the confusion of religious massacres years before, when many identities had been mixed up among refugee children. Recha, whom Nathan had reared to compensate for the loss of his own children in the massacre, is the sister of the Templar, who himself is actually the nephew of Saladin. Thus it is found that the supposedly divided groups of Christians, Moslems and Jews are closely bound by ties of blood and gratitude.

As a drama *Nathan the Wise* (1779) is stiff and artificial, inferior to Lessing's two previous tragedies, *Miss Sara Sampson* (1755) and *Emilia Galotti* (1772), and contrary to most of his own theories on the art of drama which he had published while the official critic of the German National Theatre in Hamburg. However, the spirit of tolerance as exemplified in the figure of the patriarchal Jew and in the beautiful story of the rings, makes *Nathan the Wise* one of the most impressive documents of the philosophy of enlightenment in German literature. The play, banned during the Nazi regime, is now again in the repertory of the German stage. It was last performed in English by the Dramatic Workshop in New York during the 1940's in an adaptation by Ferdinand Bruckner.

NATIVE SON (1940), by Richard Wright. Bigger Thomas, an embittered young Negro, works hard for the barest subsistence, and lives in squalor in a single room with his mother, sister and brother in Chicago's South Side. He is painfully aware of his status in a white man's world. Through Home Relief, Bigger gets a job with Mr. Dalton, a wealthy realtor. Although well intentioned, Dalton and his daughter, Mary, have an inadequate understanding of Bigger, and show their friendliness to him in a neurotic social-service fashion. The first climax in the novel is reached when, in a state of intoxication, Bigger unintentionally smothers the equally drunk Mary Dalton, after meeting her Communist friends. Bigger's flight over the roofs of the Chicago Black Belt is terrifying. Without any real motive, through panic, Bigger murders his Negro girl, Bessie. When he is finally captured, he realizes that his murderous defiance has done him no good. It was a deceptive freedom he had achieved. He is as helpless facing death as he had been in facing life. There is no escape for his caged spirit in a society which hates him. The novel concludes with a long account of Bigger's trial and his defense by a Communist lawyer.

Wright is one of this country's leading Negro authors. His other works include *Uncle Tom's Children* (1938), a volume of four short melodramatic stories concerning race prejudice; and *Black Boy* (1945), a short but poignant account of his own boyhood.

NATURAL HISTORY (1749–1804), by Georges Louis Leclerc, Comte de Buffon. See HISTOIRE NATURELLE, by Georges Louis Leclerc, Comte de Buffon.

NATURAL HISTORY (77), by Pliny the Elder (Gaius Plinius Secundus). The working habits of this erudite and industrious author are vividly described in the letters of his nephew, the younger Pliny, who also tells how he died in the midst of his humanitarian and scientific efforts at the time of the eruption of Vesuvius which destroyed Pompeii in 79. His encyclopedic *Natural History* in 37 books makes little pretense to originality. It contains some 20,000 excerpts from about 2000 separate works of almost 500 authors, to all of which Pliny gives due credit in his first book. The second book deals with astronomy and physics. Books III–VI discuss the geography and ethnography of Europe, Africa and Asia, progressing from the straits of Gibraltar east to India. Book VII is concerned with anthropology and human physiology. Books VIII–XI are devoted respectively to the zoölogy of land animals, sea creatures, birds and insects. Books XII–XIX treat the botany of forest trees and fruit trees, and horticulture. Books XX–XXVII survey pharmaceutical derivatives from botanical sources and XXVIII-XXXII those from zoölogical sources. The last five books are on mineralogy and the use of minerals in medicine and in painting, sculpture and the engraving of gems. They also include important chapters on the history of ancient art. Modern science has made much of Pliny's information useless, and his work is read only for its antiquarian and historical interest. For men of the Renaissance, however, and for early scientists it was a highly respected reference work, and its popularity is proved by the fact that there are about 200 medieval and Renaissance copies of it.

NATURAL HISTORY AND ANTIQUITIES OF SELBORNE, THE (1789), by Gilbert White. Gilbert White was an ordained clergyman who spent most of his life in the parish of Selborne, devoting his time to reading, writing and scientific observation. He kept a careful record of the weather, the migration of birds and the habits of animals. These notes, copied into letters to his friends Pennant and Barrington, were later published in book form as *The Natural History of Selborne*. His interest had nothing to do with the outside world, and his observations, founded on a personal knowledge of nature, need very few corrections today. Detailed and leisurely, his notes make entertaining reading for the layman as well as the naturalist.

NATURE AND DESTINY OF MAN, THE (1932), by Reinhold Niebuhr. See NIEBUHR, REINHOLD.

NAZARENE, THE (1939), by Sholem Asch. This panoramic portrayal of the life period of Jesus was first written in Yiddish, the medium always employed by the author. It attempts to reproduce every element of that day's life and history. The selfish splendors of the wealthy class and the despairing situation of the Palestinian populace under Rome are contrasted; this disparity helps to explain the emergence of a Messianic Saviour. The three parts of the story are related as seen by three divergent types. In the first, Cornelius, military governor of Jerusalem under Pontius Pilate, is seen as the symbol of privilege and power, feted by the high priests in their palaces, and indulging in every Hellenic pleasure. At Herod's' palace he witnesses the dance of Salome with the head of John the Baptist. Cornelius has heard of the appearance of the inspired Galilean, and senses the peril to his mode of living and reigning that must result. The second part is a new "Gospel fragment" as written by Judas Iscariot. In part three the Gospel story reaches its dramatic conclusion under the observation of Joseph, young disciple of Nicodemus, one of the most learned of the Pharisees.

Asch has also written a novel on Paul, *The Apostle* (1943); but he is best known to his Jewish readers for his many novels and short stories of Jewish life in Europe and America, and many dramatic works, largely untranslated. Most of his works are of an epic character, rugged, prophetic, grand. Among his books still in print, all translated from the Yiddish, are *Mottke the Vagabond* (1917); *God of Vengeance* (1918); *America* (1918); *Kiddush Hashem* (1926); *Sabbatai Zwi* (1930); *The Mother* (1930); *Three Cities* (1933); *Salvation* (1934); *Three Novels* (1938); *The War Goes On* (1936); *Song of the Valley* (1939); *Children of Abraham* (1942); *East River* (1946).

NED McCOBB'S DAUGHTER (1926), by Sidney Howard. See THEY KNEW WHAT THEY WANTED, by Sidney Howard.

NERUDA, PABLO (1904–   ). It is generally agreed that the Chilean Pablo Neruda is the greatest poet writing in the Spanish language today. In technique he has assimilated and blended the best elements of Whitman, the French symbolists and the vanguard poets; in content, his ideology is revolutionary, believing as he does in scientific socialism. Neruda was in Madrid during the Civil War. The experience profoundly affected him, and much of his finest work is an expression of his hatred for oppression, Fascism and imperialism.

NEST OF GENTLEFOLK, A (1858), by Ivan Sergevich Turgenev. Sometimes translated as *A House of Gentlefolk* or *Liza,* this novel makes the most of the old Orthodox ideals and the ideals of the old gentry in Russia. When Fyodor Ivanitch Lavrétsky is a student in Moscow, he is older than the other students. He falls in love with Varvara Pavlovna and marries her without knowing her at all well. The studious husband finds no companionship with this woman, who is taken up with social frivolities. He withdraws more and more into his own inner life. By accident he discovers his wife to have been unfaithful to him. He returns to the country and tries to pick up the threads of his former life. While visiting relatives he meets Liza Kalitine, a young woman, deeply religious, with his own ideals of behavior, and rather appealing. Liza has a suitor, Panshin, a worldly man chosen by her mother. She would have married him, had not Lavretsky urged her to follow the dictates of her own heart. A deep sympathy develops between the older man and Liza. At this time he reads of his wife's death. He suddenly feels light and happy; he tells Liza he loves her. When he finds that Liza loves him his cup of happiness overflows, but not for long. His wife appears as alive and as tormenting as ever. She forces him to live with her as husband and wife. Both the gentle folks are crushed. But they exhibit strength of character. Liza enters a convent; Lavretsky devotes himself to the management of his estate. His humanitarian efforts save him from the natural bitterness inherent in the situation.

NET OF THE TRUE FAITH, THE (1440–1443), by Peter Chelčický. Peter Chelčický (1390–1460) was one of the most ardent followers of Jan Hus, but unlike many of them, he refused to co-operate with the nationalist movement as soon as it showed signs of trying to conquer by force of arms. He retired to his native village and lived there the life of the peasants, while he continued his preaching and teaching. These are chiefly summed up in the *Postilla* or *Book of Interpretations of the Gospel for the Whole Year* (1441) and *The Net of Faith*.

The latter takes its title from the account of the net used in the miraculous draught of fishes (St. Luke 5, vv. 4–6). In the first part the author points out how Christianity lost its purity when Emperor Constantine and Pope Sylvester set up a divided civil and religious power. In the second part he describes the various rots that have entered the church. Among these he classes the clergy, the men of property, scholars, the cities, etc., and maintains that the true Christian must avoid all participation in government, all acts of violence, no matter how justified, all study of subjects other than the Gospels, and must live the simple and hardworking life of the common people.

Chelčický was a forerunner, in many of his ideas, of Leo Tolstoy. Out of his teachings evolved the Church of the Bohemian Brethren, the Unitas Fratrum, and no one has pleaded more eloquently the idea that the true Christian can be found only among the uneducated and laboring masses of the peasants—an idea that has left its indelible mark upon much of later Czech literature, even including the works of Karel Čapek.

NETS TO CATCH THE WIND (1929), by Elinor Wylie. See WYLIE, ELINOR.

NEUROTIC PERSONALITY OF OUR TIME, THE (1937), by Karen Horney. See HORNEY, KAREN.

NEW ASTRONOMY WITH COMMENTARIES ON THE MO-. TIONS OF MARS (1609), by Johann Kepler. See ASTRONOMIA NOVA. by Johann Kepler.

NEW ATLANTIS, THE (published 1627), by Sir Francis Bacon. This fable, inspired by More's *Utopia*, tells of a visit to the island of Bensalem, where the government is paternalistic and Bacon's hopes for the future of science are fulfilled in the research college called Solomon's House. Here various inventions and techniques are presaged, including refrigeration, oxygen tanks, vivisection, cross-breeding of plants, telephones, artificial flavors, airplanes, submarines, and optical illusions. In order to bring news of experiments and discoveries outside the island, ambassadors are sent out called Merchants of Light, but otherwise the island—to which by a special miracle Christianity has come—exists in happy isolation.

NEW DRAMA, A (1867), by Manuel Tamayo y Baus. In gratitude for his help and encouragement, the young actress Alicia marries Yorick, aged comedian in Shakespeare's company. Edmundo, a promising young actor, is Yorick's adopted son. Alicia and Edmundo fall in love. They both idolize the old man, however, so that growing remorse and a constant effort to dominate their passion for each other fill their lives. Shakespeare and the actor Walton discover the secret. The former believes them when they assure him that they have not yielded, and he promises to help them win their battle. Walton, whose wife deceived him, believes them guilty of the worst. To avenge himself on Yorick for having taken from him the great tragic role in a new play, he plans to inform him of the lovers' passion. Edmundo, terror-stricken, writes Alicia a note begging her to flee with him. Walton intercepts the note and reveals it to Yorick during a scene they are playing in which all the characters and situations are similar. Yorick in a rage actually kills Edmundo, making it necessary for Shakespeare to make the proper apologies to the audience, saying that the play cannot go on, and adding that Walton has just been murdered in the streets.

NEW ENGLAND: INDIAN SUMMER (1940), by Van Wyck Brooks. See FLOWERING OF NEW ENGLAND, THE, by Van Wyck Brooks.

NEW ESSAYS ON HUMAN UNDERSTANDING (1701), by Gottfried Wilhelm Leibnitz. See LEIBNITZ, GOTTFRIED WILHELM.

NEW EXPERIMENTS PHYSICO-MECHANICAL TOUCHING THE SPRING OF AIR AND ITS EFFECTS (1660), by Robert Boyle. See SCEPTICAL CHYMIST, THE, by Robert Boyle.

NEW FOES WITH AN OLD FACE (1853), by Charles Kingsley. See HYPATIA, by Charles Kingsley.

NEW GRUB STREET (1891), by George Gissing. Edwin Reardon, a sincere artist, is contrasted with Jasper Milvain, who is frankly basing his career on opportunistic standards. Jasper wins fame and Edwin finally dies of ill health caused by poverty and heartbreak. Writers of artistic integrity starve in garrets while the superficial eat and live well. Amy, Edwin's wife, and their son, Willie, leave him. When Amy inherits a fortune and Edwin dies, Jasper gives up his fiancée, Marian Yule, to marry Amy and her money. Harold Biffen, another struggling writer, is in love with Amy. When he finds he can neither win her nor make a living, he commits suicide. Other characters depicted are: Jasper's sisters—Maud, who marries Dolomore, and Dora, who marries Tom Whelpdale. The novel is a realistic picture of the effects of poverty on artistic endeavors and the easy success of the materialist and opporutnist conditions which exist in every age. It is laid in London in the 1880's.

NEW HAMPSHIRE (1923), by Robert Frost. See FROST, ROBERT.

NEW HÉLOÏSE, THE (1761), by Jean Jacques Rousseau. Julie, the daughter of an aristocratic family, falls in love with her tutor, Saint-Preux, a man of no fortune, and a commoner. Her family disapprove of him emphatically. She is faced with the heartbreaking choice between causing her invalid mother's death and giving up her lover. She does what all perfect women are expected to do, but rejects him only after a bitter soul struggle. She then weds Wolmar, the man chosen for her by her father, and, being a perfect woman, she is a wonderful wife to him. Here the theme of *La Nouvelle Héloïse* enters. Like the original Héloïse, who loved Abélard even after she entered the convent, so Julie continues to love her bourgeois after her dutiful marriage. She dies young, in an accident, thus saving the author the difficult task of resolving the moral impasse.

The New Héloïse is at once a novel and a tract. Rousseau, an incorrigible preacher, injects into the framework of his novel his social, religious and pedagogical views, vindicating natural love and innate virtue. Julie herself breaks into impassioned sermons upon the slightest provocation. Above all things, she preaches about the sentiment of the heart: "Is true love not the most chaste of all bonds? Is not love itself the purest and at the same time the most vital aspiration of our nature?" His novel owes much to Richardson.

NEW LAOKOÖN, THE (1910), by Irving Babbitt. See BABBITT, IRVING.

NEW MONDAY CHATS (1863–1870), by Charles Augustin Sainte-Beuve. See MONDAY CHATS, by Charles Augustin Sainte-Beuve.

NEW ORGANON (1620), by Sir Francis Bacon. See NOVUM ORGANUM, by Sir Francis Bacon.

NEW POEMS (1894), by Gustav Fröding. See FRÖDING, GUSTAV.

NEW POEMS (1844), by Heinrich Heine. See HEINE, HEINRICH.

NEW POEMS (1838–1840), by Nikolaus von Lenau. See LENAU, NIKOLAUS VON.

NEW SPOON RIVER, THE (1924), by Edgar Lee Masters. See SPOON RIVER ANTHOLOGY, by Edgar Lee Masters.

NEW SYSTEM OF CHEMICAL PHILOSOPHY (1808–1827), by John Dalton. The so-called "chemical revolution" of Lavoisier had introduced modern terminology and theories into chemistry, but it left virtually untouched the basic question of the ultimate constitution of matter. In antiquity the atomism of Democritus had been opposed by the infinite divisibility postulated in the Aristotelian doctrine. During the medieval period atomic views lingered among the Arabs, but Latin Christian theology favored the Peripatetic doctrine over the materialism of Democritus. During the seventeenth and eighteenth centuries, however, a revival of atomism appeared in the corpuscular views of Gassendi, Boyle, Newton, Voltaire, and others. Up to that time the question was largely one of philosophy, for quantitative evidence was wanting; but the precise chemical measurements of Black and Lavoisier suggested the possibility of a new attack on the problem, and it was here that Dalton did his greatest work.

Dalton did considerable investigation in meteorology, but his first real contribution to physical science was his "law of partial pressures" (1801), a result which he saw might be explained on an atomic basis. Proust's "law of definite proportions" pointed in the same direction. Dalton therefore started with the assumption that chemical combination takes place in the simplest possible way, one atom of one element combining generally with one atom of another. He erroneously assumed at first that water was composed of oxygen and hydrogen in equal numbers of atoms. Only later did he discover that there are twice as many atoms of hydrogen as of oxygen; and he enunciated the principle that atoms combine in ratios which are simple whole numbers— the "law of multiple proportions."

Dalton had been working on his atomic theory since the beginning of the century, and in 1808 he enunciated it formally in the first volume of his celebrated *New System of Chemical Philosophy*. In it he pointed out that atoms are far too small to see or weigh singly, but that it is possible to determine their relative weights through measures of chemical composition. His experimental results were very incomplete, and at first he gave oxygen an atomic weight only seven times that of hydrogen (instead of about sixteen), due to errors in measurement and to the false assumption that water is HO instead of H_2O. Gradually, as more and more quantitative studies were reported, tables of atomic weights were corrected and Dalton's theory gained adherents. However, the atomic theory was hampered by the failure to distinguish between the atoms of a chemical element and its molecules. That is, the smallest unit of oxygen as a *physical* entity is a molecule containing a pair of atoms. This distinction was made in 1811 by Avogadro, but it was overlooked until reiterated in 1858 by Cannizzaro. From then on the opposition to atomism melted before an overwhelming mass of experimental verification. Dalton, through his *New System of Chemical Philosophy,* had become the "father of modern atomic theory."

NEW WAY TO PAY OLD DEBTS, A (1633), by Philip Massenger. This domestic drama has long been popular. The play emphasizes the character of Sir Giles Overreach, a cruel extortioner, who lets nothing stand in the way of his one ambition: to pile up wealth for his only daughter, Margaret, and marry her off to a great nobleman. He does not consult her, but selects Lord Lovell, an honorable gentleman whose page, Allworth, is in love with Margaret. Lord Lovell, sympathetic with the young people, determines to help them by letting Sir Giles think he intends to marry his daughter. Sir Giles has ruined his nephew, Wellborn, who has lost all his money to the old man. Wellborn, determined on revenge, goes to the widow of his old friend,

Allworth, and enlists her help in his scheme. Lady Allworth, stepmother of young Allworth, living in retirement since her husband's death, now suddenly appears in public with Wellborn. Overreach, thinking Wellborn is going to marry the rich widow, offers him money to pay off his debts. He reveals to Lord Lovell, supposedly his future son-in-law, his plan to obtain Lady Allworth's lands by fraud. Overreach insists on a clandestine marriage, and Lovell sees to it that Margaret and Wellborn are wed. After more perfidy on the part of Overreach, the shock of his daughter's marriage unhinges his mind. At the end Wellborn discovers his uncle has unlawfully taken his estate.

NEW WAYS IN PSYCHOANALYSIS (1932), by Karen Horney. See HORNEY, KAREN.

NEWS FROM NOWHERE (1890), by William Morris. See EARTHLY PARADISE, THE, by William Morris.

NEWCOMES, THE (1855), by William Makepeace Thackeray. Narrated by Pendennis, *The Newcomes* is more sentimental than Thackeray's earlier novels. He is also more sympathetic with his characters and less intolerant of their human frailties. Colonel Newcome, an old-fashioned gentleman and kindhearted soldier, is a thoroughly lovable character. Thackeray is said to have aimed to draw attention away from worldly meanness by portraying great and commanding goodness of heart in characters such as Ethel and Colonel Newcome. His son, Clive, is a worthy but by no means perfect young man. Clive falls in love with his cousin, Ethel, but finds his suit despised by her wealthy father, Brian Newcome. Ethel's grandmother, the worldly and embittered Countess of Kew, also wants Ethel to make a more auspicious match. Barnes Newcome, Ethel's brother, a contemptible snob, does everything to discourage Clive's suit. Ethel yields to the demands of her family and becomes engaged to Lord Kew, her cousin; this she soon breaks off, and for a while is betrothed to a foppish young man, Lord Farintosh. However, she ends this, too. Clive, in the meantime, marries a pretty young girl, Rosey Mackenzie. Mrs. Mackenzie, her mother, is a treacherous, scheming person; when Colonel Newcome loses his fortune she finally drives him to an almshouse with her sharp tongue. Here the Colonel dies. The story closes with the inference that since Rosey has died Clive and Ethel will be married.

NEWER ALCHEMY, THE (1937), by Ernest Lord Rutherford. This little volume of 67 pages, published in the very year of Rutherford's death, may be taken as symbolic of the author's important work on the structure of the atom. Belief in the possibility of the transmutation of matter arose early in the Christian era; and the search for the "philosophers' stone" to transmute one element into another was pursued throughout the Middle Ages. The alchemists' search was encouraged by the Aristotelian view that the basic elements differed from each other only in possessing in varying proportions the qualities hot, cold, moist, and dry. With the rise of the atomic theory during the nineteenth century, the old idea of transmutation appeared untenable; but the discovery in 1902 of radioactivity lent plausibility to a new mechanism of atomic transformation. Radioactivity is a sign of spontaneous transformation or of atomic instability; and after a study of the radiations known as alpha, beta, and gamma rays, Rutherford in 1919 found that atoms of nitrogen could be converted, through bombardment by alpha particles (helium nuclei), into atoms of oxygen. Since then many other artificial transformations have been observed. Only rarely is the quantity of matter thus produced visible or weighable, but the certainty of methods of detection is greater than in ordinary chemical analysis. Rutherford made significant discoveries and wrote a number of important books on such transformations. His *Radioactivity* (1904) and *Radioactive Substances and Their Radiations* (1913) present the scientific data for specialists. *The Newer Alchemy* (1937) summarizes in less technical language the background of modern atomic structure and transmutation. Rutherford was in great part responsible for recent work in nuclear physics, for he suggested that the atom is made up of a heavy nucleus surrounded by small rotating charged particles known as electrons. This picture, modified by Bohr and others, has resulted in the present atomic or electronic age.

NIBELUNGENLIED (ca. 1200). A mixture of distorted historical fact and pure legend, the *Nibelungenlied,* written by an Austrian monk of the twelfth century, is one of the most important literary monuments of medieval times. Originally an oral tradition, it passed through the several phases of Germanic history absorbing many influences until it was recorded in its present epic form. The fundamental themes are unswerving personal loyalty and uncompromising revenge. Brunhild, Gunther's wife, arranges for the murder of Siegfried after she has discovered that it was not her husband, but Siegfried, who overcame her amazon powers upon which her virginity depended. Previously, Gunther had arranged for Siegfried with his magical cape to overcome her and to conquer her at various chivalric games. Hagen is the actual murderer of Siegfried, who had been rendered invulnerable, except for one spot between the shoulder blades, by a bath in dragon's blood. Kriemhild, Siegfried's wife, broods over the treacherous deed and plans for revenge. Hagen son robs Kriemhild of Siegfried's treasure—the gold of the Rhineland Nibelungen elf-men—and thus incites Kriemhild further. She marries Etzel (Attila of the Huns, historically), invites her kin—the Burgundian Royal House, among them Hagen—only to provoke a conflict in which they are all slain. Kriemhild, too, meets death, and Etzel, confused and unaware of the underlying treachery, remains.

This Middle High German folk epic, extant in three varying manuscripts and written in strophes (verses) of four lines, is highly valued for its depiction of manners and morals. It preserves the characteristics of the pre-Christian age despite an imposition of a thin veneer of chivalric and Christian elements. The motivations of the actions as well as the detailed gory descriptions of slaughter testify to the fact that the *Nibelungenlied* is thoroughly heathen in character. It has become the national epic of the German people. The best known modern versions of the legend are Hebbel's cycle of plays (cf. *Gyges and His Ring,* by Hebbel) and Richard Wagner's musical tetralogy.

NIBELUNGS, THE (1862), by Christian Friedrich Hebbel. See GYGES AND HIS RING, by Christian Friedrich Hebbel.

NIBELUNGEN RING, THE (1856), by Richard Wagner. See WAG-NER, RICHARD.

NICHOLAS NICKLEBY, THE LIFE AND ADVENTURES OF (1839), by Charles Dickens. Money-mad Ralph Nickleby balks at helping his high-spirited, independent nephew, Nicholas, who has been left penniless at the death of his father. Nicholas, who is the support of his mother and his sister, Kate, finally secures a position as tutor at Dotheboys Hall. Here the master, Wackford Squeers, beats and starves the forty pitiable boys left in his care. He particularly plagues Smike, an unfortunate half-wit. Nicholas becomes so horrified at Squeers' inhumanity that he eventually beats him and leaves the school, taking the now adoring Smike with him. He becomes an actor with Vincent Crummles' theatrical company, and finally gets a good post in a counting house owned by the benevolent Cheeryble brothers. In the meantime Kate has secured a position with Madame Mantalini, a dressmaker. Ralph takes advantage of her innocence and beauty to encourage the unwelcome and uncouth advances toward h·r of his friend, Sir Mulberry Hawk. Nicholas discovers this and frees his sister after trouncing Sir Mulberry. Gride, Ralph's partner in crime, is pursuing a lovely girl, Madeline Bray. In this he is helped by Ralph, who hopes to force her marriage to Gride. Nicholas meets Madeline and falls in love with her. Ralph, infuriated by Nicholas' interference with all his plans, tries to injure him through Smike, who finally dies, partly as a result of fear of his persecutors. Ralph's final defeat is brought about by Newman Noggs, his odd clerk, who succeeds in thwarting all his conspiracies. Facing ruin and overcome with despair at the disclosure that Smike was his own son, Ralph commits suicide. Madeline and Nicholas marry. So do Kate and the Cheerybles' nephew, Frank. Squeers and Gride get their just deserts: the former is transported, the latter murdered.

NICOLÒ DEI LAPI (1841), by Massimo D'Azeglio. See D'AZEGLIO, MASSIMO.

NICOMACHEAN ETHICS, THE, by Aristotle (384–322 B.C.). The *Nicomachean Ethics* of Aristotle, named after its editor, Aristotle's son Nicomachus, is a profound and stimulating introduction to moral philosophy. It treats of moral problems in terms of the capacities as well as of the potentialities of men to do good. At the outset Aristotle clarifies his position: "In every pursuit and art the Chief Good is that for the sake of which all that we do is done; this in medicine is health, in war victory, in house-building the house. In every action, in every moral choice, this is the End, all and everything else is directed and subordinated to achieving it. So if in all action there is an End proposed, this End will be the practical Good." Happiness, states Aristotle, is pre-eminently the final end of human aspiration. We choose it for its own sake and for no other purpose. There are, of course, ends which are not final, such as pleasure, honor, intellect, wealth, etc. These are merely subordinate aims directed toward happiness.

The question naturally follows: "If Happiness is the object of life, what is Happiness?" The answer is: "Happiness is the activity of the highest part of our nature, i.e., reason." For Aristotle the intellectual life is the happiness thinking men should strive for. It is pleasant; it is desired for itself and not as a means to a final end. Also it can be enjoyed more sustainedly than any-thing else. While not needing any outside adjuncts to complete it, it is also the highest faculty in man.

Other ancient philosophers attempted to unite all virtues in one. Aristotle prefers to define each one separately as a mean between two extremes, e.g., bravery as the mean between cowardice and rashness. As for happiness—it is not a state but an activity, not pleasure but the exercise of the virtues. Book I of the *Ethics: The Good for Man* states the subject of the inquiry. Books II-V discuss *Moral Virtue;* Book VI, *Intellectual Virtue;* Book VII, *Continence and Incontinence; Pleasure;* Books VIII and IX, *Friendship;* and Book X, *Pleasure; Happiness.*

NIEBUHR, REINHOLD (1892–   ). Reinhold Niebuhr is an impor-tant figure in contemporary Christian thought. After a thirteen-year ministry in Detroit, during the years of America's great industrial growth, Niebuhr's re-actions to economic problems led him to espouse socialism. He received the chair of Applied Christian Ethics at New York's Union Theological Seminary, where it became apparent that although he was a leftist in politics, he was a rightist in religious orthodoxy, maintaining that the church is by nature opposed to the world. During 1939–1940, he delivered the famous Gifford Lectures, pub-lished in 1941 as *The Nature and Destiny of Man.* These volumes named man's reason, thwarted by society, as the agent of egoism and the cause of materialism. Man is free in spirit, but bound by necessity, producing anxiety, the Christian environment for temptation and sin. Original sin is thus described not as an animal heritage, but as the distinct characteristic of man's self-consciousness.

Moral Man in Immoral Society (1932) is a criticism of contemporary civili-zation. The decency of the individual is contrasted with the behavior of man in the mass. Niebuhr attributes the apparent contradiction to the unsatisfactory guides and checks which exist in human groups, and the small comprehension of the needs of others. Thus arise the non-ethical attitudes of classes and na-tions, and the impossibility of justice through non-revolutionary means.

Beyond Tragedy (1932) is a Christian interpretation of history, maintaining the relativity of judgments and facts.

NIELS KLIM'S SUBTERRANEAN JOURNEY (1741), by Ludvig Holberg. See ERASMUS MONTANUS, by Ludvig Holberg.

NIELS LYHNE (1880), by Jens Peter Jacobsen. See MARIE GRUBBE, by Jens Peter Jacobsen.

NIETZSCHE, FRIEDRICH (1844–1900). Writing in a half-poetical, half-philosophical style and using allegorical devices, Nietzsche leveled a bitter and caustic attack on the complacency of the last half of the nineteenth century. Democracy (equality, concern for the welfare of the herd) and Christianity (the morality of the weak) were the special objects of his criticism. He dis-liked mediocrity in all its forms and defended aristocracy, conceived as the self-assertion of those who have talents and accept the challenge of life. Unfor-tunately history shows that the tendency is for the weak and mediocre to tri-umph through sheer weight of numbers. This pessimism seems to go back to Nietzsche's reading of Schopenhauer. Nevertheless he felt that aristocrats should assert themselves and conceive of society as existing for their use. Charity, compassion and concern for social welfare find no place in Nietzsche's ideal society. It is thought by some that these views stimulated the development of German nationalism, and the use made of them by the Nazis seems to support this judgment. However, Nietzsche's genuine interest in culture and his contempt for mobs, militarists, and racialists, tend to refute this view. Most famous of his writings is *Thus Spake Zarathustra* (q.v.), which is a collection of discourses and sermons spoken by a mythical Persian prophet. Other important books are *Beyond Good and Evil* (1885), *Genealogy of Morals* (1887), and *The Will to Power* (1909–1910).

NIGGER OF THE NARCISSUS, THE (1898), by Joseph Conrad. James Wait, a huge West Indian Negro, is "the nigger of the *Narcissus*." In an almost plotless tale, his destiny is followed from the moment he goes aboard the *Narcissus* at Bombay. He is dying of tuberculosis, and his rapid physical disintegration is accompanied by curses at life and mankind. His dying is watched with compassion and terror by his crew-mates: "He speaks . . . to the sense of mystery surrounding our lives; to our sense of pity, and beauty and pain; to the latent feeling of fellowship with all creation—and to the subtle but invincible conviction of solidarity that knits together the loneliness of innumerable hearts, to the solidarity in dreams, in joy, in sorrow, in aspiration, in illusions, in hope, in fear, which binds men to each other, which binds together all humanity—the dead to the living, and the living to the unborn." To the dying Wait are closely linked the thoughts and dreams of Singleton, "a sixty-year-old child of the mysterious sea," of Belfast, of the cook Podmore, of the three ship's officers, and most strikingly of the spiritually soiled Donkin, the cockney. When the "Nigger" finally dies, a part of them has died with him. The *Narcissus* is merely the ship of life in which the destinies of all varieties of men are irrevocably linked.

NIGHT IN THE LUXEMBOURG, A (1906), by Rémy de Gourmont. In this philosophical novel, a god walks in the gardens behind the Odéon, and a winter's night becomes a summer morning. James Rose, the journalist, hears this divinity proclaim that "the Gods are born and die," though their life is long. Where there is God, He will not have Love absent. Beautiful women come and go, kiss and are kissed sensuously, because He, "like the gods whose stories are written by the poets . . . desires a multiplicity of embraces." Our roses and our women make us the equals of the gods, and even envied by them. Most of the book is written in dialogue, and the conversations between "I" and "He" are vehicles for Gourmont's Epicurean philosophy. In his eyes, virtue means to be happy. "Human wisdom is to live as if one were never to die, and to enjoy the present minute as if it were to be eternal."

NIGHT RIDER (1939), by Robert Penn Warren. See WARREN, ROBERT PENN.

NIGHT THOUGHTS (1745), by Edward Young. For a long time Young enjoyed great popularity, almost European in its scope, and these reflections in blank verse had as immense and enduring popularity as was ever conceded to such unexciting poetry. Today it is hard reading, except to the quietly meditative, but the taste and temper of people in the eighteenth century was more tolerant of Young's sentimental faults. The full title is *Night Thoughts on Life, Death and Immortality.* Eight of the *Nights* are "Complaints": the ninth, with its vision of Christian eternity, is "The Consolation." The poem originated in family bereavement.

NIGHT'S LODGING, THE (1903), by Maxim Gorky. This, the best known of Gorky's plays, has been translated under other titles, such as *The Lower Depths,* and *At the Bottom.* The play is not essentially dramatic in its structure, but it is one of the finest character studies in Russian literature. The action takes place in a basement resembling a cavern, which is presided over by Kostilioff, a lodging house keeper, who is also a receiver of stolen goods. The Actor, a drunkard, is always dreaming about the theater and forgetting the lines he begins to recite. Wassilissa, the young wife of Kostilioff, is in love with Pepel, a thief. Pepel, in turn, has taken a fancy to Wassilissa's younger sister, Natasha. Other lodgers are Kvaschnya, a market woman; Bubnoff, a capmaker; Alyoschka, a shoemaker; and the Baron, a young man who has once been a nobleman. Into this assemblage of quarreling, wretched people comes Luka, an old pilgrim. Wassilissa approaches Pepel and suggests that he help free her of her husband and she will raise enough money for him to marry Natasha. Wassilissa beats Natasha and Kostilioff interferes. In the struggle they upset the samovar, and Natasha is badly burned. The others call Pepel, who strikes Kostilioff and kills him. Natasha is taken out, calling hysterically to the police that her sister and Pepel have killed Kostilioff. Luka leaves and after his departure the lodgers discuss him. Sahtin, a man of forty, remarks: "He worked on me like acid on a dirty old coin." The play ends with the Baron going out into the court and finding that the Actor had hanged himself.

NIGHTINGALE OF WITTENBERG, by Hans Sachs. See SACHS, HANS.

NIGHTMARE ABBEY (1818), by Thomas Love Peacock. This is an immensely amusing satirical novel of early nineteenth-century England and its writers. Scythrop is the poet Shelley; Mr. Flosky is Coleridge; Mr. Cypress is Byron. Nightmare Abbey in Lincolnshire is the family mansion of Christopher Glowry and his son, Scythrop. There are many visitors: Mr. and Mrs. Hilary, Mr. Cypress, Mr. Flosky, Mr. Toobad, Reverend Mr. Larynx, Asterias and son, Aquarius, Honorable Mr. Listless. Scythrop falls in love with two women: his cousin, Marionetta Celestina O'Carroll, and Stella, a stranger who moves into a secret compartment of his tower. She is discovered to be Celinda Toobad, and Scythrop's dual loves are exposed. Everyone leaves, and Scythrop orders a pint of port and a pistol. His father talks him out of suicide and rushes off to get one of the girls. Both, however, have been married: Celinda to Mr. Flosky, and Marionetta to Mr. Listless. Scythrop accepts his father's advice to have but one string to his bow in the future, and temporarily contents himself with Madeira.

NIM-E-CHIMMUK (1925), by Han Yong-woon. See MEDITATIONS OF THE LOVER, by Han Yong-woon.

1919 (1932), by John Dos Passos. See U.S.A., by John Dos Passos.

NINETY-FIVE THESES (1517), by Martin Luther. See LUTHER, MARTIN.

NINETY-THREE (1873), by Victor Hugo. See MISÉRABLES, LES, by Victor Hugo.

NJÁL SAGA, THE (late 13th c.). Known in G. W. Dasent's translation as *The Saga of Burnt Njál* (Everyman Edition), it is probably the greatest and certainly the most widely circulated of that vast array of unique prose writings, the Icelandic Sagas. Of their many varieties—mythological, royal, ecclesiastical, fictional, and family—this is the last type. It represents not only the culmination of the tales of violent old Icelandic feuds, but also the beginning of their decline, for here, near the end, Christian sentiments appear. The work is a composite of two, maybe three, large parts, united by the friendship of the noble Gunnar of Litharendi, of the first part, for the upright, law-abiding Njál of the second; and action is based on historical events that took place in Southern Iceland between the years 960 and 1016, after Christianity had been introduced. The *Saga* is occasionally verbose and repetitious, but has extraordinarily vivid descriptions of feuds, lawsuits, passions, and blood revenge, told impersonally in simple, impressively forceful language, through understatement and terse bits of conversation, but mostly through external action. Excellently drawn are Njál's son Skarphedin; his loyal and heroic mother Bergthora, who refuses to leave her sons and husband in their final extremity; and Gunnar's hard-hearted wife Hallgerda, who after quietly watching her husband fight his last battle against his enemies singlehanded and having his bowstring cut by one of them, refuses him a lock of her hair for a new one. She reminds him of the slap in the face which he once, in moral indignation, had given her when he had caught her stealing butter; and Gunnar dies. The tragic pathos, fearlessness, and dramatic intensity of the final scenes of the heroes' deaths have scarcely been equaled in narrative literature.

Other Sagas of permanent value worth special study are the *Egil's Saga,* based on the life of the poet Egil Skallagrimsson; the *Grettis Saga,* about an outlaw; the *Laxdaela Saga;* and the *Hrafnkel's Saga Freysgoda,* about a priest and a lawsuit. There are many others. The *Njál Saga* is judged to be the best.

NO SAFE HARBOR (1941), by Katherine Anne Porter. See PORTER, KATHERINE ANNE.

NO STAR IS LOST (1938), by James T. Farrell. See STUDS LONIGAN, by James T. Farrell.

NO TIME FOR COMEDY (1939), by S. N. Behrman. See BEHRMAN, S. N.

NOA NOA (1919), by Paul Gauguin. Tired of living in France and tempted by the tropics, Gauguin embarked for Tahiti early in 1891. *Noa Noa* is the account of his first year on the island, his disappointment in the European colonial snobbery of Papeete, his delight in the simple, native life of the interior. In this Eden, the jaded European becomes a new man. Critics agree that Gauguin's art gained a new grandeur and intensity from his two-year stay in the islands.

The self-portrait which emerges from *Noa Noa* is more explicitly delineated in Gauguin's *Intimate Journals,* published in 1921 by the painter's son Émile.

NOAH PANDRE (Eng. tr. 1936), by Zalman Shneiur. See SHNEIUR, ZALMAN.

NOCHE DEL SÁBADO, LA (1903), by Jacinto Benavente. See SATURDAY NIGHT, by Jacinto Benavente.

NOCTES ATTICAE (169), by Aulus Gellius. This work is so called because, as Gellius tells us in his preface, it was begun during the winter nights of his sojourn in Athens, whither he had gone from Rome to study philosophy. He had been gathering curious and recondite bits of learning for it since his earliest youth. It is one of those miscellanies of erudition so popular with the learned antiquarians of the age of the Antonines. Gellius lumps the excerpts from about 250 authors, some of whom are otherwise little known, into the twenty volumes of his scrapbook on no principle except that of variety of subject. Chapters on questions of philosophy, medicine, law, language, history and literature jostle one another and are interlarded with anecdotes of great men of the past and of his own day. Only the dramatic settings in which he presents his lore are original with Gellius. Even when he seems most learned, the numerous authorities he quotes are taken from similar compilations rather than from the individual authors cited. The value of the work lies in these quotations from works no longer extant and in the picture he gives of the society of his day.

NOH PLAYS OF JAPAN (ca. 15th. c.). The *Noh Plays of Japan* were essentially court theater pieces, deeply permeated by religious feeling and folkways. They have that artless simplicity and stylization with which all sacred and semisacred art expression in the Orient is endowed. This, in fact, is their great limitation; rigidity and lack of reality kept the *Noh Plays* from developing into a great art form or from achieving that depth and plasticity which characterized the early dramas of ancient Greece, which they resemble. Perhaps an even more important difference between the Japanese and the Greek play is that of intention and world view. The Greeks were humanists and concerned with reality, with the destiny of men's lives. The nobility, who formed the audience at *Noh* productions, were opposed to reality, which they regarded as vulgar.

The *Noh Plays* were composed partly in prose but largely in verse form, using the formal court language of the time. At the time of their origin the prose sections were recited or sung, the verses were sung, and the chorus chanted in unison. Already existing art materials were used to embellish or extend their play architecture. The *Noh* authors frequently built an entire play around well-known dance ballads, poems or series of poems.

Seami Motokiyu, who, with his father, Kwanami Kiyotsuga, brought the *Noh* drama to its most classic expression during the fourteenth century under the discriminating patronage of the Shogun Yoshimitsu, has left a record of his dramaturgical ideas.

The best English translations of the *Noh Plays* are by Arthur Waley, who aimed to approximate the subtlety and lyricism of the Japanese originals. Included in his collection are nineteen plays and summaries of fourteen others. An exceptionally intelligent introduction by the translator gives an illuminating historical, religious, and technical description of the *Noh Plays* and the manner of their theatrical production.

NON SUM QUALIS ERAM BONAE SUB REGNO CYNARAE (1896?), by Ernest Dowson. Written in unusual metre with a singular haunting quality, this famous poem might be a symbol of the romantic-tragic writers of the 1890's. The author, who died at thirty-three, spent much of his life in France. His verse is exquisitely finished but lacks virility. Yet this is a beautiful poem, with its pathetic refrain: "I have been faithful to thee, Cynara! in my fashion." The very name Cynara will always recall the poet who celebrated her. Dowson is chiefly known by this one poem; but others of similar nostalgic vein fill his one small book of verse. There is an appealing quality about most of the poems included which impels re-reading.

NONSENSE NOVELS (1911), by Stephen Leacock. Here Leacock parodies ten types of novel: first, in *Maddened by Mystery,* the detective novel; then, in *"Q.",* the supernatural; next, in *Guido the Gimlet of Ghent,* the novel of knights and ladies. This is followed by *Gertrude the Governess,* the sentimental Victorian novel; then *A Hero in Homespun,* a satire on Americans' admiration for important criminals; *Sorrows of a Super Soul,* the Russian novel; a Scotch novel, *Hannah of the Highlands;* a sea story, *Soaked in Seaweed; Caroline's Christmas,* the melodramatic novel of the mortgage on the old homestead; and finally, *The Man in Asbestos,* subtitled *An Allegory of the Future.*

NORMA ASHE (1942), by Susan Glaspell. See GLASPELL, SUSAN.

NORN GUEST (1919), by Johannes V. Jensen. See LONG JOURNEY, THE, by Johannes V. Jensen.

NORTH OF BOSTON (1914), by Robert Frost. See FROST, ROBERT.

NORTHANGER ABBEY (1818), by Jane Austen. This novel parodies the absurd Gothic romances popular in England at the end of the eighteenth century, particularly those of Mrs. Ann Radcliffe. The humor and gaiety bubble over as Jane Austen describes Catherine Morland, who, being "from fifteen to seventeen . . . in training for a heroine," has read all of Mrs. Radcliffe's hair-raising tales. As a result her imagination runs wild when her friends, Eleanor and Henry Tilney, invite her to visit with them at their medieval home, Northanger Abbey. During Catherine's first night at the Abbey a storm breaks. The long passages in the house and the imaginary dungeons underneath become mixed with her recollections of her reading, so that her overcharged mind begins to have "experiences." She sees ghosts, hears terrifying cries, and discovers a mysterious manuscript, which, upon closer scrutiny, turns out to be only a bundle of laundry lists. The sad climax is reached when the old General Tilney, who has been encouraging his son Henry's romantic feelings for Catherine under the impression that she is rich, discovers his mistake and sends her away. Henry, however, is in love and loyal. Defying his father, he follows Catherine and marries her, his father becoming reconciled to the situation when Eleanor announces her engagement to a peer.

Catherine met the Tilneys at Bath, which is also the scene of *Persuasion*, also published in 1818. It tells of Anne Elliot's selfishness in being persuaded to give up Captain Frederick Wentworth. More than eight years pass before the Captain realizes his mistake.

Mansfield Park (1814) has another self-effacing heroine in Fanny Price, adopted by a rich and frivolous family. Her character is variously tested before her worth is recognized by her cousin Edmund.

NORTHWEST PASSAGE (1937), by Kenneth Roberts. This historical novel tells the story of the career of Major Robert Rogers and his Rangers, the most doughty of all the Indian fighters, whose exploits during the French and Indian War are famous. At the battle of Crown Point Rogers is joined by Langdon Towne, a Harvard-educated artist. The two become bosom friends. As disaster follows disaster for Rogers' men, the leader loses heart and presents a dejected figure. Not so young Towne; he rises above adversity with matchless courage and tenacity throughout the disintegration of his hero Rogers, who after all his martial glory, ends in Fleet Prison, a broken man.

Among many other historical novels, Roberts wrote *Arundel* (1930), a novel of Benedict Arnold's attack on Quebec; and two sequels, *Rabble in Arms* (1933) and *Captain Caution* (1934).

NOSTROMO (1904), by Joseph Conrad. This is the tempestuous story of a South American revolution. Nostromo, an Italian, is the most feared man in Sulaco, headquarters of the "Gould Concession," a great silver mine. During the revolution that breaks out, he is told to remove the silver treasure, which he succeeds in hiding safely on a desert island in Placid Gulf. He lets it be known later that the ship carrying the precious metal had sunk to the bottom of the sea. From that day he grows discreetly richer. A lighthouse is built on the island, its keeper being Giorgio Viola. The old man lives with his daughters Linda and Giselle. Although the unscrupulous Nostromo is engaged to Linda, he is actually in love with Giselle. One night Giorgio sees Nostromo and Giselle together in a love tryst, and kills Nostromo.

NOT PEACE BUT A SWORD (1939), by Vincent Sheean. See PERSONAL HISTORY, by Vincent Sheean.

NOT SO DEEP AS A WELL (1936), by Dorothy Parker. See PARKER, DOROTHY.

NOTEBOOKS OF SAMUEL BUTLER, THE (1912), Samuel Butler. Early in life, Butler began to jot down his random thoughts and observations in notebooks, which were published posthumously. They offer a variety of interesting reflections on his childhood, school days, art, religion, and evolution. The philosophy revealed in these piquant notations is well illustrated by the following excerpt: "A sense of humor keen enough to show a man his own absurdities, as well as those of other people, will keep him from the commission of all sins, or nearly all, save those that are worth committing."

NOTEBOOKS OF LEONARDO DA VINCI, THE (ca. 1500), by Leonardo da Vinci. Leonardo has been so idolized that often he is regarded as an almost superhuman genius far ahead of his day. A more judicious evaluation of his position would show him as a great transition figure from late medieval to early modern times. The ingenuity of his ideas, the precision of his observations, and his extraordinary versatility are well known; but Leonardo's limitations are generally overlooked. His chief deficiency was linguistic. He knew little Latin, the universal language of learning, and even his vernacular is rough and ungrammatical. His brain was full of ideas, but he failed to express them clearly. He covered the whole field of science from astronomy to physiology, making many original contributions; but he left his results in confused and incomplete form. His output as an artist consisted of a few works of great perfection; but as a scientist he left a great and unorganized mass of papers, totaling several thousand pages. Everywhere he turned he found things which roused his scientific curiosity: human anatomy, embryology, the structure of the eye, the flight of birds, parachutes, the movement of blood, the nature of fossils, the earth's crust, the new-moon-in-the-arms-of-the-old, the camera obscura, perspective, perpetual motion, the simple machines, hydraulic engineering, quick-firing guns, fortifications. His mind teemed with thoughts on these and countless other topics, and he jotted his ideas down in his notebooks, together with innumerable diagrams and sketches. Leonardo had a passion for knowledge for its own sake, and he showed a clear grasp of scientific method with its interplay of empirical observation and mathematical formulation. Had he organized and published his results, his influence on the course of scientific development might have been profound; but his ideas were for the most part buried in a mass of notes in vernacular mirror writing. Leonardo says of at least one manuscript that he hoped to arrange things in order afterward; but this was never done. Instead of rearranging, he kept adding to the notebooks over a period of some forty years, from early manhood to old age. Most of the manuscripts were in his possession when he died in 1519, but subsequently they became scattered. Today original manuscripts of Leonardo are found in many libraries of Europe, including the Ambrosian Library in Milan, the Bibliothèque Nationale in Paris, and the British Museum at London, as well as in many private collections. The notebooks have never been published in complete form, but transliterations and translations of portions have appeared in many languages, including English.

NOTES FROM UNDERGROUND (1864), by Feodor Dostoevsky. See MEMOIRS FROM UNDERGROUND, by Feodor Dostoevsky.

NÔTRE DAME DE PARIS (1831), by Victor Hugo. *Nôtre Dame de Paris* is Hugo's historical romance of medieval Paris. The great church is the central figure of the novel. Hugo devotes much of his book to describing its aisles and galleries, towers, carvings and gargoyles, and to exploring medieval Paris, the city of François Villon, with its thieves' dens, masques, guilds and witch trials. Against this historical background, he sets a melodramatic action. The hero is Quasimodo, the deaf, deformed, grotesque bell-ringer of the cathedral, hopelessly in love with beautiful, innocent young Esmeralda, the Bohemian singer and dancer. The villain is the stern, calculating arch-deacon of the cathedral, Claude Frollo, who, desiring Esmeralda and unable to have his way with her, turns her over to the authorities for a crime he has himself committed. She is hanged. The frantic Quasimodo pushes Frollo off one of the towers of the church, and goes to die himself in the charnel house where Esmeralda's body has been thrown.

NOUVELLE HÉLOÏSE, LA (1761), by Jean Jacques Rousseau. See NEW HÉLOÏSE, THE, by Jean Jacques Rousseau.

NOVALIS (1772–1801). The German Romantic poet Friedrich von Hardenberg, who used the pseudonym "Novalis," was born in 1772 and died of pulmonary consumption before he had attained the age of twenty-nine. An intensely religious environment and the tragic passion for a young girl, com-parable to Dante's love for Beatrice, were the stimulating influences of his lyrical genius. His *Hymns to the Night* (1800) in free rhythms of exquisite beauty were the passionate outpourings of a grieving soul longing for death as the portal to a higher life. In his later years the poet turned more and more toward Catholicism. The unfinished romance *Heinrich von Ofter-dingen* was meant by Novalis to dethrone Goethe's *Wilhelm Meister* (q.v.), a novel which he loved and called at the same time "too modern and too prosaic," a book which had become an obsession with him. Like *Wilhelm Meister* the romance is an "Entwicklungsroman" (educational novel) which describes the gradual unfolding and maturing of the hero's mind. Novalis' book displays a poet's life from the first spark of inspiration in youth to ripe-ness, a life destined to bring about the age of poetry, the reign of wisdom and love. Heinrich, the poet, is in search of the Blue Flower, the symbol of love, wisdom, poetry, and bliss eternal. He is predestined to pick the blue flower at last. However, fate did not permit Novalis to execute this crowning chapter of his book. Despite the fragmentary character of *Heinrich von Ofterdingen,* it must be considered the most representative novel of early German Romanticism.

NOVELAS EJEMPLARES (1613), by Miguel de Cervantes. See CAU-TIONARY TALES, by Miguel de Cervantes.

NOVUM ORGANUM (1620), by Sir Francis Bacon. The time interval from about 1250 to 1600 sometimes is referred to as "the period from Bacon to Bacon." This designation of the transition stage from medieval to modern science serves to point out that the ideas of Roger Bacon and Francis Bacon are important parts of a connected pattern. The *Opus Majus* (q.v.) of Roger had proclaimed the importance of experimentation and mathematics in sci-ence, although he was unable to make much progress in this direction himself. Reliance upon authority continued to dominate thought for several hundred years, until Ramus, Paracelsus, Copernicus, Vesalius—and many others—broke with tradition in the middle of the sixteenth century. With the decline of Aristotelianism, however, there arose a need for a new methodology. Thus it was that Francis Bacon, with his insistence upon empiricism and induction based upon experimentation, became "the high priest of modern science." All through the turmoils of his political life he was planning what he called a

Magna Instauratio or *Great Reconstruction* of philosophy in general and of science in particular. This was to consist of seven parts or topics: 1) introductory treatises; 2) classification of sciences; 3) scientific methodology; 4) actual investigations into natural science; 5) historical development of science; 6) anticipations of scientific results; and 7) the application of science to bring about the Utopia which he confidently expected to follow upon the conquest of nature. In each of the above categories Bacon actually composed one or more treatises. *The Advancement of Learning* (q.v.), under 2, and *The New Atlantic* (q.v.), under 7, are perhaps the best known of his scientific works; but the *Novum Organum,* belonging to the third category, undoubtedly represents his greatest contribution to science. It is in the first book of this work that he makes his strongest plea for induction—for spending more time in the observation of nature and less in logic-chopping. His four "idols" of the mind recall the four "impediments" to learning of Roger Bacon; but Francis follows these with a far clearer description of the scientific method: "commencing as it does with experience duly ordered and digested, not bungling nor erratic, and from it educing axioms, and from established axioms again new experiments."

It should be noted that Francis Bacon was not a great scientist. He was essentially a literary figure, and though his phrases have a modern ring, his views on specific phenomena were far from clear. In the *Novum Organum* (Book II, section xxi), for example, he adopted the essentially modern notion of heat as a form of motion, but his heterogeneous grouping of thermal phenomena confuses more than it clarifies. He overemphasized classification at the expense of mathematical and deductive methods; and he failed to appreciate the work of great contemporaries like Gilbert and Kepler. Yet his *New Organon* exerted a deeper and more positive influence on science than did any other single work of the time. It made Bacon the prophet of the new age.

NOW WE ARE SIX (1927), by A. A. Milne. See WINNIE-THE-POOH, by A. A. Milne.

NOYERS DE L'ALTENBURG, LES (1943), by André Malraux. See MAN'S FATE, by André Malraux.

O DI UNO O DI NESSUNO (1929), by Luigi Pirandello. See PIRANDELLO, LUIGI.

O. HENRY. See PORTER, WILLIAM SYDNEY.

O. HENRY ENCORE (1939), by William Sydney Porter. See PORTER, WIILLIAM SYDNEY.

O PIONEERS! (1913), by Willa Cather. *O Pioneers!* narrates the heroic battle for survival of simple pioneer folk in the Nebraska country of the 1880's. John Bergson, a Swedish farmer, struggles desperately with the soil but dies unsatisfied. His daughter Alexandra resolves to vindicate his faith, and her strong character carries her weak older brothers and her mother along to a new zest for life. Years of privation are rewarded on the farm. But when Alexandra falls in love with Carl Linstrum, and her family objects because he is poor, he leaves to seek a different career. After Alexandra's younger brother

Emil is killed by the jealous husband of the French girl Marie Shabata, however, Carl gives up his plans to go to the Klondike, returns to marry Alexandra and take up the life of the farm.

O SHEPHERD SPEAK! (1949), by Upton Sinclair. See JUNGLE, THE, by Upton Sinclair.

OBERON (1780), by Christoph Martin Wieland. See WIELAND, CHRISTOPH MARTIN.

OBLOMOV (1857), by Ivan Alexandrovich Goncharov. Begun ten years before publication, this book made an immediate success, and has established itself as a national classic. "Oblomov is more than a character; he is a symbol. He was...the embodiment of a whole side of the Russian soul...its sloth and its ineffectiveness," Mirsky claims. "Oblomovism" became a part of the language as a result of Goncharov's creation. This state of being and of mind belonged particularly to the old gentry, but at the time the book was written it had affected even the peasants. As a foil to Oblomov we have Stoltz, the methodical, systematic, businesslike German; but it is Oblomov who wins the hearts of the readers, not Stoltz. There is a memorable scene between these two, where Oblomov tries to convince Stoltz that their ideals are identical. "Why," he asks Stoltz, "isn't it the purpose of all your running about, your passions, war, trade, politics—to secure rest to attain this ideal of a lost paradise?" But Stoltz refuses to admit that everyone seeks peace and rest; he even insists that ten years before Oblomov had had very different desires. But it was too late for Oblomov to change; he was a victim of Oblomovism.

OBSERVATIONS PREFIXED TO THE SECOND EDITION OF "LYRICAL BALLADS" (1800), by William Wordsworth. See DEFENCE OF POETRY, by Percy Bysshe Shelley.

OCTAVIA, by Seneca. See TRAGEDIES, by Seneca.

OCTOPUS, THE (1901), by Frank Norris. This novel concerns the exploitation of wheat by monopolistic interests. The antagonists are the farmers, and the Pacific and Southern Railroad. The latter engages in corrupt legislative practices to rob the farmers of their savings from the crops. The individual characters are of minor importance; they are so numerous and diversified as to represent almost an entire social order. Magnus Derrick, leader of the farmers, compromises with his conscience, then disintegrates morally during the betrayal of his trusting friends. Others are Annixter, the rancher; Hilma Tree; the poet Presley; the romantic shepherd, Vanamee; Father Sarria of the Spanish mission; the proletarian Hooven family; the saloonkeeper Caraher; the engineer Dyke; the plutocratic Cedarquist family of San Francisco; Shelgrim, the railroad president; and the rogues Delaney, Ruggles, editor Genslinger, Derrick's son Lyman, and railroad agent Behrman. In the end, Magnus is ruined and forced to take a position with Behrman when the railroads win domination. Behrman is accidentally killed, however, by a landslide of wheat.

The Pit (1903), second of a projected trilogy about wheat, is a story of manipulations in the Chicago Exchange. Curtis Jadwin, a stock speculator, is so absorbed in making money that he neglects his emotionally starved wife Laura. Into this situation steps Sheldon Corthell, dilettante artist, to console her. Laura loves her husband, and postpones for awhile going away with the aesthete. Meanwhile, Jadwin engages in a struggle with the Crookes gang of speculators. He beats them, but is crushed by fluctuations in wheat production. He and Laura effect a reconciliation.

ODE ON INTIMATIONS OF IMMORTALITY FROM RECOL-LECTIONS OF EARLY CHILDHOOD (1807), by William Wordsworth. This poem has as its motto:

> The Child is father of the Man;
> And I could wish my days to be
> Bound each to each by natural piety.

What most regard as Wordsworth's greatest lyrical achievement, the eleven irregular, predominantly iambic stanzas, are dedicated to the Platonic concept of pre-existence, of the child as being nearer to heaven than the man, since "Our birth is but a sleep and a forgetting"—and the forgetting of that original glory naturally increases with age. Thus there is nostalgia in most of the poem, and the child is called the "best Philosopher." But much can be recaptured by the adult, especially in the presence of nature, and certain basic mature experiences bring new wisdom.

ODES (23-13 B.C.), by Horace (Quintus Horatius Flaccus). Horace rested his right to fame entirely upon these four slender volumes of lyric poetry, and claimed as his proud achievement that he had adapted the measures of the great lyric poets of Greece to the Latin tongue. His success in his own generation, the brilliant Augustan Age, is indicated by the fact that as poet laureate he was called upon to write the choral ode for the celebration of Augustus' secular games. Horace combines the art of the great lyric poets, his debt to whom he freely admits, with that of the Alexandrians. The odes are composed in the most varied meters, and average about twenty lines in length. The subject matter varies widely from slight occasional trifles on love, wine and good fellowship to mild but serious Epicurean admonitions on the wise enjoyment of life, and patriotic celebrations of the greatness of Rome. Everywhere his genius for compressed and studied effectiveness of expression is evident in his use of the most commonplace words in striking phrases that are still quoted.

ODES (written 1819), by John Keats. Four of Keats' *Odes* are among the greatest poems in the English language. All four appeared in *Lamia, Isabella, The Eve of St. Agnes, and Other Poems* (1820). The mood of the "Ode to a Nightingale" is melancholy, with a sense of the burden of life accompanied by a longing for extinction: "I have been half in love with easeful Death." But the bird's voice also conjures up

> Charm'd magic casements, opening on the foam
> Of perilous seas, in faery lands forlorn.

The "Ode on a Grecian Urn" is sculpturesque, fixing antique figures beyond the bounds of time, lifted above human passion. It glories in silence. All know the final message: "Beauty is truth, truth beauty." The "Ode on Melancholy" begins, "No, no, go not to Lethe . . . ," and recommends the exquisite natural sights "when the melancholy fit shall fall." The last stanza deals with the paradox that Melancholy has her shrine "in the very temple of Delight." "To Autumn" is, like the preceding ode, in three stanzas, of which the second personifies the "season of mists" and the third shows that it, like Spring, has its music too.

ODES, by Pindar (ca. 522–443 B.C.). A proud Theban aristocrat, Pindar was the most celebrated and sought-after poet of his day. His poetic genius expressed itself in all the lyric forms cultivated in his time, but we know him only for his victory odes, written upon commission to celebrate the athletic victories of his fellow blue bloods in the contests of such Greek festivals as the Olympic Games. The four books of the *Odes* are known as the Olympian, Pythian, Nemean and Isthmian, from the names of the four Panhellenic festivals. Pindar thought of victory in the games as the most glorious goal of the strivings of those of noble birth and as a symbolic expression of their innate excellence. Therefore he cherished his own position as the chosen immortalizer of such fame, and often expresses his unabashed pride in poesy. The *Odes* are composed in free metrical form with accurate responsion of strophe, antistrophe and epode in keeping with the music with which they were originally sung. They generally follow a scheme which opens after an introductory passage with a brief reference to the victory which occasions the ode. The central portion of the ode is devoted to a myth which may be appropriate to the individual who is honored or to his family or to the festival of the occasion. The closing passage usually embodies some moral reflection upon the myth and upon the obligations of the victor as a vessel of nobility. Pindar's rich and musical vocabulary often does not appear favorably in translation, and we can have no notion of the effect his melodies must have produced, but the dazzling imagery of his poetic fancy may readily be seen.

ODI BARBARE (1877–1887), by Giosue' Carducci. See CARDUCCI, GIOSUE'.

ODYSSEY, THE (9th c. B.C.), by Homer. The *Odyssey* is a companion piece to the *Iliad* (q.v.). Its poetic style is the same but its interests are far different. The *Iliad* is truly heroic in its devotion to martial incident, whereas the *Odyssey* shows a more romantic interest in adventure. The story covers the ten years of Odysseus' return to Ithaca after the capture of Troy. At the opening a council of the gods determines to restore Odysseus to his home despite Poseidon, who has delayed him. In Ithaca Penelope, his faithful wife, is plagued by a host of overbearing suitors who hope that Odysseus is dead. Books I-IV tell of the quest of the faithful Telemachus for his father. Books V-VIII recount how Odysseus was released from the island of the beauteous Calypso at the command of the gods and was shipwrecked on the island of the Phaeacians, where he is warmly received. In Books IX-XII Odysseus relates to his Phaeacian hosts all the adventures that befell him after his departure from Troy until he reached their shore. Books XIII-XVI describe how he was miraculously returned to Ithaca by the Phaeacians, and his welcome in the hut of the swineherd Eumaeaus, where Telemachus meets and recognizes him. In Books XVII-XX

Odysseus returns to his own house in the disguise of a beggar, and endures for a time the insolence of the suitors. The last four books tell of his vengeance in slaying the suitors and his re-establishment in his realm with Penelope. Odysseus is always presented as the man of many wiles and ever-ready cunning under the sternest buffetings of misfortune. Always fascinating are the tall tales of his adventures in strange and distant lands amid fanciful men and monsters, which served for the model of Virgil's account of the wanderings of Aeneas. This central point of interest is reserved for the midpoint of the poem by use of the device of the narrative flashback. Among the famous English translations may be mentioned those of Pope and William Cullen Bryant. The most popular and useful is the prose version of Butcher and Lang.

ODYSSEY OF HOMER, THE (1871–1872), translated by William Cullen Bryant. See THANATOPSIS, by William Cullen Bryant.

OEDIPUS, by Seneca. See TRAGEDIES, by Seneca.

OEDIPUS AT COLONUS (ca. 406 B.C.), by Sophocles. Oedipus, once King of Thebes, is under a curse because he had unwittingly killed his father and married his own mother, and has been banished from his native city. The younger son of Oedipus, Eteocles, had persuaded the citizens to banish his elder brother, Polynices, who took refuge in Argos. There he married the daughter of Adrastus and levied an army of auxiliaries to support his pretensions to Thebes. Before going into exile Oedipus had cursed his sons for failing to protect him. When the play opens, Oedipus, old, blind and practically a beggar, is wandering from place to place led by his faithful daughter, Antigone. He feels that his involuntary crimes have been atoned for and that the avenging deities will now take pity on him. Father and daughter come to the village of Colonus just outside Athens and stop to rest. The village elders enter, and finally on Oedipus' request they send for King Theseus, who offers him the hospitality of Athens, and Oedipus promises a boon to that city. Ismene, his other daughter, arrives unexpectedly with word from the oracle at Delphi, and tells her father that if he dies in a foreign land the enemies of Thebes will overcome her. She warns him that Creon is approaching. Creon does his best to persuade Oedipus to return to Thebes. He tries to carry off Antigone and Ismene, but they are saved and brought back by Theseus. Polynices, who has heard that his father is near Athens, then comes to ask for the latter's blessing on his expedition against Thebes to overthrow his brother. But Polynices had been instrumental in banishing Oedipus, and the old man in a fine burst of rage renounces his son and curses his expedition. A thunderstorm threatens, and Oedipus, who feels that his death is imminent, tells Theseus that he will confer his promised boon on Athens by being buried in her soil. The old King, his two daughters, and Theseus retire.

Soon a Messenger announces to the Chorus that after certain rites had been performed the two weeping girls had left their father with Theseus. Antigone and Ismene enter, mourning their father, and when Theseus returns, Antigone falls at his feet and begs to know Oedipus' burial place. He replies that it is a mystery, that no man may go near the spot, and bids them lament no more. "His destiny hath found a perfect end."

This is the last play of Sophocles' old age, and was produced after his death.

It is full of the beauty of Colonus, which was Sophocles' birthplace, and is based on the local lore of the deme. In 407 the Athenians had defeated the Boeotians at this spot, and this event recalled the legendary promise of Oedipus.

OEDIPUS THE KING (ca. 430 b.c.?), by Sophocles. *Oedipus the King* is Sophocles' masterpiece. Structurally the play is unrivaled in dramatic liter-ature. The characters are drawn with humanity and warmth. Creon is a manly character, though in *Antigone* (q.v.) and *Oedipus at Colonus* (q.v.) Sophocles represents him as mean, treacherous, and a braggart. Jocasta, Oedipus' Queen, the widow of the former King, Laius, is portrayed as a duti-ful wife, with a slightly maternal attitude toward her younger husband. She tries vainly to comfort him and to convince him that the gods govern wisely. Oedipus dominates the play. In the beginning he is rash, proud, and obsti-nate and, as the drama mounts in horror, is overcome by the awfulness of his fate. The play opens in Thebes before the royal palace where Oedipus rules, having won the throne and the hand of the widowed Jocasta years before by ridding the city of the Sphinx. In front of the central doors is an altar, and seated on the steps are men and youths dressed as suppliants. The elderly priest of Zeus stands facing the palace. Oedipus comes forth and asks the priest why the suppliants are there. The priest replies that the city is suffering from a plague and they have appealed to their gods. Oedipus has sent his brother-in-law, Creon, to the shrine of Apollo; Creon now returns with word that the murderer of Laius, the former king of Thebes, is in their midst and must be driven forth from the city before the plague will pass. The King has also sent for the blind old seer, Teiresias, who tells Oedipus that he is the slayer of Laius, the man whom they seek. He also tells Oedipus that he is the unwitting slayer of his father, who was Laius, and that he is the incestuous husband of his own mother. The very suddenness of the revelation makes it incredible to all. Oedipus thinks Creon is in league with the seer, and unjustly accuses him of wishing to seize the kingdom. Creon answers with restraint and dignity, but Oedipus' unrestrained rage brings them close to blows until Jocasta comes out from the palace and stops the quarrel between the two men. Now the story sweeps forward with rapidly accelerating dramatic pace. The very things Jocasta tells Oedipus to reassure him that Teiresias' charge cannot be true arouse Oedipus to apprehension. He had been reared as the son of Polybus, King of Corinth, but the oracle of Delphi had warned him he would kill his father and wed his mother. To avoid such a hideous fate, he refused to return to Corinth. As he departed from Delphi, however, he had encoun-tered an unknown man and killed him and his retinue in a quarrel on the road, allowing only one survivor to escape. The circumstances of the killing seem to correspond with those of the death of Laius. A messenger now arrives with word of the death of Polybus, at which Oedipus rejoices, since he thinks he cannot now kill his father. To still his fear that he may yet wed his mother, the messenger reveals that Oedipus is not the true son of these parents. Under questioning he tells how he had found Oedipus as an abandoned child and taken him to Corinth and Polybus. Jocasta now perceives the full truth that Oedipus is indeed her son, for Laius had abandoned their child in fear of a prophecy that he would die at the child's hand. She rushes into the palace and leaves Oedipus to piece together the rest of his story. The missing link is provided by the survivor of Laius' murder, who proves to be the same servant who had exposed the child Oedipus to die. At this discovery of the complete fulfillment of the dreaded oracle Oedipus rushes into the palace after Jocasta. A servant soon reports that Jocasta has hanged herself and Oedipus has struck out his own eyes so as to look no longer upon the scene of his abomination. Oedipus himself soon reappears with blood-stained cheeks, cursing his fate and calling upon Creon to send him into the exile he had himself decreed for the murderer of Laius.

OEUVRES, by Louis Pasteur (1822–1895). Pasteur, a "mere chemist," brought about a revolution of biological science, and was primarily responsible for the most important unifying principle in medicine—the germ theory of disease. His early work in physics and chemistry centered on optics and crystallography, and his investigations on the crystals of the salts of tartaric acid, and especially on molecular dissymmetry, led him to the study of ferments and physiology. At Lille, where Pasteur became professor of chemistry in 1855, a local distillery was troubled by lactic acid in its fermentations for alcohol. Pasteur in 1857 found the cause of the trouble to be a living ferment; and this discovery brought him into conflict with Liebig, a prominent scientist who regarded alcohol fermentation as a purely chemical process. Liebig was supported in his attack by parasitologists who attempted to revive the doctrine of spontaneous generation. To meet the opposing views, Pasteur performed his well-known experiments with a swan-neck flask which admitted air but excluded dust from a solution boiled in the flask. His results effectively established the doctrine of biogenesis, proving that spontaneous generation does not occur and that air contains minute organisms. Pasteur consequently became the founder of modern bacteriology. In studying the "diseases" of wine and beer, he was led to the important law of specific ferments—each kind of fermentation is due to a particular type of bacteria. His method of preventing the development of undesired bacteria through heating has been perpetuated in the word "pasteurization." The study of fermenation led Pasteur naturally to the investigation of disease in animals and man. From the diseases of silkworms he turned to the study of anthrax in cattle, and then to his famous treatment of rabies. The germ theory of disease which he propounded has been the foundation of medicine ever since.

The work of Pasteur exhibits such an unusual degree of unity that his *Oeuvres* may be thought of as one great book. At the time they were presented, his contributions were scattered in the *Comptes Rendus* of the Académie des Sciences and the Académie de Médecine, as well as in other scientific journals. Only his studies on wine, beer, and the silkworm were collected into volumes—*Études sur le Vin* (1866), *Études sur la Maladie des Vers à Soie* (1870), and *Études sur la Bière* (1876). Only in the present century were his collected works published, from 1922 to 1939, in seven volumes, averaging over five hundred pages each, and including numerous plates and figures. The first volume is on his physical and chemical papers from 1847 to 1857; the second is on studies on fermentation and spontaneous generation from 1857 to 1863. The next three volumes are republications of his books on wine, the silkworm, and beer. Volume VI contains his important studies on "maladies virulentes," including rabies; and the final volume is on "mélanges scientifiques et littéraires." It is probably not too much to say that the *Oeuvres* of Pasteur did for biology what Newton had done for astronomy and Lavoisier for chemistry; and the name of Pasteur lives not only in the *Oeuvres* but also in the "Pasteur Institutes" which have been established in virtually all civilized lands.

OF ALL THINGS (1921), by Robert Benchley. See BENCHLEY, ROBERT.

OF EDUCATION (1644), by John Milton. Milton outlines briefly in a letter to Samuel Hartlib his views on education. The end of learning, he says, is to know, God aright; he stresses also the need to prepare students "to perform justly, skillfully, and magnanimously all the offices, both private and public, of peace and war." He advocates more rapid learning of Latin and Greek, reading to be mastered long before composition is attempted. He gives definite specifications for the house and grounds of his proposed academy and its amazingly (to us) extensive curriculum. Students should learn as much by doing as by reading; theology is to be made a pleasantly sociable study; wrestling and swordplay should not be neglected.

OF HUMAN BONDAGE (1915), by William Somerset Maugham. Philip Carey, orphaned in 1895 at the age of nine, goes to live with his aunt Louisa and uncle William Carey, vicar at Blackstable. Shy and afflicted with a clubfoot, Philip is difficult to understand, and the middle-aged Careys can only think of sending him to the King's School at Tercanbury to study for the ministry. Here he again is unhappy, and shortly before graduation, forces his elders to send him to Heidelberg. There he learns to admire art under the tutelage of the dilettante Hayward. Returning to Blackstable, Philip has his first affair with an older woman, Emily Wilkinson. Unwilling to be ordained, he next is articled to a chartered accountant in London, but leaves before the end of his apprenticeship to study art in Paris. On the Left Bank he makes friends with the indigent students Lawson, Clutton, Cronshaw, and Fanny Price. Discovering he has at best only facility, he returns to London to follow his father in medicine. At St. Luke's Hospital Philip at last finds his niche and studies intensively. He meets two women, the waitress Mildred Rogers and the penny novelette writer Norah Nesbit. Unhappily, Philip's infatuation for Mildred estranges him from Norah, seriously affects his studies, and finally uses up all his money, so that he has to leave St. Luke's. A new friend, Thorpe Athelny, temporarily aids Philip and enables him to find work as floorwalker in a large establishment. After many months of torment, Philip inherits his uncle's small estate and renews his studies. His friendship with the Athelny family and his aptitude for medicine finally bring peace to him. He marries Athelny's daughter Sally and takes a small country practice. This long novel of a slavish infatuation for an unworthy woman has become something of a classic in English literature. It has been filmed.

OF MICE AND MEN (1937), by John Steinbeck. See GRAPES OF WRATH, THE, by John Steinbeck.

OF THEE I SING (1931), by George S. Kaufman and Morrie Ryskind. John P. Wintergreen is nominated for president. As the party can find no other satisfactory issue, it is decided that he shall run on a platform of love. A beauty contest is held, the winner to be wooed by Wintergreen. But in the meantime the candidate has met and fallen in love with Mary Turner, a campaign worker. Accordingly it is she whom he woos, in each of the forty-eight states, and they are swept into office on the strength of the campaign, being simultaneously inaugurated and married by the Supreme Court. Complications arise after the election, and impeachment of Wintergreen is threatened due to a breach of promise suit brought by Diana Devereaux, jilted beauty contest winner. This crisis is avoided by the birth of twins to the presidential couple, uniting the hearts of the American people behind them. Diana is turned over, as a compromise, to the eager Alexander Throttlebottom, the vice-president and forgotten man. This Pulitzer Prize play revolutionized the genre of American musical comedy, heretofore stylized and unprogressive. George Kaufman and various collaborators have written many other classic comedies, such as *You Can't Take It with You* (with Moss Hart; 1936), *Dulcy* (with Marc Connelly; 1921), and *Dinner at Eight* (with Edna Ferber; 1932).

You Can't Take It with You introduces the household of eccentric Grandpa Vanderhof of New York City. The various personalities conduct themselves according to their own tastes, attending circuses, manufacturing fireworks, and so forth. Alice, the younger daughter, is somewhat more conventional, and is much distressed at her family's effect upon Tony Kirby, the son of her employer. When Grandpa finally converts Mr. Kirby to his philosophy, the lovers marry.

Dulcy is a light comedy about Dulcy Smith, whose erratic efforts to help her husband Gordon's business plans succeed in spite of much confusion. After a week end at the Smiths, with assorted guests invited by Dulcy, Gordon's employer, Mr. Forbes, makes him a handsome offer; Dulcy's brother Bill marries Angela Forbes; and all ends happily.

Dinner at Eight concerns a social affair held during a moment of personal crisis in the lives of the various guests of Millicent Jordan. Although many calamities are precipitated by these events, the dinner continues uninterrupted.

OF TIME AND THE RIVER (1935), by Thomas Wolfe. See LOOK HOMEWARD, ANGEL, by Thomas Wolfe.

OFFICERS (1912), by Fritz von Unruh. See UNRUH, FRITZ VON.

OIL! (1927), by Upton Sinclair. See JUNGLE, THE, by Upton Sinclair.

OLD COUNTRY, THE (1946), by Sholom Aleichem. See SHOLOM ALEICHEM.

OLD CURIOSITY SHOP, THE (1841), by Charles Dickens. This sentimental story deals with pathetic Little Nell, her grandfather who lives at the Old Curiosity Shop, and Christopher (Kit) Nubbles, a faithful friend. The grandfather has borrowed money from Quilp, a vicious dwarf, and has gambled with it in order to amass some money for Nell. He has lost his savings through a spendthrift son-in-law and through Nell's reckless brother, Fred. To save him from Quilp, who finds out where his loans are going, Little Nell goes off with him on the road to beg. They meet Thomas Codlin and his traveling puppet show, and work for Mrs. Jarley's Wax Works. Nell and the old man suffer much misery and hardship. Through it all she remains loyal and loving. Mr. Marton, a schoolmaster, befriends them and gives them a house near an old church. Little Nell tends the graves and slowly declines. When Kit and the grandfather's kindly brother finally find them, the child is dead; her grandfather dies soon thereafter. Kit's story is happier. He marries Barbara and keeps the story of Little Nell alive by relating it to his children. Other characters are: Sampson, the lawyer; his sister, Sarah Brass; Dick Swiveller, Fred's dissipated friend; the Marchioness, a servant of the Brasses; and Mrs. Jarley of the Wax Works.

OLD-FASHIONED GIRL, AN (1870), by Louisa May Alcott. See LITTLE WOMEN, by Louisa May Alcott.

OLD GORIOT (1834), by Honoré de Balzac. See HUMAN COMEDY, THE, by Honoré de Balzac.

OLD HOUSE, THE (1915), by Feodor Sologub. In a spacious old country house set in a garden, Boris' grandmother, mother, and sister Natasha await his return. Though it is over a year since he had been hanged they still cannot comprehend it. The grandmother orders his favorite dishes, Natasha plans how she will gather his favorite flowers. The story is told in flashbacks. Boris and Natasha were young revolutionists. She had been sent on a dangerous mission, but had been number three, and returned her bomb to headquarters unsuspected. During the Christmas holidays in the capital Boris had made an excuse that he had to go out of town. It was Natasha who received the telegram announcing his arrest. In vain his mother had pleaded for mercy. Boris was sentenced to be hanged; he faced death calm and unafraid. The three women are left to mourn.

OLD MARE, THE (1873), by Mendele Mocher Sefarim. See MENDELE MOCHER SEFARIM.

OLD SOAK, THE (1921), by Don Marquis. See archy and mehitabel, by Don Marquis.

OLD SWIMMIN'-HOLE AND 'LEVEN MORE POEMS, THE (1883), by James Whitcomb Riley. See RILEY, JAMES WHITCOMB.

OLD WIVES' TALE, THE (1908), by Arnold Bennett. According to Bennett himself he set out in this novel to write an English *Une Vie*, but decided to go Maupassant one better by writing the life history of two women instead of only one. It is a long book, and usually considered his best. Placed in the pottery district of the Five Towns Bennett was to make famous (*The Clayhanger Family,* q.v.), the household of the draper is vividly and realistically described. The family consists of two sisters, very unlike, the prosaic mother, the dying paralytic father, whom Sophia leaves to glimpse her exciting young man and returns to find dead. Sophia's young romanticism betrays her when she falls madly in love with the weakling Gerald Scales. Constance, the older, envies Sophia, but with her steadier and more conventional ways she makes a suitable marriage, if one rather beneath her, by wedding her father's chief clerk, the dull Mr. Povey. Their one son, Cyril, is the only bright aspect of their drab middle-class existence. Meanwhile Sophia has eloped with Scales, and nothing is heard of her for many years. Actually her lover leaves her stranded in Paris after four years of marital infidelity. She is alone with French friends during the terrible days of the Commune. Bennett had been struck by the fact that ordinary people live through world-shaking historical events and remain scarcely aware of them, so he shows Sophia and her friends in the time of the Commune. It is long after those days that through a college friend of Cyril's she is discovered. When she returns to her old home she and Cyril realize they are far more alike than either is like Constance. It is a shock to both the sisters to meet as stout middle-aged women when they parted slim, breath-taking girls. Sophia does not live long after her return, though long enough to upset the even tenor of Constance's existence, and to see Scales after he has died, a sick abandoned tramp. Constance's husband has died, too, and her son gone to more exciting places. The stout old lady with grey hair, a dowdy hat and expensive clothes, goes limping about Bursley forgotten, and dies alone and unattended. Cyril arrives three days after the funeral, in time to receive his substantial inheritance. There is a three-dimensional quality about Bennett's characters, a solidity which makes them memorable and vivid as friends one has known long and well.

OLD WIVES' TALE, THE (1595), by George Peele. Antic, Frolic, and Fantastic are lost in a wood, and Clunch the Smith takes them back to his cottage, where his wife, Madge, entertains them with a tale. Two brothers are seeking their lost sister, Delia. They meet an old man, who is a man by day and a white bear at night. He, with Delia, is under the spell of Sacrapant, a sorcerer. The two brothers likewise become Sacrapant's prisoners. The release of all is brought about by the wandering knight, Eumenides, who is squired by Jack, a ghost, to whose burial expenses he had contributed. Huanebango, a braggart character, is supposed to represent Gabriel Harvey, a well-known writer of the period. Folklore and fairy tale form a background for the whole invention, which pokes fun at the then prevailing traditions of romantic drama.

OLIVER TWIST (1838), by Charles Dickens. This novel of London in the first part of the nineteenth century is a story of poverty, crimes, and the horrors of the workhouse and the underworld. The boy, Oliver Twist, whose family is unknown, is born in a workhouse. Mr. Bumble, the cruel parish beadle, apprentices him to the undertaker, Mr. Sowerberry. Oliver runs away to London, where he meets the pickpocket, Jack Dawkins, known as the Artful Dodger, who takes him to a den of thieves. Fagin, the leader, with the aid of Charley Bates, Nancy and Bill Sikes, tries to make Oliver a successful thief. First Mr. Brownlow helps him, but the robbers kidnap him; and he is particularly persecuted by a mysterious person known as Monks. He finally falls into the hands of Rose and Mrs. Maylie, who treat him kindly. Nancy, unable to leave her life of crime, assists in uncovering the boy's parentage, by revealing what she knows to Rose. Sikes is suspicious of her motives and viciously murders her. All the criminals are finally brought to justice. and Oliver's parentage is disclosed. He finds he is related to Monks, who has been trying to deprive him of his fortune, and also to Rose Maylie. Mr. Brownlow adopts Oliver and educates him. This remains one of Dickens' most popular works.

OMOO (1846), by Herman Melville. See MOBY DICK, by Herman Melville.

ON BALANCES OR LEVERS, by Archimedes. See ARCHIMEDES.

ON CENTERS OF GRAVITY, by Archimedes. See ARCHIMEDES.

ON CONOIDS AND SPHEROIDS, by Archimedes. See ARCHI. MEDES.

ON DIVINATION, by Cicero. See PHILOSOPHICAL ESSAYS, by Cicero.

ON DUTIES, by Cicero. See PHILOSOPHICAL ESSAYS, by Cicero.

ON FLOATING BODIES, by Archimedes. See ARCHIMEDES.

ON FORSYTE' CHANGE (1930), by John Galsworthy. See FORSYTE SAGA, THE, by John Galsworthy.

ON FRIENLSHIP (De Amicitia; 44 b.c.), by Cicero (Marcus Tullius Cicero). The ideal time of this dialogue is 129 b.c. The interlocutors are the Roman, Gaius Laelius, and his two sons-in-law, Gaius Fannius and Mucius Scaevola, the Augur. They discuss Laelius' best friend, the younger Scipio, who has just died. Laelius dwells on the virtues of his dead friend and on the fullness of his life, and Fannius requests his father-in-law to discourse, for their instruction, on friendship. Laelius holds that "friendship cannot exist except among good men." Furthermore, life without friends would be hardly worth living. Cicero's definition of friendship, which he makes Laelius utter, is widely quoted: "For friendship is nothing else than an accord in all things, human and divine, conjoined with mutual goodwill and affection, and I am inclined to think that, with the exception of wisdom, no better thing has been given to man by the immortal gods." The discussion covers the value, nature and laws of friendship, and examines the opinions of the philosophers, particularly Epicurus, on these points.

ON HEROES, HERO-WORSHIP AND THE HEROIC IN HIS-TORY (1841), by Thomas Carlyle. These essays were originally presented by Thomas Carlyle as a series of lectures which he delivered in a London lyceum in 1840. The first is on "The Hero as Divinity." For this he selected Odin of Scandinavian mythology. This was followed by "The Hero as Prophet" (Mahomet), "The Hero as Poet" (Dante and Shakespeare), "The Hero as Priest" (Luther—Reformation; Knox—Puritanism), "The Hero as Man of Letters" (Samuel Johnson, Jean Jacques Rousseau and Robert Burns), and finally "The Hero as King" (Cromwell and Napoleon). Carlyle does not hesitate to be an ardent partisan, and if thereby he frequently sacrifices calm judgment and even truth he nonetheless retains a sturdy honesty and good will which compensate. He denounces cant and quackery. He deplores the ingratitude of mankind to its heroes and great men, who to him symbolize the "divineness in Man and Nature."

ON HUMOR (1890), by Gustav Fröding. See FRÖDING, GUSTAV.

ON LIBERTY (1859), by John Stuart Mill. The essay *On Liberty* is the classic justification of individual liberty from the English Utilitarian point of view. John Stuart Mill had been educated to take over the role as leader of the Utilitarians by his father, James Mill, and by Jeremy Bentham, the founder of the school. From early childhood he had been trained as a Philosophical Radical, as the Utilitarians were then called. An apt pupil, he learned quickly, and eventually outgrew the limited confines of Bentham's school. He wrote his essay *On Liberty* when he was in his fifties, by which time he had come to question some of the basic tenets of the Utilitarians.

This work is a defense of individual liberty in terms of social utility. He says at the outset that he wishes to assert "one very simple principle," which is: ". . . the sole end for which mankind are warranted, individually or collectively, in interfering with the liberty of action of any of their number, is self-protection." He is especially concerned to defend the freedom of the individual against the power of society, and the freedom of minorities against the power of the majority. Society may interfere with the individual's freedom only if society can show that the exercise of that freedom does harm to others. Applying this principle, Mill finds three areas of human behavior which are outside the proper sphere of social control. These regions of human liberty are 1) "The inward domain of consciousness; demanding liberty of conscience in the most comprehensive sense; liberty of thought and feeling; absolute freedom of opinion and sentiment on all subjects, practical or speculative, scientific, moral, or theological"; 2) "liberty of tastes and pursuits"; and 3) "liberty . . . of combination among individuals; freedom to unite, for any purpose not involving harm to others."

Mill's most eloquent writing is devoted to a defense of the first freedom, of thought and expression. He argues that no opinion should be suppressed, even if it is generally agreed by the most competent authorities that it is in error, for it might conceivably be correct, or if actually erroneous it may contain an element of truth, and in any case the truth to be kept vital must continually have to vindicate itself against challenging opinions. Without freedom of expression, the most perfect truth is reduced to the level of a dogma, repeated by rote, and not properly understood.

Though other parts of Mill's essays have served to justify a *laissez-faire* economic philosophy, the justification of individual liberty of thought and expression still stands as a challenge to all those who would suppress free inquiry in the interest of some supposedly absolute truth.

ON OLD AGE (44 B.C.), by Cicero (Marcus Tullius Cicero). In this dialogue on old age, set in the year 150 B.C., Cato, who is eighty-four, is being visited by his friends, Scipio, who is thirty-five, and Laelius, who is thirty-six. They engage in a lively discussion, in which Cato argues persuasively that the unhappy and discontented find every age a burden. However, "to those who seek all good from themselves nothing can seem evil that the laws of nature inevitably impose. To this class old age especially belongs. . . ." Cato contends that, inasmuch as Nature is the best determinant of life, and since "She has fitly planned the other acts of life's drama, it is not likely that she has neglected the final act as if she were a careless playwright." As a realist, Cicero has Cato take a sober view of old age, not as a subject for rejoicing but for philosophical acceptance. He knows that "old age is the final scene, as it were, in life's drama, from which we ought to escape when it grows wearisome, when we have had our fill."

ON OUR SUBLUNARY WORLD (published 1600), by William Gilbert. See DE MAGNETE, by William Gilbert.

ON SPHERE-MAKING, by Archimedes. See ARCHIMEDES.

ON SPIRALS, by Archimedes. See ARCHIMEDES.

ON THE CALENDAR, by Archimedes. See ARCHIMEDES.

ON THE CREATION OF THE WORLD, by Philo Judaeus. See PHILO JUDAEUS.

ON THE CUTTING-OFF OF A RATIO (ca. 225 B.C.), by Apollonius of Perga. See TREATISE ON CONIC SECTIONS, by Apollonius of Perga.

ON THE EQUILIBRIUM OF PLANES, by Archimedes. See ARCHIMEDES.

ON THE EVE (1860), by Ivan Sergeyevich Turgenev. The author attempts, not too successfully, the portrait of a heroic girl of the "new" generation in Elena Nikolayevna. When Bersenev, a student and philosopher, brings Insarov to share his home during the holidays, he introduces this Bulgarian agitator into the society of the neighborhood and even to Elena, with whom he is half in love himself.

The critics had clamored for a more virile hero than the author had ever created before, and he attempted to create such a man. He failed. Insarov, who does not believe in "Russian love," who desires only to avoid all entanglements, is merely a strong, silent "stuffed shirt." At times he is even rather ludicrous, which is fatal to a romantic hero. Elena's love for Insarov was first stirred by Bersenev's praise of his friend. The descriptions of her feelings for the Bulgarian are unpleasant reading; Turgenev usually failed when he attempted to dissect rather than suggest character. As in most Russian novels, characterization is more important than the plot. Despite himself Insarov falls in love with Elena. He is violently ill in Moscow, where Elena is staying with her parents. When he is better they secretly marry. Their love affair, which has been conducted with the utmost secrecy, now comes into the open, and brings down on their heads the wrath of Elena's parents. Meanwhile war threatens with Bulgaria, and Insarov feels he can no longer remain away from his own country. Elena affirms she has no life apart from him, and the couple leave amid sorrowing and foreboding. Insarov never reaches his destination, nor attains his desire. He dies in Venice. Elena buries him in his native soil, then vanishes. Her family can find no clue to her whereabouts.

ON THE FABRIC OF THE HUMAN BODY (1543), by Andreas Vesalius. See DE HUMANI CORPORIS FABRICA, by Andreas Vesalius.

ON THE HIGHEST GOOD AND THE HIGHEST EVIL, by Cicero. See PHILOSOPHICAL ESSAYS, by Cicero.

ON THE IMPROVEMENT OF THE UNDERSTANDING (1655), by Benedict de Spinoza. The purpose of this fragmentary treatise is to inquire into the true good of man, that which will really promote his happiness. Spinoza analyzes and discredits riches, fame and pleasure, the goals that men usually pursue. They are unstable, uncertain, and not really satisfying. He concludes that the only road to true happiness is to direct the mind to "a thing eternal and infinite," and this means knowledge of God, that is, of the natural order of the universe. The achievement of this end involves the disinterested pursuit and dissemination of the truth for himself and for all mankind.

ON THE MAGNET (1600), by William Gilbert. See DE MAGNETE, by William Gilbert.

ON THE NATURAL FACULTIES (129-199), by Galen. Greek medicine was based on the work of Hippocrates who lived in the fifth century B.C. Galen was, however, the transmitter of the knowledge of Greek medicine to after ages. His original contributions to medicine are not ascertainable; he was an eclectic, and mingled his ideas with those of his predecessors. His reverence for Hippocrates was almost religious. He laid his finger on the essence of this master's teaching when he stated: "Hippocrates was the first known to us of all who have been both physicians and philosophers, in that *he was the first to recognize what nature does.*" This principle Galen adopted for himself, and it is clearly apparent in his treatise *On the Natural Faculties,* a work which forms an excellent introduction to his more specialized works. This "Nature," or biological principle, upon which Galen, like Hippocrates, based his entire medical teaching, meant that any living thing represented a unity. All the separate parts could be dealt with only in relation to this principle of unity. The principle, now a commonplace in medical theory, was insufficiently accepted by Galen's contemporaries, who acted on the oversimplified assumption that the whole was merely the sum of its parts. Accordingly they conceived as practical the independent treatment of any ailing organ as something entirely apart from the rest of the body. Galen expressed his concept of the unity of the human organism by saying it was governed by a *Physis* or Nature whose "faculties" or powers were within the province of *physi*—ology. This fundamental principle of medical philosophy impelled Galen to call Hippocrates, its father, "master." But Galen's conception of physiology was much broader than our own; it also included a large section of physics. A translation of this treatise is available in the Loeb Classical Library. Galen was a most prolific writer, and although many of his works are lost, those which survive fill twenty volumes, covering all phases of medicine, medical history and medical philosophy. He was long a highly respected authority in the early stages of modern medicine.

ON THE NATURE OF THE GODS, by Cicero. See PHILOSOPHI-CAL ESSAYS, by Cicero.

ON THE NATURE OF THINGS (ca. 54 B.C.), by Lucretius (Titus Lucretius Carus). Lucretius' didactic poem is an exposition of the philosophy of Epicurus. The poetic treatment of such subject matter was no novelty, for verse had been a common vehicle for the thought of the pre-Socratics, and Lucretius took Empedocles as one of his models. He surpassed by far, however, the poetic genius of his predecessors, was the idol of Virgil, and even elicited praise from Cicero, who despised Epicureanism. The invocation to Venus which opens the first book is a passage of unrivaled beauty, and there are many other fine passages throughout the book. The exposition of a close-knit philosophical system in verse makes tremendous demands on the art of any poet and sheer poetry must often yield to these demands, but nowhere does Lucretius become completely pedestrian; his varied rhythms and vivid imagery always sustain the burden of his serious task. He speaks always in terms of divine awe and reverence of the master whose system had fired his imagination. His purpose in writing the poem was to show the unhappy Roman of the generation of the Civil War the senseless folly of his ways, and reclaim him for the untroubled and philosophic calm of Epicurus' rational hedonism. To do this he must clear the ground of all manner of degrading fears and superstitions. The ethical precepts of Epicurus rested squarely upon his natural philosophy, which was a startling if oversimplified anticipation of modern atomic theory. The first book treats of the fundamental characteristics of matter and void in the universe. The second book explains the nature and properties of atoms and the effect of their combination. Next it is explained in book three that the human mind and soul are concrete realities, that their dissolution is death, and so there is no possibility of immortality and no need for fear of death. In book four the operation of our sensory perceptions is also explained on a materialistic basis. Book five is devoted to Epicurean cosmology, and unfolds a beautiful and careful theory of evolution. The final book explains numerous natural phenomena on the basis of Epicurean theories of causation. The poem is a magnificent effort to give to Rome a true picture of the always much maligned and persistently misunderstood Epicurean doctrine. It is the only systematic and complete exposition of the theory of this school which has survived.

ON THE ORIGIN OF SPECIES BY MEANS OF NATURAL SELECTION (1859), by Charles Darwin. In this book the great proponent of evolution aimed to show the probability that every species is a development from previous species, and that all life is part of a continuous pattern. His objects of investigation were domestic animals and plants, which vary from generation to generation. All life, plant and animal alike, is engaged in a fierce competition or "struggle for existence." In this conflict an animal or plant which inherits an unfavorable variation will be less likely to survive and have offspring; and, conversely, an animal inheriting a favorable variation will be more likely to survive and have offspring. The severe conditions of life accordingly tend to kill off individuals with unfavorable variations and to favor "the survival of the fittest," the strongest, the most adaptable. From all this Darwin concludes that there exists a "natural selection" of favorable variations which produces new varieties. In the course of thousands of years, the operation of natural selection succeeds in producing a remarkable variety of living things, which are categorized into species, genera, families, orders. All of these classifications are alike subject, in varying degree, to the process of evolution. The first chapter of the book explains the operation of artificial selection in the case of domesticated species, and the second takes up natural selection in consequence of the struggle for existence. Chapter three describes the struggle for existence, chapter four the survival of the fittest, and chapter five the laws of variation. The rest of the book is devoted to a closer examination of some apparent difficulties in the theory of evolution, to questions of geological succession and geographical distribution, and to a recapitulation and conclusion.

The Origin of Species, one of the world's greatest books, deeply influenced biological research for over half a century. Subsequent investigation, however, has revealed the inadequacy of some of the author's arguments. In presenting "natural selection" as the effective agent of evolution, Darwin assumes the inheritance of acquired characters in a form scarcely differing from that of Lamarck, which has been discredited. There also are traces of teleology, as the subtitle of the book, *Or the Preservation of Favoured Races in the Struggle for Life,* betrays. Darwin was at his best in the investigation of nature, weakest in philosophical interpretation. Throughout the long and arduous journey aboard the *Beagle* from 1831 to 1836, Darwin painstakingly recorded his observations on geology and natural science, publishing them in 1839 in the well-known *Voyages of the Beagle.* It was the data gathered on this expedition which laid the foundation for his later work.

The storm of opposition which the theory of evolution occasioned is alluded to by Darwin in very mild terms in the *Descent of Man* (1871). Here he wrote, "The main conclusion arrived at in this work, namely that man is descended from some lowly organized form, will, I regret to think, be highly distasteful to many." In the *Descent of Man* the author shows the special affinities of man to certain lower animals, especially the high apes, and he applies the principle of natural selection in determining the origin and probable line of genealogy of the races of mankind. A large portion of the book is devoted to what Darwin calls "sexual selection," or factors influencing the choice of a mate, both in primitive and modern societies.

ON THE PUBLIC BUILDINGS (after 575), by Procopius of Caesarea.

ON THE REVOLUTIONS OF THE HEAVENLY SPHERES (1543), by Nicolaus Copernicus. See DE REVOLUTIONIBUS ORBIUM COELESTIUM, by Nicolaus Copernicus.

ON THE SPHERE AND CYLINDER, by Archimedes. See ARCHIMEDES.

ON THE SUBLIME (1st c.), ascribed to Longinus. It is impossible to determine the true authorship of this brief Greek essay on the aesthetics of literary style. Its thesis is that literary excellence depends upon an elevation or grandeur of style which results from nobility of conception and naturalness of expression, free from all affectation and labored artifice. By way of illustration, the author quotes frequently from the classical poets, and thus preserves one of our two complete odes of Sappho. The work was little known in antiquity, but received wide attention in modern times through the translation of Boileau. It still commands serious attention from literary critics.

ON TRANSLATING HOMER (1861–1862), by Matthew Arnold. In 1857 Arnold had become professor of poetry at Oxford, and these four lectures are his earliest work in criticism after his inaugural address. They were occasioned by the publication of an eccentric translation of the *Iliad* (q.v.) in ballad measure by Francis Newman, the brother of the Cardinal. They are a detailed consideration of problems of English versification and diction. Four qualities are declared to be peculiarly Homeric—rapidity, plainness and directions of diction and syntax, plainness in thought, and nobility. Of the famous English translators, Cowper lacks Homer's rapidity, Pope his plainness of syntax and diction, and Chapman is too full of conceits to have his plainness of thought. Newman, worst of all, lacks nobility. It is insisted that Homer is a master of the grand style, which arises "when a noble nature, poetically gifted, treats with simplicity or with severity a serious subject."

ONE CLEAR CALL (1948), by Upton Sinclair. See JUNGLE, THE, by Upton Sinclair.

ONE HUNDRED DUTCH QUATRAINS (1932), by Pieter Cornelis Boutens. See BOUTENS, PIETER CORNELIS.

ONE MAN'S MEAT (1942), by E. B. White. See WHITE, E. B.

ONE MORE SPRING (1933), by Robert Nathan. See NATHAN, ROBERT.

ONE PERSON (1928), by Elinor Wylie. See WYLIE, ELINOR.

ONE WORLD (1943), by Wendell L. Willkie. Wendell Willkie, after being defeated (as Republican nominee) for the presidency in the 1940 election, traveled on a forty-nine-day tour of the world by airplane. His international concepts were epitomized by the title of his subsequent book, *One World,* which restated the important facts of our modern world's smallness and its countries' interdependence.

OP HOOP VAN ZEGEN (1900), by Hermann Heijermans. Of all the large number of dramatic works of Heijermans (1864–1924), this tragedy of the sea has been performed since 1900 more often and in more different countries than any other. He depicts in it the doleful existence of Dutch fishermen, whose lives are not only menaced by the treacherous sea, but also by the lack of the sense of responsibility of their employers, who do not hesitate to let their men go to sea in boats which they know to be unseaworthy. The social-democratic author uses this circumstance to launch an attack on capitalist society in general: owner Bos, in this play, is covered by the insurance company, which has approved his boat *Op Hoop van Zegen,* so the responsibility for possible accidents does not fall on him any more. Widow Kniertje Vermeer has two sons who have to go to sea, for the population of the fishing village depends entirely on the big owners: where else could they find work?

The youngest son Barend has a presentiment of approaching disaster; when he is told to go on board he clutches the doorpost of his mother's house in fear of death. Kniertje herself tears his fingers loose: she will not see him again. The spectator remains with the fishermen's wives, and experiences in their stories the fear for their husbands as the storm breaks. When the fate of the *Hoop* becomes known, revolt blazes up in the hearts of some. What can they do against the mighty and apparently kindhearted owner? Kniertje is allowed to fetch a bowl of soup from the owner's wife. Bos helps where he can, but business is business.

Heijermans aroused a great uproar with his fierce attack on narrow limits of faith in *Allerzielen* (1903). A year earlier he had written a drama without social implication: *Schakels,* dealing with the conflict between a father who had become rich, and his mature children, who use despicable methods to prevent his second marriage in later life. Besides his dream-picture *Uitkomst* (1907), *De Opgaande Zon* must be mentioned; it is a "drama of the middle class," showing the conflict between the small stores and the large strangling department store, culminating in a clash of conscience between the leading man Matthys and his daughter. Many one-act plays were written by Heijermans, under the pseudonym of Samuel Falkland.

OPEN BOAT, THE (1898), by Stephen Crane. See RED BADGE OF COURAGE, THE, by Stephen Crane.

OPERA OMNIA (edition completed 1929), by Tycho Brahe. See HISTORY OF THE SKY, by Tycho Brahe.

OPERA OMNIA (1651), by Albertus Magnus. Albrecht von Bollstädt or Albert of Cologne (1193?–1280) enjoyed an extraordinary reputation, both in his own lifetime and afterward. His was the unique distinction among learned men of the twelfth and thirteenth centuries of the surname "the Great." An enormously prolific writer, his collected works fill thirty-eight quarto volumes in the 1890–1899 edition. These cover almost every question of theology, philosophy, and natural science; but Albert, unlike his contemporary, Roger Bacon, did not write on the mathematical sciences. A treasury of information, his works are rather a compilation than an encyclopedia, for they do not constitute an integrated whole. Albert expresses himself differently on the same topic in different places, either because he had accumulated new information or because he had changed his mind. As might be expected in the case of so great an activity, much of his work was superficial and poorly digested; only here and there is he critical. His great achievement was scientific; as a naturalist, especially in the description of plants and animals, he ranked supreme in the Latin Middle Ages. In the *De Vegetalibus* he advocates knowledge from personal experience of plants, and, if this is impossible, then reliance on authorities who have had such experience. The first part of the *De Animalibus* is based on Michael Scot and Aristotle; but the last seven books contain matter derived partly from his own observations or from direct information, and here he rejected many old superstitions about animals. The popularity of his works is attested by the publication of 313 incunabula editions of particular treatises; but the collected works were first printed at Lyons, 1651, in twenty-one folio volumes.

OPGAANDE ZON, DE (Eng. tr. 1925), by Hermann Heijermans. See OP HOOP VAN ZEGEN, by Hermann Heijermans.

OPTICKS (1704), by Sir Isaac Newton. Newton was possibly the greatest scientist of all times, and his chief contributions to physical science are contained in two classic works—the celebrated *Principia* and his *Opticks; or a Treatise of the Reflections, Refractions, Inflections and Colours of Light.* The first of these two books contains what generally is regarded as the greatest of scientific laws, the law of gravitation; the second presents what Newton described as "in my judgment the oddest if not the most considerable detection which hath hitherto been made in the operations of nature," the discovery that colors are distinguished from each other by the extent to which they are refracted.

Newton had studied Kepler's *Dioptrice* and de Dominis' *De Radiis Visus et Lucis*, both published in 1611, the *Dioptrique* and *Météores* of Descartes (1637), Gregory's *Optica Promota* (1663), Grimaldi's *Physico-Mathesis* (1665), and Hooke's *Micrographia* (1665). These books contained what was known at the time in geometrical and physical optics, and the weakest part of the subject was the theory of color. In 1666 Newton, while seeking to improve the telescope, experimented on the colors of the spectrum formed by a beam of light passed through a prism. Observing that the length of the colored spectrum was much greater than the width, he carried out repeated observations, and came to the fundamental conclusion that white light is really a mixture of rays of every color and that the elongation which he had noticed in the spectrum was due to differences in the refractive power of the prism for rays of different color. As he expressed his crucial discovery: "To the same degree of refrangibility ever belongs the same colour, and to the same colour ever belongs the same degree of refrangibility."

Newton's great optical discovery was the subject of his first scientific paper, published in 1672 in the *Philosophical Transactions* of the Royal Society. The paper involved him in a controversy with Hooke which so upset Newton that thereafter he published results only with the greatest reluctance. Thus it was that the *Opticks*, the material for which he had collected long before, appeared only in 1704. The book opens with the statement, "My design in this book is not to explain the properties of light by hypotheses, but to propose and prove them by reason and experiments." For this reason Newton made no clear-cut statement as to the nature of light. He appears to favor the corpuscular theory, but in his explanation of the so-called "Newton's rings" he adopted the view that the phenomenon was due to a periodic vibration—somewhat similar to the wave theory which Huygens proposed in 1673. Book I of the *Opticks* contains Newton's fundamental experiments on the spectrum; the second book is on the Newton ring phenomena; and the third and last book deals with diffraction. The account closes with some important "Queries" or speculations on light and gravitation. Appended to the original edition of 1704 were two works of great mathematical significance, one on the calculus, the other on the classification of cubic curves. The *Opticks* is thus in many respects one of the great classics in the history of science.

OPTICS, by Archimedes. See ARCHIMEDES.

OPTIONS (1909), by William Sydney Porter. See PORTER, WIL-LIAM SYDNEY.

OPUS MAJUS (1266–1267), by Roger Bacon. One of the most remark-able books of the thirteenth century, the *Opus Majus* was the most important part of a trilogy sent by Bacon to Rome at the request of Pope Clement IV. It is less an encyclopedia of knowledge than a critique of contemporary schol-arship and methodology. Of the seven books of the *Opus Majus,* the first treats of the four causes of error (the *offendicula,* or impediments to learning): authority, custom, the opinion of the uneducated multitude, and a pretense of learning which covers actual ignorance. The second book considers phi-losophy as opposed to theology, and in it Bacon states that all knowledge is contained in, or at least implied by, the Scriptures. The third book, on lan-guages, makes the original assertion that logic, a quality native to man, is unimportant in the pursuit of knowledge as compared to languages. Theo-logians in his time, he says, were inadequately trained, for few of them knew Greek, Hebrew, and Arabic. Book IV, on mathematics, places this subject along with languages as one of the major prerequisites to learning. Bacon, however, valued the practical utility of the subject and had little patience with tedious, rigorous proofs. Book V, on optics or perspective, takes up a subject of which Bacon was especially proud. His views were chiefly borrowed from Ibn al-Haitham (Alhazen) with small additions and practical applications. The sixth book, on experimental science, states that this is the highest of the sciences and that all others make use of it. Bacon considers experimentation sometimes as an inductive method for discovering scientific truth and some-times as applied science. Finally, the last book treats of morals, and in it one reads that the value of knowledge lies in its service to the church and Chris-tianity. Bacon's contributions as a forerunner of present-day science and the modernity of his viewpoint have frequently been greatly exaggerated. His prophecies of modern inventions are so vague as to be of small value, and his experimentation was so limited that he cannot be credited with any one in-vention or contribution to science. Nevertheless, Bacon was a keen and systematic thinker with an original emphasis, and he deserves credit for insist-ing on the indispensability of mathematics and experimentation. Some of his ideas were copied by John Peckham and William of Saint Cloud, as well as by Cardinal d'Ailly, whose statements on the circumnavigation of the globe may in turn have influenced Columbus. However, Bacon's influence was small compared to that of some of his contemporaries. The lack of interest in his works is well illustrated by the fact that there is no incunabulum edi-tion. An alchemical work by Bacon was published in 1541, but the *Opus Majus* was not printed until 1733 (at London).

OPUS OXONIENSE, by John Duns Scotus (c. 1265–1308). The *Opus Oxoniense* by Duns Scotus, the greatest of the English Franciscan Schoolmen, who was known as the "subtil Doctor," is a commentary on the "Sentences" of ₊Peter Lombard. It is essentially a theological work, but it also contains treatises on metaphysical, logical, grammatical and scientific subjects. Duns Scotus was a universal genius. However, unlike Alexander of Hales, Albertus

Magnus, and his rival contemporary Thomas Aquinas, he did not write a *summa theologica.* The *Opus Oxoniense,* and for that matter all his other writings, were merely commentaries on controversial matters. He presented no unified system, and is generally regarded today as having been primarily a critic, but one who formulated several original theories.

Duns Scotus was an Aristotelian in philosophy, but was also influenced by St. Augustine. He was a critic of Thomas Aquinas. Scotus advocated the doctrine of the immaculate conception of the Virgin Mary against Aquinas and his Dominican followers. He asserted that individual things of the same kind differed in essence as well as materially, in contrast to the theory of Aquinas that individual things of the same kind differ in number and location but not in essence.

At the beginning of his prologue to the *Opus Oxoniense,* Scotus asks the question whether man in his earthly state stands in need of a special, supernatural form of knowledge to which he could not attain by the natural light of reason. He answers his own question affirmatively. Man is not merely an automaton; he acts for the sake of an end. For this he needs a threefold knowledge. First, he must find out how he may attain his end; secondly, what means he should employ; and finally, he must have absolute assurance that these means are sufficient for reaching his objective. Here he begins to clash with the rationalist St. Thomas: these conditions, says Scotus, cannot be fulfilled by natural reason. Supernatural happiness (beatitude) is the ultimate end of man, God's reward to him for his virtue. Consequently this is not scientifically knowable since it is contingent on the free will of God. It follows then, that in order to fulfill his destiny man must have some supernatural knowledge. The truth, insists Scotus, may be perceived, but it cannot be deduced, because it has its source in the free will of God.

Duns Scotus also differed from Aquinas on the question of the kind of proof that may be offered for God's existence. He attempted to show that from the possibility of existence one can divine the necessity.

ORBIS PICTUS (collected 1657), by Comenius. See DIDACTICA, THE, by Comenius.

ORDEAL OF MARK TWAIN, THE (1920), by Van Wyck Brooks. See FLOWERING OF NEW ENGLAND, THE, by Van Wyck Brooks.

ORDEAL OF RICHARD FEVEREL, THE (1859), by George Meredith. The question of education is the essential theme of the first published novel by this English writer. Sir Austin Feverel, a proud and opinionated man, attempts to make his son into a perfect specimen of manhood by a peculiar system of education which is fated from the beginning to end in disaster. Richard at fourteen first defies the system when he sets fire to a farmer's hayrick; later he falls madly in love with Lucy Desborough, a girl beneath his station, and is forced to elope with her. They are happy at first, but soon Richard leaves his wife to live in London, where he awaits word of forgiveness from his father. Here, totally unprepared for the world, he is seduced by Mrs. Mount, a charming lady of low repute whose husband, Lord Mountfalcon, is plotting to betray Lucy. Horrified at what he has done, Richard flees to the Continent. He returns to Lucy, to whom Sir Austin has become reconciled when he discovers that she has borne Richard a son, but leaves immediately to challenge Lord Mountfalcon to a duel. He is wounded, and Lucy, forbidden to see him, dies of brain fever. Richard recovers, but is so broken mentally that it is clear he will never be what his father had hoped.

The hero of *Beauchamp's Career* (1876) also has a dominating relative and falls victim to the attractions of two women.

OREGON TRAIL, THE (1849), by Francis Parkman. See PARKMAN, FRANCIS.

ORGANON (384–322 B.C.), by Aristotle. Aristotle's separate works touching on what we call logic were early collected by some of his followers, the Peripatetics, and came to be known collectively as the *Organon*, i.e., the Instrument. The works were not originally conceived as chapters of a single work, for Aristotle's own conception of what he calls logic is much narrower than that represented by the collection.

The treatises included in the *Organon* deal with two problems, viz., the principles under which proof operates and the technique of presenting it. The basis of all of Aristotle's logical works is the syllogism. Though Socrates and Plato used the syllogism, it did not achieve importance or wide application until Aristotle. As conceived by him the syllogism required an emphasis on terms which he characterized as univocal, namely: words which have the identical meaning each time they are used, and the attempt to construct propositions and arguments from the combination of such words.

The first treatise in the *Organon*, the *Categories*, treats of simple, uncombined terms arranged in ten categories: *substance, quantity, quality, relation, place, time, situation, condition, action* and *passion*. These categories represent classes of things expressed by isolated words, i.e., words which do not form part of a proposition, and correspond to questions one might ask in trying to learn the character of an object.

In *De Interpretatione* Aristotle analyzes the *proposition* and the *judgment* and distinguishes their different kinds. The *Analytica Priora* is the treatise on deductive and inductive reasoning wherein he presents the syllogism, which he declares to be based on the *Law of Contradiction* and the *Law of Excluded Middle*. In the *Analytica Posteriora* Aristotle takes up the study of *demonstration*, which he states consists in showing causes, the middle term in a demonstration expressing the cause. The *Topica* has for its subject matter the *dialectical* or *problematic* syllogism and the commonplaces of argument. The treatise *De Sophisticis Elenchis* contains Aristotle's study of *fallacies* or *sophisms*. Out of all these works emerges Aristotle's theory of knowledge: that *experience* is the true source and true cause of all our knowledge.

ORIGIN AND DEVELOPMENT OF THE QUANTUM THEORY, THE (1922), by Max Planck. This little work of only twenty-three pages is a translation of the Nobel Prize Address delivered before the Royal Swedish Academy of Sciences in 1920. In it the author describes his own epoch-making discoveries. Though the relativity theory has captured the imagination of the world, the quantum theory has been a more fundamental force in bringing about the modern revolution in scientific thought. Planck was led to his theory by a study of the spectral distribution of radiation for different temperatures. He first presented the results of his discoveries to the German Physical Society on December 14, 1900, in a paper entitled "On the distribution of energy in a normal spectrum." In observing a beam of radiation issuing from a small opening in a hollow body heated to incandescence, Planck found that "radiant energy is not a continuous flow, for it is not indefinitely divisible." "It must be defined," he said, "as a discontinuous mass made up of units all of which are similar to one another." Energy is emitted in "quanta"; i.e., it is always found in integral multiples of hv, where v is the frequency of the radiation and h is a universal constant, now known as "Planck's constant," having the value 6.55×10^{-27} erg-seconds.

At first the new conception of radiation appeared to scientists to be fantastic, but soon physicists began "quantizing" in other connections. Einstein, for example, in 1921 was awarded the Nobel Prize primarily for having applied the quantum idea in 1905 to the photoelectric effect. Planck had assumed that energy is emitted, but not necessarily transmitted, in bundles; Einstein's application of Planck's idea to photoelectricity indicated that the quantum retains its identity while travelling from source to destination. This had a profound influence upon the theory of light, which had been presumed to be a wave phenomenon. Photons are not easily reconciled with waves, and a partial return to the Newtonian corpuscular theory seems to be implied. There are other respects in which classical physics and the quantum theory are in sharp conflict. One of these is concerned with atomic structure, in which Bohr applied Planck's work to the atom as visualized by Rutherford.

Planck has written several other important books, as well as numerous scientific papers. His *Treatise on Thermodynamics,* first published in German in 1897, has appeared in numerous editions in several languages. His *Theory of Heat Radiation* (1906) has also been translated into English. Essays by Planck on the philosophical implications of his work have been published and translated in 1932 in the book *Where Is Science Going?*

ORIGINS OF CONTEMPORARY FRANCE, THE (1875–1893), by Hippolyte Taine. The outcome of the war of 1870 had greatly distressed Taine. Even before the fighting had finished he wrote his wife that he felt that he should undertake a study of the country's history which would lay bare the reasons for its ignominious collapse. To the task he brought the method which he had spent a lifetime developing and which had produced his famous *History of English Literature* (q.v.). An artist, a nation, or an institution is the product of the race, the environment, and the historical moment at which it appears. "I have confronted my subject," he wrote later, "as I would the metamorphosis of an insect." Later historians have suspected that Taine was nowhere near so much the detached scientist as he claimed to be, that his use of documents was conditioned by his *a priori* conclusions, and that what he really wrote was a justification of his own reactionary politics.

The Ancient Regime (1875), probably the best known of the *Origins* series, is an analysis of the French monarchy and of the causes of the Revolution. Taine reconstructs the grandeurs of the old system, and finds its greatest cultural weakness in a growing tendency to generalize ideas; he points out that it was not intellectually respectable, or even gentlemanly, under Louis XIV, to know too much about anything or to pay attention to specific detail. This mania for generalization combined disastrously with new political ideas imported from England during the eighteenth century. Application of democratic theories to a completely abstract notion of man drove French political thinking to wild extremes. Instead of gradual social change in the English fashion, the French had the Revolution.

The Revolution (1884), in Taine's view, was sheer disaster. He had devoted two volumes of the original edition to the old monarchy. It took him three for the depiction and analysis of the "orgy" of blood, lust and political irresponsibility which, he thought, the French had brought upon themselves.

The Empire (1878) reveals considerable bitterness against Napoleon. The order which the Emperor had brought out of the Revolutionary chaos was not, to Taine's mind, a solution. It continued to pervert the good tradition, and was fundamentally in conflict with the character of the French as a people and nation.

The Modern Regime (1891) reveals the instinctive conservatism of the author even more than do the earlier books. He sees democracy and instability as synonyms, dreads the effect of destroying traditional institutions, and seems quite willing to give up the liberal advances of the nineteenth century if by so doing the chances of social upheaval can be lessened.

Taine died before he could finish his analysis of contemporary institutions, but not before he had come to realize that his work had pleased few and angered almost everyone. Conservatives disliked his unflattering picture of the "classical" mentality of the Ancient Regime. Bonapartists found his ideas characteristic of the timorous, middle-class *rentier*. The liberals of the Third Republic attacked him as a hopeless stand-patter. But the series sold well in France and abroad, and stands next to the *History of English Literature* in the general estimate of Taine's work.

ORLANDO FURIOSO, by Ludovico Ariosto (1532). Ariosto's *Orlando Furioso,* one of the most important poems of Italian literature, reveals the benevolent disposition of the author toward a world of heroes and knights belonging to a different time. Although that imaginary world is ridiculed, the author reveals that he deeply loves its fictitious charm. If a comparison can be drawn, Cervantes' *Don Quixote* (q.v.) is Orlando's only possible counterpart. *Orlando Furioso's* scenic background is constantly shifting, although the unifying factor is the war between the Christians and the Saracens, in which the redoubtable warrior Orlando—or Roland—takes one of the leading parts. The hero's love for Angelica and his bitter disappointment when she marries the Moor Medoro lead to his madness and earn him the title "Furioso." Equally important is the love between Ruggiero and Bradamente, supposedly the ancestors of the House of Este. The trials they so patiently and superhumanly endure, all for the sake of true love, end with a fanfare of verbal trumpets as they are united to the lasting glory of the House of Este.

ORONOKO (1688), by Aphra Behn. Mrs. Behn's novel, which was dramatized successfully, has historical value in the development of realism in English fiction. It recounts the adventures of the mighty Indian hunter,

Oronoko, in Coromantien, and describes his subsequent enslavement in Surinam, his reunion with his bride, Imoinda, his insurrection, and the dramatic events that led to his violent death, after he had slain Imoinda to save her from the vengeful slave drivers.

ORPHAN, THE (1680), by Thomas Otway. See VENICE PRESERVED, by Thomas Otway.

ORPHAN ANGEL, THE (1926), by Elinor Wylie. See WYLIE, ELINOR.

OSANJIP, by Cha Chullo. See SHIJO-YUCHIP.

OSMAN (ca. 1630), by Ivan Gundulic. Ivan Gundulic (1598–1638) was by far the most representative of that school of poets which flourished in the independent Republic of Dubrovnik-Ragusa on the eastern shore of the Adriatic Sea and developed there a special variation of the Italian Renaissance. Besides conventional mythological dramas and adaptations of the *Psalms,* he wrote this one long epic poem in twenty cantos largely on the model of Tasso's *Jerusalem Delivered* (q.v.). Two cantos are missing, and it is not known whether they were ever finished.

The theme of the poem is the Polish victory over the Sultan Osman at Khotin in 1621 and the subsequent deposition of the Sultan, which took place the next year, largely because of his attempts to restrict the power of the Janissaries and to strengthen the power of the army and of the Ottoman Empire. Yet the real hero of the poem is the Polish prince Vladyslav, who was later to become King of Poland. A close second to him was Samuel Korevsky, who had been taken prisoner by the Turks and whose wife made a trip to Constantinople in disguise to try to rescue him. There are accounts of a mission of Ali Pasha to Warsaw in an effort to make peace, and one of Kizlar Aga through the Ottoman Empire in a search for new brides for the harem. Both trips give Gundulic the opportunity to introduce historical material both of the past of Poland and of the Balkan Christians. There are the usual epic pictures of plots of the devils against the Christians, and at the end there is the prophecy that Vladyslav will ultimately be the rescuer of all the Christians oppressed by the Turks.

Osman is a call for the unity of the Christians against the Turks, and it is one of the few great epics that follow the old pattern but deal with almost contemporary events.

OSSIAN, POEMS OF (1765), by James Macpherson. These purport to be translations from the Gaelic of a legendary third-century warrior and bard, the son of Finn (Fingal). The main work, *Fingal, an Ancient Epic Poem, in Six Books,* had appeared separately in 1762. Swaran, king of Lochlin, Denmark, invades Ireland during the reign of Cormac II. Ireland is saved through the intervention of King Fingal of Morven. In the beginning, Swaran defeats Cuthullin, leader of the Irish forces; at the end, Swaran is driven back to his own land. The poet deliberately tries to introduce a primitive effect, in keeping with the period of his story. *Temora, an Epic Poem in Eight Books* (1763) is a sequel. Probably the best short example of Macpherson's loose rhythmical prose is *The Songs of Selma,* originally published with *Fingal* and inserted by Goethe in *The Sorrows of Young Werther* (q.v.). One can see here in this wild scenery, in these incantations involving natural phenomena, and in this lyrical melancholy both an influence on the European Romantic movement and the germ of the Celtic Renaissance.

OTHELLO, THE MOOR OF VENICE (1604; Quarto 1622), by William Shakespeare. In this great tragedy, taken from Cinthio, we find the skill of Shakespeare at its peak. It has a compactness and unity that sweeps the reader and spectator along so compellingly that only scholars have haggled over the technicalities of the actual time element in the play. We are almost persuaded, emotionally, that we are witnessing an unbroken continuity—actually impossible in the framework of the action.

In point of characterization the play is vivid. Othello and Iago are, of course, the primary focal points. Shakespeare has more or less taken for granted their respective attributes, and stated them as sufficient cause for the events that follow: gullibility and a quick-responding jealousy on the one hand, native treachery and malice on the other. Indeed, tenuous threads of conventional motivation are passingly alluded to, in respect to Iago, but they are frail for so forceful a character. It is easier for us to accept Coleridge's view: "Iago's soliloquy, the motive-hunting of a motiveless malignity—how awful it is!"

Othello, a Moorish general in the service of Venice, secretly marries Desdemona, having won her love by his tales of great exploits and valor. Iago, one of his henchmen, wishes to undo him. Using many cunning devices, including a stolen handkerchief, he begins to spin a web of deceit around the simple-hearted and trusting Othello. He causes Cassio, Othello's lieutenant of whose preferment Iago is jealous, to fall into disgrace through a minor brawl. He persuades Cassio to sue for Othello's favor through the intercession of Desdemona, then urges Desdemona to plead for Cassio. This done, he implies to Othello that Desdemona is unfaithful to him and in love with Cassio. Every innocent word of Desdemona's and every move of Cassio's now seem, to the inflamed Othello, confirmations of his suspicion.

With masterly skill Iago feeds the flame he has kindled, using many tricks and devices to advance his game. At last, at the height of his jealous madness, utterly convinced of her infidelity, Othello smothers Desdemona. Swift upon the heels of this irrevocable act comes the truth exposing Iago's cunning and vindicating Desdemona. In anguish and despair Othello stabs himself, and Iago is led away to punishment, after stabbing Emilia, his wife, who has helped to uncover his villainy.

Othello is one of the great tragedies, whose popularity is constant. It has been made into an opera by the composer Giuseppe Verdi.

OTHER MAIN-TRAVELLED ROADS (1910), by Hamlin Garland. See SON OF THE MIDDLE BORDER, A, by Hamlin Garland.

OUR INNER CONFLICTS (1945), by Karen Horney. See HORNEY, KAREN.

OUR KNOWLEDGE OF THE EXTERNAL WORLD (1914), by Bertrand Russell. See RUSSELL, BERTRAND.

OUR MUTUAL FRIEND (1865), by Charles Dickens. John Harmon, "our mutual friend," will inherit a fortune if he marries Bella Wilfer. He assumes the names of Julius Handford and later John Rokesmith, and his supposed death helps him conceal his identity. John's father's foreman, Nicodemus Boffin, and his wife, Henrietta, help him with the ruse. He enters the employ of Boffin, who has adopted Bella. Bella has had her head turned by wealth, but reforms when her eyes are opened to its evils; she marries Harmon. Other characters are: Jesse Hexam; his son, Charley, and daughter, Lizzie; Bradley Headstone, schoolmaster, who is jealous of Eugene Wrayburn's love for Lizzie Hexam; Fanny Cleaver (Jenny Wren), a doll's dressmaker; one-legged Silas Wegg, the villain in the main plot, as Headstone is in the secondary one. Here again Dickens protests against the poor laws through the character Betty Hidgen, who fears the workhouse.

OUR TOWN (1938), by Thornton Wilder. This Pulitzer Prize play of "Daily Life," "Love and Marriage," and "Death," is one of Wilder's most appealing poetic dramas. When the curtain rises, the stage is bare except for a few chairs. The Stage Manager enters and begins to narrate the story of Groves Corners, beginning May 31, 1901. The plot revolves about two neighboring families, that of Editor Webb and that of Dr. Gibbs. Dr. Gibbs comes in from a maternity case. The Webbs cook breakfast and send their children off to school. George Gibbs and Emily Webb, in the same class at school, lean out of their windows and call across to each other in the moonlight. In the second act, three years later, the youngsters are about to be married. There are scenes of their courtship and wedding. In the third act, nine years later, Emily has died in childbirth. At the cemetery the dead sit apart while Emily enters and leaves the living to sit among them. She tries to reminisce, but the dead are wise; they warn her to forget, and to prepare for what is ahead.

Another experimental play, *The Skin of Our Teeth* (1942), is a dramatic metaphor of humanity's progress. The Antrobus family represents Man. Through Ice Age and war they escape annihilation, and George Antrobus preserves the continuity of culture by such inventions as the alphabet and the wheel.

OUTCAST, THE (1926), by Samuel Joseph Agnon. See BRIDAL CANOPY, THE, by Samuel Joseph Agnon.

OUTLINE OF HISTORY (1920; revised 1931), by H. G. Wells. Written clearly and simply for the general reader, this book opens with the origin of the earth and the beginnings of life on this planet, and ends with a discussion of the post-World War I state of the world and Mr. Wells' dream of a future world federation. He attempts to show the increasing interdependence of life from earliest times up to the present day of airplane and radio, and to lead the reader to the conclusion that a world federation must come about if civilization is to continue. The book, frowned on by experts and specialists, is of particular significance for the reader of today in the light of World War II and the atom bomb, and has not lost its value as a popular survey.

OVER THE TEACUPS (1891), by Oliver Wendell Holmes. See AUTO-CRAT OF THE BREAKFAST TABLE, THE, by Oliver Wendell Holmes.

OVERCOAT, THE (1842), by Nikolay Vasilievich Gogol. See CLOAK, THE, by Nikolay Vasilievich Gogol.

OWL AND THE NIGHTINGALE, THE (ca. 1210–1220), by John or Nicholas de Guildford. This poem, in one thousand octosyllabic couplets, may have been written by either Nicholas or John de Guildford. The gay Night-ingale and the melancholy Owl are heard by the poet debating systematically, employing charge and countercharge, attack and rebuttal, their comparative value and standing as birds. The Owl is accused of being dismal and filthy and of preferring dark and woeful things. The Nightingale is accused of a lack of proper piety, and of implanting lustful thoughts in the minds of men. Many theories have been advanced regarding the significance of these two birds. It has been claimed that the Owl represents realism in literature, whereas the Nightingale represents romance; that they represent didactic and lyrical poetry; or that they represent the ecclesiastical as against the worldly way of life.

OWL IN THE ATTIC, THE (1931), by James Thurber. See THURBER, JAMES.

OX-BOW INCIDENT, THE (1940), by Walter Van Tilburg Clark. This is an unusual "Western" about cowboys, rustlers, and a lynching, which describes psychologically the effects on the men involved. The action occurs during one day in Nevada, in 1885. Art and Gil, cowboys, come to Bridger's Wells; after a poker game they hear talk of rustlers and the murder of Kinkaid. A posse is formed, some joining reluctantly. Among them is Ma (Jenny Grier). They leave during a night snowstorm, almost wrecking a stage coach, one of whose passengers is Rose Mapen, Gil's sweetheart. In Ox-Bow Valley three men are discovered: Donald Martin, and his helpers, a harmless old man and a Mexican. Tetley, the posse leader, immediately as-sumes they are guilty; others are dubious. At sunup they lynch the three. The last chapter describes the effects of the gruesome scene on the participants. Davies is pitifully remorseful. Young Gerald Tetley, son of the leader, com-mits suicide.

The City of Trembling Leaves (1945) concerns a youth who yearns to write music. *The Track of the Cat* (1949) is a novel of the Nevada Sierras, in which the Bridges brothers hunt a panther—an ordinary cattle-killer as some believe it to be, a huge, supernatural creature symbolizing to others the power of evil.

PABLOS DE SEGOVIA, THE SPANISH SHARPER (1626), by Fran-cisco de Quevedo. *El Buscón,* probably written in 1608 but not published until 1626, whose full title is *Historia de la vida del Buscón, llamado Don Pablos, ejemplo de vagabundos y espejo de tacaños,* is a cynical, vitriolic picaresque novel, frequently considered one of the most heartlessly cruel books ever written. Pablos, the son of a Segovian barber and a woman of ill repute, flees from his home and enters the service of a young gentleman, Don Diego Coronel. Pablos accompanies him to a boarding house in Salamanca kept by

Licenciado Cabra, a stingy dominie who may be considered a predecessor of Dickens' Squeers. Starved to the point of death, master and servant are taken out of the Licenciado's claws by Don Diego's parents and sent to study in Alcala, where Pablos assiduously patronizes the gaming dens and achieves the dubious distinction of being the most intolerable of students. Leaving his master to collect an inheritance left him by his father (hanged for thievery), Pablos moves to Madrid, where he joins a gang of thieves. Shortly thereafter he finds his way to Toledo as actor in a company of strolling players. Finally after "working" with a fencing master, he departs for America hoping to improve his luck.

PAINTED VEILS (1920), by James Gibbons Huneker. See IVORY APES AND PEACOCKS, by James Gibbons Huneker.

PAL JOEY (1940), by John O'Hara. See APPOINTMENT IN SAMARRA, by John O'Hara.

PALAMAS, KOSTES (1859–1943). Kostes Palamas even during his lifetime was recognized as the foremost poet of modern Greece. He did more than any other man by his example and influence to make the ordinary speech of the people the literary medium, and to break the hold on literature of the artificial literary tongue that preserved many of the traditions of antiquity. A deeply philosophical writer, he was fully conscious of the continuity of the Greek tradition throughout the ages, and he emphasized this in almost all of his major works. Among these are: *Life Unshakable* (Eng. tr. 1921, 1923), a study of the continuity of the Greek feeling; and similarly, *Flute of the King* (1910), and a lyric drama, *Triseryene* (1903). He is not easy to read, but he reflects the impact of the modern European world upon Greece, and he broadened in every way the modern literature. Many of his works have been translated into English by the late Aristides Phoutrides.

PALATINE ANTHOLOGY, THE (10th c.). See GREEK ANTHOLOGY, THE.

PALE HORSE, PALE RIDER (1939), by Katherine Anne Porter. See PORTER, KATHERINE ANNE.

PALGRAVE'S GOLDEN TREASURY, THE (1861), edited by Francis Turner Palgrave. The editor of this famous anthology of English lyric poetry was from 1886 to 1895 Professor of Poetry at Oxford. Tennyson was his lifelong friend, and helped him in selecting the 339 exquisitely chosen lyrics, divided into four "books." Book I contains Elizabethan songs and lyrics; Book II, lyrics between 1620 and 1700; Book III, the eighteenth century; Book IV, chiefly from the first third of the nineteenth. *Tottell's Miscellany* (1557) was the first anthology of English poetry. *The Golden Treasury,* the second, followed by Sir Arthur T. Quiller-Couch's superb *Oxford Book of English Verse* (1900), has had an incalculable influence in all English-speaking countries in making familiar the most beautiful lyric poetry in the language. Palgrave edited in 1897 a "Second Series" of 190 lyrics; largely from Matthew Arnold, the Brownings, Arthur O'Shaughnessy, the Rossettis, and especially Tennyson.

PALINGENESI POLITICA (published 1809), by Vincenzo Monti. See MONTI, VINCENZO.

PALLIETER (1916; Eng. tr. 1924), by Felix Timmermans. See TIMMERMANS, FELIX.

PALNATOKE (1807), by Adam Gottlob Oehlenschlaeger. See ALADDIN, by Adam Gottlob Oehlenschlaeger.

PAMELA (1740), by Samuel Richardson. *Pamela,* a domestic novel of sentiment, is regarded as the first modern novel. Its emphasis is on character and manners, rather than on incident. The story is told through a series of letters written by Pamela Andrews to her parents, a form of narration used by Richardson in all three of his novels. Pamela, a maidservant of a wealthy woman who dies at the opening of the story, is dishonorably pursued by the son and heir of the family. Pamela resists his advances and attempts to escape from them by leaving the house. Her pursuer follows, however, kidnaping Pamela and requiring her to use a great deal of ingenuity to preserve her virtue. Finally, the young aristocrat condescends to forget her lowly birth and station in life and marry her. After Pamela has been "rewarded" for her virtue with a wild profligate young man for a husband, she proceeds to reform him by her gentle, expedient, and judicious conduct. The book is divided into two parts, the much more interesting part being the first, in which Pamela exerts all her strength and cleverness to repel the disgraceful advances. The second part, published in 1741, deals with the way in which Pamela bore sweetly and without complaint the trials—for her spouse, Mr. B., is in danger of relapsing—of her marriage. The book was very popular. It was translated into several languages, and made the basis for several skits. Richardson made a distinct contribution to literature with *Pamela*. It was a novel idea to use such a humble person for a heroine; it was also novel for a work of fiction to make use of scenes common to ordinary life.

PAN (1916), by Herman Gorter. See MEI, by Herman Gorter.

PAN TADEUSZ (1834), by Adam Mickiewicz. The subtitle of this epic poem—"The Last Foray in Lithuania. A Story of the Nobles in 1811 and 1812"—well suggests its contents. But it is more than this, for it is a picture of the old life of the noble families of Lithuania after the downfall of Polish independence, on the eve of the entrance of Napoleon and the Polish Legions of General Dombrowski into their native land. The plot is simple. There has long been a feud between the families of the Horeszkos and the Soplicas. Years before, the head of the Soplicas, Jacek, had killed the lord of the Horeszkos under conditions that made it seem that Jacek was pro-Russian. He then vanished. His young son Tadeusz is now grown up, and his uncle wishes him to marry Zofia, the heiress to the Horeszko fortune. The Count, a Horeszko, wins a lawsuit, giving him a disputed property, and with his friends tries to acquire the estate by force. This gives the Russians a chance to intervene, but they are defeated by the joint action of both factions of Poles. Prominent in the action is a mysterious monk, Father Robak, who works for peace and reconciliation. Only on his deathbed does he explain that he is the missing Jacek Soplica; he has sought this method of expiating his impulsive crime. Through his confession all is straightened out, and Tadeusz and Zofia marry, while the Polish Legions arrive and are splendidly entertained with feasting and dancing.

The poem is a true epic of the life of the nobility at the beginning of the nineteenth century, and Mickiewicz, then in exile, threw into it all his poetic talent, all his memories of his early life, and of the national feeling for which he sacrificed so much. The poem has been well translated in prose by George Rapall Noyes (1917) and is now in Everyman's Library.

PAN WOLODYJOWSKI (1888), by Henryk Sienkiewicz. See WITH FIRE AND SWORD, by Henryk Sienkiewicz.

PANDORA'S BOX (1903), by Frank Wedekind. See AWAKENING OF SPRING, by Frank Wedekind.

PANEGYRIC (ca. 380 B.C.), by Isocrates. Isocrates has, through his influence especially on Cicero, exerted a lasting influence on prose style. He was something of a statesman of Athens, but exerted his influence rather as a professional writer of speeches and a teacher of rhetoric. He was not himself effective as a public speaker, and often published his speeches as pamphlets or open letters. That is the case with the *Panegyric,* which is written as though for delivery at one of the great national gatherings (*panegyris*) of the Greeks such as the Olympic Games. The theme of the speech is one which was dear to the heart of Isocrates. He advocates an active Panhellenism, a union of all Greek states, but especially of Athens and Sparta, against Persia, the ancient and common enemy. The leadership in such a union should, he argues, fall to Athens, whose claims he justifies by a long and brilliant encomium of her cultural achievements as a spiritual leader. As practical politics the *Panegyric* is of slight importance, but as an expression of idealism in statesmanship it is unrivaled. The beauty of Isocrates' simple and lucid periodic style is perfectly exemplified in this speech. It is because of the glowing praises of Athens in the *Panegyric* that this name has come to be a synonym for encomium.

PANIC (1935), by Archibald MacLeish. See MacLEISH, ARCHIBALD.

PANORAMA AND OTHER POEMS, THE (1856), by John Greenleaf Whittier. See SNOW-BOUND, by John Greenleaf Whittier.

PARACELSUS (1835), by Robert Browning. This verse-play eulogizes the courageous spirit and the passionate quest for knowledge and truth of the father of modern chemistry, Paracelsus. He met with opposition and hostility, but never wavered when the hue and cry was raised against him. In Part I Paracelsus leaves his monastery cell against the wishes of his friends Festus and Michal, to go out into the world for first-hand knowledge of life. In Part II, he is a successful professor but still not happy, since his greatest wish, to know God, has not been fulfilled. The disheartened scientist wanders from country to country, no longer seeking book knowledge, but concerned with achieving understanding through the senses. He finally dies at Salzburg, and with his departure from the world comes a flash of insight. Truth alone, knowledge alone, are insufficient; he has let love for man slip by him.

PARACELSUS (1899), by Arthur Schnitzler. See SCHNITZLER, AR-THUR.

PARADISE LOST (1667), by John Milton. This great epic poem is characterized by a sonorous nobility of expression and a compelling moral fervor. *Book I.* There is a short reference to the fall of man and a statement of the purpose of the work, "to justify the Ways of God to men." The poem opens with Satan and his army of rebellious angels already cast from Heaven into the Abyss of Hell. Satan rises from the Burning Lake and assures his followers that they will have a kingdom rivaling that of Heaven. They build the Palace of Pandemonium. *Book II.* The rebels meet to determine how they may best revenge themselves upon God. Abandoning the idea of waging further open war, they determine to seek the newly created Earth and God's most favored creation, Man. They hope to pervert him and wreck the great plans made by God for him. Satan alone fares forth on this quest. He escapes from Hell with the connivance of his progeny, Sin and Death, to whom he promises rich feasts upon Earth. *Book III.* God sees Satan's flight to Earth, and to His Son He foretells the fall and necessary punishment of Man. The Son expresses His desire to sacrifice Himself for Man's redemption. Meanwhile Satan reaches the outskirts of Earth. He flies to the sun, and Uriel, not recognizing him, shows him the pathway to the world. *Book IV.* In the earthly Paradise of Eden, Adam and Eve are living an idyllic life, unspoiled by Sin, Guilt, or Death. All the fruits of the Earth are theirs, with the exception of the fruit of the Tree of Knowledge, expressly forbidden by God. Satan steals into the garden, listens to them discussing the forbidden fruit, and seizes upon it as a means of seducing Man from his state of grace. He begins to tempt Eve in disturbing dreams, but is apprehended by the angels and expelled from Paradise. *Book V.* In order to give Adam and Eve every opportunity for resistance, God sends Raphael, who explains to them the full details of the revolt and war in Heaven, informing them of the person and nature of their foe. *Book VI.* Raphael tells Adam how the Angels of God fought the Legions of Satan, and of how the Son of God alone finally defeated the enemy. *Book VII.* Raphael explains that when the ranks of Heaven were depleted by the loss of Satan and his followers, God sent His Son to create a new world, peopled by new creatures. *Book VIII.* Adam asks Raphael about the movements of the sun, stars, and moon. He speaks of his own creation. *Book IX.* The wily Satan returns to Eden in the body of a Snake. He subtly seduces Eve to taste of the fruit of the Tree of Knowledge. He tells her God is jealous, and that she and Adam may become as gods. Eve yields, and the Snake slips away. Adam is appalled when he learns of her act, but, nevertheless, deliberately eats of the fruit so that they may share together whatever punishment is visited upon them. *Book X.* The Son of God judges fallen man, and Sin and Death are allowed to enter the world. The victorious Satan is hailed by his waiting comrades, but they are all transformed into serpents, and doomed to assume such form at stated intervals. *Book XI.* Michael is commanded to expel Adam and Eve from Paradise. Their day of death is deferred, and the angel comforts them by giving a vision of what shall happen up to the time of Noah. *Book XII.* The vision of the future continues. The coming of the Redeemer is predicted by Michael. He tells of the Incarnation, Death, Resurrection, and second coming of Christ. Adam and Eve then leave Paradise. "The world was all before them, where to choose. . . ."

PARADISE REGAINED (1927), by Hendrik Marsman. See MARSMAN, HENDRIK.

PARADISE REGAINED (1671), by John Milton. The Quaker Elwood flattered himself by fancying that his suggestion was responsible for this sequel to *Paradise Lost*. If Elwood's story is true, the poem must have been kept complete and unprinted for about five years. It did not have the sale of *Paradise Lost*, and is inferior not in writing but in that the subject matter afforded far less opportunity for interest and conflict of a popular kind; moreover, the conclusion is even more foregone than in its great predecessor. It is rather long for the action involved, and the style is relatively pedestrian. Divided into four books, it deals with Christ's struggle against Satan in the wilderness and His overcoming of all temptations.

PARALLEL LIVES (ca. 110), by Plutarch. The *Parallel Lives* were so called by their author because he wrote them in pairs, the biography of a great Greek corresponding to that of a great Roman, and linked each pair together by a comparison at the end. Thus Theseus and Romulus, Demosthenes and Cicero, Alexander and Caesar are linked. In all there are forty-six such parallel biographies of great and near great men from Greek and Roman history, and in addition four separate lives. Plutarch is one of few ancient biographers whose works have survived. He was a man of wide and varied learning, thoroughly versed in ancient history and philosophy. His writing shows an intimate acquaintance with a truly astonishing range of authorities. His use of his authorities is not always up to modern standards of historiography, but the information he preserves is often invaluable. His primary interest was not in history but in character, and he presents the subjects of his lives from the point of view of a moralist, tending to portray them as either remarkably good or remarkably bad. It is perhaps for that reason as well as because of the inherent interest in his subjects and of his engaging style that he has won the acclaim of such writers as Shakespeare, Montaigne and Browning, to say nothing of a much more general popularity.

PARIS BOUND (1927), by Philip Barry. See BARRY, PHILIP.

PARKER, DOROTHY (1893–   ). Dorothy Parker, after a brief career as literary and dramatic critic, began free-lance writing in 1920. She had already become famous in her native New York for her brilliant conversation and malicious *mots*. *Not So Deep as a Well* (1936), a collection of her poetry, is characterized by a facile cynicism and emphasis on such subjects as frustration and personal disillusion. In 1929, her O. Henry Memorial Prize short story, "Big Blonde," appeared. This depressing commentary on society traces the spiraling deterioration of a friendly, pretty and not too bright girl. *Here Lies* (1939) is a collection of her short stories. As in her poems, technical dexterity and sardonic observation of life mark the pieces.

PARKMAN, FRANCIS (1823–1893). Parkman, a distinguished young Bostonian, journeyed in 1846 from St. Louis westward to Fort Laramie, Wyoming, over the Oregon Trail. He lived for several weeks with the Sioux Indians, and his subsequent book, *The Oregon Trail* (1849), became a classic on frontier life. Despite bad health, he persevered for more than forty years to produce an eight-volume study of the English-French struggle for power in the New World. These volumes—the first a *History of the Conspiracy of Pontiac* and the last *A Half-Century of Conflict*—were published at intervals from 1851 to 1892. The series is a lively combination of historical research and literary color.

PARLIAMENT OF FOWLS, THE (ca. 1375), by Geoffrey Chaucer. See BOOK OF THE DUCHESS, by Geoffrey Chaucer.

PARSIFAL (1882), by Richard Wagner. See WAGNER, RICHARD.

PARZIVAL (1202), by Wolfram von Eschenbach. This epic, written about 1202, and considered to be the first of the typically German "Bildungsroman" (novel of educational development), deals with the life story of the knight Parzival—a life of blundering and failures which finally teach him the wisdom necessary for achievement. Parzival is brought up by his mother Herzeleide in the seclusion of a forest far away from the chivalric life which she and his father had known. Soon, however, he is stirred by a desire to venture forth. With complete innocence of conduct and behavior, Parzival reaches the castle of Gurnemanz, where his host instructs him in practical and knightly subjects. As a knight, he now rescues and wins for his wife the lady Kondwiramur. At the castle of Anfortas—in reality Parzival's uncle and King of the Holy Grail—the young warrior finds his host suffering from an incurable wound and awaiting the unprompted question of a strange knight to bring about his cure. The fateful question never issues forth from Parzival's lips, since he has been taught by Gurnemanz to refrain from questions. Too late he learns the importance of his visit. Then follow five years of wandering, accompanied by rebellion against himself and God and filled with remorse and doubt. Yet Parzival never wavers from the ideal of the Grail nor from faithfulness to his wife. After several adventures he proves himself worthy again. In his newly won understanding of others, he makes restitution for his previous mistakes at the castle of Anfortas, is reunited with Kondwiramur and becomes King of the Holy Grail.

Parzival finds continued reinterpretation in its symbolism of the striving toward purity of heart and soul through development of both personality and an inner synthesis of worldly and religious ideals—attained only after a life of conflict and uncertainty.

The epic, written in couplets in an irregular meter, is available in the English translation by Jessie L. Weston. *Parsifal*, Richard Wagner's music drama, is the best known among the several succeeding versions.

PASSAGE TO INDIA (1924), by E. M. Forster. Laid in Chandrapore, this novel deals with the social and political relations of the English and the people of India. The principal characters are Cyril Fielding and Dr. Aziz. Their struggle to reach a common ground of understanding and friendship is the main theme. Adela Quested falsely accuses the Indian doctor Aziz of attacking her. At the trial she retracts the charge. The doctor becomes embittered and tries to hate all Englishmen. However, he retains a feeling of love and friendship for Mrs. Moore, mother of Heaslop, who is the fiancé of Adela. Mrs. Moore leaves at the time of the trial and dies aboard ship. Later Aziz comes in contact with her two other children, Ralph and Stella (now Mrs. Cyril Fielding). The doctor has the same feeling and understanding for them that he had for their mother. In the last chapter, Aziz and Fielding discuss their positions, accuse one another, and argue. Nothing, naturally, is solved. "No, not yet, . . . No, not there."

PASSION FLOWER, THE (1913),by Jacinto Benavente. Esteban, a well-to-do farmer, loves his stepdaughter, Acacia. She unconsciously returns his passion, though she thinks she hates him because he has come between her and her mother, Raimunda. Acacia was to have married her cousin, but she jilts him and prepares to marry Faustino, the son of a neighboring landowner. Shortly after their engagement Faustino is killed. At first the cousin is suspected, but he is cleared of the charge; and gradually it becomes evident that Esteban's servant is the murderer. Raimunda, who loves her husband, is willing to shield him and sacrifice Acacia. But when he embraces Acacia and the two resolve to leave together, she calls him a murderer and threatens to expose him. He shoots her; but in the end Acacia turns to her mother.

PAST AND PRESENT (1843), by Thomas Carlyle. Opposing *laissez faire,* Carlyle argues for more social and economic organization, and contrasts the England of his day with the England of the twelfth century as depicted in Jocelin of Brakelond's *Chronica.* Looking around him, Carlyle sees only irresponsible classes. At top are the aristocracy, consisting mostly of "Denizens of Mayfair" and "rosy fox-hunting squires," master unworkers, dilettanti, "do-nothings." These people no longer govern, nor are fit to govern, and so too the priests no longer guide the nation spiritually. Organized religion is just stage-machinery. The man of power in the modern world is the Captain of Industry, and he is under the dominion of Mammon. Underneath are the oppressed workers, victims of factories, of Poor-law prisons, of mass unemployment, of dirt and disease. "We have more riches than any nation; we have less good than any other nation." The Manchester Insurrection was a warning. With this chaos is contrasted the monastery of St. Edmundsbury under the strong Abbot Samson. Here are the order and religion to which England must return. Under the present notion of democracy, government is a negative rather than a directing force.

PATHFINDER, THE (1840), by James Fenimore Cooper. See LEATHERSTOCKING TALES, by James Fenimore Cooper.

PATIENCE (ca. 1370). See PEARL.

PATTERNS OF CULTURE (1934), by Ruth Benedict. This is a distinguished anthropological study of the cultural patterns of the Zuni Indians of New Mexico, the natives of Dobu in Melanesia, and the Kwakiutl of Vancouver. It attempts to show how varied customs and traditions result in diverse institutions, and how these in turn produce different standards of individual and social behavior. This popular book in cultural anthropology utilizes material from sociology, psychology and philosophy as well, and has become something of a classic for students in anthropology.

PAUL AND VIRGINIA (1787), by Jacques Henri Bernardin de Saint-Pierre. This is a nature idyl in the form of a novel. The scene is the Isle of France—now Mauritius Island—some years before the French Revolution. Madame de la Tour, a widow, has a daughter, Virginia. Marguerite, her neighbor, has a son, Paul. The two children grow up in an atmosphere of ideal simplicity. They are completely happy and love each other tenderly. Their marriage is forestalled, however, by a letter from Madame de la Tour's aunt, who offers to make Virginia her heir, provided she visit her in France. Virginia goes to France, refuses a marriage arranged for her, is disinherited by her aunt, and comes back to the Island. But a hurricane wrecks her ship, in sight of land, and she is drowned. Paul dies of grief two months later.

The novel is at once a tract against the corruption of French society, and a sermon on the virtues of simplicity. The descriptions of tropical nature are considered classics of the type.

PEARL (ca. 1370). The four poems: *Pearl, Gawain and the Green Knight* (q.v.), *Purity,* and *Patience* occur in the same manuscript and are believed to be by the same author, some great contemporary of Chaucer. *Pearl* consists of one hundred and one twelve-lined octosyllabic stanzas in alliterative verse, with rhyme and a refrain. The poet has lost his Pearl, his Margaret (Latin for pearl), an only child who died when she was under two. (This may be entirely an allegory, however.) Walking by her grave disconsolate, he has a vision of her in Paradise, where her shining clothes are adorned with pearls. Now a bride of the Lamb of God, she tells him his grief is unnecessary, and gives him a glimpse of the New Jerusalem. He tries to plunge into the river after her, but awakens and is comforted by what he has heard and seen.

Purity (or *Cleanness*) is an alliterative unrhymed poem praising lawful love through stories from Scripture: the Flood, the destruction of Sodom and Gomorrah, the fall of Belshazzar. *Patience* tells the story of the prophet Jonah.

PEARL (1923), by Israel Joshua Singer. See BROTHERS ASHKENAZI, THE, by Israel Joshua Singer.

PEARL, THE (1948), by John Steinbeck. See GRAPES OF WRATH, THE, by John Steinbeck.

PEASANTS, THE (1904–1909), by Wladyslaw St. Reymont. Wladyslaw St. Reymont (1868–1925) won the Nobel Prize shortly before his death with the four-volume novel *The Peasants,* a study of peasant life in Poland and a glorification of the everlasting vitality of the Earth. In each of its four volumes —*Spring, Summer, Autumn* and *Winter*—is reflected the effort of the peasants to carry out the traditional round of seasonal occupations. German officers stationed in Poland during World War I were ordered to read and study this book in order to handle the peasants intelligently and profitably.

The widower, old Matthew Boryna, is unwilling to hand his estates over to his married son Anton in accordance with the law of the soil. Instead of doing this, he marries an attractive girl, Jagna, a creature of passion who is proud of her conquest and cannot be indifferent to the call of Nature. It is not long before she becomes the mistress of the married Anton. In the meantime, old Boryna has been badly hurt leading the peasants in a march against the lord of the manor, who is breaking the tradition of the village by forbidding them their ancestral rights. In this clash Anton kills a man and is arrested. Finally spring comes, and old Boryna dies trying to sow seed in his fields. Anton is released from prison, and Jagna, who has continued to seek men where she found them, is thrown out of the village and beaten until she is nearly dead.

The novel expresses the age-old conflict between law and nature, between the rights of the master of the estate and those of the peasants who till the soil, between the older generations seeking to perpetuate their power and create a new life for themselves, and the younger who try on coming to maturity to take over what is naturally theirs.

The intensity of all these conflicts in the village far overshadows other work by Reymont, such as *The Promised Land* (1927), which deals with urban life, for in *The Peasants* he has touched a theme that is eternal. In a later series dealing with the revolt of Kosciuszko to recover Polish independence he has done well, but he never repeated the intensity and effectiveness of *The Peasants,* one of the great stories of European peasant life.

PECK'S BAD BOY (1883), by George W. Peck. The episodic stories of a mischievous youth's practical jokes played upon his father first appeared in Peck's own newspaper, then in a series of books from 1883 to 1907. The non-literary style is a true reflection of the speech of Americans. The author became so popular that in 1890 he was elected governor of Wisconsin.

PEER GYNT (1867), by Henrik Ibsen. *Peer Gynt* is Ibsen's best known poetic drama, and was written during his romantic period. Really an epic, it tells the story of Peer Gynt, a Norwegian peasant boy, whose father had spent all the family money. He lives alone with his old mother, Aase. Peer is a roisterer, a braggart, and a liar. He goes off on a spree and tells Aase how he rode a reindeer buck into the fjord. While he has been away his girl, Ingrid, has become engaged to be married. Peer puts his scolding mother on the mill-house roof and goes to the wedding. He is not well received. None of the girls will dance with him, and so he asks a stranger, Solveig. The bride has locked herself in the loft, and the bridegroom asks Peer for help. Peer ends by carrying her off up the mountainside, much to the consternation of the guests, including old Aase, who has managed to get to the wedding. Ingrid breaks from him and returns to the valley below. Now virtually an outlaw, he wanders in the forest. He has an episode with three mountain farm girls, and then he encounters the troll king's daughter, and returns to her father's kingdom with her. But he has not the makings of a troll, and the trolls attack him when he tries to escape. He calls on his mother for help. The church bells in the valley start to ring, and the frightened trolls scatter. He builds himself a hut in the woods. In the meantime the Haegstads, Ingrid's parents, have seized all his available property, and left Aase only the house she lives in. Solveig comes to his hut and says she has deserted her family for him. But his happiness is short-lived, for the troll princess, now an old woman, appears with her brat, and threatens to claim her share of his affections. He flees, leaving Solveig in the hut. He comes to his mother's house as she is dying, and in one of the finest scenes in the play pretends that he is driving her to a party at Sol-Moria Castle, a game they had often played in his childhood. After her death he emigrates to America and becomes prosperous as a slave trader. Twenty-five years pass, and Peer is on the southwest coast of Morocco, dining with some international friends, guests on his steam yacht. He goes through a series of adventures in ·Africa, passing himself off as the Prophet, and has a love affair with an Arab girl, Anitra. He finds his way to Egypt and the Sphinx, and is offered an emperor's crown in an insane asylum. Finally, an elderly man, he returns to Norway and is wrecked in a storm. His past begins to catch up with him. A mysterious being, the Button-Moulder, tells him that he must be put in the Casting-Ladle and be melted down like every other Tom, Dick, and Harry; Peer has not enough soul to be of intrinsic value. He tries desperately to prove that he has sinned enough to go to hell. But it is Solveig, who has remained in the hut all these years, who saves him, as Peer's real self had lived in her faith, her hope, and her love.

PEG WOFFINGTON (1853), by Charles Reade. See CLOISTER AND THE HEARTH, THE, by Charles Reade.

PELLE THE CONQUEROR (1906–1910; Eng. tr. 1913–1917), by Martin Anderson Nexo. The four-volume novel by the Danish country schoolmaster Martin Anderson Nexo, which has been favorably compared with *Jean Christophe* (q.v.) by Romain Rolland as one of the greatest of modern works of fiction, is essentially a novel of workers, their lives, hopes and struggles. The hitherto obscure author was astonished to receive the Nobel Prize in Literature.

The four volumes deal with four separate phases in the turbulent life of its hero, who seeks a better life and social justice in the world. The boy Pelle and his father emigrate from Sweden to the Danish island of Bornholm in the Baltic Sea. They become farmhands on Stone Farm, owned by harsh landowners, the Kongstrups. Pelle is a cattle herder. On the one hand his honest imagination unfolds under the influence of the mystery and beauty of Nature; on the other hand the hard cruel world of reality, the violent clashing of wills about him, the humiliation he suffers as a despised child of a farm laborer, sear his soul and stimulate grave doubts about the goodness in man.

The second volume describes the life of Pelle as an apprentice in the town, for he had found his lot on the farm unendurable. The simple country lad falls into much trouble in the corrupt town. Trial and error lead him progressively to greater understanding. His character in the difficult process of adjustment becomes firmer. Soon he begins to find his life growing stagnant and false; so he decides to move on.

The third volume shows Pelle in the capital, Copenhagen. The plight of the workers has led him to throw himself passionately into the labor movement. He falls in love, marries, and rears a family; he is faced by the dilemma of conflicting loyalties, to the labor movement and to his family, the former calling for sacrifices and the latter obliged to make them. At the height of his success as a labor leader, after having won a general strike, the vengeful employers "frame" him and send him to prison on the charge of forgery.

The fourth volume recounts his desperate struggle to find a place for himself in the world after he has left prison with the stigma of a criminal. With a new outlook he engages in a severe struggle to establish the co-operative movement in industry. The book ends on a mystic note of optimism.

PELLEAS AND MELISANDE (1892), by Maurice Maeterlinck. See BLUEBIRD, THE, by Maurice Maeterlinck.

PENAL COLONY, THE (1919), by Franz Kafka. See TRIAL, THE, by Franz Kafka.

PEÑAS ARRIBA (1895), by José María de Pereda. See ASCENT TO THE HEIGHTS, by José María de Pereda.

PENDENNIS, THE HISTORY OF (serialized 1848–1850), by William Makepeace Thackeray. Thackeray plots a character study of Arthur Pendennis, a young Englishman of his own era. He is not the usual hero of the author's former works, but a commonplace young man with weaknesses and passions, adored by his mother, Helen, and adopted sister, Laura. He falls in love with two women outside his social caste: Emily Costigan (Miss Fotheringay), an Irish actress ten years older than himself, and Fanny Bolton, a pretty and innocent maid servant. His uncle, worldly Major Arthur Pendennis, saves him from the first, and Pen honorably saves himself from the second. Laura loves him and pays off his debts incurred at college. After life in London as a writer and man of the world, Pen becomes infatuated with Blanche Amory, who is broth flirtatious and wealthy. When Blanche jilts him, Pen's eyes are opened to true values, and he turns to Laura and enters a mature life as husband and father.

PENGUIN ISLAND (1908), by Anatole France. This novel is an allegory. The Penguins receive baptism, learn civilization, build churches, wage wars. The Napoleon of Penguins, Trinco, conquers half the world and then loses it again. The Penguins have their Dreyfus case, too—the Pyrot affair. They have their unglorious Third Republic and a succession of falling cabinets. Finally the Penguins perfect explosives which destroy Paris, and civilization has to start all over again. Generally France's irony is gentle even when most corrosive, but in *Penguin Island* it turns bitter; his Olympian detachment had been upset by the Dreyfus case.

PENROD (1914), by Booth Tarkington. The incidents recounted in this novel of juveniles for readers of all ages occur in the twelfth year of Penrod Schofield, typical boy in a middle-class Midwestern family. Penrod believes himself to be a much misunderstood boy; nor is he always to blame, after all. Take, for instance, the escapade of the slingshot. His father determines to punish him for the damage he has done—until wise old great-aunt Sarah Crim points out that she had taken the same instrument from Mr. Schofield thirty-five years before. Characteristic scrapes include a school pageant in which Penrod has to play Child Sir Lancelot; a flirtation with little Marjorie Jones; a home-made circus enterprise; minor blackmail of his sister's suitor; and a grand tar fight.

Penrod and Sam (1916) and *Penrod Jashber* (1929) continue the adventures.

Seventeen (1916) is another novel about adolescents. William Sylvanus Baxter, age seventeen, falls in love with Lola Pratt of the calf-like eyes. Mrs. Baxter, an understanding and romantic soul, patiently watches Willie slowly sober up.

PENSACI GIACOMINO (1916), by Luigi Pirandello. See PIRAN-DELLO, LUIGI.

PENSÉES (1670), by Blaise Pascal. Pascal's *Pensées,* a collection of random thoughts which were taken from his notes by his friends and published post-humously, was an apologia for the Christian religion addressed to a rising class of intellectual freethinkers among the French aristocracy. To bring these stray-ing sinners back to a knowledge of God through faith was his fervent under-taking. Pascal expressed his sympathetic understanding of the religious skeptics who look upon their doubt as the worst of evils, and knowing it as such, spare no pains to dissipate it. But he had no patience with those who neglect to seek an answer elsewhere. A feeling of interest and self-love should prompt such individuals to seek enlightenment, he maintained. There is little question that Pascal was a religious zealot. He wrote his *Pensées* with missionary intent, and he attacked the problem with sincere forthrightness. Because of the clarity and brilliance of its discussion of universal moral and religious problems, his work has become a source of inspiration for those who feel the need of faith and are troubled by doubts.

PENTHESILEA (1808), by Heinrich von Kleist. See KLEIST, HEIN-RICH VON.

PEOPLE, THE (1846), by Jules Michelet. This is a panegyric essay on the qualities and spirit of the French working class, written in an eruptive prose which at times approaches poetry. An enthusiastic democrat, Michelet looked to the people to unify France and make her great; he felt that they were the true custodians of the spirit of Joan of Arc, and that their Revolution had been a revelation of the inherent nobility of mankind. Michelet's contempora-ries considered this one-time working man who had become a professor at the Sorbonne a great historian. His clashes with the government of Napoleon III made him something of a political figure and more than something of a nuisance. Today works like *The People* and his *History of France* (q.v.) are read largely as examples of oratorical prose in the French Romantic tradition.

PEOPLE OF JUVIK, THE (1918–1923; Eng. tr. 1930–1935), by Olav Duun. This series of six relatively short novels, describing in general the battle of man against outside forces that threaten to dominate him, has in construc-tion been compared to that of an Icelandic family saga. It is written in the dialect of the author, the Norwegian Landsmaal, and is monumental in scope. It is the story of a family through several generations, over a century and a half, and portrays, through self-sacrifice and self-assertion, the gradual develop-ment from barbarism to high morality. Christian and humanitarian impulses prevail.

PEOPLE OF SELDWYLA, THE (1856, 1874), by Gottfried Keller. See GREEN HENRY, by Gottfried Keller.

PEOPLE OF THE ABYSS (1903), by Jack London. See LONDON, JACK.

PEOPLE, YES, THE (1936), by Carl Sandburg. This is a sprawling, kaleidoscopic glorification of the common people of America, written by Sandburg at the time of the great democratic revival which swept through the country before World War II. The work has great variety, written in scores of different styles and meters, and in prose and poetry; several hundred fragments achieving unity by the thread of the poet's love for the people. The episodic structure represents all America. It is humorous, sentimental, savage, tragic, and ironic in turn. It is informal, plain, idiomatic—filled with folk sayings, street songs, legends, slang expressions, wise saws, and riddles. Much of it is directed against social injustices, and it is a stirring defense of democratic idealism.

PEOPLE YOU KNEW (1903), by George Ade. See ADE, GEORGE.

PEPITA JIMENEZ (1874), by Juan Valera. Pepita Jimenez is nineteen, rich, beautiful, and a widow. She falls in love with Luis de Vargas, a young man of twenty-two, who is preparing for the priesthood. He in turn begins to find her irresistible. With quietness and subtlety, Valera shows his growing friendship for the charming widow against the background of Andalusian orchards gay with sunlight, cheerful, delightful. The outstanding qualities of the novel are the simplicity of the plot, the purity of the style, and the deft analysis of the main characters.

PEREGRINE PICKLE, THE ADVENTURES OF (1751), by Tobias Smollett. Smollett's longest novel has his usual vigor and so-called lack of morality. Peregrine is a rogue and not too disturbed about it. In his elegant, witty fashion, he is a bully possessed of as refined cruelty as any villain. Pickle's father, his aunt, Grizzle, and her husband, Commodore Trunnion, show Smollett's superb character drawing. He is also a humorist, and his savagery does not diminish this quality. There is no plot—the many episodes are strung together loosely. There is much incidental realism.

PERETZ, ISAAC LOEB (1852–1915). Known mainly for his remarkable stories of Jewish life in Russian Poland, where he spent all his days, Peretz was fortunate in having been permitted to engage in general secular studies while pursuing the intensive Jewish studies of his time and locale. So great was his fame among his coreligionists that when he died in Warsaw during World War I 100,000 persons followed his coffin. At various times a lawyer, brewer, teacher of Hebrew and the sciences, and communal official, he earned very little throughout his life from his abundant writings in fiction, drama, poetry, and scholarly articles. Though his first book was a collection of poems in Hebrew, and he contributed regularly to Russian Hebrew periodicals, he received his earliest recognition from a long narrative poem in Yiddish, on East European life, called *Monish* (1887). After this his creative efforts were almost entirely in Yiddish. He wished to show his fellow Jews the circumstances of their own weaknesses and misery, and what opportunities awaited them if they but educated themselves in the ways and knowledge of the outside world. To this end he edited and in large measure wrote the annual *Yiddishe Bibliothek,* and in 1894 began issuing his *Yomtov Bletter* (Festival Journals), containing stories, essays, poems, plays, learned articles, and editorials. Many of the stories that made Peretz's fame have been translated into English; and there is an excellent one-volume synopsis of the author's work and life by Maurice Samuel, *Prince of the Ghetto* (1948). The most moving and best known of Peretz's short stories are "Bontche the Silent," the tale of the little-known timid Jew who endured a lifetime of hardships uncomplainingly, and when offered his choice of a reward in Heaven, answered, "If it is really so, I want, every morning, a hot roll with fresh butter"; and "And Even Higher," concerning the rabbi reputed to go up to Heaven each morning; a scoffer follows him, and sees him cutting wood and warming the home of a sick old widow. When he asks if the rabbi really goes up to Heaven, he is told, "Yes, and even higher!"

PERIBÁÑEZ AND THE COMMANDER OF OCAÑA (1612?), by Lope de Vega. The Comendador of Ocaña falls in love with Casilda, the wife of a rich peasant named Peribáñez. His love having been rejected, the Comendador sends Peribáñez to Toledo as captain of the army, and manages to enter Casilda's room during the night. But Peribáñez, who suspects the Comendador's guilty intentions, unexpectedly returns and surprises and kills the Comendador. The King not only pardons Peribáñez but makes him captain of the army. This is one of Lope de Vega's best known plays. It was written some time between 1609 and 1614, and is probably based on a legend or historical episode briefly summarized in a ballad (Act II, Scene 21) which refers to the reign of King Enrique III, el Doliente (1309–1406). *Peribáñez y el Comendador de Ocaña* is a social play, clearly showing the independence of action of the peasantry. Besides its remarkable social content, it is an actable drama of tremendous power and dynamic action. It is a realistic play and quite sincere in its depiction of rural life, not country life as seen (quite universally at this time) through the eyes of a courtier, but as felt by a peasant himself.

PERICLES, PRINCE OF TYRE (ca. 1605; Quarto 1609), by William Shakespeare. Critics generally agree that the first two acts of this play, and perhaps the brothel scene in the fourth act, were written by some author other than Shakespeare. The sources of this drama are Twine's *Patterne of Painful Adventures* (1576) and the tale "Apollonius, Prince of Tyre," part of Gower's *Confessio Amantis* (q.v.).

Antiochus, King of Antioch, is in love with his own daughter. To prevent anyone else marrying her, he evolves a riddle which must be guessed by her suitors or they will lose their heads. Pericles, Prince of Tyre, guesses the riddle, which is the King's incestuous love. Fearing for his life, Pericles departs hastily from Tyre. Helicanus, his faithful minister, urges him to go on a long journey to avoid the King's vengeance. Pericles' ship is wrecked on the coast of Pentapolis; the sole survivor, he goes to the court of King Simonides and wins the hand of his daughter, Thaisa.

After a year of happy marriage, he hears from Helicanus that he must return to Tyre. He embarks with his wife and boy. A daughter is born to Thaisa during a storm, and she falls into a deep trance. The superstitious mariners, thinking her dead, insist her body be thrown overboard, in a chest. Pericles, grieving for his beloved wife, puts in at Tarsus, and leaves his little girl, Marina, in charge of his friends Cleon and Dionyza, who bring her up with their own child. She grows up to be so lovely that Dionyza is jealous for her own daughter and is going to murder her. Marina, however, is snatched away by pirates. Pericles comes for his daughter, but finds only a monument erected to her memory. In the meantime Marina has been carried to Mitylene, where her captors sell her to a brothel. Her beauty and innocence win the favor of the governor, Lysimachus, who frees her.

Pericles' ship stops at Mitylene. Marina is brought on board to distract the mournful king, and father and daughter are joyfully reunited. Diana appears to Pericles in a vision and tells him to go to Ephesus, where his wife, who was rescued from the sea by a physician, is a priestess in her temple. Marina marries Lysimachus, and Cleon and Dionyza are burned for their planned murder of Marina.

PERIQUILLO SARNIENTO, EL (1816; complete in four volumes, 1830), by José Joaquín Fernández de Lizardi. See ITCHING PARRROT, THE, by José Joaquín Fernández de Lizardi.

PERSIAN LETTERS (1721), by Montesquieu. Purportedly, the *Persian Letters* are the correspondence among several Persians visiting Europe and their friends in Ispahan. The two principals are Usbek and Rica. Usbek, the older, is the more serious and reflective of the two. His virtuous character has led him to forsake the court of Persia, and he has taken the good-humored Rica with him for company. In France the pair go everywhere and see everything. With naïve wonder they remark on the strange ways of the nobility, of the rulers, and of the church, and marvel at the insularity of these people who seem to think that their customs and manners are universal. Although often labeled satirical, the *Persian Letters* teach the same lessons of philosophical relativism which is also the foundation of Montesquieu's *Spirit of Laws* (q.v.).

PERSIANS, THE (472 B.C.), by Aeschylus. *The Persians,* written to celebrate Athens' victory over the Persians at Salamis in 480 B.C., is the earliest extant example of a historical play. It is simple in staging and construction, a tableau almost, rather than a play. There is no hero, no conflict, only tragic discovery. The scene is Persia. The Chorus of Persian elders enters and describes the departure of Xerxes' host, how the flower of the Persian youth had set out to chastise and subjugate Greece, whence no messenger has yet returned. Queen Atossa, Xerxes' mother, then appears with her retinue. She has had an ominous dream about her son and is sorely troubled. She inquires about Athens, and the Leader tells her it is a city far to the west, whose inhabitants have never been slaves. Soon a Messenger enters with the dire news that the Persians have suffered an overwhelming defeat at Salamis. He gives a long and detailed description of the battle, how the Greeks had tricked the Persians into thinking they were fleeing and then turned and fallen on them with frightful slaughter, and how Xerxes has fled. Grief-stricken, Atossa and her attendants pour libations on the tomb of Darius and his ghost rises. Dismayed at the lamentation, he asks the Chorus and Atossa what has befallen Persia and learns of the disaster. He then predicts the disaster of the Persian land forces at Plataea and vanishes. At last Xerxes enters with his robe torn, and he and the Chorus lament the loss of his ships and leaders. Weeping and mourning, the procession passes slowly into the palace. This play with its strong patriotic appeal for Athenians was staged by the rising statesman, Pericles, and is thought to have been produced to win favor for his rising star. Its interest for us is heightened by the fact that Aeschylus was probably an eyewitness of the great naval battle which he describes.

PERSON, PLACE AND THING (1942), by Karl J. Shapiro. See SHAPIRO, KARL J.

PERSONS AND PLACES (1943), by George Santayana. See LAST PURITAN, THE, by George Santayana.

PERSONAL HISTORY (1935), by Vincent Sheean. This autobiography of the American foreign correspondent is both a record of its author's intellectual evolution, and, through the spectacles of his remarkable experiences, a living history of our time. The book begins with the 1918 armistice, when the author was eighteen, and races along through an exciting journalistic course of crises in foreign lands. A large portion of the book concerns Sheean's amazing life among the Rifs during the Abd-el-Krim revolt against Spain. His treatment of China in the early struggles of the Kuomintang and the Communists, and his relationship in China and Moscow with the extraordinary and unfortunate American girl, Rayne Prohm, are other highlights of the book, which set the style for numerous memoirs of foreign correspondents.

Among other books is *Not Peace but a Sword* (1939), an account of the heroic struggle of the Spanish Loyalist armies against Franco's fascist legions, who were aided by Nazi aviation and Italian divisions. The author, an eyewitness, is bitter in his denunciation of the pre-Munich democracies and revelation of the sinister forces behind the dress rehearsal of World War II.

Lead, Kindly Light (1949) might be called Vincent Sheean's latest chapter in his own personal history. But it is much more, for it is a revelation of the meaning of the life of Mahatma Gandhi, written by a man to whom the Mahatma gave meaning in life that he had never before known.

PERSONAL RECOLLECTIONS OF JOAN OF ARC (1896), by Mark Twain. This most successful and most acclaimed American man of letters, whose books sold at the rate of 40,000 before publication a half-century before high-pressure book clubs were invented, said of this book: "I like the *Joan of Arc* best of all my books, and it *is* the best; I know it perfectly well. . . . Possibly the book may not sell, but that is nothing—it was written for love." He spent twelve years reading in preparation; "the others," he said, "needed no preparation and got none."

The *Joan of Arc* is remarkable for several reasons. Mark Twain's name has never appeared in it. He knew that his books were expected to produce nothing but laughs; and in this book—as in *The Prince and the Pauper* and *A Connecticut Yankee* (q.v.)—he was in dead earnest, determined to reveal bitter injustice and right ancient wrongs. Therefore he published the *Joan of Arc* as written by the Sieur Louis de Comte, Joan's page and secretary, at eighty-two setting down the story of the Maid as he had lived it with her; and "translated" by "Jean François Alden."

Mark has the "translator" prefix a note which remarks that "the life of Joan of Arc . . . *is the only story of a human life which comes to us under oath,* the only one which comes to us from the witness-stand." And in a powerful "Translator's Preface" Mark summarizes for all time the amazing story of this inspired but ignorant seventeen-year-old village girl—"perhaps the only entirely unselfish person . . . in profane history"—who "laid her hand upon this nation, this corpse," France, and led it to victory after victory until the power of England was completely overwhelmed.

Mark Twain's purpose in this masterpiece of his was clearly to show not only the saintliness of the Maid, but her reality and humanness. He does all this not only with the realistic vividness he always achieved, but with an adoring reverence which was astonishingly new.

Of course the book has its share of the uproarious Mark Twain humor. The Paladin, Joan's standard-bearer, is as splendid a liar as heart could wish. Other dominating figures are the cursing giant La Hire; the Duke of Alençon; the Bastard of Orleans; Charles the Dauphin; de Boussac, Marshal of France; de Culan, Admiral of France; the English leaders, the Earl of Suffolk, Fastolfe, and Talbot; and at the trial, the English Cardinal of Winchester, the Earl of Warwick, and Cauchon, Bishop of Beauvais, who presided, and who allowed no friend of the Maid to be heard.

The story is complete: Joan's girlhood at Domremy; her angel Voices; her unerring recognition of the disguised King; her convincing the French court that she has been "sent of God"; then her amazing victories—at Orléans, at Jargeau, and at Patay (that finally "broke the back" of the Hundred Years' War); the magnificent coronation of Charles VII at Rheims; the march on Paris; the tragedy of Burgundy—the capture of the Maid. Then the long-drawn-out agonies and desperate injustices of the trial, unrelentingly detailed from the author's long study of the official records—but told as only he could tell it; the martyrdom; and even (briefly) the Rehabilitation.

PERSUASION (published 1818), by Jane Austen. See NORTHANGER ABBEY, by Jane Austen.

PERUVIAN TRADITIONS (1860–1906), by Ricardo Palma. For almost half a century Peru's most popular writer sent to press delectable tales depicting the mores, scandals and sundry frivolities of his native city. But the Lima of his pageant was not the relatively dormant city of his lifetime. It was, rather, the Colonial Lima, seat of the richest and greatest Spanish Viceroyalty in America, which he, inveterate bookworm, dug out from dusty chronicles and gazetteers—a proud, religious, aristocratic, peccant metropolis, seething with amorous intrigues, superstitions, processions, duels. In his four hundred-odd *Traditions,* as he called his sketches, he wreathed in his metaphoric, often rococo utterance, the poignant deeds and misdeeds of his motley protagonists. In his *Tradiciones* are found side by side the miracles of saints, the escapades of society matrons, the murders, truancies and exultations of haughty and meek alike. In short, Palma became to a generation devoid of the "blessings" of movies and radio the most reliable purveyor of witty entertainment and quiet excitement. He has been called the Peruvian Boccaccio.

PETER IBBETSON (1891), by George du Maurier. This romantic novel is laid in England and France, in the first part of the nineteenth century. The introduction explains that the book comprises Ibbetson's memoirs, found by his cousin, Madge Plunket, in a criminal lunatic asylum. The story opens when Gogo Pasquier de la Marière (later Peter Ibbetson) and his childhood sweetheart, Mimsey Seraskier (later Mary, Duchess of Towers) are children living outside of Paris. At the death of his parents, Peter goes to live with an uncle, Colonel Ibbetson, in England, and takes his name. Mimsey leaves for Russia and later marries the Duke of Towers. They meet only once, and discover that they both have dreamed the same dream of love for each other. They then agree to separate forever. Later Peter kills Colonel Ibbetson in a rage when he claims to be his natural father. He is jailed and sentenced to hang, and Mary comes to him in his dreams the night before his execution. She reveals to him that his execution will not take place and that he will be sentenced to prison instead; she will eventually be separated from her husband and will come to comfort him. Together, in this dreamworld, they find happiness in revisiting childhood scenes and seeing strange countries of the past and present. Mary dies; their dream life ends and Peter becomes insane. He regains his sanity for one night only when Mary revisits him to comfort him and give him strength to write his story.

PETER PAN (1904), by James M. Barrie. The Darling family is unconventional and whimsical. The children, Wendy, Michael and John, are irrepressibly imaginative. One night, an elfin boy named Peter Pan appears, accompanied by Tinker Bell, a fairy. Peter tells Wendy that he ran away from home the day he was born because he overheard his parents discussing his future as a man. He teaches the children to fly; they soar away to the wonderful realm of Never-Never Land. Here they have remarkable adventures and meet unforgettable characters, among them the pirate Captain Hook, Tootles, Slightly, Nibs, Smee and Tiger Lily. Captain Hook tries to poison Peter, but Tinker Bell saves him by drinking the potion, and is saved, in turn, by Peter's appeal to the audience to believe in fairies. Upon the children's return home, Mrs. Darling offers to adopt Peter, but he declines, saying: "No one is going to catch me and make me a man. I want always to be a little boy and have fun."

In a story that is a sequel to the play, years later, Peter returns to take Wendy back to Never-Never Land, just for the Spring Housecleaning, but Wendy has grown up. She sees her own daughter Margaret fly away with Peter, just as she had once done.

PETER SCHLEMIHL (1814), by Adelbert von Chamisso. Widely read as a minor literary classic is Chamisso's *Peter Schlemihl*. An aristocratic refugee from the French Revolution, the author became one of the foremost lyric poets of German Romanticism. However, it was with *Peter Schlemihl* that he won his greatest fame. It is the didactic story of a man who sells his shadow to the devil for an inexhaustible bag of gold and then rues the bargain. The sly old gentleman from whom Peter obtained his accursed riches appears mockingly before him again, and proposes to return the shadow provided he will give him his soul in exchange. Horrified, Schlemihl throws away his purse of gold and, putting on a pair of seven-league boots, he wanders through the world in search of his shadow and his peace of mind. Narrated with the self-ironic gaiety of other Romantic poets like Heine, Chamisso's story is partly autobiographical of the author's suffering in his transplanted German environment.

PETÖFI, ALEXANDER (1823–1849). Alexander Petöfi was the greatest Hungarian lyric poet, and he stands out among the great Romantic poets of his age. An ardent patriot, he lost his life in the Hungarian revolution of 1848–1849 fighting against the invading Russian Cossacks. His poems express his fervent love of his country, and his equally firm belief in the right of the individual to freedom and self-development. He was bitterly opposed to the Hungarian political order of the day and he fearlessly attacked it, both in his lyrics and in such narrative poems as "Knight John" and "Stephen the Fierce." Petöfi was a firm believer in that Hungarian democracy which aimed to liberate and upraise the downtrodden, even at the cost of the traditional mode of life and the traditional privileges of the gentry.

PETRIFIED FOREST (1935), by Robert Sherwood. See SHERWOOD, ROBERT E.

PHAEDO, by Plato (ca. 428–348 B.C.). This dialogue reports the last hours of Socrates in prison before his execution, as told by Phaedo to Echecrates. It is both a moving, dramatic account and a noble philosophical discourse on the immortality of the soul. About fifteen of Socrates' friends came to be with him in the prison on this day. When his fetters had been struck off, Socrates welcomed his friends and asked one of them to see his wife and children home. Socrates himself was in good spirits, but the conversation naturally drifted toward death. He maintained that "a man who has really spent his life in philosophy is naturally of good courage when he is to die and has strong hopes that when he is dead he will attain the greatest blessings in that other land." In the day-long argument over the immortality of the soul Phaedo remarks: "That he had an answer ready was perhaps to be expected; but what astonished me more about him was first, the pleasant, gentle and respectful manner in which he listened to the young men's criticism, secondly, his quick sense of the effect their words had upon us, and lastly, the skill with which he cured us, and as it were, recalled us from our flight and made us face about and follow him and join in his examination of the argument." The last sad scene is described with direct simplicity, and Plato makes Phaedo remark at last: "Such was the end, Echecrates, of our friend, who was, as we may say, of all those of his time whom we have known, the best and wisest and most righteous man."

PHAEDRA, by Seneca. See TRAGEDIES, by Seneca.

PHENOMENOLOGY OF MIND, THE (1807), by Georg Wilhelm Friedrich Hegel. With the exception of his *Philosophy of History,* Hegel's most significant work is *The Phenomenology of Mind.* His principle of synthesis, unique to his own philosophy, was at one and the same time the presupposition, the outcome, and the completion of the theories of his predecessors. Specifically, it opposes Kant's theory of dualism. The elaboration of this conception is achieved in this book.

The subject matter of Hegel's work embraces the entire range of human experience in various forms and at different stages, particularly in Western

Europe. It is an exhaustive analysis of the life history of the human spirit. Entire movements in history, which have marked epochs in the history of mankind, are treated as if they were embodiments of attitudes of mind or principles of the spirit of man. The importance of religion in the life of man is not exaggerated in the scheme of things. It appears as only one act in the drama of our race. Similarly with the various philosophies; each is merely an aspect of a single mood of the mind, a single comprehensive truth which dominates all.

The Phenomenology of Mind treats of the following subjects: On Scientific Knowledge in General, Consciousness, Self-Consciousness, Reason, Spirit, Religion and Absolute Knowledge.

PHÈDRE (1677), by Jean Baptiste Racine. One of the best known plays of Racine, this is based upon the *Hippolytus* (q.v.) of Euripides, with an added subplot involving an affair between Hippolytus and a captive princess. Phèdre, second wife of the hero, Theseus, has the misfortune to fall in love with Hippolytus, her husband's grown son, during Theseus' prolonged absence. When Theseus is falsely reported dead, she feels free to confess her love, but is spurned by the horrified youth. Shortly thereafter Theseus returns. Phèdre's maid, Oenone, thinking to save her mistress from exposure, charges Hippolytus with attempting to seduce Phèdre. Theseus, outraged, banishes the young man and invokes the curse of Neptune on him. Shortly afterward Hippolytus' chariot horses, terrified by a sea monster, bolt, and he is dragged to his death. Theseus learns too late of his son's innocence, and Phèdre kills herself in remorse.

Like all of Racine's work, the play is written in a fluent and often beautiful verse, but yields so completely to the rigid rules of the classical French drama that it lacks real life and vigor. The speeches are long and the movement slow.

PHILADELPHIA STORY, THE (1939), by Philip Barry. See BARRY, PHILIP.

PHILASTER, OR LOVE LIES A-BLEEDING (acted ca. 1610; published 1620), **by Francis Beaumont and John Fletcher.** This Elizabethan tragicomedy is filled with lively incident, intrigue, jealousy and narrow escapes. Its dialogue, however, and the characterization of the self-effacing heroine, are far superior to its plot, which tells the story of Euphrasia, daughter of Lord Dion, and her ardent love for Philaster. To be near him, she disguises herself as his page, calling herself Bellario. Unfortunately for her, Philaster is in love with Arethusa, daughter of the usurper King of Sicily. Philaster, rightful heir to the throne, presents his beloved with Bellario as a servant, but grows jealous because he suspects Arethusa of being in love with the supposed youth. The latter's sex is finally discovered, and she devotedly serves the Princess after Arethusa and Philaster straighten out their misunderstandings and marry.

PHILIP NOLAN'S FRIENDS (1867), by Edward Everett Hale. See MAN WITHOUT A COUNTRY, THE, by Edward Everett Hale.

PHILIPPICS (351–340 B.C.), by Demosthenes. These twelve speeches by the great Athenian statesman, the most celebrated of the Attic orators, represent the bulk of his extant addresses on foreign policy. They are called *Philippics* after Philip of Macedon, father of Alexander the Great, whose systematic conquests of independent Greek states Demosthenes urged the Athenians to oppose before it was too late. Demosthenes led the opposition to Philip, but was plagued by an Athenian policy of false economy which resulted in aid that was too little and too late for threatened allies. Selfish interest led to vacillation between the appeasement of Philip and desperate military opposition to his encroachments. It was his firm conviction that no honorable friendship could exist between a king and a democratic state. The completion of the subjugation of Greece by Macedon is ample evidence of the farsightedness of Demosthenes' policy. The *Philippics* are masterpieces of eloquence, but not in the conventional sense. The speeches show no striving for elegance, no pretense to learning, no rhetorical embellishment nor any of the conventional appeals to emotion. Their power lies rather in their able and straightforward expression of a deeply felt and inflexible conviction that was Demosthenes' guiding principle from beginning to end. When Cicero launched on his fatal opposition to Mark Antony, he called the bitter speeches which he delivered, Philippics, and the name has come to stand for any bitter invective. Each generation rediscovers for itself the truth of Demosthenes' warnings against isolationism or co-operation with imperialist powers.

PHILO JUDAEUS (ca. 20 B.C.–A.D. 50). Philo Judaeus, a Jewish philosopher who flourished in Hellenic Alexandria during the first century of the Christian era, was, in effect, one of the founders of Christian theology. As a neo-Platonic philosopher he attempted to fuse the idealism of Plato with Jewish religious concepts current in his day and entirely syncretistic in their nature. He invented an allegorical method of interpreting Hebrew Scripture which was readily borrowed by the Jewish converts to Christianity for application to the Gospels. A highly cultured, Hellenized Jew, he found it difficult to reconcile the anthropomorphism of the *Bible* (q.v.) with the dictates of reason. As a religious Jew he refused to question the genuineness of revelation, and assumed that only by an allegorical, not a literal, interpretation of the *Bible* was it possible to make Judaism intelligible and intelligent. In this use of allegory he imitated the Greek and Roman Stoics, who had also met with a similar obstacle in their acceptance of the traditional Greco-Roman religion. From Plato and the Stoics Philo derived his doctrine of divine attributes or emanations. These are merely the expressions of God's relation with the universe. It is through these emanations, sometimes conceived as what the Greeks called *daimones,* or, after the Hebrew fashion, angels, that the ideal, perfect and immaterial god controls the material and imperfect world. Philo's conception of these "ideas" or "forces" (Platonic terminology) is not worked out with definitive clarity, but he tends to think of them collectively as manifestations of the *logos* ("word" or "reason"—Stoic terminology) of God. This is the *logos* familiar to all Christians from the opening line in the Gospel according to St. John: "In the beginning was the Word (Logos)." Patristic literature is profoundly tinctured with Philo's mystic speculations about the various emanations of God. In fact, his ideas had much to do with the formation of the Christian idea of the Holy Ghost and of the Trinity.

There is extant a large body of Philo's writings both in the original Greek and in Armenian translation. Among the best known and most important are his *Questions and Answers on Genesis and Exodus, Allegorical Interpretation of the Laws, On the Creation of the World,* and *The Embassy to Gaius.* This last describes a mission on which he was sent from Alexandria to the Emperor Caligula, and is of special interest as one of the earliest documents on the troubles of the Jews of the Diaspora with Gentiles.

PHILOSOPHIA BOTANICA (1751), by Carl Linnaeus. See SYSTEMA NATURA, by Carl Linnaeus.

PHILOSOPHIAE NATURALIS PRINCIPIA MATHEMATICA (1687), by Sir Isaac Newton. This book is recognized universally as the greatest single contribution to science of all time. It is built around Newton's discovery of the law of gravitation; but it includes also a profound treatment of many other topics in science and mathematics, from the laws of motion to the differential calculus. In the opening sentence of the preface to the first edition Newton wrote: "Since the ancients (as we are told by Pappus) esteemed the science of mechanics of greatest importance in the investigation of natural things, and the moderns, rejecting substantial forms and occult qualities, have endeavored to subject the phemomena of nature to the laws of mathematics, I have in this treatise cultivated mathematics as far as it relates to philosophy." The whole burden of philosophy he felt to consist in this— "from the phenomena of motions to investigate the forces of nature, and then from these forces to demonstrate the other phenomena." The *Principia* therefore opens with definitions of mass, momentum, inertia, centripetal force, and acceleration, and with Newton's three well-known laws of motion. The first two of these laws—on inertia and the proportionality of force and acceleration —were implied by the work of Galileo, but Newton clarified them and added the law on the equality of action and reaction. Following these introductory ideas, the body of the work is divided into three "books," of which the first two are on "The Motion of Bodies," first without a resisting medium, and then with resistance varying as the velocity or as the square of the velocity. One of the most difficult portions of these two books (I, 13), concerns the attractive forces of bodies which are not spherical. It appears that Newton delayed his publication of the law of gravitation for some twenty years because he was at first unable to prove the critical theorem that in calculating the force of attraction of an ellipsoidal body upon an external point, the entire mass of the body can be regarded as concentrated at the center of gravity. Book III of the *Principia* is entitled "The System of the World (in Mathematical Treatment)." It is Proposition IV of this book which presents the most striking aspect of the work—the law of gravitation as applied to the moon. Making use of Kepler's laws and of the formula for centrifugal force, Newton in 1665 or 1666 had made a preliminary earth-moon test of the law; but not until 1684 or 1685 was he satisfied with his calculation of the force of attraction of an ellipsoid. It was then, encouraged by Halley, that Newton undertook to write the *Principia*. Proposition XIX also is significant for the Newtonian theory, subsequently verified, of the oblate spheroidal shape of the earth.

The *Principia* contains a wealth of material on topics indirectly related to astronomy—the velocity of light and sound, reflection and refraction, the tides, hydrodynamics, the properties of conic sections. These and other problems are treated with a mathematical skill which excited the admiration of his contemporaries and successors. The *Principia* includes a short section (Book II, Lemma II) on the calculus, the earliest publication by Newton of his invention of this important method. In spite of Newton's great contributions to analysis, however, the *Principia* is cast in the older synthetic form. There is one striking omission in the *Principia,* and that is any indication of the *nature* of gravitation. Near the close of the work there occurs the famous phrase, "*Hypotheses non fingo*" (I do not frame hypotheses). Newton would not commit himself either to action at a distance or to propagation of the force of gravity in a medium.

The scientific importance of the *Principia* was quickly recognized by Newton's contemporaries and successors. The work passed through many editions in various languages, and it became the basis for a new age in science—the Newtonian Age.

PHILOSOPHICAL DICTIONARY (1764), by Voltaire (François Marie Arouet). The germ of the *Philosophical Dictionary* was suggested to Voltaire at Frederick the Great's intellectual salon in 1752 but did not come to fruition until 1764. There had been two illustrious predecessors in this field: Bayle's *Dictionary* and the *Encyclopedia* of Diderot and D'Alembert. The *Philosophical Dictionary* was characteristically Voltairean. He could hang his sharp wit on any trifling hook: Abraham, Abuse, Academy, Adoration, Adultery, Allegories, Altars, Amazons, Ambiguity, Anecdotes, Angels, Apocalypse, Apostate, Appearance, Ass, Atheism, Austerities, Avarice. The *Dictionary,* which for decades was the bourgeois-liberal Bible of Europe, consists of a series of brief essays, in the alphabetical order of their subjects. From time to time Voltaire abandons the conventional essay form and discourses on his subject in dialogue, and even in gay, witty verse. Objectivity was no concern; Voltaire was always fiercely and caustically himself. He doubts that Moses ever existed and is suspicious of the genuineness of the alleged Pentateuch authorship. He questions the moral conduct of Abraham, Isaac and Jacob as well as that of the New Testament heroes. And in the fascinating essay, "Laws, Civil and Ecclesiastical," he proposes the complete separation of Church and State, the latter to become free and secular.

PHILOSOPHICAL ESSAYS, by Cicero (Marcus Tullius Cicero; 106–93 B.C.). The great Roman orator never tired of the study of Greek philosophy, and always turned to it in the most trying moments of his political career as to a welcome refuge. Most of his essays were written in the period between Caesar's rise to power and his assassination, when he found himself eclipsed and blocked from active leadership in the state. They are all part of a large project to popularize Greek philosophy with the Roman reading public, a project aimed at overcoming the natural distrust of Romans for what they felt to be the unnecessarily abstruse and impractical intellectual preoccupation of the Greeks. The task involved many difficulties, not the least of which was the development of an elaborate philosophical vocabulary for Latin, which was, as he complains, very poor in this respect. Cicero was not in fact an adherent of any of the recognized schools of Greek philosophy, but took what he found useful from the works of the Academy, the Lyceum and the Stoa, rejecting emphatically the doctrines of Epicurus and the Garden school. This eclecticism was to become typical of Roman acceptance of Greek thought. In addition to his essays *On Old Age* (q.v.) and *On Friendship* (q.v.) there are ten works which are classified as Philosophical Essays. The *Academics* is his treatise on human understanding, and is a defense of the doctrines of the later Academy. In the *De Finibus* (*On the Highest Good and the Highest Evil*) he discusses the ethical goals set up by the various schools. Also of ethical content is the *De Officiis* (*On Duties*) in which he treats of the moral obligations of man in society. In the field of political philosophy we have his *Republic* and his *Laws,* both of which are obvious, but far from slavish, imitations of Plato's dialogues by the same name. In them he brings the Roman genius for political organization to bear upon the more theoretical and speculative Greek doctrines. Three other works deal with religious subjects. The most important of the three is *De Natura Deorum* (*On the Nature of the Gods*), to which *De Divinatione* (*On Divination*) forms a sort of appendage. The third is also of a supplementary nature and deals with the Stoic conception of fate, *De Fato* (*Fate*). The *Tusculan Disputations,* written as a consolation on the death of his beloved daughter, Tullia, are a noble discourse on death and the immortality of the soul. Finally there is the brief essay on the *Stoic Paradoxes.* The literary form chosen for these treatises is that of the dialogue. For dramatic quality they are not to be compared with those of Plato, tending as they do to be discursive, but they are incomparable for their blend of rich and periodic Ciceronian prose with the familiar tone of conversation. There is little original thought in the essays, but their ardent devotion to high moral principles helped to assure their preservation through the Middle Ages and recommended them to the scholars of the Renaissance, for whom they were the introduction to ancient philosophy.

PHILOSOPHIE ZOOLOGIQUE (1809), by Jean Baptiste de Monet de Lamarck. This work, published just half a century before Darwin's *Origin of Species* (q.v.), is one of the landmarks in the history of evolution. Its outstanding feature is the defense of the theory of the mutability of species through the inheritance of acquired characteristics. Lamarck was a great systematist and had a fertile imagination, but some of his views were so fanciful that his work was lightly esteemed by most of his contemporaries. Cuvier, who adhered to the fixity of species, attacked his ideas so vigorously that it was only long after the deaths of these two men that the importance of Lamarck's *Zoölogical Philosophy* was fully appreciated. The book is divided into three parts. The first part is devoted to zoölogy—to the natural history of animals, their characteristics, affinities, organization, classification, and species. Part Two treats of physiology, and concerns the physical causes of life, the conditions required for its existence, the exciting force of its movements, and the faculties which it confers on bodies possessing it. The third part is devoted to psychology, and this includes the physical causes of feeling, the force which produces actions, and the origin of the acts of intelligence observed in various animal species.

Lamarck held that there are no sharp boundary lines between species, and for this reason it seemed highly improbable that these should remain permanently fixed. He laid stress upon the great differences between domesticated animals and their wild counterparts. Just as different characteristics are developed by man's selective breeding, so in nature species are constantly changing under the influence of environment. The mechanism of these changes he described as the "law of use and disuse." Changes of environment, he held, lead to special demands on certain organs, and consequently these organs become specially developed. This development he believed to be transmitted to the offspring. On the other hand, useless organs, such as the eyes of animals that live in darkness, gradually become without function and in time disappear with subsequent generations. It now is certain that, in the sense suggested by Lamarck, acquired characters are not inherited; but Lamarck's insistence upon the transformation of species has earned for him the distinction of being a founder of the theory of evolution.

PHILOSOPHY OF COMPOSITION, THE (1846), by Edgar Allan Poe. See POE, EDGAR ALLAN.

PHILOSOPHY OF HISTORY, THE (1823–1827), by Georg Wilhelm Friedrich Hegel. In his *Philosophy of History,* a work consisting of lectures he had given in the 1820's, Hegel advanced a new approach to history. He attempted to see it in terms of abstract ideas encompassing entire periods and civilizations. The one difficulty experienced in reading Hegel is his baffling mysticism. He apprehended a World-Spirit in history, a spirit embodied in the destiny of one dominant people in each era of civilization. Part I of this work thus treats of the dominant peoples of the Oriental world of antiquity; Part II, of the Greek world; Part III, of the Roman world; Part V, of the German world.

What was the World-Spirit? "It is only an inference from the history of the world," says Hegel, "that its development has been a rational process; that the history in question has constituted the rational, necessary course of the World-Spirit—that Spirit whose nature is always one and the same, but which unfolds thus its one nature in the phenomena of the world's existence."

"The philosophy of history," says Hegel, "is nothing but the thoughtful consideration of it." He makes an earnest appeal to the student of human affairs to approach history rationally and not supernaturally: "If the clear idea of Reason is not already developed in our minds, in beginning the study of Universal History, we should at least have the firm, unconquerable faith that Reason *does* exist there; and that the world of intelligence and conscious volition is not abandoned to chance, but must show itself in the light of the self-cognizant Idea."

The Philosophy of History is the most popular of all of Hegel's works. It greatly influenced the social sciences and the political movements of his day in Germany. It is generally recognized as a popular introduction to his philosophic system.

PHILOSOPHY OF LOYALTY (1908), by Josiah Royce. See ROYCE, JOSIAH.

PHOENICIAN WOMEN, by Seneca. See TRAGEDIES, by Seneca.

PHORMIO (161 B.C.), by Terence (Publius Terentius Afer). This comedy, adapted from the Greek of Apollodorus of Carystus, is one of Terence's most successful plays. In it the double plot is most skillfully handled, and results in a maximum of complication, suspense and amusement. The principal characters are two Athenian brothers, Demipho and Chremes, and their respective sons, Antipho and Phaedria. In the absence of the fathers, Phaedria has become involved with a slave girl, and Antipho, through the machinations of the clever rogue, Phormio, has got himself married to a penniless girl. Demipho, upon his return, insists on a divorce, to which Phormio naturally objects. Since, however, his fertile brain sees hope of accommodating both the boys, he agrees to the divorce if Demipho will pay him a very substantial sum so that he may marry the girl himself. This money goes immediately for the purchase of the freedom of Phaedria's slave girl just in time to save her from a fate worse than death. At last the truth comes out that Antipho's bride is after all the daughter of Chremes by a clandestine marriage to a woman in Lemnos. The woman had come to Athens looking for Chremes but had died during his absence. Thus the daughter becomes a more than acceptable bride for Antipho, the old men have lost the money they paid to Phormio since they cannot give him the wife agreed upon, and Phaedria has his lady love to himself. The general hilarity of the end of the play is made complete by the situation of Chremes, whose deep, dark secret is exposed, so making him a prey to the tender mercies of his lawful and righteously indignant Athenian wife.

PHYSICIAN IN SPITE OF HIMSELF, THE (1666), by Molière. Sganarelle, a woodcutter, is compelled against his will to represent himself as a physician, and, in this imposture, he treats a supposed case of dumbness in a young girl. He discovers that the young lady is actually shamming because her father stands in the way of her marriage to her sweetheart. Sganarelle succeeds in straightening matters out for the young couple and apparently effects a wonderful cure. For this he is rewarded with a heavy purse, which he accepts with alacrity, at the same time saying, "I do not practice for money. I am not a mercenary physician." In fact, he finds the whole business so profitable that he determines to give up woodcutting and continue his career in "medicine."

The play is simple but exceedingly entertaining when played with the lavish buffoonery intended by the playwright. It is one of several plays in which Molière gives vent to a seeming grudge against the medical profession, the others being *The Doctor in Love* (1665), and, more especially, *The Imaginary Invalid* (q.v.).

PHYSICS (335–323 B.C.), by Aristotle. The Greek word *physis* may be translated *nature,* and physics, in the language of Greek philosophy, refers to what we should call natural philosophy. Ionian philosophy had begun with inquiry directed toward an understanding of the phenomena of our natural environment. From this effort to grasp fundamental reality on a material level Socrates and Plato had turned aside, through a primary interest in ethics, to idealism. In the eight books of his *Physics* Aristotle returns to the attack with his elaborate logical equipment. In the first book he discusses the theories of his predecessors as to the elements of matter. This book is an invaluable source for the history of early Greek philosophy. Then he proceeds in the second to set forth his own concept of nature on a materialistic and causal basis, developing fully his four-fold theory of causality. Book three takes up the fundamental concepts of movement, change and infinity, book four those of space, void and time. Books five and six treat of the kinds of movement, which for Aristotle includes change in a very large sense, and the condition under which it takes place. In the last two books are developed the theory of the Prime Mover, the causal force in all natural phenomena which plays so large a part in the *Metaphysics* (q.v.).

PHYSICS AND POLITICS (1872), by Walter Bagehot. The subtitle of this book is *Thoughts on the Applicability of the Principles of "Natural Selection" and "Inheritance" to Political Society*. In it Bagehot attempted to apply the theories of Darwin to social history (Social Darwinism). He gave an account of the development of society from a condition of conflict to one involving complex forms of cooperation. He ascribed this development to the operation of the principles of "natural selection" and "inheritance." He distinguished three states of civilization, the age of isolation, the age of imposed uniformity, and the age of free discussion.

PIAZZA TALES, THE (1856), by Herman Melville. See MOBY-DICK, by Herman Melville.

PICKWICK PAPERS: POSTHUMOUS PAPERS OF THE PICKWICK CLUB (1837), by Charles Dickens. These humorous episodes of the doings and foibles of the Pickwick Club have delighted generations. Its founder, genial Samuel Pickwick; romantic Tracy Tupman; poetic Augustus Snodgrass; sporting Nathaniel Winkle, are as familiar as any nineteenth century fictional characters. The book is made up of letters and manuscripts about the club's actions. Among the incidents are: the army parade; trip to Manor Farm; the saving of Rachel Wardle from the villain, Alfred Jingle; trip to Eatonswill; Mrs. Leo Hunter's party of authors, including Count Smorltork and Charles Fitz-Marshall; ice skating. Pickwick's landlady, Mrs. Bardell, faints in his arms and compromises the unsophisticated gentleman. She sues him for breach of promise and an amusing court trial follows. Pickwick refuses to pay damages and is put in Fleet prison. Sam Weller, his faithful servant, accompanies him. Mrs. Bardell is also incarcerated for not paying the costs of the trial. When Pickwick is released, he retires to a house outside London with Weller, and the latter's new bride, Mary, as housekeeper. He dissolves the club and spends his time arranging its memoranda. Some of the other characters are: Mrs. Cluppins; Wardle, his sister, Rachel, and daughters, Emily and Isabella. The characters are exaggerated and mostly caricatures. Filled with laughter, it is one of Dickens' most quoted books.

PICTURE OF DORIAN GRAY, THE (1891), by Oscar Fingal O'Flahertie Wills Wilde. Were it not for its prose style and crackling aphorisms, this fictional fantasy would be in danger of degenerating into the merely sensational. Filled with confusing symbolism, its ambiguity of purpose brought about a tempest in a teapot when the work was first published. The author was forced to defend his work against charges of immorality and degeneracy. Actually, the novel is a moral preachment against the crimes of soulless hedonism. The story concerns a beautiful youth, Dorian Gray, who has his portrait painted by Basil Hallward, an artist with a flair for the morbid. The portrait proves to have supernatural qualities, and becomes the mirror of its subject's inner life, so that whatever Dorian feels or thinks is reflected in the portrait, Dorian himself retaining his youth and beauty. Through Hallward, Dorian meets Lord Henry Wotton, a cynic and *bon vivant,* who has mastered all the secret vices. Under his influence he deteriorates rapidly. For a while he is fired with a pure love for a little Shakespearean actress, Sybil Vane, but he spurns her out of monstrous vanity, and she commits suicide. He degenerates still further, and his portrait mirrors all his hideous vices. Finally, overcome by conscience, Dorian kills Hallward, the man who had opened for him the road to evil. Afterward he stabs his now unspeakably revolting portrait. Forthwith he himself is found dead with a knife through his heart, a ghastly wreck of a man, all his sins on his face, while over him hangs the portrait of the youthful and innocent Dorian restored to what it was in the beginning.

PIED PIPER OF HAMELIN, THE (1842), by Robert Browning. Based on an old legend, this poem tells the story of a piper who agreed to rid the town of Hamelin of its plague of rats for a thousand guilders. He played his pipe, and the enchanted music lured the rodents to their death by drowning in the Weser River. The burghers, however, refused to pay the piper. In revenge, the later enticed all the children of the town into a mountain cave with his magic music. They were swallowed up, and the citizens never saw them again.

PIERRE (1852), by Herman Melville. See MOBY-DICK, by Herman Melville.

PIERRE AND JEAN (1888), by Guy de Maupassant. This novel is the story of two brothers, one dark and temperamental, the other fair and placid. A family friend leaves his fortune to Jean, the fair one. Pierre is hurt, then becomes suspicious. After much suffering on all sides, the mother admits that the suspicions are well-founded: Jean is her child by the family friend. Pierre leaves home to become a ship's doctor. Jean marries the girl they both love, but agrees that after the death of the man, who does not suspect that he is not the father of both boys, they will straighten out the question of the family fortune. More interesting than the novel is Maupassant's preface, in which he explains his debt to Flaubert and sets forth his theory of the novel as a literary form.

Other novels of Maupassant include *Bel-Ami* (1885) and *A Life* (1883). They have been eclipsed by the fame of his short stories.

PIERS THE PLOWMAN, THE VISION OF WILLIAM CONCERNING (ca. 1362–ca. 1399), by William Langland (?). This allegorical.

alliterative poem is the most significant work of the Middle English period outside of Chaucer. There are three versions of widely varying length (2500 to
7300 lines), known as the *A, B,* and *C* texts. Different dates are assigned to
their time of composition: *A,* 1362; *B,* 1377; *C,* 1395–1398. Authorship of the
poem is disputed by critical authorities. Some attribute the poem to William
Langland or "Long Will," as he calls himself in the text of the poem. Langland
appears to have been a man of some learning who lived first in Malvern, later
in London. Others believe that the differing versions are works of different
authors, or even that each single version is the work of more than one author.
There is no conclusive evidence, on any stand, as to the authorship. The *A* text
relates a vision beheld by the author on a sunny morning in Malvern Hills. In
his dream he sees the Tower of Truth and the Dungeon of Wrong, and between
them the Earth, called "a fair field full of folk." In the field all manner of
people go about their daily occupations. There are beggars, clergymen, nuns,
tradesmen, hawkers calling their wares. In a following vision, he sees Lady
Meed (Reward, or Bribery). Additional abstractions are presented. Conscience preaches to the multitude while Repentance softens them. The confession of the Seven Deadly Sins includes a lively presentation of a tavern
scene. The repentant, many in number, set out to search for St. Truth, but
the way is difficult. Piers Plowman comes to help them if they will aid him
in plowing. Some help while others remain idle. Admonition is given to
deal sternly with sturdy, lazy beggars. Workers are told not to complain of
their lot and not to demand luxurious fare. Thus ends *Passus VIII.* The
next, *Passus IX,* which some think is the work of another author, deals
with a search for "Do-well," "Do-bet(ter)," and "Do-best." Thought says:
"Do-well is the meek honest laborer; Do-better is he who to honesty adds
charity and the preaching of sufferance; Do-best is above and holds a Bishop's
crosier to punish the wicked." The clergy is scrutinized, but in vain, nor are
the Scriptures of any avail. The search is conducted with the aid of Wit and
Study, besides Thought. The additions to this work to be found in the *B*
and *C* text are confusing and numerous. In general, their author is concerned
with corruption in the Church, with the virtues of the humble life, and with
the supremacy of Love. There are seven new visions, one of which is a long
dissertation by "Ymaginatif" on riches and learning. Piers' life and the life of
Christ are recounted in part and blend in with one another, so that finally
Piers and Christ are indistinguishable from one another. There is an attack
made by Pride and Antichrist upon the Church, and an attack made by Death
upon Mankind. The additions were evidently made by a pious, thoughtful
and sincere man who had the power to express himself with strength and
clarity.

PIETER BREUGHEL (1928), by Felix Timmermans. See TIMMER-
MANS, FELIX.

PILGRIM'S PROGRESS, THE (Part I, 1678; Part II, 1684), by John
Bunyan. Probably no other book in the English language, after the *Bible,*
with the possible exception of Defoe's *Robinson Crusoe* (q.v.), has had such
sustained and world-wide popularity as Bunyan's *Pilgrim's Progress.* Since
its first appearance it has gone through hundreds of editions, has been trans-

lated into more than one hundred languages, and remains a great favorite.

The full title of the work is descriptive of its contents: *The Pilgrim's Progress, From This World To That which is to Come: Delivered under the Similitude Of A Dream, Wherein is Discovered, The manner of his setting out His Dangerous Journey, And safe Arrival at the Desired Country.* In the quaintly naïve "Author's Apology for his Book," written in doggerel, Bunyan states his moral aim in composing the work:

> This Book it chalketh out before thine eyes,
> The Man that seeks the Everlasting Prize:
> It shews you whence he comes, whither he goes;
> What he leaves undone; Also what he does:
> It also shews you how he runs, and runs,
> Till he unto the Gate of Glory comes.
>
> It shews too, who sets out for Life amain,
> As if the lasting Crown they would attain:
> Here also you may see the reason why
> They lose their labour, and like fools do die.

Pilgrim's Progress was begun by Bunyan during a prison sojourn in 1675–1676. As a stubborn nonconformist he had been lodged in the Bedford jail to expiate a crime of conscience. While there he experienced his dream, which so shook him that he sat down to record it, together with all his reflections.

His prose style is distinguished for its simplicity. Almost the only book he ever read was the King James version of the *Bible* (q.v.). In a few words he can sketch a place, such as Vanity Fair, or a character, such as the terrible Apollyon. His description of the Celestial City is memorable, full of piety and poetic rapture. The hero, Christian, is no allegorical shadow, but very much alive; despite the author's moral sensitiveness to "the wilderness of this world" he makes him humorous and gay on occasion. There is much natural talk. The names of the characters, places and things are themselves eloquent: Mr. Worldly Wiseman, the Shining One, Faithful, Giant Despair, Mr. By-Ends-of-Fair-Speech, Hopeful, Enchanted Ground, House Beautiful, Delectable Mountains, City of Destruction. In the sequel, the Pilgrim's wife, Christiana, and their children make the same journey to salvation, with trials hardly less exciting than those Christian himself experienced.

PILGRIMAGE OF HENRY JAMES, THE (1925), by Van Wyck Brooks. See FLOWERING OF NEW ENGLAND, by Van Wyck Brooks.

PILGRIMAGE TO THE WEST, THE (16th c.), by Wu Ch'eng-en. See HSI YU KI, by Wu Ch'eng-en.

PILLARS OF SOCIETY (1877), by Henrik Ibsen. Into the narrow circle of a small, self-righteous community enter Lona Hessel and her younger half-brother, Johan Tönnesen, both returned on the *Indian Girl* from America. Johan had gone to America fifteen years before, reportedly taking funds belonging to Karsten Benick, his brother-in-law, with him. Karsten, a prosperous shipbuilder, had actually been guilty of embezzlement, but Johan had been willing to take the blame to save his friend's reputation. However, Johan did not know that Karsten had also cast suspicion on him in the matter of an intrigue with an actress, the mother of Dina Dorf, who has been reared by Karsten's sister. Johan falls in love with Dina, but Rörlund, a sanctimonious schoolmaster who is also in love with her, tells her of the supposed intrigue between Johan and Dina's mother. Johan demands that Karsten clear his name, but Karsten, engaged in a complicated business deal, tells him it is impossible. Angry, Johan threatens to go back to America on the *Indian Girl* and put his affairs in order so that he can sue Karsten. Aune, an elderly foreman at Benick's shipyards, tells his employer that the *Indian Girl* is not fit for the voyage to America, but Karsten, knowing that Johan is planning to sail on it, orders its departure in a heavy storm. In the meantime, Johan had changed his plans and had left on the *Palm Tree* with Dina. Benick's only son, a boy of thirteen, had hidden himself as a stowaway on the unseaworthy *Indian Girl,* and Benick, overcome with remorse and anxiety for his child's life, confesses his guilt and clears Johan's reputation in the eyes of the townspeople. He is rewarded by the recovery of his son by Aune and Mrs. Benick, who manage to stop the ship.

PILNYAK, BORIS (Boris Andreyevich Vogau, 1894–   ). Though he had been writing since 1915, Pilnyak, novelist and short story writer, won his first recognition with *The Naked Year* (1922), a powerful novel influenced by Biely and Remizov, which presents a panorama of Russia in 1921 in its state of chaos, after she had been ravaged by civil war and famine. The individuals are minimized. It is Russia herself that is the real heroine, presented here as an elemental force and historical entity. The revolt of peasants and lower classes is described in a vivid, if complex, prose, full of innovations. An outstanding as well as characteristic chapter is "Train No. 58," impressive as a brutally frank picture of the desperate travel conditions in Soviet Russia in 1919. Sometimes translated *The Base Year,* it was one of the earliest attempts to portray the Russian Revolution. In its English version it appeared in 1928.

The Volga Falls to the Caspian Sea (Eng. tr. 1931), another successful novel, deals with the building of a dam with the object of diverting the course of the Volga as a part of the first Five-Year-Plan. *Tales of the Wilderness* (1925) demonstrates features of Pilnyak's most fruitful period; while if a single outstanding short story is to be named, the choice might fall on "The Human Wind," a story of moving pathos. Pilnyak influenced writers who followed his first success; but he has had the reputation of not being a full-fledged Bolshevik, and has in the past been criticized by the orthodox critics.

PILOT, THE (1823), by James Fenimore Cooper. See SPY, THE, by James Fenimore Cooper.

PINOCCHIO, THE STORY OF A PUPPET (1881), by Carlo Lorenzini (Collodi). To *Pinocchio,* a favorite story of children in many lands, Carlo Lorenzini, better known under the pseudonym of Collodi, owes most of his fame. The story begins when Master Cherry, the carpenter, finds a piece of wood that laughs and cries like a child. He makes a gift of it to his friend Geppetto, who fashions of it a wonderful puppet that knows how to dance, fence and perform like an acrobat. Geppetto gives the puppet the name Pinocchio. The puppet, it turns out, is a very naughty "boy"—headstrong, mischievous and reckless. The book is full of the wonderful experiences of Pinocchio, which essentially are the experiences of every child. Of course Pinocchio, and with him the entire universe of children, learns wisdom through trouble and with wisdom achieves reformation. And of course Pinocchio not only tries to do better but actually is better, so the Good Fairy turns the wooden puppet into a real boy.

PIONEERS, THE (1823), by James Fenimore Cooper. See LEATHER-STOCKING TALES, by James Fenimore Cooper.

PIPPA PASSES (1841), by Robert Browning. The theme of this verse-drama is: "God stands apart to give man room to work." Yet God is omnipresent; his hand is in everything if only man wishes to see it. The heroine, Pippa, is a silk-winder in a Northern Italian town. On New Year's Day she pretends, in turn, that she is four people whom she admires. They are Ottima, Phene, Luigi, and the Bishop. Her fate then becomes inextricably intertwined with theirs. Ottima and her secret lover, Sebald, have murdered her husband. As Pippa passes, she sings, "God's in his heaven," and Sebald is filled with remorse. Similarly, Pippa is the cause for reconciliation between the sculptor Jules and Phene; her magical song dispels all misunderstanding between them. She then saves the life of the revolutionary youth, Luigi, by inspiring him to escape the suspicious police. Pippa admires the Bishop most of all. She nearly becomes the victim of his plot to do away with her, for she is the daughter of the Bishop's murdered brother, and he wants her inheritance. But his heart and conscience are open when he hears Pippa sing, "Suddenly God took me." Pippa is completely unaware of the effects her songs have had.

PIRANDELLO, LUIGI (1867–1936). Luigi Pirandello was internationally known for his many and original dramatic plays which were innovations for modern theater. He started with descriptions of lives and characters of his native Sicily. Celebrated among these early works are *Pensaci Giacomino* (1916), *Lumie di Sicilia* (1913), and *Il Berretto a sonagli* (1916). Later, when he developed a wider range, he wrote plays in which the central theme is the examination of man in his real and genuine personality, above convention and class prejudices—man as an eternally primitive and instinctive being. These plays include: *Sei Personaggi in cerca di autore* (1921), *Enrico IV* (1922), *La Vita che ti diedi* (1923), *L'amica delle Mogli* (1927), *O di uno o di nessuno* (1929), and *L'uomo, la bestia e la vertù* (1919). Pirandello's plays express the conflicts of the bourgeoisie, with its dissolving civilization, with the inevitable re-emergence of the fundamental and irrepressible characteristics of nature and instinct.

PIT, THE (Eng. tr. 1922), by Alexander Ivanovich Kuprin. See DUEL, THE, by Alexander Ivanovich Kuprin.

PIT, THE (1903), by Frank Norris. See OCTOPUS, THE, by Frank Norris.

PITCAIRN'S ISLAND, by James Norman Hall and Charles Bernard Nordhoff. See MUTINY ON THE BOUNTY, by James Norman Hall and Charles Bernard Nordhoff.

PLAIN DEALER, THE (1677), by William Wycherley. Wycherley based his well-known comedy upon *Le Misanthrope* of Molière. But his hero, Captain Manly, is more cynical than Alceste, and has more reason to be. Fidelia, who follows Manly to sea in men's clothes, is an echo of Shakespeare's Viola. Manly has just returned from sea duty, and has lost part of his fortune in a vessel that was sunk. Before his departure, he had placed money and jewels in the care of his mistress, Olivia. Olivia's interest in Manly is purely mercenary. She and her circle rail at him, and during his absence she has betrayed him by secretly marrying his best friend, Vernish. Manly sends Fidelia to woo Olivia for him; she exposes the treachery of his mistress and his friend, and wins Manly for herself. Two other notable characters are the elderly lady, the Widow Blachacre, and her son, Jerry, whom she, to her eventual sorrow, has brought up in an atmosphere of courts and litigations.

PLAIN LANGUAGE FROM TRUTHFUL JAMES (1870), by Bre Harte. See LUCK OF ROARING CAMP AND OTHER SKETCHES THE, by Bret Harte.

PLAIN SPEAKER, THE (1826), by William Hazlitt. As Charles Lamb said of him, Hazlitt's ruling passion was a love of truth, and in his constant search for this "no personal relationships were ever allowed to stand in its way." These essays are as outspoken as any Englishman's, not excluding the "gloomy Dean's" (Inge of St. Paul's).

Several of these essays have had frequent reprintings, appearing in anthologies. "On Personal Character," which first came out in 1821, the positive author starts off with this sentence: "No one ever changes his character from the time he is two years old; nay, I might say from the time he is two hours old." He admits we "may with instruction and opportunity, mend our manners, or else alter them for the worse," and continues with his inimitable flair for association of ideas, often, too often perhaps, resorting to quotations from the great and near-great. Another delightful essay in this collection is "Is Genius Conscious of Its Powers?" Commencing as usual with a straight statement of what he saw as incontrovertible fact, Hazlitt says: "No really great man ever thought himself so." His own admiration for Burke and Milton, Shakespeare and Cervantes appears as one reads on. Then he switches to painters, and having entertained his readers he resumes the general subject with another pertinent statement: "The greatest pleasure in life is that of reading, while we are young." This introduces a digression about personal experiences, so that the essay ends on an intimate note. It is this intimacy as much as anything that makes Hazlitt so popular; he appeals to no special group or decade but to all.

Other outstanding essays in this collection are: "On Depth and Superficiality"; "Hot and Cold"; "On the Spirit of Obligations"; "On the Conversation of Authors"; "On the Prose Style of Poets"; "On Old English Writers and Speakers"; "On Reading Old Books"; "On Sitting for One's Picture"; "On the Difference between Writing and Speaking," and that one of the two or three best known of all the author's well-known essays, "My First Acquaintance with the Poets," about Coleridge and Wordsworth.

PLAIN TALES FROM THE HILLS (1888), by Rudyard Kipling. This volume of stories relates experiences of Anglo-Indian soldiers and their associates in India. Mulvaney, Ortheris, and Learoyd, the soldiers of Kipling's *Soldiers Three,* appear in some of these stories. One of the most amusing of the tales is "A Germ Destroyer," which involves mistaken identity and a fumigatory which nearly suffocates the Viceroy. "The Taking of Lungtungpen" is also farcical. At the other extreme are such tragedies as "Thrown Away," the story of a sheltered English youth who is unable to adjust himself when he is sent to India. Scolded by his colonel for offensive conduct, he commits suicide; his family is notified that he has died of cholera. Some of the other stories: "Three and—an Extra," a marital interlude, serious in nature; "False Dawn," another story based on mistaken identity; "The Three Musketeers," introducing Mulvaney, Ortheris, and Learoyd; "Consequences," an example of successful blackmail; "The Broken-Link Handicap," which tells how an unbeatable jockey is cruelly caused to lose a race; and "Tod's Amendment," in which a precocious youngster who is not abashed by rank contributes to the changes in the Land Acts because of his knowledge of what the natives think.

PLAYBOY OF THE WESTERN WORLD, THE (1907), by John Millington Synge. This is one of the most poetic plays in the English language. Synge has embodied the fire and beauty of Irish speech in his dialogue. The action takes place in a public house near a village on the coast of Mayo. Pegeen, the daughter of Michael Flaherty, the innkeeper, is about to marry Shawn, a timid young farmer. Christy Mahon, a fugitive, enters the inn hesitatingly, asks for a glass of porter, and then asks whether he is safe from the police. Michael, suspicious, questions him and discovers that Christy had struck his dominating father, and thought he had killed him. His father had tried to marry him to an elderly widow. Michael and Pegeen are greatly impressed. No one in the village had ever seen a man who had killed his father, and Christy becomes a hero. Christy, who had never looked at a girl or had one look at him, finds them flocking round him, and bringing gifts. Old Mahon turns up with a broken head, looking for his son. He starts to beat him, but Christy lets him know that from now on he is the master. They go off together, and Pegeen mourns that she has lost "the only Playboy of the Western World."

PLUTOCRAT, THE (1927), by Booth Tarkington. See TARKINGTON, BOOTH.

PLUTUS (388 B.C.), by Aristophanes. The form in which we have this comedy is that of its second presentation, the latest extant production of Aristophanes' pen. It is markedly different from the poet's earlier comedies, and has much in common with Attic comedy of the next generation. Gone is his old vital concern with the contemporary political scene, to make way for a purely fanciful plot with a setting of common domestic life. Chremylus, a poor but honest Athenian citizen, finds himself suddenly the protector and benefactor of a blind old man who turns out to be Plutus, the personification of wealth. Being blind, he has hitherto found his way frequently to the houses of the undeserving. Chremylus therefore, with the assistance of a trusted friend, takes Plutus to the temple of Asclepius, the god of healing, and has his sight restored. The second half of the play is a succession of scenes in which the possibilities of this situation are exploited. The honest get their just deserts, the reprobates are discomfited, and even Zeus, whose worshipers have deserted him for Plutus, is forced to do homage to the new god. In conclusion, Plutus is enthroned in the sadly depleted treasury of Athens.

PO CHU-I (772–846). Po Chu-i was the most popular poet of China in his day. His poems were inscribed on the walls of schools, monasteries and ships' cabins, and were in the mouth of everybody, young and old. He was born in T'ai-yuan in Shansi; his childhood was spent at Jung-yang in Honan; but he permanently settled in Ch'angan, the political capital of the country. His poetry is characterized by its verbal simplicity. "The Everlasting Wrong" and the "Lute-Girl" are best known. His poems were translated by Arthur Waley.

POD IGOTO (1893), by Ivan Vazoff. See UNDER THE YOKE, by Ivan Vazoff.

POE, EDGAR ALLAN (1809–1849). The unfortunate life of Edgar Allan Poe, which has been long treated as a legend, is of importance only in relation to his literary output. Generally speaking, his personal tragedies may be presumed to have given his mind and his work the somber tone which is his literary characteristic. A penniless orphan, unhappy in his adopted home, Poe was dismissed from West Point, married a thirteen-year-old cousin, and did hack work in New York until his wife's death. His erratic mental and personal habits continued until his own death, shortly after.

Poe produced a body of serious literary criticism which has been the center of many controversies. *The Philosophy of Composition* (1846) purports to detail his writing of "The Raven." The *Rationale of Verse* (1843) and *The Poetic Principle* (1850) are the technical dicta which lie at the heart of the matter.

As for Poe's poetry, "The Raven" (1844) is a typical short piece (eighteen six-line stanzas) syncopated with double rhyme and alliteration, with a refrain. The subject, told through a raven's visit to a weary student's study, is grief caused by the death of a beautiful woman. "The Bells" (1849) is a technical tour de force relating the ways in which bells influence moods. "Annabel Lee" is a lyric masterpiece inspired by the loss of a beautiful woman.

Poe's short stories are of two kinds. First, horror tales. "The Fall of the House of Usher" (1839) narrates the death of Roderick Usher, a recluse distressed by strange nervous maladies, and his twin sister Madeline, who had been placed, while suffering a cataleptic trance, in the family vault. The decayed old mansion crumbles in a terrific storm. "The Black Cat" (1843) tells how Pluto, a black cat, discloses a murderer who has walled the animal up with the corpse of his wife. "The Pit and the Pendulum" concerns a prisoner of the Spanish Inquisition who is bound to a table and menaced, first by a gradually lowering blade; then, escaping his bonds, by the heated metal walls of his cell, which move inward and force him toward a pit. "The Casque of Amontillado" (1846) tells how Montresor lures his enemy Fortunato into a wine cellar during a carnival and walls him up. "The Tell-Tale Heart" (1843) describes a homicidal maniac's terror when he seems to hear the beating of his victim's heart beneath the floorboards, while he is being questioned by police.

The other type of short tale is the reportorial detective story. "The Gold Bug" (1843) is the story of William Legrand, who interprets a rare scarab and a cryptogram, and with his Negro servant Jupiter discovers a treasure buried by Captain Kidd. "The Murders in the Rue Morgue" (1841) tell how the eccentric Dupin discovers that the perpetrator of a series of brutal murders is an orang-utan. "The Mystery of Marie Rogêt" (1842) is a sequel, a Dupin tale taken from an actual New York murder case of the day.

POEMA DEL CID (1140), Anonymous. See POEM OF THE CID, Anonymous.

POEM OF THE CID (1140), Anonymous. The epic poem, *Poema del Cid,* marks the beginning of Spanish literature. Written about 1140 (author unknown), it extols the deeds of Spain's national hero, Ruy Díaz de Bivar (1043–1099). This temporal proximity between hero and poet lends the *Poema del Cid* remarkable historical and geographical realism, setting it apart from all the other epic sagas of European literature, so fraught with exaggerated fantasies and weird improbabilities.

The historical background of the poem is the period of the Reconquista, when the Spaniards were trying to regain their peninsula from the hands of the Moors, who had held it since the early eighth century. In these operations of reconquest Ruy Díaz played a role of paramount importance. In a series of brilliant victories he captured town after town, leading his doughty warriors all the way down to the Mediterranean coast and crowning his campaign with the capture of Valencia (1094). His Moorish enemies in admiration of his valor called him the Cid (in Arabic *Sidi* means Lord).

The *Poema del Cid* follows history closely, without greatly idealizing its main character, but stressing or dramatizing certain events which struck the poet's fancy. As the poem opens, Ruy Díaz, who has been sent into Moorish territory to collect tributes owed to his King, Alfonso VI of Leon, is accused by intriguing courtiers of withholding some of the money. The King exiles him. Ruy Díaz places his wife, Ximena, and two daughters, Elvira and Sol, in safety in the Monastery of Cardeña, where he takes leave of them. His trusty henchman, Martín Antolínez, finances the departure by negotiating a loan from the Jews Raquel and Vidas, offering as security a sand-filled coffer which, they are told, contains the Cid's treasures. With a little band of sixty lancers Ruy Díaz raids the Moorish territories southwest of Zaragoza, where they gain great booty. As news of his successes spread, adventurers flock to his banner and victory follows victory, until finally the Cid captures the coveted city of Valencia, where he establishes himself with his wife and daughters. Meanwhile the Counts of Carrion, the nephews of King Alfonso, scheme to marry Elvira and Sol in order to acquire some of the wealth won by their father, the Cid. A conference between Díaz and the King is held on the banks of the Tagus, where Alfonso, acting for the Counts, pardons the Cid and arranges the marriages. Despite forebodings that the marriages will come to no good, the Cid loyally obeys the King's wishes.

The Cid bestows wealth upon his sons-in-law and presents them with his dearest possessions: his swords Colada and Tizona. But the Counts prove themselves cowards in battle, and when a captive lion escapes in the Cid's palace they flee like frightened children. They are so ridiculed by the Cid's vassals that they resolve to withdraw to their estates, taking with them their wives dowries and presents. Upon reaching the oak grove of Corpes they strip their wives, bind them to trees, flog them and ride away, leaving them for dead The ladies are rescued by a cousin and restored to their father.

The Cid now seeks redress from the King. The nobles of the realm are convoked in Toledo, and before them the Cid demands: first, the return of his two swords, to which the Counts readily agree, and secondly, the restitution of the dowries, to which they consent, reluctantly, under compulsion. Finally, the Cid demands that his sons-in-law be tried by judicial combat. This last request is granted by the King, and the Counts are conquered in the lists by the champions of the Cid. The triumph proves the sons-in-law traitors and the Cid a man of honor. His daughters marry the Kings of Navarre and Aragon, and thus the Cid becomes connected with the royal houses of Spain.

This epic was first published in 1779 from a fourteenth-century manuscript copied, probably in 1307, from some earlier text, by one Per Abbat. It contains 3735 assonant lines of varied length, the most common being 8 syllables in each half-line, as in ballad meter. Its simple and clear style depicts with sincerity and austerity those sentiments and feelings of pride and pity and honor which have been long associated with the Spanish soul.

POEMS (1832), by William Cullen Bryant. See THANATOPSIS, by William Cullen Bryant.

POEMS (1920), by T. S. Eliot. See ELIOT, THOMAS STEARNS.

POEMS (published 1918), by Gerard Manley Hopkins. Hopkins has written a few poems, as lovely as anything in English, which can be enjoyed without understanding his theories; unfortunately, the bulk of his poetical accomplishment needs some knowledge of "inscape." It is this theory of Hopkins which makes some of his work difficult and forbidding. The effect of "inscape" on the mind and emotions Hopkins sometimes called "instress." He maintained that a poet is one who can describe "inscape" accurately and his own "instress"; that is, a poet must be aware of what is individually distinctive in himself. "God's Grandeur" is a fine poem, written from the heart, without strain or contortion. "The Wreck of the Deutschland" is, on the other hand, a magnificent, long, fully orchestrated poem to which Hopkins applied "the new prosody." When his friend Bridges wrote a parody, Hopkins' bland response was: "Your parody reassures me about your understanding of the meter!" "Sprung rhythm" (meaning abrupt) is one of Hopkins' often-used devices. "Pied Beauty" and "Windhover" are two of the most beautiful and most individual of the famous poems. Unfortunately they must be recited to get the effect desired by the poet, or his great labor is wasted. This explains his slow impression on the public. It took his friend Bridges' best efforts for ten years before the artistic crowd accepted him, although now he is the darling of the élite. Among religious poets none has excelled him in deep emotion and utter sincerity.

POEMS (1880), by Sidney Lanier. See LANIER, SIDNEY.

POEMS (1832), by Nikolaus von Lenau. See LENAU, NIKOLAUS VON.

POEMS (1689, etc.), by Sor Juana Inés de la Cruz (Juana de Asbaje). Juana de Asbaje, the charming and brilliant Mexican girl who entered a convent at the age of sixteen, is better known as Sor Juana Inés de la Cruz. During her short life this extraordinary nun wrote scientific and philosophical treatises, plays and poetry, but it is above all for her exquisite sonnets and ballads that her name will be remembered. She had great technical skill; and her baroque and at times difficult poetry shows her now witty and caustic in her criticism of men's attitude towards women, now reflective and melancholy in her analysis of love, now serious and profound in her intimations of death. The Mexicans call her The Tenth Muse.

POEMS (1631), by Luis Ponce de Leon. Fray Luis de Leon's greatness is found not in one poem but in his whole lyrical output, which consists of scarcely thirty pieces. Of these the most memorable are his Odes to Francisco Salinas (El aire se serena . . .); to Felipe Ruiz (En vano el mar . . .; Cuando será que pueda?); to Oloarte (Noche serena), and such admirable short lyrics as "On a Life of Retirement," "On Immortality," "On the Starry Heavens," and "Hymn on the Ascension." Every line of Fray Luis breathes an intense longing for nature and peace. In him are found qualities which are rarely encountered in Spanish poetry: a harmonious classic purity of form together with sincerity and depth of feeling. Some forty years after Fray Luis' death, his original poems and his translations from the Psalms, Virgil, Horace and the Greek and Italian poets were collected by Quevedo under the title *Obras propias y traduciones latinas, griegas y italianas.*

POEMS (1543), by Garcilaso de la Vega. Posthumously published in 1543 by the widow of the poet Juan Boscán, Garcilaso de la Vega's work comprises three eclogues, five conzones, two elegies, an epistle in verse, and thirty-eight sonnets. Yet, little as this output is, it was brilliant enough to win its author the name of "Prince of Spanish Poets." During his brief life, a great part of which was spent on the battlefields of Europe in the service of his friend and protector the Emperor Charles V, Garcilaso transplanted into Spain the poetical genius of Renaissance Italy, acclimating there the metrical patterns and thematic discoveries of Petrarch, Bembo, Tansillo, Ariosto and Sannazaro: the bucolic strain, the sonnet, the Petrarchan stanza, the tercet, the octave and the lira. Garcilaso was hopelessly in love with the Portuguese lady Isabel Freyre, who married and died during the lifetime of the poet; there is to be found in his verse a melancholy note fraught with tender grace. Few poets surpass the beauty of his imagery, his felicitous turns of phrase and the sweetness and depth of his sentiment. Eclogue I is perhaps the best known of his works. It opens with an address to Pedro de Toledo, the uncle of the Duke of Alba, asking him to listen to the complaints of two shepherds: Salicio, who is recalling despondently the faithlessness of his mistress, and Nemoroso, who is mourning the death of his. Both shepherds really speak for Garcilaso and their mistress is Isabel. The eclogue closes gently with a description of the approach of evening.

POEMS AND BALLADS (First series, 1866; Second series, 1878), by Algernon Charles Swinburne. See SWINBURNE, ALGERNON CHARLES.

POEMS BY KABIR (1916), by Rabindranath Tagore. See TAGORE, RABINDRANATH.

POEMS IN PROSE (1879–1883), by Ivan Sergeyevich Turgenev. See RUDIN, by Ivan Sergeyevich Turgenev.

POEMS OF IMAGINATION (1916), by Rabindranath Tagore. See TAGORE, RABINDRANATH.

POET AT THE BREAKFAST-TABLE, THE (1872), by Oliver Wendell Holmes. See AUTOCRAT OF THE BREAKFAST-TABLE, THE, by Oliver Wendell Holmes.

POETIC EDDA, THE (ca. 900–1050), Anonymous. This collection of thirty-four ancient poems in Old Norse or Old Icelandic is the "original storehouse of Germanic mythology. . . . It is, indeed," asserts their translator, Bellows, "in many ways the greatest literary monument preserved to us out of the antiquity of the kindred races which we call Germanic." We do not know specifically when, where, or by whom these poems were composed; but some undoubtedly originated in Norway among cultured emigrants to foreign parts; others probably among Norse settlers on the islands of the North Atlantic; and one, or two perhaps, in Greenland. They were, however, collected and written down in Iceland, presumably in the latter part of the twelfth and in the thirteenth centuries. No doubt there were written copies of an earlier date. The subject matter had for generations been preserved through oral transmission, parts of it being of remote antique origin. It is the raw material of a huge tradition, complex in poetic form, which in the thirteenth century gave birth in Germany to the *Nibelungenlied,* and, in the nineteenth century, to the operas of Richard Wagner.

The poems may be divided into two large groups: mythological and heroic. The former includes the famous "Voluspá" (The Wise-Woman's Prophecy), dealing with the creation and final destruction of the world, and the didactic "Havamal" (The Ballad of the High One), a collection of precepts and proverbs; also, the unique, humorous "Thrymskvitha" (The Lay of Thrym), which treats of the recovery of Thor's hammer, one of the best poems ever written. The heroic group center on the Germanic idol Sigurd (Siegfried). The meaning of the title "Edda" is somewhat obscure, but probably signifies "poetry," because of a possible linguistic connection with the proper name "Oddi" (the genitive form of it), a cultural settlement in Iceland, where Snorri Sturluson lived for many years. (See *The Prose Edda.*) There are three principal verse-forms in *The Poetic Edda,* all in four-line stanzas, with alliteration or initial rhyme, each line having a certain number of accented syllables, and usually separated into two half-lines by a caesural pause, the Ljothahattr ("Song Measure") being the only exception, with the second and fourth lines shorter than the others and the caesura omitted. The other two verse-forms are the Fornyrthislag ("Old Verse") and the later Malahattr ("Speech Measure"), the difference between the two consisting chiefly in the number of possible un-accented syllables in the half-line. The former has two or three unaccented ones; the latter three or four. Both have two accented syllables in a half-line. The Eddic poems are "folk poetry" only in a limited sense; their authors were cultured artists who knew both the background, with its details, and the art of verse-making. A good English translation of them is that by H. A. Bellows (The American-Scandinavian Foundation, 1923).

POETIC PRINCIPLE, THE (1850), by Edgar Allan Poe. See POE, EDGAR ALLAN.

POETICS, by Aristotle (384–322 B.C.). Of all the works of Aristotle none has had so wide and lasting an influence as the *Poetics*. As we have it, it is fragmentary, dealing only with epic and tragic poetry, but it originally con-tinued with an analysis of comedy. The general principles deduced by Aristotle from familiar Greek literature contain much that is of general if not universal application, and his theory of poetry as an imitative art still com-mands the respect of critic and theoretician. After differentiating the arts according to the character and object of their imitation, he distinguishes be-tween tragedy and comedy. Then he discusses the origin of poetry and gives a brief history of the rise of comedy and tragedy. After his famous definition of tragedy as "an imitation of an action that is serious, complete, and of a certain magnitude; in language embellished with each kind of artistic orna-ment . . . in the form of action, not of narrative; through pity and fear effecting the proper purgation of these emotions," he proceeds to enlarge upon the details of this definition. In this discussion he is principally concerned with plot, character and diction, and it is here that he advances the theory of dra-matic unity which was to affect the composition and criticism of drama even into modern times. The final sections of the treatise as it is preserved contain a comparison of tragedy and epic, and Aristotle's canons of criticism.

POETRY AND TRUTH (1811–1833), by Johann Wolfgang von Goethe. See GOETHE, JOHANN WOLFGANG VON.

POINT COUNTER POINT (1928), by Aldous Huxley. Generally regarded as the best of Huxley's novels, this book in the relatively short time since its appearance has become firmly established as a modern classic. Lucy Tantamount, daughter of a distinguished, titled biologist, and Spandrell, are each in separate ways studies in advanced moral degeneracy. In Burlap is found the pseudo-intellectual, a pretentious, hypocritical *poseur* possessed of sufficient cunning and opportunism to shine as an eminent critic and *littéra-teur*. Mark Rampion is the modern pagan, proud of a dubiously "healthful" freedom from the common social fetishes. Philip Quarles is a novelist, phys-ically and emotionally restricted and apathetic, consequently rendered esoteric in his intellectual processes. Everard Webley, a man of sinister forcefulness and political skill, leads an ever-growing green-shirt Fascist movement. The behavior of all of them and of a myriad of other characters is clearly presented as the product of, or reactions from, their basic environmental background.

For a "plotless" book it is extraordinarily filled with movement and interest-binding developments. Its action possesses an intensity of its own, culminating in at least two incidents, the murder of Everard Webley, and the death of Quarles' child from meningitis.

Following the implication of its title, the book is orchestrated, rather than plotted in a conventional sense. It weaves the threads of the behavior patterns of its many characters into a complex fabric. The characters are types, recognizable and authentically familiar in the social framework of the book. But they are not types in terms of shallow characterization, but vigorously projected, rounded, and intensely individualized personalities.

In Huxley's ruthlessly satiric observation of this *milieu* there is discernible a conscious social commentary reminiscent of the best of Balzac.

POLAND (1926), by Samuel Joseph Agnon. See BRIDAL CANOPY, THE, by Samuel Joseph Agnon.

POLITICAL PALINGENESIS (published 1809), by Vincenzo Monti. See MONTI, VINCENZO.

POLITICAL TINKER, THE (1722–1731), by Ludvig Holberg. See ERASMUS MONTANUS, by Ludvig Holberg.

POLITICS, by Aristotle (384–322 B.C.). The *Politics* is not concerned with politics as we understand the term nor yet with government in any limited sense of that term, but is Aristotle's philosophy of the state. It is an extension of his ethics to communal life; and his judgments are based upon an exhaustive study of the constitutions and institutions of all the states known to him. He begins with a consideration of the nature of the state, rejecting the idea of a social contract and preferring to regard it as a development from the family. He progresses from the discussion of household management to that of state economy, wherein he recognizes the operation of the law of supply and demand. Communism of property as proposed by Plato he rejects. As to forms of government, he classifies them in order of desirability as Monarchy, Aristocracy, Constitutional Republic, Democracy, Oligarchy and Tyranny. The difficulty with the first two is that proper kings and aristocrats are seldom found. Practically, therefore, he considers the Constitutional Republic as the most desirable. On the question of an ideal state he concludes that it must be adapted to the character and needs of its citizens so as to make it capable of realizing the good life. To this end Aristotle argues that education of the citizen must be provided for, and should be a function of the state.

POLYEUCTE (1643), by Pierre Corneille. See CID, THE, by Pierre Corneille.

POOR FOLK (1846), by Feodor Dostoevsky. Sometimes translated *Poor People,* this first novel by Dostoevsky gained him instant fame, winning the praise of Russia's greatest contemporary critic, Belinsky, who, with singular penetration, foresaw the direction which Dostoevsky's genius would take. It was evident that here was a writer who did not write so much from experience and observation as from a profound intuition. A blend of the sentimental and naturalistic, the novel tells a story in a series of letters between

Makar, a poverty-stricken clerk in a St. Petersburg government office (somewhat reminiscent of Akaky Akakievitch in Gogol's *Cloak*), and Varvara, a frail, poor orphan who finds it hard to make ends meet as a seamstress. Makar loves the unfortunate girl, and denies himself essential needs in order to provide her with luxuries which he can ill afford. He gets heavily into debt, and is forced to pawn his uniform and to leave his room for nonpayment of rent. He tries unsuccessfully to borrow money, he takes to drink, and is saved from total penury only by the generosity of his chief, who gives him a hundred rubles. Varvara criticizes Makar's extravagance. Tired of the struggle to make a precarious livelihood, the ailing Varvara yearns to return to the country, where in better days she had been moderately happy. But at this moment Bykov, a well-to-do man, turns up with an offer of marriage which, if accepted, would make her the mistress of his estate. Reluctantly she consents, for this is the only way by which she may escape from the drabness of her life. Makar is left heartbroken.

POOR PEOPLE (1846), by Feodor Dostoevsky. See POOR FOLK, by Feodor Dostoevsky.

POOR RICHARD'S ALMANACK (1773-1758), by Benjamin Franklin. See AUTOBIOGRAPHY OF BENJAMIN FRANKLIN, THE, by Benjamin Franklin.

POOR WHITE (1920), by Sherwood Anderson. See WINESBURG, OHIO, by Sherwood Anderson.

PORGY (1925), by DuBose Heyward. The scene is laid in Charleston, S. C., along Catfish Row, where poor Negroes live in ruined grandeur. Porgy is a sweet-natured cripple who begs and throws dice for a livelihood. In a crap game Crown, a huge man, kills one of the players. He flees to a palmetto island, while his woman, Bess, seeks refuge with Porgy. Under his influence, she decides to reform. When Crown returns for Bess, Porgy, who is in love with her, stabs him to death. Porgy is arrested, and, true to her old ways, Bess attaches herself to a dope peddler and runs away with him to New York. Unable to live without her, Porgy follows her to the great city in his little goat cart.

The story has become an American classic. Heyward and his wife dramatized it, and in 1927 it won the Pulitzer Prize. Later, with music by George Gershwin, *Porgy and Bess* was presented in opera form (1935).

Mamba's Daughters (1929) depicts the life and misadventures of three generations of Southern Negroes, from Charleston to Harlem. The novel also follows "Saint" Wentworth, a member of a moribund patrician family who marries a wealthy Northerner, and Mamba, an amiable Negro attached to the Wentworths.

PORT ROYAL (1840-1859), by Charles Augustin Sainte-Beuve. See CAUSERIES DE LUNDI, by Charles Augustin Sainte-Beuve.

PORTER, KATHERINE ANNE (1894–   ). The author of fiction and poetry, Katherine Anne Porter has traveled widely as a journalist. *Pale Horse, Pale Rider* (1939) is a collection of five novelettes; *No Safe Harbor* (1941) is a novel.

Flowering Judas (1930) is her most popular collection of short stories. Six pieces make up the volume: "Flowering Judas," "María Concepción," "Magic," "Rope," "He," and "The Jilting of Granny Weatherall." (The 1935 edition contained four additional pieces.) There is great diversity of locale: Mexico, New Orleans, the Connecticut countryside, and New York. All stories are written in a terse, economical style. Insignificant individuals and trifling situations are given dramatic importance by the universality of their experience. The themes are characteristic of the author's endorsement of Maupassant's and Chekhov's philosophy of the art of the short story: the predicament of a young American schoolteacher in Mexico, a humorously pathetic lovers' quarrel, an Irish immigrant woman's passionate infidelities on a too quiet Connecticut farm.

PORTER, WILLIAM SYDNEY (1862–1910). William Sydney Porter had little schooling. After working in a drugstore in his native North Carolina, he went to Texas. He tried various jobs, and at length was indicted for embezzlement from a bank where he had been teller. He fled the country to Honduras, but returned when his wife was dying, and served a three-year prison term. Previously a columnist, by the time he left prison he was an author. The country acclaimed "O. Henry," who was able to produce short stories for periodicals at the rate of one a week. Although his first collection, *Cabbages and Kings* (1904), employed a general novel form, with a loose plot and a single group of characters, O. Henry did not afterward attempt longer forms of fiction. His masterpiece is the short vignette of life: stories of simple people, ironic coincidence, and the surprise ending; the unpredictable fluctuations of fortune. His best milieu is that of the everyday lives of average New Yorkers.

Perhaps the typical O. Henry tale is "The Gift of the Magi" (1906). One Christmas in New York, a young couple find themselves without money to buy presents for each other. Deeply in love, each one sacrifices his dearest possession: the wife sells her long locks, of which both are proud, to a haircutter and buys a watch chain for the husband; he sells the watch to buy her a pair of combs.

Other volumes are: *Heart of the West* (1907), *The Trimmed Lamp* (1907), *The Gentle Grafter* (1908), *The Voice of the City* (1908), *Options* (1909), *Roads of Destiny* (1909), *Whirligigs* (1910), *Strictly Business* (1910); and posthumous collections including *Sixes and Sevens* (1911), *Rolling Stones* (1913), *Waifs and Strays* (1917), *Postscripts* (1923), and *O. Henry Encore* (1939).

PORTRAIT OF A LADY, THE (1881), by Henry James. Isobel Archer, a pretty Albany girl, is assiduously courted by Casper Goodwood. To escape his attentions, she accompanies her eccentric aunt, Mrs. Touchett, to Italy. Stopping over in England, she is the focus of admiration for many men. Her invalid cousin Ralph falls in love with her, and even old Mr. Touchett, his father, cannot resist her. When she reaches Italy, now the heir of Ralph's father, she encounters the sinister Madame Merle, who introduces her to the poor but fascinating Gilbert Osmond. She marries him, but there begins a swift disillusioning process, climaxing in the discovery that her stepdaughter Pansy is the illegitimate child of her husband and Madame Merle. Casper

Goodwood reappears and again courts her. She remains loyal to Gilbert and her duty to Pansy, however, and returns home.

PORTRAIT OF THE ARTIST AS A YOUNG MAN, A (1916), by James Joyce. This work of fiction by the Irish writer is a landmark in the history of literature. It ushered in a new art form—the stream-of-consciousness novel—which later Joyce carried further in *Ulysses* (q.v.) and in *Finnegans Wake* (q.v.). The mind of the hero, Stephen Dedalus, with its various fluctuations and nuances of subconscious thought, is at least as important to the reader as his actions. The book is a story of spiritual growth, the growth of a young and sensitive man, stirred by the creative urge, and finding everything in his environment antagonistic. From his childhood amid poverty and sordidness, through his schooldays of ridicule and discipline, witnessing his struggles to free himself from the hysteria of religion and the compromises of love, the reader follows Dedalus to the point at which, having thrown off all human ties, he faces life accepting isolation from his fellow man and dedicated to his art.

POSITIVE PHILOSOPHY (1830–1842), by Auguste Comte. Published in six volumes, this was the principal work of the French philosopher and humanist whose identification with the socialism of the Saint-Simon school has frequently been overstated. In *Positive Philosophy* Comte develops the idea of the worship of humanity to the highest degree. He presents it in the form of a cult with a ritual all its own. Regeneration can come only as a result of the spiritual unification of all mankind. A follower of Saint-Simon at first, he rejected much of his mysticism. An evolutionist in social theory, he conceived the human mind as unfolding in stages according to definite scientific laws. He wrote: "The race, like the individual, necessarily passes through three intellectual stages—the theological, the metaphysical, and the positive." Until the thirteenth century, states Comte, theology dominated mankind; metaphysics ruled Western Europe until the nineteenth century; positivism, the highest development, concerns itself with the achievement of verified scientific knowledge. In the first or theological stage God was the dominant social force; in the second or metaphysical stage the concept of God was destroyed, but nothing was discovered to take its place in the beliefs of mankind. Rationalism of this type, Comte declared, was arid, destructive, and purposeless. However, he finds the constructive answer in positivism. He advocated the application of the methods of science to the study of society. Sociology must not seek its validity in God or the nature of man but only in demonstrable facts. Society was to be based on the all-powerful State ruled by a scientific priesthood. He discovers in the instinct for material self-preservation the vital life forces which engage in a struggle between humanity and animals, a contest in which humanity is bound to be victorious.

Comte's positive religion of humanity was essentially a system of ethics. He was criticized by the advanced thinkers of his day for reversion to Catholicism in his detailed arrangement of institutionalized positivism with a hierarchy, ritual and priesthood, merely substituting scientific concepts and scientists for their ecclesiastical models. The Catholic Church and the academicians on the other hand charged him with blasphemy, and he was deprived of his official

post at the university and of his livelihood. To add to his misfortune, his orthodox wife deserted him in his hour of need. John Morley wrote about Comte's
intellectual firmness: "Neither Franklin nor any man that ever lived, could surpass him in the heroic tenacity with which, in the face of a thousand obstacles,
he pursued his own ideal of a vocation."

POSSESSED, THE (1873), by Feodor Dostoevsky. The hero of this
novel (sometimes translated as *The Devils*), is Nikolai Stavrogin, a handsome,
brilliant aristocrat, with great sensibility but scarcely any heart. His mother,
Varvara Petrovna, a wealthy and domineering widow, lives on an immense
estate on the outskirts of a provincial capital. This is where the action for
the most part takes place.

When the story opens Stavrogin has already been degraded from his rank
in the army, due to several unsavory episodes, including marriage with the
feeble-minded cripple, Marya Timofyevna. He is a man who cannot find
himself; his extraordinary behavior causes doubts of his sanity to circulate.
But his powerful influence is never absent from the novel, even when he remains in the background of the main actions. His chief tool is Pyotor Verkhovensky, an unscrupulous, insolent fellow, who poses as an organizer of the
revolutionary Nihilists. He idolizes Stavrogin, and manages to insinuate himself into the company of more normal people. Kirillov, who offers to sacrifice
his life, if need be, for the "cause"; the student Shatov, an ex-serf on the estate
of Varvara Petrovna, as well as several others, are mixed up in the plot. Vir-
ginsky, a government clerk, and his brother-in-law, Shigalov, and a Jew, Lyam-
shin, with some musical ability, also play parts in the revolutionary movement.

Verkhovensky meanwhile wins the favor of the new Governor's wife, Yulia
Mikhailovna von Lembke. She is a vain and ambitious female who is determined to be in the forefront of all "advanced movements." She thinks she has
got onto the most fashionable band wagon, and happily puts on a fête at Verkhovensky's urging, the proceeds of which were to go to the poor governesses
of the Province. The fête comes to grief; disgrace follows, and the Governor
loses his mind as a result.

Meanwhile, with Stavrogin's knowledge, if not consent, the revolutionary
group set fire to a section of the provincial capital to conceal the murder of
Stavrogin's feeble-minded wife and her brother. The removal of the cripple,
Marya Timofyevna, leaves Stavrogin free to marry Lizaveta Drozdov, a charming girl of good family, who is madly in love with him. After Stavrogin ruins
her reputation he tells her he doesn't love her; that he can never love her.

The criticism of socialism and godlessness, interrelated by Dostoevsky, are
implicit in this novel, which is a sort of exposition of the Parable of the
Gadarene Swine. It is also in this novel that the author propounds his famous
exposition of the man-god, i.e., man as god unto himself, the antithesis of the
God-man of Christianity.

POSSESSION (1925), by Louis Bromfield. See GREEN BAY TREE,
THE, by Louis Bromfield.

POSTHUMOUS MEMOIRS OF BRAZ CUBAS (1881), by Joaquim
Maria Machado de Assis. See DOM CASMURRO, by Joaquim Maria Machado de Assis.

POSTILA (1412–1413), by Jan Hus. See HUS, JAN.

POSTILLA (1441), by Peter Chelčický. See NET OF THE TRUE FAITH, THE, by Peter Chelčicky.

POSTSCRIPTS (1923), by William Sydney Porter. See PORTER, WILLIAM SYDNEY.

POT OF BASIL, THE (written 1818; published 1820), by John Keats. See ISABELLA, by John Keats.

POT OF EARTH, THE (1925), by Archibald MacLeish. See MacLEISH, ARCHIBALD.

POT OF GOLD, THE or AULULARIA, by Plautus (Titus Maccius Plautus; 254–184 B.C.). This is one of the most successful of Plautus' comedies. It is the story of the comic miser, Euclio, who is too stingy to give his own daughter a dowry so that she may make a decent marriage. He has the remarkable fortune to find a pot of gold buried in his house, but instead of enjoying the blessings it could buy him he reburies it deeper than ever, and then lives in a torment of fear that someone else will discover it. His unhappy daughter, it appears, finds herself with child by some unknown culprit, but a solution of that difficulty seems to present itself. Megadorus, a confirmed and wealthy bachelor, is given a good lecture by his prim and old-fashioned sister, as a result of which he decides to marry, and asks Euclio for the hand of his daughter. Meanwhile Euclio, now suspicious of everyone, decides to rebury his treasure outside his own house. But as he buries it he is seen by a slave, who gleefully walks off with it. Now Lyconides, the nephew of Megadorus, was the young man responsible for the daughter's condition, and at this juncture he decides to do the right thing by her, persuades Megadorus to give up his suit, and goes to Euclio to make a clean breast of it. Euclio, however, has discovered the loss of his treasure, and when Lyconides tries to confess, he assumes the confession has to do with the theft, of which he proceeds to tell the young man. In the following scene Lyconides' slave, the same one who had stolen the treasure, tells his master of his great good fortune. The slave's joy is but short-lived, for Lyconides, recognizing the identity of the treasure, forces him to make restitution. Our text of the play breaks off before the end, but it is clear that Euclio learns his lesson, has a change of heart, and gives his daughter to Lyconides with the treasure for a dowry.

POTGIETER, E. J. (1808–1875). Criticism forms the major part of Potgieter's early literary works. He founded a monthly, *De Gids,* in 1837, which until the present day has remained one of the leading periodicals of the Netherlands. In his well-balanced but uncompromising essays he turned against the mediocrity in the reigning classicism of his day and in the same measure against the sentimentality and unbalanced tendencies of Romanticism. That his criticism covers a wider field than literature appears from his essays "Jan, Jannetje en hun jongste Kind" and "Het Rijksmuseum." In both he contrasts the energetic Hollander of the seventeenth century with the spiritless generation of his own day. A strong social consciousness is evident from his sketches " 't Is maar seen pennelikker," depicting the colorless existence of office employees, and "Blauwbes!," in which the sorrow of a peasant woman for her wayward daughter in the city is described with tenderness without sentimentality.

Potgieter's retreat in 1860 from this type of writing was followed by a period of rich poetry. He felt himself akin to Dante—for him the ideal citizen— expelled from his own birthplace. To Dante he dedicated his "Florence," in which he reproduced the life of the Italian poet in 20 cantos. The versification by terzas is finely manipulated. The poem "Gedroomd Paardrijden" is an historic vision of the heroic year 1672, when Holland was attacked by France and England. "Mount Vernon" gives a picture of the United States at the death of Washington, who is honored as the ideal patriot, fighting for justice and liberty. Great sympathy was felt by Potgieter for energetic and democratic America, and in several of his poems thoughtful attention to the struggle between North and South is evident. The poem "Abraham Lincoln," broadly conceived after the death of the President he so ardently admired, remained unfinished. Through his pure and well-balanced poetry, Potgieter has greatly influenced later generations in the Netherlands.

POUND, EZRA (1885–   ). Ezra Pound's educational career in this country ended in 1907 when Wabash College, Indiana, decided that his European points of view were too unconventional. He returned to Europe, therefore, first settling in London. He became a name to conjure with in the literary world, championing the poetry of the Imagists and Orientalists. He later moved to Paris, then to the Italian Riviera. His own works, translations, adaptations, and contributions, have increased his stature steadily in the field of modern verse. After World War II, Ezra Pound was charged with treason, due to pro-Fascist broadcasts. Even during this troubled time, when the declaration that he is insane has halted federal prosecution, the Bollingen committee has voted his *Pisan Cantos* the finest poetry of 1948.

Following his early poetic experiments, Pound set himself major creative tasks. *Hugh Selwyn Mauberly* (1920) illustrates the theory of modern verse which has been accepted by such followers as T. S. Eliot: conversational tone and free association, combined with complex allusiveness and deliberate dissonance.

The *Cantos* began appearing in 1925. Intended as a long series representing a human comedy, they reveal the poet himself as the main character. This fragmentary, esoteric autobiography is supposed to chronicle the progress of history, from ancient times to the present. Pound, with his semi-assimilated cultures of many countries, pictures the wrecks of several civilizations, and suggests that our society, which suffers by contrast with past eras, must regulate itself along humanitarian lines.

POWER (1925), by Lion Feuchtwanger. See FEUCHTWANGER, LION.

POWER OF A LIE, THE (1920), by Johan Bojer. Johan Bojer's short novel runs with the irresistibility of an avalanche to its disastrous conclusion. Bojer is a psychological moralist of a very austere order. Like most of his other novels, this is primarily a fervent preachment against untruth, which, no matter how innocently intended, is bound to bring misfortune. The style of the writing also is naïve and direct, like a deeply felt sermon, and these are the very qualities which give the unfolding of the simple tale a moving power. Bojer, regardless of the effect of his didactic compulsion, is a superb artist.

The principal protagonists are Norby and Wangen. Both regard themselves as being eminently virtuous men; both become criminals in fighting each other because of this self-righteousness. Norby is an active and capable man and he flourishes in the world. He is most uncharitable, however; his own success makes him vainglorious, and other people's successes make him envious and bitter. He feels let down and cheated when informed that his fellow-townsman Wangen has gone bankrupt, because Norby had signed a note for two thousand kroner for him. When a busybody informs him that Wangen had spoken of his endorsement of a note for two thousand kroner, Norby, out of a businessman's vanity for infallible judgment, dismisses the matter impatiently with a half lie, i.e., that he does not recall ever having stood bond for Wangen. Gossips accordingly conclude that Norby had not signed the note at all.

Rumor now begins its destructive course. If Norby had not endorsed the note then Wangen must have forged the signature. Norby is too slow in putting a brake on the rumor, and finally, when pricked by a guilty conscience he tries to do so, it is already too late. What was said so casually by him has now become an ever-widening wave of misfortune. Matters go so far that Fru Norby goes to the justice of the peace and accuses the unfortunate Wangen of forgery. The latter becomes embittered, and in his helplessness to clear his befouled name he sinks to unworthy defenses, and in turn slanders Norby's reputation. Both become subsequently involved in questionable intrigues. Finally Wangen, overwhelmed by persecution, in order to clear his name does commit the crime of which he was so unjustly accused: he forges Norby's signature and produces it in court on a note for two thousand kroner.

POWER OF DARKNESS, THE (1886), by Count Leo Tolstoy. *The Power of Darkness* is Tolstoy's best known play. Written in the crabbed, staccato speech of the Tula peasant, the play loses much of its atmosphere in translation. It is a gruesome and powerful story, at times reaching heights which place it on a level with the Greek tragedies. Pyotr, a rich, sickly muzhik, has married again, and his second wife Anisya is fond of finery. She has a love affair with Nikita, a stupid, pleasure-loving laborer in their employ, and when there is talk of marrying him off to Marina, a girl he has wronged, Anisya tells his mother, Matriona, an evil, scheming old woman, that she loves him. The two women plot that when Pyotr dies Anisya shall marry Nikita. Pyotr has money which Anisya tries vainly to find. Realizing he is dying, Pyotr sends his daughter by his first marriage, Akulina, to call his sister Marfa, and Anisya is afraid he will give her the money. Finally Anisya finds it, and on Matriona's advice gives it to Nikita. The women poison Pyotr and Anisya marries Nikita, who gets drunk and spends her money on a present for Akulina. The latter is betrothed by the matchmakers, but has a child by Nikita. Anisya and Matriona wish the marriage to go through and determine to get rid of the child. The play ends with a grim and horrible scene in which they compel Nikita to kill and bury his own offspring.

PRAGMATISM (1907), by William James. See JAMES, WILLIAM.

PRAIRIES, THE (1827), by James Fenimore Cooper. See LEATHER-STOCKING TALES, by James Fenimore Cooper.

PRAISE OF FOLLY, THE (1509), by Desiderius Erasmus. Erasmus wrote *The Praise of Folly* while indisposed with lumbago at the home of his friend Thomas More, in England. He wrote it in seven days. If not the most important of his works, it is the one through which he achieved international renown. It went through forty editions during his lifetime. Holbein illustrated it with pen-and-ink sketches. It is the most popular of all Renaissance classics. Speaking in the name of Folly, Erasmus criticizes the institutions, customs, men and beliefs of his time. The objects of his satire include marriage, self-love, war, the corruption in the Church, national pride, the competition for material goods, the wordiness of the lawyers, the speculations of the scientists, the logic-chopping and hairsplitting of the theologians, the ignorance and diversity of the religious orders, the pride of kings and the servility of courtiers, the neglect of spiritual duties and responsibilities to their flocks of bishops, cardinals and popes. All are held up to ridicule; the true duties and interests of all are shown. Erasmus professed a simple, humanistic form of Christianity, and though he was severely critical of the Church, he refused to leave it and join the Protestants.

PRÉCIEUSES RIDICULES, LES (1659), by Molière. Molière's first success was this satire on affectation and pedantry. Madelon and Cathos—the daughter and niece of bourgeois Gorgibus—have just rejected La Grange and Du Croissy, two young noblemen, because they have not served a long apprenticeship of courtship according to the current rules of elegant behavior. The suitors dress their valets, Mascarille and Jodelet, in rich clothing, and send them to these *précieuses,* who are completely taken in by the masquerade and the high-sounding words of the valets. Madelon, Cathos, Mascarille and Jodelet spend some time discussing fine clothes and the merits of Mascarille's latest "poetic" effort. Just as they are about to start a dance, the masters suddenly come back and force the valets to take off their rich clothes.

PRECIOUS BANE (1926), by Mary Webb. Prudence Sarn, born with a harelip in the region of England north of the Shropshire meres, tells the story of her brother Gideon's lust for money and power—and the destruction he wreaks thereby—and of her own love for Kester Woodseaves, the weaver. Gideon forces his mother and sister to work for years on his farm, promising them a fine house and riches once he has made his fortune. When his mother's illness keeps her from working, he poisons her with foxglove tea. He loves Jancis Beguildy, the beautiful daughter of the Wizard Beguildy, and would have married her, but when the Wizard sets fire to his crops in anger at Gideon's seduction of her, Sarn drives her from his mind. A year later she returns to him with their small son; he drives them both from the house. Jancis drowns herself and the baby, and Gideon, haunted by her, drowns himself a few months later. Tivvy Sexton, who loved Gideon, denounces Prue at the market as the murderer of her mother, and as the crowd is setting upon her to kill her—she also is considered something of a witch because of her harelip—Kester Woodseaves, whom she once had saved from a wild dog when he had stopped a bull baiting at the fairs, rides into town and carries her away. The novel is written in a simple but richly descriptive style, presenting an honest and living picture of the English countryside in the early nineteenth century.

PREFACE TO MORALS, A (1929), by Walter Lippmann. In this examination of the moral ideas and practices of mankind, seen within the context of our complex socio-economic world, there are three divisions: Part I discusses the problems of unbelief, the breakdown of authority, and the lost provinces of business, the family, and art; Part II considers the struggle of humanism and ultramontane religion; Part III is an appeal for the abolition of moral sanctions long frozen by custom, but now anachronistic. The author endorses a realistic approach to all ethical problems, rather than loyalty to traditions or persons. In *A Preface to Politics* (1913), Lippmann had a simple liberalism and faith in the judgment of the people. His progressive distrust, however, was shown by 1922 in *Public Opinion,* a challenge to the press and the way it contrives to mold public opinion.

PREFACE TO THE "LYRICAL BALLADS," WORDSWORTH'S (1800). See DEFENCE OF POETRY, by Percy Bysshe Shelley.

PRELUDE, THE (published 1850), by William Wordsworth. In beautifully descriptive and meditative blank verse Wordsworth gives his poetical autobiography. From animal enjoyment he passes to a conscious love of nature and a belief in its divinity. Then he develops an interest in humanity and becomes aware of his mission as a poet. He goes through a period of revolutionary fervor, loses faith, despairs, and finally regains his perspective through the influence of his sister and his love of nature. The work was begun in 1791, finished in 1805, and later revised considerably.

PRESIDENTIAL AGENT (1944), by Upton Sinclair. See JUNGLE, THE, by Upton Sinclair.

PRESIDENTIAL MISSION (1947), by Upton Sinclair. See JUNGLE, THE, by Upton Sinclair.

PRIDE AND PREJUDICE (1813), by Jane Austen. Jane Austen wrote *Pride and Prejudice* when she was twenty years old. Her father, recognizing its possibilities, submitted it to a publisher, but it was rejected. However, after the publication of another of her books, it was printed; and is the most popular of her works. Mr. and Mrs. Bennet of Hertfordshire have five daughters, all of marriageable age. Because of the lack of a male heir to the Bennet estate, their property is to pass by entail to a cousin, William Collins. William enjoys the favor of the haughty Lady Catherine de Bourgh, who has bestowed on him a living near her estate in Kent. Mr. Bennet is the harassed husband who must perforce retire to his study as his only escape from a female world. His wife is wholly occupied in the business of getting her daughters suitable husbands. Mr. Bingley, a charming and kindly young man, moves to the Bennets' neighborhood, bringing with him his two sisters and Mr. Fitzwilliam Darcy, the proud and wealthy nephew of Lady Catherine. Mr. Bingley falls in love with Jane Bennet, the oldest sister, and Darcy finds himself attracted to Elizabeth, the next sister, but incurs her dislike by his unpleasant and overly-proud attitude. She is further prejudiced against him through a false story she hears from George Wickham, a young officer whose father had been one of the Darcy stewards. According to Wickham, who is a thorough scoundrel, Darcy had dealt with him in an unjust fashion. Mr. Darcy believes that Bingley would lower himself by an alliance with the Bennet family, and, with the aid of Bingley's sisters, persuades him to leave Jane. Bingley's love for Jane is not enough to blind him to the vulgar conduct of Mrs. Bennet and the younger sisters, Lydia and Mary. The garrulous Mrs. Bennet has been openly desirous of a match between Jane and Bingley. In spite of the fact that she might save the family estate, Elizabeth refuses an offer of marriage made by Mr. Collins, who therefore proposes to and is accepted by Charlotte Lucas, one of Elizabeth's friends. She invites Elizabeth to spend some time with her in Kent; while there Elizabeth meets Lady Catherine de Bourgh. Here she again sees Darcy, who proposes to her but in such an insolent manner that she angrily rejects him. She accuses him of separating Jane and Bingley, and reveals to him the story told her by Wickham, letting him see that she considers him guilty of injustice. Darcy, stung by her refusal, writes her and reminds her of the improper conduct of her mother and sisters and denies Wickham's accusations. Some time later Elizabeth takes a trip to the north of England with an aunt and uncle, and here she visits Darcy's estate, where she and her relatives meet with kind and polite treatment at his hands. Elizabeth finds herself changing her opinion of him, but receives sudden and disturbing news of Lydia's elopement with Wickham, and returns home. Darcy helps locate the two, and saves Lydia from disgrace by forcing Wickham to marry her. He also is influential in bringing Jane and Bingley together again. Elizabeth and Darcy are finally engaged. Mrs. Bennet is overjoyed by the fact that three of her daughters have made successful matches. The novel was dramatized in New York in 1935 and filmed in 1940.

PRIMITIVE CULTURE (1871), by Edward B. Tylor. The full title of this book is *Primitive Culture: Researches into the Development of Mythology, Philosophy, Religion, Art, and Custom,* and its publication raised Tylor to the first rank of British anthropologists. Coming at a time when interest in "primitive man" was taking hold, Tylor's comprehensive treatise was an attempt to put the results of many investigations and field trips into scientific form. For this purpose he utilized a number of concepts and theories which have been much criticized since his time. The assumption that "primitive" peoples of our time represent earlier stages in the development of our civilization, the concept of "survival," the tracing of religion to animism are not accepted today as Tylor conceived them. Nevertheless this was a pioneering work, and by means of it and through his teaching at Oxford Tylor influenced a long line of anthropologists.

PRINCE, THE (1513), by Niccolò Machiavelli. A handbook of advice on the acquisition, use, and maintenance of political power, dedicated to Lorenzo de Medici by the Florentine Machiavelli, once active in government, but at the time of writing out of favor. Rules are set down for governing the various kinds of monarchies as well as conquered territory. Methods for insuring military strength are proposed. The young Prince is advised, further, in such matters as the type of personal behavior which will gain him respect without incurring hatred; whom to trust; how to make his ministers competent and faithful; how to be prepared for changes of fortune. The final chapter is an exhortation to liberate Italy from the barbarians. Although written in the formal style of the time, this book maintains an attitude of realism in government and politics. The Prince is urged to make the interests of his subjects his own. However, expediency is the standard for the conduct of a ruler, and "what ought to be" is rejected for "what is." Great importance, moreover, is attached to centralization of power, which Machiavelli saw as an aid to the unification of the Italian city-states. This, in turn, would result in the ending of internecine strife, expulsion of invaders, and enjoyment of the benefits of trade. Therein lay the germs of the nation-state of the modern Western world.

PRINCE AND THE PAUPER, THE (1882), by Mark Twain. See TOM SAWYER, THE ADVENTURES OF, by Mark Twain.

PRINCE LOUIS FERDINAND (1913), by Fritz von Unruh. See UNRUH, FRITZ VON.

PRINCE OF HOMBURG (1810), by Heinrich von Kleist. See KLEIST, HEINRICH VON.

PRINCE OF INDIA, THE (1893), by Lew Wallace. See BEN HUR, by Lew Wallace.

PRINCESS, THE (1847), by Alfred Tennyson. This blank-verse narrative poem is composed of seven parts of a continuing story, supposed to have been told by as many different men, with lyrics by the ladies between the parts. The tale itself is fantastic, with elements of classical, medieval, and modern thought. It concerns the efforts of Princess Ida to establish a college for women only, its invasion by three men, the ultimate straightening out of all difficulties, and the abandoning of the idea. The poem is richly colorful and melodious; the verse, smooth; the imagery, delightful. The interspersed lyrics (eg., "The Splendor Falls on Castle Walls" and "Sweet and Low") are among Tennyson's best. It is the basis for Gilbert and Sullivan's operetta, *Princess Ida.*

PRINCESS OF CLEVES, THE (1677), by Madame de Lafayette. In this brief novel there is little action, but much discussion of motives. A noble lady of the court of Henry II discovers that she has fallen in love with the distinguished Count de Nemours. After long consideration she tells her husband what has happened and asks for his aid. Assuming that this can only mean that he has been betrayed, the husband is so grief-stricken that, in spite of his wife's assurances, he dies. The princess is now free to accept the lover of her choice, but after further soul searching decides against this course and devotes the remainder of her life to good works. The interest of the piece is in the workings of an aristocratic mind under great stress; in Madame de Cleves' great self-control in moments of high emotion French readers see what they call "Corneillian" sublimity. The kind of psychological analysis exploited in this novel has been a favorite ingredient in French fiction from the seventeenth century to the present.

PRINCIPIA (1867), by Sir Isaac Newton. See PHILOSOPHIAE NATURALIS PRINCIPIA MATHEMATICA, by Sir Isaac Newton.

PRINCIPIA MATHEMATICA (1910–1913), by Bertrand Russell and Alfred North Whitehead. This three-volume treatise is a most important work in the history of symbolic logic and the foundations of mathematics. Its major purpose is to show that mathematical concepts are all capable of formulation in purely logical terms. In the course of this work, Russell and Whitehead made many signal contributions to the techniques of symbolic logic. No book for the layman, this is required reading for logicians and analytical philosophers.

PRINCIPLES, by Archimedes. See ARCHIMEDES.

PRINCIPLES OF GEOLOGY (1830–1833), by Sir Charles Lyell. See ANTIQUITY OF MAN, by Sir Charles Lyell.

PRINCIPLES OF HUMAN KNOWLEDGE, THE (1710), by George Berkeley. Berkeley's theory of knowledge is the result of a critique and elaboration of the views presented by Locke in his *Essay Concerning Human Understanding* (q.v.). Berkeley argues that all the reasons used to show that secondary qualities (colors, smells, etc.) exist only as ideas in the mind can also be applied to the primary qualities (solidity, extension, figure, etc.) which Locke had averred exist in matter. If the distinction between primary and secondary qualities is denied and all qualities are held to be secondary qualities, then matter becomes an unnecessary addendum to the theory of knowledge. Thus for Berkeley all reality is mental. However, this raises other problems. If objects depend for their existence on a perceiver, must we say that objects cease to exist when no one perceives them? Berkeley avoids this solipsistic consequence by asserting that God continually perceives all objects, so that all things continue to exist even if no human perceiver is present. This latter point was subsequently challenged by Hume. Berkeley also developed these views in a more popular form in his *Three Dialogues Between Hylas and Philonous* (1713).

PRINCIPLES OF POLITICAL ECONOMY AND TAXATION (1817), by David Ricardo. By profession a broker who became independently wealthy at the age of twenty-five, Ricardo devoted much of his life to the study of economic problems. Adam Smith and Malthus influenced him strongly. He is best known for his theory of rent, which asserted that the price of commodities determines rent, and it is not rent that determines prices. His Iron Law of Wages (that in general wages will not rise above the level of bare subsistence) helped to fasten on economics the description of "dismal science." He also formulated a labor theory of value which made the value of a product dependent on the amount of labor expended on it. Many of his ideas were taken over by Marx and used to support socialist theory, though in general he is in the main line of classical economists. He was associated with the Philosophical Radicals, and J. S. Mill's *Principles of Political Economy*, the standard economics text in the second half of the nineteenth century, was a reworking and elaboration of the principles of Ricardo.

PRINCIPLES OF PSYCHOLOGY (1890), by William James. See JAMES, WILLIAM.

PRISONER OF CHILLON, THE (1816), by George Gordon, Lord Byron. The dungeon of Chillon was on Lake Geneva, and there the historical Swiss patriot Bonnivard was imprisoned for years because he resisted tyranny. This poem in octosyllabics tells the story of his imprisonment—how the three brothers were chained together in utter darkness, how first the middle brother and then the youngest pined away and died and were buried on the spot. The survivor wanted to die and could not. One day he is given false hope by the song of a bird. Later his keepers allow him to walk about his cell, and he is able to glimpse the mountains through the bars after climbing the high wall. At last he is rescued, and almost regrets leaving, so familiar has his horrible dwelling become—the heavy walls, the spiders, the mice, the chains.

PRISONER OF ZENDA, THE (1894), by Anthony Hope. Rudolf Rassendyll, an Englishman, makes a three months' visit to the kingdom of Ruritania. He arrives on the eve of the coronation of King Rudolf. The King has an enemy in his brother, Duke Michael, who aspires to the throne himself. During the festivities at Zenda Castle, the Duke drugs King Rudolf so that he is unable to attend his own coronation. Later, Rassendyll, aided by Colonel Sapt, Fritz von Tarlenheim, and Antoinette de Mauban, the Duke's jealous sweetheart, succeeds in impersonating the King and is crowned in his stead. In the meantime, Princess Flavia, the king's betrothed, falls in love with Rassendyll, who in turn loves her. After many dramatic and dangerous escapades, duels, and intrigues King Rudolf is rescued from Zenda Castle where he is held prisoner by Duke Michael. Rassendyll and Princess Flavia renounce each other when the King is restored, and Rassendyll returns to England. The story has been dramatized, and was filmed in 1913, 1922, and 1937.

PRIVATE LIFE OF THE MASTER RACE (1944), by Bertolt Brecht. See BRECHT, BERTOLT.

PRIVATE PAPERS OF HENRY RYECROFT, THE (1903), by George Gissing. The first part of the book is a preface, a short "biography" of "Henry Ryecroft" and an account of the supposed finding of his diary, which Gissing decides to publish. Ryecroft, a struggling author, is bequeathed an annuity by an acquaintance. He leaves London and retires to a cottage at Exeter to enjoy a contemplative life. "Spring," "Summer," "Autumn," "Winter" are the four parts of the diary, in which we learn of the author's likes and dislikes, his everyday doings, his ideas of life, food, books, art, philosophy, nature, his childhood, and England. Each section follows the mood of the season. In the last, "Winter," we find Ryecroft lonely but feeling that he has lived a rounded life and looking tranquilly toward his last hour. The book, very quiet and contemplative, is a mirror of Gissing's personal moods and opinions.

PROCESS AND REALITY (1929), by Alfred North Whitehead. See WHITEHEAD, ALFRED NORTH.

PROFESSOR AT THE BREAKFAST-TABLE, THE (1860), by Oliver Wendell Holmes. See AUTOCRAT OF THE BREAKFAST-TABLE, THE, by Oliver Wendell Holmes.

PROFESSOR BERNHARDI (1912), by Arthur Schnitzler. See SCHNITZLER, ARTHUR.

PROFESSOR'S HOUSE, THE (1925), by Willa Cather. See CATHER, WILLA.

PROGRESS AND POVERTY (1879), by Henry George. George argues that wealth is the product of human labor, but that the land, paraphrasing the Mosaic law, belongs to God. Land values are not determined by any act of the owners but by increased population pressure. Monopoly of land appropriates "unearned increment of value," and keeps the common man poor and dependent. As the population grows, monopoly grows—then poverty increases and labor becomes helpless. A single tax derived from land, claimed George, would be ample to run the governmental machine. With such a tax everyone, presumably, would have equal opportunity; access to natural resources would be easier for society; employment would be ample; economic crises would be eliminated. The Single Tax movement grew out of this book.

PROGRESS OF THE HUMAN MIND, by Condorcet. See SKETCH OF AN HISTORICAL PICTURE OF THE PROGRESS OF THE HUMAN MIND, by Condorcet.

PROMETHEUS (1797), by Vincenzo Monti. See MONTI, VINCENZO.

PROMETHEUS BOUND (478 B.C.?), by Aeschylus. This tragedy is one of a trilogy of which the other two, *Prometheus Unbound* and *Prometheus Firebringer,* are lost. Prometheus was one of the Titans who had helped establish Zeus in his supremacy. Then the ruler of the gods, harsh and tyrannical in his new-found power, designed to destroy mankind and create a better race, but Prometheus defied his will, saved man and taught him all useful arts. This Zeus could not forgive. When the play opens, Prometheus is being brought to a rocky solitude high in the Caucasus and chained to a cliff, but he is not bowed by his punishment. The chorus of Oceanides, sea nymphs, come flying through the air to comfort him. To them he tells how he had aided Zeus and the reason for his punishment. He tells them too that one day Zeus will be obliged to call on him for help, but that he will not reveal the secret of Zeus' salvation until he is released. Then Oceanus, father of the nymphs, arrives in his chariot drawn by winged steeds. The proud Prometheus wants none of his pity nor of his council of prudence and submission. The next to come before the unrepentant Titan is Io, another victim of Zeus' heartlessness, a maiden of Argos who had found favor in Zeus' eye but was now changed into a cow and driven by the sting of a gadfly to wander the world over. To her Prometheus foretells the tribulations that still await her, and that finally she will be restored to her own form and bear offspring to Zeus, a line from which eventually shall come the hero who will free him from this rock where he is chained. Now word of Prometheus' contumacy and of his vaunted secret have reached Zeus' ears, and he sends Hermes to learn it from him. This messenger of Zeus the Titan also turns away with scornful words. Despite the threats of Zeus that an eagle shall be sent to prey upon his vitals, Prometheus remains adamant. Till the last he stands undismayed as the thunderbolt of Zeus blasts and smashes the crags all about him. The true significance of the play as Aeschylus intended it to be understood must remain a riddle so long as we do not have the final play of the trilogy wherein the resolution was presented.

PROMETHEUS UNBOUND (1820), by Percy Bysshe Shelley. A lyrical drama in four acts, this profound but often obscure philosophical poem reveals Shelley's virtuosity in the perfection of many different verse forms. Prometheus is both an ideal and an allegorical representative of man's desire for intellectual fulfillment and spiritual liberty. Chained to a rock, he is threatened and tortured by Jupiter, or Despotism. He is supported by his mother, Earth, and sustained by the thought of his bride, Asia, Spirit of Nature. When Prometheus renounces hatred and revenge and accepts eternal Love, his unshackling begins. Jupiter is dethroned by Demogorgon, the Spirit of Necessity, or Eternity, and Prometheus is released by Hercules. The final act, added as an afterthought, offers a sanguine view of future man, "sceptreless, free, uncircumscribed," and "unclassed, tribeless . . . nationless" —man finally "the king over himself."

PROMISED LAND (Eng. tr. 1927), by Wladyslaw St. Reymont. See PEASANTS, THE, by Wladyslaw St. Reymont.

PROMISED LAND, THE (1891–1895), by Henrik Pontoppidan. See LUCKY PER, by Henrik Pontoppidan.

PROPHET, THE (1923), by Kahlil Gibran. Consisting of twenty-eight prose poems or preachments by "The Prophet," who calls himself "Prophet of God, in quest of the uttermost . . . ," this work is composed in the highly embroidered style common to Near-Eastern literature. Its tone is lofty, its ideas vague, resplendent in glittering metaphor and lush imagery. The prose poems have the following titles: "The Coming of the Ship," "Love," "Marriage," "Children," "Giving," "Eating and Drinking," "Work," "Joy and Sorrow," "Houses," "Clothes," "Buying and Selling," "Crime and Punishment," "Freedom," "Reason and Passion," "Pain," "Self-Knowledge," "Teaching," "Friendship," "Talking," "Time," "Good and Evil," "Prayer," "Pleasure," "Beauty," "Religion," "Death" and "The Farewell."

PROSE EDDA, THE (ca. 1215), by Snorri Sturluson. This is a textbook for skaldic poets, written in Iceland and published in Copenhagen in the original Icelandic, with Latin and Danish interpretations, in 1665. The highly artificial Scandinavian skaldic poetry was very popular in Northern Europe, especially at the courts, during the early Middle Ages, and young skalds needed a guide; Snorri furnished one. It deals with both subject matter and form. The Icelanders, though Christians at this time, had a keen historical sense, and felt it a duty to preserve the national traditions of heroic deeds and the old heathen religion. Aspiring young poets must know the necessary background. Consequently, prefaced by a prologue containing a summary of the

Biblical story of the Creation and Deluge, the work then gives a *"rationalized* account of the rise of the ancient pagan faith, according to which the old gods appear, not as deities, but as men." The handbook proper has three divisions: first, the "Beguiling of Gylfi," an "epitome of Odinic mythology, cast in the form of a dialogue between Gylfi, a legendary Swedish king, and the triune Odin." This part supplies the required heathen pattern, and is primarily based on the Eddic poems. The two remaining sections discuss the rules of composition, metaphorical expressions, and meter, the latter being exceedingly complex and needing all the explanation that the author could give. "Each of the hundred and two stanzas of the work," says an authority, "belongs to a distinct metric type or subtype; and between stanzas Snorri has inserted definitions, occasionally longer notes, or comments." The book contains some fascinating tales, and concludes with a mythological account of the skaldic art.

PROTHALAMION (1596), by Edmund Spenser. This "spousall verse" celebrates the double marriage of the two daughters of the Earl of Worcester. Evidently the party proceeded up the Thames in barges to London; the brides-to-be are compared to two white swans. Each stanza ends with the couplet:

> "Against the brydale day, which is not long:
> Sweete Themmes, runne softly, till I end my song."

The "noble victory" of the Earl of Essex at Cadiz is commended, since he is the host on this occasion.

PROVINCIAL LETTERS (1656–1657), by Blaise Pascal. These eighteen letters originated in a theological dispute over the nature of Grace. The Jansenists believed in predestination; a coalition, led by the Jesuits and Dominicans, attacked their doctrines first in the Sorbonne and then in Rome, gradually winning over a majority of theologians to a view which allowed for the possibility of free will. At this point the Jansenists could only carry their cause to the public, and enlisted the brilliant Pascal as their advocate. Appearing one at a time, the *Letters* exposed the issues of the dispute, argued the rightness of the Jansenist position, and flayed the Jesuits—all to the great delight of a lay audience which was at least as ready to applaud vigorous writing as to espouse correct theology. Pascal's brilliant prose is said to have set the standard at which French writers have aimed ever since. But the Jesuits eventually won their point and the Jansenist views were condemned as heretical.

PRUFROCK AND OTHER OBSERVATIONS (1917), by T. S. Eliot. See ELIOT, THOMAS STEARNS.

PSYCHOLOGY, by Avicenna. See AVICENNA.

PSYCHOPATHOLOGY OF EVERYDAY LIFE (1904; Eng. tr. 1914), by Sigmund Freud. See FREUD, SIGMUND.

PUBLIC OPINION (1922), by Walter Lippmann. See PREFACE TO MORALS, by Walter Lippmann.

PUCELLE, THE (1762), by Voltaire. The full title of this poetic work is *Lu Pucelle d'Orléans*. It deals irreverently with Jeanne d'Arc. The story of the national heroine of France is merely a pretext on which to hang the most impossible, diverting incidents, drolleries, railleries, and buffooneries. Voltaire was fully aware that if he was to convey his social, philosophic, antiprivilege and anticlerical message he would first have to win and hold the attention of people. To do so, he presented his serious ideas in hilarious, Rabelaisian form. The book was popular, despite the disfavor of the Royal Court and the anathemas of the Church. Voltaire had outwitted them, and to this very day is unforgiven by religious circles in France.

The work is dazzling in its quips, epigrams, ironies and *doubles entendres*, full of rollicking humor and of the spirit of eighteenth century sophistication.

PURCHAS, HIS PILGRIMS (1625), by Samuel Purchas. Purchas, a London minister, carried on where Hakluyt left off, in compiling this interesting anthology from letters and accounts of over thirteen hundred travelers, who tell in their own words the English ideas current in the early part of the seventeenth century concerning travel in Europe, Africa, Asia and America. The work includes maps, inaccurate now of course, but interesting indications of the notions of the time. The work, originally in four volumes, is a rich storehouse of source material on early exploration by sea and land.

PURITY (ca. 1370). See PEARL.

PURPLE LAND, THE (1885), by William Henry Hudson. The land that lies between Buenos Aires and Montevideo is the exotic setting for Hudson's first novel. This beautiful country, called the Banda Oriental, was inhabited by half-sophisticated, half-wild Spaniards and Indians. Richard Lamb, an Englishman traveling through this dangerous country, is the hero of a pseudo-Gothic story of mystery and romance. Narrow escapes, both in love and in battle, provide the suspense. Besides his beautiful wife, seven other lovely women provide diversion for the lone traveler, as do also some villains. More important than the story of Richard Lamb, however, is Hudson's portrayal of the beauty of nature and the romance of native customs in a strange land.

PUSS IN BOOTS (1797), by Ludwig Tieck. See TIECK, LUDWIG.

PYGMALION (1912), by George Bernard Shaw. Henry Higgins, an eccentric Professor of Phonetics, hears Liza Doolittle, a cockney flower girl, speak with an atrocious accent. He makes notes on her speech, Liza and the bystanders taking him to be a policeman. In the crowd is Colonel Pickering, retired India officer, an authority on Indian dialects, who has come to London especially to meet Professor Higgins. Pickering gives Liza a handful of money to stop her whining, and she leaves. However, she has heard Higgins say that in three months he could pass her off as a duchess, so the next morning she taxis to his house on Wimpole Street in order to take voice lessons. Pickering bets Higgins all the expenses of Liza's training that he cannot do it. Higgins flatters, cajoles, and threatens her by turns, and finally wins her acceptance of the plan. Alfred Doolittle, her father, a rascally dustman, calls to see what has become of his daughter, but Higgins buys him off with five pounds. After a period of rigorous training, Liza is sent off to Higgins' mother's home in Chelsea. When she arrives Mrs. Eynsford Hill, her son,

Freddy, and daughter, Clara, are calling. Liza, beautifully gowned and speaking with pedantic correctness, sticks to her two topics, the weather and people's health. She gives Freddy a studied account of the former, and his mother a vivid report of her aunt's "doin' in." The Eynsford Hills are enchanted with what they believe to be a new kind of small talk. Finally Higgins presents Liza at a garden party and wins his bet from Pickering. The two men discuss her so coldly and scientifically that Liza is roused to fury. She throws Higgins' slippers in his face and demands to know what he plans to do with her now. She then takes refuge with Mrs. Higgins, who berates her son for his lack of consideration. Liza is in love with Higgins. When he shows up at her mother's house and asks her to return home with him, they quarrel a little, but the audience gets the impression that he will never let her go, even though they do not marry. In his preface to the play, Shaw explains that Liza and Higgins will not marry. In 1939 *Pygmalion* became the first Shaw play to be filmed.

PYUNGKEJIP, by Yun Pongku. See SHIJO-YUCHIP.

QUADRATURE OF THE PARABOLA, by Archimedes. See ARCHIMEDES.

QUALITY STREET (1902), by Sir James M. Barrie. See BARRIE, SIR JAMES MATTHEW.

QUEEN VICTORIA (1921), by Lytton Strachey. The story of the very womanly woman who was also a queen is told in this biography, which opens with Victoria's family origins and childhood and follows her through marriage, widowhood, old age, and the vicissitudes of a sixty-four-year reign. Strachey does not idealize his subject. He attempts to present her as she was, as evidenced by her words and acts, and emphasizes the interaction of circumstance and character. Victoria is shown as a ruler who was unaware of the economic, social, scientific, and constitutional changes going on about her, but who—with her solid domestic virtues, respect for power and property, and persistent vitality—became a fitting symbol of Britain's imperial greatness, wealth and security. She is shown, above all, as a human being—proud of her place, ingenuous, courageous, highly emotional, respectable yet attracted by the colorful and strange, intellectually limited, essentially female, and possessed of a sincerity underlying the whole.

QUENTIN DURWARD (1823), by Sir Walter Scott. The scene of the novel is France in 1468, when the feud between the crafty King Louis XI and his most powerful vassal Charles the Bold, Duke of Burgundy, was at its height. Quentin Durward, a young Scot, has come to France to seek his fortune. He impresses King Louis, and is employed by him to escort the beautiful Countess Isabelle de Croye to the castle of the bishop of Liége. The secret plan is that the villainous William de la Marck, the Wild Boar of the Ardennes, will attack the party and carry off Isabelle, who had formerly been protected by the Duke of Burgundy. But Quentin succeeds in foiling this plot, though there is trouble after they reach the castle, for William besieges it and murders the bishop. Quentin and Isabelle escape to Burgundy, only to find that the treacherous king pays a bold visit to Charles and effects a temporary reconciliation. It is agreed that Isabelle shall be the prize of whoever conquers de la Marck. Quentin finally gets credit for this and marries Isabelle.

QUEST FOR CERTAINTY, THE (1929), by John Dewey. See DEWEY, JOHN.

QUESTIONS AND ANSWERS ON GENESIS AND EXODUS, by Philo Judaeus. See PHILO JUDAEUS.

QUINCAS BORA (1892), by Joaquim Maria Machado de Assis. See DOM CASMURRO, by Joaquim Maria Machado de Assis.

QUO VADIMUS? (1939), by E. B. White. See WHITE, E. B.

QUO VADIS? (1896), by Henryk Sienkiewicz. *Quo Vadis?* is without doubt the most widely read Polish novel; it has been reprinted oftener in all languages of Europe than any other similar work, and through half a century won a definite place in world literature in the broadest sense. It is based on the life of the early Christians in Rome during the time of the Emperor Nero. The heroine Ligia, the ideal of a Romantic heroine, is a Christian, but in love with a Roman tribune, Vinicius, who is a pagan and a relative of the arbiter elegentiae, Petronius. Ligia visits his palace, but is rescued from its orgies by her faithful servant, Ursus, a simple-minded but devoted man of enormous physical strength, and hidden by him among the Christians. Vinicius pursues her, but again Ursus prevents him from carrying her away. In the effort Vinicius is wounded, but is cared for by the Christians and finally accepts their faith. Later he endeavors to rescue Ligia from burning Rome. Ligia, as a Christian, is captured and carried into the arena tied to the horns of a wild bull. Here Ursus, likewise condemned to martyrdom, kills the bull with his bare hands by grasping its horns and breaking its neck. Thrilled by the exploit, the spectators demand the release of both Ligia and Ursus, and the story ends with the happy reunion of Ligia and her beloved Vinicius. The thrilling scenes and the pictures of the ancient world and of St. Peter take precedence over the psychological development of the characters. In his own way, Sienkiewicz presents a plea for his native Poland, for the Ligi were a tribe mentioned by Tacitus as inhabiting the area of modern Poland. The novel shows a rare combination of real erudition and of narrative skill.

RAABE, WILHELM (1831–1910). Though a prolific writer, Raabe is appreciated mostly for a small part of his literary output. It was his idyl, *The Chronicle of Sparrow Street* (1857), which gained fame for him. Here he pictures the world of the "Kleinbürger," the petty bourgeoisie. The best-known among his other works are the novels *The Hunger Pastor* (1864), a story of two boys, one seeking power and wealth and the other the ideal of clerical life; *Abu Telfan* (1865–1867), and *The Schüdderump* (1867–1869). He calls the ideal of soul and feeling into the world of reality. Despite an attachment to an earlier Romanticism, Raabe includes elements of the realistic style. His chief significance lies in, the fact that he is a forerunner of a later school of more pronounced realism.

RAB AND HIS FRIENDS (1858), by John Brown. This sentimental tale is based on an incident which had happened to the author and his friend Bob Ainslie during their boyhood days. One day they were interested spectators at a fight between a small bull-terrier and Rab, a huge brindled mastiff. Thirsting for blood and emboldened by the fact that the larger dog was muzzled, the terrier fastened his teeth in his throat. Bob then came to the rescue and cut the mastiff's muzzle with his knife. Rab seized the terrier and broke its back. Six years later, when the author was interning at Minto House Hospital, Rab's owner, James Noble, brought his wife, Ailie, to the hospital. Dog and master faithfully stood by during the critical hours of her operation. When Ailie died, her husband went out of his mind with grief. Rab was given away, and his new owner killed him because he resisted orders.

RABBLE IN ARMS (1933), by Kenneth Roberts. See NORTHWEST PASSAGE, by Kenneth Roberts.

RABDOLOGIA (published posthumously 1617), by John Napier, Baron of Merchiston. See MIRIFICI LOGARITHMORUM CANONIS CONSTRUCTIO, by John Napier, Baron of Merchiston.

RACE, LANGUAGE, AND CULTURE (1940), by Franz Boas. See MIND OF PRIMITIVE MAN, THE, by Franz Boas.

RACHEL (1891), by Hviezdoslav. See HVIEZDOSLAV.

RADIOACTIVE SUBSTANCES AND THEIR RADIATIONS (1913), by Ernest, Lord Rutherford. See NEWER ALCHEMY, THE, by Ernest, Lord Rutherford.

RADIOACTIVITY (1904), by Ernest, Lord Rutherford. See NEWER ALCHEMY, THE, by Ernest, Lord Rutherford.

RAGE TO LIVE, A (1949), by John O'Hara. See APPOINTMENT IN SAMARRA, by John O'Hara.

RAGGED DICK (1867 ff.), by Horatio Alger, Jr. See ALGER, HORATIO, JR.

RALPH ROISTER DOISTER (ca. 1553), by Nicholas Udall. The earliest English comedy, modeled after Plautus and Terence, was probably written to be performed by schoolboys. The plot is simple, full of horseplay, and the characters elementary. The play is adjusted to its original performance in a great hall. The scene opens in front of the house of Dame Christian Custance, a wealthy widow. Ralph Roister Doister, a conceited numskull, wishes to woo her but has not the courage to do so unaided. He consults his friend, a clever parasite, Matthew Merrygreek, who promises to help him. Dame Custance is annoyed at Roister Doister's attentions, as she is affianced to Gawyn Goodluck, who is away on a journey and who on his return hears she is about to marry another man. Merrygreek and the Dame plot to have sport with Roister Doister. Urged on by his false friend, the latter tries to take her by storm, and he and his servants are routed by her and her maids.

Technically an interlude rather than a comedy is *The Four PP* (ca. 1533), by John Heywood, named for the quartet of characters in it. The Palmer, the Pardoner, and the 'Pothecary take turns displaying their skill as liars, while the Pedlar acts as judge. The Pardoner wins when he says he has known five hundred thousand women, and not one out of all this half million did he ever see "out of patience."

RAMAYANA, THE (ca. 1000 B.C.). *The Mahabharata* (q.v.) and *The Ramayana* form the epic literature of India. Unlike the former poem, which treats of heroes and battle and struggle for power, *The Ramayana* mirrors the gentle domestic life of ancient India. It may have been written by a single poet in its final version, but like all epics must have grown through the centuries. It is assumed that the epic poem began about 1000 B.C. and that it was completed in the form we know several centuries before the Christian era. The work consists of six books and a supplemental book, and contains 500 cantos and 24,000 couplets. The civilization it delineates is obviously one its authors, looking nostalgically back, regarded as belonging to the Golden Age when men were wise and strong and women were faithful and virtuous. The hero Rama, who is heir to the throne of the Videhas, is an ideal prince, valorous in war but goodness itself in peace. The King of the Videhas is a saint. His daughter Sita, with whom Rama is in love, is the Indian ideal of womanhood.

The Ramayana has been compared to the *Odyssey* (q.v.), but it is a far gentler poem, full of haunting music and subtle fragrances. It represents the spirit of India—even of the India of today.

RAMEAU'S NEPHEW (1821), by Denis Diderot. See DIDEROT, DENIS.

RAMONA (1884), by Helen Hunt Jackson. Ramona Ortegna, a maiden having (unknown to herself) Indian ancestry, is reared as a member of the patriarchal Moreno family, who are trying to hold their estate in spite of American conquests. Their heir, Felipe, falls in love with her, but conceals it from Ramona and from his mother, the aged Señora, who alone knows the secret of Ramona's origin. Ramona marries, out of her caste, the simple Indian peasant Alessandro, and elopes with him to San Diego. Shortly after, he is killed following persecution by the advancing Americans. At the lowest ebb of her fortunes, her foster-brother Filipe comes to the rescue of Ramona and her child. Scorning the "stigma" of her Indian blood, he marries her. When their estate is lost, they go to Mexico. A passionate defense of the Indian, this novel is often compared with the plea for the Negro in *Uncle Tom's Cabin* (q.v.). It enjoyed an almost equally spectacular popularity. The Los Angeles locale of *Ramona,* which its enthusiasts claim to be a completely historical account, has become a Mecca for tourists.

RAPE OF LUCRECE, THE (1594), by William Shakespeare. Published only a year after *Venus and Adonis* (q.v.), *The Rape of Lucrece* is the poetic, sober answer to those who had thought the first poem too light and lascivious. The passions in *Venus and Adonis* are the impulse of the moment, and youthful in their abandon; those in *Lucrece* are serious and mature. Each phase of emotion is analyzed in detail, and the story works up from a simple start with a gradual crescendo of horror to its tragic climax. Collatine, husband of Lucrece, away at the wars, had boasted of her virtue and beauty. Sextus, the son of King Tarquin, is roused to the height of lustful passion. In the guise of friendship he visits Collatine's house, and is graciously received by the unsuspecting Lucrece. He comes to her chamber at the dead of night, and threatens to kill her and one of her grooms unless she yields to him. He departs at dawn, and the miserable Lucrece sends an urgent message to her husband begging him to return. He arrives with a company of friends, and she greets them dressed in mourning. After making them all promise to revenge her, she reveals Tarquin's treachery, and stabs herself. Shakespeare dedicated this work to Henry Wriothesley, Earl of Southampton. It is written in seven-line stanzas, called rhyme royal.

RAPE OF THE LOCK, THE (1714), by Alexander Pope. This mock epic, written in polished heroic couplets, contains 814 lines of finished verse. Based on an actual quarrel arising from the theft of a lock of hair by a young gallant of the day, the poem was originally intended to settle the quarrel through friendly ridicule. Pope describes Belinda's beauty preparations, her trip to Hampton Court, the game of cards, the rape of the lock as Belinda is sipping coffee, and Belinda's wrath. The attending spirits are distressed, and the problem is finally solved when the lock floats to heaven to become a new star.

RASHI (Rabbi Solomon ben Isaac. 1040–1105). Born in Troyes, France, Rashi is noted for his vast commentaries on the Old Testament and *Talmud* (q.v.), without which much of the text would be difficult to understand. After many years of study in other places, he returned to Troyes at 25. Since rabbis then received no salary, he supported himself by cultivating a vineyard, and opening a rabbinical academy. He seems to have learned foreign tongues from his students from other lands, and his comments are marked by words in Old French, German and the Slavonic languages. Though there were commentators before him, and hundreds have arisen since, no others displayed the terseness, the clarity, and the facility of expounding obscurities that he demonstrated. Rashi's commentary on the *Talmud* remains to the present day a requisite text for students and scholars; it is always printed alongside the Talmudic text. It translates difficult Aramaic words (this language was the vernacular when the *Talmud* was developed) into the better known Hebrew, and when necessary into French. The *Bible* (q.v.) commentary is not as rational as that on the *Talmud,* for it contains many homilies, legends, and similar supplementary material which the writer no doubt recalled from intensive study of the *Midrash,* the tremendous homiletic collections enjoyed and employed by Jewish preachers. All Jewish students of the *Bible* were expected to peruse Rashi's commentary as well, for full understanding of the text. Hebrew Bibles were printed with Rashi; and in fact the Rashi *Bible Commentary* was the first Hebrew book ever to be printed. The influence of this outstanding scholar extended throughout Europe. An unusual incident is the manner in which he indirectly affected Christian scholarship. Luther, not a good Hebraist, when translating the *Bible* into German, employed a work by Nicolas de Lyre, a French monk; in writing his own work, Nicolas had made copious use of Rashi's commentary.

RASSELAS, PRINCE OF ABYSSINIA, THE HISTORY OF (1759), by Samuel Johnson. A philosophical romance, this is the nearest to a novel that Johnson ever wrote. The story revolves around the Prince of Abyssinia's search for happiness. He and Imlac, an Eastern sage, dig their way out of the Happy Valley, where the children of the Emperor are confined. Nekayah, his sister, and Pekuah, her companion, accompany them. From Suez to Cairo they travel in search of what men call happiness. They visit all types of men;

find that no one is happy. At the pyramids, Pekuah is kidnaped by Arabs. On her return, the three have decided what would bring them complete happiness: Pekuah, a convent; Nekayah, knowledge; the Prince, a little kingdom where he can administer justice. All know they will never obtain these things, so they journey back home.

RATIONALE OF VERSE (1843), by Edgar Allan Poe. See POE, EDGAR ALLAN.

RAW YOUTH, A (1875), by Feodor Dostoevsky. Of all Dostoevsky's major novels, *A Raw Youth,* by common critical consent, is generally accorded the lowest place. The failure is partly attributed to the fact that in the writing of it for a periodical which held political opinions diametrically opposed to his own, Dostoevsky's genius suffered restraint and was unable to give full sway to its expression. It is the only novel of his which lacks the urge of a compelling idea to give it coherence and unity. Dostoevsky has written no novel more formless than this. The theme of *A Raw Youth* is the relation of an illegitimate son to society and to his father. The hero, Arkady Dolgoruky, has an idea of becoming a Rothschild by self-denial and persistent accumulation of money. Only second in importance to the hero is Versilov, the father, who, it is evident from Dostoevsky's notebooks, simmered in the author's mind for three decades before finding expression on paper. He is an echo of other Dostoevsky characters, notably the hero of *The Double,* of Prince Valkovsky in *The Insulted and Injured,* and of Velchaninov in *The Eternal Husband* (q.v.); but compared to them he is unformed and incoherent. The father and son, though they appear in powerful scenes, for the most part talk and act incomprehensibly. The plot itself is inordinately confusing; the action is dictated by a letter which alternately supplies now the son, then the father, with the opportunity to blackmail the woman whom they both love. Still another mysterious letter gives the son a chance to blackmail his father. Fortunately what gives interest to this novel is not the confused plot, which because of its particularly long list of characters it is impossible to convey, but its quality as a psychological study of the duality of human nature, in many aspects of which Dostoevsky had forestalled modern psychologists. It excels as a study of the subconscious.

RAYS OF THE MICROCOSM (1845), by Petar Petrovich Nyegosh. See MOUNTAIN WREATH, THE, by Petar Petrovich Nyegosh.

REBECCA (1938), by Daphne du Maurier. This novel of the 1930's is laid at the estate of Manderley in the south of England. The second Mrs. Maxim de Winter tells her own story. She is a shy person who arrives at Manderley shortly after her marriage, to find it haunted by the memory of Maxim's first wife, the beautiful and charming Rebecca. The narrator at first feels that her husband's love is still concentrated on his dead wife, but various disturbing discoveries slowly alter her opinion. She comes to realize that it is not love but hate and guilt which fill her husband's thoughts. Rebecca's death appeared to be accidental. Apparently she had drowned when sailing. But when the sailboat and her body are located in a nearby bay some time after Maxim's second marriage, Maxim confesses to his wife that he had murdered Rebecca because she had taunted him with her unfaithfulness and had announced that her coming child was not his. Jack Fevell, a former favorite of Rebecca's, discovers that something is amiss and threatens blackmail. Maxim and his wife go to a nearby town to consult Dr. Baker, Rebecca's physician, and learn that his report confirms suicidal death, because of cancer. Maxim realizes that Rebecca wanted to be murdered rather than face pain. The story of a coming child was a falsehood. The narrator and her husband start back to Manderley, but on arrival they find the place in flames. Mrs. Danvers, the cruel housekeeper, perishes, and all the tragic memories of Manderley are destroyed. The novel became a successful film.

REBECCA OF SUNNYBROOK FARM (1903), by Kate Douglas Wiggin. Rebecca Randall is a "blithe youth incarnate"; a lovable, buoyant individual who spreads joy all about her. The novel is a tenuous chronicle of Rebecca's lovableness as revealed during her sojourn at Sunnybrook Farm, where she has gone to live with her Aunt Miranda. Rebecca makes a host of friends there, and when Aunt Miranda dies, she leaves Sunnybrook to the girl.

REBELLION IN THE BACKLANDS (1902), by Euclydes da Cunha. What Sarmiento's *Facundo* (q.v.) did for Argentina, Euclydes da Cunha's *Os Sertões* did for Brazil. Although a large part of *Os Sertões* is devoted to a retelling of the uprising led by a historical figure, the fanatic Antônio Conselheiro (the subject of R. B. Cunningham-Graham's *A Brazilian Mystic*), it is not merely a literary work but a powerful study of the backlands of northern Brazil—landscape, geography, geology, fauna and flora, ethnological types—of interest to geographers, sociologists and anthropologists. An engaging masterpiece for its scientific observation and artistic spontaneity, *Os Sertões* is commonly regarded as the greatest of Brazilian classics.

RECOLLECTIONS OF SOCRATES, by Xenophon. See MEMORABILIA, by Xenophon.

RECONSTRUCTION IN PHILOSOPHY (1920), by John Dewey. See DEWEY, JOHN.

RED AND THE BLACK, THE (1830), by Stendhal (Henri Beyle). The plot of this novel is based on an actual incident that Stendhal read of in the *Gazette des Tribunaux* in 1827. Julien Sorel, the son of a carpenter, is taken under the protecting wing of the aged Abbé de Chélan, who procures for him the position of tutor to the children of M. de Rênal, the pompous mayor of Verrières. Mme. de Rênal, unhappily married, falls in love with the attractive young tutor and becomes his mistress. The husband, discovering his wife's indiscretions, sends Julien to the seminary of Besançon on a scholarship. Here the young man finds a patron in the director, Abbé Pirard, who places him as secretary to the great Marquis de la Mole. Julien carries through a successful diplomatic mission to England and is launched on a fine public career. In the meantime he has inspired a deep passion in the heart of the Marquis' daughter Mathilde. The romance, however, is terminated when the Marquis receives a letter from Mme. de Rênal exposing Julien as a base and mercenary opportunist. Swearing revenge, Julien returns to Verrières, and while Mme. de Rênal is kneeling at prayer in the church he shoots her. Julien is arrested, and, although she is only wounded, and despite her attempts to save him, he is condemned to the guillotine. *The Red and the Black* is equally famous for its exploitation of the discoveries of the late eighteenth century psychological analysts and for its satire of nineteenth century Restoration society.

RED BADGE OF COURAGE, THE (1895), by Stephen Crane. Henry Fleming, a young New York farm lad, has volunteered with the Union forces. Swaggering with mock heroics at first, he is thrown into a panic when a pitched battle at Chancellorsville becomes imminent. As the fighting enters its first stage, Henry makes a discovery. Directly the firing begins, the individual ceases to be afraid, becomes a part of the whole. But when the enemy begins to charge, Henry loses his head and flees. As in a nightmare, every turn only brings him face to face with the terrible affair. His harrowing experiences, the spectacle of the death agony, and the inexplicable courage of common men, draw at last the blinders from his eyes. In the clash and fury, all the impurities are cleansed from his being: he carries forward the regiment's colors in a crucial advance.

It is remarkable that the author was only twenty-five and had had no personal experience of war when he wrote the book.

Crane reissued his privately published *Maggie: A Girl of the Streets* (1896). This is the story of Maggie Johnson, from the New York slums, who escapes the squalor of her home only to be abandoned by Pete, with whom she had been living. Maggie tries unsuccessfully to earn a living as a prostitute, then commits suicide.

Stephen Crane also wrote verse. *The Black Riders* (1895) is a work influenced by Emily Dickinson. *War Is Kind* (1899) is a volume of free verse. The most famous collections of his short stories are: *The Little Regiment* (1896), six tales of the Civil War; and *The Open Boat* (1898), with its title story about four men who escape from a shipwreck off Florida in a dinghy.

RED CAVALRY (1926), by Isaac Babel. This collection of thirty-four brief tales deals with incidents in cavalry leader Budenny's Volhynia campaign in 1920, in which the author took part. They are written in the vernacular but are so composed as to have elements of poetry, something in the manner of J. M. Synge. These stories are lyrical, yet epic in character, and with a touch of irony. No one else since Gogol and Tolstoy, and until the appearance of Sholokhov, has written so skillfully of the Cossacks. Among his most typical stories is "A Letter," in which a Red soldier writes to his mother that his father, who had White tendencies, was captured by his company and put to death while the son mocked him. Another fine story, "Salt," consists of a similar letter addressed to the editor of a newspaper. It tells of a peasant woman who was assisted kindly onto a train by the soldiers, only to discover that what she was carrying in her arms was not a baby but a *pood* of salt, which was contraband. "So taking from the wall my faithful rifle, I wiped this infamy from the face of the workers' earth and the republic." "The Death of Dolgushov" is another famous story, dealing with a heroic but cruel episode.

Previous to the publication of *Red Cavalry* (the English translation of which appeared in 1929), Babel published the *Story of My Dove-Cote*, which contains an impressive reminiscence of a pogrom.

RED LAUGH, THE (1904), by Leonid Andreyev. Written under the impact of the Russo-Japanese war, this short novel is a terrifying evocation of the horrors of armed conflict. It presents the hideous dementia of the mass battlefield. The agonies and blood lusts, the warping of reason and the inexorable march of Fate upon battlefields, are personified by Andreyev as a gruesome, mocking Red Laugh. Pure impressionism and stream-of-consciousness mark the style of the novel. The narrative is divided into two parts, and then into nineteen fragments of varying length. Part One follows the stream of consciousness of a soldier in the field, through terrible experiences which culminate in the loss of his legs. Once home, he seeks to return to normal life, but is hopelessly, incurably mad, and as a frantic madman he dies. Part Two continues the stream of consciousness of the soldier's brother, who becomes revealed as the actual narrator of Part One. This section portrays the mental decay of the civilian population under the impact of war. Madness pervades everything in war time—such is Andreyev's theme. The story ends in a despairing hallucination, with prophetic overtones of the abortive revolution which followed in 1905. Death and madness, usually as social symptoms, are Andreyev's preoccupation. His stories are often the very embodiment of one or the other of these. A Russian critic has said of him: "In all the range of our literature, past and present, he is the gloomiest of Russian authors." Tolstoy said of him: "He wants to frighten me, but I am not frightened."

RED ORM, THE (1941), by Frans Gunnar Bengtsson. This Swedish novel of Viking adventure is localized principally about the shores of the Baltic, during the reigns of King Harald Blue-Tooth of Denmark and King Ethelred of England, and is written in the simple style of the ancient sagas. It is a story where pagans, Christians, Jews, and Mohammedans clash, and Viking heathens without inner conviction adopt Christianity or Mohammedanism, as necessity demands. In the Göinge district of Scania, "shaven men" (Christian priests) were occasionally sacrificed to Odin; more often they remained unmolested as of no great consequence; and, again, others were bartered on the border of Smaaland for steers. But they brought no high price. The hero, Orm—Serpent —was called Red Orm because he had red hair. One day, defending his flock of sheep against Viking raiders, he was captured and became one of them. Their expedition to the South won great booty, later lost to a superior force when its members were sold as galley slaves. Ultimately freed through the influence of a formerly befriended Jew, Orm obtained a precious sword, entered the service of Almansur of Cordova, where he became a chieftain, once saved his master's life, and won a treasured necklace. The Northmen finally made their escape to Denmark, bringing with them the largest bell suspended in the tower above the grave of St. James the Apostle. Orm took heroic part in the Yule feasting at the court of King Harald, and wooed his daughter Ylva, who received the necklace. They were separated, but after Harald's death were reunited in England; Orm was baptized and married to Ylva as a Christian; and they returned to Scania to live a life of peace. The value of the novel lies in the realistic descriptions of the Viking deeds, customs, and philosophy, and, artistically, in its humor and dramatic directness.

RED ROVER, THE (1827), by James Fenimore Cooper. See SPY, THE, by James Fenimore Cooper.

REDBURN (1849), by Herman Melville. See MOBY-DICK, by Herman Melville.

REDSKINS, THE (1846), by James Fenimore Cooper. See SPY, THE, by James Fenimore Cooper.

REFLECTIONS ON THE REVOLUTION IN FRANCE (1790), by Edmund Burke. *Reflections,* written in the form of a letter to a French gentleman, is the first one of a series of writings discussing the progress of the French Revolution. The immediate occasion of this pamphlet was a meeting of an English society in support of the revolutionary cause in France. It was claimed by English sympathizers that the French Revolution was accomplishing in France what the Glorious Revolution of the previous century had accomplished in England. Burke begins by attacking this comparison, and ends by attacking the French Revolution, its leaders, its method, and its philosophy. The major point at issue between Burke and the Revolutionists was not whether liberty was desirable, but rather how liberty is to be attained, and what its limitations are. Burke, as a traditionalist and conservative, conceived of the state as an organic growth, and saw liberty as gradually achieved within the structure of the state. He opposed the rationalistic view of the philosophers of the Revolution. According to this view, there are certain simple and self-evident principles of government, immediately apparent to reason. Just and good government can, therefore, be attained simply by destroying the old state and constructing a new one in accordance with these principles. Burke was skeptical of the ability of the human mind to penetrate into the mysteries of social organization, and felt that the less tampering the better. If change is necessary, the attempt should be made to preserve as much of the old order as possible. In developing this line of criticism, Burke seems to have been unaware of the terrible plight of the French people under the monarchy. He glorified aspects of the old order that had fallen into decay, and he exaggerated the abuses of the new system. He did, however, predict quite accurately certain of the future developments of the Revolution, including the subsequent military dictatorship. The publication of this book made an enormous impression both in England and in France, alienated many of Burke's former friends, and brought forth many answers from the revolutionary side, of which Paine's *Rights of Man* is the most famous.

REFLECTIONS ON THE WORLD OF TODAY (1931), by Paul Valéry. This is a small collection of essays on the place of man, and especially of the Frenchman, in a world which has suddenly become very small. There are no more open spaces on the map, Valéry notes. "Backward" peoples have been awakened; Asia is in competition with Europe; contact between nations is continuous, so that there is no knowing where any movement, once started, will ever stop. Wars can no longer be local; any real peace must include the whole planet. In such circumstances what sort of primacy can Europe, and particularly France, enjoy? He discusses the influence of history in perpetuating patterns of thought long after they have been thoroughly outmoded, the lag between political behavior and the conditions which actually exist, the particular intellectual values by which only France can be defined and by which she may survive, the meaning of Paris as a symbol of spiritual values, the contrast between East and West, the nature of progress, the nature and inherent danger of future wars. If much that is in these essays seems trite today, it is largely because events of the intervening years have so frequently borne Valéry out.

Best known to his time as a profound and enigmatic poet, Valéry seems to be emerging, in the current perspective, as a philosopher who sometimes also writes verse.

RÈGNE ANIMAL, LE (1817), by Georges Cuvier. In the introduction to this work Cuvier, permanent secretary of the French Academy of Sciences, says that it is the result of thirty years devoted to comparative anatomy. In surveying the whole of animate nature, he stressed internal structure rather than external characteristics; and he fixed upon the nervous system as the basis for his classification of "animal functions" as opposed to "vegetative functions." He divided the animal kingdom into four great divisions, each built upon its own peculiar plan: I. Vertebrata (with a backbone); II. Mollusca (oysters, snails, etc.); III. Articulata (insects, spiders, etc.); IV. Radiata (all other animals). Cuvier had a high regard for detailed research and minute observation coupled with an equal appreciation of the unity of all branches of learning. He continually emphasized the problem of organization, and he was one of the first great scientific writers to undertake a historical survey of the different natural sciences. During the years 1804 to 1808 he investigated fossil remains in the Paris basin, and was forcibly struck by the extent to which they differed from existing species. He perceived that vast numbers of species, many no longer existing, had appeared upon the earth in earlier periods. Having lived through the French Revolution, Cuvier applied the idea of cataclysmic change to the animal kingdom. He maintained—against Lamarck, Goethe, and others, who partly anticipated the ideas of Darwin—the fixity of species, and explained the changes in form which fossils present as due to successive revolutions through which some forms of life became extinct and new ones were created. He believed that the last of these catastrophes was the flood recorded in the Book of Genesis. In spite of this view he laid the foundations of what later became known as paleontology, and this fact entitles him to an important place in the history of biology. In his day he was the foremost naturalist of France—the "dictator of biology"—a favorite of Napoleon, later a baron. His principle of the "correlation of parts"—by means of which he constructed, with surprising accuracy, an entire creature from a few bony fragments—has been of great value in paleontology. Thus *Le Règne Animal,* beautifully illustrated, remained for many years a standard work in comparative anatomy.

REGRETS, THE (1858), by Joachim Du Bellay. See DU BELLAY, JOACHIM.

RELAPSE, THE, or **VIRTUE IN DANGER** (acted 1696; published 1697), by John Vanbrugh. Vanbrugh in this comedy continues Colley Cibber's *Love's Last Shift;* it contains a more cynical attitude toward the question of marital fidelity. Loveless, once a rake but now virtuous, comes to town with his wife, Amanda. He sees her cousin, Berinthia, and falls in love with her.

Berinthia, a heartless beauty, encourages him in an affair. She plots with Worthy, a gentleman who admires Amanda, to induce her to be unfaithful to Loveless. However, they are not successful, for though Amanda resents her husband's fall from grace, she will not indulge in iniquity herself. Another and more lively intrigue recounts the adventures surrounding the engagement of Sir Novelty Fashion, recently created Lord Foppington by purchase, to Miss Hoyden, a country heiress. Neither she nor her father, Sir Tunbelly Clumsey, has ever seen his lordship. Young Fashion, Foppington's brother, has run into debt, but his brother spurns his pleas for assistance. Young Fashion, in revenge, repairs to the country house of Sir Tunbelly and passes himself off as Lord Foppington. He arranges a clandestine marriage with Miss Hoyden before his brother's arrival. When Foppington does arrive he is, at first, looked upon with scorn as an impostor. When the truth is learned, Miss Hoyden resolves to say nothing of her previous marriage, and so weds Lord Foppington. The two go to London, where Young Fashion appears to claim the lady as his wife. Her nurse and the parson confess the previous marriage, and Miss Hoyden is obliged to return to her true husband, somewhat more satisfied with her fate when she learns that Fashion is Foppington's brother.

RELATIVITY: THE SPECIAL AND GENERAL THEORY (1920), by Albert Einstein. The experiments of Michelson and Morley in America in 1881 and 1887 had failed to detect any motion of the earth relative to a stationary ether. Fitzgerald in England suggested that the paradox could be resolved by assuming that objects in motion contract, the length while in motion being given by the length when at rest multiplied by the factor $\sqrt{1 - \dfrac{v^2}{c^2}}$ where v is the velocity in the direction of the length and c is the speed of light. As v approaches c, the length approaches zero. Lorentz in Holland related this contraction to the electronic constitution of matter. Einstein in the special theory of relativity reconciled the phenomena of mechanics with those of electromagnetism through the Lorentz equations of transformation and the relativistic view of motion. One of the consequences of the theory was that energy possessed an inertia, and light had mass, indicating the equivalence of matter and energy. The special theory was published in 1905, and attempts soon were made to extend the relativity principle to include gravitation. In his general theory of 1916, Einstein made this extension on the assumption that inertial force and gravitational force are equivalent and interchangeable. This led him to substitute for Newtonian gravitation an equivalent curvature of Minkowski's space and time or space-time. By attributing accelerated motions to this space-time curvature, Einstein gave a relativistic account of celestial motions and of electromagnetic phenomena. His theory implied that light is propagated linearly only if the curvature is zero—i.e., if space is "flat" or Euclidean. In the neighborhood of large masses, such as the sun, light should follow a curved path. This suggested an important empirical test of the theory, and this was met by observations in 1919 showing that rays of light actually are deflected by the sun. The general theory also accounted for certain unexplained perturbations in the motion of the planet Mercury, and for the shift of stellar spectral lines toward the red end of the spectrum.

The mathematical foundations of the special theory of relativity are found in the original papers of Lorentz, Einstein, and Minkowski. The general theory, as well as the necessary mathematical theory of invariants, is found in Einstein's *Die Grundlagen der allgemeinen Relativitätstheorie* (1916). The present work is a translation of a German work completed also in 1916. It is intended to give an insight into the theory from a general and philosophical point of view, but without the mathematical apparatus of theoretical physics. Part I, "The special theory of relativity," includes a discussion of co-ordinates, the addition of velocities, the propagation of light, the relativity of simultaneity, the Lorentz transformation, and Minkowski's four-dimensional space. Part II, "The general theory of relativity," includes the gravitational field, the equality of inertial and gravitational mass, a critique of Newtonian mechanics and the inferences of general relativity, and the space-time continuum of relativity as a non-Euclidean continuum. Part III, "Considerations on the universe as a whole," includes cosmological difficulties of Newton's theory, the possibility of a finite and yet unbounded universe, and the structure of space in general relativity theory. An appendix by the author includes, among other things, experimental confirmation of the general theory through the motion of the perihelion of Mercury, the deflection of light by a gravitational field, and the displacement toward the red of spectral lines.

R. E. LEE (1934–1935), by Douglas Southall Freeman. This four-volume biography, twenty years in the writing, is the most thorough work done on the life and activities of the Confederate commander-in-chief. Its principal concern is to delineate Lee as a great man and a military genius. The bulk of the work deals with the campaigns planned and directed by Lee. Operations are detailed. Freeman addresses himself in part to the professional soldier, and unfolds step by step Lee's strategy. The general reader is offered fresh incidents in Lee's life, in a non-military context.

This Pulitzer Prize work was followed by *Lee's Lieutenants* (1942–1944), which brings the commander's military collaborators into prominence. Freeman points out that many of Lee's military disasters were inherited from the incompetent General Joseph Johnston, while Lee's own appointed men proved able. Among those treated are: Pierre G. T. Beauregard, John B. Magruder, Daniel A. Hill, Gustavus W. Smith, Thomas J. Jackson, James Longstreet, Richard S. Ewell, A. P. Hill, "Jeb" Stuart, Jubal A. Early, the colorful Wade Hampton, John Pelham, Fitzhugh Lee, and many others.

RELIGIEUSE, LA (1796), by Denis Diderot. See DIDEROT, DENIS.

RELIGIO LAICI (1682), by John Dryden. See DRYDEN, JOHN.

RELIGIO MEDICI (authorized edition 1643), by Sir Thomas Browne. *Religio Medici,* the religion of a physician, is a confession of Browne's own creed of religious mysticism. Browne was a physician of encyclopedic learning, who was as interested in religious meditations as in science. He loved to read and ponder odd and unusual bits of information and to combine such knowledge with his own investigations. He carefully separated science and religion, accepting revealed religion as a mystery to be taken on faith. In *Religio Medici,* Browne characterizes himself thus: "Methinks there be not impossibilities enough in religion for an active faith." And again, "I love to lose myself in a mystery."

RELIGION AND THE RISE OF CAPITALISM (1926), by R. H. Tawney. Tawney is intent on showing how the attitude that trade is one thing and religion another ("Render unto Caesar the things which are Caesar's . . .") has brought about a state of affairs where the unbridled indulgence in the acquisitive appetite has all but devoured Christianity. Once religion influenced to an almost unbelievable degree the outlook of society. Then economic and social changes reacted strongly on religion. There has been action and reaction; it is this working of very subtle change, the one on the other, with which Tawney is concerned. He starts with the medieval outlook and the sin of avarice; then he considers the effect of the reformers Luther and Calvin, then the land question in England, the religious theory and the contrasting social practice and the growth of individualism. When the Puritans came on the scene with godly discipline, the religion of trade was also on hand. The economic virtues Tawney sees as triumphant. Poverty is no longer a virtue in the sight of God, it is a vice in the sight of economic man. The Puritans held, as do the Russians today, that man must work if he would eat. Slavery seems natural enough in these circumstances. Today there is a reaction to all this. As Tawney sees it: "Economic efficiency is a necessary element in the life of any sane and vigorous society, and only the incorrigible sentimentalist will depreciate its significance. But to convert efficiency from an instrument into a primary object is to destroy the efficiency itself. . . . Compromise is as impossible between the Church of Christ and the idolatry of wealth, which is the practical religion of capitalist societies, as it was between the Church and State idolatry of the Roman Empire." The late J. Maynard Keynes, who was Britain's leading economist, was at one with Tawney in his condemnation of "snatching to hoard and hoarding to snatch."

REMEMBRANCE OF THINGS PAST (1913–1927), by Marcel Proust. This elaborate work, in six parts and peopled by a cast of two hundred characters, re-creates an epoch. A central observer, Marcel, who is also an active character in the book, watches the working of time on a whole group of Parisian aristocrats and would-be aristocrats. By the technique of involuntary memory— through which any stimulus connected with his past experience will set in motion the stream-of-thought process—he summons up and reconstructs the past. What takes place before his eyes, with excruciating slowness, is the decadence and death of a society.

Swann's Way is the first volume in this long and complex work. Lying sleepless in bed Marcel recalls vividly the days he, a sensitive and delicate child, had spent in the country. He would be in bed every evening while his family were sipping their liqueur and gossiping below on the terrace. He longed to say good-night to his mother. He loved and clung to her, but she recoiled from his affection as a sign of emotional weakness. When he is older it becomes clear that his childhood attachment for his mother had a psychopathological element in it. There is even a hint of homosexuality, too—a suspicion more than justified by events in such cases as that of Swann's degenerate friend, Baron Charlus. The character of Swann is searchingly drawn. He is a neighbor and friend of the family, a gifted, philandering, fashionable man, a favorite of women, who has made an unfortunate marriage to Odette, a beautiful but stupid cocotte. His surprising passion for this *demi-mondaine* is fatal; jealousy finally wrecks his life. Swann, the sensitive Jew, achieves the nobility of pathos in his agony and downfall.

Within a Budding Grove is the second part. As he grows up, Marcel falls in love with Swann's daughter, Gilberte. It is a deep and poetic attachment, but she gradually tires of him; his ardent nature and his attentions begin to irritate her. Out of wounded pride he avoids her, although he continues his friendly relations with the Swanns. Two years later he feels he is thoroughly cured of his hopeless passion, when he becomes involved with Albertine, a beautiful brunette he meets in Balbec. But he eventually discovers that she is interested only in platonic relations with men, and so he suffers another disappointment.

In *The Guermantes Way,* the third part, Marcel's next infatuation is for the beautiful Duchesse de Guermantes. He waits for her in the park constantly in order to bow to her as she passes, although they are but slightly acquainted. This attention, he is informed by someone, is proving very distasteful to Mme. Guermantes. Again he meets Albertine, now matured, sophisticated and a young divorcée. Marcel's final social acceptance by the Duchesse opens the doors of all Parisian society. He suddenly awakens to find it vulgar, trivial and malicious.

In *Cities of the Plain,* the fourth part, Marcel again meets Swann at a reception given by the Princesse de Guermantes, a cousin of the Duchesse. Swann is now suffering from a deadly ailment. He is an ardent adherent of Alfred Dreyfus. Swann urges Marcel to write to Gilberte, since she speaks of him frequently. But Gilberte no longer has any enchantment for Marcel; Albertine again holds his affections. She offers herself to him, but, distracted by physical attachments for other women, he desires her company only at intervals to titillate his jaded senses. Eventually he is drawn closer to her, but now his suspicion that she is a Lesbian causes him jealousy and endless torment.

The Captive, part five, reveals Marcel determined to end his emotional insecurity by marrying Albertine. He watches her closely and has others watch her and report her movements to him. Finally the thought of marriage again becomes intolerable for him, although his passion for her grows compulsive. He discovers that his emotional need of her is similar to that for his mother during his childhood. He drives her frantic with his suspicions and accusations of illicit passions, and finally she leaves him.

In *The Sweet Cheat Gone,* part six, we learn that now that Albertine is gone, Marcel, in the perverse way usual to him, desires to have her back again. Almost driven to suicide, he begs her to return. He receives a reply from her aunt informing him that Albertine had been thrown from her horse and killed. Months later he receives a telegram reading: "I am quite alive, should like to see you, talk about marriage . . . Love, Albertine." Marcel is amazed by the game Albertine is playing, but she no longer means anything to him. However, he discovers later, when it is too late for him to do anything about it, that the telegram was genuine.

In *Time Regained* the World War has come. Marcel still mingles with the decayed *haut-monde,* undeflected by its mania for pomp and pleasure even during such terrible days. Again he meets Gilberte, a stout, middle-aged woman who strikes Marcel as having the appearance of an ancient whore. And the other corrupt aristocrats seem ill and tottering toward the grave, an observation which fills Marcel with panic. Time, the precious, is fast ebbing. Marcel can delay no longer. He must devote the remainder of his life to recording the account of their lives and characters while he can still remember things past: "It did not seem as if I should have the strength to carry much longer attached to me that past which already extended so far down and which I was bearing so painfully within me!"

REMINISCENCES OF A STUPID BOY (1935), by Arthur van Schendel. See SCHENDEL, ARTHUR VAN.

RENAISSANCE, THE (1873), by Walter Pater. Pater was the founder of the aesthetic movement in England; his *Renaissance* was its evangel. Here French influence entered into English art and letters. Echoes of Baudelaire are found in Pater's observation that the artist does his sincerest work when he remains oblivious to moral considerations, and in the reference to "the love of art for its own sake." Pater calls for Spartan suppression of passion in art: "Self-restraint, a skilful economy of means, *ascesis;* that too has a beauty of its own." The Greeks had achieved this ideal, which sprang from a unity of life within the individual. The men of the Renaissance, too, had been moved by a passion for integration, i.e., form plus spirit. Pater was an eclectic and *The Renaissance* reveals him as such. He prefers "poetic or suggestive philosophies," in short, those which are preoccupied with other-worldliness. This explains his partiality for the idealism of Plato and the neo-Platonists. Besides a preface and the famous conclusion, which invites to aesthetic living, "to burn always with this hard, gemlike flame," these studies in art and poetry include the following essays: "Two Early French Stories," "Pico della Mirandola," "Sandro Botticelli," "Luca della Robbia," "The Poetry of Michelangelo," "Leonardo da Vinci," "The School of Giorgione," "Joachim du Bellay," and "Winckelmann." Pater's style is elegant, melodious, perfectly controlled.

RENASCENCE AND OTHER POEMS (1917), by Edna St. Vincent Millay. See MILLAY, EDNA ST. VINCENT.

RENÉ (1802), by François René de Chateaubriand. See ATALA, by François René de Chateaubriand.

RENÉE MAUPERIN (1864), by Edmond and Jules de Goncourt. See JOURNALS, by Edmond and Jules de Goncourt.

RENOVATION OF BUDDHISM (1928), by Han Yong-woon. See MEDITATIONS OF THE LOVER, by Han Yong-woon.

REPPLIER, AGNES (1858–1945). Agnes Repplier published both fiction and biography (mostly of ecclesiastical personages), but is especially known for her graceful essays. Early advised by an editor to adopt this literary form for her witty and scholarly writings, she lived quietly in Philadelphia and produced many volumes of distinguished work. *In Our Convent Days* (1905) is a typical book of reminiscence written in later life by the Catholic writer, full of nostalgia for her own happy years spent with the French nuns in a convent. She contrasts unfavorably the age of enlightenment and sophistication of the younger generation of the early twentieth century with her own youth, which she characterizes as zestful, innocent and obedient. She regrets the intrusion of too much liberty, of non-Catholic writers and intellectuals like Walter Pater and Matthew Arnold, into the study syllabus; and recalls the beautiful, disciplined age of faith, sentiment and purity.

REPRESENTATIVE MEN (1850), by Ralph Waldo Emerson. See ESSAYS, by Ralph Waldo Emerson.

REPUBLIC, THE, by Plato (427–347 B.C.). This dialogue is in many respects the crown of Plato's works. It is the application of his ethical theories to the delineation of an ideal state. The whole is set forth as a discussion which Socrates reports having had with the sophist Thrasymachus, two of Plato's brothers, Glaucon and Adeimantus, Polemarchus and his aged father, Cephalus, at whose house in the Piraeus they were met in casual and friendly gathering. The conversation drifts to the question of the nature of justice. In the first book attempts are made by several of those present to give a definition, but none of them stand up under Socrates' scrutiny. He suggests that it may be easier to find justice writ large in the state; and so proceeds throughout books two to four to trace the evolution of an ideal state. This state turns out to be an aristocracy, with carefully selected and trained philosophers as its guardians. Socrates then returns to the original question of justice in the individual, but his audience has been intrigued by some of the features of his ideal state; and in book five he is prevailed upon to expound his ideas on the community of women and children among his guardians. In this connection he reminds his listeners that the attempt to sketch an ideal state was undertaken only for experimental purposes, that it may or may not be capable of realization, and that perhaps the most that can be hoped for is an approximation of existing states to this ideal. On this basis he proceeds in books six and seven to discuss the character of his philosopher guardians and the type of education they must have. In the eighth book he returns to the individual, and shows how differences of character correspond to the various types of construction: aristocracy, timocracy, oligarchy, democracy, and despotism, and how these states succeed and replace one another in practice. Thence he comes in the ninth book to conclude that the just man will guide himself with reference to the ideal state. "Perhaps," he says, "in heaven there is laid up a pattern of it for him who wishes to behold it, and beholding to organize himself accordingly. And the question of its present or future existence on earth is quite unimportant." Rather surprisingly in the tenth book Socrates reverts to a subject with which he had dealt in connection with education, i.e., poetry. He finds the influence of poetry wholly bad, and decides reluctantly that it must be excluded, except for hymns to the gods and encomia of great men, from the ideal state. Then turning to the vices he argues that they cannot destroy the soul and that nothing else can, therefore the soul is immortal. The rewards that the just may expect after death are illustrated by the strange and apocalyptic myth of Er, who had witnessed life beyond death and returned to tell man of rewards and punishment and of the governance of the universe.

RESURRECTION (1872), by Joaquim Maria Machado de Assis. See DOM CASMURRO, by Joaquim Maria Machado de Assis.

RESURRECTION (1899), by Count Leo Tolstoy. This, the first full-length novel since *Anna Karenina* (q.v.), was written in Tolstoy's last period, when he was engaged in moral propaganda rather than in the creation of imaginative works. Though lacking the great art of *War and Peace* (q.v.) and *Anna Karenina,* it nonetheless has passages of genius. It is not as long as the two other works mentioned above, but it is the longest novel that he wrote after 1880, when he turned pamphleteer. It is a story of conscience. As a young man, Nekhlyudov, of the gentry—this character is commonly associated with Tolstoy himself—takes advantage of the handsome servant Maslova. Years later he is called upon to be one of the jurors in a case in which Maslova is being tried for a crime whose commission is traceable to the original injustice done her by Nekhlyudov. In the intervening years she has tried hard to make an honest living for herself and her child, but was at last forced to find a place in a brothel. On recognizing Maslova from the jurors' box, Nekhlyudov realizes that probably but for him she would not have come to this end. He undergoes a conversion, and is resolved to make amends by sharing in the punishment.

RETURN OF PETER GRIMM, THE (1911), by David Belasco. Peter Grimm, a crusty old bachelor, dies. His spirit returns, and, speaking through the boy William, grandson of Marta, an old servant, attempts to clear up the problems in his household of which he was ignorant during his life. He reveals that his nephew Frederik Grimm, who was to take over the horticultural business and marry Peter's ward Kathrien, is not to be trusted. Frederik is disclosed as the father of William, and as planning to sell the business. Peter persuades Kathrien to marry James Hartman, an employee, who she really loves; then he departs, with William.

David Belasco was famous as a manager, producer and discoverer of stars. Many of his plays were written with collaborators. (*The Return of Peter Grimm* was the result of an idea of Cecil de Mille.) A famous piece of his own, however, is *The Girl of the Golden West* (1905). This concerns a combination saloonkeeper and schoolmistress whose love for the outlaw Dick Johnson causes the miners to free him and permit the couple to start a new life in the east. Puccini wrote an opera to this libretto in 1910.

RETURN OF SHERLOCK HOLMES, THE (1905), by Sir Arthur Conan Doyle. See SHERLOCK HOLMES, by Sir Arthur Conan Doyle.

RETURN OF THE NATIVE, THE (1878), by Thomas Hardy. This intensely interesting but depressing novel is localized entirely on Egdon Heath in Wessex. The barren moor, invested by Hardy with color and warmth, is a perfect setting for the somber story. The willfulness of one person, passionate, exotic Eustacia Vye, upsets the lives of a number of people. Clym Yeobright, the native, returns from Paris, where he has been successfully engaged as a jeweler, because he is dissatisfied with the shallowness of his life abroad. He plans to study and to set up a school to improve the lot of the children in the place of his birth. Unfortunately for his idealistic plans, he falls in love with Eustacia, who, bored with her restricted life on the heath, sees in Clym the possibility of escape to a glorious life in Paris. Previously she has whiled away her boredom with Damon Wildeve, a former engineer now running the local public house. Wildeve was, at the same time, engaged in an affair with Clym's cousin, gentle, mild-mannered Thomasin Yeobright, whom he marries to spite Eustacia. Eustacia marries Clym, in the hope of inducing him to give up his idea of remaining in the county, but finds him adamant. The partial loss of his eyesight, caused by overstudy, forces Clym to turn furze-cutter, his marriage to Eustacia having estranged him from his mother. Eustacia seeks outlets once more in renewing her interest in Wildeve, who has inherited a fortune since his marriage. They are hampered somewhat by the humble reddleman, Diggory Venn, who has long loved Thomasin unselfishly, and therefore does what he can to spare her the tragedy of her unfortunate marriage. Eustacia, after unintentionally causing the death of Clym's mother, decides to escape from the heath with Wildeve. In attempting to flee, both are drowned. Clym, feeling some responsibility for the deaths of his wife and mother, becomes an itinerant, open-air preacher, thus returning to his ideal of a life of usefulness. Thomasin, after a long interval, marries Diggory Venn, whose love for her has remained steadfast throughout all her troubles. The tragic incidents of the book are relieved somewhat by numerous minor rural characters, whom Hardy has drawn with delightful skill and accuracy. Local customs and practices are woven into the story, forming a rich and informative background.

REUNION IN VIENNA (1931), by Robert Sherwood. See SHERWOOD, ROBERT.

REVELATION OF SAINT JOHN (1593), by John Napier, Baron of Merchiston. See MIRIFICI LOGARITHMORUM CANONIS DESCRIPTIO, by John Napier, Baron of Merchiston.

REVOLT OF THE ANGELS, THE (1914), by Anatole France. This rambling story is mainly about an angel who finds earth more attractive than heaven. His presence in Paris is first felt when precious books began to disappear from the Esparvieu library, to the great dismay of the librarian. The thief turns out to be the guardian angel of young Esparvieu, to whom he appears while the latter is actively engaged in an adultery. The angel, Arcade, announces that he is organizing a revolt against the Most High—but like so many revolutionaries, he seems more bent on enjoying life in Paris than in getting on with his revolution. When the revolt finally does come to a head it fizzles. But meanwhile Anatole France has had time to have his ironic say on subjects ranging from Parisian society, ecclesiastical art, current morals and the ineptitude of the French police to the organization of the cosmos.

By many this story is considered the best of a list which includes *Penguin Island* (q.v.), *At the Sign of the Reine Pédauque* (1893), *The Red Lily* (1894), and *The Crime of Sylvestre Bonnard* (q.v.). France was also famous for the short stories "Crainquebille" (1901); "The Procurator of Judea" (1902); "The Juggler of Notre Dame" (1906); he wrote a *Life of Jeanne d'Arc* (1908) which has been called infamous, and was a gifted literary critic.

REVOLUTION, THE (1884), by Hippolyte Taine. See ORIGIN OF CONTEMPORARY FRANCE, THE, by Hippolyte Taine.

RHETORIC, THE, by Aristotle (384–322 B.C.). Aristotle defines rhetoric in terms of its objective as "the power of discovering in each case the possible means of persuading." Thus rhetoric is distinguished from dialectic by its employment of argument where logical proof is impossible, and closely related to ethics by its interest in the psychology of personality as subject to various appeals. In the first book three types of speech are distinguished: the deliberative or political, the judicial, and the display piece, the first of which is considered most important; and the subjects appropriate to each are outlined, along with the kinds of argument and proof or evidence that may be used. The second book deals with the psychology of the speaker and his audience, the character he should try to display, and the character of the audience to which he must adapt his appeals. Much attention is here given to the various emotions on which the speaker may play and the means of producing them. The third book corresponds more closely to the conventional ancient handbook on rhetoric. Its first part deals with expression or style and the last with organization or outlining of a speech. Later writers on grammar owe much to Aristotle's remarks on language in this last book, and Cicero made much use of it in his rhetorical writings.

RHYMES (1871), by Gustavo Adolfo Bécquer. The reputation of the tenderly romantic Bécquer (1836–1870) depends almost exclusively upon a sheaf of short lyrics entitled *Rimas*. Melancholy love, grief and death seem to be the recurrent themes of these seventy-six poems. Their outstanding virtue is their simplicity, though their strophic pattern reveals remarkable variety and richness. Bécquer arranged the poems according to a plan of his own, but they were not published in book form until a year after his death. Although some critics have said that *Rimas* is strikingly reminiscent of Heine's *Intermezzo*, there is no ground for alleging direct influence or plagiarism. No doubt there is much similarity in their poetical climate—which is the climate that a sector of Romantic poets had in common—but Bécquer is extremely original and personal and brought a unique utterance into the fertile field of Spanish poetry.

RICH MAN, THE (1936), by Arthur van Schendel. See SCHENDEL, ARTHUR VAN.

RICHARD CARVEL (1899), by Winston Churchill. Richard Carvel spends his early life in Maryland, brought up by his grandfather, a supporter of the English King George. He loves Dorothy Manners, but she is taken to London and expected to marry a wealthy Englishman. An uncle arranges to have pirates kidnap Richard, but he is rescued by John Paul Jones. Their experiences together follow, including Richard's imprisonment in London and eventual rescue by Dorothy. Richard then lives among such Englishmen of distinction as Fox and Walpole. He prevents Dorothy's marriage; then, learning of the loss of his inheritance, he returns to America, and becomes a real estate lawyer. At the outbreak of the Revolution he enlists with John Paul Jones. The famous victory of the *Bonhomme Richard* over the *Serapis* takes place. Richard is able to go to England and marry Dorothy, who has always loved him. They return to America, and live happily.

This was the first in the popular novelist's series examining the historical trends of America's background. *The Crisis* (1901) is a sequel, dealing with the South's problems at the time of the Civil War. Among fictional characters are Eliphalit Hopper, the carpetbagger, Judge Whipple, the idealistic abolitionist, and Colonel Carver, a true Southern gentleman. The hero is Stephen Brice, an antislavery New Englander who accepts a job in the judge's law office and meets Virginia Carvel, descendant of Richard Carvel. The young people fall in love, but Virginia, because of her Southern convictions, renounces Stephen's affection and becomes engaged to her cousin, Clarence Colfax, a Confederate cavalier. Stephen is wounded with the Union Army, and becomes an aide to Lincoln. Virginia finally breaks with Clarence, who is taken as a spy, and while visiting Lincoln to seek his pardon, is reunited with Stephen.

The Crossing (1904) tells of the Kentucky frontier's part in the Revolution. David Ritchie lives in North Carolina. His father, a dour Scotchman, joins the American Army, and the youth is left with the Temple family in Charleston. When Mr. Ritchie is killed, David returns to the farm as a worker. Later he accompanies Tom McChesney in George Rogers Clark's wilderness campaign. After the fighting at Vincennes and Kaskaskia he studies law, joined by Nick Temple, who turns out to be his cousin. In New Orleans he marries a French refugee, Hélène d'Ivry-le-Tour, and takes her back to the Kentucky frontier.

The hero of *Coniston* (1906) is Jethro Bass, a rude political figure in a Vermont village during Andrew Jackson's time. He loves Cynthia Ware, the town beauty, but they part over political issues. She marries Wetherell, has a daughter, and dies confessing her love for Jethro. Wetherell settles in Coniston. At his death Jethro, now state political boss, takes little Cynthia to live with him. She dislikes his unprincipled ways, however, and leaves to teach school. Bob Worthington, son of Jethro's political enemy, loves Cynthia. Knowing it is her wish, Jethro drops his campaign, after Worthington gives his consent to Bob's marriage.

Mr. Crewe's Career (1908) concerns a capitalist who gains the nomination for governor because Austen Vane, who has made a campaign against railroad monopolies, does not wish to hurt his father or the father of his fiancée, Victoria Flint, by accepting the nomination himself. The railroaders defeat Humphrey Crewe, but do not destroy the effects of Austen's work.

The Inside of the Cup (1913) concerns religion in a modern age. John Hodder, a minister, wishes to fight slum conditions. He denounces Eldon Parr, a wealthy church member, and is asked to resign. Alison Parr leaves her father to marry John.

RICHARD II, KING (ca. 1595), by William Shakespeare. First published in quarto form in 1597, it is based on Holinshed's *Chronicles* (q.v.), in a lesser degree on Berners' translation of Froissart, Daniel's *Civil Wars,* and the play *Thomas of Woodstock.* This historical tragedy contains some of Shakespeare's finest and most familiar poetry. Bolingbroke, Duke of Hereford, accuses Mowbray, Duke of Norfolk, of treason and challenges him before the King. They are to fight at Coventry, but Richard changes his mind, and banishes them both. He shortens Bolingbroke's banishment, because of the grief of his father, the King's uncle, John of Gaunt, Duke of Lancaster. Pining for his son, Gaunt falls ill. Dying he sends for the King, and makes the famous speech about England to his brother, the Duke of York, "Methinks I am a prophet new inspired . . ." Richard seizes Gaunt's property to pay for his Irish wars, and appoints the Duke of York regent during his absence. Bolingbroke lands in England with a large force to claim his inheritance as Lancaster. He is joined by a number of disaffected nobles, including the powerful Earl of Northumberland. Green and Bushy, two of Richard's favorites, are captured and beheaded by Bolingbroke. The Duke of York meets Bolingbroke at Berkeley Castle, and decides to remain neutral. Richard returns from Ireland a day too late, and loses twenty thousand Welsh troops who go over to his rival. Richard confers with Bolingbroke at Flint Castle in Wales, and surrenders after a parley. He ponders pathetically, "What must the king do now? must he submit?" Bolingbroke rides in triumph through London on Richard's charger "Barbary," with the King in the rear of his train, unpitied and insulted. In Westminister Hall in a touching scene, Richard takes the crown, and says, "Give me the crown.— Here, cousin, seize the crown; here, cousin, on this side my hand, and on that side thine." Then he asks for a looking glass, and continues, "Give me that glass, and therein will I read." Then he dashes the glass on the pavement. Bolingbroke orders him removed to the Tower. The Queen waits for Richard to pass, and bids her husband a sad farewell. Northumberland comes to tell Richard that he is to be sent to Pomfret instead. The former King prophesies that Bolingbroke will not trust the man who made him a king. Sir Pierce of Exton, Richard's keeper, who had heard King Henry say that he wished he were rid of the royal prisoner, murders Richard in his prison, and takes his body in a coffin to London, where Henry regrets Exton's hasty action and his cousin's death. A subplot is the conspiracy of a group of nobles headed by Aumerle, the Duke of York's son, to kill Henry at Oxford. The Duke discovers his son's treachery and rides to tell his monarch, but Aumerle gets to him first and is pardoned. The play is a remarkably subtle study of a weak and vacillating character. It was successfully revived in 1937 by Maurice Evans.

RICHARD III, KING (ca. 1594; Quarto 1597), by William Shakespeare. Here we have one of Shakespeare's most compelling character portraits, but not one of his best plays. The power and intrinsic interest of its central character have caused it to persist as one of the more popular plays, frequently performed, not withstanding its faults. These are not faults of craftsmanship, but arise from the inevitable handicap of all the historical-chronicle plays. An intolerable amount of time is consumed, especially in the first act, in recounting the involved historical background, prior events, royal relationships, and so forth. Such explanatory baggage, and the tedious, oft-repeated lamentations of the Queens, all combine to intersperse the action of the play with long, arid patches. However, crook-back Richard, the malevolent and unscrupulous usurper, will cut a figure on our stage as long as we have actors in search of effective vehicles. Shakespeare took his material from Holinshed and probably from an earlier, anonymous play on Richard III.

Richard, Duke of Gloucester, is bent upon becoming King. He has previously slain King Henry IV and Edward, Prince of Wales, whose widow, Anne, he unscrupulously woos in the face of her hatred. He is moving to supplant his brother, Edward IV, currently reigning. In achieving this he is forced to perpetrate a series of bloody and terrible crimes, from which he does not shrink. He causes the death of his other brother, the Duke of Clarence, in order to have a clear field. Edward IV, a sick man, dies. In swift succession Richard murders the two young sons of the late King (the little Princes in the Tower), and also sundry Lords of the Realm who block his path. He betrays his closest henchmen and stops at nothing in hacking his bloody way to the coveted title, King Richard III. But Richard does not long enjoy this triumph. Henry Tudor, Earl of Richmond, afterward King Henry VII, leads an army against him. Richard, after a night of tortured dreams, fights a pitched battle at Bosworth Field, where he utters the famous cry, "A horse! a horse! my kingdom for a horse!" He is betrayed by Lord Stanley, and at last is slain.

RICHTER, JOHANN PAUL (Jean Paul; 1763–1825). A prolific writer, the German Jean Paul combined elements of the classic past and the coming Romanticism in his novels, which are marked by a lack of sharply defined form. Filled with a genial humor and a youthful enthusiasm, his works demonstrate abundance and fertility of imagination—at times to a point of incredibility and absurdity. He employs a noble playfulness to describe poverty and the difficulties and aspirations of common life. The prose idyl *The Life of Quintus Fixlein* (1796) tells how a poverty-stricken schoolteacher fulfills his aspirations for happiness. In the novel *Siebenkäs,* Jean Paul flouts conventional morality to free his idealistic hero by fantastic means from his down-to-earth wife, in favor of a more intellectual woman. The novels *Titan* (1800–1803) and *Boorish Years* (1804–1805) deal with the educational development of the central figure.

RIDERS TO THE SEA (1904), by John Millington Synge. Synge's famous one-act drama is set in the Aran Islands off the western coast of Ireland. The scene opens in a fisherman's cottage, and Maurya, an old woman, is mourning her son, Michael, who has been missing nine days. Nora, her younger daughter, comes in with a bundle of clothes that the priest thinks may be Michael's. She and her elder sister hide them from their mother. Bartley, the only remaining son, is going to the mainland to sell some horses, but he too is drowned. Now that the sea has claimed her husband and sons, a great peace descends on Maurya. She knows that she has nothing else to lose and that she need have no more fears.

RIGHTS OF MAN (1791–1792), by Thomas Paine. See COMMON SENSE, by Thomas Paine.

RIGHTS OF WAR AND PEACE (1625), by Hugo Grotius. Writing during a period of dynastic and religious wars, when the universal Roman law was no longer recognized and when rulers were following the precepts of Machiavelli and admitted no limit to their prerogatives, Grotius sought a rational principle to serve as a basis for regulating the relations between sovereign nations. His fame rests on the relative success of his attempt to found an international law. He believed that sovereign nations formed an international society subject to the Law of Nature. This Law of Nature he derived from the nature of man as a rational being rather than from God. Since man is social by nature, he must rationally submit to a system of law which makes social life possible. This system of law, or Law of Nature, does not vary with time and place and hence serves as a basis for social life within individual states as well as among states, and determines rights and obligations in war as well as in peace. In his *Rights of War and Peace,* Grotius outlines this theory and considers its detailed application to such problems as the distinction between just and unjust war, how a just war should be conducted, neutrality, and treaties. This work served as a basis for future attempts to construct systems of international law in terms of relations among sovereign states.

RIJKE MAN, DE (1936), by Arthur van Schendel. See SCHENDEL, ARTHUR VAN.

RIJMSNOER OM EN OM HET JAAR (1897), by Guido Gezelle. See GEZELLE, GUIDO.

RILEY, JAMES WHITCOMB (1849–1916). James Whitcomb Riley had been a journalist and verse writer. The publication of a series of his amusing dialect poems in the *Indianapolis Journal* established his reputation. The pieces appeared in 1883 as *The Old Swimmin'-Hole and 'Leven More Poems.*

Among the sentimental Hoosier poems are the whimsical "When the Frost Is on the Punkin," the pathetic "Little Orphant Annie," and "The Raggedy Man." Riley became famous as a reader of his own compositions, which have charmed youngsters for three-quarters of a century.

RILKE, RAINER MARIA (1875–1926). One of the most important poets of the twentieth century, Rilke was constantly driven by a changing, shifting world to a search for permanency. In transcending the world of objectivity and creating a closer personal reality, he viewed life as the infinite existence where death is a continuation on a higher plane rather than a limitation or completion. Throughout his life, Rilke—the sad, solitary introvert—shied away from fame and acclaim and wandered from one part of the world to another. It was his stay in France, in association with the sculptor Rodin, which lent a plastic touch to some of his poetry. Earlier, while visiting Tolstoy, he found in the lonely Russian expanses a mirror of his own feelings. Exhibiting a profoundly religious nature which reminds us of the seventeenth century mystics, his poetry reveals subtle rhythms and delicate melodies and a consummate mastery of language. The volumes of poetry *The Book of Pictures* (1902) and *The Book of Hours* (1906) express a fervor of imagination. His prose poem, *The Tale of Love and Death of Cornet Christopher Rilke* (1906) employs a taut, intense atmosphere to relate the story of one of his ancestors. Begun in 1911 at the castle of Duino in Istria and completed in 1922 in Switzerland, the *Duinese Elegies,* while making unusual demands upon the reader, demonstrate the subtlety and power of Rilke's beliefs of the basic human problems of soul, death and the after-life. In *Sonnets to Orpheus* (1936) Rilke's subtlety reaches its peak. The music becomes more delicate, and its emotional basis—accentuated by a rare symbolism—becomes more profound.

Since his death, Rilke's popularity and importance has been growing steadily. He has been translated extensively, many of his letters have been published and the serious study of his life continually increases. The influence he exerts is important in present-day literature.

RIMAS (1871), by Gustavo Adolfo Bécquer. See RHYMES, by Gustavo Adolfo Bécquer.

RIME NUOVE (1897), by Giosue' Carducci. See CARDUCCI, GIOSUE'.

RING AND THE BOOK, THE (1868–1869), by Robert Browning. Pompilia, a beautiful young girl, is unhappily married to Count Guido Franceschini, a cruel old nobleman. Pompilia prevails upon a young priest, Caponsacchi, to guide her safely back to her parents. The Count overtakes them, and accusing them of eloping, has the priest banished and Pompilia sent to a convent. Later, when she moves home, Franceschini brutally murders her and her parents. The rest of the story is concerned with the Count's trial, the court wranglings, the sentence, and his final execution. Browning found this tale in an old book and used it as the basis for his poem, as a goldsmith mixes alloy with pure gold to form a ring, hence the title.

RIP TIDE (1932), by William Rose Benét. See BENÉT, WILLIAM ROSE.

RISE OF AMERICAN CIVILIZATION, THE (1927), by Charles A. and Mary R. Beard. See BEARD, CHARLES A.

RISE OF SILAS LAPHAM, THE (1885), by William Dean Howells. This most admired of Howells' earlier novels is a study of Boston life, and of a self-made man. The Coreys, a Brahmin family, are forced to accept the aid of plebeian but wealthy Colonel Silas Lapham. Lapham and his wife, Persis, under their influence, become social climbers. They wrongly assume that Tom Corey is courting their younger daughter Irene. He proposes, however, to Penelope. When he is at first rejected, both families are angered. The Lapham fortune evaporates because Silas refuses to take advantage of a dishonest business deal. This leads to his moral regeneration, and he returns to his simple former life in Vermont. The novel, bringing out the basic sincerity of the millionaire paint maker, and the patrician Bromfield Corey's respect for him, reveals the early Howells optimism for the American way of life in the new age of science.

Other early novels written around the "little everyday things of life" are: *A Chance Acquaintance* (1873), the story of a love affair between Kitty Ellison and egotistical Miles Arbuton. The sweet girl at last breaks her engagement with the priggish socialite. *The Lady of the Aroostook* (1879) concerns Lydia Blood. As she sails on a freighter, flashbacks illustrate her life, typical of a provincial New England village. *A Modern Instance* (1881) concerns Marcia Hubbard, who divorces her unscrupulous husband Bartley, and is admired by the minister Ben Halleck. This is a study of character and ethical problems.

RISING SUN, THE (Eng. tr. 1925), by Hermann Heijermans. See OP HOOP VAN ZEGEN, by Hermann Heijermans.

RIVALS, THE (1775), by Richard Brinsley Sheridan. Sheridan's most hilarious comedy is famous for its good acting parts. The story is laid in Bath, where Captain Absolute, under the name of Ensign Beverley, is wooing Lydia Languish, a sentimental heiress who is guarded by her aunt, Mrs. Malaprop (famous for using long words incorrectly). Sir Anthony Absolute, the Captain's father, tells him that he has arranged a marriage for him, and his son at first objects. The latter discovers, however, that the lady his father has in mind is Lydia. He still plans to elope with her as Beverley to satisfy her desire for romance. Sir Lucius O'Trigger, an impecunious, swaggering Irishman, is under the impression that he is courting Lydia with the help of her maid, Lucy. Lucy delivers his notes to Mrs. Malaprop, who thinks they are meant for her. Another suitor is Bob Acres, a boastful country squire. Sir Lucius persuades Acres to send a challenge to their supposed rival, Beverley, and he challenges Captain Absolute. The duelists all meet in a famous, rollicking scene. Sir Lucius coaches and encourages the terrified Acres, who does not want to fight. He is saved from doing so when he discovers that Beverley is his good friend, Absolute. He gives up Lydia, who decides to marry Absolute even though he does not meet her requirements for a poverty-stricken romantic hero.

RIVER BREAKS UP, THE (1938), by Israel Joshua Singer. See BROTHERS ASHKENAZI, THE, by Israel Joshua Singer.

ROAD TO ROME, THE, (1927), by Robert Sherwood. See SHERWOOD, ROBERT.

ROADS OF DESTINY (1909), by William Sydney Porter. See PORTER, WILLIAM SYDNEY.

ROBBERS, THE (1781), by Friedrich von Schiller. See SCHILLER, FRIEDRICH VON.

ROBE, THE (1942), by Lloyd C. Douglas. In an atmosphere of religious devotion and melodramatic supernaturalism *The Robe* tells the story of Marcellus, a young Roman soldier who is out of favor with the imperial court politicians and is consequently dispatched to Minos (Gaza), there to take command of the Roman troops. While in Jerusalem on official business, he is caught in a crowd which surges around an extraordinary looking man riding a white donkey. The man looks at Marcellus, and from that moment the Roman is never quite the same. Not long after, Marcellus travels to Jerusalem with a detachment to officiate at an execution. On Golgotha, he sees the one who had looked at him so strangely, now in his death agony. The Roman soldiers cast dice for the executed one's garments; Marcellus wins the brown cloak. With the acquisition of this robe, the process of spiritual purgation of the Roman is intensified. He listens to accounts of the miracles of Christ, learns at first hand about the new religion, and is at last converted to Christianity. The book was enormously popular.

Magnificent Obsession (1929) is a novel of a man's influence through good works on everyone he meets. Dr. Wayne Hudson finds the secret to happiness and success through Christ's words. His influence grows after his death. Robert Merrick becomes a surgeon, and after deciphering Dr. Hudson's secret journal continues the older man's work. He, too, is repaid; in one instance by the discovery of a device which revolutionizes brain surgery—a device which saves the life of the woman he loves, Dr. Hudson's widow, Helen.

ROBIN HOOD AND GUY OF GISBORNE (published 1765), Anonymous. This, perhaps the most popular Robin Hood ballad, tells of that gallant outlaw's encounter with the Yorkshireman, Guy of Gisborne, who had sworn to take him. After a friendly display of marksmanship, Robin Hood and Guy fight with swords. Robin Hood kills Sir Guy, changes clothes with him, and tricks the Sheriff of Nottingham into letting him free Little John, who had been captured by the sheriff's men. Little John, with Guy's bow and arrows, puts the forces of the law to flight. There are, of course, many other ballads in the Robin Hood cycle, involving such comrades as Will Scarlet, Friar Tuck, Allan-a-Dale, and (a later addition) Maid Marian. Some manuscripts date back to the fifteenth century, and the legend early broke into print, not only in ballads but in prose and in plays.

ROBINSON, EDWIN ARLINGTON (1869–1935). The poetic career of Robinson was assured when President Theodore Roosevelt became interested in *The Children of the Night* (1897). This volume of fifty-seven short pieces reveals the author's typical mood of pessimism and disenchantment. Among the well-known psychological character sketches are "Richard Cory," about a wealthy man who puts a bullet through his head for want of a valid reason for living; "John Evereldown," about an old romantic; and "Aaron Stark," about a miser.

Captain Craig (1902), contains similar studies. The title piece, a mischievous poem, tells of the death of a pauper who in his own way was really the happiest man in the town. "The Book of Annandale" considers the problem of love and self-denial. *The Town Down the River* (1910) continues these portraits. "Miniver Cheevy" tells of a dreamer who does not realize that his failure is actually due to personal inadequacies.

Robinson wrote a distinguished trilogy about Arthurian characters. *Merlin* (1917) is a portrait of the king's wizard. His own love for Vivian destroyed by ominous visions, he goes to Camelot, the doomed city. *Lancelot* (1920) tells of Lancelot's abortive kidnaping of Guinevere, and of her spurning of him after he overthrows the king. *Tristram* (1927) which won a Pulitzer Prize, is a reworking of the legend first related by Malory. Robinson's Tristram is a melancholy man, easily caught in the triangular love tragedy.

Another Pulitzer Prize winner was *The Man Who Died Twice* (1924). In this long, blank verse narrative, Fernando Nash, a gifted musician, barters his genius for the pleasures of common dissipation. At forty-five the unhappy man beats a Salvation Army drum and waits resignedly for death.

Talifer (1933), a poem novel with a mood of humor, is a tale in which Dr. Quick watches Samuel Talifer leave his fiancée Althea to mary Karen, then secure a divorce to return to Althea. The posthumous *King Jasper* (1935), however, reveals Robinson's characteristic philosophy of the futility of human effort. In it a ruthless industrialist sees his career and family life destroyed by a semisupernatural series of personal dramas.

ROBINSON CRUSOE, THE LIFE AND STRANGE SURPRIZING ADVENTURES OF (1719), by Daniel Defoe. A perennial favorite in every generation, *Robinson Crusoe* is the expression of the hunger for adventure inherent in all human beings. The main part of the story (supposed to be based upon the real adventures of Alexander Selkirk) opens in the year 1659 when Robinson Crusoe is shipwrecked on a solitary island near the Orinoco River. With self-reliance, courage and ingenuity he adjusts himself to the primitive conditions he finds, builds a hut, fortifies his cave, sows corn, constructs a raft and finds consolation in the *Bible* (q.v.).

For twenty-four years he lives in solitude. Then he acquires as his companion the Negro Friday, whom he has saved from the cannibals' cauldron on a Friday. In his twenty-seventh year on the island a Spaniard and a Negro, survivors of a shipwreck, join him. Later the little community is increased by a captain, his mate and a passenger, after a mutinous crew had seized their ship from them. Robinson Crusoe helps them to recapture the ship and returns with them at long last to England.

In Part II, the much inferior sequel, after an interval of eight years of a happy life Crusoe's wife dies; he then decides to revisit his beloved island. So he takes with him a priest, several mechanics, and his good friend Friday, and puts out to sea. When they reach the island Crusoe has the priest marry off the sailors to the native girls. With a substantial Christian colony thus established, but grieved at the slaying of Friday by cannibals, he returns to England to spend his declining years.

ROCK, THE (1934), by T. S. Eliot. See ELIOT, THOMAS STEARNS.

RODERICK HUDSON (1876), by Henry James. See JAMES, HENRY.

RODERICK RANDOM, THE ADVENTURES OF (1748), by Tobias Smollett. Semiautobiographical, this picaresque novel tells of the death of Roderick's mother at his birth and of his cruel treatment by his grandfather and the schoolmaster. His mother's brother, Tom Bowling, a sailor, gives him financial aid until Tom is forced to exile himself, having killed an officer in a duel. Roderick becomes an apothecary's apprentice, goes to London with Strap, his friend, becomes a sailor and, finally, a surgeon's mate. Enduring battle, suffering, and shipwreck, he is enabled at last to work as a servant to an eccentric old woman with whose niece, Narcissa, he falls in love. She encourages him, but he has to run away to escape the revenge of Sir Timothy Thicket, a rival for Narcissa. Roderick goes to France, where he meets his uncle, Tom Bowling. Robbed of what little he has by a reprobate friar, he enlists in the French army. His old friend, Hugh Strap, has inherited some money which he shares more than generously with Roderick, who manages (after participating in some battles) to be discharged from the army. He attempts to win Miss Melinda Goosetrap by pretending to be wealthy, but her mother interferes. Gambling and bribery of officials having failed to replenish his borrowed fortunes, he next plans to marry wealthy Miss Snapper, a deformed woman. At Bath he meets Narcissa and is unable to conceal the fact that he still loves her. His renewed wooing of her is impeded by her brother, who wants her to marry Lord Quiverwit, and by the indignant Melinda, now also at Bath, who spreads scandalous stories about Roderick's origin and character. Narcissa is carried away by her brother. Roderick, in despair, joins his uncle's crew as surgeon and lands in South America, where he is befriended by Don Roderigo, a wealthy trader, who turns out to be Roderick's father. Roderick returns to England, marries Narcissa, and settles down on his father's estate, where he enjoys true happiness on earth.

ROLAND BLAKE (1886), by S. Weir Mitchell. See HUGH WYNNE, FREE QUAKER, by S. Weir Mitchell.

ROLLING STONES (1913), by William Sydney Porter. See PORTER, WILLIAM SYDNEY.

ROMANCE OF THE ROSE, THE (ca. end of 13th c.), by Guillaume de Lorris and Jean de Meun. This famous verse idyl is in two parts, the first by de Lorris and the second by his imitator, de Meun. The story is a simple allegory of the love of a young man for a beautiful girl. It contains charming pastoral descriptions, but is mainly concerned with the vices and passions of mankind. There is no clearly defined plot, although there are lifelike portraits of the jealous husband and of the duenna who tells the tale of her own wasted life. De Meun's part introduces a more realistic treatment of the problems and foibles of the people of the age. The characters, all allegorical, are grouped around The Lover, who bemoans his misfortune and disillusionment. The principal characters are: The Dreamer, afterward called The Lover, The God of Love, Fair Welcome, The Friend, Danger, Reason, Franchise, Pity, Courtesy, Shame, Fear, Idleness, Jealousy, Wicked Tongue, Venus, Wealth and Hypocrisy.

The poem had a great influence on Chaucer.

ROMANCE OF THE THREE KINGDOMS, THE (13th c.), by Lo Kuanchung. See SAN KUO CHIH, by Lo Kuanchung.

ROMANCERO, THE (15th-16th c.), Anonymous. The word "Romancero" is here used for the body of anonymous ballads (romances) which flourished in Spain during the 15th and 16th centuries and are still recited and sung by Spanish-speaking people the world over: in Spain, Latin America, North Africa, the Near East, among Christians and Jews and Indians and Negroes. A romance is a brief epico-lyric poem, fragmentary in style, generally portraying some dramatic moment in a hero's career. The romance has a fixed metrical pattern: lines of eight syllables, those of odd number being rhymeless, those of even number assonanting, with one fixed accent on the seventh syllable. As the romance's popularity increased, its subject matter widened to include Arthurian legends (King Arthur and the Round Table, Launcelot, Tristan, etc.), the Breton Cycle, the Carolingian Cycle, as well as the history of Spain, folklore, mythology, frontier warfare, the lives of highwaymen and smugglers. *The Romancero* is truly a never-failing source of pleasure; no wonder the Spanish critic Azorín has called it Castile's most inspired literary work.

Originally the romances were transmitted orally or in broadsides, but from the sixteenth century on many editors have compiled them in collections: *Cancionero General* (1511), *Cancionero de romances* (1550), *Silva de varios romances* (1550), *Romancero General* (1600), and countless others.

ROMANTIC COMEDIANS, THE (1926), by Ellen Glasgow. See BARREN GROUND, by Ellen Glasgow.

ROMANTIC YOUNG LADY, THE (1918), by Gregorio Martínez Sierra. Rosario is a romantic young lady. Having been spoiled all her life by three brothers and a kind, understanding grandmother, she is determined to go modern and shift for herself. She is alone in her parlor when apparently by accident a man's hat comes flying through the window, and, much to her surprise, a man comes after it. Presently, after some explanations, and a conversation in which Rosario confesses to this unknown man her desire for feminine independence, he advises her to apply as secretary to a well-known author. The next morning, armed with a letter of introduction, she inquires for the position. She is deeply offended when she learns that the famous author is none other than her unknown midnight intruder. Rosario even becomes jealous of his many admirers; especially a gaudy foreign dancer. Wrathfully she leaves his house. That night he attempts to visit her by the same surreptitious entrance: the window. Unfortunately, the maid spots him first and bashes his head with a statuette. He thereupon enters by the more conventional way, the front door, to have his head bandaged and his heart repaired and then to marry the girl.

ROMANY RYE, THE (1857), by George Borrow. See LAVENGRO, by George Borrow.

ROME HAUL, (1929), by Walter D. Edmonds. See DRUMS ALONG THE MOHAWK, by Walter D. Edmonds.

ROMEO AND JULIET (written ca. 1595; first Quarto 1597; second Quarto 1599), by William Shakespeare. This tragedy is based on a poem by Arthur Brooke which in turn was taken from a romance by Bandello. The Montagues and the Capulets, two powerful families in Verona, have an ancient grudge; their followers often quarrel in the streets. Prince Escalus warns them that if they break the peace again their lives shall be forfeit. Old Capulet gives a feast to which his friends are bidden, and by mistake a servant shows the list to Romeo, heir of the House of Montague. His friend, Mercutio, persuades him to go. Tybalt, nephew of Lady Capulet, recognizes him and wishes to challenge him but old Capulet forbids it. Romeo had been sighing over the fair Rosaline, but when he sees Juliet, Capulet's only daughter, he forgets Rosaline. He is aghast when he discovers who his new love is. Juliet in turn falls in love with him. Romeo climbs the wall of the Capulets' orchard and overhears Juliet on the balcony confessing her love to the moon. They plight their troth in one of the most beautiful love scenes in the English language. They plan to marry secretly, and the ceremony is performed the next day by Romeo's friend, Friar Laurence. Tybalt, who had been looking for Romeo to challenge him because of his presence at the feast, meets Mercutio and Benvolio. He starts a quarrel, as Romeo arrives fresh from his wedding. The latter tries to placate Tybalt by answering him gently. But his submission is too much for Mercutio, who starts a fight with Tybalt. Romeo tries to intervene, and in the struggle Mercutio is wounded and dies. Revengeful, Romeo turns on Tybalt and kills him. By a mandate of the Prince he is banished from Verona. He spends one night with his bride. Lady Capulet comes to announce to her daughter that her father has be-throthed her to Paris, a young nobleman. Juliet refuses to wed at first, but at last, desperate, consults Friar Laurence. The Friar thinks he sees a way out. She is to consent to her nuptials with Paris, and drink a potion, which he gives her the night before. It will give her a semblance of death; she will be laid away, according to custom, in the Capulets' burial vault. And at the time of her awakening the Friar and Romeo will rescue her. Juliet, full of forebod-ings, drinks the potion. The Friar's message to Romeo is misdirected and Romeo believes the report that Juliet is dead. Despairing, he goes to an apothecary, and purchases a powerful poison. He returns to Verona to die beside Juliet. At the tomb he encounters Paris, who had gone to lay flowers at Juliet's grave. They fight and Romeo kills Paris, who requests to be laid with Juliet. Romeo places him in the tomb and then drinks the poison. Friar Laurence hastens to the tomb and calls Juliet, who wakens to find Paris and Romeo dead. He is frightened by a noise and says he must go away but will return for her. Overcome with grief, Juliet kills herself with Romeo's dagger. Paris' page spreads the alarm and the Montagues and Capulets meet at the tomb. They are reconciled by the tragedy their feud has caused.

ROMOLA (1862–1863), by George Eliot (Mary Ann, or Marian, Evans). George Eliot thought of *Middlemarch* (q.v.) as her masterpiece, but a large proportion of her readers put *Romola* first. She visited Florence twice, and is said to have read more than three hundred volumes in preparation for her writing of the novel, which re-creates the life of Florence in the last years of the fifteenth century. *Romola* is several things: it is the first notable example in English of an ever increasingly popular genre—historical fiction; it is a movingly sympathetic yet objective analysis of the great Florentine reformer and martyr, Savonarola, forerunner of the Protestant Reformation; and it is a vivid, powerful study of the moral degeneration of a husband and of the spiritual maturing of a wife.

Tito Melema, a handsome young Greek castaway, appears in Florence with a few valuable gems, which he sells; though he feels he ought to keep them to ransom his foster-father Baldassare Calvo, who is reported to be in slavery in Turkey. Tito ingratiates himself with everyone he meets, including Bardo, the blind scholar, and his golden-haired daughter Romola. These two fall in love, and after a proper interval are married. Bardo dies; Tito, fishing in the troubled waters of Florentine politics, sells Bardo's scholarly library and plans to get safely out of Florence. Romola, shocked out of her love and even her respect for her husband, sets out from Florence, but is met and dissuaded by the famous reformer Savonarola.

Meantime Tito's abandoned foster-father, Baldassare, appears in Florence, sees Tito and is seen by him; buys a dagger, but is made helpless by age and weakness and loss of memory. At length Tito, caring only for pleasure and popularity and safety, playing both the Medicean party and their bitter opponents against each other, is caught: he leaps into the Arno to escape the mob, but falls into the avenging arms of old Baldassare, who throttles the traitorous, lying Tito, and falls dead on his body.

Romola, strengthened and ennobled by the way she takes her suffering, leaves Florence again, but returns to use her strength and sweetness to help others; and takes to her home and her heart Tito's other wife, the "baby-faced" Tessa and her two children.

Through this story runs that of the powerful and benevolent dictator of Florence, Savonarola; and it ends with his excommunication, imprisonment, torture, and martyrdom, at the instigation of the Borgia Pope, Alexander VI.

Other major characters in this famous historical novel are Fra Luca, Romola's brother; Bernardo del Nero, her godfather; Piero de' Medici and Cardinal Giovanni de' Medici; and Niccolò Machiavelli.

RONSARD, PIERRE DE (1524–1585). Like Rabelais, this Renaissance scholar, courtier and poet was intoxicated by the new learning. He combined a taste for ancient literature with a great lyric gift. As a scholar he delighted in the great Latin and especially the Greek poets; as a poet he wanted to revive the classical poetic forms, particularly the epic and the ode, and to enrich the French language to the point where it would be an adequate literary instrument. *The Defence and Illustration of the French Language* (q.v.), generally ascribed to his friend Du Bellay, is largely a statement of Ronsard's ambitions. His poetry, apart from an unreadable epic, *The Franciad* (1572–1578) is largely bucolic and amatory. Much of the love suggests the lovely *carpe diem* poems of Herrick. Ronsard's best-known single poem, the much translated "Sonnet to Helen," seems to have inspired Yeats' "When you are old and gray and full of sleep."

Around Ronsard gathered a group of lyric and dramatic poets, the "Pléiade," which included, in addition to Du Bellay, talented figures like Étienne Jodelle, Rémy Belleau, and Baïf. These last have survived changes in taste only in classroom texts. In his own time Ronsard was regarded as one of the great poets of the world. The more disciplined seventeenth century considered him barbaric, and his reputation stayed in eclipse until resurrected by the school of Hugo (ca. 1830), and its revolt against the classic doctrines. He since has had a prominent place in anthologies.

ROOSEVELT AND HOPKINS (1949), by Robert Sherwood. See SHERWOOD, ROBERT.

ROOTABAGA STORIES (1922), by Carl Sandburg. See SANDBURG, CARL.

ROSSETTI, CHRISTINA GEORGINA (1830–1894). The first book by the sister of Dante Gabriel Rossetti was *Goblin Market and Other Poems* (1862). The title piece is an allegorical fairy tale about worldly pleasures. *The Prince's Progress* (1866) is a similar allegory, employing the theme of a young prince delayed by alluring distractions while traveling to meet his bride.

The bulk of Christina Rossetti's poetry is religious in subject matter, polished in technique, and melancholy in tone.

ROUGHING IT (1872), by Mark Twain. See INNOCENTS ABROAD, THE, by Mark Twain.

ROUGON-MACQUART, THE (1871–1893), by Émile Zola. Zola's long series of violently realistic novels grew out of his great respect for biological science, and more particularly from his reading of Claude Bernard's *Experimental Medicine* and the works of Taine. From them he got the notion that the human being was determined by his heredity and environment and that the novel could acquire some of the authority of science if it adopted an experimental method and became, in theory, a demonstration of what variations in heredity and environment do to the human animal. His series would present "The Social and Natural History of a Family under the Second Empire." He intended the greatly ramified Rougon-Macquart family to represent different combinations of "good" and "bad" blood; its members, on the several social levels, would be submitted to the influence of all kinds of environments. Scientifically his theory was vulnerable—the "bleeding slice of life" is a product of the imagination, not of the laboratory. But Zola succeeded in producing novels which by their strength and vividness present an arresting picture of the life of his time.

The Dram Shop (1877) is set in the slums of Paris. Gervaise Macquart has quit the provincial town of Plassans to come to Paris with her lover, Auguste Lantier, who is the father of her two natural children, Étienne and Claude. Lantier abandons Gervaise shortly after they arrive in Paris and she sets up a laundry. She takes up with Lantier's friend Coupeau, marries him, has a daughter, Nana. Lantier returns. Both he and Coupeau are out of work and Gervaise has to support them both. Then she loses her customers, and has to go to work in a big laundry by the day. Both men cause her great grief. Coupeau takes to drink and winds up in an asylum, demented by alcohol. Gervaise also begins to drink heavily, gets delirium tremens, and at last dies in starvation and filth.

In *Germinal* (1883) her illegitimate son Étienne becomes a socialist and leads a strike at a coal mine near Lille. Hunger drives the miners to despair. The strike is broken; several miners are killed; Étienne is driven away. Zola's description of bad social conditions, heavily documented and graphic in the extreme, his expert manipulation of mob scenes, and his use of such symbols as mining machinery, make this story his masterpiece.

Nana (1880) is the story of the daughter of Gervaise by Coupeau. She grows up in the streets, becomes a third-rate actress; she has no talent, but her lethal sexuality attracts men. She breaks hearts and dissipates fortunes. Zola uses her as a symbol of social corruption, calls her a beautiful fly spawned in a dunghill.

The Downfall (1892) pictures the collapse of the society which produced such people. The subject is the war of 1870 and the Paris Commune, with the siege and capitulation of Sedan as the central episode. Another Macquart, Jean, goes through the war as a corporal, witnesses the debacle and "cleansing" of France, and emerges as one of those who will go out to rebuild the country.

Other familiar titles in the series are *The Soil* (life among the peasants; 1888), *The Human Beast* (railroading; 1890), *The Belly of Paris* (life in the food markets; 1873), and *Money* (the financial world; 1891).

"Naturalism," as Zola called his theory of the novel, was flayed by contemporary critics and, as theory, was short-lived. His practice, however, has inspired novelists in France and abroad, and such disparate types of writers as Maupassant, Huysmans, George Moore, Celine, Frank Norris, Dreiser and James Farrell have acknowledged their debt to him.

ROUSSEAU AND ROMANTICISM (1919), by Irving Babbitt. See BABBITT, IRVING.

ROWLEY POEMS, THE (published 1777), by Thomas Chatterton. Chatterton invented a fifteenth-century Bristol poet and named him Thomas Rowley. He wrote verses and passed them off as Rowley's. To give authenticity to his make-believe creation, Chatterton first composed "Rowley's" poems in English and then translated them into a quaint linguistic hodge-podge of Middle English, Elizabethan English, Scotch and folk expressions. Some scholars actually swallowed the hoax; the more judicious recognized them as mere impressionistic imitations of old-time poetry. The best known of the Rowley Poems are: "Bristowe Tragedie," "Excelente Balade of Charitie," "Songe to Ella," and "Battle of Hastings." After seeing only "Elinoure and Juga" in print—he had written it when he was about twelve—Chatterton, desperate and starving, committed suicide before reaching eighteen.

ROXANA, THE FORTUNATE MISTRESS (1724), by Daniel Defoe. Roxana is an upper-class counterpart of the author's earlier Moll Flanders, and this story too traces autobiographically the rise and fall of a woman led morally astray by circumstance. In the time of Charles II, Roxana, of French origin, marries in England "a fool" of a husband, who leaves her destitute after eight years with five children. Her only friend and ally is Amy, her maid. She becomes the mistress of her landlord, and she and her maid each has a child by him. This benefactor is set upon by robbers in France, however, and slain. Roxana takes up with a French prince and is richly rewarded. She tours Italy with him. This connection is followed by other amours in Holland and in England. At last Roxana marries a kindly Dutch merchant who had formerly been her lover and their first son is legitimized. Her daughter by her first husband pursues her out of the shady past. At the end calamities come to Roxana and Amy, giving them reason to repent their sins.

ROYAL FAMILY (1927), by Edna Ferber and George Kaufman. See SHOW BOAT, by Edna Ferber.

ROYAL HIGHNESS (1909), by Thomas Mann. See MANN, THOMAS.

ROYAL WAY, THE (1930), by André Malraux. See MAN'S FATE, by André Malraux.

ROYCE, JOSIAH (1855–1916). Royce was perhaps the strongest exponent of idealistic philosophy (in metaphysics and morals) in America. Strongly influenced by Kant and Hegel, he nevertheless developed a system of some originality because of his acquaintance with the logical theories of C. S.

Peirce and with the psychology of William James. Although his metaphysical position was one of absolutism, he did not consider it necessary that the Absolute swallow up the individual. Much of his writing is devoted to showing the terms of the reconcilation of the one and the many. His emphasis on will rather than intellect and his conception of experience in emotional rather than in scientific terms indicate the influence of the Romanticists and Schopenhauer. The most important books in which he develops these themes are *The Spirit of Modern Philosophy* (1892) and *The World and the Individual* (1900–1901). He was also concerned with problems of morality, which he approached from the point of view of the individual's relation to the ideals of his community. His theory on this matter is set forth in his *Philosophy of Loyalty* (1908).

RUBÁIYÁT OF OMAR KHAYYÁM, THE (early 12th c.), translated 1859 by Edward Fitzgerald. One of the most widely read single poetical works in English-speaking countries is the translation of these quatrains from the Persian by Edward Fitzgerald. Despite the obvious scepticism of *The Rubáiyát,* modern readers have never stopped to take issue with the poet over his "vanity-of-vanities" motif. They love the quatrains for their beauty, grace, symmetry, delicate imagery, subtle phrasing, and above all for their *fin-de-siècle* languor and insouciance. The quatrains are among the most quotable verses in all poetry. Each one of them has some underlying thought, mood, observation, or sentiment that is of universal truth and applicability.

RUDDER GRANGE (1879), by Frank R. Stockton. See LADY, OR THE TIGER? THE, by Frank R. Stockton.

RUDIN (1856), by Ivan Sergeyevich Turgenev. The hero, who gives title to the story, is a man of ideals and education; but he is not a practical man. When the story opens, he is conversing at the home of Darya Mikhailovna, who is much taken with his oratorical powers. He feels so much at home here that he falls in love with her daughter Natalya. With the romantic fervor of youth, Natalya is ready to sacrifice security for the man she loves. She discovers that Rudin is not a man cast in a heroic mold. For his part, Rudin must now abandon his sinecure and wander. He dies on the barricades in the Paris insurrection of July, 1848. As in the case of Liza, who, in *Nest of Gentlefolk,* sacrifices everything, so also does Natalya possess the power for sacrifice which fires so many of Turgenev's heroines. This moral beauty of his young women gives them their singular appeal. Dmitry Rudin, a typical man of his period, is both a victim and a hero of sorts: a Titan in words, a pigmy in deeds; eloquent in debate, puerile in action. Natalya, suffer as she did, remained radiant. She marries Alexandra Petrovna's brother, Seryozha. In the words of the author: "Natalya suffered terribly, she suffered for the first time—but first sorrow, like first love, does not come again —and thank God for it."

Only the poet Lermontov wrote such beautiful Russian prose as Turgenev. Much of the fascination of his novels lies in his mastery of the rich, flexible, musical Russian language; of which he wrote in his last work, *Poems in Prose (Senilia)* in 1879–1883: "In days of doubt, in days of sad brooding on my country's fate, thou alone art my rod and my staff—mighty, true, free Russian speech! But for thee, how not fall into despair, seeing all that happens at home? Yet who can think that such a tongue is not the gift of a great people!"

RUGGLES OF RED GAP (1915), by Harry Leon Wilson. Egbert, a cow-puncher from Red Gap, Washington, visits Paris and wins in a poker game the valet Marmaduke Ruggles. Back in Egbert's home town, Ruggles becomes a social lion. At length he becomes quite Americanized. His former master, the Honorable George, also comes to Red Gap, and marries a local girl.

Merton of the Movies (1922) is a comedy about a stage-struck youth who becomes a comedy star while attempting to act dramatic roles.

RUIN, THE (10th c.). Along with "The Seafarer," "The Wife's Complaint," "The Wanderer," "The Husband's Message," this old poem appears in the *Exeter Book*. It differs from the others in that it deals not with a person but a place—probably Bath. The description might be that of a town after an air raid. Vividly and realistically the poet describes the buildings, deserted, tottering, with no roofs to protect from wind and weather. Yet once these buildings were full of feasting and gaiety. So are the proud stones fallen.

RULE AND EXERCISE OF HOLY LIVING, THE (1650), and **RULE AND EXERCISE OF HOLY DYING, THE** (1651), by Jeremy Taylor. Among the devotional works that have attained a permanent position in English literature are these religious treatises. The first gives rules for proper, chaste conduct during life under the topic headings of "Sobriety," "Justice," and "Religion." The second presents detailed instruction by which one may prepare in life for "a holy and blessed death." Many beautiful prayers are included.

RULE OF NUNS (13th c.). See ANCRENRIWLE.

RUNYON, DAMON (1884–1946). Damon Runyon, who began to write as a newspaper man and sports columnist, became known for his short stories, in "Americanese," of certain New York types: athletes, gamblers, underworld characters and other colorful personages. Such collections as *Guys and Dolls* (1932), *Take It Easy* (1938), and *My Wife Ethel* (1940), contain pieces involving Harry the Horse, Little Isadore, Last Card Louie, Society Max, Good Time Charlie Bernstein, and others. The tales of the Roaring Forties are whimsical, sentimental, and often have a surprise ending, such as in "The Snatching of Bookie Bob." In this anecdote, a kidnaped horse player takes his abductors for their rolls by making book at the hide-out. They hardly have enough money left to pay a bonus to the person who had given them the tip that their man would be a profitable victim—the bookie's wife!

R.U.R. (1922), (by Karel Čapek. This is the best known play by the Czech dramatist, Karel Čapek (1890–1938), and it has won a lasting position not only at home, but on the world stage, for its unique and effective combination of melodrama and social analysis and philosophy.

The firm of Rossum's Universal Robots manufactures in huge numbers synthetic men and women for all kinds of occupations; finally they replace all human labor. The robots are in human form, but with a minimum of a nervous organization, and are therefore impervious to most human feelings except rudimentary pain. The wife of one of the managers of the firm persuades one of the technicians to produce more sensitive and alert robots. When this is done, the improved brand lead a revolt of their fellows and finally wipe out the human race, except for one architect who has had no scientific training. Then the robots discover that the formula for their construction has been destroyed. Just as it appears certain that the robots will follow the human race into extinction, the architect learns that some of the improved robots are the equivalent of men and women, and so a new race can be raised.

The ordinary dramatist would have maintained to the end the contrast between man and the robot, but this transformation is typical of Karel Čapek. In other plays, such as *The Makropulos Secret* (1925) and *Adam and Eve* (1930), and his novels *Krakatit* (Eng. tr. 1925), and the *Factory of the Absolute* (1927), or the very successful *Insect Comedy* (Eng. tr. 1923), written with the collaboration of his brother Joseph, Karel Čapek maintains his belief in the ultimate triumph of the ordinary man living in accordance with the laws of nature, as they have been handed down through the ages. It led him to a denial of the machine age, for he never accepted the idea that man could use his inventions for a beneficent purpose. He refused to visit the United States, and he almost literally died of a broken heart during the months before Hitler's occupation of Prague. Also well known for his whimsical travel sketches and his *Conversations with Thomas G. Masaryk* (Eng. tr. 1938), he was easily the most interesting and influential of the writers of the Czechoslovak Republic.

RURAL RIDES (1830), by William Cobbett. This is a record of many journeys made by the English economist and reformer from 1821 to 1830. He had made this extensive tour through twenty-seven counties of England partly for pleasure, and partly in order to improve his mind by observation and contact with the common people. Interested in the political philosophy of agricultural workers, he wished to see at first hand how the farmers lived. *Rural Rides* is thus a collection of Cobbett's ideas, prejudices and interests. He makes it clear that he admires tidy homes, neatly kept farms and healthy, well-fed farmers.

RUSLAN AND LYUDMILLA (1820), by Alexander S. Pushkin. Alexander Sergeyevich Pushkin, Russia's foremost poet, began writing *Ruslan and Lyudmilla,* the poetic drama that was to make him renowned in his native land, in 1817, when he was only in his eighteenth year and a student at the Lyceum. It was his first experiment with narrative verse, and it was based on a popular folk tale. Glinka, the eminent composer, in the grip of the new nationalism that was asserting itself in Russia, used the poem as a libretto for his best-known opera *Ruslan and Lyudmilla.* The story of the poem is about the princess Lyudmilla, who was carried off on her wedding night by the wizard Chernomor. It relates the adventures of Ruslan, her bereft husband, in his search for her. The poem is arranged in six cantos and consists of some 3,000 lines. When the work was published in 1820 it created a popular sensation. Its folklore story, animated by witty and charming narrative and written in musical verse sparkling with gaiety, won the hearts of the younger generation, who were dissatisfied with the stilted classicism of the day.

RUSSELL, BERTRAND (1872–   ). This Englishman's main contribution to the history of ideas was the work he did with Whitehead in the *Principia Mathematica*. His philosophic position is the attempt to apply the techniques of symbolic logic to the data of experience and thereby develop a scientific philosophy. He has been much concerned with the problem of knowledge (how do we know the external world?) and with the relation of mind and matter. He developed a theory which involved the existence or subsistence of a variety of independent entities: physical things, relations, mathematical entities, and values. He is severely critical of traditional theological beliefs, which he feels have been rendered untenable by modern science and logic. However, his notion of "A Free Man's Worship" is a religious view without the postulation of a supernatural God or immortal souls. His philosophical writing is best approached through *The Problems of Philosophy* (1911) and *Our Knowledge of the External World* (1929). His contributions to the foundations of mathematics and to social and political philosophy make him one of the most influential philosophers in the contemporary world.

RUSSIA AND EUROPE (1913), by Thomas G. Masaryk. Thomas G. Masaryk (1850–1937), President and liberator of the Czechoslovak Republic, was far more than a successful political figure. He was the foremost educator and philosopher of his people, and renewed that intellectual tradition of devotion to the truth that had been the distinguishing feature of the old Hussite period and of the Bohemian Brethren. He had a broad knowledge of Europe and of European philosophy, and all his life he had a special sympathy for Anglo-Saxon culture.

Russia and Europe, which appeared in German in 1913, and in Czech in 1919–1921, and has since been translated into English as the *Spirit of Russia* (1919), is almost an encyclopedia of Russian political and religious thought, written from the point of view of Masaryk's critical realism and strong ethical bent. He reviews the influence on Russian life of such theories as Moscow being the Third Rome, and points out the results of the secularizing into an autocracy of this religious conception. Then he analyzes the products of the autocracy, and the ideas of the leading members of the Russian intelligentsia and of the revolutionary critics. He does not accept the theories of those who stress the peculiarities of the Russian soul, or who try to explain the Russian character by geographical or physical conditions, but emphasizes the need of the Russians to overcome their tendencies toward autocracy and nihilism by a reconsideration of the achievements of great thinkers of the past like Kant and Hume, and by a clearer perception of the meaning of religion and ethics.

The two volumes of this work (a third on Dostoevsky was never completed) form one of the most penetrating studies of Russian life and thought that has ever been prepared, and amplify and complete the author's studies of Czech history and philosophy and the problems of Austria-Hungary, all of which are considered in this same light of truth and of a practical religious-ethical outlook.

RUSSIAN GENTLEMAN, A (1846–1858), by Sergei Timofeyevich Aksakov. See FAMILY CHRONICLE, A, by Sergi Timofeyevich Aksakov.

RUSSIAN SCHOOLBOY, A (1846–1858), by Sergei Timofeyevich Aksakov. See FAMILY CHRONICLE, A, by Sergei Timofeyevich Aksakov.

R.V.R. (1930), by Hendrik Willem van Loon. See STORY OF MANKIND, THE, by Hendrik Willem van Loon.

SABBATAI ZWI (1930), by Sholem Asch. See NAZARENE, THE, by Sholem Asch.

SABBATH SONGS (1875), by Mendele Mocher Sefarim. . See MENDELE MOCHER SEFARIM.

SACCHETTI, FRANCO (1335–1410). In his short stories Franco Sacchetti gives a clear and humorous picture of the Italian middle class of his time, a society turning more and more toward demagogy. The majority of Sacchetti's stories are founded on real occurrences, and are written with an unpretentious style; some of them are tragic. A man of solid and humorous wisdom, Sacchetti frequently delivers religious and moral discourses, displaying, however, a great liberalism of feeling. The stories, describing mostly events happening to jesters, artists or common people, are recounted with such simplicity that the author gives the impression of writing only for a limited circle of friends, with no special care for artistic effects. However, it is just in this simplicity and spontaneity that the principal merit of Sacchetti's work is found. Aside from literary qualities, the two hundred and seven complete short stories are important as a document of Italian, and especially Florentine, life in the thirteenth century.

SACHS, HANS (1494–1576). Hans Sachs, long-lived and prodigiously prolific shoemaker and poet, representative of the civilization of homely sixteenth-century burghers, flourished while his native Nuremberg was on the crest as a center of commerce, trade, and intellectual life. Both in the bulk of his poetical output and his poetical talent, Hans Sachs was an impressive personality of the age of the Reformation. In his autobiography Goethe recalled with gratitude what in his youth he owed to the old poet, and Richard Wagner made his name famous by making him the central character of his comic opera *The Mastersingers,* in which he also set to the music of the grandiose chorus in the third act the initial lines of Sachs' "Nightingale of Wittenberg," a long poem in praise of Luther's religious fight.

The unevenness of his eight-syllable doggerel in rhymed couplets serves to heighten Hans Sachs' simple naturalness, naïve good nature, sense of humor, comfortable ease, keen observation of everyday life, and homely morality, traits which show best in his eighty-one surviving Shrovetide plays and his numerous merry tales. The best known of his Shrovetide plays is the delightful farce *The Wandering Scholar from Paradise,* which has also been translated several times into English.

SACRED BOOKS OF THE EAST, THE, edited by Max Müller (1886–1895). The largest collection of Eastern religious lore is that edited by Max Müller under the comprehensive title of *The Sacred Books of the East*. It is in fifty volumes, containing authoritative translations by leading Orientalists; the religious texts being carefully annotated and illuminated by explanatory introductions. They may be roughly divided into six categories: The Sacred Books of the Brahmans; The Sacred Books of the Buddhists; The Sacred Books of the Zoroastrians; The Sacred Books of Confucius; The Sacred Books of Lao-tse, The Sacred Books of Islam. Except for Orientalists, few Westerners probably have heard of such religious books as: *The Sacred Laws of the Âryas; Pahlavi Texts; Institutes of Vishnu; The Dhammapada; Satapatha Brahmâna; Vinaya Texts; The Saddharma; Pundarîka; The Fo-Sho-Hing-Tsan King; The Questions of King Milinda; Buddhist Mahâyâna Texts;* and similar works. All these, and many others, are included in this monumental library of Eastern religious literature.

SACRED WOOD, THE (1920), by T. S. Eliot. See ELIOT, THOMAS STEARNS.

SAGA OF BURNT NJÁL, THE (late 13th c.). See NJÁL SAGA.

SAINT, THE (1880), by Conrad Ferdinand Meyer. See MEYER, CONRAD FERDINAND.

SAINT, THE (1905), by Antonio Fogazzaro. One of the most eminent novelists since Manzoni, Antonio Fogazzaro established his reputation with *The Saint*. Translations into other European languages quickly followed publication in Italian, and the novel became the object of tense debate in religious and literary circles. Benedetto, the Saint, is a mixture of a Saint Francis of Assisi and of an enlightened socialist. *The Saint* is largely a chronicle of his zeal, ecstasies, visions, depressions and doubts in his quest for God and a social philosophy based on service. His relation to the magnetic Jeanne only emphasizes the antihumanism of his philosophy of religion. Especially remarkable is the scene of his temptation when he is alone with her in her carriage. Across the path of Benedetto's varied experiences pass before the reader all classes of Italian society. The monk's reputation for saintliness stimulates the ladies of fashion to lionize him in their drawing rooms. The peasants, more sincere and less sophisticated, kiss the hem of his coat and have faith in his ability to work miracles. The climax of the novel is the Saint's interview with the Pope. The monk ardently appeals to him to heal the wounds of the Church, wounds from which it is rapidly dying. The wounds are "falsehood," "avarice," "clerical domination" and "spirit of immobility." The Pope, a prisoner himself of the institution he heads, sighs deeply and reveals a defeatist resignation, for he has no power to reform the Church.

SAINT JOAN (1923), by George Bernard Shaw. In his preface Shaw writes that to understand Joan's trial, which he considers remarkably fair according to the times, "it is necessary to understand Christendom, the Catholic Church, and the Feudal System as they existed and were understood in the Middle Ages." He describes Joan as a healthy, shrewd, pious girl of a bourgeois family. Her voices, which came from her imagination, were the dictations of common sense. She had a passionate love for the soldier's life, and as a child her father had had to threaten to punish her severely if she ran away with the soldiers. She wanted to lead a man's life and to wear men's clothes. The play opens with her appeal to Robert de Baudricourt to give her armor and a horse. She asks them to send her with a small escort to the Dauphin at Chinon so that she may raise the siege of Orleans. He is finally won over and she sets out. The Dauphin decides to test her by seeing if she can pick him out; she selects him from among all the men in the room. He receives with apathy her enthusiastic suggestion to crown him at Rheims, but places her in charge of the army. Joan joins Dunois, who is waiting for a favorable breeze to cross the Loire and attack the British at Orleans. With her arrival the breeze shifts.

The Earl of Warwick and the Bishop of Beauvais plot Joan's destruction. Warwick wishes her burnt for political reasons, and the Bishop considers her a heretic. Joan's friends soon tire of her voices, which are always right; they are weary of being told what to do. Charles welcomes the idea of her going back to her father's farm. The Archbishop of Rheims warns her to be careful or she will be burned as a witch. Her friend, Dunois, tells her he must leave her to her doom if she is captured.

She is taken prisoner by the Burgundians. Warwick buys her for a large sum, and she is brought to Rouen and turned over to the Church. She is tried for heresy. The Chief Inquisitor does his best to save her, but she refuses to say that the Church is above God. She feels she gets her authority directly from Him, and she will not recant. They tell her eight hundred British soldiers are waiting to escort her to the stake. She weakens and recants. When she learns she faces life imprisonment she decides to choose the stake instead. The play ends with an account of how twenty-five years later a re-inquiry into her trial cleared her name. An epilogue reveals Joan in 1920; she is honored at her canonization and she pleadingly asks God when the world will be ready to receive His saints.

SAKUNTALA (ca. 5th c.), by Kalidasa. Kalidasa, whom the Hindus enthusiastically called "The Bridegroom of Poetry," is the best known of Hindu dramatists. His classic work, *Sakuntala,* has maintained its popularity and has had a number of contemporary revivals. It has also been source material for ballets and for program music.

Sakuntala, a beautiful young girl, is the ward of a holy sage. Duschyanta, the King, discovers her in the garden of the hermitage during a hunting trip. He woos her and weds her secretly. When he is recalled to court for affairs of state, he gives her a ring as a token and promises soon to return and take her back to the capital as his queen. While he is gone, Sakuntala quite unsuspectingly offends a saint, who places the curse upon her that Duschyanta shall forget about her completely. Sakuntala knows nothing of this. Some of her friends plead with the saint for mercy on her behalf. He consents to modify his curse, saying that if Sakuntala shows the King her ring he will remember her again.

Because the King does not return as he promised, Sakuntala's guardian sends her with an escort to the court. She still does not know of the curse, and is grief-stricken when the King refuses to recognize her or acknowledge her as his wife. She thinks of her ring and is about to show it to him when she discovers that the ring has been lost. The King is puzzled when a nymph, or goddess, carries Sakuntala off to the home of the gods for protection. The ring turns up in the hands of a fisherman, who returns it to the King. It had been lost in a pool and swallowed by a fish. Duschyanta then remembers everything and is remorseful, fearing that he has forever lost Sakuntala and been dishonored. The story wanders while Duschyanta, at the request of the gods, goes off to kill a race of giants. Finally, in a sacred grove, the lovers are reunited and all the questions and misunderstandings straightened out. In the meantime, Sakuntala has borne a young son, who in infancy matches the feats of the infant Hercules for wisdom and strength. He is destined to be the equal in splendor and might of his noble father.

Like all Hindu dramas the play was written originally in Sanskrit, the written language of classical Hindu scholars. In performance the more common dialects were used. The language of the play is stilted and artificial, with an exaggerated and flowery sentimentality.

SALAMMBÔ (1862), by Gustave Flaubert. Flaubert's famous archaeological novel is a tale of ancient Carthage, in which archaeology is perhaps more important than fiction. The plot revolves around Salammbô, the daughter of Hamilcar, and her anxiety to possess and assure the safety of the Tanite, a veil of extremely occult religious significance. Salammbô finally attains possession —and then dies. Meanwhile Flaubert, a master of precise and colorful description, has had the opportunity to paint a series of grandiose spectacles, an imaginative reproduction of what must have been the most colorful life of the Ancient World. In Flaubert's *Correspondence* is a fascinating letter to the critic Sainte-Beuve in which, replying to Sainte-Beuve's charge that the archaeological detail was fictitious, Flaubert furnishes chapter and verse references justifying all of his material.

SALOMÉ (1893), by Oscar Wilde. One of Wilde's most widely known dramas, it was written in French. Lord Alfred Douglas made the English translation, and Richard Strauss used the play as the libretto for his famous opera. The scene opens on a terrace in the palace of Herod, who is giving a feast. Salomé comes out and hears the imprisoned John the Baptist denouncing Herodias, her mother, who committed incest by marrying Herod, her husband's brother. Salomé, curious, insists on seeing the prophet, and makes love to him. He repels her, and tells her to repent. Herod comes out and asks Salomé to dance for him, but first she makes him promise to grant whatever she may request. She dances and then asks that the head of John the Baptist be brought to her in a silver basin. Herod begs her to choose anything else, but she insists that he keep his word. Reluctant, he gives the order for John's execution. Salomé takes John's head and mockingly makes love to it. Herod orders his soldiers to kill her.

SALVATION (1934), by Sholem Asch. See NAZARENE, THE, by Sholem Asch.

SAMSON AGONISTES (1671), by John Milton. The scene of this poetic drama is the prison at Gaza where Samson, blinded, is held captive by his enemies, the Philistines. Samson is allowed to rest in the open air in front of the prison because it is a pagan holiday. He bemoans his weakness in revealing his secret to Dalila, his wife, and complains of all his afflictions, especially his loss of sight. He is visited by a group of his friends, acting as a Greek chorus, who endeavor to comfort him. Manoa, Samson's father, comes and is made miserable by the condition in which he finds his son. Manoa has been trying to arrange a ransom, but Samson says he does not wish to escape the punishment he deserves; he refuses to pray for his life, though he is willing to implore God's pardon. Dalila appears, avowedly repentant and apparently eager to compensate for her misdeed. Samson spurns her, however. Dalila leaves, her attitude now defiant. Harapha, the giant of Gath, next arrives to see the man of whose strength he had heard so much. Angry at his taunts, Samson offers, in spite of his blindness, to fight him in a narrow place, let his opponent wear whatever armor he wishes. They quarrel about the nature of Samson's God. Again challenged by the man he came to taunt, Harapha goes away, muttering threats. An officer then comes to command Samson to amuse his enemies at their festival by his feats of strength. At first refusing, Samson finally goes, feeling the call of God. Manoa enters, and is telling the chorus that his attempts to ransom his son are making headway, when a great noise is heard. A messenger tells them that Samson has pulled the temple down, destroying his enemies and himself.

SAMUEL JOHNSON (1944), by Joseph Wood Krutch. See KRUTCH, JOSEPH WOOD.

SAN KUO CHIH (13th c.), by Lo Kuanchung. China's outstanding historical novel, the *San Kuo Chih*, is based on the war events of the Three Kingdoms (221–265). The most famous heroes are the trio, Liu Pei, Chang Fei, and Kuan Yu, sworn brothers by the "Peach-Garden oath." This oath of friendship thrilled the Chinese mind. Kuan Yu became a god of War in the Orient, and all three warriors performed prodigious deeds of valor. In addition there was the premier of the Shu Han, Chu-ko Liang, famous for his magic inventions and military machines. Once Chu-ko sent a force of some twenty ships to feign an attack on a powerful enemy fleet commanded by Ts'ao Ts'ao. Each ship of Chu-ko Liang's held only a few soldiers with gongs and impressive weapons of noise, but all the decks were packed with straw figures to imitate soldiers. Chu-ko calculated his time of attack to coincide with a dense fog, and effectively deceived the enemy. The entire novel deals with bloodstained warriors and cunning tactics. It is written in an easy and lively style with vivid characterization.

There is an English translation, *The Romance of the Three Kingdoms,* by C. H. Brewitt-Taylor.

SANCTUARY (1931), by William Faulkner. This story of cruelty and perversion concerns an eighteen-year-old college girl, Temple Drake, who falls under the spell of Popeye, gangster bootlegger and degenerate scion of a "good" Southern family. Temple is abducted and attacked by Popeye and his gang, and later taken to Miss Reba's brothel. At the time of the attack, Popeye had murdered one of his own men. Goodwin, another member of the gang, is arrested, and defended in court by Benbow, a lawyer who is trying to make a comeback. Benbow has Temple testify, but she is now mentally unbalanced and merely convinces the jury of the prisoner's guilt. He is lynched. Popeye escapes to Florida, where he is later hanged for a murder of which he is innocent.

SANDBURG, CARL (1878–   ). The genius of Carl Sandburg has been expressed in both poetry and prose, and has masterfully illuminated two American eras—the time of Lincoln, and his own. He was born in Illinois, of immigrant parents. His education was limited, and his boyhood spent in itinerant work in the west. After serving in the Spanish-American War, he attended Lombard College, and found an admirer of his first writings in Professor Philip Green, who aided him to print privately in 1904 a small volume of verse. Sandburg continued to work in journalism and politics until 1914. That year, *Poetry* published a number of his pieces, including "Chicago." That poem, published in 1916 in the *Chicago Poems* collection, elevated Sandburg to the leadership of a group of new writers. In the vigorous, colloquial language of the harsh city whose impact on the poet had been great, Sandburg denounces social injustice, but affirms the strength, beauty and goodness of the ordinary man of the American industrial city. Included also are effective impressionistic pieces, such as "Fog," and "Grass," and provocative pieces outlining the writer's liberal position.

Sandburg continued to move about. In 1919 and 1921 he shared the Poetry Society of America award, and traveled about the country giving lectures and readings of his own work. He was also gathering folk music; in 1927 *The American Songbag* gave the country more than a hundred songs never before printed or recorded. And in 1922 his *Rootabaga Stories* appeared, revealing a sympathetic and original feeling for the literature of children.

By 1936, when he published *The People, Yes* (q.v.), Sandburg had retired to his home in Michigan, the possessor of many honors and distinctions. His great prose epic, a biography of Lincoln, appeared first in 1926, with *Abraham Lincoln: The Prairie Years* (q.v.). *The War Years* followed in 1939, and Sandburg was awarded a medal by the Roosevelt Memorial Association, and the Pulitzer Prize. *Remembrance Rock* (1948) is a novelized history of the United States, with all the sweep and grandeur of Sandburg's prose.

SAND-RECKONER, THE, by Archimedes. See ARCHIMEDES.

SANDY HILL, THE (1919), by Samuel Joseph Agnon. See BRIDAL CANOPY, THE, by Samuel Joseph Agnon.

SANIN (1907), by Mikhail Petrovich Artsibashev. This, a mediocre novel, created a sensation at the time of its appearance, a time of disillusionment among the intelligentsia as a result of the abortive Russian revolution of 1905. The primary idea of Sanin, the amoral hero, is that "first and foremost it is necessary to gratify one's natural desires," irrespective of its effect on other people. He held that what men called "love" was something untrue and unreal, the result of false ideas taught by our civilization. Sanin ridicules all conventional institutions and does his best to break them, and encourages others to do the same. Not that Sanin manages his own life too well. He is ever in fear of losing his income and "cream for the morning tea." He regards workers with contempt, and loathes their sordid conversations about their exploiters. He lightly counsels his sister to get rid of her infant, encourages Soloveichik to suicide, rapes Karsavina, beats up Sarundin, who ends his life by suicide, provoking the comment from Sanin that it is not at all surprising, and that it would be well for others if they did the same. Again, when his friend Yurü, in love with Karsavina, commits suicide and Sanin is called upon to say something nice at the funeral, all he has to say is, "One fool less in the world. That's all." The example of Sanin was promptly followed by a host of disillusioned young men and women, who gave themselves to "free love" and licentiousness. The novel contributed further to the moral disintegration of Russian society.

SANTA CLAUS (1946), by E. E. Cummings. See ENORMOUS ROOM, THE, by E. E. Cummings.

SAPPHIRA AND THE SLAVE GIRL (1940), by Willa Cather. See CATHER, WILLA.

SAPPHO (7th c. B.C.). About Sappho, the lyric poetess of Lesbos, there has grown up an elaborate and unreliable body of romance. Her name was placed by the Greeks beside that of Homer, and they paid her honors due a goddess, erecting memorials to her and stamping her portrait on coins. She was called "Sappho the beautiful" and counted as "the tenth muse." Actually she was a daughter of aristocratic Lesbian parents, and trained the daughters of other noble Aeolian families in the amenities of music, art and manners before their marriage. These pupils she loved with a warmth that often finds expression in her poems. In antiquity there were nine books of her poems, but of these only two complete poems and a large number of stray lines have come down to us by quotation in later writers. To this has been added a very considerable number of fragments discovered on papyrus in Egypt about 1900. The most recent discoveries are two beautiful odes which came to light only about ten years ago, one written on papyrus and the other scribbled on a broken piece of pottery. She composed in a rich variety of meters, including the stanza which bears her name, but the rich music of these measures is lost in translation. In English one may still enjoy the simple directness of her language and her wide range of emotional tone, from that of jest and sport at a clumsy individual's big feet to the trembling passion of love, the heartfelt bitterness of an exile, and the quiet rapture of moonlit night or noonday hush.

SAPPHO (1884), by Alphonse Daudet. *Sappho* is the moving story of a young man's love for a woman with a past. Jean Gaussin, a young man from the Midi, meets Fanny Legrand, an attractive woman in her middle thirties, in Paris at a literary party. She soon becomes his mistress. Fanny is sweet, reserved, has musical talent, but she also has a strain of weakness, and her life before meeting Jean had been neither upright nor pure. She had been kept by the novelist Dejoie, the sculptor Caoudal, the poet La Gournerie, the engraver Flamant and others. Because of her, Flamant turned counterfeiter and was condemned to ten years in prison. Fanny herself had been in jail for a short period. She tries to live up to Jean, but she has not completely overcome her weakness, and Jean, after a time, has the feeling of being "chained." The lovers break and are reconciled several times. Then Jean meets a younger girl, a real *jeune fille*, and thinks of marrying her. Realizing that she cannot hold him forever and that she is too old, too "weary" to start a new life, Fanny gives him back his freedom. She will marry Flamant, who has just left prison, and who will idolize her for the rest of their lives.

SARTOR RESARTUS (magazine publication 1833–1834), by Thomas Carlyle. This work (the title means "the tailor restored") consists of a variety of reflections ostensibly on clothes, their origin and influence, with a romantic interlude on the pretended author. Carlyle's humor is elephantine. Nonetheless, it is caustic when it reflects on the strange make-believe antics of a world concerned with external appearances. It is probably Carlyle's most discussed work, especially the chapters on "The Everlasting No," "Centre of Indifference," and "The Everlasting Yea." The subtitle reads: "The Life and Opinions of Herr Teufelsdröckh." Teufelsdröckh of Weissnichtwo (Don't-Know-Where) is, of course, the author himself in disguise. A devout Germanophile, Carlyle uses this whimsical German character and the German background as a canvas upon which to superimpose his own views. At the time of writing, Carlyle was almost forty, but he had not yet gained the attention of his generation. Possessing great intellectual energy and a love of truth as he comprehended it, he found a useful vehicle for his resentment in the character of Teufelsdröckh and his philosophy of clothes. America was the first to recognize the great English author; the first edition of *Sartor Resartus* was published in Boston in 1836.

SARTORIS (1929), by William Faulkner. See FAULKNER, WILLIAM.

SATANSTOE (1845), by James Fenimore Cooper. See SPY, THE, by James Fenimore Cooper.

SATIRES (35–30 B.C.), by Horace (Quintus Horatius Flaccus). The *Satires* of Horace are hardly satires in the modern sense of the word. They are rather uninspired but witty discourses full of chatty, homely wisdom. Horace was too kindly and genial a man to indulge in personal lampoon, and preferred to "comment with a smile" on the folly and foibles of humankind, including his own. In the first *Satire* of the second book, he says to a friend: "There are many men in the world and just as many varieties of taste and ambition. My own personal pleasure is to string words together in verse, as Lucilius, a better man than you or I, did before me. It was his way to tell all his secrets to his poems, which he regarded as his trusty and faithful friends. Whether things went well or ill with him, he always flew to his own verse for sympathy. Thus it comes about that the whole life of the old bard is there set down for all the world to look at as in a picture." What Horace says of his model, Lucilius, is largely true of himself. He reveals his own life and personality in the *Satires* with a captivating confidence. The matter of the *Satires* is varied. Horace says that he is concerned with whatever men do. He devotes his verse to a critique of the manners and morals of his times, but the approach is frequently surprising. One of the earliest of the *Satires* is simply an amusing anecdote, another gives a picturesque account of a trip from Rome to Brindisi, and still another is a dramatic narrative of Horace's encounter on the streets of Rome with an unmitigated bore. The meter is always dactylic hexameter of an intentionally rough and casual sort, and dialogue is often used for dramatic effect.

SATIRES, by Juvenal (Decimus Junius Juvenalis; ca. 60–140). A bitter and sharp-tongued moralist, Juvenal etches with the acid of his style an unrelievedly gloomy picture of his age and particularly of the reign of Domitian. In the first *Satire,* in which he discusses the reasons for writing this kind of poetry, he asks: "How can one refrain from writing satire?" There is no humor or irony in the sixteen *Satires* of Juvenal such as that which is so characteristic of Horace. It is his deliberate intention to arouse horror and revulsion at Rome as a cesspool of iniquity. He creates vivid as well as lurid pictures of life in the city, as in the famous sixth *Satire,* the so-called "Legend of Evil Women." The tenth, on "The Vanity of Human Wishes," is well known from Samuel Johnson's imitation of it. Both poor and rich alike felt the lash of his tongue, but his cruelest blows are reserved for the ignoble nobility and the unwise philosophers. Poetic satire tends at best to be informal, but Juvenal is remarkably loose in the organization of his poems. The earlier *Satires* utilize the dramatic dialogue which is characteristic of Roman satire, but the later ones are rather in the form of epistles. It is as an epigrammatist that Juvenal is at his best. He is a creator of phrases, and many of his lines are still familiar though we are not conscious of their authorship. Such proverbial expressions are: "a sane mind in a sound body," "bread and circuses," "who will watch the watchman?," "honesty is praised and starves."

SATIRICON (1st c.), by Petronius. The author of this work is probably the Petronius mentioned by Tacitus as a familiar associate of the Emperor Nero. He calls him Nero's arbiter in matters of taste, and says of him: "Indolence had raised him to fame as energy raises others. . . . The emperor thought nothing charming or elegant in luxury unless Petronius had expressed to him his approval of it." The *Satiricon* is the work of just such a cultured cynic as Tacitus describes, who could look on the spectacle of human decay with amused and only mildly censorious indifference. The work originally consisted of some twenty books, of which we now have only fragments, the most considerable of which is known as the *Cena Trimalchionis* or *Feast of Trimalchio,* the manuscript of which was found in a monastery in Dalmatia. The whole *Satiricon* belongs to no well-defined literary type, but is a sort of *chronique scandaleuse* of the adventures of a pair of disreputable perverts named Encoplius and Ascyltus in the raucous and bawdy Greco-Roman society of the time. The narrator of the feast is Encolpius. He tells how he and his friend were invited to dinner in the house of a disgustingly wealthy former slave named Trimalchio, and describes the stupefying banquet, the conversation and entertainment. The descriptions of the gross and uninhibited guests, the ignorant and pretentious host, the revolting surfeit of courses and the fantastic surprises in entertainment, all reaching a climax in maudlin stupor, are unforgettable for their realism. Touching and gently ironic are the futile efforts of Trimalchio to lead the conversation to literary and philosophic heights. His blissful ignorance makes him utterly ridiculous, and his guests barely listen to him. The vulgar orgy grows wilder and more reckless as the hours pass, and the conversation is interlarded with appropriate stories. Trimalchio finally bursts into drunken tears and launches into a recitation of his will and the epitaph he has composed for his own tombstone: "Here lies Gaius Pompeius Trimalchio, the new Maecenas. . . . He left thirty million sesterces, and never attended a course in philosophy. Stranger, go thou and do likewise." The characterizations are brilliantly realistic, depending largely upon a skillful use of the vulgar Latin idiom, which is strikingly different from literary Latin and of which this text is a unique example.

SATURDAY NIGHT (1903), by Jacinto Benavente. This play is the story of Imperia, a rich, aging woman who attempts to recapture the emotions of her youth. This youth, together with her happiness, she has sacrificed for wealth and power. Now that these are almost within her grasp, she seeks out her love child, Donina, who personifies to her her own lost youth. The daughter is in a circus. She is involved in a fiery love affair, and, half mad with jealousy and despair, she commits a murder for the sake of her young lover, Nunu. Imperia saves her daughter from the law only to have her die in her arms—heartbroken, her youthful spirit gone. The mother, stunned by this tragedy, calls to her aid Leonardo, an artist from whom, long ago in the dawn of her womanhood, she had derived her vision of the ideal. Under his wise guidance Imperia wins mastery of herself. The material world fades away and she achieves an ideal.

SATURDAY'S CHILDREN (1927), by Maxwell Anderson. See WINTERSET, by Maxwell Anderson.

SAUL (1785), by Vittorio Alfieri. Of the many tragedies written by Vittorio Alfieri (1749–1803) *Saul* is the masterpiece. Alfieri was especially inspired, in writing his tragedies, by great historical events or figures of Rome, Israel and Greece. Though his style is noble and lofty, Alfieri's tragedies, in general, lack the intimate force of real drama, and express only externally the pathos which a genuine tragedy has. In writing *Saul* Alfieri was inspired by the stern Jewish interpretation of divinity. The tyrant is God, against whom Saul is in conflict because he has sinned and there is no force which will prevent his being punished. The reader passes through Saul's remorses, torments and even madness. Especially impressive is the beautiful song by David, improvised to soothe Saul's tormented spirit.

SCARLET LETTER, THE (1850), by Nathaniel Hawthorne. The scene of this novel, to which Hawthorne owes his chief fame, is the superstitious Puritan community of Boston in early New England. It is the story of Hester Prynne, doomed to wear the scarlet letter "A" for adultery; of her wild elf-child Pearl, whose father is the minister Arthur Dimmesdale; and Roger Chillingsworth, Hester's husband, who tortures the minister with the knowledge of his sinful secret. Hester and her lover plan to flee together, but he finally resolves his fears and publicly confesses. He dies, and Roger's mental health breaks; but Hester lives on to bring happiness to Pearl and others in distress.

SCEPTICAL CHYMIST, THE (1661), by Robert Boyle. This book, the best known chemical work of its century, was without doubt the most influential of Boyle's numerous scientific treatises. It is an analysis and criticism of the two chief chemical theories of his day, the Aristotelian (or Peripatetic) idea of four elements (earth, water, air, and fire) and the Paracelsan (or Spagyric) concept of three principles (mercury, sulphur, and salt). Boyle opposed both theories and substituted a definition of chemical elements which is close to that of Lavoisier and of modern chemistry (prior to the discovery of radioactivity). The book is written in the form of a discussion (as in Galileo's dialogues) among a group of scientific friends. Carneades represents the sceptical chemist, Themistus explains the Aristotelian viewpoint, Philoponus defends the Paracelsan doctrine and Eleutherius is an open-minded scholar. The conversation is reported in the first person by an anonymous participant, presumably the author. From the text it appears that Boyle espoused an atomic theory which he doubtless derived, through Gassendi, from the ancient ideas of Leucippus, Democritus, Epicurus, and Lucretius.

Boyle was a prolific (and prolix) writer and published works on a wide variety of subjects—from *Seraphic Love* (1660) to *Feeling a Dog's Pulse* (1664). An edition of his works in five folio volumes was published in 1744 and another in six quarto volumes appeared in 1772. Boyle did important work in physics, improving the air pump and publishing an important work entitled *New Experiments Physico-Mechanical Touching the Spring of Air and its Effects* (1660). The second edition of this book (1662) contains the principle known as "Boyle's law." But his greatest influence was in the field of chemistry. Here he performed numerous experiments and made specific discoveries, such as the combustion of gas (hydrogen) evolved when acid is dropped on iron filings. His most important contribution probably lay in his view of chemistry as an independent and critical science, thus freeing it from the limitations which had been imposed by alchemy and iatrochemistry. He was more interested in the facts of nature than in applications to medicine or the arts. It was in this respect that *The Sceptical Chymist* exerted a profound effect upon the development of chemistry in the eighteenth century.

SCEPTICISMS (1919), by Conrad Aiken. See AIKEN, CONRAD.

SCHAKELS (1902), by Hermann Heijermans. See OP HOOP VAN ZEGEN, by Hermann Heijermans.

SCHENDEL, ARTHUR VAN (1874–1947). The refined and totally introvert Romanticism of Van Schendel put an end to the dominance of naturalism in Dutch literature. His first work, *Drogon* (1896), like most of the novels of his first period, deals with the Middle Ages, and describes the doomed life of a nobleman, predestined for evil. He obtained lasting popularity with *Een Zerver Verliefd* (1904), which describes the adventures of the dreamer and wanderer Tamalone, who, having become infatuated with cloister life, first joins the Franciscans and later marches with the military chief Rogier through Italy. Tamalone abducts for him Mevena, the daughter of Rogier's enemy Lugina. As Rogier marches on with the Emperor, he leaves Mevena in Tamalone's care. His infatuation for the beautiful woman causes Tamalone to kill his lord, when Mevena is discarded by him. As Rogier's soldiers avenge his death on Mevena, Tamalone adopts their child and travels with it through the world. In very subtle language, Van Schendel narrates in an extensive series of works the history of lonely dreamers, living under conditions which are determined neither by time nor space—*De Berg der Droomen* (1913), etc. In 1930, he turned to the inner realities of more modern times, first with *Het Fregatschip Johanna Maria,* the history of one of the last big sailing ships. Owners, captain and crew are proud of the fine ship, but everybody considers it a thing and nothing more. The sailmaker Brouwer alone has feeling for the ship as a living creature; thus it becomes for him the only object of affection in his life. Captains and crews change, but he remains, saving through the years in honest and dishonest ways enough money to be able to buy the ship, which, old and superseded by steamships, cannot be used any longer as an ocean carrier. Moored in the Amsterdam outer harbor, they end life together.

Thereafter a series of superb novels follows: *De Waterman* (1933), *De Rijke Man* (1936), *Grauwe Vogels* (1937), describing the nineteenth-century lower middle class in their outward tranquility, often restrained by strict Calvinism, but inwardly swept and possessed by passions and inherited inclinations and lusts. The romantic style regained domination in the profound novels in fairy-tale spirit: *Mijnheer Oberon en Mevrouw* (1940) and *De Menschenhater* (1941). Van Schendel shows himself a master of short stories in "Maannacht" (in which a moonsick person tells his dream, which has become his life) and many other stories, which have been collected in *Herinneringen van een dommen Jongen* (1935).

SCHILLER, FRIEDRICH VON (1759–1805). Johann Christoph Friedrich Schiller, born in a small Swabian town, intended to study theology but was forced to attend a military academy, where he studied law and medicine instead. After writing his first play, the young poet escaped from the rigid school discipline and devoted himself to a strenuous, restless and often depressing career as free lance writer and dramatist that led him all over Germany. Appointed professor of history on Goethe's recommendation, Schiller moved to the Thuringian university town of Jena, where he soon married. However, his health failing rapidly, he soon gave up his academic duties and continued to write and edit exclusively. The last years of his life he spent in Weimar near Goethe, whose friendship was the stimulating inspiration of his last decade. Physically frail and long a victim of pains and diseases, Schiller died in 1805, only forty-five years old.

Although not too influential outside of Germany, Schiller's work is symbolic of the climax of the classic period of German literature and marks the climax of German drama. Schiller surpasses even Goethe in popularity in Germany. The intellectual exchange between these two men, revealed in their published letters, shows the golden age of Germany.

The first drama by the youthful genius, *The Robbers* (1781), stands in debt to the Storm and Stress Movement and displays all the weaknesses and extravagances of the time. Over-long, wordy, violent and exaggerated, the play revolves around the archvillain Franz Moor and his unconventional outcast brother Karl, whom sad circumstances force into the role of a leader of a band of roaming robbers. Interwoven into the plot are the senile, ill-treated Count Moor, their father, and Amalia, who is loved by both brothers. Despite its obvious weaknesses, the drama is full of effective scenes, and breathes an almost irresistible emotional force. It made the young author famous immediately. Schiller's other dramatic creations of his early period include *Intrigue and Love* (1784) which shows him as a craftsman of theatrical instinct. In the center of the plot is Louisa, the daughter of the town musician Miller. Her love for a young man above her social class, Ferdinand von Walter, is destroyed by powerful intrigue. The play throws a bright light on the society of the despotic little states of Germany in the eighteenth century. At the end of Schiller's early period came *Don Carlos* (1787), which marks the transition to the years of maturity. The chief protagonists of this verse drama are Philip II of Spain, his son Carlos, and the liberty-loving Marquis Posa.

A decade of historical and philosophical studies passed before Schiller wrote in quick sequence his classical dramatic masterpieces. The spirit of Kant's idealistic philosophy and the harmonizing influence of Goethe were the new elements of his work. His most gigantic undertaking was the trilogy *Wallenstein* (1799), based on the historic Bohemian general of the Thirty Years' War. This tragedy, displaying a new realism and fuller characterizations, made Schiller the favorite German poet. Other historic verse dramas in a classical vein are *Mary Stuart* (1800); *Maid of Orleans* (1801), a romantic-heroic version of Saint Joan; and *Bride of Messina* (1803), modeled after Sophocles. His last completed play, *William Tell* (q.v.), based on the legend of the famous archer, was a tremendous success. It is still Schiller's most popular drama.

Although it is mainly as a dramatist that Schiller has an unsurpassed hold on his nation, his achievements in the fields of historical and philosophical prose are by no means insignificant. His treatise on "Naïve and Sentimental Poetry," for instance, has stimulated critics and writers up to our day, including Thomas Mann. It is, however, as a poet of ballads that Schiller lives in the hearts of the German people. Poems like "The Diver" or "The Ring of Polykrates" are recited by every school child. The crown of his lyric and didactic poetry is *The Song of the Bell* (1800), which is composed of two parts moving in parallel lines: the manual processes in casting a bell, and the accompanying reflections on human life.

SCHLEGEL, AUGUST WILHELM (1767–1845), and **FRIEDRICH** (1772–1829). The Schlegel brothers are considered responsible for starting German literary Romanticism. Although not outstanding as literary creators, they were versatile in their output. Friedrich served to inject the idealism of the philosopher Fichte into the new movement, and provided the stimulus for the beginnings of the study of comparative philology. His achievements in criticism and in original creation were not outstanding. It was he, however, who effectively stated the doctrine of Romantic art. August, the elder, was by far the more original and influential of the two. His greatest service to literature was a remarkable translation (1797–1810) of several of Shakespeare's dramas, which served to establish the Bard as a German literary figure. His skill as a critic was largely responsible for a revival of interest in early German literature.

SCHNITZLER, ARTHUR (1862–1931). Containing a delicate irony and showing an absolute mastery of subtlety of style, the works of the Austrian, Schnitzler, enjoy great popularity. Characteristic of the *fin de siècle*, his works are marked by a highly refined atmosphere, a deeply felt melancholy and a devotion to illusion as more desirable than truth, coupled with a somewhat blasé sophistication. A physician by profession, he was influenced by psychoanalysis and a concern with the occult. His characters are usually portrayed in a preoccupation with the moment. Each lives his life in a series of detached episodes.

It is this spirit which pervades one of his best known dramatic works, *Anatol* (1893), which is hardly definable as a play, being a succession of seven witty dialogue scenes in the life of the lady's man Anatol. In the drama *The Lovely Way* (1904) Felix Wegrath learns that his father is really his dead mother's youthful lover, Julian Fichtner. Felix proceeds to denounce Julian as a father for his callousness to his mother.

Schnitzler brought forth several plays in the one-act form, including *The Green Cockatoo* and *Paracelsus* (both 1899). *Fräulein Else* (1925) is a novella (long short story) in which Else, in an attempt to solicit a loan to save her embezzler father, agrees to a show of indecency. In the process of completing the bargain the girl commits suicide. The drama *Professor Bernhardi* (1912) relates the incidents which grow around the refusal of the Jewish physician, Bernhardi, to allow a priest to visit a dying girl who is under the illusion of recovery. Among his prose works is the novel *The Way to Freedom* (1908) and the novella *Lieutenant Gustl* (1901), a penetrating psychological study.

SCHOLA LUDUS (collected 1657), by Comenius. See DIDACTICA, THE, by Comenius.

SCHOLA PANSOPHICA (collected 1657), by Comenius. See DIDACTICA, THE, by Comenius.

SCHOOL DER POËZIE (1897), by Herman Gorter. See MEI, by Herman Gorter.

SCHOOL FOR PRINCES (1872), by Multatuli. See MAX HAVELAAR, by Multatuli.

SCHOOL FOR SCANDAL, THE (1777), by Richard Brinsley Sheridan. Sheridan's spritely, polished comedy is still one of the most popular in the English language. Lady Sneerwell has a coterie of friends who gather at her house in London for the purpose of inventing and spreading malicious gossip. Lady Teazle, the pretty young wife of elderly, obstinate Sir Peter, belongs to the circle. Joseph Surface, a sanctimonious, hypocritical young man, is wooing Sir Peter's ward, Maria, an heiress who is in love with his brother Charles, a generous, extravagant fellow. Sir Peter favors Joseph's suit. Joseph, to gain access to Maria, makes advances to Lady Teazle, and tells her he is indifferent to her ward. Lady Teazle and Sir Peter quarrel, and she keeps an appointment at Joseph's rooms. Sir Peter is announced suddenly, and Joseph hides her behind a screen, later telling Sir Peter she is "a little French milliner." When Lady Teazle overhears Sir Peter, who thinks his wife in love with Charles, consult Joseph about a generous settlement he intends to make on her she is remorseful. Charles is shown in, and Sir Peter hides in a closet. Charles reveals to Joseph, and of course to Sir Peter, that his interest is entirely in Maria. Sir Peter comes out of his closet and Joseph is called away. The screen is upset and exposes a chastened Lady Teazle. Sir Oliver Surface, wealthy uncle to Joseph and Charles and an old friend of Sir Peter's, returns from India determined to test the characters of his nephews. On the advice of Rowley, an old servant, he calls on Charles as a usurer, Mr. Premium. Charles and his friends auction off the family portraits to Premium, but Charles refuses to sell the picture of his Uncle Oliver. He sends part of the money to Stanley, a deserving old relative of the family who had applied to him for assistance. Uncle Oliver calls on Joseph disguised as Stanley, and is politely turned down on the grounds that his Uncle Oliver is parsimonious. Joseph's duplicity is fully revealed; Sir Peter and Lady Teazle are reconciled; and Maria and Charles are united.

SCHOOL FOR WIVES, THE (1662), by Molière. Arnolphe, a crabbed and jealous old man, is the guardian of young and pretty Agnes, whom he intends to marry. He keeps her closely guarded within his house. During Arnolphe's brief absence on a journey, a young man, Horace, sees Agnes, courts her, and wins her love. Arnolphe returns. Horace, who has not met the old man before and does not know his house, is the son of one of Arnolphe's close friends and bears letters of introduction to him. He meets Arnolphe on the street, makes himself known, and before long has confided in Arnolphe with great glee of his love for the closely guarded girl and his intention of stealing her out from under the nose of her guardian. Arnolphe is furious but is smart enough to keep silent, and even promises to help Horace. In the meantime, Arnolphe instructs Agnes should any suitor appear beneath her window, to throw stones at him. Agnes obeys implicitly and throws a stone at Horace, but she has wrapped a lover's message around it first. Horace arranges an elopement. Meeting Arnolphe, he eagerly unfolds his plan, and confesses that he does not know where to take Agnes for safekeeping when he has smuggled her from her guardian's house. Arnolphe is beside himself, but he owns another house and offers it to Horace. Horace is delighted. He proceeds to steal Agnes away from one of Arnolphe's houses and takes her straight to another, giving her over unwittingly to the keeping of the very man from whom he has stolen her. The vexed Arnolphe prepares to marry her immediately. But Horace's father arrives simultaneously with the arrival of Agnes' father. It is revealed that Horace and Agnes have been unknowingly betrothed since childhood. Arnolphe relinquishes his claims and all ends happily.

SCHUDDERUMP, THE (1867–1869), by Wilhelm Raabe. See RAABE, WILHELM.

SCIENCE AND CHRISTIAN TRADITION (1893), by Thomas Henry Huxley. See EVOLUTION AND ETHICS, by Thomas Henry Huxley.

SCIENCE AND HEALTH (1875), by Mary Baker Eddy. *Science and Health* is the doctrine of Christian Science. It propounds an original system of "divine healing." Its main thesis is the conviction that Christ came not only to redeem men from sin, but from sickness as well. All sick people can heal themselves and others if they are permeated with His consciousness, for disease is created by the mind and can be cured by suggestion. Appended is a section called "Key to the Scriptures" which consists of interpretations of Genesis and the Apocalypse, a glossary, and testimonials of cures.

SCIENCE AND HEBREW TRADITION (1893), by Thomas Henry Huxley. See EVOLUTION AND ETHICS, by Thomas Henry Huxley.

SCIENCE AND THE MODERN WORLD (1925), by Alfred North Whitehead. See WHITEHEAD, ALFRED NORTH.

SCIENCE OF ENGLISH VERSE, THE (1880), by Sidney Lanier. See LANIER, SIDNEY.

SCOTTISH CHIEFS (1810), by Jane Porter. See THADDEUS OF WARSAW, by Jane Porter.

SEA GULL, THE (1896), by Anton Chekhov. This play is perhaps best described as a study of frustrations and unfulfilled ambitions, associated with the deterioration of a class of Russian society. The successful novelist Trigorin, bored with his life and empty triumphs, is tormented by the knowledge that he has fallen short of real and lasting fame. Irina, a middle-aged actress already beginning to lose popularity, is vaguely troubled by the knowledge that her public success is vanishing and that she has spent no time making a success of her human relationships. Her son, Constantin, writes obscure novels and plays which are not understood by his mother and are scorned by Trigorin. He loses Nina, whom he loves, to the more sophisticated, glamorous Trigorin. Nina, filled with ambition for the theater, is soon abandoned by Trigorin, who returns to Irina, his former mistress. Nina is left to pursue what she is already beginning to realize will be a hollow life on the stage. Constantin, when he is again refused by Nina, escapes by killing himself. Yet this play is not wholly a message of despair and denial. It is a criticism of the society and way of life which produce such people.

Superficially Chekhov's plays seems almost motionless as far as dynamic dramatic movement is concerned. They are not easy to perform, which explains why they were not understood until the Moscow Art Theatre produced them with an appropriately natural and unpretentious style of acting. The title of the play is symbolical. The actual Russian word is *chaika* (which means gull, not sea gull). Nina says to Irina's son: "Like a gull, I am drawn to this lake. . . . I have lost my heart to you."

SEA OF GRASS, THE (1937), by Conrad Richter. The sea of grass is the Cross B Ranch, rude cattle empire of Colonel Jim Brewton in the 1880's when the "nesters"—homesteaders—are arriving and trying to take root on the government land. Hal, the Colonel's nephew, narrates the story which begins with the arrival from the East of Luti Cameron, the Colonel's bride, and the fight of young district attorney Brice Chamberlain in behalf of the nesters. After having three children, Lutie leaves the Colonel and the way of life so alien to her—and leaves a suspicion that her son Brock's real father is Brice (now a judge). Brock becomes an outlaw in the years that follow. He is finally trapped and shot. The era is changing. Nesters, protected by federal troops, have settled the area. At last Lutie returns to the old Colonel.

SEA-WOLF, THE (1904), by Jack London. See LONDON, JACK.

SEAL IN THE BEDROOM, THE (1932), by James Thurber. See THURBER, JAMES.

SEAMAN'S FRIEND, THE (1841), by Richard Henry Dana, Jr. See TWO YEARS BEFORE THE MAST, by Richard Henry Dana, Jr.

SEASONS, THE (1726–1730), by James Thomson. A long blank-verse poem descriptive of natural beauty, *The Seasons* is pointed up by humanitarian references. Several sentimental narratives make an especial appeal to the reader's interest; the style is consciously impressive. Sound is often linked to sight, as in the snow-scene in "Winter." In "Spring" fragrance pervades the lines. "Summer" includes the well-known picture of the caravan engulfed by a sandstorm, and two narratives: one about Celadon, and Amelia who is struck by lightning; and the other about Musidora, who bathes while Damon watches. In "Autumn" the poet presents vivid pictures of hunting, shooting and reaping. The story of Palemon, who falls in love with Lavinia, a gleaner, is also included here. The poem concludes with "A Hymn on the Seasons."

SECOND INAUGURAL ADDRESS (1864), by Abraham Lincoln. See GETTYSBURG ADDRESS, THE, by Abraham Lincoln.

SECOND MAN, THE (1927), by S. N. Behrman. See BEHRMAN, S. N.

SECOND MRS. TANQUERAY, THE (1893), by Arthur Wing Pinero. This play was one of the first of Pinero's social dramas, and one of his most popular. Aubrey Tanqueray, an idealistic widower, marries Paula Ray, a lady with a past. Ellean, Aubrey's nineteen-year-old daughter, returns from her convent school in Ireland to live with her father and Paula in Surrey. Paula, shunned by the neighbors and bored with country life, is jealous of Ellean, who is cool to her advances. Mrs. Cortelyou, a neighbor and a friend of Ellean's mother, asks the girl to go to Paris with her. They return unexpectedly as Ellean becomes engaged to a young soldier, Captain Hugh Ardale. When she meets him Paula recognizes him as one of her former lovers. She tells her husband and Ardale leaves for Paris. Aubrey forbids Ellean to see her lover again, and she guesses the truth about Paula. Paula, feeling she has no future and overcome by Ellean's coldness, kills herself.

SECOND SHEPHERD'S PLAY, THE (ca. 13th or 14th c.), Anonymous. This play, the earliest English farce, remains one of the most hilarious in the history of the English drama. It is one of the thirty-two "mysteries" or "miracles" in the Towneley or Wakefield cycle, produced near Wakefield. Few dramatists have succeeded in making their comedy derive so naturally from character. It is a good example of a play within a play. The First Shepherd enters and sets the stage by speaking of the bitter weather and the sad state of shepherds. He is joined by the Second and Third Shepherds. Mak, who has a reputation for stealing sheep, comes along, and they are at first suspicious of him. But he is a good talker and lulls them with assertions that he is true as steel. Then he waits till the shepherds are asleep and steals a fat ewe to take back to his wife. They put it in a cradle, wrapped up like a newborn infant. The shepherds wake in the morning, and, discovering the loss of their sheep, go to see Mak. He sings a lullaby, and his wife moans as though recently delivered of a child. Mak invites the shepherds to search the house, but of course, they find nothing. The shepherds leave; one of them returns, however, wishing to give the newborn child a sixpence. Against protests that he'll wake the baby, he uncovers it to take a look and recognizes his ewe. The shepherds toss Mak in a sheet until they are weary. They leave to sleep on the moor, and the Angel appears, telling them to go to Bethlehem and view the Christ child in the manger.

SECOND WORLD WAR, THE (1948–   ), by Winston S. Churchill. See GATHERING STORM, THE, by Winston S. Churchill.

SECRET HISTORY (after 575), by Procopius of Caesarea.

SECRET OF FATHER BROWN, THE (1927), by Gilbert Keith Chesterton. See FATHER BROWN, THE INNOCENCE OF, by Gilbert Keith Chesterton.

SEI PERSONAGGI IN CERCA DI AUTORE (1921), by Luigi Pirandello. See PIRANDELLO, LUIGI.

SEJANUS (1603), by Ben Jonson. Sejanus, a favorite of Tiberius, is jealous of the Emperor's son, Drusus, who, when his father erects a statue of Sejanus in Pompey's theatre, strikes Sejanus in public. To revenge himself Sejanus conspires with Drusus' wife, and has him murdered. Thus emboldened, he continues with his ambitious project of becoming Emperor. Next he intrigues to remove Nero and Drusus, Tiberius' young nephew, by arousing their uncle's suspicions against them and their mother. He hopes to marry the widow of Drusus, who is above him socially. He encourages the Emperor to indulge his vices and neglect public life. Tiberius finally becomes suspicious. He sets spies on this favorite who is planning his overthrow. When Sejanus feels most secure, on the pretext of doing him an unwonted honor in the Senate, the Emperor has him accused and condemned; he is torn to pieces by the people.

SELAMBS (1920), by Sigfrid Siwertz. See DOWNSTREAM, by Sigfrid Siwertz.

SELECTED ESSAYS (1932), by T. S. Eliot. See ELIOT, THOMAS STEARNS.

SELECTED POEMS (1929), by Conrad Aiken. See AIKEN, CONRAD.

SELECTED POEMS (1935), by Marianne Moore. See MOORE, MARIANNE.

SELECTED POEMS 1923–1943 (1944), by Robert Penn Warren. See WARREN, ROBERT PENN.

SELECTED PREJUDICES (1927), by H. L. Mencken. See AMERICAN LANGUAGE, THE, by H. L. Mencken.

SELF ANALYSIS (1942), by Karen Horney. See HORNEY, KAREN.

SELF-TORMENTOR, THE (163 B.C.), by Terence (Publius Terentius Afer). This comedy was adapted from the Greek of Menander, with the addition of some details from a second play. It has all the complications of plot made possible by a parallel set of characters: Menedemus and Chremes, the two fathers; Clinia and Clitipho, their respective sons, and Antiphila and Bacchis, the sons' mistresses. By his old-fashioned sternness about Clinia's philanderings Menedemus had driven his son to join the army, but now he lives a life of self-imposed toil and misery as penance for having so misunderstood and mistreated the boy. His neighbor, Chremes, is very patronizing, for he is sure he understands his son and enjoys his confidence. All the time, however, Clitopho has been keeping a desperately expensive slave girl. Now Clinia returns, and, fearing to face his father, stops with Clitopho. They scheme that Clinia's Antiphila shall come as the handmaiden of Bacchis to stay at Clitopho's house and Bacchis shall pose as the mistress of Clinia. Chremes will wink at the deception because he thinks Clitopho is in the clear. The two young schemers even get Chremes to put up enough money to free Bacchis. The reversal comes about when it is discovered that Antiphila is actually a long-lost daughter of Chremes. Menedemus joyfully welcomes Clinia's return, and gives a paternal blessing to his marriage. At last the tables are completely turned, so that Chremes must eat humble pie, acknowledge the subterfuges of Clitopho and the fact that he has paid to free a gold-digger to be his daughter-in-law.

SENILIA (1879–1883), by Ivan Sergeyevich Turgenev. See RUDIN, by Ivan Sergeyevich Turgenev.

SENSE AND SENSIBILITY (1811), by Jane Austin. The story tells of two sisters: Elinor, who has sense; and Marianne, who has sensibility. Their unfortunate love affairs form the basis of the narrative. Edward Ferrars, with whom Elinor is in love, is entangled with a sly, avaricious girl, Lucy Steele. His mother, upon learning this, disinherits him. Lucy, being without scruple, then jilts him for his younger brother, now the heir. So Edward returns to Elinor, who takes him back. Marianne's lover, the handsome and dashing John Willoughby, is a heartless rascal. He leaves her and goes to London. Romantic by nature, she follows him to the city, but his insolent conduct soon disillusions her. She then sacrifices her childish and absurd romanticism for the joys of a sensible marriage with the staid, middle-aged Colonel Brandon.

SENTIMENTAL EDUCATION, THE (1869), by Gustave Flaubert. The background of this novel is the decline and fall of the Monarchy of Louis Philippe and the Revolution of 1848. Against this backdrop Flaubert projects the figures of his own youth. The hero, Frédéric Moreau, has many of the traits of young Flaubert. Madame Arnous, with whom he falls in love, is very like a Madame Schlesinger whom Flaubert had admired at Trouville as early as 1836. The subject of the novel is really the futility of existence. Moreau's love ends in disillusionment. Exciting events end in complete monotony. Life merely goes on—but it is precisely this picture of the flow of the life of a time which gives the novel its strength. Émile Zola called it "the only truly historical novel I know."

Many critics today prefer this novel to *Madame Bovary* (q.v.). Its influence on the naturalistic school, and in particular on pessimists like Huysmans and Maupassant, was paramount.

SENTIMENTAL JOURNEY, A (1768), by Laurence Sterne. This book was published as *A Sentimental Journey through France and Italy by Mr. Yorick*. Though Saintsbury, the distinguished English critic, called it "dirty-trivial-pattering art," he also called it "perfect of its kind." Each little episode is complete. Others than Saintsbury have found delight in such sentences as: " 'Then I solemnly declare,' said the lady, blushing, 'that you have been making love to me all this while.'" France and Italy merely form a background for the *fille de chambre* and other damsels whom the hero, the philandering Sterne, encounters on his travels. It was his second effort at travel on the continent which resulted in the *Journey*, which is but an expansion of the seventh book of *Tristram Shandy* (q.v.), decorated with divertissements.

SENTIMENTAL TOMMY (1896), by Sir James M. Barrie. Jean Nyles, mother of Tommy and Elspeth, dies impoverished in the London slums. She has fired her children with nostalgia for their native Scottish heaths, and places them in the care of Aaron Lotta, her old lover in Thrums, Scotland. Emotionally unstable, Jean had deserted Aaron years before for an attractive blackguard who had left her and their children to starve to death in London. Lotta dislikes Tommy but loves the delicate, sweet Elspeth. In Thrums, Tommy meets Grizel, the illegitimate child of a woman known disrespectfully as "The Painted Lady." The boys of Thrums throw stones at Grizel, but Tommy defends her and wins her undying devotion. The sad sequel to this is *Tommy and Grizel* (1900), in which Tommy's success as a writer changes him into a philanderer who abandons Grizel for a married woman, Lady Pippinworth.

SEPULCHRES, THE (1807), by Ugo Foscolo. Ugo Foscolo, a celebrated poet of the Italian revolutionary period, was a man deeply imbued with Greek culture and classical enthusiasm. In his poem *The Sepulchres* the author opposes a law established by the newborn Italian Republic—for which Foscolo had fought—ordering equality of burial for all its citizens. The basic theme of the poem is that religion and the worship of Death are the two pillars of civilization. Progress and spiritual achievements are inconceivable without deep respect and admiration for those who accomplish great deeds. When this vision is dead, when men are all equalized in life as well as in death, civilization itself perishes. How is it conceivable for a people aware of their spiritual values to bury the thief and the hero, the poet and the villain, in the same grave? People cannot go on unless they are inspired by the example of their great champions. Through all centuries the tombstones of the immortals inspire and stimulate mankind to advance. The living turn to Death for inspiration and spiritual leadership. Foscolo's *Sepulchres,* together with his novel, *Letters by Jacopo Ortis* (1798), are fundamentally inspired by a genuine passion for liberty. This lofty inspiration, added to Foscolo's greatness as a poet and to his adventurous and wandering life, make of him one of the most celebrated and loved literary figures of Italy's poetical world.

SERAPHIC LOVE (1660), by Robert Boyle. See SCEPTICAL CHYMIST, THE, by Robert Boyle.

SERMONS (published 1640–1660), by John Donne. See DONNE, JOHN.

SERMONS (1412–1413), by Jan Hus. See HUS, JAN.

SERTOES, OS (1902), by Euclydes da Cunha. See REBELLION IN THE BACKLANDS, by Euclydes da Cunha.

SERVICE, ROBERT W. (1874–   ). The personal experiences of Robert Service in various parts of the world are expressed in his writings. The Yukon area, particularly during the Klondike gold rush, furnished the vigorous verses in *The Spell of the Yukon* (1907). The title piece concerns a successful prospector who, after striking it rich wastes his time in idle dissipation, but who yearns to return to the land he has fallen in love with, and to the elemental battle, not for gold, but "just finding the gold." "The Shooting of Dan McGrew" is an episode in a northern saloon. A stranger stalks in and discovers Dangerous Dan, who once stole his girl, Lou. The men shoot it out, and both are killed. Lou takes the opportunity to remove the gold from the pockets of her former lover. "The Heart of the Sourdough" tells of the irresistible lure of the northern wilds, which can be conquered again and again, but which finally wins.

The novel *Trail of '98* (1910) uses the same local color material. *Bar-Room Ballads* (1940) is a further volume of verse about people Service met in the Yukon, and elsewhere in his travels.

SESAME AND LILIES (1865), by John Ruskin. Of these two lectures the first, "Sesame—Of Kings' Treasuries," deals with the treasures hidden in books and how they may yield a fuller, more abundant life. "Whatever bit of a wise man's work is honestly and benevolently done, that bit is his book or his piece of art." But proper reading demands much of the reader. Ruskin analyzes a passage in Milton's *Lycidas* (q.v.) by way of example. The reader must bring not only the right mind but the right heart. Ruskin sees mere advancement in life as the root of all modern effort. Materialism and crude self-indulgence are rampant. There may be some patronizing of the arts, but there is more concern over the contents of wine-cellars than of books. The second lecture, "Lilies—Of Queens' Gardens," discusses the education of women. Shakespeare and Scott and Dante provide heroines showing that when man falls the redemption, if any, is wrought by a woman. It is this guiding, counseling function of a woman that is to be developed. First she must be trained to be healthy. Then "fill and temper her mind with all knowledge and thoughts which tend to confirm its natural instincts of justice and refine its natural tact of love." Except for the dangerous subject of theology, a girl will study approximately what a boy studies. In 1869 Ruskin added a third lecture, "The Mystery of Life and its Arts," which had such a tone of gloom that the author withdrew it.

SEVEN LAMPS OF ARCHITECTURE, THE (1849), by John Ruskin. Ruskin was only thirty years old when this book appeared. It is divided into seven chapters, on the lamps of Sacrifice, Truth, Power, Beauty, Life, Memory, and Obedience. It was the studies and meditations which are embodied in this work that first turned John Ruskin from art to man, history and social institutions. From an unworldly aesthete living in an ivory tower he was converted into a social moralist who made it his life's mission to regenerate society by a new gospel of work, piety and beauty. Ruskin was a Deist but mystically religious. *Seven Lamps* engages in a bewildering variety of religious discussions, oscillating between theology and philosophy.

In the first chapter Ruskin defines the nature of sacrifice; inquires into God's interest in man's work. He concludes that the best gifts are the works of love.

In the second, Ruskin declares that the flattering lie is worse than the malicious one.

In a startling transition Ruskin introduces his principal subject, architecture: "So fell the great dynasty of mediaeval architecture"—because it had lost its vitality, had disobeyed its own laws, and therefore could not oppose any resistance to the rush of overwhelming innovation. It had surrendered its integrity, and there "arose the multitudinous forms of disease and decrepitude, which rotted away the pillars of its supremacy." This destructive force was, according to Ruskin, the spiritual decay of Christianity during the opulent centuries of the Renaissance.

SEVEN PILLARS OF WISDOM, THE (privately printed, 1926; published, 1935), by Thomas Edward Lawrence. The beginning of World War I found Lawrence in the British service in Egypt. He had already acquired a vast knowledge of the Near East, especially of Arabia. The entry of the Turks into the war on the German side brought into focus the question of the position of the Arab populations of the desert. Lawrence persuaded them to enroll themselves on the British side and rise in revolt against their Turkish political masters, so that they would procure their freedom after the war. The revolt materialized under the leadership of Lawrence and Feisal, one of the sons of the Emir Hussin Ibn Ali. The story is an adventure tale of the first order. Its accounts of hardship, desert warfare, feats of personal valor, train-wrecking expeditions, and all the other exigencies of the campaign make thrilling reading. For the student the book further offers remarkable dissertations on military stategy and history, on many aspects of the Arab peoples, and upon various abstruse questions of philosophy and personal integrity. The campaign ended in victory, with the conjunction of the Arab forces under Lawrence and Feisal with Allenby's British forces at Damascus. One of the most stirring actions found in the book is the description of the joint entry into Jerusalem.

The Seven Pillars of Wisdom is a monumental work. An abbreviated popular version, consisting merely of the swift-paced adventure sequences, was published in 1927 under the title *Revolt in the Desert*. Lawrence changed his name to T. E. Shaw and lived obscurely as an aviation mechanic until his death in 1935 in a motorcycle accident. Violent revulsion against his remarkable success as a warrior arose out of the fact that his duties as a British soldier compelled him knowingly to betray the Arab revolt.

SEVEN THAT WERE HANGED, THE (1908), by Leonid Andreyev. This is a short novel concerned wholly with the awareness of death. But it is not an abstract, symbolic death with which Andreyev here concerns himself. It is the impact of certain, impending death upon eight persons. The first of these is a minister of state, who is informed by the police that an attempt upon his life has been planned for "one o'clock in the afternoon" of the following day. Although he is saved by the discovery and frustration of the plot, he spends a night of miserable terror at the realization of how close death has come to him, and how it may yet lie in wait for him. He is obsessed by the thought of the fatal hour, "one o'clock in the afternoon." Five of the characters are revolutionary conspirators, three men and two women, who had plotted the death of the minister. The remaining two are a flamboyant brigand

and a terrified, sordid murderer. It is these seven whose emotional reactions to the approach of death Andreyev scrutinizes minutely, revealing profound capacities as an observer of humanity. Although the several emotional charts range from the most abject fear to the most sublime calm, they are not constant and unvarying states; nor are they always assigned in the quarters expected. Andreyev pursues his many threads patiently up to the very moment of execution. Expressed in his fabric is a clearly implicit denunciation of the brutal social framework within which his story is unrolled.

SEVENTEEN (1916), by Booth Tarkington. See PENROD, by Booth Tarkington.

SEVENTH RING, THE (1907), by Stefan George. See GEORGE, STEFAN.

SEX AND TEMPERAMENT IN THREE PRIMITIVE SOCIETIES (1935), by Margaret Mead. See FROM THE SOUTH SEAS, by Margaret Mead.

SEXUAL BEHAVIOR IN THE HUMAN MALE (1948), by Drs. Alfred C. Kinsey, Wardell B. Pomeroy, and Clyde E. Martin. Many critics think that this volume will go down in history with such important and influential books as Karl Marx's *Das Kapital* (q.v.), Darwin's *Origin of Species* (q.v.) and Adam Smith's *Wealth of Nations* (q.v.). Pretense and concealment were the essence of the Victorian attitude toward sex. At the midpoint of our century this has long since changed. *The Kinsey Report* is as frank and complete as possible, and scientifically objective. Facts long known to specialists are graphed and catalogued for a wider public. Prevailing habits, sexual experiences, and the sexual capacities of American males in all walks of life, at all ages and stages of intellectual and cultural development, are documented. Dr. Kinsey's group plans further volumes, the next one to concern sexual behavior in the human female.

Drs. Kinsey, Pomeroy, and Martin, research scientists, have gathered and published the facts; they are cautious about interpretations. Others, however, have been less reluctant. Soon after *The Kinsey Report* a flood of books came from the press, explaining and interpreting the original statistics, which were the result of more than twelve thousand confidential interviews.

SHADOWS ON THE ROCK (1931), by Willa Cather. See DEATH COMES FOR THE ARCHBISHOP, by Willa Cather.

SHAH-NAMEH (10th c.), by Firdusi. A mirror of Persian life and intellectual currents of a bygone age, *The Book of Kings* contains some 60,000 couplets. Some have called it an epic poem, others a series of epic poems. In reality it is a historical chronicle embroidered with fables and poetic conceits. It runs through the entire course of Persian history from King Kaiumeras, the first Persian monarch, to King Yezdeherd, who was subjugated by the Arabs.

The records and chronicles which Firdusi drew upon were limited, and for the most part he utilized legends and folklore as background material for this poetic chronicle.

SHAKESPEARE (1939), by Mark Van Doren. See VAN DOREN, MARK.

SHAPIRO, KARL J. (1913–   ). Karl Shapiro is an energetic creator and a fresh critical judgment in the field of contemporary American poetry. *Person, Place and Thing* (1942), written while he was on active duty in the Pacific, contains many short pieces describing individual types, such as "The Snob," or "Waitress," and colorful vignettes of scenes, such as "Hollywood," or "Honkeytonk."

V-Letter, and Other Poems (1944), also written while Shapiro was fighting in Australia and New Guinea, was a Pulitzer Prize winner. There are war pieces, such as "Elegy for a Dead Soldier," but it is not a volume devoted exclusively to the war. "Nigger" is a compressed expression of the Negro's problems of adaptation to society. "V-Letter" is a love lyric to the poet's wife.

Essay on Rime (1945) is a decasyllabic criticism of modern poetry, attacking confusions in prosody, language and beliefs. The author uses illustrations from the works of poets as diverse as Browning, Whitman, Milton and Eliot.

Trial of a Poet (1948) includes autobiographical sequences ("Recapitulation") and a poetic drama (the title work) in which characters symbolic of government, science and religion, attack poetry, which is defended by the author.

SHAW, IRWIN (1914–   ). Irwin Shaw has made his mark in various literary media. Among his dramas is *Bury the Dead* (1936), a pacifistic fantasy about six dead American soldiers who cause a rebellion by refusing to be buried. A leading magazine short story writer, Shaw's pieces have been collected in such volumes as *Act of Faith* (1946), in which the title story is a trenchant treatment of discrimination and hopelessness.

The Young Lions (1948) is Shaw's first novel, about World War II. It deals with the German soldier Christian Diestel, and the American soldiers Noah Ackerman and Michael Whitacre. In the moral climate of war, the stories of these three are the stories of all soldiers: Diestel's slow disintegration, the efforts of the confused liberal Whitacre to find himself, and the gradual hardening of the character of the gentle Ackerman. Their destinies are intertwined up to their final acts of violence, and there emerges also a fine chronicle of World War II.

SHE STOOPS TO CONQUER, or, THE MISTAKES OF A NIGHT (1773), by Oliver Goldsmith. This gentle comedy is the story of bashful young Marlow, forward only with barmaids and serving-girls, who reluctantly sets forth to win the hand of Miss Hardcastle. He is tricked into believing that her father's house is an inn. He proceeds to treat the dignified Mr. Hardcastle, who has a predilection for everything old, as though he were merely an impudent and eccentric landlord. The consternation resulting from this is enormous; Hardcastle nearly has a stroke from rage and indignation. Miss Hardcastle takes advantage of the situation by pretending first to be a barmaid, then a poor relation of the family. In this humble guise she conquers Marlow. When the mistakes of the night have been unraveled by the arrival of Marlow's father, who had arranged the match, Hardcastle's natural indignation is mitigated by understanding. All ends happily. The play has always been deservedly popular. It is rich in ingratiating characterizations, one of the most notable of which is that of Mrs. Hardcastle's adored son by a former marriage, lazy, mischievous Tony Lumpkin, who misdirects Marlowe. The play is still produced.

SHEEP WELL, THE (1619), by Lope de Vega. The people of the village of Fuente Ovejuna are being abused by a cruel, lecherous Comendador. He tries to entice the women into his house for his own pleasures. However, led by the beautiful peasant girl Laurencia, daughter of the peasant mayor, they outwit him and escape. One day as the young peasant Frondoso is asking Laurencia to be his wife, they are interrupted by the Comendador, who seizes her and attempts to take her off. Frondoso picks up a crossbow that the Comendador had dropped and threatens him with death. The Comendador is forced to release Laurencia and retreats, cursing Frondoso, and vowing vengeance.

The peasant girl Jacinta declares that the Comendador is planning further villainies. The Comendador enters and attempts to attack her. When the peasant Mengo tries to save her honor, he is arrested and ordered flogged by the Comendador's men. The Comendador then proceeds to dishonor Jacinta.

Hiding from the Comendador and his men, Frondoso arrives at the house of Laurencia. They decide to get married. Her father, the mayor, consents and promises them a generous dowry. On the day of the wedding, when gaiety is at its peak, the Comendador breaks in with his men. Esteban, in whose house the festivities are taking place, defends his daughter for having resisted the Comendador's advances, and Frondoso for having saved her, whereupon the Comendador takes away the mayor's staff and breaks it over the old man's head. Frondoso is arrested, and Laurencia captured.

In a mass meeting in the plaza of Fuente Ovejuna, the peasants discuss what steps to take against the intolerable cruelty and injustice of the Comendador. Laurencia, disheveled, enters and declares that she has been raped by the Comendador and calls upon Fuente Ovejuna to avenge her. Even the women take up arms. They storm the Comendador's castle and kill him. Informed of the revolt, the King sends a judge to punish the slayers. Although the judge puts many villagers to the torture and relentlessly cross-examines them all, men, women and children alike give but one answer to the question who killed the Comendador: "Fuente Ovejuna!" The village killed him, they insist, and the judge must either hang no one or wipe out the entire town! Impressed by the courage and heroism of the villagers, the King pardons them all and takes the village under his personal protection.

Fuente Ovejuna was inspired by the peasants' revolt of 1464–1484, when the King joined hands with the oppressed in an effort to stem the dangerous power of the landed aristocracy. The play makes good theater, and many critics consider it Lope de Vega's major work. Because of its revolutionary ideology, it has been often produced in France, in the Soviet Union, and in Spain before and during the Civil War.

SHELBURNE ESSAYS, THE (1904–1935), by Paul Elmer More. See MORE, PAUL ELMER.

SHELLEY, PERCY BYSSHE (1792–1822). Although he produced such masterpieces on a large scale as *Prometheus Unbound* and *The Cenci* (qq.v.), Shelley's genius is mostly seen in lyrics, sometimes as short as the ten lines of

"O World! O Life! O Time!" (1821); a lament that Lafcadio Hearn regarded as the most perfect in the language. In four stanzas "When the Lamp is Shattered" (1822) mourns the frailty of the heart that love chooses as its abode. "To Night" (1821) strikingly begins, "Swiftly walk over the western wave, Spirit of Night!" and continues with memorable imagery. "Music, when soft voices die" (1821) works by analogy, as so commonly in Shelley's short pieces. "One word is too often profaned" (1821) contains the famous line: "The desire of the moth for the star." The most famous sonnet is "Ozymandias" (1818), showing the defeat of human arrogance with time. "A Dirge" (1822) is the opposite of Browning's Pippa's "Song." "The Indian Serenade" (1819) presents a lover fainting with passion.

Longer are the popular odes, "To the West Wind" (1819) and "To a Skylark" (1820), in both of which Shelley shows a remarkable power to identify himself with his subject. The first, in *terza rima,* asks the wind to "Drive my dead thoughts over the universe," and the last line is certainly not free of political connotation: "If Winter comes, can Spring be far behind?" The latter, beginning "Hail to thee, blithe spirit!", also draws a moral from this "scorner of the ground!" "The Cloud" (1820) shows again Shelley's myth-making facility. The poet's philosophic idealism is apparent in "Lines Written among the Euganean Hills" (1818) and "The Sensitive Plant" (1820), a fable. Still more Platonic is the "Hymn to Intellectual Beauty" (1816).

Among larger works three stand out. "Epipsychidion" (1821) is a bold and ingenuous declaration of Shelley's love for Emilia Viviani, culminating in an elopement proposal. Shelley employs the symbols of Sun, Moon, and Earth to represent respectively Emilia, Mary Shelley, the poet's wife, and the poet himself. His conceptions of love are here set forth in an advocacy of passionate free love as well as Platonic love. The title means "soul upon a soul." In Emilia, Shelley believed he had found a soul which reflected and harmonized with his own. "Alastor: or, The Spirit of Solitude" (1815) is Shelley's first important work. Its hero is a young idealistic bard, a lover of nature, philosophy, and literature, who sets forth "to seek strange truths in undiscovered lands." He dreams of an idealized "veiled maid," with whom he falls in love; the impossibility of possessing her in reality drives him to his death. The poet condemns self-centered idealism, and at the same time laments a soulless world. The Preface stresses the implication of the poem, that men, attempting to live without love for society, are swiftly destroyed. "Alastor" is Greek for "avenger." "Adonais" (1821) commemorates in Spenserian stanzas the death of John Keats, using the characteristic devices of the pastoral elegy. There is a long invocation to the Muse Urania, of Dreams and Desires, of Sorrow and Pleasure and other abstractions, of Morning and Spring. The poem urges the abandonment of sorrow for joy in the dead poet's removal from "the contagion of the world's slow stain" to a position of immortality. Shelley attacks literary critics, whose scurrilous and vindictive reviews, he implies, contributed to the death of Keats. English literature does not contain a more famous or elevated simile than:

> The One remains, the many change and pass;
> Heaven's light forever shines, Earth's shadows fly;

Life, like a dome of many-coloured glass,
Stains the white radiance of Eternity.

SHEPHEARDES CALENDER, THE (1579), by Edmund Spenser. This series of twelve pastoral eclogues dedicated to Sir Philip Sidney did not bear Spenser's name but were signed "Konmerito." It is his first independently published poem, and it was at once apparent that a metrical virtuoso who excelled in harmony, whether in the lyric or in iambic rhythm in uniform stanzas, had arrived. The eclogues, which offer great scope for allegorical interpretation, are loosely related to the months of the year, for which they are names. Four tell of the unrequited love of Colin Clout (Spenser) for Rosaline (the unknown lady who faintly, less passionately, corresponds to Laura or Beatrice). The lamentations of Colin Clout run to some extent through all the seasons. In December the complaint is distinctly literary, influenced as it is by a passage in Marot's *Eglogue au Roy,* closely imitated here. In the March eclogue, in the dialogue between two shepherds, Thomalin and Willie, Spenser was imitating Bion. The idea of love here is purely pagan. Four eclogues criticize ecclesiastical and political conditions of the period, though "E.K.," the commentator, denies that they do. Here again the influence is traditional and literary. Spenser extends the images suggested by Mantuan (who had built on Virgil's first eclogue), who praises mountains because monasteries are built on them, so that *his* mountains become types of ecclesiastical pride and luxury. The August eclogue has a controversy between Willie and Perigot, with Cuddie as umpire (in imitation of Theocritus) ending with a delightful song. The eclogues for November and April are given to courtly compliment and courtly elegy. "April" contains a beautiful lay in praise of Queen Elizabeth; here again the influence of Virgil and Marot can be detected. The atmosphere of *The Shepheardes Calender* is completely artificial. On the technical side it is an important achievement. The poet exhibits great skill in providing suitable form for his matter. His verbal harmony is astonishing when the immaturity of the language before the publication of this poem is considered. He revived obsolete words from Chaucer and Lydgate. With these archaisms he blended dialect, turning from the southern, which was more courtly, to the midland and northern varieties of the tongue, which were more rustic. He often coined words suitable to the style of his verse.

Spenser's object, despite the Platonism here, is artistic rather than ethical; he is concerned with expression of thought, rather than with thought itself.

SHEPHERD OF THE HILLS, THE (1907), by Harold Bell Wright. See WINNING OF BARBARA WORTH, THE, by Harold Bell Wright.

SHERLOCK HOLMES (1887–1927), by Sir Arthur Conan Doyle. This collection of stories makes up the history of an amateur consulting detective of England, told by his friend and far less keen associate, John Watson, M.D. Sherlock Holmes has uncanny powers of induction, with a background of anatomy, chemistry, geology, botany, and British law.

In the first book in the series, *A Study in Scarlet* (1887), John Watson, M.D., has returned wounded from war service and meets Sherlock Holmes. The two bachelors share rooms at No. 221 B, Baker Street. Their first case is the

Lauriston Garden Mystery. Enoch J. Drebber and Joseph Stangerson are found murdered. It is a crime of revenge going back to Utah and the Mormons. Jefferson Hope's sweetheart, Lucy, and her father, John Ferrier, met their death at the hands of the two Mormons, and Hope followed them to England to avenge their deaths.

The *Sign of the Four* (1890) is the case of missing Captain Morstan, his daughter, Mary, the East Indians Thaddeus and Bartholomew Sholto. This story takes Holmes and Watson to the city of Agra in India to seek the missing treasure. Dr. Watson falls in love with Mary Morstan and marries her.

Adventures of Sherlock Holmes (1892), is a collection of twelve short stories: "A Scandal in Bohemia," "The Red-headed League," "A Case of Identity," "The Boscombe Valley Mystery," "The Five Orange Pips," "The Man with the Twisted Lip," "The Adventure of the Blue Carbuncle," "The Adventure of the Speckled Band," "The Adventure of the Engineer's Thumb," "The Adventure of the Noble Bachelor," "The Adventure of the Beryl Coronet," "The Adventure of the Copper Beeches."

Memoirs of Sherlock Holmes (1894) is a collection of eleven short stories: "Silver Blaze," "The Yellow Face," "The Stock-Broker's Clerk," "The *Gloria Scott,*" "The Musgrave Ritual," "The Reigate Puzzle," "The Crooked Man," "The Resident Patient," "The Greek Interpreter," "The Naval Treaty," "The Final Problem."

The Return of Sherlock Holmes (1905). Holmes is supposed to have been pushed over a cliff, but he comes back for these thirteen short stories: "The Adventure of the Empty House," "The Adventure of the Norwood Builder," "The Adventure of the Dancing Men," "The Adventure of the Solitary Cyclist," "The Adventure of the Priory School," "The Adventure of Black Peter," "The Adventure of Charles Augustus Milverton," "The Adventure of the Six Napoleons," "The Adventure of the Three Students," "The Adventure of the Golden Pince-Nez," "The Adventure of the Missing Three-Quarter," "The Adventure of the Abbey Grange," "The Adventure of the Second Stain."

The Hound of the Baskervilles (1902) is the case of the eerie howling on the moor and strange deaths at Baskerville. Sir Charles Baskerville is murdered, and Holmes and Watson move in to solve the crime. The murderer worked on an old superstition of death on the moor by a gigantic hound. Selden, an escaped convict, is killed by mistake, the murderer thinking him to be Sir Henry Baskerville—a case of an heir wanting property and title.

The Valley of Fear (1915), is a story in two parts: "The Tragedy of Birlstone" and "The Scowrers." In the first, Douglas of Birlstone Manor House is found murdered. The second part is laid in America twenty years earlier, and tells the story of the murdered man, John Douglas. He reappears to tell his own story of being hunted by the Scowrers and the plot of his murder.

His Last Bow (1917) contains eight short stories: "The Adventure of Wisteria Lodge," "The Adventure of the Cardboard Box," "The Adventure of the Red Circle," "The Adventure of the Bruce-Partington Plans," "The Adventure of the Dying Detective," "The Disappearance of Lady Frances Carfax," "The Adventure of the Devil's Foot," "His Last Bow."

The Case Book of Sherlock Holmes (1927) is the final collection of twelve short stories: "The Adventure of the Illustrious Client," "The Adventure of the Blanched Soldier," "The Adventure of the Mazarin Stone," "The Adventure of the Three Gables," "The Adventure of the Sussex Vampire," "The Adventure of the Three Garridebs," "The Problem of Thor Bridge," "The Adventure of the Creeping Man," "The Adventure of the Lion's Mane," "The Adventure of the Veiled Lodger," "The Adventure of Shoscombe Old Place," "The Adventure of the Retired Colourman."

SHERWOOD, ROBERT E. (1896–   ). Robert Sherwood was a journalist who became a leading American playwright with his comedy success *The Road to Rome,* in 1927. This play is a burlesque on Hannibal's siege of Rome, and a plea for world peace. The only person in Rome brave enough to cope with the threat of the approaching legions is the lovely Amytis, wife of Rome's inept dictator, Fabius Maximus. She determines to find the secret of Hannibal's invincibility, not from patriotism, but merely because she loves to play with fire. Accordingly she proceeds to Hannibal's camp, and guilefully convinces him that so great a man should not waste his genius on needless conflict.

Among Sherwood's other distinguished plays are: *Reunion in Vienna* (1931), a nostalgic comedy of the exiled Hapsburgs in which the psychoanalyst Dr. Krug's wife Elena is cured of her complexes about her former lover, Archduke Rudolph, by an evening alone with him; *Idiot's Delight* (1936), another plea for peace, in which a variegated group of people in a hotel in the Italian Alps pursue various paths when war breaks out; *There Shall Be No Night* (1940), a play of the contemporary Finnish political and sociological scene; and *The Petrified Forest* (1935), a melodrama in an Arizona desert filling station which introduces the bandit Duke Mantee and his effect on the lives of several frustrated persons.

Roosevelt and Hopkins (1949) is a rich book of political reminiscences charting the events of the United States Government during World War II; and *Abe Lincoln in Illinois* (q.v.) is a dramatization of the president's early life.

SHIJO-YUCHIP (1923), edited by Choi Nam-Sun. This *Anthology of Korean Poems* contains 1405 songs or poems by Korean poets, mostly of the Koryu period (918–1392) and early Li dynasty (1392–1910). In these Korean poems the outstanding feature is the use of nature and of symbols to express a philosophical thought. The attitude of certain poets on death is somewhat like that of Walt Whitman. There are also many poems on love and wine expressing the philosophy of life. Some of these poems have been translated by Younghill Kang.

Many of these songs are by anonymous poets, and others have their complete works in many volumes, including novels, plays and essays. Some of the poets represented are: Li Jip, author of *Dun Chon Jip* (*Exile in the Country*), who died in 1387; Kwun Pil (1572–1612), *Sukjujip,* in 8 vol.; Sung Taejung (1732–1832), *Chungsungjip,* in 10 vol.; *Song Ikpil* (1534–1599), *Kupongjip;* Kim Chung (1486–1521), *Choongamjip;* Yun Pongku, (1683–?), *Pyungkejip,* in 60 vol.; Park Chiwon (1737–1805); Kim Changjip (1648–1721), *Mongwajip* (*Dreams of House*), in 10 vol.; Cha Chullo (1556–1615),

Osanjip (Five Mountains); Kwun Moonhae (16th century), *Taedongwunok,* *(Dictionary of Rhymes)*; Su Kujung (1420–1488), *Yujiseungnam,* in 55 vol.; Chung Yakyong (1762–1836), *Mokminsimsoo, (How to Govern),* in 48 vol.; Kim Pusik (1075–1151); *History of Three Kingdoms,* in 50 vol. Many songs in the anthology are by Chung Mongchu (1337–1392) and his mother.

SHIP, THE (1912), by Johannes V. Jensen. See LONG JOURNEY, THE, by Johannes V. Jensen.

SHIRLEY (1849), by Charlotte Brontë. Against the background of a changing world at the beginning of the nineteenth century, the story of a spirited heiress, Shirley Keeldar, is told. The author patterned her after her own sister, Emily. Robert Moore, millowner in Yorkshire, introduces labor-saving devices which cause workmen's riots. He persists, in spite of financial and physical hazards, and wins his point with a promise to give more jobs, and provide better housing. Caroline Helstone, his gentle cousin, is seeking a meaning to her life. Dissatisfied with doing nothing, she marries Robert, whom she adores, and finds direction in her decision to help him. Shirley also is a new type of woman. She marries Robert's brother, Louis, a tutor, who has as much spirit as she. Other characters are three curates whom the author satirizes: Mr. Donne, Mr. Malone and Mr. Sweeting; Joe Scott; Hortense Moore, Robert's sister; Caroline's uncle, Rev. Matthewson Helstone; Mrs. Pryor, later discovered to be Caroline's mother.

SHNEIUR, ZALMAN (1887–   ). This Russian-born poet and novelist, who was distinguished for his literary talents even as a child, has written approximately fifty volumes in Hebrew and Yiddish. He was equally facile in both languages. It was his good fortune in his teens to know Bialik, Peretz, and other noted Jewish writers; they encouraged and guided him. He was a published poet in 1902, and an assistant editor in 1904. His collection of verses, *At Sunset,* published in 1906, gave him his first taste of fame. Other later collections in Hebrew include *Gesharim* (Bridges; 1912); *Hezionot* (Visions; 1921); and *Bametzar* (In Distress; 1921). Shneiur's work is marked by modernism, individualism, and universality. It has also been affected by his youthful years of struggle and homelessness. Shneiur lived in various European countries. After being held prisoner by the Germans during World War I, he wandered throughout Europe, and to the United States and Palestine, fleeing Paris for America when the Germans overran France in World War II. His Yiddish works comprise *Collected Writings* (1909); *A Toit* (A Death; 1909), a tragic diary; and a number of novels also in English translation, most notable of which is *Noah Pandre* (Eng. tr. 1936). Some of his books and criticisms have appeared in almost a score of languages. Shneiur characterizes himself as a poet of rebellion and strife. He found struggle in everything, including his own opposition to what he thought of as "anti-quated" Judaism. Life meant only doom—and he prophesied the doom of European Jewry as early as 1913, rightly averring that advances in civilization had not slain the evil of anti-Semitism. Like many of his literary associates, he set down his memories of life in the small European town in which he was reared.

SHOEMAKER'S HOLIDAY, THE (1600), by Thomas Dekker. The play is significant in that it celebrates the ascendancy of the new class of merchants and traders and craftsmen who were rapidly rising to the level of the blooded nobility. In a frolicking and rowdy spirit it traces the rise of Simon Eyre, the genial "mad shoemaker of Tower Street," to the high office of Lord Mayor of London. The skein of actions incidental to this involves a titled heir, who disguises himself as a shoemaker in order to pursue his courtship of a middle-class girl in defiance of the opposition of his noble uncle. A contrasting upset of class alliances is found in the person of a lame but valiant apprentice who retains the affection and loyalty of his pretty wife against the competition of a nobleman. It is a gallery of refreshingly lively, vivid characters, the greatest of whom is Simon Eyre himself, with his constant refrain of "Prince am I none, yet am I Princely born," who captures the respect of the King of England himself.

Orson Welles added *The Shoemaker's Holiday* to the triumphs of his Mercury Theatre in a production which proved Dekker's play to be thoroughly alive for the modern stage.

SHOLOM ALEICHEM (1859–1916). This is the pseudonym of Solomon Rabinowitz, born in Russia, died in New York City; it is the customary Jewish greeting meaning "Peace be unto you." He was called the "Jewish Mark Twain"; when Mark Twain learned of this, he announced he was the "American Sholom Aleichem." Despite a sad home life, with an impoverished innkeeping father and a harsh stepmother, the boy was cheerful and studious. An early failure in the business world, he finally devoted all his energies to writing, in Russian, Hebrew, and Yiddish. It was in the latter medium that he achieved his greatness. He best presented the picturesque and idiomatic riches of a language that had been looked down upon as a graceless jargon, became the most successful of Yiddish writers, and has already become a classic writer, acclaimed by Gorky, Tolstoy, and many others, and compared to Gogol and Dickens. It was the very circumstance of the drabness of Russian-Jewish small town life, and his humorous reactions thereto, that made it possible for him to compose what is perhaps the best laughter-through-tears body of fiction in literary history. His major characters have become classics in Jewish lore and conversation. One is Menachem Mendel, the hopeless "schlemiehl" who is always writing his wife about his novel business enterprises to circumvent czaristic repressions; the best known incident is that where, having assured himself of a reward for an essay in matchmaking, he discovers that both parties happen to be girls. Another is Tevye (Tobias) the dairyman, a trusting, pious soul who forever misquotes Scripture, and is largely concerned with marrying off his treasure of seven beautiful daughters. Sholom Aleichem was the first Yiddish author to write for children. The principal works of this author are not available to English readers; but one may turn to Maurice Samuel's *The World of Sholom Aleichem*, and the Frances & Julius Butwin translations of *The Old Country* (1936) and *Tevye's Daughters* (1949) for a magnificent sampling of his extensive literary production.

SHORT HISTORY OF THE ENGLISH PEOPLE (1874), by John Richard Green. This history delineates with unusual color and vivacity the social, constitutional and intellectual progress of the English people from the earliest times up to the second ministry of Disraeli in 1874. Departing radically from the methods of previous historians in his increased emphasis on people— thinkers, poets, merchants, common men of the gradually rising middle-class—and in his decreased emphasis on kings, nobles and courtiers, John Richard Green succeeded in producing the most readable and most thoroughly modern account of the development of the English nation that had been written up to his time. The shortness of the work resulted in occasional oversimplifications of the causes and consequences of complex events, but the book is nevertheless clearly the work of an intelligent and devoted scholar, and is authoritative in all main respects. The interpretation of controversial periods in England's past from the liberal point of view, together with the emphasis on the development of social institutions, and the familiar, imaginative, easy style, have served to make this a popular history not only in Green's own time, but to the present day.

SHOW BOAT (1926), by Edna Ferber. A strange company of variety actors sails twice a year down the Mississippi and its tributaries on Captain Andy Hawks's floating theater, *Cotton Blossom*. At various stops between St. Louis and New Orleans they moor and give spirited performances of *St. Elmo, East Lynne,* and other theatrical standbys. The troupe's leading lady is Magnolia, Andy's daughter. Other members of the company are Julie, Elly, Schultzy, and Parthy, the puritanical New England schoolteacher. At length Gaylord Ravenal, a fascinating gambler, joins the troupe and becomes its star. Magnolia falls in love with him and they leave for Chicago. Their life there depends upon his precarious profession. Finally Ravenal deserts her. Thereafter the novel traces the meteoric singing career of Kim, their daughter. *Show Boat* was made into an operetta classic (Kern and Hammerstein, 1927). Edna Ferber has written several plays with Kaufman, including *Royal Family* (1927), which burlesques the Barrymore dynasty; and *Dinner at Eight* (1932).

Besides many volumes of short stories, Edna Ferber wrote other novels of the American scene. *So Big* (1924) tells of the struggles of Selina, a truck gardener, for her son Dirk. *Cimarron* (1930) concerns the adventures of Yancey Cravat in an Oklahoma land rush of the 1890's; *American Beauty* (1931) deals with Polish immigration to Connecticut.

SHOW-OFF, THE (1924), by George Kelly. See CRAIG'S WIFE, by George Kelly.

SHROPSHIRE LAD, A (1896), by A. E. Housman. Composed mostly in the early months of 1895, these sixty-three poems are chiseled in clean lines into a beauty and memorableness which make them unique. "When I was one and twenty," " 'Tis Spring, come out to ramble," "With rue my heart is laden," are among the best known. Fastidious Housman (an eminent classical scholar) certainly was; the most exacting professional skill was necessary to fashion these poems, famous for their simplicity. Housman himself has said, "Meaning is of the intellect; poetry is not." By poetry he seems to mean short lyrics. They are all filled with a sort of Spartan sense of tragedy, the emotion there but controlled. He sings of liquor, love, and fights, and the gist of it is that if death is cruel, life is more cruel still. To religion and its consolations Housman pays no heed. The subjects of love and youth and doom also dominate *Last Poems* (1922), and the posthumous *More Poems* (1936).

SHUI HU CHUAN (14th or 15th c.), by Shih Nai-an. *The Shui Hu Chuan* (*A Cycle of Brigand Stories*) is a Chinese novel said to have been written by Shih Nai-an in the fourteenth or fifteenth century. Very little is known of the author, except that he was born in Huaian in the province of Kiangsu, and passed the literary examination in the Yuan dynasty.

The story is set in the thirteenth century, when the Sung dynasty was falling into decadence and disorder under the reign of the Emperor Hung Chung. There are 108 men in the story, 36 as main characters and 72 as minor. Leaving the evil society of men, 36 chiefs took refuge on a lofty mountain, surrounded by a reedy marsh, which was threaded with winding, hidden waterways, perfect for ambush and attacks. In this ideal solitude, a robber band was organized with its own law, ethics, and social code. The band of the 36 chiefs ravaged central China and defied the authority of the government, taking from the rich to give to the poor.

The novel was translated by Pearl Buck as *All Men Are Brothers*.

SICILIAN LIMES (1913), by Luigi Pirandello. See PIRANDELLO, LUIGI.

SIEBENKÄS (1796–1797), by Johann Paul Richter. See RICHTER, JOHANN PAUL.

SIGN OF THE FOUR, THE (1890), by Sir Arthur Conan Doyle. See SHERLOCK HOLMES, by Sir Arthur Conan Doyle.

SIGNIFICANCE OF SECTIONS IN AMERICAN HISTORY, THE (1932), by Frederick Jackson Turner. See TURNER, FREDERICK JACKSON.

SILAS MARNER (1861), by George Eliot. This is a classic story of a bewildered man who regains his lost faith in humanity through the love of a child. Silas Marner, a linen weaver, comes to Raveloe, after being ostracized from a small, religious community because of a false charge of theft. Betrayed by his best friend, deserted by his fiancée, benumbed by injustice, Silas withdraws into a lethargic state, living his days in ceaseless toil and misanthropic solitude. The accumulation of his daily earnings becomes his prime interest in life. After fifteen years of miserly isolation, his routine is disrupted by the stealing of his hoarded gold. The culprit is Dunstan, reprobate son of the town's richest and most respected citizen, Squire Cass. During this period of new despair, Silas discovers a stray child, Eppie, in his cottage. Eppie is the offspring of the unhappy secret marriage of a common woman and Godfrey, elder son of Squire Cass. The death of Eppie's mother at this time leaves Silas free to keep the child and permits Godfrey to marry Nancy Lammeter.

Eppie, growing rapidly into womanhood, brings happiness and contentment into the linen weaver's life. Good fortune once more comes to Silas when the draining of a pond near his cottage reveals Dunstan's body with the stolen gold still intact beside it. Godfrey, prodded by his conscience, confesses his past to his wife. Together, they go to make amends to Eppie. Silas allows Eppie to make her own decision. She chooses to remain with him, thus making his happiness complete.

SILENT DON, THE (1934–1940), by Mikhail A. Sholokhov. This famous Soviet trilogy, written in the tradition of the Russian literary masters, notably Gogol and Tolstoy, is a vast panorama in which an entire historical epoch is depicted through the experiences of the inhabitants of the Don village of Tatarsk. The style is vivid, terse and colorful; all is uncompromisingly disciplined by a hard realism. There is nothing sentimental or romanticized about any of the great number of characters, all in the grip of environmental forces over which they have little control. The mood of the work is stated by the author in his quotation from an old Cossack song:

> Our gentle Don is adorned with youthful widows;
> Our gentle father Don is blossomed with orphans:
> The waves of the gentle Don are rich with fathers'
> and mothers' tears.

There are many intertwined plots that tell the story of the Don Cossacks of Tatarsk, but the principal one has for its hero the young Cossack, Gregor Melekhov. The Melekhov family, well off and patriarchal, is headed by old Prokoffey; he brought home from the Turkish war a little Turkish woman, Maura, much to the consternation of the other Cossacks. There was also Pantaleimon, his son, and Pantaleimon's wife Ilinichka, and their sons Gregor and Piotra, the latter's wife Daria, and a daughter Dunia.

Gregor was like his father, tall, strong, and a little savage. In the amoral atmosphere of Tatarsk he did not consider it wrong to have an affair with Aksinia, wife of Stepan Astakhov, a neighbor. Aksinia was a mettlesome young woman who had no love for her sot of a husband, who periodically thrashed her "for her own good." When Gregor crossed her path for the first time Aksinia realized with terror that she was attracted to him, and fell in love with him. Uninhibited, following the example of others in Tatarsk, they carried on illicit relations openly, while Stepan, a reservist, was away for military training. Upon his return he beat Aksinia cruelly. Gregor and his brother Piotra came to her rescue, but Stepan, the stronger, drove them off. Old Pantaleimon was unhappy about Gregor's infatuation, and found him a wife in Natalia Korshunov, the belle of the village. But Aksinia would not resign herself to the loss of her lover. She used her considerable wiles to lure Gregory away from Natalia, even if she could be only his mistress.

From this brawling, drinking little world, the Great War suddenly took the young men, famous as fighters and horsemen, Gregor, Piotra and Stepan among them. Gregor and his brother achieved officer rank because of their courage and intelligence.

The Revolution of 1917 came. Like most other Cossacks, Gregor was untamed and aggressively individualistic. He joined Denikin's army of counterrevolutionaries and fought savagely against the Bolsheviks. When Denikin's front was shattered in 1919 Gregor conveniently joined the Reds in the Polish war; his hostility to Bolsheviks was not based on principle but on loyalty to the Cossack Ataman.

Gregor's soldierly fidelity and performance won for him a pardon from the Reds. He returned to Tatarsk, eager to resume his affair with Aksinia and determined to settle down on his land and be a good farmer. At this point a new

White Cossack rebellion broke out. Owing to his former connection with the Whites, the Reds wanted to arrest Gregor, who fled and joined involuntarily with a White guerilla band. Aksinia went along. She was shot during flight, and Gregor, disheartened, flung his rifle and cartridges into the gentle Don and returned to Tatarsk to surrender to the Reds and to face the unknown future with fortitude.

The trilogy, which in the English version is given the title of *The Silent Don*, has two divisions. The first is *And Quiet Flows the Don* (1934); the second *The Don Flows Home to the Sea* (1940). The author, himself a Don Cossack, began the novel's composition when he was only twenty.

SILESIUS, ANGELUS (1624–1677). Under this pseudonym, the German Johann Scheffler played a part in the revival which was rooted in an older mysticism. Expressing a deep desire for spiritual union with God, he wrote two volumes of poetry after his conversion to Catholicism: *The Holy Desire of the Soul* (1652) and *The Cherubic Wanderer* (1657). In the first he harks back to Renaissance pastoral poetry, and in the second he exhibits, in the form of Alexandrine epigrams, an all-embracing universality of view. Pointing the way to God, his lyric, although marked by a naïve simplicity, devotes itself to the description of profound personal experience.

SILVA DE VARIOS ROMANCES (1550), Anonymous. See ROMANCERO, THE, Anonymous.

SILVER CORD, THE (1926), by Sidney Howard. See THEY KNEW WHAT THEY WANTED, by Sidney Howard.

SILVER SPOON, THE (1926), by John Galsworthy. See FORSYTE SAGA, THE, by John Galsworthy.

SIM-CHUNG-CHUN (1882), Anonymous. Sim Hak-kyu, a scholar, lives with his talented wife in the town of Whangchu, in the province of Whanghai, Korea. Late in life they have a girl baby named Sim-chung. The mother soon dies, and the father gradually becomes blind. The daughter is very beautiful, and dutiful to her blind father, who for ten years begs food from house to house to feed her. Although a rich scholar, Mrs. Chang Seungsang, tries to adopt her, she refuses. One day Sim Hak-kyu hears from the chief priest of Mongwoon Monastery that if he makes an offering of 300 bags of rice to the Buddha of his temple, his sight will be restored. Sim is poor, but he agrees that if the priest furnishes the rice, he will pay him back in installments. When Sim-chung discovers the pact her father has made she is very much distressed, and, in order to pay back the debt, she plans to have herself cast to the restless spirit of the sea of Imtangsu, the dread of sailors, as a 15-year-old maidenly sacrifice, for which she receives in advance the 300 bags of rice necessary to pay the debt. Sim-chung drowns herself on an appointed day, but finds herself in the submarine palace of the King of the Sea, Imtang. The king tells her that once she was a star in heaven who fell in love with another star, and for an action which made the King of Heaven angry with her the lovers were banished to earth. Fearing a recurrence of the affair on earth, he sent her lover first, keeping her imprisoned for a long time, after which she was sent as daughter to her former lover, the man known as Sim Hak-kyu. Heaven has seen her sincere filial piety, however, and repents. Sim-chung ascends to the surface of the Imtang sea concealed within a giant lotus-flower. Some sailors see the beautiful flower on the sea and take it to the emperor, who makes Sim-chung his queen. But she, always thinking of her blind father, is very unhappy. The king gives them a great feast at the palace for all the blind men in the country, so Sim-chung and her father are reunited.

SIMPLICISSIMUS (1669), by Hans Jakob von Grimmelshausen. One of the most valuable and important works of the seventeenth century is Hans Jakob von Grimmelshausen's *Simplicus Simplicissimus,* a picaresque novel with a background of the destruction and chaos of the Thirty Years' War. Simplicissimus is carried off by pillaging soldiers when a child. The rest of his life consists of a series of adventurous episodes, including a meeting with a hermit—in reality his father. His instruction in life is a bitter, painful apprenticeship to hardship and reality, teaching him to live by his wits and senses. With rising and falling fortune, he alternately is a hunter, a soldier for many causes, and a robber, until he finally retires to a secluded life of piety and contemplation.

The book makes its claim to greatness chiefly as a vividly realistic picture of the complete depravity and degradation which was so characteristic of Grimmelshausen's society. Similar to the early epic hero Parzival, Simplicissimus goes through a trying period of development to emerge a better man—conscious of his existence and profiting by his experience to increase his wisdom and spiritual stature. The novel is the most important German "Bildungsroman" (educational novel) of the seventeenth century.

SINCE IBSEN (1900), by George Jean Nathan. See NATHAN, GEORGE JEAN.

SINGLE HOUND, THE (1914), by Emily Dickinson. See DICKINSON, EMILY.

SINGOALLA (1858), by Viktor Rydberg. See LAST ATHENIAN, THE, by Viktor Rydberg.

SINKELI BAKKAL (1936), by Xālide Edib Adivar. See CLOWN AND HIS DAUGHTER, THE, by Xālide Edib Adivar.

SINNERS, THE (produced 1932; printed 1933), by Israel Joshua Singer. See BROTHERS ASHKENAZI, THE, by Israel Joshua Singer.

SIR CHARLES GRANDISON (1754), by Samuel Richardson. This novel came out in seven volumes between November, 1753, and March, 1754, as *The History of Charles Grandison; in a Series of Letters, Published from the Originals.* In the preface Richardson practically admitted authorship, although he had not signed his name to the novel. Of his three novels this is still the most debated, with its adherents and detractors about equally divided. The didactic purpose of the author is more glaring here than in *Clarissa* (q.v.) or *Pamela* (q.v.). Sir Charles' trials amount to but little; his embarrassment is caused by having too many designing females wanting to marry him, and because he is engaged to marry Clementina when he would far prefer to wed Harriet Byron. The only excitement in the long tale is the abduction of Harriet and her rescue by Sir Charles. There are far more characters here than in his two other novels. Sir Rowland Meredith is a fairish comic character, and Charlotte Grandison is well done and true to life. Of course Richardson's principal success is the creation of a perfect gentleman in Sir Charles—*sans peur et sans reproche.*

SIR PATRICK SPENS (published 1765), Anonymous. This robust ballad, first printed in Percy's *Reliques*, tells of a Scottish sailor (Sir Patrick Spens) whose reputation for seamanship is so great that the king orders him by letter to sail a ship in the dead of winter with the king's daughter aboard.

> The first line that Sir Patrick red,
> A loud lauch lauched he;
> The next line that Sir Patrick red
> The teir blinded his ee.

Patrick is loath to go, as are the lords who accompany him. But they set sail, and are overcome by the storm, which one of the sailors had forecast. They now lie at the bottom of the sea.

SISTER CARRIE (1900), by Theodore Dreiser. Carrie Meeber comes from her rural home in Wisconsin to Chicago at the age of eighteen. On the train she is accosted by Charles Drouet, a good-natured salesman. Refusing his friendly overtures, she proceeds to the home of her sister, Mrs. Hanson. This is drab and hopeless beyond belief, and Carrie's job at a shoe factory crushes her spirit. As an escape, she drifts into a relationship with Drouet. George Hurstwood, manager of a bar, meets Carrie and decides to win her away from Drouet. He promises her marriage, deserts his family, steals ten thousand dollars from his employers, and flees the country with her. Overwhelmed by remorse, he then returns the money and tries to start a new life back in New York with Carrie. But separated from his former life of affluence, he sinks lower and lower, finally committing suicide. Carrie, who has deserted him, enjoys a successful stage career, but remains lonely. Many think this Dreiser's finest book.

SIX BOOKS OF THE REPUBLIC (1576), by Jean Bodin. In his *Republic* Bodin attempted to do for modern politics what Aristotle had done for classical politics. Utilizing ancient, medieval, and some distinctively modern conceptions, he tries to construct a general theory of the state. He conceives of a state as an association of families which recognize a sovereign power. The right of property, based on the law of nature, belongs to the family. Sovereignty is the supreme power over citizens and subjects, unrestrained by law, but apparently limited by the right of property. It is perpetual, inalienable; and cannot be limited by law because law is the command of the sovereign. Thus two threads may be recognized in Bodin's construction: the inviolability of the family and the necessity for absolute power in the hands of the sovereign. This discrepancy has been explained in terms of the two purposes of Bodin. He wrote during a period of civil strife, and he saw the consolidation of the power of the king as necessary for the achievement of civil peace. As a constitutional lawyer, on the other hand, he was concerned to preserve the French constitutional tradition. In the latter parts of his study he considers such subjects as the nature of revolution, the influence of geography on politics, relations among sovereigns, and financial policies of the state. He concludes with a comparison of various forms of states, distinguishes them in terms of the location of the sovereign power, and defends the view that the "well-ordered state" is one in which the sovereign power resides in a single person.

SIX CHARACTERS IN SEARCH OF AN AUTHOR (1921), by Luigi Pirandello. See PIRANDELLO, LUIGI.

SIXES AND SEVENS (1911), by William Sydney Porter. See PORTER, WILLIAM SYDNEY.

SKETCH BOOK, THE (1819–1820), by Washington Irving. This celebrated collection of sketches, folklore, travelogues, essays and short stories, written by Irving during his residence in England, represent the author at his best, and constitute his principal fame as a stylist, wit and storyteller. Most of the pieces are reflections of an American in England, but half a dozen have American backgrounds. Two of these are adaptations of German legends. "The Legend of Sleepy Hollow" concerns Ichabod Crane, an ingenuous schoolmaster who courts Katrina Van Tassel, daughter of a rich pre-Revolutionary Hudson farmer. One night, Ichabod encounters the headless specter who haunts the region, and disappears under mysterious circumstances, while his rival Brom Van Brunt smilingly wins Katrina. "Rip Van Winkle" tells of the indolent Rip, who wanders in the Catskills hunting one day, and meets some strange dwarfs. After drinking their liquor, he falls into a deep sleep, awaking after twenty years. An old man, he cheerfully wins new friends in the much altered village.

Bracebridge Hall (1822) contains forty-nine romantic sketches, essays, and stories. There are European settings, but the main character group is the household of the whimsical English gentleman. The most popular tales are "Dolph Heyliger" and "The Storm-Ship," stories of a haunted house, buried treasure, and ghost ships.

Irving, whose literary career was sporadic, is remembered for two other works in particular. "Diedrich Knickerbocker's" *History of New York* (1809) is actually whimsical satire, with digressions, facetious disregard for the facts, and whimsical caricatures of historical personages. The five-volume *Life of Washington* (1855–1859) is a solid work of scholarship, uncolored by Irving's stylistic fancies, and amply documented in its attention to the military details of the Revolution.

SKETCH OF AN HISTORICAL PICTURE OF THE PROGRESS OF THE HUMAN MIND (1794), by Jean Antoine Nicolas Caritat Condorcet. Condorcet, called "the last of the encyclopedists and the most universal of all," was one of the intellectual molders and active participants in the French Revolution. About him the hostile reactionary critic Brunetière wrote: "He who knows Condorcet well has an almost complete idea of what one would call the state of mind during the period of about 1780." An aristocrat by birth, Condorcet threw in his lot with the Revolution out of moral choice. *The Progress of the Human Mind* is his best known work. It is the profession of faith of a revolutionary republican who saw the hereditary monarchy of France as a stumbling block to social progress. Essentially this is a philosophical disquisition on the nature of man. It is an attempt to sketch the whole of his past history and, on the basis of that, forecast his future, which Condorcet was convinced would be happy and glorious.

Condorcet, typical of his progressive humanitarian times, fervently believed in the infinite perfectibility of man. Human nature he regarded as fluid and modifiable, and tried to prove this with historical facts and by means of reason. Furthermore, he believed in the inherent goodness in man, and rejected the theological concept of original sin as barbarous and false.

SKIN OF OUR TEETH, THE (1942), by Thornton Wilder. See OUR TOWN, by Thornton Wilder.

SMALL TOWN TYRANT (1904), by Heinrich Mann. See MANN, HEINRICH.

SMOKE (1867), by Ivan Sergeyevich Turgenev. Irina, seventeen years old when the story opens, is one of the loveliest of all of Turgenev's lovely heroines. Passionate and fascinating, she takes what she wants. She is more than a match for young Litvinov. She only consents to an engagement after the poor fellow has given up all hope of winning her. The Osinins are an old, impoverished family; even so, they are disappointed that their eldest daughter has made no better match. Then comes the court ball in Moscow. Litvinov, of course, does not accompany Irina; he learns from her father that she proved a sensation and that now she wishes to break off the engagement. Years pass, years of suffering for Litvinov; he becomes engaged to his cousin Tatyana. In Baden he meets Irina again. She is married, and pretends to despise the wealthy aristocratic circle in which she shines. Litvinov's love returns in all its old intensity. When his fiancée reaches Baden-Baden he breaks his engagement with her. Irina has promised to leave her husband and join him. She backs out, however, unable to give up the life she pretended to despise. Wretched, aware of the futility of his love, Litvinov returns to his estate in Russia. As he is rushed along in the train he watches the smoke whirl past the window: "Suddenly it all seemed as smoke to him, everything, his own life, Russian life. . . ." For two years he lives in misery, hearing only rumors of his former fiancée. At length she invites him to visit her. Litvinov rushes to her, and falls on his knees at her feet. Except for the love passages which dominate the novel, it is primarily interesting as a picture of Russian society, not only in the sixties, but also as it was up to the Bolshevik revolution.

SNOW-BOUND (1866), by John Greenleaf Whittier. Of all Whittier's poetry, *Snow-Bound* proved the most popular. It is an idyl of New England country life experienced by the poet in his boyhood. He extols the virtues of the refined Quaker home, and describes the farm chores: bringing in the firewood, cleaning the stalls, feeding the cows and horses. He gives portraits of his uncle the storyteller, his aunt and sister, the schoolmaster and the wise old doctor. In retrospect, the poet waxes nostalgic about the transformation of the little domestic community when isolated by the season. Although Whittier was fond of portraying the romance of ordinary rural existence, in the manner of Burns ("The Barefoot Boy," from *The Panorama and Other Poems,* 1856, eulogizes the innocence of youthful pleasures), he was also interested in historical and contemporary issues: "Moll Pitcher" (1832) retells the legend of the heroine who took her husband's place at a cannon during the Revolution; "Barbara Frietchie," from *In War Time and Other Poems* (1864), recounts the gallantry of Stonewall Jackson when, upon entering Frederick, Maryland, he is confronted by the ninety-year-old patriot who snatches up the Stars and Stripes shot down by the General's soldiers. *Songs of Labor* (1850) is a selection of verses praising the work of such men as shoemakers and fishermen. In spite of further writing on such pressing issues as slavery, however, it is for his simple lyrics of country life that Whittier is best remembered.

SO BIG (1924), by Edna Ferber. See SHOW BOAT, by Edna Ferber.

SOCIAL CONTRACT (1792), by Jean Jacques Rousseau. This is one of the most influential works in the long history of political theory. It is brilliantly written, but the brilliancy covers serious confusions and ambiguities. Man is born free, but finds himself everywhere in chains, says Rousseau. How is this possible? Can a theory of society be discovered which will show how man's natural freedom can be preserved and extended in society? This Rousseau attempts to do. He uses the social contract theory (after the manner of Locke). We all put our persons and powers in common under the supreme direction of the general will, and thus become citizens, parts of the indivisible and organic whole of the state. Each of us will desire that which is best for the state as a whole. To that extent our true will is identical with the general will, which also wills the common good. As long as the state is directed by the general will, though we are subject to it we are morally free. The difficulty comes in attempting to determine what it is that the general will intends. It cannot be identified with the will of the majority, because each man in the majority may be looking out for his own interest. Yet the majority will is an indication of the general will. Another difficulty of Rousseau's position is that there seems to be no provision for safeguarding the rights of minorities. When the will of the majority is identified with the general will (which is necessary for practical purposes), the minority which opposes the majority must be considered not merely wrong but morally evil. Rousseau's fusion of morality and politics, which had its advantages as a reaction against Hobbes' amoralism, also paved the way for the total state of Hegel and later writers. Rousseau's influence was on the one hand to fan the flames of the growing revolt in France, and on the other to provide arguments for the conservative organic theory of the state. The above-mentioned ambiguities may be said to be responsible for this.

SOCIAL STATICS AND MAN VERSUS THE STATE (1884), by Herbert Spencer. See SPENCER, HERBERT.

SOCIETY AND SOLITUDE (1870), by Ralph Waldo Emerson. See ESSAYS, by Ralph Waldo Emerson.

SOHRAB AND RUSTUM (1853), by Matthew Arnold. A narrative poem in blank verse, based on a work by the Persian poet Firdusi, this is the story of Rustum, mighty chief of the Persians, who leaves his wife to go to war. She bears him a son, Sohrab, but sends word to him that it is a girl, because she fears that her husband will take Sohrab away to be a warrior. However, when the boy grows to manhood, he joins the Tartar forces in order to find his missing father. Sohrab becomes leader of the Tartars and engages in battle with the Persians. Not knowing that his father is their chief, Sohrab fights with Rustum in single combat. The old man finally overcomes Sohrab (who is hesitant and overchivalrous), only to discover in the latter's dying agony that it is his own son whom he has slain.

SOIL, THE (1888), by Émile Zola. See ROUGON-MACQUART, THE, by Émile Zola.

SOLDIER'S PAY (1926), by William Faulkner. See FAULKNER, WILLIAM.

SOLDIERS OF FORTUNE (1899), by Richard Harding Davis. See DAVIS, RICHARD HARDING.

SOLEDADES, LAS (1613), by Luis de Góngora. See SOLITUDES, THE, by Luis de Góngora.

SOLILOQUIES IN ENGLAND (1922), by George Santayana. See LAST PURITAN, THE, by George Santayana.

SOLITUDES, THE (1613), by Luis de Góngora. The plot of *The Solitudes* is of meager interest, being but a convenient peg on which Góngora hung his elaborate descriptions, superbly interspersed with lyrics fraught with metaphors and hyperboles. After a dedication to the Duke of Bejar (37 verses), there follow the 1091 verses of the "First Solitude" and 979 verses of a fragment of the "Second Solitude," all written about 1613, in *silvas* of varied patterns. The action of *The Solitudes* takes place in a world that is artificial and rich in suggestion. A young man, shipwrecked on an unknown shore, finds shelter with some goatherds. The next day an old man leading a party of young men and women invites him to a wedding. On reaching the village he enjoys the fireworks and the dances. Next morning the marriage takes place, with banquet, speeches and games. At nightfall the couple are conducted with ceremony to their home. In the "Second Solitude" the stranger returns with some fishermen in a large boat. He sings a song of unhappy love. After a picnic on a nearby island he listens to a father rave about the fishing exploits of his daughters. The fishermen Licidas and Micón serenade the two daughters, and at the stranger's request the father allows the young people to get married. Next morning the stranger is conveyed to the mainland, where he attends a hawking party.

On its first appearance *The Solituaes* caused a great deal of discussion and abuse. Since then its influence has been immense, especially after 1927, when on the occasion of the tercentenary of Góngora's death, the young poets became acquainted with the most baffling but perhaps the greatest ode in Spanish literature.

SOMBRERO DE TRES PICOS, EL (1874), by Pedro Antonio de Alarcón. See THREE-CORNERED HAT, THE, by Pedro Antonio de Alarcón.

SOME PROBLEMS OF PHILOSOPHY (1914), by Bertrand Russell. See RUSSELL, BERTRAND.

SON OF ROYAL LANGBRITH, THE (1904), by William Dean Howells. See HAZARD OF NEW FORTUNES, A, by William Dean Howells.

SON OF THE MIDDLE BORDER, A (1917), by Hamlin Garland. The middle border, of which Hamlin Garland writes from his rich experience, is the area between Wisconsin and Dakota. The book chronicles the adventures of the Garland and McClintock families and of the first thirty years of the author's life. The events depict the United States' great westward expansion in the sixties and seventies. In effect, the story of the bitter struggles, hardships, disillusionments—as well as the indomitable faith of the author's ancestors—is the record of all American pioneer families; hence the book's wide popularity and historic value.

A Daughter of the Middle Border (1921) continues the theme. The backgrounds range from West to East, from the Dakota blizzards to tranquil literary life in the New York of the nineties. The author's manhood, romance and marriage in a little Kansas town receive emphasis. A glimpse of the sophisticated literary life of New York, Chicago and London, affords intimate portraits of Mark Twain, G. B. Shaw, Oliver Wendell Holmes, and others.

Hamlin Garland in his youth wrote many realistic works of life in this same background. *Main-Travelled Roads* (1891) collects such bleak local-color stories as "The Return of a Private," bitter tale of an unknown soldier whose weary return from the war is greeted by an invitation to harness himself to the drudgery of the plow. *Other Main-Travelled Roads* (1910) is a sequel. *Rose of Dutcher's Coolly* (1895) is a problem novel of a girl's struggle against a farm existence. Rose Dutcher, unable to endure return to farm life after attending the state university, meets Warren Mason, a Chicago editor, and besides the encouragement of her writing, she finds romance.

SONS (1932), by Pearl Buck. See GOOD EARTH, THE, by Pearl Buck.

SONS AND LOVERS (1913), by D. H. Lawrence. The death of Lawrence in his forty-fifth year ended prematurely the literary career of one of the most brilliant of contemporary novelists. Curiously, what some discerning critics consider to be his outstanding work was a youthful effort, his third novel in a long list of fictional production. "The first part of *Sons and Lovers* is all autobiography," admitted Lawrence. The main theme of the novel is the relation between Paul Morel and his mother, an attachment characterized by a strong mother image or Oedipus complex. This emotional aberration proves a tragedy to the victim, for he finds it impossible to experience love and its fulfillment with any woman. Paul is unsuccessful in such struggle as he makes to break away from the emotional cord that ties him to his mother. The miner father finds himself rejected by both son and wife, whose sensibilities are incomprehensible to him, and he drinks himself into a decline. The other children go out into the world, and are lost in business, or marriage, or death. Miriam loves Paul, makes every sacrifice for him, but he feels for his mother, who is slowly dying of cancer, what he should have felt for Miriam. Paul strays into a triangular situation with Clara and Baxter Dawes. At the end he is left alone with Miriam, whom he rejects. The last chapter is entitled "Derelict." Lawrence had a sharp ear for the dialogue of simple folk and a deep sympathy for their complex lives.

SONG OF BERNADETTE (1943), by Franz Werfel. See FORTY DAYS OF MUSA DAGH, THE, by Franz Werfel.

SONG OF HILDEBRAND (800). See HILDEBRANDSLIED.

SONG OF ROLAND, THE (11th c.), Anonymous. This oldest of the French heroic songs (*chansons de geste*) is the story of a rear-guard action in the Pyrenees. Charlemagne, returning to France from war against the infidel in Spain, leaves Roland at Roncesvalles with his Twelve Peers and 20,000 troops, to cover the withdrawal. Should the Saracens come in great number, Roland is to blow his horn, Oliphant, to recall the Emperor. But Roland is proud and will not blow the horn, although, guided by the traitor Ganelon, the pagan horde threatens to engulf the outnumbered French. Blessed by their Bishop, Turpin, the Peers lay on. Carnage is great. They kill thousands, but other thousands come after, and one by one the noble peers go down. Too late Roland blows his horn. Charlemagne returns, full of grief, to find Roland dead on the field and the Moors long since in flight. Ganelon meets a traitor's end.

Extremely popular during the Middle Ages, whole cycles of such epics grew up around the names of such figures as Guillaume of Orange, Doon of Mayence and Charlemagne. They flourished for three centuries. Their vogue was European. It is said that Tallifer the Minstrel entertained William of Normandy in his tent with the singing of the *Roland* on the eve of Hastings.

SONG OF THE BELL, THE (1800), by Friedrich von Schiller. See SCHILLER, FRIEDRICH VON.

SONG OF THE CHATTAHOOCHEE, THE (1883), by Sidney Lanier. See LANIER, SIDNEY.

SONG OF THE LARK, THE (1915), by Willa Cather. See CATHER, WILLA.

SONG OF THE VALLEY (1939), by Sholem Asch. See NAZARENE, THE, by Sholem Asch.

SONGS AND SONNETS (1633), by John Donne. See DONNE, JOHN.

SONGS BEFORE SUNRISE (1871), by Algernon Charles Swinburne. See SWINBURNE, ALGERNON CHARLES.

SONGS OF INNOCENCE (1789), **SONGS OF EXPERIENCE** (1794), by William Blake. For many readers, the best-liked poems of Blake are contained in these few lyrics, intelligible on the surface but many of them holding a deeper meaning in symbols. Blake illustrated the volumes himself by his new method of illuminated printing. Some of the lyrics in the *Innocence* poems have their sombre or bitter antitypes in the *Experience* poems: "The Lamb" becomes "Tiger! Tiger! burning bright"; "Infant Joy," "Infant Sorrow." Whatever the range of mood, from the first line, "Piping down the valleys wild," to the additional poem now commonly included:

> Cruelty has a Human Heart,
> And Jealousy a Human Face;
> Terror the Human Form Divine,
> And Secrecy the Human Dress.

The Human Dress is forged Iron,
The Human Form a fiery Forge,
The Human Face a Furnace seal'd,
The Human Heart its hungry Gorge . . .

the authentic voice of a great poet speaks with a lovely distinctness it never again achieved. The lyrics magically combine love of nature with social consciousness and mysticism.

SONGS OF KABIR (ca. 1475). Kabir was a mystic and a religious reformer. Although born a Moslem, his unitarian convictions led him to seek God in all religions. His songs are full of religious rapture and idealistic striving, and are charged with the urgency of achieving the brotherhood of all men. But far more than social, they are preoccupied with a passion for the Infinite and God. The poet's theme is that "God is the breath of all breath," and is to be found neither in temple nor mosque. He employs homely metaphor and religious idioms and symbols universally understood. It is his song's delicate lyricism and simplicity that carry a great emotional impact.

SONGS OF LABOR (1850), by John Greenleaf Whittier. See SNOW-BOUND, by John Greenleaf Whittier.

SONGS OF LIFE AND HOPE (1905), by Rubén Darío. With the publication of these *Cantos,* the Nicaraguan poet Rubén Darío (1867–1916) won recognition as his country's leading poet. His verse represented a poetical revolution comparable to that of Garcilaso and Góngora in past centuries, bringing into Spanish prosody greater metric variety, suppleness and musicality. Darío re-created an artificial world out of the scattered mythologies of the Orient and of Greco-Roman civilization, and out of the materials handled by the Parnassian, Decadent and Symbolist poets of France. His ideas were limited to the beauty of the world, a rococo world of princesses and swans, and to the melancholy discovery of the frailty of love, of vanity and of death. His greatness is found, therefore, in his formalistic virtuosity: his colorful imagery, his rhythmical skill and his verbal felicity.

SONGS OF SELMA, THE (1762), by James Macpherson. See OSSIAN'S POEMS, by James Macpherson.

SONNETS (published 1609), by William Shakespeare. Shakespeare's sonnets contain much of the richest poetry in the English language. They were published in 1609, but there is evidence that some were written before 1598, some perhaps as early as 1591, and there are links that connect them with the early love plays. The sonnet sequence consists of three main sections. A, Sonnets I–CXXVI; B, Sonnets CXXVII–CLII; C, Sonnets CLIII–CLIV. Sections A and B are closely connected; Section C may be a sort of epilogue to B, but is more probably an independent exercise in sonneteering, based on a Latin version of a Greek epigram. The general theme of the sonnets is the poet's almost idolatrous love for a younger friend, perhaps the Earl of Southampton. "Friendship Triumphant" is the subject of Sonnets I-CXXVI. Some of the first lines of the best known are: "When forty winters shall besiege thy brow . . ," "Look in thy glass, and tell the face thou viewest . . ," "Shall I compare thee to a summer's day?," "As an imperfect actor on the stage . . ," "When to the sessions of sweet silent thought . . ," "Full many a glorious morning have I seen . . ," "Not marble, nor the gilded monuments . . ," "That time of year thou mayest in me behold . . ," "Or I shall live your epitaph to make . . ," "How like a winter hath my absence been . . ," "To me, fair friend, you never can be old." The first section is occupied mainly with "man right fair," the second concerns the "woman colour'd ill," the dark lady. A few of the sonnets show Shakespeare surprisingly careless, but others are among the finest poems in the world.

SONNETS FROM THE PORTUGUESE (1850), by Elizabeth Barrett Browning. Robert Browning said that these forty-four sonnets, written by his wife, were "the finest . . . written in any language since Shakespeare." Their theme is pure and disembodied love. It is the poet's husband who is the center of her spiritual scheme of things:

> The face of all the world is changed, I think,
> Since first I heard the footsteps of thy soul.

They are singularly intimate, simple and direct in their effect, a rare record of devotion. "How do I love thee? Let me count the ways."

SONNETS TO ORPHEUS (1923), by Rainer Maria Rilke. See RILKE, RAINER MARIA.

SORROWS OF A BOY, THE (1883), by Conrad Ferdinand Meyer. See MEYER, CONRAD FERDINAND.

SORROWS OF WERTHER, THE (1774), by Johann Wolfgang von Goethe. This short epistolary novel made Goethe world-famous at the age of twenty-five. Based on an unhappy love affair which he experienced as a law apprentice in the city of Wetzlar, and influenced by Rousseau's *La nouvelle Héloïse,* this slight book became the bible of eighteenth century sentimentalism. Its hero, young, unhappy Werther, with his blue coat and yellow topboots, his love of nature, and his worship of Homer and Ossian, was the idol of an age that delighted in a free display of tears and emotions. The book was discussed, analyzed, criticized and ridiculed all over Europe; even Chinese paintings on glass depicting Werner and Lotte reached Germany in 1779. Men like Napoleon are known to have read and treasured the story of Werther, who fell in love with Lotte, the betrothed of his friend Albert, and who finally shot himself because he was unable to tear himself from the intolerable and hopeless situation. Goethe in his mature years did not approve of the stormy violence of his youthful opus, and in 1787 he revised the book, removing some of the overflow of emotionalism and somewhat "classicizing" the style. The novel still retains charm, psychological depth and a powerful sweep of passionate feeling; one can understand that Goethe was for a long time "the author of Werther" to the world at large.

SOULS DIVIDED (1913), by Matilde Serao. Matilde Serao acquired wide reputation as a novelist and a journalist for the vivacity of her descriptions and the Neapolitan exuberance of her fantasy. *Souls Divided* is a love story told in the form of letters from Paolo Ruffo to Diana Sforza, who is married to

Sir Randolph Montague. Diana travels constantly from London to Nice and other fashionable places. She receives Paolo's passionate letters, but her role of dutiful wife militates against answering them, no matter how responsive she feels. She avoids him scrupulously, but he follows her, like a man possessed, from house to house, city to city and country to country. When she is preparing to leave with her English ambassador-husband for St. Petersburg, Paolo is heartbroken, and decides to visit distant lands accompanied by his sister, Lisa. In the meantime, Diana falls sick; and on the verge of dying she sends him a first and last message in which she confesses to have loved him from the very first moment.

SOUND AND THE FURY, THE (1929), by William Faulkner. See FAULKNER, WILLIAM.

SOUTH MOON UNDER (1933), by Marjorie Kinnan Rawlings. See YEARLING, THE, by Marjorie Kinnan Rawlings.

SOUTH WIND (1917), by Norman Douglas. Thomas Heard, the learned, modest and tolerant retiring Bishop of Bampopo in Central Africa, stops off at the island of Nepenthe on his return voyage to England. Here, in an atmosphere of disenchantment, he meets a variety of extraordinary characters who have come to the island because they are superfluous people, maladjusted to the world. Without a plot, the novel is a satirically good-humored description of these escaping individuals. There is Monsignor Francesco, young, sensual and cynical; Ernest Eames, whose life is devoted to compiling a history of Nepenthe; the Duchess of San Martino, a faded American widow looking for excitement; the eccentric but rich Keith; Edgar Marten, a Jewish mineralogist; Van Koppen, a spendthrift American millionaire; Miss Wilberforce, an unhappy Englishwoman who disrobes when she gets drunk; and rich Madame Steynlin, who finds a lover in the young Russian giant, Peter, a religious fanatic. Finally there are Denis Phipps, absurdly adolescent at nineteen; the amoral fifteen-year-old Angelina; Freddy Parker, president of the club; and many others. During his visit, the Bishop witnesses a funeral, a political upheaval, a murder and an earthquake. The story is written in a suave, cultivated prose.

SPADA DI FEDERICO, LA (1806), by Vincenzo Monti. See MONTI, VINCENZO.

SOUTHERN HARVEST, A (1937), by Robert Penn Warren. See WARREN, ROBERT PENN.

SPANISH TRAGEDY, THE (1592), by Thomas Kyd. Published anonymously for the first time in 1592, this play was assigned to Kyd because of a statement made by Thomas Heywood in his *Apology for Actors*. This drama is one of the best, as it is also one of the earliest, tragedies of blood derived largely from Seneca. In a war between Spain and Portugal Don Balthazar, the Viceroy of Portugal's son, is captured jointly by Horatio, son of Hieronimo, Marshal of Spain, and Lorenzo, the King of Spain's nephew. Balthazar falls in love with Bel-imperia, Lorenzo's sister, who loves Horatio. Finding the lovers in an arbor, Balthazar and Lorenzo fall upon Horatio and murder him. The body is discovered by old Hieronimo, who receives a letter from Bel-imperia, telling him that her brother and Balthazar had committed the murder. The Marshal plans to avenge his son's death. At the wedding festivities of Bel-imperia and Balthazar, he puts on a tragedy, and in the play within the play he and Bel-imperia manage to stab the guilty pair and end by doing away with themselves.

SPECIMEN DAYS AND COLLECT (1882), by Walt Whitman. See LEAVES OF GRASS, by Walt Whitman.

SPECIES PLANTARUM (1753), by Carl Linnaeus. See SYSTEMA NATURAE, by Carl Linnaeus.

SPENCER, HERBERT (1820–1903). A striking example of the application of biological categories to social phenomena is the work of Herbert Spencer. This nineteenth-century English liberal developed a theory of social progress using the notions of evolution and the organic state. Evolution for him is a process by which a simple undifferentiated whole develops into a complex and differentiated one. Applying this notion to social systems, Spencer developed a thoroughly optimistic theory of progress, predicting peace and plenty as the outcome of industrial society. The one caution he had was that the state should not interfere in economic affairs in any way. Placing his faith in natural laws governing society, he thus became an outspoken foe of socialism. This view was expounded in *Social Statics and Man versus the State* (1884; *Social Statics* was originally published in 1850). He also completed a compendium of all knowledge, his *Synthetic Philosophy* (1860–1896), in twelve volumes.

SPECTATOR, THE (March 1, 1711–December 6, 1712; June 18, 1714– December 20, 1714), by Joseph Addison and Richard Steele. This periodical, appearing daily except Sunday, was a successor to the thrice-weekly *Tatler*. Of the 555 essays, Addison wrote 274, Steele, 236. Pope and Thomas Tickell also contributed. The urbane, bantering style which characterized these informal and chatty discussions of contemporary life gained *The Spectator* enormous popularity, even with those who recognized themselves in the good-natured satires. Famous among the ironic pictures of prevailing manners and morals is the item in a Fine Lady's account of her day's activities: "Ten o'clock. Staid within all day not at home." One essay ridicules the way in which theatrical applause could over-ride the judgment of intelligent critics. Others gently mocked the English predilections for things foreign: Italian opera, French phrases artificially inserted in letters to impress. A few essays were allegorical, as "The Vision of Mirza," "Public Credit." Some were pieces of literary criticism, on the ballad, for example, and on *Paradise Lost* (q.v.). The most widely remembered in the series, however, were those grouped as the Sir Roger de Coverley Papers, which acquired the title from the main figure in an imaginary club gathered around Will's Coffee-house. Sir Roger is the prototype of the country squire, kindly, prejudiced, secretly superstitious. Others in the club were Sir Andrew Freeport, a man of commerce; Captain Sentry, the military representative; and Will Honeycomb, the fashionable man of the world, who looked down on scholars. In creating the last, Addison reveals his contempt for the society sophisticate, the narrowest sort of pedant;

the person who devotes his life to books at least offers the opportunity to learn from him. Despite his gentleness in ridiculing frivolities and his inoffensive attack upon vulgarity, Addison's seriousness cannot be doubted. He has been aptly called a "parson with a tie wig," i.e., a preacher not dressing the part.

SPEECH ON CONCILIATION WITH THE COLONIES (1775), by Edmund Burke. Burke expressed his fear of revolutionary change. It was not so much his love of justice and freedom that prompted him to plead for moderation on the part of the Crown toward the American colonies. It was, rather, his realistic concern with the maintenance of the status quo and power of the Empire. Prudently, he stated the case: "A nation is not governed, which is perpetually to be conquered." He saw the application of military measures against the unrest in America as leading into a blind alley: ". . . conciliation failing, force remains; but force failing, no further hope of conciliation is left." Besides, it was impractical: "Three thousand miles of ocean lie between you and the Colonies." Although Parliament ignored Burke's plea, his speech nevertheless remains a classic in the fields of colonial policy and oratory.

SPELL OF THE YUKON, THE (1907), by Robert W. Service. See SERVICE, ROBERT W.

SPHAERA MUNDI (ca. 1233), by Joannes de Sacrobosco (John of Holywood or Halifax). This treatise on spherical geometry and astronomy comprises four chapters: one on the terrestrial globe; a second on great and small circles; another on rising and setting stars; and the last on the orbits and movements of the planets. Only the most elementary topics, extracted from Ptolemy's *Almagest* (q.v.), are included. The *Sphere* constituted little advance over the Arabian commentaries on Ptolemy, being derived (almost slavishly) from al-Farghani and al-Battani: its importance lay in its immense popularity. The *Sphere* of Sacrobosco was the most widely read astronomical work of the time, and it exerted a deep influence for several centuries. Commentaries on it were written by numerous medieval and early modern scientists, such as Michael Scot, Cecco d'Ascoli, Pierre d'Ailly, Regiomontanus, Jacques Lefèvre, Melanchthon, and Clavius. It was the second astronomical work to be printed (in 1472). At least twenty-five editions appeared before 1500, and at least forty more between 1500 and 1647, many of them for school use. Nor was it used only in the Latin, for there was not only a Hebrew translation in 1399, but it was published in Italian, French, German, and Spanish. Sacrobosco composed also a *Tractatus de Arte Numerandi* or *Algorismus* (printed ca. 1490), which helped to popularize the Arabic numerals; and he wrote a *Compotus* (a book on the calculation of the date of Easter; composed ca. 1232 or 1244; printed ca. 1538) which pointed out errors in the Julian calendar.

SPIRIT OF THE LAWS, THE (1748), by Montesquieu, Charles Louis du Secondat. In many respects, Montesquieu ran contrary to the main currents of his time. In a period when science was held to be primarily deductive in method and based on self-evident principles, he adopted an empirical method and continually collected and collated factual data. In a period when men looked for simple and radical solutions to the social problems caused by the decay of the *ancien régime,* he urged caution and compromise. In a period in which men claimed to have found universal principles of politics, he emphasized variation and individual differences. His *The Spirit of the Laws* is the unsystematic and complex book in which he formulated his results. He believed that geographical conditions had much to do with determining the best type of constitution for each country. By temperament a moderate constitutionalist (he much admired the British Constitution), he did not feel that this type of government was best for all states. He thought he had discovered a basic principle in the British Constitution in the doctrine of "the separation of powers," and though this theory was very influential with statesmen, especially in America, it was based on a faulty understanding of the British system. For Montesquieu the various forms of government were based on the different virtues of which man was capable. Above all, he anticipated and laid the foundations for an empirical science of society which was to be the aim of nineteenth- and twentieth-century social thinkers.

SPIRIT OF MODERN PHILOSOPHY, THE (1892), by Josiah Royce. See ROYCE, JOSIAH.

SPIRIT OF RUSSIA (Eng. tr. 1919), by Thomas G. Masaryk. See RUSSIA AND EUROPE, by Thomas G. Masaryk.

SPIRITUAL SONG BETWEEN THE SOUL AND THE HUSBAND (1627), by San Juan de la Cruz. Many critics—T. S. Eliot, for instance—consider San Juan de la Cruz (Juan de Yépes Alvárez) among the world's most gifted writers. Poetic inspiration and mystical fervor are so fused in him that he has often been called the Ecstatic Doctor. San Juan wrote many lyrics and allegories ("The Ascent to Mount Carmel," "The Dark Night of the Soul," etc.), all of them outstanding, and it is difficult to single out any one of them for praise above the others. However, his most sustained achievement was, no doubt, *Cántico espiritual entre el alma y el esposo* (*Spiritual Song Between the Soul and the Husband*) which contains forty *liras* (i.e., stanzas of five verses combining seven- and eleven-syllable lines), with an elaborate and voluminous prose commentary on each. Patterned after Solomon's *Song of Songs,* the *Cantico* can be read and enjoyed by the profane on its most elementary realistic plane, even though one may not be aware of its more recondite allegorical meanings. San Juan's technique is irreproachable, and his *liras* stir with their entrancing music and oriental imagery.

SPIRITUAL YEAR, THE (1851), by Annette Elisabeth von Droste-Hülshoff. See DROSTE-HÜLSHOFF, ANNETTE ELISABETH VON.

SPLASHES AND RAGS (1896), by Gustav Fröding. See FRÖDING, GUSTAV.

SPOCK, BENJAMIN (1903–   ). Dr. Spock's illustrated volume, *The Common Sense Book of Baby and Child Care* (1945) is one of America's most popular infant guides. It covers such topics as feeding and diet, education, behavior, illness, the problem of separated parents, and adoption. Many parents rely greatly on the writings of Drs. Spock and Gesell (q.v.) for their child-rearing information.

SPOILS OF POYNTON, THE (1897), by Henry James. See JAMES, HENRY.

SPOON RIVER ANTHOLOGY (1915), by Edgar Lee Masters. This work is a sequence of epitaphs of nearly two hundred and fifty persons buried in a small Midwestern cemetery. In realistic free verse Masters discloses the stories of their secret lives, which held mostly monotony and frustration. The portraits range from "Anne Rutledge," Lincoln's youthful love, to "Petit, the Poet," the town's mediocre versifier, whose futile career involved an ignorance of all nonliterary matters, and whose poetry was second-rate.

The New Spoon River (1924), a portrayal of American towns, with their cruel standards, is a less successful sequel. Masters, in fact, never duplicated the excellence of the work which secured his fame.

SPORT OF THE GODS, THE (1902), by Paul Laurence Dunbar. See DUNBAR, PAUL LAURENCE.

SPORTSMAN'S SKETCHES (1847–1851), by Ivan Sergeyevich Turgenev. Turgenev, who once wrote an essay on Hamlet and Don Quixote, was a sort of Hamlet himself, who sometimes wished he were a Don Quixote. He loved much in the order into which he had been born, but he could not resist the admiration so natural to him for the young men and women who risked all to destroy this very order. His *Sportsman's Sketches,* it has been said, helped more than any other book to bring about the abolition of serfdom in Russia. Whether or not its importance has been exaggerated, it is certain Turgenev was always on the side of the oppressed. He loathed callousness; he despised the privileged antics of the aristocrats. He was deeply attached to country life.

Included in this collection are: "Hor and Kalinitch," "Yermolai and the Miller's Wife," "Raspberry Spring," "The District Doctor," "My Neighbor Radilov," "The Agent," "The Countinghouse," "Biryuk," "Two Country Gentlemen," "Lgov," "The Peasant Proprietor Ovsyanikov," "Kassyan of Fair Springs," "Byezhin Prairie," "Lebedyan," "Tatyana Borissovna and Her Nephew," "Death," "The Singers," "Piotr Petrovitch Karataev," "The Tryst," "The Hamlet of the Shtchigri District," "Tchertop-Hanov and Nedopyushin," "The End of Tchertop-Hanov," "A Living Relic," "The Battling of Wheels," "The Forest and the Steppe." Of these "The District Doctor" is probably the most famous. It tells of a girl who is ill, and in delirium is in love with the doctor, whose life is so humdrum that the experience forms the great dramatic highlight in his life. His heart nearly breaks as he realizes that he cannot save her life. His cry of "Alexandra Andreyevna!" will long remain in the reader's ears. His exalted emotion was alien; he married a merchant's daughter with a large dowry. She is ill-tempered, as are all rich women in Russian novels; the doctor dreams of his one romantic experience.

SPRING FRESHETS (1871), by Ivan Sergeyevich Turgenev. See TORRENTS OF SPRING, by Ivan Sergeyevich Turgenev.

SPRING OF CHILDHOOD, THE (1651), by Baltasar Gracián. See CRITICK, THE, by Baltasar Gracián.

SPRING'S AWAKENING (1891), by Frank Wedekind. See AWAK-
ENING OF SPRING, by Frank Wedekind.

SPY, THE (1821), by James Fenimore Cooper. This book, Cooper's second, was the success that founded his prolific literary career. It is a romance
of the Revolution, with the American background typical of the author. Harvey Birch is ostensibly a Loyalist spy, but is secretly in the service of George
Washington (disguised as William Harper during these events). Birch comes
to rescue his Loyalist neighbor, Henry Wharton, his son Captain Henry Wharton of the British Army, and his daughters Sarah and Frances. Many stirring
adventures occur, culminating in the death sentence of young Henry, who had
refused to leave his home and was captured by a rebel force under Captain
Jack Lawton, later escaping, and subsequently taken again as a spy with
Colonel Wellemere, an English officer who is about to marry Sarah when
Birch reveals that he is already married. Birch helps Henry to escape once
more; and Frances, sympathetic to the American cause, finds Mr. Harper and
persuades him to end the persecution of her brother. Birch takes Henry to a
British ship; Frances marries her patriot fiancé, Major Peyton Dunwoodie;
and Birch, his service to the cause over, returns to his job as itinerant peddler.

Among Cooper's sea stories are the following: *The Pilot* (1823), a tale of
the Revolutionary War in which the mysterious hero is said to represent John
Paul Jones; *The Red Rover* (1827), a story of piracy and concealed identity
during the Revolution; *The Water-Witch* (1830), concerning the pirate, "The
Skimmer of the Seas," his abduction of the beautiful Alinda de Barberie, and
his return of her to her suitor, the American sailor Captain Ludlow, in order
to join forces against the British.

Cooper also wrote a trilogy showing the rise of democracy over a decaying
feudalism (*The Bravo*, 1831; *The Heidenmauer*, 1832; and *The Headsman*,
1833). The "Littlepage Manuscripts" trilogy chronicles the class struggle of
New York (*Satanstoe*, 1845; *The Chainbearer*, 1845; and *The Redskins*, 1846).
There are works of controversial literature, and academic works as well; but
the most famous volumes are those which constitute the *Leather-Stocking Tales*
(q.v.).

S.S. SAN PEDRO (1931), by James Gould Cozzens. See LAST ADAM,
THE (1933), by James Gould Cozzens.

STALKY & CO. (1899), by Rudyard Kipling. Stalky (Arthur Corkran)
is the leader of the three boys (M'Turk and Beetle are the other two) who, in
these stories, often make life miserable for the masters of the college, and the
other boys, with their ingenious pranks. Rev. John Gilbert and the Head are
the only superiors who understand them or whom they respect, though the
latter conscientiously canes them, explaining that those who deviate from the
norm may expect "howling injustice." The general motive for the boys' actions is revenge against those who annoy them.

The scene is the United Services College, Westward Ho, Bideford, North
Devon, where Kipling as a bookish, nearsighted boy had his schooling. He is
Beetle; G. C. Beresford is M'Turk; and Lionel C. Dunsterville (later General)
is Stalky. The Head was Cormell Price, to whom Kipling dedicated the book.

STANZAS UPON THE DEATH OF HIS FATHER (1476), by Jorge Manrique. The soldier poet Jorge Manrique (1440–1479) is known today by a single poem, the *Coplas* (1476), a monument of Spanish poetry, written at the death of his father, Don Rodrigo Manrique (1406–1576), Count of Paredes and Maestre of Santiago. Instead of a mere outpouring of personal grief, the poem is, in its broadest sense, a moving complaint at the mutability of human happiness. The theme was, of course, well known to Biblical and Oriental poets, and seems to be but an echo of the Latin "ubi sunt qui ante nos in mundo fuere," of Petrarch's "Il trionfo della morte" and Villon's "Ballade des dames du temps jadis." Yet Manrique conveys it in Spanish, for the first time, in a perfect mold, in a versification admirably adapted to the sentiment: twelve-line stanzas alternating two lines of eight syllables with one line of four syllables, rhyming ABcABc DEfDEf, free and flowing but with an occasional antique air which intensifies its dramatic effect. The poem contains forty-three stanzas. In the first thirteen the poet meditates on life, death and the transitoriness of pleasure. The poet says that human happiness is elusive, that the grave is for all and respects neither fame nor wealth, and that it is only virtue which, in the last analysis, endures in men's hearts. In stanzas 14-25 he reminisces about the bright and festive days of his youth in the pomp and circumstance of the court of John II, now, alas, gone forever, and leaving, in sharper contrast, the gloomier and more despairing present. From stanza 26 on, the poet draws a moral portrait of his father, praising his courage in battle, his kindness and generosity in peace, his attachment and warmth to friends and relatives. Death appears to ask Don Rodrigo to leave the deceitful world and come into the enduring life of eternity. Don Rodrigo declares his readiness, and after saying a prayer to Jesus, sinks peacefully to his rest, surrounded by his children and rejoicing in his release.

STAR OF SEVILLE, THE (1617?), attributed to Lope de Vega. During a visit to Seville, the King falls in love with Estrella, called for her beauty "La Estrella de Sevilla" (The Star of Seville). The King summons her brother, Busto Tavera, offering him various dignities and honors. Suspicious of his King, Busto refuses. The same night, the King, in connivance with a slave girl, obtains entrance to Busto's house during the latter's absence. He is surprised by Busto's unexpected return. Busto challenges the King, and, dissatisfied with his answer, draws upon him. The King, to avoid fighting, reveals himself. But Busto refuses to believe him and the King is forced to fight in self-defense. The noise brings the servants with lights to the scene and the King escapes.

Irritated and humiliated, the King sends for Sancho Ortiz and requires him to avenge his outraged honor on a man who has been guilty of lèse majesté and whose name is written on a folded paper which he hands to Sancho. At the same time, the King hands Sancho another paper, relieving him of responsibility for the deed. This paper Sancho destroys, saying that honorable men require no bond to hold them to their word. Upon opening the other paper after leaving the King, Sancho finds to his dismay the name of his dearest friend, Busto Tavera, brother of Estrella, his betrothed. After a cruel struggle with himself, he provokes a quarrel with Busto and kills him. Estrella petitions the King to deliver up to her the slayer of her brother.

Sancho is arrested but steadfastly refuses to divulge his motive. In prison he falls prey to mental anguish which at one moment verges on insanity, but his determination is unshaken. Estrella, veiled, leads him out of prison. He is offered a horse and told to escape. He refuses. In order to encourage him to escape she reveals herself, but he is only more confused upon recognizing his liberator. He chooses to remain silent, even on the King's command to declare why he committed the crime. Finally, the King, who has exhausted every compromise, declares himself guilty. Sancho and Estrella are brought together, but both decide that happiness is impossible now. Since she cannot marry the murderer of her brother, she decides to enter a convent while he goes to war in search of death.

Attributed to Lope de Vega (1562–1635), this historical tragedy with the background of the King of Castile Sancho IV, el Bravo (1284–1295), influenced Corneille's *Le Cid* (q.v.).

STAR OF THE COVENANT (1914), by Stefan George. See GEORGE, STEFAN.

STATE AND REVOLUTION, THE (1917), by Nikolay Lenin. Lenin, the leader and founder of the Socialist society of the U.S.S.R., was that rare historical phenomenon, a man of intellect as well as of action. In this respect, in some measure at least, he approximated the dream of Plato, of the philosopher-ruler of the ideal republic. He was successful in reducing involved economic and political theories to simple, comprehensible terms. In this respect, too, he resembled Plato's ruler: he was a teacher of men, as well as their leader.

In the enormous theoretical literature that has stemmed from the writings of Marx and Engels, *The State and Revolution* of Lenin occupies a foremost place. It is the most comprehensive statement yet made concerning the revolutionary theory of the State, both capitalist and proletarian. More important, its ideas have been concretized in the actual process of establishing Socialism in Russia. This alone makes *The State and Revolution* one of the most influential documents in contemporary history.

The essay was written under highly dramatic circumstances, when, after the July rising in Petrograd and less than three months before the Bolshevik October Revolution of 1917, Lenin hid in a peasant's hut in Finland. In imminent danger of his life, he nevertheless succeeded in writing this theoretical study in the brief period of three weeks.

To understand the Communist theory of society and its blueprint of Socialist construction, *The State and Revolution* must be read. It explains historically the stages of the Russian Revolution; the nature of the dictatorship of the proletariat and the process of building a classless society. Of special interest is Lenin's treatment of Marx's conclusion of "the withering away" of the State, a theory upon which the Socialists, in opposition to the Communists, fall back to defend evolutionary versus revolutionary methods to achieve a Socialist society. To this Lenin retorts that a peaceful transition from capitalism to Socialism because of the decay of the former (i.e. "withering away") is an utter impossibility. Lenin agrees with Marx's view that a transition society has to come into being after the downfall of capitalism and before the emergence of a Communist society, and that this transition society can be no other than "the revolutionary dictatorship of the proletariat," a society best exemplified by the U.S.S.R. today. "The State" (i.e. the proletarian dictatorship now in the Soviet Union), says Lenin, "will be able to wither away completely when society has realized the rule: 'From each according to his ability; to each according to his need.'"

Lenin justifies the questionable morality of the dictatorship of the proletariat, even though he apparently considers it to be only a transition phase toward the true Communism of the dim and distant future: "Only then a really full democracy, a democracy without any exceptions, will be possible and will be realised . . . freed from capitalist. slavery, from the untold horrors, savagery, absurdities and infamies of capitalist exploitation, people will gradually *become accustomed* to the observation of the elementary rules of social life that have been known for centuries and repeated for thousands of years in all school books; they will become accustomed to observing them without force, without compulsion, without subordination, without the special *apparatus* for compulsion which is called the State."

STECHLIN, THE (1899), by Theodor Fontane. See EFFIE BRIEST, by Theodor Fontane.

STEELE, WILBUR DANIEL (1886–   ). Wilbur Daniel Steele is one of our few writers whose fame rests entirely upon the production of short stories. He used the conventional form, and took great pains to perfect his work. His predilection is for the horrifying. *Urkey Island* (1926) is one of his distinguished collections of short pieces. After a time, Steele decided that his type of short story had gone out of style. He turned deliberately, therefore, to playwriting, a field he considers to be closely allied. He has written one-act and full-length plays, and dramatized with Anthony Brown his own short story, *How Beautiful with Shoes* (1935). This play concerns Amarantha Doggett, a Southern mountain girl whose affair with a homicidal maniac makes intolerable to her her stupid fiancé, Ruby Herter.

STEEPLEJACK (1920), by James Gibbons Huneker. See IVORY APES AND PEACOCKS, by James Gibbons Huneker.

STEFÁNSSON, VILHJÁLMUR (1879–   ). Vilhjálmur Stefánsson, although born in Canada, has long been a resident in the United States, except for his trips of exploration and archaeology. He has written many books about his experiences. *My Life with the Eskimo* (1913) is the best account of those people and their lives, revealing Mr. Stefánsson's anthropological training. *The Friendly Arctic* (1921) gave the startling revelation, since corroborated, that it is possible for man to sustain himself entirely on the natural resources of that region. Some other volumes are *Iceland: The First American Republic* (1939), and *Greenland* (1942).

STEMMEN 1907), by Pieter Cornelis Boutens. See BOUTENS, PIETER CORNELIS.

STEPPENWOLF (1927), by Hermann Hesse. Coinciding with a crisis in the author's life, *Steppenwolf* is an important document of the confused twenties in postwar Europe. Shaken by the tragedy of World War I, the aging protagonist of the novel, Harry Haller, has become cynical about the spiritual values of Western civilization. Of Protestant-pietistic upbringing, he has suppressed "the wolf" in himself; and only after a radical change, after wildly embracing all the vices of the senses, including alcoholism, sexual aberration and narcotic intoxication, does he finally reach a new platform of humor and irony which makes life bearable. As a social outsider, a "lonely wolf of the steppes," Haller becomes increasingly aware of the dualism of the human personality: the spirit and the flesh, the mind and the subconscious. His transfiguration is brought about by Hermine and Maria, two girls who reveal to him the ultimate innocence of sexuality, and finally by the "Magic Theatre," which enables him to see the different "souls" of his split personality.

The novel, written with extraordinary restraint and experimental in form, is told in the first person: the author, only dimly disguised, acts as the editor of Harry Haller's abandoned diary. The tragic dualism of modern man, always especially prominent in German philosophy and literature, is viewed here by a mind deeply influenced by Nietzsche and Freud. *Steppenwolf*, reissued in English in 1947, is one of the most poignant indictments of the neurosis of Germany between the two world wars.

STOIC, THE (1947), by Theodore Dreiser. See COWPERWOOD NOVELS, THE, by Theodore Dreiser.

STOIC PARADOXES, by Cicero. See PHILOSOPHICAL ESSAYS, by Cicero.

STONES OF VENICE, THE (1851–1853), by John Ruskin. Volume I of this monumental, stimulating three-volume work on architecture is called *The Foundations*. It treats of architecture and its two divisions, function and ornament. There is a short history of Venice and its rulers, and a vivid account of the drive from Padua to Mestra and the passage by gondola through the city. Volume II, *Sea Stories*, is devoted to the Byzantine and Gothic periods, the latter being the culmination of Venetian life. Volume III, *The Fall*, treats of Renaissance architecture in Venice. The arrival of the Renaissance in that city marked its decline. Ruskin's contempt for Renaissance art as decadent and imitative knew no bounds: "This rationalistic art is the art commonly called Renaissance, marked by a return to pagan systems, not to adopt them and hallow them for Christianity, but to rank itself under them as an imitator and pupil." Concerning architectural values, Ruskin makes a profound and historically interesting point: "Wherever Christian church architecture has been good and lovely, it has been merely the perfect development of the common dwelling-house architecture of the period; when the pointed arch was used on the street, it was used in the church; when the round arch was used in the street, it was used in the church. . . ." Churches were never constructed in any distinctive, mystical and religious style, but only in the manner that was common and familiar to everybody at the time. Architecture, concludes Ruskin, is the most human of all the arts, reflecting an entire people rather than an individual. He accordingly deduces two elements of good architecture: it is expensive of some great truths commonly belonging to a whole people; it is understood or felt by them in all their work and life.

STORIES IN VERSE (1925), by Rabindranath Tagore. See TAGORE, RABINDRANATH.

STORY OF A BAD BOY, THE (1870), by Thomas Bailey Aldrich. This semiautobiographical novel relates the adventures of Tom Bailey. There is a sea voyage from New Orleans to Rivermouth (Portsmouth, New Hampshire). There Tom moves into the household of Grandfather Nutter, which includes Aunt Abigail and the Irish maid, Kitty Collins. Tom and his friends, the Rivermouth Centipedes, engage in typical young-boy activities—dramatic productions, burning of a stagecoach, and a battle with the local bully. Later Tom's friend Sailor Ben, whom he met on the voyage, proves to be the long-lost husband of Kitty Collins. At last Tom's father dies, and the lad goes to work.

In Aldrich's volume of short stories, *Marjorie Daw and Other People* (1873), the title piece is a series of letters Edward Delaney writes to a sick friend, John Flemming. These letters so enthusiastically describe the charms of Marjorie Daw, Edward's neighbor, that John, recovered, telegraphs he is on his way to court her. Edward then has to reveal that Marjorie was merely a product of his imagination, contrived to keep John interested.

STORY OF AN AFRICAN FARM, THE (1883), by Olive Schreiner. Olive Schreiner wrote *The Story of an African Farm* in 1876–1878 when she was still in her early twenties. It created an unpleasant stir. The courageous young Havelock Ellis defended the book stoutly against its detractors. It deals largely with its creator's own youthful years spent in the South African veldt. It was Olive Schreiner's attempt to arrange all her early memories into some coherent pattern. There is an intensity of feeling about it which clearly betrays its autobiographical origin. The three characters, Waldo, Lyndall and Em, move through the story under the compulsion of an inner necessity to understand themselves and to act freely and fearlessly according to the dictates of their consciences, no matter where they might lead. The novel breathes with the overtones of plain, sky and stars in the setting of a South African farm.

The opening chapters deal with the childhood years of Waldo, Lyndall and Em. As soon as the boy Waldo learns how to think for himself he is irked by the prevailing religious formalism of his environment. Straining hard to understand himself and the world, he becomes bewildered and despairing; he feels spiritually alone and grieves. But suddenly he discovers that he is not really isolated. Others had questioned and still were questioning the truth of religious and social dogmas, and were experiencing the same torments of doubt that he was experiencing. As a result of reading a certain book on economics, presumably a socialistic work, he discovers to his wild elation that he is actually one of a glorious company of minds, made free in a search for truth and social justice. A further discovery heartens him—that there are many people for whom love of truth outweighs personal interest.

After these spiritual experiences Waldo leaves the farm and journeys penniless but armed with faith into the world to seek a wider horizon. When self-knowledge comes to him in manhood he returns, pilgrim fashion, to the farm on the veldt in order to offer marriage to Lyndall, whom he loves. He is met, however, by the news that she is dead. First his spirit is overwhelmed—then peace returns. He goes out to sit on a log in the sunshine and take stock of his life: "An evil world, a deceitful, treacherous, mirage-like world it might be; but a lovely world for all that, and to sit there gloating in the sun was perfect."

STORY OF A NEW YORK HOUSE, THE (1887), by Henry Cuyler Bunner. See BUNNER, HENRY CUYLER.

STORY OF DR. DOLITTLE, THE (1920), by Hugh Lofting. See DR. DOLITTLE TALES, by Hugh Lofting.

STORY OF MANKIND, THE (1921), by Hendrik Willem van Loon. This history of the world, beginning with the Egyptians, was originally intended for children, and did in fact win the first Newberry Medal, in 1922; but its great popularity with readers of all ages made the author famous. Van Loon writes from an encyclopedic knowledge. Journalistic training equipped him with a regard for facts, and a facility to narrate panoramic stories interestingly. He uses a colloquial, often slangy style, and addresses himself to the reader in an intimate way. He illustrates his text with charming sketches. By recourse to literature of many languages, he steeps himself in his subject before he writes, and then brings out events as fresh, graphic news. And he often brings to bear startlingly original points of view. The book has for its thesis the idea that there has been little real progress in the world: "We modern men and women are not 'modern' at all. On the contrary, we still belong to the last generation of the cave-dwellers." Van Loon gives primary attention to individuals and peoples, their struggles and joys. A liberal, his interpretation is materialistic, social and nonreligious. His definition of history is "the mighty Tower of Experience, which Time has built amidst the endless fields of bygone ages."

Among many works, in several literary genres, are: *Van Loon's Geography* (1932), a companion volume to *The Story of Mankind; The Arts* (1937), a sweeping treatment of all the art forms (most of which the author has practiced) from the cave-dweller period to the Renaissance; *R.v.R.* (1930), a distinguished fictionalized biography of Rembrandt; and *Van Loon's Lives* (1942), a gossipy collection of about forty biographical-historical-philosophical-literary essays on famous personages, such as Confucius, Shakespeare, Beethoven, Napoleon and Leonardo.

STORY OF MY DOVE-COTE (1926), by Isaac Babel. See RED CAVALRY, by Isaac Babel.

STORY OF WOUTERTJE PIETERSE (1890), by Multatuli. See MAX HAVELAAR, by Multatuli.

STRAIT IS THE GATE (1909), by André Gide See COUNTERFEITERS, THE, by André Gide.

STRANGE INTERLUDE (1928), by Eugene O'Neill. See MOURNING BECOMES ELECTRA, by Eugene O'Neill.

STREET SCENE (1929), by Elmer Rice. This Pulitzer Prize play depicts a cross section of the occupants of an old-fashioned New York tenement. Mrs. Maurrant, first floor, is having an affair with the milk collector, Steve Sankey. She is an amiable woman, who needs love. Her husband Frank, a rough, hard-working stagehand, refuses to let the family move into a better neighborhood. Rose, the daughter, is in love with Sam Kaplin, a young Jewish student who also lives in the house. Frank leaves, supposedly for a few days. He returns unexpectedly, however, to find his wife and Sankey together. He shoots them both. Rose arrives home to find her mother dying, and her father being led away by the police. Bewildered, she leaves Sam, and takes her younger brother William away from New York, to start again somewhere else.

Another play showing Rice's interest in social problems was *The Adding Machine* (1923), an expressionist fantasy. Mr. Zero, twenty-five years with one firm, is to be replaced by a machine. He kills his employer in a rage. In the next world, he meets Daisy Devore, who had been a fellow worker. But the Keepers tell Mr. Zero that his soul must return to earth for further seasoning. Dismayed at the prospect, he learns that in fact he has so returned through several successive reincarnations, and will eventually be a soulless slave who works a super-adding machine deep in a coal mine.

STREETCAR NAMED DESIRE, A (1947), by Tennessee Williams. See GLASS MENAGERIE, THE, by Tennessee Williams.

STRICTLY BUSINESS (1910), by William Sydney Porter. See PORTER, WILLIAM SYDNEY.

STRIFE (1909), by John Galsworthy. One of Galsworthy's most important social dramas, it is a study of the strife and bitterness that is stirred up during a strike by the unyielding determination of the leaders on both sides to fight to the end. John Anthony, chairman of the Trengartha Tin Plate Works and founder of the company, has fought the men four times and has never been beaten. The struggle is a three-cornered affair, since the union, represented by Harness, has withdrawn its support from the men because the furnace men and engineers want more than the union wage scale. The men have been out six months and their families are starving, but Roberts, their leader, is determined to hold out at all costs. He has been paid seven hundred pounds for an invention which enabled the company to make one hundred thousand pounds. His wife Annie is very ill; as she had been the Anthonys' maid, Enid Underwood, Anthony's daughter, comes to see her and begs her husband to compromise. Roberts' wife dies, but he is still determined to fight on. Edgar, Anthony's son, is strongly for the men, and feels that his father should resign his chairmanship even though it means everything to him. The men, in despair over their starving families, finally agree to the union terms. Anthony is forced to resign, and the two defeated men regard each other with understanding. Trench, the company's secretary, and Harness draw up the same agreement that the men had previously opposed.

STUDENT OF SALAMANCA, THE (1840), by José de Espronceda. An elaboration of the Don Juan legend, this poem divided into four parts and consisting of some 750 verses of astonishing metric diversity, is generally considered the most successful work of the Spanish Byron, José de Espronceda (1808–1842). Don Félix de Montemar, a dissolute student of Salamanca, woos, dishonors and abandons the sweet, angelic Doña Elvira de Pastrana, and thereby causes her death. Challenged by Elvira's brother, Don Diego, Don Félix kills him without mercy. One night as he walks along a dark street, Don Félix meets a veiled woman and follows her. The mysterious lady drags him through unknown and fantastic regions filled with awesome tolling of bells, screeching of owls and cohorts of ghosts. As the noises subside, Don Félix witnesses a funeral cortège bearing along two corpses: that of Don Diego and that of himself. Soon thereafter the uncanny sounds begin again, and Don Félix again pursues the veiled woman, who leads him along through deserted corridors and down winding stairs into a chamber fraught with outcries and boisterous laughter. The daring Don Félix unveils the woman, only to find himself embracing a skeleton. Don Diego appears to tell him that she is Doña Elvira and that he can have her for his wife. As ghosts dance around them, the skeleton embraces him and kills him.

STUDIES (1844–1850), by Adalbert Stifter. See LATE SUMMER, THE, by Adalbert Stifter.

STUDIES IN THE PSYCHOLOGY OF SEX (1928), by Havelock Ellis. The first volume of *Studies in the Psychology of Sex* appeared in 1897 and was suppressed; but was nevertheless followed by successive volumes, terminating in 1928 with the volume *Sex in Relation to Society*. The whole of the *Studies* is now available in two volumes which have free circulation. The book is the most comprehensive and thorough study of the normal and the abnormal sexual impulse in existence at present, and is a classic in its field. The work is subdivided according to the leading phases of both normal and abnormal sexuality in men and women. The treatment follows the method of anonymous case history and analysis by the author, pursued with sincerity, admirable scholarliness and scientific detachment. While the original publication of the first volumes caused scandal and legal prosecution, it has now been recognized that far from being an obscene book, the *Studies* is not only a great pioneering work but still one of the most competent in the field—though singularly unFreudian.

STUDS LONIGAN (1932–1935), by James T. Farrell. Studs (William) Lonigan of this realistic trilogy is a lively, bright lad, healthy and essentially decent. His great misfortune is to be caught in the trap of Irish slum life in Chicago's South Side. In its sordid morass he flounders, struggling between environmental compulsions to vice and the consciousness of sin with which his Catholic parochial school has indoctrinated him. His father, an honest building contractor, wants Studs to "get ahead"; his mother hopes he will become a priest. But the odds are insurmountable: Studs joins other neighborhood boys in their idle pastimes at the corner poolroom. At fifteen, their ideal is the gangster; each tries to excel in the arts of bragging, vicious horseplay, and drinking. A false conception of sex warps their attitude toward women. Studs is sentimental. He would like to be noble and respectable. He falls in love with Lucy Scanlon, because she is refined and different from the delinquent girls he has known. In this instance, too, life proves stronger than his intentions.

The Young Manhood of Studs Lonigan (1934) is a sharply-drawn picture of character deterioration under environmental influences. The youth has learned to be critical of his ways, and although he has become outwardly a "tough guy," his burden of sin has become almost intolerable. When Studs is rejected by Lucy because of his affair with a pickup, he reverts to hard drinking. There is a terrifying scene which depicts a drunken New Year's Eve party of Studs' gang, at which he is almost incriminated in a rape.

His rapid decline is charted in *Judgment Day* (1935). Studs, twenty-nine, is thoroughly licked. He is bewildered by all that has happened to him; his life of excesses has undermined his Irish peasant vitality. He is obsessed with a premonition of early death. The economic depression finally finishes him. After his father is gulled in the Insull stock swindle, he seeks escape in the world of radio; Studs drugs himself with movies, dance halls, and horse races. He tries desperately to save himself. He hopes that the purity of Catherine Banahan will wash him clean of sin. She tries hard to reform him, but it is too late.

A World I Never Made (1936) concerns Danny O'Neill, a sensitive lad of the same Chicago slums. Some of the *Studs Lonigan* characters appear in this portrayal of the working people's struggles to make a decent living, their religion, passions, and weaknesses. Sequels include *No Star Is Lost* (1938), *Father and Son* (1940), and *My Days of Anger* (1943). *Bernard Clare* (1946) concerns a frustrated writer living in New York.

STUDY IN SCARLET, A (1887), by Sir Arthur Conan Doyle. See SHERLOCK HOLMES, by Sir Arthur Conan Doyle.

STUDY OF HISTORY, A (1933–1939), by Arnold Toynbee. A massive work (six of the nine contemplated volumes have appeared at this writing) in the tradition of the great philosophers of history, Toynbee's *A Study of History* is a survey of many past civilizations and an attempt to discover the pattern of their historical development. Operating with historical, political, sociological and religious concepts, he charts the rise, growth to maturity, undermining, and decay of civilizations. In the author's opinion Western civilization is on the downward path, but the moral values of the universal religion, Christianity, may save it. A return to faith in these values is advocated.

SU TUNG-P'O (1036–1101). The poems of Su Tung-p'o have long been memorized by Chinese scholars. Su's ancestors were Confucian, but Su was far too great a poet to surrender entirely to the inflexible rules of Confucian doctrine. He was a Taoist as well as a Buddhist, and was the first poet to inject Buddhistic mysticism into Confucian writing. The Chinese Emperor Shiaotsung in 1170 wrote of Su when conferring upon him the title of Literary Patriotic Duke: "He cultivated the noble and upright spirit born in man and elevated to a higher level of understanding the tradition of the past. His scholarship was all-embracing, like the sea and the earth, and his words of advice were like the striking of jades and bells."

There is a very popular anthology in China called *The Eight Great Masters of T'ang and Sung Dynasties*. Of the eight, three are Su Tung-p'o, his father Su Shun, and his brother, Su Chel. His sister was also a poet. Su Tung-p'o is best known by his prose poems of Red Cliff, a site near Hsia K'ou in Hupeh,

where a great battle was fought in 208.   Some of his poems have been trans-
lated by Cyril Drummond Le Gros Clark in 1935 in *The Prose-Poetry of Su
Tung-P'o.* Lin Yu T'ang wrote the biography of Su in an English work,
The Gay Genius, published in 1947.

SUCCESS (1930), by Lion Feuchtwanger.   See FEUCHTWANGER,
LION.

SUCH COUNSELS YOU GAVE TO ME (1937), by Robinson Jeffers.
See JEFFERS, ROBINSON.

SUEÑO DE UNA NOCHE DE AGOSTO (1918), by Gregorio Martínez
Sierra.   See ROMANTIC YOUNG LADY, THE, by Gregorio Martínez
Sierra.

SUEÑOS, LOS (1627), by Francisco de Quevedo.   See VISIONS, THE,
by Francisco de Quevedo.

SUKJUJIP, by Kwun Pil.   See SHIJO-YUCHIP.

SULTAN OF SULU, THE (1902), by George Ade.   See ADE,
GEORGE.

SUMMA CONTRA GENTILES (1261–1264), by St. Thomas Aquinas.
See SUMMA THEOLOGICA, by St. Thomas Aquinas.

SUMMA THEOLOGICA (1265–1272), by St. Thomas Aquinas. The
chief exponent of Aristotelianism in Christian theology was St. Thomas (ca.
1225–1274), and his *Summa* was the greatest point of its development. The
Summa is an attempt at a complete science of theology. In the author's own
words: "Whereas, the chief aim of this science is to impart a knowledge of
God, not only as existing in Himself, but also as the origin and end of all
things, and especially of rational creatures, we therefore shall treat first of God;
second, of the rational creature's tendency toward God; third, of Christ, who
as man is the way whereby we approach unto God." Thus the work is divided into three parts: I. The Natural; II. The Moral; III. The Sacramental.
In the first division St. Thomas attempts to ascertain the nature and limits of
theology, which he considers a science, although based on supernatural revelation. The second division is in two parts: the Prima Secundae and the Secunda
Secundae. The first views men from the earthly side, as moral, responsible
agents possessing passions, sentiments and mental faculties. The second describes the seven virtues that men possess: faith, hope, charity, prudence, justice, fortitude and temperance. The third division enters into elaborate exposition of the mysteries of the Incarnation and of the efficacy of the sacraments.
   St. Thomas concludes with a dissertation on the philosophy of expiation as
taught by Church doctrine and justified by Aristotelian philosophy. The tremendous influence of St. Thomas on Church thought is a recognized part of
world history and culture, and is still exerted today.
   Another book of St. Thomas, more important perhaps from a philosophic
point of view, is his *Summa contra Gentiles* (1261–1264), in which he attempted to defend the Roman Catholic philosophy against criticism from outsiders. In it he argues that there is no conflict between science and truth
revealed through faith. It is divided into four books: I. Of God as He is in

Himself; II. Of God the Origin of Creatures; III. Of God the End of Creatures; IV. Of God in His Revelation.

SUN ALSO RISES, THE (1926), by Ernest Hemingway. This famous postwar novel is a tale of escapist American and English expatriates. The central character is Lady Brett Ashley, a charming tippler who is touring the continent awaiting a divorce in order to marry Michael Campbell. In the group are the American reporter Jake Barnes, who has a love affair with Brett —unhappy and inconclusive due to a war injury which has emasculated him— and Robert Cohn, a Jewish novelist whom none of the others really like, who is tired of his mistress Frances Clyne, and loves Brett also. The party visits Spain for the bullfights. There Brett elopes with a handsome bullfighter, Pedro Romero, but leaves him. Cohn, an amateur pugilist, beats Jake, Michael and Romero, and leaves. And Brett decides to marry Michael after all.

Other works by Hemingway, who has profoundly influenced a certain group of realistic fiction writers, include the novels *A Farewell to Arms* (q.v.) and *For Whom the Bell Tolls* (q.v.); distinguished short stories (*Men Without Women*, 1927; *Winner Take Nothing*, 1933; and *The Fifth Column and the First Forty-Nine Stories*, 1938); *The Green Hills of Africa* (1935), a book about big-game hunting and literary matters; and *Death in the Afternoon* (1932), about bullfighting, containing a technical, detailed exposition of the sport, and Hemingway's reactions to it.

SUNKEN BELL, THE (1896), by Gerhardt Hauptmann. See HAUPTMANN, GERHARDT.

SUNRISE (1889), by Gerhardt Hauptmann. See HAUPTMANN, GERHARDT.

SUPPLIANTS, THE (ca. 490 B.C.), by Aeschylus. This is the earliest extant drama of the Western World. It shows clear signs of its closeness to the purely choral performances out of which tragedy developed. The chorus, composed of fifty members, has about half of the lines in the play, and only two actors are used. The chorus is composed of the fifty daughters of Danaus who have just arrived at Argos. They come in flight from Egypt pursued by their cousins, the fifty sons of Aegyptus, who seek their hands in marriage. Such a marriage they abhor, and present themselves as suppliants at Argos, whence Io, the common ancestress of their race, had come. Pelasgus, king of Argos, is loath to guarantee their safety, and yields only when they threaten to hang themselves in the very shrine of the gods. He takes Danaus to appeal to the people of Argos for their protection, which is generously granted. The ship of the pursuing sons of Aegyptus is then sighted, and Danaus goes to call on the Argives to make good their promise of protection. Meanwhile a herald comes from the ship, and is violently dragging the maidens from the altars of the gods, when the king arrives with his bodyguard and sternly sends the herald back to his ship with the warning that he will defend the Danaids. Danaus also returns with Argives in arms; and the play ends on a note of hope for the suppliants. The story of the Danaids was continued in the lost other plays of a trilogy, which must have told how Danaus was prevailed upon to give his daughters to their cousins and how the Danaids on their bridal night slew their bridegrooms, all save Hypermnestra, who spared Lynceus. These two became the progenitors of the Argive royal house. Thus is explained the substitution of Danaans (Greeks?) for Pelasgians (aborigines?) in Greece.

SUPPRESSED DESIRES (1914), by Susan Glaspell. See GLASPELL, SUSAN.

SURGEON'S STORIES, THE (1851-1866), by Zakarias Topelius. See TALES OF THE ARMY SURGEON, by Zakarias Topelius.

SWALLOWBOOK, THE (1924), by Ernst Toller. See MAN AND MASSES, by Ernst Toller.

SWAN SONG (1928), by John Galsworthy. See FORSYTE SAGA, THE, by John Galsworthy.

SWANN'S WAY (1913), by Marcel Proust. See REMEMBRANCE OF THINGS PAST, by Marcel Proust.

SWEDISH COUNTESS VON G——, LIFE OF THE (1747-1748), by Christian Fürchtegott Gellert. See GELLERT, CHRISTIAN FÜRCHTEGOTT.

SWEET CHEAT GONE (1925), by Marcel Proust. See REMEMBRANCE OF THINGS PAST, by Marcel Proust.

SWINBURNE, ALGERNON CHARLES (1837-1909). In the first series of *Poems and Ballads* (1866) the famous English lyric poet expresses his youthful revolt against the fustiness of the Victorian moral conventions of his time. Strongly under the influence of the Greek lyric poets, of the French poets Victor Hugo and Charles Baudelaire, as well as that of his compatriots, the Pre-Raphaelites, Swinburne in this volume composed before the age of twenty-nine, presents poems distinguished by an intense sensuality both of subject matter and of metric texture. Such examples as "Laus Veneris," "Dolores," "Faustine" and many others derived from the Hellenic and early medieval traditions, both in their ideas and in their verse forms, enjoyed an immense success with Swinburne's literary contemporaries and a *succès de scandale* with the reading public at large.

Songs Before Sunrise (1871), published five years later, shows a shift in emphasis from the sensual to the political and the philosophical. Poems in celebration of democratic revolution and in honor of Mazzini and Walt Whitman indicate the liberal direction of Swinburne's politics, while others, such as "Before a Crucifix" and "Hymn to Man," present Swinburne's virulent disgust with organized Christianity. The later poem proclaims man the master not only of himself but the world, and is typical of Swinburne's vague but passionate philosophical reasoning. The majestic "Hertha," which extols the Spirit of Man, a divine humanity, was Swinburne's favorite among his poems.

The second series of *Poems and Ballads* (1878) represents in such a poem as "A Forsaken Garden" the full flowering of Swinburne's lush anapaestic verse. There are poems to Baudelaire (the famous "Ave atque Vale"), Gautier, Tourneur and Villon. As well as these there are still the short and long lyrics as in the first series in a variety of meters, but in this case, while still extremely sensual, these poems are more restrained in their passion and less blatant in their insurgency. This and the two preceding volumes have secured Swinburne's place as a great innovator in prosody, who freed English verse from the tyranny of the iambic, who developed the anapaest, the dactyl and the choriambus, enriched with assonance and alliteration, to a high point, who sometimes spilled over into the monotony of mere sing-sing, but who at his best produced many fine lyrics in both the romantic and classic traditions.

SWISS FAMILY ROBINSON, THE (1813), by J. R. Wyss. Written by a Swiss, this concerns the amazing adventures of a minister, his wife and four sons, Fritz, Ernest, Francis and Jack, after they are shipwrecked and cast up on a desert island. They are able to rescue some indispensables from the ship, but they survive largely by their own ingenuity in making use of everything they find on the island. They construct a wonderful house in a large tree where they are safe from wild animals, and are so content with their island life that they refuse to leave when a ship finally comes to their rescue. The style is ponderous and the moralizing annoying, but the adventures are exciting enough to have kept this book a favorite with children for many years.

SWORD BLADES AND POPPY SEEDS (1914), by Amy Lowell. See LOWELL, AMY.

SWORD OF KING FREDERIC, THE (1806), by Vincenzo Monti. See MONTI, VINCENZO.

SYMPHONY, THE (1875), by Sidney Lanier. See LANIER, SIDNEY.

SYMPOSIUM, THE by Plato (427–347 B.C.). Gilbert Murray has said that "if the claim were advanced that the *Symposium* was absolutely the highest work of prose fiction ever composed, most perfect in power, beauty, imaginative truth, it would be hard to deny it." In the dialogue Apollodorus reports to certain interested companions an after-dinner (symposium) discussion he had heard among Socrates, Aristophanes, Alcibiades and others at the house of the poet Agathon. The topic of conversation is love, and each guest has his turn at expatiating on this set theme in the form of an encomium of Eros. The company is in high spirits and the speeches are brilliant and witty. The encomia treat of the various aspects of love from its purely physical to its most abstract manifestations. When Socrates' turn arrives, he demurs, and is loath to try to compete with such eloquence as he has heard. He compromises, however, by reporting a discourse on love he professes to have heard from the prophetess Diotima. Herein is set forth the much misunderstood idea of "Platonic love." Eros is described as beautiful himself and symbolizing love of beauty. He is inherent in every aspect of procreation, and love of physical beauty leads to love of moral beauty. Thus he is responsible for the children of the soul as well as those of the body, and the highest form of love is love of absolute, ideal beauty, which is the love of the philosopher. As Socrates finishes his speech, the gay young Alcibiades arrives in a festive mood with a wreath on his head and wine on his breath. Upon being told the subject of the conversation and invited to add his bit, he says he can praise no other in Socrates' presence, and delivers a mocking but serious encomium of his beloved but unresponsive idol. Other revelers join the party; and at dawn, as the group breaks up, only Socrates and two others are still awake and deep in discussion.

SYNNÖVÉ SOLBAKKEN (1857), by Björnstjerne Björnson. Modern Norwegian literature may be said to have begun with Björnstjerne Björnson's *Synnöve Solbakken*. It was Björnson's first novel, and its charm and freshness made a profound impression. It established his reputation as a storyteller at home and abroad, and became the foundation stone of a new school of fiction. Hitherto Norwegian literature had been almost entirely imbued with Danish culture; *Synnöve Solbakken* was a literary declaration of independence. As in the case of the old Norse sagas, portraits of the characters are not too clearly drawn. Björnson behaves like a true artist in that he allows his characters to speak for themselves, and he leaves it entirely to the reader to determine the implications. He does not stop to digress on details of features and dress, but portrays his men and women in broad swift strokes. Thus the reader knows, when he has finished the book, how Synnöve, or Thorbjörn, or Aslak must have appeared to the author. "*Synnöve Solbakken*," commented the great Danish critic Georg Brandes, "was the plastic harmony within the limitation of Norwegian life, and the hero Thorbjörn was the type of the vigorous stubborn youth, whose nature could only ripen to maturity through calming, soothing influences."

To a great extent this novel is autobiographical. Both Björnson's father and mother are reproduced in the characters of Saemund Granliden and Karen Solbakken. The story is an idyl so simple as to be almost threadbare. Its protagonists are the rough, complicated Thorbjörn Granliden and the radiant Synnöve Solbakken. After overcoming his reputation as a roughneck and reconciling himself to his austere father, Thorbjörn is enabled to win Synnöve, who has always loved him. The characters are unsophisticated but intelligent. The dialogue reveals character more than the incidents do.

SYNTHETIC PHILOSOPHY (1860–1896), by Herbert Spencer. See SPENCER, HERBERT.

SYSTEMA NATURAE (1735), by Carl Linnaeus (or Linné). This book is the most famous of all treatises on nomenclature and classification in biology. Attempts at such classifications are at least as old as Aristotle, and in 1693 John Ray had given a systematic grouping of animals; but all the earlier schemes were found unsatisfactory. Linnaeus in his early years traveled in many lands collecting material for his subsequent volumes on biology. In 1741 he became professor of botany at Upsala, where he remained to the end of his life. An indefatigable collector and systematizer of botanical specimens, Linnaeus subordinated all other aspects of biology to the problem of classification. He introduced what was virtually a new international language, placing plants and animals in a regular sequence. His arrangement of plants was based upon the characters of the flowers, especially the number and arrangement of the stamens and carpels. In this so-called sexual system of classification, plants are divided into classes, orders, genera, and species, the classes being determined by the number of stamens, while the orders are distinguished by the number of carpels. The fundamental unit in this classification is the species, and Linnaeus inflexibly maintained the fixity of species. This hindered him in developing a classification based upon natural affinity. For animals also Linnaeus was content to use merely morphological characteristics, paying little attention to internal structure or comparative anatomy. He recognized six classes of animals: mammals, birds, amphibians, fishes, insects, and worms; but he failed to distinguish between vertebrates and invertebrates. It was largely due to Linnaeus that the binomial system of class names—one for the genus, another for the species—has become an integral part of biological nomenclature. Linnaeus constantly revised and improved his botanical classification, in his *Philosophia Botanica* (1751) and more particularly in the *Species Plantarum* (1753). Changes in his zoölogical arrangement were made in the numerous editions of the *Systema Naturae,* and the tenth edition of this work (1758) has been generally accepted as the basis for the "Linnaean name" of an animal.

TABLE TALK (1821–1822), by William Hazlitt. This collection, with *The Plain Speaker* (q.v.), contains his most famous essays. For sensitiveness, generosity and honesty of purpose Hazlitt has long been famous. He was immensely popular in his own day; then his reputation was somewhat dimmed, though he was never completely neglected. Nowadays he is having a revival; his essays in recent years have been published in many and varied selections. "On the Ignorance of the Learned" is one of the more amusing in this group. He starts out with his usual vim by declaring that authors and readers have fewer ideas than any other group. He cares not for the "mere scholar," finding him no better than a parrot, though he admits that what men can really understand is in all instances "small in compass." His fervent admiration for Shakespeare is revealed; he declares if we want to find how insignificant human intelligence actually is we have but to read Shakespeare's commentators. "On the Fear of Death," "On Living to One's Self," "On the Knowledge of Character," "Why Distant Objects Please," "On Going a Journey," "On Familiar Style," "On the Pleasure of Painting," and "Character of Cobbett" are among the other outstanding essays in this collection.

TABLE TALK (published 1689), by John Selden. John Selden's secretary, Rev. Richard Milward, kept reports of the informal utterances made by Selden during the last twenty years of his life. Covering numerous topics relating to religion and the state, they reveal the opinions of this English Parliamentarian, lawyer and political philosopher on various controversial issues of the Civil War and Commonwealth period. They reflect his latitudinarian religious views and, politically, his desire for an ordered liberty which he felt could be found only in precedent and the ancient constitution of the nation.

TAEDONGWUNOK, by Kwun Moonhae. See SHIJO-YUCHIP.

TAGORE, RABINDRANATH (1861–1941). Even in his prose writings the late Bengali poet Rabindranath Tagore (1861–1941) reveals himself as a lyric poet—a musician employing words instead of tones to achieve the most haunting melodies. This characteristic is true not merely of Tagore's writing; it is the Indian heritage. The poems of Kabir carry the same subtle harmonies, the same delicate cadences, the same preoccupation with the soul, with the inner depths and the cosmic meanings in little things. It is the multi-thousand years of Hindu culture that permeate them: the native idealism, the quest for nonmateriality, the pantheistic worship of God in Nature.

Tagore was a transcendentalist. He perceived the divine spirit imminent in all things. Tagore felt that creation was a perpetual hymn of everlasting love, which is why he did not despise the pleasures of the senses and recoiled from the life-denying asceticism of many of his Buddhist coreligionists. "Verily, from everlasting joy do all objects have their birth."

The ethics of Buddhism are an integral part of Tagore's writings. The poet states: "Whatever we treasure for ourselves, separates us from others; our possessions are our limitations." And again, "Every endeavor to attain a larger life requires of man to gain by giving away, and not to be greedy." When a man is concentrated on himself he is confined within himself. "It is a spiritual sleep."

Tagore's first volume of poems was published in 1896. Following that appeared: *The Gardener* (1913); *The Crescent Moon* (1914); *Gitanjali* (1914); *Ephemera* (1915); *Poems by Kabir* (1916); *Poems of Imagination* (1916); *Narrative Poems* (1923); *Stories in Verse* (1925); *Grains* (1936). He was awarded the Nobel Prize in Literature in 1913.

TAKE IT EASY (1938), by Damon Runyon. See RUNYON, DAMON.

TALE OF A TUB, THE (1704), by Jonathan Swift. This allegorical prose satire was ostensibly intended to prove the superiority of the Church of England while attacking the Roman Catholic and Presbyterian churches, but Swift also assails the bigotry of warring religions, the pedantry of dishonest critics, and, in many brilliant digressions, various imperfections in the whole pattern of human life. Three editions were exhausted the first year; a fourth, fifth, etc., soon followed. The main body of the book concerns three brothers: Peter (Church of Rome), Martin (Lutheran and Anglican), and Jack (Calvinist), and their equivocating disobedience to their father's will (the Scriptures), whose instructions concerning his gift of coats (Christian faith) all but Martin are guilty of evading. This essay was written some eight years before its publication. When the fifth edition appeared in 1710 the "Author's Apology" was prefixed. *The Battle of the Books* and the *Discourse concerning the Mechanical Operation of the Spirit* appeared with *The Tale of a Tub*. Swift's shorter pieces are no less interesting and important than his more famous works. In his old age Swift, on rereading his own *Tale* of a Tub, exclaimed: "Good God! What a genius I had when I wrote that book."

TALE OF GENJI, THE (10th c.), by Murasaki Shikibu. *The Tale of Genji* or *Genji Monogatari* is the most celebrated of the classical Japanese romances. Its author was a woman. She defines her intentions in the following colorful explanation by her hero Genji: "Ordinary histories are the mere records of events, and are generally treated in a one-sided manner. They give no insight into the true state of society. This, however, is the very sphere in which romances principally dwell. Romances are indeed fictions but they are by no means always pure inventions; their only peculiarities being these, that in them the writers often trace out, among numerous real characters the best, when they wish to represent the good, and the oddest, when they wish to amuse."

Of the fifty-four chapters into which *The Tale of Genji* is divided, forty-one relate to the life and adventures of Prince Genji; the rest refer principally to one of his sons. The thread of the story is often tenuous, the narrative diffuse and the whole effect is disjointed. The author suffered from too much imagination which she was incapable of disciplining artistically. One decided merit of her work is that it was written in pure, classical Japanese. It seems certain that prior to its cultural decline, when Japan was obliged to accept Chinese as its aristocratic language and to substitute for its own ancient civilization a shallow imitation of the Chinese, it had enjoyed a great literary period, during which *The Tale of Genji* was composed.

The principal characters are Prince Genji, the son of the Emperor and his concubine; Princess Aoi, Genji's wife; the Emperor and Fujitsubo, his consort, who is loved by Genji; Kiritsubo, the concubine of the Emperor, i.e., Genji's mother; Murasaki, child of Prince Hyobukyo, who is adopted by Genji and becomes his second wife; Princess Rokujo, widow of the Emperor's brother, who serves as Genji's mistress from his seventeenth year onward; Utsusemi, wife of the provincial Governor, Iyo no Suke, who is courted by Genji; and Yugao, who serves as mistress first of To no Chujo, then of Genji, and who dies bewitched. To the tenth century Japanese aristocrat the morality of Genji was highly decorous and according to the code.

The translation of *The Tale of Genji* in six volumes by the polished Oriental scholar and poet Arthur Waley, is charming, delicate, full of Far Eastern flavor.

TALE OF TWO CITIES, A (1859), by Charles Dickens. Dr. Alexander Manette had been condemned to the Bastille because of his knowledge of the cruel treatment offered a peasant family by the Marquis de St. Evremonde and his brother. A peasant girl has been attacked, her husband killed, and her brother wounded. Dr. Manette has been released after eighteen years of imprisonment, as a result of which he is demented. His friend, Jarvis Lorry, reunites him with his daughter Lucie. Charles Darnay, a nephew of the Marquis, marries Lucie. Darnay has renounced his true name because of hatred of his uncle's cruelty. Sidney Carton, a dissolute barrister, also loves Lucie. Darnay, returning to Paris during the revolution, to help his faithful servant Gabelle, who is unjustly imprisoned, is arrested. Dr. Manette, Mr. Lorry, and Carton follow him to France. The Doctor, glorified as a Bastille prisoner, saves him; but he is again sentenced by the angry mob incited by Mme. Defarge of the wine shop, whose knitting is one of Dickens' inspired touches. It turns out that the peasant girl who had been attacked by the Marquis' brother was Mme. Defarge's sister. At Darnay's trial, the Doctor's secret and his early denunciation of the St. Evremonde family is revealed. Darnay is sentenced to the guillotine; his wife and daughter are in danger also. Carton, however, manages to spirit Darnay out of prison, taking his place, so that Lucie's husband can remain with her. Miss Pross, Lucie's English servant, prevents the revengeful Mme. Defarge from arresting the Doctor and Lucie and kills her in a tussle. The novel ends with Carton's unspoken prophecy of the new Paris, and the continued happiness of Lucie and her family in England.

Dickens secured his descriptions of Paris in revolt from Carlyle's *French Revolution* (q.v.).

TALES (1870, etc.), by Joaquim Maria Machado de Assis. See DOM CASMURRO, by Joaquim Maria Machado de Assis.

TALES FROM SHAKESPEARE (1807), by Charles and Mary Lamb. These twenty tales from Shakespeare's plays do not include the series of English histories or the Roman plays. Designed to interest young readers, they are told with simplicity and a faithfulness to their originals not lessened by salutary emphasis on the moral of the central situation. Lamb's preface insists that they pretend "to no other merit than as faint and imperfect stamps of Shakespeare's matchless image." Shakespeare's own language is skillfully interwoven, whenever possible, into the thread of the narrative. Mary wrote the fourteen comedies and Charles the six tragedies.

TALES OF A WAYSIDE INN (1886), by Henry Wadsworth Longfellow. See LONGFELLOW, HENRY WADSWORTH.

TALES OF ENSIGN STAL, THE (1848, 1860), by Johan Ludvig Runeberg. These tales, written in Swedish and published in two sections, twelve years apart, constitute the second great epic of Finland (the first one, the ancient *Kalevala* (q.v.), being composed in the native Finnish), and the author is one of the significant poets of modern literature. Twenty-five ballads, each one in a different meter and prefaced by "Our Land," the Finnish national anthem, form this epic cycle, which immortalizes the people, battles, and soldiers of the Finno-Russian War of 1808–1809. It is a glorification of suffering, sacrifice, bravery, resignation, and ultimate defeat, and an ardent, stirring hymn of loyalty to one's country, an unforgettable tribute to the character of the Finnish people. Sir Edmund Gosse, extravagantly perhaps, called its author "the greatest patriotic poet of all times." The heroes and heroines of several *Tales* were historical characters or based on such, fictionalized to suit the purpose. Biographical studies, peasants' stories, and interviews with war veterans contribute to the themes and action of the poems. Outstanding among the ballads are the popular "Sven Duva," a modern Horatius who made the supreme sacrifice while successfully defending a bridge against the onslaughts of an enemy force, and "The Girl of the Cottage," who longs for death when among the slain patriots on the battlefield she fails to find the body of her lover. He had ignominiously fled from combat in order to live and protect his family and sweetheart. The weal of the fatherland should have come first.

So far as the individual subjects treated in these poems are concerned, the choice is democratic: the general, the common soldier, the canteen-woman (Lotta Svärd), and even a Russian leader (Kulneff), an enemy with unusual human qualities, have won a place in this cycle of verse. Other notable ballads are "The Cloud's Brother" and "Döbeln at Jutas." The *Tales* reanimated the spirit, the soul of the nation. "It is hardly too much to say," according to a modern authority, "that these poems, published in the middle of the nineteenth century, have been the greatest single factor in creating the free Finland which rose out of the World War."

TALES OF SOLDIERS AND CIVILIANS (1891), by Ambrose Bierce. See BIERCE, AMBROSE.

TALES OF THE ARMY SURGEON (1851–1866), by Zakarias Topelius. This is a six-volume collection of fictionalized historical narratives covering the stirring Swedish and Finnish period from Gustavus Adolphus, Protestant leader in the Thirty Years' War, to Gustavus III of the second half of the eighteenth century. It is the author's chief prose work, and was written in Swedish by a patriotic Finlander, who is also well known as a lyric poet, professor of history, and writer of children's stories. The *Tales* strongly idealize the Finnish contribution to Swedish history during the time in question, and there is little doubt about Topelius's religious convictions. Yet, romantic elements predominate, among which the love of the Finnish, Lutheran Lieutenant Gustaf Bertila (Bertil) for the German Catholic, Regina von Emmeritz, holds the reader's interest for several hundred pages of the work. A prose creation of high rank, with Walter Scott as model, it is written with charm, vigor, and simplicity, and is still popular in all classes, especially, of course, in Finland and Sweden. An English translation of all six "cycles," as they were called, appeared in New York and Chicago, 1872–1891.

TALES OF THE WILDERNESS (1925), by Boris Pilnyak. See PIL-NYAK, BORIS.

TALIFER (1933), by Edwin Arlington Robinson. See ROBINSON, EDWIN ARLINGTON.

TALISMAN, THE (1825), by Sir Walter Scott. The story takes place during the Crusades when the various forces in the Holy Land are divided by petty jealousies among their leaders. Besides Richard the Lion-Hearted, there are Philip of France, the Marquis of Montferrat, the Grand Master of the Templars, and the Duke of Austria. Richard is ill, a fact which further accentuates the weakness of the Army. Sir Kenneth, known as the Knight of the Leopard, loves Edith Plantagenet, but since he is a poor Scottish crusader of lowly birth, there seems little chance for marriage. One day he meets a Saracen emir, with whom he fights, but later becomes friendly. The emir proves to be Saladin, Sultan of Egypt. Disguised as a physician sent by the Sultan, Saladin comes to the Christian camp and cures Richard by means of an amulet, from which the title of the story is taken. Saladin gives the amulet to Sir Kenneth after the cure is effected. Meanwhile, one night when Sir Kenneth is guarding the camp, Richard's wife, Queen Berengaria, sends him, in sport, a note signed with Edith's name, urging him to come at once. While he is gone, the English colors are insulted and Sir Kenneth's dog is injured. Richard orders Sir Kenneth's execution, the sentence being retracted when Saladin accepts him as a slave. He is then sent in disguise to attend Richard, and saves him from assassination. Richard recognizes Kenneth, and agrees to permit him to attempt to discover the man responsible for defiling the flag and wounding his dog. As the men file past, the dog springs upon Montferrat. A combat trial takes place, during which Montferrat is defeated by Kenneth. Kenneth is then discovered to be Prince David of Scotland, the obstacle to his marriage thereby being removed.

TALMUD (ca. 200–500). The *Talmud* is the most variegated body of religio-legal literature created by man. Based on the "Written Law," meaning the code divinely transmitted to Moses in the Bible (q.v.), it was termed the "Oral Law," that set down by the hands of man. After the Hebrew Scriptures had been canonized, supplementary material was steadily added, generally in a cryptic form that allowed of easy memorizing. This was called *Mishnah,* from a verb meaning to repeat, to study, or to teach. It consists of expository paragraphs, generally of the Pentateuch, of traditional laws, and of parables, wise sayings, stories, and legends. The legal portions are called *Halakah* from a word meaning to go or to follow; the cursive sections are known as *Aggadah,* from the verb signifying to tell. About the year 220 the *Mishnah* was authoritatively codified in sixty-three treatises by the famed Rabbi Judah the Prince, of Palestine; and this code, superseding similar collections, was the basis for all later rabbinic discussion.

Rabbinic academies arose in both Palestine and Babylonia, which employed the *Mishnah* as starting point for extended comment and argument called *Gemara*—completion or studious mastery ("Talmud" itself means study or instruction). Though these extensions created a tremendous literature, not all the treatises (or *tractates*) of the *Talmud* had their *Gemara* written down by the academy scribes. The Babylonian version is much larger than the Palestinian; and the former *Talmud* is the one most generally studied and accepted. It was completed about the middle of the sixth century. The *tractates* fall into six "orders": *Zeraim* (Seeds), agricultural and liturgical laws; *Moed* (Appointed Times), laws of festivals and fast days; *Nashim* (Women), on marriage, divorce, and kindred matters; *Nezikin* (Damages), civil and criminal law, and court procedure; *Kodashim* (Holy Things), laws of sacrifices and the temple service; and *Tohorot* (Purities), covering all manner of purity and impurity. The Babylonian *Talmud* is published in twenty or more huge folios; but in recent decades it has been cut down to sixteen, four, and even one volume. All these reproductions include the great commentaries that completely enclose an island of text on each page.

Traditionally the *Talmud* was invested with the same divinity that marked the books of the Bible. Its laws were considered implicit in the scriptural text, requiring only the elucidation and dialectic connecting links supplied by the rabbinic sages. It forms the fundament of the great legal codes of the Middle Ages, still honored and obeyed by orthodox Jews; for the discussions therein made it possible to relate all elements of later Jewish life to the original sacred Scriptures. And it is this very fact—that the *Talmud* is a reflection of life as well as a compendium of laws and legends and argument—which gives it its extraordinary and unique distinction among the writings of mankind.

TAM O'SHANTER (1790), by Robert Burns. This is a humorous narrative poem written in colorful Scottish dialect. One night, while Tam O'Shanter, a drunken farmer, is wending his intoxicated way home from the tavern, he sees an astonishing sight. In the graveyard of Kirk Alloway the corpses are standing up in their open coffins, lighting the weird scene with candles in their hands. Witches diabolically dance and cavort among the graves. They chase Tam, but he makes his escape over the bridge of Doon with only the loss of his mare's tail.

TAMAR AND OTHER POEMS (1924), by Robinson Jeffers. See JEFFERS, ROBINSON.

TAMBURLAINE THE GREAT (ca. 1587–1588), by Christopher Marlowe. This tragedy, though not perfect, is one of the greatest in Elizabethan literature. The poetry sweeps along in Marlowe's "mighty line," and the imagery is of the richest. Tamburlaine, an unscrupulous brigand chief, who began life as a Scythian shepherd, has been preying on travelers passing through the territory of Mycestes, King of Persia, who sends a force against him under Theridamas. Theridamas deserts his master and joins the brigand chief. Cosroe, brother to Mycestes, plans Mycestes' overthrow, but Tamburlaine in turn overthrows him, and proclaims himself King of Persia. Bajazeth, King of Turkey, makes war on him, and he and his wife, Zabina, are captured. Tamburlaine has the proud Turk shut in a cage, and wheeled about so that he can torment him at will. Eventually the captive couple dash out their brains against the bars of the cage. Tamburlaine has held up Zenocrate, daughter of the Soldan of Egypt, on her way to marry the King of Arabia, and fallen in love with her. Her betrothed and the Soldan attack Tamburlaine to free the princess, and he besieges the Soldan's city of Damascus. The Governor fails to surrender, and the conqueror, according to his custom, shows no mercy, in spite of Zenocrate's prayers and tears. Arabia is killed and the Soldan taken prisoner. Tamburlaine welcomes the Egyptian as the father of his beloved, with whom he solemnizes his nuptials. Some time elapses between Parts I and II. Zenocrate is dying and her husband and three sons bid her goodbye in a beautiful, moving scene. Tamburlaine loses the one person he ever loved. After her death his cruelty increases; he defeats his enemies again in a bloody battle, and does not hesitate to stab one of his sons for cowardice. Four captive kings draw his chariot, bitted and bridled like horses. His career of conquest and bloodshed continues; he lays waste Babylon and slaughters the inhabitants. An atheist, he defies the Prophet Mahomet by burning his books. Then a strange illness overtakes him. He dies still longing to conquer new territory, and advising his son to carry on in his barbarous footsteps. As in his other plays, Marlowe presents a study of an outstanding personality and its gradual disintegration.

TAMING OF THE SHREW, THE (ca. 1594; First Folio, 1623), by William Shakespeare. This is still one of the more stageworthy of the comedies. It is related to Gascoigne's *Supposes*. The work is preceded by an introduction concerning a drunken tinker who is picked up by a lord and his servants, who lead him to believe he is a lord of a manor. The play of the shrew is presented for his benefit. The central plot is simple. Petruchio, seeking a wealthy wife, is told of the handsome Katherina, whose violently shrewish disposition has led her father, her younger sister, and the latter's suitors, to despair of finding a husband for her. The doughty Petruchio marches in and courts her with a bold and heavy-handed treatment, brooking no resistance. Once married, he continues to bully, override, and frustrate her until, worn to exhaustion by his tornado tactics, she relents and becomes a gentle, dutiful, loving wife. It is not the bare accomplishment of this feat but the manner thereof that provides the rich, farcical comedy. The play is burdened with a conventional underplot, concerning the wooing of Katherina's sister, Bianca. This is of little interest and is frequently cut down in performance. The play maintains considerable currency in the modern theater. Within recent years it was given a notable revival by Alfred Lunt and Lynn Fontanne, and was the basis of a musical comedy, *Kiss Me, Kate,* with music by Cole Porter.

TANGLEWOOD TALES (1853), by Nathaniel Hawthorne. See HOUSE OF THE SEVEN GABLES, THE, by Nathaniel Hawthorne.

TANNHÄUSER (1845), by Richard Wagner. See WAGNER, RICHARD.

TAO TEH CHING (6th c. B.C.), by Lao Tze. The *Tao Teh Ching* is a Taoistic book of a little over 5000 characters, supposedly written by Lao Tze (born ca. 604 B.C.). Unlike Confucius, Lao Tze retired from public life to contemplate the immaterial realm and formulate the philosophy of Tao or Way of all life. In this book he advocates the state of simplicity, of nature and of nonactivity, or creative quietism. He was the greatest of all the quietists In him we see the spirit of his age. His criticism was ethically negative and iconoclastic. The basis of his teaching is nonexistence. "Heaven and earth and ten thousand things come from existence, but existence comes from nonexistence." By this nonexistence he meant "emptiness," the beginning of all things. "Before heaven and earth it was; it contains all . . . how silent! how solitary! Alone it stands and changes not. Around it moves and suffers not. It is the mother of the universe. I know not its name. I call it Tao."

He speaks the doctrine of political *laissez-faire* in *Tao Teh Ching.* To him the best government is non-governing; the way of nature is non-action. "The more restrictions and prohibitions there are in governing a nation, the poorer grow the people; the more inventions and weapons provided for soldiers, the more troubled is the state."

Chang Tzu (4th c. B.C.) clarified this book of Lao Tze, and advanced the theory of evolution, that all species are naturally evolved through variation in forms, and that each is adapted to its particular place and environment. Lieh Tze is another Taoistic author who wrote two volumes on the interpretation of the mystic philosophy revealed in *Tao Teh Ching.* Witter Bynner has translated *Tao Teh Ching* as *The Way of Life According to Lao Tze.*

TAO YUAN MING (372?–427). Tao Yuan Ming was a Confucian and at the same time a Taoist and a Buddhist. He loved to write on all the seasons, but preferred autumn, when the chrysanthemums bloom. He was a poet of maturity, and because of his classic perfection of idiom is one of the most quoted Chinese poets. He was quiet, even taciturn, and had no desire for wealth or fame. He amused himself with books, but never to such an extent that he would trouble himself with exact interpretations. "When he found a passage that particularly delighted him, he went without food."

His two best poems are called "The Peach Blossom Fountain" and "The Return," and have been translated by H. A. Giles.

TARAS BULBA (1834), by Nikolay V. Gogol. Sad and joyous, like the Ukrainian songs which inspired it, *Taras Bulba* (which has also appeared in English translation under the title of *The Terrible Vengeance*) has been called the one Homeric epic in Russian literature, and had no imitators in Russia until the appearance of *Red Cavalry* (q.v.) by Isaac Babel in 1923.

It is the story of the Setch, the military brotherhood of the Cossacks, who live under the open skies picturesquely and heroically, and kill in battle with zest, though they do not always wait for battle in order to kill. Taras, the hero, is a leader with the strict code of his clan, "born for warlike emotions, and distinguished for his uprightness of character." In a magnificent opening chapter, distinguished alike for its buoyant spirit and its high humor, Taras welcomes his two sons, Ostap and Andrii, promptly engages them in fights in order to test their mettle, while the mother helplessly looks on, wishing that she might have a chance to enjoy them in a mother's way. Taras will not allow them to linger, but promptly rides off with them to the Cossack camp and the adventure of war that the journey held for them.

In the narrative which follows, romance, humor, and tragedy play their roles, and the Cossacks roam far and wide, killing and carousing for the "glorious Russian land." The river Dniester itself is personified as a sort of a hero; but the river often flows red with blood, the blood of innocent people, victims of the Cossack lance. Love takes one of Taras's sons to the enemy camp, and Taras feels dishonored. Taras himself meets death by burning at the hands of the Lykhs, and in the midst of it he prophesies: "A Czar shall arise from Russian soil and there shall not be a power in the world which shall not submit to him." The author adds: "Can fire, flames or power be found on earth which are capable of overpowering Russian strength?" Gogol was to return to this prophetic mood in his famous *troika* passage in *Dead Souls* (q.v.).

TARKINGTON, BOOTH (1869–1946). Besides Booth Tarkington's popular *Alice Adams* (q.v.), he wrote several enduring novels with a Midwestern background. *The Magnificent Ambersons* (1918) had won a Pulitzer Prize. It is a family epic placed in Indiana during a period of social change. Isabel, the old Major's daughter, has made a loveless marriage. Later, her former sweetheart Eugene returns, a widower. Her son George and his daughter Lucy fall in love, and their parents experience their old affection also. George, when his father dies, prevents his mother's remarriage, however, living with her until her death. His fortune then is depleted, and his social position lowered, while Eugene's social position and wealth have increased. At last Eugene and the faithful Lucy are reconciled with him.

Another novel of the same locale is *The Gentleman from Indiana* (1899), the story of a young Easterner, Harkless, who becomes the most influential citizen of the sleepy western town of Plattsville. Harkless engages in a journalistic crusade against political corruption, and marries Helen Sherwood, the organizer of a successful Harkless-for-Congress campaign.

The Plutocrat (1927) concerns Earl Tinker, Midwestern millionaire whose supposedly boorish conduct among Europeans is in fact received with good grace by the bored aristocrats.

Tarkington also wrote the popular *Penrod* series (q.v.) for boys; *Monsieur Beaucaire* (1900), a romance of concealed identity in eighteenth century England, and plays, short stories, essays, and a book of reminiscence.

TARSHISH, by Moses Ibn Ezra. See IBN EZRA, MOSES.

TARTARIN OF TARASCON (1872), by Alphonse Daudet. Tartarin, the great man of a small town of the south of France, is partly Don Quixote, partly Sancho. While he loves his comfort and does not relish danger, he dreams and talks adventures, battles, hunting. He soon becomes a prisoner of his own fame. The rumor starts that he is soon going to Africa on a hunting trip. First he merely fails to deny it, then he confirms it; so at last he has to go. Tartarin sails for Africa, even though his previous hunting experience has been limited to shooting at caps flung into the air. In Algiers he nearly kills a peaceful bourgeois whom he mistakes for a lion. Finally, he kills a real lion, an old, blind, circus performer, and has to pay a 2500-franc indemnity to the owners. He sends the skin, however, to his friends, and comes back to Tarascon a hero. A few months later he tells of the ten, twenty lions he killed "once, in the darkest Sahara. . . ."

Tartarin de Tarascon is not only a delightful lampoon of the French Southerner, an exuberant good fellow, teller of tall tales, who sometimes lets the mirages of his imagination get the better of him, but also of all men who feed on words, dreams and illusions. This is a great story.

TARTUFFE (1664), by Molière. *Tartuffe* is a richly humorous, scathing attack upon religious hypocrites, but some took it to be an attack upon the church as well. Louis XIV himself liked the play, but would not permit a public performance for fully five years after it had been written and privately played.

Tartuffe, a rascally hypocrite, has ingratiated himself with Orgon, a wealthy business man. Orgon believes him to be a fountainhead of goodness and piety. By degrees Tartuffe dominates the household, living on Orgon's money, running the affairs of everyone in the family, and even making advances to Orgon's wife. Only the women of the household, the wife and the maid, know Tartuffe for what he is; Orgon is completely under his spell. This infatuation estranges Orgon from his family; he attempts to betroth his daughter to Tartuffe, and disinherits his son to make Tartuffe his heir; he deeds his house and property to him; and reveals to the hypocrite certain secret papers that would incriminate him politically. He is finally persuaded by his family to hide under a table while Tartuffe talks with his wife. When Orgon hears Tartuffe declare his love to her, he is at last disillusioned. But Tartuffe holds such power by now that he threatens to turn Orgon out of his house and home and even to have him imprisoned. Only the direct intervention of the King, leading to Tartuffe's imprisonment for fraud, saves the day.

TASK, THE (1785), by William Cowper. "The Sofa," "The Time-Piece," "The Garden," "The Winter Evening," "The Winter Morning Walk" and "The Winter Walk at Noon," comprise the six books in this long poem. The poet makes rambling reflections on the wearisomeness of a life of pleasure. Great cities, he says, are not conducive to virtue in men, although they give zest to civilized existence. He delights in a simple, domestic country life. In addition to eulogizing the country he discusses peace among nations and certain objectionable clergymen, attacks monarchy and modern patriotism and cruelty to animals, and praises divine grace as a liberating force.

TATTERED TOM (1871 ff.), by Horatio Alger, Jr. See ALGER, HORATIO.

TECHNICS AND CIVILIZATION (1934), by Lewis Mumford. Lewis Mumford, a leading American critic of the social scene, presents as his thesis in this book, and its two sequels (*The Culture of Cities,* 1938; *The Condition of Man,* 1944), that the machine has outstripped its human controllers, and for the preservation of civilization the monster of production must be humanized. Mumford traces the development of the machine age from the tenth century to the present. He names the clock as the first automatic machine. The forerunner of the automatic factory, it foreshadowed the dictatorship of machine over man. The necessary socialization is Mumford's system of "basic communism." Under this non-Marxist arrangement, there will be assured a minimum standard of living, regional planning, and communal ownership of land. The books reveals the author's interests in the fields of architecture, art, and sociology.

TEMORA, AN EPIC POEM IN EIGHT BOOKS (1763), by James Macpherson. See OSSIAN'S POEMS, by James Macpherson.

TEMPEL EN KRUIS (1940), by Hendrik Marsman. See MARSMAN, HENDRIK.

TEMPEST, THE (1611; First Folio 1623), by William Shakespeare. *The Tempest* is the one play by Shakespeare not derived from one or more of the many sources common to all the playwrights of the Elizabethan era. A contemporary German play has an analogous exile theme. The story of the shipwreck was probably taken from Sir George Somers' narrative of a Bermuda shipwreck of 1609. The play is a masque-like comedy, excelling some of the traditional pieces which had been done to death by countless contemporary writers. It is a tale of magic and wonderworking, of retribution and forgiveness, of shipwreck and enchanted isles. It is the last complete play by Shakespeare. Prospero, Duke of Milan, a studious man who had delegated to his ambitious brother Antonio many of the affairs of government, was "extirpated" by him and sent to sea, with his infant daughter. Providence brought him safely to an island used as a place of exile by the witch Sycorax, where he lived for many years, studying the art of sorcery. When the play opens, he has long ruled the island, commanding the spirits of the air, and enslaving brutish, misshapen Caliban, progeny of the witch. Through his spells he causes to be swept ashore by a tempest, a ship bearing the ally of Antonio, the King of Naples, and his son Ferdinand, and Antonio himself. To suit his purposes Prospero separates and bewitches the various groups of his prisoners. He works upon them through the instrumentality of his servant, the spirit Ariel. First he secures young Ferdinand as husband for his daughter Miranda, making a happy match between the two. Then he reveals himself, regains his dukedom, pardoning the penitent wrongdoers. This consummated, he restores the mariners to their ship and all prepare to embark for Naples.

The Tempest definitely is a court play, with some of the conventional aspects of such pieces. It is superbly wrought, full of grace and enriched with many of the poet's finest lines.

TEMPLE, THE (1633), by George Herbert. This group of 160 sacred poems presents a variety of meters and a multitude of ingenious metaphysical conceits. The first part of the book is headed "The Church Porch"; the rest, "The Church." "The Altar," one of the poems, is printed in the shape of an altar; the lines of "Easter Wings" decrease in length and then increase again to represent wings on the printed page. One of the best known conceits is expressed in "The Collar," which represents to the poet God's restraining tie, his struggle to shake it off, and his eventual surrender. Other well-known titles: "The Pearl," "The Pulley," "Jordan," "Virtue."

TEMPLE AND CROSS (1940), by Hendrik Marsman. See MARSMAN, HENDRIK.

TEMPTATION OF SAINT ANTHONY, THE (1874), by Gustave Flaubert. This book is an attempt to do in words what is more easily done in painting. Flaubert is trying to describe, in all possible detail, the temptations which beset a holy man. The flesh, the spirit and the will are in turn assailed, with a picturesqueness which is medieval and a wealth of documentary detail characteristic of modern realism. The subject had long tempted Flaubert, who did three versions of the story in his lifetime. As a tour de force of "plastic" writing it has great merit. Flaubert's reputation as a novelist, however, was made largely by his books on modern subjects.

TENNYSON, ALFRED, LORD (1809–1892). In addition to such well-known longer works as *Idylls of the King, Enoch Arden, The Princess,* and *In Memoriam* (qq.v.), the poet laureate under Queen Victoria wrote such favorites of anthologists as "The Charge of the Light Brigade" (1854), immortalizing a heroic and disastrous incident in the Crimean War, and "Crossing the Bar" (1889), which he wished placed last in all editions of his collected poems. "Break, Break, Break" (1842) was, like *In Memoriam,* a product of Tennyson's sorrow for the loss of Hallam. Three dramatic monologues are outstanding. "Ulysses" (1842) borrows from Dante the legend that Ulysses in old age set out once more on a voyage

> To follow knowledge like a sinking star,
> Beyond the utmost bound of human thought.

"Tithonus" is the unhappy husband of Aurora the dawn, of whom he had asked immortality—but he neglected to ask for perpetual youth. Now, shriveled in senility, he envies the men below who die. "Lucretius" (1868) gives a review of the great poet-philosopher's achievement before, in a fit of madness induced by a love philter, he stabs himself. A poet to whom Tennyson is akin is commemorated in "To Virgil." Love is the undoing of the unbalanced narrator of "Maud" (1855), whose most famous song is "Come into the garden, Maud." "The Lady of Shalott" (1842) is also remembered, gazing into her magic mirror. The idea of progress is the main theme of "Locksley Hall" (1842).

TERRIBLE VENGEANCE, THE (1834), by Nikolay V. Gogol. See TARAS BULBA, by Nikolay V. Gogol.

TESS OF THE D'URBERVILLES (1891), by Thomas Hardy. Tess Durbeyfield is the daughter of humble farm folk. Her shiftless father has his head turned when an antiquarian parson reveals that he represents the direct line of the ancient manorial family of D'Urberville, long obscured as a noble house. This information leads the foolish parents to send young Tess, much against her will, to claim relationship with a spurious, relatively *nouveau riche* family of D'Urbervilles not far away.

This vain errand throws Tess in the path of ruthless, unscrupulous Alec D'Urberville. She repulses his advances, but is finally seduced by him. She returns to her home and gives birth to a child, which dies in infancy.

Tess's life is now marked. She leaves her home and finds work as a dairymaid. In her new surroundings she is loved and courted by Angel Clare, a gentleman and a clergyman's son. She loves him deeply, but feels that she cannot marry him because of her past. But Clare will not be discouraged. He not only wins her consent to marry him but unconsciously blocks, by chance or purpose, her earnest desire to confess. The marriage takes place and that night honest Tess tells the whole story.

Clare, appalled and disillusioned, separates from her and ultimately goes to Brazil. The little money he had left Tess is soon gone. She is too proud to seek aid from his family, to whom she had never been presented, and tries to support herself, remaining ever loyal to her husband, hoping for his return. Alec D'Urberville appears and again harasses her. She resists his tempting offers of aid and comfort. But her father dies, her family is dispossessed, and at last, in despair, Tess is compelled to accept D'Urberville's terms.

Then, too late, Clare returns, chastened and humbled, ready to embrace Tess. When he finds her, she, in her wild despair, murders the worthless D'Urberville who had dogged her steps. She has a few fugitive, happy days with Clare, but is then apprehended and hanged as a murderess.

TESTAMENT OF BEAUTY, THE (1929), by Robert Bridges. This is a philosophical poem in four parts, with the headings "Introduction," "Selfhood," "Breed" and "Ethick." In loose Alexandrines it treats the eternal questions of Beauty, Art, Love, Reason, Sex, Nature and Man. The work bristles with allusions to the writings of Plato and Aristotle, the Neoplatonists and modern biologists. Bridges spurns the turbulent social stream; he writes his poem from the cool distance of a spectator. For that reason and because of the poet's temperament and education, *The Testament* is abstract, involved, and severely scholarly. Its main message has to do with the attractive force of an evolutionary spiritual love.

TESTAMENT OF THE DYING MOTHER (1650), by Comenius. See DIDACTICA, THE, by Comenius.

TEVYE'S DAUGHTERS (Eng. tr. 1949), by Sholom Aleichem. See SHOLOM ALEICHEM.

THADDEUS OF WARSAW (1803), by Jane Porter. This romantic novel deals with Poland in the latter part of the eighteenth century. Count Thaddeus Sobieski, last descendant of King John Sobieski, serves King Stanislaus during the Russian invasion of Poland. His father is killed and his mother dies in his arms just before the Russians burn his castle. Thaddeus escapes to England to seek his friend, Pembroke Somerset. He finally meets Pembroke, who had been kept in ignorance of his arrival. Thaddeus' identity is revealed: Sir Robert is his father and Pembroke is his stepbrother. He marries a wellborn relative, Mary Beaufort. Among the historical characters portrayed in the first part of the book are General Kosciuszko and Prince Poniatowski.

Another very successful romance was *Scottish Chiefs* (1810), dealing with the career of William Wallace.

THANATOPSIS (1817), by William Cullen Bryant. This blank-verse poem asserts fatalistically that the earth eventually reclaims all its living things. The object of man, therefore, is to live with dignity and majesty, so that the inevitable can be met with fortitude. Originally published when the author was sixteen, this poem appeared in the 1832 edition of *Poems,* which contains all the major poetic works of the author. By that time, thirty-two new lines substantially altered the philosophic content of the work, emphasizing Nature as a primary force. "To a Waterfowl" is a delicate brief lyric telling of Divine Power's revelation to man, through a small manifestation of beauty in Nature. The ballad "Song of Marion's Men" chronicles the exploits of Francis Marion during the Revolution.

Bryant's philosophical views were limited, as were his poetic themes, but he possessed a simplicity and nobility of style. He translated the *Iliad* (1870) and the *Odyssey* (1871–1872) (qq.v.) and wrote discourses on literary figures.

THEODICY (1710), by Gottfried Wilhelm Leibnitz. See LEIBNITZ, GOTTFRIED WILHELM.

THEOGONY (8th c. B.C.), by Hesiod. What is known of the poet Hesiod as an individual is to be found in the *Works and Days* (q.v.). For the *Theogony* he is simply the bard, and the poem is as impersonal as the Homeric epics. The title indicates that the bard's theme is the Birth of the Gods. It tells how all is created out of chaos, how Heaven and Earth begat the Titans, and two of them, Kronos and Rhea, in turn the gods, then how Zeus supplanted Kronos, led the gods against the Titans, defeated them and established his own regime. Then follows the story of early man, the fashioning of woman, the fall from grace, the flood and repopulation of the earth. The poem concludes with a series of myths of the birth of individual gods. Much of the matter of the poem suggests obvious parallels with the Hebrew Genesis, and there can be no question of their common ancestry, but it must also be remembered that there are other parallels just as striking, e.g., with the Icelandic *Edda*. The *Theogony* is not, however, a religious book like Genesis, for it was never regarded as "the word of God" and was never given the sanction of canonical acceptance, since there was no universal solidarity of Hellenic religious faith. What existed was a body of fairly generally received tradition. Much of what Hesiod tells was already implied in the *Iliad* (q.v.) and *Odyssey* (q.v.). Hesiod simply collects and systematizes existing myth and lore. The *Theogony* is probably not even the work of one man, for there are obvious signs of addition and revision.

THEORIA ET MOTUS CORPORUM COELESTIUM (1809), by Karl Friedrich Gauss. See DISQUISITIONS ARITHMETICAE, by Karl Friedrich Gauss.

THÉORIE ANALYTIQUE DES PROBABILITÉS (1812), by Pierre Simon Laplace. See MÉCANIQUE CÉLESTE, by Pierre Simon Laplace.

THEORY OF COLORS (1810), by Johann Wolfgang von Goethe. See GOETHE, JOHANN WOLFGANG VON.

THEORY OF HEAT RADIATION (1906), by Max Planck. See ORIGIN AND DEVELOPMENT OF THE QUANTUM THEORY, THE, by Max Planck.

THEORY OF THE LEISURE CLASS, THE (1899), by Thorstein Veblen. The theory of the consumer, in terms of psychology and economics, has never been examined with such blistering thoroughness as by Veblen. His book is an attempt to explain the following question which has so often disturbed thinking people: "Why do men seek to differentiate themselves from their fellows by establishing invidious distinctions based on wealth and the power wantonly to consume?" He reaches a socialist conclusion, i.e., that as long as there are inequalities among people in regard to their possessions, there will be discontent and strife. *The Theory of the Leisure Class* might actually be called the psychology of consumption. The thesis of the work is that, instead of attempting to spend wisely, economically and understandingly, people in our capitalist society spend their money in a manner calculated to impress others. His concept of "conspicuous waste" underlies the common psychology of "keeping up with the Joneses." Veblen was an original, unorthodox economist; his brilliance resides in his dissenting opinions rather than in constructive planning.

THERE IS ANOTHER HEAVEN (1929), by Robert Nathan. See NATHAN, ROBERT.

THERE SHALL BE NO NIGHT (1940), by Robert Sherwood. See SHERWOOD, ROBERT.

THESE TWAIN (1915), by Arnold Bennett. See CLAYHANGER TRILOGY, by Arnold Bennett.

THEY KNEW WHAT THEY WANTED (1924), by Sidney Howard. Tony, an Italian wine-grower, sees Amy, a pretty waitress, in a San Francisco restaurant. He has his handsome employee Joe write a proposal, enclosing Joe's picture. Amy accepts, but is distressed, on arriving at the ranch, to discover her fiancé is not Joe, but Tony, whose legs had been badly injured in an accident before her arrival. After a brief affair with Joe, she settles down to being Tony's wife, and when she confesses that she is going to have Joe's baby, Tony, furious at first, finally begs her to stay, and promises to accept the child.

Yellow Jack (1934) is a dramatization of Paul de Kruif's story of the Walter Reed Commission in Cuba. Colonel Tory tries to block the research of the men, who are constantly in danger of their lives, but at last doctors succeed in isolating the mosquito-borne microbe of yellow fever.

Other plays include *Lucky Sam McCarver* (1925), about the efforts of socialite Carlotta Ashe's attempts to influence the character of Sam McCarver, a night club owner; *Ned McCobb's Daughter* (1926), which tells of Carrie, daughter of an impoverished sea captain, and her efforts to rear the children of her worthless husband George Callahan; and *The Silver Cord* (1926), a much discussed piece about possessive mother love, told through the efforts of the widowed Mrs. Phelps to dominate her two sons, David and Robert.

THEY WENT ON TOGETHER (1941), by Robert Nathan. See NATHAN, ROBERT.

THIRTEEN O'CLOCK (1937), by Stephen Vincent Benét. See JOHN BROWN'S BODY, by Stephen Vincent Benét.

THIRTY-NINE STEPS, TH⌐ (1915), by John Buchan. Richard Hannay, returning to England after years of residence in South Africa, meets an American adventurer who takes Hannay into his confidence. The American tells him a lurid tale about an international plot that is being hatched against England. Shortly afterward he is murdered, and Hannay is strongly suspected of the act by the police. A dual hunt for Hannay ensues, by the police on one hand, and by the members of a powerful, ruthless gang on the other, for they realize that Hannay knows their secret—their plan to destroy England and their murder of the American. They must do away with Hannay. The rest of the story concerns his successful attempts to outwit both groups of pursuers in order to be able to bring to Scotland Yard his all-important information, and thus save his country from disaster. Alfred Hitchcock made a particularly brilliant moving picture from this story.

THIS SIDE OF PARADISE (1920), by Francis Scott Fitzgerald. This, a cynical though brilliant postwar novel, established Fitzgerald's reputation. It is the story of Amory Blaine. A handsome, healthy youth, spoiled by his mother, Beatrice, he lacks moral purpose, and flits aimlessly about in college life, interesting himself temporarily in literary cults, liberal student activities, and love affairs. He is an officer in France during the war. Upon his return, he enters the advertising industry, blighted in his early twenties with regret, false cynicism and world weariness.

THOREAU (1939), by Henry Seidel Canby. See CANBY, HENRY SEIDEL.

THOREAU, HENRY DAVID (1948), by Joseph Wood Krutch. See KRUTCH, JOSEPH WOOD.

THOUGHTFUL POEMS (1931), by Pieter Cornelis Boutens. See BOUTENS, PIETER CORNELIS.

THOUGHTS ON THE INTERPRETATION OF NATURE (1754), by Denis Diderot. See DIDEROT, DENIS.

THOUSAND NIGHTS AND A NIGHT, THE (ca. 1440–1550). See ARABIAN NIGHTS' ENTERTAINMENT.

THREE BLACK PENNYS, THE (1917), by Joseph Hergesheimer. See JAVA HEAD, by Joseph Hergesheimer.

THREE CITIES (1933), by Sholem Asch. See NAZARENE, THE, by Sholem Asch.

THREE COMRADES (1937), by Erich Maria Remarque. See ALL QUIET ON THE WESTERN FRONT, by Erich Maria Remarque.

THREE-CORNERED HAT, THE (1874), by Pedro Antonio de Alarcón. Just outside the Andalusian town of Gaudix there lived in 1805 a prosperous miller, Lucas, and his charming wife, Frasquita. In their pleasant garden they frequently entertain the notables of the town. Maddened by Frasquita's beauty, the Mayor of the town contrives to dispose of her husband and comes secretly by night to visit her. He accidentally falls into the millpond and calls for help. Frasquita saves him, but when he tries to make love to her, she knocks him down. Terrified at the thought that she might have harmed him seriously, she runs to town for help. A constable arrives, puts the Mayor in Frasquita's bed, hangs his clothes to dry on the back of a chair, and returns to town. In the meantime Lucas manages to escape from the hired ruffians of the Mayor and comes back to his mill. There he sees the Mayor's clothes by the fireplace, and, on peeping through a keyhole, the Mayor himself in Frasquita's bed. For a moment he thinks of saving his honor by killing him, but on second thought he dons the Mayor's clothes and proceeds to the Mayor's house, deciding to be revenged with the Mayor's wife. He is foiled, however, in his attempt to counter evil with evil, and this witty tale concludes with the virtue of Frasquita and of the Mayor's wife triumphant.

THREE DIALOGUES BETWEEN HYLAS AND PHILONOUS (1713), by George Berkeley. See PRINCIPLES OF HUMAN KNOWLEDGE, THE, by George Berkeley.

THREE LIVES (1909), by Gertrude Stein. See AUTOBIOGRAPHY OF ALICE B. TOKLAS, THE, by Gertrude Stein.

THREE MUSKETEERS, THE (1844), by Alexandre Dumas, *père*. *The Three Musketeers* is the best known historical novel of Alexandre Dumas, *père*. A young man from the Midi, d'Artagnan, arrives in Paris one day in 1605 and manages to be involved in three duels with three musketeers of Monsieur de Tréville's regiment, Athos, Porthos and Aramis. They become d'Artagnan's best friends. The account of their adventures from 1625 on develops against the rich historical background of the reign of Louis XIII and the early part of that of Louis XIV, the main plot being furnished by the antagonism between Cardinal de Richelieu and Queen Anne d'Autriche.

The Three Musketeers was followed by *Twenty Years After* (1845) and *The Vicomte de Bragelonne* (1847), which carry the adventures of the heroes up to the time of their deaths. *The Man in the Iron Mask* (1847), originally published as part of the last novel, toys with the idea that the man of mystery was the twin brother of Louis XIV. Aramis' attempt to substitute him for the real king is foiled by the faithful Superintendent of Finance, Fouquet.

THREE NOVELS (1938), by Sholem Asch. See NAZARENE, THE, by Sholem Asch.

THREE-PENNY OPERA (1928), by Bertolt Brecht. See BRECHT, BERTOLT.

THREE SISTERS, THE (1900), by Anton Chekhov. The drabness of provincial life and frustration of individual ambitions are emphasized in this play, which opens in the Prosorov home in a Russian provincial town. It is just a year since the death of the father. Olga, the oldest sister, is a schoolmistress; Masha, the second, has married a dull and uninteresting high-school teacher, Kuligin. Andrey, the brother, a student and a visionary, hopes some day to be a professor at the Moscow University. The one desire of the sisters is to return to the gay life of Moscow which they had left eleven years before. Andrey marries Natasha, a provincial girl, who gradually dominates her husband and cuts him off from his sisters. Irina, the third sister, has become a clerk in the telegraph office and has an admirer, a baron. Masha, bored with her limited, kindly husband, has a love affair with a family friend, Vershinin, but he eventually leaves her. Irina, on Olga's advice, decides to marry the baron. She passes an examination to become a schoolteacher, and they plan to start a new life together. Soleni, who loved Irina, kills the baron in a duel, thus driving Irina to near despair. The aspirations of all of them have been thwarted, partly through circumstance and partly through their own weaknesses.

THREE SOLDIERS (1921), by John Dos Passos. See U.S.A., by John Dos Passos.

THREE TALES (1877), by Gustave Flaubert. See TROIS CONTES, by Gustave Flaubert.

THREE VOYAGES OF CAPTAIN COOK AROUND THE WORLD, THE (published 1773–1784), by James Cook. In 1767, the Royal Society commissioned Cook to sail on the *Endeavour,* a coal bark of 370 tons, into the South Seas, in order to observe the passage of the planet Venus over the sun's disc, which, according to astronomical calculations, would happen in the year 1769. Captain Cook's second voyage took place 1772–1775. This time he completed the exploration of the Southern Hemisphere, sailing toward the South Pole and around the world. In 1776–1780 he went on a cruise of exploration to the Pacific Ocean. He wished to determine the position and extent of the west coast of North America, its distance from Asia and the practicability of a northern passage to Europe. The voluminous records kept by the Captain of his three voyages are full of scientific data and human adventure, He was murdered by the natives of Hawaii in 1779.

THREE WORLDS (1936), by Carl Van Doren. See BENJAMIN FRANKLIN, by Carl Van Doren.

THROUGH THE EYE OF THE NEEDLE (1907), by William Dean Howells. See HAZARD OF NEW FORTUNES, A, by William Dean Howells.

THROUGH THE LOOKING-GLASS (1872), by Lewis Carroll (Charles Lutwidge Dodgson). This tale for children follows *Alice's Adventures in Won-*

derland (q.v.). Talking to her kitten, Alice wonders about the world back of the locking-glass. Climbing the mantel, she enters the looking-glass house, where everything is turned backward. The story follows a game of chess with Alice as the White Pawn. She meets the Red and White Queens. The country is laid out in the form of a chessboard, with brooks and hedges dividing the ground into squares. She meets and talks to the flowers; on a train she encounters the looking-glass insects and a man in a white paper suit; Tweedledum and Tweedledee sing "The Walrus and the Carpenter"; a sheep, proprietor of a shop, takes her for a boat ride; Humpty Dumpty tells his story; the Lion and the Unicorn fight for the crown; she encounters the Knight Inventor. On the eighth square at last, Alice is made a Queen. At a dinner party strange things occur; Alice shakes the Red Queen, who turns into her kitten. Thereupon Alice awakes.

THUNDER ON THE LEFT (1925), by Christopher Morley. See MORLEY, CHRISTOPHER.

THURBER, JAMES (1894–   ). In 1920 James Thurber left State Department work and became a journalist. During subsequent years he has become one of our most popular sophisticated humorists. His work includes satirical books such as *Is Sex Necessary?* (1929), written with E. B. White, and spoofing popular science literature, and *Let Your Mind Alone* (1937), spoofing popular psychological literature and fantasies for children. He also wrote a play, *The Male Animal* (1940), with Elliott Nugent, concerning a professor and a former football-player-student who is in love with the professor's wife; and many volumes of inimitable essays, stories, and drawings.

My Life and Hard Times (1933) is a typical collection of nine gay autobiographical sketches. The foibles of the author's family, friends and neighbors are treated with good humor. The tone is a mixture of realism and nonmalicious absurdity. "The Night the Bed Fell" gives Thurber an opportunity to discuss hilariously the psychological quirks of his father (on whom the bed fell), mother, brother Herman, cousin Briggs Beall, old Aunt Melissa Beall, Aunt Sarah Shoaf, and Grandpa, a veteran of the Civil War and still fighting it.

Similar collections are *The Owl in the Attic* (1931), *The Seal in the Bedroom* (1932), and *The Middle-Aged Man on the Flying Trapeze* (1935).

THURSO'S LANDING (1932), by Robinson Jeffers. See JEFFERS, ROBINSON.

THUS SPAKE ZARATHUSTRA (1883–1886), by Friedrich Nietzsche. See NIETZSCHE, FRIEDRICH.

THYESTES, by Seneca. See TRAGEDIES, by Seneca.

TIECK, LUDWIG (1773–1853). Ludwig Tieck determined for a whole century the popular concept of German Romanticism through the all-pervading magic of his "moonlit night," a playful romantic irony, and his capacity to create nostalgia for his idealized Middle Ages, and through his evocation of the "forest murmurs" long before Richard Wagner set them to music. Though not a great writer he was a true poet, a fine scholar and a very effective prophet of Shakespeare in Germany. Tieck achieved a great popular success in 1797 with his dramatic satire *Puss in Boots.* Ridiculing pretentiousness, the poet attacked hypocritical bourgeois morality, the bad taste of middle-class playgoers, conventional sentimentality, and pedantic rationalism. For this purpose he adapted for the stage Perrault's seventeenth-century fairy tale of the booted cat who through his sly tricks helps his master, the miller's youngest son, to win both the king's affection and the hand of the princess. Although very "literary" and highly confusing, the play must be considered one of the best satirical dramas of German literature. From his three volumes of fairy tales only two stories have survived: "Blond Eckbert" and "The Beautiful Magelone."

TIGER-LILIES (1867), by Sidney Lanier. See LANIER, SIDNEY.

TIJDKRANS (1893), by Guido Gezelle. See GEZELLE, GUIDO.

TILL EULENSPIEGEL (between 1500 and 1540). Many are the disguises which the merry pranks of Till, the "Boor's Son," assumed during the Middle Ages and after. In England he emerged as Thyl Owlglass, a peasant's son, who was born in Brunswick; in Germany he was Till Eulenspiegel and in Holland Thyl Ulenspiegel. The first known published edition of *Till Eulenspiegel* is no longer extant. The one we know today is from the Augsburg edition of 1540. There is little question that the lusty ribaldries of Till, current at a time when robber knighthood was in flower and the common people were but oppressed serfs, had social implications. Till was the European counterpart of England's Robin Hood. Both scorned the rich and the powerful, both sympathized with the poor and the oppressed. Despite the ravages of time and the attempts to water down and mellow the indignation of the tales to conform with current social prejudices, Till Eulenspiegel's merry, often vulgar pranks retain their imperishable bite and truth.

TILL THE DAY I DIE (1935), by Clifford Odets. See WAITING FOR LEFTY, by Clifford Odets.

TIMAEUS (ca. 350), by Plato. This dialogue is the earliest work of Greek science (apart from medical treatises) which has come down to us, and it perhaps has exerted a greater influence upon posterity than any other, with the possible exception of the *Physics* of Aristotle. The investigation of nature was renounced by Socrates in the *Phaedo,* and so Plato puts this dialogue, with its speculations on physics, into the mouth of Timaeus, a Pythagorean philosopher. Here one finds a view, presumably accepted by Plato, of the universe as a whole—from the motions of the heavens to human physiology. The cosmology is essentially that of Pythagoras, with the earth at the center. The ordering and distances of the planets are estimated on the assumption that they are in harmony with the mathematical theory of means and with the properties of numbers. The four Empedoclean elements—earth, water, air, and fire—are put into correspondence with four of the five regular geometrical solids. The cube, being most stable, is assigned to the earth; the tetrahedron, being sharpest, is the essence of fire; water and air are assigned respectively to the icosahedron and the octahedron. Originally all things were a chaos, but the creator arranged the elements in order and gave to man his immortal soul, which dwells in the chest. The structure of man's body was fashioned with due regard to the functions of each part. It, too, was built of the mathematical triangles constituting the four elements. Disease is occasioned by the disarrangement of the elements of which the body is composed, resulting in a lack of balance in the four qualities—hot, cold, moist, and dry—and the four temperaments—blood, phlegm, black bile, and yellow bile. (Vestiges of this theory persist in modern times in the words sanguine, phlegmatic, melancholic, and bilious.) For proper balance between body and soul, the mathematician must practice gymnastics and the gymnast must practice music. Regimen and not medicine is the true cure.

The science of the *Timaeus* strikes a modern reader as fantastic, yet during the medieval period it was one of the most influential works. The Pythagorean-Platonic idea of universal harmony played a large role in the astronomy of Kepler, and can be traced in much of the development of cosmology. The speculations of Plato bear but slight resemblance to the discoveries of modern science, but the *Timaeus* still remains the greatest effort of antiquity to conceive the world as a whole, embracing man and the universe.

TIME AND FREE WILL (Eng. tr. 1910), by Henri Bergson. In this early work the eminent French philosopher appeals to thinking people to reject an intellectualist conception of the life and movement of reality. Instead he calls for an immersion in the living stream of things in whose inexorable sweep all difficulties and confusions are liquidated. The core of this study is the author's conception of *real concrete duration* and the *specific* feeling of duration possessed by our consciousness. Most errors in the attempts by philosophers to understand the nature of time are based on their confusion between *concrete duration* and *abstract time*. In applying these results to the moral field of free will, Bergson concludes that the difficulties arising from the evaluation of an act is that the judgment is made *after* the act on a conceptual basis.

TIME OF MAN, THE (1926), by Elizabeth Madox Roberts. Ellen Chesser, daughter of an itinerant tenant farmer, falls in love with a neighbor, Jasper Kent. After their marriage they work on the farm of Joe Phillips. Phillips' fondness for her, and Jasper's interest in Hester Shuck, threaten to disrupt the marriage, but the birth of their fifth child, Chick, and their common grief at his early death, reconcile them. They work on a small farm, with the prospect of improvement, but another tragedy occurs—in the burning of a neighbor's barn. Jasper, who had accidentally burned a barn before his marriage, is accused of this new fire and driven from the community. Ellen packs her things once more, and they set out in a wagon with their children, to find a new home somewhere.

Elizabeth Roberts, born in the Kentucky region described in her fiction, wrote also *My Heart and My Flesh* (1927), a pastoral novel about aristocratic Theodosia Bell, whose mind is tormented by the disillusions of her family's secrets and her own loneliness, but who finally finds happiness in the friendship of a cattle breeder, Caleb Burns, and the job of schoolteacher. *The Great Meadow* (1930) is a historical novel of Kentucky pioneer life in the 1770's. Diony Hall marries Berk Jarvis. He is reported killed by Indians, and she marries frontiersman Evan Muir. When Berk reappears, however, she returns to him.

TIME OF YOUR LIFE, THE (1939), by William Saroyan. This plotless comedy is a study of inner lives. The scene is a waterfront dive in San Francisco, run by the tolerant Nick. Characters sit about, drinking, playing the pinball machine, dancing, and discoursing on life and its meaning. The mysterious Joe, a wealthy eccentric, drinks champagne and plays with toys. He eases his conscience by giving away money. Tom, his devoted follower, runs Joe's errands. Kitty is a prostitute whose sensitive imagination substitutes dreams for memories. Joe helps Tom get a job so he can marry her. Another important character is McCarthy, an elderly longshoreman, and a gorgeous liar, who shoots a vice inspector for persecuting Kitty.

Saroyan became a name in the literary scene with *The Daring Young Man on the Flying Trapeze* (1934), a collection of irresponsible, rhapsodic, sentimental pieces revealing his love for all the world; and his freedom in—and from—subject matter and form. *The Human Comedy* (1943) is a novel of the Macauley family of California. Homer and Ulysses are naïve youths through whose eyes the reader sees that the world is the opposite of what it seems, and that virtue triumphs over evil.

TIME REGAINED (1927), by Marcel Proust. See REMEMBRANCE OF THINGS PAST, by Marcel Proust.

TIMES OF MELVILLE AND WHITMAN, THE (1947), by Van Wyck Brooks. See FLOWERING OF NEW ENGLAND, THE, by Van Wyck Brooks.

TIMMERMANS, FELIX (1886–1947). The most famous book of this Flemish novelist is *Pallieter* (1916), a glorification of the candidly sensuous enjoyment of earthly beauty. It immediately aroused as much admiration as commotion. In succulent, colorful language the author depicts the adventures of a rich young farmer, Pallieter, whose experiences form almost exclusively a series of discoveries concerning the glory of sensuous enjoyments. To him all life is a horn of plenty. Pallieter cannot become satiated with the beauty of the Flemish snowy landscapes, which are painted by Timmermans with the same witty heartiness as by Breughel centuries earlier; nor with the drinking parties of his bucolic friends; nor with the marriage feast which his buxom bride prepared for him. Timmermans felt himself closely akin to the naïve primitiveness of the Middle Ages, as may be seen in his *Kindeken Jezus in Vlaanderen* (1918), in which in a childlike, touching manner the birth of Christ is depicted in a Flemish environment. The great success his books had in Europe tempted him to yield to a popular art, with the sentimental story *De pastoor van den Boeyenden Wijngaerdt* (1923) and the fictional biography of *Pieter Breughel* (1928; Eng. tr. *Droll Peter,* 1930). However, in 1935, he published again a work of high quality, *Boerenpsalm,* a sober, very powerful delineation of a virile and stubborn Flemish farmer in his struggle with God. His very fine short work, *De Zeer Schoone Uren van Juffrouw Symforosa* (1918), brings to life the balanced spirit of the ancient Flemish towns; and the *Driekoningen-tryptiek* (1923), which was made into a stage play, has had a great success.

TIMON OF ATHENS (written ca. 1607; Folio 1623), by William Shakespeare. It is doubtful that this play was ever acted. There is a tendency among the critics to believe that it is only partly by Shakespeare. Some think that he worked on an older play; others that it is an unfinished piece of work. Shakespeare drew his material from Lucian's *Timon the Misanthrope* and Plutarch's *Life of Antony.* The play is a bitter satire, and the writing much inferior to the author's best work. Timon of Athens, a lord of apparently fabulous wealth, feasts and entertains his friends continuously. For a small worthless present he will send a lavish gift in return, till his hangers-on have worked it up into a sort of racket. The only people who do not fawn on him are Apemantus, a churlish philosopher; Alcibiades, an Athenian captain; and his steward, Flavius. The latter tries in vain to warn Timon in time and to check his extravagance. But at last the day of reckoning comes and creditors gather at his gates. He sends his servants to various lords and senators whom he has befriended to ask for money, but gets only rebuffs and excuses. He invites his friends to another banquet, and thinking that he has come into funds they all flock round him. But he calls them dogs, serves them lukewarm water and then chases them out of the house. He leaves Athens in great bitterness and retires to a cave in the woods near the sea; here he lives in solitude on grass and roots, and encounters Alcibiades, who has been banished from Athens and is making war on his native city. He has found gold in the cave, and gives some to Alcibiades' mistresses, Phrynia and Timandra. Apemantus comes to see him, and Flavius, who truly wishes to serve his master. Timon gives him gold and sends him away. The rumor that he has gold spreads, and some of his old flatterers try to come back; but he denounces them and drives them off. He turns down the Senators from Athens who wish him to defend the city against Alcibiades, and tells them he will save the citizens from Alcibiades' wrath by letting them hang themselves to his favorite tree. He dies and is buried in an obscure grave near his cave. Athens surrenders to Alcibiades, who avenges Timon's wrongs on his enemies.

TINTERN ABBEY, LINES WRITTEN A FEW MILES ABOVE (1798), by William Wordsworth. The theme of this great reflective poem is the close kinship of man and nature, each of which interprets and reveals the other. Revisiting Tintern Abbey, the poet compares his present attitude toward nature with that when he was five years younger. He reviews three periods in his concepts of nature: first, unthinking delight; second, active appreciation of the beauties of nature; and, finally, a meditative, philosophical attitude, bringing an awareness of the interrelationship of nature, God, and man.

'TIS PITY SHE'S A WHORE (1633), by John Ford. The scene of this bloody, incestuous tragedy is laid in Parma. Giovanni, son of Florio, loves his sister, Annabella, who returns his affection. She has a number of suitors, and among them is Soranzo, a nobleman with a servant, Vasques. Soranzo is loved by Hippolita, wife of Richardetto, whom she had persuaded to go on a journey to Leghorn to seek out an orphaned niece, hoping that he will never return, and that she will be free to marry Soranzo. Richardetto, sensing her design, gives out the news that he is dead. He returns with his niece, Philotis, disguising himself as a physician, and determined on revenge. Soranzo scorns Hippolita, who makes a compact with Vasques to be revenged on his master. Florio favors Soranzo's suit to his daughter. Annabella, meanwhile, finding herself pregnant, goes to Friar Bonaventura, a weaker edition of Friar Laurence, for confession. He advises her to marry Soranzo, be faithful to him, and break with her brother. Grimaldi, another suitor, had asked Richardetto to push his suit with Annabella. Richardetto tells him that Soranzo expects to marry Annabella at the Friar's cell that night. Grimaldi determines to kill his rival. Instead he kills Bergetto, a harmless suitor of Annabella's. Hippolita comes to her rival's wedding feast intending to poison her, but is poisoned herself by Vasques. Soranzo discovers how Annabella has deceived him, and is advised by Vasques to take a slow revenge. Soranzo shuts up Annabella and invites Florio and Giovanni to a feast. Giovanni, having beeen warned in a letter from his sister, comes to see her, and stabs her himself. He attends the feast bearing her heart. He and Soranzo fight, he kills Soranzo, and is killed in turn by Vasques.

TITAN (1800–1803), by Johann Paul Richter. See RICHTER, JOHANN PAUL.

TITAN, THE (1914), by Theodore Dreiser. See COWPERWOOD NOVELS, THE, by Theodore Dreiser.

TITUS ANDRONICUS (1594), by William Shakespeare. It is now generally held that Shakespeare collaborated with other dramatists on *Titus Andronicus* or that he revised an existing play. The tragedy belongs to the Senecan school of bloody revenge drama exemplified by the works of Kyd and Marlowe. It resembles Kyd's *Spanish Tragedy* (q.v.), and has the same motive of a father's revenge and other parallels in incident and dialogue. The scene is laid in Rome. Titus Andronicus has returned victorious from fighting the Goths. Tamora, Queen of the Goths, and her sons are among his prisoners. Titus has brought back the bodies of his sons who were killed in action, and cold-bloodedly has one of Tamora's sons slaughtered so that the shade of an enemy may go into the hereafter with them. Lavinia, daughter of Titus, is betrothed to Bassianus, the brother of Saturninus, the newly elected Emperor of Rome. Titus plans to marry Lavinia to Saturninus, but Bassianus, assisted by Lavinia's brothers, carries her off. The Emperor marries Tamora and forgives his brother and Lavinia. At a hunting party, assisted by her paramour, Aaron, a Moor, Tamora and her sons take their revenge on Titus by murdering Bassianus; the young men rape and mutilate the innocent Lavinia, who is revenged in turn by Titus. It is Shakespeare's worst play.

TO LET (1921), by John Galsworthy. See FORSYTE SAGA, THE, by John Galsworthy.

TO THE LIGHTHOUSE (1927), by Virginia Woolf. There is no plot with climax and conclusion in this English novel, but rather the gradual unfolding of human character. The story concerns Mr. and Mrs. Ramsay, their children, and several of their friends—Lily Briscoe, an artist; William Bankes, a scientist; Charles Tansley, an intellectual with an inferiority complex; and Mr. Carmichael, a poet. Mrs. Ramsay, the central figure, is a charming and beautiful woman with a deep understanding of other people. The first section, "The Window," presents a day at the Ramsays' summer house on the sea where they are giving a houseparty. A visit to the lighthouse is planned and then canceled. Gradually the reader becomes acquainted with the various characters and particularly Mrs. Ramsay's effect upon them. The middle section, "Time Passes," is a record of the passage of ten years, told mainly in poetic descriptions of the abandoned house. Through interpolation the reader discovers that Mrs. Ramsay has died, Andrew and Prue, two of her children, are dead also, Mr. Carmichael has become a famous poet, and a marriage has failed. The last section, "The Lighthouse," presents another morning at the house. Mr. Ramsay takes Cam and James on the trip to the lighthouse; Lily Briscoe finally completes the picture of the house she had started ten years before. Throughout the book the reader is conscious of the lighthouse as the symbol of the changing light and darkness of human relationship and the alternating joy and despair in human life.

TOBACCO ROAD (1932), by Erskine Caldwell. The Georgia back country is the squalid setting for this novel (later a most popular play) of the degraded family of sharecropper Jeeter Lester and his sick wife, Ada. There is no proper plot, but an episodic chain of events which include the following: Neighbor Lov Benson, husband of twelve-year-old Pearl Lester, calls on Jeeter and is robbed by him while Jeeter's ugly daughter Ellie May distracts him; Jeeter's widowed preacher sister Bessie Rice bribes his sixteen-year-old son Dude to marry her by purchasing a new automobile; Jeeter makes vain attempts to gain credit to farm his sterile acres; Dude crashes the automobile, causing the death of his grandmother; and at length a fire destroys the house and the Lesters.

God's Little Acre (1933) concerns the Georgia mountaineer Ty Ty Walden, who has been digging for gold for fifteen years, but always retains the proceeds of one acre for the church. In his family are daughter Darling Jill, who invites the advances of all men; and daughter Rosamund, whose husband Will Thompson is enamored of Griselda, wife of Buck Walden. Will dies in a miners' strike, and Buck commits suicide after shooting his brother Jim, also enamored of Griselda. Ty Ty is grief-stricken, but primarily concerned with his prospecting.

The distinguished short stories of Caldwell have been collected in *Jackpot* (1940).

TOILERS OF THE SEA (1866), by Victor Hugo. See MISÉRABLES, LES, by Victor Hugo.

TOM (1935), by E. E. Cummings. See ENORMOUS ROOM, THE, by E. E. Cummings.

TOM BROWN'S SCHOOL DAYS (1857), by Thomas Hughes. This story of school life at the great English public school of Rugby is interestingly and accurately done. The author spoke from first-hand experience, for he was an "old boy" himself. He wrote the story when he was still young enough to remember and appreciate the feelings of the schoolboy. Tom Brown's life is depicted from his very early childhood at home before he enters the public school until his graduation from Rugby. An all-round, typical middle-class English boy, Tom enters Rugby's lowest form, where he is subjected to the hazing of the older boys and is required, according to the system of the day, to fag for them. Homesick and shy at first, Tom soon becomes a part of the school. He forms some oddly contrasting friendships. His best friend, East, is an irresponsible, mischievous fellow like Tom, impetuous, boisterous, and with a sincere belief that rules are made to be broken with impunity. On the other hand, Tom is greatly influenced by Arthur, a gentle, intelligent, idealistic boy. Arthur has a decidedly good effect on Tom, teaching him by example and pleading that learning can be accomplished without cribbing. Tom shows both his love of fair play and his pluckiness when he fights a much bigger boy to defend

Arthur. The character of the headmaster, Dr. Arnold, is also well drawn, with a sincere appreciation of the influence of this great educator on the lives of his boys. Never exceptional in his studies, Tom develops into a husky, athletic young man of eighteen, the head of his school; he prepares to enter Oxford. (*Tom Brown at Oxford* is the inferior sequel—1868.) The book abounds in refreshing and vigorous scenes of school life on the playfield and in the living halls. It gives as well a realistic picture of the teaching methods and social life of nineteenth-century Rugby.

TOM JONES, A FOUNDLING, THE HISTORY OF (1749), by Henry Fielding. One of the great realistic novels in the English language, the story of Tom Jones opens inauspiciously when Squire Allworthy finds him, an infant, crying in his bed. This extremely honest and kindhearted man believes that a young village girl, Jenny Jones, is the mother of the child. although actually it is his vinegary sister Bridget's. Jenny is paid by Bridget to keep up the pretense. Later Bridget, who cannot help showing her love for Tom, marries the fortune-hunter, Captain Blifil, who dies shortly afterward of a stroke. Their only son, William, is a wretch who behaves in a mean and jealous way toward the unfortunate Tom. As they grow older they both fall in love with Sophia Western, the daughter of a hearty neighboring squire. The cards are consistently stacked against Tom. Although he is sincerely in love with Sophia, he is a sower of wild oats and has an affair with Molly Seagrim, a worthless hussy, whom he defends when all turn from her. His misfortunes finally lead his uncle, Squire Allworthy, to disinherit him. Tom wanders aimlessly about; he has an affair with Jenny Jones, now Mrs. Waters, in an inn. His grief is indescribable when he is untruthfully informed that Jenny is his mother. Tom has a good heart; he gives his last two guineas to a highwayman when he discovers that he has been driven to crime by desperate poverty. Tom also has a sensitive conscience; he regards himself as a low blackguard unworthy of the virtuous Sophia. But after many troubling as well as diverting experiences, amours, duels and unconscious chivalrous acts, he is finally revealed to the world as Tom Allworthy. He marries Sophia and makes a devoted husband and a good citizen. Squire Allworthy is one of the most famous characterizations in English fiction.

TOM SAWYER, THE ADVENTURES OF (1878), by Mark Twain (Samuel L. Clemens). This nostalgic tale of young adventure in the small Mississippi River town of St. Petersburg is an American classic. Mischievous Tom and his serious brother Sid live with generous Aunt Polly. After a childish quarrel with his sweetheart, Becky Thatcher, Tom goes with his friend Huck Finn on a nocturnal adventure. By chance they see Injun Joe, a half-breed, stab to death the town doctor, and place the knife in the hands of Muff Potter, a drunkard. Later the two and Joe Harper hide on Jackson's Island. A funeral service for the lost boys ends in reconciliations with Aunt Polly and Becky; next the lovers, while lost in a cave after a school picnic, discover Injun Joe's hiding place. The criminal is later discovered dead, and the boys divide the reward. Huck reluctantly permits himself to be adopted by the Widow Douglas, upon Tom's promise that he will be admitted to his robber gang anyway. An early sequence is Tom's trick, when made to whitewash a fence as punishment, of inducing friends to do the work, by pretending that it is fun and a great privilege.

There were two unimportant Tom Sawyer sequels, neither so famous as the original, *Tom Sawyer Abroad* (1894) and *Tom Sawyer, Detective* (1896). The companion piece, *The Adventures of Huckleberry Finn* (q.v.), a picaresque classic of the Mississippi, and certainly the best of this group, is also a book for readers of all ages.

The Prince and the Pauper (1882), contains much social criticism of Tudor England, but has been thoughtlessly considered only a book for children. In sixteenth-century England there are two boys who chance to be "doubles" in appearance, Edward, Prince of Wales (later Edward VI), and Tom Canty, a pauper. In a speculative mood, Edward exchanges clothes with Tom. The young prince then wanders through London slums, living with beggars, thieves, and murderers; while Tom idles luxuriously in the King's palace. Tiring of this enlightening experience, Edward tries to reveal again his true identity, whereupon he is thrown into jail as an imposter. Just as Tom is about to be crowned king, however, Edward enters and succeeds in convincing all that he is the rightful heir. His experiences have taught him the necessity of being a just ruler.

TOM SAWYER ABROAD (1894), by Mark Twain. See TOM SAWYER, THE ADVENTURES OF, by Mark Twain.

TOM SAWYER, DETECTIVE (1896), by Mark Twain. See TOM SAWYER, THE ADVENTURES OF, by Mark Twain.

TOMCAT MURR'S VIEWS OF LIFE (1820–1822), by E. T. A. Hoffman. See HOFFMAN, E. T. A.

TOMMY AND GRIZEL (1900), by Sir James M. Barrie. See SENTIMENTAL TOMMY, by Sir James M. Barrie.

TOMORROW AND TOMORROW (1931), by Philip Barry. See BARRY, PHILIP.

TOMORROW WILL BE BETTER (1948), by Betty Smith. See TREE GROWS IN BROOKLYN, A (1943), by Betty Smith.

TONG-MOON-SUN (1478). *Tong-Moon-Sun,* published in 1478 by a royal commission of 23 scholars, is a selection of Korean writers from the close of the Silla Dynasty to the middle of the fifteenth century. It is in 130 books, usually bound in 50 volumes, containing all the best known Korean writers in *belles lettres* up to that time. A supplementary collection of the original 1478 edition came out in 1518. It is very difficult today to get a complete set of the original printing. In 1914 a reprinting of this book in small type with very thin paper produced seven closely printed volumes.

Some of the writers represented in this collection are: Sul Chong (ca. 700); Choi Chiwon (858–910), regarded as the father of Korean literature; An Yu (1243–1306); Im Kandsoo (ca. 660); Wang Ichun (1088); Li Ryung (ca. 1124).

TONIO KROEGER (1903), by Thomas Mann. See MANN, THOMAS.

TONO-BUNGAY (1909), by H. G. Wells. Through a deceptively art-less, confidential style, illustrated by the divulgence of the main events of the plot in the opening paragraphs and many digressions, Wells makes this both an interesting novel and an impressive attack upon irresponsible capitalism. George Ponderevo tells his own story, first recalling Bladesover, the "Great House" where his mother was housekeeper, from which at fourteen he was banished for thrashing a young nobleman, brother of Beatrice, his first love. He goes to live with his uncle, Edward Ponderevo, a struggling chemist, who squanders George's inheritance in foolish speculation. George wins a scholar-ship to the University of London. Edward Ponderevo, now a druggist's clerk in London, launches Tono-Bungay, "slightly injurious rubbish at one-and-three half-pence a bottle." He begs George to use his business ability to "make Tono-Bungay hum." George, knowing it a swindle, accepts the opportunity to make money so that he can marry Marion, a dull, conventional girl from whom he is later divorced. The phenomenal success of Tono-Bungay is due to Edward Ponderevo's genius for dishonest advertising as well as to George's business management; both uncle and nephew grow wealthy and powerful. But Susan, Edward's loyal wife, whom George has always admired, recognizes that her husband is so intoxicated by his imagination that he believes his own extravagant fictions about the patent medicine and others, developed as side lines. She is afraid. George, interested in airplanes, neglects business. He meets Beatrice again, but their love for each other is rendered futile by Beatrice's clandestine relation with another man. Suddenly the Tono-Bungay dream collapses. George fruitlessly attempts to save his uncle from bankruptcy in a mysterious, dangerous trip to Africa to get quap, a valuable radioactive sub-stance, which sinks the returning boat. Collecting the quap, George murders an unknown, overcurious native. He rescues his dying uncle from certain im-prisonment, flying him across the channel in his airship.

TORQUATO TASSO (1789), by Johann Wolfgang von Goethe. See GOETHE, JOHANN WOLFGANG VON.

TORRENTS OF SPRING (1871), by Ivan Sergeyevich Turgenev. Sometimes translated as *Spring Freshets,* this short novel is one of the most exquisite of its period. As in *Smoke* (q.v.), a young man loves a pure, sweet young girl, but forsakes her for the woman of thirty, knowledgeable and lascivious, mature in the ways of sex, a woman loved by many men, who uses the hero for a plaything. Gemma, the Italian girl in this novella, is one of the most beautiful in Turgenev's gallery of lovely girls. When the story opens, Sanin, the young man, has stopped off in Frankfort on his way home from Italy. He enters a confectionery shop and assists a youth in a swoon, earning the gratitude of the mother and sister, who own the shop. The sister is the heroine, Gemma. At the time she is engaged to a worthy and prosperous Ger-man clerk, Herr Kluber. On a Sunday excursion, when Sanin accompanies Gemma and her fiancé, she is accosted by a drunken German officer. It leads to a duel, but the duel is a farce, the officer firing in the air. Gemma, however, now breaks her engagement, and shortly announces to her mother that she loves Sanin. Sanin decides to sell his estate in Russia and raise funds for their marriage. While he is looking for a buyer he runs across Poltsov, a former school friend. Poltsov has married a wealthy and beautiful woman. Sanin hopes he can get her to buy his estate. He accompanies Poltsov to Wiesbaden, where his wife, Maria Nikolaevna, is staying. Madame Poltsov proves to be as sensuous as she is beautiful. She defers the purchase of the estate until she has Sanin under her thumb. The skill of Maria Nikolaevna is so great that this does not take long. Sanin now forsakes Gemma and goes back to Italy with the Poltsovs.

Years later, middle-aged, weary and bitter, Sanin goes to Frankfort to try to find Gemma. The officer with whom he had fought the duel so long ago helps him. He ultimately discovers that Gemma has married a merchant and is living in America. He writes to her. She answers, not disagreeably, as she feels that Sanin has in a small way contributed to her present happiness. She sends him a picture of her eighteen-year-old daughter, who is the image of Gemma as she was when Sanin met her. The girl is about to be married. Sanin sends her a gorgeous pearl necklace, to which he attaches a tiny garnet cross which Gemma gave him at the time of their engagement. This romantic idyl is comparable to Turgenev's finest work of the sixties.

TORTILLA FLAT (1935), by John Steinbeck. See GRAPES OF WRATH, THE, by John Steinbeck.

TOTTEL'S MISCELLANY—SONGS AND SONNETS (1557). This is a famous anthology of love lyrics, most of which were written by Sir Thomas Wyatt (1503–1542) and Henry Howard, Earl of Surrey (1516–1547), pioneers in the English sonnet. Wyatt wrote in addition many delightful songs, such as the three quatrains of octosyllabic lines, "Madame, withouten many words. . . ." Surrey's sonnets are nearer Shakespeare's in form certainly, Wyatt's perhaps nearer in content. The important collection of 271 poems names only four other contributors, Nicholas Grimald, Edward Somerset, Thomas Lord Vaux, and John Heywood, the dramatist, it still being the period of shy or careless anonymity. Published a year before Queen Elizabeth began her long reign, *Tottel's Miscellany* foreshadows the great flowering to come.

TOWARD FREEDOM (1941), by Jawaharlal Nehru. Often men of celebrity write their autobiographies out of a desire to carve themselves a niche in immortality. Jawaharlal Nehru's autobiography, *Toward Freedom,* is instead the modest story of his life and suffering, a mirror in which the vast tragedy of India's plight and problems are reflected. For twenty-five years a leader of the Indian movement for independence, and for more than twelve years a prisoner in British jails to expiate for his ardent love of country, he has emerged as one of the great moral personalities of our time. *Toward Freedom* is the personal narrative of a man who loves humanity. The scion of a great and wealthy Brahmin family, he was at first inclined toward aestheticism and the "charming life," but the massacre at Amritsar by General Dyer shocked him into an awareness of the rape of his country. Nehru was then thirty, but he became transformed. Together with other patriotic and generous spirits he flung himself into the Indian independence movement. Though educated in England, and despite his hereditary wealth, he sees the final solution to his country's troubles in a socialist society. He was opposed in this to Gandhi. He deplored Gandhi's bourgeois nationalism and religious fanaticism, which he regarded as an obstacle to India's progress. Nehru was also revolted by Gandhi's glorification of poverty as a virtue; the plight of the starving millions in India fills him only with wretchedness and anger.

TOWARD THE FLAME (1926), by Hervey Allen. See ANTHONY ADVERSE, by Hervey Allen.

TOWARD THE MORNING (1948), by Hervey Allen. See ANTHONY ADVERSE, by Hervey Allen.

TOWER, THE (1928), by William Butler Yeats. See YEATS, WILLIAM BUTLER.

TOWN DOWN THE RIVER, THE (1910), by Edwin Arlington Robinson. See ROBINSON, EDWIN ARLINGTON.

TRACK OF THE CAT, THE (1949), by Walter Van Tilburg Clark. See OX-BOW INCIDENT, THE, by Walter Van Tilburg Clark.

TRACTATUS DE ARTE NUMERANDI (printed ca. 1490), by Joannes de Sacrobosco.

TRACTATUS THEOLOGICO-POLITICUS (1670), by Benedict de Spinoza. In a letter to Oldenburg, the Secretary of the Royal Society of England, Spinoza wrote in the autumn of 1665: "I am now writing a Treatise about my interpretation of Scripture." This was the *Tractatus,* the most important document in the establishment of Biblical criticism. Written in Latin, it was prudently published under the imprint of a fictitious printer of Hamburg in order to elude the inquisitorial Calvinists. Spinoza, however, was not adept at deception. When he was detected, religious zealots denounced the *Tractatus* as a work "forged in Hell by a renegade Jew and the Devil." The Synod of Amsterdam condemned it; the other synods followed suit, and asked the authorities to suppress it. Instead, the *Tractatus* went through five editions in a short time, each edition appearing under a different fictitious title, one as a medical book, another as a history, etc.

The *Tractatus* was originally planned as a political treatise to be put into the hands of Spinoza's liberal friend, the Grand Pensionary De Witt, as a potent weapon with which to fight the Calvinists. Its thesis, dispassionately propounded, was: only through the unceasing extension of knowledge can freedom of thought and religion be achieved. The choice of Holy Scripture was only a convenient springboard for the attack against the theologians. Spinoza, in analyzing the Bible, applied to it the methods of natural science so that thereby he might the better expose the self-righteous clergy. He drew freely upon history, grammar and lexicography for his refutation. He denied that the Bible was an esoteric work, or contained supernatural truth, or was in any conceivable way miraculous. He regarded it as a compendium of practical and precise social and moral laws and as a code of behavior.

Spinoza went to great lengths to prove that the functions of theology and philosophy are different, and called for a permanent divorce of the two. He defended the State against the unwarranted interference in its affairs by the Church, and *vice versa,* declaring that that State alone can be free and happy which rests on the freedom of the individual citizen. Bigotry and oppression encourage hypocrisy, destroy truth and mutilate virtue. The *Tractatus* concludes with a moving plea for freedom of speech and thought and for freedom of conscience.

TRADICIONES PERUANAS (1860–1906), by Ricardo Palma. See PERUVIAN TRADITIONS, by Ricardo Palma.

TRAGEDIES, by Seneca (Lucius Annaeus Seneca; ca. 4 B.C., 65 A.D.). The nine tragedies written by the great Roman moralist bear names and deal with mythical subjects familiar from Greek tragedy of the fifth century B.C., but his style and dramatic technique is something far different. In making comparisons, however, we must remember that Seneca was not trying to write Greek tragedy. The plays were probably not intended for production on the stage but rather for reading. Though there are many spectacular scenes, the place of action is often taken by description. The characters are made to philosophize like veritable Stoics in long and tedious speeches which often make a great parade of learning. The dominant note throughout the tragedies is that of horror, upon which Seneca dwells with a truly Roman predilection. The titles are: *Mad Hercules, Hercules on Oeta, Trojan Women, Phoenician Women, Medea, Phaedra, Oedipus, Thyestes* and *Agamemnon.* The *Octavia,* which is preserved along with these, is the only extant Roman tragedy on a historical subject, but it is almost certainly not by Seneca. These tragedies exercised a very strong influence on drama in Italy, France, and England for centuries after the Renaissance. The *Phaedra,* e.g., was imitated by Racine in his *Phèdre* (q.v.) and by d'Annunzio in his *Fedra.*

TRAGEDY OF PUDD'NHEAD WILSON, THE (1894), by Mark Twain. See LIFE ON THE MISSISSIPPI, by Mark Twain.

TRAGIC SENSE OF LIFE, THE (1912), by Miguel de Unamuno. As an adherent of feeling and intellectual skepticism Unamuno expounds here his philosophy of pessimism that is dipped in Catholicism. Because he is skeptical he cannot reach any conclusion; he therefore falls back on mystical feeling. The only true philosopher, according to him, is he who feels and lives in the world. Such a man derives a tragic sense from life because of his compassion for human suffering. In history there have been many such: Marcus Aurelius, St. Augustine, Pascal, Rousseau, James Thomson, Kierkegaard, Amiel and De Vigny. There are also "peoples who possess this tragic sense of life," states Unamuno. For these it is no longer possible to reconcile faith with reason. Therefore like Don Quixote they go a-questing not for ideas but for spirit.

TRAGICOMEDIA DE CALIXTO Y MELIBEA (1499), by Fernando de Rojas. See CELESTINA, by Fernando de Rojas.

TRAIL OF '98 (1910), by Robert W. Service. See SERVICE, ROBERT W.

TRAIL OF THE LONESOME PINE, THE (1908), by John Fox, Jr. June Tolliver is the barefoot, illiterate daughter of a mountaineer. Into her life comes engineer John Hale, coal prospecting and searching for industrial sites. He is appalled by the absurdity of feuding, especially since June's father, "Devil" Judd Tolliver, is involved. Physical symbol of romance is a giant pine tree on a mountain. The lovers find their way to it. June's cousin,

Dave, who is in love with her, swears to kill the interloper, and misunderstandings inevitable to romance occur; but in the end, after Dave and Judd are dead, the lovers are united.

Another sentimental melodrama of the mountains is *The Little Shepherd of Kingdom Come* (1902), about Chad Buford. Mountain girl Melissa Turner loves him, and saves his life during the Civil War, at the expense of her own. Chad clears up a mystery concerning his parentage, and marries Margaret Dean of Lexington.

TRAITÉ DE LA LUMIÈRE (1690), by Christiaan Huygens. Christiaan Huygens, the "Dutch Archimedes," published his celebrated *Treatise on Light* at Leyden in 1690. It consisted of an explanation in terms of wave motion of reflection and refraction, especially of the remarkable double refraction noted by physicists when light passes through Iceland spar. Huygens was at work on this epoch-making volume for twelve years. In his preface the author ventures the hope "that those who enjoy finding out causes and who appreciate the wonders of light will be interested in these various explanations and in the new explanation of that remarkable property [refraction] upon which the structure of the human eye depends and upon which are based those instruments which so powerfully aid the eye." He apologizes for being baffled by various optical problems and especially by the whole question of color: "Finally, there is much more to be learned by investigation concerning the nature of light than I have yet discovered; and I shall be greatly indebted to those who, in the future, shall furnish what is needed to complete my imperfect knowledge."

In Huygens' day there were two chief views as to the nature of light. One of these, inherited from the Pythagoreans and given modern scientific form by Newton, looked upon an optical ray as a stream of tiny particles or corpuscles traveling from the luminous object to the eye of the observer. The other, derived from Aristotle and maintained by Hooke, regarded light as a disturbance propagated in a medium. In 1678, spurred by Roemer's discovery of the finite velocity of light, Huygens fashioned the second doctrine into a clear-cut undulatory theory. He assumed that all space is pervaded by an exceedingly subtle and elastic medium, the ether, through which light waves are propagated in all directions from a source. He proposed an ingenious theory, known as "Huygens' principle," to explain the phenomena of reflection and refraction. He looked upon a source of light as emitting a series of spherical waves in the ether; and any point on the surface of such a wave in turn may be thought of as a source of new spherical wavelets; and so on indefinitely. At any distance from the original source the surface of all these waves can be regarded as combining together to form a "wave-front," and it is this which is the basis of optical phenomena. His theory accounted for the known facts in the science of optics (except for polarization); but it implied—contrary to the corpuscular theory—that the velocity of light is less in a dense medium, such as water, than it is in air. Not until over a hundred and fifty years later (in about 1850) was it possible for Foucault to perform the crucial experiment of determining the relative speeds of light in air and water, the results of which clearly confirmed the theory of Huygens. Meanwhile, the prestige of Newton so dominated eighteenth-century thought that the wave theory found few supporters until Thomas Young in 1801 explained interference phenomena. When Young and Fresnel introduced the idea that light waves are transverse periodic vibrations, the wave theory was firmly established.

Huygens contributed extensively to the fields of mathematics, astronomy, and mechanics, as well as to optics, and his collected works fill over a score of large volumes. He is well known for the discovery of the rings of Saturn and for the invention of the pendulum clock; but the wave theory of light was his greatest contribution to science. In 1690 he amplified his early work of a dozen years before and published it in his classic *Traité de la Lumière*. This great volume, translated into English in 1912, is one of the high spots in the history of optics.

TRAITÉ ÉLÉMENTAIRE DE CHIMIE (1789), by Antoine Laurent Lavoisier. The publication of this celebrated *Elementary Treatise of Chemistry* marks what often is referred to as the beginning of modern chemistry. The book is divided formally into three parts, of which the first deals with the formation and properties of gases and of caloric ("the cause of heat, the highly elastic fluid which produces it"), with oxidation, fermentation, and putrefaction, and with the composition of air, water, acids, bases, and salts. The second part opens with Lavoisier's well-known description of a chemical element or "simple substance," and includes the first clear-cut list of substances regarded then as elements. This table includes thirty-three substances, of which about half a dozen are known now not to be true elements. Lavoisier himself was skeptical of the nature of lime, magnesia, silica, baryta, and alumina, but he counted them among the elements because they had not yet been decomposed. Heat and light, which he included, also are no longer regarded as elements. The second part of the *Traité* consists largely of tables of nomenclature of chemical compounds. The new chemical terms, essentially those still in current use, had been devised by de Morveau, Berthollet, de Fourcroy, and Lavoisier, and had been published in their *Méthode de Nomenclature Chimique* two years before. The third part of the *Traité* deals with apparatus and methods of chemical experimentation, and includes many engraved plates drawn up by Lavoisier's wife.

The *Traité* summarizes material and ideas upon which Lavoisier had worked for a score of years. At the age of twenty-two he had presented his first paper, on the analysis of gypsum, to the Académie des Sciences in 1765. In 1770 he had shown that water is not converted, even partly, into earth by repeated distillation. In 1774 he had demonstrated that the increase in weight in the calcination of tin (and of other metals) is at the expense of the air, the gain in weight of the one being equal to the loss in weight of the other. The law of the conservation of mass, which Lavoisier here emphasized, has been a cornerstone of modern chemistry. This makes it possible to express chemical changes in the form of equations in which the combined weight of materials used must be equal to the total weight of the products. This scheme, his colleague Lagrange said, makes chemistry as simple as algebra. Lavoisier's experiments on the composition of air and water were subsequent to those of Priestley and Cavendish, but his interpretation of these, especially in a memoir, "Réflexions sur le Phlogistique," presented to the Académie in 1783, virtually destroyed the phlogiston theory, replacing it by the modern oxygen theory of combustion.

The success of the *Traité Élémentaire de Chimie* was enormous. Lavoisier's ideas and terminology were almost universally adopted, and the doctrine of phlogiston, upon which much of the earlier chemical work had rested, quickly disappeared. So rapid was the transformation that it often is referred to as the "chemical revolution," and Lavoisier frequently is hailed as the "father of modern chemistry."

TRANSLATIONS OF HOMER (1715-1726), by Alexander Pope. Pope's keen instinct for the wants of the new middle class, who were eager to appear cultured, yet could not read the original Greek of the classics, led him to translate Homer's *Iliad* (q.v.), a project particularly ambitious, as Pope was not a sound Greek scholar, and his health was poor. But, aided by his natural facility for writing impeccable verse and by the use of previous translations, Pope finished the task in five years. He went on, in 1725, to translate (with the assistance of Fenton and Broome, who did half of it) the *Odyssey* (q.v.), and the profits from the two publications made him a wealthy man. The translations, in heroic couplets, are smooth and effective, but, as Bentley told Pope, they are not Homer. Pope, in translating, expands his original about fifteen per cent. In many instances he misses the meaning of his original. He is artificial and elegant where Homer is direct and primitive. But his translations were perfectly suited to the taste of the times in which he made them. His faults were not unaccompanied by reverence for Homer. He felt, as he said in his preface, "utterly incapable of doing justice to Homer."

TRAVELER FROM ALTRURIA, A (1894), by William Dean Howells. See HAZARD OF NEW FORTUNES, A, by William Dean Howells.

TRAVELS (ca. 1298), by Marco Polo. The book tells the story of Marco's fabulous voyages in Asia. At the age of twenty-one, in company with his father, the rich Venetian merchant Nicolo, and his uncle Matteo, Marco made, for the purpose of trade, an unprecedented voyage. They wandered through the Gobi desert, the Pamir range, Tibet, China, Mongolia, Burma, Siam, Sumatra, Java, Ceylon, India and a number of hitherto unknown countries. In Bokhara the Tartar Khan Kublai soon became fond of Marco's talents and attached him to his court. Later Marco became the Khan's ambassador and Governor of Yangchow. Although the *Travels* often met with incredulity, in recent years a closer re-examination tends to corroborate the veracity of Marco's reports in most instances. The book is of no great importance from a literary viewpoint, but it is significant because it was the first report that gave some knowledge of the East to Europeans.

TRAVELS OF BENJAMIN III (1878; Eng. tr. 1949), by Mendele Mocher Sefarim. See MENDELE MOCHER SEFARIM.

TRAVELS OF SIR JOHN MANDEVILLE, THE (14th c.). By the best evidence there was no such person as Sir John Mandeville, and the experiences recorded here are purely fictitious, having been compiled from a number of sources, dating back in some instances at least as far as Pliny. Pretending to be a sort of guide for pilgrims to Jerusalem, Sir John describes various routes, which gives the author an opportunity for all manner of odd episodes and for the inclusion of fables of both a devout and secular nature. The author gives riot to his fancy; we read about a woman turned into a dragon, and about a giant bound in chains before Noah's flood. This portion of the book also includes some legends of Sinai and Egypt, and is followed by an animated account of the courts of the Great Cham and Prester John. India comes into the picture, as well as China, and other Eastern countries, to which the author irrationally refers as "islands." The entire narrative is a mixture of reality and fantasy. This book was known in several languages for several centuries, and was accepted as the authentic experience of an authentic person. Its manner of writing, however, is sufficiently impressive to have deceived its many readers.

TREASURE ISLAND (1883), by Robert Louis Stevenson. Stevenson says that he drew a treasure map first and labeled it Treasure Island. When he looked at the map the characters seemed to come to life for him, and their adventures formed themselves in his mind. The story is told in the first person by Jim Hawkins, whose mother kept the Admiral Benbow Inn, and who shared in the adventures from start to finish. An old sea dog comes to this peaceful inn one day, apparently intending to finish his life there. He hires Jim to keep a watch out for other sailors, but despite all precautions, he is hunted out and served with the black spot that means death. Jim and his mother barely escape death when Blind Pew, Black Dog, and other pirates descend on the inn in search of the sea dog's papers. Jim snatches up a packet of papers to square the sailor's debt, when they were forced to retreat from the inn. The packet contains a map showing the location of the pirate Flint's buried treasure, which Jim, Doctor Livesey, and Squire Trelawney determine to find. Fitting out a ship, they hire hands and set out on their adventure. Unfortunately, their crew includes one-legged Long John Silver, a pirate also in search of the treasure, and a number of his confederates. Jim, hidden in an apple barrel, overhears the plans of the crew to mutiny, and he warns his comrades. The battle between the pirates and Jim's party is an exciting and bloody one, taking place both on the island and aboard ship. Jim escapes from the ship, discovers the marooned sailor, Ben Gunn, who has already found and cached the treasure, and finally the victors get safely aboard the ship with the treasure. All this is told in the simple classic prose, clear and rhythmical, which has made Stevenson famous.

TREASURER'S REPORT, THE (1930), by Robert Benchley. See BENCHLEY, ROBERT.

TREASURY OF AMERICAN FOLKLORE, A (1944), by Benjamin A. BOTKIN. See BOTKIN, BENJAMIN A.

TREASURY OF NEW ENGLAND FOLKLORE, A (1947), by Benjamin A. Botkin. See BOTKIN, BENJAMIN A.

TREASURY OF SOUTHERN FOLKLORE, A (1949), by Benjamin A. Botkin. See BOTKIN, BENJAMIN A.

1REATISE ON CONIC SECTIONS (ca. 225 b.c.), by Apollonius of Perga. The geometry of the straight line and the circle goes back to the ancient Egyptians and Babylonians, but only with the Greeks was it developed as a logically organized field of study—one of the seven liberal arts. By the middle of the fifth century b.c. this development had reached the point where Hippocrates of Chios is said to have composed a book of *Elements* on the circle and straight line. It was shortly after this that a new stage was initiated in mathematics through the introduction of the three famous "classical problems": the trisection of the angle, the squaring of the circle, and the duplication of the cube. The original intention was that these problems were to be solved by the use only of circles and straight line; but failing to solve them in this way, Greek geometers looked about for other curves to use in the solution. It was not long before the first new curve, known as the trisectrix or quadratrix, was discovered and applied in the solution of the first two problems. The duplication problem at first resisted all efforts to solve it, but in the following century Menaechmus, tutor of Alexander the Great, discovered curves which sufficed to solve the third problem. These were the conic sections—the parabola, ellipse, and hyperbola— a family of curves which has played an essential role in mathematics and science ever since. What Menaechmus wrote on the conics has been lost, as has also the treatise on the same curves written a little later by Euclid, author of the famous *Elements*. However, there is extant, almost in its entirety, the work which marks the culmination of the Greek study of these curves—the *Treatise on Conic Sections* of Apollonius. Of the eight books in this treatise only the first four have survived in Greek; the next three have been preserved in Arabic translation, and the last is lost. The subject of conics is taken up from the very elements; but the treatment advances rapidly, and roughly the last half of the work is on original results contributed by the author. Apollonius is responsible for obtaining all three types of conics from a single oblique circular cone of two nappes, and it was he who introduced the names ever since used for the three curves—parabola, ellipse, and hyperbola. So far did he carry the development of the subject of conics that some of his theorems are equivalent to the theory of evolutes.

There are about a dozen mathematical works ascribed to Appolonius; but, apart from his *Conics,* only one, *On the Cutting-off of a Ratio,* is extant (through the Arabic). In the case of the others, only fragments, brief descriptions, or mere titles have come down to us. Nevertheless, so admirable is his *Treatise on Conic Sections* that this has been sufficient to earn for him, rather than for Euclid, the title "the great geometer" of antiquity.

TREATISE ON ELECTRICITY AND MAGNETISM (1873), by James Clerk-Maxwell. In 1855 Clerk-Maxwell (1831–1874) published a paper on "Faraday's lines of force," and for a score of years thereafter he devoted himself to a study of the nature of electrical phenomena. For Faraday's lines, Maxwell substituted the concept of rotating cylinders. At the time of his early work, there was a wide separation between mathematical theory and experimental results. Faraday had not been an analyst, and it was Maxwell who translated his results into mathematical language. The final presentation of Maxwell's views is given in his greatest work, the *Treatise on Electricity and Magnetism.* In the preface he wrote: "I was aware that there was supposed to be a difference be-tween Faraday's way of conceiving phenomena and that of the mathematicians, so that neither he nor they were satisfied with each other's language. I had also the conviction that this discrepancy did not arise from either party being wrong. I was first convinced of this by Sir William Thomson." He says that he has confined himself almost entirely to the mathematical treatment of the subject, but he recommends that the student "read carefully Faraday's *Experimental Researches in Electricity*" (q.v.). Maxwell postulates little about the nature of elec-tricity, and the doubt he expressed about its atomicity has proved to be mistaken. However, in his *Treatise* are found the famous "Maxwell equations" from which the modern radio has arisen. The most striking consequence of Maxwell's the-ory is that electrical disturbances are propagated as transverse waves of electrical and magnetic force. His calculation showed that the velocity of these should be equal to the speed of light; and this suggested that light waves are electro-magnetic waves. Maxwell's electromagnetic theory of light met the test of ex-periments performed by physicists. Not until after his death, however, was the production and detection of electromagnetic waves (other than light waves) car-ried out. Helmholtz was one of the first Continental scientists to accept the Maxwell theory, and he proposed to his student, Hertz, the experimental verifica-tion of the existence of electromagnetic waves. Using the electrical discharge between two metal balls, Hertz in 1888 produced the Hertzian or radio waves which Maxwell in his *Treatise* had predicted, and he showed that they have properties similar to those of light waves.

TREATISE ON HUMAN NATURE (1739), by David Hume. Hume's *Treatise on Human Nature* was a product of his youth; published when he was 28, it failed to make any impression on the public. Later versions of the first part (*Inquiry concerning the Human Understanding,* 1749) and of the second part (*Inquiry concerning the Principles of Morals,* 1751) were better received. Hume's influence on subsequent philosophy was enormous. He awakened Kant "from his dogmatic slumbers." He posed the central problems for the British empiricist school in the eighteenth and nineteenth centuries. Contemporary log-ical positivists and analytic philosophers continue to study and restate his ideas. The problems that Hume was concerned with were the origin of knowledge, its limits, and its relation to morality. Continuing the empiricist tradition of Locke and Berkeley, he believed that all knowledge starts with sensation. How-ever, Berkeley's use of God to account for the stability and persistence of phe-nomena did not satisfy Hume. The problem of the connections between phenom-ena becomes incapable of solution in empirical terms. How do we know that one phenomenon causes another? We cannot immediately sense the causal rela-tion, since we sense only atomic phenomena, individual sense impressions. Hume accounts for the belief in causation, that certain events produce subsequent events, in terms of psychological habits resulting from the association of ideas. This philosophic conclusion leads Hume to develop a naturalistic moral theory. He bases morality on the natural interests and propensities of men. His religious ideas are not clear from his *Dialogues on Natural Religion* (1779), though his critique of the belief in miracles has become famous.

TREATISE ON LIGHT (1690; Eng. tr. 1912), by Christiaan Huygens. See *Traité de la Lumière,* by Christiaan Huygens.

TREATISE ON RESURRECTION (1191),by Maimonides. See GUIDE FOR THE PERPLEXED, THE, by Maimonides.

TREATISE ON THE JEWISH CALENDAR (1158), by Maimonides. See GUIDE FOR THE PERPLEXED, THE, by Maimonides.

TREATISE ON THE SPHERE (ca. 1233), by Joannes de Sacrobosco. See SPHAERA MUNDI, by Joannes de Sacrobosco.

TREATISE ON THERMODYNAMICS (1897), by Max Planck. See ORIGIN AND DEVELOPMENT OF THE QUANTUM THEORY, THE, by Max Planck.

TREATISE ON TOLERANCE (1763), by Voltaire. The immediate provocation of this work was the tragic execution in 1762 at Toulouse of Jean Calas. This old Huguenot had been charged with the murder of his son, whose conversion to Catholicism he thus allegedly tried to frustrate. The *Treatise* is not a philosophical work in the strict sense; it is mainly an impassioned attack on bigotry and a plea for the free conscience. Voltaire begins with a moving narrative of the Calas case and employs it as a springboard for his subject: "People in Languedoc have religion enough to hate and persecute, but not enough to love and succor." Fanaticism steeped in dogma was the real murderer of old Calas, he insists. A review of history shows that man has never been so cruel as when he has waged war in the cause of religion. Voltaire compares unfavorably the cruelty, fanaticism and persecution of the Christian Church with the tolerance and civilized mellowness of pagan antiquity. On the constructive side, he illustrates the practical good of tolerance in human relations.

The *Treatise* had some intellectual influence on the American and French Revolutions.

TREE GROWS IN BROOKLYN, A (1943), by Betty Smith. This novel is the story of the Nolans, who live in a Williamsburg tenement. Johnny, the father, is a singing waiter whose weakness is drinking to forget his problems. Kate, the hard-working mother, represses her natural sentimentality because she does not want the children, Francie and Neeley, to inherit their father's dreams. At length, while Kate is pregnant, Johnny dies. The children work in McGarrity's saloon so that Francie does not have to leave school and get working papers. After Annie Laurie is born, Kate accepts the proposal of kind police officer McShane, a widower. Francie and Neeley feel that their childhood is over.

Tomorrow Will Be Better (1948) is also about the poor section of Brooklyn, in the middle 20's. It is the story of Margy Shannon, a shy but optimistic girl just out of school who dreams of a husband, home, and family better than her own dreary background. She does find a husband, young Frankie Malone, but their dream fades into the reality of life's bitter struggle, and after a slow process of disenchantment Margy becomes hardened to the same sort of existence she has always known.

TREE OF THE FOLKUNGS, THE (1905–1907; Eng. tr. 1925), by Verner von Heidenstam. See CHARLES MEN, THE, by Verner von Heidenstam.

TREK OF THE CIMBRI, THE (1922), by Johannes V. Jensen. See LONG JOURNEY, THE, by Johannes V. Jensen.

TRELAWNY OF THE "WELLS" (1898), by Arthur Wing Pinero. One of Pinero's few costume plays, the scene is laid in London in 1860. Rose Trelawny, the youthful lead of the Wells Theatre, becomes engaged to Arthur Gower, grandson of Vice-Chancellor Sir William Gower, and retires to private life. Rose finds life in Cavendish Square extremely dull and depressing; when some of her theatrical friends call one evening she permits the butler to let them in. Her father-in-law interrupts the party; Rose decides she wants to go back to the stage and parts from Arthur. She finds on her return that Tom Wench, one of the company, has written a comedy in which he wants Rose to star. He has a manager but needs capital. Sir William calls to see how Rose is getting on, and ends by supplying the necessary funds for the production.

TRIAL, THE (1925), by Franz Kafka. The novel opens when Joseph K. awakes one morning to be arrested for a crime of which he is completely unaware. Despite the fact that he is under arrest, K. may still go about his daily business. The inquiry to which he is summoned takes place in a dim tenement house garret where nothing is definite but everyone knows of K. —"it is only a trial if you recognize it as such" is the pronouncement of the presiding magistrate before a strange crowd of spectators. At home, K. finds it difficult to get to see Fräulein Bürstner, a fellow rooming-house lodger. Soon K.'s uncle, Karl, takes him to see a lawyer and judge, who happens to be ill and is attended by a girl, Leni. The lawyer offers no immediate aid but advises resignation to fate. Other quests for advice also seem fruitless. While at the Cathedral, K. observes a priest mount the steps to the pulpit. The cleric turns out to have been sent by the prison to discuss the case. He relates a parable about the guard at the entrance of the law and the newcomer who waits for admittance until the last moment of his life, only to learn just as the door is shut forever that it is meant only for him. In comment the priest states, "It is not necessary to accept everything as true, one must only accept it as necessary." Finally, two plump, formally-dressed men enter K.'s lodgings, escort him to the outskirts of the city, and plunge a knife into his heart.

Also in a fragmentary and abstruse, symbolic style are Kafka's two other posthumously published novels *The Castle* (1926) and *Amerika* (1928). Of his shorter prose the most outstanding piece is the nightmarish *Metamorphosis* (1916), the allegorical tale of a man who finds himself one morning transformed into a huge insect, is gradually excluded from human intercourse, and undergoes slow deterioration and disintegration. Prophetic of the scientific, hellishly efficient, frozen inhumanity of the police state and extermination camp is *The Penal Colony* (1919), in which a visitor to a prisoner's island inspects a sadistically ingenious execution appartus.

The Bohemian Jew Kafka, who wrote in German and died almost totally unknown in 1924, gradually is being recognized as one of the most remarkable writers of our time. His work is symbolic of the frustration of modern man.

TRIAL OF A POET (1948), by Karl J. Shapiro. See SHAPIRO, KARL J.

TRIALS AND TRIBULATIONS (1888), by Theodor Fontane. See EFFIE BRIEST, by Theodor Fontane.

TRILBY (1894), by George Du Maurier. This novel of Bohemian life in Paris in the 1890's is drawn from the author's own experiences. It relates the tragic story of Trilby O'Ferrall and Little Billee Bagot, who are parted, meet five years later, and, through fateful circumstances, both die early deaths. Trilby is an artist's model, and her friends are the artists who dub themselves "The Three Musketeers": Little Billee Bagot, Taffy (Talbot Wynne), Sandy (The Laird) McAllister. Mrs. Bagot hears of her son's engagement to Trilby and tells the girl that their marriage will ruin Billee's career. Trilby disappears and is befriended by the sinister Svengali, a musician. He hypnotizes her and teaches her to sing. She becomes his creature. Under this baleful influence she gains renown on the continent. Five years later "The Three Musketeers" find her, but she does not recognize them. At Svengali's death, in the midst of a concert she comes out of her trance, not realizing she was once a famous singer, and no longer possessing her gifts. They think her mind is affected. Trilby goes into a decline and dies. Little Billee, himself a famous artist now, dies soon after. The last part of the story is told twenty years later. Gecho, who had been violinist with Svengali and Trilby, explains the girl's strange life to Taffy and his wife, Blanche Bagot, sister of Billee. The book, illustrated by the author, had an immense vogue, introducing styles in feminine clothing and giving rise to endless popular misconceptions about the nature and powers of hypnotic influence.

TRIMMED LAMP, THE (1907), by William Sydney Porter. See PORTER, WILLIAM SYDNEY.

TRIPITAKA: THE PALI CANON OF BUDDHISM (3rd c. B.C.). *The Book of Dhammapada* and the *Dialogues of Buddha found in the Pali Canon* both belong to the same collection. There is no claim that any of the words were written by the Buddha himself, but after his death his disciples repeated and discussed what he had taught them. Probably it was in the third century B.C. that all this material was assembled, arranged in three groups called *The Three Baskets Tripitaka,* and accepted as the orthodox canon.

The most celebrated of Buddhist ethical teachings, *The Book of Dhammapada,* consists of a collection of aphorisms, and reaches a level of culture and thoughtfulness unequaled in almost any other collection of wise sayings. It is included in the canon of Buddhist Scriptures like the Book of Proverbs in the Judaeo-Christian *Bible* (q.v.), and is divided into twenty-six chapters. Its keynote is the statement: "The virtuous man is happy in this world, and he is happy in the next; he is happy in both. He is happy when he thinks of the good he has done; he is still more happy when going on the good path." The good path is described as follows: "Earnestness is the path of immortality (Nirvana), thoughtlessness the path of death; those who are in earnest do not die, those who are thoughtless are as if dead already." The moral emphasis of Buddhism can be read in the following delicate bit of irony: "Like a beautiful flower, full of color, but without fragrance, are the fine but fruitless words of him who does not act accordingly."

In the doctrinal section of the *Pali Canon,* the only complete set of Buddhist Scriptures, there are contained discourses attributed to Buddha as well as poems, legends and commentaries. Like other teachers of his time, Buddha taught by conversation. He followed, therefore, the literary custom of his period by embodying his doctrines in set phrases or *suttas* on which he enlarged on different occasions in different ways. In the sermon at Benares, in which the Buddha first outlined his teaching of the four great certainties and the eightfold middle path by which a man may secure his own salvation, he said: "Be a refuge to yourself; look not to another. . . . As a mother watches over her own child, so cultivate a loving mind toward all beings."

The Buddha thought of his religion as a religion of monks; his teachings were adapted to those who were giving up all ordinary commitments of life. Yet even in his lifetime laymen wished to learn from him, and he planned a less exacting regulation of life, asking for goodwill and compassion toward all living things.

TRIPLE THINKERS, THE (1938), by Edmund Wilson. See AXEL'S CASTLE, by Edmund Wilson.

TRISERYENE (1903), by Kostes Palamas. See PALAMAS, KOSTES.

TRISTRAM (1927), by Edwin Arlington Robinson. See ROBINSON, EDWIN ARLINGTON.

TRISTRAM AND ISEULT (1852), by Matthew Arnold. This poem takes up the story at the last stage when Tristram is dying in Brittany. Tended by Iseult of Brittany and a page, he waits eagerly for Iseult of Ireland to come and meanwhile dreamily recalls that past love. In Part II, Iseult of Ireland and Tristram have their last conversation, comparing their unhappy lots. Both die, to be buried in King Marc's chapel in Tyntagel. In Part III the surviving Iseult pensively tells her three children the story of the wily Vivian's trapping Merlin into a perpetual sleep.

TRISTRAM OF LYONESSE (1882), by Algernon Charles Swinburne. Episodes from the famous romantic story are unified in this poem by Love, the theme of the prelude. It tells in nine cantos of rhymed couplets of Tristram's visit to the Irish court of King Mark, of his love for Iseult of Ireland, and of her marriage to King Mark. Tristram and Iseult of Ireland separate and Tristram eventually marries Iseult of Brittany. When he lies dying Iseult of Ireland comes to him, but he is dead when she arrives. Most lovers of Swinburne's poetry agree that this volume is "the crown of his mature work."

TRISTRAM SHANDY, THE LIFE AND OPINIONS OF (1759–1767), by Laurence Sterne. Many readers will not regard this as a novel at all. The nominal hero is not even born until Book IV, and he soon becomes submerged in the author's whimsical digressions. Some of the little that does happen in the course of this sprawling masterpiece (to which Sterne gave the last years of his life) cannot be baldly recited, for this is a book famous for prurient innuendo. But the most memorable features are the highly original characters, such as Dr. Slop, the Widow Wadman the patient Mrs. Shandy, and above all that trio of the hero's father, uncle Toby, and Corporal Trim. Sterne called Cervantes his model, and from others (Rabelais, Montaigne, Burton) he had learned much. But by himself he looks forward to the stream-of-consciousness school of the present century. There are interpolated stories, after the manner of earlier narrative—the "Story of Le Fever" is notable; and typographically it is a hodge-podge of dashes, asterisks, foreign languages, index hands, and even a memorial slab for poor Yorick and a blank page for the reader to do his own composing on.

TRISTAN (ca. 1210), by Gottfried von Strassburg. Based upon a French model, Gottfried von Strassburg's unfinished version of the Tristan epic is supposed to have been written about 1210. Both his parents dead, Tristan is brought up by his father's vassal. He is brought to Kurnewall by kidnaping pirates and adopted by King Mark. During his adventures in disguise, Tristan meets Isolt, who heals a wound inflicted upon him by her uncle. On his return to Kurnewall Tristan tells of the wondrous beauty of Isolt; King Mark decides to take her for his queen and sends Tristan to Ireland to fetch her. On the return voyage, Tristan and Isolt accidentally drink a love potion, and her hate for him as her uncle's slayer turns to consuming passion. All semblance of honor and principle are abandoned by both. Even after Isolt's marriage to King Mark, the two continue deceit and cunning in their love affair. In hope of forgetting, Tristan flees and marries Isolt of the White Hands, but his heart is still with the other Isolt.

[Because of Gottfried's death the rest of the epic was written by Ulrich von Turkheim and Heinrich von Freiberg.] Tristan receives a wound which only the Isolt from across the sea can treat. She is summoned, and if the ship which returns bears her it is to fly white sails; if she has refused to come, black sails. The jealous Isolt of the White Hands falsely reports black sails at the sight of the ship, at which Tristan expires. Upon her arrival, Isolt dies of grief over her lover's death.

Despite Gottfried's superb rhyme, language and superior artistic sense, *Tristan* marks the beginning of the decline of chivalric culture. The epic's deftly portrayed love motif has been an inspiration for many artistic endeavors, including the music drama *Tristan and Isolde* by Richard Wagner. Gottfried's *Tristan* is available in an English version by Jessie L. Weston.

TRISTAN AND ISOLDE (1865), by Richard Wagner. See WAGNER, RICHARD.

TRIUMPH OF THE EGG, THE (1921), by Sherwood Anderson. See WINESBURG, OHIO, by Sherwood Anderson.

TROILUS AND CRESSIDA (1602?; Quarto 1609), by William Shakespeare. Shakespeare took the story from Chaucer's *Troilus and Criseyde* (q.v.), and the "camp story" from the *Recuyell of the historyes of Troye*. *Troilus and Cressida* is one of the most puzzling and most discussed of Shakespeare's plays. Coleridge remarks: "There is no one of Shakespeare's plays harder to characterize." It seems to be a satire, with Thersites as the main railer. All the Homeric heroes lose stature here. The scene is laid in Troy. Troilus, a younger brother of Paris, has fallen in love with Cressida, daughter of Calchas, the prophet who sided with the Greeks against Troy. Troilus woos her through her uncle, Pandarus, and they are separated when Calchas asks for the return of Cressida in exchange for an important Trojan prisoner, Antenor. Cressida proves faithless to her vows of true love, becoming Diomedes' mistress. The subplot deals with the intrigue of Ulysses in the Greek camp, the final conflict between Hector and Achilles, and the shamefully contrived death of Hector.

TROILUS AND CRISEYDE (1385), by Geoffrey Chaucer. This narrative love poem in the seven-lined rhyme-royal stanza has as its main source Boccaccio's *Filostrato,* but expands it by some twenty-five hundred lines, reaching eight thousand two hundred and forty lines and constituting in length, subject matter, and psychological analysis a novel in verse. The time is the siege of Troy. Calchas, Criseyde's father, is a seer who knows that Troy will fall and accordingly goes over to the Greeks, leaving behind his daughter, a pretty widow. Troilus, son of King Priam of Troy, sees her at the Temple of the Palladium and falls desperately in love with her. Troilus' friend, her uncle Pandarus, acts as intermediary, arranging first that Criseyde should in turn get a private glimpse of her admirer as he comes from battle with the Greeks, and carrying messages back and forth. He advises both parties fully. He tricks Criseyde into visiting him one night, assuring her that Troilus will not be there. But he lets Troilus in secretly. For the lovers, however, trouble is brewing. Calchas sends for his daughter through an exchange of prisoners. With a thousand vows to return in ten days, she leaves the city. Calchas does not intend to let her go back to the doomed city, however; moreover she is wooed by Diomed, her escort, and eventually yields to him. Meanwhile Troilus waits for her return. Day after day he mounts the walls to look for her. He sends her desperate letters; her replies are equivocal. One day Deiphebe captures Diomed's cloak, and on it Troilus sees the brooch he, Troilus, had given Criseyde. He is ready for death. He sallies out and is slain by Achilles.

TROIS CONTES (1877), by Gustave Flaubert. The three tales are unrelated. The first story, "The Legend of Saint Julian," has a medieval background, inspired by the stained glass of a cathedral. It is the legend of Julian, a mighty hunter who unwittingly kills his parents and cannot rest until God has accepted his repentance. The last, "Herodias," relates the martyrdom of Iaokannan (Saint John the Baptist), put to death by Herod, to please his wife Herodias and stepdaughter Salomé; it is a symbolic vision and colorful resurrection of Judaeo-Roman antiquity. The middle story, "A Simple Heart," has a modern and realistic setting. It narrates the obscure life of Félicité, a humble Norman servant. Félicité, is, in the author's words, "pious but not mystical, devout but without exaltation." Nothing, or hardly anything, happens to her. She loves a man; she loves the children of her employer; she loves her nephew; she loves her parrot. When the parrot dies, she has it stuffed. Her whole life has been devoted to other people—who have accepted the devotion but not returned it. Now the parrot becomes her consolation, and, as she becomes senile, she confuses it with the Holy Ghost.

Flaubert wrote "A Simple Heart" at the suggestion of George Sand, who had reproached him for the chill impersonality of his other work It thus strikes a new and pleasing note. The other two stories are not greatly different in mood and subject from *Salammbô* (q.v.) and *The Temptation of Saint Anthony* (q.v.).

TROJAN WOMEN, THE (415 B.C.), by Euripides. The tragedy opens upon a scene at Troy the morning after its capture. The men of Troy have all been put to the sword, and only the wretched women remain, waiting to be assigned as slaves to the victorious Achaeans. The play is full of the lyric grief and lamentation of these women. The action follows no plot but presents a series of scenes of suffering. First a herald brings Hecuba word that her daughter, Cassandra, has fallen to the lot of Agamemnon, a happy chance as the herald sees it but an abomination to Hecuba. Cassandra, however, accepts her fate, foreseeing in her prophetic mind that she shall witness the murder of Agamemnon. The word is then brought that Hector's wife, Andromache, has fallen to Pyrrhus, Achilles' son. To this lot Hecuba tries to reconcile her daughter-in-law, but close upon the heels of her persuasion comes the third blow. Hector's son, Astyanax, must be surrendered up as a dangerous male heir, to be cast to death from a tower. Upon this piteous scene the proud victor, Menelaus enters. He has come to claim Helen from among the Trojan women, for the army has left her punishment to him. She pleads her innocence and begs Menelaus to spare her life. Hecuba, however, rises above her grief to argue Helen's guilt and urge Menelaus to take her life. Her guilt Menelaus recognizes, but sends her aboard ship to await her punishment in Greece. There is only time for Hecuba to give hasty burial to the broken body of Astyanax before the torches are put to the dead city. When she would cast herself into the flames, even that escape is denied, for she is the prize of Odysseus. Thus while the city flames, the wife and daughters of Priam are led off to slavery. All this barbaric cruelty makes a sad travesty of the proudest victory of Hellenic legend. At the opening of the play even Athena, the champion of the Achaeans, in revulsion at their acts of violence and impiety in sacking Troy, plans with Poseidon to wreck their fleet on the homeward voyage. The tragedy is a bitter indictment of the brutality of war in general, but was aimed specifically at the unnecessary and unforgivable brutality of the Athenians in their treatment of the people of Melos as described by Thucydides. Only the year before they had put all the males of this island to the sword and enslaved the women and children for refusal of an alliance.

TROJAN WOMEN, by Seneca. See TRAGEDIES, by Seneca.

TRUE RELATION, A (1608), by Capt. John Smith. *A True Relation of Such Occurrences and Accidents of Note as hath hapned in Virginia since the first planting of that Colony,* written in Elizabethan style, is the earliest treatment of Jamestown, North America's first permanent English settlement. Captain Smith, the dominant force in the colony, recorded his eyewitness observations of the events from the arrival of the settlers at Cape Henry, April 26, 1607, to Captain Nelson's return in the *Phoenix,* June 2, 1608. The author, known for his choleric character, stood in belligerent opposition to other colony leaders; his account, it is assumed, reflects his prejudices. The story of Pocahontas does not appear.

TRUTH AND JUSTICE (1926–1933), by Anton Hansen Tammsaare. Anton Hansen Tammsaare (1878–1940) is recognized as the foremost Estonian novelist. He was a relatively prolific writer, but best known for his five-volume novel *Truth and Justice,* an attempt to portray all sides of Estonian life at the beginning of the twentieth century.

The story describes the efforts of the young farmer Andres Paas to improve his swampy land by draining it. He meets with opposition from a neighbor, and fails to find justice in the courts. His wife dies in giving birth to a son, Indrek. A devoted maid brings him up, but very soon becomes attracted to the father, and marries him when her husband commits suicide. Indrek is sent to a school in Tallinn, and passes through a phase of unbelief; from which he is rescued by his mild infatuation with a crippled girl Tiina, who is almost miraculously cured by a denial by Indrek of his irreligious thoughts. Indrek joins the revolutionary forces in 1905, but is offended by their violence and returns to his home in Vargamae. Here he finds his father heartbroken at his son's revolutionary actions. His stepmother Mari is suffering so badly from an illness that Indrek yields to her entreaties and gives her a poison. Then Indrek returns to Tallinn and marries the wealthy daughter of a business man, Karin, and is introduced to a frivolous society. Soon his wife begins to carry on affairs; when she realizes that she has finally disgusted her husband, she commits suicide. Indrek returns to his home, and after his father dies peacefully, he marries Tiina, who has followed him around as a servant and whom he has not previously recognized. He solves the problem of the drainage of the swamps, and then returns to the city with his wife.

TRYPTYCH OF THE THREE KINGS, THE (Eng. tr. 1936), by Felix Timmermans. See TIMMERMANS, FELIX.

TSODANG (1931), by Younghill Kang. See GRASS ROOF, THE, by Younghill Kang.

TU FU (713–770). Many Chinese consider Tu Fu the greatest Chinese poet. He was born in Tu Lin in the province of Shansi, although his scholar ancestors lived in Hsiangyang, Hupeh. At 15 he attracted the attention of great poets with his fantastic poems. After ten years of wandering and studying, he went to the capital, Ch'ang-an, to take his government examinations. His written papers were excellent, but because of his radical views he failed to get an appointment. Once more he became a wanderer in Ching-hsien, where he met his poet friend Li Po (q.v.). In 749 he went to the capital when the Emperor invited all scholars. Four years later, his three great prose-poems (*fu*) attracted the Emperor, and he was given a position in the Chih Hsien Library, then was promoted to another post at Feng Hsien. When the An Lushan rebellion drove the Emperor away, Tu Fu went to live with a relative at the White Water Village, where he wrote many poems. When a new emperor ascended the throne, his work fell into disgrace. His family in Kansu was very poor; some of his children died of hunger. In 768 he once more left his family to become a wanderer, but was caught by floods. Forced to take refuge in a ruined monastery, he lived for ten days without food. Upon issuing he was given a banquet by a local governor and died of overeating.

Tu Fu wrote on simple things, but he was very serious, contemplative, sometimes ironic, and his poems possess an extraordinary tenderness and sensitivity.

He is a difficult poet to translate, and no one has been able to convey his images exactly in Western language. Witter Bynner's translations of Tu Fu in *The Jade Mountain* are good. *Tu Fu: the Autobiography of a Chinese Poet* (1928) was translated by Florence Ayscough.

TUNNING OF ELYNOURE RUMMYNGE, THE (ca. 1508), by John Skelton. Exceptional only in its coarseness, this poem is written in a short, lively meter which is very effective. It is a fantastic narrative about an old alewife and her guests. No plan can be discerned. Tipsy women come and go, gossip and quarrel, and generally misbehave, all in bawdy ease. Inevitably there are touches of humor and even suggestions of dramatic action, but the poem is too long drawn out. Skelton is also the author of *The Book of Phyllyp Sparowe, Colyn Cloute, why come ye nat to Courte? Garlande of Laurell,* and many other poems, as well as the morality play, *Magnificence* (ca. 1516).

TURKISH ORDEAL (1928), by Xālide Edib Adivar. See SINEKLI BAKKAL, by Xālide Edib Adivar.

TURN OF THE SCREW, THE (1898), by Henry James, Jr. A classic of its genre, this short horror novel relies chiefly on the haunting intangibles of mystery, to stir the reader's imagination. James described it as "a piece of ingenuity pure and simple, of cold artistic calculation." The tale concerns a curse of evil which has been drawn about two beautiful children, Miles, aged ten, and Flora, eight. The supernatural forces of two "ghosts" of former servants, steward Peter Quint and governess Miss Jessel, are felt through the consciousness of a new, neurotic governess who desperately tries to protect her charges. They appear to her as real people, but are invisible to the children and the housekeeper. Her efforts with Flora succeed only in arousing the girl's terror; and in the final scene Miles dies in her arms while the specter she tries to exorcise stands looking on through the window.

The Awkward Age (1899) concerns Nanda Brookenham, English society girl, in the period between adolescence and marriage. Her mother's rival in love for young Vanderbank, she is subjected to the plotting and scheming of older persons. Vanderbank marries neither, at last; Nanda, disillusioned by her friends, goes to live at the country place of Mr. Longdon, an older man who had once loved Nanda's grandmother.

What Maisie Knew (1897) is a different treatment of children, told through the perceptions of little Maisie Farange. The girl, suffering the complications of divorced parents, befriends Mrs. Wix, a sentimental old woman, and grows into a precocious understanding of the problems of the adult world.

TURNER, FREDERICK JACKSON (1861–1932). A scholar and teacher in the field of American history, Frederick Turner's classic analysis of the importance of the frontier was included, along with a dozen short essays, in *The Frontier in American History* (1920). The essence of his interpretation is that the Westward advance of civilization into a dwindling area of free land kept furnishing new strength to American democracy. To the frontier, where savagery and civilization met, the American mind owes its chief characteristics of individualism, practicality, and great energy. The Pulitzer Prize was awarded, posthumously, to his work *The Significance of Sections in American History* (1932).

TUSCULAN DISPUTATIONS, by Cicero. See PHILOSOPHICAL ESSAYS, by Cicero.

TWELFTH NIGHT, OR WHAT YOU WILL (1600–1601; First Folio 1623), by William Shakespeare. This comedy clearly shows the master hand in its spontaneous, delightful lines. In substance it is one of the variations on the mistaken identity theme, so hard ridden in all early comedy. Viola and Sebastian, twin brother and sister, are shipwrecked in Illyria, but separated and unaware of one another's survival. Viola, taking the name of Cesario and clad in male attire, finds favor with Duke Orsino. She falls in love with him but is sent by him to plead his love to Olivia. Olivia, in turn, falls in love with the supposed young man. This predicament is, of course, resolved when Sebastian turns up and willingly marries Olivia, who had previously found his *alter ego* unresponsive. Some confusion ensues until Viola reveals her true sex and wins at last the love of Orsino. Subordinate to this romance is the farcical story of pompous, lovesick Malvolio, steward to Olivia, who entertains hopes of winning his mistress' hand. An elaborate hoax, leading him to suppose his suit successful, is perpetrated upon him by Olivia's uncle, Sir Toby Belch; his friend, Sir Andrew Aguecheek, and Olivia's woman, Maria. Though slight, the play is charming and popular. It has great currency on the contemporary stage. The character of Malvolio has been played by many famous actors, including Henry Irving and Maurice Evans.

TWELVE, THE (1918), by Alexander Blok. Blok was the greatest of all Russian Symbolist poets. One of his finest poems, the one by which, through translation into many languages, he is best known abroad, is *The Twelve,* which commemorates the Bolshevik Revolution. It is difficult to convey the superlative melodious beauty of this poem, which can be truly appreciated only by those who know Russian and love music in words. The Twelve are twelve Red soldiers marching through a blizzard in Petrograd streets, giving short shrift to the bourgeoisie and settling all quarrels with the bullet. The twelve are, of course, symbolic of the Twelve Apostles; in the end the figure of Christ appears at their head to lead them, against their will. Blok's idea of Christ was, of course, by no means the same as a Christian's; his is a decidedly irreligious mysticism. The greatness of *The Twelve,* however, does not consist in its idea, but in the quality of "pure poetry." Its impression of music is based on dissonances, and on various other devices in combination. Several English translations have been made, but none conveys adequately the spirit of the original.

20,000 LEAGUES UNDER THE SEA (1869), by Jules Verne. This yarn of scientific speculation introduces the submarine to literature, many decades before it made its appearance in reality. In 1867, an unknown monster is roaming the seas. A U.S. Navy ship, commanded by Captain Farragut, is sent to find it, carrying as passengers French scientist P. Aronnax (the narrator), his servant, Conseil, and a famous harpooner, Ned Land. One night the monster is sighted, but Captain Farragut comes off badly in the encounter. During the fight, Aronnax, faithful Conseil and Ned Land go overboard. They find refuge on the back of the monster, which turns out to be a submarine propelled by electricity and working along principles very similar to those of the modern submarine. The three men are taken into the *Nautilus* and become the prisoners of Captain Nemo, who gives them the liberty of the ship, but declares his intention of keeping them forever. Nemo is a genius with a grievance against men. The *Nautilus* cruises the waters of the world until at last, while she is in the maelstrom, Arronax escapes, is rescued by Norwegian fishermen, and returns to Paris to tell his story to incredulous ears.

TWENTY YEARS AFTER (1845), by Alexandre Dumas, *père*. See THREE MUSKETEERS, THE, by Alexandre Dumas, *père*.

TWICE TOLD TALES (1837), by Nathaniel Hawthorne. See HOUSE OF THE SEVEN GABLES, by Nathaniel Hawthorne.

TWILIGHT OF THE SOULS, THE (1901–1903), by Louis Couperus. See COUPERUS, LOUIS.

TWIN MENAECHMI, THE, by Plautus. See MENAECHMI, THE, by Plautus.

TWO CHIEF SYSTEMS (1632), by Galileo Galilei. See DIALOGUE CONCERNING THE TWO CHIEF SYSTEMS OF THE WORLD, by Galileo Galilei.

TWO GENTLEMEN OF VERONA, THE (ca. 1594; First Folio 1623), by William Shakespeare. This is one of the least vigorous and distinguished of the comedies. It is regarded as one of the earliest of Shakespeare's works, and does not contain much that could be held to represent his matured talents. Shakespeare found the material for this in the pastoral romance of Montemayor, *Diana*. Valentine and Proteus, two young men of Verona, are firm friends. Valentin travels to Milan, but Proteus, because of his love for Julia, remains at home. Proteus' father, however, desiring that his son should have the education of travel, insists that he follow Valentine to Milan. There, in the meantime, Valentine has fallen in love with Silvia, who reciprocates his passion. But Silvia's father, Duke of Milan, desires her to wed the stupid, wealthy Thurio, so their love is clandestine. Proteus falls in love with Silvia, forgets Julia, and treacherously betrays to the Duke Valentine's plan to elope with Silvia. In consequence Valentine is banished. He takes refuge in the forest with a band of gallant outlaws. Proteus next plans to outwit Thurio in his suit to Silvia. She spurns him, both for his betrayal of his friend and of Julia. The latter, meanwhile, has come to Milan in male attire and attached herself to Proteus as a follower. Silvia secretly escapes from Milan. She is captured by Valentine's outlaws, rescued from them by Proteus, but at last encountered by Valentine himself. Proteus, overcome with shame, repents. Julia discloses herself. Thurio disavows his love for Silvia in the face of danger. Both pairs of lovers are united and all ends happily.

TWO LIVING AND ONE DEAD (1931; Eng. tr. 1932), by Sigurd Christiansen. This Norwegian novel won in 1931 the Scandinavian prize in the Gyldendal competition of that year. It is a brilliant work of psychological analysis, a satire on a community's false concept of heroism. A postoffice has been robbed; one postal employee has been killed, one wounded, and another uninjured. The man killed, Kvisthus, is hailed at once as a hero-martyr, and his widow gets a small pension. The injured man, Lyderson, recovers, and for years enjoys the rewards of hero worship and promotion, eventually becoming a full-fledged postmaster. The uninjured employee, Berger, who has, like Kvisthus, wife and child, felt instinctively that life is worth more than money, and knowing that, faced with a revolver at the scene of the robbery, the postoffice funds would be lost anyway, gave up his receipts—and survives. As a result he is ostracized; his life becomes well nigh intolerable; and his chances of promotion in the postoffice department are gone forever. Officials of the town treat him with suspicion, as though a criminal, and even his wife, in a strange dilemma, wishes her husband had been a hero instead of the coward the community says he is. Is a person necessarily a hero because he is a fool or the product of circumstances, or a coward because he has common sense? Where does duty lie? Berger eventually gets a satisfying revenge, and without murder.

TWO NEW SCIENCES (published 1638), by Galileo Galilei. See DISCOURSES ON TWO NEW SCIENCES, by Galileo Galilei.

TWO NOBLE KINSMEN, THE (ca. 1613; printed 1634), by John Fletcher and William Shakespeare. As the prologue to this drama says, "Chaucer, of all admir'd, the story gives," this being an adaptation of *The Knight's Tale* (q.v.). Theseus, Duke of Athens, wins a war of liberation against Thebes and takes prisoner Palamon and Arcite, cousins who have pledged each other friendship until death. But from their prison window they glimpse Emilia, sister-in-law of Theseus, and immediately become rivals. Arcite's sentence is banishment, but he remains in Athens in disguise to be near Emilia. The jailer's daughter has fallen in love with Palamon and releases him. Palamon and Arcite meet in the forest and arrange to duel, but Theseus and his hunting-party interrupt, demand and receive explanations. The Duke forgives the two and provides for a formal trial by combat to settle the rivalry. Arcite wins, but his horse crushes him to death, and Palamon marries Emilia. The jailer's daughter, who has gone mad while wandering in the wood looking for Palamon, regains her faculties when a wooer comes to her dressed like Palamon; she accepts him.

TWO TREATISES OF GOVERNMENT (1690), by John Locke. In these two essays Locke attempted to lay the foundation of constitutional government on a basis similar to that on which Hobbes had founded absolutism. The first essay is a detailed refutation of the "divine right of kings" theory as formulated by Sir Robert Filmer in his *Patriarcha or the Natural Power of Kings*. As this theory was almost completely discredited by the time Locke wrote, this essay is not very important. The second essay, in which Locke outlined the main principles of his own theory, is considered by many historians to be the justification of the Glorious Revolution of 1688, and was extremely influential on eighteenth-century political thinkers, including Rousseau, Jefferson, and the revolutionists in France and America. The main features of Locke's theory are these: Man is born into a state of nature in which he is free and has the rights of life, liberty, and property. (Property is defined as that with which a man mixes his labor.) The law of nature requires that, all being equal, "no one ought to harm another in his life, health, liberty or possessions." Men have the natural responsibility to punish wrongdoers. Civil society is set up to make rights more secure and to relieve man of this latter responsibility. Men give up their natural powers to the community, and the community through the government is entrusted with the responsibility of maintaining rights. If the government violates this trust, the subjects have the right to rebel and set up a new government. The ambiguity and incompleteness of Locke's theory led to a variety of interpretations by subsequent thinkers.

TWO YEARS BEFORE THE MAST (1840), by Richard Henry Dana, Jr. The author joined the crew of the brig *Pilgrim* in 1836 on her voyage from Boston to San Francisco, negotiated around Cape Horn, in the hope that his weak eyes would be strengthened by the invigorating sea life. He describes in minute and vivid detail the routine of shipboard during the hundred-and-fifty-day voyage and return trip, as well as the characters of officers and men, such as the brutal Captain Thompson, and Hope, his noble Kanaka friend. He also gives realistic, local color pictures of shore life at ports where the gathering and curing of hides is the chief activity. *Two Years Before the Mast* laid bare the barbarous treatment meted out in those days to sailors, an exposé which shocked the nation and did much to institute reforms in our merchant marine. However, young Dana was not insensitive to the exhilarating experiences of the adventure. He recorded everything in an exciting narrative which has remained a perennial favorite. In later years, the author was bitter that this "boy's work" was his outstanding success in a life which he wished to devote to international law. In *The Seaman's Friend* (1841) Dana compiled a reference volume of terms, customs, and legal rights of common sailors.

TYPEE (1846), by Herman Melville. See MOBY-DICK, by HERMAN MELVILLE.

TYPHOON (1903), by Joseph Conrad. The *Nan-Shan,* skippered by Captain MacWhirr, is on her way to Fu-chau with some cargo and two hundred Chinese coolies going back home after work in various tropical colonies. The barometer is ominously falling, and the Chinese are seasick in the growing swell. The captain stalwartly refuses to change his course on the chance of avoiding the storm. The typhoon, when it breaks, tumbles some of the money chests of the coolies, and the Chinese begin fighting and scrambling and rolling in the reeking 'tween-deck. Jukes, the chief mate, and others of the crew are commanded to force peace on them, but there is danger of mutiny after the steamer has barely weathered the storm. But the captain, who passes even among his crew for a stupid man, cleverly and bravely redistributes the coolies' money, such of it as can be found. His wife at home, virtually a stranger, yawns over MacWhirr's unexpressive letter about a typhoon and "miserable objects."

UHLAND, LUDWIG (1787–1862). Ludwig Uhland was the best known and most beloved poet of later German Romanticism. The first edition of his poetry in 1815 contained the great majority of those poems which won for him fast-spreading fame: "The Blind King," "The Minstrel's Curse," "Suabian Legend," "Taillefer," "Song of a Mountain Boy," and "The Castle by the Sea," the last of which was later masterfully translated by Longfellow. In 1829 Uhland became a professor of German language and literature at the University of Tuebingen, and in 1848 he was elected delegate to the National Parliament at Frankfurt. His scholarly and political activities made him give up poetry. Among his last poems were "Bertran de Born" and "The Luck of Edenhall," the latter also known to the English-speaking world through Longfellow's adequate translation. Uhland admirably reproduced the peculiar tone of folk songs. His "Good Comrade" is sung by many who do not know the poet's name. His ballads rank among the finest of this genre, and some of his lyrical poems reach an almost classical sweetness and harmony. And yet Uhland has not kept his rank with the younger generations. Although he still arouses the enthusiasm of high-school students, he is nowadays rarely read or relished by adults.

UITKOMST (1907), by Hermann Heijermans. See OP HOOP VAN ZEGEN, by Hermann Heijermans.

ULI THE SERF (1841), by Jeremias Gotthelf. See GOTTHELF, JEREMIAS.

ULI THE TENANT FARMER (1846), by Jeremias Gotthelf. See GOTTHELF, JEREMIAS.

ULTIMA THULE (1929), by Henry Handel Richardson. See FORTUNES OF RICHARD MAHONY, by Henry Handel Richardson.

ULYSSES (1922), by James Joyce. This huge experimental work, the masterpiece of the stream-of-consciousness school, has been regarded as the most important and influential novel of the century. The time is June 16, 1904—the whole novel covers approximately sixteen hours. The place is Dublin. The framework of the story follows Homer's *Odyssey* (q.v.) closely and ingeniously. The modern allegory tells of Stephen Dedalus (Telemachus) in search of his father, with the Jew Leopold Bloom, typical of the wanderer, as Ulysses. During the day these two cross each other's path twice without recognition. Stephen lives with Buck Mulligan, a medical student, in an old tower near the coast. His conscience is troubled over his conduct at his mother's death-bed; his father is such an aimless drunkard as not to count at all. At the schoolhouse he gets advice from Mr. Deasy. Meanwhile Bloom, of Hungarian origin, prepares breakfast for his unfaithful wife, Marion Tweedy Bloom (Penelope), and then sets out on various errands, including the paying of last respects to Paddy Dignam. At the funeral he thinks of Rudy, his son, who died eleven days after birth.

Among the more striking parts of this day's odyssey of the two characters are Stephen's visit to the library, where he speculates on Shakespeare's relation to his father, and Bloom's temptation by the adolescent Gerty MacDowell, who stands for Circe. Bloom and Stephen meet in a brothel, and suffer various nightmares and fantasies, the latter becoming so drunk that Bloom (who, in bending over him, sees his own child Rudy) must take care of him. They go to Bloom's house, but Stephen refuses to stay the night.

The novel ends with Mrs. Bloom's unpunctuated and unexpurgated musings as she lies in bed after midnight.

Many techniques are employed, including styles sharply different for the different characters, newspaper headlines, parodies of English authors, dialogue with stage directions, interior monologues, free association, question-and-answer form. The external world, Dublin with its sights and sounds, is often bewilderingly interfused with the thoughts and emotions of the characters. The work was long banned in the United States—and is still banned in England—as obscene. The United States District Judge who allowed its present wide circulation remarked: "Whilst in many places the effect of *Ulysses* on the reader undoubtedly is somewhat emetic, nowhere does it tend to be an aphrodisiac." Joyce's experimentalism went still further in his last work, *Finnegans Wake* (q.v.).

UNCLE REMUS (1880), by Joel Chandler Harris. This book, the first of a series, introduced a new school of Negro folk literature. The central figure of the stories and verses is humorous old Uncle Remus, a family servant. A former slave, he tells his authentic dialect tales to a group of his employers. In the tales, animals are given human characteristics. There are Brer Rabbit, Brer Fox, Brer Wolf, and other beloved characters. Harris wrote more seriously of the plantation background, and Southerners of all classes, in several novels and volumes of tales such as *Mingo* (1884). *Mingo* includes four local color tales; the title piece concerns a Negro servant who remains loyal to his mistress when she marries beneath her class, and who, after her death, cares for her child.

UNCLE TOM'S CABIN (1852), by Harriet Beecher Stowe. When the Shelbys are forced to sell their slaves, the mulatto girl Eliza and her child escape across a frozen river; but Uncle Tom, a Christian slave, remains. Young George Shelby promises to redeem Tom when he is sold to a trader. Tom's first master is the genial St. Clair, whose charming daughter Eva he saves while sailing down the Mississippi; but after the death of these two Tom is acquired by the cruel planter, Simon Legree. This master becomes fearful of Tom's independent spirit, and has him beaten to death for refusing to give information about two escaped fellow slaves. George Shelby arrives too late, and declares that his life will be dedicated to abolition. Mrs. Stowe found herself the author of America's most popular and controversial novel. In 1853 she published *A Key to Uncle Tom's Cabin,* to defend herself from charges of inaccuracy. *Dred, A Tale of the Great Dismal Swamp* (1856) is a novel portraying slavery's degrading influence upon the masters. The tale concerns the cruel Tom Gordon, who forces his mulatto half brother Harry off his lands, and later kills Dred, a religious Negro who shields Harry. The author also wrote several other novels, less propagandizing in intention, with a New England background; and some verse.

UNCLE TOM'S CHILDREN (1938), by Richard Wright. See NATIVE SON, by Richard Wright.

UNDER THE YOKE (1893), by Ivan Vazov. Ivan Vazov (1850–1921) is the outstanding Bulgarian author in all fields of literature. Poet, dramatist, novelist, critic—for more than a half century he produced extensively. His works cover the history of Bulgaria and of Bulgarian life from the great days of the First Bulgarian Empire in the ninth century, to the period of despair that followed Bulgaria's failure in World War I.

Under the Yoke is his most successful and certainly his best known work, for it has been widely translated. It is a rather short novel based on Bulgarian life in the little city of Bela Tserkva on the eve of the Bulgarian uprising of 1876.

Into it comes Ivan Kralich, a Bulgarian revolutionist who has just escaped from the Turkish prison of Diarbekir. He settles down as a schoolteacher under the name of Boyko Ognyanov and continues his work, aided by Dr. Sokolov and the teacher Rada Gospozhina, whom he loves. All their efforts are thwarted by the rich friends of the Turks, especially Stefchov. They find, however, sympathetic support from the monks, who can always be relied upon to find the necessary money for the purchase of military supplies, even though they ostensibly are neutral and uninterested in affairs of the world. The revolution breaks out in neighboring towns and is quickly suppressed. Ognyanov, Rada and Dr. Sokolov are the last survivors, and they are killed in a last desperate battle in a mill.

The story well illustrates life in prerevolutionary Bulgaria and the shifting moods of the population during the fateful years which won the independence of the country. No author has expressed better, not only the life, but the atmosphere in those critical times.

UNFORTUNATE TRAVELLER, THE (1594), by Thomas Nashe. This picaresque novel, which is sometimes called *The Life of Jack Wilton,* is the most unusual thing of its kind before Defoe. The hero is a rogue, who wanders abroad and meets with various people and many experiences. He frequents taverns and palaces. He strikes up an acquaintance with a magician, and in Venice he pauses to elope with the wife of a magnifico but is overtaken by the earl in Florence. In Florence he encounters the plague. The English hero is properly depressed by "the modern Sodom" (Rome) and gladly returns to the less gruesome country of his birth. A review of Italy and Germany of the day passes before the reader's eyes.

Though Nashe is indebted to the Spanish picaresque novel and derived a definite stimulus from *Lazarillo de Tormes* (q.v.), his work is a spontaneous English growth. There are many similar points, the same humor and satire, the same realism, similar rough character sketches, but in Nashe the animating motive is not avarice—it is merely an indigenous love of mischief.

UNRUH, FRITZ VON (1885–   ). Von Unruh is one of the most remarkable figures of contemporary literature. Son of a Prussian general, a veteran of Verdun, wounded and highly decorated for bravery, the young officer renounced war and the unholy spirit of militarism as early as 1912 and 1913 in two plays that made him famous throughout Germany: *Officers* and *Prince Louis Ferdinand.* Connected with the Expressionistic Movement, friend of the statesman Walter Rathenau and founder of the Republican party in postwar Germany, Von Unruh went into voluntary exile after 1933 and now lives in the United States. His partly autobiographical novel *The End Is Not Yet* (1947) is a Dantesque modern descent into the hell made by Hitler.

UNVANQUISHED, THE (1938), by William Faulkner. See FAULKNER, WILLIAM.

UP FROM SLAVERY (1901), by Booker T. Washington. Booker T. Washington was born a slave on a Virginia plantation in 1856. After years of maladjustment, poverty, and maltreatment, his vows to dedicate himself to the service of the colored race were rewarded. He founded Tuskegee Institute, where young Negroes are taught trades and scientific farming. He became the friend of important leaders of the country, and by indirect influence helped advance his cause. The autobiography is a simple, though dramatic, record of a great Negro leader.

URKEY ISLAND (1926), by Wilbur Daniel Steele. See STEELE, WILBUR DANIEL.

URN BURIAL (1658), by Sir Thomas Browne. See HYDRIOTAPHIA, by Sir Thomas Browne.

URUPÊS (1918), by José Bento Monteiro Lobato. With the appearance of this short-story collection, Brazilian fiction took a distinct turn toward the realistic depiction of rural life. Previously the tendency had been to romanticize the landscape and the peasantry, but in *Urupês* the creative artist joined hands with the social critic, and the result is a vigorous analysis of the poor and decadent populations generally neglected by politicians and romantic literati. *Urupês* is therefore a milestone and also a work of permanent value.

U. S. A. (1938), by John Dos Passos. This trilogy tells the story of the United States during the early twentieth century, when a new commercialism was causing a profound shift of social values. Contemporary newspaper items, songs, and short biographies of leading public figures, as well as Dos Passos' stream-of-consciousness sections, provide a distinctive and colorful historical background.

The 42nd Parallel (1930) opens in Chicago in 1896, introducing the following characters: Fainy McCreary, a social idealist whose abortive business and domestic experiences end in a flight to Mexico; J. Ward Moorehouse, a poor boy whose shrewdness makes him a public relations power in the pre-World War I capital-labor picture; Eleanor Stoddard, an interior decorator who becomes his platonic mistress; Eveline Hutchins, her former partner; Janey Williams, Moorehouse's secretary during a trip to Mexico to bribe McCreary, and later lover of G. H. Barrow, a labor leader; Charley Anderson, a youth disillusioned by such men as Moorehouse, whose capitalistic propaganda is aimed at suppressing socialism.

1919 (1932) continues to weave these, and new narrative threads, into the epic texture through World War I and the Peace. Against the background of Moorehouse's successful promotional schemes and social rise, we meet Richard Savage, a poor youth sent to Harvard by a politician. Using influence, he becomes an officer during the war, and afterward gets a job with Moorehouse. Ben Compton, who appeared in the earlier volume, is a bright young Jew who emerges as a socialist worker and radical agitator.

The Big Money (1936) traces the decline of Charley Anderson, whose unhappy marriage to an heiress, and exciting business promotions, at first honest, but later fraudulent, cause complete disintegration of character and violent death. Margo Dowling is a young girl whose disillusioning affair with Charley leads her to Hollywood, where she enjoys brief success. Mary French, intimate friend of Barrow, and later Compton, is a labor worker during the turbulent days of the Sacco-Vanzetti affair. The only "successful" personality is the renegade radical

Savage, who meets the challenge of the age and uses its own opportunistic standards to carve a career for himself.

Dos Passos' *Three Soldiers* (1921), a controversial and popular book, is a cynical antiwar story of three doughboys. Dan Fuselli is a smug young private who tries vainly to rise through merit. Christfield is a pacifistic-minded Midwesterner who murders an enemy during the confusion of battle. John Andrews is a sensitive musician who at length deserts with Chrisfield. Apprehended, he faces death with defiance.

Manhattan Transfer (1935) is a mass of episodes depicting a kaleidoscopic New York of the 1890–1925 period. Dos Passos' naturalism and impressionism focus on such persons as Jimmy Herf, a reporter, and Ellen Thatcher, a neurotic actress. There is a motley crowd of Broadway misfits and characters broken by society in this now-brutal, now-sympathetic book.

USE OF POETRY AND THE USE OF CRITICISM, THE (1933), by T. S. Eliot. See ELIOT, THOMAS STEARNS.

UTILITARIANISM (1861), by John Stuart Mill. This essay is a mature statement of the principle of utility made famous by Bentham. The principle that the good and the right are to be defined as that which promotes happiness, was the dominant naturalistic theory of the nineteenth century. It provided a basis in moral theory for nineteenth-century liberalism. Mill did not have the same simple faith in the principle that Bentham evinced, and his treatment of the subject is cautious and moderated by qualifications.

UTOPIA (1516), by Sir Thomas More. Though the literary history of Utopias starts with Plato's *Republic* (q.v.), it is Moore's famous book which gave us the word—Greek for "nowhere." Written in Latin, the work quickly became popular and was translated into English as early as 1551. More assigns the narrative to a Raphael Hythloday ("Hythloday" is Greek for "talker of nonsense"), supposed to have traveled with Amerigo Vespucci, and, oddly enough, many of the practices in Utopia do in fact correspond with those long current in the centuries-old empire of the Incas of Peru. Book I treats of the evils of the world and asserts the need for an ideal commonwealth, which Book II describes. Utopia has the advantages of isolation, being a completely self-contained island almost immune to external forces. As the author regards property as the root of all evil, he banishes private property and all luxuries in his ideal state, and cuts the working day to six hours. There is a regular alternation of function between city dwellers and farmers, and at harvest time all lend a hand. The produce is held in vast storehouses placed at strategic points throughout the land. All dwellings are uniform, and the doors have no locks, since everything is shared in common. The government is at once democratic and paternalistic, with special arrangements for the higher education of the gifted. Among the startling social reforms are the banning of cosmetics, provision for mutual naked inspection by men and women contemplating matrimony (lest there be concealed defects), euthanasia, freedom from strife among religious sects, material rewards for virtue, and slavery as the punishment for crime.

V-LETTER, AND OTHER POEMS (1944), by Karl J. Shapiro. See SHAPIRO, KARL J.

VALLEY OF FEAR, THE (1915), by Sir Arthur Conan Doyle. See SHERLOCK HOLMES, by Sir Arthur Conan Doyle.

VALLEY OF THE MOON, THE (1913), by Jack London. See CALL OF THE WILD, THE, by Jack London.

VAN BIBBER AND OTHERS (1892), by Richard Harding Davis. See DAVIS, RICHARD HARDING.

VAN DOREN, CARL (1885–   ). Carl Van Doren, who now devotes himself entirely to writing, is a former Columbia University professor and literary editor of the *Nation* and the *Century*. *The Cambridge History of American Literature* (1917–1920), of which Van Doren was managing editor, is a discriminating, comprehensive, and basic reference work.

Contemporary American Novelists, 1900–1920 (1922) is a series of distinguished essays. *Three Worlds* (1936) is an autobiography, revealing not so much a spiritual progress as a re-creation of New York's literary and artistic society, seen from the perspective of a Midwestern youth. *Benjamin Franklin* (1938) is a Pulitzer Prize biography. A well-documented work, it does not attempt to interpret, but illuminates in bold relief the life and works of America's uninhibited, articulate humanist. Quotations from letters and writings reveal Franklin's originality, wit, grace, and learning.

VAN DOREN, MARK (1894–   ). The gifted brother of Carl Van Doren, Mark Van Doren is a literary editor and distinguished critic. Among his studies in *Shakespeare* (1939). Most interested in creative writing, Mark Van Doren has published volumes of poetry from 1924 to 1936; *Collected Poems* (1939) was awarded the Pulitzer Prize.

VAN LOON'S LIVES (1942), by Hendrik Willem van Loon. See STORY OF MANKIND, THE, by Hendrik Willem van Loon.

VAN LOON'S GEOGRAPHY (1932), by Hendrik Willem van Loon. See STORY OF MANKIND, THE, by Hendrik Willem van Loon.

VANITY FAIR (1847–1848), by William Makepeace Thackeray. *Vanity Fair* is a great novel of life and manners in the Georgian Age. Secondarily it is a social satire lampooning the *haut monde* of an England grown fat and corrupt on easy prosperity; it is rendered with inimitable wit and fullness. Jane Carlyle wrote her famous husband that *Vanity Fair* was "very good indeed, beats Dickens out of the world." While Thackeray possessed less of imaginative genius and human sympathy than Dickens, he had a vastly superior wit, greater sophistication and more brilliance of style. This novel is a scintillating, lively tale of Mayfair society, profound in its character analyses. The story centers in the entrancing little minx, Becky Sharp. She is an adventuress, capable of brilliant improvisation; when intrigue and a sharp wit fail her in her materialistic designs, she does not hesitate to throw in her reserves of feminine charm and a facile use of her sex. Contrasted with her is the gentle and womanly Amelia Sedley, whose friendship constitutes one of Becky's first steps up the social ladder. Amelia's sad story runs parallel to Becky's. While Becky is intriguing for a brilliant marriage with Rawdon Crawley, whose inheritance she loses for him in the process, Amelia devotes herself to worthless George Osborne, who finally marries her although her family has lost both money and position. The marriage is brought about by Captain Dobbin, an officer who worships Amelia and longs to see her happy. George is killed shortly thereafter at Waterloo, but not before he has had an affair with Becky, now the fashionable Mrs. Rawdon Crawley. Becky has climbed to the heights of Paris and London society, but loses her husband when he discovers her in the company of disreputable Lord Steyne, who is fascinated by her. After ten years of worshiping her idealized vision of George, Amelia is finally disenchanted by Becky, who tells her of George's infidelity. She puts the past behind her and marries her faithful Dobbin. Becky, in the meantime, sinks to a low level in continental society. As if writing with tongue in cheek, Thackeray looks at the foibles of English society through the penetrative and cynical eyes of Becky.

VATHEK (1786), by William Beckford. *Vathek* is an Oriental fantasy, originally written in French, supposedly about the grandson of Haroun-al-Raschid, the caliph-hero of the *Arabian Nights* (q.v.). Unlike Mohammed Caliph, Vathek did not think it necessary "to make a hell of this world in order to enjoy Paradise in the next." He was a king who had "the boldness to prolong his childhood and be happy." His mother, Carathis, a sorceress, influences Vathek to renounce his faith and to commit wicked crimes. Vathek then induces his new wife, Nouronihar, to accompany him in his search for the treasure of the pre-Adamite sultans. For this search he sells his soul to Eblis, supreme ruler of evil spirits. He discovers the futility of wealth when Eblis finally brings him into his kingdom, an underground abyss in which Vathek is condemned to live in eternal damnation for his crimes. The story ends: "Thus the Caliph Vathek, who for the sake of empty pomp and forbidden power had sullied himself with a thousand crimes, became a prey to grief without end and remorse without mitigation."

VATICAN SWINDLE, THE (1914), by André Gide. See COUNTER-FEITERS, THE, by André Gide.

VEDAS, THE (ca. 500 B.C.). The *Vedas* are the Sacred Books of the Hindus. However, the word "Veda," meaning "sacred knowledge," is more often limited to the first four collections of the Vedic books, so treasured by the Brahmins, priestly class of Hinduism, that they memorize them end to end and chant them in the old Sanskrit tongue in which they were originally composed. Especially given this peculiar sanctity is the *Rig-Veda*, oldest and holiest of the four, antedating the Hebrew Scriptures by some one thousand years.

These earliest four collections consist of ancient songs, hymns and magic charms. Some of them date back to prehistoric times long before there was a written language to record them. They were used for religious ceremonies and therefore carefully handed down from priest to priest through the ages. Later, the developments of Indian society and culture produced a second series of sacred books, known as the *Brahmanas*. Still later arose a third series known as the *Upanishads*. These latter were of a philosophical, mystical cast, and revealed more advanced thought and deeper religious experience than the earlier Vedas.

The *Rig-Veda*, earliest hymns, describe a simple, honest and valiant race of men. They are fighters and farmers, living in the temperate mountain regions of northern India. Supreme among the gods are two: Indra, lord of the winds, clouds and storm—a tempestuous fighting hero; and Agni, lord of fire and of the gentle, protecting hearth of man. There is a remarkable hymn which speaks of one Supreme Deity who exists behind and above all gods, who is unknown and omnipotent. This monistic concept continued to develop in the later Vedic hymns, and culminates in the *Brahmanas* and the *Upanishads* as a pure, abstract spirituality. The God Brahma, although still retaining his ancient name, emerges clearly as the one fundamental reality.

VEIN OF IRON (1935), by Ellen Glasgow. A novel with human fortitude as its central theme, the story centers in Shut-In Valley in Virginia, weaving forward and backward in time to show the unity of family character. Against an ancestral background of austere Scotch Presbyterians who endured the rigors of frontier life and Indian warfare, the Fincastles face the dangers of modern life. The connecting link between the past and present is Grandmother Fincastle. Her son John, a gentle and intelligent nonconformist minister, has been cast off by his community; but his family retain the respect of the neighbors. Ada, his proud and intense daughter, envies Janet Rowan, who has married Ralph McBride, John's student. After six years of unhappiness, Janet divorces him to marry a wealthy man. Ada then has an affair with him, and to spare him as he goes off to war, does not tell him she is pregnant. When Grandmother Fincastle dies, Ada is forced by community criticism to leave. In Queensborough Ranny is born. When Ralph returns from Europe, she marries him. An accident which temporarily paralyzes him embitters Ralph. And John's health breaks after he receives little notice for his long-worked-at metaphysical treatise. But Ada, in whom runs the family "vein of iron," encourages the family. When John dies, his insurance permits her to buy back the Shut-In Valley house, and she and Ralph return there.

VENICE PRESERVED (1682), by Thomas Otway. Otway based his play on L'Abbé Saint-Réal's *La Conjuration des Espagnols contre la république de Venise en 1618*. Jaffeir, a Venetian noble, is secretly married to Belvidera, daughter of Priuli, a Venetian senator, who has cast her off. When Jaffeir loses his money, his friend, Pierre, persuades him to join a group of conspirators who plot to overthrow the Venetian senate. Jaffeir agrees, and as a pledge of good faith gives Belvidera into the custody of the conspirators. When Renault, the leader, makes advances to her, Belvidera flies to her husband. He tells her of the plot, but she persuades him to warn the senate. This he does, but begs first for pardon for himself and friends. The faithless senators break their word, and Jaffeir finds himself exposed to the bitter contempt of the betrayed conspirators. He forces Belvidera under threat of death to go to Priuli and secure a pardon. Priuli grants it, but too late, and Belvidera goes mad. Pierre is condemned to a tortured death, but Jaffeir manages to stab him and then himself. The distracted Belvidera dies of sorrow. In the character of Antonio, a foolish old senator, Otway satirizes the Earl of Shaftesbury, leader of the Whig opposition.

The Orphan (1680) is an eloquent drama about twin brothers who love the orphan Monimia, with fatal though well-intentioned consequences. All three parties commit suicide.

VENUS AND ADONIS (1593), by William Shakespeare. This poem, which Shakespeare calls "the first heir of my invention," is dedicated to Henry Wriothesley, the youthful Earl of Southampton. It is often compared to Marlowe's brilliant fragment *Hero and Leander*. Coleridge did justice to *Venus and Adonis* when he remarked: "His 'Venus and Adonis' seem at once characters in themselves, and the whole representation of those characters by consummate actors." The story could have been taken from Golding's translation of Ovid's *Metamorphoses,* but Shakespeare was doubtless familiar with the original. The poem is written in six-line stanzas. Venus spies Adonis hunting in the forest, and is violently enamored of the beautiful boy, who is cold to her ardent advances and tender pleadings. When evening comes he insists on leaving her; he is meeting friends the next day to hunt the boar. She begs him to pursue less dangerous game. The next morning she hears the hounds and the hunter's horn, and following the sound she comes upon her lover, gored in the side and dead, as she had feared. She grieves over him and turns him into a flower.

VERDAD SOSPECHOSA, LA (1619), by·Juan Ruiz de Alarcón. See DOUBTFUL TRUTH, THE, by Juan Ruiz de Alarcón.

VERDI (1920), by Franz Werfel. See FORTY DAYS OF MUSA DAGH, THE, by Franz Werfel.

VERGETEN LIEDJES (1909), by Pieter Cornelis Boutens. See BOUTENS, PIETER CORNELIS.

VERSUS (1949), by Ogden Nash. See NASH, OGDEN.

VERY PLEASANT HOURS OF MISS SYMFOROSA, THE (1918), by Felix Timmermans. See TIMMERMANS, FELIX.

VESTIGES OF THE NATURAL HISTORY OF CREATION (1844), by Robert Chambers. This book, usually known as the *Vestiges of Creation,* was issued anonymously at a time when the idea of the fixity of species, upheld by Cuvier, had triumphed over the evolutionary views of Lamarck and St. Hilaire. Only after the death of Chambers, an Edinburgh publisher noted for *Chambers' Encyclopedia* (1859–1868), was his authorship of the controversial volume generally acknowledged. The author was a dilettante in science, and professional scientists were annoyed by the book's inadequacies; but general readers were startled by the daring with which ideas on evolution were presented. The *Vestiges* swiftly became a best seller. It is a compact little "outline of science" in which an attempt is made by the author, a sincerely religious man, "to connect the natural sciences into a history of creation." The book therefore opens with an astronomical section and an account of the nebular hypothesis, followed by sections on physics and chemistry, with the application of these to the constitution of the earth. Geology and palaeontology are presented on the basis of the writings of Cuvier and Lyell. Part II of the *Vestiges* is on the "origin of the animated tribes," in which life is assumed to have come into being spontaneously on the earth and other planets and to have followed a predestined pattern of evolution. The book quickly ran through edition after edition. If it did not win many adherents to the doctrine of evolution, it at least prepared the public mind for the reception of Darwin's *Origin of Species* (q.v.) fifteen years later. One reader particularly strongly influenced by the *Vestiges* was Alfred Russel Wallace, co-discoverer of the theory of natural selection.

VICAR OF WAKEFIELD, THE (1766), by Oliver Goldsmith. Goldsmith's purpose in this pastoral in prose is to teach the values of virtue, simplicity, and contentment in life. The Vicar, who tells the story, is completely guileless, charitable, and unworldly. His wife, ambitious for her two daughters, Olivia and Sophia, is eager to maintain the family's gentility. There are four sons: George, Oxford bred; Moses, whose smattering of home education failed to sharpen his wits much; and two small boys. Because of financial reverses, the Primrose family moves to a humble living near the estate of the unprincipled Squire Thornhill, who abducts and seduces Olivia after a mock marriage ceremony. The Vicar's cottage burns down, and he is imprisoned for debt. Sophia is also abducted, and George is thrown into prison for attempting to avenge his sister. Dr. Primrose bears all these misfortunes bravely. Sophia is rescued by the Squire's uncle, Sir William Thornhill, an eccentric vagabond. Sir William straightens out the family affairs and marries Sophia; Olivia's marriage is discovered to be legal despite the Squire's intentions; George marries his true love; the Vicar's fortune is restored; and the unscrupulous Squire is brought to terms by his uncle.

VICOMTE DE BRAGELONNE, THE (1847), by Alexandre Dumas, *père*. See THREE MUSKETEERS, THE, by Alexander Dumas, *père*.

VICTORY (1915), by Joseph Conrad. In this tale of the South Seas, Axel Heyst, a Swede, who wanders footloose over the world in search of diversion, possesses neither faith nor aim; he passes through life not as an actor but as a spectator. He becomes associated with the Tropical Belt Coal Company on Sanburan Island, entertains a visionary scheme, serves as the Company's manager, and sees it burst like a bubble. After that he remains alone on the deserted island. One day he rescues from the sea the girl Lena. She ultimately loves him, but he sees her only as a disturbing factor in his peace. The only feeling he actually is capable of is pity, and for that reason alone he befriends Lena. It is only in death that he at last discovers his love for her. " 'Who else could have done this for you?' asked Lena. 'No one in the world,' he answered. With a terrified and gentle movement Heyst hastened to slip his arm under her neck . . . he was ready to lift her up in his arms and take her into the sanctuary of his innermost heart forever! . . ."

VIDA ES SUEÑO, LA (1635), by Pedro Calderón de la Barca. See LIFE IS A DREAM, by Pedro Calderón de la Barca.

VILLAGE, THE (Eng. tr., 1923), by Ivan Bunin. See GENTLEMAN FROM SAN FRANCISCO, THE, by Ivan Bunin.

VILLAGE, THE (1783), by George Crabbe. Making a clean break with the artificial neoclassic view of country life as an idyl, this poem, in two books of heroic couplets, goes in for sturdy realism, and shows the sorrows and the hardships of the agricultural poor. The lot of the young rustics is only less miserable than that of the old, who end up in the parish poorhouse with a charlatan apothecary and an indifferent priest to speed their death. The only glimmer in the week is Sunday, which is likely to degenerate into drinking and riot. Of course the rich have their troubles too, the author notes, if there is any small comfort in that.

VILLETTE, (1853), by Charlotte Brontë. See JANE EYRE, by Charlotte Brontë.

VILLON, FRANÇOIS (1432?–1464?). Villon, the greatest French poet of the fifteenth century, was an educated man who led a vagabond life after being first condemned to death, then expelled from Paris, for killing a priest. The remains of his nimble verse are contained in two volumes. *The Small Testament* (1456), forty witty eight-line pieces, and *The Grand Testament* (1461–63), 173 eight-line pieces varied with about twenty ballads. In this latter group are the more delicate, deeply felt of Villon's verses, serious poems such as his "Regrets of Youthful Folly," and "The Ballad of Women of Yore," with its lamenting refrain, 'Where are the snows of yesteryear?' Condemned to death a second time in 1463, Villon composed during his imprisonment the famous "Ballad of Hanged Men," in which the pendent corpses address curious onlookers, complain of their fate, and pray for divine mercy.

VIRGIN SOIL (1876), by Ivan Sergeyevich Turgenev. Turgenev has attempted here to present a picture of the revolutionary movement of the seventies. By many it is considered the "last word of his greater testament." Again we have a youth, one of that series of psychological portraits so delicately traced, a Russian dreamer, incompatible with stable society, not unlike Rudin. It happens that Alexey Dimitrovitch Nezhdanov is the natural son of a nobleman. At once this makes him an outcast; he can hope for no place in society. He accepts the position of tutor to the son of the wealthy Sipiagin. While his radical views repel Sipiagin, they fascinate his young niece Marianne, who also cherishes revolutionary views. Soon they declare love for one another and plan to leave. They consult Solomin, a friend of Nezhdanov, who is manager of a factory near the Sipiagin estate. Solomin, a sensible fellow, suggests that the couple move in with him. Marianne adapts herself easily and happily; Nezhdanov, on the other hand, feels increasingly thwarted. He postpones the marriage. The government is on his trail, and it is essential that they marry at once and flee. Realizing his incapacity for playing the part he has cast for himself, Nezhdanov shoots himself. To save her reputation, Solomin marries Marianne and takes her away. We assume they are happy.

VIRGINIAN, THE (1902), by Owen Wister. Apparently pieced together from several independent stories, this novel is laid in the vast regions of the virgin West. The author asserts the real need of the rude frontier code which ruled the West. The hero, a handsome Wyoming cowpuncher, forces on a turbulent community his idea of law and order—"getting the drop" on an enemy, vigilante committees, and lynch law. He also wins the girl, Molly Wood.

VIRGINIANS, THE (1857–1859), by William Makepeace Thackeray. This sequel to *Henry Esmond* is valuable as a picture of colonial life in Virginia. It follows the life of Colonel Esmond in Virginia, where he takes his wife, Lady Castlewood. In the Virginia Castlewood, Esmond's twin grandsons also live with their widowed mother, Rachel Warrington. Colonial life before the Revolution is realistically portrayed. Famous historical characters, including young George Washington, visit Castlewood, where Madame Warrington rules rather tyrannically after Esmond's death. George Warrington, the Castlewood heir, is believed to have been killed in the French and Indian Wars. His brother Harry inherits and goes to England to live. There his wealth and generous nature make him a prey to all sorts of folly. The now elderly Baroness Bernstein, formerly Beatrix Esmond, whom Henry Esmond once loved, helps to lead him into dissipation. He is saved from debt and an unfortunate marriage by George, who arrives safely to rescue his brother and resume his inheritance.

VISION, A (1925), by William Butler Yeats. See YEATS, WILLIAM BUTLER.

VISION OF SIR LAUNFAL, THE (1848), by James Russell Lowell. See LOWELL, JAMES RUSSELL.

VISIONS (1921), by Zalman Shneiur. See SHNEIUR, ZALMAN.

VISIONS, THE (printed 1627), by Francisco de Quevedo. Written intermittently after 1607 but printed for the first time in 1627, *Los Sueños* is a series of mordant prose satires which bring to memory Jonathan Swift. In "El sueño de las calaveras" (Dream of the Skulls), the author dreams that he is witnessing the Last Judgment; in "El alguacil alguacilado" (The Bedevilled Constable), he satirizes the inferior officers of justice, one of whom is possessed, the demon complaining bitterly of his disgrace in being sent to inhabit the body of a creature so infamous. In "Las zahurdas de Plutón" (Pluto's Pigsties), perhaps his outstanding satire, he sees two paths: one, to the right, narrow and rugged, leading to Paradise and traveled only by a few soldiers and beggars, while the other, to the left, wide and comfortable, leading to Hell, swarms with people. Following the latter path, which eventually becomes extremely rough, the author goes right into Hell and examines one by one the pigsties occupied by each member of the various trades and professions: bookdealers, tailors, doctors, lawyers, poets, merchants. In "El mundo por de dentro" (The World from Within) he sees into the intentions of men as if they were something tangible: how much sadness do attendants at a funeral really feel, how true are the tears of the deceased relatives, etc. Finally, in "Visita de los chistes" (A Visit in Jest), Death invites the author to her kingdom to join in a conversation with legendary characters, but Quevedo declares that he is familiar with their crimes and follies, having been accustomed to them on earth.

In all of these sketches, which became popular in Europe and were frequently imitated, Quevedo exposes the men and institutions of his time. And there is no doubt that the bitterness of his invectives can be justified in terms of the hypocrisy and corruption of his age. Yet his sense of humor is never absent, even if it be the grim humor of his scenes in Hell, where lost poets are doomed to hear each other's verses for eternity, doctors and mur-, derers end their careers as brethren, and comic men dwell in a separate inferno lest their jokes dampen Hell's fires.

VITA CHE TI DIEDI, LA (1923), by Luigi Pirandello. See PIRAN-DELLO, LUIGI.

VITA NUOVA, LA (1295), by Dante Alighieri. *La Vita Nuova* was written by Dante as a noble literary tribute to his beloved Beatrice and to his own exalted feeling for her. The book was written in 1295. It consists of three central *Canzoni,* the first of which is a portent of his love for Beatrice, the second a vision of Beatrice's death, and the third an expression of sorrow at her passing. Between the first and second *Canzone* there are four sonnets, and likewise between the second and third there are four minor compositions. One ballad and nine sonnets precede the first *Canzone;* likewise ten other minor compositions follow the third. Each poem is preceded by a prose piece explaining the meaning and spiritual origin of the poetical composition. Dante begins with the description of his first encounter with Beatrice, when he was nine years old. He met her the second time when he was eighteen. Following this second encounter, he began to have visions of her. To hide his feelings, he used a "screen," and pretended not to be in love with Beatrice but with several gentle ladies. Beatrice, offended, no longer responded to his greetings as she used to do. From that moment Dante decided to eliminate the fiction of his "screen" and to devote the best part of his talent to praising her. *La Vita Nuova* reveals the profound spirituality of young Dante, for whom love and mysticism were combined, as part of his organic religious conception of the universe and of human life.

VITA SOMNIUM BREVE (1902), by Ricarda Huch. See HUCH, RI-CARDA.

VOCATION OF MAN (1800), by Johann Gottlieb Fichte. This is a highly moral and emotionally charged philosophic tract written by a somewhat erratic idealistic follower of Kant. At first orthodox in Kant's opinion, Fichte later diverged widely and was repudiated by Kant himself. Other followers of Kant also rejected him. The concept of struggle or striving was fundamental to Fichte's view of human life. In the *Vocation of Man* he shows that all men are in a continual state of striving. We strive toward ideal ends but can never realize them. This does not matter. What is important is the process or activity of striving itself, the overcoming of obstacles. Man is free to the extent that he is self-determining in the struggle. He also has a responsibility to respect the freedom of others. Man is moral to the extent that he subordinates the physical to the spiritual. This philosophy, which makes the will, its strivings, and its obstacles basic, was influential on Hegel and other nineteenth- and twentieth-century philosophers. In his *Addresses to the German Nation* (1807–1808) Fichte argued strongly for the superiority of the Germans in language, literature, religion and philosophy. He saw a German mission in the world, the first phase of which was the union of all Germany, and the ultimate aim of which was the Germanizing of the whole world. This work did much to fan the flames of German nationalism in the nineteenth century.

VOICE OF THE CITY, THE (1908), by William Sydney Porter. See PORTER, WILLIAM SYDNEY.

VOICES (1907), by Pieter Cornelis Boutens. See BOUTENS, PIETER CORNELIS.

VOICES OF THE NATIONS IN SONG (1778–1779), by Johann Gottfried Herder. See HERDER, JOHANN GOTTFRIED.

VOLGA FALLS TO THE CASPIAN SEA, THE (Eng. tr. 1931), by Boris Pilnyak. See PILNYAK, BORIS.

VOLPONE (1606), by Ben Jonson. Ben Jonson did not possess Marlowe's poetic power, but his career on the whole was more productive and better rounded. One of the best of his plays is *Volpone*. It is a harsh and scathing exposure of human greed in terms which are at the same time horrifying for their baseness and yet mockingly humorous. The rich and avaricious Volpone, aided by his wily servant, Mosca (The Fly), pretends that he is dying. He tricks his equally greedy friends into giving him costly gifts of gold and jewels, leading each one to believe that he has a chance of becoming heir to Volpone's great wealth. When the friends have been bled, one of them having disinherited his son in Volpone's favor, another having offered him his wife, Volpone spreads the rumor that he has died, and confounds the hopefuls by a will making Mosca his heir. Mosca, seizing the upper hand, tries to keep Volpone legally dead, but succeeds only in bringing the house of cards down upon the heads of the whole unsavory crew. *Volpone* is an impressive play, similar in quality and texture to the almost forgotten plays of Machiavelli. In 1928 the Theatre Guild produced it in an adaptation for the modern stage by Stefan Zweig, and it has since been made into a French film.

VÖLSUNGA SAGA, THE (ca. 1140–ca. 1220). Of all the stories kept alive by the oral means of the saga-tellers, the Scandinavian bards, none so fully expresses the temper and genius of the Northland as that of the Völsungs and Niblungs. Richard Wagner has immortalized them in the music dramas of the *Ring of the Nibelungen*. The tales from *The Völsunga Saga* have entered into the literature and thinking of central and northern Europe.

The stories of the Volsungs belonged to the common ancestral folk of all the Teutonic or Scando-Gothic peoples in the earliest days of their wanderings. The only historical name found in these sagas is that of Attila, the Scourge of God, who with his Huns had left a frightening impression upon the memory of the many peoples he had outraged and conquered. Like all folklore, it is rich in the wisdom and experience of the people in both good and evil.

Fragments of the original songs remain in the Icelandic *Poetic Edda* (q.v.).

VONDEL, JOOST VAN DEN (1587–1679). The most popular work of Vondel is his tragedy *Gijsbreght van Aemstel,* which since 1637 has been performed every year in the first half of January in the Municipal Theatre at Amsterdam. The play was written for the inauguration of this theater, and deals with the fictitious downfall of the town about 1300. Virgil's tale about

Troy's destruction inspired Vondel. The town is besieged for a year by the lord of Haarlem and other enemies of Gijsbreght, Knight of Amsterdam. To his amazement, the enemy has retreated suddenly the day before Christmas. The inhabitants of Amsterdam carry the abandoned weapons and a ship made of twigs into town as booty. While at night the entire population celebrates triumphantly the feast of Christmas in the cathedral, the soldiers of the enemy leave the hold of the ship, open the gates for the returning Haarlem troops, and fire the city. Gijsbreght fights desperately for the preservation of his castle, but is forced to flee with his family. Through the refusal of his wife Badeloch to leave without him, the poet is able to portray true connubial love in the midst of disaster. Vondel gave his tragedy a spiritual background by placing it at Christmas time; after the acts the superb chorus sings about Christ's birth. The downfall of worldly power is synchronized with the rise of the power of Christ. The *Gijsbreght* is one of Vondel's earliest tragedies and is of a fairly weak structure. Of his twenty-four other tragedies, composed after the Greek pattern, the Biblical plays, which are regularly performed, are:

Joseph in Dothan, written in 1640, under the influence of the expectation of the downfall of West Europe through the conquests of the Turks, according to the poet to be blamed on the enmity among Christian brother nations.

In 1654, Vondel wrote the tragedy *Lucifer,* a work of rare, majestic vision and dramatic power. The drama is set in Heaven, and describes in the radiant art of the baroque how a section of the angels are dissatisfied with the creation of man and jealous over the glory given him by God. They assemble in droves, and with cunning speech persuade Lucifer to become their leader. The charitable and forgiving Raphaël causes him to hesitate, but the strong words of the inexorable Gabriel drive him on in fury, over the path that leads to his destruction. In his old age, Vondel wrote as sequel to this tragedy: *Adam in Ballingschap* (1664). After a lyrical description of the nuptials of Adam and Eve, the fall of man and the expulsion from Paradise are depicted.

Vondel has participated passionately in the political and social life of his times. He wrote panegyrics about the martial deeds of the scions of Orange and to the glory of Amsterdam; satirized sharply the corruption in administrative circles (*Roskam*), and exhibited an increasing loathing for strict Calvinism and its dictatorial dominies. After he had left the Baptist Congregation in 1641 and embraced Roman Catholicism, he wrote long didactic poems in defense of his new faith. He also wrote many simple, short poems about the joys and sorrows of life. Often they remind one of the heart-stirring sketches by his contemporary and fellow townsman Rembrandt, with whom he had otherwise nothing in common in conception or style.

VORAGINE, LA (1924), by José E. Rivera. See VORTEX, THE, by José E. Rivera.

VORSTENSCHOOL (1872), by Multatuli. See MAX HAVELAAR, by Multatuli.

VORTEX, THE (1924), by José E. Rivera. The great Colombian novel, *La Vorágine,* describes the wanderings of Arturo Cova and his lover, Alicia, who in a romantic revolt against bourgeois conventions flee from the city. They make their way through the wide, hot savannahs of Casanare to a cattle ranch. The pregnant Alicia is sweet and naïve; Cova, tired of her, dreamily seeks some vague chimera. At a ranch the couple meet Griselda and her lover, Fidel Franco, who tell them of a fellow named Barrera who has come in search of rubber tappers for the Vichada river section. Barrera's persuasive solicitations have completely disrupted the normal activities of the ranch, and the workers, in anticipation of a lucrative trip, have caroused in wild and drunken fashion. Barrera leaves surreptitiously, taking with him Alicia and Griselda.

The description of the trek of Arturo and Fidel through the tangled labyrinth of the jungle in search of the abducted women fills absorbing pages. During their wanderings they meet a certain Clemente Silva, who becomes their guide; and from him they learn the tragic story of the rubber tappers, of enslavement that outlasts the life of the individual, extending after his death to his children and heirs. After surmounting innumerable obstacles, Arturo and Fidel finally manage to get to Griselda and to escape with her by boat. She tells them the whereabouts of Alicia and Barrera. When Arturo reaches the Yaguarani he immediately seeks out Barrera, and, after a ghastly fight, succeeds in throwing him into the river, where he is devoured by the caimans. That night Alicia gives birth to a seven-months child. With the young mother in a hastily prepared litter, Arturo and his companions depart from the plague-infested Yaguanari to seek shelter in the jungle. They leave in their shack a note for Clemente Silva describing the direction in which they are fleeing and begging that he follow them immediately. For five months Clemente seeks in vain. No traces of them remain: the jungle has swallowed them.

VOYAGE OF DR. DOLITTLE (1922), by Hugh Lofting. See **DR. DOLITTLE TALES,** by Hugh Lofting.

VOYAGES (1582), by Richard Hakluyt. The full title of this book is: *Divers Voyages Touching the Discovery of America and the Islands Adjacent to the Same.* It stimulated discovery of distant lands. Throughout his life the author and editor of innumerable books on navigation and voyages, Hakluyt was devoted to research, traveling far and wide to interview travelers and examine records. It was the scientific aspect of navigation which interested him most. His major collection, *The Principall Navigations,* was first published in 1589. In all his books he describes bays, straits, rivers and kingdoms in an intriguing yet practical manner, speaking of commodities and of the benefits of traffic among peoples.

VOYAGES OF THE BEAGLE (1839), by Charles Darwin. See **ON THE ORIGIN OF SPECIES,** by Charles Darwin.

WAGNER, RICHARD (1813–1883). Having written his own librettos, Wagner deeply influenced the theater of his time, and there is no question that he was a great dramatist in his own right. It is primarily the world of German legends and folklore from which he derived his material. In his tetralogy *Ring of the Nibelungen* (published without the music in 1856) he went back to old Nordic sources prior to the medieval version of the *Nibelungenlied* (q.v.). From a purely literary point of view, Wagner's best creation is *The Master-*

singers of Nuremberg (1868), one of the few genuine comedies German litera- ture can boast of. Although indebted to E. T. A. Hoffman, the story is Wag- ner's own: the young knight, Walter von Stoltzing, gains admittance to the guild of the Mastersingers and wins Eva, the daughter of a burgher, for his wife. In the old and genial poet Hans Sachs, Wagner has created one of his most charming characters, while the malicious "Stadtschreiber" Sixtus Beck- messer is a satirical caricature of the pedantic critics against whom the com- poser fought all his life long. Some of Wagner's other most famous musical dramas are: *The Flying Dutchman* (1843), *Tannhäuser* (1845), *Lohengrin* (1850), *Tristan and Isolde* (1865) and *Parsifal* (1882).

WAIFS AND STRAYS (1917), by William Sydney Porter. See POR- TER, WILLIAM SYDNEY.

WAITING FOR LEFTY (1935), by Clifford Odets. The opening scene of this one-act play portrays a group of cab drivers who have met to decide whether to strike; they await Lefty Costello, their leader. An agent for the capitalists, Harry Fatt, speaks to the men to dissuade them. But six short flashbacks reveal trenchantly the men's reasons for action. A taxi driver and his wife trying desperately to support their family, and a young driver who cannot afford to marry his girl, show the struggle to maintain human dignity under the pressure of financial difficulties. A laboratory assistant fired for not spying on his superior, and an intern dismissed for speaking too frankly, and for being a Jew, symbolize the ethical degeneration of the ruling class. A young actor struggles against the commercialism of art, and a spy perjures himself to defeat the unions. At the end, the men learn that Lefty has been murdered, and, urged on by their speaker Agate Keller, they decide to strike.

Odets, his position firmly established by two additional plays, *Awake and Sing!* and *Till the Day I Die* (both 1935), has devoted himself to ideologically- oriented work for the theater. *Golden Boy* (q.v.) is another of his successes.

Awake and Sing! describes the Bergers, poor Jewish family of the Bronx. Bessie, the mother, skimps to establish "respectability." Myron, her husband, is a sententious failure. Jacob, her father, is a gentle old barber who plays Caruso records, reads Karl Marx, and dreams of revolution. He tells his grandson, Ralph, to act.

When Bessie learns that her daughter Hennie is pregnant, she forces her to marry her gullible immigrant suitor, Sam Feinschreiber. In a fit of despair- ing rage, however, Bessie smashes old Jacob's records. He commits suicide, leaving his insurance money to Ralph, who has lost his girl because they are too poor to defy their elders. Ralph inherits the old man's books also, and decides they are more important than the money, which he gives to his mother- He then decides to devote himself to the improvement of society.

Hennie and Moe Axelrod, an embittered veteran of the last war, determine to save something of themselves, and go off together.

Till the Day I Die describes the struggle of the German Communists at the start of Hitler's rise to power.

WALDEN (1854), by Henry David Thoreau. This is the spiritual auto- biography of a rebel wearied by the machine age, but too much of a practical Yankee to escape into the fog of mysticism. Thoreau gave up his trade of

pencil maker and set up house at Walden Pond, outside Concord, Massachusetts. He hoped to prove to the world that the tyranny of many things is
necessary, that man can live with very little and find contentment. At Walden
the author lived in elegant simplicity. He was wonderfully able with his
hands—an excellent carpenter, mason, surveyor and mechanic. For two years
he stayed at his hermitage. His book is a record (in the form of eighteen
essays) of his life, his painstaking observations of nature, and his reflections
about the world's troubles.

During this period, Walden wrote *A Week on the Concord and Merrimack
Rivers* (1849). Tremendously stimulated by new places, he had taken notes
during an excursion on a boat built by a brother and himself. The book sings
the praise of American self-reliance, and presents a picture of the wholesome
outdoors. Frequent digressions comment on literature, religion and social relations.

Typical of Thoreau's outspoken attitude is the essay "Civil Disobedience"
(1849), largely an attack on what he called an unjust, imperialistic war against
Mexico, on the institution of slavery, and on our treatment of the Indians.

WALLENSTEIN (1799), by Friedrich von Schiller. See SCHILLER,
FRIEDRICH VON.

WALTHER VON DER VOGELWEIDE (ca. 1200). Of all medieval
poets the wandering nobleman Walther is still nearest to the heart of the German people. His lyrical gem "Under the Linden Tree" is as popular as are
some of his short rhymed maxims. About Walther's life little is known, except
that he must have been born around 1170 in South Germany or Austria and
that he probably died in the city of Würzburg not later than 1230. Some biographical conclusions can be drawn from his poetry, because he supported the
German Emperors against the Pope; and in the last years the poet, who often
complained of his poverty, received some landed property from Frederick II.
His meeting with the rival poet Wolfram at the Court of the Thuringian
Duke forms the nucleus of many legends and literary adaptations, most notable
among which is Richard Wagner's opera *Tannhäuser*. Walther is the most
outstanding poet of the so-called German "Minnesang" (poetry based on the
courtly love code of the Middle Ages). In addition, he took part in the political and religious controversies of his time. His poetry is simple, natural, sincere, beautiful, strangely free from the conventionality of his age. He is generally conceded to be the greatest lyrical genius of German literature before
Goethe.

WANDERER IN LOVE, A (1904), by Arthur van Schendel. See
SCHENDEL, ARTHUR VAN.

WANDERING JEW, THE (1845), by Eugène Sue. This romance
was one of the most popular specimens of the *roman feuilleton,* the episodic,
melodramatic novel published by the cheap dailies of the mid-nineteenth
century. The Jew who refused hospitality to Jesus has been doomed to a
life of sorrow and wandering until his last descendant shall have died. Sue's
novel relates the story of the last seven members of that ill-fated family. Those
seven happen to be the heirs to Marius Rennepont's fortune. This wealth is

coveted by the Jesuits. One of the Renneponts is persuaded to enter the Society of Jesus and give over his share to the Society. The six others die, because of the machinations of Père Rodin, an ambitious, "dissembling, crafty, patient, energetic, opinionated and wonderfully intelligent being," who destroys those people "by merely playing with their passions, good or bad, which he has artfully called into motion." Rodin's machinations, however, are finally frustrated. The treasure is destroyed by Samuel, its faithful guardian. And Rodin himself is poisoned, just as he is about to reach the goal of his ambitions and become the head of the Society of Jesus. In the concluding chapters, the seventh descendant of Marius Rennepont dies, and the Wandering Jew, at last redeemed and freed, attains "the happiness of eternal sleep."

The Wandering Jew is not quite fair to the Society of Jesus, accused throughout the book of many revolting deeds. But it is an interesting, very compelling story, as good as the best of Alexandre Dumas, *père*.

WANDERINGS OF OISIN, THE (1899), by William Butler Yeats. See YEATS, WILLIAM BUTLER.

WAR AND PEACE (1865–1869), by Count Leo Tolstoy. The clear place of *War and Peace* as one of the cornerstones of world literature must be attributed to the epic scope of the novel, and the quality of the writing. It is not a novel of plot but of historical progression. Tolstoy took as his material the Russian role in the Napoleonic wars, from the Austrian campaign of 1805 to the great war of 1812. He chronicled the chief military and political currents swirling over Europe in this era. He projected upon this vast background many fictional, individual lives. With power and firmness the author weaves his great pattern, producing a complex panorama of the life of the time, rich in social observation and analysis of all events as they affected the various classes of society.

The chief characters are Prince Andrey Bolkonsky and his friend, Pierre Bezuhov. They are not linked in any highly developed plan. Prince Andrey's story deals with the attempt of a noble and dignified spirit to serve his country in the traditional manner. He is dismayed by the corrupt self-seeking and crass stupidity manifest in military and civil affairs. We follow him through Austerlitz, the death of his first wife in childbirth, his unfortunate love for Natasha Rostov, to his death after Borodino. For Tolstoy, however, Prince Andrey represents the type of sophisticated man he does not approve of; and in contrast, he created Natasha and Nikolay Rostov, who for him represent the "natural man" whom he glorifies. Bezuhov is an amiable, bungling fellow, possessor of a title and a vast fortune. He muddles through the turmoil of historic events, making a bad marriage, becoming absorbed in Freemasonry, being captured by the French at the destruction of Moscow, surviving all to marry, at last, Natasha. She is one of the most impressive characters of fiction.

Through the Bolkonsky, Bezuhov and Rostov families we encounter a broad cross section of Russian society. Tsar Alexander I, General Kutuzov, and Napoleon are the chief historical figures. Tolstoy's scornful and searching study of Napoleon has long stood as a refutation of the "great man" theory of history. The penetrating portrayal of Kutuzov, flanked by jealous intrigues, often scorned, but more than any other man the savior of Russia, is memorable. Tolstoy interprets history as a blind force which makes short shrift of the deliberate designs of men. For this reason he juxtaposes the "natural man," Kutuzov, with the military genius, Napoleon, whose defeat is brought about by causes which his deliberate planning has failed to foresee.

WAR GOES ON, THE (1936), by Sholem Asch. See NAZARENE, THE, by Sholem Asch.

WAR IS KIND (1899), by Stephen Crane. See RED BADGE OF COURAGE, THE, by Stephen Crane.

WAR OF CATILINE, THE, by Sallust (Gaius Sallustius Crispus; 86–ca. 35 B.C.). In this essay Sallust (cf. *Jugurthine War*) recounts and interprets the conspiracy of Catiline to overthrow the government of Rome (63 B.C.) from the point of view of the popular party and as a supporter of Caesar. The essay is therefore in a sense a counterblast against Cicero's account of his management of the calamity as given in the famous Catilinarian orations. The work is prefaced by remarks on Sallust's philosophy of history in general and on the course of Roman history in particular, tending to show how the continuing course of Roman imperial expansion had resulted in a weakening of moral fiber and in political corruption. Sallust then points out how Catiline, an impoverished noble with a taste for luxury and power, a child of his age, could appeal to many dissatisfied and disgruntled elements in the state for support in his revolutionary schemes. He gives an unrelievedly dark picture of the viciousness of Catiline's youth and young manhood. The account of the actual conspiracy begins at election time in June of 64 B.C. with the convoking of the conspirators, and follows its course through the disclosure of its existence, the prosecution and execution of those members who remained at Rome, to the final defeat and death of Catiline at Pistoia. Sallust's account is on the whole more sober and certainly no more biased than that of Cicero. It fills in many gaps left by Cicero's speeches, which, even though rewritten for publication, could not deal with matters other than those discussed on the occasions when they were delivered. Thus Sallust gives us the gist of the counterproposals of Caesar on the punishment of the conspirators, and describes the battle of Pistoia, concluding his narrative with a most generous description of the bravery of Catiline and his followers on the field of battle.

WAR, PEACE, AND THE FUTURE (1914), by Ellen Key. See KEY, ELLEN.

WARDEN, THE (1855), by Anthony Trollope. This is Trollope's fourth novel, the first of the famous Barsetshire series, and the author's first real success. The book is a progressive character study of mellow old Rev. Septimus Harding, preceptor of Barchester Cathedral and warden of Hiram's Hospital, which is a charity home for twelve old bedesmen. Harding has two daughters: the elder married to Rev. Theophilus Grantly, archdeacon of Barchester, and son of Harding's superior, the bishop; and Eleanor, who is in love with John Bold, a young doctor who begins a crusade against Hiram's Hospital and the wardenship—which he characterizes as a sinecure. To the consternation of the realistic Grantly, Harding feels twinges of doubt and guilt, and resigns as warden. Although Eleanor at length persuades Bold to withdraw his action (later marrying him), the hospital remains neglected, for the Bishop does not name a new warden. The twelve old men, who had been persuaded to allege ill treatment, thus become victims of the affair.

WARREN, ROBERT PENN (1905–   ). Robert Penn Warren's writings have encompassed many fields. His first book was *John Brown* (1929), a scholarly biography of the martyr. *Selected Poems 1923–1943* (1944) placed the author as a regionalist and lyricist of the rural Southern earth, as did his contributions to *Fugitive,* the Southern verse magazine.

In *A Southern Harvest* (1937), Warren edited a volume of Southern short stories, and in 1948 there appeared a volume of his own shorter pieces, *The Circus in the Attic.* As editor of *The Southern Review* he became known as an outstanding literary critic.

Warren has written three novels. *Night Rider* (1939) is about Percy Munn, farmer-lawyer who slowly develops into a character capable of committing violence, during the vicious activities of a greedy tobacco growers' association.

At Heaven's Gate (1943) concerns Bogan Maddox, a Southerner whose business difficulties are tragically averted by the sympathy accorded him when his daughter, Sue, is murdered.

All the King's Men (1946), a Pulitzer Prize winner, is a brilliant novel on the career of a Southern governor obviously patterned after Huey Long.

WASTE LAND, THE (1922), by T. S. Eliot. See ELIOT, THOMAS STEARNS.

WATCH ON THE RHINE (1941), by Lillian Hellman. See HELLMAN, LILLIAN.

WATER BABIES, THE (1863), by Charles Kingsley. Subtitled *A Fairy Tale for a Land Baby,* this is the story of a dirty little chimney sweep who runs away from his hard master, falls into a stream, and is turned into a water baby by the fairies. Tom's adventures under the water on his journey to the sea, his life among the other water babies, and his long trip to the Shiny Wall, where he meets Mother Carey, are told with charm and imagination.

WATERMAN, THE (1933), by Arthur van Schendel. See SCHENDEL, ARTHUR VAN.

WATER-WITCH, THE (1830), by James Fenimore Cooper. See SPY, THE, by James Fenimore Cooper.

WAY HOME, THE (1925), by Henry Handel Richardson. See FORTUNES OF RICHARD MAHONY, by Henry Handel Richardson.

WAY OF ALL FLESH, THE (published posthumously in 1903), by Samuel Butler. The theme is the hypocrisy and smug complacency of English middle-class life, and particularly the relationship between parents and children, which is traced through several generations of the Pontifex family. There is John, the village carpenter; George, the domineering publisher; his son Theobald, who marries the weak, colorless Christina; and their son, Ernest. Although a skeptic, Theobald accommodates himself to his comfortable calling as a minister. He bullies his wife, whom he never loves, and his son as well. Ernest suffers from suppression by his father all through his childhood, and after his ordination as a minister he rebels. He insults a Miss Maitland, whom he takes for a prostitute, and is sentenced to six months' imprisonment. Upon his release, he marries his father's drunken servant girl, Ellen, but he abandons her when he discovers that she is already married. Ernest's aunt, Alethea Pontifex, his only friend, leaves him a fortune. This enables him to turn his fine intelligence to literature, and ultimately his life becomes pleasant and worthwhile. *The Way of All Flesh* is generally regarded as a very original work; it exercised considerable influence on later English writers. "It contains records of the things I saw happening rather than imaginary incidents," said the author. Undoubtedly this novel has a strong vein of autobiography.

WAY OF THE WORLD, THE (1700), by William Congreve. The best and most sparkling of Congreve's comedies was not highly acclaimed when it first appeared on the stage. Mirabell, a witty, ironic gentleman, wants to marry the coquette, Millamant. To accomplish this he has to placate her aunt, lovesick old Lady Wishfort, who controls her niece's estate. He makes love to the old lady, who is highly pleased with his attentions, but his stratagem is discovered by Mrs. Marwood, who hates Mirabell because he has slighted her offers of love. She spitefully reveals his plot to Lady Wishfort, who indignantly declares that Millamant will get only half of her estate if she marries Mirabell. Mirabell induces his man, Waitwell, who loves Foible, Lady Wishfort's maid, to pretend to be Sir Rowland, Mirabell's uncle, and in this character woo Lady Wishfort. Waitwell complies, having first married Foible. This deceit, too, is discovered by Mrs. Marwood, who reveals it to her new lover, Fainall, Lady Wishfort's son-in-law. Mrs. Marwood knows that Mrs. Fainall and Mirabell were formerly lovers. Fainall plans to threaten to expose Lady Wishfort and disgrace her daughter by divorcing her unless he receives control of her property and Millamant's. However, Mrs. Fainall reveals her knowledge of her husband's affair with Mrs. Marwood, while Mirabell proves that Mrs. Fainall had previously made him her trustee. Lady Wishfort is so overjoyed by his help in defeating her son-in-law that she gladly permits him to marry Millamant. Millamant, throughout the action, proves herself to be a cool, witty and intelligent young lady. She is one of Congreve's finest creations.

WAY TO FREEDOM, THE (1908), by Arthur Schnitzler. See SCHNITZLER, ARTHUR.

WEALTH OF NATIONS, INQUIRY INTO THE NATURE AND CAUSES OF THE (1776), by Adam Smith. One of the great masterpieces of eighteenth century individualism, this book exercised a tremendous influence on the development of economic theory in relation to the material affairs of society. Adam Smith was not a mere theorist; he was a shrewd, practical man of business, with a crusading spirit.

Wealth of Nations is an astonishing book in the sense that it was the creation of a universal mind. It is the first full-length, systematic treatise against state intervention in economic affairs. It treats abundantly not only of economic theory but also of philosophy, work history, social ethics, etc. In his own day Adam Smith's teachings were regarded as revolutionary. He appealed to history to complete his case against "the folly of human laws" that impeded enlightened self-interest, proving that no intellectual obstacle impeded his own conclusion that private and public interests harmonized. He asserted that social progress results from the full play of man's natural instincts. Up to this time the regulation of industry had been almost universally admitted to be a government function. The ideas and arguments of Smith went beyond his own time; they were influential at a later date in establishing the system of free trade in Great Britain.

In his most famous passage he writes that economic man "neither intends to promote the public interest nor knows how much he is promoting it . . . ; he intends only his own security; and by directing that industry in such a manner as its produce may be of the greatest value, he intends only his own gain, and he is in this, as in many other cases, led by an invisible hand to promote the end which was no part of his intention."

Meanwhile, his idea that wealth consists not in precious metals, but in the goods men consume and use and the source of these goods, which is labor, was revolutionary for that period. Smith was a genius at exposition, and it is this which has determined the continued popularity of his book; but he has fewer defects and is less dated than most writers on economic and political philosophy. This doughty Scotsman is often called the founder of political economy.

WEARY BLUES, THE, (1926), by Langston Hughes. See HUGHES, LANGSTON.

WEAVERS, THE (1892) by Gerhardt Hauptmann. This drama, originally written in Silesian dialect, was Hauptmann's fourth play, and made him the undisputed leader of the German Naturalistic movement. Based on the uprising of the Silesian weavers in 1844, the loose plot is very simple. The badly abused workers in a textile weaving town can no longer endure the conditions under which they have been laboring in dire misery. Led by the ex-soldier Moritz Jaeger, they revolt against their cruel and indifferent employer, the rich manufacturer Dreissiger. Finally, after an old weaver who had not even been among the rebels has been slain by the constabulary, they begin to wreck the mills and the machinery. *The Weavers* is a mass drama—a tragedy in which the hero is not an individual but a strongly knit group of clearly cut realistic types. Because of this bold departure from the usual dramatic formula Hauptmann's play has wielded great influence upon modern social drama.

WEB AND THE ROCK, THE (1939), by Thomas Wolfe. See LOOK HOMEWARD, ANGEL, by Thomas Wolfe.

WEEK ON THE CONCORD AND MERRIMAC RIVERS, A (1849), by Henry David Thoreau. See WALDEN, by Henry David Thoreau.

WEIR OF HERMISTON (written 1894), by Robert Louis Stevenson. See MASTER OF BALLANTRAE, THE, by Robert Louis Stevenson.

WELL OF DAYS, THE (Eng. tr., 1933), by Ivan Bunin. See GENTLE-MAN FROM SAN FRANCISCO, THE, by Ivan Bunin.

WEST CHAMBER, THE (Eng. tr., 1936), by Wang Shih-fu. See HSI HSIANG CHI, by Wang Shih-fu.

WESTERN STAR (1943), by Stephen Vincent Benét. See JOHN BROWN'S BODY, by Stephen Vincent Benét.

WESTWARD HO! (1855), by Charles Kingsley. The English novelist re-creates here the glorious days of Queen Elizabeth, when her subjects sailed the seas of the New World searching for gold and the Spaniard, or wrote sonnets in her honor at court. Amyas Leigh, the hero, represents the soldier, explorer and sailor in the Elizabethan man; his brother, Frank, who finally goes to his death romantically for love and religion, portrays the delicate, witty courtier. Amyas' adventures on the Spanish main, where he sails to find his lady love, the beautiful Rose of Torridge; his encounters with Spanish traitors, Indians, the Inquisition and the white girl Ayacanora whom he finds in the forest, make an exciting story. Among the minor characters are Salvation Yeo, a rough but faithful seaman; the Leighs' weak cousin, Eustace, who plots with the Jesuits; witty Will Cary, who accompanies Amyas on his voyages; and Don Guzman, the Spanish cavalier who carries Rose off to the Governor's House in Guayra. Raleigh, Spenser, Sir Richard Grenville, Sir Humphrey Gilbert all appear, and the final climax concerns the dramatic defeat of the Spanish Armada. The colorful style and ready wit of the writer capture the spirit of Elizabethan England excellently.

WHAT EVERY WOMAN KNOWS (1908), by Sir James M. Barrie. See BARRIE, SIR JAMES MATTHEW.

WHAT I BELIEVE (1884), by Count Leo Tolstoy. See CONFESSION, A, by Count Leo Tolstoy.

WHAT MAISIE KNEW (1897), by Henry James. See TURN OF THE SCREW, THE, by Henry James.

WHAT PRICE GLORY (1924), by Maxwell Anderson and Laurence Stallings. Marine First Sergeant Quirt and Captain Flagg are old-time service men. During World War I they continue their private feuds and rivalries, which in this case center on the favors of Charmaine, a French lass. While Flagg is away, Quirt double-crosses him; the returning Captain seeks revenge by attempting to marry the pair off. Quirt escapes this as the two move up to the front lines with their men. This play, the first realistic presentation of fighting men as human beings instead of stuffed-shirt heroes, encouraged Anderson to quit journalism and become a writer.

In 1939 he wrote another sort of "war" play. *Key Largo* concerns an American who has lost his idealism while fighting for the Spanish loyalist cause. He regains it after being involved by chance with a gangster who is preying upon several helpless people on one of the Florida Keys. In rediscovering his own courage, he finds that there are, after all, ideals worth fighting for.

Anderson has written three historical verse dramas. *Elizabeth the Queen*

(1930) concerns the love of Elizabeth and the Earl of Essex. The queen struggles to subdue her feminine temperament in the interest of her nation—eventually condemning to death her rebellious lover. *Mary of Scotland* (1933) is a version of the Mary Stuart–Earl of Bothwell romance. He proves powerless to save the unfortunate girl from Elizabeth's order of execution. *Anne of the Thousand Days* (1948), retells the story of Henry VIII and Anne Boleyn.

WHEN THE WHIPPOORWILL (1940), by Marjorie Kinnan Rawlings. See YEARLING, THE, by Marjorie Kinnan Rawlings.

WHEN WE WERE VERY YOUNG (1924), by A. A. Milne. See WINNIE-THE-POOH, by A. A. Milne.

WHERE IS SCIENCE GOING? (1932), by Max Planck. See ORIGIN AND DEVELOPMENT OF THE QUANTUM THEORY, THE, by Max Planck.

WHERE THE BLUE BEGINS (1922), by Christopher Morley. See MORLEY, CHRISTOPHER.

WHILE ROME BURNS (1934), by Alexander Woollcott. See WOOLLCOTT, ALEXANDER.

WHIRLIGIGS (1910), by William Sydney Porter. See PORTER, WILLIAM SYDNEY.

WHITE BUILDINGS (1926), by Hart Crane. See CRANE, HART.

WHITE COMPANY, THE (1891), by Sir Arthur Conan Doyle. The author of the Sherlock Holmes stories turns to adventure and romance in a novel of knights and ladies of England in the fourteenth century. Alleyne Edricson at the age of twenty leaves the Cistercian Abbey, where he was educated, to seek his way in the world. He is joined by Hordle John and Samkin Aylward. The three friends attach themselves to a band of Saxon yeomen, known as the White Company, headed by Sir Nigel Loring. Here follow the wars and adventures of the brave knights in France and Spain. Alleyne is knighted for chivalry by the Black Prince. He and John return to England, thinking that Sir Nigel and Aylward are dead. However, they also have found their way back. Alleyne arrives in time to save Lady Maude Loring, heartbroken daughter of Sir Nigel, from the convent. They are happily married.

WHITE DEVIL, THE (1612), by John Webster. Webster is famous for his two tragedies, *The Duchess of Malfi* and *The White Devil* or *Vittoria Corombona*. The source of the latter play he found in the historical story which stirred Italy in the 1580's, that of the marriage of the Duke of Bracciano to Vittoria Accoramboni, after the assassins of the duke had murdered her husband. Webster changed the duke's name to Brachiano, and gave Vittoria a brother, Flamineo, an utterly unscrupulous villain. Flamineo urges his sister to betray her husband, Camillo, with Duke Brachiano, who loves her. The Duke arranges to have his wife, Isabella, murdered. And Flamineo puts Camillo out of the way. Vittoria is tried for taking part in her husband's murder, and is sentenced to confinement in a house for fallen women. Brachiano rescues her, and they elope. Francisco, Duke of Florence, determines to avenge Isabella's death. He and several of his followers disguise themselves as Moors, enter Brachiano's service, and administer a stern and bloody justice to the lovers.

WHITE, E. B. (1899–   ). The satirical Mr. White has always been concerned with the problems of rural living and human conflicts, illustrated in his pieces done in collaboration with James Thurber (q.v.) and in *Quo Vadimus?* (1939), sketches of life's humorous complications. *One Man's Meat* (1942), a book of pieces from White's magazine column, contains reflections on such diverse topics as children's books, a pet dog, hot weather, and the World's Fair. Polished in style, these urbane commentaries usually have serious overtones. *The Wild Flag* (1946) contains editorials about peace and world government, which originally appeared in *The New Yorker* magazine.

WHITE FANG (1906), by Jack London. See LONDON, JACK.

WHITE MONKEY, THE (1924), by John Galsworthy. See FORSYTE SAGA, THE, by John Galsworthy.

WHITEHEAD, ALFRED NORTH (1861–1947). This English mathematician who became a philosopher rather late in life is in many ways a unique figure. After making a name and career for himself in the field of mathematics, he turned his attention first to problems in the philosophy of science and later to speculative metaphysics, where he earned perhaps an even greater reputation. He collaborated with Bertrand Russell on the *Principia Mathematica* (q.v.). His early philosophical work (*The Concept of Nature*, 1920) is an attempt to develop an empirical philosophy of science that does not fall into the difficulties of Hume's atomistic approach. Using mathematical techniques, he attempts to derive the abstract concepts of science from the conditions of concrete human experience. His *Science and the Modern World* (1925) contains the early form of his metaphysical system together with its historical background. Whitehead is concerned with refuting scientific materialism, which he considers the dominant philosophy of the modern scientific era. He feels that it is guilty of taking an abstraction, matter, for concrete reality. As a result, materialism not only makes moral, religious, and aesthetic problems unintelligible, but slows up scientific progress because of the inadequacy of its abstractions. In this book he presents some of the concepts and categories which he feels to be more in line with scientific developments. This metaphysical system received its full development in his *Process and Reality* (1929). Because of its technical character and abstruse language of his own devising, much of his work is difficult for the general reader. *Science and the Modern World*, a series of popular lectures, is as good an introduction as any to Whitehead's philosophy.

WHITMAN (1943), by Henry Seidel Canby. See CANBY, HENRY SEIDEL.

WHO IS HAPPY IN RUSSIA? (ca. 1870), by Nikolay Alexeyevich Nekrasov. Nekrasov (1821–1877) was Russia's greatest nineteenth century proletarian poet, whose sympathy with the peasants and the poor was expressed in many poems, extremely popular with the Russian people. *Who Is Happy* *in Russia?*, written during the seventies, in the folk song style, is his greatest and most famous achievement, satirical in vein. It tells about seven peasants who take a journey on foot to discover who lives happily in Russia. They meet members of all classes of society. The long narrative tells of the lives of these varied people and their achievements, whether moral and heroic or evil. In the end faith is expressed in the future of the Russian people and in the part the democratically minded intelligentsia is playing in their redemption. The poem is written in a singularly racy style, which is at once realistic and original, and, on the whole, happy in mood. There is a translation by Juliet M. Soskice.

WIDE IS THE GATE (1943), by Upton Sinclair. See JUNGLE, THE, by Upton Sinclair.

WIELAND, CHRISTOPH MARTIN (1733–1813). The prolific German writer Wieland began as a devotee to a strongly rooted pietism. Reversing his opinion, his attack upon the tendency toward over-serious and theoretical religious views often distorted his work to the extreme of superficiality and frivolity. Wieland attempted to expose the unreasonableness and uselessness of purely ethereal and unnatural motivations. His best known work is the youthful and imaginative verse romance, *Oberon* (1780; available in the English of John Quincy Adams), which provided the text for the opera by von Weber. The fantastic story deals with the adventures of Huon of Bordeaux, who must journey to Bagdad to carry off a handful of hair from the Caliph's beard and four teeth from his mouth. He must also win the Caliph's daughter for his bride. Oberon, the elf, aids Huon to carry out his task, only to see him suffer later through his own shortcomings.

Among Wieland's other writings is the psychological novel *The History of Agathon* (1767). He was also publisher of the influential periodical *The German Mercury*.

WILD DUCK, THE (1884), by Henrik Ibsen. *The Wild Duck* is one of Ibsen's most symbolic dramas; the dialogue is packed with meaning. The play opens at the home of Werle, a wealthy merchant and manufacturer. Among the guests at a dinner party is Hjalmar Ekdal. Gregers, Werle's son, and a boyhood friend of Hjalmar's, has been away at the mines for many years, but has just returned at his father's request. Hjalmar tells Gregers that he is in the photography business, and that he has married Gina, a former housekeeper of Werle's. Gregers had heard from his mother that his father had had an affair with Gina. Gregers finds Hjalmar happy and content in his family life, but he feels it his duty to inform his old friend of the affair between Gina and Werle. Cross-questioned, Gina admits it is true. Hjalmar's happiness is gone forever. Gregers persuades Hjalmar's daughter, Hedvig, bewildered at the air of tension in her home, that the best way to regain her father's love is to sacrifice the thing she loves most, her adored pet, a wild duck. The next day a shot is heard in the attic; Gregers thinks Hedvig has made the great sacrifice and killed her duck, but instead the child has killed herself. Gregers, with his insistence on the everyday virtues of truth and sacrifice, has ruined a once happy family.

WILD FLAG, THE (1946), by E. B. White. See WHITE, E. B.

WILHELM MEISTER'S APPRENTICESHIP (1821–1829), by Johann Wolfgang von Goethe. In the long line of the German novel of education the two volumes of *Wilhelm Meister* constitute the most important link between Grimmelshausen's *Simplicissimus* (q.v.) and Thomas Mann's *Magic Mountain* (q.v.). Goethe's work represents what is generally thought of as the national German novel. Epic in scope, the book concerns man's adventure in the art of life.

The theme of *Welhelm Meister's Apprenticeship* is the development and growth of a young man who oscillates between the respectable world of business and the glitter of the stage, and who, after concerning himself with the problems of literature, aesthetics and religion, finally gives up the theater in order to devote himself to the education of his son. A well-to-do merchant's son, Wilhelm falls in love with the actress Marianne, and is entranced by the strolling players and artistic gypsies whom he joins as an actor. It is at this point that the famous Mignon episode is interwoven—immortalized by Thomas opera based on Goethe. Wilhelm saves the young Italian girl Mignon from maltreatment at the hands of a brutal trapeze artist, for which she generously rewards him with her adoration. In the meantime he becomes more deeply involved in the activities of the theatrical company, which reach their climax in a production of Shakespeare's *Hamlet* (q.v.). Finally convinced that he is not made for the theater, Wilhelm leaves the slowly deteriorating company and spends some time as a guest of Lothario in his castle. The last stage of his apprenticeship now takes place, and he learns much about the world from the members of the lower nobility. He marries Natalie, with whom he has had a previous affair, and who turns out to be Lothario's sister. He learns that Marianne had left him a child, and the task of educating this newly found son finally helps him to find himself.

Though *Wilhelm Meister's Apprenticeship* may be called the culmination of the eighteenth century idea of humanistic self-development, the much later completed second part, *Wilhelm Meister's Travels,* is deeply entrenched in the spirit of the nineteenth century. Even more loosely constructed than its predecessor, the book is formless and fragmentary in character. While Wilhelm and his son Felix wander from place to place, their personalities become more shadowy and their lives more uninteresting. Their wanderings provide the framework for discussions of the individual's role in society and his duties as a member of the social organism. Interjected with no relevance to the novel are several separate stories from Goethe's more productive earlier years. The work is the testament of Goethe, the sage and foreseeing social philosopher of the nineteenth century. While the often surprising modernity of his ideas is nowhere more sharply revealed, it is rather the first volume, *Wilhelm Meister's Apprenticeship*, which holds a key position in the history of the European novel.

WILHELM MEISTER'S TRAVELS (1796), by Johann Wolfgang von Goethe. See WILHELM MEISTER'S APPRENTICESHIP, by Johann Wolfgang von Goethe.

WILL TO BELIEVE, THE (1897), by William James. See JAMES, WILLIAM.

WILL TO POWER, THE (1909–1910), by Friedrich Nietzsche. See NIETZSCHE, FRIEDRICH.

WILLIAM TELL (1804), by Friedrich von Schiller. The little state of Switzerland lies under the harsh hand of the Governor Gessler. In an arrogant attempt to humiliate the Swiss, Gessler causes his cap to be stuck on a pole, with the order that all who pass it must bow to it in subservience. Tell refuses to do this, and shoots the cap from the pole with an arrow. Seized by Gessler's troops, Tell is defiant. Cruelly the tyrant orders Tell to demonstrate his skill by shooting an apple from the head of his young son at a great distance. If he does this successfully he is to go free. Tell insists upon having two arrows. He shoots, and successfully splits the apple. Asked by Gessler why he had needed the other arrow, he says that had he missed and injured his son the other would have been for Gessler. One of Tell's arrows ultimately does account for Gessler, when the people of Switzerland at last rise in revolt and overthrow him. Through the play runs the romance of a young nobleman, on Gessler's side by birth and position, who, under the combined influence of his sweetheart and William Tell, joins the cause of the people.

William Tell is Schiller's last and most popular play. Based on the legendary fame of the Swiss archer, the drama is a stirring call for political freedom. Next to Goethe's *Faust* (q.v.) it is the most prominent national dramatic creation of the German people. The best known English translation is the one by Samuel Taylor Coleridge.

WIND IN THE WILLOWS, THE (1908), by Kenneth Grahame. In these animal stories for children and adults, the Mole, Water Rat, Toad and Badger act, talk and philosophize like human beings. The four friends represent different types of men, and have many adventures before they settle down in harmony at Toad Hall. The Toad is the egotistical reprobate who is finally saved after stealing a motor car and being jailed. The weasels, ferrets and stoats take over his ancestral home. The four friends discover an underground passage, conquer the invaders, and live in contentment in Toad Hall. They are pointed out by the wood folk as great heroes.

WINESBURG, OHIO (1919), by Sherwood Anderson. Consisting of twenty-three stories, this book is unified by the theme of tragic destiny that overtakes unoffending, upright but impractical individuals in the backwash of small-town American life. The author goes beneath the surface of his undistinguished characters in order to expose their spiritual dream lives, which come to an inglorious end in conflict with shackling provincialism and materialism. Anderson's frustrated characters are never bitter in their defeat, however. In "Hands," the teacher Wing Biddlebaum's gentle habit of caressing his students is misunderstood, and he is driven from town. In "Godliness," farmer Jesse Bentley prays for the destruction of his Philistine neighbors; he is himself seriously wounded by the slingshot of his own grandson, David.

Winesburg, Ohio stimulated the growth of regional literature in the post-war decade. *The Triumph of the Egg* (1921) also contains tales of maladjustment with an American local color background. "The Egg" is a humorous study of a Midwestern couple who fail at every project they attempt.

Poor White (1920) is an episode novel of the Midwest with the same themes of aspiration and disenchantment. Hugh McVey is an inventor who sees that the success of his industrial plans is also the misery of his environment. *Dark Laughter* (1925), a novel of emotionally repressed whites and unrestrained Negroes, tells of John Stockton, who returns to his home town under an assumed name, becomes a factory hand, and elopes with the wife of his friend.

Home Town (1940), the author's latest work, is a collection of essays which constitute a rediscovery of the American soul in the unhurried life of the small town.

WINGS OF THE DOVE, THE (1902), by Henry James. Milly Theale, a charming, wealthy American girl, is dying of a mysterious illness. Kate Croy, a Londoner, encourages her own lover, the journalist Merton Densher, to court Milly, a former acquaintance. Milly's happiness, which doctors call her only possible cure, will thus be promoted; and Kate assumes that she will die anyway, leaving Densher her fortune and making their own marriage possible. Lord Mark, a British adventurer, is rejected by Milly while Densher's suit progresses; he then vengefully tells the sick girl about the deception of which he has learned. This knowledge kills Milly, as Densher will not further deceive her by denying the plot. Densher does receive a legacy, but he and Kate are prevented from marrying by their tormented consciences.

WINNER TAKE NOTHING (1933), by Ernest Hemingway. See SUN ALSO RISES, THE, by Ernest Hemingway.

WINNIE-THE-POOH (1926), by A. A. Milne. In this charming volume of stories about Christopher Robin and his animal friends, the English writer describes the adventures of Winnie-the-Pooh, a bear who is very fond of eating honey and hasn't many brains; Piglet, his close friend; Eeyore the melancholy donkey; Rabbit and his friends and relations; and Kanga and Baby Roo, who come to live in the forest. The book includes stories about Pooh and his efforts to trap a Heffalump (elephant), the kidnaping of Baby Roo, the discovery of the North Pole, and a flood. Mr. Milne's understanding of children and their imaginative world makes this book an outstanding children's classic that adults also love.

A sequel, *The House at Pooh Corner* (1928), contains further adventures of these delightful characters—and the advent of a new one, Tiger. Milne's almost equally popular volumes of verse for children include *When We Were Very Young* (1924) and *Now We Are Six* (1927).

WINNING OF BARBARA WORTH, THE (1911), by Harold Bell Wright. This sentimental romance of the Colorado River desert region in the time of the first frontiersmen is written along epic lines. The hero is Jefferson Worth, a rough and ready Westerner, who, confronted by greedy land manipulations, pits his inferior financial power and intelligence against the brutal New Yorker James Greenfield. He purchases a valuable stretch of land in the very heart of the King's Basin, southern California, with water rights to transform it into a flowering area. Anxious to set an example of benevolence, he offers attractive concessions to settlers on the reclamation project. The romance of Barbara Worth, who as a child had been found nearly dead in the desert by some of his men, is of incidental importance.

The Shepherd of the Hills (1907) is a sentimental melodrama of the Ozark country, concerning mountaineers old Matt and Young Matt, and the latter's rivalry with fearless Jim Lane for the girl Sammy. *The Calling of Dan Matthews* (1909) is a tale of the spiritual disillusionment of a clergyman. Harold Bell Wright's stories are largely adventure tales of the rugged Southwest.

WINTER OF OLD AGE, THE (1657), by Baltasar Gracián. See CRITIC, THE, by Baltasar Gracián.

WINTER'S TALE, THE (1609–1610?; first Folio 1623), by William Shakespeare. Dowden says of it: "The versification is that of Shakespeare's latest group of plays; no five-measure lines are rhymed; run-on lines and double-endings are numerous." It belongs in the same period with *The Tempest* and *Cymbeline*. The story is taken from Robert Greene's *Pandosto,* or *The History of Dorastus and Fawnia.*

The scene is laid in Sicilia and Bohemia. Leontas, King of Sicilia, and Polixenes, King of Bohemia, had been childhood friends; Polixenes comes to visit Leontes. Leontes, causelessly jealous of his wife, comes to suspect her of having an affair with Polixenes, and orders Camillo, a gentleman, to murder the latter. Camillo warns Polixenes and flees with him to Bohemia. Leontes takes their son, Mamillius, from Hermione, has her arrested and tried for high treason. Leontes has sent to the oracle at Delphi, and his messengers bring back word that Hermione is chaste, Polixenes blameless, and that the King shall live without an heir till what is lost is found. However, Leontes ignores this message. Meanwhile Mamillius dies of grief at his mother's misfortune. News is brought to the King that Hermione has died in prison, and he becomes remorseful. Antigonus, a lord of Sicilia, has taken the Queen's infant to Bohemia, and is about to abandon it according to Leontes' directions when he is chased off by a bear. She is found by a shepherd and brought up as his daughter, Perdita. A number of years elapse, and Prince Florizel, Polixenes' son, meets her at a sheepshearing and falls in love with her. His father does not approve of the match, and on the advice of Camillo the young prince takes Perdita to Sicilia, where he is warmly welcomed by Leontes, who is grieving for the loss of his wife and daughter. Leontes discovers to his great joy that Perdita is his lost child; Paulina, the wife of Antigonus and Hermione's faithful attendant, offers to show the King and his daughter a lifelike statue of the Queen. This turns out to be Hermione herself; Paulina had reported her death in order to save her from the wrath of the King. All ends happily, as Polixenes is reconciled to his son's marriage when he learns that Perdita is Leontes' daughter.

WINTERSET (1935), by Maxwell Anderson. Mio is the son of a man framed and executed for a crime he did not commit. He is bent upon avenging this injustice upon Trock, a gang leader chiefly responsible. His search brings him to Garth Esdras, the witness who held the secret of the case but was never called upon to testify, and the presiding judge Gaunt, now insane from guilt and remorse. After a fleeting, unworldly sort of romance with Miriamne, Garth's sister, he is brought face to face with Trock. He perceives the futility of revenge, and almost wantonly permits himself to be shot—Miriamne going to her death with him. For this play, Anderson drew upon the details of the Sacco-Vanzetti case, as he had done in the more realistic *Gods of the Lightning* (1928), written with Harold Hickerson.

Among Anderson's plays dealing with contemporary problems are the following three: *Saturday's Children* (1927). This comedy of modern marital relations concerns Bobbie Sands and Rims O'Neil. *Both Your Houses* (1933) is a satire on modern politics, describing the disillusion of young Congressman Alan McClean as he discovers the internal corruption and external apathy rampant. *High Tor* (1937) is a fantasy involving the threat of encroaching industrialism upon individualism, personified by Young Van Dorn, who fights to prevent the sale of his mountain retreat, High Tor.

WISDOM OF FATHER BROWN, THE (1914), by Gilbert Keith Chesterton. See FATHER BROWN, THE INNOCENCE OF, by Gilbert Keith Chesterton.

WISHING RING, THE (1879), by Mendele Mocher Sefarim. See MENDELE MOCHER SEFARIM.

WITH FIRE AND SWORD (1884; Eng. tr. 1890), by Henryk Sienkiewicz. Henryk Sienkiewicz (1846–1916) revived through his historical novels the past of his country and made it live in the minds and hearts of his contemporaries at a time when its future seemed dark and dismal. He had the gift of recounting marvelous and heroic deeds performed by sincere and human individuals. *With Fire and Sword* is the first part of his trilogy on the three stages of the Polish wars in the seventeenth century, and is by far the most striking.

The story deals with the Cossack revolt of Bohdan Khmelnytsky (Chmielnicki) against the Poles in 1648, and the efforts of Prince Jarema Wiśniowiecki to rouse the Poles to a realization of their danger and to bring them victory in the field. Against this historic background we have the Polish officer Jan Skrzetuski, who falls in love with the beautiful Helena Kurcewiczowna. The lovers are separated when Helena is captured by Colonel Bohun, and Skrzetuski takes an active part in the campaign against Chmielnicki. Finally Skrzetuski succeeds in escaping from the besieged Polish camp near Zbaraż; with great danger makes his way to the Polish king, and returns with assistance and the assurance of final victory. Only then can he marry his beloved. Side by side appear also such figures as Zagloba, a good-hearted and Falstaffian nobleman, and Podbipieta, who has sworn to remain unmarried until he can cut off three heads with one stroke of his sword. The exploits of these men furnish a lighter and more humorous aspect of the life of the times, without detracting from the high tone of patriotism and of heroic self-sacrifice for the cause of the nation.

With Fire and Sword illustrates the Polish side of the struggle in the seventeenth century against the Zaporozhian Cossacks; the *Deluge* (1891) continues the story of the defense of Poland against the Swedes in the following years; and the third volume, *Pan Wołodyjowski* (1888) carries on the theme of the warfare against the Turks and Tatars until their defeat by King Jan Sobieski. Thus the trilogy covers Polish history from 1648 to 1673.

In addition to these works and *Quo Vadis?* (q.v.), Sienkiewicz treated other periods, such as that of the struggle against the Teutonic Knights in the

Crusaders, and he gave pictures of the modern Polish situation in *Without Dogma* (1893). Until his death in 1916 he was the conscious and unconscious spokesman of the Polish desire for independence.

WITHIN A BUDDING GROVE (1918), by Marcel Proust. See REMEMBRANCE OF THINGS PAST, by Marcel Proust.

WITHOUT DOGMA (Eng. tr. 1893), by Henryk Sienkiewicz. See WITH FIRE AND SWORD, by Henryk Sienkiewicz.

WITIKO (1864–1867), by Adalbert Stifter. See LATE SUMMER, THE, by Adalbert Stifter.

WITNESS TREE, A (1942), by Robert Frost. See FROST, ROBERT.

WIVES' FRIEND, THE (1927), by Luigi Pirandello. See PIRANDELLO, LUIGI.

WOE FROM WIT (1822–1823), by Alexander Sergeyevich Griboyedov. See MISFORTUNE OF BEING CLEVER, THE, by Alexander Sergeyevich Griboyedov.

WOE UNTO THE LIAR (1838), by Franz Grillparzer. See GOLDEN FLEECE, by Franz Grillparzer.

WOMAN IN WHITE, THE (1860), by William Wilkie Collins. The eerie story is told by different characters in succession. A vastly complicated and intricate plot relates the tale of Walter Hartright, who meets, on a lonely road at night, a woman dressed completely in white, whose eccentricities cause him to believe she is demented. Walter has been hired as tutor to Marion Halcombe and her half-sister, Laura Fairlie, by the elderly Mr. Fairlie. The tutor is struck by the marked resemblance between Laura and the mysterious woman in white. He falls in love with Laura, but leaves for abroad in despair when she promises her father on his deathbed that she will marry Sir Percival Glyde of Blackwater Park. The villainous Sir Percival hopes to obtain Laura's inheritance. It is revealed that he will never be able to obtain this if a certain secret, known only to Anne Catherick (the woman in white) and her mother, is disclosed. When he and his ally, Count Fosco, find that they cannot force Laura to part with her money, they confine her in the asylum which holds Anne. Because of the resemblance between the two, he is able to pass Laura off as Anne, and upon Anne's death he gives out false information that the deceased is Lady Glyde. Marion comes to the rescue of Laura, and both are taken into the care of Walter, who returns from the continent. He learns that Sir Percival's secret is the fact that he is illegitimate and has no right to his position. Sir Percival dies when the church in which he has been tampering with his birth registration is burned. It is discovered that Anne Catherick was Laura's half-sister, the illegitimate child of Mr. Fairlie. Anne's mother and Sir Percival had confined her to the asylum because she knew the secret of his birth. Anne dressed in white in remembrance of Laura's mother, who had been kind to her in her childhood and who had once dressed her in white. Count Fosco is killed by his Italian associates, but only after he is made to reveal the truth about Laura. Laura and Hartright are married.

WOMAN KILLED WITH KINDNESS, A (1603), by Thomas Heywood. In this unusual domestic tragedy, Master Frankford, a country gentleman, marries Anne Acton, a goodly lady. Master Wendoll, a poor young man, is kindly treated by Frankford and offered the hospitality of his home; he returns his host's kindness by seducing his morally weak wife. Frankford discovers their guilt and banishes her to a lonely manor, where she is surrounded by luxury but denied the sight of her husband and children. Her heart is broken, but just before she dies she receives her husband's forgiveness and blessing.

WOMEN AT POINT SUR, THE (1927), by Robinson Jeffers. See JEFFERS, ROBINSON.

WONDER WORKING MAGICIAN, THE (1637), by Pedro Calderón de la Barca. In the city of Antioch a young student named Cipriano spends his time enquiring about the existence and nature of God. When Satan tries to take advantage of his doubts, Cipriano defeats him with the strength of his reasoning powers. Afterward Cipriano falls in love with the chaste and fair Justina, who is secretly a Christian. Rejected by her, he grows desperate, and sells his soul to Satan for the possession of Justina, but all the stratagems and machinations of the Spirit of Evil designed to tempt Justina fail before her innocence and faith. Satan confesses himself conquered by the God of the Christians, and Cipriano, converted to the new religion, suffers martyrdom by her side: both are beheaded by the order of the Governor, Cipriano's father. Based on the story of Saint Cyprian of Antioch (4th century), Calderón's play is one of the best treatments of the Faust theme, and is worthy to be considered with Marlowe's *Doctor Faustus* (q.v.) and Goethe's *Faust* (q.v.). It is generally considered Calderón's best religious play.

WONDERS OF THE INVISIBLE WORLD, THE (1693), by Cotton Mather. See MATHER, COTTON.

WOODCUTTER'S HOUSE, THE (1927), by Robert Nathan. See NATHAN, ROBERT.

WOODLANDERS, THE (1887), by Thomas Hardy. When she learns that Giles Winterborne, whom she secretly loves, wishes to marry Grace Melbury, daughter of a rising timber merchant, the poor and simple Marty South sells her hair to add to the adornment of Felice Charmond, a widow and the wealthy landowner of the district. But the engagement of Grace and Giles is broken when the latter, a yeoman who makes cider, feels crude and unworthy in the presence of this girl who has just returned from finishing school, hardly recognizable in her comparative elegance and sophistication as his boyhood sweetheart. She has been attracted to the bright young Dr. Fitzpiers, who, though only recently come to Blackmoor Vale, has already had an affair with the wanton Suke Damson. Grace's ambitious father helps to persuade her to marry Fitzpiers. Soon after, the restless widow Mrs. Charmond summons the young doctor on the pretense that she needs medical help, and they become lovers. Melbury and Grace separately accost Mrs. Charmond and touch her conscience. Fitzpiers is thrown from his horse and badly injured and in danger of dying in the forest, while all three of the women who have loved him mourn. Mrs. Charmond takes him to the continent, while Grace, believing that her divorce is near, encourages Giles again, who has become very poor. At the news that divorce is legally impossible, and that her husband is returning to claim her, Grace runs to Giles' hut, asking him to escort her to the town, where she can stay with a schoolmate. But it begins to rain hard, and Giles, though he has been stricken with fever, decorously abandons his hut to her, and stays outside under "a wretched little shelter of the roughest kind, formed of four hurdles thatched with brake-fern." The storm lasts for days, and when Grace finally discovers his whereabouts and his condition, he is dying, as Fitzpiers, who has found his way to the hut, tells her. For a while Grace and Marty mourn at Winterborne's grave, but, Mrs. Charmond being dead, the wife at last returns to her husband, though she has had some revenge by letting him draw his own conclusions when he found her and Winterborne together.

WOOLLCOTT, ALEXANDER (1887–1943). Alexander Woollcott, originally a drama critic and book reviewer, turned to radio broadcast and magazine column work for a freer expression of his arbitrary yet sophisticated tastes and enthusiasms. *While Rome Burns* (1934) and *Long, Long Ago* (1934) are whimsical collections of essays and short stories, written in a rich prose consistent with the indulgent sentimentality of Woollcott's reminiscences. There are several short macabre pieces, artistic versions of horror tales familiar in American folklore. Woollcott has given screen performances, collaborated on dramas, and acted in *The Man Who Came to Dinner* (1939), by Kaufman and Hart, a comedy based on his own personality. He was known in literary circles as a conversationalist and raconteur of great charm.

WORD OF THE CAMPAIGN OF IGOR (probably early 14th c.). First discovered in manuscript in 1795, this poem, which has become a popular classic familiar to every literate Russian, is a combination of the epic, the lyric and political oratory. A piece of authentic literature, unique of its kind, the first part tells of Prince Igor's disastrous campaign against the Polovtsi, of his initial victory and later defeat, captivity and escape. It records substantially the same historical events as the earlier Kievan *Chronicle,* to which it is in every way superior. In the interlude of Igor's captivity the poet apostrophizes; several great Russian princes are introduced; they are implored to save Igor. Then Igor's wife comes into the picture; in one of the most beautiful passages in the poem she laments from the walls of her town of Putivl. The third part describes Igor's escape.

The poem was at one time thought to be a forgery, but this notion has proved to be a false one. Nature symbolism plays a large part in the poem, which has had a great influence on the style of the prose poems of Alexis Remizov. English translations of this poem are available, the most adequate of which is perhaps that of Leo Wiener, published in his *Anthology of Russian Literature.*

WORKS, by Louis Pasteur. See OEUVRES, by Louis Pasteur.

WORKS AND DAYS (8th c. b.c.), by Hesiod. The poetry of Hesiod is next in antiquity to that of Homer in the history of Greek literature, but far below it in finish and sophistication. From the *Works and Days* emerges the first historical personality in Greek poetry. Hesiod's father, a poor Boeotian farmer, had left his two sons a small farm. The brother, Perses, had taken his own share and tried to get that of Hesiod too. The poem is a sermon to Perses, urging him to mend his ways and live by hard work rather than by his wits. This suasion is given force by the addition of a large didactic section on the *Works* of the farm and a poetic calendar of the *Days* suited for various activities. Hesiod's moral earnestness and dark view of contemporary society is reminiscent of the Hebrew prophets. He uses the myth of Prometheus and Pandora to account for the tribulations of mankind, and describes the fall from a golden age to that of iron. Virgil recognized Hesiod as the father of that type of poetry represented by the *Georgics* (q.v.).

WORLD AND THE INDIVIDUAL, THE (1900–1901), by Josiah Royce. See ROYCE, JOSIAH.

WORLD AS WILL AND IDEA, THE (1818), by Arthur Schopenhauer. The chief influences on Schopenhauer's philosophy are Kant, Plato and the Buddhist philosophers. From Kant he borrowed the transcendental element, the critical method and grouping all thought under the absolute will; Plato contributed his theory of ideas; the Buddhists supplied him with their nerveless pessimism, their denial of will. In *The World as Will and Idea* Schopenhauer underscored the notion of causality. When we analyze our experiences, he argued, we find only sensation or idea. By combining internal with external experience we recognize that *will* is the ultimate and real cause of the idea. By *will* the philosopher means not merely the faculty of choice but of blind, unreasoning impulse. This makes itself manifest in the various emotions that distress the human animal: love, hatred; hope, fear; pleasure and pain. Knowledge he morosely subordinates to questionable impulse.

In the second book of this treatise Schopenhauer examines the external world, which is will in the form of objectivity. He states axiomatically that the body of man is merely the external manifestation of the inner force which is the human will; the inner will and the outer bodily action are aspects of the same reality. In the world of Nature he also finds that will is a natural force. But of all forms of will in creation, intellect is the most perfect weapon with which will has endowed all creatures.

Schopenhauer, by temperament and outlook, was a chronic pessimist. He asserted that the only positive feeling was pain—pleasure was an illusion, a temporary appeasement. He advanced no rational system. His theory of knowledge, identity of will with reality, his pessimism and doctrine of deliverance from suffering are more a world attitude than a world view.

WORLD I NEVER MADE, A (1936), by James T. Farrell. See STUDS LONIGAN, by James T. Farrell.

WORLD IN FALSEFACE, THE (1923), by George Jean Nathan. See NATHAN, GEORGE JEAN.

WORLD OF WASHINGTON IRVING, THE (1944), by Van Wyck Brooks. See FLOWERING OF NEW ENGLAND, THE, by Van Wyck Brooks.

WORLD TO WIN, A (1946), by Upton Sinclair. See JUNGLE, THE, by Upton Sinclair.

WORLD'S END (1940), by Upton Sinclair. See JUNGLE, THE, by Upton Sinclair.

WORLD'S ILLUSION, THE (1918; Eng. tr. 1920), by Jacob Wassermann. The dominating figure in this most popular of Wassermann's novels is Christian Wahnschaffe, a young German who, at the beginning of the novel, is insulated from the world's suffering by his great wealth, handsome appearance, and circle of pleasure-seeking friends, chief among them Crammon (Bernard Gervasius Crammon von Weissenfels), and Felix Imhof. But Christian, in a more instinctive than rational way, moves slowly away from them. Painfully he breaks away from his love, the dancer Eva Sorel; and, befriending a prostitute, Karen Engelschall, moves to successively poorer and poorer quarters in Berlin, begins medical studies, and renounces his fortune. Through his probing of Karen's life history—a progressive degeneration—and in his friendship with the pure Ruth Hofmann, he begins to appreciate the full measure of unhappiness that poor people contend with. He comes closest to finding peace and understanding when, through the force and deep goodness of his personality, he moves Niels Heinrich, Karen's brother, to confess to the murder of Ruth.

The stories of Christian's friends—all eager for wealth, power or merely continued indolence—are counterpointed to the main theme. Where Christian finds fulfillment through renunciation, they suffer. Eva, attaining too quickly the influence and glory she wanted, dies at the hands of an angry Russian mob. Johanna Schöntag, hurt by Christian's indifference, drifts into a sordid affair with Amadeus Voss, a fanatical ex-theology student who hopes to find salvation through Christian, but instead is frustrated by his own bitterness toward the world. Beautiful Letitia von Febronius, seeking excitement and love, marries a rich Argentinian, but finally escapes from South America, the brutality of her husband and his family, only to enter a circle of false flirtations and affairs in Europe. Christian's sister, Judith, leaves her husband, Imhof, and after obtaining a divorce, marries the actor Edgar Lorm, ruining his life with her alternating extravagance and miserliness, both stemming from complete selfishness. In contrast to these characters is Ivan Michailovitch Becker, the revolutionary who helps Christian become aware of the poverty about him.

WORTHIES OF ENGLAND, THE (published 1662), by Thomas Fuller. A great deal of the literature of Renaissance England was concerned with a description of the realm and its actual resources of various sorts. Fuller in his *Worthies* gives an admirable coverage for each county in turn, supplementing the work of Harrison, Camden, Speed, etc. It was published after the death of the royalist divine, and like his other work suffers or amuses by its endless witticisms and encyclopedic oddities—depending on the point of view of the reader. As Coleridge has said, "Wit was the stuff and substance of Fuller's intellect." Famous is his account of the "wit-combats" between Shakespeare and Ben Jonson, "which two I behold like a Spanish great galleon and an English man-of-war; Master Jonson (like the former) was built far higher in learning, solid, but slow in his performances; Shakespeare was the English man-of-war, lesser in bulk, but lighter in sailing, could turn with all tides, tack about, and take advantage of all winds by the quickness of his wit and invention."

WOUTERTJE PIETERSE (1890) by Multatuli. See MAX HAVE-LAAR, by Multatuli.

WOZZECK (published 1879), by Georg Büchner. See DANTON'S DEATH, by Georg Büchner.

WUTHERING HEIGHTS (1847), by Emily Brontë. Set against a somber background of the moorlands, this novel about Catherine Earnshaw and Heathcliff starts at Wuthering Heights, Catherine's childhood home.

Mr. Earnshaw, Catherine's father, finds a waif on the streets of London. He brings him home, and from the beginning Heathcliff causes disruption in the household. Catherine forms a passionate attachment to the boy; Hindley, her brother, regards him as a usurper, and resents the affection displayed toward the boy by his father and Catherine. After the death of Mr. Earnshaw, the household becomes completely demoralized.

Accidentally Catherine is thrown into the company of the elegant Edgar Linton and his sister, Isabella. Despite her love for Heathcliff, she lets fall a chance remark that it would degrade her to marry him. This he hears and shortly thereafter disappears.

After three years Heathcliff returns to the neighborhood, driven by the desire to see Catherine and to wreak his vengeance against the Earnshaw family. He finds her married to Edgar Linton. He gambles with Hindley, acquires liens on the property of Wuthering Heights, and gradually drives Hindley to his death. Isabella, Edgar's sister, falls in love with him, and Heathcliff, knowing that the event would cause Catherine and Edgar great unhappiness and would also place him in control of Isabella's properties, marries her. Catherine, driven to distraction by her own unhappy thoughts, and knowing in her heart that she has been the cause of Heathcliff's attitude, breaks down. She becomes mentally and physically ill, and, beaten by the cross currents of Edgar's love for her and her love for Heathcliff, she sinks into a decline. She recovers sufficiently to give birth to a daughter; then, without ever holding her infant in her arms, she dies.

Isabella, driven to despair by Heathcliff's cruel treatment, runs away from him. She bears a son, and rears him in ignorance that Heathcliff is his father. However, upon her death, Heathcliff claims his boy and brings him to Wuthering Heights. Years pass. Catherine's daughter, little Cathy, and Heathcliff's son, a weak-willed sickly boy, are thrown together, and finally, through Heathcliff's machinations, are married. A few weeks after this unhappy alliance, the boy dies, and Heathcliff now holds the last of the Earnshaws within his power. He is master of both Wuthering Heights and Thrushcross Grange. Hindley's son Hareton and Catherine's daughter live under his roof and are beholden to him for all their needs.

Heathcliff at last dies, alone in his room, as friendless and lonely as the day that Mr. Earnshaw picked him up in the streets of London. Little Cathy and Hindley's son are to be married, thus thwarting Heathcliff's plan to destroy both houses, and will move to Thrushcross Grange. Wuthering Heights is to be closed, and the unhappy memory of Catherine and Heathcliff locked within it.

WYLIE, ELINOR (1885–1928). During Elinor Wylie's youth, art and literature had been strong interests. In 1929 her prize-winning volume of poetry,

Nets to Catch the Wind, appeared, and established her as an important writer in New York circles.

The verses employ conventional meters and rhymes, but frequently juxtapose the formal and the fantastic; they are notable for their craftsmanship. The pieces reflect the author's ivory-tower attitude toward art and her escapist attitude toward life. She deals much with the beauties of nature—but largely as a means of expressing personal disillusionment. *Black Armour* (1923) is a similar collection. *One Person* (1928) is an intense sonnet sequence.

Miss Wiley's novels, the products of careful research and writing, include *Jennifer Dorn* (1923), about English eighteenth-century aristocracy; *The Orphan Angel* (1926), a speculative account of Shelley's life among American frontiersmen; *Mr. Hodge and Mr. Hazard* (1928), a tale of England during the 1830's, mixing realism and lyric reminiscence of the romantic period.

XERXES (1919), by Louis Couperus. See COUPERUS, LOUIS.

YAMA (1912; Eng. tr. 1922), by Alexander Ivanovich Kuprin. See DUEL, THE, by Alexander Ivanovich Kuprin.

YEAR OF DECISION: 1846, THE (1943), by Bernard DeVoto. See DEVOTO, BERNARD.

YEARS, THE (1937), by Virginia Woolf. This is the story of almost sixty years and three generations of an English family. The central figure is Eleanor Pargiter, and it is really her life that is the subject of the novel. Her father, Colonel Pargiter; her aunt, Eugenie; her brothers and sisters, Rose, Delia, Milly, Edward and Martin; her cousins, Sara and Maggy; Maggy's husband Renny; and finally Peggy and North, the younger generation, are all portrayed from within, both in relation to Eleanor and as separate people. The book is a series of episodes from 1880 up to the present day. The war, the suffragette movement, economic conditions, the Irish question—all play their part in the lives of the characters. Some marry, some die, some travel; a new generation grows up. But in the final scene, when all the family are gathered at a party, and Eleanor, an old woman, reviews her life, she sees it not as a compact whole, but as a formless series of impressions.

YEARS OF CHILDHOOD (1846–1858), by Sergey Timofeyevich Aksakov. See FAMILY CHRONICLE, A, by Sergey Timofeyevich Aksakov.

YEARLING, THE (1938), by Marjorie Kinnan Rawlings. In this Pulitzer Prize novel the hero is a little boy who looks at life not with the mature perceptions of the writer, but with his own childish understanding. Jody Baxter grows up in the hummock country of Florida, where he sees nothing but scrub and swamp. His parents eke out a wretched living from the uncompassionate soil. The sensitive Jody roams the countryside, ardently seeking the wonders of nature. He becomes deeply attached to a tame fawn, Flag. When the Baxters are forced to kill Flag to protect their crops, Jody is heartbroken. The experience marks the end of his childhood and the beginning of his adolescence.

The author has written much about the frontier life of the Florida wilderness. *Cross Creek* (1942) is a humorous introduction to life there. *When the Whippoorwill* (1940) is a collection of stories about its folk—moonshiners, fishermen, farmers. *South Moon Under* (1933) is a novel of Lant Jacklin, a latter-day Deerslayer; it contains much local woodlore and interesting material about the bare living conditions of the lonely farmers.

YEATS, WILLIAM BUTLER (1865–1939). Yeats is that rarest of phe-nomena, a poet who wrote his greatest poetry in old age. In his early work he was a Romantic and a Pre-Raphaelite, achieving an exquisite music, sensuous and indistinct. He escapes into the world of the imagination, particularly the Irish fairyland. Typical collections are *The Rose* (1893) and *The Wind Among the Reeds* (1899). His long narrative poem, *The Wanderings of Oisin* (1889), was based, he said, "upon the Middle Irish dialogues of S. Patrick and Oisin and a certain Gaelic poem of the last century." While hunting, Oisin meets the demon woman Niamh, who bears him off to three island paradises, in each of which he dwells a century, first among carefree dancers immune to death or change, then in victorious struggle with a demon to be conquered with the sword Manannan, and then to the Island of Forgetfulness. But he has thought of sad humanity, and when he tells his story to Saint Patrick, the weight of his three hundred years has fallen upon him.

After the turn of the century Yeats became dissatisfied with his early work and began revising it, and no longer tolerated in his poetry either the Romantic rhetoric or the Symbolist mistiness. As a poet he faced life with a new firm-ness, and some of his finest poems refer openly to himself. His mature phase is best seen in *Responsibilities* (1914), with its motto "In dreams begins respon-sibility," in *The Wild Swans at Coole* (1919), and in *The Tower* (1928)—though Yeats continued to develop as a great poet until his death, as shown in the *Collected Poems* of 1933 and the posthumous publication, *Last Poems and Plays* (1940).

Two poems from *The Tower* are regularly singled out by anthologists and critics—"Sailing to Byzantium" and "Among School Children," both inspired by the poet's consciousness of old age. "Byzantium" is a rich symbol for the sources of wisdom whence the soul may learn to sing all the louder—may, now fastened to a dying body, be gathered "into the artifice of eternity," since the country of bodily beauty has had to be given up. *Among School Children* shows the poet "a sixty-year-old smiling public man" visiting a school where nuns teach, and being reminded, as he gazes at the children, that the woman he had loved had told him an anecdote of her childhood. He puts her—she was his Helen of Troy—in his imagination as a girl like one of these children. This is in contrast with himself now, "a comfortable kind of old scarecrow." The last three stanzas show the inseparableness of beauty and the particular forms that express it.

With Lady Gregory, Yeats founded the Irish Literary Theatre, which be-came the Abbey Theatre, for which he wrote plays. The best of his early plays is *The Land of Heart's Desire* (1894), which tells of the childlike fairy that lures away Shawn's newly-married bride, Maire. *Deirdre* (1907) is a poetical retelling of the Gaelic legend that John Millington Synge was to treat more idiomatically two years later in *Deirdre of the Sorrows*. Old King Con-chubar of Uladh found the beautiful child, Deirdre, and reared her "till at last she put on womanhood, and he lost peace." Then he married her, but his happiness was short-lived. Young Naisi ran off with her. At last Fergus prevails upon King Conchubar to forgive the pair, but the crafty king only plots their undoing thereby. When the two lovers discover they have been trapped, Naisi challenges Conchubar to personal combat. The old king offers to release him, provided Deirdre returns to him. When he spurns this offer, Naisi is slain. Thereupon Deirdre stabs herself.

Yeats also produced some of the most exquisite prose in the language. His growing interest in the mystical and the supernatural can be traced from *Ideas of Good and Evil* (1903), where in the essay on "Magic" he writes excitingly about "the Great Memory," a concept which, a quarter of a century later, was to enter the poem called *The Tower,* through the elaborate mystical-metaphysical system set forth in *A Vision* (1925), where types of personality are shown at stages in a circular journey between the poles of complete objectivity and complete subjectivity, and souls are transformed in this world and the next.

His less systematic autobiography appeared in three parts, *Reveries over Childhood and Youth* (1916), the most poetical part in style and also not lacking in supernatural visitation; *The Trembling of the Veil* (1922), dealing with his early years as a writer, when he was part of the tragic, *fin de siècle* group and infatuated with Maud Gonne, the Irish nationalist; and *Dramatis Personae* (1936)—the whole published as *Autobiographies* (1938).

YEGOR BULITCHEV AND OTHERS (1932), by Maxim Gorky. See GORKY, MAXIM.

YELLOW JACK (1934), by Sidney Howard. See THEY KNEW WHAT THEY WANTED, by Sidney Howard.

YOSHE KALB (produced 1932; printed 1933), by Israel Joshua Singer. See BROTHERS ASHKENAZI, THE, by Israel Joshua Singer.

YOU CAN'T GO HOME AGAIN (1940), by Thomas Wolfe. See LOOK HOMEWARD, ANGEL, by Thomas Wolfe.

YOU CAN'T TAKE IT WITH YOU (1936), by George S. Kaufman and Moss Hart. See OF THEE I SING, by George S. Kaufman and Morrie Ryskind.

YOU KNOW ME, AL (1916), by Ring Lardner. See LARDNER, RING.

YOU NEVER CAN TELL (1898), by George Bernard Shaw. In this, one of Shaw's earliest and most popular comedies, Valentine, a young dentist, has just set up in practice at a seaside resort. Here he meets the Clandon family, consisting of Mrs. Clandon, a strong believer in woman's rights, and her three children, Gloria, Dolly and Philip. Mrs. Clandon has long since left her dictatorial husband, and has brought up her children under a name other than that of their father. The Clandons invite Valentine and his landlord to lunch. However, when Valentine arrives for lunch, she discovers to her dismay that his landlord, Mr. Grampton, is her former husband. Dolly and Philip appeal to William, a tactful waiter, who gently informs Mr. Grampton that he is dining with his family after eighteen years of separation. Valentine, in love with Gloria, proposes marriage. Mr. McComas, Mrs. Glandon's solicitor, calls on Mr. Grampton, who is resentful of his family's casual attitude. He believes that they and Valentine are plotting to annoy him, and demands the custody of the younger children. McComas engages the services of Bohun, a famous barrister, and arranges for a conference with Grampton that evening. The hotel is giving a fancy-dress ball, and Bohun arrives in costume. It develops that he is the son of William, who has discovered that his son's successful career hampers him as a waiter, and so spells his name Boon. Bohun straightens out Grampton's difficulties with his family, and Valentine's engagement to Gloria is accepted. All ends happily.

YOUNG HENRY OF NAVARRE (1935), by Heinrich Mann. See MANN, HEINRICH.

YOUNG JOSEPH (1934), by Thomas Mann. See JOSEPH AND HIS BROTHERS, by Thomas Mann.

YOUNG LIONS, THE (1948), by Irwin Shaw. See SHAW, IRWIN.

YOUNG LONIGAN (1932), by James T. Farrell. See STUDS LONIGAN, by James T. Farrell.

YOUNG MANHOOD OF STUDS LONIGAN, THE (1934), by James T. Farrell. See STUDS LONIGAN, by James T. Farrell.

YOUTH AND THE BRIGHT MEDUSA (1920), by Willa Cather. See CATHER, WILLA.

YUJISEUNGNAM, by Su Kujung. See SHIJO-YUCHIP.

YULHA ILKA (18th c.), by Park Jiwon. See HUH SAING CHUN, by Park Jiwon.

YUSIMLON (1929), by Han Yong-woon. See MEDITATIONS OF THE LOVER, by Han Yong-woon.

ZADIG (1747), by Voltaire. See CANDIDE, by Voltaire.

ZEER SCHOONE UREN VAN JUFFROUW SYMFOROSA, DE (1918), by Felix Timmermans. See TIMMERMANS, FELIX.

ZEND AVESTA (ca. 10th–7th c. B.C.?), by Zoroaster. Although Islam has long been the national religion of Iran, beneath the surface many of the old ideas and practices survive. Zoroastrianism in its purity is scarcely found except among the Parsees; their prayer book and Bible is still the *Zend Avesta,* the original document of the religion of Zoroaster (whose traditional date is ca. 1000 B.C.). The *Zend* (i.e., "interpretation") *Avesta* is the collective name of the prophet's scriptural writings (consisting principally of the *Gathas,* the *Vendidad,* the *Nasks,* the *Sirozahs,* the *Yashta* and the *Nyasis*).

The *Yasna* is the chief liturgical work of the *Avesta.* The *Gathas,* written in metrical form, constitute the most important section of the *Avesta.* They are 17 hymns, and contain the teachings, exhortations and revelations of Zoroaster—mainly in connection with the eternal conflict between the powers of good and evil, truth and falsehood, light and darkness, Ahura Mazda and Ahriman. Ahura Mazda, the Supreme Deity, is identified with the sun, and therefore the worship of the rising and setting sun is the most characteristic feature of the ritual. Fire, as symbol of the sun, is also sacred. Ultimately Ahura Mazda will emerge victorious at the Last Judgment. The *Yashta* are 21 poems in which the angels and heroes of Iran are exalted. The *Nyasis* are litanies addressed to the moon, sun, water, fire, and to the angels who rule over these elements. The *Vendidad* is a priestly code prescribing the various purifications, penalties and expiations. In addition there are a considerable number of fragments, including formulas and prayers, messianic incantations for the Day of Judgment against Ahriman and his evil cohorts.

The religion presented in the *Avesta* is a summons to take sides for all that is good against all that is evil. It is strongly moral in its emphasis. In the ancient confession of faith, the Zoroastrian is called upon to pledge to Ahura Mazda "well thought thought (clarity), well spoken word (truthfulness), well done deed (kindliness)."

Some modern scholars say that the present material is about one-quarter of the original content, and that which survives was in the present form in the third century. These sacred books of Zoroastrianism are the sole known literature of an extinct language of the East Iranian division of the Indo-Iranian linguistic family.

It is well known that both the Old and New Testaments are replete with Zoroastrian doctrine and even with almost exact Biblical phraseology. This is due to the fact that the Jewish captives of the Persians and the Medes carried back with them to Jerusalem the religious knowledge they had assimilated during the period of their exile.

ZOHAR, THE (ca. 13th c.), by Simeon ben Yohai. In cabalistic literature the *Zohar* takes a predominant place. Its origin is obscure. It is a pseudo-epigraphic work which pretends to be a revelation from God received directly in Biblical times by Simeon ben Yohai, who in turn communicated its esoteric wisdom to his disciples. Written partly in Hebrew and partly in Aramaic, the Syrian dialect in general use among Jews in ancient times, the *Zohar* contains a complete cabalistic theosophy. It treats of the nature of God, the creation of the world, the soul, sin, redemption, etc. Many regard it as the production of Moses of Leon, a thirteenth century Jewish mystic. It appears to be much older, however, and not the work of a single author but actually an anthology of mystical science.

The central theme of the *Zohar* is that the Biblical narratives and ordinances have an esoteric as well as an obvious meaning. Its alleged author, Simeon ben Yohai, is quoted as having said: "Woe unto the man who asserts that the *Torah* intends to relate only commonplace things and secular narratives; for if this were so, then in the present times likewise a *Torah* might be written with more attractive narrative. In truth, however, the matter is thus: the upper world and the lower are established upon one and the same principle. In the lower world is Israel, in the upper world are the angels. When the angels wish to descend to the lower world, they have to don earthly garments. If this be true of the angels, how much more so of the *Torah*, for whose sake, indeed, the world and the angels alike were created and exist."

Thus armed with insight into Scripture, the authors of the *Zohar* and all cabalists that followed have reinterpreted Scripture to fit into their mystical schemes. By means of numerology and the esoteric arrangement of letters of the alphabet they developed a mystic allegorism, a special kind of speech and abracadabra. However, it must be stated to its credit that the *Zohar* was opposed to religious formalism, and stimulated the imaginations and feelings of its followers. Unfortunately it had an escape motivation, and many people were deluded into believing that they would achieve happiness and illumination by means of its secret formulae and calculations.

ZOÖLOGICAL PHILOSOPHY (1809), by Jean Baptiste de Monet de Lamarck. See PHILOSOPHIE ZOOLOGIQUE, by Jean Baptiste de Monet de Lamarck.

ZULEIKA DOBSON (1911), by Max Beerbohm. Hardly a novel in the conventional sense, this is an extravaganza in which satire and burlesque wit play important parts. Zuleika is a beautiful and clever young lady whose most dazzling trick is her own charm. She visits her grandfather, who is the Warden of Judas College at Oxford, and turns undergraduate life upside down. The Duke of Dorset falls desperately in love with her at a dinner party. Zuleika visits his rooms and he makes a solemn proposal of marriage. She attends the meetings of The Junta, the select wine club, and listens to the absurd speeches of Mr. Oover, the Rhodes scholar. Zuleika has many talents. When she is complimented upon her fine writing style, she modestly says that she picked it up from a Mr. Beerbohm who once sat next to her at dinner.

ZWEIG, STEFAN (1881–1942). Stefan Zweig, although highly successful as a writer, took his own life at the age of sixty after he realized that the world of decency and humanism for which he had fought was doomed. A life rich with professional rewards, travels and friendships came to an end in a self-chosen exile in Brazil. Translated into as many as thirty languages, Zweig's literary work chiefly consists of the biographies or interpretations of outstanding personalities from Erasmus to Casanova, Stendhal, Fouché, Dostoevsky, Tolstoy, Nietzsche and Freud. Some of his shorter essays in this vein are collected in the two volumes *Mental Healers* (1931) and *Master Builders* (1935). Strongly psychoanalytical in approach is his widely read biography of *Marie Antoinette* (1932). The posthumously published *Balzac* (1944) is the result of a lifelong veneration for the great French novelist. The secret of Zweig's success is a rare fusion of deep psychological insight, profound erudition, and noble style.

Index of Authors

Character Index

CHARACTER INDEX

Note: *Etc.* after an entry indicates other characters of the same surname.